ENCYCLOPEDIA OF THE
HARLEM RENAISSANCE

ENCYCLOPEDIA OF THE
HARLEM RENAISSANCE

VOLUME 1
A–J

CARY D. WINTZ
PAUL FINKELMAN
EDITORS

ROUTLEDGE
NEW YORK · LONDON

Published in 2004 by

Routledge
An Imprint of the Taylor and Francis Group
270 Madison Avenue
New York, NY 10016
www.routledge-ny.com

Published in Great Britain by
Routledge
An Imprint of the Taylor and Francis Group
2 Park Square
Milton Park, Abingdon
Oxon OX14 4RN
www.routledge.co.uk

10 9 8 7 6 5 4 3 2 1

Printed on acid-free, 250-year-life paper
Manufactured in the United States of America

Library of Congress Cataloging-in-Publication Data

Encyclopedia of the Harlem Renaissance/edited by Cary D. Wintz and Paul Finkelman
      p. cm.
Includes bibliographical references and index.
ISBN 1-57958-389-X
1. African American arts—New York (State)—New York—History—20th century—Encyclopedias.
2. Harlem Renaissance—Encyclopedias. I. Wintz, Cary D., 1943– II. Finkelman, Paul, 1949–
NX512.3.A35E53 2004
700′.89′9607307471—dc22   2004016353

DEDICATION

We dedicate this work to John Wright, agent par excellence. He was a part of this endeavor from the beginning and guided the project through difficult times.

CONTENTS

PREFACE

The Harlem Renaissance today is a topic of great interest, celebrated as the most creative period in African American cultural life. Yet even now, some seventy-five years later, there still is little agreement about the extent of the renaissance, either in time or in content, and there is still debate about the quality of the creative work it spawned, its impact on African American and American history, and how it affected race relations. Part of the problem is that even the African American intellectuals who created and tried to define the movement, and who provided its critical framework, disagreed among themselves and with the African American writers and artists who provided its creative force. During the Harlem Renaissance, as well as today, participants and scholars alike disagreed about when it began; when it ended; what its artistic, political, and aesthetic focus should be; whether it was a success or a failure; whether it was a positive or a negative development in African American culture; and, ultimately, whether it served the interests of blacks, the interests of whites, or both.

Although the *Encyclopedia of the Harlem Renaissance* will not resolve these debates, it is based on the belief that the Harlem Renaissance was one of the most significant developments in African American history in the twentieth century. It also takes a very broad view of the renaissance and the connection of this movement to the major social, political, and intellectual developments in early twentieth-century African American history. Consequently, the encyclopedia not only addresses the artistic and cultural events directly related to the Harlem Renaissance but also examines the political, economic, and social environment in which the movement took place. Placing the Harlem Renaissance within this broader context is necessary in order to fully understand the movement and its achievements, and to understand the work of individual artists, writers, and performers. With this in mind, we structured the encyclopedia to provide deep coverage of the literary and artistic aspects of the movement as well as broad coverage of the political, social, economic, and legal issues that confronted African Americans during the early twentieth century.

Our coverage of the artistic elements of the Harlem Renaissance includes essays on the literature, art, and music of the movement. There are extensive essays on major writers, artists, and performers, as well as pieces on most of the lesser-known figures. In addition, there are discussions of the major creative works, especially those that had an impact on the development of the Harlem Renaissance. Along with the so-called higher arts (poetry, literature, painting, sculpture, theater, classical music, and dance), expressions of popular culture are covered, especially musical theater, musical reviews, and motion pictures. In other areas, the line between popular culture and art is not entirely clear. Jazz, blues, and spirituals are treated as art forms, although they were also an expression of folk or popular culture. Although not everyone who wrote a poem, sang a song, or performed onstage is covered in this encyclopedia, we have attempted to include everyone who played a significant role in the renaissance, and those whose activities reflected or influenced some aspect of African American culture in the early twentieth century.

The Harlem Renaissance was, of course, situated in time and place. We see the movement as a phenomenon of the 1920s and the 1930s, beginning at about the end of World War I and fading out in the late 1930s. Its temporal boundaries are not exact, however; they vary somewhat from one artistic category to another, and there are powerful antecedents existing as early as the turn of the century. For example, we include entries on individuals such as Paul Laurence Dunbar and Henry Ossawa Tanner, whose major work predates World War I but who had a significant influence on later writers and artists. Furthermore, the social, political, and economic developments intertwined with the movement are much less easy to contain; accordingly, various entries can range back into the late nineteenth century and extend into the 1940s. The focus, though, is on the two decades following World War I.

The geographic boundaries of the Harlem Renaissance are also complicated. Clearly Harlem was central to the movement, and a large number of entries examine multiple aspects of Harlem's life and history. The Harlem Renaissance was not confined to one location, however. For example, blues and jazz, two developments in music that helped define the renaissance, had their origins in a number of locations—New Orleans, Memphis, St. Louis, the Mississippi delta—and were transported north by people who migrated to Chicago, New York, and other cities. Likewise, most of the writers, poets, actors, and artists moved to Harlem from other parts of the country; many emerged from artistic and cultural movements in places like Los Angeles, Houston, Dallas, New Orleans, and Atlanta. Also, African American communities in other Northern cities like Washington, Philadelphia, Boston, and Chicago had their own cultural movements, which contributed to the Negro Renaissance. Furthermore, neither the movement nor its influence was confined to the United States. Caribbean writers and artists immigrated to the United States and participated in the movement; others from this region influenced the political and cultural life of Harlem. African American writers, artists, and performers traveled to the Caribbean, Africa, and Europe, where they interacted with the artistic and political life of Europeans and immigrants from the European African and Caribbean empires. A number of entries examine the connection of the Harlem Renaissance to this broader world.

Finally, race in all its complexity is fundamental to the Harlem Renaissance. Each African American writer or artist confronted in his or her own way the racism and colonialism of the United States and the Western world; at the same time, each was connected to the emergence of the struggle for civil rights and the anticolonial movements. These issues had an impact on the Harlem Renaissance and on the lives and work of those who participated in it. This encyclopedia contains numerous entries that examine race and racism, both within the United States and abroad, especially in terms of how these issues defined the African American experience in the early twentieth century and how they affected the life and work of the participants in the Harlem Renaissance.

One aspect of the racial experience that is the subject of several entries is the role of whites in the Harlem Renaissance: White authors writing about African Americans; white patrons and supporters of the Harlem Renaissance; white publishers, producers, and booking agents; white critics and promoters—they all influenced African American culture for better or worse. A closely related subject is the interaction between blacks and whites: most often black artists reacting with white publishers, promoters, and critics, but also the more complex interaction between the black intelligentsia and black writers and white publishers and intellectuals. Both W. E. B. Du Bois and James Weldon Johnson were black civil rights leaders, novelists, and poets in their own right, and both published, promoted, and critiqued the work of black artists and writers. Carl Van Vechten, a white novelist, wrote a major Harlem novel of the period and also served as a patron and promoter of black literature, art, and music, and as a documenter of the Harlem Renaissance.

The *Encyclopedia of the Harlem Renaissance*, then, examines all phases and all aspects of the Harlem Renaissance, as well as the broader cultural, political, social, and economic environment in which the renaissance, and indeed African Americans, functioned in the first half of the twentieth century. Entries address individual participants and major works and a wide range of related issues that fall into several large categories. Entries on individuals include participants in all aspects of the creative arts as well as journalists, political and cultural figures, and others who were simply personalities in Harlem and contributed to the ambience of the era. Entries on creative works cover all artistic fields but focus on books, anthologies, plays, motion pictures, and musical shows or revues. The encyclopedia also includes entries on significant newspapers, literary magazines, and periodicals that either were directly connected to the Harlem Renaissance or helped define the political and social milieu. Likewise, we provide entries on artistic and cultural organizations along with political and civil rights groups. Harlem itself is covered in essays on its history and social and economic issues, as well as its nightlife and specific institutions and places in the neighborhood. Finally, a number of thematic and interpretive essays provide a general overview of specific aspects of the renaissance such as music, literature, and the visual arts, and several somewhat shorter essays address specific concepts, events, and movements.

Through its breadth and diversity, this encyclopedia attempts to meet a common demand. Students, scholars, and the public at large are looking for information on the rich and complex culture of the Harlem Renaissance. Whether readers seek the broad outlines or the fine details of the era, they will find here, in one work, an unparalleled resource—contributed by those dedicated to studying its achievements.

Organization

The *Encyclopedia of the Harlem Renaissance* is divided into two volumes. The entries are organized alphabetically. Volume 1 contains entries from A to J, and Volume 2 contains K to Z and the index. To assist the user in finding material, each entry has cross-references ("See also") to related entries, and, as necessary, blind entries ("See") direct the reader to the proper essay. An extensive index also assists the reader in finding specific information that may not have its own entry or may be found in several entries. Each entry also includes a relatively short bibliography directing the reader to further information. The illustrations provide visual material for specific entries and for the Harlem Renaissance in general.

Contributing Authors

The encyclopedia includes some 640 entries, representing the work of about 260 contributors. The contributors represent academic faculty members and independent scholars, writers, and artists. They include specialists in history, art, music, theater, dance, politics and political theory, economics, sociology, and African American studies; and they come from across the United States as well as from abroad. Their work reflects the latest scholarship in their respective fields.

Language

This encyclopedia, in general, uses the terms "African American" and "black" interchangeably. It also uses "Negro," "Afro-American," "Aframerican," and similar terms of the early twentieth century in direct quotations and when these terms are appropriate to reflect the usages of the time and place. "Negro" is always capitalized, unless it was lowercased in a source that is quoted directly. The use of the term "nigger" and its derivations is more complicated. This term has not been used here to denote a pejorative attitude toward African Americans. As necessary and appropriate, however, it has been used in direct quotations to capture accurately the language of poetry or literature, or to reflect and understand racist language. Phrases like the book title *Nigger Heaven*, and terms like "niggerati" and "negritude" that refer to specific concepts, have been used as they were during the Harlem Renaissance. Our approach to the use of words is to be true to the language of the period, maintain a language appropriate for scholarly discourse, and address racial issues accurately and honestly while avoiding needlessly offensive phrases.

Acknowledgments

A number of people have contributed to this project. First, our associate editors provided the broad knowledge of the period necessary to review the entries. They, along with our advisory board, also reviewed the list of entries and helped identify contributors. Vincent Virga provided us guidance and significant insight during a conversation at the Library of Congress. Rita Langford at the University of Tulsa performed some of the initial work in organizing the entry list. We want to add a special word of thanks to Arnold Rampersad, who served as an associate editor during the early phases of the project but had to withdraw as the demands of his administrative duties at his university increased. We also received a great deal of assistance from the publishers. First, at Fitzroy Dearborn, where the project began, Paul Schellinger embraced our vision of this encyclopedia, and Robin Rhone and Audrey L. Berns guided the project during its initial phase. When Routledge took over from Fitzroy Dearborn, it committed the resources to help us complete the project quickly. Sylvia Miller, Mark Georgiev, and Kate Aker provided overall leadership, while Susan Gamer worked directly with us on an almost daily basis. We especially appreciate Susan's energy and hard work that kept the project moving and brought it to its completion. Finally, we wish to thank all our contributing authors for the expertise they brought to their essays; for completing their work in a timely manner; for completing revisions or taking on new assignments, often on a short schedule; and for maintaining their belief in the project as we moved toward its completion.

CARY D. WINTZ
PAUL FINKELMAN

Alphabetical List of Entries

THEMATIC LIST OF ENTRIES

Greene, Lorenzo
Hamid, Sufi Abdul
Harrison, Hubert
Haynes, George Edmund
Herskovits, Melville
Johnson, Charles Spurgeon
Johnson, James Weldon
Johnson, John Arthur
Jones, Eugene Knickle
McGuire, George Alexander
Mencken, H. L.
Miller, Kelly
Moore, Frederick Randolph
Moore, Richard B.
Morton, Ferdinand Q.
Moton, Robert Russa
Nail, John E.
Ovington, Mary White
Owen, Chandler
Padmore, George
Patterson, Louise Thompson
Payton, Philip A.
Powell, Adam Clayton, Sr.
Randolph, A. Philip
Rogers, Joel Augustus
Schomburg, Arthur A.
Scott, Emmett Jay
Spingarn, Arthur
Talbert, Mary Burnett
Trotter, William Monroe
Villard, Oswald Garrison
Walker, Madame C. J.
Washington, Booker T.
Wise, Stephen Samuel
Woodson, Carter G.
Work, Monroe Nathan
Wright, Louis T.

Promoters and Patrons
Barnes, Albert C.
Braithwaite, William Stanley
Brawley, Benjamin
Campell, Elmer Simms
Cunard, Nancy
Draper, Muriel
Holstein, Casper
Locke, Alain
Loggins, Vernon
Mason, Charlotte Osgood
Meyer, Annie Nathan

Nance, Ethel Ray
Redding, J. Saunders
Van Vechten, Carl

Publishers
Buttitta, Anthony J.
Calverton, V. F.
Eastman, Crystal
Eastman, Max
Isaacs, Edith
Kellogg, Paul U.
Knopf, Alfred A.
Knopf, Blanche
Liveright, Horace
Pace, Harry H.
Spingarn, Joel
Van Doren, Carl

Singers
Anderson, Marian
Baker, Josephine
Bentley, Gladys
Bledsoe, Jules
Brooks, Shelton
Brown, Ada
Burleigh, Harry Thacker
Clough, Inez
Cox, Ida Prather
Hall, Adelaide
Hayes, Roland
Hegamin, Lucille
Holiday, Billie
Hunter, Alberta
Lovinggood, Penman
Mills, Florence
Mitchell, Abbie
Rainey, Gertrude "Ma"
Smith, Ada
Smith, Bessie
Smith, Clara
Smith, Mamie
Smith, Trixie
Snow, Valaida
Spivey, Victoria
Ward, Aida
Washington, Isabel
Waters, Ethel
Wilson, Edith

xxiii

Runnin' Wild
Saint Louis Blues
Servant in the House, The
Show Boat
Shuffle Along
Stevedore
Taboo
They Shall Not Die
Three Plays for a Negro Theater
Within Our Gates

Books
Autobiography of an Ex-Colored Man, The
Batouala
Birthright
Black Manhattan
Blues: An Anthology
Cane
Color
Conjure Man Dies, The
Copper Sun
Dark Laughter
Dark Princess
Ebony and Topaz
Fine Clothes to the Jew
Fire in the Flint, The
God's Trombones
Harlem: Negro Metropolis
Harlem Shadows
Home to Harlem
Infants of the Spring
Negro: An Anthology
New Negro, The
Nigger
Nigger Heaven
Not Without Laughter
Passing: Novel
Porgy: Novel
Quicksand
Their Eyes Were Watching God
There Is Confusion
Tropic Death
Walls of Jericho, The
Weary Blues, The

TOPICS

Topics, Concepts, Ideologies, Events, Themes
Algonquin Roundtable
Amenia Conference, 1916

Amenia Conference, 1933
Anglophone Africa and the Harlem Renaissance
Anglophone Caribbean and the Harlem Renaissance
Antilynching Crusade
Art Criticism and the Harlem Renaissance
Artists
Atlanta University Studies
Authors: 1—Overview
Authors: 2—Fiction
Authors: 3—Nonfiction
Authors: 4— Playwrights
Authors: 5—Poets
Black Bohemia
Black History and Historiography
Black Press
Black Zionism
Blackface Performance
Blacks in Theater
Blues
Blues: Women Performers
Civic Club Dinner, 1924
Civil Rights and Law
Community Theater
Crisis, The: Literary Prizes
Crisis: The Negro in Art—How Shall He Be
    Portrayed? A Symposium
Cullen–Du Bois Wedding
Cultural Organizations
Dance
Dark Tower
Europe and the Harlem Renaissance: 1—Overview
Europe and the Harlem Renaissance: 2—Berlin
Europe and the Harlem Renaissance: 3—London
Europe and the Harlem Renaissance: 4—Paris
Europe and the Harlem Renaissance: 5—Soviet Union
Federal Programs
Federal Writers' Project
Film
Film: Actors
Film: Black Filmmakers
Film: Blacks as Portrayed by White Filmmakers
Francophone Africa and the Harlem Renaissance
Francophone Caribbean and the Harlem Renaissance
Garveyism
Great Migration
Great Migration and the Harlem Renaissance
Gumby Book Studio
Harlem: 1—Overview and History
Harlem: 2—Economics
Harlem: 3—Entertainment
Harlem: 4—Housing

MAP

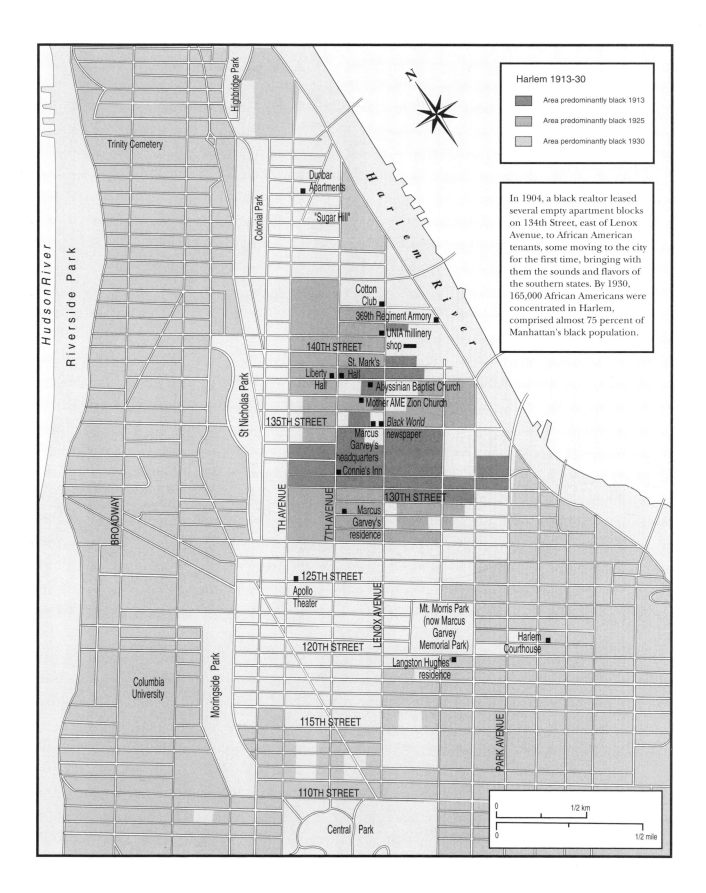

Harlem 1913-30

- Area predominantly black 1913
- Area predominantly black 1925
- Area perdominantly black 1930

In 1904, a black realtor leased several empty apartment blocks on 134th Street, east of Lenox Avenue, to African American tenants, some moving to the city for the first time, bringing with them the sounds and flavors of the southern states. By 1930, 165,000 African Americans were concentrated in Harlem, comprised almost 75 percent of Manhattan's black population.

Highbridge Park

Trinity Cemetery

Hudson River

Riverside Park

Colonial Park

Dunbar Apartments

"Sugar Hill"

Harlem River

St Nicholas Park

Cotton Club

369th Regiment Armory

UNIA millinery shop

140TH STREET

St. Mark's Hall

Liberty Hall

Abyssinian Baptist Church

Mother AME Zion Church

135TH STREET

Black World newspaper

Marcus Garvey's headquarters

Connie's Inn

7TH AVENUE

7TH AVENUE

130TH STREET

Marcus Garvey's residence

BROADWAY

125TH STREET

Apollo Theater

LENOX AVENUE

Mt. Morris Park (now Marcus Garvey Memorial Park)

Harlem Courthouse

120TH STREET

Langston Hughes' residence

Columbia University

Moringside Park

115TH STREET

PARK AVENUE

110TH STREET

Central Park

0   1/2 km

0   1/2 mile

Abbott, Robert Sengstacke

Robert Sengstacke Abbott was born in Fredericka, Saint Simon's Island, Georgia. His parents—Thomas, his father; and Flora, his mother—were both former slaves who worked in agriculture. As a youngster, Abbott became interested in the situation of African Americans when his stepfather, John Hermann Henry Sengstacke, encouraged him to consider the plight of former slaves. Abbott had to struggle to get an education. During his time in law school, he reinvented himself by taking Sengstacke's surname as his own middle name and concentrating on the practice of law.

In 1905, Abbott used twenty-five dollars to start the *Chicago Defender* in his home on State Street, proudly announcing the newspaper as the "World's Greatest Weekly." His entrance into journalism was evidently a result of disappointment with law. Several stories explain his sudden change of career. According to one story, he had been told that he was too dark to succeed in Chicago's courts; according to a second, he could not pass the Illinois bar; according to a third, he never really made much money in law and needed to earn his living some other way.

At first, the *Chicago Defender* was a one-man operation. When the earliest versions appeared, Abbott was serving as editor, business manager, and staff and tried to sell the paper to homes along Twenty-ninth and Twenty-fifth streets in Chicago. These original versions consisted of only four pages, printed in his kitchen. The first few years of operation saw modest growth. Abbott encouraged friends to write columns, and he increased the paper's circulation by selling it in local barbershops, churches, and pool halls—places that he

also used, brilliantly, as sources of news. Through these venues the *Defender* was able to gain a reputation as the voice of Chicago's African American community.

Abbott used the *Defender* to fight against discrimination, segregation, and disenfranchisement. It became a protest newspaper, highly respected among African Americans in and around Chicago. The *Defender* reported abuses against African Americans and focused on unfair treatment of minorities. It developed a controversial reputation because Abbott published articles on police brutality, racial violence, and bigotry against African Americans. Also, Abbott had copied the masthead of William Randolph Hearst's *Chicago Evening American*; this often confused readers, and he was eventually forced to change the masthead to avoid a lawsuit.

The most important factor in the growth and expansion of the *Chicago Defender* was the mass migration of African Americans from the South after 1915. These emigrants bought the *Defender* and sent it South to relatives, transforming it into a national paper. The *Defender* encouraged African Americans to fight back against racism and injustice. It responded to lynching by adopting the slogan "An eye for an eye" in 1916. By 1917, the paper was encouraging African Americans to leave the South and settle in what Abbott called the "promised land," the North.

Abbott used his success as a newspaperman to become part of Chicago's African American elite. In 1917, he joined other leading African Americans—although unsuccessfully—in trying to make real estate agreements that would be acceptable to whites. The *Defender* supported African American strikebreakers against the American Federation of Labor because the union

1

discriminated against African Americans. The paper accused the police and local leaders of failing to enforce the law and failing to investigate crimes against African Americans, particularly a rash of bombings: During the migration period of 1917–1921, there were fifty-eight unsolved bombings of African Americans' dwellings.

By 1918, the huge migration had increased the *Defender*'s circulation dramatically, to well more than 230,000. At one time the *Defender* opposed the migration because Abbott feared the effect of the emigrants on the morals and social standing of Chicago's black community. However, he later switched sides and began to write columns of advice—do's and don'ts—aimed at emigrants. Abbott used his paper to criticize the Jamaican leader Marcus Garvey and Garvey's movement; he also joined a group of prominent African Americans in encouraging the attorney general to investigate that movement.

During the Red Summer of 1919, the *Defender* played an invaluable role by presenting the African American side of the story. Abbott was rewarded for his actions during the riot by being named to the Chicago Commission on Race Relations, which issued a report, *The Negro in Chicago*, in 1922. Abbott supported this report, even though it criticized the African American press for overreacting to the riot.

During the 1920s and 1930s, Abbott lent his name and prestige to several causes, including most of the major efforts to improve the condition of African Americans in and around Chicago. He was a board member of the Young Men's Christian Association (YMCA), National Urban League, Hampton Alumni Association, Masons, and Lincoln Memorial Congregational Church. For most of his life, he was politically aligned with the Republican Party. He publicly supported Oscar DePriest, the first African American elected to Congress from the North.

After Abbott's death, the *Defender* was run by his nephew John Sengstacke.

Biography

Robert Sengstacke Abbott was born on 28 November 1868. He attended Beach Institute in Savannah; Claflin University in Orangeburg, South Carolina; and, from 1892 to 1896, Hampton Institute, where he learned the printer's trade. After completing his studies at Hampton, he earned an LL.B. at Kent College of Law in Chicago. He practiced law in Gary, Indiana, and Topeka, Kansas,

before retuning to Chicago in 1903. He started the *Chicago Defender* in 1905. Abbott was married twice, each time to a widow. His first marriage, on 18 September 1918, was to Helen Thornton Morrison; they were divorced in June 1933. In August 1934 he married Edna Rose Brown Denison, who had five grown children. Abbott died in Chicago on 29 February 1940, of Bright's disease; he was eulogized by all the major papers of Chicago and the *New York Times*.

ABEL A. BARTLEY

See also Black Press; DePriest, Oscar; Garvey, Marcus; Garveyism; Journalists; Riots: 2—Red Summer of 1919

Further Reading

Bontemps, Arna, and Jack Conroy. *Anyplace But Here.* New York: Hill and Wang, 1966.

Ottley, Roi. *The Lonely Warrior: The Life and Times of Robert S. Abbott.* Chicago, Ill.: Regnery, 1955.

Tuttle, William. *Race Riot: Chicago in the Red Summer of 1919.* New York: Atheneum, 1970.

Abyssinian Baptist Church

The Abyssinian Baptist Church is internationally recognized as a symbol of black spiritual and political power. During the Harlem Renaissance, Abyssinian relocated uptown, after having made several expansive moves from lower Manhattan.

The church was founded in 1808, when a group of African Americans at the Gold Street Baptist Church decided that they would no longer accept segregated pews. After their initial application for autonomy was rejected as too threatening, a core group of four men and twelve women invited Thomas Paul, who had founded the Joy Street Baptist Church in Boston a few years earlier, to petition church officials. Paul, an African American preacher of great renown, prevailed, and the necessary papers were granted. Some Ethiopian merchants in the founding group suggested the name Abyssinian. In its early years, the church moved often. It remained for several years on Anthony Street (now Worth Street), then moved to the Broadway Tabernacle, and later moved to Thompson and Spring streets, all the while following the progression of the African American population northward through the city.

During the 1840s, the church took a strong—and, at the time, radical—stand against slavery. At the turn of the century, Abyssinian owned church property on Waverly Place in Greenwich Village. In the first decade of the twentieth century, the church moved again and acquired additional property on Fortieth Street in the Tenderloin section.

In 1908, when the church could look back on its first hundred years, Adam Clayton Powell Sr. assumed leadership. For roughly the next three decades, he would guide Abyssinian through its most expansive period. He was at the helm when the congregation erected a church on 138th Street in Harlem in the early 1920s, then discharged its indebtedness to the bank about a decade earlier than required. The Gothic and Tudor structure with its imported stained-glass windows, fully paid for through tithing contributions from parishioners, represented the solidity and fidelity of the church membership, which had more than doubled, expanding from 3,000 to 7,000 during the 1920s through 1937, when Powell retired.

Then Powell's only son, Adam Clayton Powell Jr., stepped into the pulpit. He drew new attention to the church and inspired new energy. From the foundation his father had built, the son was able to extend the Abyssinian ministry further into the realm of politics. The younger Powell led a highly publicized labor protest to pressure white owners of stores on 125th Street to employ African Americans. A few years after becoming pastor at Abyssinian, Powell was elected to the City Council. His next step was Congress, where he served fourteen terms in the House of Representatives, championing the legal and social rights of African Americans.

Funeral at the Abyssinian Baptist Church, 1920s. (Schomburg Center for Research in Black Culture, New York Public Library.)

Like the founders of Abyssinian, he never shrank from protesting against injustice or from the light of publicity.

Following the younger Powell's tenure and that of Pastor Samuel Proctor, Rev. Calvin Butts maintained the church's respected status into the twenty-first century.

BARBARA BREWSTER LEWIS

See also Powell, Adam Clayton Sr.

Further Reading

Baer, Hans A., and Merrill Singer. *African-American Religion in the Twentieth Century: Varieties of Protest and Accommodation.* Knoxville: University of Tennessee Press, 1992.

Billingsley, Andrew. *Mighty Like a River: The Black Church and Social Reform.* New York: Oxford University Press, 1999.

Gore, Bob. *The Abyssinian Baptist Church: A Photographic Journal.* New York: Stewart, Tabor, and Chang, 2001.

Haskins, Jim. *Adam Clayton Powell: Portrait of a Marching Black.* Trenton, N.J.: First Africa World Press, 1993.

Powell, Adam Clayton. *Against the Tide: An Autobiography.* New York: R. R. Smith, 1938.

Sobel, Mechal. *Travelin' On: The Slave Journey to an Afro-Baptist Faith.* Westport, Conn.: Greenwood, 1979.

African Blood Brotherhood

The Blood Brotherhood was created by Cyril Valentine Briggs, a Jamaican African nationalist and socialist. Briggs was born on 28 May 1888 in Chester Park, Nevis, British West Indies. He had a very light complexion and was called the "angry blond Negro" in some newspapers. He worked in the printing trade in Saint Kitts and was inspired by the works of the social critic Robert Green Ingersoll (1833–1899), the "great agnostic," who attacked not only religion but also much else that was dear to Americans.

Briggs immigrated to the United States in July 1905. In 1912 he was hired as a writer by the *New Amsterdam News.* In 1915 he served one term as editor of the *Colored American Review,* the mouthpiece of Harlem's black business community. Briggs's writings emphasized racial pride and economic cooperation. Briggs was impressed by the Easter Rebellion of 1916 in Ireland and began to discuss plans for the decolonization of

Africa. During World War I, as a reporter for the *New Amsterdam News*, he was an outspoken critic of what he considered to be the United States' hypocritical aims. Because of his denunciations of American policies regarding African American soldiers and citizens, the paper was officially censured by the federal government. The issue of 12 March 1919 was detained by the U.S. Post Office because of an editorial written by Briggs in which he denounced the League of Nations as a "league of thieves." In May 1919, Briggs severed his ties with the *New Amsterdam News*.

A few months earlier, in December 1918, Briggs had begun publishing the *Crusader*. This newspaper emphasized self-government for African Americans, and Africa for the Africans. It focused on and expressed the ideas of the radical element in the New Negro movement.

After the events of the Red Summer of 1919, Briggs and others came to believe that protecting African American rights required armed resistance. His ideas fit the postwar New Negro movement. The racial violence that followed the war shocked African Americans and made them more aware of their vulnerability. Briggs's response was the African Blood Brotherhood for African Liberation and Redemption (ABB), created in October 1919 after an article was published in the *Crusader*. ABB was made up principally of native Caribbeans, young intellectuals, workers, veterans, and marginal businessmen, and it preached radical revolution; thus it was never able to gain a mass following. Briggs envisioned ABB as an alternative for those who were sophisticated enough to resist the hollow charm of Marcus Garvey and the Universal Negro Improvement Association (UNIA).

At its peak, ABB claimed to have 3,500 members and more than 100 branches. However, membership was by enlistment only, and it is virtually impossible to determine the number of members accurately. After 1920, when the leadership of ABB came under communist influence, the *Crusader*—the organization's official mouthpiece—became increasingly anticapitalist, focusing less on African issues and more on the benefits of bolshevism.

Briggs was recruited into the Communist Party with the help of another West Indian, Claude McKay. McKay introduced Briggs to Robert Minor, a famous cartoonist from Texas; and Rose Pastor Stokes, a leading Jewish activist. They were committed to the struggle for black liberation, and they convinced Briggs of the concept of parallel communism: that is, two communist parties—one legal and aboveground, the other secret and underground. As a result, during the 1920s, Briggs increasingly moved his movement toward communism and began to give his rhetoric communist overtones.

Originally, ABB was a semisecret organization with a highly centralized governing structure. Although its name was derived from the blood brotherhood ceremonies of African peoples, ABB was actually modeled after the Irish Republican Brotherhood, which dated from 1858 and led to the Fenian movement. Briggs was also impressed by the Hamitic League, with its system of passwords, secrecy, and oaths. The Hamitic League was founded by George Wells Parker of Omaha, Nebraska; and the *Crusader*, in its first few issues, proclaimed itself the publicity organ of the league.

Briggs served as the executive head of ABB, sharing power with the supreme executive council, which included Ben Burrell (director of historical research), Richard Moore (educational director), Theo Burrell (secretary), Otto Huiswoud (national organizer), W. A. Domingo (director of publicity and propaganda), Grace P. Campbell (director of consumers cooperatives), and William H. Jones (physical director).

ABB was the first black organization in the twentieth century to advocate armed self-defense. It came to national prominence in June 1921, when about 500 of its members—armed with shotguns—surrounded a jail in Tulsa, Oklahoma, to protect Dick Rowland, an African American shoeshine boy who had been accused of assaulting a white woman. In response, white mobs raided gun stores, randomly attacked African Americans, and eventually burned and looted the black section of Tulsa. ABB was widely blamed for this racial violence, but Briggs defended his organization's actions in Tulsa as community self-defense.

In 1921–1924 the leaders of ABB concentrated on criticizing Marcus Garvey and his UNIA. In 1921, at the national convention of UNIA, members of ABB had lobbied outside Liberty Hall, seeking an official link to Garvey's organization, but the UNIA delegates had ignored them. In 1922, Briggs stopped publishing the *Crusader*, creating the Crusader News Agency in its wake. In 1924, ABB was an official participant in a movement called Negro Sanhedrin, which met in Chicago under the leadership of Kelly Miller. Miller wanted to create a federation of black organizations that could coordinate protest activities and develop a unified agenda.

In 1925, ABB was disbanded on orders of the Communist Party of the United States. It was replaced by the American Negro Labor Congress and the League of Struggle for Negro Rights. Symbolically, ABB had been a very important organization. Its insistence on African American rights and protection had placed it in the forefront of the New Negro and black liberation movements. Although its tangible accomplishments were negligible, its psychological effects continue today.

ABEL BARTLEY

See also Briggs, Cyril; Domingo, Wilfred Adolphus; Garvey, Marcus; Jones, William H.; McKay, Claude; Miller, Kelly; Moore, Richard B.; New Negro Movement; Riots: 2—Red Summer of 1919

Further Reading

Foner, Philip S., and James S. Allen, eds. *American Communism and Black Americans: A Documentary History, 1919–1929.* Philadelphia, Pa.: Temple University Press, 1986.

Hill, Robert A. *The Crusader*, 3 vols. New York and London, 1987.

Negro History Bulletin, July–August 1978, p. 862.

Samuels, W. D. *Five Afro-Caribbean Voices in American Culture, 1917–1929.* Boulder, Colo.: Belmont, 1977.

Afro-American Realty Company

In the early twentieth century, Harlem became the spiritual center of a new black cultural identity and a famous center of black expression. During the 1920s and 1930s, its writers and artists gave it a worldwide reputation, and the critic Alain Locke described Harlem as an ideal locale for black self-determination. But before all of this talent could descend on Harlem, a series of changes in infrastructure and great foresight were required, beginning in the late nineteenth century. The Afro-American Realty Company, in 1904–1908, illustrates how black businesspeople provided opportunities in Harlem, leading to patterns of migration that permanently altered the community and established an era of expression.

Afro-American Realty was founded in 1904 by Phillip A. Payton, who capitalized on factors that included an economic downturn and the availability of real estate in Harlem. Vast speculative development had penetrated Harlem after the Civil War, when many single-family row houses, tenements, and luxury apartment houses were built. Businesses and religious, educational, and cultural institutions followed. Growth continued in 1873, when Harlem was annexed by

New York City and planning for elevated rail service was announced. Proposed subway routes to west Harlem set off another wave of real estate speculation and further inflated market values. By the end of the nineteenth century, virtually all of Harlem was covered by commercial and residential buildings.

The effects of years of overbuilding were exacerbated by a local real estate recession at the beginning of the twentieth century. Loans were withheld, mortgages were foreclosed, rents fell, and residences sat vacant as building owners scrambled to recover their investments. Eventually, landlords sought the services of Payton, who offered to provide regular tenants for buildings on the east side of the district if the landlords would accept black applicants. The landlords agreed, and one of New York's great internal migrations began. Thousands of families began pouring into houses and apartments between Fifth and Seventh avenues, despite opposition from the white Property Owners Protective Association of Harlem. Previously, black newcomers to Harlem had been abetted by real estate speculators seeking to extract high mortgages or rents in a discriminatory process; now, however, nonresident owners gradually realized that Payton's clients were good tenants who were willing to pay higher rents. Afro-American Realty acquired five-year leases on properties owned by whites and rented these properties at 10 percent above deflated market prices. Pent-up demand for new housing and newly created jobs in industry in New York drew thousands to Harlem.

As more black residents moved into Harlem, Afro-American Realty received considerable attention in the national press and considerable support from black leaders, such as Booker T. Washington, who was an associate and business partner of Payton's. The company also lured customers with an innovative advertising program aimed at riders on subways and elevated trains across New York City. Soon, successful black business owners and families who could pay higher rents for a higher standard of living were establishing residences and commercial spaces in Harlem. The migration continued as Afro-American Realty bought more sections of Harlem, whites fled, and a wave of immigrants from the southern United States and the Caribbean arrived, tripling New York's black population. Harlem—no longer a distant community in Manhattan—bustled with activity and a new cosmopolitan culture.

Perhaps Payton's greatest feat was his accumulation of investment capital for his operation. When the

Pennsylvania Railroad bought the property of an African American undertaker, James C. Thomas, at 493 Seventh Avenue for $103,000, Payton induced Thomas to invest much of his profit in Harlem real estate. Over time, Thomas accrued a vast fortune. Payton recruited other investors as well, people who were excited about the rapid growth of Harlem. Afro-American Realty was also boosted by the New York press corps and by the dislocation of residents in other parts of the city. For example, during the construction of Pennsylvania Station in 1906–1910, families and individuals were displaced from the Tenderloin district of Manhattan—historically one of New York's over-crowded nonwhite ghettos—and many of them made their way to Harlem. From 1900 to 1910, T. Thomas Fortune's newspaper, *New York Age*, began to depict Harlem as a vibrant, progressive neighborhood.

Payton had trouble managing his own riches, and he dissolved Afro-American Realty in 1908, but op-portunities for black migrants to Harlem continued after his company ceased operations. A new firm, Nail and Parker, began to buy rows of five-story apart-ments, which it sold to eager newcomers. John Nail and Henry Parker had both been salesmen for Afro-American Realty, and they understood the market. They brokered the move of the black Young Men's Christian Association (YMCA) and Equitable Life Assurance Properties, which included the sophisticated town houses of Striver's Row. Along with the Harlem Property Owners' Improvement Association (founded by John G. Taylor in 1913), these real estate experts continued Payton's legacy of local ownership. The efforts of businesses were matched by those of residents who focused on sustaining their community. To pay landlords, many black tenants took in boarders or gave rent parties on Saturday nights. Many homes were partitioned to create rooming houses; some lodgers even slept in bathtubs. As housing costs stabilized, this dense neighborhood contained the majority of African Americans in New York; in fact, Harlem had the highest concentration of black people anywhere on earth at the time.

The Afro-American Realty Company has not been forgotten by residents or historians of black Harlem. The firm ushered in a new era of direct investment among local renters and buyers and initiated black cultural assimilation in Harlem. Payton firmly believed that the best way for blacks to succeed in New York, and in America, was by establishing economic inde-pendence. According to Cruse (1967), Harlem was founded on the basis of "black economic nationalism by the Afro-American Realty Company." This economic gain created a climate for black expression and black cultural life.

R. JAKE SUDDERTH

See also Harlem: 4—Housing; House-Rent Parties; Locke, Alain; Nail, John E.; New York Age; Payton, Philip A.

Further Reading

Cooper, Wayne F. *Claude McKay: Rebel Sojourner in the Harlem Renaissance*. Baton Rouge: Louisiana State University Press, 1996.

Cruse, Harold. *The Crisis of the Negro Intellectual*. New York: Morrow, 1967.

Draper, Theodore. *The Rediscovery of Black Nationalism*. New York: Viking, 1970.

Huggins, Nathan Irvin. *Harlem Renaissance*. New York: Oxford University Press, 1990.

Johnson, James Weldon. *Black Manhattan*. New York: Da Capo, 1991.

Kiser, Clyde V. *Sea Island to City: A Study of Saint Helena Islanders in Harlem*. New York: Atheneum, 1969.

Lewis, David Levering. *When Harlem Was in Vogue*. New York: Penguin, 1997.

Locke, Alain, ed. *The New Negro: An Interpretation*. New York: Albert and Charles Boni, 1925.

McKay, Claude. *Harlem: Negro Metropolis*. New York: Harcourt Brace Jovanovich, 1968.

Osofsky, Gilbert. *Harlem, the Making of a Ghetto: Negro New York, 1890–1930*. New York: Harper and Row, 1966.

Scheiner, Seth M. *Negro Mecca: A History of the Negro in New York City, 1865–1920*. New York: New York University Press, 1965.

Thurman, Wallace. *The Blacker the Berry*. New York: Simon and Schuster, 1996.

Algonquin Roundtable

The Algonquin Roundtable, an institution of the literary scene in the 1920s, was a group of writers and artists who met for lunch at the Algonquin Hotel in New York. When they first gathered in 1919, all but a few of the critics and columnists who were members of this unofficial club were struggling to establish themselves. Years later, nearly all of them had achieved fame, although amid accusations of back-scratching and logrolling. Scholars often contrast the Algonquin group with other American writers of the period, such as Ernest Hemingway, F. Scott Fitzgerald, and John Dos Passos, who constituted and gained stature as an expatriate "lost generation." The Algonquin Roundtable can also be contrasted with contemporaries who were not expatriates, and particularly—for our purposes—with the writers who personified the Harlem Renaissance. Although some of the individual humorists and essayists in the Roundtable did produce significant work, their famous lunches were characterized by biting, elitist wit, whereas the Harlem Renaissance produced more meaningful and relevant work.

How the Roundtable began is not entirely clear, but according to most accounts, its inception was at a lunch meeting at the Algonquin between John Peter Toohey, a theatrical press agent, and Alexander Woollcott, an influential theater critic and columnist for the *New York Times*. Murdock Pemberton, the press agent who had arranged this meeting, later decided to have a second gathering at the same place. He invited a large group of theater professionals and writers to a party, purportedly in honor of Woollcott's return from World War I, but actually mocking Woollcott's self-indulgent personality. (Pemberton printed a program of speeches related to wartime exploits—all of them to be presented by Woollcott.) Among others, Pemberton invited Franklin P. Adams, a columnist for the New York *Tribune*; Robert Benchley, then an editor at *Vanity Fair*; Heywood Broun, drama critic at the New York *Tribune*; and George S. Kaufman, at the time a drama editor for the *New York Times* and an aspiring playwright.

When Woollcott refused to let Pemberton's joke embarrass him but instead enjoyed the meal and the company, the tradition of dining at the Algonquin began. Later, the group included other writers who were still on their way up, such as Harold Ross, a magazine editor who later founded the *New Yorker*; Dorothy Parker and Robert E. Sherwood, who were beginning their careers as writers for *Vanity Fair*; Maxwell Anderson, a playwright who would later write an antiwar classic, *What Price Glory?*; Ring Lardner, a successful syndicated columnist; and Marc Connelly, a playwright who was Kaufman's collaborator and who struggled as a newspaper writer before achieving success on Broadway.

As Woollcott and his friends began meeting regularly, the group gained considerable fame around New York. Columnists, many of whom were Roundtable regulars, recounted anecdotes and quips from the lunches, boosting the careers of all involved. The owner of the Algonquin Hotel, Frank Case, did not fail to appreciate this free publicity. The group members had at first called themselves "the Board"; they acquired their permanent name when Case replaced the original rectangular dining table with a large round one. Soon afterward, a cartoonist for the *Brooklyn Eagle* drew a caricature of the gathering with the caption "Algonquin Round Table."

Droll wit and sarcasm were criteria for success at the Roundtable; as a result, some visitors attended it only once. Clare Booth Luce found the environment "too competitive," claiming that "you couldn't say 'Pass the salt,' without somebody trying to turn it into a pun or trying to top it." Some other writers of the period saw the Roundtable as elitist and self-enchanted. According to the screenwriter Anita Loos, the members were "self-styled intellectuals . . . concerned with nothing more weighty than the personal items about themselves that were dished up in the gossip columns."

Those outside the circle also said that the members of the Roundtable promoted each other's work, excluding new thinkers and writers. The only figure of the Harlem Renaissance known to have joined the Roundtable was Paul Robeson, and even he was not a regular. For all their presumed conceit and cronyism, however, the members of the Roundtable did sometimes write critically about each other's work. Once, after Adams gave a novel by Broun a negative review, Woollcott supposedly remarked that one could "see Frank's scratches on Heywood's back yet."

Whether or not the Algonquin regulars convened for their own professional advantage, they did like one another's company. On Saturdays, the men—calling themselves the Thanatopsis Literary and Inside Straight Club—would extend the meetings beyond lunch, moving upstairs to a suite to play poker, often until the early hours of Sunday morning. The group members also spent time together in their own homes, at restaurants and speakeasies, and on vacations. In 1922, the Algonquin writers collaborated on a musical revue, *No Sirree!* (mocking a popular Russian revue called *Chauve Souris*), which played for one night to an audience of theater insiders. *No Sirree!* featured Broun as master of ceremonies, Sherwood as a song-and-dance man, and Benchley in a solo sketch that eventually led to a career as a comedian in Hollywood. The following day's newspapers completed the role reversal, allowing the performers to roast their critics in printed reviews.

The Roundtable lunches ended some time in the early 1930s, although few sources mention an exact date or give any particular reason for the demise of the circle. In the years that followed, the group became legendary—so much so that many of the writers who had lunched at the Roundtable tried to play down its cultural impact in an effort to move on with their careers. Eventually, over time, the works of the "lost generation" and the Harlem Renaissance overshadowed even the best literature of the Algonquin group. The myth that persisted, therefore, arguably inflated both the significance of the Roundtable and the legacy of the writers who dined there.

JOSHUA A. KOBRIN

See also Robeson, Paul

Further Reading

Calhoun, Randall. *Dorothy Parker: A Bio-Bibliography*. Westport, Conn.: Greenwood, 1993.

Drennan, Robert E., comp. *The Algonquin Wits*. New York: Citadel, 1968. (Also published as *Wit's End: The Best of the Brilliant Humor of the Celebrated Round Table*. London: Frewin, 1973.)

Gaines, James R. *Wit's End: Days and Nights of the Algonquin Round Table*. New York: Harcourt Brace Jovanovich, 1977.

Harriman, Margaret Case. *The Vicious Circle: The Story of the Algonquin Round Table*. New York: Rinehart, 1951.

Meredith, Scott. *George F. Kaufman and His Friends*. Garden City, N.Y.: Doubleday, 1974.

O'Connor, Richard. *Heywood Broun: A Biography*. New York: Putnam, 1975.

Alhambra Theater

The Alhambra Theater building was constructed in 1905 and (as of this writing) still stands at the intersection of 126th Street and Adam Clayton Powell Boulevard (Seventh Avenue) in Harlem. At first it was a vaudeville house; it became part of the Keith vaudeville circuit, featuring such leading performers as Julian Eltinge and the young Groucho Marx. The managers of the Alhambra clung to segregationist policies as long as they could, confining black audience members to the balcony and failing to book African American acts, long after the two other major theaters, the Lincoln

and the Lafayette, had adapted their policies to accommodate the changing community. On 4 September 1920, *New York Age* reported that the treasurer of the Alhambra had been arrested for refusing to sell orchestra tickets to two black men. By the mid-1920s, however, the Alhambra was catering to African American audiences. A highlight during this period was the Harlem premiere of *Blackbirds of 1926*, a musical revue produced by Lew Leslie to showcase the prodigious talents of Florence Mills. After a six-week engagement at the Alhambra, *Blackbirds* went on to a highly successful six-month European tour. The show that followed it at the Alhambra starred Bill "Bojangles" Robinson. Also in 1926, a ballroom for dances and cabaret performances was added to the theater building, at a reported cost of $100,000; white and black audiences attended on alternate nights. In May 1927, the theater introduced a stock troupe, the Alhambra Players, briefly billed as the All Star Colored Civic Repertory Company. Its inaugural production was *Goat Alley*, by the white playwright E. H. Culbertson; this full-length drama of life in a black slum had opened on Broadway in 1921 and was well received. However, the Alhambra Players were more likely to perform nonracial plays, such as *The Cat and the Canary* or *Rain*.

Despite good reviews and good houses, the Alhambra closed briefly beginning in June 1927 because of a lack of capital. When it reopened in late August of that year under the management of Milton Gusdorf, the theater featured musical reviews and motion pictures until legitimate drama was again incorporated into its programs, in the form of short plays complementing the reviews and films, in 1928. Actors who had appeared with the Lafayette Players, including Evelyn Preer, Charles H. Moore, Edward Thompson, J. Lawrence Criner, Susie Sutton, and Alice Gorgas, appeared as Alhambra Players. The company presented a new thirty-minute production, usually described as light drama based on contemporary themes, each week through 1929 and remained active through 1931, when the Alhambra became exclusively a movie theater.

A casualty of the Depression era, the Alhambra closed in 1932, and its ballroom and theater were never again to be used for those purposes. After standing empty for decades, it was converted into an office building. However, it was used once more for a performance on 22 May 2000, when Ingo Maurer, a German lighting designer, presented a happening and light show for an audience of 600 called *Harlem Lights: A Night at the Alhambra*.

FREDA SCOTT GILES

See also Blackbirds; Lafayette Players; Mills, Florence; New York Age; Preer, Evelyn; Robinson, Bill "Bojangles"

Further Reading

Anderson, Jervis. *This Was Harlem: 1900–1950*. New York: Farrar, Straus and Giroux, 1982.

Johnson, James Weldon. *Black Manhattan*. New York: Atheneum, 1977. (Reprint.)

Kellner, Bruce, ed. *The Harlem Renaissance: A Historical Dictionary for the Era*. Westport, Conn.: Greenwood, 1984.

Mitchell, Loften. *Black Drama: The Story of the American Negro in the Theatre*. New York: Hawthorn, 1967.

Monroe, John Gilbert, "A Record of the Black Theatre in New York City: 1920–1929." Ph.D dissertation, University of Texas–Austin, 1980.

Ali, Duse Mohamed

Duse Mohamed Ali was born in Alexandria, Egypt, to an Egyptian father, Abdul Salem Ali, an army officer who was later killed during an abortive nationalist uprising in 1881–1882; and a Sudanese mother. When he was nine years old, his father sent him to study in England, and eventually he lost his knowledge of Arabic and lost contact with his family. From then on he would live away from his country of birth, traveling widely throughout the African diaspora and residing variously in England, the United States, and Nigeria.

In 1885, at age nineteen, he started a career as a stage actor that would last for twenty-four years. He began in Wilson Barrett's theatrical company, adopting the non-Arabic name Duse; the following year, he left England for tours and performances in the United States and Canada. He quit the company in the United States and worked as a clerk for several years before returning to Britain in 1898 to resume acting.

In 1909 he began a new career in journalism, publishing articles on Egyptian nationalism and the oppression of Africa in *New Age*, an influential socialist weekly literary journal. In 1911 he published a short history of Egypt, *In the Land of the Pharaohs*, reputedly the first history of that country written by an Egyptian. The book received critical acclaim, catapulting him into international prominence.

In July 1912, in London, he founded *African Times and Orient Review*, a political, cultural, and commercial journal that advocated pan-African-Asian nationalism and was a forum for African intellectuals and activists from around the world. The journal covered issues in the United States, the Caribbean, West Africa, South Africa, Egypt, and Asia, including India, China, and Japan. Marcus Garvey, who was then living in London, briefly worked for Duse Mohamed Ali and contributed an article to the journal's issue of October 1913. *African Times and Orient Review* ceased publication in October 1918 and was succeeded by *African and Orient Review*, which operated through most of 1920.

In 1921, Duse Mohamed Ali traveled again to the United States, and thereafter he never returned to Britain. In the United States, he worked briefly in Garvey's Universal Negro Improvement Association movement, contributing articles on African issues to *Negro World* and heading a department on African affairs.

Having come to the United States to promote his vision of economic pan-Africanism, he sought to set up a commercial link between West Africans and African Americans. In the 1920s he repeatedly but unsuccessfully tried to obtain financing to enable West African produce farmers to secure markets and exports to the United States so as to wrest control from major British firms, such as Lever Brothers. In the 1930s he failed to gain European-American capital for the same purpose.

In 1931 he left the United States for West Africa, settling in Lagos. He founded and was the editor of *The Comet*, which in 1933 became Nigeria's largest weekly. In 1934 he serialized his novel *Ere Roosevelt Came,* which touched on his experiences in the United States. From June 1937 to March 1938 he also serialized his autobiography, *Leaves from an Active Life*. He retired from the newspaper's managing directorship in 1943 and died in Lagos two years later.

Biography

Duse Mohamed Ali was born in Alexandria, Egypt, on 21 November 1866. He was sent to England for schooling in 1875 or 1876. His father was killed during a nationalist uprising in 1882. Duse Mohamed Ali pursued an acting career in England (1885–1909) and traveled to and lived in the United States (1886–1898, and later in 1921–1931). He began a career in journalism in London and wrote for *New Age* (1909). He published *In the Land of the Pharaohs* (1911). He founded and edited *African Times and Orient Review* (1912–1918) and *African and Orient Review* (1920), both in London. He worked for Marcus Garvey's United Negro Improvement Association (UNIA) in the early 1920s. He settled in Lagos, Nigeria (1931–1945); there, he founded, edited, and managed *The Comet* (1933– 1943). In *Comet*, he serialized a novel, *Ere Roosevelt Came* (1934); and an autobiography, *Leaves from an Active Life* (1937–1938). He died in Lagos, on 26 February 1945.

AHATI N. N. TOURE

See also Garvey, Marcus; Negro World; Pan-Africanism; Universal Negro Improvement Association

Selected Works

In the Land of the Pharaohs: A Short History of Egypt. 1911. (Reprint, 1968.)
Ere Roosevelt Came. 1934.
Leaves from an Active Life. 1937–1938.

Further Reading

"Biographical Supplement: Duse Mohamed Ali." In *The Marcus Garvey and Universal Negro Improvement Association Papers*, Vol. 1, *1826–August 1919*, ed. Robert A. Hill and Carol A. Rudisell. Berkeley: University of California Press, 1983.

Duffield, Ian. "The Business Activities of Duse Mohamed Ali: An Example of the Economic Dimension of Pan-Africanism." *Journal of the Historical Society of Nigeria*, 4(4), June 1969.

———. "Duse Mohamed Ali and the Development of Pan-Africanism, 1866–1945." Ph.D. dissertation, University of Edinburgh, 1971.

———. "John Eldred Taylor and West African Opposition to Indirect Rule in Nigeria." *African Affairs*, 70(280), July 1971.

———. "Duse Mohamed Ali: His Purpose and His Public." In *The Commonwealth Writer Overseas: Themes of Exile and Expatriation*, ed. Alastair Niven. Brussels: M. Didier, 1976.

———. "Some American Influences on Duse Mohamed Ali." In *Pan-African Biography*, ed. Robert A. Hill. Los Angeles: African Studies Center, University of California–Los Angeles; and Crossroads, African Studies Association, 1987.

Hill, Robert A. "The First England Years and After, 1912–1916." In *Marcus Garvey and the Vision of Africa*, ed. John Henrik Clarke and Amy Jacques Garvey. New York: Random House, 1974.

Mahmud, Khalil. "Introduction to the Second Edition." In Duse Mohamed, *In the Land of the Pharaohs: A Short History of Egypt*, 2nd ed. London: Frank Cass, 1968.

Alston, Charles

Charles H. "Spinky" Alston (1907–1977) was a major figure in the art scene in New York City for fifty years—a trailblazer as a painter, muralist, sculptor, illustrator, and art educator. He had come to Harlem in 1915 when his stepfather, Harry Bearden (Romare Bearden's uncle), moved the family there. In Harlem, Alston's artistic interests were nurtured and blossomed into a professional career that would significantly influence African American art.

After graduating from Columbia University, Alston became the director of the boys' program at Utopia House, which cared for the children of working mothers; one of his students was Jacob Lawrence, who became an important African American artist. Alston was employed next at the Harlem Arts Workshop, run by the African American sculptor Augusta Savage at the 135th Street branch of the New York Public Library; this workshop was later incorporated into the Works Progress Administration (WPA). He was introduced to African art by the philosopher and cultural critic Alain Locke, whom he helped install an exhibition of African sculpture at the Schomburg Collection at the 135th Street Library.

As classes at the workshop in the library became too crowded, because of increasing demands for cultural education in Harlem, Alston found new space for the school and himself in an old stable at 306 141st Street. During the next four years, "306" became an interdisciplinary artistic salon as well as a school for the visual arts. In 1935, Alston, Savage, Elba Lightfoot, and others came together to form the Harlem Artists Guild. Also in 1935, Alston became the first black WPA supervisor. He was assigned to the WPA's Federal Arts Project Commission and was in charge of the murals to be painted at Harlem Hospital. These murals became a source of controversy in 1936, when the white director of the hospital and the city's commissioner of hospitals sought unsuccessfully to block their display. In 1938, Alston obtained a Rosenwald fellowship and began a tour of the South that became the basis of his *Family* series, renderings of the life of southern blacks.

During World War II, Alston worked for the Office of War Information, creating posters and cartoons to mobilize support among blacks for the war effort. In 1950, his career in the fine arts was revitalized when the Metropolitan Museum mounted an exhibition of contemporary art, and his submission, *Painting*, was one of the few works purchased by the museum. Alston soon became an instructor at the Art Students League. His social and racial consciousness led him to join other black artists, such as Hale Woodruff, Norman Lewis, Romare Bearden, and Emma Amos, to form Spiral, an organization concerned about the relationship of black artists to the civil rights movement. Charles Alston died in 1977, leaving behind a legacy as a pioneering artist and educator whose work was quite varied in style, but always expressive and interesting.

Biography

Charles H. Alston was born on 28 November 1907 into a prominent black family in Charlotte, North Carolina. His mother was Anna Elizabeth Miller Alston; his father was Rev. Primus P. Alston, an Episcopalian minister. Primus Alston died of a cerebral hemorrhage in 1910. Three years later, Anna Alston married Harry Pierce Bearden (the uncle of the artist Romare Bearden), who moved the family to New York. In New York, Alston attended DeWitt Clinton High School and Saturday classes at the National Academy of Art. In 1925, he received a scholarship to the Yale University School of Fine Arts but decided to attend Columbia University; there, he was introduced to modern art, including the work of Modigliani. Alston graduated from Columbia in 1929 and received his M.A. from the university's Teachers College in 1931. He worked with Utopia House, the Harlem Arts Project, and the WPA during the 1930s; with the Office of War Information during World War II; and with the Art Students League in the postwar years. He was the recipient of a Julius Rosenwald fellowship and one of the founders of Spiral. Mayor John V. Lindsay appointed him to the New York City Art Commission in 1969. Alston died in 1977.

LARRY A. GREENE

See also Artists; Bearden, Romare; Harlem Hospital; Lawrence, Jacob; Locke, Alain; 135th Street Library; Rosenwald Fellowships; Savage, Augusta; Woodruff, Hale; Works Progress Administration

Further Reading

Bearden, Romare, and Harry Henderson. *A History of African-American Artists: From 1792 to the Present.* New York: Pantheon, 1993.

Coker, Gylbert Garvin. "Charles Alston: The Legacy." In *Charles Alston: Artist and Teacher.* New York: Kenkeleba Gallery, 1990.

Henderson, Harry. "Remembering Charles Alston." In *Charles Alston: Artist and Teacher.* New York: Kenkeleba Gallery, 1990.

Hotton, Julia, ed. *Charles Alston and the "306" Legacy.* New York: Cinque Gallery, 2000.

Linden, Diana L., and Larry Greene. "Charles Alston's Harlem Hospital Murals: Cultural Politics in Depression Era Harlem." *Prospects: An Annual of American Cultural Studies*, 2001.

Amenia Conference, 1916

Arriving at Troutbeck, the setting for the three-day Amenia Conference of August 1916, W. E. B. Du Bois "knew it was mine. It was just a southern extension of my own Berkshire Hills." Troutbeck, in Amenia, New York, was the home of Joel Spingarn, chairman of the National Association for the Advancement of Colored People (NAACP); it was just thirty miles South of Du Bois's hometown, Great Barrington, Massachusetts. Not only were the sylvan surroundings familiar to Du Bois, but he also sensed that this rural estate would inspire the conference, marking the end of one era and the beginning of another.

Although the Amenia Conference was described as an "independent" retreat for the national civil rights leadership held "under the auspices" of the NAACP, the association had a clear investment in sponsoring the meeting. In just its sixth year, the NAACP—and in particular its officers Du Bois and Spingarn—perceived an opportunity to unify civil rights leaders and to fortify its own role in the struggle for freedom for African Americans. Before 1916, unity had been all but unachievable. For more than a decade, meaningful cooperation had been prevented by deep fissures and contention between African American leaders who sympathized with Booker T. Washington's program of accommodation and those who were committed to confronting Jim Crow squarely. Even within the NAACP, unity had involved a struggle. Since its founding in 1909, the association had grown in strength and numbers, yet it continued to experience internal conflict and uncertainty. Although communities from Los Angeles to Boston had responded to the appeal of the NAACP's strategy of protest and had founded local branches, Du Bois acknowledged in 1916 that the association was "a precarious thing without money, with some influential members" yet "never quite sure whether their influence would stay with us if we 'fought' for Negro rights." But when Washington died in late 1915, Du Bois and Spingarn believed the moment had arrived to ensure the NAACP's survival within a more unified civil rights movement.

Spingarn offered to hold the conference at his estate and mailed 200 invitations—an ambitious number—to a wide spectrum of activists, philanthropists, and politicians ranging from the radical Bostonian William Monroe Trotter to Robert Russa Moton, the conservative bearer of Washington's legacy. President Woodrow Wilson and former presidents William Howard Taft and Theodore Roosevelt were among those who replied with regrets, but more than fifty of the invitees arrived in Amenia on 24 August, an unusually cool and misty morning. They included the novelist Charles Chesnutt; Mary White Ovington of the NAACP; John Hope, the president of Atlanta University; Emmett Scott, who had been an associate of Washington's; Kelly Miller, a sociologist at Howard University; and Mary Burnett Talbert, president of the National Association of Colored Women. In a short while, in Du Bois's words, the conferees were having a "rollicking good time." It had taken considerable delicacy to persuade leaders of "all shades" of opinion to convene at all, let along in this unique setting. The NAACP had arranged for Spingarn's guests to camp among several canvas army tents pitched on the lawn at Troutbeck. If this rusticity had at first raised eyebrows, the congenial atmosphere—hikes through the woods, turns on the tennis court, and comedy on the croquet pitch—eventually charmed the delegates and created a cooperative spirit. "Now and again, of course," Du Bois observed, "there was just a little

sense of stiffness and care in conversation when people met who for ten years had been saying hard things about each other; but not a false word was spoken."

What *was* said, however, was meant to remain private—conducing not to secrecy but rather to candid discussion. Over three days, the participants in the Amenia Conference discovered, with little surprise, their common conviction about the principal goals of their work. Although—again, to no one's surprise—disagreement arose over how to reach these goals, no conflict prevented a united statement of purpose. The group expressed a collective belief, summarized in the resolutions of the conference, in the need to support education for African Americans, "every form" of which "should be encouraged and advanced." They also considered it essential to achieve "complete political freedom" and to abandon factionalism.

Looking back on the Amenia Conference a decade later, Du Bois asserted that "on account of our meeting, the Negro race was more united and more ready to meet the problems of the world." His words may suggest hyperbole, but the NAACP had emerged from the meeting of 1916 with renewed vitality. Following the Amenia Conference, the association founded local branches in the South, backed litigation that protected citizenship rights for blacks, and lobbied for federal antilynching legislation. By the mid-1920s the NAACP had become the nation's foremost civil rights organization.

EBEN MILLER

See also Amenia Conference, 1933; Chesnutt, Charles Waddell; Du Bois, W. E. B.; Miller, Kelly; Moton, Robert Russa; Ovington, Mary White; Scott, Emmett Jay; Spingarn, Joel; Talbert, Mary Burnett; Trotter, William Monroe

Further Reading

Du Bois, W. E. B. "The Amenia Conference." Troutbeck Leaflet 8. Amenia, N.Y.: Troutbeck, 1925. (Privately printed. See also Herbert Aptheker, ed. *Pamphlets and Leaflets by W. E. B. Du Bois*. White Plains, N.Y.: Kraus-Thompson, 1986.)

Kellogg, Charles Flint. *NAACP: A History of the National Association for the Advancement of Colored People*. Baltimore, Md.: Johns Hopkins University Press, 1967.

Lewis, David Levering. *W. E. B. Du Bois: Biography of a Race, 1868–1919*. New York: Holt, 1993.

Ross, B. Joyce. *J. E. Spingarn and the Rise of the NAACP, 1911–1939*. New York: Atheneum, 1972.

Amenia Conference, 1933

On Friday, 18 August 1933, Abram Harris, an economist at Howard University, arrived at Troutbeck, Joel Spingarn's estate in Amenia, New York, for the second Amenia Conference, along with W. E. B. Du Bois; Virginia Alexander, a physician in Philadelphia; and Pauline Young of Wilmington, Delaware, who was a librarian and an activist in the National Association for the Advancement of Colored People (NAACP). These four had traveled together in Du Bois's automobile. They were soon joined by more than two dozen fellow delegates and observers of the three-day conference to discuss the past, present, and future of the NAACP within the struggle for civil rights.

The idea of reprising the Amenia Conference had come to Du Bois and Spingarn, who were officers of the NAACP, in 1931. Fifteen years earlier, they had also arranged for a conference of civil rights leaders at Troutbeck, in the southern Berkshires. That meeting had resulted in a newfound unity of purpose, which helped the NAACP to become a powerful nationwide organization. By the early 1930s, however, the association's future appeared uncertain. For several years membership had been dwindling, leaving formerly dynamic branches from Boston to Baltimore nearly moribund. One board member of the NAACP argued in the spring of 1932 that even the appeal of the association as a civil rights organization had diminished significantly. The association was "losing ground with the average man on the street" and was just as clearly failing to "attract and hold the minds of the young people." In the context of the Depression, the NAACP's historic commitment to the legal and political rights of African Americans seemed to fall short—especially in contrast to the radical left, particularly affiliates of the Communist Party such as International Labor Defense and the League of Struggle for Negro Rights, which articulated the need for social progress through economic transformation. The leaders of the NAACP had long debated developing an economic program, and in 1933 the association accepted Spingarn's offer to host a second Amenia Conference devoted to this concern, among others.

Unlike the conference of 1916, the retreat of 1933 was limited by the NAACP to a small group representing the up-and-coming generation of African American leaders. Of the twenty-seven conferees who met in Amenia in August 1933, the youngest (Juanita Jackson, an activist from Baltimore) was twenty, and the oldest (the sociologist E. Franklin Frazier of Fisk University) was thirty-eight. Five of the conferees, including Harris, Emmett Dorsey, the lawyer Charles Houston, the political scientist Ralph Bunche, and the "New Negro" poet Sterling Brown, taught at Howard University. Frances Williams, Marion Cuthbert, Wenonah Bond, and Anna Arnold represented the Young Women's Christian Association (YWCA). Most of the group—like the attorney Louis Redding of Delaware, a graduate of both Brown University and Harvard University's law school—held degrees from prestigious northern universities and conformed to Du Bois's vision of a well-educated and socially responsible elite upper stratum of racial leadership.

Among the remaining delegates, Abram Harris had perhaps looked forward most keenly to the second Amenia Conference. Harris had spent the past decade arguing that the struggle for civil rights would succeed only by fostering a cooperative movement for economic justice between black and white workers. Until the publication of *The Black Worker* in 1931, Harris's analytical work had never earned him the stature of his celebrated contemporaries, who were poets of the Harlem Renaissance. At Amenia in 1933, however, Harris was among the most recognized intellectuals of his generation; during the election of conference officers, he was given the responsibility of formulating the group's Findings Report.

As in 1916, the deliberations of the conference were kept private to allow frank conversation. During morning, afternoon, and evening sessions held among the tents at Troutbeck, the delegates, as well as several older observers from the NAACP, such as Du Bois and Spingarn, vigorously debated the future shape of the struggle for civil rights. Whereas Harris and Emmett Dorsey (his colleague at Howard University) enunciated the power of interracial working-class unity, E. Franklin Frazier stressed the need to take black nationalism seriously. Armed with charts, graphs, and visual aids, Du Bois similarly argued for the necessity of separatism as a means to end segregation. Although the final consensus leaned toward accepting Harris's point of view, it was only after a conversation ranging from New Deal politics to the delegates' personal experiences.

The NAACP leaders had hoped that the conferees at Amenia would offer specific guidance for shaping the association's program, but the problems discussed that weekend proved too vast to address in such terms. Rather, once Abram Harris began to develop the Findings Report, he was purposefully broad—and he unabashedly drew on arguments he had already made in *The Black Worker*. Considered in the black press as the statement of a new generation, the idea that civil rights leaders needed to cooperate with the labor movement went back to the 1920s and even earlier, but it had taken on new significance during the Depression. Harris, in particular, would continue to work with the NAACP to implement an economic program, but the challenge of uniting black and white workers in a broad effort for social change remained unfulfilled over the next generation.

EBEN MILLER

See also Amenia Conference, 1916; Brown, Sterling; Du Bois, W. E. B.; Frazier, E. Franklin; Spingarn, Joel

Further Reading

Holloway, Jonathan Scott. *Confronting the Veil: Abram Harris Jr., E. Franklin Frazier, and Ralph Bunche, 1919–1941*. Chapel Hill: University of North Carolina Press, 2002.

Lewis, David Levering. *W. E. B. Du Bois: The Struggle for Equality and the American Century, 1919–1963*. New York: Holt, 2000.

Ross, B. Joyce. *J. E. Spingarn and the Rise of the NAACP, 1911–1939*. New York: Atheneum, 1972.

Wolters, Raymond. *Negroes and the Great Depression: The Problem of Recovery*. Westport, Conn.: Greenwood, 1970.

Young, James O. *Black Writers of the Thirties*. Baton Rouge: Louisiana State University Press, 1973.

American Mercury

The magazine *American Mercury* (1924–1980) began monthly publication in January 1924 under the editorship of Henry Louis (H. L.) Mencken (1880–1956) and George Jean Nathan (1882–1958). At its peak in 1927, more than 77,000 copies were sold each month. The editorial team and the content went through several major changes, especially after 1933, when Mencken's resignation led to a drastic drop in readership; but the magazine continued to come out each month, in green-covered 128-page issues, until November 1950. In 1952 it was reorganized as a right-wing journal with no resemblance to its founders' original vision; publication stopped in 1980.

American Mercury was founded, as announced in a press release before the appearance of the first issue, to "offer a comprehensive picture, critically presented, of the entire American scene." That scene included a nonconformist spectrum of ideas in diverse fields, including literature, science, politics, economics, and "industrial and social relations." The magazine devoted itself to debunking platitudes, challenging assumptions about authority and propriety, and providing an educated and discerning readership with the best available writing in a variety of genres and on a wide range of topics.

Mencken approached many of the best writers of the day to ask for contributions to the magazine: among the first were Theodore Dreiser, Upton Sinclair, and James Weldon Johnson. Realist writers, whether or not they had achieved popular or critical success, were prominently featured throughout Mencken's editorship. Volume 1, number 1 of the *Mercury* presented four poems by Theodore Dreiser; number 2 included *All God's Chillun Got Wings (A Play)* by Eugene O'Neill and "Caught (A Story)" by Sherwood Anderson. Later issues would include work by Ambrose Bierce, Sinclair Lewis, Carl Sandburg, William Faulkner, and others.

The *Mercury* widely publicized its interest in discovering new writers; it encouraged and accepted submissions by housewives, convicts, panhandlers, and many others whose stories were otherwise unlikely to be told. The magazine was also well known as a showcase for writings about racial tension and featured many contributions by African Americans, including W. E. B. Du Bois, Langston Hughes, James Weldon Johnson, Countee Cullen, George S. Schuyler, and Kelly Miller.

In addition to short stories, poems, plays, and essays, the *Mercury* was read for its regular features. Editorial essays and monthly columns on "The Theatre" and "The Library" provided strongly opinionated recommendations. The popular and much copied column "Americana" featured brief sketches of scenes from city or country life, as well as samples of entertaining sayings heard on the street or reprinted from American newspapers.

American Mercury, especially in its first decade (1924–1933), is credited with challenging and changing expectations of what a magazine could be. By actively seeking contributions from a wide variety of writers, and by providing a hearing for unpopular viewpoints, the *Mercury* served as a forum in which members of the "civilized minority," as Mencken described his varied readership, could explore and debate the social constraints under which they lived.

ROSEMARIE COSTE

See also Anderson, Sherwood; Cullen, Countee; Dreiser, Theodore; Du Bois, W. E. B.; Hughes, Langston; Johnson, James Weldon; Lewis, Sinclair; Mencken, H. L.; Miller, Kelly; Schuyler, George S.

Further Reading

Harrison, S. L. *Mencken Revisited: Author, Editor, and Newspaperman.* Lanham, Md.: University Press of America, 1999.

Scruggs, Charles. *The Sage in Harlem: H. L. Mencken and the Black Writers of the 1920s.* Baltimore, Md.: Johns Hopkins University Press, 1984.

Singleton , M. K. *H. L. Mencken and the American Mercury Adventure.* Durham, N.C.: Duke University Press, 1962.

American Negro Labor Congress

African Americans in the Workers (Communist) Party of America organized the American Negro Labor Congress (ANLC) in Chicago on 25–31 October 1925. Increasing conservatism in the United States after 1920 had brought the collapse of all-black organizations such as the African Blood Brotherhood, and ANLC was intended to fill the gap. Its principal founder was Lovett Fort-Whiteman, an African American Marxist who had studied at Tuskegee and who also initially edited ANLC's journal, *The Negro Champion*. ANLC eschewed black nationalism and separatism; it sought to achieve black liberation by concentrating on the working class and on economic issues. However, this communist emphasis often conflicted with African American sensibilities; for example, ANLC believed that lynching was caused by capitalist exploitation and control and could best be countered in the economic arena.

ANLC wanted to eliminate discrimination in employment, to open segregated unions to black members, and to create all-black unions when necessary; it repeatedly cited the failure of the American Federation of Labor (AFL) to organize black workers. ANLC demonstrated its goals in 1926 through its support for striking black theater projectionists at the white-owned Lafayette Theater in Harlem. Unfortunately, ANLC's agenda, which was extremely unfocused, also included the global elimination of discrimination against all black peoples and the liberation of victims of American and European imperialism overseas. Such sweeping objectives held little appeal to workers, who were more immediately concerned with earning a living; as a result, the membership of ANLC was never very large. William Green, the president of AFL, made ANLC's objectives even harder to attain: He considered ANLC so radical that he threatened member unions with expulsion if they participated in it. Labor activists in Harlem such as A. Philip Randolph, who was launching the Brotherhood of Sleeping Car Porters at the time ANLC met in Chicago, also gave the congress a wide berth.

ANLC made an effort to incorporate black nationalism and racial issues with its communist focus on the class struggle but failed miserably. At the founding convention in Chicago, the emphasis on communism (and Russia) overshadowed African American concerns. For instance, the thirty-two black delegates and one Mexican-American delegate met before a primarily white audience and were entertained by Russian ballet and theater groups, but no black artists. Lovett Fort-Whiteman attended the congress dressed in a *rabochka* (a Russian peasant blouse) and announced that a group of black young people had been selected for revolutionary training in Moscow and would study Marxism and Leninism at the University of the Toilers of the East. Also, in the United States ANLC focused on large eastern cities and industrial centers, failing to represent the masses of southern black workers.

Within one year, in an attempt to focus on issues more important to average African Americans, Richard Moore replaced Fort-Whiteman as the leader of ANLC and as editor of *The Negro Champion*. ANLC moved its headquarters from Chicago to New York in 1928. Although ANLC was nearly moribund after its move to Harlem, the desire for a black labor organization resulted in intermittent calls for its resurrection. In late 1930, ANLC dissolved and was replaced by the League of Struggle for Negro Rights (LSNR). Lovett Fort-Whiteman emigrated to Russia in 1930; he was arrested in 1937, during the Stalinist purges of the Bolshevik leadership, and he died in 1939 in a Soviet gulag, at age forty-four.

JOHN CASHMAN

See also African Blood Brotherhood; Communist Party; Lafayette Theater; Moore, Richard B.; Randolph, A. Philip

Further Reading

Foner, Philip S. *History of the Labor Movement in the United States*, Vol. 10, *The T.U.E.L.: 1925–1929*. New York: International, 1994.

Foner, Philip S., and Herbert Shapiro, eds. *American Communism and Black Americans: A Documentary History, 1930–1934*. Philadelphia, Pa.: Temple University Press, 1991.

Maxwell, William J. *Old Negro, New Left: African-American Writing and Communism between the Wars*. New York: Columbia University Press, 1999.

Naison, Mark. *Communists and Harlem during the Depression*. Urbana, Ill.: University of Chicago Press, 1983.

Solomon, Mark. *The Cry Was Unity: Communists and African Americans, 1917–1936*. Jackson: University Press of Mississippi, 1998.

Wesley, Charles H. "Organized Labor and the Negro." *Journal of Negro Education*, 8, July 1939.

Amos 'n' Andy

The face of entertainment was changed forever by the comedy series *Amos 'n' Andy*, originally called the *Sam 'n' Henry Show*, which was broadcast on radio from 1928 to 1960 and on television from 1951 to 1953. On radio, the white actors Charles Correll (1890–1972) and Freeman Gosden (1899–1982), who wrote and performed the shows, won audiences over with slapstick comedy and buffoonery as two southern black men hoping for success and prosperity in the city of Chicago. Correll and Gosden had begun as "harmony boys" at WGN, the radio station in Chicago where they developed what became *Amos 'n' Andy*. They made their program popular among black and white audiences alike with a combination of music, minstrel comedy, and dramatic dialogue.

Although *Amos 'n' Andy* emerged during the later part of the Harlem Renaissance, this form of entertainment worked against what many artists and scholars were attempting to achieve for blacks. As the radio program continued, black audiences became more perplexed by offensive connotations that mocked the progress of black Americans. Correll and Gosden skillfully imitated black vernacular English to give the characters authenticity and alert audiences to each character's social status—"dialect" indicated a black person, "nondialect" a white person. Also, there were mixed responses to their use of racial stereotypes as central characters. The episodes centered on Amos, who was presented as shiftless and inept; and Andy, who was lazy and pompous. Both characters reflected stereotypical minstrel caricatures that had been popularized during the nineteenth century. Still, the series continued to remain a favorite in American households.

In 1927, Correll and Gosden entered a critical period that led them to examine the future of their radio program. Their popularity had been growing not only because of the program but also because of promotional offerings such as recordings, books, and toys. Correll and Gosden decided that they wanted to distribute the program to other radio stations in order to expand their audience; however, WGN rejected this proposal.

WGN's refusal aroused the interest of WMAQ, the radio station of the *Chicago Daily News*. WMAQ offered Correll and Gosden a contract with distribution rights, which they accepted. They changed the name of the program to *Amos 'n' Andy* when WGN refused to release the original name, *Sam 'n' Henry*. On 19 March 1928, *Amos 'n' Andy* made its debut at WMAQ.

Amos 'n' Andy was similar to *Sam 'n' Henry* in centering on the adventures of two southern black men who come to the North seeking success and fortune. But now the two black men were from Atlanta, were blundering businessmen, and were members of a fraternal order, Mystic Knights of the Sea. Although the new radio series received some harsh criticism for its portrayal of blacks, it continued to be very popular on the east and west coasts, running six days a week, sometimes twice a day to accommodate time differences.

As *Amos 'n' Andy* reached the peak of its fame during the 1930s, the controversy surrounding it intensified. Correll and Gosden's uncensored use and imitation of facets of black culture disturbed black audiences and black comedians, and protesters argued that the program was baneful and demeaning to blacks. In 1931, reportedly, some 750,000 signatures were gathered by the *Pittsburgh Courier* in an effort to have the radio show canceled; this petition alleged that the program inflated misconceptions about black culture and defamed black women. Nevertheless, the program continued to be broadcast and was converted from a daily serial into a weekly half-hour presentation.

The growing popularity of the radio program led to the development of a television series, which began in the summer of 1951 on CBS. The television program was produced by Correll and Gosden, but they did not act in it: There had been an intense search, lasting more than a year, for the most appropriate black actors for the television version. The television program also differed from the radio program in that many of its episodes focused on George "Kingfish" Stevens (played by Tim Moore), the head of the Mystic Knights of the Sea lodge; Stevens typically placed Amos Jones (played by Alvin Childress) and Andy Hogg Brown (played by Spencer Williams) in situations where they—or at least Andy—might be revealed as hapless and artless. The characters in the television version also included Kingfish's wife, Sapphire (played by Ernestine Wade), and his overbearing mother-in-law, "Mama" (played by Amanda Randolph). This pro-

gram was television's first all-black comedy, and the story lines involved the lives of two types of characters: stereotypical and true-to-life. Some of the characters, as on the radio program, were reincarnations of figures in nineteenth-century minstrel shows—the coon, the Uncle Tom, the mammy. Such types, of course, precluded authentic representations of black life and reaffirmed notions of segregation and inequality.

The CBS network received criticism from various civil rights groups, such as the National Association for the Advancement of Colored People (NAACP), which believed that the show promoted racial stereotypes and negative images of blacks. Walter White of the NAACP led a significant protest and filed a lawsuit against the CBS network. This protest, however, deterred sponsors from supporting not only television comedies that exploited blacks but also comedies that featured blacks; thus the efforts of the civil rights group may have been a factor in the failure of CBS to cast any blacks as main characters in dramatic series. (After the cancellation of *Amos 'n' Andy*, no television network cast a black person in a dramatic series until 1965, when Bill Cosby starred in *I Spy*.)

The television series *Amos 'n' Andy* was canceled at the end of its second season in 1953. But during the following decade, *Amos 'n' Andy* appeared occasionally in at least 218 markets across the world, including Australia, Bermuda, Kenya, and western Nigeria; and it continued to thrive afterward through syndication. There is still debate about whether the show was actually racist, because while it did incorporate common stereotypes, it also portrayed blacks in positive, professional roles—for example, as attorneys and entrepreneurs. Eventually, though, as a result of widespread civil rights demonstrations and continued protest against local broadcasts of *Amos 'n' Andy*, CBS removed the show from the television circuit permanently in 1966. Correll and Gosden had meanwhile continued the radio series, with new material, until the program went off the air in 1960.

GENYNE HENRY BOSTON

See also National Association for the Advancement of Colored People; White, Walter

Freeman Gosden and Charles Correll as Amos and Andy.
(Photofest.)

Further Reading

Andrews, Bart, and Ahrgus Julliard. *Holy Mackerel: The Amos 'n' Andy Story*. New York: Dutton, 1986.

Barlow, William, *Voice Over: The Making of Black Radio.* Philadelphia, Pa.: Temple University Press, 1999.

Douglas, Susan J. *Listening In: Radio and the American Imagination.* New York: Random House, 1999.

Ely, Melvin Patrick. *The Adventures of Amos 'n' Andy: A Social History of an American Phenomenon.* New York: Free Press, 1991.

Harmon, Jim. *The Great Radio Heroes*, rev. ed. Jefferson, N.C.: McFarland, 2001.

Leonard, William Torbert. *Masquerade in Black.* London: Scarecrow, 1986.

Amsterdam News

Amsterdam News, the leading African American weekly in New York City since the Harlem Renaissance, was established in 1909 at a site close to Amsterdam Avenue—hence its name. With an expense account of $10, James H. Anderson assembled the paper in his apartment on 65th Street in San Juan Hill, where many African Americans lived before relocating to Harlem. One year later, the paper joined the exodus to Harlem. Between 1910 and 1920, Harlem was evolving into a hub of black America, and the *Amsterdam News* chronicled the change.

That a newspaper begun with such minimal resources managed to survive and thrive suggests the demand in the community for its image in print. The limited funds also indicate the strong odds against the black press. This was a difficult, although heady, time. World War I helped create a distinction between "old" and "new" Negroes, but the soldiers of color who participated in the Allies' victory were rarely allowed to benefit from their efforts. Some soldiers were lynched, and bloody riots erupted in several cities, with hundreds of casualties among African Americans. Decent jobs were scarce. But African Americans transformed themselves in the urban market, and they were ambitious to learn and improve, with the black newspaper as their secular bible. They read it religiously to find out where they were and what they were doing within and outside their own communities, and a single copy often passed from hand to hand.

Much of the newfound excitement of African Americans as they remade themselves in their new environment was expressed artistically. This expression culminated in the Harlem Renaissance, which was largely the work of their hands and pens. In the 1910s and 1920s, T. Thomas Fortune, then a dean of journalists,

wrote regularly for the *Amsterdam News*. In later years, so did John Henrik Clarke, W. E. B. Du Bois, Roy Wilkins, and Adam Clayton Powell Jr. Two women who were pioneers in arts journalism—Nora Holt and Marvel Cooke—contributed to the paper during and after the Harlem Renaissance, as did the novelist Ann Petry.

Sara Warren, whose husband had worked with its founder, bought the *Amsterdam News* in 1926. A decade later, it was in receivership and was sold for several thousand dollars to two physicians. Under the Powell-Savory partnership, younger writers were hired, and coverage became national as well as local. The paper also became one of the first in the country to unionize. In the 1950s and 1960s, the *Amsterdam News* was in the vanguard of civil rights journalism and was quick to recognize Malcolm X, with a column called "God's Angry Man." In 1971, a consortium of businesspeople and politicians, including Clarence Jones, John Procope, and Percy Sutton, bought the paper for $2.3 million. Twelve years later, it was sold to another group of businesspeople, headed by Wilbert Tatum, who practiced hands-on control. In 1997, Tatum retired and turned the reins over to his daughter Eleanor, who then served as publisher and editor-in-chief.

BARBARA BREWSTER LEWIS

See also Black Press; Du Bois, W. E. B.; Fortune, Timothy Thomas; Holt, Nora

Further Reading

Dodson, Howard, Christopher Moore, and Roberta Yancy. *The Black New Yorkers: The Schomburg Illustrated Chronology.* New York: Wiley, 1999.

Freedom's Journals: A History of the Black Press in New York State. New York: Public Library, 1986.

Jordan, William G. *Black Newspapers and America's War for Democracy, 1914–1920.* Chapel Hill: University of North Carolina Press, 2001.

Pride, Armistead S., and Clint C. Wilson II. *A History of the Black Press.* Washington, D.C.: Howard University Press, 1997.

Senna, Carl. *The Black Press and the Struggle for Civil Rights (The African American Experience).* New York: Watts, 1993.

Vincent, Theodore G., ed. *Voices of a Black Nation: Political Journalism in the Harlem Renaissance.* San Francisco, Calif.: Ramparts, 1973.

Wolseley, Roland E. *The Black Press, U.S.A.* Ames: Iowa State University, 1990.

Anderson, Charles W.

Charles W. Anderson was born in Oxford, Ohio; he was educated in public schools, and after brief training at business and language schools, he arrived in New York in the late 1890s. There, he quickly rose to prominence as the recognized leader of state Republican politics; by the time of his death, he was one of the most famous black politicians in the country.

Anderson held a variety of minor posts in New York early in his career—at the customs house, as private secretary to the state treasurer (and later chief clerk of the treasury), and with the state racing commission— all the while building a network of political contacts within Manhattan, mainly through his presidency of the Colored Republican Club. He was thus positioned to receive political appointments near the top of the civil service hierarchy.

The Colored Republican Club had been formed in the early 1900s, primarily to get out the black vote for Theodore Roosevelt, which it succeeded in doing; and when Roosevelt became president in 1905, Anderson was appointed collector of internal revenue for New York's second district (which included Wall Street). He was also a member of the New York State Republican Committee (for a long while, the only African American) for ten terms and a delegate-at-large to three Republican conventions. His influence on the political empowerment of African Americans was so pervasive that at his death in 1938, *New York Age* commented, "You just can't think of Republicanism in New York without remembering Charlie Anderson."

Anderson's forceful rise in Republican politics was largely a result of his friendship with Booker T. Washington, with whom he had aligned himself in the late 1890s. Anderson, like Washington, believed that solutions to the emerging "Negro problem" could be found by doing what could be done, within existing limitations, as soon as possible. This set him at odds with W. E. B. Du Bois and the Negro Democrats, a group that Anderson characterized as people "to whom nothing is desirable but the impossible." Anderson was so faithful to Washington's beliefs that he even planted spies in rival black organizations that he thought might threaten Washington's goals and carefully reported on their activities to his ally.

In character and temperament Anderson was distinctive. Savvy and freewheeling, he had a reputation as a classy dresser and as a master of the endgame in political deal-making. Versatile and apparently of inexhaustible energy, he seemed never to stop working. According to his friend and admirer James Weldon Johnson, Anderson's solution to fatigue was to stop in the nearest hotel bar for a pint of champagne, and then press on. As an astute politician, Anderson was also well read and fond of discussing contemporary culture, drawing widely on his self-taught knowledge of the English poets, the Irish patriots, and the contemporary leaders of the British parliament.

Ill health forced Anderson to retire in 1934, but there can be little doubt that he was one of the most important African American politicians of either party in the nineteenth century and the early twentieth.

Biography

Charles W. Anderson was born on 28 April 1866 in Oxford, Ohio, to Charles W. and Serena Anderson. After attending public school, he received further training at Spencerian Business College, Cleveland; and Berlitz School of Languages, Worcester, Massachusetts. He was private secretary to the state treasurer of New York in 1893–1895; he was appointed collector of internal revenue for the Second District in New York City in 1905 and for the Third District in New York City in 1922. He died in 1938.

JAMES M. HUTCHISSON

See also Du Bois, W. E. B.; Johnson, James Weldon; New York Age; Politics and Politicians

Further Reading

Osofsky, Gilbert. *Harlem: The Making of a Ghetto, Negro New York, 1890–1930.* New York: Harper and Row, 1966.
Meier, August. *Negro Thought in America, 1880–1915: Racial Ideologies in the Age of Booker T. Washington.* Ann Arbor: University of Michigan Press, 1963.

Anderson, Edmund Lincoln

Edmund Lincoln (Eddie) Anderson's career as a comedian and actor stretched from stage roles during the latter days of the Harlem Renaissance to stardom on radio, in films, and on television during the 1950s and 1960s. Anderson was always called Eddie in private, but in public he was often referred to as "Rochester," the name of the character he made famous in radio and television programs and in films with the white comedian and actor Jack Benny.

Anderson's mother, Ella Mae, was a circus tightrope artist; his father, Ed, was a minstrel performer. Although Anderson would later be most famous for his role as Rochester, he had gotten his start on the stage. One of his earliest stage appearances was in the chorus of *Struttin' Along*, an all-black revue, in 1919. He traveled the vaudeville circuit, singing and dancing with his brother Cornelius and another performer as the Three Black Aces in the show *Steppin' High*; their bookings included the Roxy on Broadway and the Apollo and the Cotton Club in Harlem. After *Steppin' High*, Anderson struck out on his own, touring as a solo song-and-dance act and eventually incorporating comedy into his routine.

His big break came when he auditioned for and won the role of a porter in a train sketch for Jack Benny's radio program. The character of the porter and Anderson's performance in the role were hugely popular with the audience, and in 1937 Anderson became a regular on Benny's radio show. His character was now Jack Benny's valet, Rochester, and in this role he stole the show on Benny's radio and television programs as well as in Benny's films. Audiences loved the fun-loving, quick-witted servant who often had the last laugh with regard to Benny's miserly character. One factor contributing to Anderson's success was the comic effect of his raspy voice, a result of damaging his vocal cords while hawking newspapers as a boy. The character of Rochester might seem stereotypical by today's standards, but at the time it was considered a step up from the antics of black characters on the vaudeville and Broadway stage in the 1920s and 1930s. Anderson became so identified with this role on Benny's program that he was sometimes credited only as "Rochester" in his subsequent films and public appearances, and he achieved such success as Rochester that for several years during the 1940s he was the highest-paid black actor in Hollywood.

In addition to radio and television, Anderson appeared in more than fifty films. His first film was *What Price Hollywood?* (1932); he also played Noah in *The Green Pastures* (1936). His biggest starring role was Little Joe Jackson in the critically acclaimed *Cabin in the Sky* (1943), a film that also featured other veterans

Eddie "Rochester" Anderson in a photo from Paramount Pictures, 1940. (Photofest.)

of vaudeville and Broadway, including Ethel Waters and Lena Horne. Anderson continued to appear with Jack Benny on radio and television and in films until 1965.

Biography

Edmund Lincoln Anderson was born in Oakland, California, on 18 September 1905. He studied at public schools in Oakland, San Francisco, and San Mateo, California. His work as an actor included Jack Benny's radio and television series, 1937–1965; *The Green Pastures*, 1936; *Jezebel*, 1938; *You Can't Take It with You*, 1938; *Gone with the Wind*, 1939; *Cabin in the Sky*, 1943; *Brewster's Millions*, 1945; and *It's a Mad Mad Mad Mad World*, 1963. He was a member of the Screen Actors' Guild, Actors Guild of Variety Artists, and Motion Picture Academy of Arts and Sciences. Anderson was married first to Mamie Sophie Wiggins, who died in 1954, and then, in 1956, to Eva Simon, with whom he had three children. His second marriage ended in divorce. Anderson died of a heart ailment at the Motion

Picture Country House and Hospital in Los Angeles, California, on 28 February 1977.

HEATHER MARTIN

See also Film; Film: Actors; Waters, Ethel

Further Reading

"Anderson, Eddie [Edmund Lincoln]." In *The National Cyclopedia of American Biography*. Clifton, N.J., 1981.

Bogle, Donald. *Toms, Coons, Mulattoes, Mammies, and Bucks: An Interpretive History of Blacks in American Films*. New York: Continuum, 1973. (New expanded ed., 1989.)

———. *Primetime Blues: African Americans on Network Television*. New York: Farrar, Straus and Giroux, 2001.

Douglas, George H. "Anderson, Eddie." In *American National Biography*, ed. John A. Garraty and Mark C. Carnes. New York: Oxford University Press, 1999.

Sampson, Henry T. *Blacks in Blackface: A Source Book on Early Black Musical Shows*. Metuchen, N.J.: Scarecrow, 1980.

Thomas, Robert McG., Jr. "Eddie Anderson, 71, Benny's Rochester." *New York Times*, 1 March 1977.

Anderson, Garland

The playwright Garland Anderson (1886–1939) was a former shoe shiner, singer, dancer, and bellhop (he was called the "San Francisco bellhop playwright"), a philosopher advocating constructive thinking, and a minister and lecturer. He was the first African American to have a serious full-length play produced on Broadway, *Appearances* (1924), which opened doors for other African American dramatists. This work is an autobiographical "courtroom melodrama in which a morally upright bellhop"—Anderson himself—"is tried and exonerated of the charge of raping a white woman" (Peterson 1990, 1997).

Anderson achieved success against considerable odds. At a young age, he ran away from home after his mother died. He set up a shoeshine stand and sang and danced for money. The hoboes he met taught him how to cadge meals, find a place to sleep, and "steam a ride on a moving train." Passengers on trains hid him beneath their seats; black hotel workers gave him food, money, and a bed. He educated himself by reading the Bible and studying books on Christian

Science, psychology, metaphysics, practical psychology, and constructive thinking.

Anderson's philosophy of constructive thinking was criticized as reflecting an "Uncle Tom" mentality. *Appearances* drew the same criticism; Anderson was accused of selling out in order to appeal to white audiences. As a bellhop at the Braetum Hotel in San Francisco, he had impressed the guests with his optimism: He believed that all things were possible through faith and that he was called to serve mankind. After seeing Channing Pollock's moralistic drama *The Fool*, Anderson decided to write a play to convey his own philosophy, although he had no training in playwriting or stage technique. He completed it in only three weeks but then spent seven months finding a producer; during this time, Al Jolson paid Anderson's expenses in New York and helped him seek financing for the play. Anderson gave public readings of his play (inviting the governor of New York to one of them); he also went to Washington, D.C., to get support from President Calvin Coolidge.

Appearances opened at the Frolic Theater on Broadway on 13 October 1925. In 1925, the policy on Broadway was to avoid mixed casts by having white actors play "colored" roles in blackface. (In 1924, the press had demanded that an off-Broadway production, *All God's Chillun Got Wings*, be banned because Paul Robeson kissed the hand of the white actress.) However, *Appearances* succeeded with a cast of fourteen white and three "colored" performers and a Negro as the principal character. In 1927–1929, the play toured Los Angeles, Seattle, Chicago, and San Francisco. On 1 April 1929, it opened again in New York City, at the Hudson Theater. In March 1930, it opened at the Royalty Theater in London, where Anderson would become a celebrity.

Anderson also became famous as a minister of constructive thinking and a lecturer to white audiences in the tradition of Booker T. Washington. His message that hard work could overcome social obstacles was well received in America and elsewhere. He and his wife, Doris, a white Englishwoman, had met when she went to a lecture of his at the International New Thought Alliance on Oxford Street in London, where he spoke twice a week. At one of Anderson's Mayfair Tea Talks, "Dick" Sheppard (then the canon of Saint Paul's and royal chaplain) was the guest of honor. In London, Anderson lived in Lowndes Square, an exclusive neighborhood; became a member of the Poets' Club; and had his portrait painted by A. Christie. He left London for America in 1935 and published a book on his philosophy, *Uncommon Sense*, in 1937. An excerpt from it suggests why African Americans rejected his teachings:

> The white race is the superior race of this age. In making this statement I do not feel that it is a reflection on my own race. The white race has centuries of civilization behind it, while the Negro race has less than a hundred years since its slavery in America in which it can lay claim to any civilized status.

Another passage, however, suggests Anderson's sense of serving humanity:

> Service to me is the rent I pay for the space I occupy on earth. . . . I realized that if I succeeded, in spite of apparently unsurmountable obstacles, in writing a play, . . . the production of that play would prove to my audience, that they would be able to do the thing they wanted to do.

Biography

Garland Anderson was born c. 1886 in Wichita, Kansas. He completed only four years of schooling there before his family moved to Sacramento, California; he was mainly self-educated. He worked as a bellhop in the Braeburn Hotel in 1907–1924 and began writing *Appearances* in 1924. He also wrote three other plays; the only one whose title is still known is *Extortion* (it was not produced). He was ordained by Rev. Netta Holmes of the Church of Constructive Thinking in Seattle, becoming the first African American ordained in a white church to minister to a white congregation. He served as a minister at the Truth Center in 1929–1939. He visited Honolulu, speaking to Japanese, Chinese, Korean, and Hawaiian Christian churches. Anderson opened a "colored" café in San Francisco and eventually bought the Braeburn Hotel, although he later sold it back to his boss. Anderson died in New York Hospital of heart disease in 1939.

FELECIA PIGGOTT MCMILLAN

See also Appearances

Selected Works

Appearances. In *Black Theater U.S.A.: Forty-Five Plays by Black Americans 1847–1974*, ed. James V. Hatch. 1974.

"How I Became a Playwright." In *International Library of Negro Life and History Anthology of the American Negro in the Theatre: A Critical Approach*, ed. Lindsay Patterson. 1967.
Uncommon Sense. 1933.

Further Reading

Abdul, Raoul. "The Negro Playwright on Broadway." In *International Library of Negro Life and History Anthology of the American Negro in the Theatre—A Critical Approach*, ed. Lindsay Patterson, 1967.
Abramson, Doris E. *Negro Playwrights in the American Theatre, 1925–1959*, 1969.
Anderson, Doris. *Nigger Lover*, 1938.
The Harlem Renaissance: A Historical Dictionary for the Era, ed. Bruce Kellner, 1984.
Hicklin, Fannie Ella Frazier. *The American Negro Playwright, 1920–1964*, 1965.
Howard, Stephanie M. "Garland Anderson and His Appearances." Master's thesis, Winston Salem, N.C., Wake Forest University, 1995.
Johnson, James Weldon. *Black Manhattan*, 1968.
Lewis, David Levering. *When Harlem Was in Vogue*, 1981.
Locke, Alain. "The Negro and the American Stage." In *International Library of Afro-American Life and History Anthology of the American Negro in the Theatre*, ed. Lindsay Patterson, 1987.
Mitchell, Loften. *Black Drama: The Story of the American Negro in the Theatre*, 1967.
Peterson, Bernard L. Jr. *Early Black American Playwrights and Dramatic Writers: A Biographical Directory and Catalog of Plays, Films, and Broadcasting Scripts*, 1990.
———. "Drama." In *The Oxford Companion to African American Literature*, eds. William L. Andrews, Frances Smith Foster, and Trudier Harris, 1997.
Potter, Joan, and Constance Claytor. "Garland Anderson." In *African Americans Who Were First*, 1997.
Sanders, Leslie Catherine. *The Development of Black Theatre in America: From Shadows to Selves*, 1988.

Anderson, Marian

The career of the contralto Marian Anderson concided during its early years with the period of the Harlem Renaissance and continued long afterward, until 1965, when she retired from the concert stage with a final performance at Carnegie Hall.

In 1923, Anderson won a competition for soloists held by the Philadelphia Philharmonic Society. In 1925, as a result of winning a competition at Aeolian Hall in New York City, she appeared at Lewisohn Stadium with the New York Philharmonic. In 1930 and 1933, she received fellowships from the Julius Rosenwald Fund. In 1933–1935, she undertook a concert tour of Europe that established her career. After her performance at at the Salzburg Festival in June 1935, the conductor Arturo Toscanini told her, "Yours is a voice such as one hears once in a hundred years." Anderson had already been well received by African Americans, but her successes abroad gave her an entrée into mainstream American concert halls, theaters, and university auditoriums.

Anderson grew up in an environment filled with music—at home, at church, at school, and in the community. She was born into a happy, close-knit "black bourgeois" family in Philadelphia and showed a natural talent for singing at a tender age, although her parents—who had little money—did not seek professional instruction for her. When she was eight years old, her father, John Anderson, bought a piano. She at first took little interest in it, but one day, as she strolled along a street, she heard a piano being played eloquently by a "dark woman" and became inspired to study the instrument. There was no money for lessons, so she used a note chart propped above the keys. She also bought a violin in a pawnshop for $3.98 and struggled with it, helped by musical acquaintances who tuned it for her until the strings wore out. Anderson, who was in some ways self-taught, played the piano and the violin by ear and matched her voice to the tones. At about this time, an aunt who was arranging a concert to raise funds for a ministry included Anderson on the program. Anderson knew nothing of the plan until she found a flier on the street with her photograph and name: "Come and hear the baby contralto, ten years old." Actually, she was still only eight, but she was tall and looked older (later, she would join her church's adult choir at age thirteen, while still keeping her membership in the junior choir, which she had joined at age six). When Anderson was ten, her father died, and she and her mother and sisters went to live with his parents, who owned an organ that she played while singing spirituals.

John Anderson had been a supervisor of ushers at Union Baptist Church, and the child Marian was introduced to choir music there. She gave her first public performances in church at about age eight: a duet with her neighbor Viola Johnson, who sang the upper part while Anderson sang the lower part, the range that would become her comfort zone; and a duet with her father's sister as the soprano and herself as the alto. Anderson soon joined a girls' church quartet. These early performances led to solo pieces, as Anderson filled in for absent soloists in the senior choir. Soon she was representing Union Baptist Church at various events as a soloist or in ensembles. One such event was at the Abyssinian Baptist Church in Harlem. When Anderson was a teenager, the tenor Roland Hayes gave a fund-raising concert for Union Baptist, and she was permitted to appear on the program. Hearing Hayes sing French songs, German lieder, and Italian airs inspired her to take up classical song. (Anderson later said that Hayes was one of three musicians who most decisively influenced her style; the others were Sigrid Onegin and Ernestine Schumann-Heink.) Hayes recommended his own vocal instructor, Arthur J. Hubbard, in Boston, but Anderson's grandmother would not allow her to travel there, so Anderson approached a music school in Philadelphia, where she was snubbed.

At William Penn High School, where she studied typing and shorthand in preparation for the civil service, Anderson sang in the school choir, often performing brief solos. After she sang at a school assembly, the principal was persuaded to transfer her to South Philadelphia High School, which had a college preparatory track that might lead to a music scholarship.

Anderson belonged to the Camp Fire Girls and performed in their chorus. She gave amateur performances—sometimes for a stipend of a dollar or two—at Baptist, Episcopal, and Methodist churches; the Young Men's Christian Association (YMCA); and the Young Women's Christian Association (YWCA). When she realized that people would pay to hear her sing, she began to charge at least five dollars a performance. Anderson also joined the Philadelphia Choral Society, a professional group. Her name became known in and around Philadelphia, and she began to give frequent concerts in nearby towns. Roland Hayes helped by recommending her to churches and colleges.

Anderson's studies with her first vocal teacher, Mary Saunders Patterson (who charged no fee), culminated in a performance in an operetta that Patterson presented for promising students. Anderson next studied with the contralto Agnes Reifsnyder; then, the musician Lisa Roma—who had heard Anderson sing at William Penn and had recommended her transfer to South Philadelphia High—arranged an audition with the tenor Giuseppe Boghetti. When Anderson became Boghetti's student, Roland Hayes performed in a concert that raised $600 to pay the fees. She then studied with Frank La Forge, on a scholarship, for more than a year.

After graduating from high school, Anderson decided to make a career of singing. William ("Billy") King became her accompanist and later her manager. On tour, she met R. Nathaniel Dett, choir director at the Hampton Institute, who took an interest in her career. After a performance at Howard University, Anderson felt confident enough to have a promoter book her at New York City's Town Hall, but her appearance at Town Hall was poorly attended and received unfavorable reviews, and she went home to ponder her next step. Encouraged by her family, she signed on with Arthur Judson's prestigious management firm. Her fees rose, and she appeared at the Academy of Music in Philadelphia and at Carnegie Hall as a soloist with the Hall Johnson Choir; but her career remained stagnant, and she felt that she could establish herself only in Europe.

Anderson's first trip abroad was in 1930: She went to England for about a year. There, she stayed in the homes of the expatriate African American actor John Payne and the painter Vicky Newburg; met, among others, Amanda Ira Aldrich (the daughter of the actor Ira Aldrich); studied German at the Hugh Institute; and performed at Wigmore Hall and the Promenade Concerts directed by Sir Henry Wood. However, her performances were more as a student than as an accomplished artist, and she did not achieve greater recognition from booking agencies in the United States after her return.

In 1933, Anderson returned to Europe for two years. She went first to Germany to perfect her performance of lieder, and after studying with Michael Raucheisen and Sverre Jordan, she financed her own appearance at the Bachsaal in Berlin. She received mostly favorable reviews, but this was the beginning of the Nazi era, and she would not perform again in Germany until 1950. During this trip she also sang in many other cities: Salzburg, Vienna, Brussels, Copenhagen, London, Helsinki, Paris, Tiflis, Leningrad (Saint Petersburg), Moscow, Kharkov, Kiev, and Odessa.

When Anderson returned to the United States, her new manager was the famous Sol Hurok, who wanted to broaden her audiences beyond African Americans. His ambition led to a legendary episode. In 1939,

Hurok tried to arrange for a concert in Washington, D.C., at Constitution Hall, which was controlled by the Daughters of the American Revolution (DAR). The DAR said that it had "no available dates" and, furthermore, that its policy was "concerts by white artists only." This rejection aroused widespread anger from many individuals and organizations that were working to end racism, and the injustice to Anderson became a cause célèbre even in the White House—the first lady, Eleanor Roosevelt, resigned from the DAR in protest. Harold Ickes, secretary of the interior, then invited Anderson to sing to the people of America in a public concert at the Lincoln Memorial on Easter Sunday, 9 April 1939. On the platform with Anderson were senators, representatives, cabinet members, a Supreme Court justice, Walter White of the NAACP, and representatives from Howard University and African American churches; the diverse audience numbered 75,000, and the concert was broadcast on radio to millions more. (Eventually, the DAR amended its policy, and Anderson appeared at Constitution Hall in 1943.)

Anderson's star rose after the Easter Sunday concert. The general manager of the Metropolitan Opera, Rudolf Bing, approached her about performing in an opera. She accepted, although with some trepidation, and studied with Max Rudolf, the artistic administrator, who prepared her to audition with Dimitri Mitropoulos, the conductor of the opera orchestra. Anderson's opera debut on 7 January 1955, at age fifty-seven, was a milestone: She was the first African American opera singer to appear onstage at the Metropolitan.

In addition to her contributions to classical music (in which she was especially renowned for her interpretations of Bach, Brahms, Handel, Schubert, Schumann, Strauss, Rachmaninoff, and Wolf), Anderson presented classical renditions of African American spirituals—the socioreligious folk songs of an enslaved people, which W. E. B. Du Bois called "sorrow songs." She brought this art form, cherished by African Americans, to international audiences in places where spirituals might otherwise not have been heard. Her performances of "Crucifixion," "Deep River," "Go Down, Moses," "He's Got the Whole World in His Hands," "My Lord, What a Morning," "Oh, What a Beautiful City," and "Were You There?"—mostly in arrangements by Harry Thacker Burleigh—are memorable for her interpretation of dialect and her embellishment, phrasing, rhythm, and tempo, which remained true to the nature of the spiritual. Anderson, who

Marian Anderson, 1940. (Library of Congress.)

Temple University and several colleges. Anderson was married in 1943 to the artist and architect Orpheus H. "King" Fisher. She died in Portland, Oregon, on 8 April 1993.

GERRI BATES

See also Burleigh, Harry Thacker; Dett, Robert Nathaniel; Hayes, Roland; Johnson, Hall; King, Billy; Music; Rosenwald Fellowships; White, Walter

Further Reading

Anderson, Marian. *My Lord, What a Morning: An Autobiography*. New York: Viking, 1956.

Ferris, Jeri. *What I Had Was Singing: The Story of Marian Anderson*. Minneapolis, Minn.: Lerner, 1994.

"Grounded in Faith, Free to Fly." *New York Times*, 18 April 1993.

Keiler, Allan. *Marian Anderson: A Singer's Journey*. New York: Scribner, 2000.

Livingston, Myra C. *Keep on Singing: A Ballad of Marian Anderson*. New York: Holiday House, 1994.

always sang with her eyes closed, opened the eyes of the international community to the value of this music.

Biography

Marian Anderson was born in Philadelphia, Pennsylvania, on 17 February 1897. She studied voice with Mary Saunders Patterson, Agnes Reifsnyder, Giuseppe Boghetti, Frank La Forge, Raimund von zur Mühlen, Mark Raphael, Amanda Ira Aldrich, Michael Raucheisen, Sverre Jordan, Madame Charles Cahier, and Steffi Rupp. Her many awards included the Spingarn Medal from the NAACP in 1930. She sang the national anthem at the inauguration of President Dwight D. Eisenhower in 1953; made her debut at the Metropolitan Opera in New York City in 1955, as Ulrica in Verdi's *Un Ballo in Maschera*; was the United States' goodwill ambassador to Asia in 1957; was appointed by President Eisenhower as an alternate delegate to the American delegation to the United Nations in June 1958; sang at another presidential inauguration—John F. Kennedy's—in 1961; and sang at the Lincoln Memorial as part of the March on Washington in 1963. She received honorary degrees from

Anderson, Regina M.

Regina M. Anderson Andrews was instrumental in the development of the Harlem Renaissance because of her vision of community cultural awareness and her ability to inconspicuously implement the ideas of others.

Anderson shared an apartment with Ethel Ray Nance and Louella Tucker in Sugar Hill, at 580 Saint Nicholas Avenue, which became known as the Harlem West Side Literary Salon or simply "580." Andrews began promoting the arts by opening the apartment to community gatherings and cultural activities. She helped organize the famous Civic Club dinner of 1924, which evolved from an event at "580" and was attended by 110 guests, including W. E. B. Du Bois and Langston Hughes. Readings at the dinner inspired Alain Locke, who edited the anthology *The New Negro* in 1925; this collection of rising African American writers is sometimes considered to mark the birth date of the Harlem Renaissance and to be its definitive work. Gatherings and events at "580"—and a similar salon in Harlem's East End, that of Dorothy Peterson and her brother Jerome Bowers Peterson—were reflected in Carl Van Vechten's fifth novel, *Nigger Heaven* (1926).

Anderson, a librarian, worked at several branches of the New York Public Library, notably as an assistant to Ernestine Rose at the 135th Street branch (renamed the Schomburg Center for Research in Black Culture). She felt that her career as a librarian was an opportunity to educate the community about its artists and the scope of its arts, and in that capacity she instituted a series of cultural events within the library system. These included Family Night, which was a setting for activities such as art exhibits and lectures (one of the guest speakers was Marcus Garvey). The cultural initiative also provided homes in the basement of the 135th Street Library for the Crigwa Theater (which moved to the parish house of Saint Philip's Protestant Episcopal Church in 1931), the Harlem Suitcase Theater, and the Harlem Experimental Theater.

Anderson was a significant figure in theater in several ways. She helped Du Bois with the work of the Crigwa Theater (founded 1924–1925), later known as the Krigwa Theater or Krigwa Players. (Its original name was an acronym for Crisis Guild of Writers and Artists, after the official publication of the NAACP, *Crisis Magazine*.) When the Krigwa Players disbanded, Anderson and Dorothy Peterson founded the Negro Experimental Theater in 1929, on the same principle—as theater by, for, about, and near blacks. Their first production, in June 1929, was Georgia Douglas Johnson's *Plumes*. This group was later called the Harlem Experimental Theater, and Anderson served as its second executive director. She was also a playwright: The Harlem Experimental Theater produced her one-act dramas *Climbing Jacob's Ladder* (written under the pseudonym Ursula Trelling) and *Underground* (also pseudonymous) in 1931 and 1932, respectively. *Climbing Jacob's Ladder* was about a lynching coinciding with a church service and was profoundly influenced by the activist Ida B. Wells. The Harlem Experimental Theater was a factor in the decision of the Federal Theater to come to New York.

Biography

Regina M. Anderson Andrews was born on 21 May 1901, in Chicago, Illinois. Her parents were William Grant Anderson (an attorney in New York) and Margaret Simons Anderson. She was educated at Normal Training School, Hyde Park High School, Wilberforce University in Ohio, the University of Chicago, and City College of New York; she received a master of library science (M.L.S.) degree from Columbia University Library

School. She married William T. Andrews (an attorney and assemblyman) in 1926; they had a daughter, also named Regina. In 1936, Anderson was the first African American to be appointed acting supervising librarian, at the 135th Street branch of the New York Public Library. She was recognized for her contributions at the World's Fair of 1939 in New York. In 1947, she became the supervising librarian at the Washington Heights branch of the New York Public Library. She retired from the New York Public Library system in 1967. Anderson wrote a two-volume work (unpublished) about black New Yorkers, originally intended for "Harlem on My Mind," an exhibition at the Metropolitan Museum of Art in 1968; and coedited *Chronology of African Americans in New York, 1621–1966* with Ethel Ray Nance. Anderson served as the second vice president of the National Council of Women, represented the National Urban League with the United States Commission for UNESCO, and worked with the State Commission for Human Rights. She was a recipient of the Musical Arts Group award, Community Heroine award, and Asia Foundation award. At the time of this writing, she was apparently still living, in upstate New York.

JULYA MIRRO

See also Barnett, Ida B. Wells; Civic Club Dinner, 1924; 580 Saint Nicholas Avenue; Johnson, Georgia Douglas; Krigwa Players; Nance, Ethel Ray; Negro Experimental Theater; Nigger Heaven; 135th Street Library; Peterson, Dorothy Randolph; Saint Philip's Protestant Episcopal Church; Salons; Van Vechten, Carl

Further Reading

Anderson, Jervis. *This Was Harlem: A Cultural Portrait, 1900–1950*. New York: Noonday, 1983.

Andrews, Regina M. Anderson. Oral History Videotape, Personal Documents, Professional Work. Schomburg Center for Research in Black Culture, New York.

Huggins, Nathan Irvin. *Harlem Renaissance*. Oxford: Oxford University Press, 1973.

Lewis, David Levering. *When Harlem Was in Vogue*. New York: Penguin, 1997.

Mitchell, Lofton. *Black Drama: The Story of the American Negro in the Theatre*. New York: Hawthorn, 1967.

———. *Voices of the Black Theatre*. Clifton, N.J.: White, 1975.

Perkins, Kathy A. *Black Female Playwrights: An Anthology of Plays Before 1950*. Bloomington: Indiana University Press, 1991.

Roses, Lorraine E., and Ruth E. Randolph. "Regina M. Anderson [Ursala Trelling]." In *Harlem Renaissance and Beyond: Literary Biographies of 100 Black Women Writers, 1900–1945*. Cambridge, Mass.: Harvard University Press, 1997.

Anderson, Sherwood

Sherwood Anderson had an important role in the development of modern writing in the United States. His immense influence was based largely on a myth that developed around his life, on his extraordinary fourth book, *Winesburg, Ohio* (1919), and on several enduring short stories. At a time when the short story was a generally moribund form, Anderson revolutionized it by rejecting what he called the "poisoned plot"—the artificially pat narrative used by O. Henry—and turning it into a vehicle for a serious examination of American realities. Anderson was a tutor and mentor to Ernest Hemingway and William Faulkner, and he influenced the vision and style of such diverse writers as Jean Toomer, Thomas Wolfe, John Steinbeck, William Saroyan, and Henry Miller.

Two towns where Anderson's family lived—Camden and Clyde, Ohio—figured large in Anderson's imagination, providing him with themes and characters for his many novels and poems. Camden gave him images (largely invented) of preindustrial America: attractively human in its relations and proportions, a utopia that would be ravaged by capitalism. Clyde gave him a wealth of complex American characters who balanced repression and meanness with generosity and untrammeled imagination. Almost all of Anderson's writing was woven from this material.

Anderson, who became the president of a manufacturing company, was never happy with the moral and ethical compromises he had to make as a businessman; and on 28 November 28, 1912, the pressures of his life intensified. He walked out of his office in the middle of the morning and did not turn up until four days later, when he wandered into a drugstore in Cleveland, not knowing where he was. This episode became a legend in American literary history, a moment when an important writer turned his back on American materialism and worldly success and took up a quest for creative accomplishment.

Anderson eventually left his first wife and their children and started a new life in Chicago as a writer. What became known as the Chicago renaissance was then in full swing, and Anderson found himself in the company of important writers and publishers, who welcomed and encouraged him. Anderson immersed himself in the tumult of ideas circulating in bohemian Chicago, including current notions of socialism and psychoanalysis, as well as the writings of Gertrude Stein, who became a close friend, and James Joyce.

Anderson had already written three novels when his first story, "The Rabbit-Pen," was accepted for publication by *Harper's* in 1913. He published *Windy MacPherson's Son* in 1916 and *Marching Men* in 1917. He was forty-three years old in 1919 when his masterpiece, *Winesburg, Ohio*, was published by B. W. Huebsch and became an immediate critical success. In this work, Anderson pioneered a new form, the unified short-story collection, that later in the century represented a significant alternative to the traditional novel. The language of *Winesburg, Ohio*—inspired, according to Anderson, by Stein's *Tender Buttons*—is spare and direct; and the narrative is honest, provocative, and indefinite: Anderson represents with stark simplicity and power the alienation that pervaded life in small-town America when industrialization began. This work strongly influenced a generation of younger writers that included Hemingway (whom Anderson introduced to Stein and Faulkner, and whose first novel Anderson got published) and Toomer, among many others.

Over the next several years, Anderson, at the height of his powers and his reputation, published in quick succession *Poor White* (1920), the story collections *The Triumph of the Egg* (1921) and *Horses and Men* (1923), *Many Marriages* (1923), the autobiographical *A Story Teller's Story* (1924), and *Dark Laughter* (1925).

With *Dark Laughter*, Anderson joined a few writers who were trying to cross the deeply entrenched color line in American culture, by drawing on and recounting the experience of African Americans. Given the political climate of the United States in the 1920s, his attempt was definitely progressive. However, it was hobbled because his treatment of African Americans never went beyond the symbolic. African Americans came to stand for all the vital impulses of the body that Anderson felt were stifled and repressed by American Protestantism. (In this regard his work was not unlike Ishmael Reed's representation of Jes' Grew and The Wallflower Order some fifty years later in *Mumbo Jumbo*, but without Reed's humor.) Ernest Hemingway parodied *Dark Laughter* in his own *Torrents of Spring* (1926), and Toni Morrison subjected both books to critical scrutiny in her essay "Whiteness and the Literary Imagination."

Sherwood Anderson, photographed by Carl Van Vechten in 1933.
(Library of Congress.)

During his remaining years Anderson published some twenty books, but none of them matched the creative accomplishment of his earlier works.

Biography

Sherwood Anderson was born in Camden, Ohio, on 3 September 1876. His family moved to Clyde, Ohio, in 1883 after living briefly in Mansfield and Caledonia. Anderson's father, a harness maker, was never very well off. When his mother died in 1893, Anderson moved to Chicago and worked as an unskilled laborer. After serving in the Spanish-American War, he went back to school for a year, then got a job writing advertising copy in Chicago. In 1904 he married Cornelia Lane, the daughter of a successful businessman. After working his way up in several manufacturing companies, in 1906 he took over and became president of Anderson Manufacturing, later renamed American Merchants Company, in Elyria, Ohio. In 1916 he and his first wife (with whom he had three children) were divorced. He then married Tennessee Mitchell; in 1924

that marriage also ended in divorce—as did his third marriage, to Elizabeth Pral, in 1932. Anderson then traveled from Chicago to New York to Reno to New Orleans and eventually settled in Virginia. In 1933, he married Eleanor Copenhaver. In 1941, on a trip with his wife to South America, he died of peritonitis in Panama.

MICHAEL BOUGHN

See also Dark Laughter; Toomer, Jean

Further Reading

Anderson, David D. *Sherwood Anderson: An Introduction and Interpretation.* New York: Holt, Rinehart and Winston, 1967.

Crowley, John W. *New Essays on Winesburg, Ohio.* New York: Cambridge University Press, 1990.

Dickerson, Mary Jane. "Sherwood Anderson and Jean Toomer: A Literary Relationship." *Studies in American Fiction,* 1, Autumn 1974, pp. 163–175.

Faulkner, William. "Sherwood Anderson: An Appreciation," *Atlantic Monthly,* 191, June 1953, pp. 27–29.

Howe, Irving. *Sherwood Anderson.* Stanford, Calif.: Stanford University Press, 1966.

Lewis, David Levering. *When Harlem Was in Vogue.* New York and Oxford: Oxford University Press, 1981.

Morrison, Toni. "Whiteness and the Literary Imagination." In *Playing in the Dark: Whiteness and the Literary Imagination.* Cambridge, Mass.: Harvard University Press, 1992.

Rideout, Walter B., ed. *Sherwood Anderson: A Collection of Critical Essays.* Englewood Cliffs, N.J.: Prentice-Hall, 1974.

Small, Judy Jo. *A Reader's Guide to the Short Stories of Sherwood Anderson.* New York: G. K. Hall, 1994.

Townsend, Kim. *Sherwood Anderson.* Boston, Mass.: Houghton Mifflin, 1987.

Anglophone Africa and the Harlem Renaissance

Anglophone Africa—which consisted of British colonies in western, eastern, and southern Africa; and the independent country of Liberia, founded by freed American slaves in 1847—occupied a central place in the discourse of the Harlem Renaissance. Like its counterpart, francophone Africa, anglophone Africa provided an imaginative resource that contributed to the cultural and aesthetic base of the Harlem Renaissance. Also, one focus (if not a preoccupation) of the renaissance movement was racial origin and pride, and in this regard the idea of Africa represented many possibilities, of which anglophone Africa provided one. The Harlem Renaissance, for its part, provided anglophone Africa with avenues of self-expression to oppose British colonial rule, develop an agenda for self-rule, and intervene in discourses about a pan-African and pan-Negro philosophy and movement that promoted a unifying agenda for racial self-determination and political freedom. The themes of self-determination, self-assertion, and black pride that defined the Harlem Renaissance resonated favorably in anglophone Africa as it struggled against British colonization. The exchange of ideas about politics, culture, racial roots, and heritage defined the relationship between anglophone Africa and the Harlem Renaissance and their opposition to colonial and racial suppression and domination. The English language, which provided a readily available means for intercultural and transatlantic communication, facilitated this connection between anglophone Africa and the Harlem movement.

In the consciousness of the Harlem Renaissance, anglophone Africa was a rallying point for envisioning racial equality and self-determination. In "The Negro Mind Reaches Out" in Alain Locke's *The New Negro* (1925), W. E. B. Du Bois drew attention to racial and political imbalances in anglophone Africa, with an emphasis on British colonial rule in west Africa (Sierra Leone, Nigeria, and the Gold Coast, later Ghana), British East Africa (Kenya, Uganda, and Sudan), and South Africa. He implied that there was a contradiction in Harlem's appropriation of the idea of Africa as a route to envisioning the New Negro while the African continent was subjected to colonial exploitation and domination. He highlighted Britain's brutal colonial policies, which he characterized as the "shadow of England"—policies that, for example, displaced Africans from their lands in Kenya and South Africa. Du Bois's essay, published in the representative text of the renaissance movement, explained that anglophone Africa was more than a geographical entity. Du Bois portrayed anglophone Africa as a culturally and economically diverse territory marked by economic exploitation, political subjugation, and racial oppression; the Harlem Renaissance addressed these issues in the United States and should also confront them in the wider context of the African diaspora. To do so, and to appeal to the mind of Harlem, Du Bois interpreted British colonial rule in anglophone Africa

as fundamentally racist, with white British rulers and black African subjects. However, Du Bois was not alone in focusing on anglophone Africa as an aspect of the aesthetics of the Harlem Renaissance.

The magazines and newspapers of the Harlem Renaissance provided the best indicators of its interest in anglophone Africa. Publications such as books, edited volumes, and anthologies that dealt with topics ranging from folklore to the ancient and modern history of anglophone Africa were highlighted in reviews and articles in *Opportunity*, *The Crisis*, and Marcus Garvey's newspaper *Negro World*. Regular columns in *Opportunity* variously titled "Africana," "Africana and Exotica," and "Anthropology and Africana" listed books on anglophone Africa. Two columns that Du Bois wrote for *The Crisis*—"Opinion" and "The Looking Glass"—covered culture, politics, and aesthetics in anglophone Africa. Editorials, opinions, and letters to the editor in Garvey's *Negro World* promoted an agenda for anglophone Africa that insistently opposed British rule and affirmed African self-governance. At the time of the Harlem Renaissance, the International Institute of African Languages and Culture began to publish a journal in English, *Africa* (1928–1929), which offered scholarly and intellectual materials on Africa and anglophone Africa, and was therefore favorably reviewed in publications of the renaissance. In addition, reviews of texts on adventure, religion, geography, missionary activities, apartheid in South Africa, art in west Africa, and the "natives" and "primitives" of anglophone Africa appeared regularly in the newspapers and magazines of the renaissance.

For some anglophone Africans, Harlem's newspapers and magazines provided opportunities to question and oppose British colonial rule. Because of British censorship, newspapers in the colonies did not publish anticolonial writings. Not surprisingly, then, anglophone Africans in the colonies sent letters, opinion pieces, stories, and poems to publications in Harlem, calling for political self-representation and self-determination. Through their contributions, anglophone Africans shared in the aspirations of the Harlem Renaissance, which linked its ideology of racial equality in the United States to a call for the end of colonial rule in Africa. Harlem reciprocated not only by publishing the contributions of writers from anglophone Africa but also by espousing anticolonialism. Harlem's newspapers published profiles of various anglophone African countries, such as Sierra Leone, Uganda, and Kenya. Moreover, some of the major figures of the Harlem Renaissance—for example,

W. E. B. Du Bois and Langston Hughes—visited anglophone African countries, particularly in west Africa, and wrote about their experiences; these accounts were also published in the magazines and newspapers of the renaissance. Writers of the Harlem Renaissance also used anglophone Africa in their works, although their depictions were sometimes stereotyped. For example, Langston Hughes set the major action of his short story "Luani of the Jungle" in Lagos, Nigeria.

Literary works of anglophone Africans were also printed in publications of the Harlem Renaissance. For example, in 1922, *Negro World* published "The Sojourner," a poem by William Essuman Gwira (Kobina) Sekyi of the Gold Coast—a lawyer, nationalist, Africanist, and pan-Africanist. The anglophone African strain in the Harlem Renaissance was evident in *Caroling Dusk: An Anthology of Verse by Negro Poets* (1927), edited by Countee Cullen. This anthology included poems by Gladys Casely Hayford (1904–1950), west Africa's first modern female poet. *The Messenger* and *Opportunity* also published poems by Hayford. Her poetry captured the cultural and aesthetic mood of the Harlem Renaissance, and in particular the discourse on racial uplift through celebrating and affirming Africa and black beauty, praising individuality, and debunking Western myths and stereotypes of Africans.

In her biographical entry for *Caroling Dusk*, Hayford said that she was born in Axim, Gold Coast (Ghana), and that her parents were Ephraim Joseph Casely Hayford (1866–1930), a Ghanaian; and Adelaide Smith Casely Hayford (1868–1960), a Sierra Leonean. Hayford's parents were prominent in the culture and politics of west Africa and had contacts with important figures of the Harlem Renaissance; Du Bois stayed in the Hayfords' home when he visited Freetown in 1924. Hayford's mother visited Harlem twice—in 1920 and in 1927—to raise money for a vocational school in Freetown, Sierra Leone, and during these visits she promoted African culture among African Americans. On her first visit, the *Crisis* of 20 August 1920 informed its readers in Harlem that Mrs. Casely Hayford was the "first West African woman to lecture in America" (169). With her niece, a Miss Easmon, she contributed to the production and performance of a pageant, *Asheeko* (1922), about the contributions of African Americans to the greatness of America. As a political activist, she was one of the black women (the only African) in Harlem who organized to raise funds for the fourth Pan-African Congress, held in New York in August 1927. The African countries represented at this congress, drawn primarily from anglophone west

Africa, were Sierra Leone, the Gold Coast, Nigeria, and Liberia.

Gladys Casely Hayford's father, Joseph Casely Hayford, was a prominent politician in the Gold Coast; because of his anticolonial, nationalist, and pan-Africanist views, he had contacts with significant figures of the Harlem Renaissance, such as Du Bois and Marcus Garvey. In 1920, he founded the National Congress of British West Africa (NCBWA), the first political movement in colonial west Africa, which comprised the British colonies of Sierra Leone, Nigeria, the Gold Coast, Nigeria, and the republic of Liberia. The main goal of NCBWA was the liberation of anglophone west Africa from British colonial rule; thus the organization was a natural ally of the anticolonialists of the Harlem Renaissance. Du Bois and Garvey saw NCBWA in west Africa and the pan-African and pan-Negro movements in Harlem as part of a global effort by black people to unify Africa and the African diaspora in the struggle against racial and colonial domination.

Politics was no doubt the most significant aspect of the relationship between the Harlem Renaissance and anglophone Africa. The political vision of self-determination and self-governance, articulated in the aesthetics of Harlem and transformed into political capital by Du Bois and Garvey, became very influential in anglophone Africa. Du Bois's pan-African movement was initiated at about the time—the 1920s—when modern political consciousness and nationalism were taking shape in anglophone west Africa (as is evident in the formation of NCBWA); and Garvey's vision and ideology of black empowerment were defined by his call "Africa for Africans."

From Harlem, Garvey transformed his United Negro Improvement Association (UNIA) into an anticolonial movement, demanding that whites leave Africa; this position appealed to anglophone Africans under colonial rule. In 1922, Garvey told the British government that UNIA stood for the liberation of African colonies, particularly the British colonies of Nigeria, Sierra Leone, the Gold Coast, and southwestern and east Africa. In the 1920s, branches of UNIA were established in anglophone west Africa, although the British colonial governments disapproved of UNIA and monitored its activities in the region. In 1924, Garvey negotiated with Liberia for an immigrant settlement by UNIA in southern Liberia; but this attempt was thwarted by the English and French, who feared anticolonial Garveyite ideas in Africa, especially near their colonies. Garvey's anticolonial *Negro World* was very popular in anglophone Africa; the British considered it seditious, disloyal, and a threat to their interests in Africa, and therefore banned it in most of their African colonies. But despite government regulations and monitoring, *Negro World* was being received by African nationalists in South Africa as late as 1933. Garvey's political and anticolonial philosophy had an especially strong influence on anglophone west African political consciousness during its formative period, the 1920s. NCBWA, in defining its anticolonial position, incorporated Garvey's ideas on African and racial self-determination. On the eve of Ghana's independence, Kwame Nkrumah expressed his allegiance to Garvey's philosophy; and in his autobiography, he noted that as he formed his political ideas, he was influenced by Garvey's *Philosophy and Opinions*. Jomo Kenyatta, the leader of the Mau Mau and later president of Kenya, described

> how in 1921 Kenyan nationalists, unable to read, would gather round a reader of Garvey's paper the *Negro World*, and listen to an article two or three times. Then they would run various ways through the forest, carefully to repeat the whole, which they had memorized, to Africans hungry for some doctrine which lifted them from their servile consciousness in which Africans lived. (James 1963, 397)

Garvey's wife recounted how the king of Swaziland had stated that the only two black men he was aware of in the Western world were the boxing champion Jack Johnson and Marcus Garvey.

Music was another link between anglophone Africa and the Harlem Renaissance, and in this regard, the music of Samuel Coleridge-Taylor (1875–1912) was particularly significant. Coleridge-Taylor, who was born to a British mother and a Sierra Leonean father, was a famous composer of choral music, including *Hiawatha's Wedding Feast* (1897); Du Bois, in *Darkwater*, eulogized him as the "immortal child." In his work, Coleridge-Taylor expressed his African and black identity, a theme many Harlem Renaissance musicians would later incorporate into their own compositions. He based some of his compositions on African and African American subjects and melodies. His *African Romances* (1897) and *African Suite* (1898) reflected his African heritage; *Sorrow Songs* (1904) and *Six Negro Melodies* (1905) drew on both African and African American song traditions. Coleridge-Taylor wanted to reclaim black identity—and even more, the dignity of the black man—through music; and he inspired

African American composers of the period leading to and including the Harlem Renaissance who used their music to inquire into their cultural roots and heritage. He directly influenced composers of the Harlem Renaissance such as Harry T. Burleigh (1866–1949) and, especially, Clarence Cameron White (1880–1960).

Anglophone Africa and Harlem shared a vision that was anticolonial and antiracist. The Harlem Renaissance contributed significantly to the development of political consciousness and activism in anglophone Africa, either through pan-Africanism and pan-Negroism, which provided political capital for self-empowerment and opportunities for addressing oppression and subjugation; or through art, which provided aesthetic capital for transatlantic contacts and cultural awareness. For its part, anglophone Africa became one of the many regions in Africa that the Harlem Renaissance used to conceptualize the meaning of heritage, roots, and history and to articulate racial pride. It should be noted, though, that the discourse of the Harlem Renaissance occasionally reproduced uncritically the stereotypical rhetoric about anglophone Africa that was part of the colonial representation of Africa as a whole.

PATRICK S. BERNARD

See also Burleigh, Harry Thacker; Crisis, The; Cullen, Countee; Du Bois, W. E. B.; Francophone Africa and the Harlem Renaissance; Garvey, Marcus; Hughes, Langston; Messenger, The; Negro World; Opportunity; Pan-African Congresses; Pan-Africanism; United Negro Improvement Association; White, Clarence Cameron

Further Reading

Adebayo, J. Babington. "The British West African Congress: Marcus Garvey's Pan-Negroism and the Universal Negro Improvement Association." *Lagos Weekly Record*, 27, November 1920, p. 7.

Agard, J. E. "Some Impressions of Uganda." *Crisis*, 30, May 1925, p. 22.

Brown, Lloyd. "The African Heritage and the Harlem Renaissance: A Re-Evaluation." *African Literature Today*, 9, 1978, pp. 1–9.

Clarke, John Henrik, ed. *Marcus Garvey and the Vision of Africa*. New York: Vintage, 1974.

Coleman, James. *Nigeria: Background to Nationalism*. Berkeley and Los Angeles: University of California Press, 1965.

Cromwell, Adelaide M. *An African Victorian Feminist: The Life and Times of Adelaide Smith Casely Hayford,*

1868–1960. Washington, D.C.: Howard University Press, 1992.

Cullen, Countee. *Caroling Dusk: An Anthology of Verse by Negro Poets*. New York: Harper and Row, 1927.

Du Bois, W. E. B. "Little Portraits of Africa." *Crisis*, 27, April 1924, p. 274.

———. "The Negro Mind Reaches Out." In *The New Negro*, ed. Alain Locke. New York: Simon and Schuster, 1992. (Originally published 1925.)

———. "The Immortal Child." *Dark Water: Voices from within the Veil*. Toronto: Dover, 1999, pp. 114–127. (Originally published 1920.)

Garvey, Marcus. *Philosophy and Opinions of Marcus Garvey*, ed. Amy Jacques-Garvey. New York: Atheneum, 1969.

Hughes, Langston. "Ships, Sea, and Africa." *Crisis*, 27, December 1923, p. 72.

———. "Luani of the Jungle." *Harlem: A Forum of Negro Life*, 1, November 1928.

———. *The Big Sea: An Autobiography*. New York: Hill and Wang, 1963.

Hodgkins, T. *Nationalism in Colonial Africa*. London: Muller, 1956.

James, C. L. R. *The Black Jacobins*. New York: Vintage, 1963.

"Kenya: A Study of English East African Conditions as Revealed by Norman Leys." *Crisis*, 31, February 1926, p. 91.

Langley, Jabez Ayodele. "Garveyism and African Nationalism." *Race*, 2, April 1970, pp. 157–172.

Obadende, I. M. "An African Program." *Crisis*, 24, May 1922, p. 33.

Ojo-Ade, Femi, ed. *Of Dreams Deferred, Dead, or Alive: African Perspectives on African-American Writers*. Westport, Conn.: Greenwood, 1996.

Sekyi, Kobina. "The Sojourner." *Negro World*, May 1922.

Shepperson, G. "Pan-Africanism and 'Pan-Africanism': Some Historical Notes." *Phylon*, 4, 1962, p. 356.

"Sierra Leone." *Crisis*, 26, June 1923, p. 76.

Weisbord, Robert G. "Marcus Garvey, Pan-Negroist: The View From Whitehall." *Race*, 2, April 1970, pp. 419–429.

"Zion in Africa: An Open Letter on Missions in West Africa by a Native Christian Secondee, Gold Coast, West Africa." *Crisis*, 31, April 1926, p. 293.

Anglophone Caribbean and the Harlem Renaissance

The Harlem Renaissance and the anglophone Caribbean presence in the United States are intimately and inextricably bound together. Claude McKay, Eric Walrond, Marcus Garvey, Hubert Harrison, Cyril Briggs, Amy Jacques Garvey, Wilfred A. Domingo, and Joel A. Rogers are only a few of the better-known Caribbean immigrants who were closely associated with the renaissance, which was as much a political as a cultural movement.

Caribbeans (especially those from English-speaking territories) distinguished themselves during the Harlem Renaissance as writers, editors, publishers of newspapers and magazines, organizers of political and cultural forums, street-corner orators, founders of dissenting political movements, and raisers of political consciousness. Their contribution is all the more remarkable when one considers that during this period, the foreign-born component never exceeded 1 percent of the black population in the United States. And were we to include those of Caribbean descent born in the United States, other notable figures of the period would be among them, such as W. E. B. Du Bois (whose father was born in Haiti but had roots in the Bahamas), James Weldon Johnson (whose mother was Bahamian), William Stanley Braithwaite (whose father was from British Guiana), and Grace Campbell (whose father was Jamaican)—all of whom expressed pride in their Caribbean background.

McKay's role as poet and novelist was pivotal in the renaissance. Eric Walrond's collection of short stories *Tropic Death* (1926) was an artistic triumph; but perhaps because the stories are set in the Caribbean and Central America and because the author was a pioneer in using regional creole languages for artistic expression, *Tropic Death* is less known and less appreciated in the United States than in Caribbean literary history and criticism. Although Walrond also wrote short stories set in the United States, he is recognized there more as a journalist and editor. Between 1921 and 1923, he served as associate editor of *Negro World*, the organ of the Universal Negro Improvement Association (UNIA) founded and led by Marcus Garvey. Two years after his break with Garvey, Walrond was the business manager and contributing editor for *Opportunity*, founded and edited by Charles Johnson under the auspices of the National Urban League. In all his writings—short stories, book reviews, essays—Walrond revealed himself as a master prose stylist and a serious thinker. Wallace Thurman, the enfant terrible of the Harlem Renaissance and the most unsparing critic of his contemporaries (and himself), showered Walrond with praise. Of the renaissance writers, observed Thurman, "None is more ambitious than he, none more possessed of keener observation, poetic insight or intelligence. There is no place in his consciousness for sentimentality, hypocrisy or clichés. His prose demonstrates his struggles to escape from conventionalities and become an individual talent." Thurman, however, felt that Walrond's talents were not fully realized, even in *Tropic Death*. He hoped that Walrond's promised novel on the Panama Canal, "The Big Ditch," which Walrond had received a Guggenheim fellowship to write, would prove an even greater triumph. But Walrond left for Britain in 1928 and never returned to the United States; he worked with the exiled Marcus Garvey in London on the latter's journal, *Black Man*, but the "The Big Ditch" was never finished. Resident mainly in Britain, Walrond traveled widely in Europe, despite failing health. He collapsed and died of a heart attack, his fifth, on a London street in 1966.

Caribbeans not only founded but also edited radical journals and newspapers such as *Voice*, *Crusader*, *Negro World*, *Promoter*, *Emancipator*, and *New Negro*. Hubert Harrison, an immigrant from the Virgin Islands, was a pioneer in this area of New Negro radical journalism; A. Philip Randolph called him the "father of Harlem radicalism." Harrison, a legendary orator, created *Voice*, the first journal of its type, in 1917. Two years later he brought out a short-lived magazine, *New Negro*, and before his own sudden death (from a ruptured appendix) in 1927 he had founded another journal, *Voice of the Negro*. Ephemeral though Harrison's magazines and journals were, his writings and example had a vast influence on the journalism of the time. Hodge Kirnon, in his obituary of Harrison, noted that *Voice* "really crystallized the radicalism of the Negro in New York and its environs." Kirnon, an immigrant from Saint Kitts, would draw on Harrison's example in founding his own magazine, *Promoter*.

Another Caribbean immigrant, Cyril Briggs, founded the magazine *Crusader* in 1918; it was the organ of the African Blood Brotherhood, which Briggs organized and led, between 1919 and 1923. W. A. Domingo (from Jamaica) and Richard B. Moore (from Barbados), two black socialists, founded *Emancipator* in 1920 mainly as a challenge to Garvey's movement. But *Emancipator*, although it had some influence over the black movement, especially through a famous exposé of the finances of Garvey's shipping company, the Black Star Line, was no match for UNIA; and unlike its black nationalist rival, *Negro World*, it lasted for only a few months.

Negro World, founded in 1918, was by far the most influential of these organs. During Garvey's tenure, each issue carried on the front page an editorial by him addressed to the "Negroes of the World"; this newspaper would outlast Garvey's departure in the late 1920s, although it died slowly as UNIA imploded and disintegrated in the 1930s. During its heyday, *Negro World* attracted the writing of some of the most talented figures of the Harlem Renaissance: Zora Neale Hurston, Claude McKay, J. A. Rogers, Arturo Schomburg, Walrond, and others. Distinguished African American intellectuals such as T. Thomas Fortune, a firebrand from the 1880s; William Ferris, a graduate of Yale; and John Edward Bruce, the venerable black nationalist, served as editors on *Negro World* during the 1920s; and it was in the pages of *Negro World* that Hubert Harrison, who was its managing editor and later a contributing editor between 1920 and 1922, reached his widest audience. Harrison revamped *Negro World*, included more book reviews, and regularly ran "Poetry for the People," a forum, often filling an entire page, that carried a wide variety of poems by ordinary black people in the United States and around the world. Perhaps the most remarkable feature of *Negro World* was "Our Women and What They Think," a deliberately unorthodox women's page, edited by Amy Jacques Garvey (a Jamaican immigrant, Garvey's second wife), which ran in 1924–1927. Amy Jacques, who combined militant black nationalism and feminism, won the admiration of black women within and outside UNIA and alienated some of its more conventional male leaders; the movement killed her column in 1927.

Apart from their involvement in publications owned and run by Caribbeans, the immigrants made significant contribution to others. Domingo was Garvey's first editor of *Negro World* but was fired by Garvey in 1919 for his socialist writing and immediately became a contributing editor for the *Messenger* magazine, edited and run by the African American socialists A. Philip Randolph and Chandler Owen. Claude McKay returned from a yearlong sojourn in Britain in 1921 and became associate editor of the influential revolutionary socialist magazine *Liberator*, edited by Max Eastman. Rogers, Walrond, McKay, and especially Harrison contributed to a wide range of mainstream and black periodicals during the 1920s. Additionally, several of these Caribbean writers contributed to major anthologies. Alain Locke's influential *New Negro* (1925) included the work of McKay, Walrond, Rogers, and Domingo; V. F. Calverton's *Anthology of American Negro Literature* (1929) included McKay (poetry and prose) and Walrond. McKay's poems appeared in all of the anthologies of black poetry published in the

1920s: James Weldon Johnson, *The Book of American Negro Poetry* (1922); Robert Thomas Kerlin, *Negro Poets and Their Poems* (1923); Countee Cullen, *Caroling Dusk: An Anthology of Verse by Negro Poets* (1927); and Alain Locke, *Four Negro Poets* (1927).

McKay and Walrond were among the immigrants who published volumes of their own work. The prolific McKay produced two highly influential and acclaimed volumes of poetry—*Spring in New Hampshire and Other Poems* (1920) and *Harlem Shadows* (1922)—and two pioneering and controversial novels: *Home to Harlem* (1928) and *Banjo* (1929). Hubert Harrison published two remarkable and influential collections of his essays: *The Negro and the Nation* (1917) and *When Africa Awakes: The "Inside Story" of the Stirrings and Strivings of the New Negro in the Western World* (1920). J. A. Rogers published several antiracist books before publishing, in 1931, the antiracist classic *World's Great Men of African Descent* (later revised as *World's Great Men of Color*). His most influential work in the 1920s was *From "Superman" to Man*, a Socratic dialogue in the form of a novel that first appeared in 1917 and was reprinted several times during the next decade. This book was acclaimed by all of the factions engaged in the black struggle, a rare accolade; UNIA made it required reading for members; and Du Bois wrote: "The person who wants in small compass, in good English and an attractive form, the arguments for the present Negro position should buy and read and recommend to his friends" Rogers's book. Hubert Harrison, who dished out praise sparingly, described *From "Superman" to Man* as the "greatest book ever written in English on the Negro by a Negro."

The great comedian Bert Williams (from Antigua) was a pioneer of black theater and helped open up Broadway to blacks. Williams received both praise and criticism. Theophilus Lewis, the theater critic for *Messenger*, averred that Williams "rendered a disservice to black people" by encouraging Broadway not to "countenance the Negro in serious, dignified, classical drama." Walrond, writing in *Negro World*, disagreed. He held that Williams had made it possible for black shows such as *Shuffle Along* to be staged on Broadway and also had been "directly responsible" for bringing to Broadway more serious dramas, such as *The Emperor Jones*: "There is no doubt about it—Bert Williams will go down in history alongside the great artists of the theatre of all time. To us, to whom he meant so much as an ambassador across the border of color, his memory will grow richer and more glorious as time goes on."

Much of the literature on the Harlem Renaissance focuses on the role of white patrons. Consequently, the role of the only notable black patron—Casper Holstein, born in the Virgin Islands—is often overlooked. Holstein made his money as a "numbers king" in Harlem; he was the most successful and most honest practitioner of this gambling game (unlike many others, he paid out when bettors won), and by far the most generous. Beginning in 1925, Holstein put up the prize money for *Opportunity*'s annual contest for Negro writers (which extended to composers of music as well). In 1926, this amounted to more than $1,000—a not inconsiderable sum. Holstein explained that he had always been a "firm and enthusiastic believer in the creative genius of the Negro race, to which I humbly belong." He congratulated *Opportunity* for organizing the contest, which he believed would "go far towards consolidating the interests of and bridging the gap" between black and white people in the United States. The contest, he wrote, "will encourage among our gifted youth the ambition to scale the empyrean heights of art and literature." Holstein also made individual gifts to needy young artists. Eric Walrond was one of his beneficiaries and dedicated *Tropic Death* to him. Another was Holstein's compatriot Hubert Harrison, who endured a mainly hand-to-mouth existence; Holstein also paid for Harrison's funeral. When Garvey's Liberty Hall was threatened with repossession, Holstein came to the rescue. From his associations, it is discernible that Holstein was not a conservative, despite his success in business. He had time and money for some of Harlem's most radical citizens, and he spoke out in uncompromising terms against American rule in his native Virgin Islands (purchased by the United States from Denmark in 1917), publishing articles on the subject in *Opportunity* and *Negro World*. Through his various efforts, Holstein contributed to the artistic and political culture of the Harlem Renaissance.

Caribbean immigrants also distinguished themselves as some of Harlem's and Afro-America's most accomplished orators. Harrison was by far the most erudite and experienced, but Garvey was more popular as a platform speaker. Richard B. Moore quickly earned a reputation as a great orator—passionate, eloquent, and informed—surpassed only by his elders Garvey and Harrison at their best. In the 1920s and 1930s, Moore's oratorical talents would be exploited to good effect by the Communist Party, which he had joined by 1923. J. Edgar Hoover's spies from the Justice Department were not only alarmed but also impressed by these men's eloquence, force, and impact as orators.

Men dominated the speakers' platforms in Harlem, on the street corners as well as indoors, but women were by no means absent. An African American, Henrietta Vinton Davis, the highest-ranking woman in UNIA, was among the very best orators of either sex. The fact that she had a successful stage career before devoting herself full time to Garvey's movement probably contributed to her effectiveness on the podium at Liberty Hall. Amy Jacques Garvey was a highly effective and popular public speaker, although she seldom spoke, preferring to devote her time to writing. Among the black socialists, Elizabeth Hendrickson, a Virgin Islander, was also considered among the best by her contemporaries.

But it was in radical politics, both black nationalist and socialist, that the Caribbean presence was most conspicuous during the Harlem Renaissance. Hubert Harrison once again stands out as a pioneer; amazingly, he won black converts to both revolutionary socialism and black nationalism. This apparent paradox is explained by the fact that Harrison was a member of the Socialist Party between 1909 and 1914 and subsequently moved toward black nationalism but never abandoned his deeply ingrained Marxism. Harrison left the Socialist Party because of the racism he encountered within it, even among its leaders. He felt that the party preached "class first" but practiced "race first," discriminating against the black working class, especially in the South; and that so as not to offend its southern white working-class members, the party had compromised its principles and succumbed to what he called "southernism"—the trumping of working-class solidarity by white supremacy. Harrison was suspended by the party in 1914 and subsequently resigned. (He apparently rejoined in 1918 but left again soon thereafter, never to return.) He insisted that because white socialists, except for the Industrial Workers of the World, practiced "race first and class after," African Americans should also practice "race first," if only in self-defense. To forward this ideology, Harrison formed the Liberty League of Negro-Americans in the summer of 1917. As Harrison put it, this league was part of Afro-America's "bold bid for some of that democracy for which their government [had] gone to war."

Moore, Domingo, McKay, and Frank Crosswaith first encountered Harrison during his socialist phase and were deeply affected by him. A. Philip Randolph recalled that when he and Chandler Owen encountered Harrison, they explained to him: "We want to develop a street forum comparable to yours. We don't plan to have any competition, but we want to extend your work, what you're doing." The extension of Harrison's work would go beyond the street forum into the publication of *Messenger*, and by 1926 Randolph would also embark directly on the organization of the black working class in the Brotherhood of Sleeping Car Porters, in which Caribbean immigrants such as Ashley Totten, Thomas Patterson, and Frank Crosswaith would play leading roles.

When Garvey arrived in the United States in 1916, Harrison (then in his black nationalist phase) was the first to offer him a public platform in Harlem. Harrison would later work with Garvey, especially on *Negro World*, but apparently never joined UNIA. It was from Harrison that Garvey borrowed the slogan "race first," and much else. Garvey developed the largest black organization the world had ever known and mobilized ordinary African Americans to an unprecedented degree, especially in the South. The leadership of UNIA in the United States and abroad was disproportionately of anglophone Caribbean origin (Vincent, 1970)—as was Cyril Briggs's African Blood Brotherhood (ABB). ABB, founded in Harlem in 1919, began as a classical black nationalist organization. But its leaders, increasingly attracted by the anti-imperialism and antiracism of the Russian revolution and the Communist International, dissolved the organization and joined forces with the Communist Party of the United States in 1923.

At both the cultural and political levels, anglophone Caribbeans played a disproportionate role during the Harlem Renaissance. The reason for this is complex, but we can briefly outline some of its key components.

Approximately 143,000 black people immigrated to the United States between 1899 and 1932. About 80 percent of these came from the Caribbean. Although they made up less than 1 percent of the black population in the United States, Caribbean immigrants and people of Caribbean descent constituted 20 to 25 percent of the black population in Harlem during the 1920s. Thus their weight was far greater, and they were more conspicuous, in Harlem and New York City than nationally.

Far more than their African American counterparts in Harlem and elsewhere, Caribbean immigrants, especially those who came to New York, had a high level of literacy and professional training. These black immigrants were far more literate than European immigrants entering the United States at the time, and they were also more literate and generally better-educated than the native-born white population. Some, such as McKay, Walrond, and Garvey, had begun their literary and journalistic careers before emigrating to the United States. By the time McKay left Jamaica, he was a well-known literary figure who was widely published in newspapers there and abroad and had written two highly acclaimed volumes of poetry. Walrond had started out as a journalist in Panama, where he grew up; Garvey had started in this field during his stay in Costa Rica and London, and then in Jamaica, before he came to the United States.

In the British Caribbean, the population was overwhelmingly black, and immigrants who came from there to the United States found it difficult to adjust to a minority status, or to being maligned, persecuted, and considered pariahs. McKay's reaction was typical: "It was the first time I had ever come face to face with such manifest and implacable hate of my race, and my feelings were indescribable. . . . I had heard of prejudice in America but never dreamed of it being so intensely bitter." When Hugh Mulzac first came to the United States, he was barred from entering a church because of his color; he quickly concluded of white America: "These people are not Christians, but savages!" Shock and frustrated hopes (especially among the most highly educated) contributed to Caribbean immigrants' radicalization and their disproportionate involvement in dissident political projects. McKay, in particular, would express bitterness and anger in his literary work and his politics. Moreover, the immigrants' shock and outrage were exacerbated by certain entrenched features of American society at the time they arrived, particularly Jim Crow (which was official in the South and unofficial in the North) and lynching.

The extensive travel and international experience of many of these migrants contributed significantly to the pan-Africanist and race-conscious thrust of the Harlem Renaissance. Contemporary commentators, black and white, attributed this internationalist dimension of the movement largely to the Caribbeans. Garvey, in particular, movingly recalled his travels to and experiences in Central America, Europe, and Jamaica, where he found that blackness was "the same stumbling block." He asked himself: "Where is the black man's Government? Where is his King and his kingdom? Where is his President, and his ambassador, his army, his navy, his men of big affairs?" He could not find them, and vowed: "I will help to make them."

Relations between Afro-Caribbeans and Afro-Americans were by no means untroubled. Ethnic epithets such as "monkey chaser" and "coon" were not unknown. Wallace Thurman, McKay, and especially Rudolph Fisher scrutinized this tension in their fiction and elsewhere, making intraracial interactions a subject of the literature that emerged during the Harlem Renaissance. The moment of greatest tension was during the "Garvey must go" campaign of 1922–1923. But the historical literature on the relations between these two parts of the African diaspora in Harlem have tended to overstate ethnic conflict and understate the remarkable level of collaboration and cooperation between them. Afro-Americans and Afro-Caribbeans married one another; shared their culture (including cuisine, music, and sartorial tastes); learned to live with one another in a very densely populated place; and joined forces, fighting shoulder to shoulder, in political movements against racism and class oppression. The tension that did exist was largely confined to the petit bourgeois and professionals of both groups, and this tension abated significantly during the Depression, which was a calamity shared by Caribbeans and African Americans alike and brought the exuberance of the Harlem Renaissance to a sudden end.

The Caribbean legacy of the Harlem Renaissance in the arts and politics would continue in subsequent generations: Paule Marshall, Shirley Chisholm, Kenneth Clark, Malcolm X, Louis Farrakhan, Harry Belafonte, St. Clair Drake, Lani Guinier, and Constance Motley Baker are some of the direct descendants of those who arrived and settled during the renaissance. In their work and contribution to the black struggle and the life of the republic generally, one discerns the continuation of a tradition.

WINSTON JAMES

See also African Blood Brotherhood; Briggs, Cyril; Brotherhood of Sleeping Car Porters; Calverton, V. F.; Domingo, Wilfred Adolphus; Emancipator; Garvey, Marcus; Harrison, Hubert; Holstein, Casper; Liberator, The; McKay, Claude; Messenger, The; Moore, Richard B.; Negro World; Numbers Racket; Opportunity; Rogers, Joel Augustus; Thurman, Wallace; Tropic Death; Walrond, Eric; *other specific individuals*

Further Reading

Anderson, Jervis. *A. Philip Randolph: A Biographical Portrait.* Berkeley: University of California Press, 1986.

Cooper, Wayne, ed. *The Passion of Claude McKay: Selected Poetry and Prose, 1912–1948.* New York: Schocken, 1973.

Harrison, Hubert. *When Africa Awakes: The "Inside Story" of the Stirrings and Strivings of the New Negro in the Western World.* New York: Porro, 1920.

Holder, Calvin. "The Causes and Composition of West Indian Immigration to New York City, 1900–1952." *Afro-Americans in New York Life and History,* 11(1), January 1987.

James, Winston. *Holding Aloft the Banner of Ethiopia: Caribbean Radicalism in Early Twentieth-Century America.* New York: Verso, 1998.

———. "Explaining Afro-Caribbean Social Mobility in the United States: Beyond the Sowell Thesis." *Comparative Studies in Society and History,* 44(2), April 2002, pp. 218–262.

———. "Being Red and Black in Jim Crow America: On the Ideology and Travails of Afro-America's Socialist Pioneers." In *Time Longer Than Rope: A Century of African American Activism,* ed. Charles Payne and Adam Green. New York: New York University Press, 2003, pp. 336–399.

Martin, Tony. *Race First: The Ideological and Organizational Struggles of Marcus Garvey and the Universal Negro Improvement Association.* Westport, Conn.: Greenwood, 1976.

———. *Literary Garveyism: Garvey, Black Arts, and the Harlem Renaissance.* Dover, Mass.: Majority, 1983.

———, ed. *African Fundamentalism: A Literary and Cultural Anthology of Garvey's Harlem Renaissance.* Dover, Mass.: Majority, 1991.

McKay, Claude. *Harlem: Negro Metropolis.* New York: Dutton, 1940.

Mulzac, Hugh. *A Star to Steer By.* New York: International, 1963.

Parascandola, Louis J. *"Winds Can Wake Up the Dead": An Eric Walrond Reader.* Detroit, Mich.: Wayne State University Press, 1998.

Perry, Jeffrey B. *A Hubert Harrison Reader.* Middletown, Conn.: Wesleyan University Press, 2001.

Turner, W. Burghardt, and Joyce Moore Turner, eds. *Richard B. Moore, Caribbean Militant in Harlem: Collected Writings, 1920–1972.* Bloomington: Indiana University Press, 1988.

Vincent, Ted. *Keep Cool: The Black Activists Who Built the Jazz Age.* London: Pluto, 1995.

Vincent, Theodore. *Black Power and the Garvey Movement.* Berkeley, Calif.: Ramparts, 1970.

———, ed. *Voices of a Black Nation: Political Journalism in the Harlem Renaissance.* San Francisco, Calif.: Ramparts, 1973.

Walrond, Eric. *Tropic Death.* New York: Boni and Liveright, 1926.

Watkins-Owens, Irma. *Blood Relations: Caribbbean Immigrants and the Harlem Community, 1900–1930.* Bloomington: Indiana University Press, 1996.

Anita Bush Theater Company

The Anita Bush Theater Company—also known as the Anita Bush All-Colored Dramatic Stock Company and the Anita Bush Players and eventually renamed the Lafayette Players Stock Company—developed during the period 1910–1917, when Negroes were exiled from the downtown theaters of New York, as a setting in which black performers played to almost exclusively black audiences. This atmosphere offered a new freedom from the constraints of performing to white or predominantly white audiences. The performers in Bush's company came from the days of shows by Isham, Williams and Walker, and Cole and Johnson; they included Anita Bush, Ida Anderson, Andrew Bishop, Laura Bowman, Tom Brown, Jack Carter, Inez Clough, A. B. Comathiere, Cleo Desmond, Evelyn Ellis, Charles Gilpin, Lottie Grady, Sidney Kirkpatrick, Abbie Mitchell, Lionel Monagas, Charles Moore, Clarence Muse, Charles Olden, Susie Sutton, Edna Thomas, Walter Thompson, "Babe" Townsend, and Frank Wilson.

Anita Bush (1883–1974), a pioneer in black theater, founded her company in 1912, after an injury forced her to stop performing as a dancer. The Anita Bush Players toured the vaudeville circuit, presenting dramatic sketches based on life in the Old West and staged plays at the Lincoln Theater at 135th Street and Lenox Avenue until the company moved to the Lafayette Theater. Bush had taken her idea for a new stock company to Eugene "Frenchy" Elmore, assistant manager of the Lincoln Theater, which was newly renovated but was experiencing an economic slump. Elmore quickly signed a contract with Bush, who assured him that the company would be ready to perform in two weeks. Bush also persuaded Billie Burke, a white male director-playwright, to direct the group in his comedy *The Girl at the Fort.* The Anita Bush Players opened in this play at the Lincoln Theater on 19 November 1915, with Charles Gilpin as the leading man and Dooley Wilson in a supporting role. For the next six weeks, the company presented different plays at two-week intervals. However, Elmore left to take a position at the rival Lafayette Theater, and Maria C. Downs, who then managed the Lincoln, demanded that Bush change the name of the company to the Lincoln Players. Bush refused and, with the help of the drama critic Lester A. Walton, moved to the Lafayette, at 132nd Street and Seventh Avenue.

The company, still bearing Bush's name, opened at the Lafayette on 27 December 1915 in *Across the Footlights* and for a while presented short plays each week. Many of the presentations were adaptations of Broadway melodramas and old favorites such as *The Gambler's Sweetheart* (adapted from *The Girl of the Golden West*); the company also produced a version of Dion Boucicault's *The Octoroon*.

By March 1916, as a result of financial difficulties, Bush sold the company, and with her consent its name was changed to the Lafayette Players Stock Company. She remained with the company until 1920, establishing new groups of Lafayette Players at other theaters on the touring circuit. By 1917, there were four troupes of Lafayette Players.

FELECIA PIGGOTT-MCMILLAN

See also Bush, Anita; Clough, Inez; Ellis, Evelyn; Gilpin, Charles; Kirkpatrick, Sidney; Lafayette Players; Lafayette Theater; Lincoln Theater; Mitchell, Abbie; Muse, Clarence; Thomas, Edna Lewis; Walton, Lester; Wilson, Arthur "Dooley" Wilson, Frank

Further Reading

Huggins, Nathan Irvin. *Harlem Renaissance*. New York: Oxford University Press, 1971.

Johnson, James Weldon. *Black Manhattan*. New York: Antheneum, 1968.

Kellner, Bruce, ed. *The Harlem Renaissance: A Historical Dictionary for the Era*. Westport, Conn.: Greenwood, 1984.

Mitchell, Loften. *Black Drama: The Story of the American Negro in the Theatre*. New York: Hawthorn,1967.

Peterson, Bernard L. *The African American Theatre Directory, 1816–1960: A Comprehensive Guide to Early Black Theatre Organizations, Companies, Theatres, and Performing Groups*. Westport, Conn.: Greenwood, 1997.

Antilynching Crusade

The crusade to end lynching in the United States began in the final decade of the nineteenth century and continued relatively unabated until the middle of the twentieth. During that time, organizations such as the Council on International Cooperation (CIC), Young Women's Christian Association (YWCA), National Association of Colored Women (NACW), United Negro Improvement Association (UNIA), National Citizens Rights Association (NCRA), National Equal Rights League (NERL), and American Civil Liberties Union (ACLU) worked toward the eradication of lynching through programs of education, investigation, and publicity and through advocacy for a federal antilynching statute. Sometimes these groups cooperated in their efforts to end lynching, but more often than not, they found themselves at odds with each other over the best means to apply. While activists such as Ida B. Wells Barnett and organizations such as the National Association for the Advancement of Colored People (NAACP) and the Association of Southern Women for the Prevention of Lynching (ASWPL) fought valiantly for the enactment of federal antilynching legislation, they were never successful. The antilynching crusade nevertheless paved the way for the equal rights movement that followed, and it helped establish the NAACP as a national force to be reckoned with in the pursuit of political and social justice. Accompanying these efforts to eradicate lynching was the work of writers of the Harlem Renaissance, who dramatized the horrors of lynching in their poetry and prose and united to form the Writers' League against Lynching in 1933.

Between 1892 and 1940, there were approximately 3,000 lynchings in the United States; of those lynched, more than 2,600 were African American. This remarkable number and the terrible violence that characterized the lynchings compelled Ida B. Wells Barnett, among others, to organize in resistance. Wells Barnett eloquently challenged the most prominent myth about lynching—that most lynchings were justified as a response to the rape of white women by black men—by investigating lynchings throughout the South. In *A Red Record* (1895), she published her findings: that rape was seldom the charge for which black men were lynched and that the numerous lynchings of African American women directly challenged the connection between rape and lynching. Wells Barnett argued that lynching was more accurately described as a mechanism for depriving African Americans of their constitutional rights. This text—by debunking the myths that were used to justify lynchings, by publicizing the number and violent nature of lynchings, and by seeking to create economic disincentives for southern jurisdictions that were permissive regarding "lynch rule"—set a precedent for subsequent antilynching campaigns (Brown 2000).

When the NAACP was founded in 1909, a vigorous antilynching effort was already under way. However, two of the NAACP's leaders—James Weldon Johnson and, later, Walter White, whose *Rope and Faggot: A Biography of Judge Lynch* (1929) remains an indispensable account—made lynching a primary focus of the organization. Using many of the techniques pioneered by Wells Barnett, the NAACP made its campaign against lynching the basis for numerous fund-raising activities, lobbied for federal antilynching legislation, and used its new prominence in the antilynching effort to draw attention to other racial inequalities. The NAACP hired Johnson in 1916, and by 1918 he had helped launch a five-year, high-priority attack on lynching. This undertaking included conferences, letter-writing campaigns, and countless editorials in the organization's newspaper, *The Crisis*; but the most visible effort was support of the Dyer bill, antilynching legislation introduced by Leonidas Dyer (Republican, Missouri) in April 1918. Although the Dyer bill and others like it—including the Costigan-Wagner bill of 1937—would pass the House of Representatives, no federal antilynching bill ever received the approval of the Senate. Between 1918 and 1923, and again between 1933 and 1937, a large proportion of the NAACP's operating budget and organizational efforts was directed toward the crusade to end lynching (Zangrando 1980).

Other organizations, some occasionally affiliated with the NAACP, worked hard to eradicate lynching. In 1922 the NAACP supported the creation of the Anti-Lynching Crusaders, a group headed by Mary Talbert (of the NACW) and dedicated to raising $1 million from one million members to combat lynching. Although they never reached this goal, the Anti-Lynching Crusaders did raise nearly $70,000. The ASWPL, founded in 1930 by Jessie Daniel Ames, attempted to combat lynching through investigations and publicity, and by seeking pledges from southern law enforcement officials to work against lynching. Despite their shared goal, the ASWPL and the NAACP were frequently at odds because the ASWPL was segregated and did not support federal antilynching legislation. In 1937, the NAACP's field secretary Daisy Lampkin oversaw a "Stop Lynching" button campaign that raised awareness and nearly $10,000.

In addition to these organized endeavors to end lynching through direct political action, there were numerous literary attacks. James Weldon Johnson not only addressed lynching in his official duties for the NAACP but also vividly described the effects of lynching in his *Autobiography of an Ex-Colored Man*. Other literary responses came from figures such as W. E. B. Du Bois (in his work for *The Crisis*), Jean Toomer (the poems "Blood-Burning Moon" and "Portrait in Georgia" in *Cane*), Claude McKay (the poems "If We Must Die" and "The Lynching"), Georgia Douglas Johnson, Angelina Weld Grimké, and others. Nella Larsen, Jessie Fauset, Mary White Ovington, Dorothy Parker, Sinclair Lewis, and Upton Sinclair were among the members of the Writers' League against Lynching.

Although its inability to get federal legislation enacted was an important factor in its demise, the antilynching crusade had lost momentum for other reasons as well: a general decrease in lynchings during the period of World War II; widespread interest in atrocities abroad, rather than at home; and the NAACP's shift in focus to more pressing matters—notably, segregation in the armed forces, housing, and the workplace. Despite the explicit failure of many of the antilynching crusaders, their work drew attention to the horrors of lynching, gained recognition for the NAACP, and laid the groundwork for other efforts on behalf of equal rights.

MATTHEW R. DAVIS

See also Barnett, Ida B. Wells; Johnson, James Weldon; National Association for the Advancement of Colored People; Talbert, Mary Burnett; White, Walter

Further Reading

Ames, Jessie Daniel. *The Changing Character of Lynching: Review of Lynching, 1931–1941*. Atlanta, Ga.: Commission on International Cooperation, 1942.

Brown, Mary Jane. *Eradicating This Evil: Women in the American Anti-Lynching Movement, 1892–1940*. New York and London: Garland, 2000.

Gunning, Sandra. *Race, Rape, and Lynching: The Record of American Literature, 1890–1912*. New York and Oxford: Oxford University Press, 1996.

Hall, Jacquelyn Dowd. *Revolt against Chivalry: Jessie Daniel Ames and the Women's Campaign against Lynching*. New York: Columbia University Press, 1979. (Rev. ed., 1993.)

Harris, Trudier. *Exorcising Blackness: Historical and Literary Lynching and Burning Rituals*. Bloomington: Indiana University Press, 1984.

Terborg-Penn, Rosalyn. "African-American Women's Networks in the Anti-Lynching Crusade." In *Gender,*

Class, Race, and Reform in the Progressive Era, ed. Noralee Frankel and Nancy S. Dye. Lexington: University Press of Kentucky, 1991.

Wells-Barnett, Ida B. *On Lynchings: Southern Horrors, A Red Record, Mob Rule in New Orleans*. New York: Arno and New York Times, 1969.

White, Walter. *Rope and Faggot: A Biography of Judge Lynch*. New York: Knopf, 1929.

Zangrando, Robert L. *The NAACP Crusade against Lynching, 1909–1950*. Philadelphia, Pa.: Temple University Press, 1980.

Apollo Theater

When the building that would become the famous Apollo Theater was erected in 1913, at 253 West 125th Street, it was an Irish music hall. By 1919 it became Hurtig and Seamon's Burlesque Theater, featuring white female performers, most notably Fanny Brice. Few African Americans were allowed to perform there, and the few black members of the audience had to sit in the balcony, which was poorly lit and often dirty. Another, much smaller burlesque theater, the Apollo, named for the Greek god of music and poetry, was also situated on 125th Street. Both theaters were shut in 1932 when Fiorello La Guardia, who was then a congressman, ordered all burlesque theaters to close. In 1934, Sidney Cohen bought the Hurtig building specifically to provide live entertainment by African Americans for African Americans in Harlem. He was the first to do anything like this on 125th Street, which was still catering to whites and still segregated. Cohen appropriated the name of the earlier small Apollo for the Hurtig building, naming his new venture the 125th Street Apollo Theater. It came to be known simply as the Apollo, and from 1934 to the present, it has been a center of African American entertainment.

Cohen's Apollo was newly decorated and had high-fidelity RCA sound equipment—an innovative system also used at Radio City Music Hall. The first show at the Apollo, *Jazz à la Carte*, opened in 1934 and was very successful. However, neither this show nor the regular appearance of talented performers such as Bessie Smith persuaded Harlem's residents to come to 125th Street, which remained segregated. In an effort to attract larger audiences, Ralph Cooper suggested that the Apollo host weekly amateur nights. Accordingly, in 1935, when the Apollo was on the verge of bankruptcy, the first amateur night took place, with Cooper as the master of ceremonies.

Ralph Cooper's Harlem Amateur Night, as it was called, was intended not only as entertainment but also to provide an opportunity for talented residents of Harlem. However, Cooper knew that he had to find some way to handle the less talented entrants. He enlisted the aid of Norman Miller, a comic stagehand, to appear in eccentric costumes and gently and humorously usher the losing contestants offstage. Cooper made it clear that Amateur Night was not meant to denigrate any of the contestants or to hurt their feelings. Miller's job, then, was to make sure that everyone, including the losers, had a good time. Amateur Night quickly became a Harlem institution, just as well-known for its rowdy, booing crowds and its dancing clown as it was for the talent that graced the stage. That talent was often impressive: Early winners of amateur nights included Ella Fitzgerald, Sarah Vaughan, and Pearl Bailey.

An interesting tradition of the amateur nights had to do with the Tree of Hope. Nearly since the beginning of these events, each amateur performer touched a special piece of wood before going onstage. This chunk of wood had been taken from the Tree of Hope, a legendary shade tree behind the Lafayette Theater and Connie's Inn. The tree had been an informal meeting place for people in show business, where Harlem's stars told anecdotes about themselves and their tours and aspiring performers listened and dreamed. When Seventh Avenue was expanded around 1935, the Tree of Hope was cut down; but Ralph Cooper took a piece of the tree as a souvenir, had a set designer at the Apollo shellac it and mount it on an Ionic column, and placed it onstage where the audience and performers could see it, as a symbol of show business in Harlem. Contestants in the amateur nights began touching it for good luck, creating a new custom at the Apollo.

The Apollo's earliest competitor was the Lafayette Theater, owned by Leo Brecher and managed by Frank Schiffman. Later it became the Harlem Opera House, still owned by Brecher and Schiffman. Although Lafayette had been opened, strategically, only half a block from the Apollo, a campaign by the Harlem Opera House to lure Harlem's audiences away from the Apollo failed. However, when Sid Cohen died of a heart attack in 1935, Morris Sussman, the general manager of the Apollo, sold it to Brecher and Schiffman. Schiffman then took over as general manager of the Apollo, and another era of its history began.

Apollo Theater, 1920s. (Schomburg Center for Research in Black Culture, New York Public Library.)

Further Reading

Cooper, Ralph, and Steve Dougherty. *Amateur Night at the Apollo: Five Decades of Great Entertainment*. New York: HarperCollins, 1990.

Fox, Ted. *Showtime at the Apollo*. New York: Holt, Rinehart, and Winston, 1983.

Schiffman, Jack. *Uptown: The Story of Harlem's Apollo Theatre*. New York: Cowles, 1971.

———. *Harlem Heyday*. New York: Prometheus, 1984.

Appearances

The events that led to the presentation of Garland Anderson's play *Appearances* (1925) on Broadway, and made Anderson the first African American playwright to have a full-length nonmusical drama produced there, are in themselves dramatic. Anderson, a bellhop in San Francisco, was inspired to write *Judge Not According to Appearances* (its original title) as an expression of his religious beliefs, based on the precepts of Christian Science, after attending a performance of Channing Pollock's religious melodrama *The Fool*. Anderson's protagonist is Carl, a black bellhop in a residential hotel to whom the white patrons turn for spiritual counsel. Wilson, an unscrupulous prosecuting attorney whose fiancée has faith in Carl, becomes envious and tries to frame Carl for the attempted rape of a white woman named Elsie. The second act takes place in a courtroom, where Carl refuses to mount a defense, simply trusting that his innocence will be revealed. The other black characters in the play—Carl's fiancée, Ella; and the hotel's porter, Rufus—try to give support. When Elsie is revealed as not white but mulatto, and as Wilson's mistress, Carl is exonerated. In the third act, all plotlines are resolved; the play has been a dream, but Carl's faith has made it come true.

On the advice of a friend, Anderson sent his script to the entertainer Al Jolson, who declined to produce the play but lent Anderson his press agent. Among other fund-raising efforts, the "bellhop playwright" presented a reading of the play by the actor Richard B. Harrison at the Waldorf Astoria Hotel, met with Governor Al Smith of New York, and went to the White House, where he presented a script to President Calvin Coolidge. Anderson then returned to California and set forth across the country on a promotional tour.

On 13 October 1925, after successful out-of-town tryouts and bearing a shortened title, *Appearances* finally

Under Schiffman's management, Amateur Night continued with Ralph Cooper as emcee. After his retirement in the 1960s, it still continued, as did performances by celebrities including Gladys Knight and the Pips, Patti LaBelle, the Jackson Five, and Parliament Funkadelic. By the 1970s, however, support for Schiffman's Apollo had waned; residents of the neighborhood were calling for more black-owned and black-operated businesses in Harlem. Nevertheless, Schiffman held on to the Apollo, although he sold many of his other theaters to religious organizations. When he died in 1974, the Apollo was the last of his holdings in Harlem still operating.

In 1977, the Schiffman family closed the Apollo. Its profits had been declining as the crime rate rose, and in 1975 there had been a shooting at the Apollo during a concert by Smokey Robinson. The family tried unsuccessfully to sell the Apollo to various church organizations; finally, it was bought by the Harlem Urban Development Corporation (HUDC).

In 1983, the Apollo, as Harlem's oldest theater, was registered as a National Historic Landmark. In 1984, it reopened as an auditorium, a television studio, and the home of a new weekly Amateur Night Contest. In 1992, *Showtime at the Apollo* premiered on television in national syndication, returning the theater to its former glory as a place of entertainment and opportunity.

CANDICE LOVE

See also Harlem: 3—Entertainment; Smith, Bessie; Tree of Hope

Appearances, scene from the stage performance. (Billy Rose Theatre Collection, New York Public Library, New York City. ©The New York Public Library / Art Resource, N. Y. Keysheets Box 4, Image 26. Photographer White Studio, anonymous.)

opened at the Frolic Theatre on Broadway, where it ran for twenty-three performances. Carl was played by Lionel Monagas, a veteran of the Lafayette Players; Rufus by the vaudevillian Doe Doe Green; and Ella by a newcomer, Evelyn Mason. Although two white actors withdrew from the production rather than work in an integrated cast, there was no serious controversy (such as the one that had beset Eugene O'Neill's *All God's Chillun Got Wings* in 1924) over this issue.

The critical response to *Appearances* was mixed. W. E. B. Du Bois enthusiastically supported the play, partly because of its perceived antilynching message. Other African Americans, such as the historian J. A. Rogers, denounced Anderson as an opportunist. The character Rufus and Green's portrayal of him had overtones of minstrelsy and were particularly controversial. Alan Dale's review in the *New York World* probably summarized the response of most of the white critical establishment: "It would be absurd to waste much time in analysis of this play. . . . I admit that this little play is better than some of the offerings that have made Broadway wretched this season."

Anderson refused to let *Appearances* die. He raised enough money for a tour through the western United States in 1927 and a revival (running for twenty-four performances) at the Hudson Theater on Broadway in 1929. In November 1929, Anderson sailed to London, where the play was produced at the Royalty Theater; it ran there from mid-March through the end of May 1930.

Anderson claimed authorship of another play, *Extortion*, which was never produced; became a lecturer for a religious organization, Unity; and established

Andy's Nu Snack, the first milk bar in England, in London in 1934. While he was in England, he became the first black person to be admitted to the prestigious literary organization PEN.

FREDA SCOTT GILES

See also Anderson, Garland; Lafayette Players

Further Reading

Hatch, James, and Ted Shine, eds. *Black Theatre U.S.A.: Plays by African Americans, 1847 to Today*. New York: Free Press, 1996.

Johnson, James Weldon. *Black Manhattan*. New York: Atheneum, 1977. (Reprint; originally published 1930.)

Kellner, Bruce, ed. *The Harlem Renaissance: A Historical Dictionary for the Era*. Westport, Conn.: Greenwood, 1984.

Kreizenbeck, Alan. "Garland Anderson and *Appearances*: The Playwright and His Play." *Journal of American Drama and Theatre*, 6(2, Spring; 3, Fall), 1994.

Mantle, Burns. *The Best Plays of 1925–1926*. New York: Dodd, Mead, 1926.

Patterson, Lindsay, ed. *Anthology of the American Negro in the Theatre: A Critical Approach*. New York: Publishers Company, 1967.

Armstrong, Louis

From 1925 to 1928, Louis Daniel Armstrong (a.k.a. Dippermouth, Satchelmouth, Satchmo, Pops) made a series of more than sixty recordings with his small groups the Hot Five and the Hot Seven. Jazz writers of later years hailed these recordings for their role in helping to transform jazz from an ensemble entertainment to a solo art. But observers in the 1920s admired Armstrong less for his recordings per se than for his utter dominance in a highly visible professional field. The respect and even awe that Armstrong aroused among white and black musicians alike made him a shining example of the New Negro, even though he was not involved in the more rarefied artistic aspects of the Harlem Renaissance. From his destitute youth in New Orleans to his triumphant performances on Broadway in 1929, Armstrong struggled to better himself musically and socially while stopping just short, as he put it, of "putting on airs."

Armstrong was born out of wedlock in the poorest section of New Orleans, in a neighborhood so violent that it was known as the Battlefield. His father moved out when Armstrong was a child, and his mother supported the family as a domestic worker and part-time prostitute. Louis helped by singing in the streets for pennies and scrounging for food in garbage bins. In 1912, he was arrested for firing a gun in the air on New Year's Eve and was sentenced to eighteen months in reform school. At the school Armstrong was subjected to military-style discipline and learned to play the cornet. Upon his release he began developing a reputation as a gifted cornetist. He sought out musical instruction from his idol Joe "King" Oliver, performed with parading brass bands, and played the blues in honky-tonks late at night. When Oliver moved to Chicago in 1918, Armstrong took his place in Kid Ory's band, the leading jazz band in New Orleans. From then on, Ory recalled, Armstrong "went up like a sunflower. His name went right through New Orleans." Yet some contractors still wouldn't hire him for certain events in polite society. One of them, Edmond Souchon, considered Armstrong "a rough, rough character" who blew "false" (he may have meant out of tune) and played too loudly. Most of Armstrong's role models were also rough characters. Early on he had developed an admiration for pimps, gamblers, and other figures of the New Orleans underworld, the most charismatic and influential males in his cultural milieu. The drummer Baby Dodds recalled that in 1920–1921, Armstrong dressed like "low-class hustlers" and gamblers, "because that's what he wanted to be in those days. . . . Back at that time he was always broke from gambling."

Armstrong's aspirations changed after he moved North in 1922. He began his career in the North playing with King Oliver's Creole Jazz Band in Chicago and Fletcher Henderson's orchestra in New York. Armstrong seems to have been at least vaguely aware of artistic and cultural trends in Harlem. In his first autobiography (1936), he mentioned several black celebrities active in New York while he was there in 1924–1925, including James Weldon Johnson, Charles Gilpin, Paul Robeson, and Bill "Bojangles" Robinson. Armstrong was especially impressed with Robinson, whom he had seen perform in Chicago. Above all, Armstrong admired the dignity and independence Robinson brought to his stage performance. "To me, he was the greatest comedian + dancer in my race—better than Bert Williams," he recalled. "He didn't need blackface to be funny." Robinson, unlike the performers in minstrel shows, did not wear rags or tell self-disparaging jokes; he dressed immaculately and exuded power and self-confidence. The example of prominent northerners like Robinson moved Armstrong to embark on a somewhat ambivalent quest for outward "respectability"—in manners, literacy, clothing style, and most significantly music.

A catalyst in this transformation was Oliver's pianist Lillian (Lil) Hardin, who became Armstrong's second wife. In 1918, in New Orleans, Armstrong had married a young prostitute named Daisy Parker. Their relationship was turbulent, involving brickbat fights in the streets and still more dangerous confrontations behind closed doors. After moving to Chicago, Armstrong divorced Daisy in order to marry Hardin, a woman from Memphis who had taken some classes at Fisk University. Hardin immediately began overhauling Armstrong's rough New Orleans persona, buying him new clothes, changing his hairstyle, and demanding a certain propriety in his behavior. When Daisy visited Chicago in an effort to reclaim him, Armstrong assured her that they were incompatible, especially since he had lately been trying to "cultivate" himself. Publicity photographs from the late 1920s show the results of Lil's handling: Wearing expensive clothing and jewelry, Armstrong invariably looks sophisticated. And yet despite his willingness to make changes in his appearance, Armstrong chafed under Lil's exacting standards in other realms. He ultimately rejected the highfalutin lifestyle that required, as he put it, "a certain spoon for this, and a certain fork for that." By around 1927 he had begun to live with Alpha Smith, a less pretentious working-class woman who would later become his third wife.

Armstrong may have resented Hardin's overbearing social direction, but he remained forever grateful that she had pushed him to expand his musical sensibility. From the moment he arrived in the North, Armstrong had electrified audiences with the boldness and originality of his playing. But the type of music he and other New Orleanians played—"hot jazz" and the blues—drew harsh criticism in the 1920s from moralists and social reformers. The critics denigrated such music, using epithets such as "lowdown" (or "low-class"), "gutbucket," and "barrelhouse," and worried that it inspired lewd dancing and generated business for nightclubs and speakeasies owned by mobsters. To insulate themselves from ill repute, many black musicians sought for "high-class," "dicty," or "society" credentials by working in vaudeville theaters, fashionable ballrooms, and dance orchestras that included elements of European art music in their programs. The ability to play within the European tradition demonstrated a literacy and refinement that raised the "class" quotient of any musician. The musicians who most self-consciously participated in the Harlem Renaissance—such as Robert Nathaniel Dett and

Roland Hayes—aspired to compose or perform works based on European classical practice. At Hardin's urging, Armstrong tried to acquire some classical training; he practiced concert pieces at home to Hardin's accompaniment on a grand piano, and he even studied briefly with a German trumpet teacher known in Chicago for advocating the "nonpressure" method of playing.

The bands and venues Armstrong played in after leaving Oliver show his concern for building a "high-class" musical reputation. In 1924, Fletcher Henderson's orchestra was the leading black society dance band in the country. When an opportunity came for Armstrong to join the band, Hardin encouraged him wholeheartedly, even though it meant that the two had to live separately for a year. Henderson's musicians, with their elegant deportment and thorough musical training, embodied the New Negro in popular music. In fact, Henderson, although impressed with Armstrong's solos, told him: "If you gonna be good someday, you'll take some [music] lessons." Armstrong apparently ignored this advice. But when he returned to Chicago in 1925, he bowed to Hardin's insistence that he join Erskine Tate's "Symphony Orchestra" at the Vendome Theater, an organization featuring violins and double-reed woodwinds as well as the more traditional jazz instruments. At the Vendome, Armstrong became more skilled at reading music and learned to play pieces from the classical repertoire. He even performed featured solos during transcriptions of Italian operas such as Mascagni's *Cavalleria Rusticana* and Puccini's *Madame Butterfly*. Within a year or so Armstrong was playing at the Sunset Café, one of the most exclusive nightclubs in black Chicago. At the Sunset and later the Savoy Ballroom, Armstrong accompanied floor shows in a style that would have required considerable versatility and technical polish. A mere handful of recordings document Armstrong's work with these bands: Erskine Tate, "Stomp Off (Let's Go)" and "Static Strut" (both 1926); and Louis Armstrong and His Stompers (the Sunset band), "Chicago Breakdown" (1927).

During the same period that Armstrong was performing high-class music at the Vendome and the Sunset, he was also recording plenty of New Orleans–style blues and jazz, the kind that most appealed to working-class southern migrants. These records, known collectively as the Hot Fives and Hot Sevens, show the same gradual reconciliation of high and low that was occurring simultaneously in Armstrong's personal life. The early Hot Five records—including such celebrated performances as "Cornet Chop Suey" and "Big Butter and Egg Man" (both 1926)—feature only New Orleans musicians (except Hardin), emphasize traditionally raucous polyphonic textures, and often suggest a casual spontaneity with little advance preparation. Over time, however, Armstrong gradually introduced ritzy pre-arranged elements. In "You Made Me Love You" (1926), "The Last Time," and "Once in a While" (both 1927), the band plays introductions and accompanimental figures redolent of the music of floor shows. In the Hot Fives of 1928, Armstrong replaced his New Orleans sidemen with the northern musicians he employed nightly at the Savoy. This last series of records features classical and other "society" elements in instrumentation, repertoire, texture, harmony, and form. For example, the meticulously arranged "Beau Koo Jack" has a structural complexity nowhere evident in earlier Hot Five recordings; and the band accompaniment to Armstrong's solo in "Muggles" alternately rises and falls in volume, showing a classical concern for dynamics (patterns of loud and soft). And yet Armstrong did not cut himself off from his New Orleans roots. His most famous records of the period, such as "West End Blues" and "Weatherbird," are a convincing hybrid of northern and southern, "high-class" and "gutbucket" elements.

By the late 1920s Armstrong's musical innovations—particularly his virtuosity, power, coherence, rhythmic "swing," and eccentric vocal style—had established him as a rising force in American popular music. His achievements had won over much of the black community, including those who earlier had fretted that the unsavory social aspects of jazz would have negative effects on the black cause. Dave Peyton, the chief music critic for the Chicago *Defender*, began calling Armstrong the "Great King Menalick" after Menelik II, the Ethiopian emperor who overthrew Italian domination in the late nineteenth century. Nor was Armstrong's influence limited by race. At a banquet in 1929, a group of white musicians gave Armstrong a wristwatch engraved: "To Louis Armstrong, the World's Greatest Cornetist, from the Musicians of New York." Also in 1929, he created a sensation on Broadway singing "Ain't Misbehavin'" in the musical *Hot Chocolates*. In 1930, he made his first film appearance in *Ex-Flame* (now lost), an achievement he proudly emphasized in his passport application two years later, wherein he stated his occupation as "actor and musician." He needed the passport to undertake his first tour of Europe, where an already flourishing group of fans attested to his international popularity.

In the 1930s, European and American left-wing commentators lauded the Hot Five and Hot Seven recordings as great works of art. Such praise might

Louis Armstrong. (Brown Brothers.)

until around age twelve and was confined in the Colored Waif's Home for Boys in 1913–1914. He joined Kid Ory's Brown-Skinned Babies in 1918, Fate Marable's band on the Streckfus Steamboat line in 1919, King Oliver's Creole Jazz Band in Chicago in 1922, and Fletcher Henderson's Orchestra in New York in 1924; performed in Chicago with the bands of Lil Hardin Armstrong, Erskine Tate, Carroll Dickerson, and Clarence Jones in 1925–1928; and accompanied many blues and vaudeville singers, including Bessie Smith and Alberta Hunter, in 1924–1930. He appeared in a Broadway show, *Hot Chocolates*, in 1929. He made his first European tours in 1932–1935; hired Joe Glaser to be his manager in 1935; hosted the Fleischmann's Yeast radio program on NBC in 1937; and appeared at Rockefeller Center in the musical *Swingin' the Dream* in 1939. Armstrong performed in the first Esquire All-American Jazz Concert at the Metropolitan Opera House in 1944. In 1947 he performed at Carnegie Hall and organized the septet Louis Armstrong's All-Stars. He performed at the first international jazz festival in Nice, France, in 1948, was featured on the cover of *Time* magazine in 1949, and made international tours in 1949–1968 and television appearances in 1949–1971. His television work included appearances on the shows of Horace Heidt, Ed Sullivan, Danny Kaye, Steve Allen, Mike Douglas, Jackie Gleason, Dick Cavett, David Frost, Johnny Carson, and Flip Wilson, and on *What's My Line?* He was given a seventieth (actually sixty-ninth) birthday tribute at the Newport Jazz Festival in 1970. Armstrong died in Queens, New York, on 6 July 1971.

BRIAN HARKER

See also Dett, Robert Nathaniel; Hayes, Roland; Henderson, Fletcher; Jazz; Music; Musicians; New Negro; Oliver, Joseph "King"; Ory, Edward "Kid"; Robinson, Bill "Bojangles"; Savoy Ballroom

have gratified musicians of the Harlem Renaissance who consciously sought to equal the achievements of western classical composers. Armstrong, however, had a different goal: to bring his music—which he viewed primarily as entertainment rather than art—to the widest possible audience. In the 1920s, that had entailed diversifying and refining his music and his demeanor; in the 1930s it involved singing and telling jokes as well as playing the trumpet. During this period Armstrong became a hero to the black community for his high profile in recordings, radio, and film. But after World War II, black America required a new New Negro, one not only culturally accomplished but also politically assertive. In this changed environment many accused Armstrong of Uncle Tomism because of his sincere desire to please an audience. For Armstrong, though, professional success and mass appeal represented the most significant advance a black musician could make. Such recognition may not have satisfied the generation of the civil rights movement, but it fulfilled some of the highest objectives of the Harlem Renaissance.

Biography

Louis Armstrong was born 4 August 1901, in New Orleans, Louisiana. He attended Fisk School for Boys

Selected Recordings

As a sideman: K. Oliver, "Chimes Blues"/"Froggie Moore" (1923, Gen. 5135), F. Henderson, "Copenhagen" (1924, Voc. 14926), Red Onion Jazz Babies, "Cake Walking Babies From Home" (1924, Gen. 5627), Bessie Smith, "St. Louis Blues" (1925, Col. 14064D). Hot Five/Hot Seven: "Muskrat Ramble"/"Heebie Jeebies" (1926, OK 8300), "Cornet Chop Suey" (1926, OK 8320), "Big Butter and Egg Man" (1926, OK 8423), "Potato Head Blues" (1927, OK 8503), "S.O.L. Blues" (1927, Col.

35661), "Struttin' with Some Barbecue" (1927, OK 8566), "Hotter than That"/"Savoy Blues" (1927, OK 8535), "West End Blues" (1928, OK 8597), "Muggles" (1928, OK 8703).

Duet with Earl Hines: "Weatherbird" (1928, OK 41454).

Big bands: "Sweethearts on Parade" (1930, Col. 2688D), "Star Dust" (1931, OK 41530), "I Gotta Right to Sing the Blues" (1933, Vic. 24233), "Jubilee" (1938, Decca 1635), "Struttin' with Some Barbecue" (1938, Decca 1661).

All-Stars: "Rockin' Chair"/"Save It Pretty Mama" (1947, Vic. 40–4004), "Basin Street Blues" (1954, Decca 29102), *Louis Armstrong Plays W.C. Handy* (1954, Col. CL591), *Satch Plays Fats* (1955, Col. CL708), "Hello Dolly" (1963, Kapp 573), "It's a Wonderful World" (1967, ABC-Para. 45–10982).

Selected Films

Rhapsody in Black and Blue, 1932; *Pennies From Heaven*, 1936; *Artists and Models*, *Everyday's a Holiday*, 1937; *Going Places*, 1938; *Cabin in the Sky*, 1943; *Atlantic City*, 1944; *New Orleans*, 1947; *The Glenn Miller Story*, 1954; *High Society*, 1956; *Satchmo the Great*, 1957; *Jazz on a Summer's Day*, 1958; *The Beat Generation*, 1959; *Paris Blues*, 1961; *A Man Called Adam*, 1966; *Hello Dolly*, 1969.

Further Reading

Armstrong, Louis. *Swing That Music*. New York, 1936. (Reprint, New York: Da Capo, 1993.)

———. *Satchmo: My Life in New Orleans*. New York: Prentice-Hall, 1954. (Reprint, New York: Da Capo, 1986.)

———. *Louis Armstrong in His Own Words: Selected Writings*, ed. and intro. Thomas Brothers. New York: Oxford University Press, 1999.

Bergreen, Laurence, *Louis Armstrong: An Extravagant Life*, New York: Broadway, 1997.

Berrett, Joshua, ed. *A Louis Armstrong Companion: Eight Decades of Commentary*. New York: Schirmer, 1999.

Collier, James Lincoln. *Louis Armstrong: An American Genius*. New York: Oxford University Press, 1983.

Gabbard, Krin. "Actor and Musician: Louis Armstrong and His Films." In *Jammin' at the Margins: Jazz and the American Cinema*. Chicago, Ill., and London: University of Chicago Press, 1996.

Giddins, Gary. *Satchmo*. New York: Doubleday, 1988.

Harker, Brian. "'Telling a Story': Louis Armstrong and Coherence in Early Jazz." *Current Musicology*, 1999.

Jones, Max, and John Chilton. *Louis: The Louis Armstrong Story, 1900–1971*. London, 1971. (Reprint, New York: Da Capo, 1988.)

Miller, Marc H., ed. *Louis Armstrong: A Cultural Legacy*. New York: Queens Museum of Art, with Seattle and London: University of Washington Press, 1994.

Schuller, Gunther. "The First Great Soloist." In *Early Jazz: Its Roots and Musical Development*. New York: Oxford University Press, 1968.

Art Criticism and the Harlem Renaissance

The Harlem Renaissance, with its emphasis on racial and ethnic distinctiveness, created an audience for visual art made by Americans of African descent. However, as an invention of the 1920s, the category "American Negro artist" would soon be suspended between the rhetoric of cultural nationalism and the reality of a segregated society as yet ill-equipped to fulfill its democratic promise. Within the African American community during these years, there were lively exchanges on the nature of "black creativity," typically in terms of a dynamic interaction between race and nationality. But critics writing for mainstream publications consistently emphasized that "Negro art" was separate from the overarching category "American art." As exposure to so-called Negro art grew, a set of critical constructs emerged, based on racial difference, that in effect isolated black art from the mainstream and contributed significantly to its subsequent historical neglect.

During the Harlem Renaissance and its aftermath, speculation on the relationship between race and creativity filled the pages of black periodicals and spilled over into the mainstream press. In these discussions, African Americans raised important questions about the responsibility of black artists to social (as opposed to aesthetic) issues, about the most desirable ways to represent members of the race, and about whether art should furnish cultural models or present actual individual experience. Articles highlighting the achievements of African American artists and articles about the current reappraisal of African art appeared regularly. The reader was frequently admonished to support black artists by buying their work, so that the artists would not be corrupted by too much white patronage.

But in this heady intellectual climate, black artists seeking a reputation in American art received complex and even conflicting messages. Although critics looked for growing technical facility in emerging black artists, their work was often considered interesting only to the extent that it differed from mainstream art. Critics were bored when the work of black artists appeared too derivative or too much like the work of artists who were not black. Yet critical standards were not altered to accommodate original or innovative expression when it did appear. To a certain extent, the perception of difference was encouraged by African American critics such as Alain Locke. Locke often referred to racially specific experience and culture; he urged black artists to express themselves in characteristically racial terms by drawing on the uniqueness of their experience and on their position as heirs to both an authentic American folk culture and the artistic traditions of ancestral Africa.

In considering art criticism and the Harlem Renaissance, genuine art criticism must be distinguished from what is more properly described as art journalism. These were very different modes of conveying information about African American art and artists, and most critical opinion on what is called the art of the Harlem Renaissance falls into the category of art journalism. Although critics and historians such as Locke and James Porter addressed complex issues of race, culture, identity, and nationalism, journalists writing for the popular press rarely went beyond basic questions such as what "Negro art" was and why anyone should be interested in it.

This situation reflected the state of American art criticism in general during the early twentieth century. With some notable exceptions, a good deal of the writing about art before World War II was a mixed bag of journalism and editorial commentary. Art criticism was not highly professionalized in the United States, and very few American critics applied a consistent, recognizable methodology. The writers of essays on art and culture in literary magazines and the popular press often had little background in the visual arts. Furthermore, in appraising African American visual art, these critics often relied on typologies from music and literarture, with which they were more familiar. Thus they tended to raise general issues rather than engage in complex critical analysis of specific works or artists.

Moreover, the aggressive public relations strategies of the Harmon Foundation, the institution most involved in promoting African American artists during the 1920s and 1930s, ensured its control over newspaper coverage of the Harmon awards for achievement in the visual arts and of its annual exhibitions of Negro art. In the period between the two world wars, a good deal of writing about African American art was simply the Harmon Foundation's publicity posing as art criticism; articles in the mainstream press often took the form of responses to, or paraphrases of, the foundation's promotional literature. Reviews and notices of the foundation's shows either focused on the evidence for and the merits of racial expression or dwelled on anecdote and biography. The black press stressed the professional accomplishments of successful artists; the mainstream press announced cash prizes awarded to artists who had emerged from extremely humble circumstances. In neither case was it common to find long analytical discussions of individual works of art.

Beginning in 1928, the annual exhibitions of the Harmon Foundation stimulated considerable discussion about the achievements and future direction of African American artists. Stemming from the larger debates about black creativity that were of central concern during the Harlem Renaissance, these discussions addressed many of the same issues that occupied critics in literary circles, where they were clearly articulated and hotly contested. Questions were raised about the relationship between contemporary black expression and black folk culture, about the meaning of Africa to modern American blacks, and about the transmission of racial characteristics across time and place. There was also intense concern about the proper representation of African Americans, especially in literary circles, as African American writers came to terms with a sudden fascination with black life in the 1920s. This interest in representation was coupled with an ongoing discussion about the nature of black creativity.

In this context, a set of issues emerged that provided mainstream art critics with a fairly consistent focus for considering the works of African American artists. The visual art of the Harlem Renaissance was typically evaluated according to a priori assumptions about amateurism, primitivism, Authenticity, and racial uniqueness. The fusion of these qualities created specific expectations: Authentic Negro art would be primitive because it was the product of amateurs or individuals predisposed to the primitive by virtue of their unique racial heritage; and such authenticity and uniqueness should be manifest in both the form and the content of Negro art. The ideology of racial primitivism, which often combined beliefs about authenticity, amateurism, and atavism, resulted in a clear preference among mainstream critics for black artistic expression that manifested it. The fascination with tribal art would later, in the populist climate of the 1930s, be displaced by an idealization of folk art; but insofar as Africa and rural black culture were understood as authentic subject matter for African American artists, they were welcomed. The popularity in the late 1920s of the painters Archibald Motley and Malvin Gray Johnson can in part be explained by this fascination with the primitive.

Mainstream critics looking for racial primitivism in the work of African American artists were especially pleased when they discovered evidence of emotional sensibility based on southern black folk culture and religion. They were in fact seeking the visual equivalent of the Negro spiritual. This sentiment—nearly universal among critics who followed developments in African American art and literature—emanated from a widespread belief that cultural sophistication would be the ruination of the "real American Negro." For many white Americans, the so-called sorrow songs were the most familiar, and therefore most representative, form of black expression.

Of the black visual artists of the Harlem Renaissance, Richmond Barthé and Archibald Motley were among those most consistently and favorably reviewed by the art press. By the end of the 1930s, Barthé was regarded as one of America's most promising sculptors, a truly gifted artist who was also racially authentic. Art critics also often found value in the work of seemingly naive black artists such as William H. Johnson. Nineteenth-century American folk art was widely admired during these years as an example of authentic native expression from the past. Modern black folk art and the black folk spirit in professional art were thus often received with greater enthusiasm by art critics than the more obviously sophisticated productions of academically trained artists. Ultimately, these expectations would prompt critics to express displeasure when the work of African American artists presented itself as similar to, or derived from, mainstream artistic practices. Even though many African American artists followed the same general principles as their peers who were not black, racial difference was expected to override shared national cultural ideals or similar professional training.

Notices on the Harmon Foundation shows during the 1930s rehashed many of the same issues that had emerged in the early reviews. Reviewers continued to be disappointed by an evident lack of authentic racial expression and to regard increased technical skill and the mastery of existing conventions as symptomatic of black artists' regrettable eagerness to imitate mainstream traditions rather than creating their own. Critics of these later shows consistently remarked that work by black artists resembled the work of their white counterparts. Although William H. Johnson's work was frequently considered the best in the show, it also commonly prompted (along with the work of Hale Woodruff) the observation that the Harmon collection did not differ significantly from that of any other modern art exhibition coming out of New York. Mainstream critics, straining to find distinctive racial qualities, resorted to clichés about Negroes' rhythm, spontaneous emotion, and affinity for bright colors. But more often than not, writers concluded that, were it not for the ubiquity of black subjects, the work might "pass" for that of any group of contemporary artists.

The issue of aesthetic modernity and its relationship to traditional African art is also a recurrent theme in much writing about African American art after the Harlem Renaissance. In *The New Negro*, Locke emphasized that African tribal art had invigorated European painters and sculptors, helping to free them of academic practices, and he claimed that it could be an even more potent stimulant for modern African American artists. Although in some of Locke's writing in the 1930s the emphasis shifts from the tribal antecedents of African American expression to native black American folk culture, Locke never abandoned his belief that African art could be a powerful source for black expression. The conflation of these ideals caused considerable confusion as critics and artists struggled to assess the emerging black modernist aesthetic, prompting the African American artist Selma Day to observe, in 1930:

> A few of the artists are producing what is called modern art by some, Negro art by others, and still another group will name the same paintings primitive art. I imagine that one often wonders where one style ends and the other begins, and more often questions whether or not any such thing as modern art or Negro art or primitive art really exists.

The 1920s had forecast the coming of an invigorated American culture that would be expansive and replete with possibilities, and in this context, artists of the Harlem Renaissance made their claims as important contributors to American national culture. The critical writing of Locke and other African Americans concerned with the progress of black artistic expression reflects a complex understanding of broad cultural discourse in America. Locke noted that although black artists have always sought cultural freedom through art, they have expressed themselves in artistic modes responsive to the American mainstream. Implicit in all of Locke's writing was an unswerving conviction that black Americans, by virtue of their distinctive racial heritage and singular experience, were destined to make a unique contribution to national culture at a critical moment in its development. However, mainstream art critics were more inclined to deal with the artist of African descent in the United States as an "American Negro" rather than a "Negro American," and so they typically did not acknowledge African American art as a vital manifestation of cultural nationalism. During the years between the wars, at a time when black expression, especially in music, was a powerful signifier of American culture in Europe, racism and segregation made it improbable that the visual art of African Americans would be so recognized at home.

Although visual representations of American blacks were considered authentic American subject matter, the discussions of democracy and culture that dominated the American art world, particularly during the Depression, rarely extended to the work of black artists. Instead, African American artists were constantly accused of sacrificing their birthright and were entreated to articulate their difference through archetypal images of suffering, naïveté, or racial primitivism. In an age that merged nationalistic and aesthetic issues, and in which critical discourse about art often lacked sophistication and focus, race seems to have remained the only relevant issue in considerations of African American art. The failure to fundamentally alter this fact has resulted in continued neglect and distortion of African American artists in both American art history and contemporary art; their work is rarely understood in terms that would affirm their participation in mainstream cultural ideals. In this respect, the Harlem Renaissance was a lost opportunity for American art critics, who failed to recognize the extent to which African American artists, both through their work and in their rhetoric, sought to participate in a collective project of national self-definition.

MARY ANN CALO

See also Barthé, Richmond; Harmon Foundation; Johnson, Malvin Gray; Johnson, William H.; Locke, Alain; Modernism; Motley, Archibald J. Jr; New Negro, The; Porter, James Amos; Primitivism; Woodruff, Hale

Further Reading

Calo, Mary Ann. "African American Art and Critical Discourse Between World Wars." *American Quarterly*, Fall 1999.

Conwill, Kinshasha Holman. "In Search of an 'Authentic' Vision: Decoding the Appeal of the Self-Taught African-American Artist." *American Art*, Fall 1991.

Driskell, David C., ed. *African American Visual Aesthetics: A Postmodernist View*. Washington, D.C.: Smithsonian Institution Press, 1995.

Gaines, Charles, with Maurice Berger and Catherine Lord. *Theater of Refusal: Black Art and Mainstream Criticism*. Irvine: Fine Arts Gallery of the University of California, 1993.

Hutchinson, George. *The Harlem Renaissance in Black and White*. Cambridge, Mass.: Belknap Press of Harvard University, 1995.

Johnson, Eloise E. *Rediscovering the Harlem Renaissance: The Politics of Exclusion*. New York and London: Garland, 1997.

Metcalf, Eugene. "Black Art, Folk Art, and Social Control." *Winterthur Portfolio*, 18, 1983.

Powell, Richard J. *Rhapsodies in Black: Art of the Harlem Renaissance*. Los Angeles: University of California Press, 1997.

Reynolds, Gary. "The American Critics and the Harmon Foundation Exhibitions." In *Against the Odds: African-American Artists and the Harmon Foundation*. Newark, N.J.: Newark Museum, 1989.

Sims, Lowery Stokes. "Subject/Subjectivity and Agency in the Art of African Americans." *Art Bulletin*, December 1994.

Stewart, Jeffrey C., ed. *The Critical Temper of Alain Locke*. New York: Garland, 1983.

West, Cornel. "Horace Pippin's Challenge to Art Criticism." In *Keeping Faith: Philosophy and Race in America*. New York: Routledge, 1993.

Wilson, Judith. "Shades of Grey in the Black Aesthetic, Part 1, The Myth of the Black Aesthetic." In *Next Generation: Southern Black Aesthetic*. Winston-Salem, N.C.: Southeastern Center for Contemporary Art, 1990.

Artists

During the Harlem Renaissance, the visual arts flowered with the same vigor as drama, dance, music, and literature. For a brief but resplendent moment in the

1920s and 1930s, Harlem was the center of a visual arts movement whose effects were felt across the United States and around the world, in places such as Atlanta, Chicago, Kansas City, San Francisco, Paris, Copenhagen, and Berlin. For the first time in history, there was a widespread interest in African American art among dealers, patrons, and curators. As early as 1919, an exhibit of the paintings of the African American expatriate Henry Ossawa Tanner (1859–1937), who was then living in Paris, was mounted at Knoedler Gallery in New York City. It was followed in 1921 by an exhibit of African American painting and sculpture at the 135th Street branch of the New York Public Library (later known as the Schomberg Center for Research in Black Culture). This second show featured works by Tanner as well as other accomplished artists, such as Meta Vaux Warrick Fuller (1877–1968), William Edward Scott (1884–1969), and Laura Wheeler Waring (1887–1948). In 1926, the Harmon Foundation (a philanthropic agency that awarded prizes to African Americans for achievement in the visual arts) granted the first of many annual prizes to the painters Palmer Hayden (1890–1973) and Hale Woodruff (1900–1980); and in 1927, a pivotal exhibition, "The Negro in Art," was presented by the Chicago Women's Club.

Interdisciplinary collaboration also marked this period. For example, Aaron Douglas (1899–1979) designed covers for black periodicals such as *The Crisis*, *Opportunity*, and *Fire!!*; and artists illustrated books of scholarly writing, poetry, and fiction by literati of the Harlem Renaissance, including Claude McKay, Countee Cullen, Charles S. Johnson, Alain Locke, and James Weldon Johnson.

The Harlem Renaissance was pervaded by the concept of the New Negro—someone with, in Locke's words, "renewed self-respect and self-dependence," who found a voice in the arts. Locke's sentiments were articulated in 1925, in an edition of *Survey Graphic* magazine dedicated to Harlem as the "mecca of the New Negro." The magazine, which contained drawings, poems, essays, fiction, and social commentary by young African American artists, writers, and intellectuals, sold more than 5,000 copies and helped launch the literary and artistic movement that came to be known as the Harlem Renaissance. This special issue of *Survey Graphic* became the manifesto of the era; in addition to writings, it included illustrations and portraits of notable figures of the renaissance, such as the singer and actor Paul Robeson, the tenor Roland Hayes (who appeared on the magazine's cover), and other distinguished African Americans.

The magazine's art director was the artist Winold Reiss (1886–1953), who had emigrated to the United States from Germany in 1913 and became known for his documentary-style portraits of Americans from widely varied racial and cultural backgrounds. Reiss's cover design for the Harlem issue of *Survey Graphic* featured a sensitive portrait of Hayes (as the New Negro) and a combination of African and art deco design elements. In fact, Reiss's cover, with its emphasis on African forms and abstract design motifs, embodied the modern international spirit of the Harlem Renaissance—a spirit clearly arising from both European and African culture. Many of the Harlem Renaissance artists studied abroad, particularly in Paris (where Negritude, a counterpart to the New Negro movement, was forming) and incorporated elements of German expressionism and cubism (itself inspired by African sculpture) into their own art. The Harlem Renaissance may be considered one of the first truly international art movements to take root on American soil.

An unprecedented number of African American visual artists were able to achieve some degree of success during this period, owing in no small measure to the Harmon Foundation. Aaron Douglas, Augusta Savage (1892–1962), and William H. Johnson (1901–1970), among others, gained a national and even an international reputation with the help of this foundation, whose art prizes were intended to bring African American creativity to the attention of a broad public and to lend financial support to participating artists. The winner of the foundation's Gold Medal Prize for art in 1926, and one of the first to benefit from the Harmon programs, was Palmer Hayden, who was then thirty-six. Hayden had earlier spent ten years in the armed services, during which time he enrolled in a correspondence course in drawing. After his discharge in 1920, he pursued further art study at Columbia University and at the Boothbay Commonwealth Art Colony in Maine. After winning the Harmon medal (and a $400 prize) for an impressionistic marine painting, Hayden traveled to Paris, where he lived, studied, and exhibited for five years, from 1927 to 1932.

While abroad, Hayden made the acquaintances of Tanner and of Locke (who was traveling in Europe at the time). Locke, the major interpreter of Harlem Renaissance aesthetics, had received his Ph.D. at Harvard and had the distinction of being the first African American Rhodes Scholar (at Oxford). He also headed the philosophy department at Howard University from 1912 to 1953. Locke, whose pivotal essay "The Legacy of the Ancestral Arts" urged African American artists to look to the art of their African ancestors for creative inspiration, argued that modern European art, particularly the works of Matisse, Picasso, Derain, and the German expressionists, had been substantially influenced by the abstract qualities of African sculpture. Locke believed that if African art was capable of arousing the aesthetic impulses of the European modernists, then surely it should inspire the same outpouring of creativity from the "culturally awakened" New Negro artist.

Locke's hope that black artists would take inspiration from Africa found representation in one of Hayden's best-known works, *Fétiche et Fleurs*, which won the Harmon painting prize in 1933. The painting comprised a still life of a vase of flowers, a Gabon Fang mask, and a Congo Bakuba cloth arranged in a Cézannesque design that tilted perspective and compressed the picture space. Hayden, who had by then returned to New York from Paris, continued to focus on ethnic subjects, but his style began to reveal a disturbing element of caricature that was evidently popular among the white clientele on whom most Harlem Renaissance artists depended for support. Hayden exaggerated the features of his subjects to the point, some people believed, of grotesqueness and, as a result, became a target of criticism, particularly from the respected art historian James A. Porter, the author of *Modern Negro Art* (1943). Porter objected to Hayden's new painting style as "ill-advised if not altogether tasteless" and reminiscent of billboards advertising blackface minstrel shows.

Hayden, however, maintained that his purpose was not to mock or to satirize but rather to paint, in his own "naive" style, the life and people that he knew. He compared his means to the writing style of Langston Hughes (who admired Hayden's work) and argued that the vernacular elements and characters found in Hughes's writings were similar to those that he painted. Locke praised Hayden's work and considered Porter's assessment too severe; notwithstanding these conflicts, Hayden flourished. He worked for the easel division of the Works Progress Administration (WPA) Federal Arts Project, which provided continued support to many artists of the Harlem Renaissance after the Harmon Foundation's exhibits were discontinued in 1933. Hayden's paintings, particularly those that centered on black life, had broad appeal and exerted an incontrovertible influence on perceptions of Harlem Renaissance aesthetics.

The artist most closely associated with the Harlem Renaissance was Aaron Douglas, who was born in Kansas. Douglas espoused not only Locke's ideal of art embodying African motifs but also a similar mandate set forth by the scholar and social activist W. E. B. Du Bois (in 1915, in an issue of the NAACP's magazine *The Crisis*) that black artists should depict only the most ennobling self-imagery. Douglas studied fine arts as an undergraduate at the University of Nebraska and taught art briefly in Kansas City before coming to New York in 1924. There he met Winold Reiss, who encouraged him to incorporate African abstraction into his work.

Douglas quickly developed a unique method of painting, which combined accessible narrative imagery with a complex compositional substructure of geometric abstraction. His stylized representations of African American life and history greatly appealed to patrons and literati in Harlem. In 1925, Reiss included Douglas's illustrations in the Harlem issue of *Survey Graphic*. That same year, Douglas received commissions to illustrate *Opportunity* (the publication of the New York Urban League) and *The Crisis* (for which Du Bois was a contributing editor). In 1926, Douglas helped illustrate the first issues of *Fire!!*, a cutting-edge periodical that was devoted to the works of young African American artists and writers; and in 1927, he collaborated with one of the cofounders of the NAACP, James Weldon Johnson, in creating drawings to accompany Johnson's collection of poems *God's Trombones*. In 1928, Douglas designed the jacket for Claude McKay's highly successful book *Home to Harlem*.

Also in 1928, Douglas received an award from the Barnes Foundation that enabled him to study the Barnes collection in Merion, Pennsylvania. This experience and a one-year stay in Paris from 1931 to 1932 exposed Douglas to a variety of African art objects as well as to European modernism. The influences of both are revealed in Douglas's mature style, which by the 1930s was a synthesis of African and European elements. By this time, Douglas was creating large-scale murals such as *Jungle and Jazz* for Harlem's Club Ebony, and other murals for businesses and institutions beyond the borders of Harlem, including Fisk University in Nashville (where he would later be the chairman of the art department) and the Sherman Hotel in Chicago. Douglas's most famous mural sequence was produced under the auspices of the WPA for the Schomburg Center in Harlem in 1934 and was called *Aspects of Negro Life*.

The large-scale oil compositions of *Aspects of Negro Life* comprise a chronological record of four critical moments in African American history. The first panel, *The Negro in an African Setting*, portrays African dancers, musicians, and ritual objects during an elysian time before the African slave trade began. The second, *From Slavery through Reconstruction*, shows a scene of enslaved workers behind a screen of cotton plants, men breaking their chains, and a figure holding up a copy of the Emancipation Proclamation in the shadow of the Capitol building. *An Idyll of the Deep South* depicts a time just after Reconstruction, during the period of Jim Crow, when legal segregation and widespread lynchings marred African American life. Portrayed in this complex narrative is a group of farmworkers and banjo players amid stylized flora. The figures in this group are overshadowed by the specter of a victim of lynching—the dangling feet of a body hanging from a tree. In *Song of the Towers*, the fourth mural in the series, Douglas portrays a saxophone player (a symbol of the black creative spirit) and a businessman in a towering industrial setting. The composition—a requiem for the proletariat—is crisscrossed with sinister, shadowy forms that haunt the figures, who appear to be overcome by intense emotional anguish.

Douglas's inimitable fusion of disparate elements— abstraction and figuration, Africanism and modernism, social and historical narrative—within his signature lyrical, translucent, nearly monochromatic palette appealed to both the neophyte and the connoisseur. Unlike most social realist and regionalist artists of his time, Douglas was able to embrace geometric abstraction in a way that allowed his paintings to remain accessible to the broader public. The comprehensibility of his images, and their dignified black subject matter, made Douglas one of the most popular artists of the period. In fact, one year after the completion of *Aspects of Negro Life*, Douglas was elected president of the Harlem Artists' Guild (the Harlem affiliate of the Artists Union), through which he fought for better opportunities for black artists.

Douglas's contemporary William H. Johnson was equally prolific and talented. Johnson came to New York from South Carolina in 1918, studying art and supporting himself at a variety of odd jobs until 1926, when he moved to Europe. During his years in New York, Johnson studied the visual arts, taking classes at the National Academy of Design beginning in 1921 and winning several art prizes and scholarships. He also spent summers at the Cape Cod School of Art in Provincetown, Massachusetts, where his works were included in a group exhibition at the local art associa-

tion. After studying briefly with George B. Luks, the renowned American "ashcan school" artist, Johnson went to the Montparnasse section of Paris with funds given to him by the director of the Cape Cod School of Art, Charles W. Hawthorne.

Johnson was an exceptional draftsman. His early still lifes and figure studies show a keen understanding of form and color and evoke the loose brushwork and spatial analyses of the impressionists and postimpressionists. His portraits and landscapes during his first years abroad demonstrate his own painterly expressiveness and also reveal the influence of the French artist Chaim Soutine and the Norwegian symbolist painter Edvard Munch. Johnson experimented in a variety of two-dimensional media while he was in Europe, and his works, like those of Douglas, show evidence of a broad understanding of European modernism, particularly German expressionism.

While he was abroad, Johnson met and married the Danish artist Holcha Krake; they returned to the United States in 1929. One year later, encouraged by Luks, Johnson entered his work in the Harmon Foundation's annual exhibit and was awarded a gold medal for painting. Throughout the 1930s, Johnson continued to exhibit at the Harmon Foundation and at numerous galleries at home and abroad. In 1937, he took a position with the WPA as an instructor at the Harlem Community Art Center. At about this time, his work began to undergo stylistic changes. Under pressure from the Harmon Foundation (which disapproved of his single-minded espousal of a European aesthetic), and in response to the expectations of the broader public regarding African American artists in general, Johnson turned to more deliberately ethnic themes and to a less apparently erudite formal technique. He moved away from European modernism toward a pseudo-naive *art brut* style that evoked vernacular art and African sculpture. He also began to focus on African American religious subjects and on genre scenes of couples in Harlem, street musicians, and farmworkers. In shifting toward an approach like that of folk art, Johnson was similar to Hayden, but, despite the guise of naïveté, Johnson's later works continued to show a keen sense of composition, an understanding of color and form, and an undeniable gift for complex design.

After his wife's death from breast cancer in 1944, Johnson's mental health began to deteriorate. While traveling in Norway, he was hospitalized for paresis (a disease of the central nervous system characterized by mental and emotional instability and paralytic attacks). The U.S. State Department arranged for his return home, and he was admitted to Central Islip State Hospital in New York. Johnson would never paint again; he remained confined at the state hospital until his death. However, the more than 1,000 works he had produced during the Harlem Renaissance were rescued from a warehouse in Manhattan by the Harmon Foundation, which purchased his estate and donated his paintings and prints to the Smithsonian Institution, where they remain today. The immense body of work produced by Johnson during the Harlem Renaissance reflects his complex personality and his response to life between two world wars and on two continents.

In 1927, the Newark Museum of Art mounted an exhibition, "Paintings and Watercolors by Living American Artists." A delicately rendered portrait of an elderly woman, seated at her sewing beside a lace-covered table, was voted the most popular work in the show. The painter was an alumnus of the Chicago Art Institute, Archibald Motley Jr. (1891–1981); and the painting was *Mending Socks*—a carefully constructed composition portraying Motley's grandmother in near profile within a compressed space. *Mending Socks* represented Motley's unquestionable talent, but as an early work depicting a conventional domestic subject in a naturalistic manner, it was far from indicative of the stylized forms and edgy, urban themes (influenced by his onetime mentor, the American artist George Bellows) for which Motley would become known.

Motley's penchant for realism quickly gave way to a more modernist vision, developed during a year of study in Paris at the end of the 1920s. In his new paintings, Motley generalized figures and faces, simplified forms, and subordinated details in favor of mood or ambience. He was able to capture his emotional impressions as well as his visual impressions of each scene he chose, bringing to life crowded Harlem nightclubs or cobblestoned Parisian streets teeming with French *flâneurs*. He achieved this feat through the use of vibrant colors, diffuse lighting, overlapping forms, and unique angles of vision and handling of space. The results were often visually dazzling.

Motley preferred metropolitan themes: pool halls, dance halls, and street scenes. He was also one of the first American artists to treat the black female nude as a subject worthy of "high" art, rather than as an object of ridicule or pornography. His psychologically intense *Brown Girl after the Bath* (1931) reconstitutes a seventeenth-century Dutch motif with a realism and quiet authority that conveys not only a sexualized body but also a contemplative woman whose melancholy,

enigmatic gaze holds that of the viewer. Motley, who was supported throughout the Depression by the WPA, made a definitive and lasting creative contribution to the Harlem Renaissance—a contribution which, although largely ignored after the 1930s, has been recognized in recent years as integral to our understanding of the period.

Women artists, too, thrived during the Harlem Renaissance. One was the sculptor Nancy Elizabeth Prophet (1890–1960), who graduated in 1918 from the Rhode Island School of Design, and then moved to New York, attracted by the art scene there. She developed a signficant alliance with Gertrude Vanderbilt Whitney, a member of New York's cultural elite and founder of the Whitney Museum of American Art. Whitney was responsible for some of the museum's first acquisitions of African American art: several works by the sculptor Richmond Barthé (1901–1989).

Whitney and Prophet were not only fellow artists but also close friends, and they shared a studio and exhibited together. In fact, in 1922 Whitney financed Prophet's first trip to Europe; Prophet would remain in Europe for ten years, studying and exhibiting throughout the 1920s and early 1930s—and becoming acquainted with W. E. B. Du Bois, Countee Cullen, and Augusta Savage, who were all sojourning in France. Toward the end of her stay in Paris, Prophet began to cultivate her reputation in the United States by sending two of her works to the Harmon exhibition of 1930 and winning a $250 prize for one of them.

Returning to the United States in 1934, at the invitation of John Hope, the president of Atlanta University, Prophet joined the art faculty at Spelman College—one of the southern magnets for talented figures in the Harlem Renaissance (Hale Woodruff had recently founded the art department there). For a time, Prophet's career flourished. Her elegant portraits in wood, marble, and other three dimensional media appeared in major American exhibitions, including the Whitney Biennials of 1935 and 1937, and in renowned collections such as the Philadelphia Museum of Art. In 1944, Prophet left her position at Spelman College; as a northerner, she had found the southern rural environment uninspiring. She returned to Rhode Island and made several attempts to further her professional goals; however, she found it impossible to repeat her earlier successes. To support herself, Prophet was forced to work as a housekeeper and as a live-in domestic servant. Occasionally, she made portrait busts for a ceramics factory to earn extra money, but her final years were spent in poverty and obscurity.

Another woman artist, Lois Mailou Jones (1905–1998), is a shining example of the creativity and productivity of the Harlem Renaissance. Unlike Prophet, Jones had nearly half a century of artistic success. Jones began her career in 1919 as a student at the High School of Practical Arts in Boston; her decision to pursue the arts as a profession was inspired, in part, by a meeting in the early 1920s with an older artist, Meta Warrick Fuller (whose sculpture *Ethiopia Awakening* of 1921 is considered one of the first to articulate the pan-Africanist philosophy of black enfranchisement that was integral to the New Negro and Negritude movements). Jones started by designing costumes and textiles, but she was also a prolific draftsman and painter. She held her first one-person show in 1923, when she was only seventeen. She spent her college years at the Boston Museum School on a four-year scholarship, majoring in design and winning numerous awards.

When she graduated, Jones relocated briefly to North Carolina and founded the art department at Palmer Memorial Institute in Sedalia. Her success there brought her to the attention of James V. Herring, then chairman of the art department at Howard University in Washington, D.C. (where Alain Locke headed the philosophy department). Herring invited Jones to join the faculty at Howard, and she would go on to teach design there for nearly fifty years. During her abundantly creative and productive life, Jones had more than sixty solo exhibitions, and she participated in literally hundreds of group shows, including the Harmon Foundation exhibits. Like Douglas, Jones also worked as a graphic designer, producing illustrations for a book by the African American historiographer Carter G. Woodson, *African Heroes and Heroines*, and designing covers for his *Negro History Bulletin*. Jones was a pioneer American abstractionist who combined a flair for decorative and geometric patterning with a keen understanding of human anatomy and a gift for portraiture. Responding to the inspiration of Locke and the Harmon Foundation, she focused consistently on African and African American subject matter, alternating these interests with a love of impressionist-style landscape.

The sculptor Augusta Savage—a contemporary of both Jones and Prophet—came to New York in the 1920s, like so many others, as part of the "great migration." Savage was one of the most influential artists of the Harlem Renaissance, making her greatest impact as an educator and an activist for the arts. After a period of study at New York's Cooper Union and a stay in Europe in the late 1920s, Savage returned to New York

in 1932 to establish her own Studio of Arts and Crafts. With aid from the WPA, this studio eventually evolved into the Harlem Community Arts Center, which provided art instruction to some 1,500 constituents and was a model WPA facility, visited by Eleanor Roosevelt and Albert Einstein. Savage's students included Jacob Lawrence (1917–2000), Norman Lewis (1909–1979), and William Artis (1914–1977), who were then novices but would go on to become renowned artists.

In 1939, Savage was offered a professional commission by the organizers of the New York World's Fair to create her sculpture *The Harp (Lift Every Voice and Sing)*. This monumental sixteen-foot plaster work featured a human harp consisting of singing African American figures. It also paid homage, through its subtitle, to James Weldon Johnson's song "Lift Every Voice and Sing," often known as the "black national anthem." After the World's Fair closed, Savage did not have the funds to cast or store this sculpture, and it was bulldozed when the fairgrounds were demolished. Savage also discovered that because she had been privately employed (even if only temporarily), she no longer qualified for her WPA position, and her employment with the Harlem Community Arts Center was terminated.

That year marked the last major showing of Savage's work, and her further attempts to advance her career were unsuccessful. In fact, her later career paralleled that of Prophet. The fact that neither woman could make professional progress after the 1930s was largely because of the demise, in 1943, of the WPA Federal Arts Project, which—because of its mandates against racial and sexual discrimination—had provided a short season of opportunity to women and minority artists. The unprecedented opportunities afforded to women and minorities during this period ended as congressional budgets were cut or discontinued, as abstract expressionism began to replace social realism and other narrative art, and as socialist sentiments gave way to more conservative values. Like Prophet, Savage rarely exhibited or produced art after the early 1940s; eventually, she became an embittered recluse on an old farm in upstate New York, shunning the art community altogether. Despite this unfortunate conclusion to her own artistic life, Savage's genius survived in the art of one of her most important students, Jacob Lawrence.

Lawrence's art is epitomized in images of Harlem and of African American heroes and heroism, configured in meticulously structured spaces. Lawrence was only a boy during the Harlem Renaissance, but his experiences in Harlem and in Savage's studio helped make him one of the most renowned African American artists of the twentieth century. His earliest painting cycles—*Frederick Douglass* (1938–1939), *Toussaint L'Ouverture* (1939), *Harriet Tubman* (1939–1940), *Migration* (1940–1941), *John Brown* (1941), and *Harlem* (1942–1943)—reflect his affinity with the Harlem Renaissance. Like Douglas, Lawrence was inspired by the formal principles of contemporaneous art movements such as cubism and art deco, and he produced a body of work that is visually, emotionally, and intellectually provocative.

Lawrence was born in Atlantic City and moved to Harlem when he was thirteen years old, at a time when the glittering nightlife and the social milieu of Harlem were being displaced by the harsh realities of the Depression. His series *Harlem* compassionately portrays and interprets his experiences of life in New York. The scenes, thirty in all, range from pulsating city views to intimate interiors and use an often explicit narrative vernacular that reveals the depth, breadth, and complexity of African American existence. Lawrence, who remained active into his eighties, spent a lifetime enchanting and enlightening audiences, and informing them about the African American experience; through his work, he carried the legacy of the Harlem Renaissance into the next millennium.

Romare Bearden (1912–1988), like Lawrence, was a youth in Harlem at the end of the renaissance. Bearden attended college in New York in the early 1930s and exhibited at the Harlem YMCA and at the Harlem Art Workshop (also headed by Savage). By 1940, Bearden had rented studio space on 125th Street in a building also occupied by Jacob Lawrence and Claude McKay. Bearden is seldom identified directly with the Harlem Renaissance, but his art, like the work of Lawrence, recontextualizes his experiences of Harlem. Although Bearden had left Harlem by the mid-twentieth century, remembrances of the old neighborhood would continue to appear in his art for decades.

In the true spirit of the Harlem Renaissance, Bearden took inspiration from African as well as various other sources, including medieval stylization, Chinese calligraphy, the work of the European masters, and biblical and literary themes. His later collages reflect his affinity with cubist structure and the painting of the American precisionist Stuart Davis (who was active in New York during the Harlem Renaissance), as well as his studies at the Art Students League in the 1930s with the political satirist George Grosz. Bearden was also a disciple of jazz, which he deftly translated into visual form. In his compositions, he configured complex overlays of negative and positive space with the same intuitive rectitude as a jazz musician might conceive the compound relationships between sounds and silence. Bearden also applied the methods of the dada artists of the 1920s and 1930s, combining elements of montage, collage, and photography. His images are unique visions of tenement houses, conjure women, jazz sessions, and life in Harlem. Bearden was a man of many talents and deep emotional and intellectual commitments. In addition to his career as a visual artist, he studied philosophy at the Sorbonne in Paris, spent two decades as a social worker, published poetry, and pursued a brief career as a songwriter. Bearden is recognized today as one of the great American modernists of the twentieth century and a quintessential "renaissance" man.

The artists discussed here are only a few of those whose lives and ambitions were interconnected during the years of the Harlem Renaissance. There are many others, such as the photographer James Van Der Zee (1886–1983), who recorded in pictures a crucial time in our history—creating, for example, valuable visual documents of the activities of Marcus Garvey's pan-Africanist organization, the Universal Negro Improvement Association (UNIA). Van Der Zee's photographic portraits of families and individuals in Harlem provide a breathtaking record of the age. Arriving in Harlem from Massachusetts in 1906, Van Der Zee was hired by the Gertz department store as a darkroom technician, and by 1917, he had opened his own portrait studio on 135th Street (by the early 1930s, he moved to a larger space on Lenox Avenue). Soon, Van Der Zee's talent for creative settings, elaborate props, and ennobling photographs of Harlem's citizens made him a celebrated artist in the community; ultimately, he achieved a reputation as one of the most important photographers in modern American history.

Other artists include the sculptor Richmond Barthé, who studied at the Art Institute of Chicago almost simultaneously with Motley; by the early 1930s, three of Barthé's elegant, lyrical bronze sculptures were purchased by the Whitney Museum. The painter and sculptor Charles Alston was one of the first African Americans to be given a supervisory position by the WPA. Under its auspices, Alston created murals for Harlem Hospital and opened a studio space at 306 West 141st Street. Alston's atelier, known affectionately as "306," became a hub for African American artists and intellectuals, who gathered there to discuss important issues of the day.

William Johnson, *Street Life, Harlem*, c. 1939–1940. (Smithsonian American Art Museum, Washington, D.C.; Art Resource, New York.)

Aaron Douglas, *Song of the Towers*, 1934, at the Schomburg Center for Research in Black Culture. (Schomburg Center, New York Public Library; Art Resource, New York.)

Miguel Covarrubias, *Rhapsody in Blue*, 1929. (Art Resource, New York. By permission of Fundación Covarrubias.)

Malvin Gray Johnson (1896–1934) studied at the National Academy of Design and exhibited with the Harmon Foundation. His Cézannesque portraits of African American subjects received some adverse criticism for their emphatic modernism, but they attracted the attention of commercial galleries and were given enthusiastic reviews. Sargent Claude Johnson (1887–1967), who was based in San Francisco, created African-inspired sculptural portraits that paid homage to the physical beauty of the black race; Johnson participated in Harmon shows throughout the 1920s and 1930s. Hale Woodruff, who was born in Illinois,

Jacob Lawrence, *The Migration of the Negro*, 1940–1941, Panel 12: "The railroad stations were at times so crowded that special guards had to be called in to keep order." Tempera on gesso on composition board, 12 by 18 inches; text and title revised by the artist, 1993. (© ARS, New York; © Digital Image; © The Museum of Modern Art, New York, gift of Mrs. David M. Levy, 28. 1942. 6. Licensed by Scala / Art Resource, N. Y.)

was inspired by Mexican muralists; he received one of the first Harmon Foundation awards in 1926, and went on to paint social realist murals on African American history for the libraries of both Atlanta University (where he was chairman of the art department) and Talladega College in Alabama.

Although important research has been done on many visual artists of the Harlem Renaissance, numerous others remain unsung. Many of these men and women have faded into obscurity, but their legacy has not. The painters and sculptors of the Harlem Renaissance constitute a remarkably talented group, who made possible the successes of subsequent generations of African American artists, represented by Bearden, Lawrence, and others. Serious racial, economic, and sociopolitical impediments faced the artists of the Harlem Renaissance in the pursuit of their chosen vocation. Yet the particular circumstances of the period, which allowed a momentary flowering of genius, caused Americans to sit up and take notice of African American creativity for the first time in the history of the United States.

LISA E. FARRINGTON

See also Art Criticism and the Harlem Renaissance; Crisis, The; Europe and the Harlem Renaissance: 4— Paris; Federal Programs; Fire!!; Harmon Foundation; Locke, Alain; Modernism; Negritude; New Negro; 135th Street Library; Opportunity; Porter, James Amos; Survey Graphic; Visual Arts; Woodson, Carter G.; *specific artists*

Further Reading

Bearden, Romare, and Harry Henderson. *A History of African-American Artists From 1792 to the Present*. New York: Pantheon, 1993.

Driskell, David, et al. *Harlem Renaissance Art of Black America*. New York: Studio Museum in Harlem, 1987.

Farrington, Lisa. *Creating Their Own Image: A History of African-American Women Artists*. New York and London: Oxford University Press, 2004.

King-Hammond, Leslie, and Tritobia Hayes Benjamin. *Three Generations of African-American Women Sculptors*. Philadelphia, Pa.: Afro-American Historical and Cultural Museum, 1996.

Patton, Sharon. *African American Art*. New York and London: Oxford University Press, 1998.

Powell, Richard. *Rhapsodies in Black: Art of the Harlem Renaissance*. Berkeley: University of California Press, 1997.

Reynolds, Gary A., and Beryl J. Wright. *Against the Odds: African-American Artists and the Harmon Foundation*. Newark, N.J.: Newark Museum, 1989.

Associated Negro Press

The Associated Negro Press was not the first black news service. In 1884, Colonel William Murrell, general manager of the Washington, D.C. *Bee*, announced at a meeting of the National Colored Associated Press (NCAP) that Western Union had installed wires in its office to transmit news to other black newspapers around the country. Charles C. Stewart of the Baltimore *Vindicator* chose at least one black newspaper in each state to become a member of NCAP. In 1890, the Associated Correspondents of Race Newspapers (ACRN) was established. It consisted of at least forty reporters from ten newspapers around the country who were based in Washington, D.C., and sent news from Washington to newspapers other than their own ten. Matthew M. Lewey, owner and founder of the Gainesville *Sentinel* and president of the National Negro Press Association, realized that a more efficient system of exchanging articles was necessary to improve coverage by the black press. This topic was explored at the association's convention in Little Rock, Arkansas, in 1911; later that year, Lewey arranged a meeting in Nashville, Tennessee, where a newspaper service for member weeklies was established. The service would gather news from all of the weeklies through Wednesday of each week for publication on Friday or Saturday.

In 1918, Claude Barnett, as part of a public relations campaign for the Chicago *Defender*, visited several black newspapers and learned that many of them had local coverage but lacked national and international news. He then approached Robert S. Abbott, owner and publisher of the *Defender*, and suggested starting a news service to provide stories to back newspapers. Barnett received no support, but in 1919 he launched the Associated Negro Press (ANP) in Chicago.

Barnett called ANP a news service, but its critics said that it was actually a clipping service because Barnett and his staff clipped articles from newspapers nationwide and included them in what ANP sent to its clients, along with articles rewritten from papers such as the Chicago *Defender* and only a handful of original articles from freelancers in Chicago and elsewhere. Abbott complained to a friend that Barnett was "stealing my news and selling it to other papers for a profit" (Waters 1987, 419); and in general, historians—although they believe that ANP was more than a clipping service—agree with Abbott's accusation. Barnett was short-staffed at the outset and found that the most economical means of providing his service was to rewrite material from the *Defender*, which was then the leading black newspaper in terms of circulation and coverage. In this way, his small staff produced an impressive amount of copy. However, as ANP gained more clients, Barnett was able to attract news sources and thus decrease his dependence on the *Defender*.

Barnett's criteria included accuracy, human interest, coverage of racial concerns, and appeal to a wide audience. As ANP grew, it also attracted reporters from other newspapers: Nahum Brazier (Nahum Daniel Brascher) and Percival Prattis from the *Defender*, and Frank Marshal Davis from Atlanta. They broadened the product by enlisting well-known scholarly writers and personalities as columnists, who commented on a wide variety of topics including civil rights, sports, and science. Barnett paid his writers only a meager salary, on the assumption that they would become celebrated by having their articles and columns published in numerous newspapers. This appeal to fame rather than money helped keep ANP solvent.

ANP served newspapers, schools, organizations, businesses, and individuals; newspaper clients could pay for the service by providing ANP with their local news. ANP's news was mimeographed and delivered twice a week by first-class mail and special delivery. A delivery might consist of two or three packages of fifty to seventy-five legal-size sheets of single-spaced copy, depending on the circulation of the client newspaper. This represented more than enough articles to fill all the sections of the paper except for local stories. ANP's feature stories focused on black history, entertainment, women's fashions, and other subjects. Late-breaking stories and special events were sent over the wires. ANP had its own part-time correspondents in large cities and correspondents abroad in Paris, Moscow, London, Tokyo, and elswhere.

ANP did not collaborate with its white counterpart, the Associated Press (AP); in fact, some of ANP's editors considered AP the enemy. Oswald Garrison Villard, for one, believed AP's coverage of Negroes was biased and tended to polarize whites and Negroes:

> The Associated Press (white) . . . always in its first paragraph . . . attributes the source of trouble to our people "molesting white women." That, the

Associated Press knows, is always fuel for the fire of the fury. . . . It arouses certain elements of whites to indignation by the thoughts of the ever "burly black brutes," and it stirs the people of our group to a state of fighting made by the folly of it. (Pride 1974, 51)

But ANP was like AP in at least one respect: Both helped sustain newspapers. According to Waters, "Half, maybe three-fourths, of the papers could not have existed without the copy provided by ANP, just as most white papers would have folded had it not been for AP and UPI" (420). Historians credit ANP with building the Negro press by providing reliable content. Moreover, ANP did much to orchestrate the civil rights movement by reporting on racial discrimination.

ANP reached its height after the period of the Harlem Renaissance, during World War II, when it had 225 domestic subscribers. By 1958, it had only thirty-seven domestic clients. In August 1964, Barnett retired and sold ANP to Alfred Duckett, a public relations specialist in New York City. At that time, ANP had recovered somewhat; it had seventy-five domestic subscribers and two hundred international subscribers (mostly African newspapers). But even a reasonable number of subscribers could not sustain it: With the advent of television and the increased coverage of black issues in white dailies, black newspapers and eventually ANP lost importance. In the early 1960s, though, Barnett started an extension of ANP in Africa, called World News Service (WNS). In 1967, after a series of strokes, Barnett died in Chicago. Duckett distributed feature stories through ANP until 1969.

During the years when ANP operated, 1919 through 1969, nearly fifty African American news services cropped up. However, none of these was nearly as successful as ANP; and after 1969 the black press had no news service until April 1972, when the National Newspaper Publishers Association (NNPA, based in Washington, D.C.) began to provide the National Black News Service.

GERI ALUMIT

See also Abbott, Robert Sengstacke; Black Press; Chicago Defender; Villard, Oswald Garrison

Further Reading

Hogan, A. *A Black National News Service: The Associated Negro Press and Claude Barnett, 1919–1945*. London: Associated University Presses.

Pride, Armistead S. "The News That Was." In *Perspectives of the Black Press: 1974*, ed. Henry G. La Brie III. Kennebunkport, Maine: Mercer House Press. 1974.

Pride, Armistead S., and Clint C. Wilson II. *A History of the Black Press*. Washington, D.C.: Howard University Press, 1997.

Shofner, Jerrell H. "Florida." In *The Black Press in the South, 1865–1979*, ed. Henry Lewis Suggs. Westport, Conn.: Greenwood, 1983.

Thornbrough, Emma Lou. *T. T. Thomas Fortune, Militant Journalist*. Chicago, Ill.: University of Chicago Press 1972.

Waters, Enoch P. *American Diary: A Personal History of the Black Press*. Chicago, Ill.: Path, 1987.

Association for the Study of Negro Life and History and Journal of Negro History

Scholars tend to focus on the artistic and literary manifestations of the Harlem Renaissance, neglecting its historical component. In fact, though, the black history movement led by Carter G. Woodson, the second African American to earn a Ph.D. from Harvard University, experienced growth and expansion during the time of the renaissance.

From its humble beginning in 1915, Woodson envisioned the Association for the Study of Negro Life and History (ASNLH) as a scientific and scholarly organization dedicated to the promotion and dissemination of useful information about various aspects of black history. Central to this project was the publication of a scientific historical journal, the *Journal of Negro History* (*JNH*), founded in 1916. In format, *JNH* resembled the *American Historical Review*, edited by the prominent scholar J. Franklin Jameson, which was the official organ of the American Historical Association (AHA). Both ASNLH and *JNH* represented a century-long effort to establish black history, first in black academia—historically black colleges and universities—and later in American society in general. The Harlem Renaissance was not only the backdrop but also a significant impetus for this institutionalization. Several factors made a serious study of black history possible: They included (1) white patronage, from individual donors and philanthropic organizations; (2) Woodson's single-minded leadership and his ability to attract prominent white historians and black civic leaders; and (3) the shifting demographics of black America, caused by the "great migration." These same factors also allowed the construction of an intellectual apparatus through which studies of black history could be disseminated to both African Americans and whites.

Throughout much of the nineteenth century, and up to the founding of ASNLH, black history was pursued in the narrow, parochial confines of specialized and localized black intellectual and historical associations. Among African Americans, interest in history and organization for its study were characterized by groups such as the American Negro Academy, founded by Alexander Crummell in 1897; and the Negro Society for Historical Research, founded in the early twentieth century by two black bibliophiles, John ("Grit") Bruce and Arthur Alonso Schomburg. Because their origins were in the late nineteenth century and the early twentieth century, the American Negro Academy and the Negro Society for Historical Research relied heavily on nineteenth-century notions of gentlemanly deportment and on elitist ideas about scholarship. Their members, drawn mostly from the black elite, saw their role as disseminating information to educated audiences in the form of addresses, lectures, and treatises. The American Negro Academy published occasional papers, and W. E. B. Du Bois, one of its most distinguished leaders, considered its membership representative of the best men of the race. Although the Negro Society for Historical Research was less exclusive, it, too, had only a moderate impact on the larger community. It consisted primarily of serious collectors and bibliophiles who focused on the black experience, and it proved too insular to survive in a changing intellectual environment.

ASNLH represented a significant departure from these earlier societies. By the 1920s, it emerged from its shadowy position as a small, localized historical organization and became a recognized scholarly association for the promotion of black history. Much of this change was a result of Woodson's pioneering work. Woodson was a native of Kentucky and a graduate of Berea College and Harvard University. As a professionally trained historian, he strongly believed that history and historical understanding involved not only the collection and preservation of materials but also a rigorous application of scientific objectivity to historical data. He understood, furthermore, that to be respected as a legitimate scholarly enterprise and to sustain itself financially, his organization would need the endorsement of white historians, philanthropists, and prominent African American scholars and donors. One source of such support was the presence of leading figures in the white and black communities on the executive council of ASNLH. Throughout the 1920s, prominent individuals from all walks of life served in this capacity. Historians were represented on the council by Carl Russell Fish of the University of Wisconsin and Albert Bushnell Hart of Harvard University. Philanthropists included Julius Rosenwald, chairman of Sears Roebuck and Company; and the financier George Peabody, a trustee at Hampton University. The council also included well-known white activists and black intellectuals. For example, two council members were Moorfield Storey, who served as executive director of the NAACP in the early twentieth century; and Monroe Nathan Work, a prominent black sociologist who was the editor of *Negro Yearbook*, an annual compilation of statistics regarding blacks in the United States. Perhaps the most prominent black college president to serve on the council was Robert Russa Moton, Booker T. Washington's successor at Tuskegee Institute; Moton had close ties to the Republican Party throughout the 1920s.

ASNLH also received $25,000 from the Carnegie Institute, with the help of J. Franklin Jameson, the director of the foundation; and a $25,000 grant from the Laura Spelman Rockefeller Memorial Fund. These grants were used to collect data and fund several projects on free black families in the early republic (1789–1830) and in the antebellum period (1830–1860). The grants also supported a series of investigations by Alrutheus Ambush Taylor, a graduate of the University of Michigan and Harvard University who was ASNLH's first associate investigator. Taylor collected information about African Americans during the Reconstruction period (1865–1877) and wrote two monographs: *The Negro in the Reconstruction of Virginia* (1924) and *The Negro in the Reconstruction of South Carolina* (1926). In addition, the grants facilitated the hiring of Lorenzo Greene as a part-time associate and field investigator for ASNLH. Between 1928 and 1930, Greene made important contributions to several of Woodson's book-length studies, including *African Myths*, *The Negro in Our History*, and *The Negro Wage Earner*.

ASNLH hired several African American women as research assistants. Irene Wright was hired in 1923 to conduct research in archives at Seville, in Spain. Wright investigated the struggle between the British and Spanish empires for territorial control of the Americas during the colonial period; she also examined material related to the position of blacks in Spanish colonial society. Ruth Anna Fisher, a graduate of Oberlin College who was a research assistant to J. Franklin Jameson, conducted research in the British Museum and the Public Record Office and found important letters as well as the diaries of captains of slaving vessels. Woodson's goal in having Fisher conduct research was to develop a documentary history and an anthropological portrait of Native Africans before the advent of the slave trade.

Another important component of the black history movement was the annual conventions held by ASNLH. Consistent with the overall goals of the organization and the fact that it sought to establish itself in large urban centers, meetings were held in cities with large black populations and established black communities: Baltimore, Maryland; Washington, D.C.; Chicago, Illinois; St. Louis, Missouri; Nashville, Tennessee; and elsewhere. These conventions often showcased the varied achievements of ASNLH and brought together distinguished individuals from many sectors of the population of the host city. The meetings of 1920 and 1924 can serve to illustrate the goals of ASNLH. The convention of 1920, held in Louisville, Kentucky, was devoted to the theme "Social and Economic Development of the Negro." Speakers focused on the early history of African Americans, the teaching of black history, and the specific contributions of enslaved Africans to civilization. The convention of 1924, in Baltimore, Maryland, examined (among other subjects) folklore among African Americans. Also, N. F. Mossell, author of *The Work of the Afro-American Women*, presented a paper, "History from the Point of View of a Child," in which he stressed the importance of elementary reading material in helping young students acquire a knowledge of their history.

These conferences not only highlighted black history but also addressed other concerns of ASNLH. Woodson felt that the role of the organization encompassed more than history as an academic discipline: It also extended to solving the problems of society. He hoped that ASNLH could help strengthen training in the social sciences in black schools and stimulate research and teaching about the social sciences and the economic problems of African Americans. Most important, he thought that ultimately his work could and would lead to an improvement in race relations.

One of the most enduring legacies of ASNLH was the establishment of Negro History Week in 1926. This event—celebrated in February, the month in which Frederick Douglass and Abraham Lincoln were born—highlighted the work of ASNLH and drew attention to the importance of teaching black history in primary and secondary schools and at institutions of higher learning. Woodson never wanted Negro History Week to be observed only by the black community, so he took great pains to disseminate information about it to members of the white community.

Like ASNLH, the *Journal of Negro History (JNH)* played a crucial role in the creation of a viable black historical tradition. The journal—edited by Woodson from 1916 until his death in 1950—was the organization's premier scientific publication. It was founded to meet the need for an accurate record of black people's past and, equally, to provide a forum where black scholars could publish studies challenging conventional wisdom about that past. As many scholars have noted, the major historical associations, such as the American Historical Association, rarely published scholarship by African Americans. The *American Historical Review* did not invite W. E. B. Du Bois to publish a paper until 1910; the Mississippi Valley Historical Association and the Southern Historical Association did not invite black historians to present papers until the 1940s.

JNH was also important because of its multifaceted presentation of African Americans' past. The journal featured articles, communications, informative letters from individuals, notices, and reports from the annual and spring conferences of ASNLH. Many books were first printed, in their entirety, in *JNH*. At the center of the journal's philosophy were "five ways to help the cause"—reminders about how subscribers could help promote the study of black history. They were as follows: "subscribe to the journal, become a member of the Association, contribute to the research fund, collect and send us the historical materials bearing on the Negroes of your community, and urge every Negro to write us all he knows about his family history."

JNH published a wide range of scholarship. It concentrated on revisionist history; for example, it challenged the southern historian Ulrich Bonnell Philips, whose *American Negro Slavery* depicted slavery as fairly benign; and it also offered significant revisions of the concept of Reconstruction (1865–1876) as a "tragic era." The earlier, legendary account had taken a dim view of blacks' participation in Reconstruction; blacks, who were portrayed as docile, lazy, and incompetent, were said to have been manipulated by two invidious factions: northern carpetbaggers (northerners who packed all of their belongings in a carpetbag and came South to profit from Reconstruction) and southern scalawags (native southerners who profited from the corruption of the Reconstruction era at the expense of their fellow southerners). This older view was countered in articles by John Lynch, a participant in Reconstruction in Virginia; by Alrutheus Ambush Taylor's pioneering work on Reconstruction; and by Woodson's

own *Negro in Our History*, a scholarly textbook published in several editions throughout the 1920s. Moreover, Lynch, Taylor, and Woodson offered alternative portraits of black politicians and their activities in southern legislatures during Reconstruction, and thus did significant groundwork for the contemporary view of Reconstruction.

JNH also focused on the diaspora and its implications for African American life. The journal often included articles on the African past as well as the black experience in Latin America, Europe, and elsewhere. The article "Three Elements of African Culture," by Gordon Blaine Hancock, a well-known African American educator at Virginia Union, appeared in *JNH* in 1923. Also in 1923, in a nod to European history, *JNH* published Albert Perry's article on Abram Hannibal, an African who served at the court of the Russian czar Peter the Great. Perhaps the most interesting work of this kind was produced by Zora Neale Hurston. Hurston, who was a folklorist and ethnographer, spent considerable time in the 1920s documenting the folkways of rural African Americans throughout the South. Her contributions include "Cudjo's Own Story of the Last African Slavery" and a set of her own letters on the Mose Settlement, one of the oldest black colonies in Florida. Hurston's work complemented that of Elsie Clews Parsons, who worked intensely to stimulate interest in the collection of black folklore. ASNLH offered a prize of $200 for the best material collected.

JNH also included other subject matter of importance to African Americans. Particular issues presented material on black people's feelings about World War I; letters from participatants in the "great migration," the movement of blacks from the rural South to the urban North between 1915 and 1930; reviews of the work of prominent authors, such as W. E. B. Du Bois's *Darkwater* (1920); and advertisements for black colleges and universities such as Howard, Tuskegee, Fisk, and Morris Brown.

Some issues of *JNH* were devoted to a specific topic. The issue of July 1922, for instance, was devoted to the black church; articles by Woodson, John Cromwell, and Walter Brooks focused on denominations such as the Baptists and examined churches in specific geographic locales such as the District of Columbia. An issue in 1924 was devoted exclusively to civil rights groups in the black community. Mary White Ovington, a protégé of Du Bois, wrote an article about the NAACP; L. Hollingsworth Wood, who was an active member of the executive council of ASNLH and a longtime supporter of African American causes, wrote an article on the Urban League; and the bibliophile and collector Jesse Moorland, a trustee of Howard University, wrote about the influence of the YMCA on African Americans. On important topics like Reconstruction, whole books were printed. For example, Alrutheus Ambush Taylor's *The Negro in the Reconstruction of Virginia* and *The Negro in the Reconstruction of South Carolina* were first printed in *JNH*, in 1924 and 1926.

ASNLH and *JNH* represent the culmination of a century-long effort to make black history a professional discipline. Like the Harlem Renaissance, the black history movement represented an assertive effort to reconstruct the past through viable organizations. This goal was supported by several trends in the African American community and the wider American community. Urbanization and professionalization—which facilitated the growth of institutions such as the black press, black businesses, black academic associations, and graduate training for black historians—were directly responsible for the development of the black history movement. Thus this movement, not unlike the literature of the Harlem Renaissance, created a legacy for black and white Americans.

STEPHEN G. HALL

See also Bruce, John Edward; Greene, Lorenzo; Hurston, Zora Neale; Moton, Robert Russa; National Urban League; Ovington, Mary White: Schomburg, Arthur A.; Woodson, Carter G.; Work, Monroe Nathan

Further Reading

Dagbovie, Pero Gaglo. "Black Women, Carter G. Woodson, and the Association for the Study of Negro Life and History, 1915–1950." *Journal of African American History*, 88, Winter 2003, pp. 21–41.

Franklin, John Hope. *George Washington Williams: A Biography*. Chicago, Ill.: University of Chicago Press, 1985.

———. "On the Evolution of Scholarship in Afro-American Scholarship." In *The State of Afro-American History: Past, Present and Future*, ed. Darlene Clark Hine. Baton Rouge: Louisiana State University, 1986.

Goggin, Jacqueline. "Countering White Racist Scholarship: Carter G. Woodson and the Journal of Negro History." *Journal of Negro History*, 68, 1983, pp. 355–375.

———. "Carter G. Woodson and the Movement to Promote Black History, 1915–1950." Ph.D. dissertation, University of Rochester, N.Y., 1986.

———. *Carter G. Woodson: Life in Black History*. Baton Rouge: Louisiana University Press, 1993.

Hall, Stephen G. "Alrutheus Ambush Taylor, Black Intellectualism, and the Remaking of Reconstruction Historiography, 1893–1954." *UCLA Historical Journal*, 16, 1996, pp. 39–60.

Higham, John. *History Professional Scholarship in America*. Baltimore, Md.: Johns Hopkins University Press, 1983.

McHenry, Elizabeth. *Forgotten Readers: Recovering the Lost History of African American Literary Societies*. Durham, N.C.: Duke University Press, 2002.

Meier, August, and Eliott Rudwick. *Black History and the Historical Profession, 1915–1980*. Chicago: University of Illinois Press, 1986.

Moses, Wilson Jeremiah. *Afrotopia: The Roots of African American Popular History*. Cambridge: Cambridge University Press, 1998.

Sinnette, Elinor Des Verney. *Arthur Alonso Schomburg: Black Bibliophile and Collector—A Biography*. Detroit, Mich.: Wayne State University Press, 1989.

———, et al. *Black Bibliophiles and Collectors: Preservers of Black History*. Washington, D.C.: Howard University Press, 1990.

Walker, Clarence. *Deromanticizing Black History: Critical Essays and Appraisals*. Atlanta: University of Georgia Press, 1991.

Wilson, Francille Rusan. "Racial Consciousness and Black Scholarship: Charles H. Wesley and the Consciousness of Negro Labor in the United States." *Journal of Negro History*, 81, 1996, pp. 72–88.

Atlanta University Studies

The Atlanta University Studies series lies outside the historical context of the Harlem Renaissance. Nevertheless, under the editorship of the protean W. E. B. Du Bois (1897–1914), the series provided an intellectual foundation for many of the significant themes in the ideology of the New Negro. To be more precise, the studies provided an intellectual justification for attempts by social scientists, writers of fiction and cultural and social criticism, and graphic artists to unearth African elements retained in the black population not only in North America but also in the Caribbean and South America. Furthermore, with regard to the development of black businesses, the series provided a philosophical rationale that resonated in the rhetoric of many black political leaders, such as Marcus Garvey. Finally, the studies provided factual evidence of significant enterprise among blacks (both male and female) nationwide. Thus despite the unevenness of the publications and the consequent acerbic criticism of Du Bois's efforts from white commentators who reviewed some of the studies, these works were an integral part of the philosophical rationalization of the New Negro movement.

The Atlanta University Studies series originated in 1896, at the annual Atlanta University Conference on Negro Problems. The annual conferences—the brainchild of the university's white president, Horace Bumstead; and one of its white trustees, a New Englander—were modeled after the Farmers Conferences of the Tuskegee Institute. Like Tuskegee's conferences, those at Atlanta were, in the words of the historian Leroy Davis, "laudable early attempts at meshing the needs of the community with the resources of the academy."

The studies conceived between 1897 and 1914 were edited primarily by Du Bois. His grandiose vision of the project called for a repetition of each topic every ten years. The proceedings of the studies ranged widely and (as noted above) varied in quality. Although Du Bois's plans did not reach fruition (and he did not participate in the project after 1914), his volumes in the series had a perceptible impact on the thought of people as varied as Alain Locke, Charles S. Johnson, and other patrons of the Harlem Renaissance; E. Franklin Frazier and other social and cultural critics; and sculptors and painters such as Richmond Barthé and Aaron Douglas.

As editor of and contributor to the series, Du Bois often vacillated between stereotypes of his African ancestors and genuine, lucid insights into their lives. For example, in *Efforts for Social Betterment Among Negro Americans* (1898), he referred to African religions as the "mystery and rites of . . . fetishism." As late as 1914, in *Morals and Manners Among Negro Americans*, Du Bois seemed to invent traditions, writing, "Africa is distinctly the land of the Mother." Nevertheless, Du Bois's thoughts on Africa and Africans were significant. Influenced by the immigrant German-Jewish anthropologist Franz Boas, who delivered the commencement address at Atlanta University in 1906, Du Bois again and again celebrated the contribution of blacks to world civilization, demonstrating that black Americans were descendants of peoples who had made and were perfectly capable of making essential contributions to the progress of humankind in the present and future. Furthermore, Du Bois anticipated the anthropologist Melville J. Herskovits and the works of the "father of Negro history," Carter G. Woodson, during the 1920s and early 1930s, that revealed African "retentions" in the black population in the United States. Africanism

in the African American peoples was a vital theme, promulgated time and again by major writers and artists during the Harlem Renaissance. Du Bois also overtly linked pertinent African retentions to the issue of black people's capability in business enterprises when he asserted, in 1897, that many Africans "are born men and traffickers." In 1899, in *The Negro in Business*, a work in the Atlanta series, he once again asserted that "the African Negro is born a trader." Accordingly, although one of the most renowned social critics of the Harlem Renaissance, E. Franklin Frazier, rejected the notion of Africanism as the source of some blacks' success in business, he nevertheless saw business enterprises as essential for any program of black liberation.

In sum, the Atlanta University Studies evidently provided a strong foundation for the rising New Negro ideologies of economic and cultural nationalism. That the artists and theoreticians of the Harlem Renaissance were unable to impose cultural nationalism perhaps had more to do with their economic dependence on white patronage than with any unwillingness on their part to seize the historical moment of the 1920s for black liberation.

VERNON J. WILLIAMS

See also Barthé, Richmond; Boas, Franz; Douglas, Aaron; Du Bois, W. E. B.; Frazier, E. Franklin; Herskovits, Melville; Johnson, Charles Spurgeon; Locke, Alain; New Negro; New Negro Movement; Woodson, Carter G.

Further Reading

Broderick, Francis. *W. E. B. Du Bois: A Leader in a Time of Crisis*. Stanford, Calif.: Stanford University Press, 1959.
Lewis, David. *W. E. B. Du Bois: A Biography of Race, 1868–1919*. New York: Holt, 1993.
Rudwick, Elliott. *W. E. B. Du Bois: A Study of Minority Group Leadership*. Philadelphia: University of Pennsylvania, 1960.

Attaway, William

William Alexander Attaway (1911–1986) was a novelist, songwriter, playwright, screenwriter, labor organizer, and actor. He was the son of a physician and a teacher in Greenville, Mississippi, and was born into a life of privilege, but he did not want to follow in his parents' professional footsteps. As a teenager he chose to attend a vocational school and learn automotive mechanics; and although he soon yielded to family pressure and went to a regular high school, he continued to rebel against upper-class respectability. When a high school teacher introduced him to the poetry of Langston Hughes, he immediately decided to become a writer. He attended the University of Illinois at Urbana until his father's death, whereupon he dropped out to travel around the country as a hobo for the next two years. He returned to college and graduated with a bachelor's degree in 1936.

Attaway published his first short story, "Tale of the Blackamoor," in *Challenge* in June 1935. At about the same time he joined the touring company of *You Can't Take It With You*, helped by his sister, Ruth Attaway, who had begun her acting career as Rheba in the original production. While on the road, he learned that his novel *Let Me Breathe Thunder* had been accepted for publication, immediately quit the tour, and returned home to write.

The publication date of *Let Me Breathe Thunder*—1939—puts Attaway at the end of the Harlem Renaissance and the beginning of a period of realism. He established himself as a writer with this novel, a critically acclaimed story of two white hoboes and their Mexican charge. However, neither *Let Me Breathe Thunder* nor his next novel, *Blood on the Forge*, which was also well received by the critics, sold well (the latter, though, was reprinted in 1993). The reason may be that the landmark work *Native Son* by his friend Richard Wright, the icon of realism, was published in 1940, and Attaway's novels suffered in comparison. The three tragic Moss brothers in *Blood on the Forge*, like the white characters in *Let Me Breathe Thunder*, seem tame next to Wright's Bigger Thomas. (Attaway and Richard Wright had become friends in November 1935, when both were working on the Federal Writers' Project guide to Illinois.)

Attaway later turned to more lucrative forms of writing. He composed and arranged songs for Harry Belafonte, among others, and was involved in *Calypso Song Book* (1957, a collection of songs) and *I Hear America Singing* (1967, a children's book about the history of popular music). He also wrote scripts for radio, television, and motion pictures. One of his most important scripts was *One Hundred Years of Laughter* (1966), for a television special on black humor. After its completion he took his family to Barbados for what was to have been a week's vacation; they stayed eleven years. Attaway spent the last years of his life in Berkeley and then in Los Angeles, California. In 1985, while working on a script for *The Atlanta Child Murders*, he suffered a heart attack from which he never fully recovered. He died in 1986.

Biography

William Attaway was born on 19 November 1911 in Greenville, Mississippi. His mother, Florence Parray Attaway, was a teacher; his father, William Alexander Attaway, was a physician and businessman who co-founded the National Negro Insurance Association. Dr. Attaway moved the family to Chicago when young William was about ten years old, to escape the segregated South; this migration northward became a central theme in Attaway's novel *Blood on the Forge* (1941). Attaway left college for two years and became a hobo—this experience was a theme in his novel *Let Me Breathe Thunder* (1939)—but eventually received his B.A. in 1936. He married Frances Settele on 28 December 1962, at the home of his friend Harry Belafonte. The Attaways had a son and a daughter. Attaway died on 17 June 1986, in Los Angeles.

CARMALETTA M. WILLIAMS

See also Federal Writers' Project; Wright, Richard

Further Reading: Works

Blood on the Forge: A Novel. Garden City, N.Y.: Doubleday, Doran, 1941. (Reprint, 1993.)

Calypso Song Book, ed. Lyle Kenyon Engel. New York, Toronto, and London: McGraw-Hill, 1957. (Attaway was a contributing editor.)

Carnival. (Play produced at University of Illinois-Urbana, 1935.)

"Death of a Rag Doll." *Tiger's Eye*, 1, October 1947, pp. 86–89.

I Hear America Singing. New York: Lion, 1967.

Let Me Breathe Thunder. New York: Doubleday, Doran, 1939; London: Hale, 1940. (Novel.)

One Hundred Years of Laughter. American Broadcasting Company (ABC-TV), 1967. (Television script.)

"Tale of the Blackamoor." *Challenge*, 1, June 1936, pp. 3–4.

Authors: 1—Overview

The authors of the Harlem Renaissance shared the goal of developing new forms of artistic representation of the African American experience. At the same time, they manifested a wide range of aesthetic principles and radically diverse concepts of blackness. The Harlem Renaissance meant different things to different people. The novelists, poets, dramatists, and essayists whose activity was centered in Harlem, although aware of the unique value of African American culture and art, interpreted and represented this uniqueness in many, sometimes conflicting, ways, embodying the tensions and contradictions of their American context.

In their quest to move beyond the dominant white aesthetics, black writers and intellectuals, such as W. E. B. Du Bois, Alain Locke, and James Weldon Johnson, were convinced that the Negro Renaissance was an auspicious movement in American cultural life. Johnson, among others, believed that if it succeeded it would undermine prejudice, win respect for the intellectual and artistic achievements of blacks, and consequently promote equal rights.

The new sensibility of this period, first anticipated by Du Bois in *The Souls of Black Folk* in 1903, affirmed the dignity and cultural potential of African Americans. Centuries of slavery and racial prejudice had imposed on them a "double-consciousness," to use Du Bois's term, and they were now challenged to acknowledge their own intrinsic power (such power is always closely connected to knowledge of one's own value) and to explore broader personal and artistic territories. Du Bois promoted many talented young African Americans, and as one of the organizers of the Pan-African conference in Paris in 1919, he urged black artists to create works from their own experiences and to celebrate their African and African American cultural heritage.

Du Bois was a charismatic figure who had an unquestionable influence on the New Negro, but his elitist notion of the "talented tenth" was criticized by several artists of the period (Wallace Thurman, Claude McKay, Zora Neale Hurston, and Langston Hughes in particular) as a Victorian cliché. Also, Du Bois's moral outlook contrasted with Locke's broader celebration of the New Negro. Locke saw the New Negro movement as a spiritual coming-of-age and "the finding of one another" as the greatest experience for those who gathered in Harlem. He saw Harlem as an experiment in racial welding that would enhance race consciousness. In his anthology *The New Negro* (1925), illustrated by Aaron Douglas, Winold Reiss, and Miguel Covarrubias, Locke not only showed the world the impressive impact of modern black culture but also acknowledged an emerging "common consciousness."

Many writers of the Harlem Renaissance were convinced that drama was the crucial form for the future of blacks' artistic development. As early as 1908 the first organization of African American theater professionals, the Frogs, was founded by George Walker and ten other members. Their purpose was to develop an archive of social, historical, and literary materials for a theatrical library. Around 1910 Egbert Austin ("Bert") Williams, then America's top comedian, was elected president of the Frogs.

Du Bois's idea of theater was that it should be essentially political, so that drama would teach colored people the meaning of their history and also reveal African Americans to the white world. This concept was counterbalanced by that of Locke, who had a propensity for drama concerned not so much with protest or propaganda as with a revival of folklore. In Locke's opinion, poetry and drama should reflect the soul of a people different in temperament from the "smug, unimaginative industrialist and the self-righteous Puritan." The problem facing the black playwright was how to reconcile the vitality of folklore, an oral tradition, with the written language. Zora Neale Hurston (who won second prize for both fiction and drama in *Opportunity*'s literary contest of 1925) and Langston Hughes (who won first prize for poetry) did achieve a balance between these elements and conceived works based on black folk culture. In 1926, Locke, in "The Negro and the American Stage," stressed the importance of folklore for the "complete development of the Negro dramatist"; that same year Hurston's play *Color Struck* appeared in *Fire!!*—a magazine produced by the collaborative efforts of Wallace Thurman, Aaron Douglas, Bruce Nugent, John P. Davis, Gwendolyn Bennett, Hurston, and her friend Langston Hughes. *Color Struck* was the first of Hurston's many achievements in drama, which she considered "inherent to Negro life." In her plays as well as her prose, ethnography was applied to performance as a mode of scientific investigation and artistic representation. In 1930, Hurston and Hughes—who both received the patronage, and were subject to the psychological impositions, of Charlotte Mason—wrote *Mule Bone*, intending it to be "the first real Negro folk comedy." Through a skillful use of black vernacular and black tradition, the play introduced a dramatic form that contrasted strongly with the stereotypical or ambivalent black characters in popular drama of the time, and also marked a clear departure from white American modernism.

Because of a disagreement between the authors over the copyright, *Mule Bone* could not be performed until several decades later (1991). Other African American plays, however, did have a significant impact at the time. In 1929, *Harlem*, by Wallace Thurman and William Rapp, opened at the Apollo Theater and became the most successful work written by African Americans but produced for Broadway's white audience. In 1935, Hughes's play *Mulatto* opened on Broadway; it had the longest run of any play by an African American until Lorraine Hansberry's *A Raisin in the Sun*, in 1959.

The aesthetic characteristics of the dramas of the Harlem Renaissance can also be found in its poetry and fiction. The first New Negro poets to attain recognition were Claude McKay and Countee Cullen. McKay, whose genius encompassed many contradictions, moved to Harlem from his native Jamaica in 1915; he immediately became a voice of unconventional wisdom and later was praised by Thurman as one of the few relevant artists "who had some concrete idea of style." McKay's *Harlem Shadows* (which included the famous sonnet "If We Must Die") was published in 1921, introducing him as the most fiery, radical, and powerful poet in Harlem's artistic world.

Countee Cullen was the boy wonder of the Harlem Renaissance and Du Bois's son-in-law. (He was married to Yolande, Du Bois's only daughter, in a memorable ceremony, and soon therafter escaped to Europe with a male friend, Harold Jackman.) Cullen is a striking example of the controversial aspects of the vogue for Harlem. He tried to embody the spirit that made the New Negro respectable and worthy to white audiences. Fearing the dangers inherent in yielding to the contemporary fashion for exoticism and in exposing things that should remain secret, Cullen was among those who strongly objected to Carl Van Vechten's novel *Nigger Heaven* (1926). Cullen's own poetry, although it dealt with African and African American themes, conformed to traditional middle-class taste. Thurman gave an ironic picture of Cullen in his "creative hours, eyes on a page of Keats, fingers on typewriter, mind frantically conjuring African scenes."

James Weldon Johnson, a transitional figure who later became an inspiration for the Harlem Renaissance and a renowned poet, composed many songs for Broadway musicals, together with his brother Rosamond and Bob Cole. They also wrote several popular songs, including "Lift Every Voice and Sing," which became the unofficial black national anthem. Johnson is also important for his groundbreaking preface to *The Book of American Negro Poetry* in 1922; in this preface he stressed the literary potential of the black vernacular, as well as the power, emotional endowment, and artistic originality of African American writers. At about the same time, Hughes was incorporating blues rhythms and vernacular idioms into his poetry; and his radical poems of the 1930s included realistic portrayals of black characters—the lives of plain black men and women and their struggles against injustice.

Writers of fiction often focused on a fascination with Harlem, on the complexities of interracial relations and relations among blacks, and on the black protagonist represented with all his or her uncertainties. In *The Autobiography of an Ex-Colored Man* (published anonymously in 1912 but reprinted in 1927), James Weldon Johnson prefigured what would become a pattern of other works of the Harlem Renaissance: an often unreliable narrator who tells about his moving from the rural South to the metropolitan North, experiencing the excitement of groundbreaking intellectual and artistic activity, and becoming intrigued by African American tradition and folklore—stereotypes still prevalent in white culture.

Jean Toomer's novel *Cane* (1923), a montage of prose and poetry, was the most refined modernist attempt thus far to render the black experience, individual perceptions of that experience, and the ambiguities that persisted in cultural dialogues between the South and the North. *Cane* introduced many of the themes and concerns of later Harlem Renaissance fiction, including differences of geographical origin, class, and gender within the black community. McKay's *Home to Harlem* (1928) was an immediate success, but it was harshly criticized by Du Bois for its lack of social decorum and still remains largely unappreciated despite its modern style. McKay combines the narratives of two migrants to show how a working-class African American and an intellectual Haitian immigrant overcome their class and national prejudice to develop an increasing, albeit unlikely, sense of familiarity and comradeship. The following works all appeared in 1928, an important year for the black novel: Jessie Redmon Fauset's *Plum Bun*, focusing on middle-class urban blacks in the North; Nella Larsen's *Quicksand*, which took up complex themes and issues such as female identity, class, color, and gender; Rudolph Fisher's *The Walls of Jericho* (Hughes described Fisher as the wittiest writer of the Harlem Renaissance, "whose tongue was flavored with the saltiest humor"); and Du Bois's *Dark Princess*. In 1932, Wallace Thurman's *Infants of the Spring* caused an uproar because of its uninhibited depiction of nightlife in Harlem and because Thurman sharply criticized many representative figures of the renaissance—his sarcastic bent made him disclaim the polite literature promoted by black leaders. (This inclination toward sarcasm was shared by several other authors, such as Claude McKay; Zora Neale Hurston, who dubbed Du Bois "Mr. Dubious"; Rudolph Fisher; and George S. Schuyler, who, as Hughes recalled, wrote "verbal brickbats that said sometimes one thing sometimes another but always vigorously.") McKay was not only an able critic but also an exceptionally voracious reader; as a result, the publisher Macaulay hired him as a reader—the only African American reader to be employed by any of the larger white publishing firms. Interestingly, in *The Blacker the Berry* (1929), Thurman used a dark-skinned female protagonist; he was one of very few male writers who did this (Du Bois, in *Dark Princess*, was another).

Gender remained an issue in the Harlem Renaissance. The success of Nella Larsen's cryptic, modernist fiction, such as *Quicksand* (1928) and *Passing* (1929), did not prevent her from falling into oblivion right after the crash of the stock market in 1929. The career of Jessie Redmon Fauset came to the same sad conclusion—as did the career of Zora Neale Hurston, although Hurston was one of the two literary giants of the Harlem Renaissance (the other was Toomer). The female poets Georgia Douglas Johnson, Anne Spencer, and Helene Johnson (whose "American Color Point of View" can be read as a feminine counterpart of Hughes's "The Negro Speaks of Rivers") went almost unacknowledged.

The New Negro movement seemed to decline with the crash of 1929 and the ensuing Great Depression, which led many artists and intellectuals to either an outright commitment to Marxism or an identification with American progressivism in general. Still, despite the shock caused by the Depression, the works published in the middle and late 1930s—Hurston's novels, including her masterpiece *Their Eyes Were Watching God* (1937), and her collection of tales *Mules and Men* (1935); Hughes's autobiography *The Big Sea* (1940); McKay's *Harlem: Negro Metropolis* (1940); and many others—confirmed the lasting legacy of this generous movement, which would leave its imprint on generations of writers to come. The vocabulary of color and sounds that James Baldwin borrowed from the Harlem Renaissance painter Beauford Delaney, the modernist surrealistic mode of Ellison's *Invisible Man*, the epic of the black struggle shown in the panels of Jacobs Lawrence and recounted in the novels of Toni Morrison—these are just a few examples of the inheritance left to today's black artists.

PAOLA BOI

See also Covarrubias, Miguel; Cullen–Du Bois Wedding; Delaney, Beauford; Douglas, Aaron; Lawrence, Jacob; Literature: 1—Overview; Mason, Charlotte Osgood; Modernism; New Negro; New Negro Movement; Opportunity Literary Contests; Pan-African Congresses; Reiss, Winold; Talented Tenth; Theater; Williams, Egbert Austin "Bert"; *specific writers and works*

Further Reading

Anderson, Jervis. *This Was Harlem: A Cultural Portrait, 1900–1950*. New York: Farrar, Straus and Giroux, 1981.

Bernard, Emily, ed. *Remember Me to Harlem: The Letters of Langston Hughes and Carl Van Vechten*. New York: Knopf, 1991.

Boi, Paola. *Talking Books: Zora Neale Hurston and the Power/Knowledge Philosophy in American Modernist Fiction*. Cagliari, Italy: AV, 1999.

Bontemps, Arna. *The Harlem Renaissance Remembered*. New York: Dodd and Mead, 1972.

The Book of American Negro Poetry, ed. James Weldon Johnson. San Diego, Calif.: Harcourt Brace Jovanovich, 1983. (Originally published 1931.)

Cooke, Michael G. *Afro-American Literature in the Twentieth Century: The Achievement of Intimacy*. New Haven, Conn., and London: Yale University Press, 1984.

Davis, Thadious M. *Nella Larsen, Novelist of the Harlem Renaissance: A Woman's Life Unveiled*. Westport, Conn.: Greenwood, 1997.

Douglas, Anne. *Terrible Honesty: Mongrel Manhattan in the 1920s*. New York: Farrar, Straus and Giroux, 1995.

Du Bois, William E. Burghardt. *Writings*. New York: Library of America, 1986.

———. *Dark Princess*, intro. Claudia Tate. Jackson: University Press of Mississippi, 1995. (Originally published 1928.)

Fabre, Geneviève, and Michel Feith, eds. *Jean Toomer and the Harlem Renaissance*. New Brunswick, N.J., and London: Rutgers University Press, 2001.

Fauset, Jessie Redmon. *Plum Bun: A Novel Without a Moral*. Boston: Beacon, 1990. (Originally published 1929.)

Fisher. Rudolph. *The Walls of Jerico*. New York: Knopf, 1928.

Gates, Henry Louis Jr., ed. *The Prize Plays and Other Acts: Zora Neale Hurston, Eulalie Spence, Marita Bonner, and Other African American Women Writers, 1910–1940*. New York: G. K. Hall, 1996.

Hemenway, Robert. *Zora Neale Hurston: A Literary Biography*. Urbana: University of Illinois Press, 1977.

Huggins, Nathan Irving. *Harlem Renaissance*. New York and Oxford: Oxford University Press, 1971

——, ed. *Voices From the Harlem Renaissance*. New York and Oxford: Oxford University Press, 1996. (Originally published 1976.)

Hughes, Langston. *The Big Sea*. London: Pluto, 1986. (Originally published 1940.)

Hughes, Langston, and Zora Neale Hurston. *Mule Bone: A Comedy of Negro Life*, ed. Henry Louis Gates Jr. and George Houston Bass. New York: Harper Perennial, 1991. (Originally published 1931.)

Hurston, Zora Neale. *Folklore, Memoirs, and Other Writings*, ed. Cheryl A. Wall. New York: Library of America, 1995.

——. *Novels and Stories*, ed. Cheryl A. Wall. New York: Library of America, 1995.

Hutchinson, George. *The Harlem Renaissance in Black and White*. New York and Oxford: Oxford University Press, 1996.

Johnson, Charles S. *The Negro in American Civilization: A Study of Negro Life and Race Relations in the Light of Social Research*. New York: Holt, 1930.

Johnson, James Weldon. *Along This Way: The Autobiography of James Weldon Johnson*. New York: Viking, 1968. (Originally published 1933.)

——. *Black Manhattan*. New York: Arno, 1968.

——. *The Autobiography of an Ex-Colored Man*. New York: Random House, 1989. (Originally published 1912.)

Kaplan, Carla, ed. *Zora Neale Hurston: A Life in Letters*. New York and London: Doubleday, 2002.

Kerman, Cynthia Earl, and Richard Eldridge. *The Lives of Jean Toomer: A Hunger for Wholeness*. Baton Rouge and London: Louisiana State University Press, 1987.

Larsen, Nella. *Quicksand; Passing*, ed. Deborah McDowell. New Brunswick, N.J.: Rutgers University Press, 1986. (*Quicksand* originally published 1928; *Passing* originally published 1929.)

Lewis, David Levering. *When Harlem Was in Vogue*. New York: Knopf, 1981.

Locke, Alain. *The New Negro: Voices of the Harlem Renaissance*. New York: Atheneum, 1992. (Originally published 1925.)

McKay, Claude. *A Long Way From Home: An Autobiography*. London: Pluto, 1970. (Originally published 1937.)

——. *Home to Harlem*. Boston, Mass.: Northeastern University Press, 1987. (Originally published 1928.)

Perkins, Kathy A., ed. *Black Female Playwrights: An Anthology of Plays Before 1950*. Bloomington and Indianapolis: Indiana University Press, 1989.

Rampersad, Arnold. *The Life of Langston Hughes* (2 vols.). New York and Oxford: Oxford University Press, 1986.

Redding, Saunders J. *To Make a Poet Black*. Ithaca, N.Y., and London: Cornell University Press, 1988. (Originally published 1939.)

Schoener, Allon, ed. *Harlem on My Mind: Cultural Capital of the World, 1900–1968*. New York: Random House, 1995. (Originally published 1968.)

Schuyler, Georges B. *Black No More: Being an Account of the Strange and Wonderful Workings of Science in the Land of the Free, A.D. 1933–1940*. Boston, Mass.: Northeastern University Press, 1989. (Originally published 1931.)

Thurman, Wallace. *The Blacker the Berry*. New York: Scribner, 1996. (Originally published 1929.)

——. *Infants of the Spring*. New York: Modern Library, 1999. (Originally published 1932.)

Toomer, Jean. *The Wayward and the Seeking: A Collection of Writings by Jean Toomer*, ed. Darwin T. Turner. Washington, D.C.: Howard University Press, 1982.

——. *Cane*, ed. Darwin T. Turner. New York and London: Norton, 1988. (Originally published 1923.)

——. *Essentials*. Athens and London: University of Georgia Press, 1991.

Van Vechten, Carl. *Nigger Heaven*. New York: Knopf, 1926.

Wall, Cheryl A. *Women of the Harlem Renaissance*. Bloomington and Indianapolis: Indiana University Press, 1995.

Watson, Steven. *The Harlem Renaissance, Hub of African American Culture, 1920–1930*. New York: Pantheon, 1995.

Wilson, Sondra Katryn, ed. *The Crisis Reader: Stories, Poetry, and Essays from the NAACP's Crisis Magazine*. New York: Modern Library, 1999.

Wintz, Cary, D. *Black Culture and the Harlem Renaissance*. Houston, Tex.: Rice University Press, 1988.

Authors: 2—Fiction

African American writers of fiction during the Harlem Renaissance continued a tradition that had begun in the mid-nineteenth century. In their novels and short stories, these writers developed themes of race, gender, class, justice, violence, history, migration, and cultural memory—themes that were similar to those found in the earlier fiction of, among others, William Wells Brown (*Clotel*, 1853), Harriet Wilson (*Our Nig*, 1859), Frances Harper (*Iola Leroy*, 1892), Pauline Hopkins (*Contending Forces*, 1900), Charles Chesnutt (*House Behind the Cedars*, 1900; *The Marrow of Tradition*, 1901), and James Weldon Johnson (*The Autobiography of an Ex-Colored Man*, 1912). However, the fiction writers of the Harlem Renaissance broke away from the earlier tradition in that they "gave African American culture a more urban, assertive, and cosmopolitan voice" (Andrews et al. 1997). One significant factor in this transformation of the fictional voice was the migration of African Americans from the rural South to northern urban industrial centers as well as to urban areas of the South; another factor was African Americans' travels in Europe during World War I and as part of the expatriate generation. At the same time, it is important to note that writers such as Zora Neale Hurston (in "Spunk," 1925; "Sweat," 1926; and *Their Eyes Were Watching God*, 1937) and Jean Toomer (in *Cane*, 1923) paid homage to Africans' and African Americans' southern ancestral past.

The transformed voice permeating the fiction of the Harlem Renaissance expresses strong pride in blackness, and in some instances calls directly for resistance to both subtle and overt racial oppression. In calling for social and political equality for black Americans and encouraging African Americans not to acquiesce, fiction writers—along with poets and writers of prose—contributed to the racial uplift movement.

Many fiction writers of the Harlem Renaissance disagreed about whether the purpose of art should be aesthetic or propagandistic. Much of the fiction produced during this period served a political or propagandistic purpose whether or not an author intended a work to be used in that way. The fiction of the Harlem Renaissance emphasizes the richness and diversity within African American culture. Consequently, novelists such as Nella Larsen and Jessie Fauset provide a glimpse into middle-class black America, primarily in the North; Zora Neale Hurston provides an overview of class within African American communities in the South. The fiction of the Harlem Renaissance offers a panoramic view of African American life at various levels from the black bourgeoisie to folk culture. By exploring the diversity within African American culture, these writers point out differences in the experience of African Americans based on educational background and class, despite common experiences based on racial background.

Johnson: *The Autobiography of an Ex-Colored Man*

James Weldon Johnson's novel *The Autobiography of an Ex-Colored Man* (1912) can set the stage for the fiction

of this period, because Johnson developed common themes such as the construction of identity, "passing," violence, and intraracial conflict. This novel was reissued in 1927, at the height of the Harlem Renaissance, perhaps because of those themes. Johnson examines the social construction of race through a mixed-race protagonist. Similar to several other fiction writers—such as Nella Larsen in *Quicksand* (1928) and *Passing* (1929), Jessie Fauset in *Plum Bun* (1929), and Wallace Thurman in *The Blacker the Berry* (1929)—Johnson explores the psychological consequences of blackness as a racial marker in a society that prefers biological and visible whiteness.

Johnson was a precursor of other writers of the Harlem Renaissance who examined race relations, violence, and interracial as well as intraracial conflict. For instance, Larsen, Fauset, and Toomer, like Johnson, explore interracial relationships at several levels: intimate, political, and social. Furthermore, Toomer in *Cane* (1923), Walter White in *The Fire in the Flint* (1924), and Langston Hughes in *The Ways of White Folks* (1933) examine the causes and effects of racial violence directed against African Americans.

During the Harlem Renaissance, fiction writers continued another tradition in African American literature: examining the effects of migration on black individuals and communities. Hundreds of thousands of African Americans migrated from the South to the North and within the South. Johnson's protagonist in *The Autobiography of an Ex-Colored Man* migrates from the North to the South, to Europe, and then back to the United States. Similarly, in their fiction, Jean Toomer, Nella Larsen, Wallace Thurman, and Langston Hughes focus on the movement of blacks from one cultural space to another; Larsen and Toomer shed light on how the return to the South affected African Americans.

Toomer: *Cane*

Jean Toomer's *Cane* was published in 1923. It received positive reviews for its modernist style and its examination of black migration and the connection between African Americans and their ancestral past in the South and in Africa. Many scholars associate the publication of *Cane* with the beginning of the Harlem Renaissance as a literary movement. *Cane* is certainly important in relation to other fiction of this period, given the common themes found in Toomer's text and in subsequent works. However, it is difficult to place *Cane* within any one genre, because throughout this work Toomer used elements of the short story, poetry, and the novel. *Cane* is divided into three sections, to chronicle black migration from South to North and back to the South.

Toomer explores the causes and effects of the psychic or spiritual death many African Americans underwent during this period. This theme of spiritual death is explored in both northern and southern settings. Toomer emphasizes the theme of migration to illustrate the cultural displacement and social isolation of blacks who went from the South to the urban North. The rural South depicted in *Cane* symbolizes African Americans' spirituality and strong communal bonds; the North symbolizes isolation, materialism, and individual success.

Other themes developed in *Cane* include sexual exploitation, miscegenation, generational shifts, work, violence, and resistance. Toomer develops these themes and the theme of spiritual death through individual narratives centered on archetypal characters representing a broad range of individuals. For instance, the text opens with "Karintha," in which the title character is a girl stifled by a sexually oppressive and exploitative environment; and in this part of the book, Toomer contrasts Karintha's beauty, and the beauty of certain aspects of nature, with the ugliness of the girl's poverty-stricken environment, the men who exploit Karintha, and the devastating psychological effects of sexual exploitation.

"Becky," the second vignette in *Cane*, explores the theme of interracial relationships and miscegenation. Becky is a white woman who gives birth to two African American boys. This is the first story in *Cane* to explore the tangled racial skeins in the South, but it revises the traditional narrative of miscegenation by focusing on the community's reaction to the forbidden sexual relationship between Becky and her black lover. In mainstream narratives that alluded to intimate relationships between black men and white women, the black man was more often than not described as a brute threatening the sanctity of white womanhood. Toomer challenges the stereotype of the black brute: He depicts Becky as willingly becoming involved with a black man. We know that Becky has entered this relationship willingly because in order to protect her lover from retaliatory violence by white "protectors" of womanhood, she never reveals his identity. Furthermore, the fact that she has two black sons indicates a long-term relationship with her lover.

Toomer addresses race as a social construction in "Becky," and also in "Bona and Paul." Becky's sons are described as Negro rather than biracial even though their mother is white. This accords with a practice of the time during which the story is set: the "one drop" rule, whereby people of mixed race were considered to belong to the socially subordinate race. Other fiction writers of the Harlem Renaissance—including Nella Larsen in *Quicksand* and *Passing*, Jessie Fauset in *Plum Bun*, and Langston Hughes in the short stories "Passing" and "Father and Son" from *The Ways of White Folks*—also take up the theme of race as a social construction, describing the plight of mixed-race individuals and people involved in interracial relationships in a racist society.

"Becky" also considers the hypocrisy of southerners who attempt to hide behind religion while engaging in unchristian behavior. Toomer writes: "She's dead; they've gone away. The pines whisper to Jesus. The bible flaps its leaves with an aimless rustle on her mound." The reference to the pines suggests that the crimes committed by presumably Christian yet racist southerners—in this case the death of Becky and the disruption of her sons' lives—will be revealed to a higher being. In the story, both whites and blacks isolate Becky and render her powerless. They assuage their guilt by leaving food for her and by building her a house, but the house is built on such shaky ground that it collapses, crushing her.

Each story in *Cane* builds on other stories in the text. For instance, "Fern" further develops the themes of isolation, sexual exploitation, and miscegenation found in "Karintha" and "Becky." Toomer also develops the theme of interracial relationships and sexuality and connects it to the theme of violence in "Blood Burning Moon." In "Blood Burning Moon," Toomer asks who has the right to the black woman, and he shows how this question is inextricably linked to the history of the socially condoned sexual exploitation of the black female body during the era of slavery. Although this story is set after that era, the narrator alludes to past differences in power—differences determined by race—and shows the connections between race relations during slavery and afterward.

Toomer addresses the causes and effects of racially based violence for the first time in *Cane* in "Blood Burning Moon." This story opens with a poem describing a woman's braid, which looks like a lyncher's rope. As in other stories in the text, the epigraph at the beginning foreshadows the prevalent theme. Writers such as Toomer, Hughes, White, and Larsen present lynching as a theme because this was a very real threat to African Americans of the time.

The second part of *Cane* takes place in the urban North: in Washington, D.C., and Chicago. Here Toomer contrasts the earthy southern landscape with northern coldness. Toomer associates the cold with the isolation of blacks living in this new environment and with the concrete buildings characteristic of industrialization. Toomer demonstrates in Part Two how African Americans who deny Africa and the American South as a vital part of their heritage become consumed by an emphasis on money, "machines, nightclubs, newspapers, and anything else which represents modern society" (Bontemps 1972). The acceptance of materialistic, individualistic values has a devastating impact on the African American community because the emphasis on individual success can lead to estrangement from the black community and their ancestral past. Toomer's critique of the northern urban environment suggests the disillusionment felt by many blacks who had migrated to the promised land and found that they still encountered racism and limited employment opportunities and were still subjected to violence.

Part Three of *Cane* takes the reader and Kabnis, the central character of this section, back to the South. Toomer depicts Kabnis as a man in search of his identity, and this is especially important because Kabnis rejects and hates the South upon first arriving there. In this section, Toomer chronicles Kabnis's journey toward connecting with his black ancestral past.

Cane is a seminal work of fiction. Toomer addresses themes associated with the Harlem Renaissance; he also addresses concerns of modernist writers during this era, linking the literature of the Harlem Renaissance to the American modernist movement.

White: *The Fire in the Flint*

In *The Fire in the Flint* (1924), Walter White expands on Johnson's and Toomer's use of violence as a theme. During his tenure with the National Association for the Advancement of Colored People (NAACP), White—who was able to pass as a white man—infiltrated and investigated white supremacist groups. As an eyewitness of the activities of white lynch mobs, he was able to give lawyers and others in the antilynching movement valuable firsthand information. In *The Fire in the Flint*, he not only exposes American racism

and lynching but also offers insights into the black labor movement and demolishes the myth of the African American brute.

Women Writers

African American women wrote some of the most important fiction of the Harlem Renaissance. Jessie Redmon Fauset, a prolific writer, wrote four novels—*There Is Confusion* (1924), *The Chinaberry Tree* (1931), *Plum Bun*, and *Comedy American Style* (1933)—as well as literary reviews, poems, and short stories. Nella Larsen wrote *Quicksand* and *Passing*. Zora Neale Hurston wrote short stories, plays, and novels including "Sweat," "Spunk," *Colorstruck* (1925), and *Their Eyes Were Watching God*. The playwright Georgia Douglas Johnson wrote antilynching works and dramas focused on class, miscegenation, and the sexual exploitation of black women, such as *A Sunday Morning in the South* (1925), *Blue Blood* (1926), *Safe* (1929), and *Blue-Eyed Black Boy* (1930s). Mary Burrill, another playwright of the Harlem Renaissance, addressed themes similar to those of black female novelists and playwrights. Burrill's *They That Sit in Darkness* (1919) focuses on motherhood and birth control; her *Aftermath* (1928) focuses on resistance to racial oppression and the position of black soldiers returning to the United States after fighting for American democracy.

Women authors such as Fauset, Larsen, Hurston, and Georgia Douglas Johnson provide a critique of both the "new woman" and the "New Negro" in their fiction. Fauset and Larsen illustrate the precarious position of African American women within both movements. In general, these women writers describe intersections of race, class, and gender. They create multidimensional female characters who overtly and covertly resist victimization based on their gender as well as their race.

Fauset, Larsen, and Hurston also offer a profound critique of marriage by examining the unequal power of men and women and the economic basis of marriage as an institution. As DuCille (1993) notes, writers such as Fauset, Larsen, and Hurston "use coupling as a metaphor through which to examine and critique the color consciousness, class stratification, social conventions, and gender relations of the burgeoning black middle class and working class communities." Furthermore, these writers examine how African American women react to being considered sex objects. Hurston and Larsen illustrate how African American women develop a sense of sexual agency despite living in a racist, sexist society. For instance, Hurston's novel *Their Eyes Were Watching God* is a coming-of-age story describing the social and sexual development of the heroine, Janie Crawford.

Female authors also provide a critique of the educational and employment opportunities available to women. For instance, Larsen, in her depiction of Naxos in *Quicksand*, criticizes the southern black school for attempting to train pupils to imitate whiteness. Larsen's heroine has difficulty finding employment once she leaves Naxos, because of her race and gender. Fauset demonstrates how women are constrained by societal notions of acceptable employment for unmarried black women, such as domestic service, teaching, and office work. Hurston illustrates that women of higher socioeconomic status are judged harshly by society when they pursue nontraditional work; Hurston's character Janie Crawford ends up doing migrant farm work, side by side with her husband.

McKay: Examining Black Intellectuals and Expatriates

Claude McKay—and some other writers of the Harlem Renaissance, including Larsen, Toomer, Langston Hughes, Walter White, and James Weldon Johnson—looked at the role of the black intellectual and the black expatriate in their fiction. McKay, like some of his contemporaries, experimented with writing in a variety of literary genres, and he produced poetry as well as fiction. Critics often associate McKay's fiction with cultural primitivism because of his emphasis on black, especially Jamaican, folk culture. McKay's fiction includes *Home to Harlem* (1928), *Banjo* (1929), and *Banana Bottom* (1933). In these books McKay addresses the plight of the black intellectual and the relationship between black intellectuals and the mass of black people.

McKay felt that progress and true racial uplift depended on all segments of the black community, not just the educated black elite. According to McKay, educated African Americans during the 1920s espoused the need for a racial renaissance without considering the role of the common folk in this new cultural movement. McKay writes in his novel *Banjo*: "It's the common people, you know, who furnish the bone and sinew and salt of any race or nation. . . . If this renaissance is going to be more than a sporadic scabby thing, we'll have to get down to our racial roots to create it."

Home to Harlem provides one view of life in the black urban ghetto. McKay associates Harlem—where this novel is set—with a vibrant black culture, but he also explores alienation, economic uncertainty, and negative aspects of American materialism. He contrasts two characters, Jake and Ray, to emphasize the division between common black folk and the so-called black intellectual. McKay's depiction of Jake, which is similar to Toomer's depiction of Rhobert in *Cane* and Larsen's depiction of Helga Crane in *Quicksand*, draws attention to the conflict between modern society and the vitality and passion associated with African cultural images and black life in Harlem. Ray represents the black intellectual who exchanges his humanity for a mainstream education (Bontemps 1972)—who separates the intellect from the emotions. Ray's inability to reconcile his intellectual and emotional development leads him to become an expatriate, and this decision suggests the alienation of the black intellectual and artist within the United States, largely because of American racism. Expatriation was in fact a realistic theme: Many black artists, as well as whites, were actually leaving the United States and moving to Europe to pursue their personal development.

McKay also examines the black expatriate movement and the plight of the black intellectual in *Banjo*. Ray, the character from *Home to Harlem*, reappears in *Banjo*; and McKay once again explores the causes and effects of the alienation of black intellectuals from the masses of black people and whites. The narrator notes that despite educational accomplishments and socioeconomic status, color and race shape the experiences of individuals in American society. African Americans do not particpate as equals in the American dream; rather, regardless of their intellectual acumen, they are judged first and foremost as blacks and are consequently looked down on. McKay writes in *Banjo*: "The thinking colored man could not function normally like his white brother, responsive and reacting spontaneously to the emotions of pleasure or pain, joy or sorrow, kindness or hardness, charity, anger, and forgiveness." McKay illustrates how American mainstream society views African Americans as a monolithic group, whereas whites are judged on their merits as individuals.

In *Banjo*, McKay further explores the relationship between the artist and the folk in African American culture. Ray represents the black intellectual; Banjo represents the artist. Banjo describes his instrument as a reflection of his soul and himself, and McKay's emphasis on the banjo as an important instrument elevates African American folk art. (Similarly, Zora Neale Hurston elevates African American folk culture through her use of folklore and black dialect as art forms; and Langston Hughes elevates the black artist and the spiritual tie between artists and their art through his depiction of Roy in "Home" and Oceola in "The Blues I'm Playing," in his short-story collection *The Ways of White Folks*.) McKay likens the banjo to African Americans' culture by noting that this instrument was preeminent in their creation of music. He also describes the banjo as affirming the existence of African Americans in a world where they were rendered invisible by the dominant culture. In *Banjo*, McKay celebrates African American folk culture and shows how black artists and their art help to empower African Americans in the face of attempts to displace them and despite the chaos associated with black life in the early twentieth century.

Thurman: *The Blacker the Berry and Infants of the Spring*

Wallace Thurman's novels *The Blacker the Berry* (1929) and *Infants of the Spring* (1932) develop the themes of racial consciousness, the role of the black artist, and racism. *The Blacker the Berry* is unique because Thurman focuses on the effects of internalized racism and intraracial prejudice. *Infants of the Spring* provides a first-hand critical evaluation of the Harlem Renaissance.

Thurman—like Langston Hughes in *The Ways of White Folks* (1934), Rudolph Fisher in *The Walls of Jericho* (1929), and George Schuyler in *Black No More* (1931)—was a master of both satire and irony. *The Blacker the Berry* is a scathing critique of color and class prejudice within the African American community. This novel explores the development of Emma Lou, a dark-skinned African American, as she confronts not only the prejudice to which her family and her associates are subjected because of her darkness but also her own negative self-image, a result of internalized racism. Thurman took his title from a common saying among African Americans: "The blacker the berry, the sweeter the juice." That folk saying, as well as Thurman's novel, celebrates blackness.

Emma Lou desperately tries to transform herself by straightening her hair and using creams to lighten her skin. Although these attempts are in part a consequence of the psychological abuse she has suffered because of color prejudice within the black community, Thurman suggests that her own self-hatred has played an even larger role in causing her discontent. According to the narrator, Emma Lou eventually learns that she must "accept her black skin as being real and unchangeable . . . and with this in mind begin life anew, always fighting, not so much for acceptance by other people but for acceptance of herself by herself."

Thurman's novel *Infants of the Spring* provides a critique of African American artists, specifically those associated with the Harlem Renaissance. It exposes the foibles of and conflicts between some of the major figures in the Harlem Renaissance, including Zora Neale Hurston, Langston Hughes, Alain Locke, Countee Cullen, Rudolph Fischer, and Thurman.

Fisher: *The Walls of Jericho*

Rudolph Fisher uses satire in *The Walls of Jericho* (1928) to develop a critique of social class and racial conflict during the 1920s. Like Thurman, he exposes the dangerous elitism among the African American bourgeoisie. He also satirizes the relationship between African Americans and white liberals through one of his characters, the white socialite Agatha Camp (his model for this character was Charlotte Osgood Mason, a white patron of black artists). Essentially, Fisher demonstrates how relationships between African Americans and whites can develop only so far if whites take a paternalistic attitude.

Hughes: *Not Without Laughter and The Ways of White Folks*

Langston Hughes, one of the most prolific writers of the Harlem Renaissance, produced poetry, fiction, and nonfiction during this period and afterward. *Not Without Laughter* (1933) and *The Ways of White Folks* (1934) are two of his most intriguing works. *Not Without Laughter* is a coming-of-age story about a black boy in the Midwest. *The Ways of White Folks* focuses on relationships—intimate and superficial—between blacks and whites. Hughes uses satire to expose white racism; to criticize liberal (or presumably liberal) white Americans' growing fascination with black culture, especially when this fascination stems from and perpetuates stereotypes of African Americans; and to criticize the patronage system that affected many artists of the Harlem Renaissance.

The writers discussed in this essay are among the best-known figures associated with the Harlem Renaissance. Their fiction reflects a new era in African American history: This period was characterized by the Jazz Age, the image of the New Negro, a renewed sense of radicalism among some African Americans, and a sense of pride in being black. Although the Great Depression of the 1930s marked the end of the Harlem Renaissance, the influence of the writers associated with this movement can be seen in much later works by African Americans: the "black arts movement" of the 1960s and 1970s, the renaissance of African American women's literature in the 1980s, and the fiction and poetry of African Americans today.

DEIRDRE J. RAYNOR

See also Literature: 4—Fiction; Mason, Charlotte Osgood; Modernism; Primitivism; *specific writers and works*

Further Reading

Andrews, William, et al. *The Oxford Companion to African American Literature.* Oxford: Oxford University Press, 1997.

Baker, Houston A. *Modernism and the Harlem Renaissance.* Chicago, Ill.: University of Chicago Press, 1987.

Bernard, Emily, ed, *Remember Me to Harlem: The Letters of Langston Hughes and Carl Van Vechten.* New York: Knopf, 2001.

Bontemps, Arna, ed. *The Harlem Renaissance Remembered.* 1972.

DuCille, Ann. *The Coupling Convention.* Oxford: Oxford University Press, 1993.

Fabre, Geneviève, and Michel Feith, eds. *Temples for Tomorrow: Looking Back at the Renaissance.* Bloomington: Indiana University Press, 2001.

Gates, Henry Louis, et al. *The Norton Anthology of African American Literature.* New York: Norton, 1997.

Singh, Amritjit, et al. *The Novels of the Harlem Renaissance.* 1996.

Wall, Cheryl. *Women of the Harlem Renaissance.* 1995.

Wilson, Sondra Kathryn. *The Crisis Reader: Stories, Poetry, and Essays from the N.A.A.C.P.'s Crisis Magazine.* New York: Random House, 1999.

————. *The Opportunity Reader: Stories, Poetry, and Essays from the Urban League's Opportunity Magazine.* New York: Random House, 1999.

————. *The Messenger Reader: Stories, Poetry, and Essays from the Messenger Magazine.* New York: Random House, 2000.

Authors: 3—Nonfiction

African American and Jewish-American historians, anthropologists, psychologists, and sociologists who came of age between 1877 and 1919—an era that scholars of African American history often describe as "the nadir"—laid the intellectual foundations for the nonfiction authors of the Harlem Renaissance in the 1920s and 1930s. African American historians in particular reacted against such blatant forms of racism as Jim Crow laws, disenfranchisement, extralegal violence, and the removal of blacks from positions involving skilled labor.

These nonfiction authors, figures such as W. E. B. Du Bois and Carter G. Woodson, used their writings not only in an attempt to bolster black racial pride and instill self-esteem in their people, but also to educate whites in what was a seething and sometimes explosive national atmosphere of racial conflict—despite Booker T. Washington's public policy of racial accommodation. Du Bois and Woodson were the leading historians who wrote works extolling the achievements and capabilities of their people, not only in the United States but also in Africa, the Caribbean, and South America.

Du Bois was born into a poor, female-run household in Great Barrington, Massachusetts. He received degrees from Fisk and Harvard universities, as well as graduate training in the social sciences at some of the most prestigious German universities; but in his own ideology, he vacillated between color-blind universalism and cultural pluralism. He often spoke and wrote as if there were what David Levering Lewis called "distinct racial attributes." Thus Du Bois argued—in his Atlanta University Studies and his seminal volume of African history, *The Negro* (1915), which drew on the pioneering work on Africa by Franz Boas, the great anthropologist of German-Jewish descent—that African peoples had made, and were perfectly capable of making in the present and future, achievements essential to human progress. In so doing, Du Bois discredited the claim of white supremacists that "color is a mark of inferiority." At the same time, though, he argued that black peoples were distinct from whites "to some extent in spiritual gift."

Carter G. Woodson, the son of former Virginian slaves, had lifted himself up from abject poverty to reasonable comfort through sheer pluck, hard work, and perseverance. Like Du Bois, he attended Harvard, where he received his doctorate despite being embroiled in disputes with his major professor. Woodson founded the *Journal of Negro History* in 1915. During the 1920s and 1930s he published several historical and sociological works, including five textbooks (one of which, *The Negro in Our History*, went through several editions during the years between its initial publication in 1922 and 1947). His work (as noted above) was consciously aimed at enhancing black racial pride and, as a consequence, instilling self-esteem in his black readers.

Arthur Schomburg, a Puerto Rican immigrant who lived in New York City, is known primarily as a bibliophile (he sold part of his library to the Carnegie Corporation, which in turn donated the collection to the New York Public Library). However, Schomburg also made a vital contribution to Alain Locke's monumental anthology *The New Negro* (1925). In that collection, Schomburg wrote what has become a credo for present-day autodidacts: "The American Negro must remake his past in order to make his future." Like both Du Bois and Woodson, Schomburg sought—as the recent historian Winston James has pointed out—to construct a black "vindicationist" history.

For sociologists such as Charles S. Johnson and E. Franklin Frazier, the "social problems" of blacks during the 1920s and 1930s required environmental explanations rather than the racial explanation that pervaded most of the writings of most European-American social scientists at the time. Johnson, a native of Virginia, was trained at the University of Chicago and became an educator, author, and editor (he edited *Opportunity*, the organ of the National Urban League). He believed that a revitalization of African American folk culture was necessary in order to restore the values and behavior of the mass of black people who had migrated from the South to the urban industrial North. Johnson left New York City in 1926 to become a professor and later the first African American president of Fisk University in Nashville, Tennessee; and in 1934, he published a classical sociological work, *Shadow of the Plantation*. This book documented the harsh, even brutal, conditions under which African American farmers lived in Macon County, Alabama; it was a crushing indictment of the sharecropping system—which, however, was changing because of the increasing number of literate young blacks in the country.

E. Franklin Frazier was a native of Maryland and a graduate of Howard University, Clark University, and the University of Chicago. Frazier, like Johnson, was alarmed by the anomie that characterized the northern urban industrial areas where the mass of transplanted southern immigrants lived. In *The Negro Family in Chicago* (1932) and his classic work *The Negro Family in the United States* (1939), Frazier publicized the plight of most African American migrants. Frazier, who had published essays in *Opportunity* between

1924 and 1930, intended to subvert the traditional orthodoxies regarding race and culture. Accordingly, he launched assaults against both strictly racial and strictly cultural explanations for the normlessness of black ghettos.

Anthropologists were especially fascinated by issues of race and culture with reference to blacks. Melville J. Herskovits, a Jewish-American anthropologist, believed that the discussion of race in the American social sciences had direct implications for the issue of the assimilation of blacks. At the beginning of his career, Herskovits, who was a student of the methodological puritan Franz Boas, was involved in arguments about the relative merits of the methodology of racist intelligence testers. As early as the 1900s his mentor, Boas, had attacked their empirical methodology and had concluded that there was no compelling evidence of "racial" mental differences among blacks. As a consequence, Boas argued that assimilation through miscegenation was the true solution to the problems centered on relations between blacks and whites.

In Herskovits's essay "The Negro's Americanism," published in Alain Locke's *The New Negro*, the tension between assimilation and racial essentialism was apparent. Nevertheless, the New Negro sought—with infectious enthusiasm—an essential cultural identity with bases in African and African American folk culture. As a result, Herskovits's embrace of the ideology of the intellectuals of the Harlem Renaissance led him to his own search for African "retentions" in the Western Hemisphere, a search that had begun three decades earlier in the nonfiction writings of W. E. B. Du Bois.

Finally, African American and Jewish-American psychologists such as Howard Hale Long, Horace Mann Bond, Herman Canady, Martin D. Jenkins, Joseph St. Clair Price, Doxey Wilkerson, and Otto Klineberg published articles in *The Crisis*, *Opportunity*, and the *Journal of Negro Education* that raised issues related to the sources of racial differences between the scores of whites and blacks on intelligence tests. These authors were critical of the cultural biases in the tests.

In sum, the nonfiction authors of the Harlem Renaissance contributed narratives that countered the pervasive racism of the majority group in the United States. Seeking to revitalize African American culture, nonfiction authors challenged the dominant racial and ethnocentric discourse that attempted to use history, anthropology, sociology, and psychology as the "social scientific" bases for white supremacy.

VERNON J. WILLIAMS JR.

See also Association for the Study of Negro Life and History and Journal of Negro History; Atlanta University Studies; Boas, Franz; Crisis, The; Literature: 6—Nonfiction; Opportunity; *specific authors and works*

Further Reading

Baker, Houston A. *Modernism and the Harlem Renaissance.* Chicago, Ill.: University of Chicago Press, 1987.

Fabre, Geneviève, and Michel Feith, eds. *Temples for Tomorrow: Looking Back at the Renaissance.* Bloomington: Indiana University Press, 2001.

Huggins, Nathan Irvin. *Harlem Renaissance.* New York: Oxford University Press, 1971.

———. *Voices of the Harlem Renaissance.* New York: Oxford University Press, 1995.

Hutchinson, George. *The Harlem Renaissance in Black and White.* Cambridge, Mass.: Belknap–Harvard University Press, 1995.

Lewis, David Levering. *When Harlem Was in Vogue.* New York: Random House, 1979.

———, ed. *The Portable Renaissance Reader.* New York: Penguin, 1994.

Locke, Alain, ed. *The New Negro.* New York: Albert and Charles Boni, 1925.

Wintz, Cary D. *Black Culture and the Harlem Renaissance.* Houston, Tex.: Rice University Press, 1988.

Authors: 4—Playwrights

Feeling overwhelmed by the numerous fictitious stories and plays published and produced during the early 1900s that perpetuated negative racial stereotypes, W. E. B. Du Bois made a public statement in an editorial in the February 1926 issue of *The Crisis* (the magazine of the National Association for the Advancement of Colored People, NAACP), raising questions about the liability and social responsibility of artists and authors. The acclaimed Negro actress Hattie McDaniel, who was criticized by certain members of the Negro community for portraying negative racial images (she is credited with creating the quintessential film representation of the "mammy" caricature), once remarked that it was better to play a maid than to be a maid and certainly more profitable. However, her critics—such as Jessie Redmon Fauset, the literary editor of *The Crisis*—argued that the long-term damage done by artists like McDaniel would preclude any hope of racial equality.

In his editorial in *The Crisis*—"The Negro in Art: How Shall He Be Portrayed?"—Du Bois asked artists and writers to consider seven questions: (1) What is the actor's personal responsibility in portraying black characters? (2) Can an author be criticized for depicting positive or negative characteristics of a racial group? (3) Should publishers be criticized for refusing to publish books with nonstereotypical representations of Negroes? (4) How can Negroes refute negative stereotypes that most Americans accept as cultural truths? (5) Should educated black characters receive the same sympathetic treatment from artists and audiences as Porgy received in the popular American opera *Porgy and Bess*? (6) How will white and Negro artists find the courage to create multiple representations of black characters when the world has seen only negative representations and believes that Negroes are incapable of behaving differently? (7) Who will tell the truth about the actual character of the Negro people if their young writers are tempted to follow popular trends?

Du Bois was not the only activist during the Harlem Renaissance to be concerned about the popular tendency, on most American stages, to portray Negro characters as minstrel-type clowns. Several writers, artists, philosophers, politicians, ministers, and housewives posed the same or similar questions and sometimes even tried to answer them. Those whose attempts to answer Du Bois's questions were the most successful or caused the most controversy were probably the playwrights.

The playwrights of the Harlem Renaissance were unified in their determination to solve the problem of "race" through their work for the theater but were divided with regard to strategy. Some of them advocated "folk dramas"; others advocated history or pageant plays; still others thought that propaganda plays, such as plays about lynching, were the most effective. The merits of the various forms of Negro theater were often debated not only in Harlem and elsewhere in New York state but also in Washington, D.C., at the Saturday Nighters Club. The host for these passionate discussions in Washington was the well-known playwright and poet Georgia Douglas Johnson (1880–1966), who wrote twenty-eight or more plays at her home on S Street in several genres, such as folk plays, anti-lynching plays, and history plays.

W. E. B. Du Bois

W. E. B. Du Bois (1868–1963), a widely respected Negro leader, philosopher, and playwright, greatly influenced Georgia Douglas Johnson's career and the discussions about the plight of Negro theater that were held at her house. As the editor of *The Crisis*, Du Bois sponsored playwriting contests and helped several playwrights produce their work professionally. However, when the debate over the portrayal of the Negro onstage and in film intensified, and when both the Negro masses and Du Bois's "talented tenth" became hopeless about racial oppression, he decided that further action was needed. In "Krigwa Players Little Negro Theatre: The Story of a Little Theatre Movement," an essay that also appeared in *The Crisis* in June 1926, he argued that the

> plays of a real Negro theatre must be: 1. *About us.* That is, they must have plots which reveal Negro life as it is. 2. *By us.* That is, they must be written by Negro authors who understand from birth and continual association just what it means to be a Negro today. 3. *For us.* That is, the theatre must cater primarily to Negro audiences and be supported and sustained by their entertainment and approval. 4. *Near us.* The theatre must be in a Negro neighborhood near the mass of ordinary Negro people.

On 3 May 1926, Du Bois had made his dream a reality by opening a Negro "little theater"—the Krigwa Players—in the basement of the 135th Street branch of the New York Public Library. The company staged three one-act plays: *Compromise* and *The Broken Banjo* (two tragedies by Willis Richardson), and *The Church Fight* (a comedy by Ruth Ann Gaines-Shelton). Du Bois hailed the event as an unquestionable success and said that enthusiastic audiences left the theater wanting more. His goal was to organize Krigwa Players Little Negro Theaters (KPLNTs) throughout the United States to stage works written by himself and others presenting his views about the future of Negro theater and the talented tenth. Several playwrights were influenced by Du Bois's little theater movement, including Marieta Bonner, Owen Dodson, Shirley Graham Du Bois, Zora Neale Hurston, Langston Hughes, Georgia Douglas Johnson, May Miller, Willis Richardson, and Eulalie Spence.

Willis Richardson

Interestingly, Willis Richardson (1889–1977), whose plays were staged by Du Bois's KPLNT, had somewhat different views about the goals and future of Negro theater. Richardson, as noted above, was influenced by Du Bois, who was his mentor, but he was also inspired by a controversial antilynching play called *Rachel* (1916) by Angelina Weld Grimké (his former high school teacher) and by the Irish National Theater. In 1919, Richardson had addressed concerns similar to those of Fauset, in an essay in *The Crisis* titled "The Hope of a Negro Drama." Richardson believed that the Negro had a natural predisposition for poetry, that all playwrights are poets, and that therefore all Negro poets should write Negro drama "that shows the soul of a people; and the soul of this people is truly worth showing." He considered the Irish National Theater an excellent model for Negro playwrights because of its small size and its international reputation. He wanted his vision of Negro theater to reach the entire world; and even though he strongly encouraged Negro poets to write plays, he praised the work of playwrights who were not Negroes but nevertheless wrote about the "souls" of Negro people in a suitable fashion—playwrights such as Eugene O'Neill and Ridgley Torrence. Richardson did not agree with Du Bois that Negro plays had to be written by Negro playwrights, produced near Negro communities, or aimed at exclusively Negro audiences; he felt, rather, that Negro plays should be written for theatergoers worldwide. Despite their philosophical differences, Du Bois advanced Richardson's career by staging several of Richardson's plays and by advising him to share his work with Raymond O'Neil's Ethiopian Art Players in Chicago.

Richardson wrote at least forty-eight plays, including children's plays, historical plays, and family and marital plays; a few examples are *The Flight of the Natives; The Black Horseman; The House of Sham; Attucks, the Martyr; Near Calvary; Antonio Maceo; The King's Dilemma; The Dragon's Tooth;* and *The Gypsy's Finger Ring.* His one-act drama *The Chip Woman's Fortune*—a realistic work emphasizing cohesive relationships in a family despite generational gaps—was the first nonmusical play by a Negro to be produced on Broadway; it opened on 15 May 1923 at the Frazee Theater. Richardon also edited two anthologies of drama: *Plays and Pageants from the Life of the Negro* (1930) and *Negro History in Thirteen Plays* (1935).

Richardson's distinguished career was shaped by many other mentors besides du Bois. Richardson met some of these mentors through his attendance at Georgia Johnson's Saturday Nighters Club. He was greatly influenced by the work of Alain Locke (1886–1954), a philosopher who was teaching at Howard University and was a cofounder of the Howard University Players. Richardson had originally submitted his plays to Locke, hoping that they would be produced at Howard University; but Locke's request to stage one of them was turned down by the president of the university, and Richardson then sought Du Bois's help.

Alain Locke

Locke was a mentor to numerous other playwrights of the Harlem Renaissance besides Richardson and was a judge in the playwriting contests sponsored by *Opportunity*, a publication of the Urban League. Locke published several essays on the New Negroes and their place in theater. He developed and published an extensive manifesto outlining his views on Negro folk drama and edited several anthologies that included plays representing his vision of this genre. Locke encouraged Negro artists to abandon commercial theater, in which stereotypes and caricatures of the Negro had dominated American and some European stages since the late 1800s. He believed that Negro theater should be housed at universities instead of community centers in major cities. In 1922, in an essay published in *The Crisis*, he wrote:

> We believe a university foundation will assure a greater continuity of effort and insure accordingly a greater permanence of result. We believe further that the development of the newer forms of drama has proved most successful where laboratory and experimental conditions have obtained and that the development of race drama is by those very circumstances the opportunity and responsibility of our educational centers.

Ideally, these educational centers would replicate European theatrical training schools, such as the Moscow Art Theater, where novice actors could work with a master director.

Locke and his colleague Montgomery Gregory, the cofounder of the Howard Players, produced works by professional playwrights (such as Ridgley Torrence) with professional actors (such as Charles Gilpin); they also produced plays written by students under the auspices of Howard University's theater department. Locke and Montgomery invited theater professionals, regardless of race, to help them train the Howard University Players. As time went on, Locke realized the importance not only of training actors but also of developing scripts. He began to publish a series of articles about the importance of folk drama and the stage voice of the "New Negro."

Locke argued that a problem with Negro theater was its desire to imitate western European theater. In his essay "The Negro and the American Stage," he asserted that "one can scarcely think of a complete development of dramatic art by the Negro without some significant artistic reexpression of African life and the traditions associated with it." Negroes had not been encouraged to explore cultural memory, retrieve artistic traditions from the past, or bring these traditions into their own work for the stage. Locke was interested in plays with African elements: themes, scenes, music, storytelling, ritual, and nonlinear plots. He believed that once Negro playwrights found the truth about their past, a new sense of cultural and artistic freedom would emerge and would naturally connect with American theatrical sensibilities, thereby creating a true or realistic form of Negro theater that illustrated the New Negro. Playwrights who were influenced by Locke's folk drama included Marieta Bonner, Owen Dodson, Shirley Graham Du Bois, Zora Neale Hurston, Langston Hughes, Georgia Douglas Johnson, Willis Richardson, and Eulalie Spence.

Zora Neale Hurston

Zora Neale Hurston (1891–1960) was especially intrigued by the possibilities of Locke's vision for the theater of the New Negro, and she experimented with its form throughout her life. Hurston studied with Locke and Montgomery Gregory at Howard University in the 1920s. She was greatly influenced by Locke, who encouraged her to write about Negro folklore and "Africanisms." At Columbia University, as a student at Barnard College interested in anthropology, and as a budding writer, Hurston—like Locke—refused to believe that people of African ancestry were innately inferior to whites. A popular study at this time was craniology, the size of the human head relative to the size of the brain; accordingly, she stood on various street corners in Harlem and asked passersby if she could measure their heads. This use of science to prove that African Americans were not inferior to whites may have inspired Hurston, in her plays and novels, to depict the struggles of Negroes as they attempted to "love" themselves. For instance, in 1925, while she was a student at Barnard, she wrote what may have been her first play, *Color Struck*. It focuses on the inability of one woman to love herself because of racial shame: This woman does not have light skin, and she believes in a doctrine, espoused by racist scientists of the time, that darker-skinned Negroes were inferior to whites or mulattoes. She destroys her own life and causes the death of her mulatto daughter; still, she is an object of pity, not a villain. This controversial folk drama, written in Negro dialect appropriate for that period, forces audiences to confront issues of miscegenation and racial pride. Hurston submitted *Color Struck* to *Opportunity* magazine and won an award for it. The following year, she submitted her next play, *Spears*, to *Opportunity* and received an honorable mention. In 1927, she wrote the play *The First One*, which was published in *Ebony* and *Topaz* magazines.

All together, between 1920 and 1950, this extraordinarily prolific woman wrote nearly forty plays and musical reviews, four novels, two books of folklore, an autobiography, and more than fifty short stories and essays. She received a Rosenwald fellowship and two Guggenheim fellowships and was widely recognized as a successful writer. Still, she often found herself in poverty; and although she tried to break away from the confines of patronage, she has been criticized by some historians and biographers for accepting the support of a wealthy white woman, Charlotte Osgood Mason of Park Avenue. Mason, who enjoyed Negro literature, supported not only Hurston but also Langston Hughes during most of their literary careers. Alain Locke often met with Mason, and he encouraged her to support young Negro folk dramatists. But in return for her patronage she insisted that the playwrights refer to her as their "godmother," and she also liked to be described as the "little mother of the primitive world" (Hurston 1979, 12).

In addition to experimenting with Locke's form of folk drama, Hurston was interested in Du Bois's theories of theater. She became a member of the "cabinet" for Du Bois's Krigwa Players and participated in the company's first season at the 135th Street Library. At this time she found herself under the tutelage of Locke

and Du Bois and hoped that her plays would be produced by the Krigwa Players and at Howard University. While working with Du Bois, she continued to write plays and attempted to produce Negro musical revues. She was selected to be one of nine writers for *Fast and Furious*, a Broadway musical revue in two acts and thirty-seven scenes. The famous figures involved in this production included Tim Moore and Jackie "Moms" Mabley, but when the revue opened in New York in September 1931, it was received unfavorably by several white theater critics. Hurston's next theatrical venture, *Jungle Scandals*, was also unsuccessful; this was followed by *The Great Day*, which was praised by the critics but was not a financial success. *The Great Day*, which centered on "a day in the life of a railroad work camp," incorporated themes from Negro folklore and included "Bahamian dances, conjure ceremonies, club scenes, work songs, and children's games" (Perkins 1989, 78).

Hoping to forward her career in theater, Hurston applied for faculty positions in the theater departments of two historically black schools—Bethune-Cookman College and Fisk University—but was rejected by both. She then returned (after a six-year hiatus) to writing novels and short stories, that is, to the world of Negro fiction in which she had first achieved success. However, her theatrical career seemed to be rekindled in 1935 when the New York Negro unit of the Federal Theater Project (FTP) hired her as a drama coach, a position in which she worked directly with John Houseman. While working with FTP, she submitted several plays for production, most notably *The Fiery Chariot*. She did not succeed in this regard, although she was encouraged by Houseman, who seemed enthusiastic about the possibility that FTP might produce one of her plays in the future. In his autobiography, *Run-Through*, Houseman writes:

> For a few days I thought I had found a solution in a new play by Zorah [sic] Hurston, our most talented writer on the project, who had come up with a Negro *Lysistrata* updated and located in a Florida fishing community, where the men's wives refused them intercourse until they won their fight with the canning company for a living wage. It scandalized both the Left and Right by its saltiness. (quoted in Perkins, 78)

After the short-lived FTP came to a close, Hurston was hired from 1939 to 1940 to organize a drama program at North Carolina College for Negroes in Durham. There, she developed a professional relationship with the playwright Paul Green, who was the winner of a Pulitzer Prize and worked with the drama department at the University of North Carolina in Chapel Hill. Hurston and Green discussed collaborating on a play to be called *John de Conqueror* (Perkins, 78), but this plan ended when Hurston left North Carolina College to work for a year at Paramount Studios as a story consultant. At Paramount, Hurston tried hard to persuade various producers to use one of her novels or plays as a film script, but again she did not succeed. Her last attempt to achieve success in the theater was in 1944, when she and a white theater artist, Dorothy Varing, produced a musical comedy, *Polk County*, that was supposed to appear on Broadway in the fall of that year. However, the play lost its financial backing and never opened. Disgruntled and disappointed, Hurston returned to Florida (where she had grown up) and lived there until her death on 29 October 1960.

Langston Hughes

Langston Hughes (1898–1967), like Hurston, is often thought of as a poet but was also a prolific playwright: He wrote almost one hundred theatrical pieces, ranging from short scenes to full-length plays. In fact, he and Hurston collaborated on writing a play called *Mule Bone*, although because of personal differences they were unable to finish it. One of Hughes's full-length plays, *Mulatto*, opened on Broadway on 24 October 1935. *Mulatto* is about a mulatto son, Bert, who murders his father—the father having refused to acknowledge Bert as anything more than a slave plantation worker. Hughes was disappointed with the Broadway production because the white producer, Martin Jones, altered the script after buying the rights to the text. Nevertheless, *Mulatto* was the longest-running Negro play on Broadway until Lorraine Hansberry's *A Raisin in the Sun*, which opened in 1959. Although *Mulatto* is a tragedy, Hughes primarily wrote comedies and musicals. His theater works include *The Barrier* (an opera); *Emperor of Haiti*; *Little Ham*; *Don't You Want to Be Free?*; *Limitations of Life?*; *Scarlett Sister Barry*; *The Em-Fuehrer Jones*; *Little Eva*; *Run, Ghost, Run—*; *Joy to My Soul*; *Simply Heavenly*; *The Sun Do Move*; *Tambourines to Glory*; *The Gold Piece*; *Soul Gone Home*; and *Black Nativity*.

After his experiences with having *Mulatto* presented commercially and trying to have his other plays produced professionally, Hughes wrote several essays outlining his hopes for the future of Negro theater. Hughes advocated a Negro theater similar in structure to what Du Bois envisioned. He believed that Broadway and Hollywood were too commercial, averse to experimentation, and interested only in minstrel-like caricatures of Negro life. (Hughes expressed these ideas in, for example, "The Need for an Afro-American Theatre" in *Anthology of the American Negro in Theatre*.) He also wanted Negro theater artists to be able to work in professional spaces; accordingly, he urged the formation of a national black theater. He considered it important for young playwrights to see revivals of the work of older playwrights; he also thought there should be a place like a national theater that could serve as a workshop for the next generation of artists. Hughes believed that without some sort of national African American theater, the world would have no opportunity to hear what he called "authentic" Negro voices, that is, diverse voices in the Negro community that also spanned lines of skin color and class; he also strongly believed that these voices would be heard by all Americans, regardless of color, if such a theater existed. In his own work—his poetry, his short stories, and especially his theatrical characters—he emphasized these authentic voices.

Georgia Douglas Johnson

Hughes enjoyed discussing his ideas with other Negro playwrights and artists of the Harlem Renaissance. He, Hurston, Locke, Richardson, and Du Bois all attended Georgia Douglas Johnson's Saturday Nighters Club—the salon on S Street in Washington, D.C., where the future of Negro art was debated. Johnson, who happily proclaimed herself the maternal hostess of the Harlem Renaissance outside New York City, once remarked, "I'm halfway between everybody and everything and I bring them together" (Hull 1987, 186–187). Johnson had a reputation for taking in stray animals and artists; Hurston, during her periods of financial difficulty, was a frequent and welcome guest at Johnson's house.

Johnson was a playwright as well as a hostess. She wrote dramas that reflected the political and social doctrines of Locke and Du Bois and attempted to address the questions raised by Du Bois. She was well known in the African American and white American theater communities; thus it is not surprising that she worked, although indirectly, with the Federal Theater Project (FTP) from 1935 to 1939. She submitted six plays to FTP for production: four antilynching plays (*A Sunday Morning in the South*, versions 1 and 2; *Safe*; and *Blue-Eyed Black Boy*) and two historical dramas about slaves escaping from bondage to achieve freedom, or what should have been freedom (*Frederick Douglass* and *William and Ellen Craft*). FTP decided not to produce any of these plays, but that did not discourage Johnson; she continued to write not only plays but also poetry and dozens of musical compositions. She also wrote articles and essays for various black journals and newspapers; in these essays, she discussed the plight of Negro women and the political and social struggles of the Negro community. She was a contributing editor for the magazine *Negro Women's World* and an associate editor with *The Women's Voice*, periodicals located in the area around Washington.

Georgia Douglas Johnson wrote approximately thirty plays, but only five were published, and only a few of her scripts are still extant (her family has most of the unpublished plays). The five plays that were published were *A Sunday Morning in the South* (1925), *Blue Blood* (1926), *Plumes* (1927), *Frederick Douglass* (1935), and *William and Ellen Craft* (1935). Of these, only *Plumes*, *Blue Blood*, and *Frederick Douglass* have a record of theatrical production. The one-act play *Blue Blood* was first staged in New York City, starring Frank Horne and May Miller, who was also a playwright and poet of the Harlem Renaissance; it was later performed at Howard University as part of a program featuring three one-act works. *Blue Blood* attracted attention and was critically acclaimed after it won the playwriting contest sponsored by *Opportunity* in 1926; *Plumes* took first prize in that contest in 1927. *Blue Blood* is significant because it examines black women's struggle to redefine their lives: The female characters boldly confront issues of rape, miscegenation, the Negro elite, racism and classism within the African American community, and the concept of women as objects. Johnson's commitment to the development of Negro theater is demonstrated not only in her own theatrical work but also in her influence over many playwrights and artists of the Harlem Renaissance, including Du Bois, Locke, Richardson, Hurston, and Hughes.

It is worth noting here that Johnson's activism went beyond the theater; she was also a part of the antilynching campaigns in African American communities during the 1920s.

Summary

In sum, the playwrights of the Harlem Renaissance—along with its artists and scholars—attempted to answer the questions posed by Du Bois. They were committed to demolishing the dehumanizing stereotypes of people of African descent, but they understood that changing dominant attitudes takes time. Most writers of the Harlem Renaissance were not interested in chastising an artist like Hattie McDaniel, who perpetuated the popular nineteenth-century image of the Negro as a clown from a minstrel show, because they understood the dilemma of such an artist, and they also often felt caught between the politics of the burgeoning Negro community and the white community's stereotypical perceptions of Negroes. They were more intrigued with finding a theatrical formula that would ensure "authentic" representations of Negro identity on the American stage. Du Bois argued that Negro artists who were writing about Negroes, for Negroes, in Negro communities could produce authentic Negro characters for the theater. Numerous theater artists—Marieta Bonner, Mary Burrill, Shirley Graham Du Bois, Angelina Weld Grimké, Langston Hughes, Zora Neale Hurston, Georgia Douglas Johnson, May Miller, Willis Richardson, Eulalie Spence, and others—were influenced by Du Bois's theories of theater. However, Alain Locke, although he admired Du Bois's historical pageants, had a different theory about the future of Negro theater. Locke believed that Negro theater should be produced at universities and that folk drama was the essence of cultural and artistic expression for the New Negro. He encouraged playwrights such as Zora Neale Hurston, Langston Hughes, Georgia Douglas Johnson, May Miller, and Willis Richardson to abandon western European theatrical standards for "Africanisms" or cultural memory. Hughes, Hurston, Johnson, and Richardson are just four of the playwrights of the Harlem Renaissance who transformed popular Negro theatrical characters from their predecessors in minstrelsy to diverse, realistic dramatic figures. These four playwrights experimented with Du Bois's and Locke's theories of drama but also remembered Willis Richardson's assertion that the most important goal was to create a "play that shows the soul of a people; and the soul of this people is truly worth showing."

JASMIN L. LAMBERT

See also Blacks in Theater; Crisis, The; Crisis: The Negro in Art—How Shall He Be Portrayed? A Symposium; Du Bois, W. E. B.; Ethiopian Art Players: Fauset, Jessie Redmon; Krigwa Players; Literature: 3—Drama; Mason, Charlotte Osgood; Minstrelsy; 135th Street Library; Opportunity; Porgy and Bess; Talented Tenth; Theater; *specific writers and works*

Further Reading

Brown-Guillory, Elizabeth. *Wine in the Wilderness.* New York: Praeger, 1990.

Hatch, James V. *Black Theater, U.S.A. 1847–1974.* New York: Free Press, 1974.

Hatch, James V., and Hamalian. *Lost Plays of the Harlem Renaissance, 1920–1940.* Detroit, Mich.: Wayne State University Press, 1996.

Hull, Gloria T. *Color, Sex, and Poetry: Three Women Writers of the Harlem Renaissance.* Bloomington: Indiana University Press, 1987.

Hurston, Zora Neale. *I Love Myself When I Am Laughing . . . ,* ed. Alice Walker. New York: Feminist, 1979.

Krasner, David. *A Beautiful Pageant: African American Theatre, Drama, and Performance in the Harlem Renaissance, 1910–1927.* New York: Palgrave Macmillan, 2002.

Patterson, Lindsay. *Anthology of the American Negro in the Theatre: A Critical Approach.* New York: Publishers Company, 1970.

Perkins, Kathy. *Black Female Playwrights.* Bloomington: Indiana University Press, 1989.

Turner, Darwin T. *An Anthology of Black Drama in America.* Washington, D.C.: Howard University Press, 1994.

Wall, Cheryl A. *Women of the Harlem Renaissance.* Bloomington: Indiana University Press, 1995.

Authors: 5—Poets

Judged by its quality and popularity, poetry produced by African American writers in the 1920s constitutes a bright period in American literature. In the last decade of the nineteenth century, Paul Laurence Dunbar (1872–1906) enjoyed international popularity, primarily for his humorous poems in dialect. From Dunbar's death to the early 1920s, no African American poet received a great deal of attention; but during the 1920s, with the advent of the New Negro movement, that situation changed dramatically. The high profile of poets during the Harlem Renaissance was influenced by changes in the American publishing scene as well as by the development of a more militant race consciousness in the black community.

Background

In the early decades of the twentieth century, many newspapers, including the black press, published poems on their editorial pages or in special literary columns. These poems were usually patriotic, sentimental, pleasantly philosophical, or humorous and were contributed by local readers as well as by more accomplished writers from all over the country. However, they were often regarded as filler by both editors and readers and did not get much serious attention. The critical consensus of the period was that most late nineteenth-century American poetry was undistinguished at best. There were other periodicals, though, in which poetry was taken more seriously, and by the beginning of the 1920s, such journals had created a resurgence of interest in poetry among the general public. Poets were gregarious or controversially argumentative, and poetry became fashionable for a season. That mood helped direct attention to African American poets as well.

For their part, African American readers seemed to be eager to read literature that expressed both their social and political aspirations as well as their resentment of the racial segregation laws and discriminatory customs that frustrated them. The phrase "New Negro" had been popularized around the turn of the twentieth century to indicate a new sense of self-awareness and militancy in the African American community. The young intellectuals who became the poets of the Harlem Renaissance proudly adopted that phrase, and Alain Locke (1885–1954), a professor of philosophy at Howard University, used it as the title of a groundbreaking anthology of sociological essays and literary works that he edited in 1925.

The poets who emerged in the 1920s were an incarnation of a people's hopes. The first generation of the twentieth century, children of the African American middle class, were often college-educated and were able to aspire to much greater ambitions than their elders had ever imagined. They were proud of their heritage and intent on celebrating African American culture, but they were also aware of the necessity of proving the value of that culture to the rest of the world. The work they produced illustrates two methods of accomplishing these goals: (1) some poets attempted to demonstrate their mastery of time-honored classical and traditional literary forms; (2) others, however, emphasized adapting colloquial language or folk-based motifs and investing them with artistic legitimacy.

An important aspect of the poetry of the Harlem Renaissance is the fact that it was primarily aimed at an African American readership. Although many of the works voiced a protest against the status quo, the poets attempted to avoid an attitude of supplication and what the critic John Henrik Clark has called the "literature of petition." The journals that published their poetry facilitated this polemical position.

The Crisis, published by the National Association for the Advancement of Colored People (NAACP), and the National Urban League's *Opportunity: Journal of Negro Life* were among the primary venues for the new poetry. The literary pages of the newspaper *Negro World*, published by Marcus Garvey's Universal Negro Improvement Association (UNIA), also promoted poets, as did political journals such as *The Messenger*, edited by the labor organizers Chandler Owen and A. Philip Randolph. Mainstream journals such as *Vanity Fair* and H. L. Mencken's *American Mercury* were also supportive of African American poets. Across the country, local chapters of the NAACP and UNIA, women's organizations, and churches encouraged book clubs, discussion groups, and elocution societies. Beginning in 1925, annual contests sponsored by *Opportunity* brought many talented young writers widespread attention, and celebrated judges such as Carl Van Vechten and Fannie Hurst were able to help these writers secure generous patrons or publishing contracts.

Poetry with a Purpose

The poetry of the Harlem Renaissance does not adhere to any one style, although most of it does appear to serve a particular purpose. Young poets such as Countee Cullen and Langston Hughes vociferously declared their artistic freedom to write in any way they pleased. Cullen went so far as to say that while he hoped his work would be appreciated, he didn't particularly want to be identified primarily as a Negro poet. Even so, much of the poetry produced by Cullen, Hughes, and their peers focused on issues

and experiences specific to black Americans. Other writers articulated the movement's goals in political terms. Both James Weldon Johnson and Alain Locke pointed out that literature might be a force in improving the way mainstream American society viewed African American people. In Johnson's view, no race or nationality could be considered inferior if it produced great art. As early as 1918, Johnson had written, "The world does not know a race is great until that race has produced great literature." Locke, in *The New Negro*, suggested that talented artists might emphasize African Americans' contributions to society and culture and, by reversing the negative images of African people encouraged by slavery, help eliminate the "great discrepancy between the American social creed and the American social practice."

Although it produced no uniform style of writing and followed no specific aesthetic guidelines, the New Negro poetic movement was not exactly a spontaneous or undirected development. The historian David Levering Lewis used the phrase "civil rights by copyright" to describe the strategy of improving the African Americans' status by demonstrating intellectual and artistic excellence. The literary campaign was envisioned and carefully nurtured by W. E. B. Du Bois and Jessie Redmon Fauset at *The Crisis*, by Charles S. Johnson at the National Urban League, by the NAACP's James Weldon Johnson, and by the scholars Alain Locke and Carter G. Woodson. These leaders in turn drew on the goodwill and significant connections of a network of white editors, sociologists, and charitable institutions.

The ideas that undergirded the creative activity were most clearly articulated by Alain Locke. Democracy could not succeed, Locke stated, "except through the fullest sharing of American culture and institutions." *The New Negro* announced that the talented young people in the black community were ready to make their contribution. Locke hoped that this rising generation would be able to advance "from the arid fields of controversy and debate to the productive fields of creative expression." Locke—like Du Bois and the white cofounder of the NAACP, Joel A. Spingarn—believed that the progress of an ethnic group or a nation-state depended on the leadership of cultured individuals. These leaders also firmly believed that the arts have the power to change society.

In his article "Criteria of Negro Art," published in *The Crisis* in October 1926, W. E. B. Du Bois (1868–1963) bluntly stated what Alain Locke and James Weldon Johnson had often implied. All art, Du Bois declared, should be propaganda. Literary works should support an ethical or political point of view, be persuasive, and—in the case of the art of black Americans—promote the social advancement of the group. In fact, although younger writers might have resented the constraints implied by Du Bois, they attempted to produce poetry that would examine the characteristics of black life in the United States and inspire black readers with a sense of both individual and collective self-worth. They wrote poems clearly intended to redeem African American people in their own eyes by countering racist stereotypes, and in so doing, to inspire and promote political action for achieving the rights and privileges of citizenship.

The Early Poets

The forerunners of the Harlem Renaissance poets include two writers who achieved significant national attention following Dunbar's death. William Stanley Braithwaite (1878–1962) wrote elegant, sentimental, and somewhat mystical verse. His collection *The House of Falling Leaves* (1908) was warmly received. Braithwaite's true influence, however, came later, as he established himself as a major literary editor and critic. Fenton Johnson (1888–1958) published three collections of poems between 1912 and 1916. Although his earliest work was in the dialect mode popularized by Dunbar, he experimented with poems based on Negro spirituals and later became known for poems marked by an ironic tone and written in the avant-garde style that emerged in Chicago at the time of World War I. By 1922, however, perhaps because of his controversial political militancy, Johnson had stopped publishing poetry.

Two other poets named Johnson (unrelated to each other and to Fenton Johnson) achieved recognition as well. James Weldon Johnson (1871–1938) first achieved fame and wealth as a lyricist for Broadway musicals at the turn of the century; he wrote the words for "Lift Every Voice and Sing" (1900), a song cherished by millions of people as the "Negro national anthem." He also aspired to a literary career and, modeling himself on Dunbar, published *Fifty Years and Other Poems* (1917), a book divided between dialect verses and poems in standard English. The popular and prolific poet Georgia Douglas Johnson (1877–1966) received recognition and critical praise for her finely crafted verses in *The Heart of a Woman* (1918). Georgia Johnson, who was educated at Atlanta University, Oberlin Conservatory of Music, and the Cleveland College of Music, married and settled in Washington, D.C., in 1909. Throughout the 1920s, she wrote a syndicated newspaper column and held a weekly literary salon at her home. On Saturday evenings, Alain Locke, Jessie Redmon Fauset, Jean Toomer, Anne Spencer, and others who might be visiting the city met to read their works and discuss artistic issues. After her husband's death in 1925, Georgia Johnson worked for various agencies of the federal government and raised two sons while continuing her literary activities. Her published works of poetry also include *Bronze* (1922) and *An Autumn Love Cycle* (1928).

Joseph Seamon Cotter Jr. (1895–1919), a journalist in Louisville, Kentucky, published an impressive collection titled *The Band of Gideon and Other Lyrics* (1918), but he succumbed to tuberculosis soon afterward. His poetry demonstrates his skilled approach to standard rules of versification, but some of the poems reflect the "imagist" approach of the modernists and some reflect his interest in colloquial African American idioms—an interest he shared with Fenton Johnson and James Weldon Johnson.

The multitalented W. E. B. Du Bois also published poems in the first two decades of the century. Several idiosyncratic, biblically cadenced verses were included in his book *Darkwater: Voices from Within the Veil* (1920). Focusing on events such as the mob violence that shook Atlanta in 1906, these are starkly angry, bitter poems.

Because of its stylistic innovation and racially focused subject matter, *Cane* (1923)—a book by Jean Toomer (1894–1967) that includes fictional vignettes, poems, and a play—is often considered the inaugural expression of the Harlem Renaissance. Poems such as "Song of the Son" and "Georgia Dusk" represent Toomer's lyrical attempt to capture what he felt was the beauty, as well as the memories of pain and hardship, of a southern rural way of life that was passing with the old century. Like Fenton Johnson before him, Toomer in "Song of the Son" elegantly captures the tone and flow of spirituals without resorting to dialect.

Claude McKay

The first major poetic voice of the Harlem Renaissance, however, was Claude McKay (1889–1948). McKay was born in Jamaica, West Indies, and had worked there as a policeman and published two volumes of dialect verse based on his experiences before coming to the United States to attend college in 1912. He quickly became involved in radical politics and served on the editorial board of socialist magazines such as *Liberator* and *The Masses*. His bold antilynching poem "If We Must Die," first published in *Liberator*, was a militant response to the "red summer" of racial violence in 1919. The poem's powerful effect is derived from the seeming contrast of its immediacy of subject matter, its militant content, and McKay's sonorous but meticulous Elizabethan sonnet form.

McKay could render beautiful images of nature and vibrant urban scenes, but he is primarily a poet of social engagement. He was a dedicated political activist, and in 1919 he was briefly associated with the International Workers of the World (IWW) and with socialists in Harlem such as Hubert H. Harrison and Richard B. Moore. Between 1920 and 1934 McKay lived and traveled widely in England, Europe, the Soviet Union, and Africa, writing and publishing prolifically. Although he was not actually in the United States, his work remained central to the "New Negro" movement.

McKay's poetry, as in "If We Must Die," is uncompromising in its analysis of racial bigotry and his assertion of the will to overcome it. Poems such as "America" specifically address social conflict, and "Baptism" uses the metaphor of a trial by fire. "Into this furnace let me go alone," writes McKay. This sonnet ends with the affirmation "I will come out, back to your world of tears, A stronger soul within a fine frame." Trials, in McKay's vision, strengthen the spirit of a race or an individual. In later years, McKay would seek a similar affirmation in religion.

Although he would go on to publish additional volumes of poetry, novels, journalism, and political commentary, McKay's collection *Harlem Shadows* (1922) established a high standard for other poets—a standard that would be met by major poets such as Countee Cullen (1903–1946), Langston Hughes (1902–1967), and Sterling Brown (1901–1989).

Countee Cullen

Countee Cullen, who was the adopted child of Carolyn Mitchell Cullen and the pastor of the Salem Methodist Episcopal Church, Dr. Frederick Asbury Cullen, epitomized Harlem's educated and polished upper middle class. A brilliant student and precocious writer, he received several academic and literary prizes, including the John Reed Memorial Prize from *Poetry* magazine.

His first collection of poems, *Color* (1925), published by the venerable firm Harper Brothers, was a bestseller. This book appeared just as Cullen graduated Phi Beta Kappa from New York University and went on to Harvard to earn a master's degree.

At the beginning of his career, Cullen was easily the most acclaimed and prolific poet of the Harlem Renaissance. His work appeared in a wide range of African American and mainstream journals, and he published three books in 1927: *Copper Sun*, *The Ballad of the Brown Girl: An Old Ballad Retold*, and *Caroling Dusk: An Anthology of Verse by Negro Poets*. Two years later, his own book *The Black Christ and Other Poems* provoked some controversy. From 1926 to 1928 Cullen also wrote a literary column, "The Dark Tower," for *Opportunity*.

Cullen insisted that while his subject matter might focus on African American life, his poetry was nevertheless part of a long English-language literary tradition. He argued that African American writers had more to gain from a study of that literature than from "any nebulous atavistic yearnings toward an African influence." He definitely opposed the tendency of some poets to indulge in sensationalized "primitive" imagery. Other literary critics also expressed weariness with poets who seemed to exploit tawdry urban scenes.

In the anthology he edited, Cullen applauded the stylistic diversity of his contemporaries. He praised Anne Spencer's "cool precision," delighted in Lewis Alexander's experiments with haiku, and admired McKay's rebelliousness even though he feared that it sometimes "clouds his lyricism." Above all, though, Cullen desired to "maintain the higher traditions of English verse."

He was aware of the ambivalence in his own position. In his magnificent poem "Heritage" (1925), identifying himself as "one three centuries removed," Cullen wonders, "What is Africa to me?" Self-doubt, social ostracism because of race, and skepticism about religious faith become powerfully conflicting forces. As with Du Bois's famous formulation of "double consciousness" in *The Souls of Black Folk* (1903), Cullen shows how the discrepancy between America's democratic rhetoric and the realities of race threaten to unhinge black citizens.

Langston Hughes

Beginning with "The Negro Speaks of Rivers," published in *The Crisis* when he was nineteen years old, Langston Hughes made a tremendous impact on the literary world; eventually, he achieved international fame that rivaled Dunbar's. Since his death in 1967, Hughes has been increasingly viewed by critics as a major American poet.

Hughes was born in Joplin, Missouri, and raised by his grandmother and mother in Kansas and Ohio. He was a voracious reader as a child, and while he was still in high school, he determined that he wanted to be a writer.

Influenced early on by the modernist poetics of Carl Sandburg and other practitioners of free verse, Hughes developed a terse, freely rhymed (almost syncopated) style in short lyrics and dramatic monologues that captured aspects of everyday life. Hughes found support for his early writing from luminaries such as Du Bois and the popular poet Vachel Lindsay, who helped him make contacts that led to the publication of his first book in 1926. *The Weary Blues* sounded a new note in African American poetry. Hughes celebrated the common man; chose to write about situations that many thought unpoetic; and, without apology, used the folk blues stanza as if it were as acceptable as the sonnet. When *The Weary Blues* was reviewed in the *Times* of London, Hughes was slightingly called a "poet of the cabaret" and unfavorably compared with Countee Cullen.

Such reviews might have angered him, but Hughes did not flinch before criticism. In 1928, in a letter to the editor published in *The Crisis,* he forcefully declared that he did not care if critics found the poems included in *Fine Clothes to the Jew* (1927) "low-down, jazzy . . . and utterly uncouth." He would be satisfied if his poems depicted the details and rhythms of urban African American life with lyrical realism. Hughes was concerned to show his readers—as he put it in his essay "The Negro Artist and the Racial Mountain" (1926)—that "we are beautiful. And ugly too."

Despite his capacity for generating controversy, Hughes found favor with a middle-class audience and, particularly through the appearance of his poems in newspapers, an enthusiastic working-class readership as well. A nationwide tour in 1931–1932 boosted his popularity; he traveled across the country giving readings of his work at colleges, churches, and community auditoriums. Poems such as "I, Too, Sing America" captured the community's mood of pride, determination, and impatience with second-class citizenship. The beautiful monologue "Mother to Son," more than likely drawing on Hughes's own personal childhood experiences, spoke directly to both elders and the rising generation, reinforcing the need for perseverance in the face of adversity and racism.

At the same time, Hughes's blues poems expressed the reality of hard times and bad luck. In "Po' Boy Blues," he states that "this world is weary/An' de road is long an' hard." But the blues poems also demonstrate how to use humor to survive the worst. Hughes was also capable of biting political satire. His "Advertisement for the Waldorf-Astoria" was a withering critique of the American economic system and the structural inequalities that were made apparent by the stock market crash of 1929. The poem brought him praise from the left wing but also cost him the support of Charlotte Osgood Mason, his wealthy patron. Regardless of his approach, in diction that seems both eloquent and effortless, Hughes produced a consistent stream of poems that people read with excitement and—as they had done with Dunbar's verses—memorized for their own entertainment.

Sterling Brown

Sterling Brown (1901–1989) was born in Washington, D.C., and literally grew up on the campus of Howard University, where his father was a faculty member. He graduated Phi Beta Kappa from Williams College, earned his master's degree at Harvard in 1923, and eventually became a beloved professor at Howard, serving for half a century. Under the mentorship of his colleague Alain Locke, Brown became both a formidable scholar and a public intellectual. He wrote a literary column for *Opportunity* and was an active folklore researcher. He pursued doctoral studies at Harvard and, in 1937, published two important critical surveys— *The Negro in American Fiction* and *Negro Poetry and Drama*.

Brown's folklore studies helped him develop into a marvelous storyteller, and in some ways he embodied the traits of the trickster Slim Greer, a figure he featured in a series of hilarious poetic monologues. Brown found beauty and grandeur in ordinary people, but he could evoke their sorrows, too. "Maumee Ruth," written in ballad meter, prematurely mourns the death of a rural matriarch. The reader is told, "Might as well drop her / Deep in the ground" because Maumee Ruth's children have been lost to the vices of urban life and have turned their backs on her. The use of colloquial idiom—without the usual mechanics of dialect verse—underscores the poem's ironic tone and emphasizes the tragic toll caused by prodigal sons and daughters.

Brown used dialect skillfully in poems such as "Odyssey of Big Boy" and "Long Gone." In "Southern Road," he incorporated the work song rhythms of a chain gang; and in "Ma Rainey," he alternated dialect and standard English stanzas to explore the powerful attraction of the blues.

Minor Poets

Many excellent writers, not all of whom published their work in book form, made the Harlem Renaissance truly remarkable in terms of poetic activity. Although most of the best-known writers were located in New York, the creative flowering was actually a national artistic movement, and many fine poets could be found in all parts of the United States. There were vibrant literary scenes in cities such as Chicago and Washington, D.C. Black colleges and universities also supported artistic communities and employed professors with literary interests.

Among the noteworthy but lesser-known poets of the era are Helene Johnson, Walter Everette Hawkins, Gwendolyn Bennett, Anne Spencer, Waring Cuney, Frank Horne, Arna Bontemps, Esther Popel, and Lewis Alexander. While Helene Johnson and Bennett (like McKay and Cullen) cultivated the sonnet tradition, poets such as Cuney, Horne, and Alexander explored *vers libre* and other experimental forms. Hawkins, a regular contributor to *The Messenger*, exemplifies a boldly militant voice, continuing the tradition established by Fenton Johnson, Du Bois, McKay, and others.

Anne Spencer (1882–1975), a librarian and community leader in Lynchburg, Virginia, said, "I proudly love being a Negro woman." Her poetry, however, was primarily focused on the beauties of nature and the elevating life of the mind. When she chose to write about social problems, it was often to focus attention on the quirks of human nature. In "Neighbors," for example, considering people "who ask too much," Spencer cleverly noted the dangers of friendliness: "Offered a hand, a finger-tip, / You must have a soul to clutch."

Esther Popel (1896–1958), a poet who was concerned much more with politics, was a participant in Georgia Douglas Johnson's literary salon and a frequent contributor to *Negro World*, *Opportunity*, and other journals. Popel graduated Phi Beta Kappa from Dickinson College and became a high school teacher in Washington, D.C. Her often bitterly ironic poems are as searingly effective as Claude McKay's. Her "Blasphemy—American Style" (1934), for example, is a prayer of thanks raised by a lynch mob. Popel did not, however, publish a book-length collection of her work.

Like Popel, Walter Everette Hawkins (b. 1883)—a postal clerk in Washington, D.C.—was among the more militant voices of the era. Hawkins published two collections of poems: *Chords and Discords* (1920) and *Petals From the Poppies* (1936). He was also featured in Nancy Cunard's *Negro Anthology* (1934).

Frank Horne (1899–1974) had been trained as an ophthalmologist but eventually enjoyed a distinguished career as a college and government administrator. His grimly titled "Letters Found Near a Suicide" won a prize from, *The Crisis* in 1925 and launched a series of spare but witty modernist poems that celebrate the vigor and camaraderie of youth while also attacking Victorian middle-class complacency.

Lewis Alexander (b. 1900), who had been educated at Howard University and the University of Pennsylvania, was an actor and theatrical director. As a poet, he preferred to write in traditional stanza forms but also experimented with free verse and Japanese forms such as haiku and tanka. At his best, Alexander could produce strikingly evocative images such as "The earth trembles tonight / Like the quiver of a Negro woman's eye-lids cupping tears."

Clarissa Scott Delany (1901–1927), the daughter of Booker T. Washington's secretary Emmett J. Scott, was a Phi Beta Kappa graduate of Wellesley College. In her tragically short life she wrote excellent lyric poems and was capable of brilliant and memorable lines such as "Joy shakes me like the wind that lifts a sail."

The equally talented Gwendolyn Bennett (1902–1981), a visual artist as well as a writer, graduated from Pratt Institute and studied in Paris at the Académie Julian and the École de Panthéon. Many of her poems exalted femininity and, in some cases, natural African beauty. In her poem "Heritage"—perhaps in response to Cullen—she offers romanticized images of dancers "around a heathen fire" and, in terms reminiscent of Dunbar, testifies to her desire to "feel the surging / Of my sad people's soul / Hidden by a minstrel-smile." During the 1920s, Bennett wrote a regular column for *Opportunity* and taught in the art department at Howard University.

Arna Bontemps (1902–1973) was for many years a librarian at Fisk University and collaborated with Langston Hughes on many projects, including their major anthology *Poetry of the Negro: 1746–1964*. During the 1920s, Bontemps published poems in *Opportunity*, *The Crisis*, and other journals. His powerful "Nocturne at Bethesda" received the poetry prize from *The Crisis* in 1927 and has been frequently anthologized. Perhaps drawing on a technique used in spirituals and African American sermonic traditions, poems such as this one and "Golgotha Is a Mountain" (1926) use biblical stories but carefully relocate them in a contemporary historical setting.

Helene Johnson (1906–1995) was among the youngest and most talented of the Harlem Renaissance poets. She was raised in Boston, won an honorable mention in the first *Opportunity* literary contest, and settled in New York in 1927. Her poems appeared in *Vanity Fair, The Messenger, Fire!!,* and other journals, as well as in several anthologies. Some of her poems reflect a primitivistic theme by celebrating an imagined African state of nature.

Waring Cuney (1906–1976), a member of a prominent African American family, was a classically trained musician who graduated from Lincoln University and studied at the New England Conservatory of Music and in Rome. Cuney's "No Images" (1926) is a small modernist masterpiece that is often reprinted. An attempt to encourage personal and racial pride by contrasting a vibrantly mythical Africa and the anesthetic working-class city, "No Images" is the quintessential Harlem Renaissance poem.

Conclusion

These young writers were a remarkable cohort of brilliant, creative people who exemplified the "talented tenth" that Du Bois saw as the hope of the nation's future. Their ambitious and accomplished example demonstrated that only a seriously shortsighted society would deny their contribution or reject their promise.

While the poets of the Harlem Renaissance took pride in the "newness" of their work and their role as representatives of a newly awakened generation, they were also part of a literary tradition. In their attempt to distance themselves from the anxious alternation of dialect and standard English poetry practiced by Dunbar, the younger poets adopted a kind of division of labor: McKay and Cullen demonstrated their skill in expressing African American ideas in traditional stanzas, whereas Hughes and others enjoyed creating rhythmic literary experiments in colloquial black English. The movement launched the careers of several major writers and made a lasting impact on American literature. The poets of the Harlem Renaissance won favorable attention in Europe as their work was translated into other languages, and they served as an inspiration

to African and Caribbean writers, including the founders of the *nègritude* movement. Since the 1990s, excellent annotated collections of several poets, major and minor, have appeared, and literary critics continue to publish studies and interpretations of the Harlem Renaissance group.

LORENZO THOMAS

See also American Mercury; Crisis, The; Fire!!; Harper Brothers; Literature: 7—Poetry; Mason, Charlotte Osgood; Messenger, The; Modernism; Negritude; Negro World; Opportunity; Opportunity Literary Contests; Primitivism; Riots: 2—Red Summer of 1919; Spingarn, Joel; Talented Tenth; Vanity Fair; *specific poets, writers, and works*

Further Reading

Bontemps, Arna, ed. *The Harlem Renaissance Remembered.* 1972.

Honey, Maureen, ed. *Shadowed Dreams: Women's Poetry of the Harlem Renaissance.* 1989.

Hutchinson, George. *The Harlem Renaissance in Black and White.* 1995.

Kellner, Bruce, ed. *The Harlem Renaissance: A Historical Dictionary of the Era.* 1987.

Lewis, David Levering. *When Harlem Was in Vogue.* 1981.

Locke, Alain, ed. *The New Negro.* 1925.

Martin, Tony, ed. *African Fundamentalism.* 1991.

Rampersad, Arnold. *The Life of Langston Hughes,* 2 vols. 1986, 1988.

Roses, Lorraine Elena, and Ruth Elizabeth Randolph, eds. *Harlem's Glory: Black Women Writers, 1900–1950.* 1996.

Wagner, Jean. *Black Poets of the United States: From Paul Laurence Dunbar to Langston Hughes.* 1973.

Wintz, Cary. *Black Culture and the Harlem Renaissance.* 1988.

Autobiography of an Ex-Colored Man, The

James Weldon Johnson's novel *The Autobiography of an Ex-Colored Man* (1912; sometimes spelled . . . *of an Ex-Coloured Man*) unsettles distinctions of genre just as its light-skinned narrator, who has lived on both sides of the "color line," unsettles racial distinctions. The work was originally published anonymously as an actual autobiography (the publisher was Sherman,

French of Boston) but was reissued as fiction (by Knopf) in 1927.

Johnson's text interweaves personal experience, sociological observation, and social protest. The narrator begins his life's story in the South, of which his vague memories include occasional visits from a white man he later learns is his father. When this man announces his imminent marriage to a white woman, the narrator and his mother move North, to a small town in Connecticut, where he grows up immersed in books and music. Inspired by his mother's singing of old southern melodies, he distinguishes himself by becoming a remarkable classical pianist with a distinct, "singing" style. Although his musicality seems tied to his mother's race, the narrator remains unconscious of his blackness until his teacher distinguishes him from the white students in the classroom, thus initiating a crisis of identity reminiscent of W. E. B. Du Bois's "double consciousness." His new sense of racial identity leads him back to the black South, where he plans to attend Atlanta University but instead ends up working at a cigar factory alongside black Cuban immigrants and teaching piano to middle-class black children. When the factory closes, he moves North again, to the emerging "black belt" of New York City, where he narrowly escapes the pull of gambling and other vices by discovering ragtime. After hearing a "natural" black musician play ragtime by ear, he brings his classical training to bear on this new music to develop his own ragtime style—"ragging the classics"—and quickly gains a reputation as the city's best ragtime pianist.

The narrator's playing attracts white audiences in particular, and one of his admirers, a young, disaffected millionaire, hires him as a companion and personal pianist on a trip to Europe. Although the narrator enjoys relative freedom from prejudice in London and Paris, he nonetheless leaves his employer after being inspired by a German pianist to consider a new way of combining his two musical—and racial—traditions. Instead of ragging the classics, the narrator decides to devote himself to incorporating black music into classical forms, and thereby make a name as an important black composer. This ambition takes him back to the American South, where, in search of "raw material" for his work, he finds himself moved beyond expectation by the music he hears. Before his project materializes, however, he witnesses the brutal lynching of a black man and, repulsed and "shamed" by the idea of belonging to a race that could be so demeaned, he returns to New York to live as a white man. By the end of the narrative, at the moment when he begins to write his life story, the "ex-colored man" has made his fortune in real estate, married a beautiful "lily white" woman, and fathered two light-skinned children; but none of this outweighs his growing sense of regret that he has "sold his birthright for a mess of pottage."

Johnson began writing *The Autobiography of an Ex-Colored Man* at the end of a brief stint as a lyricist in musical theater; he published it six years later, while serving as an American consul in Latin America. Although some southerners who reviewed the edition of 1912 doubted its authenticity, most accepted the narrative as genuine autobiography and praised it as a "dispassionate" revelation of modern blacks' experiences and of race relations. When the text was reissued as fiction in 1927—at the height of the "Harlem Renaissance"—it carried the author's name and had a cover designed by Aaron Douglas and an introduction by Carl Van Vechten. Echoing earlier reviews, Van Vechten praised its "calm dispassionate tone" and its continuing relevance as "a composite autobiography of the Negro race."

Not until Robert Bone's *The Negro Novel in America* (1965) did critics begin to consider Johnson's narrator as a fictional character, rather than simply a mouthpiece for the author's opinions or a "dispassionate" conveyor of truths. Bone's characterization of the "ex-colored man" as a coward, and the novel as a "tragedy," opened the door to a range of new approaches to the literary qualities of the work and to the narrator's point of view. In the 1970s, critics attempting to articulate a black literary tradition considered the novel a link between nineteenth- and twentieth-century African American narratives. Both Houston Baker (1973) and Robert Stepto (1979) hailed it as an important revision of the slave narrative and a forerunner of black protest fiction.

Much early critical discussion concerns whether and to what extent the text uses irony to undermine the narrator's point of view. This criticism tends to fall into two camps: Some scholars, such as Robert E. Fleming (1971), read the narrator as wholly unreliable and maintain that his perceptions are colored by guilt over abandoning his race; and others, such as Eugene Levy (1973), insist that the narrator embodies, without irony, Johnson's own ambivalence and biases. Joseph T. Skerrett Jr. (1980) offers a compromise between these positions, arguing that Johnson used both irony and tragedy in constructing his narrator. Invoking biographical material, Skerrett suggests that Johnson "symbolically restructured" his own vexed relationship to a college friend "D," about whose decision to pass as white he felt both envy and disapproval.

More recent critics have revisited the ambiguities of Johnson's novel with a new set of questions, interested less in defining Johnson's intentions than in exploring the text's challenges to notions of authenticity. Invoking Lacanian theory, Samira Kawash (1997) underscores the text's treatment of race as "specular image" and its rejection of any notion of racial authenticity. Donald Goellnicht (1996) draws a parallel between the fictional text's "passing" as autobiography and the narrator's passing as white, and argues that the text is a "subversion" of conventional literary and racial boundaries.

As this critical history demonstrates, Johnson's only novel has continued to inspire interest and debate since its original publication, providing evidence of the changing concerns of literary criticism and the heterogeneous resonance of this richly ambiguous text.

CRISTINA L. RUOTOLO

See also Douglas, Aaron; Johnson, James Weldon; Van Vechten, Carl

Further Reading

Baker, Houston, Jr. "A Forgotten Prototype: 'The Autobiography of an Ex-Colored Man' and 'Invisible Man.'" *Virginia Quarterly Review*, 49, 1973. (Reprinted in *Critical Essays on James Weldon Johnson*, eds. Kenneth M. Price and Lawrence J. Oliver. New York: G. K. Hall, 1997.)

Bone, Robert. *Negro Novel in America*. New Haven, Conn.: Yale University Press, 1965.

Clarke, Cheryl. "Race, Homosocial Desire, and 'Mammon' in *Autobiography of an Ex-Colored Man*." In *Professions of Desire: Lesbian and Gay Studies in Literature*, eds. George E. Haggerty and Bonnie Zimmerman. New York: MLA, 1995.

Fleming, Robert. "Irony as a Key to Johnson's *The Autobiography of an Ex-Coloured Man*." *American Literature*, 43, March 1971.

Garrett, Marvine P. "Early Recollections and Structural Irony in *The Autobiography of an Ex-Coloured Man*." *Critique*, 2, 1971.

Goellnicht, Donald. "Passing as Autobiography: James Weldon Johnson's *The Autobiography of an Ex-Coloured Man*." *African American Review*, 30, Spring 1996. (Reprinted in *Critical Essays on James Weldon Johnson*, eds. Kenneth M. Price and Lawrence J. Oliver. New York: G. K. Hall, 1997.)

Kawash, Samira. "The Epistemology of Race: Knowledge, Visibility, and Passing." In *Dislocating the Color Line: Identity, Hybridity, and Singularity in African American Narrative*. Stanford, Calif.: Stanford University Press, 1997.

Levy, Eugene. *James Weldon Johnson: Black Leader, Black Voice*. Chicago, Ill.: University of Chicago Press, 1973.

Pfeiffer, Kathleen. "Individualism, Success, and American Identity in *The Autobiography of an Ex-Colored Man*." *African American Review*, 30, Fall 1996.

Ruotolo, Cristina L. "James Weldon Johnson and the Autobiography of an Ex-Colored Musician." *American Literature*, special issue, "Unsettling Blackness," June 2000.

Skerrett, Joseph T., Jr., "Irony and Symbolic Action in James Weldon Johnson's *The Autobiography of an Ex-Coloured Man*." *American Quarterly*, 32, Winter 1980. (Reprinted in *Critical Essays on James Weldon Johnson*, ed. Kenneth M. Price and Lawrence J. Oliver. New York: G. K. Hall, 1997.)

Stepto, Robert B. "Lost in a Quest: James Weldon Johnson's *The Autobiography of an Ex-Coloured Man*." In *From Behind the Veil: A Study in Afro-American Narrative*. Urbana: University of Illinois Press, 1979; 2nd ed., 1991. (Reprinted in *Critical Essays on James Weldon Johnson*, ed. Kenneth M. Price and Lawrence J. Oliver. New York: G. K. Hall, 1997.)

B

Baker, George

See Father Divine

Baker, Josephine

Josephine Baker's performances and writings of the years 1925–1936 form an archive of the transatlantic dimensions and expressions of the Harlem Renaissance. Like many African American performers of the era, Baker found her audience in Europe, where the phenomenal popularity of black Americans came to be known as *le tumulte noir*, or "black rage." She made her debut in *La Revue Nègre* (1925), and its promotional posters, designed by Paul Colin, remain the most controversial and important images of Josephine Baker. After her *danse sauvage* with Joe Alex in *La Revue Nègre*, Baker was both hailed as a primitivist icon and denounced as an indecent savage by Parisian critics. Today, "Although many people celebrate Baker's career, many could argue that her initial success was achieved at the expense of her integrity and the principles of African Americans" (Barnwell 1997, 86). According to Sharpley-Whiting (1999), Baker doubtless "realized that her popularity . . . depended on her exploitation of French exoticist impulses . . . [and] the Black Venus narrative" (107). Baker achieved greater financial success and artistic freedom in France than she might have had in the United States, but she did not escape the problem of realizing her artistic ambitions within the limitations of stereotypical black roles. Still, like many artists of the Harlem Renaissance, Baker sought to use entertainment to improve race relations, and she consistently praised the relatively liberal racial policies of the French, as an oblique critique of American racism.

Before she became a star in Paris, Baker had learned the ways of the entertainment world through black vaudeville. She toured with the Dixie Steppers on the Theater Owners' Booking Association circuit (TOBA, widely known as "Tough on Black Asses"), for a salary of $9 per week. As a dresser for the blues singer Clara Smith, she tended to Smith's costumes and was probably influenced by Smith's preference for tight pink dresses, red wigs, and feather boas—in later years, Baker would be admired for the bravado of her own fashions. When the Dixie Steppers disbanded, Baker, who was then fifteen years old, made for New York, where she was hired to perform in the touring company of Noble Sissle and Eubie Blake's *Shuffle Along*. For $30 a week, she played the chorus line's "Funny Girl," that is, the chorine on the end who doesn't quite get the routine. To the consternation of the other performers, Baker's funny faces, out-of-time kicking, comparatively dark skin, and skinny, rubbery body drew crowds and earned her admiring reviews.

Baker was then recruited by Caroline Dudley to perform in France, as a comic dancer in *La Revue Nègre* at the Théâtre des Champs-Elysées in Paris. Dudley assembled a troupe of twenty-five dancers and musicians, including the clarinetist Sidney Bechet, and they set sail 15 September 1925 aboard the *Berengaria*, arriving at Le Havre several days later. André Daven and Rolf de Maré had the company in rehearsals almost immediately, and in consultation with the music

Josephine Baker performing "The Conga" in the Ziegfeld Follies at the Winter Garden, New York, 11 February 1936.
(AP / Wide World Photos.)

hall choreographer Jacques Charles, the directors transformed the Harlem-style tap show with the aesthetics of French colonialist fantasy. The most signficant revision of La Revue Nègre was Charles's creation of a pas de deux for Josephine Baker and Joe Alex called *La danse sauvage*. Baker and Alex danced topless in costumes consisting of feathers about the head, pelvis, and ankles that caused the show to be remembered long after its brief run (from 2 October until 19 November 1925) was finished.

In Paris, Baker added fantastic colonialist costumes of bananas, feathers, and grass to her repertoire of grimaces and dances, which included the eagle rock, turkey trot, kangaroo dip, itch, break a leg, pimp walk, through the trenches, shimmy, snake hips, black bottom, and mess around (Wood 2000, 24). She typically performed a series of dances with unexpected changes at a high speed, "violating white conventions of movement" (Rose 1989, 29). One interviewer praised her as a "black Venus, who turned our concept of rhythm and movement on its head" ("Femmes d'aujourd'hui," 3). Baker's performance style of the

1920s departed from the liquid prewar style of Vernon and Irene Castle and prefigured the scholarly choreography of Katherine Dunham, which was based on the African diaspora.

Baker's famous banana skirt was her costume for *la danse des bananes*, a scene in the film *La folie du jour* (1926). Archival footage shows Baker entering the scene on the high branch of a tree and descending to the stage laughing and shaking her bananas. Baker danced without a partner in *la danse des bananes*, but she is surrounded by black male drummers, and a lounging white explorer looks on. Baker later abandoned the bananas, except for her unfortunate performance in 1936 in the Ziegfeld Follies, in which she wore a more aggressive version of this comically sexy costume (Documents des Archives, Cinémathèque de la Danse).

After her world tour of twenty-five countries in 1928–1929, Baker would transform herself during the 1930s from a black novelty to an exotic singer of love ballads and a leading actress in colonial films, under the orchestration of Pepito Abatino, her manager and partner. Abatino engaged tutors in French, voice, and dance, and he himself gave his *vedette* (star) lessons in table manners and polite conversation. He negotiated Baker's contract to appear in a silent film, *Sirène des tropiques*, in 1927. His friend Arys Nisotti, a Tunisian casino owner, produced the films *ZouZou* (1934) and *Princesse Tam Tam* (1935). Abatino wrote the script and is credited as the artistic director for *Princesse Tam Tam*. Both films included narratives of transformation and unrequited assimilation and were meant as vehicles for the new "Parisianized" Josephine Baker. Of her movies, Baker said, "It all seems so real, so true, that I sometimes think it's my own life being played out on the sets" (Rose 1989, 163).

Baker's hope for roles in Hollywood movies did not materialize, but she did star successfully in an adaptation of Offenbach's operetta *La Créole*, realizing her goal of performing serious music in French with French actors. Thus, in the 1930s Baker struggled against the *sauvage* persona she had created in the 1920s. As a jazz empress during the 1930s she wore glamorous Poiret gowns, sang, and chatted with the audience in French; and when she danced, her movements tended to conform to the fluidity and the stationary upper body of ballet. The American vernacular dance called the Charleston would remain in her repertoire, however, and this dance and the song "J'ai deux amours" became her signature. The square near the Bobino Theater in Paris where this complex and brilliant star gave her last performance has been named in her honor.

Biography

Josephine Freda McDonald Baker was born 3 June 1906 in St. Louis, Missouri. Her parents were Carrie McDonald and Eddie Carson; her stepfather was Arthur Martin; her siblings were Richard, Margaret, and Willie Mae. Her primary education was at public schools in St. Louis; she received private instruction in French, acting, voice, and dance at Beau-Chêne, France, in 1930–1931. Baker married Willie Wells in 1919. In 1920–1921, she was a dresser for Clara Smith and a featured blues singer and substitute in the chorus line with the Dixie Steppers (a vaudeville troupe) at the Booker T. Washington Theater in St. Louis, the Gibson Theater in Philadelphia, and elsewhere, earning $9 a week. She married Willie Baker in September 1921. In 1922–1923, she was with the touring company of Noble Sissle and Eubie Blake's *Shuffle Along* as the "Funny Girl" in the chorus line, earning $30 per week. In 1924–1925, she was the "Comedic Principal" in Sissle and Blake's *Bamville/Chocolate Dandies* on Broadway and on tour, at $125 per week. Also in 1925, for several months, she was a dancer at the Plantation Theater Restaurant.

Baker emigrated to France in 1925, sailing on 22 September on the *Berengaria*. In France, she was a dancer with *La Revue Nègre*, featured in a *danse sauvage* with Joe Alex, at the Théâtre des Champs-Elysées (opening 2 October 1925, closing 19 November 1925; directed by André Daven, produced by Caroline Dudley, choreographed by Jacques Charles) at $200 per week. In 1926, she was a principal in *La folie du jour* at the Folies Bergère, featured in *la danse des bananes* (the composers were Irving Berlin, Spencer Williams, and Vincent Scotto). Baker opened Chez Joséphine on Rue Fontaine, in the Montmartre district of Paris, on 14 December 1926.

Baker's films of the 1920s include *La folie du jour*, directed by Mario Nalpas (silent, 1926); *Un vent de folie*, which opened in April 1927; and *An Excursion to Paris*. There is also a film of her performance in *La Revue des revues* (1927, directed by Mario Nalpas). She appeared in the short silent film *Le pompier des Folies Bergères/Les hallucinations d'un pompier* (c. 1927, possibly with Pierre Brasseur). She starred in *Siren of the Tropics* (silent, 1927; directed by Henri Etiévent and Mario Nalpas). In 1927, Baker published the first of five collaborative autobiographies: *Les mémoires de Joséphine Baker, recuillis et adaptés par Marcel Sauvage*, which had drawings by Paul Colin. She also endorsed a hair-straightening pomade, Bakerfix, patented by an Argentinean chemist. In 1928–1929, she undertook a tour of twenty-five countries.

During the 1930s, Baker published a novel, *Mon sang dans tes veines* (1930); was a principal in *Paris qui remue* at the Casino de Paris (1930–1931 season); recorded her signature song "J'ai deux amours" (July 12, 1930); starred in the film *ZouZou* (1934, a backstage musical with Jean Gabin, directed by Marc Allégret); starred in a remake of Offenbach's operetta *La Créole*, which opened 15 December 1934 in Marseilles; and starred in the musical comedy film *Princesse Tam Tam* (1935, directed by Edmond Gréville). Baker was the first black woman to appear in the Ziegfeld Follies (1936). On 30 November 1937, she acquired French citizenship by her marriage to Jean Lion. In September 1939, she performed in the revue *Paris-Londres* with Maurice Chevalier.

In 1940, during World War II, Baker joined the French resistance; she served as a sublieutenant in southern Europe and North Africa in 1940–1942. In 1942–1944, she organized the equivalent of the American United Services Overseas for the Free French. In 1943, *The Josephine Baker Show*, a benefit concert for the French Red Cross, was presented in Casablanca, Morocco. In 1945, Baker starred in *Un soir d'alerte/Fausse alerte*, directed by Jacques de Baroncelli. She was awarded the Croix de Lorraine by General Charles de Gaulle, in appreciation of her wartime efforts, and the Medaille de la Résistance, on 6 October 1946.

Baker toured the United States in 1951. The National Association for the Advancement of Colored People (NAACP) declared Sunday, 20 May 1951, Josephine Baker Day in recognition of her civil rights activism. She renovated her chateau in France, Les Milandes, as a tourist attraction and home, and she adopted the twelve children of her "Rainbow Tribe" in 1954–1962. In 1945, she established the Josephine Baker Foundation, hoping to use it to support the College of Brotherhood. In 1961, she was awarded the Légion d'Honneur by General de Gaulle. In 1963, she addressed the March on Washington, D.C., and starred in concerts at Carnegie Hall to benefit the Student Non-Violent Coordinating Committee (SNCC), the Congress of Racial Equality (CORE), the NAACP, and the College of Brotherhood. She sold Les Milandes on 3 May 1968 to reimburse her creditors. In 1973, she starred in concerts at the Palace Theater; in 1974, she starred in *Joséphine's Story*, a benefit for the Red Cross presented at Monte Carlo. Her last show was *Joséphine*, in 1974–1975. Baker died in Paris 12 April 1975.

TERRI FRANCIS

See also Bechet, Sidney; Chocolate Dandies; Dance; Primitivism; Shuffle Along; Smith, Clara

Further Reading

Baker, Jean-Claude, and Chris Chase. *Josephine Baker: The Hungry Heart.* New York: Random House, 1993.

Barnwell, Andrea D. "Like the Gypsy's Daughter or Beyond the Potency of Josephine Baker's Eroticism." In *Rhapsodies in Black: Art of the Harlem Renaissance*, ed. Richard J. Powell. London, Los Angeles, and Berkeley: University of California Press, 1997.

Dalton, Karen C. C., and Henry Louis Gates Jr. "Josephine Baker and Paul Colin: African American Dance Seen Through Parisian Eyes." *Critical Inquiry*, 24, no. 4 (1998): 903.

"Femmes d'aujourd'hui: perle noire, poésie noire— Joséphine Baker." *Femme de France*, 26, October 1930 (Arsenal Pressbook, Rondell 15.816).

Hammond, Bryan, comp. *Josephine Baker.* London: Cape, 1988.

Kalinak, Kathryn. "Disciplining Josephine Baker: Gender, Race, and the Limits of Disciplinarity." In *Music and Cinema*, ed. James Buhler, Caryl Flinn, and David Nuemeyer. Hanover, N.H.: University Press of New England, 2000, pp. 315–335.

Lemke, Sieglinde. *Primitivist Modernism: Black Culture and the Origins of Transatlantic Modernism.* Oxford and New York: Oxford University Press, 1998.

Rose, Phyllis. *Jazz Cleopatra: Josephine Baker in Her Time.* New York: Doubleday, 1989.

Sauvage, Marcel. *Les mémoires de Joséphine Baker.* Paris: Éditions Kra, 1927 (with drawings by Paul Colin).

Sauvage, Marcel. *Voyages et aventures de Joséphine Baker.* Paris: Éditions Marcel Sheur, 1931 (preface by Fernand Divoire; illustrated with photographs and drawings).

Sharpley-Whiting, T. Denean. *Black Venus: Sexualized Savages, Primal Fears, and Primitive Narratives in French.* Durham, N.C.: Duke University Press, 1999.

Wood, Ean. *The Josephine Baker Story.* London: Sanctuary, 2000.

Selected Films

Les hallucinations d'un pompier/Le pompier des Folies-Bergère, c. 1927 (credits unknown)

Princesse Tam Tam, 1935 (color; dir. Edmond Gréville)
Sirène des tropiques, 1927 (black-and-white, silent; dir. Maurice Dekobra)
ZouZou, 1934 (black-and-white, with Jean Gabin; dir. Marc Allégret)

Baker, Ray Stannard

Ray Stannard Baker, one of the significant journalists of the muckraking period, joined the staff of the revolutionary *McClure's Magazine* in 1892. Working alongside Lincoln Steffens and Ida Tarbell, Baker produced a variety of investigative articles that molded his political beliefs. Initially, he wrote with little sympathy for the worker, feeling that protesters and strikers failed to understand the problems of a growing nation. Soon, however, his perspective changed, as he investigated lawlessness, monopolies, and corruption. Although he was not pro-labor, he began to distrust corporations, and a series of articles that he wrote about railroads pushed him further toward progressivism. When Steffens, Tarbell, and John S. Philips resigned from *McClure's* to buy *American Magazine*, Baker joined them. A study of the nation's racial divide would be his first investigative series for this new reformist publication.

At the time of the race riots of 1906 in Atlanta, Baker traveled South to investigate America's "color line." He had previously written about racial issues in two articles for *McClure's*; for those articles, he had traveled to the sites of four widely publicized lynchings and studied the lawlessness that characterized racial problems in the United States. In his new series, however, he planned to examine the "Negro problem" in depth. His research included interviews with southern leaders, both black and white, as well as clergymen, farmers, scholars, and other citizens. At one of these meetings, Baker sat down with W. E. B. Du Bois, then a professor of economics at Atlanta University, along with the white Episcopal clergyman Cary Breckenridge Wilmer. As Du Bois and Wilmer debated racial issues, both acknowledged they had never before done so face to face with someone of the opposing race (Tuttle 1974, 242).

In April 1907, the *American* published the first article in Baker's series, which concentrated on the race riot and the situation of blacks in Atlanta. After four more pieces, which covered topics such as Jim Crow laws and black life in the city, Baker broadened his

Ray Stannard Baker, c. 1930–1946. (Library of Congress.)

life under the pseudonym David Grayson. In 1918–1919, Baker served as director of the press bureau for the American peace commission at Versailles, where his close relationship with President Woodrow Wilson enabled him to define the role of press secretary. After the war, Baker continued to write; he produced an autobiography and fifteen volumes on Wilson.

Biography

Ray Stannard Baker was born 17 April 1870 in East Lansing, Michigan. He attended public schools in St. Croix Falls, Wisconsin; received a bachelor of science degree from Michigan Agricultural College (later Michigan State) in East Lansing, Michigan, in 1889; and studied at the University of Michigan Law School in 1891 (he did not graduate). Baker was a reporter for the Chicago *News-Record* (1892–1896); an associate editor at *McClure's Magazine* (1897–1906); a part owner and editor of the *American Magazine* (1906–1915); a freelancer for *Century, Harper's Weekly, Outlook, World's Work,* and other publications; and director of the press bureau of the American peace commission (1918–1919). He received the Pulitzer Prize for Biography in 1940. Baker died in Amherst, Massachusetts, 12 July 1946.

JOSHUA A. KOBRIN

See also Great Migration; Lynching

study, examining the color line in the North. The completed series, while presenting few solutions, pointed to various trends in American racial politics. Baker considered the impact of the "great migration," divisions within the African American community, and the many societal factors that made racism a regional and national issue.

Despite their thorough—and rare—analysis of the subject, however, Baker's articles fell short of radicalism. In a conversation with Baker, his colleague John Philips had reminded him to "keep the interests and friendliness of southern readers. . . . They are the people whom we wish to reach and enlighten." Also, many scholars have noted that Baker was never particularly extreme, or even immoderate, on the issue of race. Ideologically, he was allied with the progressive philanthropists and with Booker T. Washington; as a result, his articles received compliments from white liberals and moderate black leaders, and only slight criticism from more radical leaders like Du Bois.

In 1908, Baker published the series in a book, *Following the Color Line.* During the following years, he continued to write about race relations and also published a succession of idealistic books about country

Selected Works

"Railroads on Trial." *McClure's Magazine,* November 1905–March 1905, June 1906.
Adventures in Contentment. 1907 (as David Grayson).
"Not Less Democracy, But More: A Suggestion for the Solution of the Negro Problem in America, Made After Wide Observation and Careful Study." *Christian Endeavor World,* 7 October 1909.
Following the Color Line: An Account of Negro Citizenship in the American Democracy. 1908 (new ed., 1964).
Adventures in Friendship. 1910 (as David Grayson).
"Negro Suffrage in Democracy." *Atlantic Monthly,* November 1910.
"The Problem of Race." In *Conservation of National Ideals.* 1911.
"Pressing On: Specific Cases in the Struggle Against Prejudice and Ignorance and Fear." *American Magazine,* July 1912.
"The New Head of Tuskegee." *World's Work,* March 1916.

"The Negro Goes North." *World's Work*, July 1917.
What Wilson Did at Paris. 1919.
The New Industrial Unrest. 1920.
Woodrow Wilson and World Settlement (3 vols.). 1922.
Adventures in Understanding. 1925 (as David Grayson).
The Public Papers of Woodrow Wilson (6 vols.). 1925–1927 (ed., with William E. Dodd).
Woodrow Wilson, Life and Letters (8 vols.). 1927–1939.
Adventures in Solitude. 1931 (as David Grayson).
Native American: The Book of My Youth. 1941.
American Chronicle: The Autobiography of Ray Stannard Baker [*David Grayson*]. 1945.

Further Reading

Bannister, Robert C., Jr. *Ray Stannard Baker: The Mind and Thought of a Progressive*. New Haven, Conn.: Yale University Press, 1966.

Chalmers, David. "Ray Stannard Baker's Search for Reform." *Journal of History and Ideas*, 19(3), 1958.

Grantham, Dewey W., Jr. "Introduction to the Torchbook Edition." In Ray Stannard Baker, *Following the Color Line*. 1964.

Semonche, John E. "The 'American Magazine' of 1906–1915: Principal Versus Profit." *Journalism Quarterly*, 40(1), 1964.

———. *Ray Stannard Baker: A Quest for Democracy in Modern America, 1870–1918*. Chapel Hill: University of North Carolina Press, 1969.

Tuttle, William M., Jr. Introduction to "W. E. B. Du Bois's Confrontation With White Liberalism During the Progressive Era: A Phylon Document." *Phylon*, 35(3), 1974.

Baltimore Afro-American

The outburst of literary creativity known as the Harlem Renaissance might have been little noticed or remembered were it not for black newspapers. Black newspapers publicized and provided media outlets for black novelists, poets, and essayists. Although black and white magazines of the 1920s such as *Opportunity*, *The Crisis*, and *American Mercury* did publish Harlem Renaissance artists and writers, the black newspapers exposed them to a much wider audience. One black newspaper, the Baltimore *Afro-American*, provided an invaluable if little known outlet for the Harlem Renaissance.

The Baltimore *Afro-American* was and is one of the most important black newspapers. During the 1920s, it was the most widely read black newspaper on the East Coast. It was founded in Baltimore in 1892 by a group of black entrepreneurs and ministers led by Rev. William Alexander. John H. Murphy, its printer, acquired the newspaper in 1897, and his descendants have owned and operated it down to the present. In 1918, his son Carl Murphy, who was a graduate of Howard and Harvard universities, became the editor of the *Afro-American*. When John H. Murphy died in 1922, the family chose Carl Murphy to run the newspaper. Under his leadership, which lasted until 1967, the *Afro-American* became one of the top three black newspapers in the United States, matching its competitors the Chicago *Defender* and the Pittsburgh *Courier* in circulation and influence.

During the 1920s, the *Afro-American* reported news about the black community and crusaded for racial justice locally and nationally. It also extensively publicized black artists and entertainers. This last function was its greatest contribution to the Harlem Renaissance.

The *Afro-American* endlessly publicized jazz, blues, and the concert singers and musicians of the Harlem Renaissance—figures such as Marian Anderson, Louis Armstrong, Josephine Baker, Eubie Blake, Duke Ellington, Roland Hayes, Florence Mills, and Bessie Smith. It also gave prominent coverage to the singer, actor, and activist Paul Robeson. It regularly reviewed Broadway plays with black themes, such as *The Emperor Jones*, and occasionally published excerpts from these plays. It also published excerpts from the works of black novelists of the era such as Jean Toomer; and it frequently published the poems and essays of such Harlem Renaissance figures as Countee Cullen, Langston Hughes, Alain Locke, Claude McKay, and Zora Neale Hurston. Countee Cullen became a columnist for the newspaper, and Langston Hughes, later on in the 1930s, covered the Spanish Civil War for it. The *Afro-American* encouraged young black writers by publishing serials and short stories in its magazine section; eventually these stories were published in an anthology edited by Nick Aaron Ford, *Best Short Stories by Afro-American Writers*. In addition, the *Afro-American* publicized black playwrights and advertised local presentations of their plays. It publicized and published, as well, such intellectual and political leaders as W. E. B. Du Bois, Marcus Garvey, James Weldon Johnson, and Kelly Miller. Its homegrown columnist Ralph Matthews became nationally known as the "black H. L. Mencken." In all these ways, the *Afro-American* supported the Harlem Renaissance.

HAYWARD "WOODY" FARRAR

See also American Mercury; Black Press; Chicago Defender; Crisis, The; Cullen, Countee; Emperor Jones, The; Garvey, Marcus; Hughes, Langston; Matthews, Ralph; Mencken, H. L.; Miller, Kelly; Murphy, Carl J.; Opportunity; Pittsburgh Courier; Revue Nègre, La; *specific entertainers, musicians, and writers*

Further Reading

Buni, Andrew. *Robert L. Vann of the Pittsburgh Courier.* Pittsburgh, Pa.: University of Pittsburgh Press, 1974.

Detweiler, Frederick G. *The Negro Press in the United States.* Chicago, Ill.: University of Chicago Press, 1922.

Farrar, Hayward. *The Baltimore Afro-American, 1892–1950.* Westport, Conn.: Greenwood, 1998.

Ford, Nick A. *Best Short Stories by Afro-American Writers.* Baltimore, Md.: Afro-American Co., 1950.

Huggins, Nathan Irvin. *Harlem Renaissance.* New York: Oxford University Press, 1971.

Johnson, Abby Arthur, and Ronald Mayberry. *Propaganda and Aesthetics: The Literary Politics of Afro-American Magazines in the Twentieth Century.* Amherst: University of Massachusetts Press, 1979.

Johnson, James Weldon. *Black Manhattan.* New York: Knopf, 1940. (Reprint, New York: Arno, 1968.)

Kornweibel, Theodore, Jr. *No Crystal Stair: Black Life and the Messenger.* Westport, Conn.: Greenwood, 1975.

Lewis, David Levering. *When Harlem Was in Vogue.* New York: Knopf, 1981.

Barnes, Albert C.

Albert C. Barnes established the Barnes Foundation in Merion, Pennsylvania, in 1922, having amassed the largest private collection of modern and African art in the world. Most important, Barnes appreciated African sculpture as art, not simply as artifacts that were best placed in museums of ethnography and natural history. He also understood the profound impact of African sculpture on the formal and aesthetic innovations of the European avant-garde—artists such as Pablo Picasso, Georges Braque, and Henri Matisse.

In addition, Barnes was a tireless and aggressive champion of the cultural importance of African art for African Americans: "Negro art is so big, so loaded with possibilities for a transfer of its value to other spheres where Negro life must be raised to higher levels, that it should be handled with the utmost care. . . . It involves intellectual, ethical, social, psychological, [and] aesthetic values of inseparable interactions." As a consequence, Barnes soon caught the eye of Alain Locke, the editor of *The New Negro*, who may be considered the philosophical "midwife" of the Harlem Renaissance and who was himself seeking to make the art of Africans and African Americans the locus of a new aesthetics and a new racial consciousness. Thus began a complex friendship that would also involve Barnes's relationship with other prominent figures of the Harlem Renaissance, in particular the novelist Walter White and the editor of *Opportunity*, Charles S. Johnson.

Barnes met Locke in Paris in December 1923 and the next month sought Locke's assistance with an article, "Contribution to the Study of Negro Art in America," that was to be published in both *Ex Libris* and *Les Arts à Paris*. Three months later, at Barnes's suggestion, Johnson devoted a special issue of *Opportunity* (March 1924) to African art; this issue included Barnes's own article, "The Temple," together with Locke's "A Note on African Art" and Paul Guillaume's "African Art at the Barnes Foundation." One year later, Locke included Barnes's "Contributions to the Study of Negro Art" (retitled "Negro Art and America") in a special issue of *Survey Graphic*, "Harlem: Mecca of the New Negro" (March 1925); soon afterward, he included this same article in *The New Negro*.

Barnes was an important cultural resource—a person to consult regarding African art. George Hutchinson has claimed that Locke and *Opportunity* relied on Barnes as their "house expert" on African aesthetics and its relation to European modernism. One must be careful, however, not to overstate this influence. Locke was not entirely satisfied with Barnes's "Negro Art and America," which offered little help in Locke's own effort to provide a cultural context for African art. Partly for this reason, Locke offered "The Legacy of the Ancestral Arts" to supplement Barnes's effort. For the remainder of the decade and into the next, Locke continued to champion African art. He now argued, however, that to see African art through the eyes of modernists such as Barnes, who so strongly emphasized form, was to see it "through a glass darkly."

Biography

Albert C. Barnes was born 2 January 1872 in Philadelphia, Pennsylvania. He studied at public schools in Philadelphia; at the University of Pennsylvania Medical School, 1892; and at Heidelberg in Germany, 1900. He established the Barnes Foundation in December 1922. Barnes transferred 710 paintings from his personal collection (works by Picasso, Van Gogh, Renoir, Cézanne, and Matisse) to the foundation and first purchased African sculpture in 1922. He was named an Officier de l'Ordre National de la Légion d'Honneur by the French government on 27 July 1936 and was made an honorary doctor of science by Lincoln University on 5 June 1951. Barnes died 24 July 1951. (His provisions for the Barnes Foundation have since given rise to continuing controversy.)

MARK HELBLING

See also Johnson, Charles S.; Locke, Alain; Modernism; New Negro, The; Opportunity; Survey Graphic; White, Walter

Selected Works

"The Temple." *Opportunity*, 1924.
The Art of Painting. 1925.
"Negro Art and America." *Survey Graphic*, 1925.
"Negro Art Past and Present." *Opportunity*, 1926.
Art and Education. 1929.
The Art of Renoir. 1935.
The Art of Cézanne. 1939.

Further Reading

Helbling, Mark. *The Harlem Renaissance: The One and the Many*. Westport, Conn.: Greenwood, 1999.
McCardle, Carl. "The Terrible Tempered Barnes." *Saturday Evening Post*, March 1942.
Meigs, Mark. "The Barnes Foundation and the Philadelphia Museum of Art: Bifurcated Loci of Cultural Memory." *Annales: Lieux de Mémoire aux États-Unis*, 18, 1995.
Spalding, Francis. *Roger Fry: Art and Life*. Berkeley: University of California Press, 1980.
Twitchell, Beverly. *Cézanne and Formalism in Bloomsbury*. Ann Arbor: University of Michigan Research Press, 1987.
Williams, Elizabeth. "Art and Artifact at the Trocadero: Ars Americana and the Primitivist Revolution." In *Objects and Others: Essays on Museums and Material Culture*, ed. George Stocking. Madison: University of Wisconsin Press, 1985.

Barnett, Ida B. Wells

Ida Bell Wells Barnett was born a slave in Holly Springs, Mississippi, in 1862. She began her work as a teacher in the rural schools of Mississippi but then went to Memphis, a move that radicalized her and gave her an opportunity for a new career and for leadership. In the late nineteenth century she was one of the best-known African American women in the United States and internationally.

In Memphis, Barnett became part of a politically and intellectually active community. She joined a lyceum, composed primarily of other public school teachers, whose members enjoyed music, reading together, debating issues of the day, giving recitations, and writing and presenting essays. She contributed

Ida B. Wells Barnett in a photo published in 1891.
(Library of Congress.)

essays to a periodical associated with the lyceum, the *Evening Star*, then served as its editor; she was also a columnist for another local paper, *Living Way*. An incident that informed her editorials and articles at this time took place when she was forcibly removed from a train for taking a seat in the ladies' coach (rather than in the smoking car, as Jim Crow regulations required) and led to a lawsuit against the railroad, the Chesapeake, Ohio, and Southwestern. She won the suit, and although the decision was overturned by the supreme court of Tennessee, the episode began Barnett's lifetime of outspoken activism and advocacy. Barnett also wrote articles about the poor conditions in schools in the African American community (these writings got her fired from the teaching pool), and she encouraged African Americans, including members of her own family, to leave Memphis and seek justice and political and economic opportunities in the West.

During this period, Barnett was a full-time investigative journalist; a co-owner and editor of her own newspaper, *Free Speech and Headlight* (1889), with Rev. Taylor Nightingale and J. L. Fleming; an astute businesswoman and professional woman who made her paper a successful enterprise; an active member and then secretary of the predominantly male National Press Association; a columnist syndicated in African American periodicals throughout the country; and an outspoken crusader for justice. In 1892, she wrote an editorial about the lynching of three of her friends, Thomas Moss, Calvin McDowell, and Lee Stewart, who had been co-owners and operators of the People's Grocery, in competition with a store owned and operated by whites. Barnett was a sharp-tongued political observer, and in her editorial—which, like all of her writing, was short, simple, and direct—she argued, provocatively, that these and other lynchings were not what the white establishment claimed them to be. The white power structure in Memphis reacted with threats and the actual burning of her newspaper offices, but she herself was in New York at the time and prudently remained there. In fact, she did not return to the South until January 1922, when she went to Little Rock, Arkansas, as an advocate against injustice and terrorism during a riotous period in which many African Americans were incarcerated or murdered.

Barnett's exile from the South gave her another arena for political action. Though she remained an active journalist for the rest of her life, she also began a career as a public speaker and a lifelong commitment to community development and political organization.

From 1892 on, she traveled and spoke frequently as a political activist.

Barnett had a reputation as a "difficult" woman who was often involved in public disagreements if not out-and-out feuds with a broad range of adversaries. Some of these were with highly respected white reformers: for example, in 1893, Barnett disputed with Frances Willard (of the Woman's Christian Temperance Union) and the evangelist Dwight Moody, because she considered their response to lynching inappropriate. Another adversary was a white journalist, John W. Jacks, president of the Missouri Press Association; in 1895, Jacks wrote a scathing attack on the morals of African Americans generally, and Barnett in particular. There was also tension between Barnett and some women who were part of the African American elite, such as Mary Church Terrell and Fannie Barrier Williams, who both vied with Barnett, for several decades, for leadership and power in various organizations. Some of Barnett's disagreements were with African American men, most notably Booker T. Washington during the time when he dominated the black leadership: Barnett found his political position intolerable. She also disagreed with political organizations; for instance, although she herself was a founder of the National Association for the Advancement of Colored People (NAACP), in 1910, she considered it too conservative and overly controlled by white rather than African American viewpoints.

However, not all of Barnett's activity was so contentious. She was always an active member of the African American church, most consistently in the African Methodist Episcopal Church, but in many others as well. She joined many professional, social, and community organizations whose goals were self-improvement and securing justice, equality, and empowerment for all. Before the turn of the twentieth century, she organized one of the most successful anti-lynching campaigns: documenting cases; developing careful, thorough arguments; and offering proposals to end this type of terrorism. After the turn of the century, she continued the antilynching crusade but also became active in the woman's suffrage movement and the settlement house movement. With regard to settlement houses and community development, one of her striking achievements was the founding, in 1913, of the Negro Fellowship League in Chicago; she kept this organization alive and functioning for ten years before competing organizations and a lack of resources compromised her ability to continue. By the 1920s and 1930s, Barnett was also involved in political campaigns, and she herself ran for the state senate in Illinois in 1930, although she was defeated.

Barnett died in 1931, never having lost her passion for justice, never having wavered in her commitment to people who were disenfranchised politically or economically, and leaving as her legacy a remarkable record of achievements. She was a successful and significant investigative journalist, an insightful political observer and analyst, and a creative community organizer who was able to put together a network of services in support of specific needs. She was also an intellectual with a genuine vision of possibilities for African Americans. Perhaps most important, she was a leader who helped to identify strategies for social and political action that would constitute a framework for positive change for generations to come.

Biography

Ida Bell Wells Barnett (or Wells-Barnett) was born 16 July 1862 in Holly Springs, Mississippi. Her parents, James and Elizabeth Warrenton Wells, were politically active after the Civil War; they and one of her brothers died in the yellow fever epidemic of 1878, and she was left to care for her surviving siblings. Barnett attended elementary and high school at Shaw University, later renamed Rust College. She taught in the public schools of rural Mississippi and Shelby County, Tennessee. She was a contributor to and later editor (1886) of the *Evening Star* and a columnist for *Living Way*, both periodicals in Memphis, Tennessee; was a co-owner and editor of *Free Speech and Headlight* (with Rev. Taylor Nightingale and J. L. Fleming), 1889; and was elected secretary of the National Press Association, 1889. In 1892, she wrote an editorial that made her famous as a leader of the antilynching movement and in effect exiled her from the South for the next three decades. In 1893 and 1894, she made two speaking tours of England, Scotland, and Wales. Barnett was active in several political organizations—including the National Afro-American League, Afro-American Council, National Association of Colored Women, National Equal Rights League, Ida B. Wells Woman's Club, and National American Woman's Suffrage Association—and in the Niagara movement, the woman's suffrage movement, and the international peace movement. She was a cofounder of the NAACP (1910) and a founder of the Negro Fellowship League (1910) and the Alpha Suffrage Club (1913). She ran unsuccessfully for the Illinois state senate in 1930.

Barnett died in Chicago (of uremic poisoning) 25 March 1931.

JACQUELINE ROYSTER

See also Antilynching Crusade; Lynching; National Association for the Advancement of Colored People

Further Reading

Aptheker, Bettina, ed. *Lynching and Rape: An Exchange of Views*. New York: American Institute for Marxist Studies, 1977.
DeCosta-Willis, Miriam. *Ida B. Wells: The Memphis Diaries*. Boston, Mass.: Beacon, 1994.
Duster, Alfreda M. *Crusade for Justice: The Autobiography of Ida B. Wells*. Chicago, Ill.: University of Chicago Press, 1970.
Harris, Trudier, comp. *Selected Works of Ida B. Wells-Barnett*. New York: Oxford University Press, 1991.
Humrich, Shauna Lea. "Ida B. Wells-Barnett: The Making of a Reputation." Master's thesis, University of Colorado, 1989.
Hutton, Mary M. B. "The Rhetoric of Ida B. Wells: The Genesis of the Anti-Lynch Movement." Ph.D. diss., University of Indiana, 1975.
Logan, Shirley W., ed. *With Pen and Voice: A Critical Anthology of Nineteenth-Century African-American Women*. Carbondale: University of Southern Illinois Press, 1995.
McMurry, Linda O. *To Keep the Waters Troubled: The Life of Ida B. Wells*. New York and Oxford: Oxford University Press, 1998.
Royster, Jacqueline Jones. "To Call a Thing by Its True Name: The Rhetoric of Ida B. Wells." In *Reclaiming Rhetorica*, ed. Andrea Lunsford. Pittsburgh, Pa.: University of Pittsburgh Press, 1995, pp. 167–184.
———. *Southern Horrors and Other Writings: The Anti-Lynching Campaign of Ida B. Wells, 1892–1900*. Boston, Mass.: Bedford, 1997.
Rydell, Robert W., ed. *The Reason Why the Colored American Is Not in the World's Columbian Exposition*. Urbana: University of Illinois Press, 1999.
Thompson, Mildred I. *Black Women in United States History*, Vol. 15, *Ida B. Wells-Barnett: An Exploratory Study of an American Black Woman, 1893–1930*. New York: Carlson, 1990.
Tucker, David M. "Miss Ida B. Wells and Memphis Lynching." In *Black Women in United States History*, Vol. 4, *Black Women in American History: From Colonial Times through the Nineteenth Century*, ed. Darlene Clark Hine. New York: Carlson, 1990, pp. 1085–1095.

Video

The American Experience: Ida B. Wells, a Passion for Justice. New York: Video Dub, 1990 (prod. William Greaves).

Barthé, Richmond

James Richmond Barthé (1901–1989), a formally trained academic sculptor, was one of the most widely collected and publicized artists of the Harlem Renaissance. His work was characterized by racial pride, naturalistic representation, movement, sensuality, and spirituality; it appealed to a clientele extending beyond the black American community and attracted patronage from the white American mainstream; and it helped form the image of the "New Negro."

In the 1920s, when Harlem was coming into vogue and the young Barthé was experimenting in art, he received funding from a pastor to attend the School of the Art Institute of Chicago. There, he acquired a traditional academic education strongly influenced by European art in the classical and Renaissance styles. At first, he studied painting under Charles Schroeder; later, however, an exercise in molding clay, intended to enhance his appreciation of three-dimensional forms, thrust him into the spotlight.

In 1927, the Chicago Women's Club, a progressive group interested in the fine arts as a social commentary on race, sponsored an unprecedented exhibition of art, music, and literature by black Americans and needed some three-dimensional works to be placed alongside African sculpture. Two sculptured busts that Barthé had made for an art course were included in this exhibition, which was part of the *Negro in Art Week* programs. It introduced him to the world of professional artists and led, in 1928, to his first commissions for sculptures: portrait heads of Henry O. Tanner and Toussaint-Louverture. Throughout Barthé's long career, his principal source of income would be such figurative bronze sculpture, particularly commissions for single portrait busts of Africans, African Americans, Caribbean-Americans, and European-Americans, although he also produced realistic freestanding full-length nude and clothed statues, some groups of figures (often with African themes), and some religious sculpture.

Barthé met Alain Locke during the *Negro in Art Week* programs; they developed a lifelong friendship,

and Locke became a loyal supporter of Barthé's work. During this time Barthé also met Frank Breckinridge and Julius Rosenwald, two prominent and influential businessmen in Chicago. This acquaintance led to a one-year travel grant to New York City in 1929, enabling Barthé to create works for an individual exhibition at the Chicago Women's Club in 1930. A year earlier, he had exhibited four sculptures in New York in a show sponsored by the Harmon Foundation—*The Jubilee Singer* (1927), *Toussaint L'Overture* (1928), *Head of a Tortured Negro* (1929), and *Tortured Negro* (1929)—and they received an honorable mention. *The Jubilee Singer* appeared on the cover of *Opportunity* in 1928. Barthé continued to exhibit regularly with the Harmon Foundation until 1933 and received tremendous publicity and recognition through its promotion of black American artists.

Barthé became a permanent resident of New York City in 1931, attracted by its artistic culture and especially its progressive black arts community. He met artists, writers, and intellectuals such as Aaron Douglas, Langston Hughes, Wallace Thurman, and Carl Van Vechten and attended the salon of A'Lelia Walker. Through this salon he secured work such as a sculptured portrait of Walker herself.

Barthé lived not in Harlem but on Fourteenth Street in Chelsea, where he also opened a studio. He may have found the "New Negro" arts movement too restrictive because it focused on Afrocentric imagery, and he may have wanted more exposure in mainstream artistic circles. He seems to have concluded that his primary customers and patrons would be whites rather than blacks, and that by living and working downtown he could make himself more accessible to whites. If this was his strategy, it succeeded; he received numerous commissions and exhibitions and was praised by white and black critics in the 1930s and 1940s. Still, Barthé was a figure in Harlem, enjoying its nightlife, interacting with the literati of the Harlem Renaissance, and attending dance, music, and theater performances, although he maintained some measure of anonymity.

During the time of the Harlem Renaissance, mainstream institutions in culture, entertainment, and publishing were extraordinarily open to black Americans, and Barthé evidently took advantage of this openness. His work was displayed in exhibitions at the Whitney Museum (which acquired some for its collection), the New Jersey State Museum, the Corcoran Galleries, the Pennsylvania Academy of Fine Arts, and the Carnegie Institute, among others. His acquaintance with businesspeople led to public commissions, notably a frieze for the Harlem River Housing Project, *Green Pastures: The Walls of Jericho* (1938); and the Arthur Brisbane Memorial (1939), a monument to the newspaper editor and columnist. Barthé was also acquainted with people in theater, and he created many portrait sculptures for stars such as Phillips Holmes, John Gielgud, and Katharine Cornell.

Some of Barthé's sculpture—such as *African Dancer* (1933), *Wetta* (c. 1934), *Feral Benga* (1935), and *African Boy Dancing* (1937)—had African themes that appealed to the popular culture of the day: the Afrocentric self-awareness of blacks, and the expectation of whites that black artists would infuse their work with African "primitivism." Dance was a central motif in much of Barthé's art; Barthé had enrolled in classes in modern dance to enhance his understanding of the human figure in motion. His mastery of human anatomy, acquired during his years of academic training, combined with this appreciation of dance allowed him to capture emotion, movement, and sensuality, especially in his more stylized, elongated pieces.

Recent scholars have pointed out homoerotic aspects of Barthé's sculpture and have suggested that his use of the black male nude was a way of working out of his own sexual conflicts. His sensual sculptures of nude black males, such as *Feral Benga*, *The Boxer* (1940), and the robust *Stevedore* (1937), may well have appealed to white homosexuals who saw eroticism in their interpretation of images of African male "primitivism." The suggestion that Barthé had a double life during the Harlem Renaissance—participating in an intricate network of gays, lesbians, and bisexuals—may explain his wide appeal and patronage, especially among New York's homosexual and artistic circles; it may also explain his apparent need to obtain privacy by living downtown rather than in Harlem.

Barthé did cross racial, gender, and class lines in his career. Yet he may have made his greatest contribution to the Harlem Renaissance as a role model for other black American artists, demonstrating through his life and work the heights that artistic creativity could achieve in an integrated society.

Biography

James Richmond Barthé was born 28 January 1901 in Bay St. Louis, Mississippi. He studied at Saint Rose de Lima (a parochial school) and Valena C. James High School; at the School of the Art Institute of Chicago,

1924–1928; with Charles Schroeder and Albin Polasek, privately; and at the Art Students League, New York, 1931. Barthé traveled and worked in Italy and Iolaus, Jamaica. His awards included the Eames McVeagh Prize, Chicago Art League, 1928; a Rosenwald Foundation fellowship, 1928–1929; an honorary mention from the Harmon Exhibition, for *Tortured Negro*, 1929; an honorary master of arts degree from Xavier University in New Orleans, Louisiana, 1934; a Guggenheim Memorial Foundation fellowship, 1940–1941; the Edward B. Alford Award; an award from the National Sculpture Society, 1945; the James J. Hoey Award for Interracial Justice, 1945; the Audubon Artists Gold Medal of Honor, 1945; an honorary doctorate in fine arts from Saint Francis College in Brooklyn, New York, 1947; and election to the National Academy of Arts and Letters, 1949. He died in Pasadena, California, 6 March 1989.

CLAUDIA HILL

See also Art Criticism and the Harlem Renaissance; Artists; Douglas, Aaron; Harmon Foundation; Harmon Traveling Exhibition; Locke, Alain; Primitivism; Salons; Tanner, Henry Ossawa; Van Vechten, Carl; Walker, A'Lelia

Selected Individual Exhibitions

1930: Chicago Women's Club, Chicago
1931: University of Wisconsin, Madison, Wisconsin
1931: Caz-Delbo Galleries, New York
1931: Rankin Art Galleries, Washington, D.C.
1933: Caz-Delbo Galleries, New York
1939: Arden Galleries, New York
1941: De Porres Interracial Center, New York
1942: South Side Art Center, Chicago
1945: International Print Society, New York
1947: Margaret Brown Galleries, Boston
1947: Duncan Phillips Memorial Galleries, Washington, D.C.
1947: Grand Central Galleries, New York
1948: Saint Peter College, Jersey City, New Jersey

Selected Group Exhibitions

1927: Chicago Women's Club, Chicago
1928: Chicago Art League, Chicago
1929: Fisk University, Nashville
1929: Harmon Foundation, New York
1930: Regal Theater, Chicago

1931: Harmon Foundation, New York
1933: Harmon Foundation, New York
1933: Whitney Museum of American Art, New York
1933–1934: Century of Progress Show, Chicago
1934: Salons of America, New York
1934: Howard University, Washington, D.C.
1934: New School of Social Research, New York
1934: Whitney Museum of American Art, New York
1935: New Jersey State Museum, New Jersey
1935: Whitney Museum of American Art, New York
1936: Corcoran Galleries, Washington, D.C.
1936: Texas Centennial Exposition, Texas
1938: Pennsylvania Academy of the Fine Arts, Philadelphia
1939: Baltimore Museum, Maryland
1939: Pennsylvania Academy of the Fine Arts, Philadelphia
1939: Whitney Museum of American Art, New York
1939: World's Fair, New York
1939: Harlem Art Galleries, New York
1939: Sculptors' Guild Outdoor Exhibition, New York
1940: American Negro Exposition, Chicago
1940: Pennsylvania Museum Sculpture Show
1941: Carnegie Institute, Pittsburgh
1941: Pennsylvania Academy of Fine Arts, Philadelphia
1943: Art Institute of Chicago, Illinois
1947: World's Fair, New York

Further Reading

Bearden, Romare, and Harry Henderson. "Richmond Barthé." In *A History of African-American Artists: From 1792 to the Present*. New York: Pantheon, 1993.

Billops, Camille. *The Hatch-Billops Collection*. New York: Unpublished. (Archives of Black American Cultural History, Taped Oral Interviews. See interview with Richmond Barthé at his home in St. Albans, Queens, 9 December 1975.)

Cederholm, Theresa Dickason. "Barthé, Richmond." In *Afro-American Artists: A Bio-Bibliographical Directory*. Boston, Mass.: Trustees of the Boston Public Library, 1973.

Hammond, Bert D. "Richmond Barthé and Elizabeth Catlett: An Exchange." *International Review of African American Art*, 6(1), 1984.

Hedgepeth, Chester M. "Barthé, Richmond (1901–1989)." In *Twentieth-Century African American Writers and Artists*. Chicago, Ill., and London: American Library Association, 1991.

Igoe, Lynn, with James Igoe. "Barthé, Richmond." In *Two Hundred Fifty Years of Afro-American Art: An Annotated Bibliography*. New York: Bowker, 1981.

Lewis, Samella. *Two Sculptors, Two Eras: Richmond Barthé, Richard Hunt*. Los Angeles, Calif.: Landau Traveling Exhibitions, 1994.

——. "Barthé, Richmond." In *Encyclopedia of African-American Culture and History*, ed. Jack Salzman, David Lionel Smith, and Cornel West. New York: Macmillan Library Reference, 1996.

Shaw, Thomas M. "Barthé, Richmond." In *St. James Guide to Black Artists*, ed. Thomas Riggs. Detroit, Mich.: St. James, 1997.

Smalls, James. "Barthé, James Richmond (1901–1989)." In *Glbtq: An Encyclopedia of Gay, Lesbian, Bisexual, Transgender, and Queer Culture*, ed. Claude J. Summers. Chicago, Ill.: Glbtq, 2002. http://www.glbtq.com/arts/barthe_jr.html.

Vendryes, Margaret Rose. "Expression and Repression of Identity: Race, Religion, and Sexuality in the Art of American Sculptor Richmond Barthé." Master's thesis, Princeton University, 1997.

Batouala

René Maran's novel *Batouala* (1921) is set in the French colony of Ubangui-Shari and takes the reader into the cultural practices and emotions of the people whom Maran came to know as an administrator in the French colonial empire. Sexually explicit and dramatically exotic, *Batouala* was an immediate sensation and caused a furor in France. Although it won the Prix Goncourt, the most prestigious award France has to offer a young writer, the book was banned for many years, and Maran was forced to resign his post. The most incendiary part of *Batouala* was the preface, in which Maran, who was from Martinique, attacked the French in Africa and equated colonialism with deceit and genocide: "You build your kingdom on corpses. . . . You aren't a torch, but an inferno. Everything you touch, you consume." Not only had this "brother of France" declared that assimilation was a myth but he had also used his position of authority to question the raison d'être of the French presence in Africa. After he returned to France, Maran became involved in various pan-African movements, joining the Ligue Universelle de la Défense de la Race Noire (as a member of the editorial staff of its journal, *Les continents*) and the Comité Universel de l'Institut Nègre de Paris (its literary journal was *La revue du monde noir*).

Many people consider *Batouala* the founding text of African nationalist literature. For writers and intellectuals of the Harlem Renaissance, the novel and its author evoked strong feelings of racial pride and testified to the artistic potential of Africa. In Marcus Garvey's *Negro World*, for example, *Batouala* became a cause célèbre. As a consequence, Maran's salon in Paris soon became a meeting place for African and West Indian intellectuals (most notably Aimé Césaire, Léon Damas, and Léopold Senghor), as well as African American intellectuals. In 1924, Alain Locke met Maran in Paris; this meeting was the beginning of a long friendship. Maran introduced members of the Harlem Renaissance to the French public in such articles as "Le mouvement negro-littéraire aux États-Unis"; he was also instrumental in having Walter White's *Fire in the Flint* translated into French. At the same time as Maran began to appear in *Opportunity*, the *Revue de monde noir* began to publish the writings of Locke, Jean Toomer, Claude McKay, Langston Hughes, and James Weldon Johnson.

African Americans have long considered France the "garden spot of Europe." *Batouala* served both to complicate that understanding and to bring intellectuals of the Harlem Renaissance into the larger political and cultural universe of the African diaspora.

MARK HELBLING

See also Césaire, Aimé; Damas, Léon; Europe and the Harlem Renaissance: 4—Paris; Fire in the Flint, The; Francophone Africa and the Harlem Renaissance; Francophone Caribbean and the Harlem Renaissance; Locke, Alain; Maran, René; Negro World; Opportunity; Pan-Africanism; Senghor, Léopold

Further Reading

Fabre, Michel. "Autour de René Maran." *Presence Africaine*, 1973.

Fayolle, Roger. *Batouala et l'accueil de la critique Afrique litteraire et artistique*. 1978.

Hausser, Michel. *Les deux Batouala de René Maran*. 1975.

Ikonne, Chidi. "René Maran 1887–1960: A Black Francophone Writer Between Two Worlds." *Research in African Litterature*, 1974.

Kesteloot, Lilyan. *Les écrivains noirs de la langue française*. 1965.

Miller, Christopher. "Nationalism as Resistance and Resistance to Nationalism in the Literature of Francophone Africa." *Yale French Studies*, 1993.

Ojo-Ade, Femi. *René Maran, écrivain negro-africain*. 1977.

Bearden, Romare

Among African American artists, Romare Bearden is one of the most inventive, distinctive, and famous and has received more critical acclaim and scholarly analysis than nearly anyone else. His art evolved considerably during his career: Early on, he was committed to social realism and political illustration; after World War II, he was one of the few African American painters who embraced abstract expressionism; at the beginning of the 1960s, his art became more representational but remained highly modernist in style and materials. When the civil rights movement erupted during the 1960s, he began to explore the social, economic, cultural, and political issues of African American life, through his many collages, which were made with found images from newspapers, magazines, and photographs. Although collage was hardly new at that time, Bearden was radical in his use of brutally factual photographic images to visualize the African American

Romare Bearden, photographed by Carl Van Vechten. (Library of Congress.)

experience from his personal perspective. It is for these works that he is still best known.

Bearden was born around 1912 in Charlotte, North Carolina, and was raised there and in Pittsburgh and Harlem. He came to Harlem as a child and often visited his grandmother in Pittsburgh, where he eventually lived for a few years during his childhood. In Pittsburgh he had a friend named Eugene whom he later credited with inspiring his desire to draw and therefore his career as an artist. As a youth, Bearden came into contact with many artists and writers associated with the Harlem Renaissance, because his mother worked for the New York office of the *Chicago Defender*, an African American newspaper.

After college, Bearden studied at the Art Students League with George Grosz, who was then one of the great political satirists in graphic media. Bearden himself worked as a political cartoonist in the mid-1930s, first publishing cartoons in *Medley*, a humor journal published by New York University, then having illustrations and cartoons published in *Collier's, Fortune,* the Baltimore *Afro-American,* and the *Saturday Evening Post.* Thus, early in his artistic career he was creating images weighted with social commentary and observation, undoubtedly having learned this skill from Grosz. At about this time he became associated with the 306 Group of African American artists based in Harlem; this group included Charles Alston, Aaron Douglas, Jacob Lawrence, and Augusta Savage and was named for a salon that developed at 306 141st Street.

By the mid-1940s—after the period of the Harlem Renaissance—Bearden began to receive recognition for his social realist paintings. His work was exhibited in 1945 in the Whitney Museum Annual, and in the next three years he had exhibits at the Kootz Gallery. Ironically, though, his social realist works from these years are little known today, especially compared with his later collages; and social realism was not a long phase in his development as an artist. It seems that he felt some displeasure with how African American artists were publicly received at the time and with his own identity, and this discontent led him to take new stylistic directions. Still, social realist paintings such as *Two Women in a Landscape* (1941) reveal his keen observation of the problems of ordinary people, particularly poor African Americans, during the Great Depression; and his painting *Factory Workers* (1942) was used to illustrate "Negro's War," an article in *Fortune* magazine.

In his paintings of the mid-1940s, many of biblical subjects, his style was becoming much more abstract. In the late 1940s, Bearden was deeply involved in studying the paintings and drawings of the old masters, European artists of the Renaissance and later. He did not care to sketch in public at museums; instead, he made photocopies of masterworks and hung them in his studio so that he could study them conveniently and carefully. However, during the late 1940s and early 1950s, he was not very productive as a visual artist.

Bearden, who had served in the army during World War II, was able to go to Paris in 1950 to study philosophy at the Sorbonne, thanks to the GI Bill. He was very active in Parisian artistic and intellectual circles and got to know many older artists who had been part of the rise of modern art early in the century, as well as younger expatriate American writers and artists.

From the mid-1950s to the early 1960s, he continued to paint abstractly. Abstract expressionism was then at the height of its popularity, and Bearden's works have the painterly, agitated brushwork and diverse tonal colors that were typical of this style. A characteristic technique of his own was to pull painted pieces of paper off canvases, creating rough, uneven, gritty paint surfaces. But although the abstract expressionists' philosophical introspection and self-discovery might have appealed to Bearden, he and other African American artists of this period felt alienated from the New York school, which was all-white. At the same time, they seemed to feel that representational, socially conscious painting was no longer meaningful or effective.

In the early 1960s, as the civil rights movement was advancing, Bearden's own art—and his idea of what African American art should be—changed dramatically. In 1963, he and several other African American artists in New York City, including Norman Lewis, Hale Woodruff, and Charles Alston, formed the group Spiral to help promote distinctly African American aesthetics and find a way to use art for the benefit of the civil rights movement. This group, which at its largest numbered sixteen artists, met frequently in Bearden's studio in SoHo to discuss various philosophical and political views concerning the social turmoil of the day and the members' own place as visual artists in the struggle for equality. After the march on Washington, D.C., in 1963, they organized an exhibit of their recent work; this was held in Manhattan and was called "Black and White" because all the works were done using only black and white. The exhibit was interpreted as fiercely political despite the artists' attempt to minimize polemical responses to their work.

Also in 1963, Bearden began to create his socially conscious collages about African American life and culture. He concentrated on several rather broad themes, such as the inner city, the rural South, music, and musicians. Hoping that the artists with whom he was associated would collaborate with him on these collages or follow his lead, he collected a huge number of fragmentary cutout images and brought them to the meetings of Spiral, and two members—Richard Mayhew and Reginald Gammon—did start to work with him, but they soon lost interest and stopped.

Bearden created his collages by first assembling the fragmentary images, then painting over them in scattered places, then using a brayer to work a resin emulsion adhesive over the whole. The collages were then photocopied and enlarged. It was in this enlarged format that they were first exhibited, in 1964, under the collective title "Projections." They have been described as projections (a term referring to the method of enlargement) but also as "photomontages." These works were well received by most critics, whose response encouraged Bearden to abandon painting and devote himself to collage. It should be noted, though, that the critics were reacting at least partly to the newsworthy content of the works, and this is how they have usually been interpreted by scholars. Bearden himself did not approve of that approach, however, because the collages were not meant to illustrate or be parallel to the civil rights movement.

Bearden's collages feature disparate, abruptly juxtaposed found images. Bearden cut them out of various popular magazines of the time, such as *Life*, *Ladies Home Journal*, *Ebony*, and *Look*. Abrupt shifts in depth and scale create intense, provocative scenes of ordinary people and their activities. His composites of cutout images can create extremely realistic or very distorted figures and settings. Photographic images that were originally without color or had been stripped of their color during the photocopying are sharply contrasted with colored photographs and periodical illustrations and brightly painted areas. (Color derived from found images or created with paint is seen in the later collages, but the breakthrough works of the mid-1960s are without color.) Bearden evolved his own fully realized, tonally charged aesthetics, and his collages seem to reverberate with the rhythms of jazz and the blues and the movement and speed of urban life. They were often inspired by the artist's recollections of his youth and his perceptions of the life of rural and urban African Americans. Themes of travel and motion, usually with some reference to trains, appear frequently.

Because Bearden had produced illustrations and cartoons thirty years earlier, he knew the expressive power of images in the mass media; but when he began his collages he resisted the literal, direct approach of illustration. Photographs, with their striking immediacy, were a provocative, enticing means of visualizing the reality of life for a part of America that had been historically poor and alienated from the dominant mainstream culture.

Dove (1964) shows urban dwellers on a tense, noisy, crowded street. Its title refers to a bird, in the upper center, that suggests peace, tranquillity, and spiritual release and is in sharp contrast to all else that is depicted. The faces are brutally real; scale and depth are not. *The Prevalence of Ritual—Baptist* (also 1964) includes some of the most important themes in Bearden's collages: Christian references, the concept of inclusion or exclusion, the rituals of black culture, and the ritualistic quality of making art. *Pittsburgh Memories* features two large faces of black men; these faces suggest African masks, are made up of fragments of photographs (in a way influenced by cubism), and are surrounded by assembled photographs of city buildings. As with many of Bearden's collages, the inspiration for this image was the artist's recollection of his youth. *Watching the Good Trains Go By* and *Train Whistle Blues Numbers 1* and *2* show one of Bearden's most persistent themes: the train. Bearden said that for him the train represents how white society encroached on African American society. It may well also be his personal reflection on the migration of many African Americans from the South to the North in the early decades of the twentieth century, a theme that Jacob Lawrence immortalized in his series of paintings *The Migration of the Negro*. *The Conjur Woman* depicts an African American folk mystic who could supposedly work magic and cast spells. *Summertime* (1967) contrasts the sentimental wholesomeness of a girl eating an ice cream cone with the impoverishment of people behind tenement windows, who seem to be caged in.

After the 1960s, Bearden returned to painting. He depicted socially conscious themes and scenes of African American life in vivid colors, sometimes with scratchy, agitated brushwork. Some of these works are pleasantly abstract scenes with large, bold areas of color, whereas others are violent and disturbing.

Late in life, Bearden was a mentor to younger black artists and an advocate of African American art. He received widespread recognition and acclaim for his work, becoming one of America's most famous black artists. In 1967, he was a cocurator of "The Evolution of Afro-American Artists, 1800–1950" at City College in New York City, an exhibit that was one of the first to explore the history of African American art. Bearden wrote "Rectangular Structure in My Montage Paintings," an important treatise on his own collages, in 1968. In 1969, he and the abstract artist Carl Holty wrote *The Painter's Mind: A Study of the Relations of Structure and Space in Painting*. Bearden's years of research became the foundation for *A History of African American Artists: From 1792 to the Present*, of which he and Harry Henderson were coauthors; this was one of the first major surveys of the topic. Bearden died of cancer in 1988.

Biography

Romare Bearden was probably born 2 September 1912 in Charlotte, North Carolina. (There is some disagreement among sources as to the year of his birth, with dates ranging from 1911 to 1914. According to the Register of Deeds in Charlotte, he was born in 1912.) He was brought as a child to New York, where his father was an inspector for the Department of Sanitation. Bearden studied at Boston University while playing for one of the Negro baseball leagues; he eventually received a B.S. in mathematics from New York University in 1935. He also studied at the University of Pittsburgh, the American Artists School, and the Art Students League, New York City. In the late 1930s and then again from the early 1950s to the mid-1960s, he was a social worker in New York City. Bearden served in the army from 1942 to 1945, traveled to Paris in 1950, and married Nanette Rohan in 1954. His awards include the National Medal of the Arts and numerous honorary doctorates. He was a member of Spiral, the American Academy of Arts and Letters, and the National Institute of Arts and Letters. Bearden was involved in music as well as art: he wrote music for well-known performers such as Billie Holiday; started his own business, the Bluebird music company; and had twenty of his songs recorded. Bearden died 12 March 1988 of complications from cancer.

HERBERT R. HARTEL JR.

See also Alston, Charles; Artists; Baltimore Afro-American; Chicago Defender; Douglas, Aaron; Lawrence, Jacob; Savage, Augusta; Woodruff, Hale

Individual Exhibitions

1940: "Romare Bearden: Oils, Gouaches, Watercolors, and Drawings, 1937–1940," Addison Bates Studio, New York

1944 and 1945: G Place Gallery, Washington, D.C.

1945: Duvuloy Gallery, Paris

1945: Caresse Crosby, Washington, D.C.

1945, 1946, 1947: Samuel Kootz Gallery, New York City

1948: Niveau Gallery, New York City

1955: Barone Gallery, New York City

1960: Michael Warren Gallery, New York City

1961: Cordier and Ekstrom Gallery, New York City

1964: "Projections," Ekstrom's Gallery, New York City

1965: "Projections," Corcoran Gallery, Washington, D.C.

1966: Dundy Art Gallery, Wattsfield, Vt.

1967: Michael Warren Gallery, New York City

1967: J. L. Hudson Gallery, Detroit

1968: "Romare Bearden: Paintings and Projections," Art Gallery, State University of New York at Albany

1969: Iowa State University, Iowa City

1970: Michael Warren Gallery, New York City

1971: "Romare Bearden: The Prevalence of Ritual," Museum of Modern Art, New York City

1972: Studio Museum in Harlem

1975: Gallerie Albert Loeb, Paris

1975: Madison Art Museum, Madison, Wis.

1980: "Romare Bearden: 1970–1980," Mint Museum, Charlotte, N.C.

1986: "Romare Bearden: Origins and Progressions," Detroit Institute of Arts

1991: "Memory and Metaphor: The Art of Romare Bearden, 1940–1987," Studio Museum of Harlem, New York City

1992: "A Graphic Odyssey: Romare Bearden as Printer," Cleveland Museum of Art

1997: "Romare Bearden in Black and White: Photomontage Projections, 1964," Whitney Museum of American Art, New York City

1997: "The Painted Sounds of Romare Bearden," Mount Saint Vincent University Art Gallery, Halifax, Nova Scotia

2003: "The Art of Romare Bearden," National Gallery of Art, Washington, D.C.

Group Exhibitions

1945 and 1946: Whitney Museum Annual

1946: Durand-Ruel Gallery, New York City

1948: Six American Painters, Galerie Maeght, Paris

1948: Art Institute of Chicago

1948: Barnett-Aden Gallery, Washington, D.C.

1950: "American Painting Today: A National Competitive Exhibition," Metropolitan Museum of Art, New York City

1955: Clearwater Art Museum, Clearwater, Fla.

1960: "Recent Acquisitions," Museum of Modern Art, New York City

1961: Carnegie International, Pittsburgh

1964: Farleigh-Dickinson University, Madison, N.J.

1964: "Black and White," Christopher Street Gallery, New York City

1966: New School of Social Research, New York City

1966: UCLA Art Gallery, Los Angeles

1967: City College, City University of New York

1967: Forum Gallery, New York City

1968: "International Exhibition of Posters," Sofia, Bulgaria

1968: Minneapolis Museum

1969: "New American Painting and Sculpture," Museum of Modern Art, New York City

1969: Detroit Museum

1969: Cranbrook Academy of Art, Bloomfield Hills, Mich.

1971: "Seventeen Black Artists," Newark, N.J.

1975: "Art Students League Anniversary Exhibition— 100 Artists," Kennedy Galleries, New York City

2003: "Challenge of the Modern: African-American Artists, 1925–1945," Studio Museum in Harlem

2003: "African-American Artists, 1929–1945: Prints, Drawings, and Paintings in the Metropolitan Museum of Art"

Further Reading

Fine, Ruth. *The Art of Romare Bearden*. New York: Abrams, 2003.

Campbell, Mary Schmidt, and Sharon F. Patton. *Memory and Metaphor: The Art of Romare Bearden, 1940–1987*. New York: Oxford University Press, 1991.

Driscoll, David. *Two Centuries of Black American Art*. New York and Los Angeles, Calif.: Knopf and Los Angeles County Museum of Art.

Gelburd, Gail. *Romare Bearden in Black and White: Photomontage Projections, 1964*. New York: Whitney Museum of American Art, 1997.

Gibson, Ann E. *Abstract Expressionism: Other Politics*. New Haven, Conn.: Yale University Press, 1997.

Henderson, Harry, and Romare Bearden. *African-American Artists: From 1792 to the Present*. New York: Pantheon, 1993.

Lee, Felicia R. "An American Life in Mixed Media: Bearden Is Honored With a National Gallery Retrospective." *New York Times*, 11 September 2003, pp. E1, E5.

Lewis, Samella. *African-American Art and Artists*. Berkeley: University of California Press, 1990.

Patton, Sharon F. *African-American Art*. New York: Oxford University Press, 1998.

Pomeroy, Ralph. "Romare Bearden." In *Contemporary Artists*. New York: St. James, 1977, pp. 79, 80.

Powell, Richard J. *Black Art and Culture in the Twentieth Century*. New York: Thames & Hudson, 1997.

Reynolds, Gary. *Against the Odds: African-American Artists and the Harmon Foundation*. Newark, N.J.: Newark Museum, 1990.

Schwartzman, Myron. *Romare Bearden: His Life and Art*. New York: Abrams, 1990.

Beavers, Louise

The actress Louise Beavers, like the better-known Hattie McDaniel, was a favorite "mammy" figure in American film—a wise if sometimes naive servant, cheerful and loyal, who provided her white employers, and a predominantly white audience, with sage advice, commentary, humor, and a reaffirmation of the status quo.

Beavers began her career as a member of the Lady Minstrels but soon started to get small parts in silent films. She made her feature debut in *Gold Diggers* (1923) and also appeared in the 1927 version of *Uncle Tom's Cabin*. During this period Beavers was being trained to fit into the "mammy" and "Aunt Jemima" mold; in fact, she was asked to gain weight so that her image on the screen would conform to the imagined ideal. With the advent of talkies, her career took off, and between 1929 and 1960 she appeared in more than one hundred films. The characters Beavers played generally brought comic relief or served as a counterpart of the Greek chorus, commenting on the foibles of the leading characters. She was described as conveying sincerity, authenticity, and warmth, and as seeming tamer and less cantankerous than McDaniel.

The highlight of Beavers's career was a dramatic role: she played Delilah Johnson opposite Claudette Colbert in the tearjerker *Imitation of Life* (1934). In this film Beavers and Colbert portray single mothers juggling the demands of jobs and parenthood. Beavers's character still functions as a loyal servant who makes sacrifices for her white employer. However, her conflict with her daughter (played by Fredi Washington), who tries to pass for white, suggests the influence of racism in American society. Beavers received critical praise for her role in *Imitation of Life*, but in her remaining films she once again played the stereotypical servant.

The Harlem Renaissance partly coincided with the arrival of sound films in Hollywood; and both the renaissance and the talkies opened new doors not only for African American performers who had been active in New York's theaters and nightclubs but also for those who were establishing their careers elsewhere in the United States. More work was available, and there were new avenues for artistic expression. However, Hollywood was affected by the racism and discrimination that also characterized American society as a whole; as a result, only minor roles—as servants, entertainers, or comic characters—were generally available to black actors. Moreover, these roles were stereotypical. This kind of casting drastically limited the parts that African Americans, such as Beavers, could play. Nevertheless, during the 1920s and 1930s, a performer like Beavers could still manage to create a unique screen persona within these confines.

Beavers, who had died in 1962, was posthumously inducted into the Black Filmmakers Hall of Fame in 1976.

Biography

Louise Beavers was born 8 March 1902 in Cincinnati, Ohio, and moved to Los Angeles as a teenager. She made her feature film debut in 1923 and appeared in some one hundred films between 1929 and 1960. Later, she brought her screen persona to television in the situation comedies *Beulah* and *The Danny Thomas Show*. She died of a heart attack 26 October 1962 in Hollywood, California.

DWANDALYN R. REECE

See also Film: Actors; Film: Blacks as Portrayed by White Filmmakers; Washington, Fredi

Selected Films

Gold Diggers. 1923.
Uncle Tom's Cabin. 1927.
Coquette. 1929.
Girls About Town. 1931.
What Price Hollywood? 1932.
She Done Him Wrong. 1933.
A Shriek in the Night. 1933.
Bombshell. 1933.
Imitation of Life. 1934.
Palooka. 1934.
It Happened in New Orleans. 1936.
Made for Each Other. 1939.

Further Reading

Bogle, Donald. *Toms, Coons, Mulattos, Mammies, and Bucks*. New York: Continuum, 1997.
Nesteby, James. *Black Images in American Films*. New York: Lanham, 1982.
Noble, Peter. *The Negro in Film*. London: Skelton, 1948.
Sampson, Henry. *Blacks in Black and White*. Metuchen, N.J.: Scarecrow, 1995.

Bechet, Sidney

Sidney Bechet, who has been called the "wizard of jazz," was perhaps the most prominent virtuoso to emerge from the early jazz community in New Orleans and was certainly the hottest reed man of this era. He was born a Creole in New Orleans—the city often associated with the birth of jazz—and was considered a child prodigy, having taught himself the clarinet on his brother Leonard's instrument. By age eight Bechet was performing with neighborhood bands; at age fourteen he had played with the greats in New Orleans: Bunk Johnson, King Oliver, Louis Armstrong, and Freddie Keppard. Bechet left New Orleans around 1916 and after several detours reached Chicago in 1918. There he encountered musicians from New Orleans: Keppard, Oliver, Armstrong, and Jelly Roll Morton. Bechet, who was always adventurous, set out for Europe in 1919 with Will Marion Cook's orchestra and traveled to England, France, and eventually Russia. The hotheaded Bechet was deported at one time or another from both England and France, and in 1928, he spent almost a year in jail in France for having been involved in a shooting scrape. On other trips to England and France, though, he gave command performances for royalty.

After a brief downturn in his popularity, Bechet became a significant figure in the jazz renaissance of the 1940s; he would maintain this role in the rebirth of jazz for the rest of his life. In 1951, when he took up permanent residence in France, he became an idol to the French people and played and recorded with several French jazz orchestras. A street—rue Sidney Bechet—was named in his honor.

Bechet's first love was the clarinet, but during his first trip to Europe he bought a soprano saxophone, the instrument on which he later excelled. Until John Coltrane took up this instrument in the 1960s, Bechet was the premier performer on it. The soprano saxophone is a lead and solo instrument; in sound and quality, it can pervade an ensemble much as the trumpet—the "king of instruments"—does. Many observers say that if Bechet's instrument had been the trumpet, he would have been as famous a virtuoso as Louis Armstrong.

As it was, some authorities on jazz name Bechet, Armstrong, and Duke Ellington as the three top figures in the development of jazz, with regard to improvisation and virtuosity. Although Bechet had his detractors, he was widely considered a gifted and passionate improviser and a consummate artist who inspired his fellow musicians to transcend the mediocre. According to Williams (1978, 1989), Bechet was also a great blues player. (Reportedly, Bechet performed with Bessie Smith, the "empress of the blues.") Williams also says that Bechet had impressive powers—paraphrase, invention, and adaptation to a particular musical climate—as well as an "outstanding sense of overall structure." Bechet's musical legacy includes hundreds of recordings with several groups, on American and French labels.

We may appropriately end with a quotation from about 1919 from the classical maestro Ernest Ansermet (1883–1969), then the resident conductor of the Orchestre de la Suisse Romande: "There is in the Southern Syncopated Orchestra an extraordinary clarinet virtuoso who is, so it seems, the first of his race to have composed perfectly formed blues on the clarinet. I wish to set down the name of this artist of genius; it is Sidney Bechet."

Biography

The clarinetist and saxophonist Sidney Bechet was born in New Orleans in 1897. Bechet was a child prodigy who played with the greats in New Orleans at age fourteen, in 1911. He came to Chicago in 1918 and went to Europe in 1919, playing with major jazz groups in the United States and abroad. Around 1919, he was praised by the Swiss classical conductor Ernest Ansermet. At about this time Bechet took up the soprano saxophone. He traveled back and forth to Europe, toured extensively, and recorded numerous jazz tracks. In 1951, Bechet settled in Paris; he became an idol of the French from then until his death. He married a German, Elizabeth Zeigler (an event reported in *Life* magazine), and they maintained an imposing residence near Paris; however, he also had a mistress,

with whom he had a child, Daniel. Bechet died in Paris in 1959.

MALCOLM BREDA

See also Armstrong, Louis; Cook, Will Marion; Jazz; Morton, Jelly Roll; Music: Bands and Orchestras; Oliver, Joseph "King"

Further Reading

Bechet, Sidney. *Treat It Gentle: An Autobiography*. New York: Da Capo, 1978.

(Paperback ed. See also hardback ed., Twayne and Cassell, 1960.)

Chilton, John. *Sidney Bechet: The Wizard of Jazz*. New York: Da Capo, 1996. (First printing, London, 1987.)

Hippenmeyer, Jean-Roland. *Sidney Bechet: Ou l'extraordinaire odyssée d'un musicien de jazz*. Geneva: Tribune, 1980.

Porter, Lewis, and Michael Ullman. "Sidney Bechet and His Long Song." *Black Prespective in Music*, 16(2), Fall 1988.

Williams, Martin T., ed. *The Art of Jazz*. New York: Oxford University Press, 1959.

Williams, Martin T. *Jazz Masters of New Orleans*. New York: Da Capo, 1978.

———. *Jazz in Its Time*. New York: Oxford University Press, 1989.

Zammarchi, Fabrice. *Sidney Bechet*. Paris: Éditions Filipacchi- Sonodip, 1989.

Becton, George Wilson

George Becton—the "dancing evangelist"—is perhaps most remembered today through Langston Hughes's poem "Goodbye Christ," which rails against religious hypocrisy in Harlem and across the globe. Hughes specifically indicts "Big black Saint Becton/ Of the Consecrated Dime" and laments that "The popes and preachers've/Made too much money from [the Bible]." Although Hughes mentions Becton by name only in "Goodbye Christ," he almost certainly had Becton in mind in other poems with a similar theme, such as "To Certain 'Brothers'" and "Sunday Morning Prophecy." It should be noted that the working-class people of Harlem undoubtedly remember Becton quite differently. Hughes may have best summed up Becton's life and career in one sentence in

George Wilson Becton: inset, and in his living room, 1930s.
(Schomburg Center for Research in Black Culture, New York Public Library.)

The Big Sea (1940, 275): "Dr. Becton was a charlatan if there ever was one, but he filled the huge church—because he gave a good show."

George Wilson Becton was born in Clarksville, Texas, where he was known as the "boy clergyman." From an early age he felt that he had a calling as an evangelist and began practicing the trade; eventually he went to Ohio to pursue his career. He earned degrees from Payne Theological Seminary at Wilberforce University before becoming the pastor at Zion Baptist Church in nearby Xenia. In the mid-1920s, he moved to Harlem, where he landed at the Salem Methodist Episcopal Church on the corner of Seventh Avenue and 129th Street. F. A. Cullen (father of the poet Countee Cullen) was its pastor. There, Becton became known for his upbeat services. He would swagger onto the stage wearing a pearl-gray suit, a top hat, and white silk gloves and carrying a malacca cane, followed by his "twelve disciples" and accompanied by the music of a jazz band with seven to fifteen players (reports vary). Becton was gentle-looking, baby-faced, fleet of foot, poetic, quick-witted, and charismatic. His congregation swooned, shouted, danced, and, most important, contributed to the collection basket. Becton called his show "The World's Gospel Feast Party," and the primary tenet of the organization was the "consecrated dime." Every member of this working-class congregation was to put a dime a day into an envelope, and on Sunday Becton would collect the envelopes, each containing seventy cents of hard-earned money. Becton would consecrate the dimes to God

during the worship service but put them into his own pocket afterward. He lived in an extravagant apartment, wore the finest clothes, and bought real estate. When asked about his wealth, Becton delivered the familiar refrains "If Jesus were alive, he would dress like me" and "God ain't broke!" (Anderson 1981, 249). At the height of his popularity as Harlem's favorite evangelist, he founded a magazine, *The Menu*, and took his "World's Gospel Feast Party" on the road.

Becton was visiting one of his churches in Philadelphia on 21 May 1933 when he was gunned down, presumably by members of the policy racket, a mob-run lottery system, of which he was a vocal opponent. He died four days later. Mourners piled into the Salem M. E. Church (which had a capacity of 3,000) on the morning of 30 May 1933 for the funeral, and more than 5,000 lined the street—so many, in fact, that a small riot broke out. Despite Becton's unrestrained swindling of the poor, it was clear that in both life and death "he gave a good show."

Biography

George Wilson Becton was born 15 April 1890 in Clarksville, Texas. His parents were Matthew and Lucy Ann (Bagsby) Becton. He attended Payne Theological Seminary at Wilberforce University in Wilberforce, Ohio; he received a bachelor of divinity degree in 1910, a bachelor of arts degree in 1917, and the Rust prize for oratory in 1913 and was selected as the speaker for Founders' Day in 1914. Becton was the pastor of Zion Baptist Church in Xenia, Ohio, c. 1913–1925. He then moved to Harlem, where he worked at Salem Methodist Episcopal Church (Seventh Avenue and 129th Street) under Rev. Dr. F. A. Cullen. Becton married Rev. Josephine Bufford, pastor of Allen Memorial Spiritualist Church at 135 West 120th Street, and resided at 62 West 120th Street. He was the founder and president of the World's Gospel Feast Party, Inc., and publisher of and contributor to a bimonthly magazine, *The Menu*. Becton was known for leading upbeat evangelical revivals and preaching the concept of the "consecrated dime." He was shot by mobsters in Philadelphia on 21 May 1933 and died 25 May 1933 (although some sources give the day of his death as 31 May). His funeral was held on 30 May 1933; thousands attended, and rioting broke out.

STEPHEN F. CRINITI

See also Cullen, Frederick Asbury; Hughes, Langston

Further Reading

Anderson, Jervis. *This Was Harlem: A Cultural Portrait, 1900–1950*. New York: Farrar Straus and Giroux, 1981.

Cunard, Nancy. "Harlem Reviewed." In *Negro: An Anthology*, ed. Nancy Cunard. New York: Frederick Ungar, 1970, pp. 47–55.

"5,000 Riot to See Harlem Funeral." *New York Times*, May 31, 1933, p. L13.

Hughes, Langston. "Goodbye Christ." *Negro Worker*, 2(11–12), 1932, p. 32.

————. *The Big Sea*. New York: Hill & Wang, 1940.

"Negroes Here Mourn Slain Evangelist." *New York Times*, 30 May 1933, p. L13.

Yenser, Thomas, ed. *Who's Who in Colored America, 1930–1931–1932*, 3rd ed. Brooklyn, N.Y.: Yenser, 1933.

Bennett, Gwendolyn

Gwendolyn Bennett was a graphic artist as well as a writer. Because her writing tapered off in the 1930s, she can only be considered a minor figure now; but to her contemporaries she was one of the most promising of the younger artists and a very visible part of the Harlem Renaissance.

Bennett was born in Giddings, Texas, in 1902. After her parents divorced, her father stole her from her mother, and Bennett spent much of her early life moving from place to place. Her father later remarried and settled in Brooklyn, where Bennett graduated from high school in 1921 at the top of her class. After graduation she decided to pursue art as a career, studying fine art at Pratt Institute and taking classes at Columbia University. In 1923, her poem "Heritage" was published in *Opportunity*.

In 1924, she was introduced to Harlem's literary circles at a dinner for Jessie Redmon Fauset. The poem "To Usward," which she read to the gathering, was subsequently published in both *The Crisis* and *Opportunity* and became a rallying cry for the aspirations of the "New Negro." Bennett quickly found herself caught up in a young literary group that included Countee Cullen, Langston Hughes, Eric Walrond, Wallace Thurman, and others. In 1925, her poem "Song" appeared in Alain Locke's influential anthology *The New Negro*.

In 1924, Bennett took a position at Howard University, in the fledgling fine arts department. The next year she went to Paris to study. Her letters to Cullen and others back home are full of events in Harlem but also describe buying James Joyce's *Ulysses* and visiting the famous Parisian bookseller Shakespeare and Company. France had a great effect on her art, and her two published short stories both involve Paris.

Bennett became an assistant editor at *Opportunity* in the summer of 1926, and she kept her affiliation with *Opportunity* even after returning to Howard. Most significantly, 1926 marks the beginning of "The Ebony Flute," a gossipy monthly column in *Opportunity* that would last for nearly two years. "The Ebony Flute" is filled with vivid details about the goings-on of the young literary community in Harlem and is a unique record of the avant-garde of the Harlem Renaissance.

Bennett married a doctor, Alfred Jackson, in 1927 and moved with him to rural Florida. Her marriage ended her career at Howard and also ended "The Ebony Flute," as she was no longer part of events in Harlem. The Jacksons' marriage became increasingly unhappy because of financial pressures and the young couple's isolation. By the time Bennett and her husband returned to New York in 1930, the Harlem Renaissance was nearly over. Bennett was able to resume some of her former lifestyle, but her marriage continued to be troubled, and financial problems finally caused the Jacksons to lose their home on Long Island. Dr. Jackson died in the early 1930s.

As late as 1937, Bennett corresponded regularly with Claude McKay and Cullen and was active in their literary circle. Accusations of communist affiliations cost Bennett a job with the Federal Arts Project in 1941 and brought her under investigation by the House Un-American Activities Committee. This seems to have broken her spirit, and by the early 1940s she had retreated into anonymity. Eventually, Bennett remarried and moved to Kutztown, Pennsylvania, to retire. She died there in 1981.

Biography

Gwendolyn Bennett was born in Giddings, Texas, 8 July 1902. She graduated from Pratt Institute, 1924; studied at Columbia University, 1921–1924; and studied at Académie Julian and École du Pantheon, Paris, 1925. She was an instructor in watercolor and design at Howard University, 1924 and 1926; and taught art education and English at Tennessee State College, 1927. In the 1930s, Bennett was associated with the Federal Arts Project and with the Harlem Community Art Center, as assistant director (1937) and as director

(1938–1941). She was a teacher and administrator at the Jefferson School for Democracy, c. 1941; director of the George Washington Carver School, beginning in 1943; secretary of Consumer's Union, mid-1940s; and an antique dealer in Kutztown, Pennsylvania. She received a fellowship from the Alfred C. Barnes Foundation, 1926. Bennett died in Kutztown in 1981.

STEVEN NARDI

See also Authors: 5—Poets; Crisis, The; Cullen, Countee; Fauset, Jessie Redmon; Fire!!; Hughes, Langston; Literature: 7—Poetry; McKay, Claude; New Negro, The; Opportunity; Thurman, Wallace; Walrond, Eric

Selected Works

Bennett, Gwendolyn. "Tokens." In *Ebony and Topaz: A Collectanea*, ed. Charles S. Johnson. New York: 1927, pp. 149, 150.

Bennett, Gwendolyn. "Wedding Day." *Fire!!*, November 1926, pp. 26–28.

Cullen, Countee, ed. *Caroling Dusk: An Anthology of Verse by Negro Poets.* 1927. (Collection in which Bennett appears.)

Honey, Maureen, ed. *Shadowed Dreams: Women's Poetry of the Harlem Renaissance.* 1989. (Collection in which Bennett appears.)

Hughes, Langston, and Arna Bontemps, eds. *The Poetry of the Negro, 1746–1949.* 1949. (Collection in which Bennett appears.)

Further Reading

Dictionary of Literary Biography, Vol. 51, *Afro American Writers from the Harlem Renaissance to 1940.* Detroit, Mich.: Gale, 1987.

Govan, Sandra Y. "Gwendolyn Bennett: Dramatic Tension in Her Life and Art." *Langston Hughes Review*, 6(2), 1987, pp. 29–35.

Perry, Margaret. *Silence to the Drums: A Survey of the Literature of the Harlem Renaissance.* Westport, Conn.: Greenwood, 1976.

Bentley, Gladys

Gladys Bentley once wrote: "It seems I was born different. . . . From the time I can remember anything, even as I was toddling, I never wanted a man to touch me. . . . Soon I began to feel more comfortable in boys' clothes than in dresses." She left home at age sixteen, bound for Harlem and the chance to be a jazz singer. There was a public hungry for gay and lesbian entertainers, and in Harlem Bentley carved out a niche for herself among what were known as "pansy acts" and "hot mamas." Bentley began performing at house-rent parties and in the speakeasies of the nightclub district called Jungle Alley, at 133rd Street between Lenox and Seventh avenues; and in the 1920s, she achieved international fame as a male impersonator who cultivated an image as a bulldagger. She sang at Harlem's most fashionable clubs, dressed in her signature tuxedo and top hat, and openly flirted with female patrons. Bentley would playfully transform popular tunes of the day by adding raunchy lyrics. Her popularity and her earnings were ever-increasing, and she was frequently mentioned in many of the entertainment columns of the day. Characters based on her appeared in novels such as Carl Van Vechten's *Parties* and Clement Wood's *Deep River*. Moreover, she was a major influence on the careers of other blues singers, including Bessie Smith.

Bentley's enormous popularity on the stage led to a highly successful recording career when she was twenty-one. She recorded eighteen songs for the Okeh company and a side with the Washboard Serenaders on the Victor label. Her recordings—unlike her stage act—had no homoerotic elements and no lesbian lyrics.

As the era of the "New Negro" ended and the Great Depression began, Bentley moved to Los Angeles to care for her ailing mother and to continue her career as an entertainer. She had some success during World War II, performing at Loquin's El Rancho in Los Angeles and at Mona's in San Francisco, a club whose motto was "Girls Will Be Boys" and where she was known as the "brown bomber of sophisticated songs." However, the McCarthy era brought with it a great deal of homophobia, and Bentley's act was targeted. In response, she stopped wearing her tuxedo onstage and appeared in dresses instead. In 1950, Bentley wrote an article for *Ebony* magazine, "I Am Woman Again," in which she claimed that she was no longer a lesbian, having cured herself with hormone treatments. After two marriages to men (one of which was disputed by the bridegroom, J. T. Gibson), and two divorces, she went back to performing at the Rose Bowl in Hollywood. She also recorded a song on the Flame label and appeared twice on Groucho Marx's television show.

Bentley became a member of a church called the Temple of Love in Christ, Inc., and was preparing to become a minister; but she died, at age fifty-two, before she could be ordained.

Biography

Gladys Bentley was born 12 August 1907 in Philadelphia, Pennsylvania; her father was American-born, and her mother was a native of Trinidad. She left home to go to Harlem at age sixteen and became famous as a male impersonator during the 1920s. At the beginning of the Depression, she moved to California, where she continued her career as an entertainer during World War II; but in the postwar period her homoerotic act became less acceptable. She announced in 1950 that she had been "cured" of lesbianism, and she was married twice (to men). Both marriages ended in divorce, and Bentley then returned to performing; however, at the time of her death—in 1960, during a flu epidemic—she was planning to become a minister

COURTNEY JOHNSON

See also Homosexuality; House-Rent Parties; Jungle Alley; Smith, Bessie; Van Vechten, Carl

Further Reading

Bentley, Gladys. "I Am Woman Again." *Ebony*, 1950.
Bogus, Diane. "The Myth and Tradition of the Black Bulldagger." In *Dagger: On Butch Women*, ed. Lily Burana Roxxie and Linnea Due. San Francisco, Calif.: Cleis, 1994.
Garber, Eric. "A Spectacle in Color: The Gay and Lesbian Subculture of Jazz Age Harlem." In *Hidden From History: Reclaiming the Gay and Lesbian Past*, ed. Martin Duberman, Martha Vicinus, and George Chauncey Jr. New York: Penguin, 1989.
Mitchell, Carmen. "The Oppositional Lives of Gladys Bentley." In *The Greatest Taboo: Homosexuality in African American Communities*, ed. Delroy Constantine-Simms. Los Angeles, Calif.: Alyson, 2000.

Bethune, Mary McLeod

Mary McLeod Bethune, educator, clubwoman, political appointee, and civil rights activist, believed in the power of education, the need for collective action, and political protest to gain social justice for African Americans. She was a major educational and political leader during the Harlem Renaissance. Through the institutions she founded and the posts she held, Bethune encouraged political activism and resistance to oppression. She struggled to make African American voices heard and to move black Americans from the sidelines to the center of American social, economic, and political life.

In an era of accommodation and a strong belief in industrial education, Bethune established the Daytona Normal and Industrial Institute for Negro Girls to provide a classic liberal arts education and to train young women for leadership. Through Daytona Institute Bethune became a role model in community activism—initiating outreach and cultural programs and setting up mission schools, community centers, reading rooms, summer schools, playgrounds, a hospital, a visiting-nurse service, and farmers' institutes. She organized black voters to support a mayoral candidate who had come out against the Ku Klux Klan, and on election day she marshaled 500 eligible black voters who successfully challenged and undermined the Klan's political dominance. This episode drew attention to the importance of the black vote, the power

Mary McLeod Bethune. (Library of Congress.)

of collective action, and the use of the ballot as a political weapon.

As a member of the black women's club movement, Bethune further demonstrated the importance of collective action in advancing black people's interests. She herself was president of the Florida State Federation of Colored Women's Clubs, founder of the Southeastern Federation of Colored Women, and the Circle of Negro War Relief, and a lecturer for the Red Cross. Other black clubwomen opened the Home for Delinquent Girls in Ocala, Florida; supported the United States' involvement in World War I; began interracial organizations; actively addressed the problems of black workers; and took up the cause of world peace. As a two-term president (1924–1928) of the National Association of Colored Women (NACW), Bethune established its permanent national headquarters in Washington, D.C.; she saw this as a first step toward making NACW the official, authoritative female voice for the concerns of African Americans. The permanent headquarters gave NACW legitimacy, set it on an equal footing with similar white women's organizations, gave black women a place for making international contacts, and became the official archive of NACW. Bethune, who had gained recognition through her club work, became an adviser to two administrations—those of presidents Calvin Coolidge and Herbert Hoover—on African American educational issues through the National Child Welfare Commission.

In 1935, President Franklin D. Roosevelt appointed Bethune as director of the Office of Minority Affairs in the National Youth Administration (NYA). This was the first federal office created for a black woman. In this position Bethune publicized New Deal programs to ensure participation by blacks and used NYA programs to empower African Americans politically. She diminished the control of local white administrators over programs and funds by persuading racially liberal federal administrators to appoint qualified African Americans to positions in which they could make decisions that directly affected black students. She ensured that black state administrators dispensed funds to black people and used those same administrators to build an autonomous national black field staff that reported directly to her. By creating a Special Negro Higher Education Fund, Bethune gained direct control over some $600,000 in New Deal funds that secured graduate training for African American students. Bethune also organized the "black cabinet" and used her position to arrange public conferences between civil rights activists and government officials; these conferences succeeded in putting civil rights on the national political agenda.

Personal political appointments made Bethune aware of how few African American women held decision-making positions. She soon concluded that black women should create a national coalition to effect political change; accordingly, she organized the National Council of Negro Women (NCNW) in 1935. This was an umbrella organization designed to give black women political visibility and power on the national level. Through its programs, NCNW encouraged independent action by African American women, taught self-reliance, and honed women's leadership skills. A significant portion of these programs was educative. Women investigated problems in their communities, analyzed political campaigns and party platforms, and became familiar with state constitutions and voting laws. They organized voter registration campaigns and mobilized women voters. They studied and publicized voting records and drew up and presented petitions. NCNW's programs made many black women astute political activists and lobbyists. As a result of the political education women gained through NCNW, ten of its members secured federal administrative and judicial posts between 1941 and 1946. Once in place, these women promoted legislation designed to improve conditions for the entire race, including laws against lynching and against the poll tax; and they fought for public health, equal education, and equal employment opportunities. Their politics addressed the everyday struggle for survival as well as movements intended to change power relationships. Through political education and collective action, NCNW compelled the government to recognize African American women's legitimate place in federal programs and taught black women how to effect long-term political change by giving them a voice in the national political arena.

Mary McLeod Bethune's impact was significant. She used education, clubs, government appointments, and collective action to change individual consciousness while organizing African Americans to fight collectively for the transformation of social, economic, and political institutions. She worked to improve African Americans' lives and to change the contours of American democracy. She used insight, determination, and persuasiveness to make African Americans more visible in American social, economic, and political life; and she continually fought for social justice for African Americans.

Biography

Mary Jane McLeod Bethune was born 10 July 1875 in Mayesville, South Carolina. She studied at Trinity Mission School in Mayesville; Scotia Seminary (later Barber-Scotia College) in Concord, North Carolina (1893); and Moody Bible Institute in Chicago, Illinois (1895). She taught at Trinity Mission School in Mayesville (1895); Haines Institute in Augusta, Georgia (1895–1896); Kendell Institute in Sumter, South Carolina (1897–1998); and Palatka Mission School in Palatka, Florida (1899–1903). She was founder and president of Daytona Normal and Industrial Institute for Negro Girls (1904–1923), later Bethune-Cookman College (1923–1942); Southeastern Federation of Colored Women's Clubs (1920); National Council of Negro Women (1935–1949); and the Mary McLeod Bethune Foundation (1953). Her government positions included the National Committee for Child Welfare (1924–1928); the Executive Committee of the National Youth Administration (1935); director of Minority Affairs of the National Youth Administration (1936–1943); special assistant to the secretary of war, for selection of candidates for the first officers candidate school for the Women's Army Corps (1942); and consultant to the San Francisco Conference on drawing up the charter for the United Nations (1945). Bethune received honorary degrees from Wilberforce University (1915), South Carolina State College (n.d.), Lincoln University (1935), Tuskegee Institute (1938), Howard University (1942), Wiley College (1943), Bennett College (1945), West Virginia State College (1947), and Rollins College (1949). She was affiliated with or held positions in the following: Association for the Study of Negro Life and History; International Longfellow Society (honorary president); Commission on Interracial Cooperation (vice president); National Council of Women of the United States (honorary president); Afro-American Life Insurance Company (vice president); Southern Conference for Human Welfare (vice president); Central Life Insurance Company (member of the board of directors, and president); National Association of Colored Women (president); Florida State Teachers Association (president); Florida State Federation of Colored Women's Clubs (president); Florida Council on Human Relations (state director); National Association for the Advancement of Colored People (member of the board of directors, and vice president); National Urban League (vice president); National Sharecroppers Fund (member of the board of directors);

Southern Conference Educational Fund (member of the board of directors); American Women's Volunteer Service (member of the board of directors); American Mother's Committee (member of the board of directors), Bethune-Volusia Beach (founder, treasurer). She was a member of the General Conference of the Methodist Church, Women's Army for National Defense, National Commission on Christian Education, Council of Church Women, Social Service Commission of the Methodist Church, Americans for Democratic Action, National Civil Liberties Union, First Daytona Beach Housing Authority, American Council on African Education, National Committee on Atomic Information, and Good Neighbor Association. She received the Spingarn Medal (1935); Francis Drexel Award (1937), First Annual Youth City Award (1941), Thomas Jefferson Award (1942), Haitian Medal of Honor (1952), Haitian Star of Africa (1953), and Dorie Miller Award (1954). Her writings include contributions to *What the Negro Wants*; "Spiritual Autobiography"; columns in the Chicago *Defender* and the Pittsburgh *Courier*; articles in *Journal of Negro History* and *Ebony*; and editorials in *Afro-American Woman* and *Women United*, the official publications of the National Council of Negro Women. Bethune died in Daytona Beach, Florida, 18 May 1955.

JOYCE A. HANSON

See also Harlem Renaissance in the United States: 9—Washington, D.C.

Selected Works

"The Adaptation of the History of the Negro to the Capacity of the Child." *Journal of Negro History*, 24(1), January 1939.

"The Association for the Study of Negro Life and History: Its Contribution to Our Modern Life." *Journal of Negro History*, 20(4), October 1935.

"Certain Inalienable Rights." In *What the Negro Wants*, ed. Rayford W. Logan. New York: Agathon, 1944. (Writings by Mary McLeod Bethune and others.)

"Clarifying Our Vision with the Facts." *Journal of Negro History*, 23(1), January 1938.

"My Last Will and Testament." *Ebony*, 18 September 1963.

"The Negro in Retrospect and Prospect." *Journal of Negro History*, 35(1), January 1950.

"The Torch Is Ours." *Journal of Negro History*, 36(1), January 1951.

"Spiritual Autobiography." In *American Spiritual Autobiographies: Fifteen Self-Portraits*, ed. Louis Finkelstein. New York: Harper, 1948.

Further Reading

Brawley, Benjamin G. *Negro Builders and Heroes*. Chapel Hill: University of North Carolina Press, 1937.

Daniels, Sadie Iola. *Women Builders*. Washington, D.C.: Associated Publishers, 1931.

Fleming, Shelia Y. *The Answered Prayer to a Dream: Bethune-Cookman College, 1904–1994*. Virginia Beach, Va.: Donning, 1995.

Giddings, Paula. *When and Where I Enter: The Impact of Black Women on Race and Sex in America*. New York: Bantam, 1984.

Hicks, Florence Johnson, ed. *Mary McLeod Bethune: Her Own Words of Inspiration*. Washington, D.C.: Nuclassics and Science, 1975.

Holt, Rackham. *Mary McLeod Bethune*. Garden City, N.Y.: Doubleday, 1964.

Leffall, Delores C., and Janet L. Sims. "Mary McLeod Bethune: The Educator; also Including a Selected Annotated Bibliography." *Journal of Negro Education*, 45(3), Summer 1976, pp. 342–359.

Lerner, Gerda, ed. *Black Women in White America: A Documentary History*. New York: Vintage, 1973.

McClusky, Audrey T. "Mary McLeod Bethune and the Education of Black Girls." *Sex Roles*, 21(1–2), 1989.

———. "Multiple Consciousness in the Leadership of Mary McLeod Bethune." *NWSA Journal*, 6(1), Spring 1994, pp. 69–81.

McCluskey, Audrey, and Elaine M. Smith, eds. *Mary McLeod Bethune: Building a Better World—Essays and Selected Documents*. Bloomington: Indiana University Press, 1999.

Ovington, Mary White. *Portraits in Color*. New York: Viking, 1927.

Peare, Catherine Owen. *Mary McLeod Bethune*. New York: Vanguard, 1951.

Perkins, Carol O. "The Pragmatic Idealism of Mary McLeod Bethune." *Sage,* Fall 1988, pp. 30–35.

Poole, Bernice Anderson. *Mary McLeod Bethune, Educator*. Los Angeles, Calif.: Melrose Square, 1994.

Ross, B. Joyce. "Mary McLeod Bethune and the National Youth Administration: A Case Study of Power Relationships in the Black Cabinet of FDR." *Journal of Negro History*, 60(1), January 1975, pp. 1–28.

Sitkoff, Harvard. *A New Deal for Blacks: The Emergence of Civil Rights as a National Issue—The Depression Decade*. New York: Oxford University Press, 1978.

Smith, Elaine M. "Mary McLeod Bethune and the National Youth Administration." In *Black Women in American History: The Twentieth Century*, Vol. 4, ed. Darlene Clark Hine. New York: Carlson, 1990.

———. "Mary McLeod Bethune's 'Last Will and Testament': A Legacy for Race Vindication." *Journal of Negro History*, 84(1–4), Winter 1996, pp. 105–122.

Stern, Emma Gelders. *Mary McLeod Bethune*. New York: Knopf, 1957.

Birth of a Nation, The

The Birth of a Nation, D.W. Griffith's controversial film, premiered on February 8, 1915, at Clune's Auditorium in Los Angeles. It had cost a remarkable $110,000 to make, more than had ever been spent on a film, and it was a huge box-office success. At twelve reels, it was probably the longest and most impressive piece of filmmaking to date. In it, Griffith concentrated on storytelling and characterization, and this approach would come to dominate American filmmaking.

Released fifty years after Robert E. Lee's surrender at Appomattox, *The Birth of a Nation* was Griffith's attempt to present a history of the Civil War and Reconstruction. Griffith believed that, as a medium, film could be objective and was therefore well suited to history. He wrote at the time, with regard to the historical film, "There will be no opinions expressed. You will merely be present at the making of history" (Griffith 1915). But *The Birth of a Nation* was hardly objective. It was

Scene from *The Birth of a Nation*. (Photofest.)

based on a novel, Thomas Dixon's *The Clansman* (1904), which had presented the Civil War and Reconstruction from the perspective of the Democratic Party, criticizing the radical Republicans for treating the South punitively after the war. Dixon was known to be a racist, and many people considered his novel racist propaganda. *The Birth of a Nation* would face the same accusation.

The Birth of a Nation depicts the radical Republicans of the North as villains who exploited freed slaves and used the freedmen's vote to disenfranchise and victimize white Southerners. To appeal to the viewers' emotions, Griffith chose to narrate these events not as an impersonal epic but rather as the story of two families: the Stonemans, who are liberal, abolitionist Northerners; and the Camerons, who are slaveholding Southerners living on a plantation. The cause of the rift between these two families, and between the North and the South, is clear. The first image in the film is a "tableau of a minister praying over manacled slaves to be auctioned in a town square"; and the accompanying intertitle states, "The bringing of the African to America planted the first seed of disunion," pointing to blacks as the primary threat to national unity. Through what Griffith called "historical facsimiles"—reenactments of historical events—we watch the destruction of the South at the hands of the newly enfranchised blacks. Again and again, the film shows the Civil War and Reconstruction as violations of the South, a point vividly dramatized by the attempted rape of one of the Cameron daughters by a black man. Ultimately, the nation is preserved by the union of the two families by marriage. But first, the threat from the African Americans must be contained. At the climax of the film, the Ku Klux Klan rides triumphantly through the town of Piedmont, South Carolina, signaling the defeat and ultimate eradication of African Americans there and in the world of the film. An intertitle reads, "The aftermath. At the sea's edge, the double honeymoon," and is followed by an image of the two couples: first, Margaret Cameron and Phil Stoneman; then, seated on a bluff overlooking the sea, Ben Cameron and Elsie Stoneman. The double wedding heals the breach between North and South.

From the outset, the blatant racism of *The Birth of a Nation* engendered controversy and aroused protests. The National Association for the Advancement of Colored People (NAACP) sent out thousands of pamphlets to even the smallest towns in an effort to prevent the film from opening in New York, and blacks began a nationwide campaign against a movie that "few eyes had ever seen" (Cripps 1993, 52–53). Although the protests achieved limited success on the West Coast, where some of the most gruesome and violent scenes were cut from the film, *The Birth of a Nation* did open in New York, at the Liberty Theater. And despite the protests by blacks, whites flocked to see it in record numbers. In the press, the film was lauded as "the last word in picturemaking" (Vance 1915/1994) and as "the soul and spirit and flesh of the heart of your country's history, ripped from the past and brought quivering with all human emotion before your eyes" (Greene 1915/1994).

In writing about *The Birth of a Nation*, film scholars have long faced the problem of reconciling the film's overt racism and its impressive stylistic innovations. Critics have tended to address either race or aesthetics, but primarily the latter. Because Griffith is widely considered the father of American cinema, many critics have been reluctant to take up the question of race at all. But Taylor (1996) has argued that it is indefensible to disregard racism, because the film's ideology and form cannot be separated. Griffith uses lighting, framing, costumes, and camera angles to induce the spectator to look favorably on some characters and unfavorably on others. Because this film is focused on families, it actually has more in common with the popular genre of melodrama than with the discipline of history. Melodrama neatly divides the world into good and evil. In *The Birth of a Nation*, white women, the symbols of goodness and purity, are continually threatened by black and mulatto men, who are represented as dangerous. Furthermore, Lang (1994b) argues that with the depiction of Abraham Lincoln as "the Great Heart . . . even politics becomes 'familiarized'" (22). The family rift, the Civil War, must be resolved by the joining of the white Northern and Southern families in matrimony, in preparation for the "birth of the nation." According to White (1994), history is a mere pretext in this film, "the premise or occasion for developing a story whose values and meanings extend beyond the purview of any single social-historical moment" (214). Ultimately, if Griffith is to be considered the father of American cinema, then *The Birth of a Nation* is a constant reminder of its racist heritage.

ALISON LANDSBERG

See also Birth of a Race, The; Film; Film: Blacks as Portrayed by White Filmmakers; National Association for the Advancement of Colored People

Further Reading

Carter, Everett. "Cultural History Written With Lightning: The Significance of *The Birth of a Nation*." *American Quarterly*, 12, Fall 1960, pp. 347–357.

Cripps, Thomas. "The Year of *The Birth of a Nation*." In *Slow Fade to Black: The Negro in American Film, 1906–1942*. New York: Oxford University Press, 1993.

Gish, Lillian, with Ann Pinchot. *Lillian Gish: The Movies, Mr. Griffith, and Me*. Englewood Cliffs, N.J.: Prentice-Hall, 1969.

Greene, Ward. Review. *Atlanta Journal*, 7 December 1915. (Reprinted in Robert Lang, ed. *The Birth of a Nation*. New Brunswick, N.J.: Rutgers University Press, 1994.)

Griffith, D. W. "Five Dollar 'Movies' Prophesied." *Editor*, 24 April 1915.

Lang, Robert, ed. *The Birth of a Nation*. New Brunswick, N.J.: Rutgers University Press, 1994a.

Lang, Robert. "History, Ideology, Narrative Form." In *The Birth of a Nation*, ed. Robert Lang. New Brunswick, N.J.: Rutgers University Press, 1994b.

May, Lary. *Screening Out the Past*. Chicago, Ill.: University of Chicago Press, 1980.

Rogin, Michael. "'The Sword Became a Flashing Vision': D. W. Griffith's *The Birth of a Nation*." *Representations*, 9, Winter 1985, pp. 150–195.

Schickel, Richard. *D. W. Griffith: An American Life*. New York: Simon & Schuster, 1984.

Taylor, Clyde. "The Re-Birth of the Aesthetic in Cinema." In *The Birth of Whiteness: Race and the Emergence of U.S. Cinema*, ed. Daniel Bernardi. New Brunswick, N.J.: Rutgers University Press, 1996.

Vance, Mark. Review. *Variety*, 12 March 1915. (Reprinted in Robert Lang, ed. *The Birth of a Nation*. New Brunswick, N.J.: Rutgers University Press, 1994.)

White, Mimi. "The Birth of a Nation: History as Pretext." In *The Birth of a Nation*, ed. Robert Lang. New Brunswick, N.J.: Rutgers University Press, 1994.

Birth of a Race, The

The history of the silent film *The Birth of a Race* (1918) is bound up with that of a more famous film—D. W. Griffith's *Birth of a Nation* (1915). *The Birth of a Nation* was strikingly innovative in many ways and was widely praised as the best film of its day. However, it was also blatantly racist, portraying black and mulatto characters as villainous and the Ku Klux Klan as heroic. Black critics and intellectuals were outraged by *The Birth of a Nation* and even more outraged by its huge popularity. The National Association for the Advancement of Colored People (NAACP) organized protests against it, and the backlash was so strong that Griffith filmed a prologue at Hampton Institute (or using footage from Hampton) to be included in future prints of the film (he had wanted to film the prologue at the Tuskegee Institute, but Booker T. Washington refused). Griffith's attempt at an apology seemed feeble and did not mollify the growing number of objectors, many of whom, including W. E. B. Du Bois and William Howard Taft, began to call for some other cinematic response.

Initially, the NAACP planned to spearhead the "official response" to Griffith's film. A consortium of artists, with financial backing from Carl Laemmle, the president of Universal Pictures, came together to film an adaptation of Washington's book *Up From Slavery*. From the beginning, however, there was discord. Blacks and whites had conflicting interests in the project, and there was disagreement over whether the film should be a work of art, a political statement, or a work for profit. Universal withdrew its financial support when the NAACP could not provide matching funds, and soon afterward the NAACP dropped out. The project was then taken over by Emmett Jay Scott. But Scott (who in 1917 was appointed a special assistant to the secretary of war) was more concerned about black Americans in the armed services than about responding to *The Birth of a Nation*; accordingly, the script was changed—as was the title, from *Lincoln's Dream* to, finally, *The Birth of a Race*. Scott decided not to rely on money from white-owned businesses; instead, he financed his production company by selling stock to more than 7,000 shareholders, most of them black.

At this point, the project was still supposedly a history of the black race. A later advertisement would claim that it was "[t]he true story of the Negro—his life in Africa, his transportation to America, his enslavement, his freedom, his achievements together with his past, present, and future relations to his white neighbor and to the world in which both live and labor." However, the demands of the investors changed the scope of the film, and Scott, owing to his concerns regarding World War I, moved the content more toward Judeo-Christian ideals and anti-German sentiments. Scott was eventually removed from the project, but not before directing most of the footage that appeared in the final cut. The final product, conceived by a committee and worked on by a variety of artists, was a series of loosely related vignettes associating biblical stories (the story of Noah, Moses freeing the slaves from Egypt, and the crucifixion of Jesus Christ) with events in American history (Christopher Columbus's discovery of the new world, Paul Revere's ride, and Reconstruction). The final two-thirds of the film focused on the problems faced by those involved in World War I, including a German immigrant family in the United States that was split by the conflict.

After three years of work, including numerous pauses in production caused by financial problems, *The Birth of a Race* was released in 1918. At the time of its release, it was considered a critical and popular failure, and it was a financial fiasco. The sudden jumps between eras and vignettes disoriented most audiences, who found the film sprawling and not always coherent. A review in *Moving Picture World* concluded, "The names of three men are given as the authors of the scenario. It will be a deed of charity not to reveal their identity nor the names of the members of the cast. All have well-earned reputations and are probably anxious to live down their connection with the entire affair."

The Birth of a Race quickly faded from the national consciousness and in fact was thought to be lost for many years, while *The Birth of a Nation* became one of the most noted and controversial films of all time. In the long run, however, *The Birth of a Race* proved to be effective. Although the final version was far removed from what had first been envisioned, this film demonstrated to black America that a distinct market existed for black cinema. Also, *The Birth of a Race* had a tremendous influence on young black filmmakers, encouraging Oscar Micheaux and two brothers, Noble and George Johnson, to widen their horizons. The Johnson brothers formed the Lincoln Motion Picture Company, which independently created and released films from 1916 to 1923.

In the early 1980s, a print of *The Birth of a Race* was discovered in Texas. Although (as of this writing) it has not been released to the public, several clips can be found on a DVD version of *The Birth of a Nation*, and some critics have seen it and evaluated it. In general, *The Birth of a Race* is still considered a salient moment in the evolution of black expression in cinema; but there is an undercurrent of objections. The main objection is that this film actually reinforces some unfortunate stereotypes. In certain passages, black subjectivity is linked to aggression, even prejudice; in the film's most famous scene, for instance, a black farmer and a white farmer, holding plows, fade into soldiers marching in

uniform and carrying rifles. Nevertheless, the film does imply that the army is a force for integration. And although there may have been compromises, so that the film fell far short of the initial aspirations, *The Birth of a Race* did actively seek an alternative tradition, one more racially equitable than was suggested in *The Birth of a Nation*.

ANDREW HOWE

See also Birth of a Nation, The; Film; Johnson, Noble; Lincoln Motion Picture Company; Micheaux, Oscar; Scott, Emmett Jay; World War I

Further Reading

Cripps, Thomas. "The Birth of a Race Company: An Early Stride Toward a Black Cinema." *Journal of Negro History*, 59, 1974, pp. 38–50.
Cripps, Thomas. "'The Birth of a Race': A Lost Film Rediscovered in Texas." *Texas Humanist*, 5, 1983, pp. 11–12.
———. "The Making of 'The Birth of a Race': The Emerging Politics of Identity in Silent Movies." In *The Birth of Whiteness: Race and the Emergence of United States Cinema*, ed. Daniel Bernardi. New Brunswick, N.J.: Rutgers University Press, 1996.
Leab, Daniel J. *From Sambo to Superspade: The Black Experience in Motion Pictures*. Boston: Houghton Mifflin, 1975.
Nesteby, James R. *Black Images in American Films, 1896–1954: The Interplay Between Civil Rights and Film Culture*. Washington D.C.: American University Press, 1982.

Birthright

Birthright is T. S. Stribling's first novel with a southern setting. It was initially serialized in *Century Magazine* from October 1921 to April 1922, then published by the Century Company in New York in the spring of 1922. It was filmed twice by the famous black director Oscar Micheaux: in 1924 (as a silent movie) and 1939.

With *Birthright*, Stribling became a pioneer in the southern literary renaissance. The novel is characterized by a keen social consciousness, a sympathetic and empathetic portrayal of the black race, and a high degree of realism, and it was a new departure in the treatment of race relations by a white southerner. Stribling satirizes bigotry, hypocrisy, conventional thinking, and narrow-mindedness and accuses whites of dehumanizing blacks.

The similarities between his novel and Sinclair Lewis's *Main Street* (1920) were frequently pointed out by critics; in fact, *Birthright* was called "a Negro *Main Street*," a southern rendition of Lewis's novel.

Birthright presents the spiritual journey of an educated southern mulatto, Peter Siner, after he graduates from Harvard University and returns to his hometown, Hooker's Bend. Siner comes home with idealistic plans for the education of black children in town. However, his hopes soon turn into frustration and disillusionment. Stribling describes the plight of the young protagonist realistically and sympathetically, showing how Siner becomes a victim not only of white hatred and oppression but of the entire racist caste system in the South. Siner considers himself an "evangel of liberty" to the black people. However, both his "white blood" and his "white Harvard education" create an unbridgeable gap between him and his people. *Birthright* explores Siner's difficulties in his process of self-formation. Influenced by white standards, he is profoundly disturbed by what he sees as signs of the inferiority of his race: odor, uncleanliness, sexual promiscuity, and dishonesty. He suffers from what W. E. B. Du Bois called "double-consciousness." Siner feels ashamed of his own people in Niggertown, whose real trouble is that they have adopted the white man's estimate of them as worthless, immoral, and subhuman. Considering her immoral, he rejects the girl he loved. He temporarily finds a safe retreat in the library of a white patron, Captain Renfrew, his unacknowledged father, only to find out that Renfrew is a traditional southern racist.

However, Siner's spiritual journey ends with an affirmation of his blackness and acceptance of his people. He marries Cissie, who has just come out of jail and is pregnant with another man's child, and he leaves Niggertown to find work in the North. The ethics that he acquired in Harvard proved untenable in the odd morality of Niggertown; eventually, though, Siner outgrows "white ethics," rejects the notion of absolute morality, and embraces the idea that morals are relative and that they differ from one race to another. In the end, practicality wins out over idealism and altruism. Still, Siner retains some of his idealism: as he sets out for the North with his bride, he hopes to find there the equality and opportunity that turned out to be impossible in his southern hometown.

ASLI TEKINAY

See also Micheaux, Oscar; Stribling, Thomas Sigismund

Further Reading

Becker, George J. "T. S. Stribling: Pattern in Black and White." *American Quarterly*, 4, Fall 1952.

Cleghorn, Sarah N. "Review of *Birthright* by T. S. Stribling and *White and Black* by H. A. Shands." *Nation*, 26 April 1922.

Durham, Frank. "The Reputed Demises of Uncle Tom or, the Treatment of the Negro in Fiction by White Southern Authors in the 1920s." *Southern Literary Journal*, 2, Spring 1970.

Eckley, Wilton E. *T. S. Stribling*. Boston, Mass.: Twayne, 1975.

Heywood, Brown. "Review of *Birthright* by T. S. Stribling." *New York World*, 29 March 1922.

Piacentino, Edward J. "The *Main Street* Mode in Selected Minor Southern Novels of the 1920s." *Sinclair Lewis Newsletter*, 7–8, 1975–1976.

———. "'No More Treacly Sentimentalities': The Legacy of T. S. Stribling to the Southern Literary Renaissance." *Southern Studies: An Interdisciplinary Journal of the South*, 20, Spring 1981.

Black and Tan Clubs

Black and Tan clubs were nightclubs where African Americans and whites could be found socializing and listening to jazz. These clubs were always located in the predominantly black sections of towns, notably "Bronzeville" in Chicago and Harlem in New York. African Americans rarely entered white neighborhoods after dark, but young white enthusiasts and musicians could always venture to black neighborhoods for entertainment. So, in addition to an appreciation of jazz, there was a sense of excitement among the whites who came to these clubs, which were part of a culture of jazz, liquor, and race.

Though New Orleans is often considered the birthplace of jazz, Chicago emerged as its second home. During the period of black creativity known as the renaissance, Harlem became its third. These urban centers appealed to black musicians because in the South they were rarely allowed to play on the same stage as whites, and any social mixing of the races was even rarer. World War I and growing industry in the North around 1920 led to an exodus of African Americans northward, and jazz went with them. Prohibition and the temperance movement were also important factors in the development of the culture of the Black and Tan clubs. In 1920, the Eighteenth Amendment made illegal the manufacture, sale, and transport of alcoholic beverages. Its advocates had hoped that it would foster temperance; instead, trafficking in bootleg liquor became a profitable enterprise, and crime rates soared. The illegally run clubs that sold bootleg liquor were called speakeasies, and many of these were Black and Tans, with an interracial clientele and an interracial roster of entertainers.

There is no definitive explanation of how the name Black and Tan began, but there are at least two plausible origins. The first explanation is that the name was probably coined by some of the recent immigrants who controlled bootleg liquor during Prohibition and who would no doubt have kept abreast of happenings abroad. In Ireland, the "black and tans" were British officers who aided the Irish police in quelling the Irish Republican Army in 1920 and 1921; these officers wore a distinctive uniform: khaki coat, black trousers, and black cap. The gangsters in America, therefore, may have adopted "black and tan" as an apt description of the clubs' clientele (if so, the term would have had wry connotations, since the "black and tans" in Ireland were notoriously brutal). The second explanation is that white Americans who came to the black neighborhoods were different from the whites who disavowed jazz and African American culture in general. "Tan," then, would have been slang for whites who immersed themselves in black musical culture, pretending for a brief time that they belonged to the black community, and who were thus, in a sense, neither white nor black.

The most famous Black and Tan in Chicago was the Sunset Café, which was remodeled in 1937 and renamed the Grand Terrace Ballroom (it was designated a historic landmark in 1998). The Sunset Café was a host to the elite of jazz, including Earl "Fatha" Hines and Louis Armstrong. Another notable club was the Silver Frolics. The Black and Tan clubs of note in Harlem were Connie's Inn, Small's Paradise, and Barron Wilkin's club; all three presented Ethel Waters, Count Basie, Thomas "Fats" Waller, and other famous figures. Many of these clubs were a training ground for aspiring jazz musicians—not only African Americans but also many young whites, particularly Jimmy Dorsey, Benny Goodman, and Bix Beiderbecke.

The Black and Tan clubs often seemed to symbolize racial harmony and testify to the universality of music. However, Langston Hughes noted in his autobiography, *The Big Sea* (1940), that "ordinary Negroes [did not] like the growing influx of whites in Harlem . . .

flooding the little cabarets and bars where formerly only colored people laughed and sang. . . . Thousands of whites came to Harlem night after night, thinking the Negroes loved to have them there." To accommodate this influx, some Black and Tan clubs began to follow the example of the famous Cotton Club, which—despite being in Harlem and showcasing black entertainment—discouraged black patronage and catered exclusively to whites. Still, a large part of the appeal of the Black and Tans was the thrill of watching the people of Harlem in their own environment.

By the late 1950s, a few Black and Tans were still operating, but race relations in the United States were becoming increasingly strained, and hardly anyone, black or white, frequented these clubs. This was an ironic and sad end to an institution that had fostered jazz and had contributed, in its way, to improving relations between the races.

CANDICE LOVE

See also Cotton Club; Jazz; Nightclubs; Nightlife; Small's Paradise

Further Reading

Anderson, Jervis. *This Was Harlem: A Cultural Portrait, 1900–1950.* New York: Farrar, Straus and Giroux; Toronto: McGraw-Hill Ryerson, 1982.

Erenberg, Lewis. *Steppin' Out: New York Nightlife and the Transformation of American Culture.* Chicago, Ill.: University of Chicago Press, 1981.

Fisher, Rudolph. "The Caucasian Storms Harlem." *American Mercury,* 11, 1927, 393–98.

Lewis, David Levering. *When Harlem Was in Vogue.* Oxford and New York: Oxford University Press, 1979.

Schoener, Allon, ed. *Harlem on My Mind: Cultural Capital of Black America, 1900–1968.* New York: Random House, 1968.

Watson, Steven. *The Harlem Renaissance: Hub of African-American Culture, 1920–1930.* New York: Pantheon, 1995.

Black and White

Black and White was a film project—an attempt to make a movie in the Soviet Union about the plight of African Americans in the United States. It exemplifies a growing interest among blacks during the 1930s in challenging American racism through communism and the international arena.

The project began in March 1932, when the American communist James A. Ford, acting for the Meschrabpom Film Corporation of the Workers International, recruited African American performers and intellectuals and created the Cooperating Committee for Production of a Soviet Film on Negro Life. The committee's sponsors included Whittaker Chambers, Malcolm Cowley, W. A. Domingo, Waldo Frank, and Rose McClendon; its corresponding secretary, Louise Thompson, organized the cast. (Meschrabpom gave the performers a salary and room and board in Moscow, but they had to pay for their own transportation.)

The diverse group that arrived at the Brooklyn Pier on 14 June 1932, to board the German ship *Europa* included, in addition to Thompson herself, the aspiring fiction writer Dorothy West (one of the youngest figures of the Harlem Renaissance); the journalists Henry Lee Moon and Theodore Poston of the *Amsterdam News* in New York; two social workers, Leonard Hill and Constance White; an art student from Hampton Institute, Mildred Jones; a pharmacist, Mollie Lewis; a postal clerk, Homer Smith (who had a degree in journalism); a salesman, Alan McKenzie (the only member of the Communist Party of the United States in the group); the writer Loren Miller (who was a friend of Langston Hughes and of Thompson); an agricultural worker, Laurence Alberga; an insurance clerk, Matthew Crawford; a paperhanger and house painter, Lloyd Patterson (who was a graduate of Hampton); a student at Howard University, Frank Montero; Juanita Lewis, who had sung with Hall Johnson's choir; Thurston McNairy Lewis; Katherine Jenkins, who was a tenant at Thompson's home; George Sample; and only two experienced actors: Sylvia Garner and Wayland Rudd (who had appeared in *Scarlet Sister Mary* and *Porgy*, respectively). At the last minute, Langston Hughes arrived, having agreed to help write the English dialogue for the screenplay.

During the voyage, the group studied the Russian language and some history but more often played cards, danced, and lounged on deck; Dorothy West wrote, in her letters home, about champagne parties and "congenial folks." A proposal to send a cable of support to Ada Wright, the mother of one of the Scottsboro boys, was voted down—a hint of differences between the more and less political members of the group.

On 25 June 1932, the group arrived in Leningrad (Saint Petersburg), by train from Berlin, to be greeted by representatives of Meschrabpom and a brass band playing the "Internationale"; the next day the cast members were warmly welcomed at Nikolayevski Station in Moscow, photographed, and taken to the luxurious Grand Hotel in a fleet of Buicks and Lincolns. The Soviet Union was like nowhere else these African Americans had ever known. Meschrabpom paid them 400 rubles a month each and provided ration books for shopping; Russians on crowded streetcars offered them seats; they were ushered to the front of every line; and they were guests of honor at receptions, museums, factories, and schools. "For all of us who experienced discrimination based on color in our own land, it was strange to find our color a badge of honor," Thompson (1968) recalled.

But the film itself was another matter. The German-born director Karl Yunghans found the cast inexperienced in acting and singing and uninformed about the black working class; furthermore, he himself spoke neither English nor Russian, and knew, in Langston Hughes's (1956) words, "nothing at all about race relations in Alabama, or labor unions, North, South or European." Worse, the screenplay—by a Soviet writer, in consultation with Lovett Fort-Whiteman, an African American communist who had emigrated to the Soviet Union in 1928—bore no resemblance to the sweeping history of the African American experience that the cast and their sponsors had expected. Instead, it was a fictional account of black steelworkers in Birmingham, Alabama, who try to organize a union, wrest power from their corrupt white bosses, and overcome racism and class antagonism by joining forces with oppressed white workers. This story may have expressed communist ideals, but it hardly reflected race relations in the South; Langston Hughes (1956) said it was "improbable to the point of ludicrousness."

The script had been approved by Comintern, and by the time Meschrabpom finally agreed to make revisions, the performers, bored by weeks of waiting and anxious about the film's prospects, had become edgy and quarrelsome. One woman (probably Sylvia Garner) fell in love with another (probably Constance White), was spurned, and attempted suicide; Thompson objected to the "embarrassing" behavior of Ted Poston and Thurston Lewis, who had romped naked in the river near Moscow's Park of Rest and Culture; and the political divisions became sharper as the group debated whether or not to attend a rally for the Scottsboro boys.

Meschrabpom rescheduled the filming for 15 August and took the cast to the Black Sea, at the invitation of the Theatrical Trade Unions, for sunbathing in Odessa and a cruise to Sebastopol and Yalta. But when the group returned to Odessa from the cruise, they found Henry *Lee Moon, who had not accompanied them, waving an edition of the Paris* Herald-Tribune with the headline "Soviet Calls Off Film on U.S. Negroes; Fear of American Reaction Cause," and "hell broke loose. Hysterics took place" (Hughes 1956).

Thompson, Hughes, and Loren Miller defended Meschrabpom; but Moon, Thurston Lewis, Leonard Hill, and Laurence Alberga considered Thompson gullible (they called her "Madame Moscow") and denounced Meschrabpom, the Soviet Union, and Joseph Stalin for selling out the black race under pressure from the United States. An American engineer, Colonel Hugh Cooper, was then overseeing the building of the important Dnieprostroi Dam, and one story was that he had threatened to end construction unless *Black and White* was stopped. Another story, reported by Homer Smith (1964), was that the project was canceled out of fear that the United States would withhold diplomatic recognition of the Soviet Union. An article in the *Afro-American* on 8 October 1932 offered a third reason: that the Soviet Union was courting American favor because it was threatened by Japan's aggression in Manchuria. The competing accounts were debated in the African American press for months. Moon and Poston published statements in the *Amsterdam News*, and Thompson and Hughes replied in *The Crisis, International Literature*, and the *Daily Worker*.

Nevertheless, the film project and the Soviet Union left an indelible imprint on the African American participants. Many cast members extended their visit: Hughes spent six months traveling around Central Asia on a writing assignment; Dorothy West and Mildred Jones stayed in Moscow for another year writing for an English-language newspaper; Lloyd Patterson married a Russian woman and settled there; Wayland Rudd stayed on to study singing, fencing, and dancing; Alan McKenzie accepted a job with Meschrabpom; and Homer Smith became a consultant at the central post office in Moscow and remained in the Soviet Union until 1947.

Even those who returned home immediately remained impressed. Matthew Crawford told his wife that the trip had converted him to socialism; Loren Miller wrote that "the Soviet Union is the best friend of the Negro and all oppressed people"; Louise Thompson announced in the *Amsterdam News* that "Russia today is the only country in the world that's really fit to live in"; and Henry Moon wrote in *The Nation* in 1934 that

he had "never felt more at home among a people than among the Russians."

Note: Papers of Louise Thompson Patterson and Matthew Crawford are at Emory University in Atlanta. Documents related to the film project can also be found in the papers of Langston Hughes in the James Weldon Johnson Collection at the Beinecke Library at Yale University in New Haven, Connecticut; and in the papers of Dorothy West at the Schlesinger Library at Harvard University in Cambridge, Massachusetts.

CLAIRE NEE NELSON

See also Amsterdam News; Communist Party; Domingo, Wilfred Adolphus; Europe and the Harlem Renaissance: 5—Soviet Union; Frank, Waldo; McClendon, Rose; West, Dorothy

Further Reading

Berry, Faith. *Langston Hughes: Before and Beyond Harlem.* Westport, Conn.: Lawrence Hill, 1983.

El-Hai, Jack. "Black and White and Red." *American Heritage,* 42(3), 1991.

Hughes, Langston. "Moscow and Me: A Noted American Writer Relates His Experiences." *International Literature,* 3, July 1933.

———. *I Wonder as I Wander.* New York: Hill & Wang, 1956.

Kellner, Bruce. "Black and White." In *The Harlem Renaissance: A Historical Dictionary for the Era.* Westport, Conn.: Greenwood, 1984.

Lewis, David Levering. *When Harlem Was in Vogue.* New York: Penguin, 1997.

McDowell, Deborah E. "Conversations with Dorothy West." In *The Harlem Renaissance Reexamined,* ed. Victor A. Kramer. New York: AMS, 1987.

Rampersad, Arnold. *The Life of Langston Hughes,* Vol. 1, *1902–1941.* New York: Oxford University Press, 1986.

Smith, Homer. *Black Man in Red Russia: A Memoir by Homer Smith.* Chicago, Ill.: Johnson, 1964.

Thompson, Louise. "The Soviet Film." *Crisis,* 40, February 1933.

———. "With Langston Hughes in the U.S.S.R." *Freedomways,* 8, Spring 1968.

Black Bohemia

Black bohemia, as both a place and a group of people, was a significant aspect of the Harlem Renaissance. Black bohemians were creative artists—the literati, intellectuals, writers, musicians, actors, and visual artists—who lived and worked in Harlem in the 1920s and created and critiqued the Harlem Renaissance. Black bohemians were also the political activists, nightclub owners, nightclub habitués, petty criminals, hustlers, and the other characters who defined and participated in the counterculture that flourished in Harlem during the decade or so following World War I.

"American bohemianism" refers to the men and women who turned their backs on conventional, bourgeois culture and values and instead embraced the "modern." They repudiated the economic, political, social, and cultural conventions of their day in favor of the experimental, in art and aesthetics and in their personal beliefs and lifestyle. In the United States bohemian communities sprouted in most major cities among creative and educated young people, but the center of the movement was in New York City's Greenwich Village. It grew out of a writers' colony that settled there in the late nineteenth century and the early twentieth. By 1920, these writers had transformed a once dingy neighborhood into a district that epitomized the modern and avant-garde. Writers and artists congregated in its cafés and discussed aesthetics and politics with its radicals. They adopted the life of the "intellectual," a new term coined by the political left that referred to people who supported themselves through careers in the arts or literature. Intellectuals belonged to the professional class (rather than the working class), but they generally were not men or women of wealth or social status. Indeed, a certain level of poverty usually went hand in hand with the intellectual or bohemian lifestyle.

Although bohemians might thumb their noses at most social conventions, Greenwich Village was about as segregated as other neighborhoods in New York during the early twentieth century, with no significant interaction between blacks and whites. However, a black bohemia developed, initially in the Tenderloin district, on the west side North of Greenwich Village and South of Times Square, and then—at about the turn of the century—in an area centered near West Fifty-third Street. The Tenderloin neighborhood had tenements, boardinghouses, theaters, hotels, and restaurants but also speakeasies, brothels, and gambling houses. Among the neighborhood's pimps and prostitutes, and amid its loan sharking, gambling, and assorted vices, a community of writers, musicians, and entertainers emerged. Paul Laurence Dunbar and James Weldon Johnson lived in the Fifty-third Street area during the first decade of the twentieth century

and described this early black bohemia and its habitués in two novels: Dunbar's *The Sport of the Gods* (1902) and Johnson's *Autobiography of an Ex-Colored Man* (1912). Others who frequented these neighborhoods in the prewar period included the musicians and performers Bob Cole and John Rosamond Johnson, Will Marion Cook, Willie "the Lion" Smith, Jelly Roll Morton, and Scott Joplin. The Tenderloin district between Twenty-seventh and Fifty-third streets had clubs and restaurants; and Fifty-third Street itself was the site of the Marshall and Maceo hotels, both of which were operated by African Americans and served as gathering places for black artists, performers, and sports celebrities. Musicians and entertainers frequently gathered at the Marshall Hotel, among them James Reese Europe and his Clef Club Orchestra; the comedian-songwriters Bert Williams and George Walker; the musicians Willie "the Lion" Smith, Jelly Roll Morton, and Scott Joplin; and the heavyweight champion Jack Johnson. Black literati and artists mingled with white performers at the Marshall (which was across the street from the Clef Club); Diamond Jim Brady, Lillian Russell, Florenz Ziegfeld, and Anna Held often dined there.

By the outbreak of World War I, black bohemians had followed the rapidly growing black population into Harlem. A typical example is James Weldon Johnson: When he returned to New York in 1914 after an absence of eight years, he relocated from Fifty-third Street to 507 Edgecombe Avenue in Harlem. By the mid-1920s, Harlem was home to most of the creative artists associated with the Harlem Renaissance, as well as to major African American political and civil rights organizations, publications, and institutions. Although it lacked an African American university, Harlem supplanted Washington, D.C., and Atlanta as the center of African American intellectual life. Furthermore, among its tenements, apartment buildings, and brownstones, and amid its poverty and wealth, an African American bohemian community flourished. Harlem's cafés and nightclubs nourished an artistic, intellectual lifestyle. Gatherings of artists, writers, critics, and political radicals debated aesthetics as well as politics and race.

Like their white counterparts, black bohemians embraced political and aesthetic beliefs and a lifestyle that put them in sharp contrast to both the previous generation and their more conventional contemporaries. However, connections between Harlem and Greenwich Village were limited. Radical politics led Claude McKay downtown from his home in Harlem.

The first poems that he published in the United States appeared in 1917 in *Seven Arts* and in 1918 in Frank Harris's *Pearson's Magazine*, two avant-garde literary journals. Then he linked up with Max Eastman and Crystal Eastman and the more political *Liberator*. In addition to publishing a number of poems and essays in *Liberator*, for six months in 1922 McKay coedited this radical journal with Herbert Gold. Although the relationship between McKay and Gold was occasionally stormy, McKay's radical politics, sympathy for the Bolshevik revolution, and free-spirited lifestyle fit well with the political radicalism of Greenwich Village. Jean Toomer, whose interests were more philosophical and aesthetic than political, also connected with the artistic community in the Village. During the time when Toomer was writing *Cane*, his main literary connections there were Waldo Frank and Frank's associates. Later, as Toomer entered a spiritual search that took him away from race and literature, the photographer Alfred Stieglitz and the artist Georgia O'Keeffe became his close friends.

Most of the interaction between the Village and Harlem was in the other direction. Legal and extralegal segregation, zoning laws, racism, homophobia, sexism, and resistance to conventional values linked black and white bohemians. Well before World War I black bohemia and the Tenderloin had become a playground for literary and visual artists, theater people, lesbians and gays, gangsters, and prostitutes of both races; and elite activities took place concurrently with what was generally regarded as vice. The privileged hobnobbed with the proletariat, and whites frequented black communities—although de jure and de facto segregation inhibited African Americans from making reciprocal jaunts to white neighborhoods. The law circumscribed black bohemia, and certain activities were relegated to within its circumference. By the 1920s, this activity had shifted to Harlem and had greatly accelerated. White thrill seekers joined white bohemians in the cabarets and nightclubs of Harlem.

The person most responsible for making Harlem a vogue was the author Carl Van Vechten, a product of the bohemia in Greenwich Village. Even before his best seller *Nigger Heaven* popularized Harlem as a playground, he had led groups of daring downtowners through Harlem's nightlife. To his credit, Van Vechten was sincerely interested in African American life and became a major promoter of African American music, art, literature, and theater. He also opened his home to African Americans. At the gatherings and parties in his apartment on Fifty-third Street black bohemians and intellectuals met and established contact with their white counterparts.

In the cabarets and parties of Harlem, the discouraged white youth of the "lost generation" mingled with the African American "encouraged youth"—Alain Locke's New Negroes. The former were the descendants of landed immigrants; the latter were the descendants of the African diaspora and constituted the first critical mass of educated blacks. The viewpoints of both groups had been affected by World War I, though in different ways: white young people lost their belief in humanity, whereas optimism and determination took root among black young people, who believed that their military service entitled them to the social and economic equality that their parents had waited for so patiently. One thing the two groups had in common was their commitment to art and modernity. Among the white writers were T. S. Eliot, Ezra Pound, Edith Wharton, Ernest Hemingway, Sinclair Lewis, Eugene O'Neill, Willa Cather, and F. Scott Fitzgerald. These authors produced a number of works critical of American life and society, and Eliot, Pound, Wharton, and Hemingway became expatriates in Europe. African American writers included Langston Hughes, Countee Cullen; Claude McKay, Wallace Thurman, James Weldon Johnson, Nella Larsen, Jessie Redmon Fauset, Zora Neale Hurston, and Rudolph Fisher. These black writers—and visual artists like Aaron Douglas and Augusta Savage—all met with white publishers at Van Vechten's apartment or at James Weldon Johnson's apartment in Harlem.

Harlem provided a sociopolitical milieu for black bohemia. It was home to a wide range of political ideologies, including the cultural nationalism exemplified by W. E. B. Du Bois, Marcus Garvey's "back to Africa" movement, Charles S. Johnson's sociology of racial advancement, the militant socialism of A. P. Randolph and *The Messenger*, and the radical racial politics of the African Blood Brotherhood. Harlem was also a place where the intelligentsia mingled with the criminal underground and frequented establishments owned by gangsters: the accoutrements of Prohibition allowed interracial socializing, and as in many major cities throughout the 1920s, blacks and whites transcended race, class, and gender.

Prohibition contributed the development of Harem's black bohemia. Laws prohibiting the manufacture, sale, or exportation of alcohol spawned illegal sources of alcoholic drinks and entertainment, beyond the restraint of law and convention. Speakeasies flourished in urban centers nationwide, and Harlem was a hotbed of them. Organized crime provided the management and capital for many of Harlem's legal and illegal nightspots. The presence of criminals and the potential for violence, along with the relaxation of racial and sexual mores, added to the attractiveness of Harlem for both black and white bohemians.

Not all speakeasies were backstreet dives. Some evolved into legitimate nightclubs, but racketeers tended to retain their ownership of clubs that provided black entertainment for white patrons. Many of these establishments became venues for the rapidly evolving African American music scene. Black musical styles migrated to the North and merged to engender new forms. Clubs proliferated; they included Barron's Exclusive Club, Connie's Inn (where Thomas "Fats" Waller played piano for white customers), Connor's Club, Edmond's Cellar, Ed Small's Paradise, the Manhattan Casino on West 155th Street, and the renowned Cotton Club. The Cotton Club, owned by the white gangster Owney Madden, featured "café au lait" women; Cab Calloway and his band included in their repertoire compositions with titles like "Tall, Tan, Terrific" and "Copper Colored Gal of Mine," exemplifying the audience's preference for women of color as entertainers at such a club. Duke Ellington and his orchestra had a twelve-year association with the Cotton Club, during which Ellington popularized a sound called jungle music; this was the sound that white people slumming in Harlem wanted to hear, because it fulfilled their preconceived notion of blacks as exotic. The Cotton Club was on 133rd Street between Lenox and Seventh avenues, a strip known as "Jungle Alley." It was one of eleven clubs in the area.

The Cotton Club catered to a wealthy white clientele. Indeed, it was segregated: the only African Americans who gained admittance were the performers and a handful of black celebrities. Its major patrons were the white international "high bohemian" crowd who traveled to Harlem in their Stutzes and Daimlers and reportedly included Princess Violette Murat, Cecil Beaton (the British artist, designer, and photographer), Gertrude Vanderbilt Whitney (founder of the Whitney Museum of American Art in 1930), Otto Kahn, James J. Walker (mayor of New York from 1926 to 1932), Lady Mountbatten, Libby Holman, Michael Arlen (the British novelist and short-story writer), Beatrice Lillie (the Canadian-born actress), Harry K. Thaw (infamous for murdering the celebrated architect Stanford White), Muriel Draper, and Harold Lloyd (the silent film comedian).

As a result of this surge in the black population, and as a result of the productivity of black literati, artists, and entertainers, new cultural venues such as theaters and ballrooms emerged and contributed to the culture available to black bohemians. These included a number of theaters—the Roosevelt, Douglas, West End, Lincoln, and Lafayette—as well as Hurtig and Seamon's Burlesque (which later became the Apollo Theater), Keith's Alhambra, the Harlem Opera House, and Loew's Seventh Avenue. Ballrooms were inspired by the music of the jazz age; the three most renowned were the Savoy, Renaissance, and Alhambra.

Literary and artistic salons also emerged. A'Lelia Walker held "invitation only" gatherings and soirées for writers, artists, entertainers, and statesmen in her mansion, twin town houses at 108–110 West 136th Street, generally referred to as the "Dark Tower" after Countee Cullen's column in *Opportunity*. This was an important meeting place for black and white artists and writers who came after dark, circumventing the segregation laws. There Langston Hughes, Zora Neale Hurston, Countee Cullen, and many other black literati met successfully with Carl Van Vechten, Mabel Dodge, Nancy Cunard, and other influential white writers, publishers, and philanthropists. A block down the street was one of the better-known black bohemian institutions, "Niggerati Manor," a rooming house at 267 West 136th Street where Wallace Thurman, Zora Neale Hurston, and Langston Hughes lived in the mid-1920s and held far more informal and interesting gatherings of young black writers and artists. A few blocks away Alexander Gumby's studio on Fifth Avenue between 131st and 132nd streets was a place for frequent gatherings of black and white literati where bathtub gin and stronger intoxicants flowed and racial and gender lines blurred.

Like their white counterparts in Greenwich Village, the black bohemians embraced modernity and the counterculture. They were at war with their elders and the bourgeois leadership of the race, especially anyone who attempted to restrict their life and work by imposing racial, political, aesthetic, or sexual barriers. Like their counterparts downtown, they rejected conventional sexual morality and tended toward promiscuity and experimentation. Homosexuality and bisexuality were far more open in Harlem than in Greenwich Village; this may have been one reason for Van Vechten's attraction. Although few works focused specifically on homosexuality (Richard Bruce Nugent's short story of 1926, "Smoke, Lillies, and Jade," is a notable exception), many literary works and songs of the Harlem Renaissance contained references to homosexuality, and many of the people involved in the renaissance experimented with homosexuality or bisexuality.

Homosexuality among black bohemians, especially its appearance in their creative works, was one of the issues separating African American leadership from the movement. Political and intellectual leaders like W. E. B. Du Bois and even Alain Locke argued that too much sexuality of any sort, but especially homosexuality, in black art would reinforce negative white stereotypes of black sexuality and immorality, and harm the race politically. Most of the creative artists rejected this criticism, as well as any effort by the older generation to impose limits on the creative process. Langston Hughes expressed this rejection of the aesthetics and morality of conventional black leadership in 1926, in his essay "The Negro Artist and the Racial Mountain." Also in 1926, the one-issue literary magazine *Fire!!* by Wallace Thurman and his black bohemian cohort reinforced the determination of young black intellectuals to move beyond the values and aesthetics of their elders.

The determination of black writers and artists to assert their independence from conventional values and leadership did not mean that black bohemians were apolitical. On the contrary, politics and political radicalism were at the center of the black bohemian experience. This was especially true during World War I and the immediate postwar period, when the Bolshevik revolution, the racial and social turmoil of the "red summer" of 1919, and the racial militancy associated with the "New Negro" and with Garvey's Universal Negro Improvement Association aroused unprecedented political excitement in Harlem. African American radical and political periodicals like *The Messenger* and *Negro World* joined more mainstream civil rights publications like *The Crisis* and *Opportunity* in publishing and promoting black creative arts. And although no single political viewpoint dominated black bohemia or the creative work of black bohemians, an essential part of their work was politics—generally radical politics. Claude McKay, with his connection to radicals in Greenwich Village and his reputed involvement in the Communist Party, is one example. Langston Hughes is another. Hughes, who seemed to eschew propagandistic art in his essay of 1926, nevertheless cited political differences, especially his refusal to write apolitical poetry, as a cause of his breakup with his patron, Charlotte Osgood Mason. In the 1930s, Hughes, like McKay before him, would travel to the Soviet Union, celebrate the Bolshevik revolution in his writings, and define himself as a "social poet."

Black bohemia was essential to the Harlem Renaissance. It provided a community in which black creative artists and intellectuals operated. Like all bohemian movements, it was characterized by a sense of independence from conventions and from outdated concepts and aesthetics, and it was in rebellion against traditional values and traditional leadership. It embraced modernity and rejected the bourgeois life and values of the previous generation.

ELIZABETH AMELIA HADLEY
CARY D. WINTZ

See also African Blood Brotherhood; Dunbar, Paul Laurence; Eastman, Crystal; Eastman, Max; Europe, James Reese; Fire!!; Frank, Waldo; Garvey, Marcus; Greenwich Village; Homosexuality; Hughes, Langston; Johnson, Charles Spurgeon; Johnson, James Weldon; Johnson, John Rosamond; Joplin, Scott; Liberator; Madden, Owen Vincent "Owney"; McKay, Claude; Morton, Jelly Roll; Nigger Heaven; Seven Arts; Smith, Willie "the Lion"; Tenderloin; Toomer, Jean; Van Vechten, Carl; Walker, A'Lelia; Williams, Egbert Austin "Bert"; *other specific performers, writers, and artists; specific nightclubs*

Further Reading

Anderson, Jervis. *This Was Harlem: A Cultural Portrait, 1900–1950*. New York: Farrar, Straus and Giroux, 1981.

Chauncey, George. *Gay New York: Gender, Urban Culture, and the Makings of the Gay Male World, 1890–1940*. New York: Basic Books, 1994.

Foley, Barbara. *Spectres of 1919: Class and Nation in the Masking of the New Negro*. Urbana: University of Illinois Press, 2003.

Hughes, Langston. *The Big Sea*. New York: Hill and Wang—Farrar, Straus and Giroux, 1997. (Originally published 1940.)

Johnson, James Weldon. *Along This Way: The Autobiography of James Weldon Johnson*. New York: Viking, 1933.

———. *Black Manhattan*. New York: Atheneum, 1968. (First published 1930.)

Osofsky, Gilbert. *Harlem: The Making of a Ghetto—Negro New York, 1890–1930*, 2nd ed. New York: Harper & Row, 1971.

Ottley, Roi. *New World A-Coming*. New York: Arno and New York Times, 1968.

Schoener, Allon, ed. *Harlem on My Mind: Cultural Capital of Black America, 1900–1968.* New York: Random House, 1968.

Stansell, Christ. *American Moderns: Bohemian New York and the Creation of a New Century.* New York: Holt, 2001.

Watson, Steven. *The Harlem Renaissance: Hub of African-American Culture, 1920–1930.* New York: Pantheon, 1995. (Reprint, 1996.)

Black History and Historiography

History and historiography were significant aspects of the Harlem Renaissance, along with artistic expression. The historical tradition among black Americans was informed by two parallel developments. First, black thinkers continued and refined "contributionism"—a late-nineteenth-century trend that emphasized African Americans as participants in and contributors to American life. Second, professional historical organizations and professionally trained historians emerged.

The contributionist tradition had flourished from about 1880 to 1900. Blacks used history as a marker of racial progress, and many "race histories" were published, including George Washington Williams's *History of the Negro Race* (1883), William Alexander's *History of the Colored Race* (1887), William Simmons's *Men of Mark: Eminent, Progressive, and Rising* (1887), Joseph Wilson's *Black Phalanx* (1890), Leila Amos Pendleton's *Narrative of the Negro* (1903), and John Wesley Cromwell's *History of the American Negro* (1915).

Another component of contributionism derived from the largely proto-professional projects of African American literary and historical societies. Early societies often merged the social, political, and intellectual agendas of the rising black middle class with "uplift"—the idea that, for blacks, respectability was a matter of social class and intellectual attainments. The interest in black history among the urban black elite is evident in early literary and historical societies, such as the Bethel Literary and Historical Association (1881, based in Washington, D.C.), the American Negro Academy (1897), and the Negro Society for Historical Research (1911, based in New York).

Bibliophiles were also important. One of the most accomplished collectors was Arthur A. Schomburg. He was born and educated in Puerto Rico, emigrated to the United States in 1891, and established himself as a collector of rare books and manuscripts on the African diaspora. Schomburg was an early proponent of teaching black history in colleges and universities; his widely quoted paper *Racial Integrity* (1913) was one of the first calls for a chair of black history in black colleges. Cognizant that historical work was becoming increasingly professional, Schomburg joined the American Negro Academy in 1914.

Contributionism was perhaps best expressed in Schomburg's essay "The Negro Digs Up His Past" (1925), in Alain Locke's *The New Negro.* This essay emphasizes history as a factor in group identity and describes the maturation of race history. Schomburg argues that the popularizers who simply listed blacks' achievements have been replaced by true historians who present evidence systematically. Although he was critical of white racialists who attributed all of the world's great accomplishments to Europeans, he also criticized "Ethiopian racialists," who did much the same for blacks. Schomburg always sought the contributionist goal—history as a sustainer of group pride and identity—but he also believed in merging contributionism with newer objective, scientific models.

The second development, as noted above, was a professionalized milieu for black history and historians. In the late nineteenth century, American scholars began to move away from the notion of history as an avocation for gentlemen. Drawing on German historiography, which emphasized objectivity and the methods of the natural sciences, Americans created graduate programs in history—for instance, at Johns Hopkins, Wisconsin, Harvard, and Yale universities. The American Historical Association was founded in 1884, the *American Historical Review* in 1895, and the precursor of the Organization of American Historians in 1909.

Carter G. Woodson, the second African American to earn a Ph.D. in history from Harvard University, founded the Association for the Study of Negro Life and History (ASNLH) in 1915. He established the *Journal of Negro History* (*JNH*) the following year, and later Associated Publishers, the publishing arm of the ASNLH. For the first five years of *JNH*, most of its writers were contributionists. After World War I, J. Franklin Jameson, director of the Department of Historical Research at the Carnegie Institution of Washington, supported Woodson with a $25,000 grant from the Carnegie Foundation. As a direct result of that grant, Woodson received a $25,000 grant from the Laura Spelman Rockefeller Memorial Fund, enabling him to hire several investigators who would be instrumental in recasting African American history.

Three investigators during the 1920s were Alrutheus Ambush Taylor, Charles Wesley, and Lorenzo Greene. Taylor had earned a degree in mathematics at the University of Michigan in 1916, and Woodson arranged for him to receive graduate training in history under Edward Channing at Harvard University in 1922. Taylor's studies *The Negro in the Reconstruction of South Carolina* (1924), *The Negro in the Reconstruction of Virginia* (1926), and "Negro Congressmen During Reconstruction" (in the *Journal of Negro History*) challenged the legend of the "tragic era"—John W. Burgess's and William Archibald Dunning's concept of Reconstruction as having been characterized by the political malfeasance and incompetence of blacks supported by the Republican Party. Wesley, a historian trained at Harvard, received his doctorate in 1925 and published his revised dissertation, *Negro Labor in the United States, 1850–1925*, in 1927. Also in 1927, Wesley joined Woodson's staff as a part-time investigator; later, he directed a survey on the African American church. Wesley himself was a minister in the African Methodist Church (AME) and wrote an early scholarly treatment of Bishop Richard Allen. Greene, a graduate of Howard University, joined ASNLH to work on a church research project. After that project ended, he wrote *The Negro Wage Earner* (1930); later, he wrote *The Negro in Colonial New England* (1942).

Woodson himself produced monographs and published the textbook *The Negro in Our History* (1922), one of the first scholarly treatments of the subject and one of the most widely circulated textbooks before John Hope Franklin's *From Slavery to Freedom* (1948). Monographs written or edited by Woodson included *History of the Negro Church* (1921); *The Negro Professional Man and the Community* (1924); *Negro Orators and Orations* (1925); *Free Negro Heads of Families in the United States in 1830* (1925); *Free Negro Owners of Slaves in the United States in 1830* (1925); *The Mind of the Negro as Reflected in Letters Written During the Crisis, 1800–1860* (1926); and *African Myths* (1928).

In 1926, Woodson led the movement for "Negro History Week," to be observed in February (the month when Abraham Lincoln and the abolitionist Frederick Douglass were born). This week highlighted the work of ASNLH and promoted African American history in secondary schools. As ASNLH opened chapters in cities across the country, the annual celebrations of Negro history also extended to the larger white community.

Woodson spent considerable time collecting primary documents on the black experience—scouring black newspapers and maintaining ties with black churches, fraternal organizations, bibliophiles, and literary and historical associations. Printed notices appeared regularly in *JNH*, asking individuals who possessed documents to bring them to ASNLH's offices in Washington, D.C.

In addition to these community-based activities, Woodson had relied on grants from the Carnegie Foundation and the Social Science Research Committee. However, because he insisted on autonomy and refused to affiliate ASNLH with other black organizations, his foundation support eroded. A $25,000 three-year matching grant from the Rockefeller Foundation in 1930 was his last. Thereafter, he turned almost exclusively to the community. Woodson founded the *Negro History Bulletin* in 1937. Despite his contributions to professionalization, he never entirely abandoned contributionism and "uplift."

The emergence of a professional milieu for black history is surely one of the legacies of the Harlem Renaissance. In many ways, historiography, like the renaissance itself, was an outgrowth of migration, urbanization, and industrialization—factors in the rise of urban institutions, such as the black press and literary societies, that gave expression to cultural knowledge and pride. The study and preservation of history served much the same purpose, and it has continued to offer insights into American history.

STEPHEN G. HALL

See also Association for the Study of Negro Life and History and Journal of Negro History; Greene, Lorenzo; New Negro, The; Schomburg, Arthur A.; Woodson, Carter G.

Further Reading

Franklin, John Hope. *George Washington Williams: A Biography*. Chicago, Ill.,: University of Chicago Press, 1985.

———. "On the Evolution of Scholarship in Afro-American Scholarship." In *The State of Afro-American History: Past, Present and Future*, ed. Darlene Clark Hine. Baton Rouge: Louisiana State University Press, 1986.

Goggin, Jacqueline. "Countering White Racist Scholarship: Carter G. Woodson and the Journal of Negro History." *Journal of Negro History*, 68, 1983, pp. 355–375.

———. "Carter G. Woodson and the Movement to Promote Black History, 1915–1950." Ph.D. diss., University of Rochester, 1986.

———. *Carter G. Woodson: Life in Black History*. Baton Rouge: Louisiana State University Press, 1993.

Hall, Stephen G. "Alrutheus Ambush Taylor, Black Intellectualism, and the Remaking of Reconstruction Historiography, 1893–1954." *UCLA Historical Journal*, 16, 1996, pp. 39–60.

Higham, John. *History of Professional Scholarship in America*. Baltimore, Md.: Johns Hopkins University Press, 1983.

Meier, August, and Eliott Rudwick. *Black History and the Historical Profession, 1915–1980*. Urbana: University of Illinois Press, 1986.

Moses, Wilson Jeremiah. *Afrotopia: The Roots of African American Popular History*. Cambridge: Cambridge University Press, 1998.

Sinnette, Elinor Des Verney. *Arthur Alonso Schomburg: Black Bibliophile and Collector—A Biography*. Detroit, Mich.: Wayne State University Press, 1989.

Sinnette, Elinor Des Verney, et al. *Black Bibliophiles and Collectors: Preservers of Black History*. Washington, D.C.: Howard University Press, 1990.

Walker, Clarence. *Deromanticizing Black History: Critical Essays and Appraisals*. Athens: University of Georgia Press, 1991.

Wilson, Francille Rusan. "Racial Consciousness and Black Scholarship: Charles H. Wesley and the Consciousness of Negro Labor in the United States." *Journal of Negro History*, 81, 1996, pp. 72–88.

Black Manhattan

In *Black Manhattan* (1930), James Weldon Johnson intended to provide a history of blacks' progress in theater in New York. What resulted was much more: Johnson produced a history of blacks in New York from the time of its establishment as a colony in 1626 through its heyday at the height of the Harlem Renaissance. *Black Manhattan* is an interdisciplinary history that sets the theatrical successes and global fame of Harlem in the context of many complicated historical, political, and geographical trends up to 1930, the year of its publication. In broad strokes, this book also presents a very general history of blacks in America. Johnson traces Negro life in New York in order to describe how African Americans formed a thriving black community centered in Harlem.

In *Black Manhattan*, Johnson prefers description rather than depth, argument, or analysis, although his descriptions of events and performances are at times quite detailed. The ways that Johnson contextualizes his subject, however, indicate his belief that the condition and progress of Negro culture (to use the terminology of the time and of the text) in the United States relate directly to the struggle against violence and discrimination and the struggle for full citizenship—efforts that took myriad forms throughout American history. The list of historical facts begins with the settlement of New York as a colony in 1926, slavery under the Dutch, and the number of slaves and freedmen in the area at the time. Johnson describes major events in American and African American history and the involvement of black New Yorkers in these events. Among them are the establishment of free education in New York, the manumission and abolition movements, black publications, the colonization movement, New Yorkers and the Civil War, antiblack draft riots, blacks in the military in World War I and the attending antiblack violence, attacks against blacks in cities in 1919, and Marcus Garvey's movement. In relating this history, Johnson focuses on all aspects of performance that gave blacks fame (and sometimes notoriety) in New York, including theater, sports, club life, and music.

In developing the history of theatrical performance, Johnson loosely defines three phases in the development of Negro theater that he unceremoniously names according to their order: the "start of the Negro in American theater," the "middle theatrical period," and the "third theatrical period," which lasted from about 1918 through the 1920s. Johnson categorizes black American theater chronologically and only very informally according to content and trends in performance. Since the characteristics of each theatrical period have as much to do with the state of race relations in the nation and what audiences would accept as with artistic license, the development of black audiences and a broadly visible black cultural presence that accompanied the formation of the Harlem community was a key to the maturation of black theater. Geographical and community development greatly influenced the content and character of black theatrical performance. Thus the concept of "Harlem" as a place, an idea, and a cultural community facilitated artistry and complexity in black theater and influenced the way that Johnson was able to describe theater history. Without such an environment, consistent development and evaluation of theatrical content were only faintly possible.

The first phase, the "start," occurs very roughly between about 1820 and 1880. Although this period included a burgeoning club life that nurtured black artistic talent, it was characterized primarily by black minstrel performances, which were popularized fairly late in the nineteenth century. Several "all-Negro" companies, such as Lew Johnson's Plantation Minstrel Company and the Georgia Minstrels, are described. This period is also sparsely punctuated with classical plays performed by the African Company at the African Grove Theater and the mainly international work of the actor Ira Aldridge.

The second or "middle" phase in black theater begins in the mid- to late nineteenth century. Musical revues and programs produced and performed by black artists dominated this period. Musical comedies by the famous Cole and Johnson, Williams and Walker, and Ernest Hogan are described. Other productions highlighted include *The Octoroons, Oriental America, A Trip to Coontown,* and *Clorindy—The Origin of the Cakewalk.*

The onset of the third theatrical phase was facilitated by what Johnson calls the "conquest of Harlem," a process in which African American real estate developers and residents of New York initiated a complicated and challenging move involving houses to be bought and the surplus of apartments in upper Manhattan in the early 1900s. The "invasion" of this area was the beginning; by 1930, the neighborhood had become home to 200,000 blacks. The characteristics of the third theatrical period have mainly to do with the quantity, diversity, quality, and "seriousness" of the plays and revues.

In the final third of *Black Manhattan* (the last hundred pages or so), Johnson details the theatrical, artistic, and cultural developments of the 1920s. The large amount of theatrical and literary production described in these chapters makes it clear why this decade has been considered the high-water mark of the Harlem Renaissance. Theatrical events that, according to Johnson, changed the status of the Negro in American theater include a revival of *Shuffle Along, All God's Chillun Got Wings, The Emperer Jones, Porgy,* and *The Green Pastures.* The emergence of a number of stars—Florence Mills, Charles Gilpin, Paul Robeson, Bill Robinson, and Ethel Waters, among others—is also described. Literary and poetic works and blacks' efforts in the fine arts are described, along with major productions and plays.

Johnson directly links Harlem—its location, population, community, and history—to the advent of the black renaissance in literature and performance that occurred in the 1920s. He helps us understand why this period was called the *Harlem* Renaissance.

Black Manhattan is a narrative of struggle and accomplishment in which Johnson holds up the rich, diverse culture of this massive northern community of black American citizens for the world's respect and admiration.

STEPHANIE L. BATISTE

See also Blacks in Theater; Emperor Jones, The; Gilpin, Charles; Green Pastures, The; Johnson, James Weldon; Mills, Florence; Porgy: Play; Robeson, Paul; Robinson, Bill "Bojangles"; Shuffle Along; Theater; Waters, Ethel

Further Reading

Bogle, Donald. *Toms, Coons, Mulattoes, Mammies, and Bucks: An Interpretive History of Blacks in American Films.* New York: Continuum, 1998.

Elam, Harry J., and David Krasner, eds. *African-American Performance and Theater History: A Critical Reader.* New York: Oxford University Press, 2001.

Gottschild, Brenda Dixon. *Waltzing in the Dark: African American Vaudeville and Race Politics in the Swing Era.* New York: Palgrave, 2000.

Hatch, James V. *The Black Image on the American Stage: A Bibliography of Plays and Musicals, 1770–1970,* New York: DBS, 1970.

Horton, James, and Lois Horton. *Hard Road to Freedom: The Story of African America.* New Brunswick, N.J.: Rutgers University Press, 2001.

Johnson, James Weldon. *Along This Way: The Autobiography of James Weldon Johnson.* New York, Viking, 1968. (First published 1933.)

———. *The Autobiography of an Ex-Colored Man.* New York: Knopf, 1970.

Krasner, David. *Resistance, Parody, and Double Consciousness in African American Theatre, 1895–1910.* New York: St. Martin's, 1997.

———. *A Beautiful Pageant: African American Theatre, Drama, and Performance in the Harlem Renaissance, 1910–1927.* New York: Palgrave Macmillan, 2002.

Lewis, David Levering. *When Harlem Was in Vogue.* New York: Knopf, 1981.

McKay, Claude. *Harlem: Negro Metropolis.* New York: Dutton, 1940.

Price, Kenneth M., and Lawrence J. Oliver, eds. *Critical Essays on James Weldon Johnson.* New York: G. K. Hall; London: Prentice Hall, 1997.

Wilson, Sondra Kathryn, ed. *The Selected Writings of James Weldon Johnson.* New York: Oxford University Press, 1995.

Woll, Allen. *Dictionary of the Black Theatre: Broadway, Off-Broadway, and Selected Harlem Theatre.* Westport, Conn.: Greenwood, 1983.

———. *Black Musical Theatre: From Coontown to Dreamgirls.* Baton Rouge: Louisiana State University Press, 1989.

Black Migration

See Great Migration; Great Migration and the Harlem Renaissance

Black Opals

A small group of young black intellectuals and creative writers in Philadelphia published three issues of the literary journal *Black Opals* between the spring of 1927 and June 1928. Though it was only a short series, not a true magazine, it was part of a continuing discourse about what was considered the proper direction for blacks' writings.

In almost every good-sized American city at the time, groups of African American "culture nurturers" were supporting literary publications. In Boston, for example, the Quill Club launched the *Saturday Evening Quill.* Although many of these societies were more social than literary, the journals provided a sounding board for the work of writers of the Harlem Renaissance. *Black Opals* was one of the most promising of the Afro-American "little reviews" of the 1920s.

Led by the folklorist, civil rights activist, and educator Arthur Huff Fauset, the venture was originally intended as an outlet for students of the local high school as well as the Philadelphia Normal School, Temple University, and the University of Pennsylvania. It was established because of "the desire of older New Negroes to encourage younger members of the group who demonstrate talent and ambition."

The poet Langston Hughes and the writer Alain Locke lent their influence to the enterprise. Locke wrote "Hail, Philadelphia!" for the first issue in an attempt to close the gap between conservative and radical voices among black writers and scholars. (Arthur Fauset was basically conservative but was willing to present works of either side in his publication.) The first issue also carried three poems by Langston Hughes. The poets Nellie Bright and Mae V. Cowdery were among the other significant figures associated

with *Black Opals.* Contributors to the later issues included the short-story writer Marieta Bonner; the writer Lewis Alexander; and Arthur Fauset's sister, the novelist Jessie Redmon Fauset, who was a former literary editor of W. E. B. Du Bois's periodical *The Crisis.* The poet Gwendolyn Bennett, who taught art at Howard University, was a guest editor of *Black Opals.* The journal exposed a growing reading public to these and other talented literary people.

Countee Cullen, who at that time was the new literary editor of *Opportunity* magazine, praised "some highly commendable material" in the first issue of *Black Opals,* especially two poems by Bright and Cowdery. Cullen also wrote that *Black Opals* "is a venture we should like to see sweeping the country." W. E. B. Du Bois wrote that he was happier with *Black Opals* than he had been with earlier efforts of black writers to publish a literary "little magazine."

The writers in Philadelphia planned to make *Black Opals* a quarterly, but, like other publications of its kind, it did not have sufficient support or a wide enough readership: the subscription list required that only 250 copies of each issue be printed. *Black Opals* ceased publication after the issue of June 1928, which had been prepared by an editorial board. Its presence, though brief, made the point that Harlem was not the sole locale of the black arts movement in the period after World War I.

KATHLEEN COLLINS

See also Bennett, Gwendolyn; Bonner, Marieta; Cowdery, Mae Virginia; Cullen, Countee; Fauset, Arthur Huff; Fauset, Jessie Redmon; Harlem Renaissance in the United States: 6—Philadelphia; Hughes, Langston; Locke, Alain; Saturday Evening Quill

Further Reading

Daniel, Walter C. *Black Journals of the United States.* Westport, Conn.: Greenwood, 1982.

Kellner, Bruce, ed. *The Harlem Renaissance: A Historical Dictionary for the Era.* New York: Methuen, 1984.

Lewis, David Levering. *When Harlem Was in Vogue.* New York: Penguin, 1987.

Black Press

The black press flourished during the Harlem Renaissance. There were many reasons for its success. First, the massive increase in northern black urban populations as a result of the "great migration" of black southerners in the years beginning about 1915 provided northern black newspapers with a greatly expanded circulation. For example, the circulation of the Baltimore *Afro-American* rose from 19,200 a week in 1919 to 40,432 in 1930 (from its Baltimore and out-of-town editions). Other black newspapers saw similar increases in circulation. Second, the black migrants hungered for news about themselves and the communities they had moved to. Black newspapers, especially the Chicago *Defender*, Pittsburgh *Courier*, and Baltimore *Afro-American*, satisfied this hunger by offering intensive, often sensationalistic coverage of news relevant to black audiences. Third, increased circulation made the black press more attractive to advertisers who wanted blacks to purchase their products. Fourth, the increased wealth of black newspapers enabled these enterprises to upgrade their staffs and physical plants, provide a stronger institutional base for black journalists, and create outlets for the black essayists, poets, playwrights, and novelists of the Harlem Renaissance.

It is useful to consider what a black newspaper looked like in the era of the Harlem Renaissance, and the Baltimore *Afro-American* will serve as a representative example. The *Afro-American* typifies the black press of the Harlem Renaissance. It was the most widely circulated black newspaper on the East Coast, and it matched the Pittsburgh *Courier* and Chicago *Defender* in national impact. The *Afro-American* constantly crusaded for racial reform, especially in jobs, politics, housing, and education. These topics, as well as civil rights, black uplift, crime, sports, entertainment, and society news, dominated its pages.

A typical issue of the *Afro-American* in the 1920s was that of 24 April 1926. Its front page headlined the discovery of the body of the Reverend J. E. Fitchett, who had been a prominent black minister on the eastern shore of Maryland and had been missing for three months after being caught with the wife of a parishioner. The front page also carried an account of an interracial conference in Birmingham, Alabama, at which Will Alexander, chairman of the Commission on Interracial Cooperation, called for an end to Jim Crow laws and an end to the occupation of Haiti. Also on the front page were stories dealing with a divorce suit, a conference of African Methodist Episcopal (AME) ministers, and two black students who had won Guggenheim fellowships.

Pages 2 and 3 contained news from Washington, D.C., and advertisements. The fourth, fifth, and sixth pages were the entertainment pages; they carried copious advertisements for motion picture and vaudeville theaters, dance halls, and cabarets in Baltimore that catered to blacks. Pages 7 and 8 were the sports pages; they dealt with Negro League baseball, black college baseball, boxing, tennis, and the Penn Relays track and field competition. Advertisements—mostly for cigars, clothing, and quack doctors—were also found on the sports pages. The ninth page was Baltimore society news. Page 10 was local Baltimore news, mostly having to do with crime.

Page 11 was the editorial page; this was the most serious section of the *Afro-American*. The editorials on 24 April commented on President Calvin Coolidge's inaction concerning black disenfranchisement in the South; on the appointment of a black to the executive committee of the American Federation of Labor; and on Dartmouth College's awarding of a prize for achievement in biology to Lowell Wormley, a black student. Also on the editorial page was the column of letters to the editor. Among them was one complaining about the *Afro-American*'s campaign for more black Republican patronage in the South. Another congratulated the newspaper for its championing of exploited black workers. A third described how conditions on Pennsylvania Avenue, the "main street of Black Baltimore," were leading black youngsters to crime. Completing the editorial page were columns by Kelly Miller, a dean of Howard University; William N. Jones, city editor of the *Afro-American*; and Ralph Matthews Sr.

The rest of the *Afro-American* consisted of more society news from Baltimore; a magazine section, which featured the short stories "On the Rock" and "Home Made Goods"; and miscellaneous local news. Church news and announcements, a survey of local black business, court news, and the classified section filled the final pages.

The Chicago *Defender* and the Pittsburgh *Courier*—which were the chief national competitors of the *Afro-American*—tended to publish the same type of news, though with differing emphases and in different formats. On 24 April 1926, the *Defender* and the *Courier* both headlined stories of domestic scandals: the *Defender* reported that a police raid had caught a prominent black minister in bed with a nineteen-year-old woman; the *Courier* reported that a young black woman had shot and wounded a man who was pestering her with unwanted attentions. Both the *Defender* and the *Courier*, owing to their national status and reputation, carried more national news on their front pages than the *Afro-American*. Otherwise, however, the *Defender* and the *Courier* carried the same mixture as the *Afro-American*: local news—mostly about crime, reported as sensationally as possible; society; theater; and sports—and service features.

The editorial page was not as extensive in the *Defender* as in the *Afro-American*; the *Defender* had only one signed column, on health, whereas the *Afro-American* had three. The editorial page of the *Courier* was more like that in the *Afro-American*: the *Courier* carried two signed columns dealing with current issues, one by Walter White of the National Association for the Advancement of Colored People (NAACP), and the other by George Schuyler, who fancied himself a black H. L. Mencken. All three newspapers had congruent editorial ideologies, though in depth and breadth of editorial opinion the *Afro-American* was superior to the other two.

Black newspapers such as the *Afro-American* also covered and commented on national issues such as presidential elections, which they tried to influence by endorsing candidates; Marcus Garvey's movement; and the Harlem Renaissance.

Black voters were a growing force in the North, and black newspapers attempted to harness that force through endorsements for president. In 1924, for example, the Pittsburgh *Courier* and the Chicago *Defender*—both longtime supporters of the Republican Party—endorsed Calvin Coolidge (a Republican) over the candidate of the Democratic Party, John W. Davis. The *Afro-American*, however, broke with the two major parties by endorsing a third-party candidate, Robert La Follette, a Progressive, because he supported voting rights in the South and equal employment opportunity and specifically opposed the Ku Klux Klan, discrimination in the allocation of federal patronage, and lynching. The editors of the *Afro-American* felt that neither of the other two candidates had such an impressive record on black people's concerns. In the election, Coolidge won a landslide victory over Davis, and La Follette won no electoral votes at all (though he did win some 5 million popular votes). Its maverick endorsement of La Follette in 1924 cost the *Afro-American* influence and prestige in national black Republican circles.

In 1928, the *Afro-American* again broke from the pack and endorsed the Democratic candidate for president, Governor Alfred E. Smith of New York, whose record on race relations seemed more progressive than that of his Republican opponent, Herbert Hoover. Smith was the first Catholic to run for president, and the *Afro-American* believed that the religious bigotry he had experienced made him sensitive to the plight of other oppressed minorities. In this election, the *Afro-American* was not the only black newspaper to desert the Republican Party and support a Democratic candidate; it was joined by the Norfolk *Journal and Guide*, the Boston *Guardian*, and the Atlanta *Independent*. But the two largest black newspapers—the Chicago *Defender* and Pittsburgh *Courier*—remained in the Republican fold, as did *New York Age* and the New York *Amsterdam News* in Smith's home state. These newspapers questioned Smith's commitment to racial reform, since his running mate was a segregationist senator from Arkansas, Joseph T. Robinson. As in 1924, the endorsement of the *Afro-American* did its candidate no good: Smith was buried in Hoover's landslide victory. However, the *Afro-American* was no longer isolated in its independence from the Republican Party with regard to presidential endorsements.

The black press was ambivalent toward Marcus Garvey's movement. Garvey, a Jamaican printer and social activist, emigrated to the United States in 1916. The next year he founded the Universal Negro Improvement Association (UNIA), which was based in Harlem; by 1919, he had built the UNIA to a point where it claimed to have more than 2 million members. Though its membership figures may have been exaggerated, the UNIA and Garvey, its "provisional president," had become important forces in black America. The UNIA owned a newspaper, *Negro World*; owned an auditorium, Liberty Hall, which seated some 6,000 people; and operated several businesses, the most prominent of which was the Black Star Line, a steamship venture to promote trade between black America, Africa, and the world. Nothing like Garvey's movement had ever occurred in black America. For the first time a black advancement organization was gaining widespread support among the black masses, who hitherto had made their desires known only through migration.

Some black newspapers, such as the *Courier* and the *Afro-American*, initially supported Garvey's movement, believing that it was a positive influence in its emphasis on racial pride, solidarity, and enterprise, and that its goal of an independent, powerful Africa was a worthy one. Other newspapers, such as the *Defender* and *New York Age*, were harshly critical of Garvey. For example, *New York Age* ridiculed his plans for Africa, and the Chicago *Defender*—black America's leading newspaper—disparaged him. Moreover, the editor of the *Defender*, Robert S. Abbott, signed a letter to the U.S. attorney general, Harry Daugherty, asking him to investigate Garvey for mail fraud in connection with the sale of stock in the Black Star Line.

Garvey's black nationalism was more appealing to the black masses than the assimilationist doctrines expressed by the middle class through such organizations as the NAACP. Black newspapers such as the *Afro-American*, while supporting racial integration as an ultimate goal, advocated a kind of black nationalism, constantly calling for the creation of black businesses, the establishment of an independent black vote, and black control of institutions serving blacks. This position accounts for the benign treatment that Garvey received from some of these newspapers in the years preceding his trial for mail fraud. However, by the time the trial took place, the black press had pretty much broken with Garvey. This was probably because the middle-class owners of black newspapers wanted men like themselves to lead the masses—not a man like Marcus Garvey, whose flamboyance, bombast, and financial incompetence disturbed their sensibilities.

Black newspapers in major markets, such as the *Afro-American*, encouraged the outburst of literary and artistic creativity known as the Harlem Renaissance. In its feature pages, the *Afro-American* published poems and essays by Langston Hughes, Countee Cullen, and Claude McKay. It also encouraged young black writers by publishing serials or short stories in its magazine section (in 1950, Nick Aaron Ford compiled and published a selection of these short stories). The Chicago *Defender* employed Langston Hughes, and George Schuyler—one of the leading columnists, essayists, novelists, and satirists of the era—wrote not only for the Pittsburgh *Courier* but also for A. Phillip Randolph and Chandler Owen's magazine *The Messenger*, which employed Wallace Thurman as well. Garvey's *Negro World* initially supported aspects of the Harlem Renaissance, though it turned against the renaissance from 1923 on, owing to its distaste for the more bohemian aspects of the renaissance.

Apart from the major-market black newspapers with a regional or nationwide circulation, it is not clear how, if at all, the Harlem Renaissance affected or was affected by the black press. Neither of the two main surveys of the black press in the hinterlands (Suggs 1983, 1996) mentions coverage or critiques of writers of the renaissance in black newspapers—although each survey discusses the development of these newspapers as businesses and their political and civil rights crusades. Presumably, these regional newspapers devoted some attention to the Harlem Renaissance, but the specific details are no longer known (much work needs to be done in this regard). The large-circulation black newspapers did publish some of the writers of the Harlem Renaissance, but their editorial attitude toward these writers is not clear. Presumably, given the middle-class orientation and sensibilities of the editors, the major black newspapers—especially the *Afro-American*—would not have looked favorably on such works as Carl Van Vechten's *Nigger Heaven* or Claude Mc Kay's *Home to Harlem*, which offered explicit depictions of black life. These editors would have sided with W. E. B. Du Bois, who felt that black art should uplift black life and protest against racism, since their newspapers emphasized those points as well. (Again, though, much work needs to be done on this topic.)

As noted above, the major black newspapers such as the *Afro-American*, *Defender*, and *Courier* supported the Harlem Renaissance to some extent; and the black magazines *The Crisis*, *Opportunity*, *The Messenger*, and *Fire!!* supported it even more. *The Crisis*, the magazine of the NAACP, was edited by Du Bois and employed the novelist Jessie Fauset as its literary editor. Fauset encouraged and was one of the earliest publishers of Langston Hughes and Jean Toomer. Du Bois, who was a novelist himself, favored the promotion and publication of young black writers. In 1924, *The Crisis* began a literary contest, and in 1926, it published a symposium called "The Negro in Art: How Shall He Be Portrayed?" Through such activities Du Bois and *The Crisis* hoped to determine the course of the Harlem Renaissance. However, with the publication in 1926 of Carl Van Vechten's *Nigger Heaven* and in 1928 of Claude McKay's *Home to Harlem*, Du Bois turned from a supporter to a critic of the renaissance. Though he was becoming more radical in his politics, Du Bois was culturally conservative, and both novels presented a slice of African American life that he felt should not be portrayed. Jessie Fauset, a leading supporter of the Harlem Renaissance, left *The Crisis* in 1927; with her departure, the magazine deemphasized coverage of this literary phenomenon.

Opportunity, the magazine of the Urban League, edited by Charles Spurgeon Johnson, helped to give birth to the Harlem Renaissance by sponsoring literary contests and prizes beginning in 1925. Among the winners were Sterling Brown, Arna Bontemps, Zora Neale Hurston, and Langston Hughes. Though Johnson is better known as a sociologist, he made a valuable contribution to the Harlem Renaissance by encouraging, publishing, and awarding prizes to some of the literary lights of that period.

The Messenger, a radical socialist magazine published by A. Phillip Randolph and Chandler Owen, also provided an outlet for writers of the Harlem Renaissance. Its most important contribution was

"These Colored United States," a series of articles it ran between 1923 and 1926, giving a panoramic view of black American communities at the time. *Fire!!*, which began publication in 1926, was the only periodical established and edited by members of the Harlem Renaissance. It was edited by Wallace Thurman, and its contributors and editors included Langston Hughes, Zora Neale Hurston, Aaron Douglas, Countee Cullen, and Arna Bontemps. Its unvarnished depictions of black life provoked extreme reactions in the black middle class and among black intellectuals; some loved it for its dedication to the truth, whereas others hated it for its sometimes unflattering portrayals of black life. *Fire!!* never gained enough financial support to be viable; it lasted for only a few issues.

Black newspapers were an integral resource for the black community of the Harlem Renaissance. Without the black press, that community would have been voiceless and powerless. It was black periodicals such as *Opportunity, The Crisis, The Messenger,* and *Fire!!* that provided the main print outlets for the poets, essayists, and novelists of the Harlem Renaissance. If not for black newspapers and magazines, the social, political, and cultural gains of the Harlem Renaissance would have been impossible.

HAYWARD "WOODY" FARRAR

See also Amsterdam News; Baltimore Afro-American; Chicago Defender; Crisis, The; Crisis, The: Literary Prizes; Crisis: The Negro in Art—How Shall He Be Portrayed? A Symposium; Fire!!; Garvey, Marcus; Garveyism; Harlem Renaissance: 1—Black Critics of; Journalists; Messenger, The; Miller, Kelly; Negro World; New York Age; Opportunity; Opportunity Literary Contests; Party Politics; Pittsburgh Courier; Schuyler, George S.; Universal Negro Improvement Association; White, Walter; *specific writers*

Further Reading

Baltimore *Afro-American*. 1919–1930.
Buni, Andrew. *Robert L. Vann of the Pittsburgh Courier.* Pittsburgh, Pa.: University of Pittsburgh Press, 1974.
Chicago *Defender*. 1919–1930.
Farrar, Hayward. *The Baltimore Afro-American, 1892–1950.* Westport, Conn.: Greenwood, 1998.
Ford, Nick A. *Best Short Stories by Afro-American Writers 1925–1950.* Boston: Meador Pub. Co. 1950.
Huggins, Nathan Irvin. *Harlem Renaissance.* New York: Oxford University Press, 1971.
Johnson, Abby Arthur, and Ronald Mayberry. *Propaganda and Aesthetics: The Literary Politics of Afro-American Magazines in the Twentieth Century.* Amherst: University of Massachusetts Press, 1979.
Johnson, James Weldon. *Black Manhattan.* New York: Knopf, 1940. (Reprint, New York: Arno, 1968.)
Kornweibel, Theodore Jr. *No Crystal Stair: Black Life and* The Messenger. Westport, Conn.: Greenwood, 1975.
Lewis, David Levering. *When Harlem Was in Vogue.* New York: Knopf, 1981.
———. *W. E. B. Du Bois: The Fight for Equality and the American Century, 1919–1963.* New York: Holt, 2000.
New York Age. 1919–1928.
Osofsky, Gilbert. *Harlem: The Making of a Ghetto.* New York: Harper & Row, 1966.
Ottley, Roi. *The Lonely Warrior: The Life and Times of Robert S. Abbott.* Chicago, Ill.: Regnery, 1955.
Pittsburgh *Courier*. 1919–1930.
Pride, Armistead. *A History of the Black Press.* Washington, D.C.: Howard University Press, 1997.
Stein, Judith. *The World of Marcus Garvey: Race and Class in Modern Society.* Baton Rouge: Louisiana State University Press, 1986.
Suggs, H. Lewis, ed. *The Black Press in the South, 1865–1979.* Westport, Conn.: Greenwood, 1983.
Suggs, H. Lewis. *P. B. Young, Newspaperman: Race, Politics, and Journalism in the New South.* Charlottesville: University Press of Virginia, 1988.
Suggs, H. Lewis, ed. *The Black Press in the Middle West, 1865–1985.* Westport, Conn.: Greenwood, 1996.
Vincent, Theodore G. *Voices of a Black Nation: Political Journalism in the Harlem Renaissance.* Trenton, N.J.: Africa World, 1973.
Vogel, Todd. *The Black Press: New Literary and Historical Essays.* New Brunswick, N.J.: Rutgers University Press, 2001.
Weiss, Nancy J. *The National Urban League, 1910–1940.* New York: Oxford University Press, 1974.
Wintz, Cary. *Black Culture and the Harlem Renaissance.* Houston, Tex.: Rice University Press, 1988.
Wolseley, Roland E. *The Black Press U.S.A.* Ames: Iowa State University Press, 1971.

Black Star Line

Black Star Line Steamship Corporation was founded in Harlem in June 1919 and lasted until 1922. It was established under the auspices of the Universal Negro

Black Star Line, certificate for one share, issued in November 1919. (Schomburg Center for Research in Black Culture, New York Public Library.)

Improvement Association (UNIA) and the stewardship of Marcus Garvey and was an integral part of Garvey's "back to Africa" program. The company was a manifestation of his desire to help blacks achieve economic independence and to give African migrants across the world a sense of unity.

With the enthusiastic participation of UNIA's membership, Garvey raised the money for this venture. Shares valued at $5 each were sold at UNIA meetings and through mailed circulars, traveling agents, and advertisements in the newspaper *Negro World*. Nearly $200,000 was raised in less than four months. Much of the capital came from the working poor of the Caribbean and the United States.

The available capital allowed Garvey to purchase a ship just months after Black Star's incorporation. The company's first vessel, the SS *Yarmouth*, which Garvey intended to rename the *Frederick Douglass*, set sail with an all-black crew on 31 October 1919. Thousands crowded the dock at 135th Street in Harlem to witness the event. However, the *Yarmouth*, which had transported coal in World War I, was in poor condition when the UNIA bought it for $165,000, and on its maiden voyage for Black Star, fears about poor equipment and a lack of proper insurance kept the ship's crew from venturing past the Twenty-third Street pier.

Two other ships joined the line in 1920: the SS *Shadyside*, and the steam yacht *Kanawha*, renamed SS *Antonio Maceo*. All three ships were commissioned to transport manufactured goods, raw materials, and produce for black businesses in North America, the Caribbean, and Africa. The backers hoped that the enterprise would allow African Americans to return to Africa and would also enable black people around the Atlantic to exchange goods and services. Unfortunately, in the autumn the *Shadyside* sank, after having provided only passenger travel on the Hudson River; and the *Kanawha* blew a boiler on its maiden voyage, killing a man onboard.

Mismanagement and expensive repairs severely disrupted the operations of the fleet. In February 1922, Garvey was indicted on charges of mail fraud related to promotional claims made for the Black Star Line during the company's sale of stock. Soon afterward he suspended company operations. Estimates of Black Star's losses were as high as $1.25 million. Garvey was eventually convicted of mail fraud in 1923 and imprisoned in 1925 as the Justice Department pursued legal action, bolstered by information from J. Edgar Hoover's Federal Bureau of Investigation (an organization that Garvey's supporters accused of sabotage). The government later commuted Garvey's sentence, only to deport him to Jamaica in November 1927.

The troubles of the Black Star Line were chronicled by two African American leaders—W. E. B. Du Bois and A. Philip Randolph—who cautioned black Americans about investing in schemes that required operational complexity but had no proper management. Still, Garvey was a respected advocate for African culture and progress. He believed that mass urban organization by African Americans in the North could provide the necessary wealth and unity to combat imperialism in Africa and discrimination in the United States. The Black Star Line was a symbol of unfulfilled potential during a period of dynamic change in Harlem.

R. JAKE SUDDERTH

See also Garvey, Marcus; Negro World; Universal Negro Improvement Association

Further Reading

Cronon, David E. *Black Moses: The Story of Marcus Garvey and the United Universal Negro Improvement Association.* Madison: University of Wisconsin Press, 1969.

Hill, Robert A., ed. *The Marcus Garvey and Universal Negro Improvement Association Papers.* Berkeley: University of California Press, 1983.

Johnson, James Weldon. *Along This Way: The Autobiography of James Weldon Johnson.* New York: Viking, 1961.

Meier, August. *Negro Thought in America, 1880–1915.* Ann Arbor: University of Michigan Press, 1966.

Moses, Wilson J. *The Golden Age of Black Nationalism, 1850–1925*. Hamden, Conn.: Archon, 1978.

Redkey, Edwin S. *Black Exodus, Black Nationalist, and Back-to-Africa Movements*. New Haven, Conn.: Yale University Press, 1969.

Stein, Judith. *The World of Marcus Garvey: Race and Class in Modern Society*. Baton Rouge: Louisiana State University Press, 1986.

Watson, Steven. *The Harlem Renaissance: Hub of African-American Culture*. New York: Pantheon, 1995.

Black Swan Phonograph Company

Black Swan Phonograph Company was the first record label substantially owned and operated by African Americans. It advertised its product as "the only records made entirely by colored people," though that claim was true only for the first year of its existence. The label was named after a nineteenth-century African American classical singer, Elizabeth Taylor Greenfield, who was known as the "black swan." Its proprietor, Harry H. Pace, had been a banker and insurance executive in Memphis, Tennessee, when he met the bandleader and composer W. C. Handy around 1905. The two formed the Pace and Handy Music Publishing Company in 1907, with Pace managing the business, while Handy composed the music. They had only modest success until Handy's "Saint Louis Blues" (1914), the first blues song published, was a national sensation. Business picked up, and they moved their operation to New York in 1918, considering themselves uniquely positioned to publish music by African American composers.

Immediately following World War I, recorded music became increasingly popular, and publishers and other businesspeople were scrambling to produce records. Equally important to Pace, a black entrepreneur in music, was the success of Okeh Records' "race" recordings (music performed by blacks), particularly Mamie Smith's two blues hits for the Okeh label in 1920. These records sold in the hundreds of thousands, especially among southern blacks, a fact not lost on the entire record industry, which had never seriously marketed to African Americans. Other white-owned labels rushed to follow Okeh's lead, and Pace saw an opportunity to enter the field. In 1921, he severed his ties with W. C. Handy and opened the Pace Phonographic Company to produce records under the Black Swan label. After a difficult three-month search for a pressing plant (competition was fierce, and the problem was compounded by racism), he secured a deal and began to hire a staff. Pace lured away from Handy's publishing firm Fletcher Henderson, to direct the musical operations, and the composer William Grant Still, as chief arranger. Serving on the board of directors of the upstart label were W. E. B. Du Bois and the African American real estate developer John E. Nail.

Harry Pace fundamentally agreed with many leaders of the Harlem Renaissance that the true future of African American music lay not in the "lower" folk idioms of blues and jazz but in classical genres. Black musicians would be seen as the equals of white Americans or Europeans on the concert stage, and black composers would demonstrate the value of black musical themes in works composed for orchestras and chamber and vocal ensembles. Thus Pace sought to build a varied catalog of light and serious classical music, as well as more popular dance bands and jazz and blues vocals. It is the jazz and blues recordings, however, that brought financial success and represent some of the most important documents of black popular music in New York during the early 1920s.

After a series of mediocre light classical recordings, the first important success for Black Swan came in the spring of 1921, when the black vaudeville and blues singer Ethel Waters recorded "Down Home Blues" and "Oh Daddy." Waters, Henderson, and other Black Swan artists toured black vaudeville theaters as the Black Swan Troubadours in 1921 and early 1922, bringing increased attention to the label. The outstanding sales of its blues line suddenly put Black Swan on the same level as Columbia and Okeh in the "race records" market, and Pace began to expand his catalog to include more blues artists. Alberta Hunter, Trixie Smith, and Lucille Hegamin all had hits in 1921, presenting a problem for Pace—the need for more recording facilities. In April 1922, Pace entered a partnership with John Fletcher, a white businessman who had an interest in the struggling Olympic Records, and the team purchased Olympic's former pressing plant. Also, the Olympic catalog, consisting exclusively of white popular and classical musicians, devolved to Black Swan Records.

With these moves, Pace's company seemed the mirror image of white-owned labels that had ventured into recording black musicians and had begun to hire black staff members to produce their race records. Yet the company publicly maintained the image of an exclusively African American enterprise. Its advertisement in the *Chicago Defender* in February 1923 claimed that "[A]ll stockholders are Colored, all artists are Colored, all employees are Colored"; its black clientele, however, did not know that the company featured white bands such as Fred Smith's Society Orchestra and Henderson's Dance Orchestra.

Regardless, Pace attempted to fulfill his mission to record black concert artists, and in 1922 he began an opera series featuring African American singers including the soprano Antoinette Gaines of the Chicago Grand Opera. However, the blues and jazz recordings of Alberta Hunter, Trixie Smith, and other singers were actually the mainstay of the label, as there was simply no substantial market among its African American customers for classical music or the lighter popular fare performed by white and black acts. The true market for race records was to be found among southern black audiences, where there was no interest in classical forms. White-owned companies could unabashedly sell blues and jazz to these markets while retaining their white audiences by offering more familiar fare, an option not open to Pace.

This was not the only problem for Pace and Black Swan. By early 1923, the emergence of radio had devastated the young, fragile recording industry, leaving many companies struggling for survival. Moreover, the Columbia and Paramount labels had tremendous success with Bessie Smith and Gertrude "Ma" Rainey, respectively, and Paramount had lured Ethel Waters, Trixie Smith, and Alberta Hunter away from Black Swan with more lucrative contracts. Both Columbia and Paramount had hired African Americans to run their race records lines and had created their own rosters of prominent black musicians. By late fall 1923, Pace declared bankruptcy and leased his catalog to Paramount, which reissued the recordings by the black stars.

Many Black Swan artists, who had not achieved success, never recorded again. Pace left the music business altogether and served many years as president of the Supreme Liberty Life Insurance Company.

WILLIAM J. NANCARROW

See also Hegamin, Lucille; Henderson, Fletcher; Hunter, Alberta; Nail, John E.; Pace Phonographic Company; Rainey, Gertrude "Ma"; Saint Louis Blues; Smith, Mamie; Smith, Trixie; Still, William Grant; Waters, Ethel

Further Reading

Allen, Walter C. *Hendersonia: The Music of Fletcher Henderson and His Musicians: A Bio-Discography.* Highland Park, N.J.: Walter C. Allen, 1973.

Thygesen, Helge, with Mark Berresford and Russ Shor. *Black Swan: The Record Label of the Harlem Renaissance.* Nottingham, England: VJM, 1996.

Waters, Ethel, with Samuel Charters. *His Eye Is on the Sparrow.* New York: Doubleday, and London: W. H. Allen, 1951.

Black Zionism

Black Zionism is the name given collectively to the movements among blacks of the diaspora for self-determination, economic independence, and cultural renewal. Since the mid-1960s, scholars in African American studies have used the term "diaspora," borrowed from the Jewish tradition, to refer to the historical experience of blacks who were forcibly transferred from their African homelands to the new world by European slave traders. Despite significant differences, the African diaspora and the Jewish diaspora are both understood as exile from a lost ancestral homeland. With the advent of various nationalist movements in nineteenth-century Europe, Jewish leaders such as Theodor Herzl (1860–1904), Moses Hess (1812–1875), and Leo Pinsker (1821–1891) argued that Jews needed a sovereign state of their own in order to end centuries of oppression and restore ethnic pride and unity. These leaders were called Zionists, after a biblical name for the ancient kingdoms of Israel and Judea, which the legendary descendants of the Jews had lost to the Romans and other invaders in the first century after Christ. Herzl's political tract *The Jewish State* (1896) and his astute leadership of the World Zionist Organization had a profound influence on the beliefs and practices of black leaders such as Edward Wilmot Blyden (1832–1912), W. E. B. Du Bois, and Marcus Garvey, who advocated various strategies for political and economic liberation and greater race consciousness in the African diaspora.

Since the beginning of slavery in the new world, there have been numerous efforts by individuals and groups to return slaves and free blacks to Africa. These efforts are based on a utopian belief that blacks and whites should live separately for the good of all concerned. Early instances of separatist organizing include the Free African Societies of the 1780s and Abraham Lincoln's emigration plan of 1862. After Reconstruction came to an untimely end with the Compromise of 1877, black leaders like Blyden and Bishop Henry M. Turner (1834–1915) of the African Methodist Episcopalian Church abandoned the hope that blacks could ever achieve real equality as a minority group in a racist culture. In the years before World War I, these men and others raised funds, wrote propaganda, and founded steamship companies to encourage diaspora blacks to resettle in independent West African states such as Liberia, Sierra Leone, and the Gold Coast (Ghana).

In his pamphlet *The Jewish Question* (1898), Blyden commended Herzl's bold political vision and his tremendous influence among European Jews. He also called on Jews "to come . . . to the assistance of Ishmael in the higher work for Africa which Japheth, through a few struggling representatives, is laboring heroically under great disadvantages to carry out." Blyden's invocation of biblical metaphors was not only a strategy for reaching out to religious Jews but also part of the black Protestant tradition of mythologizing the diaspora with figures borrowed from scripture. John Gibbs St. Clair Drake (Washington 1984) has suggested that the Jewish patriarchs have had a distinct resonance for diaspora blacks, who, like the ancient Israelites, longed for both political deliverance and spiritual redemption: the spirituals and sermons of black churches, the jazz songs of Louis Armstrong, and the poetry of James Weldon Johnson and Paul Laurence Dunbar are full of allusions to the Hebrew Bible.

In the Harlem of the 1920s, one of Blyden's most ardent admirers, Marcus Garvey, led a second wave of black separatist activity that was especially popular with lower-class urban blacks who could not benefit from philanthropic initiatives like Booker T. Washington's Tuskegee Institute. Garvey was born in Jamaica, where he founded the Universal Negro Improvement Association (UNIA) in 1914. He came to the United States in early 1916 and went on the lecture circuit, touring thirty-eight states before establishing a branch of the UNIA in Harlem that same year. Although he began by addressing the black elite, he soon took to the streets, where his gift for oratory drew great crowds. In Garvey's speeches, he extolled the virtues of the racially pure Negro and the superior achievements of ancient African civilization, claiming

that whites had insidiously suppressed history and had taught diaspora blacks to hate their own bodies. He also announced the goals of the UNIA, which were to encourage stronger economic, political, and cultural ties between Africans around the world; to agitate against European colonization of the African continent; and to enact "back to Africa," a massive emigration and resettlement program. To further these goals, Garvey and other executives of the UNIA—including his second wife, Amy Jacques Garvey—established a merchant marine, the Black Star Line; a newspaper, *Negro World*; and a manufacturing chain, the Negro Factories Corporation, which was operated entirely by blacks.

The driving force behind the UNIA was Garvey's vision of a prosperous, proud, unified black people, a vision that has been called pan-Africanism. Representatives of the UNIA, many of them West Indians or native Africans, often spoke of the common ground of Garvey's pan-Africanism and Jewish Zionism. Because of his charismatic and often theatrical style of leadership, Garvey was nicknamed the "black Moses" (similarly, many Jews were inspired to describe Herzl in messianic terms).

Garvey's program, like that of the Jewish Zionists, had aesthetic as well as political and economic dimensions. The newspaper of the UNIA, *Negro World*, published many leading writers of the Harlem Renaissance, including Zora Neale Hurston, Claude McKay, and Alain Locke, as well as international figures like the Egyptian nationalist Duse Mohamed Ali. These writers contributed poetry, reviews, polemical essays, and journalistic sketches of Africa, all of which exhibited a general concern for promoting pan-African consciousness in the diaspora. Tony Martin has collected some of the best writing from *Negro World*, including articles by Garvey himself, as part of the New Marcus Garvey Library series.

Garvey's incendiary comments on racial matters and his mismanagement of the UNIA's business ventures often provoked the ire of political opponents such as W. E. B. Du Bois, the chief founder of the National Association for the Advancement of Colored People (NAACP), whose own newspaper, *The Crisis*, was unsparing in its criticism of Garvey's movement. The story of Garvey's legal entanglements that led to his political demise can be read elsewhere. But it is important that Garvey and Du Bois, despite their mutual hatred, were both pan-Africanists who modeled some of their rhetorical and administrative strategies on the successes of Jewish Zionism. In fact, it was Du Bois who convened the first Pan-African Congress in Paris in 1919, a year before Garvey's own international gathering at Liberty Hall. Du Bois wrote many articles, pamphlets, and scholarly books about African culture and history, and eventually settled in Ghana as a distinguished citizen. In his essay "The Negro's Fatherland" (1917), Du Bois wrote, "The African movement means to us what the Zionist movement means to the Jews." As a committed socialist and a person of multiracial descent, Du Bois argued for the cooperation of whites and blacks in the struggle for basic human freedoms, yet he also insisted that group identity and the preservation of inherited traditions were essential to the continued progress of civilization.

Black Zionism never had much appeal for middle-class blacks of the 1920s and 1930s, who tended to favor either the pragmatic approach of Booker T. Washington or the policy of the Communist Party, "self-determination in the black belt"; however, its broad legacy extends through radicals of the 1960s like Malcolm X and the Black Panthers to contemporary pan-Africanists like Louis Farrakhan and Ntozake Shange. Furthermore, the Afrocentric aesthetic experiments of the cohort at *Negro World*, as well as similar experiments by writers like Langston Hughes and Richard Wright, were highly instrumental in shaping the black cultural revolution that is known today as the Harlem Renaissance.

DARYN GLASSBROOK

See also Black Star Line; Du Bois, W. E. B.; Garvey, Marcus; Negro World; Pan-Africanism; Universal Negro Improvement Association

Further Reading

Drachler, Jacob, ed. *Black Homeland/Black Diaspora: Cross-Currents of the African Relationship.* Port Washington, N.Y.: Kennikat, 1975.

Du Bois, W. E. B. *The Dusk of Dawn: An Essay Toward an Autobiography of a Race Concept.* New York: Schocken, 1968.

———. *The World and Africa.* Milwood, N.Y.: Kraus-Thomson, 1976.

Hall, Raymond L. *Black Separatism in the United States.* Hanover, N.H.: University Press of New England, 1978.

Hill, Robert A. "Black Zionism: Marcus Garvey and the Jewish Question." In *African Americans and Jews in the Twentieth Century: Studies in Convergence and Conflict,* ed. Grant Franklin et al. Columbia: University of Missouri Press, 1998, pp. 40–53.

Lewis, Rupert, and Patrick Bryan, eds. *Garvey: His Work and Impact.* Trenton, N.J.: Africa World, 1991.

Lynch, Hollis R. *Edward Wilmot Blyden, Pan-Negro Patriot, 1832–1912.* New York: Oxford University Press, 1967.

———, ed. *Black Spokesman: Selected Published Writings of Edward Wilmot Blyden.* New York: Humanities, 1971.

———. *Selected Letters of Edward Wilmot Blyden.* Milwood, N.Y.: KTO, 1977.

Martin, Tony, ed. *African Fundamentalism: A Literary and Cultural Anthology of Garvey's Harlem Renaissance.* New Marcus Garvey Library, 5. Dover, Mass.: Majority, 1991.

Washington, Joseph R., Jr., ed. *Jews in Black Perspectives: A Dialogue.* Rutherford, N.J.:

Fairleigh Dickinson University Press, 1984. (Includes John Gibbs St. Clair Drake's "African Diaspora and Jewish Diaspora: Convergence and Divergence.")

Blackbirds

Blackbirds was the title of a series of musicals with all-black performers, produced and directed by Lew Leslie, a white former vaudevillian. The shows were presented from the late 1920s through the 1930s. They included singing, dancing, and blackface comedy skits and were a stepping-stone to greater fame for

Blackbirds of 1928, Poker scene from the stage production. (Billy Rose Theatre Collection, New York Public Library, New York City. Photographer: White Studio.)

many of the featured performers. *Blackbirds of 1928* was the most successful version of the series; it became the longest-running all-black show of its time.

As the manager of a cabaret at Café de Paris on Broadway in 1921, Lew Leslie (whose original name was Lev Lessinsky) was inspired by the success of Eubie Blake's and Noble Sissle's *Shuffle Along*, an all-black musical hit on Broadway. Leslie began to produce and direct successful all-black shows (*Plantation Revue, From Dover to Dixie,* and *From Dixie to Broadway*) at the Café de Paris, in Broadway theaters, and at venues in London and Paris. Leslie added Florence Mills from *Shuffle Along* to the cast of his shows, to great acclaim. The title of Leslie's *Blackbirds* series came from a popular song ("I'm a Little Black Bird") performed by Mills in *From Dover to Dixie*.

After a successful run in Harlem, *Blackbirds of 1926* played to enthusiastic audiences in Paris and London. This production starred Florence Mills. Although her performance in Europe made her an international star, the show was the last before her death in 1927.

The most successful of Leslie's productions, *Blackbirds of 1928*, starred Adelaide Hall, replacing Mills. It also featured Bill "Bojangles" Robinson, whose dancing was a hit with audiences and critics alike. Other performers included Peg Leg Bates, a one-legged tap dancer. Famous songs from *Blackbirds of 1928* included "Diga Diga Do," "I Can't Give You Anything but Love," and "Doing the New Low Down" (a dance number featuring Robinson). The singing and dancing were accompanied by stereotypical sketches such as the blackface poker skit "According to Hoyle." The show also offered parodies of novels and plays, including DuBose Heyward's *Porgy,* and it featured a tribute to Florence Mills sung by Adelaide Hall. *Blackbirds of 1928* played on Broadway for 518 performances, the longest run for an all-black musical to that point.

The *Blackbirds* shows, like Leslie's earlier all-black productions, were intended for all-white audiences and were usually written by whites. The white audiences' stereotypes of blacks were reflected in formulaic numbers: plantation scenes, African primitives, black performers doing skits in blackface, and parodies of popular plays and novels, exploiting the novelty of all-black casts in versions of white works. It was typical at the time for whites to have artistic and financial control of Broadway shows with all-black casts. Despite the stereotypes and racism in the shows, though, many black performers appreciated the chance to appear in productions on the grand scale such as Florenz Ziegfeld's *Follies.*

Leslie never repeated the success he had with *Blackbirds of 1928. Blackbirds of 1930,* although it had music and lyrics by the African Americans Eubie Blake and Andy Razaf and starred Ethel Waters, played for only fifty-seven performances on Broadway. *Blackbirds of 1933* played for only twenty-five performances on Broadway, and the critics said that the dancing of Bill Robinson, who was a guest performer, was the only redeeming feature of the show. *Blackbirds of 1939* (the final edition) featured a newcomer, Lena Horne, but played on Broadway for only nine performances.

HEATHER MARTIN

See also Blackface Performance; Blake, Eubie; Hall, Adelaide; Leslie, Lew; Mills, Florence; Musical Theater; Razaf, Andy; Robinson, Bill "Bojangles"; Shuffle Along; Waters, Ethel

Further Reading

Green, Stanley. *Ring Bells! Sing Songs!—Broadway Musicals of the 1930s.* New York: Galahad, 1971.

Krasner, David. *A Beautiful Pageant: African American Theatre, Drama, and Performance in the Harlem Renaissance, 1910–1927.* New York: Palgrave Macmillan, 2002.

Moore, James Ross. "Leslie, Lew." In *American National Biography,* ed. John A. Garraty and Mark C. Carnes. New York: Oxford University Press, 1999.

Peterson, Bernard L. *A Century of Musicals in Black and White: An Encyclopedia of Musical Stage Works By, About, or Involving African Americans.* Westport, Conn.: Greenwood, 1993.

Woll, Allen. *Dictionary of the Black Theatre: Broadway, Off-Broadway, and Selected Harlem Theatre.* Westport, Conn.: Greenwood, 1983.

———. *Black Musical Theatre: From Coontown to Dreamgirls.* Baton Rouge: Louisiana State University Press, 1989.

Blackface Performance

Blackface performance emerged as a form of theatrical entertainment for American audiences who desired new and more enthralling pastimes. The early minstrel show consisted of white performers who mocked, with excessive exaggeration, the behavior of blacks. They adorned their faces with greasepaint or burnt cork to create a dark complexion; their lips were painted red, or a large, rounded white circle was left to intensify the exaggeratedly full lips and gaping mouth; the eyes were bulged. A costume of rags was added, for a more effective theatrical and comic reincarnation of the black slave. Blackface performances in the theaters of metropolises like New York, Philadelphia, and Chicago appealed to audiences partly because of the songs, dances, and comic repartee, but also because they reflected ideas about white superiority and class conflict.

Early blackface minstrel performances attracted audiences from among lower-class, middle-class, and upper-class American audiences and became very popular; this form of entertainment served as a common denominator. White audiences enjoyed the racial ambivalence of blackface performance, which reinforced not only white superiority but also black inferiority. The performances often included songs with lyrics extolling the South, dances accompanied by fiddles or banjos, and comic dialogues insisting that the black slave loved his master and plantation life. Often, the blackface roles included caricatures like Sambo, Jim Crow, and Zip Coon, whose songs, dances, and comic routines conveyed dubious interpretations of blackness as well as conflicting depictions of cultural exchange.

During the nineteenth century, some blackface productions offered literary works and new material. William Shakespeare's *Othello* was the blackface production most often performed on American stages; it was first presented in 1751 and was eventually performed more than 400 times. Other popular blackface productions included Samuel Woodworth's *The Forest Rose; or, American Farmers* (1825), which had 126 performances, and R. B. Peake's *The One-Hundred-Pound Note* (1827), which had 109 performances.

During the late 1820s and early 1830s, two main blackface roles were popularized: the first was a ragged, happy southern plantation hand eager to please and serve his master; the second was a black imitation or burlesque of the white dandy. In 1822, Charles Mathews, an English actor, based his one-man blackface act on these images; he also often used the black preacher as his main character. In 1828, Thomas Dartmouth Rice created "Jim Crow," a crippled plantation slave who sang and danced. By 1832, when Rice arrived in New York City after touring along the northeastern seaboard, he was a celebrity: Audiences were eager to see his act, and other performers tried to imitate him.

In the late 1830s, two new types of blackface performance emerged that changed the nature of this kind of theater. Whereas the stage figures Jim Crow and Zip Coon had relied on orchestral accompaniment, the redesigned acts included only the solo banjo or solo dancers. William Whitlock, known as the "king of banjo players," performed simply instrumental pieces or played a tune and sang. Whitlock and John Diamond, who was known Master Diamond and was noted for his skill at "Negro dancing," became one of the most popular blackface comedy teams during the early 1840s; this new form of entertainment became a favorite of white American audiences.

In 1843, blackface entertainment, also commonly known as minstrelsy, was changed forever by several factors. Faced with a financial crisis, the theaters in New York reduced ticket prices and performers' wages. Theatrical ensembles increased in size from duos to teams of three or four, which usually included a banjoist and two dancers. This form became more highly regarded with the success of the Tyrolese Family Ranier, who introduced a family quartet consisting of two women and two men.

Another change in blackface productions was the appearance of black performers, although this practice was not very common. Before the early 1840s, blacks did not legitimately perform on American stages for white audiences; however, they did on rare occasions appear in theaters exclusively for blacks. During the mid-1840s, William Henry Lane, known onstage as Master Juba, became the most renowned, and nearly the only, black performer to appear before white audiences. John Diamond, after being defeated by "Master Juba" in a dance competition in 1844, said that Lane was the best dancer he had ever seen.

In the 1850s, blackface performance became more controversial, and it was banned in some southern cities as issues related to slavery intensified. A financial crisis in 1858 and the onset of the Civil War in June 1861 marked a decline in public interest in blackface performance; however, this decline was temporary: interest revived as social and political unrest subsided. Some black minstrel troupes were formed in the midst of the Civil War, and such troupes became more common after 1865. At first, black minstrels did not usually wear blackface, but by the end of the nineteenth century, white audiences were demanding blackface even for black performers.

Although blacks became more widespread in blackface performance, whites still dominated the circuit for this kind of entertainment, as performers, managers, and owners. By the late 1870s, white minstrel groups had virtually cornered the market in the United States and abroad, although blacks were making great strides toward eliminating stereotypes and ambivalent interpretations of blackness onstage. Two successful shows—*Clorindy* (1898), which mainly featured a chorus line of female dancers, and *Creole Show* (1899), featuring well-dressed cakewalk teams—were instrumental in establishing new images. Vaudeville, introduced in the 1880s, also offered various opportunities for black performers, despite the fact that two vaudevilles existed, one for blacks and one for whites.

By the twentieth century, professional minstrel troupes were no longer a principal form of entertainment for American audiences. The Harlem Renaissance introduced new types of entertainment, including jazz and the blues; Dizzy Gillespie, Gertrude "Ma" Rainey, and Josephine Baker are just three of the performers who generated this transformation. Nevertheless, blackface performance had served as a foundation for black music and theater in the United States and across the world.

GENYNE HENRY BOSTON

See also Jim Crow; Minstrelsy

Further Reading

Abrahams, Roger D. *Singing the Master: The Emergence of African American Culture in the Plantation South.* New York: Pantheon, 1992.

Cockrell, Dale. *Demons of Disorder: Early Blackface Minstrels and Their World.* Cambridge: Cambridge University Press, 1997.

Levine, Lawrence W. *Black Culture and Black Consciousness: Afro-American Folk Thought from Slavery to Freedom.* New York: Oxford University Press, 1988.

Lhamon, William T. *Raising Cain: Blackface Performance in Its Lore Cycle.* Cambridge, Mass.: Harvard University Press, 1999.

Lott, Eric. *Love and Theft: Blackface Minstrelsy and the American Working Class.* New York: Oxford University Press, 1993.

Mahar, William J. *Behind the Burnt Cork Mask: Early Blackface Minstrelsy and Antebellum American Popular Culture.* Urbana and Chicago: University of Illinois Press, 1999.

Roach, Joseph. "Slave Spectacles and Tragic Octoroons: A Cultural Genealogy of Antebellum Performance." *Theater Survey,* 33, November 1992, pp. 167–187.

———. *Cities of the Dead: Circum Atlantic Performance.* New York: Columbia University Press, 1996.

Rourke, Constance. *American Humor: A Study of the National Character.* New York: Harcourt Brace, 1986.

Blacks in Theater

Ideological constructions of African American identity (what the novelist Toni Morrison in our own time has called American Africanisms) were central in the development of American and African American theater long before black people made a collective effort to shape that theater through their artistic contributions. One source of American stage history is blackface minstrelsy, which probably began in the 1820s or 1830s with the song-and-dance routines of performers like T. D. Rice. Rice is said to have created the figure "Jim Crow" after seeing a lame black man dancing on the street in a southern city, possibly Lexington. The legend is that Rice assumed this street performer's shabby clothes and dance steps, and with his own "Jump Jim Crow" humorously imitated and exaggerated them onstage. Thereafter, the stereotypical traits of this minstrel character—comical shiftlessness, laziness, and bumbling foolishness—became fixed in the American consciousness as defining characteristics of the American Negro. These perceived traits diminished black people's humanity in the eyes of the nation. Still, the origins of minstrelsy in the cultural productions of enslaved African Americans—their song, dance, and music—gives credence to the designation of minstrelsy as the first authentic American theater form.

During the Harlem Renaissance, the works of "New Negro" performing artists and intellectuals were intended to inscribe on the national consciousness a new and more progressive image of blackness. Believing that social change and racial equality could be achieved through their contributions to the arts, including theater, New Negro artists considered drama a means of waging the struggle for self-determination and self-expression. Their theatrical performances and dramatic works were created in the shadow of minstrelsy. At the same time as mainstream theatrical depictions of African Americans continued to reflect and perpetuate the stereotypical images that had emerged from minstrelsy, the dramatists of the Harlem Renaissance, whose work was often staged in smaller, less commercial spaces, challenged these debasing notions about blacks.

During the early twentieth century, it was easy to discern the continuing presence of minstrel traditions in performances by African Americans in vaudeville and on Broadway. For example, George Walker and Bert Williams—who were thought of as being among the brightest Negro stars on Broadway—frequently depicted recognizable types from the minstrel stage. They billed themselves as "Two Real Coons": Walker played a smooth, wily dandy, and Williams played a shuffling buffoon. Their talent for comedy made an impression on their audience, and they formed a company that made a successful transition from vaudeville and the minstrel stage to Broadway. The Williams and Walker Company included Jesse Ship, Alex Rogers, Will Marion Cook, and Walker's wife, the dancer and choreographer Ada Overton Walker. They created a number of musical and comic revues that did well on Broadway, including *In Dahomey* (1902–1905), *Abyssinia* (1905–1907), and *Bandana Land* (1907–1909). Overton Walker choreographed all the shows, and her introduction of the cakewalk in the production of *In Dahomey* made the dance a sensation in both the United States and Europe.

Overton Walker felt that she was in a position to contribute to the dance concert stage. In 1908, she staked a claim for black performers' participation in classical dance by choreographing a version of *Salome* from the 1907 production of *Bandana Land* and then reprising it at the Roof Garden Theater in 1912. In creating and performing a dance based on the biblical story of the seductress Salome, she joined a number of white female modern dancers who were choreographing similar pieces and who were seen as participating in a more serious classical dance tradition. Overton Walker's tentative expansion of the vocabulary of black theatrical dance anticipated a greater shift in sensibilities in the mid-1920s. By 1925, Hemsley Winfield—one of the first men to attempt to dance the role of Salome—was involved in theatrical ventures in Yonkers, in Harlem with the Krigwa Players, and in Greenwich Village with the Provincetown Players; and Edna Guy began her studies with the Denishawn School of Dance in New York. These dancer-choreographers all had to contend with an assumption on the part of critics and audiences that black bodies were suitable only for performances of more exotic fare, such as African and Caribbean dance, or for vernacular dances that made use of jazz or blues.

Bert Williams himself faced obstacles when he wanted to take roles that strayed from the limited possibilities offered to blacks in the popular imagination.

After the Williams and Walker Company disbanded in 1909, Williams spent the next nine years with the Ziegfeld Follies, performing routines that showcased his mastery of comic timing and mimicry but repeated the sad-sack type he was known for on Broadway. Williams was a well-read man whose formal speech suggested considerable complexity beneath the simple types he depicted, but he found no other vehicles for his gifts for humor and mimicry. He famously remarked: "I have never been able to discover that there was anything disgraceful in being a colored man. But I have often found it inconvenient—in America."

In the early years of the twentieth century, being a black performer in popular theater entailed other inconveniences in addition to the limited range of roles. The Theater Owners' Booking Association (TOBA), also known as "Toby"—a consortium of forty theaters, mostly in the South—was one of several outlets for black entertainers and audiences in the 1910s and 1920s. But it was controlled primarily by whites, and performers said that TOBA stood for "tough on black asses" because their wages were low and unreliable and their acts were subject to unexpected cancellation. Moreover, as performers traveled through the segregated South, they often suffered the indignities of Jim Crow in transportation and housing. Other, smaller circuits existed, including the Dudley circuit, which was run by the African American producer and theater owner Sherman "S. H." Dudley and operated from 1911 to 1916; and the Southern Consolidated Circuit (SCC), which operated from 1916 to 1925. After the demise of his own circuit, Dudley owned a controlling interest in the SCC. He attempted to provide an alternative for black performers by regulating hiring and payment practices and minimizing the corruption that characterized relations between performers and theatrical managers and agents. He also owned more than a dozen theaters and produced, wrote, and acted in several successful musicals.

Audiences in New York and around the United States showed an obvious and enduring interest in black musical and comedic performances. The Harlem Renaissance is noteworthy, however, for a groundswell of interest in serious African American drama. This shift in what American audiences were prepared to see in depictions of black life was marked by the success, in the autumn of 1917, of Emily Hapgood and Ridgely Torrence's three one-act plays. At the Garden Street Theater, Hapgood produced Torrence's *The Rider of Dreams*, a voodoo tragedy; *Simon the Cyrenian*, a passion play; and *Granny Maumee*, a comedy. The all-black casts enacted dignified characters that were the antithesis of the minstrel types mainstream audiences were accustomed to seeing onstage. The dignity of these roles made the productions notable, as did the critics' acclaim and the audience's positive response.

This landmark performance was followed by a number of other noteworthy dramatic performances by black actors. In 1920, Charles Gilpin captivated audiences in Eugene O'Neill's *Emperor Jones*. Gilpin played Brutus Jones, a con artist who becomes the emperor of an unnamed Caribbean island. Jones' subjects eventually discover his deception, and they pursue him to his death. Critics praised Gilpin for the magnetism and power of his performance; and the play eventually moved to Broadway, where it was a huge hit. Gilpin also toured the country, playing the lead in some 200 performances in more than thirty cities between 1921 and 1922. Gilpin's acting career had begun several years earlier, when he performed at the turn of the twentieth century as a singer and dancer. As his reputation grew, he was hired to start up Harlem's Lafayette Theater in December 1915. Gilpin left that position, however, and went on to play Rev. William Custis, an "old slave," in John Drinkwater's *Abraham Lincoln* on Broadway; he then took what would become his greatest role, Brutus Jones.

Paul Robeson, Gilpin's heir as the stage's great black dramatic actor, made his theatrical debut in Mary Hoyt Wilborg's *Taboo* (1921), and he was an understudy in Eubie Blake and Noble Sissle's pioneering musical *Shuffle Along*. But it was a revival of *The Emperor Jones* in 1924 that made Robeson's career—along with his star turn the same year in O'Neill's *All God's Chillun Got Wings*, which was also a sensation. *All God's Chillun Got Wings* examined miscegenation and costarred Mary Blair. After these performances, Robeson was offered roles in international and Broadway productions, including the Broadway revival of Oscar Hammerstein II and Jerome Kern's *Show Boat* in 1932. Robeson's rendition of "Ol' Man River" in *Show Boat* became a classic.

Other notable theater events included, in 1926, the Provincetown Players' production of *In Abraham's Bosom*, which won a Pulitzer Prize in 1927. The cast featured Rose McClendon, Abbie Mitchell, Frank Wilson, and Jules Bledsoe. Also in 1927, the Theater Guild produced *Porgy*, Dorothy and DuBose Heyward's adaptation of his novel of the same name. In 1930, at the end of the first decade of African Americans' participation in American legitimate theater, Marc Connelly's *The Green Pastures*—a play based on Roark Bradford's tales of southern folk life, *Old Man Adam and His Chillun*—was produced. Richard Harrison, playing "De Lawd," led an all-black cast that included Rose McClendon, Frank Wilson, Georgette Harvey, Leigh Whipper, and Jack Carter; the Hall Johnson Choir also performed. *The Green Pastures* won the Pulitzer Prize and had one of the longest runs in the history of African American theater.

In addition to these successful stage productions, which were presented in both large and small spaces, there were one-act plays written and performed in more intimate venues that offered some of the most innovative work being done in the American theater at the time. Eugene O'Neill, for example, was one of three associate directors of the Provincetown Players, a theater company in Greenwich Village that produced his "Negro drama," which included *The Emperor Jones* and *All God's Chillun Got Wings*. O'Neill and his associates hoped to rejuvenate America theater by exploring contemporary topics and using native themes such as race. He, George Cram Cook, Susan Glaspell, and Edna St. Vincent Millay initiated the "little theater" movement, which grew out of the discontent of actors, writers, and directors with the obvious commercialism of large Broadway-style productions. Experimental theater companies like the Provincetown Players strove to create alternatives to the formulaic dramas and gaudy spectacles that they considered the primary fare of more commercial venues.

These collaborations between white writers, directors, and producers and black actors and musicians left a mixed legacy. Many of these plays won popular and critical acclaim, but they still conveyed deep-rooted racial attitudes and perpetuated stereotypes of black characters as inferior and primitive. Because they kept alive negative images of African Americans, the plays often received mixed reviews from black audiences and critics. At the same time, African American playwrights had to struggle to make their voices heard in a climate of hostility or indifference. Many black writers considered themselves lucky if a church or community group staged a reading, and it was improbable that their scripts would ever make the transition from page to stage.

For example, young playwrights like Zora Neale Hurston and Marieta Bonner would have gone unrecognized if not for the support of Negro journals such as *Crisis* and *Opportunity*. Hurston is more widely known as a novelist, but in 1925, her play *Color Struck* won second prize in the drama division in a contest run by *Opportunity*. This play had originally been published in *Fire!!*, a journal produced by younger, more radical members of Harlem's literary establishment, who wrote for a primarily black audience. *Color Struck* explores the issue of "colorism" in a black community in Florida, showing the damage done to a single black woman's consciousness by the community's assignment of privilege according to degrees of darkness and lightness of complexion. This play also features a cakewalk contest as a communal ritual, underscoring Hurston's interest in vernacular culture.

Marieta Bonner's plays were rarely if ever staged. She was most widely known as a short-story writer, but in 1927, she wrote three plays: *Exit: An Illusion, The Pot Maker,* and *The Purple Flower*. Both *Exit: An Illusion* and *The Purple Flower* won first prize for playwriting in a contest in *Crisis* that year. Bonner had graduated in 1922 from Radcliffe College, where she majored in comparative literature and became fluent in German. Her education introduced her to German expressionist drama of the 1920s, and her own plays reveal its influence. Like the German expressionists, Bonner wanted to expose social truths and shock society out of its complacency. In *The Purple Flower*, for example, Bonner relies on allegory more than realism to explore the themes of racial injustice and resistance. The play centers on a character, Old Man, who is a member of the "Us's," representative of African Americans, who are pitted against the more powerful and exploitative "Sundry White Devils." Old Man eventually realizes that his passive resistance to the injustices of the White Devils is misguided and that the only avenue to liberation is violence. The play ends with a call to revolution.

Bonner's abstraction of racial themes contrasted with a dominant trend toward realism among African American dramatists as they addressed social and political themes. The theatrical counterculture that the "little theaters" represented could be found in black circles as well. By the mid-1920s, every major urban center had an African American theater. Such theaters developed because members of the black middle class were seeking spaces for cultural expression and enrichment and were also contending with apparently entrenched racial segregation and even with interracial violence. Some of the best-known theaters were the Harlem Experimental Theatre, Lafayette Players, and Hapgood Players in New York; the Krigwa Theater of New York and Washington, D.C.; the Howard University Players Theater and Dunbar Players Theater of Washington, D.C.; the Ethiopian Art Theater and Folk Theater of Chicago; the Dunbar

Theatre of Philadelphia; the Dixwell Players Theater of New Haven, Connecticut; and the Karamu House's Gilpin Players Theater in Cleveland. These spaces were situated in black communities and aimed their projects toward a black audience; they staged readings and presented plays and musicals by black playwrights.

The most influential African American theaters were the Lafayette in Harlem and the Ethiopian Art Theater in Chicago. The Lafayette opened in 1915 and for about ten years catered to a black audience, often staging plays from Broadway that had been altered to suit the tastes of this audience, and showcasing black casts in productions originally written for white actors. The Ethiopian Art Theater was founded in Chicago in 1923 by Raymond O'Neill and was sponsored by Sherwood Anderson's wife. The troupe made its debut in New York that same year at the Frazee Theatre with a series of plays that included Willis Richardson's *The Chip Woman's Fortune*, Oscar Wilde's *Salome*, and a jazz version of Shakespeare's *Comedy of Errors*. As noted above, the group's production of *Taboo*, a study of voodoo by Mary Hoyt Wilborg, started Paul Robeson on the road to stardom.

Two other theaters are worthy of notice because they were affiliated with W. E. B. Du Bois and Alain Locke, who were leaders of the New Negro movement and important supporters and shapers of African American theater. Du Bois's Krigwa Players, who met in the basement of the 135th Street branch of the New York Public Library in Harlem, had their inaugural season in 1926. In 1927, they produced two plays by Eulalie Spence (1894–1981): *Her* and *Foreign Mail*. Spence's plays were acclaimed by critics in the black press, but Spence encountered opposition from Du Bois because she refused to treat her art as propaganda. She did not believe that drama could compel white society to empathize with the victims of lynching and rape; instead, she tried to portray black life realistically. In Washington, D.C., Alain Locke and Montgomery Gregory organized the Howard University Players in order to cultivate African American drama. The Howard Players produced *Simon the Cyrenian* and *The Emperor Jones* in March 1921; in the latter play, Charles Gilpin and Jasper Deeter had the leading roles, and students filled the supporting roles. The Howard group also produced plays written by students in Howard University's drama department, as well as one-act plays by Thelma Duncan and Willis Richardson.

Du Bois and Locke were important in black theater during this period because they controlled the means of and possibilities for publication and production through their books (such as Locke's anthology *The New Negro*), journals (such as *Crisis*), and theater, which provided the primary venues for black playwrights. For this reason, Du Bois's belief in art as propaganda, Locke's insistence that authentic black drama must emphasize folk life, and their shared conviction that art can be an instrument of social change were prominent features of much drama written and produced during this era. This was particularly true of the community theaters that provided an alternative to large commercial Broadway spectacles. However, although both Du Bois and Locke believed that art could change society, Locke did resist the temptation to make art synonymous with propaganda, believing instead that the African American folk experience provided rich material for drama and gave voice to free and full self-expression. Locke was instrumental in developing black drama during this period. He attended Georgia Douglas Johnson's literary soirees at her home in Washington, D.C., and sponsored both her and Willis Richardson's plays, including Richardson's *Mortgaged* at Howard University in 1924. Locke reviewed and critiqued Georgia Johnson's and Richardson's plays and included Richardson's *Compromise* in *The New Negro*.

Du Bois's definition of "race drama" gave a nationalist dimension to the New Negro manifestation of the "little theater" movement. Referring to his Krigwa Little Theatre, Du Bois wrote in 1926 that African American theater must follow four principles: it should be "about us," that is, with plots about black life; "by us," written by African American authors who by birth, affiliation, or both had an understanding of what it meant to be black; "for us," catering primarily to black audiences; and "near us," in black neighborhoods.

New Negro dramatists tended to treat black folk culture seriously. They believed in art as propaganda, and they intended to provide alternatives to mainstream depictions of black primitivity, exoticism, and decadence. They also believed that small theaters producing work with black themes contributed more to black communities than large Broadway-style productions. In this sense, then, it would be incorrect to conclude that black dramatists were absent from the more commercial venues solely because they were unable to find a receptive audience there. They intentionally wrote one-act plays to be performed in churches, meeting halls, college theaters, and private homes.

Georgia Douglas Johnson and Willis Richardson—the most prolific playwrights of the 1920s—offer two models of dramatic creativity during the Harlem Renaissance. Although both lived in Washington, D.C., they were identified as artists of the renaissance, and their plays presented the characters' racial pride, resistance to oppression, and moral rectitude. Richardson joined luminaries such as Alain Locke, Jean Toomer, and Jessie Redmond Fauset at Johnson's weekly literary salon, which provided a fertile ground for black theater. Another source of nourishment was the existence of a solid black middle class in Washington; this middle class flourished because of the city's nonsegregated government jobs and excellent schools, including Howard University. Moreover, Washington's large black population provided a ready audience for nonmusical drama.

Georgia Johnson published two books of poetry before 1925, but she mostly deferred her creative and professional ambitions in order to raise her family and help her husband, who was a lawyer in Washington. When her husband died in 1925, Georgia Johnson began to flourish artistically. In 1926, her play *Blue Blood* received an honorable mention in a contest in *Opportunity*; in 1927, her play *Plumes* took first prize in *Opportunity*'s contest. *Plumes* introduces a mother, Charity Brown, who must decide whether to pay for an expensive operation for her daughter or bury the daughter in style; she is also torn between conventional medicine and her belief in herbalism. Ultimately, Charity's hesitation in deciding costs the daughter her life, and the mother buries the daughter in grand style. This play was produced twice in 1928, in Harlem and Chicago.

Willis Richardson studied drama, rhetoric, and English under the playwright Mary Burrill at the respected M Street High School in Washington, D.C. In 1923, his play *The Chip Woman's Fortune* was the first nonmusical drama by an African American to be produced on Broadway. He won the *Crisis* playwriting award twice, in 1925 and 1926.

Antilynching plays are an important subset of the serious dramatic productions written and performed during this period. From the mid-1910s through the 1920s, several antilynching plays by African Americans were produced. Dramatists such as Mary Burrill, Georgia Douglas Johnson, and Angelina Weld Grimké wrote in response to the mob violence that broke out in both southern and northern cities. They used realistic settings and characters and vernacular language to address social injustice. These women playwrights created strong female figures who had to contend with the effects of racial violence. Grimké's *Rachel*, the first full-length antilynching drama, was written and produced in 1916 in Washington, D.C., by the drama committee of the National Association for the Advancement of Colored People. The play was taken up and performed in regional theaters as well, including the Neighborhood Playhouse in New York, and in Cambridge, Massachusetts. It recounts the decision of a sensitive, educated African American woman to forgo motherhood rather than bring children into a world where they would be hated and effaced. Rachel has learned that, before she was born, her father and older brother were lynched in the South; she realizes that black mothers cannot protect their loved ones, and she resolves to keep future generations of black children from the fate of being victimized by racial violence. The original title of *Rachel* was *Blessed Are the Barren*.

Georgia Douglas Johnson wrote three antilynching plays: *A Sunday Morning in the South* (1925), which was submitted to the Federal Theatre Project between 1935 and 1939 but was never produced or published; *Blue Eyed Black Boy*; and *Safe*. All three plays are sentimental, portray folk life, and make a plea for society to recognize the damage wrought by lynching.

Mary Burrill, Willis Richardson's drama teacher at the M Street High School, wrote two plays—*Aftermath* (1919) and *They That Sit in Darkness* (1919)—dealing with lynching and birth control. Both were published in journals: *They That Sit in Darkness* was published in the *Birth Control Review* in September 1919, and *Aftermath* in *Liberator* in April 1919. Du Bois's Krigwa Players produced *Aftermath* in 1928.

Although many of these productions received critical acclaim when they were produced in small regional theaters, and although race dramas by white playwrights were popular, black dramatists did not find an enthusiastic reception on Broadway. With the exception of some sketch writers and an occasional librettist for musical shows, black writers did not often have opportunities to create works for Broadway. From 1917 to 1930, fifteen playwrights presented works on the Broadway stage that dealt with African American themes and characters, but only five black playwrights found a stage for their plays about black life. When blacks did manage this feat, they were met with skepticism about the interest of a mainstream audience. Willis Richardson's *The Chip Woman's Fortune* did make the leap from "little theater" venues to Broadway. It was first produced by the Ethiopian Art

Theater in Chicago, eventually moved to Washington, then moved to the Lafayette Theater in New York, and finally—in May 1923—came to New York's Frazee Theater, where (as mentioned above) it became the first drama by an African American to be produced on Broadway. It was, however, a commercial failure, as was Frank Wilson's *Meek Mose* (1928). Garland Anderson's *Appearances* (1925), which focused on Christian Science, cannot strictly be called an African American drama. However, it was performed by a mixed cast of fourteen whites and three blacks, and a black actor played the principal character. Wallace Thurman's *Harlem* (1929), written in collaboration with William Jordan Rapp, a white man, was a melodramatic treatment of a family's attempt to survive after moving to Harlem from the South.

The few plays that reached the stage were often presented on the outskirts of Broadway, in neighborhoods that raised doubts about the respectability of the productions and their casts. However, the tremendous popularity of *Shuffle Along* caused producers to reconsider their attitude toward black productions.

Shuffle Along was by far the most popular musical among both white and black audiences during the Harlem Renaissance. Before it became a hit on Broadway, it had first been given for black audiences at the Howard University Theater in Washington, D.C., and at the Dunbar Theater in Philadelphia. In 1921, *Shuffle Along* opened at the Sixty-third Street Theater. This landmark production had music, lyrics, choreography, a cast, and a production that were entirely created, made up of, or controlled by African Americans. James Hubert (Eubie) Blake had collaborated with the lyricist Noble Sissle and the comedy duo Flournoy Miller and Aubrey Lyles to write the music and dialogue for *Shuffle Along*. Blake and Sissle began their careers in vaudeville, performing ragtime, jazz, and sentimental melodies. Blake's "I'm Just Wild About Harry" and "Love Will Find a Way" were only two of the many songs from the show that became American standards, and the show was so popular that it ran continuously on Broadway until 1928. It also inaugurated the careers of Paul Robeson, Josephine Baker, and Florence Mills.

Shuffle Along takes place in "Jimtown," a fictional southern black city. The plot revolves around a mayoral election in which there are three candidates: Steve Jenkins and Sam Peck, the unscrupulous partners of a local grocery store; and Harry Walton, an honorable man whose love for Jessie Williams will go unrequited unless he wins the election, which he is expected to lose. This musical succeeded in striking an unlikely balance: it depicted black characters who had integrity while also appealing to audiences' nostalgia for minstrel humor. *Shuffle Along* had stock characters such as the "Uncle," actors performed in blackface, and the female dancers were dressed provocatively. Moreover, Miller and Lyles's comic routines used the racial humor that made their vaudeville routines so popular. But the show also had noble characters, attractive, well-dressed young people who spoke standard English, and a romantic black couple.

The audiences who flocked to *Shuffle Along* also attended other musicals, including *Put and Take* (1921); *Strut Miss Lizzie, Plantation Revue, Oh Joy, Liza*, and *Runnin' Wild* (1923); *The Chocolate Dandies* and *Dixie to Broadway* (1924); *Lucky Sambo* (1925); *Blackbirds of 1926* and *Blackbirds of 1928*; and *Africana* (1927). These musicals introduced a number of talented performers and made many songs and dances created by African Americans popular with mainstream audiences. For example, *Runnin' Wild* introduced the Charleston to America and the world and helped to define the jazz age. *Chocolate Dandies* starred Josephine Baker and was a step in her path to international stardom. Florence Mills became a star in 1924 in *From Dixie to Broadway* and went on to even greater success in Lew Leslie's *Blackbirds*. Next to Baker, Mills was the most successful African American female performer of the 1920s. Mills was a protégée of Ada Overton, from whom she learned to cakewalk. She began performing in vaudeville as a child and later joined the Williams and Walker Company. Going by the names "Little Baby Flo," "Little Twinks," and "Little Blackbird," she became popular in numerous musical comedies. At the peak of her career (1921–1927) she appeared in *Shuffle Along, Plantation Review*, and *Dover to Dixie* (which was renamed *Dixie to Broadway* when it moved to Broadway). In 1926, she performed in Paris in *La revue nègre*, the cabaret act that made Josephine Baker a star. Mills's final performance was in *Blackbirds of 1926*, which opened at the Alhambra Theater in Harlem before touring Europe. Finally, Bill "Bojangles" Robinson dazzled audiences with his complex, improvisational footwork onstage and on the screen. He appeared in a number of Broadway shows including *Brown Buddies* (1930), *Blackbirds of 1926* and *1933*, and *The Hot Mikado* (1939).

The talent, ambition, and vision of African American playwrights, actors, dancers, composers, and musicians during the first decades of the twentieth century are indisputable. More debatable is their success in achieving the social change to which so many New Negro artists aspired. Nonetheless, the period was one of newfound freedom of artistic expression and creativity. It is a historical juncture that contributed much to the emergence of a new, more modern, and more progressive image of the African American as an artist and a human being.

DAPHNE LAMOTHE

See also Antilynching Crusade; Authors: 4—Playwrights; Blackface Performance; Community Theater; Crisis, The; Dance; Du Bois, W. E. B., Fire!!; Liberator; Literature: 3—Drama; Locke, Alain; Minstrelsy; Musical Theater; 135th Street Library; Opportunity; Opportunity Literary Contests; Theater; Theater Owners' Booking Association; *specific people, plays, theaters, and theater groups*

Further Reading

Du Bois, W. E. B. "Krigwa Players Little Negro Theatre." *Crisis*, 32(3), July 1926.
———. "Criteria for Negro Art." *Crisis*, 32(6), October 1926.
Krasner, David. *A Beautiful Pageant: African American Theatre, Drama, and Performance in the Harlem Renaissance, 1910–1927*. New York: Palgrave Macmillan, 2002.
McKay, Nellie. "Black Theatre and Drama in the 1920s: Years of Growing Pains." *Massachusetts Review*, 28(4), Winter 1987.
Perkins, Kathy A., and Judith L. Stephens. *Strange Fruit: Plays on Lynching by African American Women*. Bloomington: Indiana University Press, 1998.
Woll, Allen. *Black Musical Theatre: From Coontown to Dreamgirls*. Baton Rouge: Louisiana State University Press, 1989. (Reprint, New York: Da Capo, 1991.)

Blake, Eubie

In a professional career that spanned more than eighty years, James Hubert (Eubie) Blake was celebrated, successful, and influential as a ragtime pianist, a vaudeville performer, a songwriter, and a composer of musicals. Blake wrote at least 300 compositions and also recorded hundreds of songs in arrangements for solo piano, small orchestras, and other configurations.

Blake was the only surviving child of two former slaves. When he was six, his parents bought him an organ and sent him to an instructor, hoping that he

"Charleston Rag" by Eubie Blake, c. 1917: a page of the composer's manuscript. (Library of Congress.)

would take up religious music, but he was irresistibly drawn to the ragtime and popular music that he heard blaring from neighborhood brothels, nightclubs, and parades. His professional career began when he was fifteen, in a local brothel where he composed his ragtime masterpiece "Charleston Rag" in 1899. Blake's early career as a ragtime pianist included playing in traveling shows and taverns in Baltimore and Atlantic City, New Jersey; in 1907, he worked in Baltimore's prominent Goldfield Hotel. Blake was one of the first ragtime players to publish songs: In 1911, his "Chevy Chase" and "Fizz Water Rag" were printed as sheet music. In New York he encountered flashy, competitive ragtime pianists who inspired him to develop his own virtuosic style, characterized by syncopated right-hand figures, steadily descending bass lines, and—because of his unusually long fingers—extended octave runs.

In 1915, Blake met the singer and lyricist Noble Sissle, with whom he would have a longtime partnership. Almost immediately, the two embarked on a series of collaborations that would bring them fame and fortune and make musical theater history. Their first song, "It's All Your Fault" (1915), was popularized by the legendary vaudeville singer Sophie Tucker. Sissle was responsible for Blake's move to New York in 1916 and his employment by the most famous black bandleader of the day, James Reese Europe. In 1919, Sissle and Blake formed a successful traveling vaudeville act, the Dixie Duo. They rejected the standard blackface makeup, ragged minstrel attire, and "comic darky" behavior expected of African American performers. Wearing black tuxedos, the dapper Sissle and Blake presented a classy act that featured dynamic piano playing and singing of fresh, original material—with none of the usual stereotyped clowning, exaggerated dialect, or mugging. The Dixie Duo performed on the road, in Harlem, and at New York's prestigious Palace Theater, and Blake and Sissle's act was considered among the best of the 1920s and was widely imitated.

In 1921, Sissle and Blake collaborated with the comedy team Flournoy Miller and Aubrey Lyles to produce the most acclaimed musical of the period, *Shuffle Along*. This has been widely described as a "Broadway show" that paved the way for a succession of black musicals on Broadway, but *Shuffle Along* actually had its very successful run (fourteen months, 500 or more performances) in a hastily refurbished lecture hall that opened as the Sixty-third Street Theater, far away from Broadway's main entertainment district. *Shuffle Along* was also a hit on tour throughout the United States for three years after its New York run. Its unprecedented success and its mixture of lively dancing, hilarious comedy, charismatic actors, and appealing music set a standard for the style and format of future musicals, drew attention to all forms of black entertainment (especially in Harlem), and introduced stars like Florence Mills, Paul Robeson, and Josephine Baker. *Shuffle Along* had a number of songs by Sissle and Blake that became hits nationwide, including "Bandana Days," "I'm Just Wild About Harry," and "Love Will Find a Way." Although syncopation was to remain a characteristic of Eubie Blake's music, this show gave him an opportunity to turn from ragtime to composing slower ballads influenced by light opera; he did not compose rags again for over twenty years.

Blake and Sissle were the first African Americans to appear in a sound film: they performed two songs in *De Forest Phonofilm* (1923), which premiered in New York. They also wrote other musicals together—the mildly successful *Chocolate Dandies* (1924), for which Blake was also the conductor and music director; and unsuccessful remakes of their earlier hit *Shuffle Along* in 1933 and 1952. Shortly after a European tour of their vaudeville act in 1927, Sissle and Blake split up as a team, but on rare occasions thereafter they did collaborate on some projects.

Blake continued to write songs with other lyricists, as well as record and compose for shows. The revue *Hot Rhythm* (1930) featured his hit "Loving You the Way I Do." He teamed up with the lyricist Andy Razaf and produced twenty-eight songs for Lew Leslie's *Blackbirds of 1930*, which included several hit standards: one was "You're Lucky to Me" (popularized by Louis Armstrong's recording in 1930), and another was Blake's most famous composition, the sentimental ballad "Memories of You."

During the Depression, black Broadway musicals declined. Blake then formed a studio orchestra that made recordings, performed in plays, and appeared in the films *Harlem Is Heaven* and *Pie, Pie Blackbird* (both 1930). He became somewhat less active in the 1930s, but he and Razaf produced new music for *Swing It!* (1937, a show sponsored by the Works Progess Administration) and the revue *Tan Manhattan* (1940). A song from the latter, "I'll Take a Nickel for a Dime," became a standard in lounge acts after being featured by the singer Joe Williams in the 1950s.

During World War II, Blake headed a USO touring troupe and played at hospitals and military bases throughout the United States. In 1945, Blake—now a widower, and an avid ladies' man—married for the second time; his new wife, Marion, became his business manager.

When his musical style was no longer in vogue and he was financially secure, Blake planned a quiet retirement. But he became bored by leisure and enrolled at New York University, where he studied the Shillinger system of musical composition between 1946 and 1950. In 1948, "I'm Just Wild About Harry" became a hit again (and introduced Blake's name to a new generation) when Harry Truman used it as a presidential campaign theme song. Blake's life changed unexpectedly and dramatically in the 1950s when a ragtime revival—inspired by the book *They All Played Ragtime* (1950)—focused attention on him as one of the style's few remaining original figures. Suddenly he had a new career, performing (though sporadically), lecturing, recording, and giving interviews. Blake was now recognized as the elder statesman of ragtime.

In his seventies and eighties, Blake proved to be much more than a charming relic of a bygone era. In the late 1960s, he made several appearances that proved that he had lost none of his ability. He was still

a technically adept and innovative pianist who practiced regularly and continued to develop new songs and creative ideas. Blake's later style dazzled musicians and audiences alike. It featured dramatic chord flurries, syncopated right-hand melodies and runs, dynamic improvised breaks, and steady "wobble-wobble" bass lines; it represented an original and personalized blend of ragtime, show music, jazz, classical music, and Harlem stride piano.

Blake's career reached even greater heights after the release of his recording *The Eighty-six Years of Eubie Blake* (1969, Columbia), which made him an international star during the 1970s. He was now featured on television talk shows, in newspapers and magazines, and at concert halls and music festivals around the world. He received numerous honors and awards from universities and social, civic, and professional organizations. In 1972, at age eighty-nine, he formed Eubie Blake Music (EBM), publishing music and producing records (mainly his own). A successful Broadway revue, *Eubie!* (1978), featured his music and focused even more attention on him. He maintained an active schedule of appearances until age ninety-eight. Blake died in 1983, five days after his hundredth birthday.

Blake left an important legacy. During his long, productive, and prosperous career, he had been an early ragtime virtuoso, a songwriter, a defiant vaudeville entertainer, and a trend-setting composer of musical shows. With his compositions, recordings, and performances, he transformed rags, classical pieces, marches, show music, ballads, and (rarely) blues into his own distinctive, dramatic syncopated style. Throughout his life he was a pioneer who influenced the direction, perception, and visibility of black entertainment and oversaw its leap into the American mainstream during and after the Harlem Renaissance.

Biography

James Hubert (Eubie) Blake, a pianist and composer in ragtime and musical theater, was born 7 February 1883 in Baltimore, Maryland. He studied music at New York University and received a bachelor of arts degree in 1950. He founded the music publishing and record company Eubie Blake Music (EBM) in 1972. Blake was a member of the American Society of Composers, Authors and Publishers (ASCAP) and the American Federation of Musicians. His honors and awards include the Presidential Medal of Freedom (1981) and honorary doctorates from Brooklyn College

(1973), Dartmouth College (1974), Morgan State University (1973), New England Conservatory of Music (1974), Pratt Institute (1975), and Rutgers University (1974). Blake died 12 February 1983 in Brooklyn, New York.

MICHAEL WHITE

See also Baker, Josephine; Blackbirds; Chocolate Dandies; Europe, James Reese; Lyles, Aubrey; Miller, Flournoy; Mills, Florence; Musical Theater; Razaf, Andy; Robeson, Paul; Shuffle Along; Sissle, Noble; Vaudeville

Selected Compositions

"Bandana Days." 1921. (With Noble Sissle.)
"Charleston Rag." 1899. (Originally "Sounds of Africa.")
"Chevy Chase." 1911.
"Fizz Water." 1911.
"Gypsy Blues." 1921. (With Noble Sissle.)
"I'm Just Wild About Harry." 1921. (With Noble Sissle.)
"It's All Your Fault." 1915 (With Noble Sissle and E. Nelson.)
"Love Will Find a Way." 1921. (With Noble Sissle.)
"Memories of You." 1930. (With Andy Razaf.)
"Thinking of You. 1924. (With Noble Sissle.)
"You Were Meant for Me." 1922. (With Noble Sissle.)
"You're Lucky to Me." 1930. (With Andy Razaf.)

Musicals

Blackbirds of 1930. 1930.
The Chocolate Dandies. 1924.
Shuffle Along. 1921.
Swing It. 1937.
Tan Manhattan. 1940.

Selected Recordings

The Eighty-six Years of Eubie Blake (Columbia: C2S847, 1969)
Memories of You (from Rare Piano Rolls; Biograph: BCD 112 DDD, 1990)
The Wizard of Ragtime Piano (Twentieth-Century Fox, 20CF 3003, 1958)

Further Reading

Blesh, Rudi, and Harriet Janis. *They All Played Ragtime.* New York: Oak, 1971.

Carter, Lawrence T. *Eubie Blake: Keys of Memory.* Detroit, Mich.: Balamp, 1979.
Jasen, David A., and Gene Jones. *Spreadin' Rhythm Around: Black Popular Songwriters, 1880–1930.* New York: Schirmer, 1998.
Jasen, David A., and Gene Jones. *Black Bottom Stomp: Eight Masters of Ragtime and Early Jazz.* New York: Routledge, 2002.
Levin, Floyd. *Classic Jazz.* Berkeley: University of California Press, 2000.
Rose, Al. *Eubie Blake.* New York: Schirmer, 1979.
Shaw, Arnold. *Black Popular Music in America.* New York: Schirmer, 1986.
Waldo, Terry. *This Is Ragtime.* New York: Da Capo, 1991.

Bledsoe, Jules

For two decades, Jules Bledsoe was the most famous African American singer of classical music, as well as an actor and composer. He made his professional singing debut on April 20, 1924, at Aeolian Hall in New York City, performing the music of Bach, Brahms, Handel, and Purcell, then began a career performing on concert stages throughout the United States and Europe. A baritone with a wide range, he sang evocatively in several languages. He performed with some of the leading orchestras of the day, including the Boston Symphony (1926) and the British Broadcast Company Symphony in London (1936). In 1931, he presented a program at Carnegie Hall. Bledsoe was also a talented actor, receiving critical praise for his role as Tizan, the Voodoo King, in W. Frank Harling's opera *Deep River* (1926), the first opera performed in the United States with a racially mixed cast. Bledsoe performed in Giuseppe Verdi's opera *Aida* with the Cleveland Stadium Opera in 1932, with the Chicago Opera Company in 1933, and with the Cosmopolitan Opera Company in New York in 1934; and he sang the leading role in the opera *The Emperor Jones* by Louis Gruenberg in 1934.

Bledsoe is perhaps best known for creating the role of Joe in Jerome Kern's musical *Show Boat*, in which he sang "Ol' Man River." Kern had conceived the character and written the song, which became an American classic, specifically for Bledsoe, after hearing him sing. Bledsoe played the role through the run of the show at the Ziegfeld Theater, but Paul Robeson, not Bledsoe, was eventually chosen to play the role in England and in the film version.

Bledsoe went on to other roles and other work. In 1927, he was hired as a member of the music staff at the Roxy Theater in New York City, becoming the first African American to have an ongoing position on Broadway. He left the Roxy in 1930 to resume his concert schedule in the United States and Europe. He moved to Hollywood in the early 1940s and played dramatic roles in *Drums of the Congo* (1942) and other feature films.

Bledsoe wrote several of the songs he performed, sometimes borrowing the language and style of spirituals and folk music. One of his songs, "Pagan Prayer," was based on a poem by Countee Cullen; his one opera, *Bondage*, was based on the novel *Uncle Tom's Cabin* by Harriet Beecher Stowe. He also wrote patriotic songs, including "Ode to America" (1941), which he dedicated to President Franklin Delano Roosevelt, and "Ballad for Americans." He composed a series of songs, *African Suite*, for voices and orchestra. Bledsoe was well aware of the privileges he enjoyed as a successful black artist in a segregated country. In an article he wrote for the July 1928 issue of *Opportunity*—"Has the Negro a Place in the Theater?"—he described the responsibilities that he believed accompanied those privileges.

Biography

Julius Lorenzo Cobb Bledsoe was born 29 December 1897 in Waco, Texas. He graduated (as valedictorian) from Central Texas Academy in Waco in 1914 and from Bishop College (with a B.A.) in Marshall, Texas, in 1918; was in the ROTC at Virginia Union University, 1918–1919; and studied medicine at Columbia University in New York City, 1920–1924. He was a professional singer and actor, appearing in concerts, onstage, and in films, 1924–1941; and a composer, 1931–1942. Bledsoe died 14 July 1943 in Hollywood, California.

CYNTHIA BILY

See also Cullen, Countee; Emperor Jones, The; Opportunity; Robeson, Paul; Show Boat; Singers

Further Reading

Abdul, Raoul. *Blacks in Classical Music*. New York: Dodd, Mead, 1977.

Cuney-Hare, Maude. *Negro Musicians and Their Music*. Washington, D.C.: Associated Publishers, 1936.

Fletcher, Tom. *One Hundred Years of the Negro in Show Business*. New York: Da Capo, 1954, 1984.

Geary, Lynette G. "Jules Bledsoe: The Original Ol' Man River." *Black Perspective in Music*, 17, (1, 2), 1989.

Mendosa, Patrick M. *Extraordinary People in Extraordinary Times: Heroes, Sheroes, and Villains*. Englewood, Colo.: Libraries Unlimited, 1999.

Petrie, Phil. "The Negro in Opera." In *International Library of Negro Life and History: The Negro in Music and Art*, ed. Lindsay Patterson. New York: Publishers Company, 1967.

Blues

The music known as blues (or as "the blues") can be counted among the remarkable achievements of the twentieth century, not only in its own right but as an influence on artistic production in a variety of genres and settings. To a number of writers and artists of the Harlem Renaissance—who were seeking connections with their African and African American past and a native idiom that would capture the spirit of the lives of many blacks in America—blues provided an ideal source and an ideal vehicle for their creative output. Although the influence of Europe is clear in the language (English) and strophic elements of blues, several other characteristics are derived from African modes of performance, including its strong rhythmic emphasis, syncopation, percussive techniques, call-and-response patterns, blue notes, improvised lyric moments, musical instruments, and vocal timbres. Also, the griot performers in African societies may have been figurative ancestors of the African American blues singer. Particularly in its use of integrated polyrhythms and antiphonal techniques, we can see that blues has affinities with African societal structures and life, which were communally oriented and in which art was, intentionally, an integral part of everyday life rather than an adjunct. One can also trace a number of these elements in African American music that preceded the blues, such as spirituals, jubilees, and ragtime: this earlier music surely bequeathed some African strains to the blues tradition.

In form, blues loosely follows a relatively small number of musical and lyric stanza patterns. The combination of the field holler vocal with a harmonic pattern common to European-derived ballads seems to have produced the stanza forms that are used most frequently in blues. Those stanzas most often consist formally of variations of the chord progression I–IV–V lasting for eight bars, twelve bars, sixteen bars, or occasionally some other number of bars. Most frequently, blues songs tend toward a roughly twelve-bar musical pattern. This is described as a "tendency" because the singer could frequently draw out the length of a word or line to indefinite length, as frequently occurred in the work songs and field hollers that preceded the blues. This practice was based on the feelings and exigencies of the moment, and therefore a song could be structured in emotional or social terms rather than according to strict, metronomic formal demands. With regard to the lyrics, there are also a number of pattern variations. For twelve-bar blues, there are usually three roughly equal four-bar segments that rhyme in one of the following strophic patterns: one "line" or thought repeated three times (AAA); one line repeated twice and completed by a different line that end rhymes (AAB); one line sung once and then completed by a second line, with the end rhyme repeated twice (ABB); or a rhyming couplet completed in four bars followed by a refrain of eight bars. The other eight-bar, sixteen-bar, and longer blues stanzas frequently present some kind of variation or adaptation of these patterns.

Some commentators consider this apparent simplicity a limitation; but for blues performers, the basic patterns are a challenge—the performer tries to maintain an essential historical and emotional connection to the community while creating a distinctive individual voice that, through infinite variation and invention, avoids any descent into monotony or self-caricature. Additionally, within the basic structure a great deal of variation is possible in performing techniques, instrumental combinations, and settings. In fact, a wide array of blues styles developed over the years, influenced by geographical, chronological, and social factors, including the dominance of a local musical figure in the blues community. All the while, blues has offered musicians a remarkable opportunity to explore a variety of themes and issues: the complexities of male and female relationships, domestic violence, alcoholism, natural disasters, social protest, labor difficulties, alternative sexual identities, and many others. In fact, blues can be seen as a forum for raising important issues, if not explicitly, then implicitly, and therefore as an important means of creating and sustaining a voice for those who are frequently voiceless in the African American community. These were voices that many creative artists of the Harlem Renaissance wanted to hear, represent, and express in their work.

It was no accident that the musical genre known as blues and the literary movement known as the Harlem Renaissance both emerged on the national and international scene in the 1920s. Both traced their roots back to the nineteenth century during the period when the first generation of freeborn African Americans were coming of age. At this point, most African Americans were facing for the first time the prospect of life outside the oppressive plantation system, and there was no older generation with experience in such a context to help them deal with new modes of oppression. Blues seems to have been created to explore the new experiences and new difficulties facing African Americans. It provided a flexible new structural and emotional setting that still had ties to previous African and African American musical genres. Blues focused primarily on love between men and women and on wanderlust—two major issues confronting African Americans outside the system that had controlled the slaves' sexuality and mobility—and this music gave performers ample opportunities to express in a direct, earthy, pithy way the joys, sorrows, and ambiguities of their experiences. Blues, then, provided both structural guidelines and expressive freedom.

While writers such as Charles Chesnutt and Paul Laurence Dunbar, the premier African American dialect poet, were exploring the lives and language of African Americans through the local-color tradition, musicians were creating and spreading the feelings, forms, and techniques that made up the budding blues tradition—which would receive a great deal of attention from folklorists, songsmiths, literary artists, and eventually the general public. The establishment of the American Folklore Society at Harvard University in 1888 was an impetus for the study and collection of American, including African American, folklore; shortly thereafter, reports began to surface of blues or blueslike songs heard by W. C. Handy and Gates Thomas in 1890, Charles Peabody in 1901, Gertrude "Ma" Rainey in 1902, and Howard Odum between 1905 and 1908. The first three blues songs published in history were Artie Matthews's "Baby Seals Blues" (August 1912), Hart Wand's "Dallas Blues" (September 1912), and Handy's "Memphis Blues" (late September–early October 1912). In just a few years, blues would be available on phonograph records and would inspire dance crazes (Noble Sissle claimed that Handy's "Memphis Blues" had inspired Vernon and Irene Castle's fox trot), and a flurry of activity would bring blues to the attention of the American intelligentsia and to mainstream popular culture as well.

African Americans had appeared in recordings possibly as early as 1890–1892, when the Bohee Brothers recorded titles (now unknown) for Edison cylinders (unfortunately untraced) in London; also, the white Victor Military Band had recorded instrumental blues as early as 1914; and beginning in 1916 the *Chicago Defender* had been urging African Americans to release records. However, African American vocal blues made their first appearance on phonograph records in 1920. Perry Bradford took Mamie Smith—an artist from his revue *Made in Harlem*—first to the Victor label and then to Fred Hager at Okeh, where Smith recorded "That Thing Called Love," which was successful enough to earn her another recording date the same year. At her second session, she recorded "Crazy Blues," the first vocal blues recorded by an African American artist, and its effect on the market was electrifying. "Crazy Blues" sold 75,000 copies in the first month after its release and persuaded a number of other companies in New York City to jump into what came to be called the "race" record market, even though these companies had initially been reluctant to record African American performers. Recordings by Lucille Hegamin, Lillyn Brown, Lavinia Turner, and Bessie Smith soon followed. Harlem had mounted one parade to welcome soldiers returning home from World War I, and another (10,000 strong) to protest against lynchings and racial discrimination in 1917; and Smith's recording seemed to be one more sign of the imminent emergence of the New Negro onto the American scene.

The first five years or so of blues recording were dominated by these women vaudeville blues singers, who performed blues based on folk blues but composed, arranged, and clearly aimed at a more refined audience. The recordings were in part influenced by the efforts of trained composers and musicians such as Handy, who saw a chance to make blues more "respectable" and marketable. Handy smoothed off what he saw as some of the "rough edges" and made blues more palatable by using trained, reading musicians who had a sense of timing and technique less idiosyncratic than that of the frequently untrained folk performers. Vaudeville blues often consisted of a sung narrative or lyric introduction preceding the main body of the song and setting up the situation that the singer was about to lament, followed by either twelve-bar stanzas or some sophisticated popular modification of the twelve-bar pattern, accompanied by professional musicians on piano, brass, and reeds who gave the recordings a tinge of jazz. This is not to suggest that all vaudeville blues performers sounded alike: There was a remarkable diversity in styles, vocal

timbres, and stage presence, and the tradition included a range of artists from hog-maw earthy to saccharine-sweet.

As writers sought to represent not only the lives but the spirit of African Americans, blues seemed to demonstrate how a people had been able to survive systematic oppression and discrimination by generating an art that explicitly or implicitly examined the deprivations imposed by slavery and Jim Crow—and how blacks had risen above and become superior to oppression by creating their own artistic system, which was more democratic than the putative democracy that had enslaved them. African American writers of the 1920s searching for an alternative to the worn-out literary modes and values of the previous generation found in the blues and jazz traditions a meaningful historical and cultural past that helped them deal with their own current social issues and also helped them generate art dealing with familiar modernist themes: the outsider's sense of dislocation and alienation; rejection of conventional middle-class values; rejection of rationalization for "primitive" passion and living and improvising in the moment; and the need to find a new structure and language adequate for expressing these ideas.

It was no wonder that blues musicians seized the moment in 1920. Blues—with its roots in the oral tradition among the masses of African Americans and its welter of voices frequently lacking the inhibitions and pretensions of upwardly mobile middle-class African Americans—captivated a number of "new guard" African American writers who were anxious to declare themselves liberated from what they considered (at least in some cases) the smothering influence of the American literary tradition and of the "old guard" proponents of the Harlem Renaissance. W. E. B. Du Bois, for example, was known to prefer European classical music; in *The Crisis*, he gave the most prominent space to African Americans who worked in the classical tradition and European artists who drew on African American elements to enliven their classical compositions. Moreover, in *Dusk of Dawn* (1940) he referred to jazz as "caricature"—which no doubt some of it was, pandering as it occasionally did to white popular tastes—and throughout his career he seemed to wrestle with being proud of jazz and blues but not quite able to wholly accept them as worthy of artistic appreciation. James Weldon Johnson, who was somewhat more sympathetic, appreciated the contributions of African American secular folklore and called for someone to capture its "racial flavor" (as John Millington Synge had done for the Irish); however, Johnson himself championed spirituals, not blues, as the great African American folk art. Clearly, Du Bois's and Johnson's middle-class orientation and their concentration on image as a bridge into mainstream American society prompted them to reject the earthy, even vulgar, blues in favor of genres that more definitively demonstrated that African Americans were capable of generating art just as good as (read "just like") that of white Europeans.

Among the writers of the Harlem Renaissance who were most influenced by blues were Langston Hughes, Sterling Brown, and Zora Neale Hurston. All three represented the younger generation of writers who had connections to middle- and upper-class society yet felt misgivings about allowing their work to be dominated by European aesthetics. In his famous manifesto "The Negro Artist and the Racial Mountain" (1926), Hughes praised "the low down folks" for their unpretentiousness and their unself-conscious joy, hearing in their blues and religious songs a natural alternative to the restrictions of contemporary society. He had been profoundly affected by the blues singers he heard as a child on the appropriately named Independence Avenue in Chicago in 1918; in Washington, D.C., in 1924; and in the cabarets, theaters, and nightclubs of Harlem—his frequent use of the blues idiom in his works reflects that influence. Hughes used a variety of stanza patterns, earthy language, metaphors and other imagery, dramatic situations, and references to blues performers in his poetry, prose, fiction, and drama from his first volume, *The Weary Blues and Other Poems* (1926), to his last, *The Panther and the Lash* (1967). Inherent in the blues idiom, as Hughes applied it, were call-and-response elements and a philosophy of perseverance in the face of adversity. As a professed urban poet, Hughes most frequently mentioned and made use of the works of urban blues singers, particularly women such as Ma Rainey; Bessie, Clara, and Trixie Smith; Gladys Bentley; Victoria Spivey; and Georgia White, along with sophisticated male blues singers such as Lonnie Johnson. In a review of *The Weary Blues* in *Opportunity* (February 1926), Countee Cullen called Hughes's jazz poems "interlopers" that did not "belong to that dignified company, that select and austere circle of high literary expression which we call poetry." But while some people tried to discourage Hughes from using blues in his work, he was placing in the mouth of his unpretentious folk hero Simple the last word on his love of the blues and the people who made it, putting aside personal vanity and social

self-consciousness in the face of their enduring presence: "I will not deny Ma Rainey, even to hide my age. Yes, I heard her! I am proud of hearing her! To tell the truth, if I stop and listen, I can still hear her" ("Shadow of the Blues").

Sterling Brown and Zora Neale Hurston were more familiar with southern folk blues, and more adept at using it in their works. Brown, who described himself as an amateur folklorist, studied the roots of blues more systematically than Hughes; and although Brown was less likely than Hughes to incorporate blues stanza patterns in his work, he had an unsurpassed ability to evoke the nuances of the blues experience in his stark portraits of characters such as Big Boy Davis, John Henry, Ma Rainey, and old nameless couples giving it one more try. Hurston, who was an anthropologist, also made a systematic study of African American expressive culture. She was familiar with the vivacity of folklore from her earliest years in Eatonville, Florida, where front-porch "lying" sessions had given her an unquenchable passion for the powerful language of the "folk." Sometimes accompanied by Alan Lomax and Mary Elizabeth Barnicle, she made trips to collect folklore at the behest of Franz Boas and with financial support from Charlotte Mason; these trips produced some excellent blues recordings by Gabriel Brown (who is portrayed in Hurston's folklore collection *Mules and Men* of 1935), Booker T. Sapps, and others. Significantly, Hurston attempted to consider African American folklore in context, that is, in terms of its functions in the community (something no other folklorist at the time had been capable of doing). Thus, although some readers considered Hurston's portrait altogether too rosy or too artificial, it was still neither as artificial nor as stodgy as most written material that had been generated by white folklorists. More important, Hurston's masterpiece, *Their Eyes Were Watching God* (1937), has been called a blues novel because it uses a variety of elements related to blues: the color blue, blues songs, blues performers, creative and earthy language, sexual metaphors, a setting in the bottoms or the muck, call-and-response actions and situations, and a philosophy that can be summed up as "sun gonna shine in my back door someday." In the work of Hughes, Brown, and Hurston, as well as in that of Claude McKay, Rudolph Fisher, Wallace Thurman, and others, we can see blues as an important aesthetic element informing the literature of the Harlem Renaissance.

Of course, it was not only literature that drew on blues. The jazz and pop songs of the period, as performed by such Harlem artists as Ethel Waters, Nina Mae McKinney, Duke Ellington, and Cab Calloway, frequently showed evidence of blues techniques and structures. Duke Ellington in particular worked wonders with the blues idiom; his brilliant three-minute vignettes, and some longer pieces, made him one of the most distinguished composers of the twentieth century. Performances of blues, pop-blues, and jazz were largely responsible for attracting "slumming" whites to Harlem, where they spent money in night spots, and thus for encouraging an interest in African American culture. Whether or not this interest was illusory, it helped finance a number of artists of the Harlem Renaissance.

In the visual arts, Aaron Douglas's *I Needs a Dime for Beer* (1926), paired with Langston Hughes's blues poem "Down an' Out"; Winold Reiss's *Hot Chocolates* (1929), and Archibald Motley's *Blues* (1929) were inspired by the syncopated style of blues. In Motley's *Blues*, one can almost feel the angular energy, shifting accents, and sensual pulse of performers such as Louis Armstrong, Bessie Smith, and Duke Ellington.

The Harlem Renaissance did not come to an abrupt end at the close of the 1920s; neither did blues—it continued to develop and thrive, and to adapt to and reflect its surroundings. Still, one can look back to the music and art of the Harlem Renaissance as a foundation for much African American art that followed. In the best of this later work, one can hear echoes of the rural and urban blues idiom of the renaissance era—shaped, of course, in the best blues tradition, by the genius of the individual creative artist and passed back to the community that inspired it.

STEVEN C. TRACY

See also Blues: An Anthology; Blues: Women Performers; Boas, Franz; Brown, Sterling; Chesnutt, Charles Waddell; Crisis, The; Cullen, Countee; Douglas, Aaron; Du Bois, W. E. B.; Dunbar, Paul Laurence; Fisher, Rudolph; Hughes, Langston; Hurston, Zora Neale; Jazz; Johnson, James Weldon; Mason, Charlotte Osgood; McKay, Claude; Motley, Archibald J. Jr.; Music; Musicians; Reiss, Winold; Singers; Thurman, Wallace; *specific musicians and singers*

Further Reading

Bradford, Perry. *Born with the Blues*. New York: Oak, 1965.

Cohn, Lawrence, ed. *Nothing but the Blues*. New York: Abbeville, 1993.

Dixon, Robert M. W., John Godrich, and Howard Rye, eds. *Blues and Gospel Records, 1890–1942*, 4th ed. Oxford: Clarendon, 1997.

Ford, Robert, comp. *A Blues Bibliography*. London: RIS, 1999.

Handy, W. C. *Father of the Blues*. New York: Collier, 1941.

Harris, Sheldon. *Blues Who's Who*. New Rochelle, N.Y.: Arlington House, 1979.

Harrison, Daphne Duval. *Black Pearls*. New Brunswick, N.J.: Rutgers University Press, 1988.

Oliver, Paul. *The Blues Fell This Morning*. London: Cassell, 1960.

———. *The Story of the Blues*. Philadelphia, Pa.: Chilton, 1973.

Titon, Jeff. *Early Downhome Blues: A Musical and Cultural Analysis*. Urbana: University of Illinois Press, 1978.

Tracy, Steven C. *Langston Hughes and the Blues*. Urbana: University of Illinois Press, 1988.

———, ed. *Write Me a Few of Your Lines: A Blues Reader*. Amherst: University of Massachusetts Press, 1999.

Blues: An Anthology

Blues: An Anthology (1926), edited by W. C. Handy, was one of the earliest studies of the influence of folk blues on American jazz, popular music, and classical music and remains one of the most famous published collections of commercial blues. It celebrated African American musical traditions and contributed to a growing interest in blues, and in black folk culture generally, during the Harlem Renaissance. Handy himself was among the first composers to write and publish commercial songs inspired by the newly emerging folk blues, which he heard in the Mississippi delta.

Blues: An Anthology resulted from interviews that the American music scholar Edward Abbe Niles (who was also a lawyer on Wall Street) held with Handy in 1925, about blues and black folk music. It consisted of 180 pages and contained the music and lyrics of fifty songs, selected by Handy and arranged for piano and voice. About half of the songs were Handy's own compositions or arrangements, including several of his most famous titles: "Saint Louis Blues" (1914), "Joe Turner Blues" (1915), "The Hesitating Blues" (1915), "Aunt Hagar's Children Blues" (1921, 1922), and "Harlem Blues" (1923)—though not "Memphis Blues" (1912), his earliest published commercial blues, because its publisher had refused to grant permission. Also included were songs by Spencer Williams, Will Nash,

159

Irving Berlin, Jerome Kern, and John Alden Carpenter; excerpts from George Gershwin's *Rhapsody in Blue* (1924), a work that was influenced by blues; and Gershwin's *Concerto in F* (1925), "no part of which," Handy said, "had been published elsewhere at that time." The anthology also had a critical introduction by Niles (which included a concise biography of Handy, music examples, and the first use of the term "folk blues"), notes on the origins of the songs, and eight full-page illustrations by the Mexican artist Miguel Covarrubias.

Blues: An Anthology was received warmly by critics such as Edmund Wilson, Sigmund Spaeth, and Carl Van Vechten. Langston Hughes, in his review for *Opportunity* magazine, said that the collection was "a much needed, beautiful book . . . filled with invaluable information for the student of Negro folk music and folk poetry." James Weldon Johnson, in the *Saturday Review of Literature*, praised the book as "a valuable contribution to the literature of American folk-lore and folk music." He added, "In this volume Mr. Handy has taken the first step to do [to] the Negro secular music what has been done quite fully for the Spirituals and the plantation stories."

During the 1920s, there was intense interest in African American folk music, and several important studies of black musical traditions, sacred and secular, were published. But Handy's anthology was the first devoted exclusively to blues, and except for James Weldon Johnson's *Book of American Negro Spirituals* (1925) and *Second Book of Negro Spirituals* (1926), it was the only one edited by an African American. Revised editions of *Blues: An Anthology* were published in 1949 and 1972. Since then, various editions have been reprinted under the original title by Da Capo Press (1985, 1990) and by Applewood Books (2001).

PATRICK HUBER

See also Blues; Bontemps, Arna; Covarrubias, Miguel; Handy, W. C.; Johnson, James Weldon; Van Vechten, Carl

Further Reading

Evans, David. "William Christopher Handy." In *The New Grove Dictionary of Music and Musicians*, 2nd ed., ed. Stanley Sadie. New York: Grove's Dictionaries, 2001.

Handy, W. C., ed. *Blues: An Anthology*, intro. Abbe Niles. New York: Albert and Charles Boni, 1926. (Revisions: *A Treasury of the Blues: Complete Words and Music of Sixty-seven Great Songs from Memphis Blues to the Present Day*. New York: Charles Boni, 1949; with historical and critical text by Abbe Niles. *Blues: An Anthology: Complete Words and Music of Fifty-three Great Songs*, rev. Jerry Silverman. New York: Macmillan, 1972; with historical and critical text by Abbe Niles. Reprints, New York: Da Capo, 1885, 1990; new introduction by William Ferris. Also, Applewood, 2001.)

Handy, W. C. *Father of the Blues: An Autobiography*, ed. Arna Bontemps. New York: Macmillan, 1941. (Foreword by Abbe Niles.)

Hughes, Langston. "Review of Blues: An Anthology." *Opportunity*, 4(44), August 1926.

Johnson, James Weldon, ed. *The Book of American Negro Spirituals*. New York: Viking, 1925. (With musical arrangements by J. Rosamond Johnson and additional numbers by Lawrence Brown.)

Johnson, James Weldon. "'Now We Have the Blues'— Review of Blues: An Anthology." *Saturday Review of Literature*, 19 June 1926.

———, ed. *The Second Book of Negro Spirituals*. New York: Viking, 1926. (With musical arrangements by J. Rosamond Johnson.)

Van Vechten, Carl. "Mean Ole Miss Blues Becomes Respectable—Review of Blues: An Anthology." *New York Herald Tribune*, 6 June 1926.

Blues: Women Performers

African American women were among the first popularizers of recorded blues in the 1920s and 1930s, during the Harlem Renaissance. Mamie Smith's recording of Perry Bradford's "Crazy Blues" sold 75,000 copies (at a dollar apiece) in the first month after it was released on 10 August 1920, and its success opened doors for many other African American female artists. Recording companies established "race record" divisions to tap the African American market, and eventually mainstream consumers as well. Columbia, Okeh (which merged with Columbia), and Paramount searched rural and urban areas for women who could sing the blues. Black Swan began its own effort to record, not the guttural sounds of southern blues, but African American women whose voices would contribute to cultural uplift. (Accordingly, Black Swan rejected the great Bessie Smith.)

Gertrude "Ma" Rainey

The contralto Gertrude "Ma" Rainey (26 April 1886–22 December 1939) is called the "mother of the blues." She was born in Columbus, Georgia, to the minstrel performers Ella Allen and Thomas Pridgett, who were her inspiration. She made her debut at age fourteen in a song-and-dance troupe, A Bunch of Blackberries, at Springer Opera House in Columbus. In 1902, she was intrigued by the haunting lyrics of a blues tune sung by a woman at a theater in St. Louis, Missouri, and incorporated the style into her own act. In 1904, she married a minstrel song-and-dance man and comedian, William Rainey; they billed themselves as Rainey and Rainey, or "Ma and Pa Rainey, Assassinators of the Blues." (The Raineys separated in the 1920s.)

As head of the Rabbit Foot Minstrels, Ma Rainey established herself on the Moses Stokes Company circuit (managed by Cora and Lonnie Fisher), singing blues in the earthy male minstrel style. In 1912, in Chattanooga, Tennessee, the troupe hired Bessie Smith, who was eight years younger than Rainey. Rainey and Smith became friends (and possibly lovers), and Rainey taught Smith dance steps and the art of the stage entrance, prepared her for the rigors of the road, and introduced her to blues.

In 1923, Paramount Records promoted Rainey's indigenous southern blues sound. Rainey recorded with Paramount until 1928, releasing more than ninety songs and attracting fans in the urban North and the rural South. Her accompanists included the best musicians, such as Tommy Dorsey and Louis Armstrong. Rainey composed many of her songs but received no royalties—Paramount paid her a flat fee per recorded side. Rainey's style (for example, in her rendition of "See See Rider" and "Prove It on Me Blues") was characterized by rhythmic call-and-response improvisation, distinctive phrasing and timbre, and groans, moans, and shouts; it established the standard for classic blues. The impressive sales of Rainey's records caught the attention of the Theater Owners' Booking Association (TOBA), which provided steady concert tours for her.

Ma Rainey's eventual departure from the concert circuit and the recording industry was a result of competition from talking pictures, radio, swing music, and the Depression. Paramount canceled her contract in 1928, but she continued on the vaudeville circuit until 1935.

Bessie Smith

The "empress of the blues," Bessie Smith (15 April 1894–26 September 1937), was born in Chattanooga,

Tennessee. Her career in show business was started there by her brother Clarence, who encouraged her to sing and dance for coins from passersby (with another brother, Andrew, as guitar accompanist) on the sidewalk in front of the White Elephant Saloon. Smith gave girlish but rowdy renditions of "Bill Bailey, Won't You Please Come Home?" At age nine, she entered an amateur contest at the Ivory Theater.

In 1912, again influenced by Clarence, she joined the dance troupe (managed by Cora and Lonnie Fisher in the Moses Stokes Company) in which Ma Rainey was a blues artist. Smith's salary in this troupe was $10 a week, plus money thrown onto the stage. Audiences loved her rendition of "Weary Blues" and tossed even more coins at her when she sang it.

In 1913, Smith made Charles Bailey's 81 Theater in Atlanta, Georgia, her home base; she also traveled with Pete Werley's Florida Blossoms and the Silas Green show. However, she was fired (at the suggestion of the African American producer Irvin Miller) because her complexion was too dark for a show called "Glorifying the Brownskin Girl." In 1921, Smith went to Philadelphia, where she performed at Moran's Cabaret. She also performed at the Dunbar and Standard theaters and Paradise Gardens in Atlantic City, New Jersey. She married the night watchman at Moran's, Jack Gee, on 7 June 1923.

A customer at Moran's, Charlie Carson, who owned a record shop, persuaded the pianst Clarence Williams to take Smith to Frank Walker, a manager at Columbia, for an audition. At Columbia's recording studio, Smith performed two songs on 15 February 1923. Smith also auditioned for Thomas Edison, Fred Hager at Okeh (who disliked her rural strain), and Harry Pace of Black Swan (who thought her sound too raw). She had her first recording session—three songs—at Columbia on 16 February 1923. Columbia released the hugely successful "Gulf Coast Blues" and "Down Hearted Blues" and gave Smith a one-year contract to record at least twelve usable sides. She was soon being called Columbia's "queen of the blues"; her fee increased to $200 per usuable side, and Fletcher Henderson became her studio accompanist.

Smith also continued touring. With Irvin Johns as her accompanist, she performed in 1923 at the 81 Theater in Atlanta (because of segregation, she gave a special midnight performance for whites). She broke attendance records at the Frolic Theater in Birmingham, where she sang "Nobody's Bizness If I Do" and "Gulf Coast Blues." A performance at the Beale Street Palace in Memphis was broadcast. Smith was so popular on tour that she refused to share the stage with any other blues singer.

By 1924, Smith was earning $2,000 a week and contracted for a twenty-week tour with the TOBA. She had a new musical director, Fred Longshaw. By 1925, she owned a custom-made railroad car; recorded with Louis Armstrong; and made her first appearance at the Liberty Theater in Chattanooga, including her brother Clarence in her show. She recorded (again) with Fletcher Henderson in 1926, and with James P. Johnson in 1928. By this time, nightlife in Harlem was at its zenith, and vaudeville and blues were declining, but Smith remained popular. She made her Broadway debut in *Pansy* (1929) and appeared in a film based on "Saint Louis Blues" (1932).

After the stock market crashed in 1929, audiences fell off, and so did Smith's income. Swing music and talking movies became the new sensation, but Smith, billed as the "queen of recording artists," made eight recordings for Columbia in 1930 (being paid $125 per side); she made her final recording for Columbia on 20 November 1931. Although the demand was not high, she appeared at the Lafayette Theater in New York in 1932, taking second billing to Jules Bledsoe. In 1933, she recorded four sides for Okeh (at $37.50 per side), including "Gimme a Pigfoot" and her last recording, "I'm Down in the Dumps." (As Smith left the studio, Billie Holiday, age seventeen, was in the waiting room preparing to make her recording debut.) Smith also performed at Connie's Inn in New York in 1936.

Mamie Smith

Mamie Gardener Smith (26 May 1883–16 September 1946) was born in Cincinnati, Ohio. At age ten she was a dancer with the Four Dancing Mitchells; by 1910, she was a member of the Smart Set Company, an African American minstrel troupe. In 1912, she married her first husband, the singer William "Smitty" Smith, and moved to New York, where she became a cabaret singer, pianist, and dancer. Perry Bradford, the African American entrepreneur and songwriter, discovered her in 1918 and chose her to break the color barrier in New York's recording industry. He cast her in his musical *Made in Harlem* and arranged auditions with Victor and Okeh. Smith recorded "That Thing Called Love" and "You Can't Keep a Good Man Down" for Okeh. Her recording of "Crazy Blues" (1920) made her a star, opened a new market for

vocal blues, and inspired the recording industry to go in search of other African American women blues singers. "Crazy Blues" featured Willie "the Lion" Smith on piano, Jimmy Dunn on cornet, and Dope Andrews on trombone; these musicians became known as the Jazz Hounds and established the sound of recorded blues. Smith recorded thirty more songs for Okeh and starred in vaudeville shows, including *Follow Me* (1922), *Struttin' Along* (1923), *Dixie Review* (1924), *Syncopated Revue* (1925), and *Frolicking Around* (1926).

By the end of the 1920s, blues recordings were losing momentum, but Smith recorded for Okeh through 1931. She also appeared in African American musicals such as *Sun Tan Frolics* (1929), *Fireworks of 1930*, *Rhumbaland Revue* (both 1931), and *Yelping Hounds Revue* (1932–1934), and in the films *Paradise in Heaven* (1939), *Mystery in Swing* (1940), *Sunday Sinners* (1941), *Murder on Lenox Avenue* (1941), and *Because I Love You* (1943).

Clara Smith

Clara Smith (c. 1894–2 February 1935), "queen of the moaners," was born in Spartanburg, South Carolina. She joined the vaudeville circuit in 1910, became a regular with the TOBA in 1918, and joined the Harlem club scene in 1923. She had a thinner voice than Bessie Smith (with whom she sometimes sang duets) but had a distinct comedic style, especially in double-entendre songs like "Whip It to a Jelly." Her biggest hit was "Every Woman's Blues" (1923). She also oversaw the business of the Clara Smith Theatrical Club.

Trixie Smith

Trixie Smith (1895–1943) was born in Atlanta, Georgia. In 1922, she made her first recording with Black Swan and won a blues singing contest at the Manhattan Casino, sponsored by the Fifteenth Regiment of the New York Infantry. Black Swan later merged with Paramount, and Smith recorded for the new company until 1926. Her popular recordings were her own compositions, including "Trixie's Blues," "Railroad Blues," and "Mining Camp Blues." She recorded for Decca in the 1930s. Smith worked with noted jazz musicians, including Louis Armstrong, Fletcher Henderson, and Sidney Bechet. She performed in African American musicals and appeared in one film, *The Black King* (1932).

Alberta Hunter

Alberta Hunter (Josephine Beatty, 1 April 1895–17 October 1984) was born in Memphis, Tennessee. She ran away to Chicago at age eleven and became an entertainer there in 1914, performing in cabarets and clubs. In 1921, in New York, she also appeared in clubs, and she recorded for the Gennett label, accompanied by Joe "King" Oliver, Louis Armstrong, Sidney Bechet, and Fletcher Henderson. She recorded for other labels as May Alix and Josephine Beatty. She had several musical styles and could adapt her voice to almost any musical situation. Hunter was the composer of "Downhearted Blues" (1922), made famous by Bessie Smith in 1923.

Hunter had one of the longest careers of the early African American women blues singers. From 1927 to 1953 she had lucrative engagements in the United States, as well as in Europe, where she was the first African American woman to perform blues. She made her film debut in *Radio Parade* in 1936. In London, she appeared opposite Paul Robeson in *Show Boat*. She performed in USO shows during World War II and the Korean War. Hunter was known as a shrewd businesswoman; she was also a nurse, from 1954 until 1977, when her performing career rebounded.

Ida Prather Cox

Ida Prather Cox (25 February 1896–10 November 1967), "queen of the blues," was born in Toccoa, Georgia. Her early music was inspired by the church; but in 1911 she ran away from home and joined White and Clark's Black and Tan Minstrels. She later performed with other vaudeville troupes, including the Rabbit Foot Minstrels, Florida Cotton Blossom Minstrels, and Silas Green from New Orleans. The first song she performed in public was "Put Your Arms Around Me." During her vaudeville years, she married Adler Cox, the first of her three husbands.

Cox was known for her classic blues style. She was always a lady, always regal; her shows were sophisticated and glamorous, and her music was sultry and sensuous. Her accompanists included Lovie Austin, Jesse Crump (her third husband), Jelly Roll Morton, and Joe "King" Oliver. Her recording "Wild Women Don't Have the Blues" became a feminist anthem. Between 1923 and 1929, she recorded more than forty records for Paramount. When the stock market crash depressed the blues music industry, Cox produced her own road shows, *Raisin' Cain* and *Darktown Scandals*. In 1934, she performed with Bessie Smith in *Fan Waves Revue* at the Apollo Theater in Harlem, billed as the "sepia Mae West." Cox recorded again in 1939 for John Hammond on the Okeh and Vocalion labels, with her All-Star Orchestra. She toured until 1945, when she had a stroke; in 1961 she recorded *Blues for Rampart Street* for Riverside.

Edith Wilson

Edith Goodall Wilson (6 September 1896–March 1981) was born in Louisville, Kentucky. She began performing in church and school recitals. In 1910, at age thirteen, unbeknownst to her parents, she was in a show at White City Park, earning $35 per week, more than twice her mother's salary as a housekeeper. Wilson left home at a tender age to seek a stage career in Milwaukee.

Edith appeared on the same bill as, and became friends with, the young piano player Danny Wilson (whom she would marry) and his sister Lena. Danny Wilson, a graduate of a conservatory in Charleston, South Carolina, trained Lena and Edith for the competitive stage, encouraging them to sing all kinds of songs, not just blues. As a trio, Edith, Lena, and Danny Wilson worked in cabarets and clubs in Chicago. In 1921, they went to Thomas's club in Washington, D.C.; eventually they came to New York City.

Perry "Mule" Bradford, a composer and talent scout for Columbia, had a disagreement with Mamie Smith, who was the lead singer in his musical *Put and Take*. After seeing one of Edith Wilson's performances, he decided to replace Smith with Wilson. The musical opened at Town Hall, New York City, and Wilson made a sensational impression on other talent scouts for Columbia. She recorded sides for Columbia on September 13, 1921. Bradford gave her "Nervous Blues," backed by Johnny Dunn and the Jazz Hounds, with her husband, Danny, on the piano. Wilson's next recording, "Vampin' Liza Jane," marked Columbia's entry into "race records" and the start of Wilson's climb to the top.

Wilson cut most of the sides for Columbia in 1922, producing thirty-two recordings (twenty-six were released). She joined the TOBA, billed as "queen of the blues," and performed Bradford's songs at Connie's Inn, the Lincoln Theater, and the Dixieland Plantation Room of the Winter Garden. In 1923, Wilson traveled to London with the revue, renamed *Dover Street to*

Dixie. She expanded her repertoire to include show tunes and comedy skits. In 1924, she joined *Club Alabam Revue* at the Lafayette Theater in New York City, teamed with Doc Straine in comedy skits, and returned to Columbia Records. She and Straine took their comedy routine on the road during 1924–1925. In 1926–1927, Wilson performed in *Blackbirds* in Paris and London.

Again in New York, she performed at Loew's State Theater and occasionally sang on CBS radio broadcasts, when Duke Ellington and his band were with Loew's. Her success continued into the late 1970s, when she appeared at blues festivals.

Wilson's audiences included monied Broadway patrons, affluent African Americans, and patrons of Harlem cabarets controlled by underworld figures. Wilson was a good businesswoman, and she had learned not just blues but vaudeville and cabaret style, ballads, ditties, and humorous songs. Her Creole-type yodel distinguished her sound from that of other women blues performers, and her beauty, light complexion, and charm appealed to her mixed audiences.

Ethel Waters

Ethel Waters (31 October 1896–1 September 1977) was born in Chester, Pennsylvania, and raised in Philadelphia by her grandmother. Waters married Buddy Purnsley when she was thirteen and he was twenty-three (the marriage failed). She supported herself as a domestic but performed in churches and other local venues. The producers of a vaudeville troupe discovered her at a Halloween party in 1917 (on her birthday) and billed her as "Sweet Mama Stringbean." Waters became a performer with the TOBA and in clubs in Harlem, where she arrived in 1919. She signed with Black Swan in 1921; her style, with its articulate melodic phrasing, was what the African American elite considered essential for an emerging culture. Her recordings and performances of the 1920s, under the direction of Fletcher Henderson, led to a contract with Columbia. Waters recorded many hits, notably "Down Home Blues" and "Oh Daddy."

As the blues era drew to an end, Waters embarked on a second career as an actress, making her debut in the Broadway musical *Africana* in 1927. She was a stage and screen star in the 1930s, 1940s, and 1950s and was nominated for an Academy Award for Best Actress for her work in *Pinky* (1949).

Sippie Wallace

Beulah Belle Thomas Wallace ("Sippie," 1 November 1898–1 November 1986) was born in Houston, Texas, and became known as the "Texas nightingale." Her special sound was a mix of spirited, hard-edged, southwestern rolling honky-tonk and Chicago shouting and moaning. She followed her musical brother George to the Storyville district of New Orleans, where she married her first husband, Frank Seals. Her second husband was a gambler, Matthew "Matt" Wallace. Sippie Wallace sang at local social gatherings and tent shows in Texas while working as a maid and stage assistant to a snake dancer with Philip's Reptile Show, Madam Dante.

In 1923, Wallace moved with her brother Hersal and her niece Hociel to Chicago, where George Wallace was influential in the music division of W. W. Kimball Company and directed his own orchestra. Sippie, Hersal, and George became a popular recording trio. George and Sippie also formed a songwriting partnership; they wrote "Shorty George" and "Underworld Blues." Sippie Wallace's initial recordings, "Shorty George" and "Up the Country Blues," were for Okeh. She became a regular on the TOBA circuit in 1923 and 1924. She released "Special Delivery Blues" and "Jack o' Diamond Blues" (a homage to Matt Wallace) in 1926 and performed "Dead Drunk Blues" with Louis Armstrong in 1927. She moved to Chicago in 1929 and contracted with Victor Records, recording four sides (two were released: "I'm a Mighty Tight Woman" and "You Gonna Need My Help").

The Depression hampered Wallace's career as a blues singer, and she retired, becoming the organist for Leland Baptist Church in Detroit. However, she continued to accept club bookings. Mercury Records reissued "Bedroom Blues" in 1945, Detroit's Fine Arts label reissued a recording in 1959, and Victoria Spivey encouraged Wallace to join the circuit of folk and blues festivals. In Europe in 1966, Wallace performed for a new generation of blues enthusiasts. She appeared at Lincoln Center in New York in 1977 and in Germany in 1986.

Victoria Spivey

Victoria Spivey (6 October 1906–3 October 1976) was born in Houston, Texas; performed in local clubs as a teenager; and recorded "Black Snake Blues" for Okeh and wrote songs for the St. Louis Publishing Company in 1926. Spivey popularized "TB Blues" and "Murder in the First Degree." She appeared in the

African American musical *Hallelujah!* in 1929, the touring show *Dallas Tan Town Topics* in 1933, and the touring Broadway show *Hellzapoppin'* in 1938–1939.

In the 1950s and 1960s, Spivey was a mainstay at blues festivals and college performances, recording for Bluesville and Folkways. Her voice had a Texas twang, a high nasal sound into which she incorporated a moan that she called her "tiger squall."

Other Women Performers

There were other important figures, recording for Ajax, Black Swan/Paramount, Brunswick, Emerson, Gennett, Okeh/Columbia, Pathé, Perfect, RCA Victor, and Vocalion: Fae Barnes; Bessie Brown; Eliza Brown; Josephine Carter; Martha Copeland; Helen Gross; Ethel Hayes; Lucille Hegamin, the "Cameo Girl"; Rosa Henderson; Edna Hicks; Chippie Hill; Leitha Hill; Edith Johnson; Mary Johnson; Virginia Liston; Sara Martin, the "colored Sophie Tucker"; Viola McCoy; Josie Miles; Lizzie Miles, the "Creole songbird"; Nettie Potter; Susie Smith; Grace White; Lena Wilson—and still more. The cabarets, clubs, and theaters of the Harlem Renaissance were brightened by African American women blues singers, who were, according to Daphne Duval Harrison (1988), "black pearls."

GERRI BATES

See also Black Swan Phonograph Company; Blackbirds; Blues; Columbia Phonograph Company; Hallelujah; Lafayette Theater; Lincoln Theater; Manhattan Casino; Miller, Irvin; Music; Musical Theater; Singers; Theater Owners' Booking Association; *specific musicians and performers*

Further Reading

Davis, Angela Y. *Blues Legacies and Black Feminism: Gertrude "Ma" Rainey, Bessie Smith, and Billie Holiday.* 1998.
Harrison, Daphne Duval. *Black Pearls: Blues Queens of the 1920s.* 1988.
Lieb, Sandra. *Mother of the Blues: A Study of Ma Rainey.* 1981.

Boas, Franz

Franz Uri Boas, a German-born Jewish immigrant who was chairman of the Department of Anthropology at Columbia University in New York City, was the leading American anthropologist during the germination, maturation, and demise of the Harlem Renaissance. When the Harlem Renaissance was emerging, Boas had a considerable reputation as a result of his ground-breaking research and writing on race and culture, and his financial and institutional support of talented representatives of the "New Negro." He significantly influenced the graphic artists, folklorists, writers, and critics of the renaissance in numerous and diverse ways, beginning with the publication of "Human Faculty as Determined by Race," which was his vice-presidential address to Section H at the annual meeting of the American Association for the Advancement of Science in 1894, and culminating with his monumental work *The Mind of Primitive Man*, which was brought out in 1911 and marked the zenith of his prowess as a researcher. Three aspects of his influence are especially important.

First, Boas offered a physical anthropological critique of racial formalism based on the overlapping sizes of the cranial cavities of blacks and whites. This critique convinced many people that biological racial differences were negligible, and it persuaded the leader of the "New Negro" movement, Alain Locke,

Franz Boas, c. 1930–1950. (Photo by R. H. Hoffman. Library of Congress.)

to argue in 1916 that racial inequalities were to be explained "in terms of historical, economic, and social factors," not biological factors. W. E. B. Du Bois, one of the leading custodial figures, concurred in this argument, observing that not all blacks were intellectually inferior to all whites; Zora Neale Hurston and Melville Herskovits tested Boas's conclusions by measuring the heads of black Harlemites; and Charles Spurgeon Johnson corresponded with "Papa Franz" in reference to the relative reliability of intelligence tests and drew directly on Boas's advice. Furthermore, in this regard Boas opened the *Journal of American Folk-Lore*, which he edited, to black amateur folklorists such as Locke, Hurston, Arthur A. Shomburg, Arthur Huff Fauset, and Carter G. Woodson. Eventually, though, Boas began to promote his own students instead of black writers who were attempting to promote "race consciousness."

Second—and even more significantly—Boas revealed the achievements of the western African and central African ancestors of black Americans. In his investigations into the African background and culture, which were published in numerous journals of anthropology and popular magazines between 1904 and 1909, he paid particular attention to Africa's peoples, their early successes in smelting iron, their artistic industries, and their agriculture, cultures, laws, and state building. These revelations convinced notable black thinkers such as Du Bois, Booker T. Washington, Monroe Nathan Work, and George Washington Ellis that blacks were not descended from inferior peoples. In addition, Boas introduced Americans to the disciplined, classical graphic and cultural traditions in black African art, profoundly influencing Locke, who in turn introduced black American painters and sculptors such as Richmond Barthé and Aaron Douglas to these works.

Third, Boas was instrumental in obtaining financial and institutional support for the "New Negroes." Much of this support was made possible through the beneficence of Carter G. Woodson, founder and head of the Association for the Study of Negro Life and History. Boas was successful in securing funds from Woodson for Zora Neale Hurston and the future economist Abram L. Harris. When Locke was fired by the president of Howard University in 1925, Boas provided him with the institutional support of the American Association of University Professors. (In 1926, however, Boas blocked the funding of a project by Locke on African art.)

During the Harlem Renaissance, Boas maintained his huge reputation among both black and white intellectuals, men and women. "Papa Franz" (an affectionate nickname given to him by Zora Neale Hurston) was the mentor of Herskovits, who was a major contributor to Locke's manifesto anthology *The New Negro*, as well as of Ruth Benedict, Margaret Mead, and others who became noted cultural anthropologists. These scholars would contribute to Boas's legacy as the father of Americanist anthropology, which was characterized by its revulsion against racism and its advocacy of cultural relativism.

However, since the 1980s Marshall Hyatt and the present author have raised issues in reference to the unevenness of Boas's critique of racial formalism and to his hypothesis about "men of high genius," that is, the belief that blacks would produce proportionally fewer male geniuses than whites. Also, there have been objections to Boas's cultural relativism. Nathan Huggins (1971) implied that relativistic research on Africa and African cultures contributed to the primitivism and exoticism that pervaded much of the outpourings of the Harlem Renaissance. With regard to Boas's withdrawal of his support from black amateur folklorists, Lee Baker (1998) has noted that Boas opposed these folklorists because he equated attempts to promote racial solidarity with nationalism.

Still, the controversies that have arisen about Boas's contribution to the Harlem Renaissance should not detract from his stature. Although Boas was limited by the state of knowledge about blacks' character and capabilities, his findings with respect to human differences were nevertheless far more forward-looking than those of the vast majority of his contemporaries, and the black intelligentsia seized on these findings as a means to demonstrate unequivocally that they were perfectly capable of producing great art and criticism. Although some of Boas's findings that they appropriated were used to rationalize the creation of primitive, exotic, sensationalistic work, this was no fault of his. In short, a significant part of the success that the artists of Harlem enjoyed was no doubt directly related to Boas's prodigious efforts.

Biography

Franz Uri Boas was born 9 July 1858 in Minden, Westphalia, Germany. He was educated at the Bürgerschule (an elementary school) and the Gymnasium (a secondary school) in Minden and the universities of Heidelberg (1877), Bonn (1877–1879), and Berlin (1879–1882, 1885–1886). He received his Ph.D. from the University of Berlin in 1882. Boas was temporarily employed at the Royal Ethnological Museum in Berlin; was geographical editor of *Science* in New York (1887–1888); taught at Clark University in Worcester, Massachusetts (1888–1892); was chief assistant of anthropology at the World's Columbia Exposition in Chicago (1892–1894); was assistant curator at the American Museum of Natural History in New York (1896–1901) and then curator (1901–1906); taught at Columbia University (1896–1936); served as editor of *American Anthropologist* (1898–1920) and *Journal of American Folk-Lore* (1908–1924); and was president of the American Association for the Advancement of Science (1931). He died in New York City 21 December 1942.

VERNON J. WILLIAMS

See also Association for the Study of Negro Life and History and Journal of Negro History; Barthé, Richmond; Douglas, Aaron; Du Bois, W. E. B.; Fauset, Arthur Huff; Herskovits, Melville; Hurston, Zora Neale; Johnson, Charles Spurgeon; Locke, Alain; New Negro; New Negro Movement; Schomburg, Arthur A.; Woodson, Carter G.; Work, Monroe Nathan

Selected Works

The Central Eskimo. 1888. (Reprinted, 1964.)
"Human Faculty as Determined by Race." 1894.
"Introduction." In *Handbook of American Indian Languages.* 1911. (Reprinted, 1966.)
The Mind of Primitive Man. 1911. (Rev. ed., 1938.)
Changes in Bodily Form of Descendants of Immigrants. 1912.
Anthropology and Modern Life. 1928.
Race, Language and Culture. 1940.
Race and Democratic Society. 1945.
A Franz Boas Reader: The Shaping of American Anthropology, 1883–1911, ed. George W. Stocking Jr. 1972.

Further Reading

Baker, Lee. *From Savage to Negro.* Berkeley: University of California Press, 1998.
Bay, Mia. *The White Image in the Black Mind.* New York: Oxford University Press, 2000.
Degler, Carl. *In Search of Human Nature.* New York: Oxford University Press, 1992.
Huggins, Nathan. *Harlem Renaissance.* New York: Oxford University Press, 1971.
Hutchinson, George. *The Harlem Renaissance in Black and White.* Cambridge, Mass.: Harvard University Press, 1995.
Robbins, Richard. *Sideline Activist.* Jackson: University Press of Mississippi, 1996.
Stocking, George, Jr. *Race, Culture, and Evolution.* New York: Free Press, 1968.
Williams, Vernon, Jr. *Rethinking Race.* Lexington: University Press of Kentucky, 1996.

Bojangles

See Robinson, Bill "Bojangles"

Boni and Liveright

Boni and Liveright, one of the most progressive publishing houses of the 1920s, played an important role in connecting the aspiring writers of the Harlem Renaissance to the bohemian, radical culture of white intellectuals in Greenwich Village. Under the direction of its cofounder, Horace Liveright, the firm was willing to risk publishing modern, experimental, and radical books by young, unknown writers. In publishing Jean Toomer's *Cane* and Eric Walrond's *Tropic Death*, Boni and Liveright helped to create a vogue for exotic and primitive black writers.

Boni and Liveright began in 1917 as publishers of Modern Library, a series of inexpensive reprints of modern classics, attractively bound and priced at only sixty cents. Modern Library offered hard-to-find and out-of-print titles by such authors as Nietzsche, Wilde, Gorky, Strindberg, and Dostoyevsky. With a backlist of steadily selling, profitable Modern Library titles, Boni and Liveright went about making publishing history, taking chances and fighting censorship to redefine American literature with the publication of Pound, Eliot, O'Neill, Anderson, Hemingway, Dreiser, Crane, and Faulkner. In addition, Boni and Liveright published Sigmund Freud, Bertrand Russell, Upton Sinclair, Leon Trotsky, and Jack Reed—writers who shaped the era's most progressive thought.

Given its history and reputation, Boni and Liveright was a logical choice to publish *Cane*, a highly experimental book by an unknown black author, dealing with racial themes. Jean Toomer had been introduced to the intellectual elite in Greenwich Village in 1921 by Waldo Frank, a modernist writer and critic whose

167

experimental prose Boni and Liveright had previously published. The firm published *Cane* in 1923, with an introduction by Frank. Heavily influenced by the modernist aesthetics of Frank, Hart Crane, and Sherwood Anderson (all Boni and Liveright writers), Toomer's masterpiece was praised by the critics but was financially unsuccessful, selling only 500 copies. Unhappy with the book's publicity, which touted him as a rising black author, Toomer soon sailed for Europe. He had contracted with Boni and Liveright for a second book, but it was never written.

Boni and Liveright also published two other works of fiction by blacks: Jessie Fauset's novel *There Is Confusion* and (as noted above) Eric Walrond's *Tropic Death*, a collection of short stories. Together, these books indicate that the publisher's commitment to black literature was more than a commitment to the primitive. Although *Tropic Death* is, like Toomer's *Cane*, modernist, exotic, and sensual, *There Is Confusion* is a more conventional treatment of the African American upper classes, reminiscent of Edith Wharton.

By 1927–1928, the heyday of Boni and Liveright was over. In 1925, Modern Library, the firm's most reliable source of profits, was sold to cover a series of poor investments in stocks and theatrical productions. By 1926, the Boni brothers, Albert and Charles, were operating parallel publishing ventures, including the landmark publication of Alain Locke's *The New Negro*. Liveright continued to publish important books, but the partnership ended in 1928, as the firm's financial situation worsened. Liveright, who had invested deeply in the stock market, never recovered from the crash of 1929; and by the time of his death in 1933, he had already lost control of the company to Arthur Pell, his onetime bookkeeper. After 1933, the firm continued under the name Liveright Publishing Company; it became a subsidiary of W. W. Norton and Company in 1974.

MICHAEL ZEITLER

See also Anderson, Sherwood; Boni and Liveright Prize; Cane; Fauset, Jessie Redmon; Frank, Waldo; Greenwich Village; Liveright, Horace; Locke, Alain; New Negro, The; Primitivism; Publishers and Publishing Houses; There Is Confusion; Toomer, Jean; Tropic Death; Walrond, Eric

Further Reading

Darden, Tom. *Firebrand: The Life of Horace Liveright*. New York: Random House, 1995.
Gilmer, Walker. *Horace Liveright: Publisher of the Twenties*. New York: Lewis, 1970.
Hutchinson, George. *The Harlem Renaissance in Black and White*. Cambridge, Mass.: Belknap–Harvard University Press, 1995.
Lewis, David Levering. *When Harlem Was in Vogue*. New York: Knopf, 1981.
Tebbel, John. *A History of Book Publishing in the United States*, Vol. 3. New York and London: Bowker, 1978.
Wintz, Cary. *Black Culture and the Harlem Renaissance*. Houston, Tex.: Rice University Press, 1988.

Boni and Liveright Prize

Although the Boni Prize competition is often associated with the publishing house Boni and Liveright, the contest was actually the independent work of the Boni brothers, Albert and Charles. In addition to publishing with Horace Liveright under the name Boni and Liveright, the Boni brothers made significant contributions to the Harlem Renaissance in their own right. Their most important joint venture was surely the publication of Alain Locke's anthology *The New Negro*, but they also tried to discover and develop new talent through their patronage of a much heralded literary contest similar to the contests sponsored by *Opportunity* or the Harmon Foundation.

On 29 January 1926, the National Association for the Advancement of Colored People (NAACP) held a press conference in New York announcing that the publishers Charles and Albert Boni were offering a prize of $1,000 for the year's best novel "about Negro life and written by a Negro." The NAACP also announced a sterling committee to judge the entries: Henry Seidel Canby, editor of *Saturday Review*; W. E. B. Du Bois of *The Crisis*; Charles Spurgeon Johnson of *Opportunity*; James Weldon Johnson; Edna Kenton; Laurence Stallings; and Irita Van Doren. Taken individually, this panel of judges reflected the diversity of aesthetic opinion engendered by the novelists of the Harlem Renaissance.

By early 1926, such divergent viewpoints on the representation of the African American in art were subject to vigorous debate. That spring *The Crisis* ran a symposium on "The Negro in Art: How Shall He Be Portrayed?," with responses from, among others, Alfred Knopf, Carl Van Vechten, Sherwood Anderson, and Vachel Lindsay. Du Bois himself wrote "Criteria for Negro Art," and Claude McKay wrote "Negro Life and

Negro Art." While Du Bois saw little value in promoting art that could not be used to better the conditions of the race, McKay saw such propagandistic motives as self-defeating for any serious artist.

Considering the diversity of opinion and the emotionally charged climate of debate, it is not surprising that any committee as representative as that of the Boni brothers would have difficulty in reaching a consensus. Thus, for reasons that are still unclear, although the contest was heavily advertised in early 1926, with announcements in the *New York Times*, *Publisher's Weekly*, and *The Crisis*, no novel was selected as worthy, and the prize was never awarded.

MICHAEL ZEITLER

See also Anderson, Sherwood; Boni and Liveright; Crisis: The Negro in Art—How Shall He Be Portrayed? A Symposium; Du Bois, W. E. B.; Harmon Foundation; Johnson, Charles Spurgeon; Johnson, James Weldon; Knopf, Alfred A.; Lindsay, Nicholas Vachel; McKay, Claude; Opportunity Literary Contests; Van Vechten, Carl

Further Reading

DuBois, W. E. B. "Criteria of Negro Art." *Crisis*, 32(11), October 1926.

Hutchinson, George. *The Harlem Renaissance in Black and White*. Cambridge, Mass.: Belknap–Harvard University Press, 1995.

Lewis, David Levering. *When Harlem Was in Vogue*. New York: Knopf, 1981.

Wintz, Cary D. *Black Culture and the Harlem Renaissance*. Houston, Tex.: Rice University Press, 1988.

Bonner, Marieta

Marieta Bonner (Marita Odette) was a significant contributor to the African American literary scene from the 1920s to the 1940s, producing short stories, essays, plays, and reviews. Bonner's writing first came to notice in 1925 with an essay in *The Crisis*, "On Being Young—A Woman—and Colored," which dealt with the prevailing sexism as well as racism of the times and presented a spirited critique of the assumptions of many of her "New Negro" compatriots regarding gender. (This essay is reprinted in *Frye Street and Environs*, 1987.) Bonner was awarded a literary prize from *Crisis* for the essay, and she received two more awards

in *Opportunity*'s literary competitions in 1934 (for "A Possible Triad on Black Notes" and "Tin Can"). She published in *Opportunity* and *The Crisis* in the 1930s and 1940s, producing twenty short stories and three plays, including the acclaimed *The Purple Flower* (1928), although after 1941 she turned from writing to devote herself to teaching and motherhood. Bonner was also a regular attendee at Georgia Douglas Johnson's salon on S Street in Washington, D.C., an important meeting place for many writers of the Harlem Renaissance, including Angelina Weld Grimké, Clarissa Scott Delany, Jessie Fauset, Mary Burrill, and Alice Dunbar Nelson.

Bonner herself was middle class, but she wrote almost exclusively about working-class communities. Her writing combines sociological detail, allegory, and stream of consciousness to represent the experience of urban African Americans, avoiding the folk idiom that is so familiar from the work of the better-known Zora Neale Hurston. Bonner examines the experience of urban life, racism, and reproduction for women who have little or no desire to uplift the race but simply need to get by. In her "Frye Street" stories she presents a fictional urban neighborhood (based on Chicago's South Side) where migrants' aspirations for the expanding African American community nearly always go unrealized; their difficulties are manifested in anxiety related to motherhood and the black woman's responsibilities toward her race. Bonner's stories constitute a series of jeremiads on the impact of poverty, poor education, bad parenting, female-headed households, drugs, and violence on the inner city—which, in her works, holds little of the promise of Harlem during the jazz age. As noted by Cheryl Wall (1997) and Mary Helen Washington (1987), the brutalism of Bonner's writing offers a sharp retort to those who stereotype women writers of the Harlem Renaissance as genteel and apolitical.

The limitations imposed on African American women preoccupied Bonner throughout her life as a writer. Stories such as "Drab Rambles" (*The Crisis*, 1927), "One Boy's Story" (*The Crisis*, 1927), and "Tin Can" (*Opportunity*, 1934) deal with the constrictions of the city, which is prejudiced against her protagonists, socially and economically, because they are black and female. Bonner's later stories become steadily more pessimistic; in these works, women and children find themselves trapped within, and victimized by, racialized socioeconomic structures. Bonner's "Frye Street" stories link the Harlem Renaissance with more explicitly politicized African American social protest writing of the 1930s and 1940s.

Biography

Marieta Bonner (also known as Marita Odette) was born in Boston in 1899. She studied at Brookline High School in Boston and at Radcliffe College in Cambridge, Massachusetts (1918–1922). She taught high school in Cambridge and later in Washington, D.C., and Chicago. Bonner was a member of the Krigwa Players in Washington, D.C. She died in Chicago in 1971.

MARIA BALSHAW

See also Crisis, The; Delany, Clarissa Scott; Fauset, Jessie Redmon; Grimké, Angelina Weld; Johnson, Georgia Douglas; Krigwa Players; Nelson, Alice Dunbar; Opportunity Literary Contests; Salons

Further Reading

Balshaw, Maria. "New Negroes, New Women: The Gender Politics of the Harlem Renaissance." *Women: A Cultural Review*, 10(2), 1999, pp. 127–138.

———. *Looking for Harlem: Urban Aesthetics in African American Fiction*. London and Sterling, Va.: Pluto, 2000.

Bonner, Marieta. *Frye Street and Environs: The Collected Works of Marita Bonner*, ed. Joyce Flynn and Joyce Occomy Stricklin. 1987.

Hill, Errol. "The Revolutionary Tradition in Black Drama." *Theatre-Journal*, 38, 1986, pp. 419–421.

McKay, Nellie. "What Were They Saying? Black Women Playwrights of the Harlem Renaissance." In *The Harlem Renaissance Re-Examined*, ed. Victor Kramer. New York: AMS, 1988.

Roses, Lorraine Elena, and Ruth Elizabeth Randolph. "Marita Bonner: In Search of Other Mothers' Gardens." *Black American Literature Forum*, 21(1–2), 1987, pp. 165–183.

Wall, Cheryl. *Women of the Harlem Renaissance*. Bloomington: Indiana University Press, 1997.

Washington, Mary Helen, ed. *Invented Lives: Narratives of Black Women, 1860–1960*. New York: Anchor, 1987.

Bontemps, Arna

Through his distinguished career and his contributions as a novelist, poet, and librarian, Arna Wendell Bontemps brought additional recognition to the historical and literary movement known as the Harlem Renaissance.

Bontemps spent his early formative years in Los Angeles, where, despite his father's objections, he developed a love of literature. Inspired by his uncle Buddy's penchant for folk culture, Bontemps formally began his writing career in 1923, on his graduation from Pacific Union College; in 1924, he published a poem, "Hope," in *The Crisis*, one of the leading periodicals for aspiring writers of the Harlem Renaissance.

Shortly thereafter, Bontemps moved to New York City. There, he pursued a teaching career at the Harlem Academy; simultaneously, his writing career accelerated. In 1926 and 1927, he received *Opportunity* magazine's Alexander Pushkin Poetry Prize for his poems "Golgotha Is a Mountain" (1926) and "The Return" (1927). Bontemps's poetry, which addressed the themes of racial pride and love of African civilization, brought him into contact with notable writers of the Harlem Renaissance such as James Weldon Johnson, Claude McKay, and—most important—Langston Hughes. He and Hughes would later collaborate as

Arna Bontemps, photographed by Carl Van Vechten, 1939.
(Library of Congress.)

writers on projects such as *Popo and Fifina: Children of Haiti* (1932), a travel book for young readers.

In 1931, Bontemps published his first novel, *God Sends Sunday*, the story of the pioneering African American jockey Little Augie. A few years later, Bontemps collaborated with Countee Cullen to transform the book into the play, *St. Louis Woman* (1939). Although W. E. B. Du Bois criticized *God Sends Sunday* for its description of the seamy side of black life, the novel was recognized for its unique depiction of black people's interest in sporting life and of the usages of the Creole language. Most significantly, the publication of *God Sends Sunday* marked Bontemps's emergence as an important African American writer.

Bontemps's literary success continued after he relocated to Huntsville, Alabama, to teach at Oakwood Junior College in 1931. In 1932, he won a prize from *Opportunity* magazine for his short story "A Summer Tragedy," about an elderly couple whose victimization by the sharecropping system results in their double suicide. (This story has since appeared in many anthologies.) Bontemps also continued to write juvenile books; he believed that a younger reading audience was more accessible, and he wanted to offer young people a positive literary depiction of African Americans. His works of juvenile literature include *You Can't Pet a Possum* (1934); *We Have Tomorrow* (1945); *Frederick Douglass: Slave, Fighter, Freeman* (1959); and *Young Booker: Booker T. Washington's Early Days* (1972). Later, Bontemps became involved in the Illinois Writers' Project and developed a friendship with another participant, Jack Conroy; he and Conroy then collaborated on several children's books.

In 1936, Bontemps's most widely recognized novel—*Black Thunder: Gabriel's Revolt, Virginia 1800*—was published. This historical novel tells of a fictional slave revolt, led by Gabriel Prosser, that fails because of horrendous weather and an act of betrayal. Although the book was written during an unfavorable time for black people, *Black Thunder* was recognized as a powerful statement about the relevance of African American history. Bontemps's use of language was also praised, and this novel secured his place within the African American literary tradition.

Black Thunder was followed by a third novel, *Drums at Dusk* (1938); this too is a historical novel, about a slave revolution on the island of Santo Domingo. Around this time, Bontemps accepted a Rosenwald Fellowship for travel and research in the Caribbean. Additional achievements soon followed: the publication of *Father of the Blues* (1941), a commissioned biography of

W. C. Handy; two more Rosenwald grants; the publication of *Golden Slippers: An Anthology of Negro Poetry for Young Readers* (1941); and the completion of a master's degree in library science from the University of Chicago in 1943.

From 1943 until 1965, Bontemps was the head librarian at Fisk University. In this capacity, he significantly enhanced the university's holdings of materials on African American culture by establishing the Langston Hughes and George Gershwin collections and acquiring the papers of James Weldon Johnson, Jean Toomer, and Charles S. Johnson. Later (1969), Bontemps would serve as curator of the James Weldon Johnson Collection at the Beinecke Library at Yale University. (Bontemps's own letters and other memorabilia of his long friendship with Langston Hughes are also housed at this library.) Bontemps's posts at Fisk and Yale enabled him to establish important resources for the study of African American literature and culture.

Bontemps's work as an anthologist is also significant. In 1958, Bontemps and Hughes coedited *The Book of Negro Folklore*, a collection of folklore and essays. In 1963, Bontemps edited *American Negro Poetry*. Another anthology, *Hold Fast to Dreams: Poems Old and New* (1969), includes works by black and white poets. Perhaps the most important anthology of Bontemps's career is *The Harlem Renaissance Remembered* (1972), a collection of edited essays about notable figures of the period. This book also includes Bontemps's personal reflections about the movement. Another anthology, *Personals* (1963), is a collection of Bontemps's poetry and his thoughts on Harlem Renaissance writers. Finally, *The Old South: "A Summer Tragedy" and Other Stories of the Thirties* (1973) is a collection of short fiction.

After retiring from Fisk in 1964, Bontemps held other academic posts at the University of Illinois (Chicago Circle campus) and later at Yale University. He eventually returned to Nashville, Tennessee, as a writer-in-residence at Fisk. In 1971, Bontemps began work on an autobiography, but it was left unfinished.

Although Arna Bontemps did not receive the same recognition as many of his contemporaries, such as his close friend and idol Langston Hughes, his literary accomplishments—particularly his novels, his children's literature, his anthologies, and his work as a librarian—established him as an important chronicler of African American life and culture. His work also helped to preserve the history and vibrancy of the Harlem Renaissance movement.

Biography

Arnaud Wendell Bontemps was born 13 October 1902 in Alexandria, Louisiana, to parents of Creole origin. He studied at San Fernando Academy in Los Angeles; Pacific Union College in Angwin, California (A.B., 1923); and the Graduate School of Library Science, University of Chicago (M.L.S., 1943). Bontemps taught at Harlem Academy in New York City (1924–1931); Oakwood Junior College in Huntsville, Alabama (1931–1934); Shiloh Academy in Chicago (1935–1937); and the University of Illinois (1966–1969). He married Alberta Johnson in 1926; they would have six children. Bontemps was editorial supervisor for the Federal Writers Project of the Illinois Works Progress Administration (1938); head librarian at Fisk University in Nashville, Tennessee (1943–1965); director of university relations and acting head librarian at Fisk University (1964–1965); and lecturer and curator for the James Weldon Johnson Collection at Yale University in New Haven, Connecticut (1969–1971). His awards included *Opportunity* magazine's Alexander Pushkin Poetry Prize (1926, 1927) and its short-story prize (for "A Summer Tragedy," 1932), and a Rosenwald Fellowship (1939). Bontemps died in Nashville 4 June 1973.

Larnell Dunkley

See also Crisis, The; Cullen, Countee; Handy, W. C.; Hughes, Langston; Johnson, Charles Spurgeon; Johnson, James Weldon; McKay, Claude; Opportunity; Opportunity Literary Contests; Rosenwald Fellowships; Toomer, Jean

Selected Works

God Sends Sunday. 1931.
Popo and Fifina: Children of Haiti. 1932. (Coedited with Langston Hughes.)
"A Summer Tragedy." 1932.
You Can't Pet a Possum. 1934.
Black Thunder: Gabriel's Revolt, Virginia 1800. 1936.
Drums at Dusk. 1939.
Father of the Blues. 1941.
Golden Slippers: An Anthology of Negro Poetry for Young Readers. 1941.
We Have Tomorrow. 1945.
St. Louis Woman. 1946.
The Poetry of the Negro. 1949. (Coedited with Langston Hughes.)

The Book of Negro Folklore. 1959. (Coedited with Langston Hughes.)
Frederick Douglass: Slave, Fighter, Freeman. 1959.
American Negro Poetry. 1963. (Coedited with Langston Hughes.)
Personals. 1963.
Hold Fast to Dreams: Poems Old and New. 1969.
The Harlem Renaissance Remembered. 1972.
Young Booker: Booker T. Washington's Early Days. 1972.
The Old South: "A Summer Tragedy" and Other Stories of the Thirties. 1973.

Further Reading

Arna Bontemps–Langston Hughes Letters, 1925–1967, ed. Charles H. Nichols. 1988.
Jones, Kirkland C. *Renaissance Man from Louisiana: A Biography of Arna Wendell Bontemps*. 1992.
Sundquist, Eric J. *The Hammers of Creation: Folk Culture in Modern African-American Fiction*. 1992.

Booklovers Club

The Harlem Booklovers Club was founded in the early twentieth century and flourished from the years preceding World War I through the 1940s. It was composed of university-trained black women who were members of the black middle and upper classes or were connected through marriage and family to the black elite of Harlem. This organization was a regional outgrowth of the first Booklovers Club, which had been established in Washington, D.C., in 1894. According to Mary Church Terrell (1863–1954), a founding member of the Booklovers movement, the club was "organized for the purpose of reading, reviewing, and discussing books" (Terrell 1940). Ida Gibbs Hunt (1862–1957) reported that the Booklovers met to "pursue courses of reading and study for higher culture." Meetings and programs were often devoted to Shakespeare and Wagner, and to reports on the members' travels to Europe and elsewhere abroad. Some sessions also dealt with child-rearing practices and other family-related topics. All-black female Booklovers Clubs spread as far west as the twin cities of Kansas City, Kansas, and Kansas City, Missouri, where the Inner-City Booklovers Club flourished from the 1920s through the 1990s.

During the 1920s, the Harlem Booklovers met at the 135th Street Branch of the New York Public Library on 135th Street and Lenox Avenue. (The club was one of many community organizations that used the 135th Street branch for meetings and cultural programs throughout the years of the Harlem Renaissance. This facility was a key institution for the central Harlem community, serving approximately 125,000 people in a twenty-block area.) In 1925, the Division of Negro Literature, History, and Prints was established through a community advisory committee of Harlem bibliophiles, with the assistance of the librarians Ernestine Rose and Catherine Latimer, the first black librarian hired by the New York Public Library. In 1926, the New York Public Library purchased the private library of Arthur Schomburg—Harlem's leading bibliophile, as well as a cofounder of the Negro Society for Historical Research—and integrated his materials into that special division.

The Booklovers sponsored lectures on African American history and culture, book collecting contests, book review sessions, discussions of children's literature, programs related to community concerns, family development and training sessions, and gatherings that gave individual members an opportunity to share their travel and vacation experiences. Some of Harlem's most prominent intellectuals and collectors of Africana participated in the weekly history lectures sponsored by the Booklovers. This group included Arthur Schomburg; John Edward Bruce, who was a prominent journalist, a self-trained historian, and president of the Negro Society for Historical Research; Hubert Harrison; William Ernest Braxton, a painter who was also a member of many literary societies; and Willis Nathaniel Huggins, who was the owner of the Blyden Bookstore, a leader of the Harlem History Club, the sixth black educator to be hired by the New York public school system, and eventually the first black student to finish a doctorate in history at Fordham University. Huggins was also a tireless advocate for including African history in the curriculum of New York's public schools.

Some members of the Booklovers Club were married to black men who not only were professionally accomplished but were also linked to a flourishing circle of black bibliophiles and collectors that had established regular communication between colleagues in New York City, Philadelphia, and Washington, D.C. Prominent black bibliophiles in all three cities were active in the American Negro Historical Society and the Black Opals Literary Society of Philadelphia; the American Negro Academy; the Association for the Study of Negro Life and History; the Negro Book

Collectors Exchange; the Bethel Historical and Literary Association, based in Washington, D.C.; and the Negro Society for Historical Research, the Negro Library Association, and the Phalanx Club, located in New York City. Mary Church Terrell and her husband, Judge Robert H. Terrell, were both active in the prestigious Bethel Historical and Literary Association, and she served as Bethel's first female president in 1892–1893.

RALPH L. CROWDER

See also Association for the Study of Negro Life and History and Journal of Black History; Black History and Historiography; Bruce, John Edward; Harrison, Hubert; 135th Street Library; Schomburg, Arthur A.

Further Reading

Gatewood, Willard B. *Aristocrats of Color: The Black Elite, 1880–1920*. Bloomington: Indiana University Press, 1990.

Hunt, Ida Gibbs, and William H. Hunt. Papers. Moorland-Springarn Research Collection, Howard University, Washington, D.C.

McHenry, Elizabeth. *Forgotten Readers: Recovering the Lost History of African American Literary Societies*. Durham, N.C.: Duke University Press, 2002.

Sinette, Elinor DesVerney. *Arthur Alfonso Schomburg: Black Bibliophile and Collector*. Detroit, Mich.: New York Public Library and Wayne State University Press, 1989.

Terrell, Mary Church. *A Colored Woman in a White World*. Washington, D.C.: Ransdell, 1940. (Reprint, New York: G. K. Hall, 1996.)

Booklovers Magazine

Booklovers Magazine, founded in Philadelphia in January 1903 by the journalist Seymour Eaton, was a monthly publication offering articles on a variety of subjects for a general audience. It appeared under three separate titles during a relatively short span: *Booklovers Magazine* from January 1903 to June 1905, *Appleton's Booklovers Magazine* from July 1905 to June 1906, and *Appleton's Magazine* from July 1906 to June 1909. The magazine sold for twenty-five cents an issue, and at its peak had a circulation of about 100,000, making it a serious and respectable publication but not widely read enough to turn much of a profit. Still, it was lavishly illustrated and printed on glossy paper, and its contributors included such notables as Theodore Roosevelt, Henry Cabot Lodge, Theodore Dreiser, Joseph Conrad, and John Philip Sousa. Its articles on contemporary issues and controversies were well regarded.

The July 1903 issue of the magazine included an article by W. E. B. Du Bois, "Possibilities of the Negro: The Advance Guard of the Race." Du Bois's "advance guard" comprised ten successful black men, each of whom was given a brief biographical treatment: Booker T. Washington, the writers Charles Chesnutt and Paul Laurence Dunbar, the Reverend Frances James Grimké, the painter Henry Ossawa Tanner, the legislator and attorney Edward H. Morris of Illinois, the inventor Granville T. Woods, the mathematician and teacher Kelly Miller, the surgeon Daniel H. Williams, and the businessman W. L. Taylor. Portraits of the men accompanied the biographies.

Du Bois concluded his article by discussing the issues of mixed races, pointing out that of the ten men he profiled "three are black, two are brown, two are half white, and three are three-fourths white." All represented the American Negro and his potential. In a magazine serving an overwhelmingly white readership, Du Bois's article made the simple point that blacks were capable of intellectual and artistic excellence. The editor, Seymour Eaton, included a brief profile of Du Bois, praising *The Souls of Black Folk* and Du Bois's contributions to addressing the "Negro problem."

CYNTHIA BILY

See also Chesnutt, Charles Waddell; Dreiser, Theodore; Du Bois, W. E. B.; Dunbar, Paul Laurence; Miller, Kelly; Tanner, Henry Ossawa; Washington, Booker T.

Further Reading

Aptheker, Herbert. *Annotated Bibliography of the Published Writings of W. E. B. Du Bois.* Kraus-Thomson, 1973.
Mott, Frank Luther. *A History of American Magazines*, Vol. 5, *Sketches of Twenty-one Magazines, 1905–1930.* Cambridge, Mass.: Harvard University Press, 1968.

Bradford, Perry

The songwriter, music publisher, entrepreneur, and entertainer Perry Bradford entered show business in 1906 and worked in Allen's New Orleans Minstrels in 1907. He worked as a pianist in Chicago in 1909 and played at the Grand Theatre with Alberta Perkins. He was part of a successful double act, Bradford and Jeanette, in black vaudeville from 1909 to 1918. He toured in the shows *The Chicken Trust* (c. 1913) and *Sgt. Ham, Darktown After Dark*, and *Made in Heaven* (1918).

Blues songs, beginning with those of W. C. Handy, became increasingly popular shortly before World War I. However, there were as yet no opportunities for African Americans to record this music. Bradford set out to change this situation, with great energy and determination. In 1920, he persuaded Fred Hager, recordings manager for Okeh, to record the blues singer Mamie Smith; her first recordings, featuring Bradford's own "Crazy Blues" and "That Thing Called Love," sold extremely well and precipitated a craze for blues records by African American women. During 1921–1922 Bradford was the most prominent black entrepreneur on Broadway, making money with ease and spending it with abandon. He made several recordings as both singer and pianist from 1923 to 1929, but his skill in these areas was limited; he was much more important, from 1920 to 1944, as a producer of recordings by many of the greatest musicians of the era, including Louis Armstrong, Johnny Dunn, Buster Bailey, Willie "the Lion" Smith, and James P. Johnson.

Bradford sold most of his early songs to other publishers, such as Pace and Handy, but he went into business for himself as a publisher in 1920, joining Handy and other black entrepreneurs in the Gaiety Theater building on Times Square. During the 1920s he was incorporated under several names, of which the most important was Perry Bradford Music Publishing Company. He published songs for the show *Put and Take* (1921), including several by the prolific songwriter Spencer Williams, as well as a few of his own originals. Bradford is most important for publishing numerous works by James P. Johnson, including a version of the extended concert work *Yamekraw*. He and Johnson contributed songs to more shows in the 1920s, including *Keep Shufflin'* (1928) and *Messin' Around* (1929). Bradford held frequent wild parties at his office in the Gaiety building; these meetings of the "Joy Club" included Johnson, Fats Waller, and the lyricist Andy Razaf.

Unlike Handy and Clarence Williams, Bradford experienced a boom-and-bust cycle in his business affairs: he was an erratic, undisciplined businessman, so he realized only a small percentage of the profits that his pieces generated, and he spent those profits rather than investing them. He got into considerable trouble by double-dealing other publishers on certain songs; and he was sentenced to prison in 1923 for suborning a witness (Spencer Williams) to commit perjury, in a dispute over Lemuel Fowler's hit song "He May Be Your Man, but He Comes to See Me Sometimes." Bradford wasted considerable energy from the 1920s to the 1940s on fruitless lawsuits against more powerful entities such as the publisher Southern Music and the American Society of Composers, Authors and Publishers (ASCAP).

A famously stubborn man, Bradford early on was nicknamed "Mule." Although he was a prolific songwriter, none of his compositions can be considered standards. However, his pugnacious autobiography, *Born With the Blues*, is one of the great primary documents in the history of African American music.

Biography

Perry Bradford (John Henry Perry Bradford) was born in Montgomery, Alabama, 14 February 1893; his family moved to Atlanta in 1901. He began his career in show business in 1906 and performed as a minstrel, pianist, and vaudevillian (1907–1918). He married Marion Dickerson in 1918; for a time she was in the music business with him, but the marriage ended in divorce. In 1920, Mamie Smith very successfully recorded some of Bradford's blues songs for Okeh. In 1921–1922, Bradford was a leading black entrepreneur on Broadway. From 1920 to 1944 he was a producer of recordings by many great musicians; however, he experienced economic and legal difficulties during this time. He took a day job at the Belmont Park race track in the 1940s. His autobiography was published in 1965. Bradford died in New York 20 April 1970.

ELLIOTT S. HURWITT

See also Armstrong, Louis; Handy, W. C.; Johnson, James P.; Razaf, Andy; Smith, Mamie; Smith, Willie "the Lion"; Waller, Thomas "Fats"; Williams, Clarence

Selected Songs

"Lonesome Blues." c. 1916. (All dates are approximate.)
"Broken Hearted Blues." 1918.
"Harlem Blues." 1918. (Retitled "Crazy Blues" in 1920.)
"That Thing Called Love." 1919.
"You Can't Keep a Good Man Down." 1920.

"Nervous Blues." 1921.
"I Ain't Gonna Play No Second Fiddle." 1925.
"My Home Ain't Here, It's Further Down the Road." 1925. (Retitled "Dixie Flyer Blues" by Bessie Smith.)

Further Reading

Bradford, Perry. *Born With the Blues: Perry Bradford's Own Story*. New York: Oak, 1965.

Charters, Samuel, and Len Kunstadt. *Jazz: A History of the New York Scene*. New York: Da Capo, 1981. (First published 1962.)

Hurwitt, Elliott S. "W. C. Handy as Music Publisher: Career and Reputation." Ph.D. diss., City University of New York Graduate Center, 2000.

Jasen, David A. "Perry Bradford: Pioneer of the Blues." Folkways CD FJ 2863. (Program booklet; includes an interview with Bradford by Noble Sissle.)

Jasen, David A., and Gene Jones. *Spreadin' Rhythm Around: Black Popular Songwriters, 1880–1930*. New York: Schirmer, 1998.

Braithwaite, William Stanley

"Negro poetic expression hovers for the moment, pardonably perhaps, over the race problem, but its highest allegiance is to Poetry; it must soar." William Stanley Beaumont Braithwaite published these words in *The Crisis* in 1924. He believed strongly in poetic purity, without reference to skin color; the issue of race, he felt, placed an unnecessary burden on the poet, hindering poetic rhythm and leading to self-destructiveness. (Braithwaite once advised Claude McKay not to identify his race in his writings.) The generation of poets in Harlem in the 1920s did not share his view (they wanted to write about their triumphs and struggles, and they could do that only if they acknowledged their race), but they nevertheless respected Braithwaite as a literary leader.

Braithwaite was born in Boston, but his father, William Smith Braithwaite, was a native of British Guiana who had studied in England and then immigrated to New England. The elder Braithwaite preferred all things British, disdained the struggling African Americans, and therefore limited his children's association with the descendants of slaves. The younger Braithwaite was at first tutored at home; after his father's death he went to public school, but he left school at age twelve (in 1890) to help support the family by working as a porter and errand boy. His sisters Eva and Rosie, who were musically inclined, formed a duet and toured the United States and Europe as "Sadie and Rosie"; by the turn of the twentieth century, they were members of Sam T. Jack's Creole Show.

Eventually, Braithwaite found employment as an apprentice in the pressroom of the publisher Ginn and Company. Here he read galley proofs of poets, developing an interest in poetry and books that would lead to a career path as an anthologist, editor, educator, biographer, critic, novelist, poet, and publisher. He was later promoted to compositor. His contact with the publishing industry and his exposure to creative works inspired him to write poetry himself, in the style of the British romantics.

In 1904, after covering the printing costs, Braithwaite published his first volume of poetry. Edited collections and another volume of lyrics followed, along with occasional poems and critical essays. His work appeared in periodicals such as *Atlantic Review*, *North American Review*, and *Scribner's*. Braithwaite's critical and poetic insight caught the attention of people at a newspaper, the *Boston Evening Transcript*, where he became a literary critic, a position he held for twenty-five years. He continued to compile anthologies of Elizabethan, Georgian, and Restoration poetry and to compose his own works. Soon he acquired a reputation for his scholarly approach to criticism and poetry. (He would continue to be recognized more for his critical commentary than his poetry.)

Braithwaite's annual *Anthology of Magazine Verse* made him very influential in the world of arts and letters. To be included in this anthology became a mark of recognition. Braithwaite did not focus exclusively on African American poets or themes; he published the work of black and white poets from the American North and South and from abroad: Sterling Brown, Countee Cullen, Paul Lawrence Dunbar, Robert Frost, Langston Hughes, James Weldon Johnson, Vachel Lindsay, Edgar Lee Masters, Claude McKay, Amy Powell, Carl Sandburg, and Anne Spencer, to name a few. His anthologies were so successful that they were published for more than a quarter of a century: from 1913 to 1939. Moreover, he wrote critical essays on African American poetry, and he was a contributor to Alain Locke's anthology *The New Negro* (1925). In 1921, Braithwaite headed his own publishing company, B. J. Brimmer, which issued the works of Lucius Beebe, James Gould Cozzens, and Georgia Douglas Johnson. Thus Braithwaite was a contributor to the arts during the Harlem Renaissance, was instrumental in exposing the poetry of African Americans of that period, and encouraged the literary movement of the renaissance.

In 1935, Braithwaite joined the faculty of Atlanta University as a professor of creative literature. In this position he gained greater exposure to the day-to-day experiences of educated African Americans and to African American writers and poets; until then, his contacts had been occasional and sometimes limited. He published little during this time, however, and he retired from the university in 1945.

Braithwaite studied the poetic patterns of the eighteenth- and nineteenth-century British poets, concentrating on the forms, meters, and themes of the romantics. His poetry, criticism, and compilations are not centered on race or color and do not reflect an identifiable cultural context. Because he circumvented the issue of racial identity, he himself fell into obscurity, and he has tended to be excluded from recently published anthologies that focus on African American writers. Nevertheless, he was among the first to develop the canon of African American poetry and prose.

Biography

William Stanley Beaumont Braithwaite was born in Boston, Massachusetts, 6 December 1878. He was home-schooled for a while and was later an apprentice typesetter at Ginn and Company. Braithwaite was an editor at *Colored American Magazine* in Boston (1901–1902); literary editor and columnist at the *Boston Evening Transcript* (1905); professor of creative literature at Atlanta University, Georgia (1935–1945); publisher, *Poetic Journal* in Boston (1912–1914); editor, *Poetry Review* (1916–1917); and founder and editor of B. J. Brimmer Publishing Company (1921–1927). He and Emma Kelly were married in 1903; they had four sons and three daughters. Braithwaite's awards and honors included the NAACP Arthur B. Spingarn Award for Outstanding Achievement in Literature (1918); A.M., Atlanta University, Georgia (1918); and Litt.D., Talladega College (1918). Braithwaite was a member of the Poetry Society of America, the New England Poetry Society, the Boston Authors' Club, and the editorial board of *Phylon*. He moved to 409 Edgecombe Avenue in Harlem in 1941, and died there on 8 June 1962.

GERRI BATES

See also Brimmer, B. J., Publishing House; Brown, Sterling; Cullen, Countee; Dunbar, Paul Laurence;

Hughes, Langston; Johnson, Georgia Douglas; Johnson, James Weldon; Lindsay, Vachel; Locke, Alain; McKay, Claude; New Negro, The; Spencer, Anne

Selected Books

The Canadian. Boston, Mass.: Small, Maynard, 1901.
Lyrics of Life and Love: Poems. Boston, Mass.: Turner, 1904. (Reprints, 1969 and 1971.)
The House of Falling Leaves With Other Poems. Boston, Mass.: Luce, 1908. (Reprint, 1969.)
The Story of the Great War. New York: Stokes, 1919.
Going Over Tindal: A Fragment Wrenched From the Life of Titus Jabson. Boston, Mass.: Brimmer, 1924.
John Myers O'Hara and the Grecian Influence. Portland, Me.: Smith and Sale, 1926.
The Story of the Years Between 1918–1939. 1940.
Selected Poems. New York: Coward-McCann, 1948.
The Bewitched Parsonage: The Story of the Brontës. New York: Coward-McCann, 1950.
The William Stanley Braithwaite Reader, ed. Philip Butcher. Ann Arbor: University of Michigan Press, 1972.

Selected Articles

"A Grave Wrong to the Negro." *Boston Globe,* 1906.
"Some Recent Verse." *Poet Lore: A Magazine of Letters,* January 1911, pp. 223–240.
"The Poets and the Magazines." *Boston Evening Transcript,* 9 December 1911.
"Christmas Books for Children." *Boston Evening Transcript,* 23 November 1912.
"The Year and the Writers." *Boston Evening Transcript,* 28 December 1912.
"A Foremost American Lyricist." *Lippincott's Monthly Magazine,* 1913.
"Mrs. Dargan as Lyric Poet." *Boston Evening Transcript,* 12 Dececember 1914.
"Imagists and Their Poetry." *Boston Evening Transcript,* 21 April 1915.
"The Mystery." *Scribner's,* 1915.
"Imagism: Another View." *New Republic,* 12 June 1915. (Reprint, 1954.)
"The Substance of Poetry." *Poetry Review,* May 1916.
"Poetry as a Fine Art." *Poetry Review,* October 1916.
"The Year in Poetry." *Bookman,* March 1917.
"Some Contemporary Poets of the Negro Race." *Crisis,* 1919.
"The Negro in Literature and Art." *Crisis,* September 1924, pp. 208–210.
"Some Contemporary Poets of the Negro Race." *Crisis,* April 1924, pp. 275–280.
"The Negro in American Literature." *New Negro,* 1925.
"The Poetry Clinic." *Step Ladder,* December 1926.
"The Novels of Jessie Fauset." *Opportunity,* January 1934.
"The House Under Arcturus: An Autobiography." *Phylon,* 1–3, 1941; 1–2, 1942.
"A Tribute to W. E. Burghardt Du Bois." *Phylon,* 1949.
"The First Negro Novelist." *Pittsburgh Courier,* 30 May 1953.
"The Passing of Alain Leroy Locke." *Phylon,* 1954.
"Alain Locke's Relationship to the Negro in American Literature." *Phylon,* 1957.

Further Reading

Bardolph, Richard. *The Negro Vanguard.* New York: Rinehart, 1959.
Brawley, Benjamin Griffith. *The Negro in Literature and Art in the United States.* New York: Duffield, 1918, 1929.
Brown, Sterling Allen. *Negro Poetry and Drama.* Washington, D.C.: Associates in Negro Folk Education, 1937.
———. *The Negro Caravan: Writings by American Negroes.* New York: Dryden, 1941.
Cullen, Countee, ed. *Caroling Dusk: An Anthology of Verse by Negro Poets.* New York: Harper, 1927.
Johnson, James Weldon, ed. *The Book of American Negro Poetry.* New York: Harcourt, Brace, 1931. (First published 1922.)
Redding, J. Saunders. *To Make a Poet Black.* Chapel Hill: University of North Carolina Press, 1939.
Wagner, Jean. *Black Poets of the United States: From Paul Laurence Dunbar to Langston Hughes,* trans. Kenneth Douglas. Urbana: University of Illinois Press, 1973.
White, Newman Ivey, ed. *An Anthology of Verse by American Negroes.* Durham, N.C.: Trinity College Press, 1924.

Brawley, Benjamin

Benjamin Griffith Brawley (1882–1939) was an author, a minister, and a college professor and administrator. He was born in Columbia, South Carolina, to parents who would have a profound impact on his career aspirations. In particular, his father, Edward McKnight Brawley, was a Baptist preacher and an instructor at Benedict College in South Carolina who served as president of a number of Baptist-affiliated colleges and was also a noted speaker and a proficient writer.

Benjamin Brawley, c. 1910. (Schomburg Center for Research in Black Culture, New York Public Library.)

Throughout his early years, Brawley traveled a great deal, as the family moved several times; he attended a number of elementary schools but also received home schooling. He earned bachelor's degrees from Atlanta Baptist College (later Morehouse College) and the University of Chicago and a master's degree from Harvard. As a young adult, Brawley was aware of the importance of cultural institutions such as the church and school in the African American community and began to dedicate his own professional life to preserving and promoting African American culture through the appreciation and celebration of literature. As a classroom teacher, he also tried to inspire his students with a similar hunger for African American culture. Brawley taught at Howard University, Atlanta Baptist College, and Shaw University (at Shaw, one of the oldest African American Baptist-affiliated colleges in North Carolina, he and his father were colleagues). In 1911, at Howard, he became a member of the faculty committee for the College of Liberal Arts, supervising the work of masters' candidates. In this capacity, he could instill in his students, and help them extract, ideas that would be critical to the next generation of African American scholars.

In 1920, Brawley had an opportunity to travel to Liberia, in western Africa, for six months. On this journey, he was able to explore his own religious beliefs and spread Baptist doctrine. When he returned to the United States, he was ordained as a Baptist minister. During a yearlong absence from the classroom, he served as a minister to the Messiah Baptist Church in Brockton, Massachusetts; however, an ideological conflict developed between him and the Baptist polity, and he resigned this post. The dispute had to do with the assimilationist thesis, which stressed faith over race as true patriotism; adherents of this thesis held that African Americans should develop into American citizens through American Christianity. With regard to this conflict, there was also a disagreement between Brawley and his father, who had taken a radical position but remained an active minister in the Baptist church. Still, despite their differences, Brawley esteemed his father's faith, articulate intelligence, and professionalism.

When Brawley returned to teaching, he was afforded time for scholarship and writing; this resulted in many works that captured African American cultural themes through literature, the arts, and history. Over the course of his career, Brawley produced seventeen books and more than twenty articles, including the following: *History of Morehouse College*, 1917; *Africa and the War*, 1918; *Women of Achievement Written for the Fireside Schools under the Auspices of the Woman's American Baptist Home Mission Society*, 1919; *A Short Social History of the American Negro*, 1921; *The Negro in Literature and Art in the United States*, 1921; *Doctor Dillard of the Jeanes Fund*, 1930; *Early Negro American Writers: Selections With Biographical and Critical Introductions*, 1935; *Paul Laurence Dunbar*, 1936; and *Negro Builders and Heroes*, 1937. One particularly notable work of Brawley's was *A Short History of the American Negro* (1913), a collection of essays examining social, cultural, and historical issues relevant to African Americans; it received broad attention in both African American and mainstream news media. Another popular work of Brawley's was *Paul Laurence Dunbar: Poet of His People*, which has been reprinted numerous times.

In 1927, Brawley was nominated for an award from the Harmon Foundation, a philanthropic organization that sought out African American artists and intellectuals in order to support their creative efforts. He won second place, but he rejected the award because he and many of his colleagues believed that he had deserved first place.

As part of his work in preserving and promoting African American culture, Brawley concerned himself with the education and enlightenment of white Americans. He worked hard to explain the unique position of African Americans in American society to his white audiences, and in his essays and books of poems, he sought to provide a shared educational experience for white and African American readers. He was also a collector of materials documenting African American history and culture. His personal library contained a number of books on African American literature and history, including many signed first and limited editions. He also acquired one of the largest collections of manuscripts by and about the journalist and critic Richard Le Gallienne. Brawley bequeathed his manuscript and literary collections to Howard University's Moorland Spingarn Research Center in Washington, D.C. A collection of materials pertaining to Brawley himself is housed at the Moorland Spingarn Research Center, Manuscript Division.

Biography

Benjamin Griffith Brawley was born 22 April 1882, in Columbia, South Carolina; his parents were Edward M. and Margaret Saphronia (Dickerson) Brawley. In 1898–1901, he attended Atlanta Baptist College (Morehouse College) in Georgia, receiving a B.S. degree. He received an A.B. from the University of Chicago (1906) and an A.M. from Harvard University (1908). Brawley taught in Georgetown, Florida (1901); at Morehouse College as an instructor in English (1902) and then a professor of English (1906–1910); at Howard University as a professor of English (1910–1912, 1931); and at Shaw University in Raleigh, North Carolina, as a professor of English (1923–1931). He also served as dean of Morehouse College (1912). He married Hilda Damaris Prowd, of Kingston, Jamaica, in 1912 (they had no children). In 1920, Brawley went to Liberia to do a study of the republic. On 2 June 1921, he was ordained as a Baptist minister in Boston. Brawley died 1 February 1939.

IDA JONES

See also Dunbar, Paul Laurence; Harmon Foundation

Further Reading

Dyson, Walter. *Howard University, the Capstone of Negro Education: A History, 1867–1940.* Washington, D.C.: Graduate School of Howard University, 1941.

Logan, Rayford W. *Howard University: The First Hundred Years, 1867–1967.* New York: New York University Press, 1969.

Logan, Rayford W., and Michael R. Winston, eds. *Dictionary of American Negro Biography.* New York: Norton, 1982.

Sinnette, Elinor Des Verney, W. Paul Coates, and Thomas C. Battle, eds. *Black Bibliophiles and Collectors: Preservers of Black History.* Washington, D.C.: Howard University Press, 1990.

Smith, Jessie Carney, ed. *Notable Black American Men.* Farmington Hills, Mich.: Gale Research, 1999.

Who's Who in Colored America, 1928–1929. New York: Who's Who in Colored America, 1929.

Briggs, Cyril

Although Cyril Valentine Briggs was born with a speech impediment that made it almost impossible to hold a conversation with him, he more than compensated for this disability with his deft organizational skills and his prolific pen. Briggs was at the forefront of black radical politics of the 1920s. The militant organization he founded, the African Black Brotherhood (ABB), helped advance the cause of black nationalism and advocated racial solidarity of the working classes. Briggs was also important as the author of numerous articles espousing black rights and communism, and for establishing several highly influential black radical periodicals, including the *Crusader.*

Briggs was born in Nevis, in the British West Indies. He was the illegitimate child of Mary M. Huggins, a woman of color, and Louis E. Briggs, a white plantation manager. Briggs himself was light-complexioned enough that he was later described as an "angry, blond Negro." After graduating from grade school in 1904, he worked at a newspaper on Saint Kitts.

In 1905, Briggs immigrated to New York City, where he became part of a growing West Indian population. Between 1912 and 1915 he worked in a variety of positions for the *Amsterdam News.* In 1915, he became the editor of the *Colored American Review,* a black business magazine in Harlem; however, his work with this magazine ended after only two issues, perhaps because of his militant tone. He then returned to the *Amsterdam News*, writing pieces in which he urged self-determination for blacks and argued against the United States' involvement in World War I. Perhaps his most significant piece was a two-part editorial (5 and 19 September 1917) advocating an independent black nation within the United States. The publishers' growing censorship of his articles caused his break with the *Amsterdam News* in 1919.

Briggs established the *Crusader* in September 1918. In its early years, this periodical was the organ of the Hamitic League of the World, a group espousing "race patriotism." Briggs' stance is perhaps best summed up in an editorial, "Race Catechism," published in the inaugural issue of the *Crusader*. In it, he stressed that blacks should be proud of their race and be prepared to make any sacrifice for it.

The *Crusader* continued to emphasize race patriotism, but after the "red summer" of 1919 (a season marked by several bloody race riots) it became increasingly anticapitalist and anti-imperialist, as is evidenced in the editorial "The Salvation of the Negro" (April 1921). This editorial encapsulates Briggs's beliefs about saving the race by creating an autonomous black state "in Africa or elsewhere" and by establishing "a Universal Socialist Co-Operative Commonwealth."

The *Crusader* also became the voice of the African Blood Brotherhood, a semisecret paramilitary organization attempting to blend black nationalism with an interracial working-class program. The group, never numbering more than a few thousand, consisted largely of anglophone West Indians, including Claude McKay, W. A. Domingo, and Richard B. Moore. There was a close link between the ABB and the Communist (Workers') Party, and Briggs and most of the other ABB leaders would join the communists by 1921 (ABB would be dissolved in 1924).

Briggs and other members of the ABB became increasingly convinced that black liberation worldwide would necessitate bloodshed, particularly after the riot of 1921 in Tulsa, in which more than 50 whites and 150 blacks died. Although Briggs denied that the ABB had been involved in this riot, he praised the use of force by blacks. Accusations in the *New York Times* (June 1921) that the ABB was involved gave the organization much-needed publicity, which increased its numbers.

Briggs's increasingly communistic stance put him in conflict with Marcus Garvey. Initially, Briggs had been supportive of Garvey and Garvey's Universal Negro Improvement Association (UNIA). But he had made an unsuccessful overture to Garvey in an attempt to work with the UNIA at its convention in 1921; after this rebuff, Briggs became one of Garvey's sharpest critics, using the *Crusader* to wage a harsh campaign against him.

Tbe *Crusader*—unlike Garvey's newspaper, the *Negro World*—was never able to reach a mass audience. Because of increasing government pressure and dwindling financial support, the *Crusader* ceased publication in 1922. Subsequently, Briggs headed the Crusader News Agency, which disseminated radical news items to some 200 newspapers. Briggs also published pieces in various forums for Marxist thought, including the *Daily Worker* and *The Communist*, on many of his long-term concerns.

Briggs went on to edit the *Negro Champion*, the house organ of the communist-backed American Negro Labor Congress (ANLC); and the *Negro Liberator* of the League of Struggle for Negro Rights (LSNR). Both the ANLC and the LSNR were attempts by the Communist Party to appeal to black nationalists. In these organizations, for the first time, the party began to emphasize the importance of race, not just class, in the effort to improve blacks' living conditions. The most radical proposal of the communists regarding the "Negro question" came at the Sixth World Congress, held in Moscow in 1928, when the Comintern (the international arm of the Socialist Party of Soviet Russia), declared that blacks in the American South had the right of self-determination as a "subject nation." Briggs was at the forefront of this controversial movement toward black self-determination.

By 1939, Briggs was expelled from the party because of his support of black nationalism over class issues, but he rejoined it soon after moving to Los Angeles in 1944. During the late 1950s, he worked as an editor with the *Los Angeles Herald-Dispatch* and the *People's World*. Briggs also became involved with younger black radicals in the 1960s, continuing his lifelong dedication to the cause of black nationalism until his death in 1966.

During much of his life, and during the years immediately after he died, Briggs was relegated to relative obscurity. However, a recent resurgence of interest in radical black politics and the reprinting of a full run of the *Crusader* have belatedly brought Briggs the attention he has long deserved.

Biography

Cyril Valentine Briggs was born 28 May 1888, on Nevis (or possibly, according to some sources, Saint Kitts),

British West Indies. He graduated from the Ebenezer Wesleyan grade school on Saint Kitts in 1904. He immigrated to the United States on 4 July 1905 and became a naturalized U.S. citizen on 6 August 1918. He was the founder of the African Blood Brotherhood and editor of the *Amsterdam News* (1912–1915, 1916–1919), *Colored American Review* (1915), *Crusader* (1918–1922), *Negro Champion*, *Negro Liberator*, *Los Angeles Herald-Dispatch*, and *People's World*. Briggs died in Los Angeles 18 October 1966.

Louis Parascandola

See also African Blood Brotherhood; American Negro Labor Congress; Amsterdam News; Communist Party; Domingo, Wilfred Adolphus; Garvey, Marcus; McKay, Claude; Moore, Richard B.; Riots: 2—Red Summer of 1919; Riots: 3—Tulsa, 1921; Universal Negro Improvement Association

Further Reading

Haywood, Harry. *Black Bolshevik: Autobiography of an Afro-American Communist*. Chicago, Ill.: Liberator, 1978.

Hill, Robert A., intro. and ed. *The Crusader*, 3 vols. New York: Kraus, 1987.

Hutchinson, Earl Ofari. *Blacks and Reds: Race and Class in Conflict, 1919–1990*. East Lansing: Michigan State University Press, 1995.

James, Winston. *Holding Aloft the Banner of Ethiopia: Caribbean Radicalism in Early Twentieth-Century America*. New York: Verso, 1998.

Kornweibel, Theodore Jr. *"Seeing Red": Federal Campaign Against Black Militancy, 1919–1925*. Bloomington: Indiana University Press, 1998.

Solomon, Mark. *The Cry Was Unity: Communists and African Americans, 1917–1936*. Jackson: University Press of Mississippi, 1998.

Thomas, Theman R. "Cyril Briggs and the African Blood Brotherhood: Another Radical View of Race and Class During the 1920s." Ph.D. diss., University of California, Santa Barbara, 1981.

Vincent, Theodore G. *Black Power and the Garvey Movement*. San Francisco, Calif.: Ramparts, 1972.

Brimmer, B. J., Publishing House

B. J. Brimmer Publishing House was a short-lived company, based in Boston. It was founded in 1921 under the direction of the well-known African American poet and literary critic William Stanley Braithwaite, who was also editor in chief. Braithwaite was also editor of the annual *Anthology of Magazine Verse*; he previously had been with Cornhill, but he left when Brookes More gained control and stopped publishing the works of African American poets.

Brimmer primarily published poetry, nonfiction, and drama; it issued very few novels. Along with trade printings, the firm published titles in limited, signed editions, which were printed on handmade paper. Brimmer's list (which included Benjamin Rosenbaum's and Celia MacKinnon's first books of poems) reflected Braithwaite's interest in new poetry, as well as his desire to promote the work of new black poets. Among the company's publications were *Bronze: A Book of Verse* by Georgia Douglas Johnson (1922); *The Poems of Seumus O'Sullivan* by James Starkey (1923); and *The Hills Give Promise, a Volume of Lyrics, Together With Carmus: A Symphonic Poem* by Robert Sillman. The firm also published one nonfiction book by an African American, about black soldiers during World War II; and its list for spring 1924 included a novel by Joshua Henry Jones about the "race problem."

Despite Braithwaite's desire to help African American authors, and despite his influence with poets such as James Weldon Johnson, Countee Cullen, and Claude McKay, his primary interest was in white authors from New England. The names on his list of the best contemporary American poets in 1927 (at the height of the Harlem Renaissance) included Edwin Arlington Robinson, Robert Frost, Carl Sandburg, Vachel Lindsay, Edgar Lee Masters, Amy Lowell, Conrad Aiken, and Sara Teasdale (Hutchinson 1995, 355). Braithwaite's Anglocentric position was influenced by his assimilationist political stance and his view that American culture was a whole. In terms of his literary preferences, Braithwaite also held rather old-fashioned ideas about what literature should be, and he often balked at the writings of many black authors of the time, which were overtly racial and politically charged. As a result of his literary preferences and his sometimes questionable publishing practices—which included helping to create primarily vanity presses like Brimmer to promote the works of authors for whom he acted as a kind of agent—he lost influence as a critic throughout the 1920s. In fact, Braithwaite was criticized by Claude McKay in the latter's letters to Langston Hughes during this period.

At a time when new publishing companies like Alfred A. Knopf Inc., Harcourt Brace, and Boni and

Liveright were on the rise in New York and were embracing new "modern" authors, Brimmer's list of little-known and now hardly memorable writers such as Lucias Beebe, Mary Esther Cobb, Bella Flaccus, and Zoe Patricia Hobbs, combined with his unwillingness to join current trends in literature, proved fatal to the company's financial success. B. J. Brimmer Publishing Company went bankrupt in 1927 and was ultimately of little importance to the publishing of the Harlem Renaissance, despite Braithwaite's personal hope of contributing to the success of African American poetry.

APRIL CONLEY KILINSKI

See also Braithwaite, William Stanley; Cornhill; Cullen, Countee; Hughes, Langston; Johnson, Georgia Douglas; Johnson, James Weldon; McKay, Claude; Publishers and Publishing Houses

Further Reading

Dzwonkoski, David. "B. J. Brimmer Company." In *American Literary Publishing Houses*, 2 vols., ed. Peter Dzwonkoski. Detroit, Mich.: Gale Research, 1986, p. 71.
Hutchinson, George. *The Harlem Renaissance in Black and White*. Cambridge, Mass.: Belknap Press of Harvard University Press, 1995.
Wintz, Cary D. *Black Culture and the Harlem Renaissance*. Houston, Tex.: Rice University Press, 1988.

Brooks, Clarence

Clarence Brooks was a pioneer in African American cinema, both in front of and behind the camera. Brooks was born in Texas but moved to Los Angeles after graduating from high school. In 1915, he met the brothers George P. and Noble Johnson, who would soon (in 1916) form the country's first black-owned and -operated film production firm, the Lincoln Motion Picture Company. Brooks was part of a group of blacks who wanted to make films to counter the demeaning stereotypes that were so frequently in mass culture. Their aim was to portray African Americans realistically and seriously, and in particular to show the concerns and aspirations of a budding black middle class. These same sentiments characterized African American art and culture during the Harlem Renaissance.

Brooks served as secretary of the Lincoln company and was an actor in most of its films. He had a featured role in Lincoln's first release, *The Realization of a Negro's Ambition* (1916), the story of a graduate of Tuskegee Institute who leaves the farm to find his fortune out west. This was the first black film to offer a serious depiction—with no burlesque or buffoonery—of middle-class blacks, and it was well received in black communities throughout the United States. Lincoln quickly followed with *Trooper of Company K* (1916), a film about the massacre of black troops in the U.S. Army's Tenth Cavalry. These films were a source not only of entertainment but of racial pride; for actors like Brooks, they provided an opportunity to play fully conceived characters that were in stark contrast to the unflattering stereotypes pervasive in mainstream studio films.

Brooks went into semiretirement after Lincoln went out of business in 1921. He was lured back to films, however, in 1928, when he played the part of a wounded veteran of World War I in *Absent* (produced by the Rosebud Film Corporation). Brooks would eventually become one of the most popular stars in black films. He also appeared in some big studio productions, most notably as the heroic Dr. Oliver Marchand in John Ford's *Arrowsmith* (1931). Brooks's role in *Arrowsmith* was one of the rare cases in which black actors were able to portray characters other than the standard racial stereotypes. Brooks earned strong reviews for his performance, but he was never to get another role of that caliber. Nevertheless, Brooks managed to put together a strong body of work, and he continued to appear in mostly black films, including a series of black cowboy westerns, throughout the 1930s and 1940s.

Biography

Clarence Brooks was born around 1895 in San Antonio, Texas; he moved to Los Angeles after graduating from high school. He studied dentistry for a short while at the University of Southern California before opening his own drugstore. In 1916–1921, he was the secretary of the Lincoln Motion Picture Company and appeared in most of its films. After Lincoln went out of business, Brooks returned to films in 1928 and remained a popular actor through the 1940s. The date of his death is unknown.

DWANDALYN R. REECE

See also Film: Actors; Johnson, Noble; Lincoln Motion Picture Company

Select Filmography

The Realization of a Negro's Ambition. 1916.
Trooper of Company K. 1916.
The Law of Nature. 1917.
A Man's Duty. 1919.
By Right of Birth. 1921.
Absent. 1928.
Georgia Rose. 1930.
Arrowsmith. 1931.
Murder in Harlem. 1935.
The Brand of Cain. 1935.
Lem Hawkins's Confession. 1935.

Further Reading

Cripps, Thomas. *Slow Fade to Black: The Negro in American Film, 1900–1942.* Oxford and New York: Oxford University Press, 1977, 1993.
Sampson, Henry T. *Blacks in Black and White: A Source Book on Black Films,* 2nd ed. Lanham, Md., and London: Scarecrow, 1995.

Brooks, Gwendolyn

Gwendolyn Elizabeth Brooks was born in 1917, at the very beginning of the Harlem Renaissance, was barely a teenager at its close, and spent most of her life in Chicago. While she thus cannot properly be called a participant in the renaissance, she is certainly one of its most distinguished students and heirs, receiving encouragement from such Harlem notables as Langston Hughes and James Weldon Johnson. Brooks was known for her astute blend of realism and romanticism, her striking ability with language, and her dedication to African American culture and to children; and she was the first African American to win a Pulitzer Prize.

Brooks was born in Topeka, Kansas, but grew up in Chicago. She began writing poetry in elementary school. Her mother, Keziah Wims Brooks, took her to public poetry readings and asserted that her daughter would one day be the *"lady* Paul Laurence Dunbar." In 1930, Brooks's first poem, "Eventide," was published in *American Childhood Magazine.* While in high school she became a regular contributor to the column "Light and Shadows" in the *Chicago Defender,* with more than one hundred poems in print. She met and corresponded

Gwendolyn Brooks. (Schomburg Center for Research in Black Culture, New York Public Library.)

with Langston Hughes and James Weldon Johnson during this period (Hughes, especially, would be a lifelong supporter of her writing). They urged her to read modern poetry, especially such figures as T. S. Eliot, Ezra Pound, and e. e. cummings. Brooks developed her own distinctive voice and message, always reflecting a concern for issues of oppression but with more of a turn toward the political in the 1960s. However, the attention to craft urged and modeled by Hughes and other modernists is a hallmark of her entire body of work.

Brooks's first book of poetry, *A Street in Bronzeville,* was published in 1945 by Harper and Row. It was praised by the critics and helped earn her a place on *Mademoiselle* magazine's list of "Ten Young Women of the Year." Focusing on the daily lives of urban blacks, *A Street in Bronzeville* is marked by strong individualized voices, concern for issues of racial and intraracial discrimination and the lives of women, and compassion for all the lives represented. Three of the poems from this volume that have been most frequently anthologized and quoted are "The Sundays of Satin-Legs Smith," a day in the life of an urban zoot-suiter; "Gay Chaps at the Bar," about war veterans; and "The Mother," about abortion.

Annie Allen (which won the Pulitzer Prize) appeared in 1949. Divided into sections called "Notes From the Childhood and the Girlhood," "The Anniad," "Appendix to the Anniad," and "The Womanhood," the volume traces the experiences of an inner-city girl growing into womanhood. In "The Anniad," Brooks uses a variety of poetic techniques, including what she herself called the "sonnet-ballad," with the protagonist achieving an epic heroism in her daily struggles. *Annie Allen* juxtaposes a realistic approach to life with hopes and dreams for something better, demonstrating the complexities of ordinary human lives.

Brooks's one novel, *Maud Martha*, appeared in 1953; it consists of very short chapters—practically vignettes—and was drawn in part on her experiences as a maid. *Maud Martha* was greeted with some interest but also some confusion when it was published. It has been a subject of increasing interest in recent years, especially among feminist critics.

Throughout her life, Brooks advocated for and wrote about the needs of children. Her *Bronzeville Boys and Girls* (1956), a collection of thirty-four poems with traditional rhyme schemes, explores processes of self-discovery; these boys and girls could be children of any race or region. Another example is her *Children Coming Home* (1991). Twenty children living in poverty each have a poem describing the pains, joys, and challenges they find as they come home from school. In addition, Brooks passed along the mentoring and encouragement she had received from such Harlem figures as Hughes and Johnson, becoming very active in the poetry workshop movement—and perhaps more notably in poetry classes and contests for inner-city children, to which she devoted tremendous energy and gave both financial and personal sponsorhip.

In 1967, Brooks attended the historic Fisk University Second Black Writers' Conference. She was both honored and influenced by such outspoken figures as Amiri Baraka and Ron Milner. She took an active role in the "black arts movement" from that time forward and began to host a poetry workshop in Chicago for such young poets as Sonia Sanchez, Nikki Giovanni, and Don L. Lee.

According to Cook (1993), Brooks's earlier poetry follows an "integrationist ideology," but she "turns from the image of the meek, suffering victim so well loved in earlier poetry to that of the raging, threatening avenger." But Williams (1997), among others, argues that elements of protest and an awareness of oppression were always present in Brooks's poetry, and that her radicalization in the 1960s and 1970s led rather to a shift in balance.

Brooks's more open attention to social and political issues can be seen in *The Bean Eaters* (1960), which includes such famous poems as "We Real Cool" and "A Bronzeville Mother Loiters in Mississippi. Meanwhile, a Mississippi Mother Burns Bacon," a response to the murder of Emmett Till. Notably, these poems were written before the conference at Fisk University, lending support to Williams's position. Brooks's *In the Mecca* (1968) shifts to more free verse and more black vernacular speech. The title poem traces a woman's search through a tenement for her murdered daughter. *In the Mecca* received a nomination for the National Book Award.

After many years with Harper and Row, in the 1970s Brooks switched to African American publishers, especially Broadside Press, out of Detroit. In the 1980s, Brooks established her own publishing house, the David Company of Chicago.

Brooks continued to write until the end of her life, publishing several more volumes of poetry and two autobiographies, *Report from Part One* (1972) and *Report from Part Two* (1996). Brooks received more than fifty honorary degrees, as well as two Guggenheim fellowships, the Frost Medal, and the title of poet laureate of Illinois (1968), among many other awards. In 1976, she became the first black woman elected to the 250-member National Institute of Arts and Letters. In 1985, she became a poetry consultant to the Library of Congress. The Gwendolyn Brooks Chair in Black Literature and Creative Writing was established at Chicago State University in 1990. In what she has described as her highest honor, she was named the Jefferson Lecturer by the National Endowment for the Humanities in 1994, and in 1995, she received a National Medal of Arts award. She considered the Gwendolyn Brooks Junior High School, just South of Chicago, equally important.

Through her poetry and the example of her life, Brooks carried on the legacy she herself inherited from the Harlem Renaissance and provided a bridge between it and the "black arts movement." Her influence seems likely to continue well into the future.

Biography

Gwendolyn Elizabeth Brooks was born in Topeka, Kansas, 7 June 1917. She graduated from Wilson Junior College in 1937. She worked as a maid, then as a secretary; she taught poetry workshops and creative writing at Columbia College beginning in 1963, and later at institutions including Northeastern Illinois University, Elmhurst College, Columbia University, Clay College of New York, and the University of Wisconsin. She married Henry Lowington Blakely Sr. in 1939; they had two children. Blakely and Brooks divorced in 1969, but they remarried in 1973. Brooks's awards included the following: Midwestern Writers' Conference Poetry Award, 1943, 1944, 1945; Eunice Tietjens Prize from *Poetry* (for *Annie Allen*), 1949; more than fifty honorary degrees; two Guggenheim fellowships; American Academy of Arts and Letters Grant, 1946–1947; Shelley Memorial Award; Frost Medal; the first Kuumba Award; a Senior Fellowship in Literature; Pulitzer Prize, 1950; appointment as poet laureate of Illinois, 1968; election to the National Institute of Arts and Letters, 1976; consultancy in poetry to the Library of Congress, 1985–1986; Lifetime Achievement Award, National Endowment for the Arts, 1989; Lifetime Achievement Award, National Book Foundation, 1994; Jefferson lectureship, 1994; and National Medal of Arts award, 1995. Brooks died in Chicago 3 December 2000.

KATHRYN WEST

See also Chicago Defender; Dunbar, Paul Laurence; Hughes, Langston; Johnson, James Weldon; Literature: 7—Poetry; Modernism

Selected Works

A Street in Bronzeville. 1945.
Annie Allen. 1949.
Maud Martha. 1953.
Bronzeville Boys and Girls. 1956.
The Bean Eaters. 1960.
Selected Poems. 1963.
We Real Cool. 1966.
The Wall. 1967.
In the Mecca. 1968.

Family Pictures. 1970.
Riot. 1970.
The World of Gwendolyn Brooks. 1971.
Aloneness. 1971.
Black Steel: Joe Frazier and Muhammad Ali. 1971.
Aurora. 1972.
Report from Part One: An Autobiography. 1972.
Beckonings. 1975.
A Capsule Course in Black Poetry Writing. 1975.
Black Love. 1981.
To Disembark. 1981.
Primer for Blacks. 1981.
Young Poet's Primer. 1981.
Very Young Poets. 1983.
The Near-Johannesburg Boy and Other Poems. 1986.
Blacks. 1987.
Winnie. 1988.
Children Coming Home. 1991.
Report from Part Two: An Autobiography. 1996.

Further Reading

Bloom, Harold, ed. *Gwendolyn Brooks: Modern Critical Views.* 2000.

Cook, William W. "The Black Arts Poets." In *The Columbia History of American Poetry*, ed. Jay Parini. New York: Columbia University Press, 1993.

Kent, George E. *A Life of Gwendolyn Brooks.* Lexington: University Press of Kentucky, 1990.

Melhem, D. H. *Gwendolyn Brooks: Poetry and the Heroic Voice.* Lexington: University Press of Kentucky, 1987.

Mootry, Maria K., and Gary Smith, eds. *A Life Distilled: Gwendolyn Brooks—Her Poetry and Fiction.* Urbana: University of Illinois Press, 1987.

Tate, Claudia, ed. *Black Women Writers at Work: Conversations with . . . .* New York: Continuum, 1983.

Washington, Mary Helen. "Plain, Black, and Decently Wild: The Heroic Possibilities of *Maud Martha*." In *The Voyage In: Fictions of Female Development*, ed. Elizabeth Abel, Marianne Hirsch, and Elizabeth Langland. Hanover. N.H.: Dartmouth College/University Press of New England, 1983.

———. "'Taming All That Anger Down': Rage and Silence in the Writing of Gwendolyn Brooks." In *Invented Lives: Narratives of Black Women, 1860–1960.* New York: Anchor/Doubleday, 1987.

Williams, Kenny J. "Gwendolyn Brooks" In *The Oxford Companion to African American Literature*, ed. William L. Andrews, Frances Smith Foster, and Trudier Harris. New York: Oxford University Press, 1997.

Wright, Stephen Caldwell, ed. *On Gwendolyn Brooks: Reliant Contemplation*. Ann Arbor: University of Michigan Press, 1996.

Brooks, Shelton

Shelton Brooks was a well-known vaudeville entertainer who sang, danced, acted, performed comedy, and played the piano. He is best remembered as the composer of several hit songs between 1910 and 1918—songs that helped set off America's dance craze, furthered the careers of several popular singers, and became part of the standard repertoire of early jazz. Brooks was exposed to church music at an early age and taught himself to play the organ and then the piano. By age fifteen he was playing professionally in Detroit; in 1905, he moved to Chicago, where he became active as a vaudeville performer and an imitator of the comedian Bert Williams. Over the next sixteen years he starred in several plays and composed most of the songs for which he became famous.

Brooks began to establish a reputation as a songwriter 1910, when the popular white vaudeville singer Sophie Tucker adopted his "Some of These Days" as her theme song. It was an overnight hit, sold more than 2 million copies as sheet music, and became a popular vehicle for jazz improvisation. Tucker herself recorded the tune several times and continued to sing it for the rest of her life. Brooks then wrote a string of hits that captured the spirit of the era: dancing, drinking, and good times. In 1911, Brooks wrote "All Night Long," which expressed the mood of drinking parties. The double-entendre song "I Wonder Where My Easy Rider's Gone" (1913) was popularized in performances and recordings by both Sophie Tucker and Mae West.

Brooks wrote three tunes that inspired nationally renowned dances when they were taken up by white dance troupes and shows: "Walking the Dog" (1916), "Darktown Strutters' Ball" (1917), and "I Want to Shimmie" (1918). "Darktown Strutters' Ball" became an instant dance (shimmy) favorite and was Brooks's biggest hit, eventually selling more than 3 million copies as sheet music. Despite its irresistible lyrics, "Darktown Stutters' Ball" received most attention as an all-instrumental version (1917) by the white Original Dixieland Jazz Band, which made it one of the earliest recorded jazz hits and a traditional jazz standard.

In 1922, Brooks moved to New York. He then worked mainly as a vaudeville actor on Broadway and in Europe, in popular shows such as the *Plantation Revue* and *Blackbirds* (in both of these, he played opposite Florence Mills). He also recorded during the "race records" boom of the 1920s. The majority of his nearly two dozen recordings are comedy skits. In 1923, he provided piano accompaniment for two vocal duets that he recorded on the Okeh label with singer Sarah Martin. Brooks was also Ethel Waters's piano accompanist on two Columbia recordings in 1926. In 1928, he produced and starred in the show *Nifties*. In 1927, he appeared in the short comedy film *Gaiety*.

In 1930, Brooks was the costar of a popular biweekly CBS radio show, *Egg and Shell*, and also performed on Broadway in the revue *Brown Buddies*, for which he cowrote the song "Don't Leave Your Little Blackbird Blue." Brooks also acted in and wrote two songs for the film *Double Deal* (1939). His last major appearance in New York was at Harlem's Apollo Theater in 1940. That same year, he was honored by the American Society of Composers, Authors and Publishers (ASCAP) as a composer. In the early 1940s, Brooks moved to Los Angeles, where he would perform in the burlesque tribute *Blackouts* for seven years. He continued performing into the 1960s and 1970s with other legends of his era, such as Eubie Blake and Ethel Waters.

Although Shelton Brooks spent much of his career as an entertainer on the musical stage, he wrote several of the century's best popular songs before 1920. His true legacy is that he was a member of a generation of multitalented, successful black entertainers and songwriters who pushed beyond the standard genre of minstrel and coon songs after 1910 and produced new material that inspired, influenced, and helped to shape trends in dance, show music, jazz, and twentieth-century American popular culture.

Biography

The composer, vaudevillian, and pianist Shelton Brooks was born 4 May 1886 in Amesburg, Ontario, Canada. By age fifteen he was playing professionally in Detroit; he moved to Chicago in 1905. From then until about 1920 he starred in plays and composed most of his famous songs. Brooks moved to New York in 1922 and continued to perform onstage, in recordings, and in films; he also costarred in a radio show in 1930. He moved to Los Angeles, California, in the 1940s and continued performing into the 1960s and 1970s. Brooks died 6 September 1975 in Los Angeles.

MICHAEL WHITE

See also Jazz; Mills, Florence; Singers; Waters, Ethel; Williams, Egbert Austin "Bert"

Selected Works

"All Night Long." 1921.
"Darktown Strutters' Ball." 1917.
"Don't Leave Your Little Backbird Blue." 1930.
"I Want to Shimmie." 1918.
"I Wonder Where My Easy Rider's Gone." 1913.
"Some of These Days." 1910.

Recordings

"After All These Years." 1926. (As piano accompanist to Ethel Waters.)
"I've Got What It Takes to Bring You Back." 1923. (Piano accompaniment and vocal duet with Sara Martin.)
"Lost Your Mind." 1921. (Comedy skit with cast and orchestra.)
"Original Blues." 1923. (Piano accompaniment and vocal duet with Sarah Martin.)
"Throw Dirt in Your Face." 1926. (As piano accompanist to Ethel Waters.)

Further Reading

Ewen, David. *The Life and Death of Tin Pan Alley*. New York: Funk and Wagnalls, 1964.
Jasen, David A., and Gene Jones. *Spreadin' Rhythm Around: Black Popular Songwriters, 1880–1930*. New York: 1998.
Morgan, Thomas. "Shelton Brooks: A Profile." In *Jazz Roots: Shelton Brooks Discography*. http://www.jass.com/sheltonbrooks/brooks.html
Shaw, Arnold. *Black Popular Music in America*. New York: Schirmer, 1998.
Tucker, Sophie. *Some of These Days*. New York: Doubleday Doran, 1945.

Broom

Broom: An International Magazine of the Arts, an important literary publication of the 1920s, was intended as a showcase for the best work by living writers and artists. A cartoon on the back cover of the first issue (November 1921) depicts a character with a broom, suggesting an intention to sweep things clean; later, Gordon Craig's cover drawing for the fourth issue, of a figure thumbing its nose, implies an even stronger sense of defying the norm. However, *Broom* was not solely a magazine of the avant-garde or of experimental work. Rather, its content was eclectic: The first three issues included photographs of art by Pablo Picasso, Jacques Lipschitz, Fernand Léger, and Henri Matisse, among others, as well as poems, short stories, and criticism by writers such as Conrad Aiken, Amy Lowell, Sherwood Anderson, Wallace Stevens, Malcolm Cowley, Marianne Moore, and Gertrude Stein.

Broom was first published in Rome. Its founding editor was Harold Loeb, assisted by Alfred Kreymborg, but the two became divided over questions of finances and editorial policy, and Loeb announced Kreymborg's resignation in only the fourth issue. Edward Storer became the new associate editor, and Lola Ridge became the American editor, based in New York City. In the October 1922 issue, Loeb announced that the magazine was moving to Berlin; he also announced the appointment of another new associate editor, Matthew Josephson. Loeb continued to edit *Broom* from Berlin until March 1923, when lack of funding caused him to cease publication. *Broom* was later revived in New York City, in August 1923, under Josephson's editorship (though Loeb was still listed on the masthead), but it again ceased publication—this time permanently—in January 1924.

In the May 1922 issue, Loeb published an essay, "Foreign Exchange," in which he praised American expatriate writers, claiming that they could view the United States more objectively, and he began to publish poems and prose by writers such as John Dos Passos, e. e. cummings, and Robert Coates. In an essay for the September 1922 issue, "The Mysticism of Money," Loeb argued that the objects of industrialism such as "engines, forges, . . . motors, . . . automobiles, ships, aeroplanes," can be works of art that achieve "simplification, elimination of inessentials, balance and beauty." He also argued that materialism and the pursuit of money can be as great an inspiration for art as religion.

Several new American writers were published in *Broom* before its demise, including Kay Boyle, Hart Crane, and Jean Toomer—the latter an important figure in the Harlem Renaissance. *Broom* was one of the first English-language reviews of the arts in Europe, was representative of the post–World War I "lost generation," and did much to expand artistic form and scope in the 1920s. It was judged by Kenneth Rexroth to have been the best literary magazine of the period.

J. P. STEED

See also Anderson, Sherwood; Toomer, Jean

Further Reading

Kreymborg, Alfred. *Troubadour*. New York: Liveright, 1925.
Loeb, Harold. *The Way It Was*. New York: Criterion, 1959.
Sarason, Bertram D. "Harold Loeb." In *Dictionary of Literary Biography*, Vol. 4, *American Writers in Paris, 1920–1939*, ed. Karen Lane Rood. Detroit, Mich.: Gale Research, 1980.

Brotherhood of Sleeping Car Porters

The Brotherhood of Sleeping Car Porters (BSCP) was a labor union formed in 1925 to represent the African American porters and maids who worked on the sleeping and dining cars of the Pullman railroad company. These workers were paid very little and had to rely on tips from the predominantly white passengers; moreover, their work hours were long and irregular, and their working conditions were deplorable—a situation that grew even worse after the federal government's control of the railroads ended in 1920. The increasingly discontented workers began to organize to present their demands in common. In August 1925, they gathered at the Elks Club in Harlem to form their union, choosing A. (Asa) Philip Randolph as their leader. Randolph was a brilliant speaker, a cofounder and coeditor of the socialist newspaper *The Messenger*, and a committed advocate of equality for all African Americans; he did not work for Pullman, and so he was in no danger of recriminations from the company.

However, the BSCP grew very slowly. Pullman fought vehemently against it; used spies, threats, and indiscriminate firings to try and break it; used yellow-dog contracts, which were agreements whereby employees promised not to join it; and created a rival company-sponsored union. Pullman also induced conservative members of the black community, particularly ministers and preachers, to denounce the BSCP as socialist or communist and as interfering with a

benevolent company that provided good jobs for loyal people. Moreover, while Randolph struggled for an agreement with Pullman, the BSCP also faced a battle for recognition from the American Federation of Labor (AFL), an umbrella organization that coordinated the activities of its member unions. The AFL had a long tradition of organizing only the most highly skilled workers in elite craft unions, and it had long ignored the needs of black workers. In 1928, although the federal Railway Labor Board had granted the BSCP the right to organize Pullman porters and maids, the AFL refused to grant the BSCP a charter, insisting that the right to organize porters had already been granted to the Hotel and Restaurant Employees (HRE), an AFL union. In 1934, Randolph was again rebuffed in his attempt to win an AFL charter, when the AFL's executive council awarded jurisdiction over the Pullman porters to yet another union, the Order of Sleeping Car Conductors (OSCC), a white union that excluded blacks but nonetheless planned to accept African Americans into "auxiliary" locals. Eventually, though, the AFL did embrace the BSCP, because the brotherhood, which was led by socialists, took a strong stance against communist labor organizations (such as the American Negro Labor Congress) and seemed to the conservative AFL to be a bulwark against radical communists.

The ten-year struggle for recognition of the BSCP ended in 1935, when the Pullman company began negotiations. In addition to the BSCP's own efforts and the solidarity of its members and leaders, other events helped coerce the company into cooperating. This was the Depression era, and President Franklin Roosevelt's

BSCP at the Elks' Club. (Brown Brothers.)

New Deal legislation had outlawed company unions and yellow-dog contracts, and had guaranteed workers the right to bargain collectively. Thus, in 1935, the National Mediation Board awarded the BSCP sole jurisdiction over Pullman porters; and in 1936, the AFL finally welcomed the BSCP into the federation with an international charter. In 1937, the BSCP concluded its first labor contract with Pullman—the first agreement in American history between a major corporation and a black union.

Later History

By 1940, the BSCP was the most powerful black labor organization in the United States, and A. Philip Randolph was one of the nation's most powerful labor leaders. This enabled the BSCP to expand its activities beyond the workplace concerns of Pullman porters and maids. Beginning in the 1930s, the BSCP became a major force in the civil rights movement. There were several factors in this evolution. For one thing, the union had been so successful that many members were at an economic and social peak in black America, and they used their advantages and power to contribute to their communities. Another factor was Randolph's intelligence, energy, and connections, which helped the BSCP to become a major political force. Thus the BSCP could seek civil rights by mobilizing African Americans nationwide, with solid financial backing and increasing political influence.

As World War II began in China in 1937 and in Europe in 1939, white Americans rushed to fill lucrative new jobs in war industries, but African Americans remained relegated to the lowest-paying occupations. The BSCP intervened, and in 1941 Randolph organized the March on Washington (D.C.) movement. The African American community supported him, and the scope of the planned march grew, although President Roosevelt and other leaders, who worried that such obvious internal racial divisions would weaken the United States, tried to prevent it. Roosevelt and Randolph negotiated a settlement that included Roosevelt's signing of Executive Order 8802 in June 1941—an order banning discrimination in government employment or in any private business that had contracts with the federal government. Also, Roosevelt established the Fair Employment Practices Committee (FEPC), to ensure equal access to jobs. In exchange, Randolph canceled the march. He was criticized for this by many radical blacks, who argued that black

Americans had never before organized a mass protest so successfully and that the march should proceed as planned. Randolph, for his part, argued that the government had made unprecedented concessions and that there might be a backlash among whites if blacks were seen as unpatriotic.

In 1947, Randolph again clashed with a president over civil rights. The beginning of the cold war and the expansion of the peacetime armed forces drew attention to segregation in the military. Randolph called on African Americans to refuse military service and refuse to register for the draft; he also founded the Committee against Jim Crow in Military Service and Training, which became the League for Non-Violent Civil Disobedience against Military Segregation; and he continued to lobby President Harry Truman and the Senate Armed Services Committee. On 26 July 1948, Truman signed Executive Order 9981, barring discrimination in the armed forces; in addition, he signed Executive Order 9980, establishing a new FEPC, which significantly improved on Roosevelt's earlier commission. (However, Jim Crow did not end in the military until 1953, during the Korean War, when a manpower shortage led many reluctant commanders to integrate their units.)

The BSCP continued to make its mark during the 1950s. When Rosa Parks was arrested in Montgomery, Alabama, on 1 December 1955, it was a member of the BSCP—E. (Edgar) D. Nixon—who organized a boycott of the city's public transportation. The bus boycott, which lasted for more than a year, first brought the young minister Martin Luther King Jr. into the national spotlight; this boycott also illustrates the significance of the BSCP in the civil rights movement. E. D. Nixon strongly believed that, although the civil rights movement could ensure that African Americans would have the legal right to ride on buses and Pullman cars, the labor movement was needed to ensure that they would have the money to pay the fare.

Still, the BSCP continued to encounter resistance from some longtime opponents. In 1955, the AFL and the Congress of Industrial Organizations (CIO) merged to form the AFL-CIO. Of its 15 million members, 1.5 million were black, and of twenty-nine vice presidents, Randolph was one of only two who were black. The BSCP objected to the constitution of the new AFL-CIO because, although it imposed punishments on member unions engaging in corrupt or communist activities, it provided no sanctions against unions violating workers' civil rights. During the AFL-CIO convention of 1959, Randolph and AFL-CIO president

George Meany engaged in an angry debate over the place of civil rights and desegregation in the labor movement. Meany wanted to let black local unions remain segregated and to give white unions more time to change their individual constitutions, whereas Randolph wanted all unions, black and white, ordered to desegregate within the year. (Meany made newspaper headlines when he shouted at Randolph, "Who the hell appointed you as the guardian of all the Negroes in America?")

The BSCP's efforts toward social advancement through economic security were threatened by economic downturns in the late 1950s, and during this time white unions were reluctant to admit black members. Randolph now called for a "March on Washington for Jobs and Freedom" that would highlight the interdependence of civil rights and economic self-sufficiency. The BSCP and other unions, notably the United Auto Workers (UAW), provided organizational and financial support, although Meany and the AFL-CIO refused to endorse the demonstration. The resulting march owed much to numerous groups and individuals, black and white, but the BSCP and A. Philip Randolph were the central force. More than 250,000 people took part in the demonstration, on 28 August 1963; this was the event at which Martin Luther King Jr. gave his famous "I Have a Dream" speech. In response to objections from President John Kennedy's administration, Randolph, King, and other leaders met with Kennedy to air their grievances; the march helped to ensure passage of the landmark Civil Rights Act of 1964.

The march of 1963 was one of the BSCP's last great victories. As fast, economical air travel and a new national highway system developed after World War II, the luxury train business declined steadily. The membership of the BSCP also dropped steadily; furthermore, its remaining members grew older, and their political influence and their ability to finance civil rights reform eroded. A. Philip Randolph retired from the BSCP in 1968, after forty-three years of service. In 1978, the BSCP merged with a larger union, the Brotherhood of Railway and Airline Clerks, and ceased to exist as an independent organization. Randolph died in 1979 at age ninety; his funeral was attended by numerous labor leaders, social activists, celebrities, and politicians, and by President Jimmy Carter.

JOHN CASHMAN

See also American Negro Labor Congress; Jim Crow; Labor; Messenger, The; Randolph, A. Philip

Further Reading

Bracey, John H., August Meier, and Elliott M. Rudwick. *Black Workers and Organized Labor.* Belmont, Calif.: Wadsworth, 1971.

Brazeal, Brailsford Recse. *The Brotherhood of Sleeping Car Porters.* New York: Harper, 1946.

Chateauvert, Melinda. *Marching Together: Women of the Brotherhood of Sleeping Car Porters.* Urbana: University of Illinois Press, 1997.

Davis, Daniel S. *Mr. Black Labor: The Story of A. Philip Randolph, Father of the Civil Rights Movement.* New York: Dutton, 1972.

Grizzle, Stanley G., and John Cooper. *My Name's Not George: The Story of the Brotherhood of Sleeping Car Porters—Personal Reminiscences of Stanley G. Grizzle.* Toronto: Umbrella, 1997.

Hanley, Sally. *A. Philip Randolph.* New York: Chelsea House, 1989.

Harris, William Hamilton. *Keeping the Faith: A. Philip Randolph, Milton P. Webster, and the Brotherhood of Sleeping Car Porters, 1925–1937.* Urbana: University of Illinois Press, 1977.

Pfeffer, Paula F. *A. Philip Randolph: Pioneer of the Civil Rights Movement.* Baton Rouge: Louisiana State University Press, 1990.

Reef, Catherine. *A. Philip Randolph: Union Leader and Civil Rights Crusader.* Berkeley Heights, N.J.: Enslow, 2001.

Santino, Jack. *Miles of Smiles, Years of Struggle: Stories of Black Pullman Porters.* Urbana: University of Illinois Press, 1989.

Wilson, Joseph F. *Tearing Down the Color Bar: A Documentary History and Analysis of the Brotherhood of Sleeping Car Porters.* New York: Columbia University Press, 1989.

Wright, Sarah E. *A. Philip Randolph: Integration in the Workplace.* Englewood Cliffs, N.J.: Silver Burdett, 1990.

Brown, Ada

Ada Brown, with her full, rich, mellow voice, earned a reputation as a talented vocalist during the Harlem Renaissance era, and she toured extensively on the vaudeville circuit throughout her career. She was born to a musical family in Kansas City, Kansas; her cousin James Scott was a noted ragtime composer and performer. Brown was said to have sung in clubs in Paris and Berlin as a teenager, and by 1910 she was singing at the Pekin Theater in Chicago. She had an active career singing the blues during the 1920s and 1930s, playing theater dates steadily on both coasts, recording in Chicago and St. Louis, and performing internationally as well. She toured with Flournoy Miller and Aubrey Lyles's *Step on It* in 1922, and with *Struttin' Time* in 1924. In September 1923, she recorded one of her most popular songs, "Evil Mama Blues," for the Okeh label. She performed at the Lafayette Theater in *Plantation Days* in 1927, *Bandana Land* in 1928, and *Tan Town Tamales* in 1930. After *Jangleland* in 1931 and *Going to Town* in 1932, she appeared at the Apollo Theater in *Hawaiian Moon* and *Jungle Drums* in 1934. Brown was also one of the incorporators of the Negro Actors Guild of America in 1936. In the late 1930s, she sang with the Fletcher Henderson Orchestra in Chicago and at the London Palladium. In 1938, Brown appeared in the culturally diverse production *International Rhythms* with the Cecil Mack Choir, the Chinese dancer Princess Chiyo, and Mogiloff's Balalaika Orchestra.

Brown appeared with Thomas "Fats" Waller in the film *Stormy Weather* (Twentieth Century Fox, 1943), singing "That Ain't Right," along with such acclaimed performers as the legendary Lena Horne and Bill Robinson (both of whom played leading roles in this film), Cab Calloway and his band, Emett "Babe" Wallace, Katherine Dunham and Dunham's dancers, Mae Johnson, and Flournoy Miller, among others. *Stormy Weather* was based on the story of Bill Robinson and his rise to the top of the show world. The film attracted significant attention from reviewers and audiences because, although its plot structure and content were simple, it was generously endowed with musical numbers.

In 1945, Brown returned to her hometown, Kansas City, where she died in 1950.

Biography

Ada Brown was born 1 May 1890 in Kansas City, Kansas. She toured with Flournoy Miller and Aubrey Lyles's *Step on It* (1922) and *Struttin' Time* (1924). Brown also performed in *Plantation Days* (1927), *Bandana Land* (1928), *Tan Town Tamales* (1930), *Jangleland* (1931), *Going to Town* (1932), *Hawaiian Moon* (1934), *Jungle Drums* (1934), and *Stormy Weather* (1943). She was a cofounder of the Negro Actors Guild of America (1936). Brown died in Kansas City, Kansas, 31 March 1950.

CARMEN PHELPS

See also Apollo Theater; Blues; Calloway, Cabell "Cab"; Henderson, Fletcher; Lafayette Theater; Lyles, Aubrey; Mack, Cecil; Miller, Flournoy; Robinson, Bill "Bojangles"; Singers

Selected Works

"Evil Woman Blues." 1932.
"That Ain't Right." 1943.

Further Reading

The African-American Theatre Directory, 1816–1960. Westport, Conn.: Greenwood, 1997.

Harris, Sheldon. *Blues Who's Who*. New Rochelle, N.Y.: Arlington House, 1979.

Johnson, James Weldon. *Black Manhattan*. New York: Da Capo, 1930.

Kellner, Bruce, ed. *The Harlem Renaissance: A Historical Dictionary for the Era*. Westport, Conn.: Greenwood, 1984.

Mapp, Edward. *Directory of Blacks in the Performing Arts*. Metuchen, N.J.: Scarecrow, 1978.

Peterson, Bernard. *Profiles of African American Stage Performers and Theatre People, 1816–1960*. Westport, Conn.: Greenwood, 2001.

Sampson, Henry T. *Blacks in Black and White: A Source Book on Black Films*. Lanham, Md.: Scarecrow, 1995.

Spradling, Mary Mace, ed. *In Black and White: A Guide to Magazine Articles, Newspaper Articles, and Books Concerning More Than 15,000 Black Individuals and Groups*, 3rd ed., 2 vols. and supplement. Detroit, Mich.: Gale Research, 1980, 1985.

Brown, Hallie Quinn

Educator, author, temperance advocate, and renowned public lecturer Hallie Quinn Brown was born in Pittsburgh in 1850, the child of former slaves. She attended school in Pittsburgh and later in the African American expatriate community of Chatham, Ontario, where her family moved in the early 1860s. The family returned to the United States after the Civil War, and Brown received her bachelor of science degree from Wilberforce University in 1873, becoming one of the nation's first black female college graduates.

After graduation, Brown joined the caravan of teachers going South to minister to the freedpeople. She taught first at a plantation school in Mississippi, and later in public schools in Dayton, Ohio; and Columbia, South Carolina. She served as dean of Allen University, a college of the African Methodist Episcopalian Church in Columbia; and in 1892, she accepted a position as woman principal of Booker T. Washington's Tuskegee Institute. A year later, she returned to Wilberforce, her alma mater, as a professor of elocution.

Brown epitomized the late nineteenth-century ideology of "racial uplift." She was a prime mover in the formation of the National Association of Colored Women (NACW), an organization whose interwoven class, racial, and gender politics were neatly knotted in its memorable motto, "Lifting as we climb." She led the campaign against African American women's initial exclusion from the Columbian Exposition in Chicago in 1893, and spoke at the World's Congress of Representative Women that later convened at the fair. In her speech, Brown focused on black women's education, stressing the unparalleled progress of southern freedwomen and the need for a balanced training of head, hands, and heart. Invoking the domestic assumptions of her era and social class, she reminded her audience that mothers shaped the character of their sons, and that no race could progress beyond the attainments of its women.

The high-water mark of Brown's career came in the 1890s, but she remained active in the 1920s, when she was over seventy. She served as president of the NACW from 1920 to 1924, after which she was appointed lifetime honorary president. In 1924, she spoke at the Republican National Convention, pointedly reminding the delegates of their party's historical commitment to civil rights. In 1925, she organized a black boycott of the International Council of Women's All-American Musical Festival, in protest against Jim Crow seating in the theater.

Brown made her most important contribution to the decade of the 1920s as an author, publishing five books—collections of biographies and stories intended to edify and enlighten black readers. With their emphasis on respectability, domesticity, and proper elocution, the books were distinctly out of step with the aesthetic and political temper of the Harlem Renaissance, but they rang with their author's conviction and commitment to racial service. The most widely read was *Homespun Heroines and Other Women of Distinction*, a collection of sixty short, inspirational biographies of African American women, from the poet Phillis Wheatley to the cosmetics mogul Madam C. J. Walker. In a passage as applicable to herself as to her subjects, Brown declared: "Regarded in the light of heroism, many Americans, bound and free, have passed on unhonored and unsung who yet were worthy of the olive crown and the victor's palm for their constancy, their courage and their firm belief in the ultimate triumph of justice."

Hallie Q. Brown died in Wilberforce, Ohio, in 1949.

Biography

Hallie Quinn Brown was born in 1850 in Pittsburgh, Pennsylvania. She attended public schools in Pittsburgh and Chatham, Ontario; and Wilberforce University in Wilberforce, Ohio, (B.S., 1873). Brown taught in black schools in Mississippi, Ohio, and South Carolina; was a dean of Allen University in Columbia, South Carolina (1885–1892); was woman principal at Tuskegee Institute in Alabama (1892–1893); and was a professor of elocution at Wilberforce University (1893–1903). She was also a founder of the National Association of Colored Women (1893) and its president (1920–1924), and the president of the Ohio Federation of Colored Women's Clubs (1905–1912). Brown was a delegate to the World's Congress of Representative Women, Chicago (1893); the World's Women's Christian Temperance Union, London (1895); International Congress of Women, London (1899); and the World Missionary Conference, Edinburgh, Scotland (1910). She died in 1949 in Wilberforce, Ohio.

JAMES CAMPBELL

See also Higher Education; Walker, Madame C. J.

Selected Works

Bits and Odds: A Choice Selection of Recitations. 1880.
Elocution and Physical Culture. 1910.
First Lessons in Public Speaking. 1920.
The Beautiful: A True Story of Slavery. 1924.
Our Women, Past, Present, and Future. 1925.
Tales My Father Told. 1925.
Homespun Heroines and Other Women of Distinction. 1926.
Pen Pictures of Pioneers of Wilberforce. 1937.

Further Reading

Cooper, Anna Julia. *A Voice From the South.* New York: Oxford University Press, 1988.

Fisher, Vivian Njeri. "Hallie Quinn Brown." In *African American Women*, ed. Dorothy C. Salem. New York: Garland, 1993.

Johnson, George T. "Hallie Quinn Brown." In *Dictionary of American Negro Biography*, ed. Rayford W. Logan and Michael R. Winston. New York: Norton, 1982.

Shaw, Stephanie J. "Black Club Women and the Creation of the National Association of Colored Women." *Journal of Women's History*, 3, Fall 1991, pp. 10–25.

White, Deborah Gray. *Too Heavy a Load: Black Women in Defense of Themselves, 1894–1994*. New York: Norton, 1999.

Brown, Sterling

The literary scholar, university professor, poet, and folklorist Sterling Allen Brown was a major figure in twentieth-century African American letters. His scholarly essays, anthologies, and reviews were crucial to the development of African American literature as an academic discipline. Brown was also a highly esteemed teacher and curator of African American life and culture; one former student described him as a "repository of information and inspiration" (Baraka 1976). Furthermore, Brown's poems, evoking black folk expression, have become part of the canon and appear in numerous anthologies; and his experience as folklorist helped to shape his literary and academic career. As an editor of Negro Affairs for the Federal Writers'

Sterling Brown, second from left, in the 1940s. The others are the author Chester Himes (second from right), his wife, and Backlin Moore. (Schomburg Center for Research in Black Culture, New York Public Library.)

Project of the Works Progress Administration, as a Rosenwald Fellow, and as a staff member of the Carnegie-Myrdal Study, Brown was able to document various aspects of African American folk life as part of systematic studies of American culture.

Sterling A. Brown was born in 1901. His father, Sterling Nelson Brown, a professor of theology at Howard University and pastor of Lincoln Temple Congregational Church, was prominent in black society in Washington, D.C.; much of the younger Brown's early education was influenced by his father's associations. The son was virtually reared on the campus of Howard University, which had a faculty of African American intellectuals, and his father's acquaintances included African American leaders such as Frederick Douglass. Joanne Gabbin (1985/1994) notes that the father's church was the site of several debates between Booker T. Washington and W. E. B. Du Bois and that it sponsored a major conference, "How to Solve the Race Problem," in 1903. Brown's mother, Adelaide Allen Brown, a graduate of Fisk University, was also an important influence, encouraging his literary interests.

Brown graduated in 1918 (as valedictorian) from Dunbar High School, then widely regarded as the premier secondary school for blacks in the United States. At Williams College—where he was on the debating team and the Common Club tennis team, was a member of Omega Psi Phi fraternity, and was inducted into Phi Beta Kappa—he was introduced to contemporary trends in literature such as realism and modernism, and began studying contemporary American literature, especially poetry. By the time he left Williams in 1922, he had begun to write poetry. In 1923, he earned his master's degree at Harvard University; later, he returned to Harvard for further graduate study toward a doctorate.

Brown taught English at Virginia Seminary in Lynchburg from 1923 to 1926; at Lincoln University in Missouri from 1926 to 1928; at Fisk University in Nashville in 1929; and ultimately for forty years, 1929 to 1969, at Howard University. Brown was a legendary figure at Howard during his tenure there—at one point in the 1960s, students supported an effort to rename the school after him—and many of his students became writers and literary scholars and consider him a major influence, not just as a teacher but also, in the words of one of them, as a "poet and anthologist and writer [who] gave us a great deal of inspiration" (Baraka 1976). Brown was offered posts at other institutions, such as Vassar College, but although he lectured and taught during summer sessions at Vassar and elsewhere, he remained at his beloved

Howard. He also maintained his teaching post at Howard while serving as an editor on the Federal Writers' Project and as a staff member of the Carnegie-Myrdal research project, and while writing creatively as a Guggenheim fellow. Indeed, the combination of all these duties and experiences probably enabled Brown to mine the richness of African American life and culture and infuse his poetry with it.

Undoubtedly, Brown's experience of African American folk culture—his extended stay in the rural South as a young professor, his work preserving folklore as part of the Federal Writers' Project, and his study of southern Negro life as a Rosenwald fellow—informed his creative and critical output. In particular, African Americans of the rural South would dominate his poetry as folk characters. Brown realized that this segment of American society was underrepresented or stereotyped in most American art and literature. Through his own experiences among "the folk," he developed a high regard for the vernacular tradition. He believed that folk forms such as blues, spirituals, and boasts were authentic and laudable forms of artistic expression, and he would immortalize them in his poetry. His "Southern Road," for example, uses the oral tradition of the work song:

Swing dat hammer—hunh—

Steady, bo';

Swing dat hammer—hunh—

Steady, bo';

Ain't no rush, bebby,

Long ways to go. . . .

This verse also illustrates a common feature in Brown's poetry: dialect. James Weldon Johnson, in his preface to God's Trombones, had said that dialect was "absolutely dead"; but Brown revived the tradition, filling his own dialect poems with dignified and heroic figures and forcing Johnson to reevaluate the function of dialect in African American poetry. Later, Johnson acknowledged that although dialect grounded in the minstrel and plantation traditions could evoke only pathos or humor, authentic dialect treated with fidelity—as it was treated in Brown's ballads and folk epics—could be used to great effect.

Brown himself insisted on authentic documentation of folk life in folklore studies such as the Federal Writers' Project. He and the officials of the Federal Writers' Project developed detailed guidelines for interviewing

and recording, so as to avoid intrusion and distortion by the writers and interviewers. Brown was especially concerned about presenting black dialect accurately in narratives of slavery; he recommended that "the stories be told in the language of the ex-slave, without excessive editorializing and 'artistic' introduction on the part of the interviewer" (Gabbin 1985/1994, 72–73). As a scholar, Brown also objected to inauthentic representations of black life in art and literature. His essays "A Century of Negro Portraiture" and "The American Race Problem as Reflected in American Literature" as well as his book-length text The Negro in American Fiction contrast stereotyped representations of African Americans by white authors with more accurate portrayals by blacks. Brown's insistence on realistic depictions of African American life was a profound contribution not only to the African American literary tradition, but to documenting black life in American history and consequently to creating a greater understanding of the African American experience.

Biography

Sterling Allen Brown was born 1 May 1901 in Washington, D.C. He attended public schools in the District of Columbia, including Dunbar High School; Williams College in Williamstown, Massachusetts (A.B., 1922); and Harvard University (A.M., 1923). He was elected to Phi Beta Kappa in 1921 and did additional graduate study at Harvard in 1931–1932. Brown taught at Virginia Seminary in Lynchburg, Virginia (1923–1926); Lincoln University in Jefferson City, Missouri (1926–1928); Fisk University (1928–1929); and Howard University (1929–1969). He was also a visiting professor at Vassar College (1942–1944), the University of Minnesota (1945), New York University (1949 and 1950), and the University of Illinois (Chicago Circle Campus, 1967 and 1968). Brown was an editor of Negro Affairs, Federal Writers' Project (1936–1940); a Guggenheim Fellow (1937–1938); a Julius Rosenwald Fellow (1942); and a staff member of the Carnegie-Myrdal research project. His awards included honorary doctorates from Boston, Brown, Harvard, Howard, Lincoln, Northwestern, and Yale universities; Lewis and Clark and Williams colleges; and the universities of Maryland (Baltimore County), Massachusetts, and Pennsylvania. He was poet laureate of the District of Columbia (1984). Brown died in Takoma Park, Maryland, 13 January 1989.

NATASHA COLE-LEONARD

See also Authors: 5—Poets; Federal Writers' Project; Guggenheim Fellowships; Johnson, James Weldon; Literature: 7—Poetry; Rosenwald Fellowships; Works Progress Administration

Selected Works

"When De Saints Go Ma'ching Home." *Opportunity*, July 1927.

"Negro Literature: Is It True? Complete?" *Durham Fact-Finding Conference*, 1929.

"The Blues as Folk Poetry." In *Folk-Say: A Regional Miscellany*, ed. B. A. Botkin. 1930.

"Our Literary Audience." *Opportunity*, February 1930.

"James Weldon Johnson." In *The Book of American Negro Poetry*, ed. James Weldon Johnson. 1931.

"Lonesome Valley." In *Folk-Say: A Regional Miscellany*, ed. B. A. Botkin, 1931.

Outline for the Study of the Poetry of American Negroes. 1931.

"A Literary Parallel." *Opportunity*, May 1932.

"In Memoriam: Charles W. Chesnutt." *Opportunity*, December 1932.

Southern Road: Poems by Sterling A. Brown. 1932.

"Negro Character as Seen by White Authors." *Journal of Negro Education*, April 1933.

The Negro in American Fiction. 1937.

The Negro in Washington. 1937.

Negro Poetry and Drama. 1937.

"Problems of the Negro Writer." *Official Proceedings, National Negro Congress*, 1937.

"The Negro in American Literature." In *James Weldon Johnson, a Biographical Sketch*. 1938.

"The American Race Problem as Reflected in American Literature." *Journal of Negro Education*, July 1939.

The Negro Caravan. 1941. (As coeditor.)

"The Negro Writer and His Publisher." *Quarterly Review of Higher Education Among Negroes*, July 1941.

"Out of Their Mouths." *Survey Graphic*, November 1942.

"Words on a Bus." *South Today*, Spring 1943.

"Farewell to Basin Street." *Record Changer*, December 1944.

"Georgia Sketches." *Phylon,* Summer 1945.

"Georgia Nymphs." *Phylon*, Autumn 1945.

"The Muted South." *Phylon*, Winter 1945.

"And/Or." *Phylon*, Fall 1946.

"The Approach of the Creative Artist." *Journal of American Folklore*, October–December 1946.

"Negro in American Theatre." In *Oxford Companion to the Theatre*, ed. Phyllis Hartnoll. 1950.

"In the American Grain." *Vassar Alumnae Magazine*, February 1951.

"The Blues." *Phylon*, Autumn 1952.

"Seventy-Five Years of the Negro in Literature." *Jackson College Bulletin*, September 1953.

"Negro Folk Expression: Spirituals, Seculars, Ballads, and Work Songs." *Phylon*, Winter 1953.

"The New Negro in Literature, 1925–1955." In *The New Negro Thirty Years Afterwards*, ed. Rayford Logan et al., 1955.

The Reader's Companion to World Literature. 1956. (As coeditor.)

"A Century of Negro Portraiture in American Literature." *Massachusetts Review*, Winter 1966.

"Arna Bontemps, Co-Worker, Comrade." *Black World*, September 1973.

"The Last Ride of Wild Bill" and Eleven Narrative Poems. 1975.

The Collected Poems of Sterling A. Brown, ed. Michael S. Harper. 1996.

A Son's Return: Selected Essays of Sterling A. Brown, ed. Mark A. Sanders. 1996.

Further Reading

African American Review (Fall 1997). (Various essays.)

Baraka, Amiri. "Sterling Brown: A Repository of Information and Inspiration." In *Sterling A. Brown: A UMUM Tribute*, ed. Black History Museum Committee. Philadelphia, Pa.: Black History Museum UMUM Publishers, 1976. (See also expanded edition, 1982.)

Bentson, Kimberly. "Sterling Brown's After Song: 'When de Saints Go Ma'ching Home' and the Performances of Afro-American Voice." *Callaloo*, February–May 1982.

Fuller, Hoyt W. "The Raconteur." *Black World*, April 1967.

Gabbin, Joanne V. *Sterling A. Brown: Building the Black Aesthetic Tradition*. Westport, Conn.: Greenwood, 1985. (Reprint, Charlottesville: University Press of Virginia, 1994.)

———."Sterling Brown's Poetic Voice: A Living Legacy." *African American Review*, Fall 1997.

Harper, Michael. "Sterling Brown, 1901–2001." *Parnassus*, 1980.

Henderson, Stephen. "A Strong Man Called Sterling Brown." *Black World*, 1970.

———. "The Heavy Blues of Sterling Brown: A Study of Craft and Tradition." *Black American Literature Forum*, 1980.

Palmer, Ronald D. "Memories of Sterling Brown." *African American Review*, Fall 1997.

Rowell, Charles H. "'Let Me Be With Ole Jazzbo': An Interview With Sterling A. Brown." *Callaloo*, Fall 1991.

Sanders, Mark A. *Afro-Modernist Aesthetics and the Poetry of Sterling A. Brown*. Athens: University of Georgia Press, 1999.

Tidwell, John Edgar, and John S. Wright. "Sterling A. Brown, Afro-American Poet: A Special Section." *Callaloo*, February–May 1982.

Tidwell, John Edgar, and John S. Wright. "Sterling A. Brown Tribute." *Black American Literature Forum*, Spring 1989.

Brownies' Book, The

The Brownies' Book, the nation's first magazine for African American children and young adults, was created by three people from the publication *The Crisis*: W. E. B. Du Bois, editor; Jessie Redmon Fauset, literary editor; and Augustus G. Dill, business manager. The debut issue of *The Brownies' Book* appeared in January 1920, with this description: "A monthly magazine for the children of the sun, designed for all children but especially for ours." This first issue also included a dedicatory poem by Fauset, expressing the importance of providing black children with a history and literature of their own.

While other children's magazines and schoolbooks perpetuated grotesque stereotypes of the "dark continent," *The Brownies' Book* highlighted the honor, integrity, and beauty of African and African American life. The first issue, for instance, included a photograph of African American children in the South protesting violence against blacks. In the June 1920 issue, the article "A Little Talk About West Africa" was accompanied by a full-page photograph of West African children posing in front of their school. Summer issues published the names, pictures, accomplishments, and plans of graduates of African American boys' and girls' high schools.

For fifteen cents a copy or $1.50 per year (twelve issues), readers of *The Brownies' Book* were offered an array of materials, including African, West Indian, Native American, and European legends, fables, and tales, as well as photographs, riddles, puzzles, and songs from around the globe. Each issue contained biographical profiles of historical figures, such as Sojourner Truth, Harriet Tubman, Toussaint-Louverture, Crispus Attucks, and Phillis Wheatley. Regular columns included "Little People of the Month," featuring news about individual children, particularly their academic and artistic achievements. In "The Judge," conversations between an adult and children offered lessons of love, kindness, and friendship. "As the Crow Flies" provided international news updates. "The Jury" comprised letters from young readers, while "The Grown-Ups' Corner" provided a forum for their parents' concerns, such as the lack of positive role models for African American youth and the imposition of white values on them. *The Brownies' Book* became renowned for its race consciousness, high educational standards, and mature presentation to children of complex information. The magazine's few advertisements were mainly suggestions for books and educational programs and activities.

The Brownies' Book featured work by numerous notable and up-and-coming artists and writers. Langston Hughes, who was then a recent high school graduate, published several plays, poems, and short stories in 1921; these brought him to Jessie Fauset's attention and so launched his career. Nella Larsen's first publications, articles on Scandinavian children's games, appeared in June and July 1921 under the byline Nella Larsen Imes. *The Brownies' Book* also published pieces by Georgia Douglas Johnson, James Weldon Johnson, and Arthur Huff Fauset, among others. Jessie Fauset, who was a tireless promoter of women, chose poems and stories by Mary Effie Lee and Mary White Ovington, and illustrations by Laura Wheeler, Hilda Wilkinson, and Louise Latimer. Almost all the artwork in *The Brownies' Book* was by African Americans, as were the many contributions by children of all ages. Along with selecting and editing the content of each issue, Jessie Fauset herself contributed dozens of articles, poems, and stories.

The Brownies' Book ran for two years, publishing twenty-four issues. The last issue, in December 1921, ran a full-page message to readers explaining regretfully that because it had too few subscribers, the magazine could no longer sustain itself. *The Brownies' Book* continues to stand virtually alone as a venue devoted to promoting self-respect, hope, and pride in African American children.

KRISTIN KOMMERS CZARNECKI

See also Du Bois, W. E. B.; Fauset, Arthur Huff; Fauset, Jessie Redmon; Hughes, Langston; Johnson, Georgia Douglas; Johnson, James Weldon; Larsen, Nella; Ovington, Mary White

Further Reading

Allen, Carol. *Black Women Intellectuals: Strategies of Nation, Family, and Neighborhood in the Works of Pauline Hopkins,*

Jessie Fauset, and Marita Bonner. New York and London: Garland, 1998.

Johnson-Feelings, Dianne, ed. *The Best of The Brownies' Book.* New York: Oxford University Press, 1996.

Lewis, David Levering. *When Harlem Was in Vogue.* New York and Oxford: Oxford University Press, 1981.

Sinnette, Elinor. "The Brownies' Book: A Pioneer Publication for Children." *Freedomways*, 1965, pp. 133–138.

Sylvander, Carolyn Wedin. *Jessie Redmon Fauset, Black American Writer.* New York: Whitston, 1981.

Wall, Cheryl. *Women of the Harlem Renaissance.* Bloomington and Indianapolis: Indiana University Press, 1995.

Bruce, John Edward

John Edward Bruce was a journalist, historian, writer, orator, and pan-African nationalist. He was born in 1856 in Piscataway, Maryland, to enslaved parents: Robert Bruce and Martha Allen Clark. When Bruce was three years old, his father was sold, never to be heard from again. Bruce and his mother joined a regiment of Union soldiers passing through Maryland in 1860, and so escaped to freedom in Washington, D.C. In 1864, they moved to New York state; later they moved to Stratford, Connecticut, where they remained for two years and where, at an integrated school, Bruce received his first formal education. Although he was largely self-educated, Bruce did receive private instruction in Washington, D.C., and enrolled in a three-month course at Howard University.

After leaving Connecticut, Bruce, then eighteen years old, found a job as a helper in the office of the Washington correspondent for the *New York Times* in 1874. Around the same time he became the special correspondent for the *Progressive American.* Thus began a fifty-year career in journalism, during which Bruce would write for more than forty newspapers and other periodicals in the United States and around the world. Between 1877 and 1880 he wrote for or sent letters to the *Richmond Star* of Virginia; the *Freeman's Journal* of St. Louis, Missouri; the *World* of Indianapolis; and the *St. Louis Tribune.* He then became a Washington correspondent for the *Chicago Conservator; North Carolina Republican; Enterprise* of Fayetteville, North Carolina; *New York Freeman; Reed City Clarion; Detroit Plaindealer; Christian Index;* and *Cherokee Advocate.* Many of his articles also appeared in European-American

publications such as the *Boston Transcript* and the *New York Times.*

Bruce also founded and edited several newspapers. In 1879, at age twenty-three, he founded the *Argus* of Washington, D.C., which he managed for two years. In 1880, he established the *Sunday Item*, the first Sunday newspaper ever founded and run by an African American. In 1882, he became editor of the *Republican* of Norfolk, Virginia; in 1884, he was the assistant editor and business manager of the *Commonwealth* of Baltimore; from 1896 to 1901 he was the associate editor of *Howard's American Magazine* of Harrisburg, Pennsylvania; and in 1903, he was editor of a monthly, *The Impending Conflict* of New York City. In 1884, he founded the *Washington Grit* as a campaign sheet, dedicated to Republican Party politics and African advancement. In that year he also began writing regular columns under the pen name "Bruce Grit" in the *Gazette* of Cleveland and in *New York Age*, the journal of the fiery civil rights activist T. Thomas Fortune. Grit—implying courage and resoluteness—was the name Bruce would be known by throughout his long career. In 1887, he became a special correspondent for *New York Age*. Three years later he joined Fortune's Afro-American League; in 1898, he joined its successor, the Afro-American Council. Both groups advocated African solidarity and aggressiveness in combating abuses of human rights.

Bruce was independent-minded, despite his close collaboration with Fortune, who was a fierce opponent of Booker T. Washington (Bruce would attend the conference that founded the anti-Washington Niagara movement in 1905). In 1897, Bruce cofounded the *Chronicle* in New York City with Charles Anderson, Washington's lieutenant in the city's Republican Party. In 1908, Bruce cofounded, again with Anderson, the *Weekly Standard* in Yonkers, New York. Bruce also edited the *Masonic Quarterly* in New York City. His articles and editorials appeared not only in newspapers across the United States, but also in parts of Africa, the Caribbean, and Europe, including Duse Mohamed Ali's *African Times and Orient Review*, which was based in London. Bruce also wrote essays, short stories, plays, poems, and the music and lyrics to songs.

Bruce worked Washington, D.C., until around 1900, when he moved to New York State—first to Albany, then to New York City and Yonkers. He was married twice: first to an opera singer, the contralto Lucy Pinkwood of Washington, D.C., who presumably died before his second marriage, on 10 September 1895, to Florence A. Bishop of Cleveland. He and his second wife had one child, a daughter named Olive.

Bruce was a powerful and popular orator with a strong interest in African history. Many of his speeches and articles focused on the achievements of the African past and the importance of history to counteract white supremacy and its effects on the African psyche. He wrote several pamphlets dealing with African history, as well as two books—*Short Biographical Sketches of Eminent Negro Men and Women in Europe and the United States* (1910) and a fictional work, *The Awakening of Hezekiah Jones* (1916). In 1911, in Yonkers, Bruce and the Afro–Puerto Rican bibliophile Arthur A. Schomburg founded the Negro Society for Historical Research. In 1908, Bruce was made a member of the Africa Society of England. President Arthur Barclay of Liberia also made him a Knight of the Order of African Redemption. In 1913, Bruce founded the Loyal Order of the Sons of Africa, which intended to establish its headquarters in Africa and to achieve global pan-African unity.

Bruce was not only an independent but also a fiercely nationalistic thinker. Throughout his life, he refused to join any organization run or supported by Europeans, and in his work as a journalist and activist he largely ignored them. Much of his work excoriated European-American society, and he directed his attention chiefly to the struggle for human rights of Africans in the United States and later to fostering their political and economic ties with Africa. He stood outside the mainstream thought of elite and middle-class African Americans of his day. His views combined nationalist goals—economic independence, cultural pride and solidarity, and self-directed group initiatives—with an unrelenting agitation for political, civil, and human rights. Among other things, he urged that Africans in the United States use merciless armed retaliation to combat pogroms and lynching by European mobs. He insisted that although Africans were to remain politically a part of the United States, they should resist assimilation into European-American culture and society. After World War I, when pogroms intensified, he preferred the objective of national independence on the African continent, maintaining that European-American oppression would remain inflexible. His belief in an independent national destiny led him, in the period around 1919, to embrace Marcus Garvey's pan-African nationalism. As a member of Garvey's Universal Negro Improvement Association, Bruce wrote columns for the movement's *Negro World* and the *Daily Negro Times*.

Despite his enormous productivity, Bruce found that for most of his adult life, he needed to earn a living by working for the Port Authority of New York. After he retired in 1922, he received a small pension until his death in New York City two years later.

Biography

John Edward Bruce was born in Piscataway, Maryland, 22 February 1856. He escaped with his mother to Washington, D.C., in 1860; they moved to New York state in 1864. Bruce attended school in Stratford, Connecticut. He was a helper in the office of the Washington correspondent for the *New York Times* and special correspondent for the *Progressive American* (1874) and wrote for the *Richmond Star* of Virginia; the *Freeman's Journal* of St. Louis, Missouri; the *World* of Indianapolis; and the *St. Louis Tribune* (1877–1880). He was a Washington correspondent for the *Chicago Conservator*; *North Carolina Republican*; *Enterprise* of Fayetteville, North Carolina; *New York Freeman*; *Reed City Clarion*; *Detroit Plaindealer*; *Christian Index*; and *Cherokee Advocate*. He also wrote articles for the *Boston Transcript*, *Washington Evening Star*, *New York Times*, *St. Louis Globe-Democrat*, *Buffalo Express*, *Albany Journal*, *Times Union*, *Press Knickerbocker*, the Sunday edition of the *Albany Argus*, and *Sunday Republican* of Washington, D.C. Bruce founded the *Argus* of Washington, D.C. (1879); *Sunday Item* (1880); and *Washington Grit* (1884). He was editor of the *Republican* of Norfolk, Virginia (1882); assistant editor and business manager of the *Commonwealth* of Baltimore (1884); associate editor of *Howard's American Magazine* (1896–1901); and editor of the monthly *The Impending Conflict* (1903). Bruce was also a columnist for the *Gazette* of Cleveland and *New York Age* (1884) and a special correspondent for *New York Age* (1887). He joined the Afro-American League in 1890 and the Afro-American Council in 1898, and cofounded the *Chronicle* in New York City (1897) and the *Weekly Standard* in Yonkers (1908). He published *Short Biographical Sketches of Eminent Negro Men and Women in Europe and the United States* (1910) and *The Awakening of Hezekiah Jones* (1916). He cofounded the Negro Society for Historical Research (1911) and founded the Loyal Order of the Sons of Africa (1913). He was made a member of the Africa Society, England (1908), and a Knight of the Order of African Redemption by Liberia's President Barclay. Bruce joined the United Negro Improvement Association around 1919. He was married twice (his second marriage was in 1895). He retired from the Port Authority of New York in 1922 and died in New York City 7 August 1924.

AHATI N. N. TOURE

See also Ali, Duse Mohamed; Anderson, Charles; Black History and Historiography; Black Press; Fortune, Timothy Thomas; Garvey, Marcus; Journalists; Negro World; New York Age; Niagara Movement; Pan-Africanism; Schomburg, Arthur A.; United Negro Improvement Association

Selected Works

The Blot on the Escutcheon. 1890.
Blood Red Record: A Review of the Horrible Burnings and Lynchings by Civilized White Men in the United States. 1901.
A Defense of Colored Soldiers. 1906.
Short Biographical Sketches of Eminent Negro Men and Women in Europe and the United States. 1910.
The Awakening of Hezekiah Jones: A Story Dealing With Some of the Problems Affecting the Political Rewards Due the Negro. 1916.
Tribute for the Negro Soldier. 1918.
Prince Hall: The Pioneer of Negro Masonry. 1921.
The Making of a Race. 1922.

Further Reading

Bullock, Penelope L. *The Afro-American Periodical Press, 1838–1909.* Baton Rouge: Louisiana State University Press, 1981.

Ferris, William H. *The African Abroad or His Evolution in Western Civilization: Tracing His Development Under Caucasian Milieu,* Vol. 2. New Haven, Conn.: Tuttle, Morehouse, and Taylor, 1913. (Reprint, New York: Johnson Reprint, 1968.)

Gatewood, Willard B. *Aristocrats of Color: The Black Elite, 1880–1920.* Bloomington and Indianapolis: Indiana University Press, 1990.

Gilbert, Peter. *The Selected Writings of John Edward Bruce: Militant Black Journalist.* New York: Arno and New York Times, 1971.

Logan, Rayford W., and Michael R. Winston, eds. *Dictionary of American Negro Biography.* New York: Norton, 1982.

Newkirk, Pamela. *Within the Veil: Black Journalists, White Media.* New York: New York University Press, 2000.

Penn, I. Garland. *The Afro-American Press and Its Editors.* Springfield, Mass.: Willey, 1891. (Reprint, New York: Arno and New York Times, 1969.)

Pride, Armistead S., and Clint C. Wilson II. *A History of the Black Press.* Washington, D.C.: Howard University Press, 1997.

Salzman, Jack, David Lionel Smith, and Cornel West, eds. *Encyclopedia of African-American Culture and History,* Vol. 1. New York: Simon & Schuster Macmillan, 1996.

Thorpe, Earl E. *Black Historians: A Critique.* New York: Morrow, 1971.

Wesley, Charles H. "Racial Historical Societies and the American Heritage." *Journal of Negro History,* 37, January 1952.

Wesley, Charles H. "Evaluation of the Black Studies Movement: The Need for Research in the Development of Black Studies Programs." *Journal of Negro Education,* 38, Summer 1970.

Bubbles, John

John William Sublett, better known as John Bubbles, was born in Louisville, Kentucky, in 1902. In 1919, he teamed with Ford Lee "Buck" Washington. While working at various odd jobs in carnivals and at a racetrack, they developed a theatrical act, Buck and Bubbles. It featured Bubbles' superfast rhythmic tap dancing and Buck's piano accompaniment, as well as Buck's artfully lackadaisical parody of Bubbles's dance style, all peppered with laconic dialogue.

Buck and Bubbles moved to New York in 1921 and soon broke into white vaudeville at the Palace Theatre, bypassing the black Theater Owners' Booking Association (TOBA) circuit. They were headliners on the prestigious Keith Circuit and in shows by the white producer Nat Nazarro (*Hot Chops* in 1922 and *Raisin' Cain* in 1923).

Criticism of his dancing style from the tap experts of the legendary Hoofers' Club angered Bubbles. Touring west in vaudeville, he rehearsed endlessly; and on his return he silenced his critics, establishing himself as one of the all-time greats of tap, on a par with Bill "Bojangles" Robinson—in fact, many people considered him technically superior to Bojangles. Bubbles is credited with being the originator of a style known as rhythm-tap or jazz-tap, with innovative use of the heel through the "cramp roll" step, and four-to-the-bar rhythm phrases, rather than the traditional two-to-the-bar. His creative approach to tempo was a forerunner of later developments in bebop.

Throughout the 1920s, Buck and Bubbles were popular on stage and in films. They were featured

Buck and Bubbles, c. 1937. (Photofest.)

performers in Lew Leslie's *Blackbirds of 1930* and the *Ziegfeld Follies of 1931*. In 1935, Bubbles reached the peak of his career when he created the role of Sportin' Life in the original Broadway production of *Porgy and Bess*. His status as a dancer was already assured, and this performance also showed him to be a talented dramatic actor and a singer of considerable appeal. His Sportin' Life is still considered by many to be the definitive portrayal.

In 1936, Buck and Bubbles performed in London, where they starred in a revue, *Transatlantic Rhythm*; made records; and were featured performers in the inaugural broadcast of BBC's television service. They continued to perform in films and onstage throughout the 1930s, although the film roles available to them reflected the usual stereotypical pattern for blacks in Hollywood. A notable exception was Bubbles's memorable stick-and-stair dance in the all-black movie *Cabin in the Sky* (1943).

The duo continued successfully until Buck's death in 1955. Bubbles then dropped out of the limelight for a time, but he later resumed an active career in television, as a guest on celebrity shows with stars like Lucille Ball, Bing Crosby, and Perry Como. In 1964, he formed a nightclub act with the singer Anna Maria Alberghetti and toured in Vietnam, Thailand, the Philippines, Guam, and Korea with Bob Hope's show. In 1967, Bubbles revisited his old vaudeville haunt, the Palace, as a supporting act in a comeback performance by Judy Garland; but shortly thereafter he suffered a stroke that effectively ended his career.

In 1980, Bubbles appeared, in a wheelchair, in an all-black commemorative show, *Black Broadway*; also in 1980, he received a Certificate of Approval from the mayor of New York City and a lifetime achievement award from the American Guild of Variety Artists. Bubbles died in 1986.

Bubbles' singing style can be heard on an available CD recording of *Porgy and Bess* and also in occasional compilations, including a Vee-Jay vinyl LP of 1964, "Bubbles, John W. That Is"; this LP recording has not been issued on CD but can still be found secondhand.

Biography

John William Sublett, also known as John Bubbles, was born in Louisville, Kentucky, on 19 February 1902 and attended grammar and high school there. In 1919, he formed a partnership, Buck and Bubbles, with Ford Lee "Buck" Washington. Bubbles' stage appearances included *Hot Chops* (1922), *Raisin' Cain* (1923), *Weather Clear* (1927), *Track Fast* (1927), *Blackbirds of 1930*, *Ziegfeld Follies of 1931*, *Harlem on Parade* (1935), *Porgy and Bess* (1935), *Transatlantic Rhythm* (London, 1936), *Virginia* (1937), *Frolics of 1938*, *Laugh Time* (1943), *Carmen Jones* (1944), *At Home at the Palace* (with Judy Garland, 1967), and *Black Broadway* (1980). In 1964, he toured in Asia with Bob Hope. He also had many nightclub engagements. Bubbles's films included *Foul Play*, *In and Out*, *Honest Crooks*, *High Toned*, and *Dark Town Follies* (all shorts made in 1929–1930); *Calling All Stars* (Britain, 1937); *Varsity Show* (1937); *Cabin in the Sky* (1943); *I Dood It* (1943); *Atlantic City* (1944); *Buck and Bubbles Laugh Jamboree* (1945); *Mantan Messes Up* (1946); *A Song Is Born* (1948); and *No Maps on My Taps* (1978). He appeared in the inaugural BBC television broadcast in 1936 and made many guest appearances on television. In 1980, he received the American Guild of Variety Artists Lifetime Achievement award and a Certificate of Approval from Mayor Edward Koch of New York City. Bubbles died 18 May 1986 in Baldwin, California.

BILL EGAN

See also Blackbirds; Blacks in Theater; Dance; Europe and the Harlem Renaissance: 3—London; Film; Film: Actors; Gershwin, George; Heyward, DuBose; Jazz; Musical Theater; Porgy and Bess; Robinson, Bill "Bojangles"; Vaudeville

Further Reading

Fisher, James. "Bubbles, John." In *American National Biography*, Vol. 3, ed. John A. Garraty and Mark C. Carnes. New York: Oxford University Press, 1999.

Frank, Rusty. *Tap! The Greatest Tap Dance Stars and Their Stories.* New York: Da Capo, 1990.

Goddard, Chris. *Jazz Away From Home.* New York: Paddington, 1979. (For a discussion of John Bubbles's tempo innovations, see pp. 90–103.)

Kellner, Bruce, ed. *The Harlem Renaissance: A Historical Dictionary for the Era.* New York: Methuen, 1984. (See "Bubbles, John," p. 60.)

Peterson, Bernard L., Jr. *Profiles of African American Stage Performers and Theatre People, 1816–1960.* Westport, Conn., and London: Greenwood, 2001. (See "Buck and Bubbles," p. 38.)

Sampson, Henry T. *Blacks in Black and White: A Sourcebook on Black Films.* Metuchen, N.J., and London: Scarecrow, 1977. (See especially "Buck and Bubbles," p. 229.)

Slide, Anthony. *The Encyclopaedia of Vaudeville.* Westport, Conn., and London: Greenwood, 1994. (See "Buck and Bubbles," p. 71.)

Stearns, Marshall, and Jean Stearns. *Jazz Dance: The Story of American Vernacular Dance.* London: Macmillan, 1968. (See especially ch. 22.)

Burleigh, Harry Thacker

Harry (Henry) Thacker Burleigh was the earliest African American to compose American art songs and to arrange African American choral spirituals and the so-called concert solo spiritual for solo voice with piano accompaniment. His art songs amount to some 265 vocal compositions, including three song cycles. He arranged about 187 choral spirituals, scoring them for unaccompanied mixed chorus; some of these he had heard from the grandfather who helped raise him in his hometown, Erie, Pennsylvania—his grandfather called these spirituals plantation songs. Harry T. Burleigh was also a singer of great repute. He was a baritone soloist at the wealthy and prestigious Saint George Episcopal Church in New York City for fifty years, and at Temple Emanu-El, also in New York City, for twenty-five years. He became an institution at Saint George's, where he established an annual concert of African American music and began a tradition of singing Fauré's "The Palms" at every Palm Sunday service.

Burleigh became the first American person of color to make his living through music as a composer, arranger, and singer. His first professional studies were with the Czech composer Antonín Dvořák at the National Conservatory of Music in New York. Burleigh initially made a reputation through this association with Dvořák, who said that Burleigh had given him an understanding of the music of African Americans and had inspired him to encourage American composers to develop an indigenous music and style rather than rehashing the European tradition.

Burleigh was a pioneer in the development of the concert version of African American spirituals and was the catalyst for the use of spirituals arranged for solo voice in recitals by most of the major performing artists of color, including Roland Hayes and Marion Anderson, as well as a number of prominent white artists during this period and later. Of great interest is Burleigh's setting (1917) of "Deep River" for solo voice, which helped establish him as an arranger of spirituals for solo voice and piano. However, a better-known work is his earlier arrangement (1913) of "Deep River" for a cappella mixed chorus (SATB). Burleigh's choral and solo arrangements of spirituals are considered a valuable contribution to the American choral and art song repertoire. However, his freely composed secular art songs have not been widely recognized since the early years of the twentieth century.

Whether or not it has been adequately acknowledged—and although he received some adverse criticism from African American and white colleagues—Burleigh's creative output has undeniably enriched the African American as well as the American musical tradition. He concertized extensively and was the first artist of color to demonstrate that African Americans could perform the operatic and art-song literature that was at the heart of the serious recital program.

During his last year at the National Conservatory, Burleigh had been engaged to teach voice. From 1913 until his death, he worked as a music editor for Ricordi Music Publishers. As a result, a great deal of his music was published—a reward that many composers would relish.

Biography

Harry (Henry) Thacker Burleigh was born in Erie, Pennsylvania, 2 December 1866. He attended the National Conservatory of Music in New York City; was a baritone soloist at Saint George, 1894–1946, and at Temple Emanu-El, 1900–1925; and made extensive tours as a soloist in the United States and abroad (including a recital tour in England in 1908). He also appeared with Booker T. Washington on fund-raising tours. Burleigh was an editor with G. Ricordi Music Publishers, 1911–1946. His awards included honorary degrees, a Spingarn Medal in 1917, and a Harmon Foundation award in 1929. Burleigh died 12 September 1949.

MALCOLM BREDA

See also Anderson, Marian; Hayes, Roland; Singers

Further Reading

Allison, Roland Lewis. "Classification of the Vocal Works of Harry T. Burleigh (1866–1949) and Some Suggestions for Their Use in Teaching Diction in Singing." Ph.D. diss., Indiana University, 1966. (Ann Arbor, Mich.: University Microfilms.)

"H. K. M. in Retrospect . . . Harry T. Burleigh (1866–1949): 'Deep River' Popularizes a Composer." *Black Perspective in Music*, 2 Spring 1974. (Reprinted from *Boston Evening Transcript*, 10 March 1917.)

Janifer, Ellsworth. "H. T. Burleigh Ten Years Later." *Phylon*, 21, 1960.

Lee, Henry. "Swing Low, Sweet Chariot." *Black Perspective in Music*, 2, Spring 1974.

Simpson, Anne Key. *Hard Trials: The Life and Music of Harry T. Burleigh*. Metuchen, N.J.: Scarecrow, 1990.

Synder, Jean Elizabeth. "Harry T. Burleigh and the Creative Expression of Bi-Musicality: A Study of an African-American Composer and the American Art Song." Ph.D. diss., University of Pittsburgh, 1992.

Walton, Lester A. "Harry T. Burleigh Honored Today at Saint George's." *Black Perspective*, 2, Spring 1974.

Bush, Anita

The theater entrepreneur and actress Anita Bush was born in 1883 in Washington, D.C.; she moved to Brooklyn, New York, with her parents by the age of two. Her father was a tailor for people in show business, and Bush, who made deliveries for him, soon became fascinated with the theater. As a child, she appeared onstage at the Bijou and Columbia theaters in Brooklyn and the Park Theater in Manhattan, playing bit parts in *Fatal Wedding* and *Antony and Cleopatra*. In 1903, at age thirteen, with her father's consent, she began her career with the Williams and Walker traveling show as a chorus girl in *In Dahomey, In Abyssinia*, and *Mr. Lode of Koal*. Her love of drama—and of greasepaint, costumes, and backstage life—led to a

"marriage" with the theater that would take her to Cincinnati, Chicago, and Phoenix, and on a tour of *In Dahomey* in London and Scotland. In 1909, George Walker's illness forced the Williams and Walker company to close; but soon thereafter Bush became the head of her own professional drama company. She wanted to prove to blacks and whites alike that black performers could succeed in doing what white performers were doing on Broadway, and her company disdained stereotypical comic song and dance.

The Anita Bush Stock Players, or Anita Bush Theater Company, first played at the Lincon Theater on 135th Street in Harlem, in November 1915. When the white proprietor of the theater, Maria C. Downs, insisted that the company should be called the Lincoln Stock Players, Bush refused and moved her players to a rival theater on 132nd Street: the Lafayette, which was managed by two blacks, Lester Walton and Eugene Elmore. On 2 March 1916, the company assumed the name Lafayette Players.

Bush, who became known as the "mother of Negro drama," remained an active member of the company until 1920 and received critical acclaim as a star in *The Girl at the Fort, Across the Footlights, The Gambler's Sweetheart, The Octoroon, New York After Dark, Wanted—A Family, When the Wife's Away, For His Daughter's Honor, The Lure*, and *Within the Law*. Her own talent and the sophistication of the company brought an invitation for her to start up touring Lafayette Players in major cities. These tours gave many actors across the country their start.

In 1921, Anita Bush appeared in the silent movie *The Crimson Skull*, an all-black western mystery; in 1923, she appeared in *The Bull-Dogger* and a black cowboy film, *Girl of the Golden West* (1923). The *Exhibitor's Herald* said that these films "prove conclusively that the Black cowboy is capable of doing anything the white cowboy does."

During the 1930s and 1940s, Bush appeared in a production by the Works Progress Administration, *Swing It* (1938), taught acting at the Harlem YMCA (then an important theatrical venue), and served as executive secretary for the Negro Actors Guild. She retired from the theater in 1943. Bush died in 1974, at age ninety-one.

Biography

Anita Bush was born in 1883 in Washington, D.C.; her family moved to Brooklyn, New York, in 1885. Bush was a stage and screen actress from 1903 to the 1930s and the founder of the Anita Bush Stock Players, which later became the Lafayette Players. She was also executive secretary for the Negro Actors Guild. Plays in which she was involved included *Fatal Wedding, Antony and Cleopatra, In Dahomey, Abyssinia, Mr. Lode of Koal, Across the Footlights, The Gambler's Sweetheart, The Octoroon, New York After Dark, Wanted—A Family, When the Wife's Away, Roanoke, Southern Life, For His Daughter's Honor, The World Against Him, Within the Law, Paid in Full*, and *Swing It*. He films included *The Crimson Skull* (1921), *The Bulldoggers* (1923), and *Girl of the Golden West* (1923). Bush died 19 February 1974 in the Bronx, New York.

SHIRLEY BASFIELD DUNLAP

See also Anita Bush Theater Company; Lafayette Players; Lafayette Theater; Lincoln Theater

Further Reading

Andrews, William L., Frances Smith Foster, and Trudier Harris, eds. *The Oxford Companion to African American Literature.* New York: Oxford University Press, 1997.

Haskins, James. *Black Theater in America.* New York: Crowell, 1982.

Richards, Larry. *African American Films Through 1959: A Comprehensive, Illustrated Filmography.* Jefferson, N.C.: McFarland, 1998.

Sampson, Henry T. *A Source Book on Black Films.* Metuchen, N.J.: Scarecrow, 1977.

Tanner, Jo A. *Dusky Maidens: The Odyssey of the Early Black Dramatic Actress.* Westport, Conn.: Greenwood, 1992.

Thompson, M. Francesca. "The Lafayette Players, 1917–1932." In *The Theater of Black Americans*, Vol. 2, *The Presenters—The Participators.* Englewood Cliffs, N.J.: Prentice-Hall, 1980.

Willis, Cassandra. "Anita Bush." Hatch-Billops Collection, Schomburg Center for Research in Black Culture, Harlem. New York: New York City Library, 1972. (Interview by Willis; sound recording.)

Buttitta, Anthony J.

Anthony J. Buttitta contributed to the Harlem Renaissance primarily through the literary magazine *Contempo*, which he and Milton Abernathy launched in 1931 when they were both students at the University of North Carolina. Buttitta and Abernathy envisioned *Contempo* as a forum in which to explore new ideas and encourage literary controversy. In an effort to broaden the magazine's content and establish it as a southern mouthpiece for the Harlem Renaissance, Buttitta recruited black writers to submit poetry, essays, and short fiction and also reviewed texts by black authors. Countee Cullen, Langston Hughes, James Weldon Johnson, Walter White, and Wallace Thurman were among those asked to submit work. Buttitta did not see himself solely as a patron of black writers, however. He also asked James Weldon Johnson and Langston Hughes to read a manuscript that he himself was working on and to help promote his own career.

Hughes visited Buttitta for several days in November 1931, and the two became close friends and colleagues. As a result, Hughes published four poems and one article in Buttitta's magazine, including the poem "Christ in Alabama," which was on the front page of a special issue on the Scottsboro case. The issue drew heavy criticism from outraged journalists, faculty members, and local advertisers (many of whom withdrew their support from the magazine), but Buttitta and Abernathy did not abandon their mission or their relationship with Hughes. Hughes became a contributing editor for December 1931 issue and was supposed to edit a "Negro Arts Edition" of *Contempo*, although that edition never materialized.

The idea of a southern publication of black literature appealed to many, including White and Cullen, but Buttitta had difficulty finding contributors for the "Negro Arts Edition," because some of the writers he approached were already overcommitted and were unable to write new pieces. Buttitta's special issue of *Contempo* was also beleaguered by poor timing relative to other anthologies that were already being produced. He might have succeeded a decade earlier, but by 1932, there was little room for his collection in the literary marketplace; similar issues of *Vanity Fair* and *Palms* were out, in addition to anthologies by Alain Locke, Charles S. Johnson, Countee Cullen, and James Weldon Johnson. Finally, internal struggles between Buttitta and the other editors at *Contempo* made the completion of the special issue impossible. Buttitta separated from the failing magazine by October 1932, and the division ultimately led to its end in 1934. After he left *Contempo*, Buttitta's interest shifted from African American literature to F. Scott Fitzgerald, whom he met in 1935, and to the Federal Theater Project.

Although he made an important contribution to the Harlem Renaissance through his publication of Hughes's poetry, Buttitta was never a major figure in the movement. Indeed, his failure to complete the "Negro Arts Edition" of *Contempo* suggests that the Harlem Renaissance was, to a considerable extent, a northern, urban movement, and that it had already peaked by the time he sought to bring it to the South.

Biography

Anthony J. Buttitta was born 26 July 1907, in Chicago. His parents were Giacomo Buttitta, a businessman, and Nina Buttitta, a teacher. He attended Normal College in Natchitoches, Louisiana (1926–1928), received his B.A. from the University of Texas (1929), and pursued graduate study at the University of North Carolina. He was married to Remy Horton in 1932 (they were divorced in 1941), and later to Monica Hannasch. Buttitta was the founder and editor of *Contempo* (1931–1933); a freelance newspaper correspondent (1932–1935); a press representative for the North Carolina Symphony Orchestra in Chapel Hill (1935); a staff member of the Federal Theater Project (1936–1938); a press representative for Roanoke Island, North Carolina (1938–1940); a press agent on Broadway (1939–1945); a public relations staffer in the U.S. Army (1943–1944); a press representative for the San Francisco Civic Light Opera (1931–1962); and a freelance writer (from 1962 on). His publications (as Tony Buttitta) include *Singing Piedmont* (1937); "Scott: One More Emotion" (1974); *After the Good Gay Times: Asheville, Summer of 1935: A Season With Scott Fitzgerald* (Viking, 1974, reprinted in 1987 as *The Lost Summer: A Personal Memoir of F. Scott Fitzgerald*); *Uncle Sam Presents: A Memoir of the Federal Theatre, 1935–1939* (with Barry Witham, 1982); "Contempo Caravan: Kites in a Windstorm" (1985); "Thank You, Malcolm!" (1989); *The Singing Tree* (1990); "A Memoir of Faulkner in the Early Days of His Fame" (1999); and "William Faulkner: That Writin' Man of Oxford" (1999). His other works include an unpublished novel, *No Resurrection*; a one-act play first produced in Natchitoches at State Normal College, *Barataria* (1927); a three-act play first produced in Chapel Hill at the University of North Carolina, *Playthings* (1931); and a memoir, *Never a Stranger* (forthcoming at the time of the present writing).

AMANDA M. LAWRENCE

See also Contempo; Cullen, Countee; Hughes, Langston; Johnson, Charles Spurgeon; Johnson, James Weldon; Locke, Alain; Palms; Scottsboro; Thurman, Wallace; Vanity Fair; White, Walter

Further Reading

"Anthony Buttitta." In *Contemporary Authors: A Bio-Bibliographical Guide to Current Writers in Fiction, General Nonfiction, Poetry, Journalism, Drama, Motion Pictures, Television, and Other Fields*, ed. Frances Carol Locher, Vol. 81. Detroit, Mich.: Gale Research, 1979, p. 72.

Buttitta, Tony. "Contempo Caravan: Kites in a Windstorm." In *Dictionary of Literary Biography Yearbook*, ed. Jean W. Ross. Detroit, Mich.: Gale Research, 1986, pp. 109–124.

Hutchinson, George. *The Harlem Renaissance in Black and White*. Cambridge, Mass.: Belknap Press of Harvard University Press, 1995.

Wintz, Cary D. *Black Culture and the Harlem Renaissance*. Houston, Tex.: Rice University Press, 1988.

C

Calloway, Cabell "Cab"

Cab Calloway was born into a middle-class family in Rochester, New York, and moved to Baltimore when he was eleven. A rebellious youth, he spent almost as much time at the racetrack as in school, but he did manage two years of classical voice training during his teens. He was more attracted to ragtime and jazz, and the glamour of entertainment in general, than to his studies, and picked up work as a jazz singer and drummer at speakeasies in Baltimore. He often encountered his teachers at these illegal clubs, but he and they maintained their respective silence, and Calloway continued to perform.

Calloway's sister Blanche, who had already ventured into show business in New York and sung in *Shuffle Along*, returned to Baltimore in 1927 with a touring company of *Plantation Days*. Calloway begged his reluctant sister to get him an audition with the company; she did, and it was successful. Against his mother's wishes, he traveled with the show on the Theater Owners' Booking Association (TOBA) circuit, until it closed in Chicago in 1928. A brief and insincere stint at Crane College notwithstanding, Calloway spent most of his time in Chicago hustling singing work in local clubs, until steady work at the Dreamland Café and the Sunset Club came along. Here he met Louis Armstrong, who suggested that he develop freer, scat-style singing. This accorded well with Calloway's flamboyant personality, and Calloway became as much of a showman as a singer, often serving as master of ceremonies for the night's entertainment. The highlight of an evening's show with the Alabamians at the Sunset Club, for example, was a

wild call-and-response song with Calloway and the orchestra all shouting into megaphones.

In 1929, Calloway and the Alabamians made their debut in Harlem at the Savoy Ballroom, but they bombed after the first song—their Chicago sound was not hot enough for the Harlem crowd. Desperate to salvage the two-week contract, the booking agent set up a battle of the bands between the Alabamians and the Savoy's house band, the Missourians. The Alabamians were cut to pieces, but Calloway's flamboyant stage presence stole the show. Now unemployed, Calloway, on Louis Armstrong's recommendation, was hired for the Broadway and Boston runs of *Hot Chocolates*. After it closed in early 1930, the Savoy's agent, remembering Calloway's triumph, hired him to front the Missourians, but got them a better job: opening the new Plantation Club on 126th Street. What should have been a milestone event for Calloway crumbled when the club was ransacked by mobsters affiliated with the rival Cotton Club hours before opening night. Fortunately, Calloway and the Missourians secured work at the Crazy Cat, which was frequented by an upscale clientele and broadcast on radio every night.

This brief stint drew attention to the band, particularly from the mobsters running the Cotton Club. Through implied threats, they persuaded Calloway to break the Missourians' contract with the Crazy Cat and substitute at the Cotton Club while the house band, the Duke Ellington Orchestra, toured the West Coast. The Calloway band and its flashy leader were a hit, and they filled in for Ellington during his frequent absences until they themselves became the house band in 1931. Calloway's performances at the Cotton

Club guaranteed him a national radio contract and the attention of the star-studded crowd at this prestigious Harlem venue. George Gershwin saw him there and based the character Sportin' Life in *Porgy and Bess* on Calloway. Gershwin even offered Calloway the role in the first production, in 1935, but Calloway, who was becoming increasingly popular, declined, citing scheduling conflicts. It was at the Cotton Club that Calloway adopted "Minnie the Moocher" as his theme song. After the addition of the "hi-de-hi-de-hi-de-ho" call-and-response between Calloway and the audience, it was an instant hit nationally, and it became his life-long signature piece. The Cotton Club meant stardom, national and international tours, and movie contracts, which all came between 1931 and 1936. Responses to Calloway ranged from the respect and enthusiasm of European audiences to frenzied adulation among many college students and African American fans to occasional threats and violence at segregated dances during several trips in the South.

Although Calloway was now immersed in the Harlem entertainment scene, he had had little contact with the leaders or ideas of the Harlem Renaissance. Harlem was certainly "*the* place for a Negro to be," according to Calloway, but he never felt connected to the literary movement. He observed that "the two worlds, literature and entertainment, rarely crossed. We were working hard on our thing and they were working hard on theirs." Also, Calloway's flamboyant stage show was hardly suitable for the great concert halls to which most renaissance leaders aspired for African American musicians.

During the mid-1930s, Calloway's tours and radio show helped bring both white and black swing bands, most notably those from New York, to national prominence. But though his orchestra, early in the decade, was serviceable for a Cotton Club revue, it did not approach the caliber of Ellington's or Fletcher Henderson's units. This began to change as Calloway increased the size of the band from ten to sixteen pieces, the standard complement for a swing orchestra, and added a number of hot young players to replace the Missourians. The tenor saxophonist Chu Berry, hired away from Henderson, and the legendary bassist Milt Hinton were added in 1936; the fiery (and troublesome) young trumpeter Dizzy Gillespie and drummer Cozy Cole joined the band in 1939; and the tenor sax player Ben Webster and the trumpeters Jonah Jones and Mario Bauza also played under Calloway. By 1941, Calloway had one of the great ensembles of the era, and he rode

Cab Calloway. (Brown Brothers.)

the wave of swing's popularity until after World War II. Economic problems caused the breakup of virtually all the big bands between 1946 and 1948, the year Cab Calloway's orchestra folded permanently.

Calloway performed infrequently after 1948. Between 1952 and 1954, he finally played Sportin' Life in a famous revival of *Porgy and Bess*. That plus a tour as Horace Vandergelder in *Hello, Dolly!* from 1967 to 1971 and record royalties guaranteed financial security for him and his family.

Biography

Cabell "Cab" Calloway was born in Rochester, New York, 25 December 1907. He was educated in public schools in Baltimore and at the Downing-town Industrial and Agricultural School; pursued vocal studies with Llewelyn Wilson and Ruth Macabee in Baltimore; and attended Crane College in Chicago (1928), though he did not graduate. Calloway sang in the touring company of *Plantation*

Days (1927–1928); at the Dreamland Café and the Sunset Club in Chicago (1928); with the Alabamians at the Savoy Ballroom in Harlem (1929); in *Hot Chocolates* (1929–1930); and with the Missourians, substituting for the Ellington Orchestra at the Cotton Club (1930–1931). Cab Calloway and His Cotton Club Orchestra were the house band at the Cotton Club in 1931–1934 and made occasional appearances there in 1934–1940. Calloway's first record contract was with Brunswick; he recorded his first hit, "Minnie the Moocher," in 1931. He went on national tours in 1931–1948 and a European tour in 1935. He was on the radio show *Quizzicale* (NBC Blue Network), a black version of Kay Keyser's Kollege of Musical Knowledge, in 1942. Calloway's orchestra disbanded in 1948. Calloway played Sportin' Life in *Porgy and Bess* on Broadway (1952–1954) and Horace Vandergelder in *Hello, Dolly!* (1967–1971). He died in Hockessen, Delaware, 19 November 1994.

WILLIAM J. NANCARROW

See also Armstrong, Louis; Cotton Club; Hot Chocolates; Jazz; Music: Bands and Orchestras; Musicians; Porgy and Bess; Savoy Ballroom; Singers

Selected Recordings

"Minnie the Moocher." 1931. (Dates are of recordings, not publication.)
"Bugle Call Rag." 1931.
"Reefer Man." 1932.
"Zaz Zuh Zaz." 1933.
"At the Clambake Carnival." 1938.
"Pluckin' the Bass." 1939.
"Ratamacue." 1939.
"Pickin' the Cabbage." 1940.
"Jonah Joins the Cab." 1941.
"Special Delivery." 1941.
"Let's Go Joe." 1942.

Films

The Big Broadcast. 1932.
The Singing Kid. 1936.
Saint Louis Blues. 1937.
Ali Baba Goes to Town. 1937.
Stormy Weather. 1943.
Dixie Jamboree. 1944.

Further Reading

Calloway, Cab, and Bryant Rollins. *Of Minnie the Moocher and Me*. New York: Crowell, 1976.
Dance, Stanley. *The World of Swing*. New York: Scribner, 1974. (See also 2nd ed., Da Capo, 2001.)
Gillespie, Dizzy, and Al Fraser. *To Be, or Not . . . to Bop: The Autobiography of Dizzy Gillespie*. New York and London: Quartet, 1983.
Haskins, James. *The Cotton Club*. New York: Random House, 1977; London: Robson, 1985. (See also 3rd ed., Hippocrene, 1994.)
Popa, Jay. *Cab Calloway and His Orchestra*. Zephyrhills, Fla.: Joyce Record Club, 1987.

Calverton, V. F.

The socialist V. F. Calverton was one of the most significant figures of the American intellectual left during the first half of the twentieth century. "V. F. Calverton" was a pseudonym, adopted by George Goetz so that his involvement in socialist politics would not compromise his position as a public school teacher. As Calverton, he founded, with others, *Modern Quarterly*, an influential magazine of intellectual debate with a Marxist point of view. The magazine published essays of literary criticism, book reviews, and articles exploring economics, politics, and race relations in the United States. As editor, Calverton controlled the content of the magazine, and he wrote essays and book reviews for virtually every issue. During the mid- to late 1920s, *Modern Quarterly* dealt frequently with issues of race, with both black and white writers participating. The issue of October–December 1925 included an article by W. E. B. Du Bois on the significance of the Harlem Renaissance. Other black intellectuals, including Alain Locke, the composer Clarence Cameron White, the sociologist E. Franklin Frazier, and the musicologist Carl E. Gehring also wrote articles for the magazine. Besides providing a forum for black writers, *Modern Quarterly* reviewed many books coming out of the Harlem Renaissance. Calverton's positive review of Langston Hughes's *Fine Clothes to the Jew* (1927), for example, helped ensure the book's success.

During the 1920s and 1930s, Calverton and his wife opened their home at 2110 East Pratt Street in Baltimore as a sort of a salon, a place to discuss politics and the arts. These weekly gatherings quickly became known as one of the few—and one of the most stimulating—opportunities for black and white intellectuals to mingle freely. Although Baltimore was not the intellectual center that New York and Washington, D.C., were, important leftists of the day made it a point to stop at "2110" on their way between those two major cities. Guests included the educator Charles S. Johnson, the novelist F. Scott Fitzgerald, Alain Locke, and Langston Hughes, who gave a lecture on the blues.

In 1929, Calverton published *Anthology of American Negro Literature*, which included poetry, fiction, drama, music, criticism, and historical essays, as well as an introduction in which he argued for the uniqueness and importance of black culture. Later, he published books on sexual liberation and psychology.

Biography

V. F. Calverton (whose real name was George Goetz) was born in Baltimore, Maryland, 25 June 1900. He studied engineering at the Baltimore Polytechnic High School (1914–1916) and liberal arts at City College, an academic high school in Baltimore (1918); he then studied at Johns Hopkins University (B.A., 1918–1921). He taught at Baltimore Public School 40 (1920–1929), Baltimore Labor College (beginning in 1926), and the Rand School of Social Science in New York (summers, beginning in 1926). He was the founder and editor of *Horizon* magazine (one issue, 1922) and *Modern Quarterly* (1923–1940). He died 20 November 1940 in Baltimore.

CYNTHIA BILY

See also Du Bois, W. E. B.; Fine Clothes to the Jew; Frazier, E. Franklin; Hughes, Langston; Johnson, Charles Spurgeon; Locke, Alain; Modern Quarterly; White, Clarence Cameron

Selected Works

Modern Quarterly. 1923–1940.
The Newer Spirit: A Sociological Criticism of Literature. 1925.
Anthology of American Negro Literature. 1929. (As editor.)

Further Reading

Aaron, Daniel. *Writers on the Left.* New York: Avon, 1965.
Abbott, Philip. *Leftward Ho!: V. F. Calverton and American Radicalism.* Westport, Conn.: Greenwood, 1993.
———. "Utopia by Hypnosis: V. F. Calverton's *The Man Inside* and American Radicalism in the 1930s." *Utopian Studies,* 10(2), 1999.
Diggins, John P. *Up from Communism: Conservative Odysseys in American Intellectual History.* New York: Harper & Row, 1975.
Washington, Robert E. *The Ideologies of African-American Literature: From the Harlem Renaissance to the Black Nationalist Revolt.* Lanham, Md.: Rowman & Littlefield, 2001.
Wilcox, Leonard. *V. F. Calverton: Radical in the American Grain.* Philadelphia, Pa.: Temple University Press, 1992.

Campbell, Dick

As a director, producer, and manager, Dick Campbell (Cornelius Coleridge Campbell) was instrumental in the development and promotion of black theater during the Harlem Renaissance. He himself was a singer, dancer, and former vaudevillian, and he was dedicated to training black playwrights, directing black actors, and producing plays that reflected the vitality of black life. He helped establish a community theater in Harlem that exemplified the artistic integrity of black theater professionals.

Dick Campbell was born in Beaumont, Texas. As a boy, he shined shoes, worked as a high school janitor, and took odd jobs. His involvement in high school plays inspired his early interest in theater; and in 1926, after attending Paul Quinn College, he moved to Los Angeles, California, where he began performing at local speakeasies. Campbell joined the Theatrical Owners' Booking Association (TOBA) vaudeville circuit as part of the Whitman Sisters' Show, and he arrived in Harlem in 1928 while touring with that group. He remained in New York and often performed alongside Ethel Waters, Bill "Bojangles" Robinson, Louis Armstrong, and others in theaters in Harlem and on Broadway. His credits include *Connie's Hot Chocolates* (1929), *Hot Rhythm* (1930), and *Singing the Blues* (1931). After George Gershwin did not cast him in *Porgy and Bess*, Campbell recognized the difficulty black actors faced in acquiring credible roles on Broadway. In an effort to combat racial discrimination in the theater and offer black actors more roles that were not stereotypical servants, Campbell turned his attention to producing.

Campbell spent the 1930s organizing theater companies in Harlem. In 1935, he cofounded the Negro

People's Theater with Rose McClendon, and they successfully staged an all-black production of Clifford Odet's *Waiting for Lefty*. Following McClendon's death in 1936, Campbell continued their shared vision of creating a theater in Harlem that was intrinsically connected to the community; presented plays by, about, and for blacks; promoted a dignified image of blacks; and gave black theater artists professional training and a reasonable income. Thus he founded and directed the Rose McClendon Players, a "little theater" in Harlem that was funded by audience subscriptions. The Rose McClendon Players furthered the black community's interest in and support of black drama, and, under Campbell's personal guidance, the company helped establish the careers of several black theater artists, including Abram Hill, Loften Mitchell, Frederick O'Neal, and Ossie Davis.

Campbell's unswerving commitment to black artists and the black community was lifelong. As founder of the Harlem Workshop Theater and chairman of the Coordinating Council for Negro Performers, Campbell opened doors for black artists where white institutions would not. He managed the concert career of the singer Muriel Rahn, his wife, and showcased black performers such as Alvin Ailey and Duke Ellington in more than sixty-five shows overseas while working as the producer of black USO camp shows during World War II. After working for the U.S. State Department, Campbell spent his later years raising awareness in the black community about sickle-cell anemia. Campbell died in 1994 at age ninety-one.

Biography

Dick Campbell (Cornelius Coleridge Campbell) was born in Beaumont, Texas. He was orphaned at age six and was reared by his maternal grandmother, Pauline Snow. He worked as the janitor at his high school (1918–1922) and attended Paul Quinn College in Waco, Texas (1922–1926). Campbell began his theatrical career in Los Angeles as a singer and straight man in vaudeville comedy shows (1926–1928). He then joined the Whitman Sisters' Show and traveled to New York (1928). From 1929 to 1942, he was a cast member in various shows in Harlem and on Broadway, including *Connie's Hot Chocolates*, *Hot Rhythm*, and *Singing the Blues*. In 1930–1931, he costarred with Eddie Green on radio in the comedy show "Green and Campbell" as part of the *Fleischmann Yeast Hour*. In 1932, he met and married the concert singer Muriel

Rahn. In 1935, he and Rose McClendon founded the Negro People's Theater in Harlem. He founded and directed the Rose McClendon Players (1937–1942). Campbell was appointed director of the Harlem unit of the Federal Theater Project (1939). He was a producer of the black USO camp shows (1942–1946). He was an African representative for the American National Theater Association, the administrative branch of the U.S. State Department's International Cultural Exchange Program for which he was the field consultant on African affairs (1956–1964); assistant director of public affairs for New York City Human Resources Administration (1967–1972); and executive director of the Sickle Cell Foundation of Greater New York (1972–1994). Campbell died in New York 20 December 1994.

MELINDA D. WILSON

See also Hot Chocolates; Federal Programs; McClendon, Rose

Further Reading

Gill, Glenda E. *White Grease Paint on Black Performers: A Study of the Federal Theatre, 1935–1939*. New York: Peter Lang, 1988.

Mitchell, Loften. *Voices of the Black Theatre*. Clifton, N.J.: White, 1975.

Peterson, Bernard L. *The African-American Theatre Directory, 1816–1960: A Comprehensive Guide to Early Black Theatre Organizations, Companies, Theatres, and Performing Groups*. Westport, Conn.: Greenwood, 1997.

Campbell, Elmer Simms

E. (Elmer) Simms Campbell was one of the preeminent cartoonists and illustrators of his day; his supple black-and-white drawings and lush watercolors were a regular feature in the pages of *Opportunity*, the *New Yorker*, *Life*, *Collier's*, the *Saturday Evening Post*, the Pittsburgh *Courier*, *Cosmopolitan*, *Redbook*, and *Playboy*. Through William Randolph Hearst's King Features Syndicate, Campbell's "Cuties" appeared in 145 newspapers nationwide. With his tenure as a staff illustrator for *Esquire*, beginning with its debut issue in January 1934 and lasting until 1957, Campbell became the first black artist to break into the "major" magazines. Campbell is credited with creating "Esky," the well-dressed, pop-eyed ladies' man with the white walrus mustache who appeared on most *Esquire* covers; and the parodic odalisques of his sultan-and-harem series perfectly embodied the urbane, leering men's magazine aesthetic that *Esquire* was busy defining at mid-century. Although Campbell sometimes complained that drawing was a little like ditch digging, but without the benefit of fresh air, he managed to turn out anywhere between 300 and 500 pieces a year.

Campbell's work rarely concerned itself with specifically black subject matter, and rarely featured black characters, largely sticking to the befuddled tuxedoed gents and redheaded "cuties" that assured him a mass audience. An *Esquire* cartoon of October 1934 (ostensibly making reference to the bandleader Cab Calloway, who considered Campbell his closest friend) struck a self-referential note in this respect. It depicted a white choirmaster eyeing the single black choirboy in his chorus; the caption read: "And none of that hi-de-ho stuff!" Yet his harem series had a certain critical edge to its leer: It featured a disturbingly matter-of-fact approach to the sexual economics of slavery, while at the same time, with its all-in-a-day's-work punchlines, it poked fun at his mainstream audience's fascination with exotic otherness.

In a more direct contribution to the Harlem Renaissance, Campbell illustrated a number of books by black writers: most notably Sterling Brown's collection of poems, *Southern Road* (1932); a children's book by Langston Hughes and Arna Bontemps, *Popo and Fifina: Children of Haiti* (1932); and Binga Dismond's *We Who Die and Other Poems, Including Haitian Vignettes* (1943). Campbell was also an astute observer of jazz and the Harlem scene: His jivey, idiosyncratic "Night-Club Map of Harlem" (1932) is a classic of its kind; its cat's-eye-view guide to hot spots off Lenox or Seventh Avenue ("or heaven") is full of knowing asides ("You've never heard a piano really played until you hear Garland Wilson") yet still manages to find room for the "nice new POLICE STATION" and the "Harlem Moon." And in 1936, Campbell revealed to *Esquire*'s readers what its editors described as "a happy combination of sympathetic insight and critical detachment" ("Homeland" 1936, 101) as he began to write sharply personal, beautifully illustrated articles on such topics as dancing at Harlem's Savoy Ballroom, the plight of Haitian sugarcane workers, and the history of jazz.

When *Esquire* changed its format in 1957, Campbell moved to Switzerland, but he remained an active contributor to American periodicals through the 1960s.

Biography

Elmer Simms Campbell was born in St. Louis, Missouri, 2 January 1906. He attended Englewood High School in Chicago, studied at the Lewis Institute of Chicago and the University of Chicago, and graduated from the Art Institute of Chicago (1927). He was an illustrator at the Triad Studios advertising agency in St. Louis (1927–1928). In 1928, he moved to New York, where he worked in advertising, attended the Academy of Design, studied under George Grosz at the Art Students League, and began to contribute to periodicals. Campbell was a staff illustrator and cartoonist at *Esquire* magazine (1933–1957). He moved to Neerach, Switzerland, and was a cartoonist for *Playboy* magazine (1957–1970). He won the St. Louis *Dispatch* Award for black-and-white illustration (1928) and the William Randolph Hearst Art Prize (1936), as well as an honorable mention for watercolor at the American Negro Exposition (1940). He also received honorary degrees from Lincoln, Pennsylvania (M.F.A. in art), and Wilberforce universities and from the University of Ohio (doctor of humane letters). He was a member of the Society of Illustrators, Society of Artists, and National Society of Cartoonists. Campbell died in White Plains, New York, 27 January 1971.

RYAN JERVING

See also Bontemps, Arna; Brown, Sterling; Calloway, Cabell "Cab"; Hughes, Langston; Opportunity; Pittsburgh Courier; Savoy Ballroom

Group Exhibitions

Minneapolis Artists Exhibit, Minnesota. 1924.
Painting and Sculpture by American Negro Artists, Harmon Foundation, National Gallery, Washington, D.C. 1929.
Harmon Foundation, New York. 1935.
Arthur H. Newton Galleries, New York. 1935.
American Negro Exposition: Exhibition of the Art of the American Negro, Chicago Coliseum, Chicago, Illinois. 1940.
South Side Community Art Center, Chicago, Illinois. 1941.

Selected Works

Southern Road by Sterling Brown. 1932. (As illustrator.)
Popo and Fifina: Children of Haiti by Arna Bontemps and Langston Hughes. 1932. (As illustrator.)

"Homeland of Happy Feet" and "Swing, Mr. Charlie." *Esquire*, February 1936.

"Ten Dollars a Head" and "A Portfolio of Haitian Sketches." *Esquire*, April 1938.

"Jam in the Nineties." *Esquire*, December 1938. (Reprinted as "Early Jam" in *The Negro Caravan*, ed. Sterling Brown, Arthur P. Davis, and Ulysses Lee. 1941.)

Cuties in Arms. 1942.

More Cuties in Arms. 1943.

We Who Die and Other Poems, Including Haitian Vignettes by Binga Dismond. 1943. (As illustrator.)

Ladies of the Harem. 1948. (*Esquire* calendar.)

Further Reading

Calloway, Cab, and Bryant Rollins. *Of Minnie the Moocher and Me*. New York: Crowell, 1976.

"Esky's True Paternity." *Esquire*, 124(4), October 1995.

Jordan, Casper L. "E. Simms Campbell." In *Contemporary Black Biography*, Vol. 13, ed. Shirelle Phelps. London and Detroit, Mich.: Gale, 1997.

Cane

Jean Toomer's *Cane* was first published in 1923 by Boni and Liveright, a publishing firm in New York, with a foreword by the pluralist and cultural critic Waldo Frank. From the start, the book appealed to two very different audiences—not surprisingly, given that parts of it had been previously published in magazines as different as *Crisis* and *S 4 N*. At the time, the book earned a reputation as the first modernist work of fiction by a "Negro writer," securing Toomer's place in the radical cosmopolitan set of Greenwich Village and the New Negro artists of the burgeoning Harlem Renaissance. The book itself is not so much a novel as a collection of brief literary portraits and one longer prose play.

Growing up in Washington, D.C., in the household of his grandfather, a venerable "blue veiner" and a racial chameleon of sorts, Toomer struggled for some time to discover just who and what he was. He briefly attended the University of Wisconsin, took up exercise, and tried his hand at writing poems and short dramatic pieces. In 1921, Toomer—discontented and struggling as a writer to define himself and his subject matter—was offered a job as the head of an African American school in Sparta, Georgia. He took it and

mined what he found there for the fugitive pieces that would become the first section and last story of *Cane*. As was typical of this extraordinarily autobiographical writer, for the middle and the last sections he also drew deeply from his own life and from his own sense of self.

The form of the novel was confusing enough to "irritate" W. E. B. Du Bois, the editor of *The Crisis*. Indeed, to sum up the combination of writing styles that is *Cane*, Arna Bontemps once remarked that in this work "poetry and prose were whipped together in a kind of frappé." The book has three parts, the first of which is a series of sensitive, lyrical vignettes of African American womanhood in the South. The women Jean Toomer wrote about in this section were not classic Victorian matriarchs, but compromised, even fallen, and certainly sexually complicated and alive. In breathing life into Fern, Karintha, and others, Toomer painted with words, as Du Bois put it, in the impressionist style, using a "sweep of color" to liberate black women from the restrictive confines of middle-class prudery.

The second section of *Cane* is set in the North, specifically in Washington, D.C., and Chicago. Once again, Toomer emphasized the contradictions between the modern and the primitive, the superego and the id, in Afro-America. But in contrast to the portraitures of the first section, the characters in his northern stories seem awkwardly out of place and lost. Men are given a significant role here, and they seem to suffer from an excess of self-consciousness and Victorian self-control, afflictions of the cold, prim, whitened North—not of the black South, where emotions were unbridled and human beings whole.

The third section contains the longest single piece of writing in *Cane*, an apocryphal story titled "Kabnis," in which a northern African American man named Ralph Kabnis heads to the South to find himself, only to be lost forever. His life in the North, it seems, has left him weak and incapable of balance and unity, and so he drifts into moral chaos and impoverishment. His very "northernness"—his psychological hesitation, his heady intellectualism, his emphasis on the mind over the body—renders him unable to enjoy the lives, loves, and labors of the South. As a balance to Ralph Kabnis, Toomer included another, more successfully integrated northerner, Lewis: "He is," the book suggests, "what a stronger Kabnis might have been." The ever-confident Toomer admitted to his friends and confidants that he himself was a combination of the very best of Kabnis and the very best of Lewis.

Many of Jean Toomer's contemporaries claimed that Cane was an "essential" text of some sort, but very few of them seem to have fully understood the book. The bibliophile William Stanley Braithwaite would claim in the pages of Alain Locke's *The New Negro* that Jean Toomer was "the very first artist of the race," an aesthete and folklorist creatively capturing the essence of proletarian black America in the deep South before it was ground away by modernity. Waldo Frank's original preface to the book, written after numerous conversations with Toomer, presented the author of Cane as "a poet": "The book is the South," Frank concluded; "[a] poet has arisen among our American youth who has known how to turn the essences and materials of his Southland into essences and materials of literature." "No previous writer," Montgomery Gregory (chair of the drama department at Howard University) suggested, "has been able in any such degree to catch the sensuous beauty of the land or of its people or fathom the deeper spiritual stirrings of the mass-life of the Negro. . . . [I]t IS the South, it IS the Negro."

It is also clear, in hindsight, that *Cane* captured the essence of Jean Toomer himself. Inspired by Waldo Frank's book *Our America*, with its cultural pluralism, Toomer hoped that *Cane* would reveal what "the Negro" had to offer to America, envisioning the work as part of the missionary radicalism led by the literary avant-garde. But, given his complicated upbringing and racial background, he also envisioned himself as more than a "Negro," and he saw *Cane* as a reflection of just one part of his personality. When, in the wake of its publication, few could understand his complicated racial position, he struggled to make that position understood, and then, finally, turned to the writing and rewriting of his numerous unpublished autobiographies.

MATTHEW PRATT GUTERL

See also Authors: 2—Fiction; Boni and Liveright; Bontemps, Arna; Braithwaite, William Stanley; Crisis, The; Du Bois, W. E. B.; Frank, Waldo; Literature: 4—Fiction; New Negro, The; Toomer, Jean

Further Reading

Bontemps, Arna. "The Negro Renaissance: Jean Toomer and the Harlem of the 1920s." In *Anger and Beyond: The Negro Writer in the United States*, ed. Herbert Hill. New York: Harper & Row, 1966.

Kerwin, Cynthia Earl, and Richard Eldridge. *The Lives of Jean Toomer: A Hunger for Wholeness*. Baton Rouge: Louisiana State University Press, 1987.

Turner, Darwin. *In a Minor Chord: Three Afro-American Writers and Their Search for Identity*. Carbondale and Edwardsville: Southern Illinois University Press, 1971.

Carolina Magazine

Founded in Chapel Hill, North Carolina, in March 1844, the *North Carolina University Magazine* was the official literary publication of the students of the University of North Carolina. It was designed to give the student body an "opportunity of perfecting ourselves in an equally important Department of Letters" tradition and as "a token of our devotion to Literature." Within this context, *Carolina Magazine*, as it was known in the late 1920s, linked itself with the New Negro movement, also referred to as the Harlem Renaissance and the Negro Renaissance—the artistic and cultural renaissance in Harlem that focused on "race consciousness and racial cooperation" among African Americans.

From 1927 to 1930, *Carolina Magazine* compiled a yearly issue for April or May called the "Negro Number," presenting a theme representative of black life and art. For example, John Mebane, the editor of the Negro Number of 4 May 1930, explained that the editorial staff of the magazine was happy to give the students "some idea" of what New Negroes were "doing in the field of literature." Mebane recognized that "the Negro," during the 1920s, retained in "his" literature, poetry, music, and art "a certain tint of beauty that is unrestrained by artificial limits, a beauty and an intensity of feeling that are genuine and intimate."

The first of four issues of the Negro Number was published in May 1927. Lewis Grandison Alexander (1900–1945), a New Negro writer whose works were published in the *Messenger, Opportunity,* and *Fire!!,* served as the honorary editor for this and the subsequent issues. Alexander, whose work for the magazine was deemed "indispensable," and Charles S. Johnson, the editor of *Opportunity* and a shaper of the New Negro movement, were acknowledged as the "key to this issue" and as having provided an identification for New Negro writers. Indeed, the article "The Negro Enters Literature," written by Johnson, set the tone for the entire series. This first issue contained drawings by Aaron Douglas for *The Emperor Jones* and poetry by Langston Hughes, Countee Cullen, and Angelina W. Grimké, to name a few.

The second issue, in May 1928, was dedicated to Alexander "in appreciation of his friendship and service." The editorial staff explained that the magazine would not have made its appearance without Alexander, who had given "his time unstintingly in the assembling of the material" and his "tireless assistance" in calling on his New Negro friends for contributions. This issue was noted for a pen-and-ink sketch of the "New Negro" by Allan R. Freelon and for the article "The Message of the Negro Poets" by Alain Locke, author of the anthology *The New Negro* (1925).

The third issue, "The Negro Play Number," in April 1929, is noted for having featured four playwrights, Willis Richardson among them, who all won prizes in contests run by *Crisis* and *Opportunity*.

The fourth and final issue, in May 1930, was noted for acknowledging the "rich and ancient tradition" of Negro art and literature. With these four issues, *Carolina Magazine* shed a bright light on its role as an active participant in the New Negro movement.

GLEN ANTHONY HARRIS

See also Crisis, The; Cullen, Countee; Emperor Jones, The; Douglas, Aaron; Fire!!; Grimké, Angelina Weld; Hughes, Langston; Johnson, Charles Spurgeon; Locke, Alain; Messenger, The; New Negro; New Negro Movement; Opportunity

Further Reading

"Lewis Grandison Alexander." In *Black American Writers Past and Present: A Biographical Dictionary*, ed. Theresa Gunnels Rush, Carol Fairbanks Myers, and Esther Spring Arata. Metuchen, N.J.: Scarecrow, 1975.
Carolina Magazine, 57(7), 1927, pp. 1–39; 58(7), 1928, pp. 1–4; 59(7), 1929, pp. 1–4, 44.
Carolina Magazine, Literary Supplement to the *Daily Tar Heel*, 1(12), 1930, pp. 1, 2, 1–35.
North Carolina University Magazine, 1(1), 1844, pp. 1–5.

Césaire, Aimé

Aimé Césaire was among the most illustrious Caribbean writers and statesmen of the twentieth century. In his youth he was both an acute observer of France's colonial legacy in his native Martinique, and the beneficiary of an extensive education, there and later in Paris, in the French and classical humanities. These experiences enabled him to become an active participant in French literary and civic traditions and at the same time a powerful spokesman for those traditionally excluded from such traditions. He is best known for his French lyric and dramatic poetry, although he also wrote influential essays on literary, historical, and political subjects. He played an important role in the electoral politics of Martinique for almost fifty years, before retiring from public service in 1993.

In 1939, Césaire published the first version of what would become his most famous work, the extended poem *Cahier d'un retour au pays natal* (*Notebook of a Return to the Native Land*), revisions of which were later published in book form. In this poem, Césaire brings vividly to life his narrator's complex experience of being black in French-controlled Martinique and also expounds the broader concept of *négritude*. This elusive term, which Césaire himself coined, would take on disparate meanings among those who came to be associated with the *négritude* movement instigated by Césaire and his fellow poets Léopold Senghor and Léon Damas. The three had met during their student days and had helped launch two short-lived pan-Africanist magazines: *Légitime Défense* and *L'Etudiant Noir*. The proponents of *négritude* wanted to revolutionize widespread concepts of black identity; they asserted the beauty of their African heritage and the creative potential of blacks united by ancestry and shared suffering. Senghor and Césaire were particularly influenced in the late 1930s by the German ethnographer Leo Frobenius's *Histoire de la civilisation africaine*. Frobenius celebrated African artistry and attributed it to an "African essence" in all black culture. Frobenius's Africanism broke away from widespread European assumptions that Africa was a cultural void; but his ascription of a shared essence to a diverse black population, along with the *négritude* poets' glorification of that concept, has since led many African and African American critics to reject *négritude* in favor of a multicultural approach.

In 1941, Césaire cofounded *Tropiques*, a journal of poetry and criticism, largely surrealist and directed at promoting *négritude* (as opposed to assimilation into white French culture) among black and mulatto Martinicans. The journal initially focused on the arts but then became increasingly political. In an early issue, Césaire wrote an homage to the poets of the Harlem Renaissance, who had inspired him as he developed his concept of *négritude*. In this essay, "Introduction à la poèsie nègre américaine" ("Introduction to Negro-American Poetry"), Césaire introduced French versions of poetry by James Weldon Johnson, Jean

Toomer, and Claude McKay and praised what he took to be its revelation and celebration of the innate imagination, emotionalism, and spirituality of all blacks, and of their racial and historical bonds. Césaire had admired the writers of the Harlem Renaissance at least since his second year as a student at the École Normale Supérieure, where he earned his diploma by writing a thesis (no longer extant), "Le thème du sud dans la poésie négro-américaine des États-Unis" ("The Theme of the South in the Negro-American Poetry of the United States"). Césaire especially admired McKay's novel *Banjo*, which urged blacks to resist assimilation, reclaim their lost folk traditions, and preserve their "primitive" kinship with nature.

Despite his affinity with the Harlem Renaissance writers' notions of black identity, Césaire had a strong European orientation and wrote poetry in a style very different from theirs. He inherited the French modernist poetics of Baudelaire, Mallarmé, Lautréamont, Rimbaud, and the symbolists and surrealists but extended these poets' formal and thematic innovations to new subjects. Césaire's poetry—skeptical of realism and rationality—is densely, often esoterically figurative and allusive; it frequently violates standard French syntax and is full of outlandish, logically irreconcilable juxtapositions of images and meanings. Césaire also shares the modernist concern with alienation, social and cultural upheaval, anticolonialism, and primitivism, but he transforms these themes by introducing the perspective of those who are socially and culturally repressed. In Césaire's view, this perspective is unique to the disempowered African diaspora. Another European thinker who influenced Césaire was Nietzsche. Césaire's repeated representation of a hero's voluntary self-sacrifice on behalf of the community is reminiscent of Dionysus's sacrifice in Nietzsche's *The Birth of Tragedy*, and Césaire's mythic images and allusions suggest Nietzsche's vision of history as cyclical. Arnold (1981) argues that Césaire often depicts heroes, fictional and historical, who surrender their personal well-being for the benefit of the group. For instance, Césaire was impressed by a seven-month lecture tour in Haiti in 1945, and he later wrote works inspired by the Haitian heroes Henri Christophe and Toussaint Louverture.

In 1945, Césaire unexpectedly won the mayoralty of Fort-de-France on the Communist Party ticket. Later that year he was elected to represent Martinique as a *député* in the French Assemblée Nationale. Despite his change of party affiliation thirteen years later, he retained these positions until he retired from politics just before his eightieth birthday. In 1946, his draft of a proposal to the French government to make Martinique a *département* of France (the equivalent of a U.S. state), was passed into law. Césaire received bitter criticism from the next generation of Martinican activists, who believed that he should have sought independence for the island.

With *Les armes miraculeuses* (*Miraculous Weapons*, 1946) and *Soleil cou coupé* (*Sun Cut Throat*, 1948), Césaire established his reputation in francophone avant-garde circles as a foremost surrealist poet; moreover, he was supported by leading francophone intellectuals, including the founder of surrealism, André Breton, whom he had met in Fort-de-France in 1941 and who wrote a laudatory essay about him, "Un grand poète noir" ("A Great Black Poet"). In 1949, Césaire collaborated with Pablo Picasso on a limited edition of *Corps perdu* (*Lost Body*). Earlier, in 1947, Césaire and Jean-Paul Sartre had helped found the publishing house Présence Africaine, which ever since has distributed a periodical of the same name as well as books pertinent to black studies, and has printed many of Césaire's writings. In 1956, Césaire attended the First International Congress of Negro Artists and Writers in Paris and delivered a paper—"Culture et colonization" ("Culture and Colonization")—that was more measured in tone than his well-known earlier polemic *Discours sur le colonialisme* (*Discourse on Colonialism*) but nevertheless controversial. For years Césaire's concept of *négritude* had been evolving differently from Senghor's, and in this paper he attempted to give it a historical grounding so as to challenge Senghor's essentialist vision. In the 1960s, Césaire continued his critique of colonial repression and exploitation in the more broadly accessible form of biography (*Toussaint Louverture*) and drama: *La tragédie du Roi Christophe* (*The Tragedy of King Christophe*), *Une saison au Congo* (*A Season in the Congo*), and *Une tempête* (*A Tempest*, a reworking of Shakespeare's play.) In the 1970s, he returned to lyric poetry. In 1983, after France created regional councils in overseas departments, he became president of his local *conseil régional*.

Biography

Aimé Césaire was born 26 June 1913 in Basse-Pointe, Martinique. He studied on a scholarship at the Lycée Schoelcher in Fort-de-France and was awarded his baccalaureate with distinction in 1932; in 1931, he had won another scholarship to continue his studies at the Lycée Louis-le-Grand in Paris, and in 1935, he was admitted to the École Normale Supérieure. In 1932, he cofounded the magazine *Légitime Défense*; in 1934, he cofounded another magazine, *L'Etudiant Noir*. Césaire returned to Martinique in 1939. In 1940, he began teaching at the Lycée Schoelcher; in 1941, he cofounded *Tropiques*. In 1944, he spent seven months on a lecture tour in Haiti. He returned to Martinique, and in 1945, he was elected mayor of Fort-de-France and a deputy to the French national assembly. In 1947, Césaire helped launch the publishing house and magazine *Présence Africaine*. In 1956, he resigned from the French Communist Party; two years later, he founded the Parti Progressiste Martiniquais. In 1966, he attended a production of his already widely performed play *La tragédie du Roi Christophe* at the first Festival Mondial des Arts Nègres in Dakar, Senegal. In 1972, he gave a series of lectures at the Université Laval in Quebec. He became president of his local regional council in 1983. In 1991, *La tragédie du Roi Christophe* was performed at the Comédie-Française in Paris. Césaire remained in political office until his retirement in 1993. His awards included the Prix René Laporte for his collection of poems *Ferrements* in 1960 and the Grand Prix National de la Poésie in 1982.

MARA DE GENNARO

See also Damas, Léon; Francophone Caribbean and the Harlem Renaissance; Johnson, James Weldon; McKay, Claude; Negritude; Senghor, Léopold; Toomer, Jean

Selected Works

Cahier d'un retour au pays natal. 1939. (Rev. ed., 1947, 1956. See also *Notebook of a Return to the Native Land*, trans. Clayton Eshleman and Annette Smith, 1983; from 1956 version.)

"Introduction à la poésie nègre américaine." *Tropiques*, 2, July 1941.

"Poésie et connaissance." *Tropiques*, 12, January 1945. (See also "Poetry and Knowledge," trans. A. James Arnold. In *Lyric and Dramatic Poetry, 1946–1982*. 1990.)

Les armes miraculeuses. 1946. (Rev. ed., 1970. See also *Miraculous Weapons*, trans. Clayton Eshleman and Annette Smith, 1983.)

Et les chiens se taisaient. 1946. (Dramatic poem first published with *Les armes miraculeuses*. See also rev. ed., 1956; stage version.)

Soleil cou coupé. 1948. (See also *Solar Throat Slashed*, trans. Clayton Eshleman and Annette Smith, 1983.)

Corps perdu. 1949. (With illustrations by Pablo Picasso. See also *Lost Body*, trans. Clayton Eshleman and Annette Smith, 1983.)

Discours sur le colonialisme. 1950. (See also *Discourse on Colonialism*, trans. Joan Pinkham, 1972.)

Lettre à Maurice Thorez. 1956.

"Culture et Colonisation." *Présence Africaine*, 8–10, 1956.

"L'homme de culture noir et ses responsabilités." *Deuxième Congrès des Ecrivains et Artistes Noirs*, special issue of *Présence Africaine*, 24–25, 1959.

Ferrements. 1960. (See also *Ferraments*, trans. Clayton Eshleman and Annette Smith, 1983.)

Cadastre. 1961. (Containing rev. ed. of *Soleil cou coupé* and *Corps perdu*.)

La tragédie du Roi Christophe. 1963. (See also *The Tragedy of King Christophe*, trans. Ralph Manheim, 1969.)

Une saison au Congo. 1966. (See also *A Season in the Congo*, trans. Ralph Manheim, 1968.)

Toussaint Louverture: La révolution française et le problème colonial. 1968.

Une tempête. 1969. (See also *A Tempest*, trans. Richard Miller, 1985; rev. trans., 1992.)

Noria, trans. Clayton Eshleman and Annette Smith, 1983. (Nine poems from *Noria* were republished in *Soleil éclaté: Mélanges offerts à Aimé Césaire à l'occasion de son soixante-dixième anniversaire par une équipe internationale de chercheurs*, ed. Jacqueline Leiner. Tübingen: Gunter Narr Verlag, 1984.)

Oeuvres completes, 3 vols. 1976.

"Entretien avec Aimé Césaire," with Jacqueline Leiner. *Tropiques*, 1, 1978.

Moi, laminaire. 1982. (See also *I, Laminaria*, trans. Clayton Eshleman and Annette Smith, 1990.)

Aimé Césaire: The Collected Poetry, trans. Clayton Eshleman and Annette Smith. Berkeley: University of California Press, 1983.

Lyric and Dramatic Poetry, 1946–1982, trans. Clayton Eshleman and Annette Smith. Charlottesville: University Press of Virginia, 1990.

La poésie. 1994.

Refusal of the Shadow: Surrealism and the Caribbean, trans. Michael Richardson and Krzysztof Fijakowski. London: Verso, 1996. (Includes selected essays by Césaire.)

Further Reading

Arnold, A. James. *Modernism and Negritude: The Poetry and Poetics of Aimé Césaire*. Cambridge, Mass.: Harvard University Press, 1981.

Bailey, Marianne Wichmann. *The Ritual Theater of Aimé Césaire: Mythic Structures of the Dramatic Imagination*. Tübingen, Germany: Gunter Narr Verlag, 1992.

Breton, André. "Un grand poète noir." *Hemispheres*, 2, 1943. (Reprint, Preface. Aimé Césaire. *Cahier d'un retour au pays natal*, 2nd ed. Paris: Présence Africaine, 1947. See also "A Great Black Poet: Aimé Césaire," trans. Dale Tomich. In André Breton, *What Is Surrealism? Selected Writings*, ed. Franklin Rosemont. New York: Pathfinder, 1978.)

Condé, Maryse. *Cahier d'un retour au pays natal: Analyse critique*. Paris: Hatier, 1978.

Davis, Gregson. *Aimé Césaire*. Cambridge: Cambridge University Press, 1997.

Delas, Daniel. *Aimé Césaire*. Paris: Hachette, 1991.

Hale, Thomas. *Écrits d'Aimé Césaire: Bibliographie commentée*. Montreal: Presses de l'Université de Montréal.

Irele, Abiola. "Introduction." In *Cahier d'un retour au pays natal*. Ibadan, Nigeria: New Horn, 1994; Columbus: Ohio State University Press, 2000. (Also notes and bibliography.)

Kesteloot, Lilyan. *Les écrivains noirs de langue française: Naissance d'une litterature*. Brussels: Éditions de l'Institut de Sociologie de l'Université Libre de Bruxelles, 1963. (See also *Black Writers in French: A Literary History of Negritude*, trans. Ellen Conroy Kennedy. Washington, D.C.: Howard University Press, 1991.)

Kesteloot, Lilyan, and Barthélemy Kotchy. *Aimé Césaire: L'homme et l'oeuvre*. Paris: Présence Africaine, 1993.

Leiner, Jacqueline, Mario de Andrade, et al. *Aimé Césaire ou l'athanor d'un alchimiste: Actes du premier colloque international sur l'oeuvre littéraire d'Aimé Césaire*. Paris: Éditions Caribéennes, 1987.

Ngal, M. *Aimé Césaire: Un homme à la recherche d'une patrie*. Dakar: Nouvelles Éditions Africaines, 1975.

Ngal, M., and Martin Steins, eds. *Césaire 70*. Paris: Éditions Silex, 1984.

Sartre, Jean-Paul. "Orphée Noir." In *Anthologie de la nouvelle poésie nègre et malgache de langue française*, ed. Léopold Sédar Senghor. Paris: Presses Universitaires de France, 1948.

Scharfman, Ronnie Leah. *Engagement and the Language of the Subject in the Poetry of Aimé Césaire*. Gainesville: University of Florida Press, 1987.

Toumson, Roger, and Simonne Henry-Valmore. *Aimé Césaire: Le nègre inconsolé*. Paris: Syros, 1993.

Challenge

Challenge was a literary magazine devoted to publishing high-quality literature primarily written by African Americans during the 1930s, the Depression era. Dorothy West, its founding editor and publisher, originally intended it as a monthly, but its revenues were insufficient (owing to sparse subscriptions and advertisements), and it evolved into a literary quarterly from 1934 until its demise in 1937. West nurtured *Challenge* through six issues: Volume 1, comprising issues released in March and September 1934, May 1935, and January and June 1936; and Volume 2, the issue of April 1937. Harold Jackmann served as associate editor from May 1935 until April 1937.

From its inception, West financed and edited the magazine to "challenge" the young, relatively unknown African American voices that emerged during and after the Harlem Renaissance. She had designed it for the "New Negro Voice, which is an explanation of its title, *Challenge*." She was aware that support from educators would be valuable to her attempt to edit a literary journal during the Depression, when patronage of black literature had declined or ended, and so she anticipated that *Challenge* would be established at high schools and universities across black America, where could be found "maybe much of the talent we want to challenge." In a letter of 18 December 1933, mailed to a broad group of teachers of English nationwide who she hoped would become subscribers, West explained the significance of the magazine for new, emerging writers:

> We, who are their literary elders, challenge these unknown writers to clean competition in poetry and prose. For I do not think that we, who were the lauded New Negroes of the late nineteen-twenties, quite lived up to our promise. We can in part make up our lack of lighting the literary way of the new singers and their songs may be lustier and lovelier.

Just as *Opportunity* and *The Messenger* had been beacons of hope for the "talented tenth" during the Harlem Renaissance of the 1920s, West thought that with sufficient financial support from black educators and students, *Challenge* could represent the artistic promise of the 1930s and 1940s.

Challenge included guest editorials; short stories; special articles; book reviews; poetry; and a column, "Dear Reader," in which West restated the quarterly's intention to accept and publish only high-quality literature, pleaded for the public's continued financial support, and stressed that excellent submissions had come from notable writers whose creativity exemplified an artistic synthesis of the Harlem Renaissance and the Depression. The contributing writers included Arna

Bontemps, Frank Yerby, James Weldon Johnson, West herself (she used the pen name Mary Christopher), Harry Thacker Burleigh, Zora Neale Hurston, Claude McKay, Countee Cullen, William Attaway, Paul Robeson, Richard Bruce Nugent, and others. This is an impressive list, but *Challenge* succumbed to the economic hardships of the time, publishing its last issue in April 1937.

PEARLIE PETERS

See also Messenger, The; Opportunity; Talented Tenth; West, Dorothy; *specific writers*

Further Reading

Daniel, Walter C. "Challenge Magazine: An Experiment That Failed." *CLA Journal*, 19, June 1976, pp. 494–503.

Ferguson, Sally. "Dorothy West." In *Dictionary of Literary Biography*, 76. Detroit, Mich.: Gale Research, 1988.

Genii Guinier. *Black Women Oral History Project: Interview with Dorothy West, 6 May 1978.* Cambridge, Mass.: Schlesinger Library of Radcliffe College, 1981, pp. 1–75.

Peters, Pearlie. "The Resurgence of Dorothy West as Short-Story Writer." *Abafazi: Simmons College Review of Women of African Descent*, 8(1), Fall–Winter 1997, pp. 16–22.

Chenault, Lawrence

Lawrence Chenault, who is frequently called the "dean of black film actors," appeared in twenty-four films during the Harlem Renaissance. Chenault was born in Mount Sterling, Kentucky, in 1877, but was raised in Cincinnati, Ohio. The young Chenault developed his singing voice as a soloist at Allen Temple Church, before becoming a professional stage and screen actor in Chicago, New York, and other American cities. He had established his career by the 1910s, and was a major figure in the dynamic early years of African American performance.

Chenault began his acting career in the late nineteenth century at the Pekin Theater in Chicago, and he had steady work for six or seven seasons in the long-running play *Darkest America*, staged by A. G. Fields Company. He then joined the renowned Black Patti Troubadours. With the M. B. Curtis Minstrels, Chenault toured the United States, Australia, New Zealand, and

Hawaii, before settling in San Francisco for several years. In San Francisco, he evidently sang and acted in various venues, most notably with the comedian Ernest Hogan in the Smart Set Company. Chenault next joined the Williams and Walker company and performed in its staging of *Abyssinia*. When Anita Bush organized the Lafayette Players in 1915, Chenault was among her first leading men.

The leading stage actors—comic and dramatic—of the Harlem Renaissance, who had performed or continued to perform with the Lafayette Players, also

Poster for *The Crimson Skull*, with Lawrence Chenault. (Library of Congress.)

worked as actors in race films. Chenault was already a veteran of the stage when he made his screen debut as Herbert Lanyon in Oscar Micheaux's *The Brute* in 1920. A reviewer for the *Chicago Defender* wrote that Chenault and his costars "demonstrated that we do not have to go beyond our own Race for screen artists of ability" (Sampson 1995, 243). Later in 1920, Chenault performed in Micheaux's *Symbol of the Unconquered*. Chenault went on to a challenging triple role in a popular cowboy film, *The Crimson Skull* (Richard E. Norman, 1921). The fair-skinned Chenault played the villain in many films, notably in Micheaux's *Body and Soul* (1925), in which he was a former jail mate of a crooked preacher (played by Paul Robeson). Chenault also appeared in a race film with a temperance theme, *Ten Nights in a Bar Room* (1926), a famous collaboration with Charles Gilpin. This film enjoyed the longest continuous run of any race film of the silent era: four weeks at the Grant Theater in New York.

Race films, which were made for African American audiences, included a wide range of genres: melodramas, thrillers, musicals, comedies, and westerns. They offered black viewers images of the African American experience—including romance, urban migration, social uplift, racial violence, alcoholism, and color prejudice within the black community—that were conspicuously absent from Hollywood films. Many companies were formed to produce these films, including the Colored Players Company and Robert Levy's Reol Productions, which each financed four of Chenault's films. Chenault's association with the race film industry helped make him a leading figure of the Harlem Renaissance.

Biography

Lawrence Chenault was born in 1877 in Mount Sterling, Kentucky. He received his primary education at public schools in Cincinnati, Ohio. His credits as a performer included A. G. Fields Company, *Darkest America*; Black Patti Troubadours; M. B. Curtis Minstrels; Smart Set Company, 1905; Williams and Walker Company, *Abyssinia*, 1908; three years as a member of the Pekin Stock Company, Chicago; appearances in vaudeville as a member of the teams Allen and Chenault and Martin and Chenault; and a play, *His Honor the Barber*. He was also a member of the Lafayette Players. Chenault married Evelyn Preer in 1924.

TERRI FRANCIS

See also Bush, Anita; Chicago Defender; Gilpin, Charles; Lafayette Players; Micheaux, Oscar; Preer, Evelyn; Race Films; Robeson, Paul

Selected Works

The Brute. 1920. (Directed by Oscar Micheaux; nonextant print.)

The Symbol of the Unconquered. 1920. (Directed by Oscar Micheaux; also known as *The Symbol of the Unconquered: A Story of the Ku Klux Klan.*)

The Crimson Skull. 1921. (Norman Film Manufacturing Company; nonextant print.)

The Sport of the Gods. 1923. (Reol Productions; nonextant print.)

Birthright. 1924. (Directed by Oscar Micheaux; nonextant print.)

Body and Soul. 1925. (Directed by Oscar Micheaux.)

Ten Nights in a Barroom. 1926. (Written and directed by Roy Calnek.)

The Scar of Shame. 1927. (Directed by Frank Perugini.)

Ten Minutes to Live. 1932. (Directed by Oscar Micheaux.)

Veiled Aristocrats. 1932. (Directed by Oscar Micheaux.)

Birthright. 1939. (Directed by Oscar Micheaux.)

Further Reading

Baker, Houston. *Modernism and the Harlem Renaissance.* Chicago, Ill.: University of Chicago Press, 1987.

Bogle, Donald. *Toms, Coons, Mulattoes, Mammies, and Bucks: An Interpretive History of Blacks in American Films,* 3rd ed. New York: Continuum, 1998.

Bowser, Pearl, Jane Gaines, and Charles Musser, eds. "Oscar Micheaux and His Circle: African-American Filmmaking and Race Cinema of the Silent Era." *Twentieth Pordenone Silent Film Festival Catalogue.* Sacile: Udine, 13–20 October 2001, pp. 60–61.

Bowser, Pearl, Jane Gaines, and Charles Musser, eds. *Oscar Micheaux and His Circle: African-American Filmmaking and Race Cinema of the Silent Era.* Bloomington and Indianapolis: Indiana University Press, 2001.

Diawara, Manthia, ed. *Black American Cinema.* New York and London: Routledge, 1993.

Elsaesser, Thomas, ed. *Early Cinema: Space—Frame—Narrative.* London: British Film Institute, 1990.

Everett, Anna. *Returning the Gaze: A Genealogy of Black Film Criticism, 1909–1949.* Durham, N.C.: Duke University Press, 2001.

Gaines, Jane. "'Scar of Shame': Skin Color and Caste in Black Silent Melodrama." *Cinema Journal*, 26(4), Summer 1987, pp. 3–21.

Sampson, Henry T. *Blacks in Black and White: A Source Book on Black Films*, 2nd ed. Lanham, Md., and London: Rowman & Littlefield, 1995. (See "Review," *Chicago Defender*, 28 October 1920, p. 243.)

Stewart, Jacqueline. "Migrating to the Movies: The Emergence of Black Urban Film Culture." Ph.D. diss., University of Chicago, 2000. (Ann Arbor, Mich.: UMI, 2000.)

Chesnutt, Charles Waddell

Charles Chesnutt (1858–1932) was one of the first successful African American writers of fiction. Beginning in 1887, when he published his dialect tale "The Goophered Grapevine" in the *Atlantic Monthly*, Chesnutt had a thriving career as a writer of short stories and novels. Chesnutt's stories and novels (of which three were published in his lifetime and two very recently) deal with a variety of times, places, and circumstances, but they all address the tragically absurd ideology of race prevalent in American history, law, culture, and custom. In 1905, Chesnutt completed his final published book-length project, the novel *The Colonel's Dream* (1905), but he did not stop writing. Even as he remained engaged in African American causes, he continued to write essays, to speak out on issues of the day, to write short stories, and, during the 1920s, to complete two novels, *Paul Marchand, F.M.C.* (i.e., *Free Man of Color*; 1998) and *The Quarry* (1999), both of which were published for the first time in the late 1990s. With these two novels in print and the general critical attention devoted to Chesnutt since the early 1990s, his reputation has grown as a figure engaged with the issues of the Harlem Renaissance, not just as one of its important forefathers.

Chesnutt was born in Cleveland, Ohio, in 1858, the son of two free light-skinned African Americans from Fayetteville, North Carolina. Chesnutt's father, Andrew Jackson Chesnutt, was the son of Waddell Cade, a white slaveholder who left some of his property and land to the free mulatto children whom he fathered with his mistress, Ann Chesnutt. Charles Chesnutt was of an appearance that allowed him to "pass," and many of his characters, as they struggle with the puzzling status implied by a mixed-race background, serve to raise questions about the American system of racial classification.

After the Civil War, Chesnutt's family moved back to Fayetteville, where he went to school and then became first a teacher and later a principal. In 1878, he married Susan Perry, and they soon started a family. Chesnutt and his family moved to Cleveland in 1884 after he had tried a brief stint writing for various newspapers in New York. Chesnutt studied law in Cleveland, passed the Ohio bar in 1887, and at the same time published "The Goophered Grapevine" in the *Atlantic Monthly*, probably the most prestigious literary magazine in the United States at the time. Throughout the rest of the 1880s and 1890s, Chesnutt continued publishing stories while he also opened and ran a prosperous business as a court reporter and stenographer. In 1899, he published two collections of short stories, *The Conjure Woman* (1899) and *The Wife of His Youth and Other Stories of the Color Line* (1899). Both were well received at the time, but *The Conjure Woman*, as Brodhead (1993) writes in his introduction to the reissue of these stories, "has recently been recognized as a literary creation of remarkable interest and power. In the African American tradition this book stands out as a major literary production . . . and it helped pioneer a literary use of black vernacular culture important to many later writers." "Conjure" is a term for the African magical arts that appear in many of the stories, which are set in the South after the Civil War and feature the complex figure of Uncle Julius, an enigmatic former slave who serves as guide and servant to a carpetbagging northern couple come to cultivate grapes on a desolate former plantation. During this period Chesnutt rose to the very top echelon of elite publishing, befriending the likes of William Dean Howells, the reigning tastemaker of the day, but also writing genuinely complex and what have now proved to be lasting works of serious fiction. Between 1900 and 1905, Chesnutt published three novels; but after this effort to make a serious go of writing fiction exclusively (he closed his legal business from 1899 to 1902), he became dissatisfied with limited sales and disillusioned with the book-buying public and entered a creative hiatus. Until recently, 1905 was considered the end of Chesnutt's writing career.

Remarkably, though, beginning in 1920, Chesnutt experienced a personal creative renaissance that coincided with the Harlem Renaissance. Encouraged by the sale of two of his novels to film production companies in 1920—*The House Behind the Cedars* (1900) was actually produced by Oscar Micheaux in 1923—Chesnutt began writing again. He wrote two novels, both of which have only now been published: *Paul*

Marchand, F.M.C.; and *The Quarry*. He also wrote essays that reflect his engagement with the issues of the day.

Paul Marchand is a historical novel set in antebellum New Orleans, where its hero, Marchand, is raised as an octoroon but learns that he is actually white, the son of a prominent New Orleans family. He chooses to move to France and maintain his status for the sake of his octoroon wife and children, whom he would probably have to forsake if he stayed in New Orleans as a white man. Matthew Wilson, in his introduction to the 1998 edition, suggests a reading of *Paul Marchand* as politically meaningful even within the rapidly changing world of the 1920s: "[Chesnutt] insisted that the experiences of mixed-race people break us out of the trap of the American racial binary, and that to ignore those experiences is a damaging oversimplification of our collective history." The book was rejected by a number of publishers. Chesnutt continued his involvement in local civic causes and the National Association for the Advancement of Colored People (NAACP). He also wrote essays and lectured, as a representative of a previous but still important generation.

Chesnutt's final novel, *The Quarry*, written after he won the prestigious Spingarn Medal from the NAACP in 1928, also failed to find a publisher. In this novel, the hero, Donald Glover, raised as a light-skinned African American, learns as a young adult that he in fact is white, but he chooses to continue serving his adopted people. Dean McWilliams, in his introduction to the 1999 edition, points out that Chesnutt's novel, in contrast to James Weldon Johnson's influential *Autobiography of an Ex-Colored Man* (1927), "might well be subtitled 'The Biography of an Ex-*White* Man'" because *The Quarry* "turns the novel of passing on its head by recounting the story of a white man who decides to be colored." Chesnutt takes Donald Glover on a tour of the Harlem Renaissance as Glover attends Columbia University, cavorts in bars, hangs out with a Jewish socialist, and discusses the teachings of W. E. B. Du Bois, Booker T. Washington, and Marcus Garvey. In 1930, when Chesnutt futilely submitted the novel to Houghton Mifflin, he did show some dismay and even resentment over what he saw as the general trend in the Harlem Renaissance: "I have not dredged the sewers of the Negro underworld to find my characters and my scenes" (Chesnutt to Houghton Mifflin, 29 December 1930, quoted in Andrews 1980). Chesnutt died in 1932, but his stature as a figure of the Harlem Renaissance is only now undergoing a full exploration.

Biography

Charles Waddell Chesnutt was born 20 June 1858 in Cleveland, Ohio. He studied in a Freedman's Bureau school in Fayetteville, North Carolina, 1866–1873, and began teaching in Charlotte, North Carolina, 1873–1876. He was assistant principal and later principal of the State Colored Normal School, Fayetteville, 1877–1883. Chesnutt passed the Ohio bar examination in 1887 and opened his own business as attorney, stenographer, and court reporter in Cleveland in 1888. He wrote short stories for the *Atlantic Monthly*, 1887–1904. His first novel, *The House Behind the Cedars*, was published in 1900. He was chairman of the Committee on Colored Troops, Thirty-Fifth National Encampment of the Grand Army of the Republic, 1901; president of the Cleveland Council of Sociology, 1910; a member of the Rowfant Club, 1910; a member of the Cleveland Chamber of Commerce, 1912; and a member of the National Arts Club, 1917. Chesnutt's awards included an honorary degree from Wilberforce University, Xenia, Ohio, 1913; and the Spingarn Medal, 1928. Chesnutt died in Cleveland 15 November 1932.

JOSHUA BOAZ KOTZIN

See also Authors: 2—Fiction; Autobiography of an Ex-Colored Man, The; Micheaux, Oscar

Selected Works

Frederick Douglass. 1899.
The Conjure Woman. 1899.
The Wife of His Youth and Other Stories of the Color Line. 1899.
The House Behind the Cedars. 1900. (Reissued 1993.)
The Marrow of Tradition. 1901. (Reissued 1969.)
The Colonel's Dream. 1905. (Reissued 1977.)
The Short Fiction of Charles W. Chesnutt, ed. Sylvia Lyons Render. 1974.
Collected Stories of Charles W. Chesnutt, ed. William L. Andrews. 1992.
The Journals of Charles W. Chesnutt, ed. Richard H. Brodhead, 1993
The Conjure Woman and Other Conjure Tales, ed. Richard H. Brodhead. 1993.
Mandy Oxendine, ed. Charles Hackenberry. 1997.
To Be an Author: Letters of Charles W. Chesnutt, 1898–1905, ed. Joseph R. McElrath Jr. and Robert C. Leitz III. 1997.
Paul Marchand, F.M.C., intro. Mathew Wilson. 1998.
The Quarry, ed. and intro. Dean McWilliams. 1999.

Further Reading

Andrews, William L. *The Literary Career of Charles W. Chesnutt*. Baton Rouge: Lousiana State University Press, 1980.

Brodhead, Richard H. *Cultures of Letters: Scenes of Reading and Writing in Nineteenth-Century America*. Chicago, Ill.: University of Chicago Press, 1993.

Keller, Frances Richardson. *An American Crusade: The Life of Charles Waddell Chesnutt*. Provo, Utah: Brigham Young University Press, 1978.

Molyneaux, Sandra. "Expanding the Collective Memory: Charles W. Chesnutt's 'The Conjure Woman' Tales." In *Memory, Narrative, and Identity: New Essays in Ethnic American Literatures*, ed. Amritjit Singh, Joseph T. Skerrett Jr., and Robert E. Hogan. Boston, Mass.: Northeastern University Press, 1994.

Sundquist, Eric J. *To Wake the Nations: Race in the Making of American Literature*. Cambridge, Mass.: Harvard University Press, 1993.

Wintz, Cary D. *Black Culture and the Harlem Renaissance*. College Station, Tex.: Texas A&M University Press, 1996.

Chicago Defender

Robert S. Abbott began the *Chicago Defender* in a rented room on State Street, furnished with a card table and a borrowed chair. Abbott was a graduate of Kent College of Law in Chicago and had wanted to practice law, but he was denied admittance by the state bars of Illinois, Indiana, and Kansas. Inspired by the speeches of two militant black journalists of the time, Ida B. Wells and Frederick Douglass, Abbott switched his interest to newspapers. With twenty-five cents from his financial backers he bought paper and pencils. He arranged for the newspaper to be printed on credit. On 5 May 1905, Abbott delivered door to door in Chicago 300 papers of handbill size, which became the *Defender*'s first issue.

Abbott distributed the newspaper throughout the compact ghetto in which he lived and on which he relied for his advertising. Some 44,000 people resided within a few blocks of this part of Chicago, so his delivery route was very short. Abbott remained the newspaper's sole reporter until 1910, when he hired J. Hockley Smiley, who helped boost the *Defender*'s circulation with his own brand of sensational news coverage, resembling the "yellow journalism" of

William Randolph Hearst and Joseph Pulitzer. (In the late 1890s, Hearst and Pulitzer were competing against each other for circulation size; their battleground was the front pages of the newspapers they owned, and they tried to outdo each other in terms of lurid stories, bold headlines, and graphics.)

Abbott's *Defender* also adopted another journalistic approach, called "muckraking"—a term coined by President Theodore Roosevelt to describe investigative reporting that dug into the backgrounds of people and organizations to expose corruption. Abbott and Smiley investigated problems in their neighborhood, such as prostitution; but when investigative articles fell from prominence, they often made up "wild stories." "I tell the truth if I can get it, but if I can't get the facts, I read between the lines and tell what I know to be facts even though the reports say differently" (Hogan 1984, 49). The *Defender* became known for its detailed and salacious accounts of violent crimes and its use of large headlines printed in red; it was the first African American newspaper to depart from the more traditional journalism that simply reported accurate, straightforward news and offered editorial opinions.

Abbott's penchant for sensationalism increased sales enormously: The *Defender*'s circulation rose to a height that had never been attained by a black newspaper. "In little more than a decade, the weekly Chicago *Defender* emerged as the most important black newspaper in the nation. Its unprecedented success was such [that], with the exception of the Bible, no publication was more influential among the Negro masses" (Ottley 1955, 8). The *Defender* increased sales not only in the North but also in the South, becoming a nationally known black newspaper. African Americans who had moved North sent the *Defender* to their families and friends in the South; train conductors were asked to drop copies off at certain southern crossroads.

Moreover, the *Defender* strategically targeted southern readers—for example, by printing help-wanted ads for jobs located in the North. Job opportunities abounded in the North as a result of World War I: The government closed off European immigration, and many factory workers joined the armed forces, so large numbers of new workers were needed in northern factories. At the same time, the South was facing a boll weevil infestation of its cotton crops that made work scarce there; in addition, in order to urge southern blacks to move north, Abbott reported sensationalized stories of lynchings and violence in the South. Abbott's strategy succeeded in two ways: By the end of World War I in 1918, the sales of his newspaper were higher in the South than anywhere else; and Abbott is sometimes credited with having started a "great northern drive" in which thousands of southern blacks resettled in the North. He himself set the date as 15 May 1917. Other newspapers—the *Christian Recorder*, *New York News*, *Dallas Express*, and *New York Age*—also urged blacks to migrate North. However, as the South faced a shortage of blacks to work in the fields, southern states such as Mississippi and Arkansas enacted laws against the *Defender* particularly, suppressing its printing and distribution. The Ku Klux Klan threatened harm to anyone seen with the *Defender*; two distributors of the newspaper were killed, and many others were run out of town. But as more and more southern leaders tried to stop the *Defender*, its circulation in the South kept growing.

The *Defender*'s large profits in the North and the South gave it financial stability; it also had editorial clout that was unprecedented for a black newspaper: During World War I, the *Defender* continued its activist reporting and editorials and criticized the federal government for giving substandard treatment to black military personnel. Furthermore, its success led African Americans to consider journalism as a possible, even lucrative, career. The *Defender* nurtured a number of writers, such as Langston Hughes, who wrote a column called "Simple and Me," which discussed the general attitudes of black people.

In 1919, Abbott became the first African American to build a newspaper plant. The circulation of the *Defender* remained strong: During most of the 1920s, it was about 150,000; and according to Henri (1975), at one point it climbed to 283, 571. The actual number of people who read the *Defender* was much higher than its subscription rate, because copies of the newspaper were passed on many times.

When Abbott died in 1940, his nephew John Sengstacke became the new owner and publisher of the *Defender*. Sengstacke extended the influence of the *Defender* by building it into a group of newspapers, which grew to five editions (one was the *Indiana Defender* in Gary); the group also had two subsidiaries.

GERI ALUMIT

See also Abbott, Robert Sengstacke; Barnett, Ida B. Wells; Black Press; Great Migration and the Harlem Renaissance; Hughes, Langston; Journalists; New York Age

Masthead of the *Chicago Defender*, 18 August 1917.

Further Reading

Burns, Ben. *Nitty Gritty: A White Editor in Black Journalism*. Jackson: University Press of Mississippi, 1996.

De Santis, Christopher C., ed. *Langston Hughes and the Chicago Defender*. Urbana: University of Illinois Press, 1995.

Detweiler, Frederick G. *The Negro Press in the United States*. College Park: University of Chicago Press and McGrath, 1968, pp. 20–21.

Finkle, Lee. *Forum for Protest: The Black Press during World War II*. Cranbury, N.J.: Associated University Press, 1975.

Hemmingway, Theodore. "South Carolina." In *The Black Press in the South, 1865–1979*, ed. Henry Lewis Suggs. Westport, Conn.: Greenwood, 1983.

Henri, Florette. *Black Migration Movement North, 1900–1920*. Garden City, N.Y.: Anchor/Doubleday, 1975.

Hogan, Lawrence D. *A Black National News Service: The Associated Negro Press and Claude Barnett, 1919–1945*. Rutherford, N.J.: Fairleigh Dickinson University Press, 1984.

Metz, T. P. Lochard. "Robert S. Abbott: 'Race Leader.'" *Phylon*, 8, 1947.

Newkirk, Pamela. *Within the Veil: Black Journalists, White Media*. New York: New York University Press, 2000.

Ottley, Roi. *The Lonely Warrior: The Life and Times of Robert S. Abbott*. Chicago, Ill.: H. Regnery Co., 1955.

Pride, Armistead S., and Wilson, Clint C., II. *A History of the Black Press*. Washington, D.C.: Howard University Press, 1997.

Reddick, Dewitt C. *The Mass Media and the School Newspaper*, 2nd ed. Belmont, Calif.: Wadsworth, 1985.

Simmons, Charles A. *The African-American Press: A History of News Coverage During National Crises, With Special Reference to Four Black Newspapers, 1827–1965*. Jefferson, N.C.: McFarland, 1998.

Stevens, John D. "World War II and the Black Press." In *Perspectives of the Black Press*, ed. Henry G. La Brie III. Kennebunkport, Me.: Mercer House, 1974.

Suggs, Henry Lewis. *The Black Press in the South, 1865–1979*. Westport, Conn.: Greenwood, 1983.

Toppin, Edgar A. *A Biographical History of Blacks in America Since 1528*. New York: David McKay, 1971.

Waters, Enoch P. *American Diary: A Personal History of the Black Press*. Chicago, Ill.: Path, 1987.

Wolseley, Roland E. *The Black Press U.S.A.* Ames: Iowa State University Press, 1971.

Chocolate Dandies, The

Noble Sissle and Eubie Blake's collaboration *The Chocolate Dandies* (1923–1924, originally called *In Bamville*) helped establish black musical comedy as a force on Broadway. The show was a result of a songwriting partnership between Sissle and Blake dating back to 1916, when Sophie Tucker performed their first song, "It's All Your Fault." That same year, Sissle joined James Reese Europe's Society Dance Orchestra; he then joined Europe's 369th Infantry Regiment Band as a drum major during World War I. Sissle toured with Reese's band in France and the United States in the year after the war. After Reese was murdered by a band member, Sissle rejoined Blake, and they toured as the Dixie Duo.

Before Sissle and Blake created *The Chocolate Dandies*, they had had a smash success, *Shuffle Along* (1921). Lew Payton cowrote the book for *The Chocolate Dandies* (mainly contributing additional dialogue), and the star-studded cast included Josephine Baker, Lottie Gee, Inez Clough, Valaida Snow, and Payton himself.

Although this production was far more extravagant and expensive than its predecessor (at one point, three live horses ran a race onstage), it was not as economically successful as *Shuffle Along*. It had only six profitable weeks and closed after a much shorter run of only ninety-six performances.

The Chocolate Dandies received mixed reviews. Some critics praised it as highly as *Shuffle Along*, but others said that it pandered too much to the stale ideas and expectations of white audiences. Droves of white patrons certainly did come uptown to see *The Chocolate Dandies* and many other black shows, and Harlem sent its hits downtown to Broadway. The factors in this phenomenon are complex: White patronage increased the economic and emotional support for black musical theater, but it also contributed to a situation in which black performers were limited to stereotypical roles. Scholars have sometimes wondered what types of performance might have developed if white Americans had not been watching so closely.

The African American theater critic Theophilus Lewis thought that *The Chocolate Dandies* had a high level of sophistication and an aristocratic tone, and that it could be compared to the best of white American theater. Perhaps confirming this, some white reviewers considered the show too "ambitious" and high-minded; they evidently deplored its attempt to abandon the confining notions of what black musicals could do. In other words, they raised questions about "blackness" (a controversial term) and argued that *The Chocolate Dandies* resembled white productions too closely and lacked the expected black style. (This problem was to persist: Many comedies and revues similar in style to *Shuffle Along* succeeded, whereas nonconforming productions like *The Chocolate Dandies* were doomed.) On the other hand, certain reviewers thought that *The Chocolate Dandies* was not innovative enough. Eric Walrond, reviewing the show for *Opportunity*, said that it added nothing new to the line of black shows on Broadway since *Shuffle Along*. He found *The Chocolate Dandies* neither bad nor good but dull, tiresome, and formulaic: "For a Negro show to make a bid for Broadway all that is required, it seems, is a bevy of dancing girls, a 'harmony four,' a riot of color, and a slender plot (which is unimportant), built usually around the swindling of some poor, old, illiterate 'darky.'" Walrond concurred with those who questioned the "blackness" of the show; he thought that the play was trying to cater to the desires of jaded whites who loved black musical comedies: "Sissle and Blake doubtless forgot that there are colored people who like to see their shows. . . . It didn't seem like a colored show at all." Besides the cut-out and Charleston dance numbers, "there isn't a thing in it that cannot be duplicated by any group of white actors and actresses on the road. . . . The life of the Negro as [it] is sketchily presented in a show like this is false." According to Walrond, *The Chocolate Dandies* had omitted all the particulars of race, and he considered this omission undesirable. He noted that there was ample talent in Harlem, as well as ample material, but that it was not used in *The Chocolate Dandies*.

Despite these issues of aesthetics and style, *The Chocolate Dandies* was still an important production. For one thing, it was Josephine Baker's first major show, and Baker impressed the critics with the slapstick comedy that she had begun earlier, in her embellished role in *Shuffle Along*. This work had helped her get a leading role in *The Chocolate Dandies*, and in 1924, she was billed as "that comedy chorus girl." (However, she soon abandoned her comic style for the exotic, erotic image that made her an international sensation.)

The tenor and actor Ivan Harold Browning was the romantic lead in *The Chocolate Dandies*. Alfred "Slick" Chester performed as an actor, singer, and dancer. Inez Clough played Mrs. Hez Brown, wife of the president of the Bamville Fair. Lottie Gee played Angeline Brown from 1923 to 1924, before the show went to Broadway, when it was still titled *In Bamville*. Valaida Snow played Manda. Noble Sissle played Dobbie Hicks.

According to Eubie Blake, when the production was headed to Broadway, the producers brought in Julian Mitchell, a white dance director, to give it a "Broadway touch." Mitchell received more money and credit than Charlie Davis, the black choreographer, who did more work. This was a common story at the time; the enthusiasm for blacks' contributions to musical theater often did not translate into economic gains for the artists.

NADINE GEORGE-GRAVES

See also Baker, Josephine; Blake, Eubie; Clough, Inez; Europe, James Reese; Lewis, Theophilus; Musical Theater; Sissle, Noble; Shuffle Along; Snow, Valaida; Walrond, Eric

Further Reading

Dictionary of the Black Theatre: Broadway, Off-Broadway, and Selected Harlem Theatre. Westport, Conn.: Greenwood, 1983.

Kimball, Robert, and William Bolcom. *Reminiscing With Sissle and Blake*. New York: Viking, 1973.

Woll, Allen. *Black Musical Theatre: From Coontown to Dreamgirls*. Baton Rouge: Louisiana State University Press, 1989.

Civic Club Dinner, 1924

The Civic Club dinner, a gathering of writers and editors held in Manhattan on 21 March 1924, was the first of a number of interracial promotional events organized by Charles S. Johnson to draw attention to the young writers and artists of the Harlem Renaissance. The idea for the dinner first came up among the members of a group that called itself the Writers' Guild; it met in Harlem and included Johnson and a number of other writers. The dinner originally was conceived of as a "coming-out party" that would raise awareness of the work of African American writers; the publication of Jessie Fauset's novel *There Is Confusion* was selected as the occasion. But as Johnson began to make the arrangements, he made it clear in a letter to Alain Locke that he wanted to include as many writers as possible rather than having an event focused exclusively on Fauset.

The site of the dinner, the Civic Club, had been established in 1917 by, among others, founding members of the National Association for the Advancement of Colored People (NAACP); it was one of the few places in New York City that welcomed both black and white members. The guest list was carefully interracial: It included scores of African American writers, many of the most influential white editors and publishers of the time, and key figures in a number of important organizations, such as the NAACP, the National Urban League, and the YMCA. In total, about 110 people attended.

The attendees heard a number of speeches by editors and publishers, including Charles Johnson; Locke; Horace Liveright, whose company had published Jean Toomer's book *Cane* in 1923, as well as *There Is Confusion*; W. E. B. Du Bois, the editor of the NAACP's magazine, *Crisis*; James Weldon Johnson, who had just edited the *Book of American Negro Poetry*; and Carl Van Doren, the editor of *Century* magazine. Albert Barnes also spoke, about his collection of African art. Fauset did speak, but so did Walter White, whose novel *Fire in the Flint* had recently been accepted for publication; Countee Cullen and Gwendolyn Bennett read poems. Montgomery Gregory, the chair of the drama department at Howard University, and the poet Georgia Douglas Johnson were also recognized. Fauset ended up feeling slighted because she and her book had not received more attention.

Charles Johnson, as editor of *Opportunity* magazine, was already familiar with these writers' work, and he clearly hoped that the dinner would encourage white publishers and editors to be more welcoming of this material. That seems to have been the result. Frederick Allen, the editor of *Harper's* magazine, read Countee Cullen's poems at the dinner and promptly asked to publish them. More important, immediately after the dinner Paul Kellogg, the editor of *Survey Graphic* magazine, began plans for a special issue on Harlem. Locke, who served as master of ceremonies for the dinner, became the editor of that issue, which was published in March 1925. It proved remarkably popular, and Locke expanded its contents into the anthology *The New Negro*. The Civic Club dinner, then, was the event that led to one of the most important books of the Harlem Renaissance.

The optimism of the event and the enthusiasm of the participants for the work of African American writers contributed to the energy of the Harlem Renaissance. Furthermore, a number of the speakers articulated points that became themes of the movement. Many of them offered suggestions to the young writers or made arguments about how their work should be understood. Locke, for example, argued that the quality and content of the new literature might spark reappraisals of African Americans; Liveright encouraged writers to provide well-rounded portraits of the race; White heralded the passing of stereotypes of African Americans; and Gregory emphasized the potential for African Americans in drama. Van Doren's comments seem to have been particularly well received, for they were reprinted—along with an account of the evening and a partial list of guests—in *Opportunity*'s May 1924 issue. Van Doren praised the potential of young writers and their work, asserting that they were contributing important characteristics to American literature: emotional power, as well as "color, music, gusto, the free expression of gay or desperate moods." He also offered advice to young writers, encouraging them to strike a balance between rage and complacency, passion and humor. He acknowledged that black writers had to continue to be "propagandists," but he also argued that their work must rise above the limits of propaganda.

Reprinting Van Doren's comments in *Opportunity* brought them to a wider audience. His comments are also echoed by arguments made and advice given elsewhere by other participants in the Harlem Renaissance. His tendency to emphasize the emotional characteristics of African American literature runs through a good deal of the literary criticism of the period—but so, too, does his argument that African Americans were making important contributions to American culture. Other writers and editors also offered advice to aspiring writers and artists. Du Bois and Charles Johnson, for example, laid out artistic criteria each year as they encouraged writers and artists to submit work to the annual contests sponsored by *Crisis* and *Opportunity*.

Charles Johnson also continued the tradition of the Civic Club dinner with increasingly elaborate events to celebrate the work of *Opportunity*'s contest winners in 1925, 1926, and 1927. He used both black and white writers and editors as judges for the contests. The judging and celebrations, then, followed the pattern established for the Civic Club dinner of bringing black and white Americans together, in the interest of advancing African American literature and arts. The Civic Club dinner, in short, is one event that reveals many of the issues, criteria, and strategies that characterized the work of the following years.

ANNE CARROLL

See also Barnes, Albert C.; Bennett, Gwendolyn; Crisis, The: Literary Prizes; Cullen, Countee; Du Bois, W. E. B.; Fauset, Jessie Redmon; Johnson, Charles Spurgeon; Johnson, Georgia Douglas; Johnson, James Weldon; Kellogg, Paul U.; Liveright, Horace; Locke, Alain; New Negro, The; Opportunity Literary Contests; Survey Graphic; Van Doren, Carl; White, Walter

Further Reading

"The Debut of the Younger School of Negro Writers." *Opportunity*, May 1924, pp. 143–144.

Gilpin, Patrick J. "Charles S. Johnson: Entrepreneur of the Harlem Renaissance." In *The Harlem Renaissance Remembered*, ed. Arna Bontemps. New York: Dodd, Mead, 1972.

Hutchinson, George. *The Harlem Renaissance in Black and White.* Cambridge, Mass., and London: Belknap Press–Harvard University Press, 1995. (Paperback, 1997.)

Johnson, Charles S. "The Negro Renaissance and Its Significance." In *The New Negro Thirty Years Afterward*, ed. Rayford W. Logan, Eugene C. Holmes, and

G. Franklin Edwards. Washington, D.C.: Howard University Press, 1956, 1978.

Lewis, David Lewering. *When Harlem Was in Vogue.* New York: Knopf, 1979. (Paperback, New York and Oxford: Oxford University Press, 1989.)

Long, Richard A. "The Genesis of Locke's 'The New Negro.'" *Black World*, 25(4), 1976.

Van Notten, Eleonore. *Wallace Thurman's Harlem Renaissance.* Amsterdam and Atlanta, Ga.: Rodopi, 1994.

Van Doren, Carl. "The Younger Generation of Negro Writers." *Opportunity*, May 1924, pp. 144–145.

Civil Rights and Law

The Harlem Renaissance coincided with the push among blacks, and sympathetic whites, to reverse the downward spiral of civil rights that had been taking place since the end of Reconstruction. Civil rights during the renaissance must be understood in the context of the preceding decades.

From Reconstruction to the Renaissance

The passage of the Civil Rights Act of 1875 marked the high point of the legal protection of black people's rights until the 1960s. Between 1875 and 1915, the rights of African Americans, at the national level, steadily declined. The Harlem Renaissance would coincide with new initiatives in civil rights but would come after four decades of backtracking at the national level. With a few exceptions, blacks lost case after case in the U.S. Supreme Court during this period.

In *United States v. Reese* (1876), the Supreme Court refused to allow the prosecution of whites who prevented blacks from voting, and in so doing struck down a major portion of the Enforcement Act of 1870, which had been designed to protect the right of blacks to vote. Later that term the Court refused to allow the prosecution of whites who had murdered blacks in Louisiana, in what is known as the "Colfax massacre." This case ended any hope that the Court would uphold the Enforcement Act and other statutes designed to protect blacks from violence by whites. Two years later, in *Hull v. DeCuir* (1878), the Court struck down a Louisiana statute that had required integration in steamboats, trains, and other common carriers passing through the state. The Court found that these regulations promoting integration violated the federal commerce power. Ironically, of course, less than

twenty years later, in *Plessy v. Ferguson* (1896), the Court would find that state regulations requiring segregation did not violate the commerce clause.

In a series of cases involving blacks and juries the courts held, in *Strauder v. West Virginia* (1880), that states could not specifically prohibit blacks from serving on juries. In *Neal v. Delaware* (1881), the Supreme Court further held that the states could not indirectly prohibit blacks from serving on juries by tying jury service to some other right that was denied to blacks. However, these rare victories were undercut by the decision in *Virginia v. Rives* (1880). Here the court refused to interfere in the prosecution of two black teenagers for murder, even though no blacks had ever served on grand or petit juries in the county.

Perhaps the worst year for blacks' civil rights was 1883. In January, the Supreme Court held in *United States v. Harris* (1883) that the federal government had no jurisdiction to prosecute members of a white mob who had broken into a jail and attacked three black prisoners, murdering one of them. A few days later, in *Pace v. Alabama* (1883), the Court upheld a state prosecution of a black man for marrying a white woman, on the theory that the law punished blacks and whites equally for the crime of interracial marriage. Later that fall, in *The Civil Rights Cases* (1883), the Supreme Court struck down the Civil Rights Act of 1875, which had been designed to give blacks equal access to public accommodations such as hotels, restaurants, and theaters. The Court concluded that the Fourteenth Amendment was applicable only to "state action," and thus private individuals were free to discriminate if they wished to. In a bitter dissent Justice John Marshall Harlan noted that the business involved in the case were all state-regulated and were "affected with a public interest," and thus there was a great deal of "state action" if the Court chose to see it.

By the mid-1890s, blacks faced discrimination in almost every aspect of life. More than 90 percent of all African Americans lived in the fifteen former slave states, where segregation had become a way of life. Lynching was common enough so that all blacks feared the possibility. More than 500 blacks were lynched in the 1880s, and more than 1,000 in the 1890s. Blacks voted in substantial numbers through the 1880s, but in the two decades between 1890 and 1910 they were effectively disenfranchised in most of the South. Between 1890 and 1892, the number of black voters in Mississippi declined from more than 190,000 to about 8,000. In 1898, whites rioted in Wilmington,

North Carolina, undermining the political power base of black voters in that state. Legally elected black officials in that city were forced to flee their homes and resign their positions. In 1906, bloody riots in Atlanta preceded the virtual compete disenfranchisement of blacks in Georgia. Meanwhile, in 1896, the Supreme Court in *Plessy v. Ferguson* held that state laws requiring segregation did not violate the equal protection clause of the Fourteenth Amendment as long as the separate facilities were "equal." The age of Jim Crow not only had arrived but had been sanctified by the nation's highest court.

Between 1890 and 1910, about 200,000 blacks fled the impoverished South looking for better jobs. They also left the South because it was increasingly repressive and dangerous. Tied to economic opportunity was the chance that their children would have a better education in the North. But this migration was tiny, as some 10 million more blacks—just under 90 percent of the nation's African American population—remained segregated, brutalized, and mostly impoverished in the South.

Those few blacks who made it to the North did not find nirvana but did find somewhat better conditions. In the 1880s, most of the northeastern states, including New York, passed civil rights laws that at least on their face prohibited racial discrimination in many aspects of life. Except in a few places schools were not formally segregated. In most of the North segregated schools resulted from housing patterns, but in an age before massive ghettoization, many blacks in the North lived near whites and attended schools with them. And in the period before World War I, even where the schools were formally segregated in the North, they were a vast improvement over the South, where often there were no high schools at all for blacks. In 1897, for example, the city of Augusta, Georgia, simply closed its only black high school, claiming that it could not afford the luxury of providing such advanced education for blacks. In *Cumming v. Richmond County Board of Education* (1899), the Supreme Court refused to intervene on behalf of black parents in that city. Indeed, even where private citizens wanted to provide education for southern blacks, they faced an uphill battle. Berea College, in Kentucky, was integrated after the Civil War. But in 1904, the Kentucky legislature prohibited integrated education, and in *Berea College v. Kentucky* (1908), the Supreme Court upheld the state law. During this period the Supreme Court usually protected private property from state legislation, but when it

came to the rights of blacks, the Court had no problem allowing the state to impose its racial theories on a private college.

Changing Civil Rights: 1915–1937

In 1909, black and white advocates of civil rights organized the National Association for the Advancement of Colored People (NAACP) to fight segregation and discrimination. The organization was led by a new generation of black intellectuals and activists, most notably W. E. B. Du Bois and Ida B. Wells; white reformers, such as the socialist William English Walling and Mary White Ovington; and establishment whites with ties to the abolitionist movement. These included Oswald Garrison Villard, the grandson of William Lloyd Garrison, and Moorfield Storey, a leading attorney and former president of the American Bar Association, who had once been the secretary to Senator Charles Sumner, the author of the Civil Rights Act of 1875. The NAACP investigated lynching and lobbied—though unsuccessfully—for federal antilynching legislation. The organization also initiated legal action on a variety of fronts, with Storey acting as legal counsel.

The first success came in a voting rights case from Oklahoma. In 1910, Oklahoma adopted a literacy test for voters, but under a "grandfather clause" the law exempted from the test anyone who would have been able to vote in 1867, the year before the Fourteenth Amendment was adopted. This meant that whites did not have to take the literacy test, because any white man who had been an adult in 1867 would have been able to vote; but because blacks could not vote in 1867, they had to take the test. Black voters in Oklahoma brought suit, and in 1912, President William Howard Taft instructed the Department of Justice to intervene. When the case reached the Supreme Court, as *Guinn v. United States* (1915), Moorfield Storey argued on behalf of the NAACP, but in a huge victory for the civil rights organization, the main argument was made by Solicitor General John W. Davis. The Court unanimously struck down the Oklahoma statute as violating the civil rights of blacks. For the first time in living memory civil rights advocates had won a case in the U.S. Supreme Court.

Two years later, in *Buchanan v. Warley*, Storey persuaded the Supreme Court to strike down a Kentucky law prohibiting blacks from buying houses on streets that had a majority of white residents, and also prohibiting whites from buying houses on streets that had a majority of black residents. The goal of the statute was to gradually create fully segregated neighborhoods. The Court rejected the idea that this was "separate but equal" under the precedent in *Plessy v. Furgeson*, and instead saw it as an unconstitutional infringement on the right of property owners to sell their property to whomever they wished. This was the first time that the Court had struck down a law mandating racial segregation. But what the state could not do, private parties could do. In *Corrigan v. Buckley* (1926), the Court upheld a restriction in deeds that prohibited the sale of land to blacks. In one area of Washington, D.C., some thirty parcels of land had restrictive covenants, prohibiting anyone in the area from selling land to blacks for twenty-one years. When Corrigan sold her house to a black, Buckley sued under the covenants, which he claimed were contracts binding on all landowners in the area. The Court rejected arguments that the covenants violated the Thirteenth and Fourteenth Amendments, and as it had in the *Civil Rights Cases*, concluded that private discrimination was constitutionally permissible.

In *Nixon v. Herndon* (1927), the Supreme Court struck down a Texas law that prohibited blacks from voting in primary elections. Because at the time winners of the Democratic primary were virtually assured of winning the state offices they sought, the "white primary" effectively barred blacks from meaningful political participation in the state. Texas responded by passing legislation allowing the parties to set their own rules for participation in the primary, and not surprisingly, the Democratic Party barred blacks. In *Nixon v. Condon* (1932), the Supreme Court struck down this scheme, noting that the state could not delegate to the party what it could not do itself. Texas then withdrew entirely from the process of running primary elections and left the parties free to choose candidates however they wished. In *Grovey v. Townsend* (1935), the Court concluded that the parties were "private" and that no "state action" was involved. Thus once again the primary became an all-white affair. Finally, in *Smith v. Allwright* (1944), the Court ruled that the parties were not "private" for purposes of running primaries, and that any discrimination in voting was unconstitutional.

Civil rights were also tied to criminal justice. In *Moore v. Dempsey* (1923), Storey and the NAACP persuaded the Supreme Court to reverse the convictions of blacks charged with murder for defending themselves during a race riot in Arkansas in 1919. In 1925, the NAACP teamed up with Clarence Darrow and

Arthur Garfield Hayes to successfully defend Ossian Sweet, a black physician charged with murder after he shot at a mob that attacked his home in Detroit, Michigan. These cases gave blacks some sense of fair justice. In the famous Scottsboro case, nine black boys were accused of raping two white girls. The story was entirely fabricated—there had been no rape or even consensual sex between the black youths and the two girls. But the accusations led to trials and convictions for all the defendants. In *Powell v. Alabama* (1932), the Supreme Court reversed a conviction in the case on the ground that the defendant was not properly represented by counsel. In *Norris v. Alabama* (1935), the Court reversed another conviction because no blacks had ever been in the jury pool in the county where the trial took place. These cases were brought to the Court by the International Labor Defense (ILD), which was affiliated with the Communist Party. The *Norris* case was a victory for civil rights because a unanimous court recognized that de facto discrimination—simply not putting blacks in the jury pool—violated the Fourteenth Amendment as much as a statute banning blacks from juries. After both cases the defendants were retried and convicted; officials in Alabama put blacks in the jury pool, but then never called them. Ultimately, however, all the defendants either were pardoned or escaped to the North, where they remained free. In *Brown v. Mississippi* (1936), the Court overturned the conviction of blacks based on confessions they made after they had been tortured and threatened with being lynched. This was another small step in the recognition that civil rights should be tied to a fair administration of justice.

During the 1920s and 1930s, there were no successful civil right initiatives at the national level. Antilynching legislation regularly died in committees or with the threat of filibusters in the Senate. Even without legislation during this period, however, the number of actual lynchings began to decline. The investigations of lynching by the NAACP put some public pressure on communities to try to avoid it. The fact that there was no lynching after the alleged rapes in the Scottsboro incident suggests that the NAACP and other civil rights organizations had won a cultural, if not a legal, victory in this area. However, a spate of race riots during and after World War I in the North and the South reminded blacks and their white allies that race and racial discrimination were not solely a southern problem. Hundreds of blacks died across the country in riots in Chicago, East St. Louis, Knoxville, Omaha, Houston, and Tulsa. Justice was rarely served in the aftermath of these attacks on black communities. Perhaps the best blacks could hope for was what happened after the riots in Elaine (Arkansas) and Tulsa (Oklahoma). In Arkansas, twelve blacks were sentenced to death and more than sixty to prison terms, but the convictions were all reversed after the decision in *Moore v. Dempsey* (1923). After the riot in Tulsa, the city attempted to use new zoning regulations to prevent blacks from rebuilding on the land they owned in the burned-out North side of the city. A local attorney, Buck C. Franklin, prevented this by convincing a trial court that it would effectively take property away without just compensation. During World War II the executive branch would initiate some fair employment practices as executive orders, but by and large, the era was one that offered little for blacks at the national level. The victories in the Supreme Court pointed toward the future but did little at the time except offer hope to blacks struggling against legalized inequality.

Illustrative of this is *Missouri ex rel. Gaines v. Canada* (1938). Lloyd Gaines, a black citizen of Missouri, applied to attend law school at the University of Missouri. The state offered to pay his tuition at state law schools in neighboring Illinois or Iowa, which were not segregated, but Gaines insisted on his right to attend a state-supported law school in his home state. The Supreme Court agreed and ordered Missouri to admit Gaines. However, Gaines disappeared shortly after the decision and was never found. Some scholars believe he was murdered by the Ku Klux Klan or other white terrorists; others suggest that he was too afraid to attend the law school and simply moved out of state. In the 1950s, this precedent would help lead to the desegregation of southern graduate and professional schools, but in the age of the Harlem Renaissance, it did little to change the circumstances of blacks living in the South.

Black leaders and organizations never ceased their demands for equal rights, even in the face of so few victories. A. Philip Randolph used the Brotherhood of Sleeping Car Porters—the only black-dominated union in the country—to push for greater rights and to threaten a mass march on Washington, D.C., in the 1930s and early 1940s. The Urban League (unlike the NAACP) did not have a litigation arm but nevertheless pushed for equality. The Socialist Party and the Communist Party also agitated for civil rights, and although these organizations were unsuccessful at the polls, they helped keep the issue on the table.

At the state level, particularly in the North, there were some more substantive victories. After 1915, blacks began to exert significant political power. In 1915, Oscar De Priest was elected to the board of aldermen in Chicago, and in 1928, he became the first black Congressman in the North. In 1934, he was succeeded by Arthur Mitchell. Similarly, in New York, Charles Roberts was elected to the board of aldermen in 1919. In 1941, Adam Clayton Powell Jr. began his long career with a seat on the New York City council, and three years later he went to Congress. Thus in the North voting rights and civil rights began to have a substantive meaning. By the end of the Harlem Renaissance, blacks held office in Ohio, Illinois, New York, Pennsylvania, and other northeastern and midwestern states. Blacks in these states fought for fair housing laws and other antidiscrimination laws. In 1935, for example, Assemblyman James E. Stephens, the only black in the New York state legislature, successfully sponsored a bill to prohibit any "life insurance corporation doing business within" New York state from making "any distinction or discrimination between white persons and colored persons, wholly or partially of African descent, as to the premiums or rates charged for policies" and further prohibited "a greater premium from such colored persons." Meanwhile, some blacks in Harlem and elsewhere in the North took advantage of state laws to attend public colleges and universities and participate in professional and civil life. By the eve of World War II, a significant number of blacks in the North had obtained education and skills to lead the postwar civil rights movement. The NAACP and its powerful Legal Defense and Educational division—which would successfully challenge the legality of racial segregation after World War II—had headquarters in New York City throughout this period.

PAUL FINKELMAN

See also Antilynching Crusade; Barnett, Ida B. Wells; Brotherhood of Sleeping Car Porters; Communist Party; De Priest, Oscar; Du Bois, W. E. B.; Great Migration; Great Migration and the Harlem Renaissance; National Association for the Advancement of Colored People; National Urban League; Ovington, Mary White; Riots: 1–Overview; Riots: 3–Tulsa; Scottsboro; Villard, Oswald Garrison; *other specific individuals*

Further Reading

Fairclough, Adam. *Better Day Coming: Blacks and Equality, 1890–2000*. New York: Viking, 2001a.
———. *Teaching Equality: Black Schools in the Age of Jim Crow*. Athens: University of Georgia Press, 2001b.

Kluger, Richard. *Simple Justice: The History of Brown v. Board of Education and Black America's Struggle for Equality.* New York: Knopf, 1976.

Lewis, David Levering. *W. E. B. Du Bois: The Fight for Equality and the American Century, 1919–1963.* New York: Holt, 2000.

Murray, Pauli, ed. *States' Laws on Race and Color.* Athens: University of Georgia Press, 1997. (Reprint ed.; originally published 1951.)

Shapiro, Herbert. *White Violence and Black Response.* Amherst: University of Massachsuetts Press, 1988.

Sitkoff, Harvard. *A New Deal for Blacks: The Emergence of Civil Rights as a National Issue.* New York: Oxford University Press, 1978.

Tushnet, Mark V. *The NAACP's Legal Strategy Against Segregated Education, 1925–1950.* Chapel Hill: University of North Carolina Press, 1987.

Clef Club

The Clef Club was an organization dedicated to presenting concerts of music featuring African American performers and composers in a disciplined manner; it was most active between 1910 and the late 1920s.

The Clef Club evolved from informal meetings at the Marshall Hotel, a gathering place on West 53rd Street for musicians of the ragtime era. The club held its first meeting on 11 April 1910, gave its first concert on 11 May, and was incorporated on 21 June. Its first president, music director, and guiding light was the bandmaster James Reese Europe. Other musical luminaries connected with the club at its inception included the bandleader Dan Kildare, vice president; the composer William H. Tyers, assistant music director; the show composer Henry S. Creamer; and the bandleader and impresario C. Arthur ("Happy") Rhone. The composer Will Marion Cook was soon named second assistant conductor. At the initial concert, the songwriter Joe Jordan made the biggest impression, conducting his "That Teasing Rag."

At an early gala concert at Harlem's Manhattan Casino (20 October 1910), Europe led an orchestra of about one hundred musicians, most playing plucked string instruments. These included mandolins and banjos, plus hybrid instruments that were once common but are no longer in use today, such as bandolins (banjo-mandolins) and harp-guitars. There were also seven violins, nine cellos, and two basses. Three percussionists played trap sets and timpani. Of thirty-three pianists

then listed on the roster of the Clef Club, eleven played, conducted, and entertained on this program, sometimes en masse. Several were prominent composers who had works on the program, including Creamer, Tyers, Ford Dabney, and Al Johns. The veteran minstrel Sam Lucas was on the entertainment committee for this concert, which was followed by a dance. The concert itself, which lasted three hours, was broken up into segments conducted by different composer-performers, interspersed with specialty acts. This pattern was followed for a number of later events of the Clef Club.

Old-fashioned minstrel numbers were an important component of the Clef Club's early concerts but were definitively dropped late in 1911, in favor of a more up-to-date cabaret and show repertoire. The performances also included light classics, waltzes, marches, and some ragtime. The instrumentation of the orchestra evolved during its first years under Europe's direction: Flutes, clarinets, and a pipe organ were added in 1911, and a brass section was added by the end of that year.

The Clef Club reached its apogee with a concert at Carnegie Hall on 2 May 1912, the first event of its kind held there. This concert was a benefit for the Music Settlement School for Colored People in Harlem; it had been organized by Europe with the white musician David Mannes and was enormously successful, raising almost $5,000. A second concert was held at Carnegie Hall on 12 February 1913. This time, spirituals were added to the program, in honor of the fiftieth anniversary of the Emancipation Proclamation. The biggest hit of both concerts was Cook's lovely song "Swing Along." In November 1913, the entire 125-man orchestra went on an extensive tour of the East Coast.

Remarkably, fewer than a quarter of the Clef Club's musicians were able to read music. Instead, in rehearsals small groups would form, each around a reading musician as a nucleus, with the others catching the tune from him. Some players improvised their own approximations of the written melody. This gave the Clef Club Orchestra a unique sound, synchronized but uncommonly rich in texture.

At the end of 1913, Europe had a falling-out with some other officials of the Clef Club and left to found new organizations. Other luminaries of the Clef Club, including Ford Dabney and Will Tyers, went with Europe to found the Tempo Club. These men soon dominated social dance music in the New York area—particularly Europe, through his association with the dance team of Vernon and Irene Castle. The craze for black musicians in this era benefited the Clef Club long after Europe's departure. Nevertheless, he was asked to resume leadership when he returned to New York from France in 1919—now as bandleader of the 369th New York Regiment, the "Harlem Hellfighters"—but he declined.

Following Europe's departure, the Clef Club was led at various times by most of the prominent African American musicians of the day. Europe was initially succeeded as president by Dan Kildare, who in turn was forced out in March 1915, to be succeeded by J. Wesley ("Deacon") Johnson. The songwriter J. Tim Brymn took charge of the club's orchestra in 1914. Will Marion Cook was briefly the conductor of its orchestra and chorus in 1918, but he quit before a planned tour. On 22 April 1918, the Clef Club presented the debut of the contralto Marian Anderson at the Academy of Music in Philadelphia. Also in 1918, a Clef Club orchestra, organized by Cook and renamed the New York Syncopated Orchestra, toured the United States. In 1919, Cook went to London with this band, where they met with great acclaim. In February 1919, a gala honoring the return of the 369th Regiment featured three guest conductors: Europe, W. C. Handy, and Lieutenant Eugene Mikell. Lieutenant Tim Brymn was briefly conductor in 1919; later in that year E. Gilbert Anderson was conductor. In the early 1920s, the composer Will Tyers took the Clef Club's musicians on vaudeville tours. During the same period Eugene Mikell—who, like Europe and Tim Brymn, had been a respected bandmaster in World War I—occasionally conducted Clef Club orchestras.

In the 1920s, the Clef Club was a more loosely organized outfit, with frequent shifts in its leadership and personnel. Over the years its presidents included S. S. Weeks, Alexander Fenner, Sam Patterson, and Aubrey Brooks. Under the leadership of its third president, Deacon Johnson, it became more like an ordinary booking agency for black entertainers. Johnson was the most important figure in the club's fortunes in the 1920s; by 1927, his Apex Musical Bureau was the parent body and controlling factor in the Clef Club. For a time the Apex Bureau was headed by the ragtime pianist Hughie Woolford. In 1927, Deacon Johnson was forced out as head of the Clef Club—an awkward situation, because he still controlled such named entities as the Clef Club Singers and Players.

As the jazz age evolved, the Clef Club's associations with earlier styles made it less relevant to the more forward-looking musicians in Harlem. Nevertheless, it continued to attract the best young artists of the 1920s, including the bass-baritone Paul Robeson. The noted baritone Jules Bledsoe appeared with a small Clef Club unit in upstate New York at the end of 1925. Fletcher Henderson and his Roseland Orchestra appeared at the club's sixteenth-anniversary reception in 1926. The violinist Allie Ross conducted the club's string orchestra at a memorial service for Florence Mills in 1927.

Although the Clef Club was already in decline in the late 1920s, by then it owned its headquarters at 137 West 53rd Street. This ensured its continued existence for another three decades. Eventually, however, the building had to be sold, and the last fifteen years of the Clef Club's decline were spent at 334 West 53rd Street. The club finally folded in 1957.

Although the Clef Club as an organization never moved its headquarters to Harlem from the older black district of west midtown, as a musical institution it was of the utmost importance in the years leading up to the Harlem Renaissance.

ELLIOTT S. HURWITT

See also Bledsoe, Jules; Cook, Will Marion; Europe, James Reese; Henderson, Fletcher; Jordan, Joe; Manhattan Casino; Music; Music: Bands and Orchestras; Robeson, Paul

Further Reading

Badger, Reid. *A Life in Ragtime: A Biography of James Reese Europe.* New York: Oxford University Press, 1995.

Brooks, Tim. "Dan Kildare." *Storyville*, 1976–1977.

Clef Club clippings file. Schomburg Center for Research in Black Culture, New York Public Library.

Jenkins, Sara. "Music Night and the Clef Club Contribution." *New York Age*, 28 November 1927.

Outram, Percival. "Activities Among Union Musicians." *New York Age*, 10 December 1927.

Clough, Inez

The singer and actress Inez Clough joined John W. Isham's *Oriental America* company in 1896 and toured with the show in the United States. In April 1897, Clough and the company sailed for Great Britain to participate in Queen Victoria's jubilee; over the next twelve months, they performed in many of the cities and towns of the British Midlands, in Scotland and Wales, and on the Isle of Man. When the company disbanded in the spring of 1898, Clough settled in London; as a solo act, she was seen in all the major British music halls. In addition to those appearances, she appeared in English pantomimes, including *Little Red Riding Hood, Dick Whittington*, and *Robinson Crusoe*.

In 1902, Clough returned to New York, where she joined the Williams and Walker company. She appeared with the troupe in *In Dahomey* (1902–1904), *Abyssinia* (1906–1907), *Bandanna Land* (1908–1909), and *Mr. Lode of Koal* (1909). Clough also was a member of the Cole and Johnson Brothers company for *The Shoo-Fly Regiment* in 1907. During this time, she also appeared in concerts in New York, Philadelphia, Washington, D.C., and other eastern cities. In 1913, Clough became a charter member of the original Lafayette Players in Harlem. She appeared in many of their productions, both dramatic and musical. In 1922, she joined a road company of *Shuffle Along*; two years later, she appeared in *The Chocolate Dandies* on Broadway. In 1925, she became a member of Ida Anderson's company of players, which presented dramatic plays at the Lincoln Theater in Harlem for ten weeks. Clough retired from show business in the late 1920s.

Biography

Inez Clough was born in the 1860s or 1870s, probably in Massachusetts, where she was given voice and piano lessons. It is possible that she studied voice in Europe during the late 1880s. She lived in London from 1898 until 1902, when she returned to New York and joined the Williams and Walker company. She also appeared in concerts, was one of the original members of the Lafayette Players, and performed in dramas at the Lincoln Theater. Clough died in December 1933.

JOHN GRAZIANO

See also Chocolate Dandies, The; Lafayette Players; Lincoln Theater; Shuffle Along; Singers

Further Reading

Sampson, Henry T. *Blacks in Blackface: A Source Book on Early Black Musical Shows*. Metuchen, N.J.: Scarecrow, 1980.

Southern, Eileen. *Biographical Dictionary of Afro-American and African Musicians*. Westport, Conn.: Greenwood, 1982.

Cohen, Octavus Roy

Octavus Roy Cohen was a journalist, lawyer, novelist, short-story writer, and script writer for radio and film. He wrote more than fifty novels and collections of short stories published originally in the *Saturday Evening Post, Red Book*, and *Colliers*, among other magazines. He received writing credits for more than fifteen films and several radio programs, including *Amos 'n' Andy*. Cohen was also a playwright, best known for *Come Seven*, starring Earle Foxe, who in seventy-two performances brought the character Florian Slappey to life on Broadway in 1920. Slappey, a "sepia gentleman," leaves Alabama to make his mark in Harlem; sartorially elegant, the "Beau Brummell" of Birmingham, he survives humorous adventures in Birmingham and then in Harlem.

Cohen's stories—in which Slappey is often featured—demonstrate his handling of southern black dialect and chronicle the fast-paced Harlem night scene in the 1920s and 1930s, with its con men, rent parties, fancy women, and just plain decent folk. *Highly Colored* (1920), *Bigger and Blacker* (1925), *Florian Slappey Goes Abroad* (1928), *Lilies of the Alley* (1931), and *Florian Slappey* (1938) record Slappey's major experiences.

Epic Peters Pullman Porter (1930) is a collection of short stories exploring the comic misadventures of another character, a train car porter on the Birmingham to New York run. The stories about Epic Peters are told with dialect humor highlighting class, race, and the personal relationships an African American sleeping car porter had with train officials, fellow porters, and whites in the 1920s. *Carbon Copies* (1932), a collection of short stories set in Birmingham, features the lawyer Evans Chew, "attorney at law and orator extraordinary," and his comic interactions with Slappey and Peters, among other denizens of Darktown. These caricatures reflect an ethnic humor common during the period but considered offensive today.

Among Cohen's work with black characters is a series of short films produced by Christy Studios in Hollywood in 1929: *Melancholy Dame, Oft in the Silly Night, The Lady Fare, Music Hath Harms*, and *The Framing of the Shrew*. These films, which had a black cast, were adapted from Cohen's short stories and often starred

Spencer Williams, who also cowrote many of the scripts. The films are characterized by broad satire and stereotyped, often uncouth figures who are meant to portray African American life.

Cohen's "rogue school" mystery fiction is marked by the creation of the detective Jim Hanvey, a white "good ol' boy," who constantly plays with a gold toothpick worn on a chain around his neck and who smokes pungent, cheap little black cigars. Hanvey's ill-kept raiment and slovenly manner conceal his shrewd intelligence. Hanvey made his first appearance in the *Saturday Evening Post*, and many of these stories were collected and published: *Jim Hanvey, Detective* (1923), *Detours* (1927), and *Scrambled Yeggs* (1934). Novels featuring Hanley include *The May Day Mystery* (1929), *The Backstage Mystery* (1930), and *Star of the Earth* (1932). *The Townsend Murder Mystery* (1933) is the dialogue of a radio serial about Hanvey, essentially as broadcast on NBC, published in book form.

Cohen's hard-boiled detective fiction, exploring the tawdry underside of the South, New York, and California, includes a number of novels: *There's Always Time to Die* (also published as *I Love You Again*, 1937), *Romance in Crimson* (also published as *Murder in Season*, 1940), *Strange Honeymoon* (1939), *More Beautiful Than Murder* (1948), *A Bullet for My Love* (1950), and *Love Can Be Dangerous* (also published as: *The Intruder*, 1955). These novels rely on traditional techniques of the detective story to create a sense of realism, especially concerning civic corruption, love triangles, the nightclub crowd, and murder.

Biography

Octavus Roy Cohen, a journalist, lawyer, and writer, was born 26 June 1891 of Jewish parents in Charleston, South Carolina. He graduated in 1911 from Clemson College; he married Inez Lopez on 6 October 1914 in Bessemer, Alabama. Cohen worked as a newspaperman—for the *Birmingham Ledger* and the *Charleston News and Courier* in the south, and for the *Bayonne Times* and the *Newark Morning Star* in New Jersey—before he was admitted to the bar in South Carolina in 1913. He abandoned the practice of law in 1915 to devote himself to writing. As a writer, he produced some fifty novels and collections of short stories and worked on films and in radio. He was also a playwright; his Broadway play *Come Seven* (1920) was notable for its presentation of his

character Florian Slappey. Cohen died in Los Angeles on 6 January 1959.

JAMES E. REIBMAN

See also Amos 'n' Andy

Further Reading

Brasch, Walter M. *Black English and the Mass Media.* Amherst: University of Massachusetts Press, 1981.
DeAndrea, William L. *Encyclopedia Mysteriosa: A Comprehensive Guide to the Art of Detection in Print, Film, Radio, and Television.* New York: Prentice Hall General Reference, 1994.
"Octavus Roy Cohen (1891–1959)." University of Texas Website.
Steinbrunner, Chris, and Otto Penzler. *Encyclopedia of Mystery and Detection.* New York: McGraw-Hill, 1976.
Worth, Robert F. "Nigger Heaven and the Harlem Renaissance." *African-American Review*, 29(3), Fall 1995, pp. 461–473.

Cole, Bob

Although Bob Cole (Robert Allen Cole) died before the beginning of the Harlem Renaissance, many of his innovations paved the way for the renaissance with regard to theater. According to his cocomposer, longtime partner, and friend James Weldon Johnson, "Bob was one of the most talented and versatile Negroes ever connected with the stage. He could write a play, stage it, and play a part." Cole was committed to artistic excellence and aimed to prove that blacks were capable of competing with whites in artistic creation.

Cole, a lyrist, songwriter, vaudeville entertainer, playwright, director, producer, and stage manager, was involved in a number of historical "firsts" related to the stage. As part of Sam T. Jack's *Creole Show*, Cole took part in the first black show to break from the minstrel tradition of an all-male cast. Cole served as the show's writer and stage manager and as a member of the cast. In 1894, Cole organized the first all-black stock company, the All-Star Stock Company. In 1898, Cole and Billy Johnson's show *A Trip to Coontown* opened. This was the first all-black musical comedy: It was written, performed, administrated, and owned by blacks. For this reason, and as a very early example of the genre, it changed the nature of theater.

Cole's first big hits were products of his partnership with William "Billy" Johnson. After the success of *At Jolly Coon-ey Island*, for which they received no additional remuneration from the management, Cole and Johnson set out to use an all-black troupe and management for their next show. The result, *A Trip to Coontown*, was a turning point for Cole. After the tour of this show, Cole departed from the popular coon songs and tried to elevate the image and creativity of blacks through song lyrics. He and Johnson went their separate ways, but Cole entered a successful partnership with the brothers James Weldon Johnson and John Rosamond Johnson (who were not related Billy Johnson) that would last the remainder of his life. Under the name Cole and Johnson and later Cole and Johnson Brothers, the partnership introduced elegance and an air of sophistication to the personae of black artists, as well as to the stage. Cole and John Rosamond Johnson often traveled as a performing duo; they wore fine suits and presented a diverse repertoire, including German selections and many originals. The partnership amassed more than 150 songs composed for both blacks and whites.

Cole continued to be a trailblazer in theater as he and John Rosamond Johnson introduced a love scene in the stage show *The Shoo-Fly Regiment* (1905). Before this, there were no romantic scenes involving blacks onstage. The team's next success, *The Red Moon*, used the talented Joe Jordan, and many observers at the time considered it the best black show ever.

Cole committed himself to self-empowerment and the uplift of the black race; but episodes of mental illness forced him to retire from the stage in 1910. He died in 1911.

Biography

Robert Allen "Bob" Cole Jr. was born 1 July 1868 in Athens, Georgia. He studied piano, banjo, guitar, and cello as a child and attended public schools in Atlanta. Cole is often said to have studied at Atlanta University, but research by Thomas Riis (1985) has revealed that although Cole was an employee of the university, he never enrolled there. Cole was the organizer and manager of the All-Star Stock Company, 1894; a coorganizer of the Colored Actors Beneficial Association, 1903; and a founding member of Frogs, Inc., 1908. Cole died in New York City 2 August 1911.

EMMETT G. PRICE III

See also Johnson, James Weldon; Johnson, John Rosamond; Jordan, Joe; Musical Theater

Selected Songs

"Colored Aristocracy." 1896.

"Dem Golden Clouds." 1896.

"4–11–44." 1897. (Composed with William "Billy" Johnson.)

"My Castle on the Nile." 1901. (Composed with J. Rosamond Johnson.)

"Oh, Didn't He Ramble?" 1902. (Under the pseudonym Will Handy.)

"Under the Bamboo Tree." 1902.

The Evolution of Ragtime: A Musical Suite of Six Songs Tracing and Illustrating Negro Music. New York: Edward B. Marks, 1903. (Composed with J. Rosamond Johnson.)

Musical Theater

At Jolly Coon-ey Island: A Merry Musical Farce. 1896–1897. (Written and produced with William "Billy" Johnson.)

A Trip to Coontown. 1897–1901. (Written and produced with William "Billy" Johnson.)

The Shoo-Fly Regiment. 1905–1907. (Written and produced with J. Rosamond Johnson.)

The Red Moon. 1908–1909. (Written and produced with J. Rosamond Johnson and Joe Jordan.)

Further Reading

Cole, Bob. "The Negro and the Stage." *Colored American Magazine*, 4(3), 1902.

Dennison, Sam. *Scandalize My Name: Black Imagery in American Popular Music.* New York: Garland, 1982.

Johnson, James Weldon. *Along This Way: The Autobiography of James Weldon Johnson.* New York: Viking, 1968. (First published 1933.)

Morgan, Thomas L., and William Barlow. "Bob Cole and the Johnson Brothers." In *From Cakewalks to Concert Halls: An Illustrated History of African-American Popular Music from 1895 to 1930.* Washington, D.C.: Elliot and Clark, 1992.

Peterson, Bernard L., Jr. *Profiles of African-American Stage Performers and Theatre People, 1816–1960.* Westport, Conn.: Greenwood, 2001.

Riis, Thomas L. "Bob Cole: His Life and Legacy to Black Musical Theatre." *Black Perspective in Music*, 13(2), Fall 1985.

Saffle, Michael. "Cole, Robert Allen (Bob)." In *Center for Black Music Research, International Dictionary of Black Composers*, ed. Samuel Floyd Jr. Chicago. Ill.: Fitzroy Dearborn, 1999.

Sampson, Henry T. *Blacks in Blackface: A Source Book on Early Black Musical Shows*. Metuchen, N.J.: Scarecrow, 1980.

Southern, Eileen. "Cole, Robert Allen (Bob)." In *Biographical Dictionary of Afro-American and African Musicians*. Westport, Conn.: Greenwood, 1982.

Woll, Allen. *Black Musical Theatre: From Coontown to Dreamgirls*. Baton Rouge: Louisiana State University Press, 1989.

Color

The publication by Harper and Row of *Color*, Countee Cullen's first volume of poetry, in 1925 marked the emergence of one of the most promising young writers of the Harlem Renaissance. The same year that *Color* was published, Cullen—who was then twenty-two—graduated Phi Beta Kappa from New York University and began graduate school at Harvard. At the time, Cullen "was the most celebrated and probably the most famous black writer in America" (Early 1991, 3–4). *Color* was the first volume of poetry by an African American born in the United States to appear under the imprint of a major American publishing house since Paul Laurence Dunbar's success early in the century. Many of the poems in *Color* had previously appeared in African American magazines and in magazines edited by whites; and Cullen—a talented, educated, young author from a prominent family (he was the adopted son of an influential pastor in Harlem)—was showered with awards. *Color* was in all regards a literary event.

After an opening invocation, "To You Who Read My Books," the poems in *Color* are organized in four sections: "Color," which includes the book's most widely anthologized pieces on racial matters; "Epitaphs"; "For Love's Sake," the shortest section; and "Varia"—some of which Cullen would reuse in his later volumes. "Color" begins with the sonnet "Yet Do I Marvel," originally published in *Century*; its concluding couplet is a well-known example of Cullen's pithy writing: "Yet do I marvel at this curious thing:/To

make a poet black and bid him sing!" The poems in "Epitaphs," mostly single quatrains, reflect on death, among other subjects. The eight poems in "For Love's Sake" vary in length but are composed mostly of ballad stanzas, a verse form that Cullen liked. As its title indicates, "Varia" is eclectic in subject and form, although it includes works on many themes that characterize *Color* and Cullen's oeuvre as a whole: race, alienation, sexuality, Christianity, religious faith, suicide, and death.

The section "Color" includes several poems that were printed in the March 1925 issue of *Survey Graphic* and the expanded *New Negro* (which was published less than a year after *Color*). One of these is "Tableau," which describes two boys, one black and one white, walking unself-consciously through a hostile world. This poem counterbalances its vision of interracial camaraderie with the negative attention that the two friends attract. In contrast to the companionship depicted in "Tableau," another poem, "Incident," recounts the effect on the narrator when a white boy hurls a racist epithet at him. "Tableau" and "Incident" use different rhyme patterns, but each consists of three ballad stanzas and has added syllables to effect double rhymes in select trimeters. The concluding stanza of "Incident" has a triple rhyme. Cullen masterfully uses traditional lyric forms whose poetic order suggests a somewhat ironic relationship to the racial world he is describing.

The longest poem in *Color* is "The Shroud of Color," which was first published, to much acclaim, in H. L. Mencken's *American Mercury* in 1924; it is an extended dialogue with God. This poem is followed by "Heritage," which concludes the section "Color" and is considered by many to be Cullen's finest work. *Survey Graphic* and *The New Negro* both printed another version of "Heritage," differing from the poem in *Color* in organization, length, and dedication. The version in *Color*, however, is the standard text. It is twenty-six lines longer than the alternative version and is dedicated to Harold Jackman. This poem turns on the repeated query *"What is Africa to me?"*—a question that resonated with writers such as Nella Larsen, who used lines from "Heritage" as the epigraph for her novel *Passing* (1929), and W. E. B. Du Bois, who used it as a point of departure in *Dusk of Dawn* (1940).

There has been some scholarly debate over "Heritage," illustrating the uncertainty that surrounds Cullen's legacy. Huggins (1971) considers Cullen's imaginary Africa "romantic and exotic, no more or no less real for him as a black poet than it would have been for a white one" (81). Davis (1953), on the other hand, describes this Africa as a "means of escape . . . a dream world if you will, of past loveliness," in the face of the actual world of Jim Crow (393). Redding (1939/1988), whose title *To Make a Poet Black* was taken from "Yet Do I Marvel," like Huggins, is unimpressed by Cullen's poems about Africa, concluding that Cullen's "gifts are delicate, better suited to *bons mots*, epigrams, and the delightfully personal love lyrics for which a large circle admire him" (111).

The section "Epitaphs" certainly includes the epigrams that Redding (1939/1988) notes, but it also incorporates Cullen's social commentary. For example, "For a Lady I Know," which appeared in *Poetry* in May 1924, describes a woman who imagines that the racial order of domestic service in the United States is consistent with heaven's design. This section also contains a series of literary tributes to Joseph Conrad, Paul Laurence Dunbar, and John Keats, all of which first appeared in *Harper's*, in February 1925.

"Varia" includes a second piece for Keats, "To John Keats, Poet. At Spring Time," which Cullen uses to reflect on his own relationship to the craft of poetry. Writers are not the only figures honored in Cullen's poetry. For instance, the poem "In Memory of Col. Charles Young," also in "Varia," remembers an African American in World War I who was discharged to prevent his imminent promotion to general.

Color stands out among Cullen's oeuvre and contains many of his most popular poems: for instance, seven of the eight poems in the *Norton Anthology of African American Literature* appeared in *Color*. Still, many critics find in *Color* evidence of the potential that was left unfulfilled in Cullen's later work.

At the time of this writing, *Color* was out of print— as was *My Soul's High Song: The Collected Writings of Countee Cullen, Voice of the Harlem Renaissance*, an anthology edited and with a substantial introduction by Early, which included most but not all of the poems in *Color*. Like its author, *Color* continues to be represented primarily by a handful of widely anthologized poems; the volume remains an underappreciated achievement by one of the most heralded poets of the Harlem Renaissance.

IRA DWORKIN

See also American Mercury; Authors: 5—Poets; Cullen, Countee; Cullen, Frederick Asbury; Du Bois, W. E. B.; Jackman, Harold; Larsen, Nella; Literature: 7—Poetry; New Negro, The; Survey Graphic

Further Reading

Baker, Houston A., Jr. *The Many-Colored Coat of Dreams: The Poetry of Countee Cullen*. Detroit, Mich.: Broadside, 1974. (Reprinted in *Afro-American Poetics: Revisions of Harlem and the Black Aesthetic*. Madison: University of Wisconsin Press, 1988, pp. 45–87.)

Davis, Arthur P. "The Alien-and-Exile Theme in Countee Cullen's Racial Poems." *Phylon*, 14(4), December 1953, pp. 390–400.

Early, Gerald, ed. *My Soul's High Song: The Collected Writings of Countee Cullen, Voice of the Harlem Renaissance*. New York: Anchor, 1991.

Huggins, Nathan Irvin. *Harlem Renaissance*. New York: Oxford University Press, 1971.

Lomax, Michael L. "Countee Cullen: A Key to the Puzzle." In *Harlem Renaissance Reexamined*, ed. Victor A. Kramer and Robert A. Russ. Troy, N.Y.: Whitson, 1997.

Perry, Margaret. *A Bio-Bibliography of Countee P. Cullen, 1903–1946*. Westport, Conn.: Greenwood, 1971.

Powers, Peter. "'The Singing Man Who Must be Reckoned With': Private Desire and Public Responsibility in the Poetry of Countee Cullen." *African-American Review*, 34(4), 2000, pp. 661–678.

Redding, J. Saunders. *To Make a Poet Black*. Ithaca, N.Y.: Cornell University Press. 1988. (First published 1939.)

Turner, Darwin T. *In A Minor Chord: Three Afro-American Writers and Their Search for Identity*. Carbondale: Southern Illinois University Press, 1971.

Wagner, Jean. *Black Poets of the United States: From Paul Laurence Dunbar to Langston Hughes*. Urbana: University of Illinois Press, 1973. (First published 1962.)

Colored Players Film Corporation

The Colored Players Film Corporation (CPFC), which was organized in Philadelphia in 1926, complicates the issue of racial categorization. It had white founders and a predominantly white staff and technical crew, and its financing was firmly in the hands of white investors. However, it used all-black casts; it competed with the better-known film productions of Oscar Micheaux for the attention of black audiences; and its objective was to produce more "authentic," more uplifting representations of black life and to counter minstrelsy and the debasing stereotypes that were endemic in American culture. Also, during its four years of operation, CPFC produced four films that coincided with a burst of black artistic production in New York City. Thus, if the criteria for categorizing a company as "black" were social and racial content, along with significant participation by blacks in various phases of the enterprise, CPFC would indeed qualify. However, CPFC might more accurately be described as a vehicle for interracial cooperation in the arts during a period when racial animus and rigid segregation were the norm in the United States.

The white founders of CPFC—David Starkman, Louis Groner, and Roy Calnek—were joined in 1927 by Sherman Dudley, a black businessman who was a former vaudevillian. Dudley is thought to have given the fledgling company a needed infusion of cash. The films CPFC produced were *A Prince of His Race* (1926), *Ten Nights in a Barroom* (1926), *Children of Fate* (1927), and *The Scar of Shame* (1929). Only *Ten Nights in a Barroom* and *The Scar of Shame*, which lists Dudley as producer, still survive. Dudley had a grand vision of a "black Hollywood" that may have been his original motivation in joining CPFC. Nevertheless, in 1975, in an interview with the film historian Thomas Cripps, Lucia Lynn Moses, who starred in *The Scar of Shame*, said that she always took direction "from the two white fellas." She may have been referring to the director Frank Perugina and the screenwriter David Starkman, who worked together on the project.

Although it was neither written nor directed by blacks, *The Scar of Shame* has been called the most important independent black film of the silent era. In this film, as in the other films by CPFC, the plot involves the aspiring black middle class, with its lofty idealism and its hierarchy of castes based on color. *The Scar of Shame* is the story of an ill-fated marriage between a young composer and a lower-class laundress. The film suggests that the relationship between these lovers is doomed because of class differences. After a series of disastrous events befall the laundress, suicide is her only recourse. The action thus gives rise to several questions. Is the "scar of shame" lower-class origins? Is it dark skin? In the film, lower-class, dark-skinned characters are prone to drunkenness and other moral failings, an idea that most of society accepted at that time. The film therefore conveys a version of racial uplift with a hint of biological determinism.

A Prince of His Race proposes a similar division between good and bad characters, who represent types that will either lift up or tear down the race. The plot involves a man from an upstanding family who is tricked and ultimately disgraced by unscrupulous associates. After a series of episodes, including a love triangle, the story builds to a surprising climax. In *Ten Nights in a Barroom*, the renowned actor Charles Gilpin plays a man who loses his money to, and whose daughter is killed by, a gangster. Gilpin's character pursues the perpetrator but during the pursuit undergoes an awakening that leads him to a productive life as a public servant.

With such heavily moralistic melodramas, and also with technically innovative filmmaking, CPFC offered an alternative view of black life, gave black actors an opportunity to stretch their talents, and offered black audiences entertainment that would not make them feel ashamed.

AUDREY THOMAS MCCLUSKEY

See also Dudley, Sherman H.; Film; Gilpin, Charles; Micheaux, Oscar

Further Reading

Bowser, Pearl, Jane Gaines, and Charles Musser, eds. *Oscar Micheaux and His Circle.* Bloomington: Indiana University Press, 2001.
Cripps, Thomas. *Black Film as Genre.* Bloomington: Indiana University Press, 1978.
———. *Making Movies Black: The Hollywood Message Movie from World War II to the Civil Rights Era.* New York: Oxford University Press, 1993.
Gaines, Jane. "The Scar of Shame: Skin Color and Caste in Silent Melodrama." *Cinema Journal*, 26(4), Summer 1987.
Sampson, Henry T. *Blacks in Black and White: A Source Book on Black Films*, 2nd ed. Metuchen, N.J.: Scarecrow, 1995.

Columbia Phonograph Company

Columbia was founded in Washington, D.C., in 1887 as the American Graphophone Company. The Columbia label, originally a regional subsidiary, began recording African American artists early in the twentieth century. Bert Williams, the leading black entertainer from about 1900 until his death in 1922, made most of his recordings for Columbia (although he and his partner George Walker recorded for Victor at the beginning of the twentieth century); he was featured in Columbia's promotional materials and the in-house leaflets printed for its salesmen.

As the jazz age dawned, Columbia competed with Victor records, which had the wildly popular white New Orleans quintet, the Original Dixieland Jazz Band; Columbia had let this band slip through its fingers after waxing the band's first record in January 1917. By mid-1917, during the fad for vaudeville "jazz," Columbia joined a search for other jazz bands to record the frenetic new dance music. This led to a boom for black bands on records. Columbia recorded ten sides by W. C. Handy's Memphis Blues Band (actually a pickup band consisting of Chicagoans) in September 1917. These sold moderately well, as did Columbia's recordings (1918–1920) by Wilbur Sweatman, a "novelty" musician (his tricks included playing three clarinets at once).

With the success of Mamie Smith's recording of "Crazy Blues" for Okeh in 1920, there was a sudden interest in blues records by black women. Columbia made Edith Wilson's first records in 1921, and in 1923, it signed the great Bessie Smith. Smith's recordings sold well; she recorded exclusively for Columbia for a decade. Her popularity was crucial in keeping Columbia solvent during the 1920s, when the advent of broadcast radio sank many smaller record companies. Smith's rival Ethel Waters, the blues and pop singer, recorded successfully for Columbia from 1924 until well into the 1930s. Columbia's other important commercial blues singers in the 1920s included Alberta Hunter, Clara Smith, Edith Wilson, Lena Wilson, Gertrude Saunders, and Monette Moore.

Midway through the 1920s, Columbia acquired the important "race record" label Okeh. Louis Armstrong made some of the most important small-band recordings in jazz history for Okeh, including those of the legendary "Hot Five" and "Hot Seven" (1925–1927) and the extraordinary sessions with the pianist Earl Hines (1928). The fully developed jazz solo mainly began with Armstrong's records from these sessions, such as "West End Blues." Armstrong's mentor King Oliver had already recorded for Okeh in 1923; after becoming Okeh's parent in 1926, Columbia acquired Armstrong's and Oliver's earlier records and many other important recordings. Okeh continued to issue records by black artists, including the Kansas City big band of Bennie Moten, the New Orleans guitarist Lonnie Johnson, and the classic sessions (1928) of the singer Mississippi John Hurt.

Small combos of the 1920s that recorded for the Columbia label itself included Johnny Dunn's Jazz Hounds, the Get Happy Band (including Sidney Bechet), the Gulf Coast Seven, Leroy Tibbs and His Connie's Inn Orchestra, and numerous others. By the end of the 1920s, Columbia was perhaps the leading label of New Orleans jazz, with numerous recordings of Clarence Williams in New York and field recordings of Oscar "Papa" Celestin and Sam Morgan in New Orleans, in addition to Armstrong's and Oliver's sides on Okeh.

Columbia was also important in recording big bands. Fletcher Henderson, first of the great black orchestra leaders, was with Columbia between 1924 and 1932, when his arrangers included Don Redman and Benny Carter, and his soloists included Louis Armstrong, Coleman Hawkins, and Buster Bailey. Solo pianists on Columbia included Eubie Blake and Fats Waller (more commonly a Victor artist).

Many leading black artists of the big band era recorded for Columbia, the most important being Louis Armstrong and Duke Ellington. Other groups Columbia recorded during the 1930s included Harlan Lattimore and His Connie's Inn Orchestra, Claude Hopkins and His Orchestra, Dicky Wells' Shim Shammers, Chick Webb's Savoy Orchestra, and Teddy Wilson and His Orchestra. Columbia also recorded early integrated bands, such as the Benny Goodman Sextet with Lionel Hampton and Charlie Christian.

ELLIOTT S. HURWITT

See also Blues: Women Performers; *individual recording artists*

Further Reading

Albertson, Chris. *Bessie Smith*, rev. ed. New Haven, Conn.: Yale University Press, 2003. (First published 1972.)

Anon. Program notes: *The Complete Bert Williams*, Vol. 2, *The Middle Years, 1910–1918*; Vol. 3, *His Final Recordings, 1919–1922*. Archeophone 5002, 5003.

Burford, Ray. "Columbia." In *New Grove Dictionary of Music*. London: Macmillan, 2001, Vol. 6, pp. 164–165.

Hoefer, George. Program notes: *Jazz Odyssey*, Vol. 3, *The Sound of Harlem*. Columbia C3L 33, 1965.

Kernfeld, Barry, and Howard Rye. "Columbia." In *New Grove Dictionary of Jazz*, 2nd ed., ed. Barry Kernfeld. London: Macmillan, 2002, Vol. 1, 495–496.

Sanjeck, Russell, and David Sanjek. *American Popular Music Business in the Twentieth Century*. New York: Oxford University Press, 1991.

Come Along Mandy

Come Along Mandy (1924) was a musical farce and touring show from the collaboration of the brothers Salem Tutt Whitney and J. Homer Tutt and Donald

Heywood. Tutt and Whitney wrote the book and lyrics, and Heywood composed the music. The show played at the famous Lafayette Theater in Harlem from December 1923 until 1924, during a time when vaudeville, musical comedy, and movies were the most popular fare among African American theatergoers in Harlem.

Come Along Mandy is set in Hopeville, Georgia, and centers on a dispute over land between two of the characters, Zack and Sudds (played by Whitney and Tutt, respectively). As these two characters argue, Al LaBabor steals the deeds to the property. A chase ensues, and the title character, Mandy, is invited to join the others in the hunt for the thief. Other characters include Lovey Joe, a peacemaker; and Lucinda and Krispy, detectives on the trail of the thief. The comedy ends with Al LaBabor's capture in New York and the reconciliation of Zack and Sudds.

In an article in *The Messenger* magazine in February 1924, the noted African American theater critic Theophilus Lewis marveled at the presence of brown-skinned women in the chorus of *Come Along Mandy*; most chorus girls in musicals of the time were light-skinned. Lewis considered the first part of the show the most interesting and found the rest repetitious.

Whitney and Tutt were writers, producers, and performers of musical comedies, farces, and sketches. From 1908 to 1923, they managed one of the most successful black touring groups in the United States—the Smart Set Company, also known as the Southern Smart Set Company, the Smarter Set Company, and the Tutt-Whitney Musical Comedy Company. The brothers produced more than thirty musical shows. They included blackface and slapstick in their productions. Whitney was the main writer, and Tutt worked primarily as an actor. Whitney was also a columnist for two newspapers: the *Indianapolis Freeman* and the *Chicago Defender*. Later in his life, he was in the cast of Marc Connelly's play *The Green Pastures*.

Donald Heywood also wrote music for other Tutt-Whitney shows, including *Ginger Snaps* (1929), a Broadway production. He had studied music at Fisk University and had begun his career as a performer. Heywood was also a playwright, but he was most successful as a composer and lyricist, particularly in *Africana* (1927). This production had a long run and starred Ethel Waters. Heywood later wrote for all-black films.

HEATHER MARTIN

See also Chicago Defender; Green Pastures, The; Lafayette Theater; Lewis, Theophilus; Messenger, The; Musical Theater; Waters, Ethel

Further Reading

Lewis, Theophilus. "Theatre." *Messenger*, 6(2), February 1924.

Peterson, Bernard L., Jr. *Early Black American Playwrights and Dramatic Writers: A Biographical Directory and Catalog of Plays, Films, and Broadcasting Scripts.* New York: Greenwood, 1990.

———. *A Century of Musicals in Black and White: An Encyclopedia of Musical Stage Works By, About, or Involving African-Americans.* Westport, Conn.: Greenwood, 1993.

———. *The African-American Theatre Directory, 1816–1960: A Comprehensive Guide to Early Black Theatre Organizations, Companies, Theatres, and Performing Groups.* Westport, Conn.: Greenwood, 1997.

———. *Profiles of American Stage Performers and Theatre People, 1816–1960.* Westport: Conn.: Greenwood, 2001.

Sampson, Henry T. *Blacks in Blackface: A Source Book on Early Black Musical Shows.* Metuchen, N.J.: Scarecrow, 1980.

Southern, Eileen. *Biographical Dictionary of Afro-American and African Musicians.* Westport, Conn.: Greenwood, 1981.

Communist Party

Of the complex political and ideological currents that swirled around the Harlem Renaissance, or New Negro Renaissance, communism—by which is signified the official Communist Party of the Third International—constituted an important body of thought and practice, one that influenced not only the lives of the individuals drawn into its immediate orbit, but also those of countless other workers, activists, intellectuals, writers, and artists.

In the early twentieth century, Harlem had become the magnet for "an impressive group of young African American and West Indian radicals . . . who were enthusiastic about socialism and committed to the struggle for African American liberation" (Kuykendall 2002). In the heady and contentious sociopolitical climate of World War I and postwar era, these "New Negroes" were at the forefront of the sharp debates about race, class, justice, and the future of blacks in the United States that characterized the public mood of the black community. Many "New Negroes" opposed the United States' entry into the war, arguing that it was hypocritical to fight abroad for freedoms that blacks were routinely denied at home. They cast a sharp and critical eye on anticolonial struggles in the international arena, taking particular note, for example, of the Irish rebellion. With the triumph of the Russian revolution in 1917, an earlier social and political tradition of socialism in Harlem took on new life and dimensions. The debates among socialists of many stripes over whether or not to support the Russian revolution led to sharp divisions within the Socialist Party and comparable splits among radical "New Negroes." African American socialists, led by A. Philip Randolph and Chandler Owen, rejected the appeal of the communists and remained with the socialists of the Second International; others, many of them West Indians, gravitated toward the Third International. Out of this politically fluid moment emerged the African Blood Brotherhood (ABB), "the first independent socialist/communist organization composed exclusively of persons of African descent in the United States" (Kuykendall 2002). Organized sometime between 1917 and 1919 by Cyril Briggs, publisher of the magazine *Crusader*, ABB announced itself as a revolutionary secret society for people of African descent, committed to armed self-defense and the "liberation of people of African descent all over the world." Initially setting its sights on Marcus Garvey's Universal Negro Improvement Association (UNIA), ABB sought to influence the Garveyites toward its own brand of revolutionary black nationalism, but in 1921, the UNIA expelled the ABB for its political extremism. During that same year, the ABB came to public attention in the aftermath of the rioting in Tulsa, Oklahoma, when it claimed to have played a leading role in the defense of Tulsa's black community. Around this time, also, the ABB established close working relationships with the American Communist Party. By 1925, a number of the leaders of the ABB—Cyril Briggs, Richard B. Moore, Grace Campbell, Frank Crosswaith, and Otto Huiswood, among others—had joined the Communist Party, providing the party with its first leadership cadre from the black Community.

The leadership of the ABB was generally not directly involved with literary or cultural production during the New Negro or Harlem Renaissance, but like many organizations of the period—the National Association for the Advancement of Colored People (NAACP), the National Urban League, and Garveyism—the ABB devoted considerable space to literature and culture in its publication, the *Crusader*. Furthermore, it could claim as one of its own a literary light of the renaissance: Claude McKay, one of the first black writers in the United States to be associated with the Communist Party. The publication of his best-known poem, "If We Must Die," in the left-wing magazine *Liberator* in July 1919 was a direct response to the racial upheavals of the summer of 1919, effectively capturing the angry, defiant mood of the black community. The poem won the praise of the African American cultural elite as well as the admiration of the Garveyites, and it also gained McKay entrance into the radical bohemian community of Greenwich Village. At the same time, McKay was extending his relationships with other prominent black radicals in Harlem—first developed through his close relationship with a pioneering black socialist and street-corner orator, Hubert H. Harrison—most of whom were associated with the ABB. Like his politically committed friends, McKay played a central role in interpreting the outlook of the Communist Party to the black community, and vice versa. In addition to writing radical poems about American racial injustice, such as "Baptism" and "The White House," McKay sojourned in England in 1919–1920, writing numerous essays, reviews, and letters for Sylvia Pankhurst's *Workers' Dreadnought*—in effect warning his white allies that the revolutionary movement in the United States and abroad was doomed to failure unless it honestly and directly confronted the legacy of racism. McKay's general outlook during this period seemed to conform to the broad goals of the ABB. After McKay returned to the United States in 1921, he joined the editorial staff of *Liberator*; and when Max Eastman resigned as editor, McKay and Mike Gold—who became known as the cultural commissar of the Communist Party through his editorship of *New Masses* beginning in the late 1920s—were appointed as coeditors. There was personal and political tension between McKay and Gold, exacerbated by McKay's racial militancy and sharpened by Gold's alarm when he discovered that McKay was holding meetings with the African Blood Brotherhood and other Harlem radicals at the offices of *Liberator*. McKay resigned as coeditor of *Liberator* in June 1922, but his tension and squabbles with white leftists did not prevent him from traveling to the Soviet Union later that year to attend the Fourth Congress of the Third International; the high point of his journey occurred on 22 November 1922, when he joined Grigory Yevseyeivich Zinoviev, the executive director of the Communist International (Comintern), and other leaders of the party on the platform of the Bolshoi Auditorium to address the congress about racial issues in the United States. McKay remained in the Soviet Union after the conclusion of the Fourth Congress and was treated as a celebrity. He traveled extensively, met and corresponded with Leon Trotsky, and wrote poems and articles for the Soviet press. In his autobiography, he wrote of this experience as a pinnacle in his life. After his visit to the Soviet Union, McKay spent the next decade, from 1923 to 1934, living and working abroad; he returned to the United States during the worst period of the Great Depression. Politically disillusioned, socially and culturally isolated, often poverty-stricken, McKay had become a relentless critic of the American Communist Party, embracing Catholicism before his death in 1948. Nevertheless, the potent fusion of radical political sentiment and traditional poetic forms that constituted the hallmark of McKay's creativity during the period of his most intense political involvement with communism provided an example, a model that was not overlooked by some of his contemporaries during the renaissance.

Twelve years younger than Claude McKay, and more open and experimental in his use of poetic forms, Langston Hughes—by virtue of his travels, temperament, and social outlook—gave strong indications, early in his career, of receptivity to radical politics. Hughes first came to public attention when he won a prize in a literary contest sponsored by *Crisis*, the journal of the NAACP, and his work was published often in its pages, as well as in *Opportunity*, the journal of the National Urban League. However,

James W. Ford (*right*) in 1932, at the time he was nominated as the vice-presidential candidate of the Communist Party, shown with the presidential candidate, William Z. Foster. (© Bettmann/Corbis.)

he sought a venue for his more politically radical poetry in the socialist magazine *The Messenger*, edited by A. Philip Randolph and Chandler Owen, which published early poems such as "Gods," "Grant Park," "Prayer for a Winter Night," "Johannesburg Mines," "To Certain Intellectuals," and "Steel Mills." Hughes would continue to contribute poems to *The Messenger* when his friend Wallace Thurman worked on the staff in 1927. In March and April 1925, Hughes published a number of politically stinging poems in *Workers Monthly*, a communist publication: "Drama for Winter Night (Fifth Avenue)," "God to Hungry Child," "Rising Waters," "Poem to a Dead Soldier," and "Park Benching." This vein of Hughes's poetry was so pronounced that when he published his second volume of poems, *Fine Clothes to the Jew*, in 1927, George Schuyler praised him as "the poet of the modern Negro proletariat." Although Hughes never joined the Communist Party, by late 1931 he had thrown himself wholeheartedly into the struggle to save the Scottsboro Boys, nine young southern black men falsely accused of rape in Alabama and sentenced to death. In 1932, Hughes joined a group of African Americans—among them Louise Thompson, Loren Miller, Henry Lee Moon, and Ted Poston—who traveled to the Soviet Union to make a film called *Black and White* about race relations in the United States. The film project turned into a public relations fiasco, but from that point on Hughes's work would be firmly rooted in the cultural politics of the Communist Party for the rest of the decade.

Claude McKay and Langston Hughes were the two writers whose political views sometimes converged with the outlook of the Communist Party during the heyday of the 1920s. Others were also attracted to the political left, if not to the party per se. Jean Toomer flirted with socialism early in his career; and the still neglected but highly talented Eric Walrond, whose striking collection of short stories *Tropic Death* reveals a sharply developed class consciousness, routinely contributed to Randolph and Owens's *Messenger*. As the optimistic mood of the Harlem Renaissance darkened with the onset of the Great Depression in 1929—the stock market crash that, in Langston Hughes's words, "sent Negroes, white folks, and all rolling down the hill towards the Works Progress Administration"— many of the writers associated with the period began to reassess their cultural and political views. Countee Cullen, the most celebrated poet of the New Negro movement, announced his support for the presidential ticket of the American Communist Party, William Z. Foster and James Ford, in the election of 1932.

Gwendolyn Bennett, who had contributed poetry and short fiction to *Opportunity*, *The Crisis*, and *The Messenger* during the 1920s, became increasingly prominent in communist circles in New York City during the mid-1930s. Sterling Brown, whose poems had been celebrated in communist literary circles since the publication of *Southern Road* in 1932, seemed sympathetic to the party's outlook during the 1930s but never became a member. Most notably, Alain Locke, an architect of the New Negro movement, was clearly affected by the general drift toward the left of many black writers. Throughout the 1930s, Locke's annual review, "Literature of the Negro," written for *Opportunity*, revealed a distinct preference for "proletarian fiction" and literature shaped by social realism. He took an active role in the League of American Writers and the National Negro Congress, and he turned to the *New Masses* as an important venue for his writing.

If the publication of Richard Wright's manifesto "Blueprint for Negro Writing" in 1937 can be seen as signaling the emergence of another generation of "New Negroes," it can also be said that the ideas Wright explored, and the synthesis of black nationalism and Marxism he sought, had their historical antecedents in the encounter between communism and an earlier generation of black activists, intellectuals, and writers. In this encounter with Marxist orthodoxy, African American writers sometimes contested it, sometimes reworked it, and sometimes embraced it; but there is no doubt that, as a significant body of contemporary scholarship makes clear, this encounter played a central role in shaping African American literature, from the Harlem Renaissance until well into the twentieth century.

JAMES A. MILLER

See also African Blood Brotherhood; Black and White; Briggs, Cyril; Eastman, Max; Europe and the Harlem Renaissance: 5—Soviet Union; Fine Clothes to the Jew; Harrison, Hubert; Hughes, Langston; Locke, Alain; McKay, Claude; Moore, Richard B.; Owen, Chandler; Randolph, A. Philip; Riots: 2—Red Summer of 1919; Riots: 3—Tulsa, 1921; Thurman, Wallace; Toomer, Jean; Tropic Death; Universal Negro Improvement Association; Walrond, Eric; Workers' Dreadnought; Wright, Richard; *other specific individuals*

Further Reading

Berry, Faith. *Langston Hughes: Before and After Harlem.* New York: Citadel, 1992.

Cooper, Wayne. *Claude McKay: Rebel Sojourner in the Harlem Renaissance.* Baton Rouge: Louisiana State University Press, 1987.

Cruse, Harold. *The Crisis of the Negro Intellectual.* New York: Morrow, 1967.

Dawahare, Anthony. *Nationalism, Marxism, and African-American Literature Between the Wars: A New Pandora's Box.* Jackson: University Press of Mississippi, 2003.

Denning, Michael. *The Cultural Front: The Laboring of American Culture in the Twentieth Century.* London and New York: Verso, 1996. (Haymarket Series.)

Favor, Martin. *Authentic Blackness: The Folk in the New Negro Renaissance.* Durham, N.C.: Duke University Press, 1999.

Foley, Barbara. "Race and Class in Radical African-American Fiction of the Depression Years." *Nature, Society, and Thought*, 3, 1990, pp. 305–324.

———. *Spectres of 1919: Class and Nation in the Making of the New Negro.* Urbana: University of Illinois Press, 2003.

Haywood, Harry. *Black Bolshevik: Autobiography of an Afro-American Communist.* Chicago, Ill.: Liberator, 1978.

Hutchinson, Earl Ofari. *Blacks and Reds: Race and Class in Conflict, 1919–1990.* East Lansing: Michigan State University Press, 1995.

Kelley, Robin D. G. *Hammer and Hoe: Alabama Communists During the Depression.* Chapel Hill: University of North Carolina Press, 1990.

———. *Race Rebels: Culture, Politics, and the Black Working Class.* New York: Free Press, 1994.

Kuykendall, Ronald A. "African Blood Brotherhood: Independent Marxist During the Harlem Renaissance." *Western Journal of Black Studies*, 26(1), Spring 2002, pp. 16–21.

Maxwell, William. *New Negro, Old Left: African-American Writing and Communism Between the Wars.* New York: Columbia University Press, 1999.

McKay, Claude. *A Long Way Home.* New York: Arno, 1969. (First published 1937.)

———. *The Negroes in America*, ed. Alan L. McLeod, trans. (from Russian) Robert J. Winter. Port Washington, N.Y.: Kennikat, 1979.

Miller, James A. "African-American Writing of the 1930s: A Prologue." In *Radical Revisions: Rereadings 1930s Culture*, ed. Bill Mullen and Sherry Linkon. Urbana: University of Illinois Press, 1996, pp. 78–90.

Naison, Mark. *Communists in Harlem During the Depression.* New York: Grove, 1983.

Rampersad, Arnold. *The Life of Langston Hughes*, Vol. 1, 1902–1941: I, Too, Sing America.* New York: Oxford University Press, 1986.

Rampersad, Arnold, and David Roessel, eds. *The Collected Poems of Langston Hughes*. New York: Knopf, 1994.

Robinson, Cedric J. *Black Marxism: The Making of the Black Radical Tradition*. London: Zed, 1983.

Smethurst, James. *The New Red Negro: The Literary Left and African-American Poetry, 1930–1999*. New York: Oxford University Press, 1999.

Solomon, Mark. *The Cry Was Unity: Communists and African-Americans, 1917–1936*. Jackson: University Press of Mississippi, 1998.

Tillery, Tyrone. *Claude McKay: A Black Poet's Struggle for Identity*. Amherst: University of Massachusetts Press, 1992.

Wald, Alan M. *Exiles From a Future Time: The Forging of the Mid-Twentieth-Century Literary Left*. Chapel Hill: University of North Carolina Press, 2002.

Community Theater

By the mid-1920s, there were small theaters in New York, Washington, D.C., Chicago, Cleveland, and many other major American cities. The growth of these theaters, which came to be known as the "little theater" movement, can be attributed to a great extent to the larger black community theater that already existed. As Hurston (1994) noted, community theater was not restricted to the makeshift playhouses of this period; it also appeared in the form of the "jook" (a house where men and women could dance, drink, and gamble), on street corners, and in churches. Community theater, therefore, encompasses any public artistic performance; and "little theater" encompasses professional activities—including financing and the creation of infrastructure—emanating from community theater. In other words, "little theater" is not the totality of community theater but can be considered a microcosm of it.

The genealogy of little theater is important because the movement served as an idealized model for the larger community theater. During the Harlem Renaissance, theater was transformed from something that was used to mock African Americans into an endeavor in which African Americans could claim historical agency. Throughout this period, artists, thinkers, and producers tried to transform stories about black people into communal narratives: stories by and for black people. Thus theater became innovative and experimental, not just a form of resistance.

The little theater movement was part of the aesthetics of the Harlem Renaissance, was a model for communal practice, and helped define the ethos of the "New Negro" by refuting the depictions of blacks as inferior and by exposing the mechanisms that facilitated stereotypical images in minstrelsy. The movement drew attention to the fact that degrading images of black people were a source of pleasure, and to the fact that challenging such images entailed an economic struggle. Drama, unlike prose or poetry, is necessarily experienced in performance before an audience; the little theater movement illuminates the dependence of the "New Negro" ethos not only on voices willing to speak but also on ears willing to listen. This movement shifted black theatrical production from the community to a professional realm in which theater was a commodity as well as an art, and so the movement drew attention to both the product and the modes of production. Each theater company that emerged during this movement had conflicting desires: On the one hand, it wanted to define itself and control its own art; on the other hand, it wanted to attract audiences. To explore the struggle that developed when community theater adopted a public persona, this article will focus on some distinctive movements within little theater, particularly the production of *The Star of Ethiopia* (1913–1923), the Lafayette Players (1914–1928), and the Krigwa Players (1926–1927).

The little theater movement, as the professional component of community theater, suggests the material difficulties underlying the making of the Harlem Renaissance. However, these professional activities within community theater go beyond the widely accepted span of the Harlem Renaissance—from the end of World War I until the beginning of the Great Depression—because community theater includes performances and related activities, leading up to the plays, poems, and novels that usually mark the renaissance. Frequently, the term "Harlem Renaissance" refers to artistic production during the 1920s, but a study of community theater as it relates to the renaissance must consider earlier activities, both professional and nonprofessional, that resulted in the concept of the New Negro as an identity and a community.

The Star of Ethiopia

Accounts of the black little theater movement typically begin in 1912, with the Anita Bush Stock Company, later renamed the Lafayette Players. However, in 1911, W. E. B. Du Bois had already begun work on a pageant, *The Star of Ethiopia*, that would contribute to the new African

American image. This pageant was performed only four times—in New York, 1913; in Washington, D.C., 1915; in Philadelphia, 1916; and in Los Angeles, 1923—but no preceding professional performance had better expressed the ideological desire for self-definition and communal autonomy. In *The Star of Ethiopia*, Du Bois depicts the reality of the black experience in America and the contributions of African Americans to the nation; his vision of community stems from a historical narrative in which the transatlantic slave trade is part of a much longer story of the Negro race.

Du Bois's vision countered the images that then permeated the national imagination, and the stage offered him a perfect medium for conveying it. Although Du Bois praised Bert Williams's and George Walker's accomplishments on Broadway, he himself wanted to present a historical narrative that would transcend limited images such as their performances in *The Two Real Coons*. However, *The Star of Ethiopia* had 350 people in the original cast and a script that covered 10,000 years of history in six scenes; because of the sheer grandeur of the pageant, Du Bois had to cope with unusual material realties. The vastness of the staging focused the spectators' attention on the community as a whole rather than on individual actors, and the production required coordinating a community of performers.

The pageant emerged as an art form that could set American drama apart from other traditions. At the turn of the twentieth century, African Americans were trying to distance themselves from the images of minstrelsy, and American drama was trying to distinguish itself from the English tradition. *The Star of Ethiopia* contributed to both of these goals because its narrative was situated within an American narrative and because it staged and restaged communal negotiations. On 22 October 1913, at the Twelfth Regiment Armory in New York City, Du Bois presented a performance unparalleled in African American drama. He was entirely aware of the aesthetic and social possibilities involved: His pageant was an attempt to rewrite black people's role in American history, through an idealized version of the modes of aesthetic resistance that New Negroes were practicing daily in the jook, on the street corner, and in the church. As such, *The Star of Ethiopia* marked the birth of the little theater movement.

This lofty objective was attained at a considerable price. As Diamond (1997) notes, the economics of the pageant over its twelve-year history mirrored the financial struggle experienced by the black community at that time. Unlike many of the more established commercial American theaters, the little theater movement found it difficult to balance aesthetics with the material realities of the community. *The Star of Ethiopia*—a text that demanded staging—was seriously affected by a lack of material resources. At the inception of the project, Du Bois, who was the editor of *The Crisis*, the magazine of the National Association for the Advancement of Colored People (NAACP), asked the NAACP for help but was turned down. (The NAACP was unwilling to make such a large investment in an unprecedented venture.) Instead, he had to wait for an act of Congress (Senate Bill 180, passed by the Sixty-Second Congress, Second Session, 2 April 1912) to finance the pageant. This act launched Du Bois's limited career as a playwright; and the production of *The Star of Ethiopia* was a turning point for the black community because it demonstrated the economic negotiations blacks would have to undertake in order to participate in professional theater.

Anita Bush's Lafayette Players

Around 1914, a tenacious young woman named Anita Bush shifted the emphasis of the little theater movement: As the founder of what would become the Lafayette Players, she focused on finding adequate space in the black community and training members of the community to establish a commercial theater. During this period, the little theater movement faced three main issues: It needed to develop (1) finances (including paying audiences) and an infrastructure (spaces to perform), (2) professionally trained actors, and (3) scripts that would reflect the reality of the black experience in the United States. Under Bush's guidance, the Lafayette Players tackled the first two issues; the third issue was addressed by *The Crisis*, which took an interest in the development of drama.

After achieving some success as an actress, Bush had decided to create an African American theater company. In the autumn of 1914, she needed to find a rehearsal and performance space for her troupe of black players. At that time, two theaters in Harlem catered to African Americans—the Lincoln on West 135th Street and the Lafayette on 132nd Street and Seventh Avenue—but neither of these had experienced much financial success. Bush convinced the manager of the Lincoln, Eugene "Frenchy" Elmore, that she could help him get out of a slump and persuaded him to give her players a chance. He agreed, and in November 1915, the Anita Bush Stock Company (as it was then still named) opened at the Lincoln, to enthusiastic reviews; it included Bush, Charles Gilpin, Dooley Wilson, Carlotta Freeman, and Andrew Bishop. After a few weeks, the company moved to the Lafayette Theater, where it made its debut on 27 December 1915. (This change was partly because of the company's success at the Lincoln, which had induced the manager of the Lafayette, Lester Walton, to approach Bush about making the move, and partly because of a dispute between Bush and the manager who had succeeded Elmore at the Lincoln.)

The players were as successful at the Lafayette as they had been at the Lincoln, if not more so, although they also received some criticism. The criticism arose because for the most part they presented well-known, popular Broadway shows that did not focus on the black experience; but, to repeat, it did not seem to harm the players' public image. In fact, at one point the company had to perform two shows a day of *Within the Law*, a recent Broadway hit by Bayard Veiller, to accommodate the growing crowds. Thompson (1972) notes, "According to manager Elmore, the fame of the Lafayette Players at this time had spread so far that on a certain Saturday night some 1,500 people had to be turned away, many of them having come from Philadelphia to attend a performance" (218). (Elmore had followed the players when they relocated from the Lincoln to the Lafayette.) Their popularity gave the Lafayette Players scope to develop their skills; despite the complaints that they were imitating white performers rather than reflecting the black experience, they did achieve a degree of liberation and did break away from the tradition of the minstrel show to give dignified performances for large audiences. Moreover, even though they charged only five or ten cents for matinees and only ten, fifteen, or twenty-five cents for evening performances, the Lafayette Players achieved a financial success unmatched by that of any other theater company during the Harlem Renaissance; indeed, the Lafayette group demonstrated that such success was possible for African American theater.

It should be noted, though, that the Lafayette Players had to make some ideological sacrifices for the sake of their financial success. For example, in March 1916, they presented *For His Daughter's Honor*, a four-act

"race play" with Gilpin as the star, but it was not nearly as successful as some of their other productions. Under financial pressure, the players could not both produce and perform scripts; as a result, they could not really serve as an ideal model of a successful community theater for, near, and about black people—they served mainly as a model of material success.

Players' Guild, Harlem YMCA, and Krigwa Players

Many of the theater companies that developed during the Harlem Renaissance proper (between 1919 and 1928) were responding to the accusations that the Lafayette Players, in rehashing Broadway productions, failed to present theater about black life. In October 1917, the Circle for Negro War Relief was established; its New York branch was reorganized into the Players' Guild in 1919. The Players' Guild gave several performances during the 1920s at the Harlem YMCA, including one that helped Paul Robeson rise to stardom. The guild was praised for "creating an alternative to the 'cheap melodrama and the cheaper musical comedy' which dominated Harlem theatres" (Monroe 1983, 64); as a result of its success, the YMCA became a new venue for black drama. In May 1923, under the direction of a white woman named Anne Wolter, the Acme Players gave a performance at the YMCA of Frank Wilson's two short plays *A Train North* and *The Heartbreaker*. The Acme Players had developed out of a performance given in 1922 by the National Urban League at the Lafayette Theater; because of these players' success, Wolter developed the National Ethiopian Art Theater, which later became a school. Her objectives for the school included instruction in dramatic arts, dancing, music, direction, and public speaking, and—eventually—the erection of a theater building in Harlem. The Players' Guild, the Acme Players, and the school furthered the three goals of creating a black theater, cultivating black actors, and performing black drama.

Writing contests sponsored by two magazines—the NAACP's *Crisis* and *Opportunity*, a publication of the National Urban League—gave what was perhaps the strongest push in the effort to realize the ideal of a professional community theater. These contests encouraged black drama because the winning plays would at least be published and at best be produced.

After the contests by *The Crisis* and *Opportunity*, the Krigwa Players emerged as a body affiliated with the NAACP and dedicated to performing the prizewinning plays. By the summer of 1926, the Krigwa Players Little Negro Theater was organized in Harlem. Du Bois served as the chairman of the group, although he did not participate in its productions. In July 1926, he wrote: "The movement which has begun this year in Harlem, New York City, lays down four fundamental principles. The plays of a real Negro theatre must be: *About us . . . By us . . . For us . . . Near us*. Only in this way can a real folk-play movement of American Negroes be built up" (134). Because Du Bois's principles concerned the "real Negro theater," they transcended the little theater movement. Still, little theater attracted considerable attention from the black political leaders and black political and social organizations because it provided an opportunity for the world to see the potential of the New Negro community; and the Krigwa Players used these principles as their foundation.

The Krigwa Players had a performance space in the lecture room in the basement of the 135th Street Library in Harlem. (After the group became inactive in 1930, this room was used by successive companies of players; it was later renamed the Krigwa Playhouse.) The Krigwa Players' first season opened with three one-act plays by prizewinning authors of the contest sponsored by *The Crisis*: Willis Richardson's *Compromise* and *The Broken Banjo* and Ruth Gaines-Shelton's *The Church Fight*. The performances, repeated twice, attracted capacity audiences totaling approximately 600 people. Eight months later, in January 1927, the Krigwa Players opened their second season with two critically acclaimed plays by Eulalie Spence, *Her* and *Foreign Mail*. The Krigwa Players were criticized for the long gaps between their productions, but as a practical matter they could not earn a living as full-time actors—they had to work at other jobs, and so they could not commit themselves to the rigorous performance schedules of the Lafayette Players. Although ideologically they were perhaps the most powerful players' group of the Harlem Renaissance, a financial dispute would mark their end.

After a production of Spence's *Fool's Errand* in the national Little Theater Tournament in May 1927, the company won the Samuel French Prize of $200 for original playwriting. In an interview in 1973, Spence would say that Du Bois had resented *Fool's Errand* because it was not a propaganda play and had insisted that the prize money be used to offset the expense of the production (Monroe 1983, 67). The Krigwa Players were angry about his decision and, as a result, dissociated themselves from the organization. After the Krigwa Players disbanded for a time, the space in the 135th Street Library was occupied by other groups, including the Sekondi Players, who later became known as the New Negro Art Theater. Thus other organizations were able to profit from the theatrical infrastructure that the Krigwa Players established.

The little theater movement reflected the ideals of its participants only in glimpses and spurts, if at all, but the efforts to achieve these goals suggest the difficulty of achieving the New Negroes' communal identity in the context of a resistant audience and a resistant country. The little theater movement served as a testing ground for a social struggle that would persist in Harlem's community theaters even after many of the playhouses had shut their doors.

SOYICA S. DIGGS

See also Anita Bush Theater Company; Blacks in Theater; Bush, Anita; Crisis, The: Literary Prizes; Du Bois, W. E. B.; Gilpin, Charles; Krigwa Players; Lafayette Players; Lafayette Theater; Lincoln Theater; Literature: 3—Drama; Little Theater Tournament; National Ethiopian Art Theater; New Negro; 135th Street Library; Opportunity Literary Contests; Richardson, Willis; Theater; Walton, Lester; Williams, Egbert Austin "Bert"; Wilson, Frank

Further Reading

Diamond, Elin. *Unmaking Mimesis*. New York: Routledge, 1997.

Du Bois, W. E. B. "The Drama Among Black Folk." *Crisis*, 12(4), August 1916.

———. "Krigwa Players Little Negro Theatre: The Story of a Little Theatre Movement." *Crisis*, 32(3), July 1926.

Gregory, Montgomery. "The Drama of Negro Life." In *The New Negro: Voices of the Harlem Renaissance*, ed. Alain Locke. New York: Simon & Schuster, 1997.

Hill, Errol, ed. *The Theatre of Black Americans: A Collection of Critical Essays*. New York: Applause Theatre, 1987.

Hurston, Zora Neale. "Characteristics of Negro Expression." In *Within the Circle: An Anthology of African-*

American Literary Criticism From the Harlem Renaissance to the Present, ed. Angelyn Mitchell. Durham, N.C.: Duke University Press, 1994.

Krasner, David. *Resistance, Parody, and Double Consciousness in African-American Theatre, 1895–1910*. New York: St. Martin's, 1997.

———. *A Beautiful Pageant: African-American Theatre Drama and Performance in the Harlem Renaissance, 1910–1927*. New York: Palgrave Macmillan, 2002.

Monroe, John G. "A Record of the Black Theatre in New York City." Ph.D. diss., University of Texas at Austin, 1980.

———. "The Harlem Little Theatre Movement, 1920–1929." *Journal of American Culture*, 6(4), Winter 1983.

Thompson, Sister Mary Francesca. "The Lafayette Players, 1915–1932." Ph.D. diss., University of Michigan, 1972.

Walker, Ethel Pitts. "Krigwa: A Theatre by, for, and About Black People." *Theatre Journal*, 40(3), October 1988.

Walrond, Eric. "Growth of the Negro Theatre." *Theatre Magazine*, 41, October 1925.

Conjure Man Dies, The

Rudolph Fisher's *The Conjure Man Dies: A Mystery Tale of Dark Harlem* (1932) was not the first detective novel by a black author, but it was the first "black-identified" detective novel, focused entirely on African American characters and set in Harlem during the Depression era. This novel relies on elements of classic detective stories such as the locked-room mystery and the police procedural, yet it also infuses these elements with the African American vernacular, urban rituals, and contemporary social issues. The influence of the naturalist novel of the 1930s is also apparent in Fisher's use of documentary-style exposition and in the recurring topic of social determinism. Fisher, who was a popular intellectual, scientist, and artist, bestowed his own attributes as a "renaissance man" on his multitalented, complicated protagonists.

The novel opens as Bubber Brown, a former street cleaner turned detective, rushes across 130th Street to the office of Dr. John Archer and asks Archer to examine the body of N'Gana Frimbo, "Psychist." Brown explains that he had accompanied his friend Jinx Jenkins to see Frimbo for a consultation when Frimbo suddenly fell to the floor dead; Jenkins soon becomes implicated in the murder as his fingerprints are found on the weapon. On the case is Detective Perry Dart, who is described as a street-smart product of the public schools and as one of only ten black police officers in Harlem to be promoted to detective. Dart is a friend of the more intellectual Archer, and he asks Archer to assist in the investigation. The investigators find that Frimbo was an African king, a Harvard-educated philosophy student, a laboratory scientist, and a victim of American racism. While Archer occasionally questions Frimbo's sanity, the text never entirely challenges Frimbo's belief system—a provocative combination of western science and eastern mysticism.

Fisher's characters provide him with an opportunity for comic dialogue and slapstick humor even as he complicates stereotypes and educates readers unfamiliar with the ways of mysterious "dark Harlem." At Dart's request, the seemingly inept Brown efficiently locates two of Frimbo's recent visitors, a numbers runner who intended to collect Frimbo's bet and a drug addict who wanted to kill Frimbo. Others in Frimbo's office that night are also Harlem "types": a railroad porter, the attractive wife of an undertaker, and a desperate churchgoing wife. At a crucial moment, Frimbo himself turns up alive, claiming that he has indeed been dead and asking to join the investigation of his own murder, so he becomes the fourth detective on the case. But Frimbo's walleyed African butler is later found dead by Brown, who catches Frimbo in the act of disposing of the remains, and so Frimbo is also a suspect as well as a victim and an investigator. Fisher manipulates the preconceptions of his protagonists and his readers to plant several red herrings and disguise the killer's identity until the last minute, when Frimbo stages an unmasking in the style of Hercule Poirot that results in an act of violence in the style of Chester Himes.

The Conjure Man Dies was intended to be the first in a series. It was very favorably reviewed on publication, and a dramatized version was presented by the Federal Players at the Lafayette Theater in New York on 11 March 1936, starring Arthur "Dooley" Wilson as a "song-and-dance" detective. However, as of the present writing, this novel had not received the critical attention it deserves.

KIMBERLY DRAKE

See also Authors: 2–Fiction; Fisher, Rudolph; Literature: 4–Fiction; Wilson, Arthur "Dooley"

Further Reading

Bailey, Frankie Y. *Out of the Woodpile: Black Characters in Crime and Detective Fiction*. New York: Greenwood, 1991.

Bell, Bernard. *The Afro-American Novel and Its Tradition*. Amherst: University of Massachusetts Press, 1987.

Deutsch, Leonard J. "Rudolph Fisher's Unpublished Manuscripts: Description and Commentary." *Obsidian*, 6, Spring–Summer 1980.

Heglar, Charles. "Rudolph Fisher and the African-American Detective." *Armchair Detective*, 30(3), 1997.

McCluskey, John. *The City of Refuge: The Collected Stories of Rudolph Fisher*. Columbia: University of Missouri Press, 1987.

Soitos, Stephen F. *The Blues Detective: African-American Detective Fiction*. Amherst: University of Massachusetts Press, 1996.

Woods, Paula L. *Spooks, Spies, and Private Eyes: Black Mystery, Crime, and Suspense Fiction*. New York: Bantam, 1996.

Contempo

Contempo: A Review of Books and Personalities was a literary journal, or so-called little magazine, published between 1931 and 1934 in Chapel Hill, North Carolina. It was founded by a group of five young men; Milton Abernathy and Anthony J. Buttitta were the primary forces behind it. Although both Abernathy and Buttitta were students at the University of North Carolina during part of the lifetime of *Contempo*, the magazine was not officially associated with the university—a fact that university officials were quick to point out, owing to the radical positions the editors took. During its three years and forty-one issues of publication, *Contempo* developed a reputation for leftist politics and for being a first-rate little magazine that published significant writers of the era, including James Joyce, William Faulkner, Langston Hughes, Kay Boyle, Wallace Stevens, and William Carlos Williams.

The importance of *Contempo* to the Harlem Renaissance is primarily its relationship with Langston Hughes, who published four poems and one article in the magazine during 1931–1932. The article and one of the poems—"Christ in Alabama"—were published on the front page of a special issue devoted to the Scottsboro case; this issue also contained a poem by Countee Cullen. The issue had been timed to correspond with a visit by Hughes to the University of North Carolina during his speaking tour of the South in 1931. Abernathy and Buttitta were instrumental in bringing Hughes to Chapel Hill and planned to be his hosts in the apartment they shared. A scandal ensued when their landlord discovered their plans and evicted them; they had to find other accommodations for Hughes, and they themselves had to sleep on the floor in a bookshop they ran. Hughes's visit and "Christ in Alabama"—with its opening line, "Christ is a Nigger"—attracted a great deal of hostile attention to the poet, the editors, and the magazine. One official of the University of North Carolina called the editors "half-baked, uneducated, and wholly reprehensible adolescents." During the visit, Abernathy and Buttitta took Hughes to a popular local restaurant and broke the color line there.

Contempo was published sporadically in its final years and finally ceased publication after a split between Abernathy and Buttitta.

ERIK BLEDSOE

See also Buttitta, Anthony J.; Cullen, Countee; Hughes, Langston

Further Reading

Cunard, Nancy. "A Note on *Contempo* and Langston Hughes." In *Negro: An Anthology*. London: Nancy Cunard with Wishart, 1934. (See also reprint, ed. and abridged Hugh Ford. New York: Frederick Ungar, 1970.)

Hughes, Langston. *I Wonder as I Wander: An Autobiographical Journey*. New York: Rinehart, 1956.

Meador, Judith Hay. "A History and Index of *Contempo*." Master's thesis, University of Louisville, 1968.

Rampersad, Arnold. *The Life of Langston Hughes*, Vol. 1, *1902–1941: I, Too, Sing America*. New York and Cambridge: Oxford University Press, 1986.

Cook, Will Marion

One of the most important questions confronting black intellectuals at the turn of the twentieth century was how to raise the image of the Negro as a writer, composer, and performer. A number of distinguished black composers, writers, and performers—including Harry T. Burleigh, Bob Cole, Will Marion Cook, Paul Laurence Dunbar, James Weldon Johnson, and J. Rosamond Johnson—held serious discussions about this at Marshall's Hotel on West 53rd Street in Manhattan, where they would gather for an evening of southern food, syncopated music, and stimulating dialogue. In effect, they were pondering how to elevate the old Negro minstrel show to the "New Negro" musical.

Even in this stellar group, the composer Will Marion Cook was considered an especially original genius. He was respected for his pioneering achievements in popular songwriting, black musical comedies, and syncopated orchestral music—genres that he dramatically transformed. After matriculating at the Oberlin Conservatory and at the Hochschule für Musik in Berlin (where Joseph Joachim taught him violin), Cook studied at New York's National Conservatory with the Bohemian Antonín Dvořák, who urged American composers to stop copying European models and take a new path, using the indigenous music of America. Cook accepted the challenge and wrote pioneering black musical comedies under the tutelage of Bob Cole at Worth's Museum (a theater in New York) at the corner of Sixth Avenue and Thirteenth Street.

In the summer of 1898, the musical production *Clorindy: The Origin of the Cakewalk*, by Cook and the poet Paul Laurence Dunbar, opened at the Casino Roof Garden. A story in song and dance, it helped bring syncopated African American music to Broadway and helped introduce the high-stepping cakewalk dance to the stage. Cook declared that blacks had finally arrived on Broadway and were there to stay.

The success of this venture led Cook to write a stream of other musicals, notably *In Dahomey*, which featured "back to Africa" as a theme. This work made theatrical history in 1903 as the first full-length musical written and performed by blacks to be presented at a major Broadway theater—the New York Theater in Times Square. It was also given more than 250 times in London; these presentations included a command performance in Buckingham Palace. Other musicals followed, including *In Abyssinia* (1906), *Bandanna Land* (1908), and *Darkydom* (1915).

During the years when Cook was involved in theatrical work, he was also intermittently conducting various ensembles. He became active with a group known as the Memphis Students, who were neither students nor from Memphis. This playing-singing-dancing orchestra was organized by Ernest Hogan; however, in 1905, Cook took the members on tour to Europe for several months. An outgrowth of this ensemble was the Clef Club Orchestra, led by James Reese Europe and assisted by Cook. The historic debut of the Clef Club Orchestra at Carnegie Hall on 12 May 1912 featured Cook's compositions "Swing Along," "The Rain Song," and "Exhortation."

In 1918, Cook established the New York Syncopated Orchestra (better known as the Southern Syncopated Orchestra), an all-black group of fifty formally attired men and a few women, who played and sang a diverse repertoire of light classics, popular songs, ragtime, spirituals, and waltzes. They toured the United States and abroad, featuring the clarinetist Sidney Bechet, who introduced characteristic blues.

In the 1920s, Cook freelanced with his orchestra, assisted Abbie Mitchell at the piano in performances at the Lafayette Theater, and presented a series of programs devoted to "all-Negro" music in Manhattan. In 1929, he trained the chorus for Vincent Youmans's "Great Day"

Will Marion Cook. (Schomburg Center for Research in Black Culture, New York Public Library.)

and assisted with Miller and Lyles's *Runnin' Wild*. He furthered the careers of many musicians, most notably Josephine Baker, Duke Ellington, Hall Johnson, Eva Jessye, and Clarence White.

Cook's life and music suggest a prototype of the New Negro, a generation before Alain Locke's volume on this subject in 1925. His background as a member of the black middle class, his international exposure, and his musical education in the European and African American idioms well prepared him for the role of uplifting African Americans' lives and music. His means were identification with Africa; the use of more realistic, more positive images of blacks in song lyrics; and his willingness to use aggression, assertiveness, and agitation for the sake of racial equality. Cook revealed in his memoirs that his ultimate challenge was to try to redress social injustices, and at the same time write beautiful music.

Biography

William Mercer Cook was born 27 January 1869 in Washington, D.C. He studied at public schools in Oberlin, Ohio; at Oberlin Conservatory (violin, 1884–1888); in Berlin, Germany (violin, 1888–c. 1889); and at the National Conservatory of Music, New York (under director Antonín Dvořák, 1895). Cook made his debut as concert violinist in 1889 in Washington, D.C. In 1890, Cook was the director of a new orchestra with Frederick Douglass as president. Cook's *Clorindy, or The Origin of the Cakewalk*, the first major black show at a major theater, was performed at the Casino Roof Garden in New York City in 1898. Cook was musical director and composer for George Walker and Bert Williams's company, which produced *In Dahomey*, *In Abyssinia*, and *Bandanna Land* (1899–1908). He performed at Buckingham Palace for the birthday celebration of Prince Edward of Wales in 1903 and in the musical *The Southerners*, with a white cast and black chorus, on Broadway in 1903. He took the Memphis Students to Europe in 1905. Cook collaborated on many musicals, including *The Traitors* and *Darkydom*, from 1912 to 1915; in 1912, at Carnegie Hall, he participated as performer and composer in a concert by the Clef Club. In 1918–1922 he organized and toured widely with the New York Syncopated Orchestra (also called the Southern Syncopated Orchestra, American Syncopated Orchestra, and Will Marion Cook Syncopated Orchestra), which included Sidney Bechet, Tom

Fletcher, Abbie Mitchell, and Arthur Briggs. In 1929, he collaborated with Will Vodery on the musical *Swing Along*. Cook was an adviser, teacher, coach, and patron of many musicians in New York, and a founding member of the American Society of Composers, Authors, and Publishers (ASCAP), 1914. He died in New York City 20 July 1944.

MARVA CARTER

See also Burleigh, Harry Thacker; Clef Club; Cole, Bob; Dunbar, Paul Laurence; Ellington, Duke; Europe, James Reese; Jessye, Eva; Johnson, Hall; Johnson, James Weldon; Johnson, John Rosamond; Locke, Alain; Music; Music: Bands and Orchestras; Musical Theater; New Negro, The; White, Clarence; *other specific musicians*

Selected Works

"Bon Bon Buddy." 1907. (From *Bandanna Land*.)
"Brown-Skin Baby Mine." 1902. (From *In Dahomey*.)
"Darktown Is Out Tonight." 1898. (From *Clorindy, or The Origin of the Cakewalk*.)
"Down de Lover's Lane." 1900. (From *The Traitor*; *Jes Lak' White Fok's*; *The Sons of Ham*; *The Casino Girl*.)
"Exhortation: A Negro Sermon." 1912. (From *Bandanna Land*.)
"Jump Back, Honey, Jump Back." 1898. (From *Clorindy, or The Origin of the Cakewalk*.)
"A Little Bit of Heaven Called Home." 1933.
"The Little Gypsy Maid." 1902. (From *The Wild Rose*.)
"Mammy." 1916. (From *Darkydom*.)
"Molly Green." 1902. (From *In Dahomey*.)
"My Lady's Lips Am Like de Honey." 1915. (From *Darkydom*.)
"On Emancipation Day." 1902. (From *Clorindy, or The Origin of the Cakewalk*; *In Dahomey*.)
"Rain Song." 1912. (Also arranged for men's chorus.)
"Red, Red Rose." 1908. (From *Bandanna Land*; *The Man from 'Bam*.)
"Society." 1903. (From *The Sons of Ham*; *In Dahomey*.)
"Swing Along." 1902. (Also arranged for men's chorus; from *The Southerners*; *In Dahomey*.)
"Wid de Moon, Moon, Moon." 1907. (From *In Zululand*.)

Further Reading

Carter, Marva Griffin. "The Life and Music of Will Marion Cook." Ph.D. diss., University of Illinois, 1988.

———. "The 'New Negro' Legacy of Will Marion Cook." In *Afro-Americans in New York Life and History*, 23(1), January 1999a, pp. 25–37.

———. "Will Marion Cook." In *International Dictionary of Black Composers*, ed. Samuel A. Floyd Jr. Chicago, Ill.: Fitzroy Dearborn, 1999b, pp. 297–302.

———. "Removing the 'Minstrel Mask' in the Musicals of Will Marion Cook." In *Musical Quarterly*, 84(2), Summer 2000, pp. 206–220.

Cook, Will Marion. "Clorindy, or The Origin of the Cakewalk." In *Theater Arts*, 31, 1947, pp. 61 ff. (Reprinted in *Readings in Black Music*, ed. Eileen Southern, 2nd ed. New York: Norton, 1983.)

Green, Jeffrey. "'In Dahomey' in London in 1903." In *Black Perspective in Music*, 11(1), 1983, pp. 22–40.

Johnson, James Weldon. *Along This Way: The Autobiography of James Weldon Johnson*. New York: Viking, 1933. (Reprint, 1968.)

Riis, Thomas L. *Just before Jazz: Black Musical Theater in New York, 1890–1915*. Washington, D.C.: Smithsonian Institution Press, 1989.

———. *The Music and Scripts of In Dahomey*. Madison, Wisc.: A-R Editions, 1996.

Copper Sun

Countee Cullen's *Copper Sun* was published in 1927 by Harper Brothers, two years after his first volume of poems, *Color* (1925). Most critics had found *Color* promising, if perhaps occasionally trite or flawed; but they felt that in *Copper Sun*—with its lofty diction, excessively neat rhyme and meter, and uncritical borrowings from older masters—Cullen had failed to develop a personal style. Another perceived shortcoming was Cullen's tendency to focus on traditional apolitical, metaphysical topics rather than on social problems related to race; many readers believed that this leaning had intensified in *Copper Sun*. Most critical studies of Cullen therefore center on poems from *Color* and from his well-received third volume, *The Black Christ* (1929); as a result, there is something of a gap in the scholarship on Cullen, despite periodic references to various poems from *Copper Sun*, most notably "From the Dark Tower," "Uncle Jim," and "Threnody for a Brown Girl."

For some time after Cullen's death in 1946, critics perceived a conflict between his interest in racial problems and folk idioms on the one hand, and his interest in the genteel romanticism of poets like John Keats on the other. *Copper Sun* is most often faulted for Cullen's tendency to muse abstractly on love and death rather than address race relations and racial inequality. Scholars, for their part, have tended to focus on Cullen's celebrated race poems and to read his poetry as a clue to various facets of his enigmatic identity; in particular, they have been interested in the relationship between Cullen's poetic "investment" and what was considered his duty to write about race.

Davis (1953) examined the role of Africa in Cullen's poetic imagination as a set of characteristics against which the poet plots his own identity. Reimherr (1963) looked at Cullen's relationship with Christianity. Cullen was the adopted son of a Methodist minister, and like many black artists whose work had social protest as its raison d'être, he was known for finding or devising biblical parallels in order to expose the hypocrisy and tyranny of racist philosophies. Reimherr notes that Cullen often identified heroic black characters with biblical figures, casting the suffering of blacks so as to appeal to white audiences. Some readers have seen a link between Cullen's desire to appeal to whites and his preference for western literary forms and traditions. Baker (1974), however, observes that Cullen's preference for traditional "white" forms would not necessarily have attracted whites in an era when white patrons sought authentic "blackness" expressed in exotic folk forms. Baker himself sees *Copper Sun* as a work characterized by tension between stasis and change, in which the poet never reconciles his taste for voluptuous sentiment with his concern for sociopolitical racial equality. Lomax (1974) suggests that the demand for an authentic black "folk voice" actually prevented Cullen from developing a more personal style. Primeau (1976) believes that Cullen's attraction to romanticism was a way to explore feelings of alienation stemming from racism.

During the 1990s, critics often examined how race overlaps with other categories of identity, and some began to analyze Cullen's poetry in light of his homosexuality. Kelley (1997) noted that Cullen's attraction to primitivist imagery (especially in poems from *Color* such as "Heritage") might be understood as a homoerotic attraction to idealized decadence and might also be related to a consideration of urbanity and savagery as categories invoked in support of racial supremacy. Powers (2000) has theorized that in Cullen's psyche and poetry there was a profound split between private, forbidden homoerotic desires and the demand for a normative heterosexual lifestyle—that is, for a public persona aligned with Christian uprightness and institutional academic credentials and validation. According to Powers, Cullen's own culture made no allowance for the possibility that these two realms might coincide in the persona of an emblematic black artist and public role model; therefore, Cullen had to live and write on both sides of the divide. Although *Copper Sun* was a somewhat anomalous critical failure, and although it has had only a minor role in the changing considerations of Cullen's life and art, it may suggest interesting problems in the political climate of the arts during the Harlem Renaissance.

VICTORIA A. ELMWOOD

See also Authors: 5–Poets; Color; Cullen, Countee; Homosexuality; Literature: 7–Poetry

Further Reading

Baker, Houston A., Jr. *A Many-Colored Coat of Dreams: The Poetry of Countee Cullen*. Detroit, Mich.: Broadside, 1974.

Davis, Arthur P. "The Alien-and-Exile Theme in Countee Cullen's Racial Poems." *Phylon*, Winter 1953, pp. 73–86.

Early, Gerald, ed. *My Soul's High Song*. New York: Doubleday, 1991, pp. 3–73.

Kelley, James. "Blossoming in Strange New Forms: Male Homosexuality and the Harlem Renaissance." *Soundings: An Interdisciplinary Journal*, 80, 1997, pp. 499–517.

Lomax, Michael L. "Countee Cullen: A Key to the Puzzle." *Studies in the Literary Imagination*, 7(2), 1974, pp. 39–48.

Powers, Peter. "'The Singing Man Who Must Be Reckoned With': Private Desire and Public Responsibility in the Poetry of Countee Cullen." *African-American Review*, 34(4), 2000, pp. 661–678.

Primeau, Ronald. "Countee Cullen and Keats's 'Vale of Soul-Making.'" *Papers on Language and Literature: A Journal for Scholars and Critics of Language and Literature*, 12, 1976, pp. 73–86.

Reimherr, Beulah. "Race Consciousness in Countee Cullen's Poetry." *Susquehannah University Studies*, 7(2), 1963, pp. 65–82.

Cornhill

The Cornhill Company was a small vanity press based in Boston, owned by Walter Reid and William Stanley Braithwaite during the early Harlem Renaissance. In 1918, the poet Brookes More made the acquaintance of the owners when Cornhill published his work *The Lover's Rosary*. In 1919, More decided to retire and concentrate on writing. To facilitate publication of his own works, he acquired control of Cornhill in 1921 from Reid and renamed the firm the Cornhill Publishing Company. Reid initially stayed on as manager, but his policies landed the company in serious financial difficulties, and in 1922, More had to dismiss him.

Before More acquired it, Cornhill had been important in making known to larger publishers, and to the reading public, the work of some talented African American poets who would have an impact on black American literature. In the years after World War I, the publishing industry was still controlled by major white publishing houses; African American writers and poets might submit their work to small black magazines and newspapers, which were sometimes affiliated with the black church, but they could not achieve real success unless they published with a major white firm. Although the leading black writers tended to have little or no difficulty finding a white publisher, lesser black writers had to struggle to prove themselves to white companies. Cornhill, as a vanity press, was open to publishing African American literature, and it became a local center of black publication, together with a number of other small presses in the Boston area. However, these local companies had limited resources; very often the writers had to subsidize the printing as well as the promotion of their own work, and both distribution and promotion were rather poor. Nevertheless, for struggling black writers these almost self-financed publications did serve to open the door to white publishing companies.

During the early years of the Harlem Renaissance, Cornhill published a number of works by black writers who later became significant figures in the artistic movement. These included James Weldon Johnson's first volume of poetry, *Fifty Years and Other Poems* (1917); Angelina Weld Grimké's play *Rachel* (1917); Joseph S. Cotter's *The Band of Gideon and Other Lyrics* (1918); and Joshua Jones's *Poems of the Four Seas* (1921). Other works of African Americans published by Cornhill during this period were Maud Cuney-Hare's *The Message of the Trees*, Charles Bertram Johnson's *Songs of My People*, and Georgia Douglas Johnson's *The Heart of a Woman and Other Poems*.

This list of publications suggests the significance of Cornhill as a stepping-stone for African American writers during the early period of the Harlem Renaissance: Their work did attract attention from major white publishing houses. After 1922, however, under More's management, Cornhill no longer specialized in black literature. More reduced the size of the company; gave particular attention to binding, paper and other technical details; and produced popular works of literature for the general public.

AMY LEE

See also Braithwaite, William Stanley; Cotter, Joseph Seamon; Cuney-Hare, Maud; Grimké, Angelina Weld; Johnson, Georgia Douglas; Johnson, James Weldon; Publishers and Publishing Houses

Further Reading

Brawley, Benjamin. *The Negro Genius: A New Appraisal of the Achievement of the American Negro in Literature and the Fine Arts.* New York: Biblio and Tannen, 1966.

Brewer, Wilmon. *Life and Poems of Brookes More.* Boston, Mass.: Marshall Jones, 1940.

Hutchison, George. *The Harlem Renaissance in Black and White.* Cambridge, Mass.: Belknap Press of Harvard University Press, 1995.

Kramer, Victor A., and Robert A. Russ, eds. *Harlem Renaissance Reexamined.* Troy, N.Y.: Whitston, 1997.

Wintz, Cary D. *Black Culture and the Harlem Renaissance.* Houston, Tex.: Rice University Press, 1988.

Corrothers, James D.

The career of James D. Corrothers predated the Harlem Renaissance; however, themes in his writing and struggles in his life prefigured the spirit and strivings of the renaissance. W. E. B. Du Bois remarked that Corrothers's death in 1917 was "a serious loss to the race and to literature."

After receiving the best education available to an impoverished black youth in a rural area (in the public schools of South Haven, Michigan), Corrothers became an itinerant laborer in western Michigan, Indiana, and Ohio, and in Chicago and Springfield, Illinois. While he was working in Springfield as a coachman, his poem "The Deserted Schoolhouse" was published in Springfield's *Champion City Times.* The general reaction among whites was disbelief that Corrothers had actually composed the poem—an ominous sign of the difficulties Corrothers would later face in trying to pursue a writing career. Nevertheless,

Springfield was important to Corrothers's development as a writer.

In Springfield, Corrothers met Albery A. Whitman, then known as the "colored poet of America"; attended a lecture by Frederick Douglass; and joined the Young Men's Republican Club, where he met several of Booker T. Washington's associates and where, although he was not yet old enough to vote, he became immersed in politics and was encouraged to write and make speeches. Corrothers then headed back to Chicago, hoping to publish his work; but he was unable to find a publisher for the patriotic songs he had written, and he took a series of menial jobs, eventually working as a porter and bootblack in a white barbershop. One distinguished-looking customer happened to be Henry Demarest Lloyd, part-owner of the Chicago *Tribune*; Lloyd had one of Corrothers's poems published in the *Tribune* and gave Corrothers a job in the newspaper's counting room.

From his menial but secure job at the *Tribune*, Corrothers wrote poetry, studied the paper's writing style, and waited for a chance to break into journalism—though he soon learned that the editor would not give an African American a permanent position as a reporter. Repeatedly, Corrothers's career as a journalist was stymied by newspaper editors who refused to give him permanent work while at the same time publishing his articles and dialect poetry at space rates.

At the time—the 1890s—black dialect in speech and writing was generally used to demean African Americans. Consequently, Corrothers had an aversion to it; but audiences and readers relished it and were accustomed to finding it in minstrel skits, local-color writing, and plantation nostalgia. After meeting Paul Laurence Dunbar and reading Dunbar's works, Corrothers gained a different perspective on black dialect; ultimately, to appeal to readers and support his family, he began to use it. Corrothers contributed dialect poetry to leading magazines and published a series of complex yet minstrel-like character sketches in dialect, which were later collected in his first book, *The Black Cat Club* (1902). However, as Corrothers's career was gaining momentum, the heyday of dialect writing was coming to an end: James Weldon Johnson defined a new agenda for poets in *The Book of American Negro Poetry* (1921) and assailed black dialect.

Corrothers was never able to support himself and his family as a full-time writer, and he finally had to retire from writing. His disappearance from the literary scene left a gap in African American literary history that current scholarship on Corrothers and on African American writing preceding the Harlem Renaissance has begun to fill.

Biography

James D. Corrothers was born 2 July 1869 in Chain Lake Settlement, Cass County, Michigan. He attended public schools in South Haven; a Northwestern University preparatory school in Evanston, Illinois; and Bennett College in Greensboro, North Carolina. Corrothers contributed news and poetry to the *Bee, Tribune, Times-Herald, Journal, Daily Record,* and *Daily News* in Chicago; to the *Mail, Express, Herald,* and *Sunday Herald* in New York; to the *Inquirer* in Philadelphia; and to the *Globe-Democrat* in St. Louis. He also contributed to magazines: *Truth, Criterion, Southern Workman, Century, American, Colored American,* and *The Crisis.* He entered the ministry and was a pastor of Methodist congregations in Rochester (New York) and Red Bank and Hackensack (New Jersey); of Baptist congregations in Jersey City (New Jersey), South Haven (Michigan), and Lexington (Virginia); and of a Presbyterian congregation in West Chester (Pennsylvania). Corrothers died 2 February 1917 in West Chester, Pennsylvania.

VETA TUCKER

See also Dunbar, Paul Laurence; Johnson, James Weldon

Selected Works

"Way in de Woods, and Nobody Dar." *Century,* 57, April 1899, p. 959.
"A Dixie Thanksgivin'." *Century,* 59, November 1899, p. 160.
"Me 'n' Dunbar." *Colored American,* 3, July 1901, pp. 163–164.
The Black Cat Club. New York and London: Funk and Wagnalls, 1902.
"An Awful Problem Solved." *Colored American,* 6, November 1903, pp. 793–795.
"Paul Lawrence Dunbar." *Century,* 85, November 1912, p. 56.
"The Negro Singer." *Century,* 85, November 1912, p. 56.
"At the Closed Gate of Justice." *Century,* 86, June 1913, p. 272.
"A Man They Didn't Know." *Crisis,* 7, December 1913, pp. 85–87; 7, January 1914, pp. 136–138.
"The Dream and the Song." *Century,* 87, January 1914, p. 398.
"At the End of the Controversy." *American,* 77, March 1914, pp. 36–41.
"In the Matter of Two Men." *Crisis,* 9, January 1915, p. 138.
"The Black Man's Soul." *Crisis,* 10, October 1915, pp. 304, 306.
"An Indignation Dinner." *Century,* 91, December 1915, p. 320.
In Spite of the Handicap: An Autobiography. New York: Doran, 1916.

Further Reading

Barton, Rebecca Chalmers. *Witnesses for Freedom: Negro Americans in Autobiography.* New York: Harper, 1948.
Brown, Sterling. *Negro Poetry and Drama.* Washington, D.C.: Associates in Negro Folk Education, 1937.
Bruce, Dickson D., Jr. *Black American Writing from the Nadir: The Evolution of a Literary Tradition, 1877–1915.* Baton Rouge: Louisiana State University Press, 1989.
———. "James Corrothers Reads a Book: Or, the Lives of Sandy Jenkins." *African-American Review,* 26(4), Winter 1992, pp. 665–673.
Dictionary of Literary Biography, Vol. 50, *Afro-American Writers Before the Harlem Renaissance.* Detroit, Mich.: Gale, 1987, pp. 52–62.
Gaines, Kevin. "Assimilationist Minstrelsy as Racial Uplift Ideology: James D. Corrother's Literary Quest for Black Leadership." *American Quarterly,* 45(3), September 1993, pp. 341–369.
Johnson, Abby Arthur, and Ronald Maberry Johnson. *Propaganda and Aesthetics: The Literary Politics of Afro-American Magazines in the Twentieth Century.* Amherst: University of Massachusetts Press, 1979.
Johnson, James Weldon, ed. *The Book of American Negro Poetry.* New York: Harcourt, Brace, 1931.
Payne, James Robert. "Griggs and Corrothers: Historical Reality and Black Fiction." *Explorations in Ethnic Studies,* 6, January 1983, pp. 1–9.
Redmond, Eugene B. *Drumvoices: The Mission of Afro-American Poetry.* Garden City, N.Y.: Anchor/Doubleday, 1976.

Cotter, Joseph Seamon Jr.

The poetic range of Joseph Seamon Cotter Jr. extended from well-crafted sonnets to poems grounded in the biblical allusions of the time-honored African American sermonic tradition. His poems also addressed the pressing social and political issues of his time. Considering his skillful use of free verse, some critics have seen Cotter as a transitional figure who, like Fenton Johnson, established a pattern for African American poets of the 1920s.

Cotter was an avid reader before he began first grade. A fine student, intelligent and athletic, he received a good academic foundation at Central Colored High School in Louisville, Kentucky, where he excelled in Latin, English, history, and mathematics. He graduated at age fifteen, second in his class. In 1911, Cotter followed his older sister Florence to Fisk University in Nashville, Tennessee. There he worked on the staff of the student magazine, the *Fisk Herald*. In his sophomore year, however, Cotter contracted tuberculosis and was forced to return to Louisville. Florence also contracted the disease; she died in December 1914, shortly after graduating from Fisk and beginning a teaching career.

Under close medical supervision, Cotter worked as an essayist for the weekly *Louisville Leader* and began writing poems that were collected as *The Band of Gideon and Other Lyrics*, published in June 1918 by the Cornhill Company in Boston. Reviewing the book in *New York Age*, James Weldon Johnson declared, "Cotter is free and bold. He has imagination and fine poetic sense," coupled with "a splendid mastery of the tools that every poet must know how to use." Years later, Sterling Brown praised Cotter's "concern for social themes, done with quiet persuasiveness," and noted that Cotter shared this focus with younger poets of the Harlem Renaissance.

Cotter's most widely known poem, "Sonnet to Negro Soldiers," dedicated to the all-black Ninety-second Division of the United States Army, was reprinted in *The Crisis*, the journal of the National Association of Colored People where it had the force of an editorial. African American soldiers, facing enemy fire in France in World War I, "walk unafraid within that Living Hell,/Nor heed the driving rain of shot and shell." Their willing sacrifice, says the poet, serves as "a glorious sign,/A glimmer of that resurrection morn," when racial prejudice and second-class citizenship will be a thing of the past. Other poems, such as "Moloch" and "O Little, David, Play On Your Harp," sound an angrier, less optimistic tone. "The Mulatto to His Critics" and "Is It Because I Am Black?" are eloquent free-verse expressions of racial pride.

Cotter was terminally ill in the autumn of 1918 when he wrote his final poems. Impressive in technique though adhering to syncope and archaic verb forms, "Out of the Shadows: An Unfinished Sonnet-Sequence" appeared posthumously in the *AME Zion Quarterly Review* in 1920 and 1921.

In his poem "A Prayer," Cotter described his own fragile condition and ended with the pathetic supplication "O God, give me words to make my dream-children live." For about a year that prayer was answered. The sixty-five poems that make up his collected works are testimony to Cotter's talent. Some are good enough to suggest that his early death was, indeed, a loss for literature.

Biography

The poet and journalist Joseph Seamon Cotter Jr. was born in Louisville, Kentucky, on 2 September 1895. He was the second of three children; the third, Leonidas, died in infancy in January 1900. His father was a school principal and a published poet; his mother, Maria Cox Cotter, was a schoolteacher. The Cotters, who were respected community leaders, admired Booker T. Washington and were acquaintances of luminaries such as Paul Laurence Dunbar. Cotter briefly attended college and worked as a journalist. He died of tuberculosis 3 February 1919, but his father saw to it that his poems continued to be published and anthologized.

LORENZO THOMAS

See also Authors: 5–Poets; Brown, Sterling; Cornhill; Johnson, Fenton; Johnson, James Weldon

Further Reading

Cotter, Joseph Seamon, Jr. *Complete Poems*, ed. James Robert Payne. Athens and London: University of Georgia Press, 1990.

Johnson, James Weldon. "Some New Books of Poetry and Their Makers." In *Selected Writings of James Weldon Johnson*, 2 vols., ed. Sondra Kathryn Wilson. New York: Oxford University Press, 1995, Vol. 1, pp. 271–277. (This essay was first published in 1918.)

Payne, James Robert. "Joseph Seamon Cotter, Jr." In *Dictionary of Literary Biography*, Vol. 50. Detroit, Mich.: Gale Research, 1986, pp. 70–73.

Redmond, Eugene B. *Drumvoices: The Mission of Afro-American Poetry*. Garden City, N.Y.: Anchor, 1976, pp. 155–169.

Shockley, Ann Allen. "Joseph S. Cotter, Sr.: Biographical Sketch of a Black Louisville Bard." *CLA Journal*, 18, March 1975, pp. 327–340.

Cotton Club

The Harlem cabaret is perhaps the most fabled intersection of the jazz age and the Harlem Renaissance, and no cabaret was more fabled than the Cotton Club—the "aristocrat of Harlem"—at the northeast corner of Lenox Avenue and 142nd Street: Between its opening in September 1923 and its relocation downtown in February 1936, the Cotton Club would boost the early careers of Edith Wilson, Bill "Bojangles" Robinson, Aida Ward, Adelaide Hall, Earl "Snakehips" Tucker, Mantan Moreland, Ethel Waters, Lena Horne, the Nicholas Brothers, and the bands of Duke Ellington (in 1927–1931 and 1933), Cab Calloway (in 1930–1933), and Jimmie Lunceford (in 1934–1936). As famous for its exclusionary racial policies as for its fast-stepping revues, the Cotton Club embodied many of the contradictions of the popular Harlem Renaissance; its cultural meaning was shaped by the combined forces of Prohibition economics, postwar trends in musical theater, black performance traditions and innovations, white patronage, and the mass media.

The Douglas Casino—a large, underused dance hall space over a movie house—had been built at 644 Lenox Avenue in 1918. It was sold in 1920 to the former heavyweight champion Jack Johnson, refurbished as an intimate supper club seating 400, and renamed the Club Deluxe. In 1923, the struggling club was resold to Manhattan's most powerful underworld figure, Owen "Owney" Madden, who was then in prison, having been convicted of manslaughter. Madden had made his fortune on sales of Madden's No. 1 beer during the national experiment with enforced sobriety; he also owned a number of other nightclubs in Manhattan, including the Stork Club and the Silver Slipper. Initially, most of the personnel of the Cotton Club, including cooks, waiters, busboys, the management, and entertainers, were imported from Chicago. George "Big Frenchy" DeMange managed the club, while Walter Brooks, who had brought *Shuffle Along* to Broadway in 1921, served as front. Lew Leslie produced the first floor shows; and Andy Preer's Missourians, renamed the Cotton Club Syncopators, provided music. Madden himself rarely visited the newly baptized Cotton Club, and although

federal authorities padlocked the club's doors for three months in 1925 for forty-four violations of the Volstead Act, he faced little trouble from the police before his voluntary return to Sing Sing prison and semiretirement in July 1932.

Madden spared little expense in creating an exclusive, titillating uptown destination for a well-heeled downtown crowd. The club was renovated to fit 700, with seating surrounding the dance and show floor that extended from the horseshoe-shaped stage. Joseph Urban, Florenz Ziegfeld's celebrated set and costume designer, redesigned the interior in what Singer (1992) describes as "a brazen riot of African jungle motifs, Southern stereotypology, and lurid eroticism" (100). The gangsters themselves were an attraction; DeMange was expected to be present and visible. Admission to the club cost $2.50, and, except for Madden's beer, drinks were expensive. Strict decorum and studied elegance were expected of both staff and customers. Shows (generally three per night) were scheduled to allow performers at other locations to drop in after work; Sunday night became "Celebrity Night," with everyone from Jimmy Durante to New York's mayor Jimmy Walker asked to take a bow and perhaps do a number. New floor shows opened twice each year and were budgeted to rival Ziegfeld's *Follies* (indeed, some—such as Lew Leslie's long-running *Blackbirds of 1928*—would eventually find their way to Broadway). Following the closing in 1925, Harry Block replaced Brooks as front, Herman Stark began a fifteen-year run as stage manager, Dan Healey replaced Leslie as floor-show producer, and Jimmy McHugh composed the music (McHugh was joined in 1927 by the lyricist Dorothy Fields). Healey established the formula: a top-billed singer or comedian; specialty acts in eccentric dances and "adult" songs; a chorus line attired in elaborate, or elaborately brief, costumes; and behind it all top-notch jazz—particularly once Duke Ellington's Washingtonians became the house band in December 1927 (some commentators remember it as an offer the band couldn't refuse). At the Cotton Club, where he had to write not only dance tunes but also overtures, transitions, accompaniments, and "jungle" effects, Ellington developed much of his distinctive orchestral composition style.

A key innovation in creating the Cotton Club's exclusive atmosphere was Madden's seemingly paradoxical introduction of a strict color line into the heart of Harlem. In establishing a whites-only policy regarding customers, Madden was following the practice at Connie's Inn, a rival Harlem club favored by moneyed whites. At the Cotton Club, the concept was extended to the division of labor, creating a strict divide between the whites who ran the club and produced, wrote, and choreographed its shows, and the blacks who cooked, waited and bussed tables, and entertained. Women in the chorus line faced their own color bar; they were essentially conceived as part of the club's decor, and they were expected to be "tall, tan, and terrific": at least 5 feet 6 inches, no darker than a light olive tone, and under twenty-one. Then, in 1927, the Columbia Broadcasting System, one of the emerging radio networks, began to broadcast from the Cotton Club. By 1930, half-hour programs might be broadcast over several stations and networks five or six nights a week, giving bandleaders a chance to build a national—and mixed—audience and greatly increasing their opportunities to tour and record. In deference to Ellington's new clout and his expressed regret that friends and family of the performers were unable to see them play, the club relaxed its whites-only policy for customers, at least for light-skinned celebrities willing to sit near the kitchen.

Though the Cotton Club experienced a number of changes in the early 1930s, the Depression had trouble catching up with it. For the revue of spring 1930, *Brown Sugar—Sweet but Unrefined*, Cab Calloway's orchestra replaced Ellington's, and the composer Harold Arlen and the lyricist Ted Koehler replaced McHugh and Fields, who were then (like Ellington) leaving for Hollywood. However, the repeal of Prohibition and the increasingly visible poverty of Harlem eventually created insurmountable problems for many mob-run uptown clubs. The Cotton Club pulled up stakes after the close of its show for spring 1936

and reopened in September at 200 West 48th Street and Broadway, the former site of the Palais Royale and the future site of the Latin Quarter. After four years of high midtown rents, the rising cost of mounting elaborate floor shows, changing tastes in jazz, and renewed federal attention to income tax evasion among New York's nightclubs, the Cotton Club closed its doors permanently on 10 June 1940.

RYAN JERVING

See also Blackbirds; Fields, Dorothy; Harlem: 3–Entertainment; Johnson, John Arthur "Jack"; Leslie, Lew; Madden, Owen Vincent "Owney"; Nightclubs; Nightlife; Organized Crime; *specific entertainers*

Further Reading

Burns, Ken, dir. "Our Language." In *Jazz*. PBS Home Video, 2000, Episode 3.

Calloway, Cab, and Bryant Rollins. *Of Minnie the Moocher and Me*. New York: Crowell, 1976.

Ellington, Duke. *Music Is My Mistress*. Garden City, N.Y.: Doubleday, 1973; New York: Da Capo, 1988.

Haskins, Jim. *The Cotton Club*. New York: Random House, 1977.

Hasse, John Edward. *Beyond Category: The Life and Genius of Duke Ellington*. London and New York: Simon & Schuster, 1993.

Singer, Barry. *Black and Blue: The Life and Lyrics of Andy Razaf*. New York and London: Schirmer—Simon & Schuster Macmillan, 1992.

Tucker, Mark, ed. *The Duke Ellington Reader*. Oxford and New York: Oxford University Press, 1993.

Cotton Club, c. 1920s. (© Underwood and Underwood/Corbis.)

Covarrubias, Miguel

Miguel Covarrubias (1904–1957) was never formally trained as an artist; he began drawing as a boy and perfected his technique through constant work. During his youth, he became well acquainted with artistic circles in Mexico City and began to do caricatures of their members. His images of well-known artists such as Diego Rivera, Dr. Atl, and Carlos Mérida, as well as of politicians and intellectuals, were frequently seen in Mexican publications such as *La Falange*, *Fantoche*, *El Heraldo*, *El Mundo*, and *El Universal Ilustrado*. He was equally adept at caricaturing the signature styles of other visual artists, something he first did in the art journal *Zig-Zag* in 1921, when he incorporated Aubrey Beardsley's style into a caricature of the work of the Mexican painter Roberto Montenegro.

In 1923, Covarrubias arrived in New York City, through the sponsorship of the Mexican Ministry of Foreign Relations. This move would have tremendous significance for his artistic career, and his period in New York (lasting until 1936) was his most prolific. In September 1923, he made the acquaintance of the photographer, writer, and socialite Carl Van Vechten, who introduced him to Frank Crowninshield, editor of *Vanity Fair*. At Van Vechten's suggestion, Covarrubias began to contribute illustrations featuring black figures; these illustrations aroused interest in Harlem, which had already come to the attention of the white intelligentsia, and were later (1925) exhibited at the New Gallery in New York. By 1924, Covarrubias was the head caricaturist at *Vanity Fair*, sometimes contributing as many as eight illustrations per issue; he continued to work with this magazine even after it merged with *Vogue* in 1936. Covarrubias's friendship with Van Vechten also led to close connections with others who were significant in the Harlem Renaissance. In 1926, he illustrated the cover of Langston Hughes's *The Weary Blues* and the pages of W. C. Handy's *Blues: An Anthology*. Later, he illustrated books such as René Maran's *Batouala* (1932), Herman Melville's *Typee* (1935), Harriet Beecher Stowe's *Uncle Tom's Cabin* (1938), and numerous ethnographic studies.

Covarrubias had a distinctive style that combined a sense of design with simplicity of line, and his work was much in demand; in fact, he, Ralph Barton (1892–1932), and Al Hirshfeld (1903–2003) defined American caricature in the 1920s. He relied on integrity of line to create his caricatures, and his manipulation of abstract patterning gave them a decidedly modernist appeal; in his attention to line, careful geometry, and exaggeration of particular features he was inspired by cubism. In addition to *Vanity Fair*, he published caricatures in other prominent publications such as *World* and the *New Yorker*. He worked in theater as well; in 1925, he designed the set for the musical number "Rancho Mexicano" in the *Garrick Gaieties*, the set and costumes for George Bernard Shaw's *Androcles and the Lion*, and the set for Josephine Baker's *Revue nègre*. Also in 1925, the publisher Alfred Knopf issued Covarrubias's first book of caricatures, *The Prince of Wales and Other Famous Americans*.

In 1927, Covarrubias published what may be his most significant book, *Negro Drawings*. These works grew from his direct experience of Harlem; they depict a broad variety of "types" found in Harlem—flappers, musicians, dancers, street preachers, socialites, blues singers, mothers and children, waiters, and others—and convey the feel of the neighborhood. Some of the drawings are of single figures; others are scenes with entertainers, parties, and fashions in appropriate settings. The figures are weighty, nearly monumental, although they are created from a few linear forms. Covarrubias would start a portrait with two circles for eyes and then add a few curved lines or angles, instantly creating the syncopated rhythm of a dancer or the movement of a dandy through Harlem's streets.

Covarrubias's images serve as complete narratives even when they show only one figure. This is particularly true when the single figure, like someone sitting for a photograph, seems aware of the viewer. Unlike his other illustrations, which were intended particularly to entertain, these portrait images present a careful, profound consideration of various facets of Harlem's cultural life, as seen through a modernist's eyes. Stylistically, the works have been described as postcubist by some art historians; Covarrubias always remains interested in depicting the movement of the human figure.

Negro Drawings foreshadowed Covarrubias's interest in examining marginalized cultures throughout the world. Later, he would turn to Bali and his native Mexico for inspiration, taking an anthropological approach to doing research for his images. Once he left New York, Covarrubias abandoned the style of his caricatures in favor of a more documentary style that would inform the work of his later years, beginning with a yearlong trip to Bali in 1933, funded by a Guggenheim fellowship.

Covarrubias's interest in material culture continued to manifest itself in his love of crafts and the indigenous arts of Mexico. He organized an exhibition of Mexican applied arts at the Art Center in New York in 1928. His impressive collection of books, photographs, and other documents of Mexican art and craft allowed him to study these objects closely and illustrate them meticulously. It would seem that Covarrubias's interest in Harlem was part of a larger commitment to studying and depicting a variety of cultural "others." The fascination of the white majority with the culture of Harlem might have given him the idea of bringing Mexican, African American, and Balinese culture to wider audiences.

Along with his caricatures, Covarrubias did numerous paintings. These were large, colorful canvases

Miguel Covarrubias with two Balinese men, c. 1930–1935.
(Library of Congess.)

that featured Mexican peasants as well as portraits of patrons and acquaintances. Created with the same sense of monumentality as his caricatures, the figures in his paintings have a quiet dignity that is suggested by their posture, their clothing, and their surroundings. His images of Mexican women vendors are particularly heroic and seem to reflect something of the *costumbrista* paintings—featuring vendors of wares and foodstuffs in colorful landscapes—that were popular in Mexico at the turn of the twentieth century. Other images, such as his portraits of women, put the sensuality of his drawn lines at the service of the nude female body.

Biography

Miguel Covarrubias was born in Mexico City in 1904 to a wealthy family. Both his father and his uncle held prominent positions in the Mexican government. Covarrubias began drawing in his boyhood and started his artistic career doing caricatures. He came to New York in 1923 and soon became a caricaturist for *Vanity Fair*. Covarrubias was also an illustrator and cover artist for books by a number of writers of the Harlem Renaissance, a designer for theatrical productions, and a painter on canvas. He died in 1957.

ROCIO ARANDA-ALVARADO

See also Batouala; Blues: An Anthology; Guggenheim Fellowships; Modernism; Van Vechten, Carl; Vanity Fair; Weary Blues, The

Further Reading

Cox, Beverly J. *Miguel Covarrubias: Caricatures.* Washington, D.C.: National Portrait Gallery, 1985.
"Miguel Covarrubias: Homenaje." Mexico City: Centro Cultural de Arte Contemporaneo, 1987. (Exhibition catalog.)
Navarrete, Sylvia. *Miguel Covarrubias: Artista y explorador.* Mexico City: Consejo Nacional para la Cultura y las Artes, 1993.
Williams, Adriana. *Covarrubias.* Austin: University of Texas Press, 1994.

Cowdery, Mae Virginia

Mae Virginia Cowdery (1909–1953) was part of an artistic and literary milieu, based in Philadelphia during the early twentieth century, that also included many of her contemporaries who were, then and later, better-known figures of the Harlem Renaissance. Cowdery was born into an upwardly mobile middle-class family, the only child of a social worker and a caterer, and she benefited from an environment of racial uplift that valued talent in the arts and in letters as a means of promoting equality and opportunity for black Americans. In 1927, while still a student at the prestigious Philadelphia High School for Girls, Cowdery published writing and poems in *Black Opals*, a briefly successful black intellectual journal that had been founded by "older New Negroes to encourage younger members of the group who demonstrate talent and ambitions." In writing for *Black Opals*, Cowdery was in good company: The journal also printed work by Langston Hughes, Jessie Fauset, Alain Locke, and other notables. Also in 1927, Cowdery won first prize in a poetry contest run by *The Crisis*, for her poem "Longings"; and another of her poems, "Lamps," won a Krigwa Prize for poetry.

As a winner of its poetry contest, Cowdery had her picture printed in *The Crisis*; her biographers all note her unique style, which today might be described as gender bending. In this picture, she wears a tailored suit and a bow tie, and her hair is slicked back, perhaps suggesting her integration into Harlem's bohemian circle. Actually, though, very little is known of Cowdery's personal life, and her artistic life is only somewhat less obscure. It appears from her three-part work "Three Poems for My Daughter" that Cowdery may have had a daughter; but there are no other known records of this child, and other poems—such as "Spring Lament"—may indicate that the child was not born alive. For unknown reasons, Cowdery committed suicide in 1953, at the age of forty-four.

Cowdery was one of the few African American women poets in the first half of the twentieth century to publish her own volume of poetry: This was *We Lift Our Voices and Other Poems* (1936). This work, a visually stunning limited edition (350 copies) of delicate yet intensely powerful verse, had an introduction by the literary editor William Stanley Braithwaite and a frontispiece by the artist Allan Freelon, and it was critically well received. Its date is well after the period that many scholars consider the height of the Harlem Renaissance, the 1920s; however, Cowdery had published a substantial amount of poetry during the late 1920s, in journals, magazines, and collected anthologies. Cowdery's history of publication in black journals is similar to that of other women writers of the Harlem Renaissance; her older contemporaries Jessie Fauset and Zora Neale Hurston, for example, also built a reputation by publishing their work in black journals.

Despite the obscurity surrounding her personal life and her participation in the Harlem Renaissance, Cowdery clearly arose out of and was intimately connected with an artistic and literary upsurge articulated by a northern, black, middle-class, urban sensibility.

Biography

Mae V. Cowdery was born in 1904 in Philadelphia, Pennsylvania. She studied at Philadelphia High School for Girls and the Pratt Institute, New York. Her awards included first prize in *The Crisis* poetry contest and the Krigwa Poetry Prize, both in 1927. She published *We Lift Our Voices and Other Poems* in 1936. Cowdery committed suicide in 1953.

LAURA ALEXANDRA HARRIS

See also Black Opals; Braithwaite, William Stanley; Crisis, The: Literary Prizes; Fauset, Jessie Redmon; Hughes, Langston; Literature: 7—Poetry; Locke, Alain

Further Reading

Braithwaite, Willian Stanley. Introduction. In *We Lift Our Voices and Other Poems*. Philadelphia: Alpress, 1936.

Brawley, Benjamin. *The Negro Genius*. New York: Bilbo and Tannen, 1972.

Cowdery, Mae V. *We Lift Our Voices and Other Poems*. Philadelphia: Alpress, 1936.

Honey, Maureen, ed. *Shadowed Dreams: Women's Poetry of the Harlem Renaissance*. New Brunswick, N.J., and London: Rutgers University Press, 1989.

Jubilee, Vincent. "Philadelphia's Afro-American Literary Circle and the Harlem Renaissance." New Haven: J. W. Johnson Collection at Yale, 1980.

Kellner, Bruce, ed. *The Harlem Renaissance A Historical Dictionary for the Era*. Westport, Conn.: Greenwood, 1984.

Lewis, David Levering. *The Portable Harlem Renaissance Reader*. New York: Penguin, 1995.

Cox, Ida Prather

The blues singer Ida Prather Cox (1896–1967) started her career in vaudeville at age fourteen. Before she began recording with Paramount in 1923, she sang with Jelly Roll Morton, and she was occasionally accompanied by Louis Armstrong and King Oliver when she sang in clubs in Chicago for a time in her late teens. She had a longtime musical partnership with the woman pianist Lovie Austin and recorded several songs with Austin and Tommy Ladnier on trumpet. Although the music that Cox recorded was blues in its lyrical form, her musical arrangements did not rely on the classic blues instrument, the guitar. In the early years she sang with a band that usually consisted of a piano; trumpet, clarinet, or cornet; and occasionally percussion, drums, or a banjo.

Ida Cox was a unique woman blues singer—for one reason, because she wrote most of her own songs, including the classic "Wild Women Don't Have the Blues" (1924). In addition, she had a strong sense of the music business. She produced all her own stage shows through her touring company, which she named Raising Cane. She also hired her own musicians.

During the 1930s Cox toured extensively but did not record much in the studios. In 1939, at the height of her career, she appeared in John Hammond's revue *From Spirituals to Swing* at Carnegie Hall. In 1945, onstage at the Moonglow Nightclub in Buffalo, New York, she suffered a stroke that would halt her singing career for fifteen years. In 1961, she recorded her final session, "Blues for Rampart Street," with the legendary jazz musicians Coleman Hawkins, Milt Hinton, Roy Eldridge, and Jo Jones.

Biography

Ida Prather Cox was born on or around 25 February 1896 in Toccoa, Georgia. The precise date of her birth is disputed, as are details of her early childhood; but it is known that she left home and began singing in vaudeville shows at age fourteen. Cox recorded at least sixty-five records and hundreds of songs between 1923 and 1940 on various labels; she was called the "uncrowned queen of the blues" by Paramount Records when she sang for its label for six years in the early 1920s. In addition to the many songs she recorded under her own name, she recorded under pseudonyms such as Kate Lewis, Julia Powers, Velma Bradley, and Jane Smith. Throughout her thirty-five-year musical career, Cox she was also popular as a live performer. She died of cancer on 10 November 1967 in Knoxville, Tennessee, where she lived with her daughter and sang in the church choir.

ASALE ANGEL-AJANI

See also Armstrong, Louis; Blues; Blues: Women Performers; Morton, Jelly Roll; Oliver, Joseph "King"; Singers

Selected Works

"Any Woman's Blues." Paramount, 1923.
"Lawdy, Lawdy Blues." Paramount, 1923.
"I've Got the Blues for Rampart Street." Paramount, 1923.
"Wild Women Don't Have the Blues." Rosetta, 1924.
"Coffin Blues." Paramount, 1925.
"Jail House Blues." Paramount, 1929.
"Four Day Creep." Vocalion, 1939.
"Blues for Rampart Street." Riverside, 1961.

Further Reading

Cowley, John, and Paul Oliver. *The New Blackwell Guide to Recorded Blues*. London: Blackwell, 1996.
Harris, Sheldon. *Blues Who's Who: A Biographical Dictionary of Blues Singers*. New Rochelle, N.Y.: Arlington House, 1979.
Oliver, Paul. *Conversation With the Blues*. London: Cambridge University Press, 1997. (First published 1965.)
———. *The Story of the Blues*. Boston, Mass.: Northeastern University Press, 1998. (Reprint.)
Santelli, Robert. *The Big Book of the Blues*. New York: Penguin, 2001.

Crescent Theater

The Crescent Theater, at 36–38 West 135th Street and Lenox Avenue, was built in 1909, slightly later than its rival, the Lincoln Theater. Because the Lincoln was considered a movie house with live entertainment added, the Crescent is generally acknowledged as the first black theater in Harlem. The Crescent was also considered more middle class, as opposed to the working-class Lincoln.

The creation of new venues for theater in Harlem was a major advance for black performers. In the words of James Weldon Johnson (1939/1991):

> The Negro performer in New York, who had always been playing to white or predominantly white audiences, found himself in an entirely different psychological atmosphere. He found himself freed from a great many restraints and taboos that had cramped him for forty years. . . . Colored performers in New York experienced for the first time release from the restraining fears of what a white audience would stand for. (171)

The Crescent's original white managers, Flugelman and Johnson, followed a policy of light entertainment featuring top-drawer black vaudeville acts from established groups or companies like Smart Set and Mr. Load of Kole. These were sometimes supported by promising local talent, such as the fourteen-year old Florence Mills with her sisters in the Mills Trio in 1910.

The middle-class orientation of the Crescent was demonstrated by the production, in 1911, of *The Tryst*, an opera by the black composer H. Lawrence Freeman. *The Tryst* dealt with a tragic theme and starred Freeman's wife Carlotta, who later became prominent with the Lafayette Players.

Sometime in late 1911 or early 1912, the Crescent passed into the hands of two white liquor dealers, Martinson and Nibus. To compete with the Lincoln, they called on the talents of the comedian Eddie Hunter. He appeared regularly during 1912 and 1913 in sketches that involved commentary intercut with moving pictures—"talking pictures before they talked," according to Hunter. His presentations "Goin' to the Races" and "The Battle of Who Run" were highly successful.

The Crescent had also acquired a drama company, the Crescent Players. Their "Twenty Minutes in Hell," featuring the comedian Emmett Anthony, shared the bill with Hunter's "Battle of Who Run" in March 1913. Sometime in 1914, Clarence Muse and his wife, Ophelia, merged their own stock company with the Crescent

Players. They starred in several plays, including *Another Man's Wife*.

In 1912, when the Lafayette Theater was built in Harlem, Martinson and Nibus leased it also. Though they used black acts, they sought to operate the Lafayette on a segregated basis; however, they soon found this impractical, and they relinquished the lease in 1914. The new operator appointed Lester Walton as manager, ending segregation. Before they left, Martinson and Nibus switched many acts, including Eddie Hunter's, away from the Crescent. The Muses also switched from the Crescent Players, initially to the short-lived Lincoln Players and ultimately to Anita Bush's new Lafayette Players. The Crescent now found itself squeezed between the Lincoln and the Lafayette. By 1915, the Crescent was out of business, and the Lafayette had become the vanguard of black drama. Nevertheless, in its brief tenure the Crescent had created vital opportunities for many developing black performers.

BILL EGAN

See also Black Manhattan; Blacks in Theater; Bush, Anita; Harlem: 3: Entertainment; Hunter, Eddie; Lafayette Players; Lafayette Theater; Lincoln Theater; Mills, Florence; Muse, Clarence; Musical Theater; Theater; Vaudeville; Walton, Lester

Further Reading

Anderson, Jervis. *Harlem: The Great Black Way*. London: Orbis, 1982. (See "Towards a Black Theatre," p. 110.)

Johnson, James Weldon. *Black Manhattan*. New York: Knopf, 1939. (Reprint, New York: Da Capo, 1991. See ch. 15, p. 170.)

Mitchell, Loften. *Black Drama*. New York: Hawthorn, 1967.
———. *Voices of the Black Theatre*. Clifton, N.J.: White, 1975. (See "The Words of Eddie Hunter.")

Peterson, Bernard L., Jr. *The African-American Theatre Directory, 1816–1960*. Westport, Conn.: Greenwood, 1993. (See "Crescent Theatre, Harlem.")

Sampson, Henry T. *Blacks in Blackface: A Source Book on Early Black Musical Shows*. Metuchen, N.J., and London: Scarecrow, 1980.

Crisis, The

The Crisis—the monthly publication of the National Association for the Advancement of Colored People (NAACP)—was the leading vehicle for bringing the grand ideas of the Harlem Renaissance to the provinces, and also for generating and reflecting those ideas. It occupied a central position in setting the agenda of the renaissance: social uplift, promoting literature and the arts, ensuring voting rights and equal funding for education, ending lynching, ending legalized segregation, and seeking equal treatment in the courts. *The Crisis*, situated at the center of the renaissance, served as a gathering place and a central distribution point for ideas; it printed news coming in from the provinces and then—through its nationwide distribution—spread that news throughout the country. Many observers considered its activities "agitation."

W. E. B. Du Bois served as the editor of *The Crisis* from its first issue, which appeared in November 1910, until he was forced to resign in 1934. In that first issue, he set the tone of the journal. *The Crisis* cataloged recent triumphs and defeats in regard to racial discrimination. It printed pages of news, broken down under headings such as political, education, social uplift, judicial decisions, science, and art. Du Bois told his readers in the first issue that the journal sought to alert the nation to the crying evil of racial prejudice. In its early years it printed articles by leading social reformers like Professor Franz Boas of Columbia University's anthropology department and Jane Addams of Chicago's Hull House. Other key contributors included Oswald Garrison Villard, Charles Edward Russell, Arthur Schomburg, and M. D. Maclean. In later years, mostly after 1915, the journal continued to include commentary by social scientists, but it also included more work on literature and the fine arts. With guidance from its literary editor, Jessie Fauset, it published work by Langston Hughes, Charles Chesnutt, Countee Cullen, and Claude McKay, and extensive excerpts from W. D. Howells and Mary White Ovington.

The Crisis provided a systematic critique of mainstream racial attitudes. Some articles articulated grievances; and in an editorial in April 1911, Du Bois identified five key problems: lack of opportunity to save money, local discrimination, discrimination in wages, mob violence, and legal violence. Much of the power of *The Crisis* came from its monthly catalog of injustices. An example is the case of Pink Franklin, who was serving a life sentence in a prison in South Carolina for killing a white man who had invaded Pink's house to try to enforce an arrest warrant; Franklin had violated South Carolina's "debt peonage" statute, which was subsequently struck down. *The Crisis* asked in February 1911: If a white man had

Cover of the first issue of *The Crisis*. (Corbis.)

committed a similar offense, would he ever have been convicted? In June 1916, an article entitled "Progressive Oklahoma" compared the rape of a black girl by a white man with a burglary committed by a black man in the same town on the same day: The rapist was free on bond, whereas the burglar was being severely punished.

Other articles exposed the hypocrisy of white Americans' attitudes. In November 1917, for instance, *The Crisis* pointed out contradictory statements in southern newspapers, such as a statement that blacks in Alabama were safe juxtaposed with a threat to punish any "Negro in any community who dares raise his hand against white men, no matter what the cause." Such statements showed that newspapers often exaggerated stories, making blacks who defended themselves against attack appear to be criminals, and exonerating whites from culpability for crimes. In one article, *The Crisis* cataloged how newspapers called attention to crimes by black people but failed to note the race of criminals when no blacks were involved.

According to a story in *The Crisis* in April 1911, these tendencies of the white press manufactured prejudice.

Often, *The Crisis* provided sophisticated social science critiques of inequality. In a series of long articles in the 1920s, it explored differences in quality between white and black schools in the southern states. Through meticulous analysis of such issues as expenditures per pupil, these articles demonstrated the shameful lack of educational opportunity for black students. Side-by-side pictures of schools for blacks and whites, along with graphs and tables, brought home the reality of separate educational systems. Baltimore, where segregated housing was required by zoning laws, received extended treatment, such as an article in November 1911, "A Year of Segregation in Baltimore."

Over the years, through close analysis of problems with voting rights, lynching, and legalized (or required) discrimination, Du Bois articulated a philosophy of equal treatment. This philosophy was captured in his statement in an article of April 1915: "The American negro demands equality—political equality, industrial equality, and social equality; and his is never going to rest satisfied with anything less." *The Crisis* built many of its arguments around the idea of equal treatment. That idea was central to American jurisprudence and had extraordinary power; thus there were frequent articles summarizing discrimination in voting rights, discrimination by police officers and prosecutors, and the persistence of lynching. One particularly contentious issue was legislation preventing marriage between blacks and whites; an editorial in February 1913 urged that such laws stamped blacks as inferior to whites and left black women subject to exploitation by white men.

The campaign against lynching was one of the most important throughout Du Bois's leadership of *The Crisis*. Lynching represented the worst breakdown of law; it also represented, according to a statement by James Weldon Johnson to the NAACP's annual meeting (reported in the September 1927 issue), "the seizing of black America's body and of white America's soul." Du Bois focused special attention on lynching, citing statistics, giving accounts of individual lynchings, and highlighting the complete failure of law enforcement agencies and prosecutors to punish lynchers. He also used photographs to attack lynching: These were a particularly compelling way to depict the gruesome details. White participants often took photos in order to celebrate lynchings (and then made postcards of these photos); Du Bois turned those same pictures to a different purpose. As he said in "Lynchers Triumphant" in December 1911, printing the photographs would show the world "what semi-barbarous America is doing." Similarly, in July 1916, the article "The Waco Horror" combined sociological inquiry with appalling photographs. "Jesus Christ in Georgia," published in December 1911, was a short story about a Christlike victim of a lynching.

As Congress was considering antilynching legislation, *The Crisis* printed legal analyses supporting such legislation. Lynching was the centerpiece of Du Bois's campaign for a new understanding of the equal protection of the law; he asked that blacks as well as whites be given the protection of laws against lynching. Moreover, equal treatment under the law promised to improve the lives of blacks in general: It promised economic opportunities and opportunities in housing, business, and education.

The rhetoric of democracy that prevailed during World War I was a key component of Du Bois's campaign for equal protection; he emphasized the differences in treatment that blacks received at home. However, under pressure from the NAACP and the war department, which had temporarily banned *The Crisis* from soldiers' reading rooms, Du Bois published a brief editorial in July 1918, entitled "Close Ranks." This editorial pointed out the benefits blacks could expect from defeating Germany and urged them to "close ranks" with whites and fight for democracy.

Still, Du Bois did not retreat from his demand for equal treatment; and after the war, his agitation landed him in trouble again. The post office delayed delivery of the May 1919 issue, which contained controversial material, including the article "Essay Toward a History of the Black Man in the Great War," describing the heroism of black soldiers during the war and exposing their mistreatment. The editorial "Returning Soldiers" promised that, although blacks had closed ranks during the war, they were now ready to demand equal treatment. It contained the ominous statement "We return. We return from fighting. We return fighting." A report to the U.S. Senate, "Radicalism and Sedition Among Negroes as Reflected in Their Publications," prepared by J. Edgar Hoover, who was then a young lawyer, quoted this editorial as an example of the objectionable material in *The Crisis*. Hoover paid *The Crisis* and other black periodicals—such as A. Philip Randolph's *Messenger*—the compliment of warning the Senate that "the influence of the Negro press" should not be "reckoned with lightly."

In February 1919, Du Bois went to Paris for the Pan-African Conference, which he had largely coordinated and which he reported on in the issues of April and May. This conference laid out a broad agenda for self-determination for African nations and opportunities for educational and economic advancement, as well as basic protections such as public health and decent working conditions. Du Bois's coverage of the conference marked a widening of focus for *The Crisis*, which now looked to Africa and the rest of the world, including Russia, Japan, and India.

The Crisis also celebrated the many triumphs of African Americans. Frequently, articles in *The Crisis* discussed legal victories: the United States Supreme Court's invalidation of debt peonage in 1911, of the "grandfather provision" in Oklahoma in 1915, and of zoning that segregated cities in 1917; the Interstate Commerce Commission's requirement of integration on certain railroad cars; and lower courts' decisions invalidating other racially restrictive covenants and punishing police officers who turned prisoners over to lynch mobs. Some articles noted economic successes; there were accounts, with pictures, of successful black professionals, educational achievements, college and professional athletes, and advances in art and music. The record label Black Swan received attention, as did Josephine Baker. Even the advertisements in *The Crisis* emphasized opportunities for economic advancement. Insurance companies, banks, real estate companies, and clothiers appealed for customers; colleges and technical schools sought students. One can see how, through the pages of *The Crisis*, the Harlem Renaissance was pushing back many frontiers.

By the end of World War I, the circulation of *The Crisis* reached approximately 80,000 copies per month; in 1919, circulation peaked at just over 100,000. *The Crisis* resumed its radical stance, examining, for instance, mob violence against African Americans and the unequal treatment that they received at the hands of the police. The issue of October 1919—a particularly radical edition—gave an account of how the black community in Longview, Texas, had armed to protect itself against lynching after one black man was lynched there. A riot in which several whites died had ensued, but the article described the black community's resort to "self help" in terms of admiration and concluded with a somber warning that "Negroes are not planning anything, but will defend themselves if attacked."

Throughout the 1920s, *The Crisis* increased its coverage of literature, art, and African culture; modern art, portraits, and scenes of Egypt and other African civilizations often appeared on its covers. At the same time it continued its efforts against lynching, focusing on the vicious riots that took place from 1917 through 1921. *The Crisis* campaigned relentlessly to free black tenant farmers who had been sentenced to death following a particularly heinous attack on the black community around Elaine, Arkansas, in 1919. The campaign culminated with Justice Oliver Wendell Holmes's landmark decision in *Moore* v. *Dempsey* in 1923; in the issue of April of that year, Walter White wrote an article entitled "The Defeat of Arkansas Mob Law."

Du Bois' socialist attitudes had often caused problems with the board of the NAACP, and he angered the board further with two editorials in 1934: "Segregation" in January and an elaboration, "Segregation in the North," in April, which seemed to oppose integration. As a result, Du Bois tendered his resignation and was replaced by Roy Wilkins. Thereafter, *The Crisis* continued to be published, but without the intellectual leadership that had made it so important to the Harlem Renaissance. Du Bois had crisply described the hypocrisy of whites with regard to race and had identified inconsistencies in the nation's treatment of blacks and whites. His theme of equal treatment, developed persistently for twenty-four years, bore extraordinary fruit. It was ultimately adopted and extended by courts and legislatures, so that ideas expressed in *The Crisis* became central parts of American law and culture. Ralph Ellison, in his essay "What Would America Be Like Without Blacks," listed contributions by African Americans to American culture; one is tempted to add to that list "the idea of equal protection under law." When Du Bois resigned, the board of the NAACP said that his ideas, particularly as expressed in *The Crisis*, had "transformed the Negro world as well as a large portion of the liberal white world, so that the whole problem of the relation of black and white races has ever since had a completely new orientation."

ALFRED L. BROPHY

See also Antilynching Crusade; Baker, Josephine; Black Swan Phonograph Company; Boas, Franz; Crisis, The: Literary Prizes; Du Bois, W. E. B.; Fauset, Jessie Redmon; Messenger, The; National Association for the Advancement of Colored People; Pan-African Congresses; Schomburg, Arthur A.; Villard, Oswald Garrison; *specific writers*

Further Reading

Investigation Activities of the Department of Justice, Sixty-sixth Congress, First Session. *Senate Docs.*, 153, 1919.

Jordan, William G. *Black Newspapers and America's War for Democracy, 1914–1920.* Chapel Hill: University of North Carolina Press, 2001.

Kornweibel, Theodore, Jr. *Seeing Red: Federal Campaigns Against Black Militancy, 1919–1925.* Bloomington: Indiana University Press, 1998.

Lewis, David Levering. *W. E. B. Du Bois: Biography of a Race, 1868–1919.* New York: Holt, 1993.

Lewis, David Levering, ed. *W. E. B. Du Bois: A Reader.* New York: Holt, 1995.

Lewis, David Levering. *W. E. B. Du Bois: The Fight for Equality and the American Century, 1919–1963.* New York: Holt, 2000.

Litwack, Leon. *Trouble in Mind: Black Southerners in the Age of Jim Crow.* New York: Vintage, 1998.

Washburn, Patrick S. *A Question of Sedition: The Federal Government's Investigation of the Black Press During World War II.* New York: Oxford University Press, 1986.

Crisis, The: Literary Prizes

The Crisis, the monthly magazine of the National Association for the Advancement of Colored People (NAACP), was first published in 1910. Its first editor was W. E. B. Du Bois, who was director of publicity and research when the NAACP was established, also in 1910, and who would remain the editor until 1934. Du Bois used the magazine to champion the rights of American blacks and people of color worldwide, but he also emphasized the promotion of African American arts—literature, music, fine art, and drama. His efforts with regard to the arts helped launch the careers of many figures who are now considered leaders of the Harlem Renaissance, including Zora Neale Hurston, Jean Toomer, Gwendolyn Bennett, and Anne Spencer.

The Crisis promoted the arts in various ways. First, through the arts it presented issues having to do with politics and social and civil rights. Second, it encouraged its readers to participate in and celebrate the arts. Third, it offered discussions of various aspects of the arts: art as propaganda, appropriate subjects for writing, appropriate styles of writing, and ways of portraying blacks in art. All these issues were debated between the covers of the magazine during the early decades of the twentieth century. Fourth, the well-known novelist, poet, and essayist Jessie Fauset was the literary editor of *The Crisis* from 1919 to 1926, and under her leadership many writers of the Harlem Renaissance were introduced to American audiences. Fifth—and of particular importance—*The Crisis* showcased the arts by sponsoring literary contests.

The Amy Spingarn Contest in Literature and Art was named for its benefactor, the poet Amy E. Spingarn, who was the wife of Joel Spingarn, the literary critic and chair of the NAACP from 1914 to 1919. The Spingarns were responsible for funding the first two literary contests. Amy Spingarn donated $600 in 1925 and 1926 for first-, second-, and third-place winners in fiction, drama, poetry, essays, and artwork. In 1927, she provided $350 for the literary prizes, while women's and commercial groups donated more than $1,600 for further literary awards. These additional patrons wanted the entries to have more themes related to finances and insurance, and to offer examples of financial industriousness among American blacks.

Judges of the contests included respected black and white writers such as Charles Chesnutt, Sinclair Lewis, H. G. Wells, James Weldon Johnson, William Stanley Braithwaite, Eugene O'Neill, and Du Bois himself. Winners included Arna Bontemps, Countee Cullen, Aaron Douglas, Rudolph Fisher, and Langston Hughes. In the poetry contest of 1926, for example, Arna Bontemps won the first prize of $100 for "A Nocturne at Bethesda," and Countee Cullen won second prize for "Thoughts in a Zoo."

The entries and judges declined in stature in 1927, and the annual contests were ended in 1928. Thereafter, Amy Spingarn and the business groups awarded the Charles Waddell Chesnutt Honoraria of $50 each for the best poetry and short story published each month. They also planned to have monthly economic prizes, but these were never actually awarded, owing to the small number of participants.

Another prominent editor, Charles S. Johnson of the National Urban League's magazine, *Opportunity*, also encouraged young black writers by offering cash prizes for literature. In addition, both *The Crisis* and *Opportunity* were very generous about publishing the work of aspiring writers; Du Bois also included in *The Crisis* the judges' remarks about the winning entries. Thus, although the contests sponsored by these magazines were of relatively short duration initially—about three years—they were important vehicles for talented figures of the Harlem Renaissance.

At *The Crisis*, literary prizes returned in the 1930s, funded by Louise Mathews, the mother-in-law of Oliver La Farge, the trustee of the awards, who wanted them to be called the Du Bois Literary Prizes. Each year, $1,000 was to be awarded; the rotating categories were prose fiction, prose nonfiction, and poetry. In 1932, no prize was given for prose fiction, because no entry was considered suitable. In 1933, the award for prose nonfiction was given to James Weldon Johnson's *Black Manhattan* (1930). In 1934, no award was given for poetry, because Du Bois resigned from *The Crisis* that year, and the awards were closely associated with him. When Roy Wilkins became the editor of *The Crisis* in 1934, the NAACP asserted its editorial control and insisted on reducing the magazine's literary content. Thereafter, *The Crisis* was never as essential an outlet for literary talent as it had been during the Harlem Renaissance.

LOU-ANN CROUTHER

See also Bennett, Gwendolyn; Crisis, The; Douglas, Aaron; Du Bois, W. E. B.; Fauset, Jessie Redmon; Hurston, Zora Neale; Johnson, Charles Spurgeon; Opportunity Literary Contests; Spencer, Anne; Spingarn, Joel; Toomer, Jean; *other specific writers*

Further Reading

Andrews, William L., Frances Smith Foster, and Trudier Harris, eds. *The Oxford Companion to African-American Literature*. New York: Oxford University Press, 1997.

Aptheker, Herbert, ed. *The Correspondence of W. E. B. Du Bois*, Vol. 1, *Selections, 1877–1934*. Amherst: University of Massachusetts Press, 1973.

Daniel, Walter C. *Black Journals of the United States*. Westport, Conn.: Greenwood, 1982.

Hutchinson, George. *The Harlem Renaissance in Black and White*. Cambridge, Mass.: Belknap Press of Harvard University Press, 1995.

Johnson, Abby Arthur, and Ronald Mayberry Johnson. *Propaganda and Aesthetics: The Literary Politics of Afro-American Magazines in the Twentieth Century*. Amherst: University of Massachusetts Press, 1979.

Kramer, Victor A., and Robert A. Russ, eds. *Harlem Renaissance Re-Examined: A Revised and Expanded Edition*. Troy, N.Y.: Whitson, 1997.

Lewis, David Levering. *When Harlem Was in Vogue*. Toronto: Random House of Canada; New York: Knopf, 1981.

Moon, Henry Lee. "History of 'The Crisis.'" *Crisis*, 77(9), 1987.

Crisis, The: The Negro In Art—How Shall He Be Portrayed? A Symposium

W. E. B. Du Bois did not set out to transform *The Crisis* into the premier African American literary journal, but under his editorial leadership it became one of the most important showcases for the early work of many young writers of the Harlem Renaissance. Du Bois viewed this new literature in terms of its potential for improving race relations. An extended example of his view of literature as a tool for racial progress begins with his editorial in February 1926 issue of *The Crisis*, in which he calls for a symposium, "The Negro in Art: How Shall He Be Portrayed?," and lists seven questions. These questions were reprinted with each of the seven installments of the symposium appearing in the journal in the months that followed:

1. When the artist, black or white, portrays Negro characters, is he under any obligations or limitations as to the sort of character he will portray?
2. Can any author be criticized for painting the worst or the best characters of a group?
3. Can publishers be criticized for refusing to handle novels that portray Negroes of education and accomplishment, on the ground that these characters are no different from white folk and therefore not interesting?
4. What are Negroes to do when they are continually painted at their worst and judged by the public as they are painted?
5. Does the situation of the educated Negro in America with its pathos, humiliation, and tragedy call for artistic treatment at least as sincere and sympathetic as "Porgy" received?
6. Is not the continual portrayal of the sordid, foolish, and criminal among Negroes convincing the world that this and this alone is really and essentially Negroid, and preventing white artists from knowing any other types and preventing black artists from daring to paint them?
7. Is there not a real danger that young colored writers will be tempted to follow the popular trend in portraying Negro characters in the underworld rather than seeking to paint the truth about themselves and their own social class?

These questions reflected Du Bois's legitimate concerns about the effect of white patronage on African American art and about the reinforcement of negative images of black people in the white popular imagination, but what begins in this symposium as a call to dialogue ends in rhetorical posturing. The first three, open-ended questions are followed by two that assume a particular stance toward recent literature and its impact on public opinion (question 4, for instance, implies that African Americans indeed were being "continually painted at their worst" and that they were viewed accordingly by a large number of readers). The list then ends with two closed-ended questions. Several participants in the symposium openly criticized the formulation of the questions. H. L. Mencken replied that the fifth question was "simply rhetorical"; Alfred A. Knopf found the third one "to be senseless" and the others rarely to deserve more than a one-word reply.

The symposium included an impressive list of names, and many of the responses deserve closer attention. As the first contributor to the first installment, Carl Van Vechten did not address the questions directly, but his reply anticipated the speech of the white editor in his novel *Nigger Heaven*; he argues that the "wealth of novel, exotic, picturesque material" found in lower-class African American life will be used to the point of exhaustion by the white artist unless the African American succeeds in representing it in art first. Other white intellectuals and artists, addressing Du Bois's questions more systematically, agreed with Van Vechten that the black artist should be free to choose any subject matter. Mencken stated that the artist should be "under no obligations or limitations whatsoever." Vachel Lindsay rejected the idea of obligations and maintained that the artist must only be "honest." DuBose Heyward also held that the "sincere artist" is not obligated in any way and that art "destroys itself as soon as it is made a vehicle for propaganda." Julia Peterkin agreed: "The minute anyone becomes an advocate he ceases to be an artist." The "true artist, black or white," Peterkin continued, "will search for these tokens of racial worth and weave around them his contribution to literature."

Black writers were far less unified in their responses. In his brief reply, Langston Hughes—like the white respondents—insisted on the freedom of the "true literary artist." Similarly, Walter White maintained that "the artist should be allowed full freedom in the choice of his characters and material." Other black writers, however, identified more closely with Du Bois's concerns. Jessie Fauset was in emphatic agreement with the implication of Du Bois's final question, regarding pressures on the young black writer to portray only the sordid side of black life. She added: "This is a grave danger making for a literary insincerity both insidious and abominable." Countee Cullen's response was more measured but still in line with Du Bois's concerns: "Negro artists have a definite duty to perform in this matter [of reconstructing the image of black people in literature], one which should supersede their individual prerogatives without denying their rights." Cullen also noted that the young black writer should choose material freely, even from among lower-class blacks, but he then added "only let him not pander to the popular trend of seeing no cleanliness in their squalor, no nobleness in their meanness, and no commonsense in their ignorance."

The varied responses to the questions in this symposium mirror a larger debate in the Harlem Renaissance about the responsibilities and freedoms of the African American artist and the proper roles of white critics and publishers. In its May 1926 issue, *The Crisis* carried the third grouping of responses to the questions and announced briefly that Jessie Fauset had stepped down from her position as the journal's literary editor. The fourth installment of the symposium coincided with the publication of Langston Hughes's essay "The Negro Artist and the Racial Mountain" in *The Nation* (23 June 1926), in which Hughes most famously develops his position on the responsibilities and freedoms of the African American writer. Along with the second-to-last set of responses (October 1926), Du Bois issued his own manifesto on blacks' creative production, "Criteria of Negro Art," in which he famously asserts: "All art is propaganda and ever must be, despite the wailing of the purists. . . . I do not care a damn for any art that is not used for propaganda." In the December 1926 issue of *The Crisis* (the issue following the last of the set of printed responses to the symposium), Du Bois published his scathing review of Carl Van Vechten's novel *Nigger Heaven* (1926). Subsequent novels by others, including Julia Peterkin's *Black April* (1927) and Claude McKay's *Home to Harlem* (1928), also drew Du Bois's sharp

criticism for their unsavory representations of African American life.

The symposium "The Negro in Art—How Shall He Be Portrayed?" remains of interest as an example of Du Bois's concerns about literary tastes and publishing trends and as a concise record of the views of many other artists and intellectuals important to the Harlem Renaissance.

JAMES B. KELLEY

See also Crisis, The; Cullen, Countee; Du Bois, W. E. B.; Fauset, Jessie Redmon; Heyward, DuBose; Knopf, Alfred A.; Lindsay, Vachel; Mencken, H. L.; Nigger Heaven; Peterkin, Julia Mood; Van Vechten, Carl

Further Reading

Kelley, James. "Blossoming in Strange New Forms: Male Homosexuality and the Harlem Renaissance." *Soundings*, 80(4), Winter 1997.

"The Negro in Art: How Shall He Be Portrayed—A Symposium." *Crisis*, 31(4), February 1926; 31(5), March 1926; 31(6), April 1926; 32(1), May 1926; 32(2), June 1926; 32(4), August 1926; 32(5), September 1926; 33(1), November 1926.

Rampersad, Arnold. *The Art and Imagination of W. E. B. Du Bois*. Cambridge, Mass.: Harvard University Press, 1976.

Cullen, Countee

Concerning Countee Cullen (1903–1946), there is a sense of expectations unfulfilled. Cullen was one of the most respected poets of the Harlem Renaissance; but although the publication of *Color* in 1925 announced a young poet full of promise and potential, this first volume would turn out to be his best, so much so that critics and Cullen himself often noted the underachievement of his subsequent publications. As the author of several evocative and poignant lines about not only African Americans but also "universal" topics, such as life, death, and love, Cullen demands more serious appraisal and evaluation than he has yet received.

Cullen's early background consists of puzzling ambiguities. There is, for example, some discrepancy about the place of his birth: Louisville, Kentucky; Baltimore, Maryland; and New York City have all been cited at various times. In addition, little is known about his real parents. Records suggest that as a young child he lived with his grandmother. After she died, he lived with Rev. Frederick A. and Carolyn Cullen of New York. By 1918, when he may have been adopted by the Cullens, he identified himself as Countee P. Cullen; and eventually he called himself simply Countee Cullen.

Cullen had a classic literary education that influenced his poetry. He attended Dewitt Clinton High School, and his first published poems appeared in the high school literary journal, *The Magpie*, of which he was the associate editor during his senior year. He attended New York University from 1921 to 1925, after which he received his master's degree in English and French from Harvard University. From 1926 to 1928, Cullen wrote an editorial and book review column for *Opportunity* magazine called "The Dark Tower."

In April 1928, Cullen married Nina Yolande Du Bois, the daughter of W. E. B. Du Bois; Rev. Frederick A. Cullen performed the ceremony, which was well publicized, at his church. This union of two young members of the "talented tenth" appeared to be successful. Nina Yolande Du Bois received her master's degree from Columbia University and taught art and English at Frederick Douglass High School in Baltimore, and Cullen had recently won a Guggenheim fellowship; this fellowship sent him to France, and Yolande followed later. However, they divorced in March 1930 after being married for less than two years. Cullen was married again in 1940, to Ida Mae Roberson, whose scrapbooks concerning her husband have offered a wealth of information for scholars.

Cullen was a successful writer of sonnets, and the early nineteenth-century English poet John Keats was his model. But Cullen's usual choice of subject matter has tended to draw harsh criticism. Huggins (1971) described Cullen as "forever true" to a "genteel" straitjacket (211), and Shucard (1984) said that "Cullen's voice sometimes sounds effete" (16). Cullen himself held his writings to a high standard. His own definition of "good poetry" expresses his idealistic criteria:

[G]ood poetry is a lofty thought beautifully expressed. . . . Poetry should not be too intellectual; it should deal more . . . with the emotions. The highest type of poem is that which warmly stirs the emotions, which awakens a responsive chord in the human heart. Poetry, like music, depends upon feeling rather than intellect, although there should of course be enough to satisfy the mind, too. (quoted in Perry 1971, 29)

Perhaps because of his artistic ideals, Cullen explicitly rejected a poetic identification solely with African Americans; in this, he differed from his contemporaries Claude McKay and Langston Hughes, who both made explicit references to their racial background (in McKay's case, that background was Caribbean). Cullen (1927) revealed his reluctance to be identified only as a "Negro poet" in the preface to an anthology he edited, *Caroling Dusk*:

I have called this collection an anthology of verse by Negro poets rather than an anthology of Negro verse, since this latter designation would be more confusing than accurate. . . . The attempt to corral the outbursts of the ebony muse into some definite mold to which all poetry by Negroes will conform seems altogether futile and aside from the facts. . . . As heretical as it may sound, there is the probability that Negro poets, dependent as they are on the English language, may have more to gain from the rich background of English and American poetry than from any nebulous atavistic yearnings toward an African inheritance. (xi)

These comments reveal the extent to which Cullen perceived the primitive as an unwelcome, anachronistic legacy for black people. Indeed, one of Cullen's best-known poems, "Heritage," evokes the divided response of the African American to his African past. Cullen's more "universal" poems were attempts not to deny his racial background but to assert the poet's right to compose lines on subjects not explicitly dealing with race:

Must we, willy-nilly, be forced into writing of the old atavistic urges, the more savage and none too beautiful aspects of our lives? May we not chant a hymn to the Sun God if we will, create a bit of phantasy in which not a spiritual or a blues appears, write a tract defending Christianity, though its practitioners aid us so little in our argument; in short do, write, create what we will, our only concern being that we do it well and with all the power in us? (1929, 373)

Cullen perceived the interest of the (usually white) public in the primitive and the salacious as a limitation for the black writer. Indeed, in his review of Langston Hughes's first book of poems, *The Weary Blues*, Cullen (1926) expressed a belief that Hughes was indulging in sensuality. He said, for instance, that Hughes's jazz poems "tend to hurl this poet into the gaping pit that lies before all Negro writers, in the confines of which they become racial artists rather than artists pure and simple. There is too much emphasis here on strictly Negro themes" (74). For Cullen, Hughes' "spontaneous" poems coincided too well with the public's expectations of blackness.

Although Cullen resisted the title "black poet," some of his most memorable and most often anthologized poems are those that deal with the experience of race. In addition to "Heritage," other well-known poems such as "Incident," "Uncle Jim," and "From the Dark Tower" continue to resonate with readers decades after they were first published. The sonnet "Yet Do I Marvel," contains the classic couplet "Yet do I marvel at this curious thing:/To make a poet black and bid him sing!" One of Cullen's later poems, "Karenge Ya Marenge" (1942), evokes the frustrated desire for liberty that impelled the leader Mohandas Gandhi:

> Is Indian speech so quaint, so weak, so rude,
>
> So like its land enslaved, denied, and crude,
>
> That men who claim they fight for liberty
>
> Can hear this battle-shout impassively . . . ?

Cullen also wrote several long, narrative poems. *The Black Christ* was the story of a lynching, and *The Ballad of the Brown Girl* told the story of a young maiden whose lover leaves her for another.

Cullen's novel *One Way to Heaven* (1932) is sometimes taken as a response to Carl Van Vechten's novel of Harlem, *Nigger Heaven* (1926). Though frequently dismissed in favor of his poetry, *One Way to Heaven* does exhibit Cullen's strong writing skills. The opening chapter, for example, offers a quite dramatic and perceptive description of an African American church revival. In addition, Cullen's emphasis on a lower-class black couple, the usually unemployed Sam Lucas and the maid Mattie Johnson, makes this work stand out from the other novels of the period that dealt with the educated members of the talented tenth or with the familiar issue of racial passing. Unlike Van Vechten's Scarlet Creeper in *Nigger Heaven*, Sam, with his illegal escapes, inspires the reader's comprehension and sympathy.

Less known though equally intriguing are Cullen's children's stories: *My Lives and How I Lost Them*, about the adventures of a cat; and *The Lost Zoo*, about the animals that missed the opportunity to board Noah's ark. Cullen apparently had a strong interest in cats: He "cowrote" these children's books with a feline, Mr. Christopher Cat.

From 1934 until his death, Cullen taught French and English at Frederick Douglass High School in New York, where the young James Baldwin was one of his students. At the time Cullen died, he was in the process of collecting what he considered his best poems; this collection was published posthumously as *On These I Stand*. One of his other final projects was his work with Arna Bontemps on a dramatic version of Bontemps's novel *God Sends Sunday*. It was produced as *Saint Louis Woman* several months after Cullen's death.

One of the more recent issues in scholarship on Countee Cullen has been his sexual orientation. When Cullen left the United States on his Guggenheim fellowship, his best friend, Harold Jackman, went with him; there has been speculation that the two may have been lovers. Cullen's poem "Tableau" (1925) may support these conjectures: It presents two boys, one black and one white, "locked arm in arm." Although passersby are "indignant that these two should dare/In unison to walk," the boys are "oblivious to look and

Countee Cullen in Central Park, New York, 1941. (Library of Congess.)

word." However, Early (1991) notes that "nothing conclusive" has been presented to substantiate these claims (19, n. 21), and Cullen did have a strong relationship with second wife, Ida. In brief, there are some scholars who take Cullen's homosexuality as a given, whereas others have been more resistant to this idea.

Cullen died 9 January 1946, never having produced another volume that would receive as much critical acclaim as his first, *Color*. Bontemps (1947) noted that "Cullen did not live to see another springtime resurgence of his own creative powers comparable with the impulse that produced the first three books of poetry, the books which give his selected poems most of their lilt and brightness" (44). Nor has Cullen received as much retrospective attention as other writers of the Harlem Renaissance, such as Hughes. As Early (1991) suggests, this may have more to do with "the dynamics and politics of the making of a black literary reputation" (6) than with the perception that Cullen's writing is not worthy of new criticism. Although Cullen has been criticized for not being bolder in experimenting with his gift, he was unequaled in his talent for creating what one can politely call the formal poetry of the Harlem Renaissance.

Biography

The poet Countee P. Cullen (originally named Countee Porter) was born in 1903; the place of his birth is not certain, and little is known of his parents. He evidently lived with a grandmother; after her death, he lived with Rev. Frederick A. and Carolyn Cullen of New York, who may have adopted him by 1918. He then identified himself as Countee P. Cullen, and eventually simply as Countee Cullen. He attended Dewitt Clinton High School, and his first published poems appeared in its literary journal. He attended New York University (1921–1925) and then received a master's degree in English and French from Harvard University. In 1926–1928, he wrote an editorial and book review column, "The Dark Tower," for *Opportunity* magazine. In April 1928, he married Nina Yolande Du Bois, the daughter of W. E. B. Du Bois; this marriage ended in divorce in March 1930, and in 1940, he married Ida Mae Roberson. In addition to poetry, Cullen wrote a novel and children's stories. From 1934 to his death in 1946, he taught French and English at Frederick Douglass High School in New York.

MIRIAM THAGGERT

See also Authors: 5—Poets; Bontemps, Arna; *Color*; Cullen, Frederick Asbury; Cullen–Du Bois Wedding; Guggenheim Fellowships; Homosexuality; Hughes, Langston; Jackman, Harold; Literature: 7—Poetry; McKay, Claude; Primitivism; Talented Tenth; Van Vechten, Carl; *specific works*

Selected Works

The Ballad of the Brown Girl: An Old Ballad Retold. New York: Harper, 1927.
The Black Christ and Other Poems. New York: Harper, 1929.
Color. New York: Harper, 1925.
Copper Sun. New York: Harper, 1927.
Caroling Dusk: An Anthology of Verse by Negro Poets. New York: Harper, 1927.
The Medea, and Some Poems. New York: Harper, 1935.
On These I Stand: An Anthology of the Best Poems of Countee Cullen. New York: Harper, 1947.
One Way to Heaven. New York: Harper, 1932.

Further Reading

Bontemps, Arna. "The Harlem Renaissance." *Saturday Review of Literature*, 22 March 1947, pp. 12 ff.
Cullen, Countee. "Poet on Poet." *Opportunity*, February 1926, p. 73.
———. "Countee Cullen on Miscegenation." *Crisis*, November 1929, p. 373.
Early, Gerald, ed. *My Soul's High Song: The Collected Writings of Countee Cullen, Voice of the Harlem Renaissance*. New York: Doubleday, 1991.
Huggins, Nathan. *Harlem Renaissance*. New York: Oxford University Press, 1971.
Perry, Margaret. *A Bio-Bibliography of Countee Cullen, 1903–1946*. Westport, Conn.: Greenwood, 1971.
Shucard, Alan R. *Countee Cullen*. Boston, Mass.: G. K. Hall, 1984.

Cullen, Frederick Asbury

Frederick Asbury Cullen served for forty-two years as minister of Salem Methodist Episcopal Church in Harlem, but he is now remembered primarily as the foster father of the poet Countee Cullen. Having unofficially adopted the teenage Countee Porter, Cullen and his wife, Carolyn, raised the boy and introduced him to Harlem's prestigious social circles, which would eventually celebrate him as Harlem's poet laureate. Frederick Cullen promoted his son's achievements as any father might do, attending readings and reprinting two of his son's poems in his self-published autobiography. Yet Frederick Cullen's significance hardly turned solely on his son's prestige. Indeed, as a minister, Cullen was clearly a more influential figure in Harlem than a poet could ever hope to be.

Arriving in 1902, Frederick Cullen began a ministry to Harlem under the aegis of Saint Mark's Methodist Episcopal Church. The Salem mission began with a service attended by three women, who left nineteen cents in the offering plate. But riding the wave of the "great migration," and inspired by Cullen's indefatigable evangelism, Salem swelled to more than 2,500 members by the 1920s. Along with churches such as Abyssinian Baptist, Salem became one of the most significant social institutions in Harlem, and its minister one of the most influential leaders. Prodded by Cullen, Salem began a variety of social ministries. Further, unlike some ministers, who catered to the tastes of the black bourgeoisie, Cullen changed the culture of worship at Salem in order to welcome southern immigrants. For instance, at the risk of some ridicule, he welcomed the flamboyant evangelist George W. Becton to his pulpit.

While insisting that the ultimate cure for Harlem's social ills was conversion to Christianity, Cullen also participated energetically in the political events of his day. He helped organize the Silent Parade of 1919 and headed a delegation to President Woodrow Wilson to protest against the execution of black soldiers following riots in Brownsville, Texas. Cullen was also an early member of the National Association for the Advancement of Colored People (NAACP); he served as president of the Harlem chapter and helped send W. E. B. Du Bois to the first Pan-African Congress. Thus, while Cullen's ideology and path to leadership mark him as a member of a more conservative generation of black leaders, he can also be seen as an early prototype of New Negro activism, paving the path for his son and other writers of the Harlem Renaissance.

This having been said, it remains true that Cullen's most direct significance to the Harlem Renaissance was through his influence on his son. A vigorous proponent of the traditional moral strictures of Methodism, Frederick Cullen often preached against the vices and entertainments of Harlem that he feared would lead his flock astray. Clearly, Frederick Cullen's devotion accounted for much of Countee Cullen's self-proclaimed

struggle between his "Christian upbringing" and the "pagan inclination" that he associated with poetry, with Africa, and with his homoerotic desires. Some commentators have suggested that the younger Cullen's struggle reflected tension having to do with Frederick Cullen's own ambiguous sexuality. Nevertheless, the son deeply appreciated his father's benevolence, penning several poems in his father's praise. The two remained lifelong companions, often traveling together to Europe and the Middle East. This intimate bond was symbolized when father and son died in the same year, 1946.

Biography

Frederick Asbury Cullen was born c. 1868 in Somerset County, Maryland. He was educated in Somerset County public schools and at Maryland State Normal School (later Towson University); he studied theology at Morgan College (1901). Cullen was converted to Christianity at Sharp Street Methodist Church in Baltimore, Maryland, in September 1894; he was ordained as a minister in Delaware County, Maryland, in 1900. He served as minister of the Methodist Episcopal Church in Catlin, Maryland (1900–1902) and of Salem Methodist Episcopal Church (later Salem United Methodist) in Harlem (1902–1944). He served as president of the Harlem branch of the NAACP and helped organize the National Urban League (1910). Cullen died 25 May 1946.

PETER POWERS

See also Abyssinian Baptist Church; Becton, George Wilson; Cullen, Countee; Lynching: Silent Protest Parade; National Urban League; Saint Mark's Methodist Episcopal Church

Further Reading

Anderson, Jervis. *This Was Harlem: A Cultural Portrait, 1900–1950*. New York: Farrar, Straus & Giroux, 1982.
Cullen, Frederick Asbury. *From Barefoot Town to Jerusalem*. N.d.
Early, Gerald, Introduction. In *My Soul's High Song: Collected Writings of Countee Cullen, Voice of the Harlem Renaissance*. New York: Doubleday, 1991.
———. "About Countee Cullen's Life and Career." In *Modern American Poetry: An Online Journal and Multimedia Companion to Anthology of Modern American*

Poetry, ed. Cary Nelson. New York: Oxford University Press, 2000. (Web site.)

Sernett, Milton C. *Bound for the Promised Land: African-American Religion and the Great Migration.* Durham, N.C., and London: Duke University Press, 1997.

Cullen–Du Bois Wedding

The wedding of Yolande Du Bois (1900–1961) and Countee Cullen took place on Easter Monday, 9 April 1928, at Salem Methodist Episcopal Church in Harlem. It had the aura of a royal wedding and became known as the single most important social event of the Harlem Renaissance. Yolande Du Bois, who was then twenty-five, was the only surviving child of the scholar and activist William Edward Burghardt (W. E. B.) Du Bois and his wife, Nina; she had been educated at Fisk University and was a teacher in the Baltimore public school system. Countee Cullen, then twenty-four, was one of the leading poets in the Harlem Renaissance ("Yet Do I Marvel" is among his best-known poems) and was one of the rare artists of the period who had actually grown up in Harlem; he was the adopted son of Rev. Frederick Cullen and Frederick's wife, Carolyn.

It appears that Yolande Du Bois and Countee Cullen had been introduced in the mid-1920s by Cullen's best friend, Harold Jackman, a debonair and charming man about town who encouraged their acquaintance. The courtship was somewhat rocky. With the support of her father, Cullen proposed to Yolande Du Bois during the Christmas holiday season of 1927; then, Cullen and W. E. B. Du Bois spent the next few months planning the wedding, with some input from her.

Extensive coverage by the African American press kept readers informed of virtually every detail of the wedding. Everything associated with the wedding was news—including the special rail car used to transport Yolande Du Bois and her bridesmaids from Baltimore, and Countee Cullen's receipt of the marriage license four days before the ceremony so as to not be inconvenienced by any potential closing of the office for the Easter holiday. On the day of the wedding, the church was overcrowded, perhaps because of a banner headline that had appeared in the Baltimore *Afro-American* on the Saturday before—"5,000 to See Her Married Monday"—above a large photograph of Yolande Du Bois. There

were actually 1,200 invited guests, but 3,000 people attended the ceremony. This seems to have put Frederick Cullen, the minister who was to perform the marriage, in an awkward position; he was compelled to state "This isn't my wedding!"—explaining that the bride's parents were in charge of it and that he himself could not include additional guests. Yolande Du Bois was attended by sixteen bridesmaids. Countee Cullen was attended by nine groomsmen, including Edward Perry, Langston Hughes, Arna Bontemps, and Sydney Peterson; Harold Jackman served as his best man. After the wedding, the couple left New York City on Tuesday, 10 April 1928, for visits to Philadelphia; Atlantic City, New Jersey; and Great Barrington, Massachusetts. By the following week both were back at their jobs in New York City and Baltimore, respectively; however, their brief honeymoon was followed by a more extensive vacation later that summer.

Gossip spread when the African American press reported that Countee Cullen and Harold Jackman left for Europe in June 1928 and then that Yolande Cullen joined her husband in August. By September–October, W. E. B. Du Bois was counseling his son-in-law on maintaining the marriage. Presumably, the issue was not Yolande Cullen's inexperience or her ways as a spoiled child but rather that Countee Cullen eventually admitted his preference for men, and the marriage was over. The separation and divorce were negotiated by Countee Cullen and W. E. B. Du Bois. The divorce became final in France in the spring of 1930.

JACQUELINE C. JONES

See also Cullen, Countee; Cullen, Frederick Asbury; Du Bois, W. E. B.; Jackman, Harold

Further Reading

Belles, A. Gilbert. "Du Bois: The Father." *Crisis*, November 1980, pp. 389–391.

Du Bois, W. E. B. "So the Girl Marries." *Crisis*, June 1928, pp. 192–193, 207–209.

———. "Dr. Du Bois, 93, Writes Daughter's Obituary." *Baltimore Afro American*, 18 March 1961.

Ferguson, Blanche. *Countee Cullen and the Negro Renaissance.* New York: Dodd, Mead, 1966.

Lewis, David Levering. *When Harlem Was in Vogue.* New York: Random House, 1981.

———. *W. E. B. Du Bois: The Fight for Equality and the American Century, 1919–1963*. New York: Holt, 2000.
Shucard, Alan. *Countee Cullen*. Boston, Mass.: Twayne, 1984.

Cultural Organizations

A wide range of cultural organizations existed during the Harlem Renaissance to support the arts. They functioned in both formal and informal capacities. Black institutions such as the National Association for the Advancement of Colored People (NAACP) and the National Urban League gave significant support to the arts, although their main purposes were broader social and political missions. Public libraries served as informal community centers; the 135th Street branch of the New York Public Library (now known as the Countee Cullen Regional Branch) was a central gathering place during the 1920s, with a series of forums that attracted a wide audience. Groups such as the Young Men's Christian Association (YMCA) located in black neighborhoods offered cultural events and provided spaces for plays and exhibitions. Wealthy white philanthropists ran foundations that benefited black artists directly. Last, interested African American individuals sponsored culture broadly within the black community.

Black associations played a critical role in encouraging young African American writers, artists, and musicians. Although not specifically created as cultural organizations, the National Urban League and the NAACP celebrated literature and the fine arts and recognized the achievements of African Americans through award programs. The magazines of both these organizations, *Opportunity* and *The Crisis*, published significant amounts of poetry and art by up-and-coming African Americans. In 1914, Joel E. Spingarn, chairman of the board of the NAACP, established the Spingarn Medal; it was given annually to an African American of note who had made significant contributions in "any field of elevated or honorable human endeavor." A decade later, Spingarn's wife, Amy Spingarn, established the Amy Spingarn Prizes for literature and the arts. The awards were announced in *The Crisis*, and the magazine sponsored the first awards ceremony at a dinner at the Renaissance Casino at 138th Street in August 1925. Several months earlier, the National Urban League sponsored the *Opportunity* Literary Contest, which gave prizes for short stories, poetry, and drama. The first *Opportunity* awards were given in May 1925 at a dinner at the Fifth Avenue Restaurant. Among the winners were Zora Neale Hurston, Langston Hughes, and Countee Cullen, all young writers who formed the epicenter of the Harlem Renaissance.

Although it was not so well recognized in this regard, Marcus Garvey's Universal Negro Improvement Association (UNIA) published literature and poetry in its official weekly newspaper, *Negro World*, and sponsored literary clubs for its members. *Negro World* was an outlet for the young Zora Neale Hurston and Eric Walrond and for other aspiring writers from Africa, the Caribbean, and Central America. Branches of the UNIA established literary clubs in Boston, Portland (Oregon), Norfolk (Virginia), Philadelphia, and New York as well as in Montreal, Cuba, and the West Indies. These clubs arranged for members to attend concerts, poetry readings, and plays and participate in debates. Members of the UNIA frequently held functions at the 135th Street Library. The Booklovers Club met regularly at this library, and intellectuals associated with the UNIA presented lectures on topics such as "Negro Prose Writers," "Books and How to Read Them," and "Nordic Culture and the Negro" (Martin 1983).

The 135th Street Library was created with funds from Andrew Carnegie (he had donated $5.2 million to New York City to build sixty-seven library branches, which were completed between 1901 and 1929). It opened on 14 January 1905 in a three-story classical revival building, designed by McKim, Mead, and White, with large windows, a wood-paneled vestibule, round plaster columns, and a main staircase with iron railings. The location of the 135th Street branch was central to its success: The 135th Street YMCA, Harlem Hospital, Abyssinian Baptist Church, and an elementary school were located within a radius of a few blocks.

The 135th Street Library was a repository for African and African American materials and an important place for the study of black culture. In 1920, Ernestine Rose was appointed librarian, with Catherine Allen Latimer as assistant librarian. Latimer, the first black librarian hired by the New York Public Library, began to create clipping files on black history and established a separate collection of books on African American life. Rose and Latimer eventually established, on the third floor of the library, a separate reference collection called the Division of Negro History. In 1926, the New York Public Library, with a $10,000 gift from the Carnegie Corporation, purchased the bibliophile Arthur Schomburg's collection of rare books, prints, and manuscripts, making this division one of the most significant collections of such materials in the United States.

In the evenings, the 135th Street Library was alive with activity; it was a facility where one could see African American art and attend various cultural events. Rose, with the assistance of Jessie Fauset, Ethel Ray Nance, and Gwendolyn Bennett, organized poetry readings, book discussions, and other literary activities at the library. The 135th Street Library also lent its space for the annual Harmon Foundation exhibits. Writing about the importance of local library branches, Rose said that "the function of a library in any community is to act as a natural center for the development of the community's intellectual life" (Sinnette 1989). In the pursuit of this development of the mind, the library sponsored a Library Forum. One such forum took place in March 1923 with Countee Cullen, Bennett, Langston Hughes, Sadie Peterson, and the sculptor Augusta Savage reciting their poetry, Eric Walrond reading a short story, and Arthur Schomburg sitting in the audience (Martin 1983).

The "colored branches" of the YMCA also provided spaces for exhibitions, concerts, lectures, and literary and educational programs. African Americans had a long history of participation in the YMCA, which was established in the United States in 1852. Although the YMCA focused primarily on improving the spiritual and intellectual life of its members, its "colored branches" served broader goals in the African American community. The Washington, D.C., YMCA, one of the oldest branches in the nation, articulated the mission as the "mental, moral, and spiritual improvement of our race" (Mjagkij 1994). In segregated America, the "colored branches" offered, among other things, swimming pools, gymnasiums, reading rooms, dormitories, and cafés solely for the use of African American men. They provided opportunities for professional and personal development through organized sports, father-and-son events, and classes. Women attended evenings dedicated to cultural activities.

Between 1912 and 1933, twenty-four "colored branches" of the YMCA were built around the United States in such cities as Chicago (1913), Philadelphia (1914), and Cincinnati (1916). Most were constructed with substantial funding from Julius Rosenwald, the president of Sears, Roebuck, who was a committed philanthropist. In 1918, a new YMCA opened in Brooklyn on Carleton Avenue; the following year, the newly built 135th Street YMCA opened to much fanfare. The 135th Street YMCA became a center of activity in Harlem. Paul Robeson performed there in 1920, in a production of Ridgely Torrence's *Simon the Cyrenian*, and W. E. B. Du Bois's Krigwa Players presented a full repertoire of dramas that attracted wide attendance in the YMCA's new auditorium. The Krigwa Players performed works by the black playwrights Angelina Weld Grimké, Willis Richardson, Georgia Douglas Johnson, and Eulalie Spence. Branches in Washington, D.C., Chicago, and Brooklyn were early locations for exhibitions devoted to the work of African American artists.

One of the key cultural organizations to emerge during the Harlem Renaissance was the Harmon Foundation, established in 1922 by the philanthropist and real estate tycoon William E. Harmon. This organization's original mission was to encourage individual self-help. Harmon later acknowledged African Americans' accomplishments when he established, in 1926, a five-year award program: the William E. Harmon Awards for Distinguished Achievement Among Negroes. Awards were offered in eight categories: literature, music, fine arts, business and industry, science and invention, education, religious service, and race relations. The Commission on Race Relations of the Federal Council of Churches of Christ in America under the guidance of George Haynes administered the Awards for Distinguished Achievement from 1926 to 1930. Harmon selected Haynes because of his dedicated service to interracial cooperation (Reynolds and Wright 1989).

From 1928 to 1933, the Harmon Foundation sponsored annual juried exhibitions to show the work of African American artists. The director, Mary Beattie Brady, established that a jury of five experts would evaluate the work. Artists submitted a portfolio that included art completed within the competition year, letters of recommendation, biographical information, and a recent photograph. Titled "Exhibit of Fine Arts Productions of American Negro Artists," the first three Harmon exhibitions opened in New York City at International House, located at 500 Riverside Drive. In 1931, the annual exhibition was moved to a better space for exhibiting art, the Art Center at 65–67 East 56th Street. With the assistance of the Commission on Race Relations, Brady also sponsored traveling exhibitions of the work; these went to art museums, colleges such as Fisk University and Spelman College, libraries, and "colored branches" of the YMCA. The last Harmon

Cultural Organizations

Foundation exhibition took place in 1933. At the end of its five-year commitment, the organization decided to redirect its attention by supporting smaller group and solo exhibitions and providing small stipends directly to artists.

Although it clearly presented opportunities for exhibition, the Harmon Foundation and more particularly its director came under attack in the 1930s for including artists who appeared to lack ability, for segregating African Americans from the mainstream art world, and for assuming that black artists shared innate "racial qualities." The most noted critique came from the artist Romare Bearden in an article entitled "The Negro Artist and Modern Art" for *Opportunity* in December 1934. He accused the Harmon Foundation of coddling and patronizing black artists and of creating a standard of inferiority by which African Americans would be judged as lesser artists in relation to the mainstream art world.

The Barnes Foundation would appear to have been less directly involved in the Harlem Renaissance, but it was an important place that encouraged art education, African art, and African American music. In 1922, Albert C. Barnes, a well-to-do pharmaceutical businessman and physician, established the Barnes Foundation on a 12-acre arboretum in Merion, Pennsylvania. Barnes created the educational institution "to promote the advancement of education and the appreciation of the fine arts." Along with the foundation, Barnes had a residence and a gallery constructed to house his large collection of work, which was dominated by European and American modernist paintings and African art. A central part of Barnes's mission was educating students in how to look at paintings and teaching them to understand the "plastic" relationship of art to nature. Classes at the Barnes Foundation actively involved studying works of art by such modernists as Paul Cézanne, Pablo Picasso, and Amedeo Modigliani as well as a variety of other artistic traditions including African sculpture; ancient Egyptian, Greek, and Roman carvings; and Chinese drawings and watercolors.

From the outset, Barnes himself was actively involved in the Harlem Renaissance. He attended the Civic Club dinner in March 1924 and was impressed with the range of talented authors and poets. After this encounter, he decided to support educational work among African Americans and contacted Alain Locke. Locke and Barnes had first met in Paris in January 1924, and it was Locke who invited Barnes to the Civic Club dinner. Barnes discussed with Locke

possible opportunities for young African American artists to study using his collection. One of the first individuals to benefit from this relationship was the graphic artist and painter Aaron Douglas, who received a stipend to study at the Barnes Foundation in 1925. Douglas wrote: "Gosh, but it is a marvelous place. He undoubtedly has the largest single collection of modern paintings in America and certainly the finest collection of Negro sculpture." Charles Spurgeon Johnson, editor of *Opportunity*, reproduced selected pieces from Barnes's collection of African art in the May 1924 issue. Locke also illustrated key pieces in his influential anthology *The New Negro* (1925). Barnes wrote an essay entitled "Negro Art and America" for this anthology that helped to define the Harlem Renaissance. Although this fact is infrequently noted, Locke took much of his understanding of African art from his interactions with Barnes (Clarke 1998).

Starting in 1925, Barnes also began to hold concerts of black spirituals at his foundation. Charles Spurgeon Johnson developed a cordial relationship with Barnes after the publication of his African art collection in *Opportunity* and in 1926 introduced Barnes to the Bordentown School Choir from Bordentown, New Jersey. From the first concert, Barnes was impressed, and he invited the choir to sing annually at the foundation. Barnes, who saw a strong link between music and art, included an annual lecture on the relationship between African sculpture and African American spirituals, giving his lecture between the sets of spirituals sung by the choir (Clarke 1998).

Other organizations and societies outside Harlem actively celebrated and promoted the culture of the 1920s. In such cities as Chicago and Washington, D.C., the black intelligentsia attended events similar to those of their counterparts in Harlem. Chicago's Arts and Letters Society, the Chicago Art League, and the Tanner Art Students' League in Washington, D.C., all supported exhibitions of the art of African Americans and also served as gathering places for those interested in literature and fine arts. The National Black Women's Club Movement, with more than 1,000 clubs in American cities, sponsored numerous lectures and educational and cultural programs. In November 1927, the Chicago Woman's Club organized the "Negro in Art Week," a one-week extravaganza that included a concert, lectures, and an exhibition at the Art Institute of Chicago. This groundbreaking show included work by contemporary African American artists and the Blondiau Collection of African Art from the Belgian Congo. The concert included Bach and

Ravel and traditional black spirituals sung by the Fisk Jubilee Singers. Both Alain Locke and James Weldon Johnson were invited to the exhibition, and Johnson gave a lecture entitled "The Art Approach to the Negro Problem." The Chicago Woman's Club is just one illustration of commitment by an organization to underscoring black culture and using culture as a tool to "uplift the race" (Meyerowitz 1997).

Individuals also were essential in promoting culture during this time: A'Lelia Walker stands out for her attempt to bring together both black and white literati. In 1928, Walker, the heiress of the hair-straightening magnate Madame C. J. Walker, established the Dark Tower, a literary salon held in her mansion at 108–110 West 136th Street in Harlem. The invitation to the opening of the Dark Tower stated, "We dedicate this tower to the aesthetes. That cultural group of young Negro writers, sculptors, painters, music artists, composers, and their friends." The Dark Tower, which was for members only, functioned as place where one could mingle with the literati, hear poetry read, and see art. Walker decorated the walls of the salon with the written text from Countee Cullen's poem "The Dark Tower" and Langston Hughes's "The Weary Blues." Although Walker's sponsorship of literary conversation appealed primarily to an elite audience, she supported a venue where aspiring and established writers—including Cullen, Hughes, and Richard Nugent—could express themselves creatively.

Music flourished during the Harlem Renaissance, and several cultural organizations stand out for their dedication to promoting concert music and musicians. The National Association of Negro Musicians (NANM), organized in 1919, helped to establish black concert and recital music as critical components of the New Negro movement. The NANM, which was based in New York, said that its purpose was "stimulating progress, to discover and foster talent, to mold taste, to promote fellowship, and to advocate racial expression." Its members included music teachers, professional musicians, and music clubs. By 1933, it had twenty-eight branches in the United States; it continues to function as an organization based in Chicago (Cuney-Hare 1936/1974).

Two important choral societies were established early in the twentieth century and continued to thrive during the Harlem Renaissance. The Choral Study Club was organized in 1900 and provided instruction and opportunities for performance and music appreciation to African Americans of Chicago. The Samuel Coleridge-Taylor Society gave its first concert in 1903 at the Metropolitan African Methodist Episcopal Church in Washington, D.C. Like the Choral Study Club, the Samuel Coleridge-Taylor Society fostered a choral music program but focused primarily on the work of African American composers. It was disbanded in 1915 after the death of its founders but was revived in 1921 and continued to perform into the 1930s. Choral societies abounded during this period, including many based on the Samuel Coleridge-Taylor Society. Other prominent choirs included the People's Choral Society of Philadelphia, Festival Chorus of Atlanta, and Musergia of Louisville, Kentucky.

Symphonic organizations also blossomed during this time. The Negro String Quartet and the Harlem Symphony Orchestra performed a wide range of music in New York City. The Negro String Quartet, founded in the same year as the NANM, performed show music, compositions by contemporary black composers, and classical work by European composers such as Beethoven, Haydn, and Tchaikovsky. The Harlem Symphony Orchestra performed the composer and songwriter James P. Johnson's *Yamekraw* and a later concert of music by Weber, Beethoven, and Mendelssohn. Musicians and performers received their share of formal recognition as well. For a three-year period beginning in 1925, Casper Holstein donated monies for the Holstein Prizes for composition, awarded through *Opportunity*. The Spingarn Medal also acknowledged outstanding musicians and singers: Harry T. Burleigh received the prize in 1917 and Roland Hayes in 1925 (Floyd 1993).

The organizations, societies, and associations that supported cultural activity during the Harlem Renaissance were broad in range and deep in scope. The 135th Street Library and the 135th Street YMCA gave immeasurable assistance through their public programming and their nurturing of the arts. Organizations such as the NAACP and the National Urban League publicly acknowledged, through their various prizes, talented authors, poets, and playwrights. And the unflagging support of individuals and smaller groups proved that African American culture was vividly alive and dynamic and worthy of notice.

RENÉE ATER

See also Barnes, Albert C.; Booklovers Club; Civic Club Dinner, 1924; Crisis, The: Literary Prizes; Harmon Foundation; Haynes, George Edmund; Johnson, Charles Spurgeon; Krigwa Players; Locke, Alain; National Association for the Advancement of Colored People; National Association of Negro Musicians;

National Urban League; Negro World; 135th Street Library; Opportunity Awards Dinner; Opportunity Literary Contests; Schomburg, Arthur A.; Spingarn, Joel; Spingarn Medal; Universal Negro Improvement Association; Walker, A'Lelia; *specific actors, artists, musicians, and writers*

Further Readings

Campbell, Mary Schmidt, et al. *Harlem Renaissance: Art of Black America*. New York: Studio Museum in Harlem and Abrams, 1987.

Clarke, Christa. "Defining Taste: Albert Barnes and the Promotion of African Art in the United States." Ph.D. diss., University of Maryland, 1998.

Cuney-Hare, Maud. *Negro Musicians and Their Music*. 1936. New York: Da Capo, 1974.

Dierickx, Mary B. *The Architecture of Literacy: The Carnegie Libraries of New York City*. New York: Cooper Union for the Advancement of Science and Art, 1996.

Floyd, Samuel A., Jr. *Black Music in the Harlem Renaissance: A Collection of Essays*. Knoxville: University of Tennessee Press, 1993.

Lewis, David Levering. *When Harlem Was in Vogue*. New York: Oxford University Press, 1979.

Martin, Tony. *Literary Garveyism: Garvey, Black Arts, and the Harlem Renaissance*. Dover, Mass.: Majority, 1983.

Meyerowitz, Lisa. " 'The Negro in Art' Week: Defining the New Negro Through Art Exhibition." *African-American Review*, 31(1), Spring 1997, pp. 75–89.

Mjagkij, Nina. *Light in the Darkness: African-Americans and the YMCA, 1852–1946*. Lexington: University of Kentucky Press, 1994.

Reynolds, Gary A., and Beryl J. Wright. *Against the Odds: African-American Artists and the Harmon Foundation*. Newark, N.J.: Newark Museum, 1989.

Sinnette, Elinor Des Verney. *Arthur Alfonso Schomburg: Black Bibliophile and Collector: A Biography*. New York: New York Public Library, 1989.

Watson, Steven. *The Harlem Renaissance: Hub of African-American Culture, 1920–1930*. New York: Pantheon, 1995.

Cunard, Nancy

The British heiress Nancy Cunard (1896–1965) was a writer, editor, and printer who actively rebelled against the economic and racial ideologies of her class. Her chief connection to the Harlem Renaissance is her massive anthology *Negro* (1934), which contains works by a number of its leading writers.

Early on, Cunard tried to escape the world of her mother, the famous socialite Emerald Cunard, by settling in France, where she became part of avant-garde circles in Paris and began her own printing press. In 1928, she met an African American jazz musician, Henry Crowder, in Venice; they became lovers, and one evening they discussed the state of American blacks. Crowder reported being amazed at Cunard's ignorance about this, but he found her immensely interested. Thereafter, racial justice became a passion for Cunard.

Her first public writings on race appeared in 1931. Upon hearing that her mother had learned about Crowder and was disgusted by the relationship, she wrote "Does Anyone *Know* Any Negroes," which was published in the magazine *The Crisis* in September of that year and in which she excoriated the racism of her mother's class and described instances of racial prejudice that she herself had encountered since she became involved with Crowder. A few months later, her privately printed pamphlet *Black Man and White Ladyship: An Anniversary* contained an even more vehement attack. Its first part was a vicious personal assault on Cunard's mother; its second part summarized the historic and current mistreatment of black people and argued passionately against racism and imperialism, but most readers agreed that the valuable points made in this second part were overshadowed by the personal hatred expressed in the first. Even Crowder (1987) called the pamphlet "an atrocious piece" (119).

As early as 1930, Cunard had considered compiling an anthology of black history and culture to challenge racial prejudice. In April 1931, she sent out a circular requesting submissions, and she spent the next three years assembling the work. She made two trips to Harlem during which she met some of her contributors, including Walter White, Langston Hughes, and Countee Cullen; continued raising money for the defense of the Scottsboro boys (a project she had taken up while in Europe); and was dogged by reporters who seemed interested only in salacious tidbits about her black lovers. These trips also gave her an opportunity to observe Harlem; she recorded her impressions in an article entitled "Harlem Reviewed" for the anthology. In this essay she criticizes Harlem's nightclubs for refusing to admit black patrons and accuses white writers such as "[Carl] Van Vechten and Co." of presenting the public with a narrow, negative vision of Harlem as nothing more than "a round of hooch-filled night-clubs after a round of 'snow'-filled boudoirs."

Negro was published in England on 14 February 1934, at Cunard's expense. It is a large book (855 pages), with more than 250 contributions: long and short articles, songs, poems, and illustrations. In addition to White, Hughes, and Cullen, contributors associated with the Harlem Renaissance include Zora Neale Hurston, Alain Locke, W. E. B. Du Bois, Arna Bontemps, and Sterling Brown; the book also contains pieces by black social scientists, musicologists, and historians as well as works by whites. Among Cunard's own contributions—in addition to "Harlem Reviewed"—are a long report on the Scottsboro case, a harsh critique of the National Association for the Advancement of Colored People (NAACP) as bourgeois and reactionary, and a sampling of the "hate letters" she had received during her visits to Harlem.

Negro is wide-ranging, divided into sections on the United States, black stars, music, poetry, the West Indies, South America, Europe, and Africa; titles of articles include "Flashes From Georgia Chain Gangs," "A Negro Film Union, Why Not?" and "French Imperialism at Work in Madagascar." In fact, *Negro* was so broad in scope that many readers found it an unwieldy hodgepodge, difficult to read and assess. Cunard was disappointed that it was not widely reviewed and that it did not sell well; an additional reason for this lack of public support may have been its communist slant. Cunard was never a member of the Communist Party, but she supported the communist agenda; the foreword to the anthology notes that "it is Communism alone which throws down the barriers of race. . . . The Communist world order is the solution to the race problem for the Negro." Still, Cunard received private praise from many people, including Langston Hughes, and Arthur Schomburg; Alain Locke wrote, "I congratulate you—almost enviously, on the finest anthology in every sense of the word, ever compiled on the Negro" (quoted in Chisholm 1979, 293).

Original copies of *Negro* are now scarce, but an abridged version was published in 1970 and reprinted in 1996. The anthology has received limited attention in the primary studies of the Harlem Renaissance. Huggins (1971) makes no mention of Cunard and *Negro*, although Lewis (1981) and Wintz (1988) address them briefly. More recently, scholars such as Jane Marcus (1995) and Holly McSpadden (1997) have sought to recover *Negro* as a landmark text on race.

Cunard's role as an advocate of racial justice is sometimes difficult to evaluate. In the early twentieth century, she was one of the most outspoken European supporters of equality for blacks, and few others so willingly condemned the racism of their own group. But one must also ask whether she was completely able to escape the influence of her class. For example, although she professed a distaste for primitivism, she often told Henry Crowder that she wished he were darker and admonished him to "be more African" (Chisholm 1979, 186), and he believed that she often chose lovers because of the darkness of their skin. She also sometimes saw racial politics in rather simplistic terms. To confront prejudice head-on, for instance, she would often take a black lover or a black friend to places that excluded African Americans, overlooking the real risk to her black companions in such encounters. Some commentators allow Cunard's flamboyant personal life to preclude an objective analysis of her work on race; the fact that she had a sexual interest in black men is sometimes seen as undercutting the seriousness of her commitment to racial equality. Cunard herself, however, never doubted this commitment. In

Nancy Cunard in an inscribed photograph, 1927. (Library of Congress.)

making notes for an autobiography, she wrote that her work for the equality of the races was predominant in her life. She regarded her relationship with Crowder as life-changing; on learning of his death, she wrote to a friend, "Henry made me. I thank him."

Biography

Nancy Clara Cunard was born 10 March 1896 in Leicestershire, England, and was educated at private girls' schools in London, Munich, and Paris (1911–1914). She contributed a poem to *Wheels: An Anthology of Verse* in 1916 and published *Outlaws* (poems) in 1921, *Sublunary* (poems) in 1923, *Parallax* (a long poem) in 1925, *Poems* in 1930, *Grand Man: Memories of Norman Douglas* in 1954, and *G. M.: Memories of George Moore* in 1956. Cunard founded and ran the Hours Press in La Chapelle-Réanville, France (1928). She was a correspondent for the Associated Negro Press (1935–1950); and she reported on the Spanish Civil War (1936–1939) for the Associated Negro Press, *New Times, Spanish Newsletter, Spain at War, Voice of Spain*, and *Manchester Guardian*. She edited *Authors Take Sides on the Spanish War* (1937) and *Poems for France* (1944). Cunard died 16 March 1965 in Paris.

CHRISTINA G. BUCHER

See also Bontemps, Arna; Brown, Sterling; Crisis, The; Cullen, Countee; Du Bois, W. E. B.; Hughes, Langston; Hurston, Zora Neale; Locke, Alain; Negro: An Anthology; Primitivism; Schomburg, Arthur A.; Scottsboro; Van Vechten, Carl; White, Walter

Selected Works

"Does Anyone *Know* Any Negroes." *Crisis*, September 1931, p. 300.
Black Man and White Ladyship: An Anniversary. 1931. (Abridged in *Nancy Cunard: Brave Poet, Indomitable Rebel, 1896–1965*. 1968.)
Negro. 1934. (Abridged ed., 1970, reprinted 1996.)
The White Man's Duty. 1943.
These Were the Hours. 1969.

Further Reading

Chisholm, Anne. *Nancy Cunard,* New York: Knopf, 1979.
Crowder, Henry. *As Wonderful as All That?* Navarro, Calif.: Wild Trees, 1987.
Douglas, Anne. *Terrible Honesty: Mongrel Manhattan in the 1920s*. New York: Farrar, Straus and Giroux, 1995.
Fielding, Daphne. *Those Remarkable Cunards: Emerald and Nancy*. New York: Atheneum, 1968.
Ford, Hugh, ed. *Nancy Cunard: Brave Poet, Indomitable Rebel, 1896–1965*. Philadelphia, Pa.: Chilton, 1968.
Lewis, David Levering. *When Harlem Was in Vogue*. New York: Knopf, 1981.
Marcus, Jane. "Bonding and Bondage: Nancy Cunard and the Making of the *Negro* Anthology." In *Borders, Boundaries, and Frames: Essays in Cultural Criticism and Cultural Studies*, ed. Mae Henderson. New York: Routledge, 1995.
McSpadden, Holly. "Transgressive Reading: Nancy Cunard and *Negro*." In *Essays on Transgressive Readings: Reading Over the Lines*, ed. Georgia Johnston. Lewiston, N.Y.: Edwin Mellen, 1997.
Moynagh, Maureen. "Cunard's Lines: Political Tourismus and Its Texts." *New Formations*, 34, 1998, pp. 70–90.
———. *Nancy Cunard: Essays on Race and Empire*. Peterborough, Ontario, Canada: Broadview, 2002.
Wintz, Cary D. *Black Culture and the Harlem Renaissance*. Houston, Tex.: Rice University Press, 1988.

Cuney, Waring

Although Waring Cuney is today considered one of the minor poets of the Harlem Renaissance, and although he lived a quiet, private life that defies the efforts of biographers, his use of language and the rhythms of urban African Americans gave credibility to a kind of writing that was echoed throughout the twentieth century and into the twenty-first. With his friend Langston Hughes, Cuney worked hard at being a poet during their years at Lincoln University; much later, in 1954, they coedited an anthology, *Lincoln University Poets: Centennial Anthology, 1854–1954*.

Cuney's first love was music, but his singing voice was weak, and so he was led to choose writing as a career. Still, his poetry was often influenced by his music education and his musical sensitivity. His poems are strongly rhythmic, and many of them are in ballad stanzas. He is especially known for creating poetic forms echoing blues. He also wrote song lyrics, some of which were recorded by Josh White. Many of Cuney's works are vivid character sketches of people living in black American inner cities, and their vernacular speech and folk rhythms are affirming and energetic. Attention is paid to the smallest and most humble details of daily life. Religion is a recurring theme.

Cuney's most famous poem, "No Images," which he wrote at the age of eighteen, has been called a minor masterpiece and has been widely anthologized. "No Images" won first prize in the literary contest sponsored by *Opportunity* magazine in 1926; and his poems "A Traditional Marching Song" and "De Jail Blues Song" won honorable mentions in 1927. Cuney's poetry and criticism were published in magazines such as *The Crisis, Fire!!, Harlem Quarterly, Negro Quarterly, Black World*, and *Opportunity*. His poetry was also selected for inclusion in anthologies such as *An Anthology of Magazine Verse for 1926*; Countee Cullen's *Caroling Dusk: An Anthology of Verse by Black Poets of the Twenties* (1927); James Weldon Johnson's *Book of American Negro Poetry* (1931); Sterling Brown's *Negro Caravan* (1941); and Arna Bontemps's *American Negro Poetry* (1963).

By the 1950s, Cuney was largely forgotten in the United States, but his work had been translated into German and Dutch and had a small following in Europe. In 1960, his poems were collected and published for the first time as a book, *Puzzles*, in the Netherlands. Shortly afterward, Cuney stopped writing and publishing and became a recluse. A second book, *Storefront Church*, was published in London in 1973.

Biography

William Waring Cuney was born in Washington, D.C., 6 May 1906. He was educated in public schools in Washington, D.C.; at Howard University; at Lincoln University, Pennsylvania (B.A.); at the New England Conservatory of Music, Boston; and at the Conservatory of Music, Rome. He was active as a poet from 1927 to 1962. Cuney served in the U.S. Army as a technical sergeant during World War II (1941–1945); he was awarded the Asiatic Pacific Theater Ribbon and three Bronze Stars. His poem "No Images" won first prize in *Opportunity*'s contest of 1926. Cuney died in New York City 30 June 1976.

CYNTHIA BILY

See also Authors: 5–Poets; Crisis, The; Fire!!; Hughes, Langston; Literature: 7–Poetry; Opportunity Literary Contests

Selected Works

Lincoln University Poets: Centennial Anthology, 1854–1954. 1954 (As coeditor.)
Puzzles. 1960.
Storefront Church. 1973.

Further Reading

Bell, Bernard W. "Contemporary Afro-American Poetry as Folk Art." *Black World*, 20(5), 1973.
Bontemps, Arna. *The Harlem Renaissance Remembered.* New York: Dodd, Mead, 1972.
Brown, Sterling A. *Negro Poetry and Drama.* Washington, D.C.: Associates in Negro Folk Education, 1937.
Hayden, Lucy. *Dictionary of Literary Biography*, Vol. 51, *Afro-American Writers From the Harlem Renaissance to 1940*, ed. Trudier Harris. Detroit, Mich.: Gale Research, 1987.
Hughes, Langston. *The Big Sea: An Autobiography.* New York: Knopf, 1940.
Woodson, C. G. "The Cuney Family." *Negro History Bulletin*, March 1948.

Cuney-Hare, Maud

Maud Cuney-Hare (1874–1936) was a concert pianist, music historian, folklorist, writer, educator, playwright, producer, and lecturer. She was the author of a biography of her father, *Norris Wright Cuney: A Tribune of the Black People* (1913); editor of *Six Creole Folk Songs: With Original Creole and Translated English Text* (1921), a subject she was the first to bring to the attention of American concertgoers; and editor of a collection of poems, *The Message of the Trees: An Anthology of Leaves and Branches* (1918). She also contributed articles on music to *The Crisis* (where she edited the column on music and the arts), *Musical Quarterly, Musical Observer, Musical America*, and the *Christian Science Monitor*.

As a folklorist, Cuney-Hare traveled to Mexico, Puerto Rico, Cuba, Haiti, and the Virgin Islands, collecting songs and doing research on sources of African American music. She owned a famous collection of African American, Creole, and early American music that included instruments, photographs, scores, and programs. The National Association for the Advancement of Colored People (NAACP) sponsored an exhibit of this collection at the Wanamaker store in Philadelphia; the exhibit was also shown in other libraries and museums in the Northeast and on the West Coast.

Cuney-Hare's authoritative reference work *Negro Musicians and Their Music* (1936) was published two months before her death and is still used today. In it, she traced the African influence on the music of black people; described African instruments, songs, and dances; and discussed the origin, variants, and applications of spirituals, folk music, sea chanteys, and work songs. Her work covered minstrelsy, vaudeville, musical comedy, classical music, and some blues and jazz and included detailed biographies of famous and less well-known musicians, singers, and composers of African descent from Arabia, Europe, the Americas, the Caribbean, and the United States.

Cuney-Hare as pianist and the baritone William Howard Richardson developed a very popular lecture and concert series that they presented—sometimes in costume—in the United States and abroad from 1913 to the early 1930s. They specialized in African American and Creole music. Cuney-Hare and Richardson also gave concerts, especially of spirituals, with the violinist Clarence Cameron White and the singer Roland Hayes; in one of these concerts, Arthur Fiedler, the famous conductor of the Boston Pops orchestra, played the viola.

Cuney-Hare founded the Allied Arts Center in Boston, Massachusetts, which had a little theater group (c. 1926–1935). The center also offered children's theatrical workshops, concerts, art, music study classes, and drama classes; all races were invited to participate, but it was especially a training ground and showcase for young black performers and

playwrights. Although Cuney-Hare had begun this organization with only her own money, it later received outside donations and revenues from its activities. The black League of Women for Community Service found a site for the center in downtown Boston, opposite the New England Conservatory of Music.

The Allied Arts Players presented *Plumes* by Georgia Douglas Johnson; *Tambour* by John Frederick Matheus (1929); *Dessalines, Black Emperor of Haiti* by William Easton (on 15 May 1930); and Cuney-Hare's own original play, *Antar of Araby, Negro Poet of Araby* (1926), about a historical figure of the sixth century. The music for *Antar of Araby* was provided by Clarence Cameron White and Montague Ring (a pseudonym of Amanda Ira Aldridge, the daughter of Ira Aldridge, a prominent black Shakespearean actor of the time).

Biography

Maud Cuney-Hare was born 17 February 1874 in Galveston, Texas. In 1890, she was one of the first graduates of Central High School there, a school that was a direct result of efforts by her father to ensure an education for blacks. After graduating from the New England Conservatory of Music in Boston, she studied English literature at Lowell Institute, Harvard University; and studied music privately with two famous European piano teachers: Edwin Klahre and Emil Ludwig. She also studied music theory with Martin Roeder. She became the director of music (1897–1898) for the Deaf, Dumb, and Blind Institute for Colored Youth in Austin, Texas. She worked at the settlement house of the African Methodist Episcopal Church in Chicago and was a music instructor at Prairie View Agricultural and Mechanical College (1903–1904). She was a noted lecturer and concert artist and was the founder of an arts center in Boston, that included a theater. Cuney-Hare died 13 February 1936 in Boston.

MARVIE BROOKS

See also Crisis, The; Hayes, Roland; Johnson, Georgia Douglas; Matheus, John Frederick; New Challenge; White, Clarence Cameron

Maud Cuney-Hare, c. 1910. (Schomburg Center for Research in Black Culture, New York Public Library.)

Further Reading

African-American Registry. *Maud Hare, Texas Original!* (Web site.)

"Cuney-Hare, Maud." In *Handbook of Texas Online*. 2003. (Joint Project of University of Texas at Austin and Texas State Historical Association; Web site.)

Du Bois, W. E. B. "Opinion." *Crisis*, 28(5), September 1924, pp. 196–238. (On the Maud Cuney-Hare Exhibit.)

Hales, Douglas. *A Southern Family in White and Black: The Cuneys of Texas*. College Station: Texas A&M University Press, 2003.

Logan, Rayford W., and Michael R. Winston, eds. *Dictionary of American Negro Biography*. New York: Norton, 1982, p. 152.

Peterson, Bernard L., Jr. *Early Black American Playwrights and Dramatic Writers: A Biographical Directory and Catalog of Plays, Films, and Broadcasting Scripts*. Westport, Conn.: Greenwood, 1990, p. 56.

Quinlan, Elizabeth. "African-American Women in Jamaica Plain History." *Jamaica Plain Gazette*, 28 August 1992.

Salem, Dorothy, ed. *African-American Women*. New York: Garland, 1993, pp. 134–136.

Southern, Eileen. *Biographical Dictionary of Afro-American and African Musicians*. Westport, Conn.: Greenwood, 1982, pp. 166–167.

White, Clarence Cameron. "Maud Cuney-Hare." *Journal of Negro History*, 21(2), April 1936, pp. 239–240. ("Notes" section.)

D

Daddy Grace

Bishop Charles Manuel "Sweet Daddy" Grace was the founder, in 1919, of the United House of Prayer for All People of the Church on the Rock of Apostolic Faith. His denomination was based on the "apostolic faith" that emerged from the Azusa Street Revival in Los Angeles (1906); he emphasized God's power to heal and advocated worship filled with the spirit. Daddy Grace drew attention from the press for his flamboyant attire, long painted fingernails, and extensive investments in real estate.

Grace, whose original name was Marcelino da Graca, left the Portuguese Cape Verde Islands for New Bedford, Massachusetts, in 1904; he anglicized his name within five years of his arrival. He was one of thousands of Cape Verdeans who immigrated to this area between 1900 and 1921, and like many of the others, he was puzzled by American racial categories. He did not accept the American classification "black" or "Negro" but insisted that he was a white citizen of Portugal. This claim led some critics, who were unaware of his Cape Verdean heritage, to describe him as a "race-rejecter."

Dismayed by the limited options available to a man society viewed as "black," Grace looked for a new occupation. In 1919 he founded his ministry in West Wareham, Massachusetts. He soon headed out in his "gospel car," spreading his message throughout the southern United States. While his House of Prayer was explicitly created "for all people," most of his followers were African Americans. Grace, however, did hold "mixed-race" meetings and was consequently a target of intimidation by the Ku Klux Klan in the South. The press found it difficult to classify Grace, calling him variously a "Portuguese faith healer" and the "black Christ."

In 1927 Grace formally incorporated the church in Washington, D.C., making that city his headquarters. His early successes in the South encouraged him to expand into Philadelphia and Harlem. In 1938 the writer Dorothy West documented a worship service in one of Grace's Houses of Prayer in Harlem for the Works Progress Administration (WPA). She captured the integral role of music in the House of Prayer, including a forerunner of the church's unique trombone shout bands. Also in 1938, Grace challenged Father Divine's power in Harlem when he purchased Divine's "Number One Heaven."

As Grace's ministry grew, he offered his followers a line of products, including *Grace Magazine*, Grace writing paper, and Grace hair pomade. He invested the money he raised in real estate, including a plantation in Cuba and the El Dorado apartment building on New York's Upper West Side. He also created low-income housing and affordable dining options for his congregations; however, this aspect of his activity rarely received attention in the press, and, despite it, his critics charged that he was duping his followers out of their money. When Grace died, he was somewhat vindicated: he left the bulk of his holdings to his followers and the United House of Prayer.

Grace's followers held an elaborate funeral for him. His body traveled from Los Angeles to Charlotte, North Carolina, and was then escorted to Newport News (Virginia), Washington (D.C.), Philadelphia, and Newark (New Jersey) before arriving in New Bedford

285

Daddy Grace, photographed by James Van Der Zee, 1938. (Library of Congress.)

for burial. In the years after Grace's death, the United House of Prayer for All People continued to thrive.

Biography

Charles Manuel Grace (Marcelino da Graca) was born in Brava, Cape Verde Islands, on 20 January 1881. He immigrated to and permanently settled in New Bedford, Massachusetts (1904). Grace began his formal ministry in 1919; made a trip to the Holy Land in 1923–1924; and incorporated his church, the United House of Prayer for All People of the Church on the Rock of Apostolic Faith, in Washington, D.C., in 1927. He died in Los Angeles, California, on 12 January 1960.

DANIELLE BRUNE

See also Father Divine; Fauset, Arthur Huff; West, Dorothy

Selected Works

Bishop Grace from the Holy Land. "You May Be Healed By the Power of God" and "The Power of God

Can Raise His Friends from the Dead." In *Preachers and Congregations,* Vol. 4, *1924–1931.* DOCD-5548. (Recording.)

Further Reading

"America's Richest Negro Minister." *Ebony,* January 1952, pp. 17–23.

Davis, Lenwood G. *Daddy Grace: An Annotated Bibliography.* New York: Greenwood, 1992.

Fauset, Arthur Huff. *Black Gods of the Metropolis.* Philadelphia: University of Pennsylvania Press, 1945.

Halter, Marilyn. *Between Race and Ethnicity: Cape Verdean American Immigrants 1860–1965.* Chicago: University of Illinois Press, 1993.

West, Dorothy. "Temple of Grace." In *A Renaissance in Harlem,* ed. Lionel C. Bascom. New York: Avon, 1999.

Dafora, Asadata

Asadata Dafora (1890–1965) was born in Sierra Leone; his mother was a concert pianist who had studied in Vienna and Paris, and his father was a city treasurer. As a student, Dafora traveled throughout west Africa, Europe, and Russia, and then studied voice at La Scala in Milan, Italy, for two years. He emigrated to the United States in 1929 to pursue a career in opera, but he found greater success during the Harlem Renaissance as a dancer and choreographer. He formed the company Shogola Oloba, with other African émigrés, to perform songs and dances of the Temini ethnic group.

Shogola Oloba performed at the Communist Party Bazaar in New York in 1933, as well as at the opening of the New YMCA Little Theater at 180 West 135 Street. In May 1934 Dafora presented *Kykunkor, or the Witch Woman*, the seminal African dance opera, which told of a bridegroom cursed by a scorned lover. Dafora arranged the libretto, music, and dances, and oversaw the entire production. This work combined operatic dramatic conventions with African dancing and singing by a large company of African and African American performers who were costumed with great theatrical flair according to his specifications; the production was accompanied by an orchestra of three drummers. *Kykunkor* confirmed the viability of African arts as American entertainment and awakened a broad interest in traditional west African performance practice.

Artists from many disciplines saw *Kykunkor* and appreciated the implications of Dafora's vision. Among these artists were Leopold Stokowski, conductor of the Philadelphia Orchestra; Lawrence Tibbett of the Boston Symphony; the composer George Gershwin; the novelists Sherwood Anderson and Theodore Dreiser; the choreographer George Balanchine; and the eminent literary critic Carl Van Doren. The work made its way to Broadway, where it ran for three months.

Following this resounding success, Dafora created several more works in the same vein, including *Bassa Moona* (1937) and *Zunguru* (1938), which were also performed on Broadway, at Carnegie Hall, at the Ninety-Second Street YM-YWHA, the New York Museum of Natural History, the Brooklyn Museum, the Brooklyn Botanical Gardens, and the Bronx Zoo. Dafora also toured throughout the southern and western United States. In 1936, he served as choreographer for Orson Welles's production of *Voodoo Macbeth*.

In 1943, Dafora organized "African Dance Festival," a program held at Carnegie Hall on 13 December as the first arts project of the African Academy of Arts and Research. The academy's purpose was to "foster goodwill between the United States and Africa through a mutual exchange of cultural, social, and economic knowledge." Two guests of honor, Eleanor Roosevelt and Mary McLeod Bethune, spoke during the intermission in support of the academy and its artistic project.

Dafora's influence as a teacher and proponent of African music and dance has been underestimated. Throughout his career, he taught many significant dance and drum artists, including Ismay Andrews, Pearl Primus, Josephine Premice, Katherine Dunham, Norman Coker, Alphonse Cimber, Jean-Léon Destiné, Alice Dinizulu, Michael Olatunji, and Charles Moore. Shangola Oloba remained in existence until 1960, when Dafora returned briefly to Sierra Leone.

Biography

Asadata Dafora Horton was born on 4 August 1890 in Sierra Leone. He attended the Wesleyan Boys' High School and studied in England and Russia and at La Scala in Milan, Italy. He was artistic director of the Shogola Oloba company (1933–1960), choreographer for Orson Welles's *Voodoo Macbeth* (1936), and organizer

of the program "African Dance Festival" at Carnegie Hall on 13 December 1943. He died in New York City in March 1965.

THOMAS F. DeFRANTZ

See also Anderson, Sherwood; Bethune, Mary McLeod; Dance; Dreiser, Theodore; Van Doren, Carl

Selected Works

Awassa Astrige/Ostrich. 1932.
Voodoo Macbeth. 1936. (Directed by Orson Welles.)
Zoonga. 1933.
Kykunkor, or the Witch Woman. 1934.
Bassa Moona. 1937.
Zunguru. 1938.
Batanga. 1949.

Further Reading

"Asadata Dafora." In *Dictionary of Blacks in the Performing Arts*, ed. E. Mapp. Metuchen, N. J.: Scarecrow, 1978.

Beiswanger, George W. "Asadata Dafora and Company." *Dance Observer*, January 1944.

Heard, Marcea E., and Mansa Mussa. "African Dance in New York City." In *Dancing Many Drums: Excavations in African American Dance*, ed. Thomas F. DeFrantz. Madison: University of Wisconsin Press, 2001.

Lloyd, Margaret. "Dancer from the Gold Coast." *Christian Science Monitor*, 26 May 1945.

Needham, Maureen. "*Kykunkor, Or The Witch Woman*: An African Opera in America, 1934." In *Dancing Many Drums: Excavations in African American Dance*, ed. Thomas F. DeFrantz. Madison: University of Wisconsin Press, 2001.

Damas, Léon

Léon Gontran Damas (1911–1978), poet, storyteller, pamphleteer, and lecturer, is remembered, with Aimé Césaire and Léopold Sédar Senghor, as a member of the "trinity" that formulated *négritude* (negritude) in Paris in the 1930s and spread the concept throughout the world.

Negritude meant acceptance of one's blackness and glorification of African history and culture. The concept enabled Damas to discover his own identity, to move beyond being simply "an object of domination and a consumer of culture" and to become "a cultural actor in history." Taking pride in one's own culture would, he believed, lead not to racism and rejection of the other, but rather to the universal. Thus, while remaining profoundly Antillean and dedicated to the progress of blacks in his native Guiana, Damas insisted on the ties that bound blacks of the diaspora to each other and to African blacks. He stressed, in particular, that poets of negritude were indebted to musicians and writers of the Harlem Renaissance.

Damas had been born into an interracial, dysfunctional Guianan bourgeois family that was bent on assimilation with all things French, but his newfound roots led him to reject assimilation completely. *Pigments* (1937), his most famous work, records the revolt of a young black man who has discovered his identity in African-Guianan traditions. The poems accentuate a rhythm reminiscent of the tom-tom; their tone is nostalgic, humorous, at times bitingly ironic. Many lines are confrontational: black-white, slave-master, innocence-cruelty, love-hatred, truth-falsehood.

The same themes underlie his report (*Retour de Guyane*, 1938) on a trip to Guiana that he undertook for the French anthropologist Paul Rivet to document the state of black culture there. He chastises the French for viewing Guiana as merely a penal colony, rather than a region with major agricultural and human potential.

Damas later illustrated this human potential by publishing his French transcription of Guianan-African tales collected during his trip (*Veillées noires*, 1943). Tales of animals, humans, or supernatural beings, in which the weak but intelligent triumph over the powerful, are passed on to a new generation by an old woman, Tétèche, who clearly symbolizes Guiana. Damas helps her reach a wider audience.

In his next major work, *Black Label* (1956)—which followed his portrayal of a failed love affair in *Graffiti* (1953)—the poet combines the personal and the polemic. "Black label" is the whiskey in which he drowns his sorrow, but also the mark of the branding iron on the slave. The now-mature poet creates dramatic tension by alternating themes of negritude with songs of love and nostalgia.

However, while important, Damas's literary production is rather limited. The man and his spoken words greatly enhanced his role in the creation of an international black community and in the fight against racism. After World War II Damas traveled repeatedly to the United States and solidified the ties he had established in Paris with black American intellectuals. Among his friends were Countee Cullen, Claude McKay, Mercer Cook, and Langston Hughes. In 1966 he settled in the United States, lecturing at various universities. He also continued to travel extensively throughout Europe, the Caribbean, and black Africa, lecturing on behalf of international organizations and becoming a bridge between Africans on several continents.

Biography

Léon Gontran Damas was born on 17 July 1912 in Cayenne, Guiana. He studied in Guiana, in Martinique (Lycée Victor Schoelcher), in Paris (School of Oriental Languages, School of the Humanities, Law School, 1929–1933), and again in Guiana (anthropology, 1934). In Paris in 1930–1933, he met Senghor, Césaire, and the Martinican students editing *La Revue du Monde Noir* (*Review of the Black World*). Damas was drafted into the colonial infantry in 1939 and demobilized in 1940. He returned to Paris in 1942; traveled to Guiana via New York and Washington, D.C.; was elected a deputy in the French national assembly as a socialist (1948–1951); married Martinican Isabelle Victoire Vécilia Achille (1948); was divorced (1951); went on cultural missions to Jamaica, Cuba, the Dominican Republic, Haiti, French West Africa, and French Equatorial Africa on behalf of French ministries of foreign affairs and of "overseas France" and participated in conferences in Europe, Africa, and the Caribbean and Latin America (1953–1963); married Marietta Campos (1964); continued traveling and lecturing, often for UNESCO (1965–1970); and taught in American universities and went on traveling and lecturing (1970–1977). He died on 22 January 1978 in Washington, D.C.; his ashes were brought to Guiana via Martinique, receiving great honors along the way.

L. NATALIE SANDOMIRSKY

See also Césaire, Aimé; Cullen, Countee; Francophone Caribbean and the Harlem Renaissance; Hughes, Langston; McKay, Claude; Negritude; Senghor, Léopold

Selected Works

Pigments. 1937. (Published by Senghor and other friends; rev. ed., 1962; combined ed. with *Névralgies*, 1972.)
Retour de Guyane (*Return from Guiana*). 1938.

Veillées noires (Black Vigils). 1943. (2nd ed., 1972.)

Poètes noirs d'expression française (*Black Poets Writing in French*). 1947.

Poèmes nègres sur des airs africains (Negro Poems Based on African Songs). 1948.

Graffiti. 1953.

Black Label. 1956.

Névralgies (*Neuralgias*). 1966. (Combined ed. with *Pigments*, 1972.)

African Songs of Love, War, Grief, and Abuse by Léon Damas, trans. Miriam Koshland and Ulli Beier. 1981.

Further Reading

Hommage posthume à Léon-Gontran Damas, 1912–1978 (*Posthumous Homage to Léon-Gontran Damas*). Paris: Présence Africaine, 1979.

Jack, Belinda. *Negritude and Literary Criticism: The History and Theory of "Negro-African" Literature in French.* Westport, Conn.: Greenwood, 1996.

Ojo-Ade, Femi. *Léon-Gontran Damas: The Spirit of Resistance.* London: Karnak House, 1993.

Racine, Daniel. *Léon Gontran Damas, 1912–1978, Founder of Negritude: A Memorial Casebook.* Washington, D.C.: University Press of America, 1979.

———. *Léon-Gontran Damas, l'homme et l'oeuvre* (*Léon-Gontran Damas, the Man and His Works*). Paris: Présence Africaine, 1983.

Warner, Keith Q., ed. *Critical Perspectives on Léon Gontran Damas.* Washington, D.C.: Three Continents, 1988.

Dance

Dance of the Harlem Renaissance during the 1920s and 1930s was a flowering of artistic creativity that led to later innovations and to periodic revivals. In the context of dance, it is useful to note, briefly, the nature of the Harlem Renaissance, which has been one of the most intensely studied periods in the history of African American life. This renaissance was an intellectual awakening involving literary and visual artistic expression and a spiritual experience; the basis of the movement was equality, pride, and conscious recognition of being black. Beginning in 1916, there was a mass migration of blacks from the South to Harlem, which had formerly been an exclusive residential area for wealthy whites fleeing the congested lower-class immigrant neighborhoods of downtown Manhattan. During the renaissance, Harlem became known as the black capital of America and was seen by African Americans as a symbolic mecca—and certainly, by young aspiring artists, as a beacon of light.

In examining the significance of dance in the Harlem Renaissance, it is also appropriate to consider the context of evolving knowledge about dance. Not until 1926 was dance recognized as a subject worthy of study in universities. In the 1950s, psychologists began to do research on nonverbal communication, a key element of dance. As more was learned about dance as a means of sending and receiving messages, the traditional split between mind and body was no longer accepted. Many scholars came to stress the "mentality of matter": the merging of the physical, emotional, and cognitive in dance. One cannot create mindlessly; dance—like speaking and writing—requires an underlying faculty in the brain for conceptualization, innovation, and memory. Dance is actually in many ways like language: it has a vocabulary (steps and gestures), grammar (justifying how one movement follows another), and meaning—the multiple symbolic meanings of dance more often resemble poetry than prose. Also, dance has purposeful, intentionally rhythmic, culturally influenced sequences of body movements that are selected in much the same way as a person would choose sequences of verbal language.

In the Harlem Renaissance, new dances emerged out of the cultural mixing of African Americans from different parts of the South and the north; and Harlem became the fountainhead of the social dances that were a craze during America's "roaring twenties." As a result, racial agency, appropriation of cultural dance forms, and the commodification of black stereotypes were at issue. Also at issue was the purpose of art, including dance: many participants in the Harlem Renaissance valued art for its service to civil rights; others, however, believed that artistic freedom was the most important civil right.

During the intellectual fervor of the renaissance, the dances performed in Harlem influenced African American writers, who tried to capture the lives of the unsophisticated masses in rural areas and inner cities. But certain leaders of the Harlem Renaissance considered dance as something apart from the intellectual movement because to them, as to Americans in general, dance seemed merely emotional and physical. The old proverb "Good dancers mostly have better heels than heads" conveys a common misconception about dance. Mainstream society tends to distrust the body and view it as separate from the mind that creates vocal and written discourse; and schools measure knowledge in words and numbers, not kinetic images.

Still, even when their significance went unrecognized by the leadership of the Harlem Renaissance, the dances of this era—in the street, at house parties, in theaters, in ballrooms—altered the course of dance in America and the world. Dances originated by blacks permeated established forms and influenced the emerging American repertoire of jazz dance and dance in theater and film, much as peasant folk dances had influenced European ballet. Dances popularized during the Harlem Renaissance continue to reverberate widely today, in new and old versions. Some of these indigenous American dances blossomed and then faded but eventually reseeded themselves, particularly in the 1990s, when a revival of swing dance swept the United States and also reached the United Kingdom, Scandinavia, and Germany.

The Harlem Renaissance, in effect, opened a window for—or gave an imprimatur to—the African American dance heritage, which came from the cultures of many African groups. The continent of Africa has some 1,000 different language groups and probably as many constellations of dance patterns. Blacks in America, uprooted from their homes in Africa, had been enslaved not only personally but also culturally. Ethnic groups, clans, and families were broken up, and as a result, African dances specific to these units were constrained and transformed in the new world. Even so, the styles of many African dances persisted in the diaspora. Asadata Dafora, a dancer from Sierra Leone who came to the United States in 1929, identified many black dance movements of the time as common in his homeland. Dancers in Harlem used different parts of the body, undulated the spine, rotated the hips, bent the knees, fluidly extended and flexed the legs, and moved on flat feet with the torso oriented earthward.

In 1921, the black musical *Shuffle Along* broke through to Broadway, entered the American imagination, and electrified the Harlem Renaissance. Great African American dancers had been known in vaudeville, but many of them performed on the segregated southern circuits and had remained unknown to the wider American public. *Shuffle Along* opened new doors for talented blacks and proved that money could be made with native, homegrown dancing; this was the first outstanding African American musical to play in white theaters nationwide. It ran a full year

on Broadway and continued in various revivals across the country into the 1940s.

The influence of minstrelsy and blackface performance on dance was perhaps somewhat mixed. White minstrels mastered African American expressive styles of performance, but they did this for the purpose of mockery. African American dancers, if they wanted to have opportunities to perform in mainstream society, often had to black up like white minstrels playing Negroes and say they were white. On the other hand, black minstrelsy—in which the black performers wore blackface just as white minstrels did—distinguished itself from its white counterpart by including women, and in this regard it was a precursor of the transition to vaudeville.

White audiences' preconceptions were a factor not only in minstrelsy and blackface entertainment but in other areas as well. To appeal to white audiences, black men and women portrayed themselves as primitive dancing fools, a white fantasy. Duke Ellington's band, for instance, played "Jungle Music." Earl "Snakehips" Tucker (who became famous among other dancers) and the tap dancer Bill "Bojangles" Robinson performed in a happy, sensual way, playing powerless fools. Also, there was a widespread assumption that blacks were natural dancers rather than performers who had learned their art and craft as any other artists do: through observation, coaching, and practice. This assumption could hardly be applied to blacks in general, even though it might have been appropriate for someone like Bill Robinson, who never did take dancing lessons as we understand them.

Robinson was one of several black dancers who became widely famous during the 1920s and 1930s. His nickname, Bojangles, may have come from a hat he wore as a signature piece—the hatmaker's name was Lion J. Boujasson, which sounds rather like it. In Harlem, both the elite and ordinary people were so crazy about Robinson that he was called the "mayor of Harlem," although at the same time he was fighting for a foothold in American society as a whole. Bojangles had begun his career as a "pick," that is, one of the pickaninnies in choruses of African American children, aged four to the early teens, who appeared in white minstrel shows. He performed the buck dancing style, a full-footed shuffle that was a forerunner of modern tap. "Buck and wing" was a minstrel term referring to a combination of jig and pigeon wing or chicken wing in which the neck was held still and arms and legs flailed like a bird's wings. Robinson also further popularized the cakewalk, a dance that whites, for their blackface minstrel shows, had appropriated from enslaved blacks, who in turn had been mocking the pompous strutting mannerisms of whites. When Bojangles appeared on Broadway in *Blackbirds* in 1928, he achieved instantaneous success with his "stair dance," in which he moved up and down a staircase, changing the tempo and dance movements on each step. Robinson could and did socialize with white people. In 1935, he costarred with Shirley Temple in *The Little Colonel*. In 1939, he was a hit in *Hot Mikado* at the New York World's Fair. Robinson is known for his comment, "I'm copacetic. Everything is better than fine."

Clayton "Peg Leg" Bates, another legendary tap dancer, could execute nearly any tap step with one leg. He wanted to surpass two-legged dancers, and he performed acrobatic turns, graceful soft-shoes, buck-and-wings, and powerful rhythm dances. With a regular tap shoe on his right foot and the peg leg covered with leather on the inside and rubber on the outside, he created a unique combination of sounds. Throughout the 1930s, he played at the top Harlem nightclubs.

John Bubbles is best-known for his portrayal of Sportin' Life in George Gershwin's *Porgy and Bess* (1935) and as half of Buck and Bubbles, a singing and dancing comedy act; Buck was Ford Lee Washington. Buck and Bubbles were headliners in vaudeville, and Bubbles became more broadly appreciated on Broadway in the *Ziegfeld Follies* of 1931. They were the first black artists to appear at Radio City Music Hall in New York. Instead of dancing on his toes, as most tap dancers did, Bubbles dropped his heels to create gradations of tone and complex syncopations. He changed his routine for each show, to prevent other dancers from stealing his steps.

Earl "Snakehips" Tucker arrived in Harlem in the mid-1920s and performed "jungle ritual dances" to accompany the theme of Duke Ellington's band. Snakehips slithered menacingly, like a cobra; his hips described wide circles, and he performed the belly roll, an undulation of the torso. Snakehips appeared briefly (along with Bill Robinson) in *Blackbirds*. The first male headliner who did not tap, he was ahead of his time with "outrageous" pelvic movements.

The Nicholas brothers, who played the Apollo in 1928, were acclaimed for a multiunit torso; thrust hips; shuffles with bent knee; movement with "jazz hands," fingers outstretched; syncopations; and partnering steps from the lindy hop.

Audiences in the United States and Europe were extraordinarily fascinated with the dancer Josephine Baker, who was even more acclaimed abroad than in her homeland. Baker performed wild renditions of the Charleston as well as her trademark *danse sauvage* at the Folies Bergère and elsewhere. Actually, she parodied the image of a savage sex goddess that had been cast for her. Her dance movements and rhythm influenced George Balanchine of the New York City Ballet.

The Charleston—which came from Charleston, South Carolina—had been introduced to New York by Elida Webb in 1923, in the Broadway show *Runnin' Wild*. It became a huge national hit. Trendy young white women were called "flappers," a term referring to their flailing limbs as they danced the Charleston. It was a fast dance in which the whole body was used in shimmying motions with a kicking step both forward and backward; the hands were crossed on the knees as they moved toward and away from each other. The shimmy was of African derivation: it was common among Igbo girls and mature warriors in Nigeria, and among the Ibibio people, Ghana's Ashanti, and numerous other African groups.

Partly because of dance, Harlem was a site of diffusion as whites ventured uptown. These whites came to Harlem for the same reason as some other Americans went to Cuba: to be in touch with what they saw as primal authenticity, to feel the pulse of life. Many whites thought that blacks had sensate superiority and that blacks were sensual, lewd, libidinous, and licentious—a quintessential representation of the exotic, erotic, and primitive. Blacks were supposed to be incredibly potent, perhaps even a menace to morality. Whites saw these qualities as manifested in dance, in which, as in sex, the body is the instrument.

To whites, blacks seemed to have a provocative dance vocabulary: swinging hips; a rotating, thrusting pelvis; an undulating torso; and shimmying shoulders. Also, blacks appeared to take unabashed delight in the primacy of the body, to believe in the importance of the spiritual in dance, and to express universalized personal experience in their dances. Whites in Harlem nightclubs were thrilled to partake of a sense of illicit sexuality in a socially protected environment.

In the years after World War I, prosperity and economic growth meant not only more disposable income but also a shorter workweek and longer vacations: that is, more leisure time to pursue personal entertainment. The 1920s were a time of cultural transformation, shifting moral boundaries, and changing lifestyles. The Volstead Act of 1919 had ended the legal sale and distribution of alcoholic beverages; most of the big Harlem clubs were owned by whites and flourished when liquor became illegal. As a result of all these factors, whites who lived downtown saw Harlem as a playground. Harlem witnessed a boom in cabarets from 133rd Street to 135th Street between and on Lexington and Seventh avenues. The Cotton Club, Connie's Inn, Ed Small's Paradise Nest, the Plantation Club, and the Savoy Ballroom were prominent; and the Cotton Club in particular took pride in being the source of new social dances.

Harlem revues were a saturnalia of humor, big bands, vocalists, and dancers. Revues produced for white audiences showcased light-skinned women who appealed not only to these audiences' concept of beauty but also to their taste for exoticism and animality. (Many blacks at the time of the Harlem Renaissance had the same notion of beauty and felt contempt for darker-skinned people.) Dances such as the truckin', Susie-Q, peckin', and scrontch gained recognition in production numbers and then caught on as ballroom fads. Interestingly, though, the lindy hopper George "Shorty" Snowden originated the "shorty George" step at the Savoy Ballroom; it then made its way to nightclub and vaudeville stages.

The lindy hop was the rage across black and white America and Europe for about twenty years. In one of the dance contests at the Savoy, George Snowden, its all-time champion, did a breakaway, flinging his partner out and improvising a few solo steps of his own. The effect was electric, and Snowden called the step the lindy, after Charles Lindbergh, who made a historic nonstop airplane flight from New York to Paris in 1927. In this dance, women actually did take flight; the lindy hop involved rocking and turning moves with freewheeling, flowing, improvised steps to an eight-beat count. At the Savoy, the lindy hop had a democratizing effect, offering emotional freedom and individual expression: race and class boundaries temporarily dissolved.

White dancers often achieved recognition by performing dances that had been originated by blacks, although the whites transformed these dances by toning down the original uninhibited display of sexuality. This appropriation of African American dances by outsiders was sometimes resented and even considered a form of theft, but it did often evoke a sense of pride in black people—a sense of having created something that others valued.

Furthermore, this appropriation of black dances by whites motivated blacks to create new dances, frequently in the sensual African tradition. For African American dance, the locus of creativity was in streets, homes, and clubs. Style makers and rule breakers, African Americans could reinvent their identity through dance, presenting a new view of their American experience. This association of dance and identity is not unique to blacks: people everywhere may consciously use dance symbolically, as an identity marker, as they might use flags, uniforms, and hairstyles.

Clayton "Peg Leg" Bates, 1927. (© Bettmann Corbis.)

Josephine Baker *en pointe*. (Library of Congress, n.d.)

In most social dance settings, the participants would say they are dancing to have a good time. Some would also say that they are seeking social or sexual partners; and some would think in terms of health— "It's good exercise." Black dance also simultaneously conveyed messages having to do with identity: "This is who I am. This is how creative I am." Dance was, like swearing, a form of release; it was also an assertion that the body is beautiful. It was a component of cultural identity; it encoded messages about hierarchy, inclusion and exclusion, and exchanges across social boundaries. It might also be a covert political challenge, because dance involves a symbolic, stylistic breaking of rules. Thus artistic freedom for African Americans dancers during the Harlem Renaissance was a historically meaningful civil right.

Vocabulary: Terms in Song Accompanying Dance

Balling: having fun, sex

Belly rub: sexy dance

Boogie-woogie: a kind of dance

Bread, cabbage, cookie: vagina

Charleston: popular dance of 1925 with movements common to several dances of the Igbo of Nigeria

Dogging: dancing

Fishtail: movement in which the hips create a figure eight

Fungshun: crowded, sweaty dance

Jagging jig: a black person; people dancing

Jig and clog: body held upright

Jooking: dance style

Pecking: neck and shoulder movement similar to the Yanvallou dance of Dahomey

Rug-cutter: a person too cheap to frequent dance halls; also, a good dancer

Scronch: to dance with sexual innuendo

Shaking the shimmy: a slow walk with frequent twitching of the shoulders (movement common among Igbo warriors of Nigeria)

Shim-sham shimmy: erotic dance

Shout: a ball or prom; one-step dance

Stomp: raucous dance party

Strut: stylized walk with attitude

Trucking: dance step resembling a stroll

Wobble: dance

JUDITH LYNNE HANNA

See also Baker, Josephine; Blackbirds; Bubbles, John; Cotton Club; Dafora, Asadata; Ellington, Duke; Harlem: 3—Entertainment; Nightclubs; Primitivism; Robinson, Bill "Bojangles"; Shuffle Along; Tucker, Earl "Snakehips"

Further Reading

Dagan, Ester, ed. *The Spirit's Dance in Africa.* Montreal, Canada: Galerie Amrad, 1997.

Gottschild, Brenda Dixon. *Waltzing in the Dark: African American Vaudeville and Race Politics in the Swing Era.* New York: St. Martin's, 2000.

Hanna, Judith Lynne. *To Dance Is Human: A Theory of Nonverbal Communication.* Chicago, Ill.: University of Chicago Press, 1987.

Miller, Norma, with Evette Jensen. *Swingin' at the Savoy.* Philadelphia, Pa.: Temple University Press, 1996.

Perron, Wendy. "Dance in the Harlem Renaissance: Sowing Seeds." In *EmBODYing Liberation: The Black Body in American Dance*, eds. Dorothea Fischer-Hornung and Alison D. Goeller. London: Lit Verlag, 2001.

Stearns, Marshall, and Jean Stearns. *Jazz Dance: The Story of American Vernacular Dance.* New York: Macmillan, 1968.

Dark Laughter

Sherwood Anderson's novel *Dark Laughter* (1925)— his most popular work of fiction during his lifetime— demonstrates the influence of Jean Toomer's *Cane* (1923) in its language and imagery. In *Dark Laughter*, Anderson presents an America racially divided between the sterile materialism of the white world and the more sensual indulgences of the African American world. Against this backdrop, the novel records the struggles of two white Americans to escape the neurosis and impotence of a society damaged by overindustrialization and world war. Serving as a Greek chorus to this rebellion is the "dark laughter" of African Americans, a sound that represents to Anderson a primitive state of sensual enjoyment now lost to the modern world.

One of the main characters, John Stockton, dissatisfied with his career and his marriage, leaves his wife and home and takes a new identity as Bruce Dudley, a drifter. He first wanders down to New Orleans, where he becomes enthralled by the easy movement and laughter of the African American workers on the docks. He envies their apparent freedom from the obsessions of the white world and tries to embrace a more sensual life. After this journey South, he settles in Old Harbor, Indiana, and earns a modest living painting carriage wheels. Aline Grey, the wife of the owner of the wheel factory, is also seeking to escape—in her case, from a stifled existence and a passionless marriage.

293

Aline's husband, who has been physically and psychologically wounded by the war, concerns himself only with plans to expand his business. Dudley's newfound easy manner attracts Aline, who hires him as a gardener. The consummation of their relationship takes place before the amused gaze of the African American servants, who laugh at the repressive sexuality of white people.

When it was published in 1925, *Dark Laughter* received mixed reviews and no notice from African American publications. Some reviewers disapproved of the novel's apparent immorality and its sometimes incomprehensible experimentalism; others praised Anderson's critique of modern American materialism. A few reviewers saw in Anderson's simple construction of racial difference an attempt to construct a primitivism that could serve as an antidote to a European civilization gone awry. Waldo Frank (1925) warned that Anderson's African Americans should not be read as an attempt to represent real African Americans accurately. Anderson's romanticized vision of blackness, Frank wrote, was merely an expression of white people's longing for redemptive laughter. More recent scholars have wrestled with issues raised by the African American presence in this novel. Howe (1951) found the depictions of African Americans "oversimplified and patronizing." But Fanning (1977), in an article about the reception of *Dark Laughter* by French critics in the 1920s, found the novel a valuable document reflecting the racist views of some progressive white people. Dickerson (1973) argued, in an important article, that Anderson's attempt to portray a lush, sensual world of African Americans in New Orleans bears the imprint of Jean Toomer's *Cane*. She did not consider *Dark Laughter* as convincing in its execution as Toomer's work, but she noted that Anderson's novel demonstrates the lasting influence of *Cane* on American literature.

CHARLES D. MARTIN

See also Anderson, Sherwood; *Cane*; Frank, Waldo; Toomer, Jean

Further Reading

Anderson, David D. *Sherwood Anderson: An Introduction and Interpretation*. New York: Holt Rinehart and Winston, 1967.
Burbank, Rex. *Sherwood Anderson*. New York: Twayne, 1964.
Dickerson, Mary Jane. "Sherwood Anderson and Jean Toomer: A Literary Relationship." *Studies in American Fiction*, 1(2), 1973.
Fanning, Michael. "Black Mystics, French Cynics, Sherwood Anderson." *Black American Literature Forum*, 11(2), 1977.
Frank, Waldo. "Laughter and Light." *Dial*, 79, December 1925.
Howe, Irving. *Sherwood Anderson*. Stanford, Calif.: Stanford University Press, 1951.

Dark Princess

W. E. B. Du Bois's *Dark Princess: A Romance* (1928) was his second novel (the first, *The Quest of the Silver Fleece*, had appeared in 1911). *Dark Princess* can be read as dramatizing the problem of culture for the Negro—an issue of the Harlem Renaissance, the New Negro movement, and modernism.

This novel relates the journey of Matthew Towns from America to Europe and back, from one thwarted profession to another, and, after considerable struggle, from brooding isolation to happiness in marriage and fatherhood. When he is barred from completing a residency in obstetrics because he is black, Matthew goes to Berlin. There he falls in love with an Indian princess, under whose tutelage he joins an organization of "darker peoples"—Indians, Chinese, Japanese, and Egyptians—who want to dismantle European imperialism. Matthew returns home to track the progress of black Americans toward nationhood; under the guise of a Pullman porter, he becomes involved with a militant black leader in a drive to unionize black porters and then in a terrorist plot. Matthew is jailed but is then rescued by a businessman and launched into a political career that is at first brilliant but then hypocritical. Matthew enters a loveless marriage with his political manager and then a scandalous illicit affair; ultimately, though, he balances the personal with the social by marrying the Indian princess and becoming the parent of an African-Asian child who is called "king," "maharajah" and "messenger and messiah to all the darker worlds." The novel combines the conventions of social realism and romance; portrays a "new" black man; and depicts the many facets, personal and political, of desire.

The critical reception of *Dark Princess* reflects shifts in literary and cultural analysis and also suggests the specific challenge that Du Bois—a man with manifold and sometimes contrasting creative and social commitments—represents for readers and scholars. Alain

Locke, reviewing the novel for the *New York Herald Tribune*, gave it measured praise; but he called it a "not wholly successful" mixture of "pure romance" and "rich deposits of sociology," and in a private letter to Langston Hughes he expressed graver doubts. Other reviews in the black press were more favorable. In *The Crisis* of October 1928, Allison Davis described *Dark Princess* as "propaganda at once eloquent and sane"; and Alice Dunbar Nelson, in her literary column, "As in a Looking Glass," found it "complete and eminently soul-satisfying." Reviews in the white press were also mixed: some considered the novel too romantic, whereas others thought its realistic portrayal of black humanity was not really "art."

During the 1930s and 1940s, *Dark Princess* was overshadowed by novels of social protest, but it continued to receive attention from critics then and later (e.g., Broderick 1959; Redding 1939). Aptheker (1976) gives insight into Du Bois's own view of this novel; in the publisher's advertisements, Du Bois described it as a "story of the great movement of the darker races for self-expression and self-determination" and as a "romance with a message" about the "defense and self-development of the best in all races." Moses (1982) locates *Dark Princess* in the tradition of African American messianic redemption. Beavers (2000) also reads it as a "messianic discourse," and as reminiscent of the biblical parable of the prodigal son. Tate (1998) notes that it puts romantic and erotic elements at the service of racial propaganda and is disturbed by its celebration of racial hybridity and its idealization of Asian rather than African beauty; but Gilroy (1993) considers the merging of African and Asian cultures valuable and also finds in *Dark Princess* a "politics of transfiguration." With regard to the aesthetics conveyed in *Dark Princess*, Byerman (1994) considers this element "play" (as opposed to the real "work" of the laborer); but others, including Gilroy and Posnock (1998), find deeper meaning in this theme. *Dark Princess* will probably continue to raise questions about race and culture, individuality and community, and politics and aesthetics.

ERIKA RENÉE WILLIAMS

See also Du Bois, W. E. B.; Locke, Alain; Modernism; Nelson, Alice Dunbar; New Negro Movement

Further Reading

Aptheker, Herbert. "Introduction." In *Dark Princess*. Millwood, N.Y.: Kraus-Thomson, 1976.

Beavers, Herman. "Romancing the Body Politic: Du Bois's Propaganda of the Dark World." *Annals of the American Academy*, 568, March 2000.

Broderick, Francis L. *W. E. B. Du Bois: Negro Leader in a Time of Crisis*. Stanford, Calif.: Stanford University Press, 1959.

Byerman, Keith. *Seizing the Word: History, Art, and Self in the Works of W. E. B. Du Bois*. Athens and London: University of Georgia Press, 1994.

Gilroy, Paul. "'Cheer the Weary Traveller': Du Bois, Germany, and the Politics of (Dis)placement." In *The Black Atlantic*. Cambridge, Mass.: Harvard University Press, 1993.

Lester, Julius, ed. *The Seventh Son: The Thoughts and Writings of W. E. B. Du Bois*, Vol. 2. New York: Vintage, 1971.

Lewis, David Levering. *W. E. B. Du Bois: Biography of a Race, 1868–1919*. New York: Holt, 1993.

Marable, Manning. *W. E. B. Du Bois: Black Radical Democrat*. Boston, Mass.: Twayne, 1986.

Moses, Wilson Jeremiah. *Black Messiahs and Uncle Toms: Social and Literary Manipulations of a Religious Myth*. University Park: Pennsylvania State University Press, 1982.

Posnock, Ross. *Color and Culture: Black Writers and the Making of the Modern Intellectual*. Cambridge, Mass., and London: Harvard University Press, 1998.

Rampersad, Arnold. *The Art and Imagination of W. E. B. Du Bois*. Cambridge, Mass.: Harvard University Press, 1976.

Redding, J. Saunders. *To Make a Poet Black*. Ithaca, N.Y: Cornell University Press, 1988. (Originally published 1939.)

Sundquist, Eric J., ed. *The Oxford W. E. B. Du Bois Reader*. New York and Oxford: Oxford University Press, 1996.

Tate, Claudia. "'Dark Princess, a Romance,' by W.E.B. Du Bois." In *Psychoanalysis and Black Novels: Desire and the Protocols of Race*. New York: Oxford University Press, 1998.

Zamir, Shamoon. *Dark Voices: W. E. B. Du Bois and American Thought, 1888–1903*. Chicago, Ill., and London: University of Chicago Press, 1995.

Dark Tower

The Dark Tower, a literary and artistic salon, would have been impossible without the sponsorship of A'Lelia Walker. She had, in 1919, inherited a fortune from her mother, Madame C. J. Walker, the inventor of

295

a very popular hair-straightening process. Whereas her mother had supported African American charities, A'Lelia Walker enjoyed spending her money on jewelry, card games, parties, and cars. As Richard Bruce Nugent, an eccentric among the younger Harlem Renaissance artists, suggested, A'Lelia Walker had two motives in sponsoring the Dark Tower. First, there certainly was a wish to support African American artists, many of whom she knew personally from parties and other social occasions. Another fact may also have played a decisive role: A'Lelia Walker could, as Nugent put it harshly, be described as a "social failure" in that she was not part of the mostly class-oriented black elite. She had become rich not because of an elevated class background but through inheritance, and she was furthermore far from the African American upper-class ideal of near-white. She may have thus viewed the organization of the Dark Tower as a potential gateway to higher social circles.

The Dark Tower, planned as a setting where young artists of the Harlem Renaissance could meet and discuss their plans, was much needed because no regular meeting place existed for them. Before the inception of this salon, they occasionally met at places like Jessie Fauset's home, for formal occasions with poetry recitals; or, in contrast, at the house of Wallace Thurman, where their meetings were usually characterized by drunkenness and chaos. What the black artists and A'Lelia Walker intended to create was "a sufficiently sympathetic place . . . completely informal, a quite homey, comfortable place to which they could bring their friends for a chat and a glass of lemonade, coffee, or tea." Walker would thus occupy a position like Mabel Dodge, who had opened her home to the artists of Greenwich Village.

A'Lelia Walker chose her twin limestone townhouse at 108–110 West 136th Street in Harlem as the location for the Dark Tower. Countee Cullen served as the inspiration for the name of her salon. He had written the popular poem "From the Dark Tower," published in 1927 in *Copper Sun*, in which he described the suffering of the suppressed "dark" race; and from 1926 to 1928 he had also contributed "The Dark Tower," a literary and cultural column in *Opportunity* magazine. To create an adequate framework, Walker dedicated an entire floor to the salon and made extensive plans for redecoration. In accordance with her desire to sponsor African American artists, she wanted Aaron Douglas, the best-known painter of the Harlem Renaissance, to decorate the main room, with Nugent as his assistant. According to Nugent, numerous meetings were

arranged, but no specific plans for redecorating were ever agreed on. It thus came as a surprise when formal invitations on stylish cards were issued for the grand opening of the Dark Tower in the autumn of 1928:

> We dedicate this tower to the aesthetes. That cultural group of young Negro writers, sculptors, painters, music artists, composers and their friends. A quiet place of particular charm. A rendezvous where they may feel at home to partake of a little tidbit amid pleasant, interesting atmosphere. Members only and those whom they wish to bring will be accepted. If you choose to become one of us you may register when first attending "The Dark Tower." One dollar a year. Open nine at eve "til two in the morn." (quoted in Watson 1995, 143)

The younger artists to whom the place was explicitly dedicated were astonished: the salon was characterized by what Nugent described as "stiff dignity" rather than, as planned, by a casual, relaxed atmosphere. The cream-colored walls had been decorated not by Aaron Douglas but by Paul Frankel, a local sign painter, who had put up passages from Cullen's "From the Dark Tower" and Langston Hughes's "The Weary Blues" in gold lettering on facing walls. Nor did the furniture correspond to earlier plans for an informal air: it consisted of stylish rosewood chairs and tables, a rosewood piano, rose-colored curtains, and a blue Victrola. More decisive for the future development of the Dark Tower, however, were the arrangements regarding prices. Before the opening of the salon, the plan had been to consider the young artists' lack of money—"Food was to be so reasonably priced that the artists would be benefited"—but now everything was set up differently: Everyone turned up in evening clothes; hats had to be checked for 15 cents; and food was expensive. As Nugent remembered it, there was only one option when the guests "saw the menus. Coffee—10 cents, sandwiches anywhere from 25 to 50 cents; lemonade a quarter—and on and on. They left hungry." Moreover, it seemed that the focus was not really on black artists. According to Nugent, "the place was filled to overflowing with whites from downtown who had come up expecting that this was a new and hot nightclub."

Although some artists of the Harlem Renaissance returned to the Dark Tower on other occasions, it was clear that the vision of a regular meeting place had failed. Nevertheless, the Dark Tower survived for roughly one year. As is evident from newspaper reports by Geraldyn Dismond, the gossip columnist for the *Inter-State Tattler*, its social status was significant; and Dismond therefore bemoaned its closing. Moving from West 136 Street to her apartment on Edgecombe Avenue, A'Lelia Walker decided to reopen the Dark Tower—this time, however, not as an artists' venue but as a nightclub and restaurant in the studio below the actual Dark Tower salon. The new venture, which opened, rather optimistically, on 27 October 1929, three days after Wall Street's "black Thursday," apparently continued until A'Lelia Walker's death on 16 August 1931. Eventually, the place was leased to the city.

Although it did not achieve its actual purpose of serving African Americans artists, the Dark Tower still stands out as a symbol of an unprecedented upsurge of black self-confidence and creativity.

CHRISTA SCHWARZ

See also Cullen, Countee; Douglas, Aaron; Fauset, Jessie Redmon; Hughes, Langston; Inter-State Tattler; Nugent, Richard Bruce; Salons; Thurman, Wallace; Walker, A'Lelia

Further Reading

Cullen, Countée. "From the Dark Tower." In *Copper Sun*. New York: Harper, 1927.

Lewis, David Levering. *When Harlem Was in Vogue*. New York: Knopf, 1981.

Nugent, Richard Bruce. "The Dark Tower." N.d. (Probably late 1930s; private collection of Thomas H. Wirth, Elizabeth, N.J.)

Rampersad, Arnold. *The Life of Langston Hughes, Vol. 1, 1902–1941: I, Too, Sing America*. New York: Oxford University Press, 1988.

Watson, Steven. *The Harlem Renaissance: Hub of African-American Culture, 1920–1930*. New York: Pantheon, 1995.

DePriest, Oscar

When Oscar Stanton DePriest came to Chicago in 1889, the city was rapidly changing and expanding as a result of migration from the American South and immigration from Europe; between 1880 and 1930, Chicago's African American population would increase from 6,480 to 233,903. Although discrimination and de facto segregation existed in Chicago, racial issues were not as virulent there as in the South.

DePriest became active in local politics, joining the Republican Party. His service to the Republicans was rewarded in 1904, when he was nominated for and elected to the Cook County Commission; he served consecutively until 1908. After 1908, he concentrated on his real estate business.

Between 1906 and 1915 DePriest worked with leading African American politicians to form a black political organization centered in two predominantly black wards in Chicago's South Side. In this effort, they were aided by the large migration of blacks to Chicago during World War I; and they succeeded in organizing a voting bloc capable of settling factional disputes within the party.

In 1915 DePriest ran for the city council, backed by a progressive coalition that elected him as the first African American alderman in Chicago. As an alderman, he became part of William "Big Bill" Thompson's political machine. When the Republican U.S. Congressman Martin Madden died, DePriest ran for the open seat; in November 1928, attracting the rapidly rising African American constituency, he was elected and became a member of the Seventy-First Congress. He thus also

Oscar DePriest at his desk at the Capitol in Washington, D.C., 1929. (© Bettmann Corbis.)

became the first African American elected to Congress in the twentieth century, the first elected from a northern state, and an inspiration to politically minded Harlemites. He served three consecutive terms before leaving office on 2 January 1935, after the Democratic landslide in the election of 1934.

As an African American Congressman, DePriest was subjected to several personal slights, and his congressional career received mixed reviews. He was criticized, for example, for opposing federal aid to the unemployed; he was unable to get an antilynching bill passed; and he could not achieve a law changing the venue of a trial if the defendant believed that a fair trial was impossible in the designated jurisdiction. However, he was praised for demanding equal treatment in the House of Representatives and for eating in the Senate dining room. He also defended the right of students at Howard University to be served in the House restaurant; and he obtained approval of an increase from $240,000 to $460,000 in federal aid for Howard University's power plant. Ignoring death threats, he delivered speeches in the South. His most recognized legislative achievement was an amendment prohibiting discrimination in the Civilian Conservation Corps.

After serving in Congress, DePriest returned to Chicago and his real estate business. An ardent anticommunist, he remained politically active: he won a seat on the Chicago city council in 1943 and served until 1947. He died in 1951.

Biography

Oscar Stanton DePriest was born on 9 March 1871, in Florence, Alabama; his mother worked part time as a laundress; his father was a farmer. In 1878 the family settled in Kansas; Oscar DePriest was educated in local schools there and then studied business for two years at Salina Normal School. In 1888 he left home; he spent a year traveling and then moved to Chicago, working as a painter, a decorator, and eventually an independent contractor and realtor. He became active in the Republican Party and was commissioner in Cook County in 1904–1908. In 1906–1915 he participated in forming a black political organization in Chicago; in 1915, he was elected to the city council. He was elected to the U.S. Congress in 1928 and served until 1935. DePriest died in 1951, after having been hit by a bus.

ABEL BARTLEY

See also Politics and Politicians

Further Reading

Chicago Defender. 19 May 1951.

Gossnell, Harold F. *Negro Politicians: The Rise of Negro Politics in Chicago.* 1967.

New York Times. 13 May 1951.

Spear, Allan. *Black Chicago: The Making of a Negro Ghetto 1880–1920.* Chicago, Ill.: University of Chicago Press, 1967.

Dean, Lillian Harris

Lillian Harris (Lillian Harris Dean, 1870–1928), known as "Pig Foot Mary," was an entrepreneur in Harlem. Unlike her famous contemporary, the businesswoman Madame C. J. Walker, Dean was known to few people outside Harlem. Yet in Harlem, she was a legendary success story: unable to read or write, she had achieved prosperity through inventiveness, hard work, and business savvy.

Pig Foot Mary was described as a black woman with a pleasant face and a deep voice, and physically immense–she was often called "Goliath" and "Amazonlike." From early morning until late at night, her towering figure could be seen stationed on a segment of the sidewalk at Sixtieth Street and Amsterdam Avenue in front of Rudolph's Saloon. There, wearing one of her starched, checked gingham dresses, she sold the delicacies that many southern-born Harlemites had grown up eating: pigs' feet, chitterlings, corn on the cob, and hogmaws.

Pig Foot Mary had run away from her impoverished home as a teenager and had eventually come to New York City in 1901. She began her business shortly after arriving in Harlem, selling her wares at first from a dilapidated baby carriage. Taking five dollars that she had earned working as a domestic during her first week in Harlem, she spent three of the dollars for the baby carriage and a large wash boiler and spent the other two on pigs' feet. She persuaded the proprietor of Rudolph's saloon to allow her to use his stove each day to boil her wares, and by the end of a month, her business was a stunning success. She then progressed from the baby carriage to selling her wares over a specially constructed portable steam table that she had designed.

In 1917, in an effort to find better living conditions, many black people started moving farther uptown into Harlem. Pig Foot Mary then moved her business to the corner of 135th Street and Lenox Avenue, next to

John Dean, who had a flourishing newspaper stand and shoeshine stall there. She and Dean were married shortly afterward.

It has been said that one reason why Pig Foot Mary worked so hard was to save money for her old age: she wanted to afford a place for herself in a respectable old folks' home. After marrying Dean and evidently feeling somewhat more secure, she began to invest the income from her food business in Harlem real estate. Her first acquisition was a $44,000 apartment on Seventh Avenue, which she sold six years later for $72,000. She then bought more buildings at 69–71 West 138th Street, and then still more at 2324 Seventh Avenue, as well as houses in Pasadena, California. She was considered a tough, no-nonsense landlord; tenants and agents who fell behind in their rent would receive letters admonishing them to "Send it and send it damn quick!" By 1925, her real estate holdings were valued conservatively at $375,000.

Biography

Lillian Harris Dean (Pig Foot Mary) was born in 1870, in a shanty on the Mississippi delta, to a large, poverty-stricken family. Longing for a better life, she ran away from home as a teenager and wandered to many northern cities before she arrived in New York City in the autumn of 1901. In Harlem, where she became a prosperous and legendary figure, she sold southern food on the street, married John Dean c. 1917, and invested profitably in real estate. She died in 1928 in California, at age fifty-eight.

JANICE TUCK LIVELY

See also other businesses

Further Reading

Bascom, Lionel C., ed. *A Renaissance in Harlem*. New York: Avon, 1999.

Bontemps, Arna. *The Harlem Renaissance*. New York: Dodd, Mead, 1972.

Bundles, A'Lelia. *On Her Own Ground: The Life and Times of Madam C. J. Walker*. New York: Scribner, 2001.

"Dean, Pig Foot Mary." In *The Harlem Renaissance: A Historical Dictionary of the Era*, ed. Bruce Kellner. New York, 1987, p. 97.

Fisher, Walter. "Sarah Breedlove Walker." In *Notable American Women*, ed. Edward T. James et al. Cambridge, Mass.: Harvard University Press, 1971.

Huggins, Nathan. *Harlem Renaissance*. New York: Oxford University Press, 1971.

Lewis, David Levering. *When Harlem Was in Vogue*. New York, 1981, pp. 109–110.

"Pig Foot Mary." In *The Negro in New York: An Informal Social History*, eds. Roi Ottley and William J. Weatherby. New York, 1967, p. 187.

Defender

See Chicago Defender

Delaney, Beauford

Beauford Delaney, an expressionist painter, whose brother Joseph was also an artist, was born in Tennessee in 1901 and studied in Boston. In the midst of the Harlem Renaissance, Beauford Delaney went to New York and found work as a bellboy. He lived in Greenwich Village during the 1930s and 1940s. During that period, he was highly productive; he exhibited at the Whitney Studio Gallery in 1930 and at the Harmon Foundation in Harlem, and he had his first one-man show at the Harlem branch of the New York Public Library. In 1936, under the auspices of the Federal Arts Project, he assisted Georgette Seabrooke Powell on a mural for the nurses' recreation room at Harlem Hospital.

In 1947 Delaney exhibited at the Pyramid Club in Philadelphia; in the 1950s he had a successful show at the RoKo Gallery in New York. At the time, his subjects were mainly urban scenes and portraits. Gregarious and endowed with an engaging personality, Delaney met many important people who recognized his talent and sat for portraits. Among his sitters were W. E. B. Dubois, the New Orleans jazz musician Billy Pierce, Louis Armstrong, Duke Ellington, W. C. Handy, the cartoonist Al Hirschfeld, and the author Henry Miller.

Just as Delaney's subjects were inspired by the white community as well as by the African American community—he was at home both in Harlem and in the Village—so his style reflected influences from both groups. He was impressed by the painterly possibilities of abstract expressionism, which he combined with the rhythms of jazz. His *Can Fire in the Park* (1946), for example, has affinities with expressionism; the impasto paint is thickly applied, and the color is vivid. It shows a group of blacks gathered around a fire in a garbage can. Illuminated with Delaney's unique light, the canvas pulsates with shimmering reds, yellows, blues, and greens. The outlines vibrate as if to the rhythm of music.

Like Jackson Pollock, Delaney studied for a time with Thomas Hart Benton at the Art Students League and was apparently influenced by his teacher's dynamic painted figures. With a fellowship to Yaddo in the 1950s, Delaney found the time and space to experiment with abstraction. From then on, nonrepresentational paintings would become part of his repertoire.

In the 1950s Delaney went to Paris, where he would spend the rest of his life and would become a magnet for other black artists living abroad. Constantly in need of money, he was helped by his friends among the expatriate American intellectuals in Paris. In addition to Miller, Delaney painted portraits of James Jones, James Baldwin, and Jean Genet. But sometimes he painted distinctively black themes, as in his portrait *Rosa Parks* (1970). He shows the defiant civil rights activist in a perky yellow hat and dress, seated confidently on a park bench, surrounded by his signature white impasto light. In the background the silhouette of a black man echoes a barren tree at the right.

In 1973, Delaney had a major retrospective in Paris, but by then his mind and his health were deteriorating as a result of alcoholism and Alzheimer's disease. He died in 1979.

Biography

Beaufort Delaney was born in Knoxville, Tennessee, on 31 December 1901. His mother, Delia, had been born a slave in Virginia and later worked as a domestic. His father, part African American and part Native American Creek, was a Methodist Episcopal preacher who built churches in rural Tennessee and Virginia. Delaney attended an all-black high school in Knoxville before moving to Boston. There he studied art at the Massachusetts Normal School, the South Boston School of Art, and the Copley Society; frequented the Boston Museum of Fine Arts and the Isabella Stewart Gardner Museum; and developed an interest in classical music and opera. He moved to New York during the Harlem Renaissance and navigated between the white artists in Greenwich Village and the blacks who frequented Harlem. In the 1950s he went to Paris, where he remained until his death. He is best-known for his portraits, mainly of well-known intellectuals, and for his urban scenes. His style is expressionist, but he had a uniquely vivid color sense that he combined with musical rhythm, making his pictures seem to vibrate. Delaney died in 1979 and is buried in Paris.

LAURIE ADAMS

See also Artists; Greenwich Village; Harmon Foundation

Further Reading

Beauford Delaney: A Retrospective. New York, 1978. (Exhibition catalog.)

Leeming, David. *Amazing Grace: A Life of Beauford Delaney*. New York and Oxford: Oxford University Press, 1998.

Beauford Delany, photographed by Carl Van Vechten. (Library of Congress.)

Lewis, Samela. *African-American Art and Artists*. Berkeley: University of California Press, 1990.

Miller, Henry. *The Amazing and Invariable Beauford Delaney*. New York, 1941. (Reissued 1978.)

Patton, Sharon F. *African-American Art*. New York: Oxford University Press, 1998.

Delany, Clarissa Scott

Although she is best-known for her poetry, Clarissa Scott Delany was active in several professions. She contributed essays, book reviews, and poems to *Crisis*, *Opportunity*, and *Palms*, but she also traveled in Europe, taught at the prestigious Dunbar High School, and collected statistical data as a social worker in New York City. Some insight into her varied experiences may be found in her poem "Solace," in which she writes "my life is fevered/and a restlessness at times . . . possesses me." In each endeavor, she addressed the concerns of African Americans from all walks of life.

Delany's social consciousness was probably inspired by her father, Emmet Jay Scott, who was Booker T. Washington's secretary. Delany was raised in the "black belt" in a middle-class family; she left home at age fifteen to study at the Bradford Academy in New England. Upon graduation, she entered Wellseley College, where she studied poetry and social economics and was a member of the varsity field hockey team, as well as many clubs. It was during this time that Scott began attending meetings of the Literary Guild in Boston, where she heard Claude McKay speak and made connections with other socially minded and artistically inspired African Americans.

Her literary and political interests blend in "A Golden Afternoon in Germany," an essay inspired by a postgraduation trip through Europe and published in *Opportunity* in 1925. This piece profiles two German artists whose works show, in Delany's words, "a recognition of soul, of spirituality in the African." Although the essay explicitly discusses major issues of the Harlem Renaissance, such as pan-Africanism, art, and essentialism, Delany's poetry is more subtle and personal, revealing her private struggles through the imagery of nature. For example, in "Solace," the speaker discovers in the "shifting/Pageant of the seasons" a way that she can "Take meaning from all turmoil/And leave serenity/Which knows no pain." Throughout her poetry, rain and wind seem to be a counterpart to the speakers' emotions and seem to offer the writer some distance from anguish. Such distance is addressed more directly in "The Mask," which features a speaker so detached from emotion that she refers to herself as "she," until a betrayal causes the mask to fall and the "I" to emerge. However, Delany writes not only of masking the "bitter black despair" of social and personal defeat, but also of transcendence, as in her often-quoted "Interim": "Another day will find me brave/and not afraid to dare."

After three years of teaching at Dunbar High School, Clarissa Scott married Hubert T. Delany, a lawyer, and moved to New York City. She continued to work as a poet, critic, and social worker until her death of kidney disease in 1927. Although she published only four poems, her work was lauded by W. E. B. Du Bois, Alice Dunbar Nelson, and Countee Cullen, who included her poems in his anthology *Caroling Dusk*. Upon her death, Delany's Dunbar colleagues Angelina Weld Grimké and Anna Julia Cooper wrote moving tributes to her.

Biography

Clarissa Mae Scott Delany was born on 22 May 1901, in Tuskegee, Alabama. She studied at Bradford Academy, Haverhill, Massachusetts (1916–1919); and Wellesley College, Wellesley, Massachusetts (B.A., Phi Beta Kappa, 1919–1923). Delany taught at Dunbar High School in Washington, D.C. (1923–1926), and was a social worker with the National Urban League and the Women's City Club of New York (1926). Her husband was Hubert T. Delany, a lawyer. Her poem "Solace" won fourth place in the literary contest sponsored by *Opportunity*. She died in New York City, on 11 October 1927, at age twenty-six.

Rebecca Meacham

See also Authors: 5–Poets; Crisis, The; Cullen, Countee; Grimké, Angelina Weld; Nelson, Alice Dunbar; Opportunity; Opportunity Literary Contests; Palms

Selected Works

"A Golden Afternoon in Germany." 1925. (Essay.)
"Solace." 1925.
"Interim." 1926.

"The Mask." 1926.
"Joy." 1926.

Further Reading

Cullen, Countee, ed. *Caroling Dusk: An Anthology of Verse by Negro Poets.* New York: Harper and Row, 1927. (See also 2nd ed., 1974.)

Grimké, Angelina Weld. "To Clarissa Scott Delaney [sic]." In *The Selected Works of Angelina Weld Grimke,* ed. Carolivia Herron. New York: Oxford University Press, 1991.

Honey, Maureen. *Shadowed Dreams: Women's Poetry of the Harlem Renaissance.* New Brunswick, N.J.: Rutgers University Press, 1989.

———. "Survival and Song: Women Poets of the Harlem Renaissance." In *The Harlem Renaissance 1920–1940: Analysis and Assessment, 1980–1994,* ed. Cary D. Wintz. New York: Garland,1996.

Roses, Lorraine Elena, and Elizabeth Randolph, eds. *Harlem's Glory: Black Women Writing, 1900–1950.* Cambridge, Mass.: Harvard University Press, 1996.

Roses, Lorraine Elena, and Elizabeth Randolph, eds. *Harlem Renaissance and Beyond: Literary Biographies of 100 Black Women Writers, 1900–1945.* Boston, Mass.: G. K. Hall, 1990.

Shockley, Ann Allen. *Afro-American Women Writers, 1746–1933: An Anthology and Critical Guide.* Boston, Mass.: G. K. Hall, 1988.

Wilson, Sondra Kathryn, ed. *The "Opportunity" Reader: Stories, Poetry, and Essays from the Urban League's "Opportunity" Magazine.* New York: Modern Library (Random House), 1999.

Dett, Robert Nathaniel

I am a musician whose ambition in life is the advancement of my people, and who believes absolutely in equality of opportunity for all peoples, regardless of race, creed, or color, or previous condition of servitude. (Excerpt from *Annual Report to President Gregg,* Hampton Institute, 1918)

Robert Nathaniel Dett was born in Canada and raised in New York. He had been a child prodigy, and as an adult he worked for the advancement of "his people" through his roles as educator, pianist and organist, composer, conductor, and intellectual.

Dett's commitment to education was apparent not only in his personal academic studies and accomplishments but also through his teaching: he was a professor at numerous black institutes and colleges. His longest tenure was at Hampton Institute (1913–1932), where he served as the first black chair of music and introduced the B.S. degree in music. He was a protégé of the black educator and soprano E. Azalia Hackley; and one of his students—among other noted artists—was the acclaimed soprano Dorthy Maynor.

As a pianist and organist, Dett performed at numerous prestigious venues, including Carnegie Hall, Boston Symphony Hall, and the Library of Congress. He also performed for two presidents: Herbert Hoover and Franklin Delano Roosevelt. Dett's rapid success during the early 1920s gained him the attention and support of the banker and philanthropist George Foster Peabody, who was his benefactor for more than a decade.

Dett was one of the most celebrated composers of the period; his nearly 100 compositions include works for piano, chorus, solo voice, orchestra, and organ. Many of his compositions reflect his love of black folk music, especially the spiritual. Dett's compositional style was characterized by traditional harmonies and rhythms and was often classified as neoromantic. He received some criticism because of this style, which was seen as an imitation of white classical composers. Nevertheless, along with Harry T. Burleigh, Will Marion Cook, and J. Rosamund Johnson, he paved the way for subsequent black composers; and Penman Lovinggood described Dett as "our most characteristically racial composer." Dett's most noted pieces during the period include the motet *The Chariot Jubilee* (1919), based on the spiritual "Swing Low, Sweet Chariot"; "Let Us Cheer the Weary Traveler" (1926); and the oratorio *The Ordering of Moses* (1931–1932, 1937).

Dett was also an esteemed leader within the music community. In the spirit of self-empowerment, he formed the Musical Arts Society in 1919 as a way to invite distinguished artists such as Marian Anderson, Percy Grainger, Roland Hayes, Clarence Cameron White, and Burleigh to the Hampton-Norfolk area to give lectures, concerts, and performance clinics. Also in 1919, motivated by his love of black folk music and by his desire to preserve this music and to foster talent, he cofounded the National Association of Negro Musicians (NANM) with Nora Holt, Henry Grant, and White. Dett served as chair of NAMN's advisory board and later as its president.

Many of Dett's thoughts on black music are expressed in his prize-winning four-part essay "Negro Music" (1920), and in numerous published and unpublished articles.

Biography

Robert Nathaniel Dett was born on 11 October 1882, in Drummondville, Ontario (Canada). He studied at Halstead Conservatory of Music in Lockport, New York, with its founder, Oliver Willis Halstead (1901–1903); at Oberlin College Conservatory of Music in Ohio, with Howard Handel Carter (piano), J. W. Horner (voice), F. Lehman (theory), Edward Dickinson (history of music), Arthur E. Heacox (theory), George Carl Hastings (piano), George W. Andrews (organ and composition), and J. R. Frampton (organ), receiving a bachelor of music degree in piano and composition (1908); again at the Oberlin Conservatory with Karl Gehrkens (musical pedagogy, summer 1913); at Columbia University in New York with Peter Dykema (summer 1915); at the American Conservatory of Music in Chicago (summer 1915); at Northwestern University in Evanston, Illinois, with Lawrence Erb (summer 1915); at Harvard University with Arthur Foote (1919–1920); at Fontainebleau School of Music in France, with Nadia Boulanger (1929); and at the Eastman School of Music in Rochester, New York, with Max Landow (piano), Bernard Rogers (composition and orchestration), Edward Royce (counterpoint), and Howard Hanson (modern harmony) in 1932. Dett taught at Lane College in Jackson, Tennessee (1908–1911); at Lincoln Institute in Jefferson, Missouri (1911–1913); at Hampton Institute in Virginia (1913–1932); at the Eastman School of Music (1931–1933); at Sam Houston College in Austin, Texas (summer 1937); and at Bennett College in Greensboro, North Carolina (1937–1942). He was the founder of the Musical Arts Society (1919); a cofounder (1919) and president (1924–1926) of the National Association of Negro Musicians; and director of the Hampton Institute Choir (1913–1931) and of the Hampton Institute School of Music (1928–1932). His awards included the Francis Boot Music Award (1919), Bowdoin Literary Prize (1920), and the Harmon Foundation Award (1928). He received honorary doctorates from Howard University (1924) and Oberlin College Conservatory of Music (1926). He was a member of Phi Beta Kappa, American Society of Composers, National Association of Negro Musicians, and National Association of Teachers in Colored Schools. Dett died in Battle Creek, Michigan, on 2 October 1943.

EMMETT PRICE III

See also Anderson, Marian; Burleigh, Harry Thacker; Cook, Will Marion; Hayes, Roland; Holt, Nora; Johnson, John Rosamond; Lovinggood, Penman; Music; National Association of Negro Musicians; White, Clarence Cameron

Selected Writings

"Emancipation of Negro Music." *Southern Workman*, 47, 1918.

"Musical Standards." *Etude*, 15, 1920.

"John W. Work." *Southern Workman*, 54, 1925.

"As the Negro Sings." *Southern Workman*, 56, 1927.

Religious Folk Songs of the Negro as Sung at Hampton Institute. Hampton, Va.: Hampton Institute Press, 1927. (As editor.)

"Musical Invasion of Europe: Hampton Institute Choir Abroad." 1930.

The Dett Collection of Negro Spirituals, 4 vols. Chicago, Ill.: Hall and McCreary, 1936. (As editor.)

"From Bell Stand to Throne Room . . . ." *Etude*, 52, 1934; reprinted in *Black Perspective in Music*, 1(1), 1973.

Selected Compositions

"America the Beautiful." New York: Fisher, 1918.

"Go On, Mule!" New York: John Church, 1918.

"A Thousand Years Ago or More." New York: John Church, 1919.

Concert Waltz and Ballad. 1919. (Unpublished.)

"Magic Moon of Molten Gold." New York: John Church, 1919.

The Chariot Jubilee. New York: John Church, 1919. (Recorded: Audio House AHS 30F75.)

"Enchantment." New York: John Church, 1922.

"Nepenthe and the Muse." New York: John Church, 1922.

"Oh, the Land I'm Bound For." New York: John Church, 1923.

"The Winding Road." Bryn Mawr, Pa.: Theodore Presser, 1923.

"Cotton Needs Pickin'." 1924. (Unpublished.)

Sonata No. 1 in F Minor. 1924. (Unpublished.)

"The Voice of the Sea." New York: John Church, 1924.

"Were Thou the Moon." New York: John Church, 1924.

Sonata No. 2 in E Minor. 1925. (Unpublished.)

"Fair Weather." Bryn Mawr, Pa.: Theodore Presser, 1926.

"God Understands." New York: John Church, 1926.

"Let Us Cheer the Weary Traveler." New York: John Church, 1926.

Cinnamon Grove Suite. New York: John Church, 1928.

"Lord Gently, Lord, and Slow." New York: John Church, 1929.

"My Day." New York: John Church, 1929.

"As Children Walk Ye in God's Love." New York: Schirmer, 1930.

"Ave Maria." New York: Schirmer, 1930.

The Ordering of Moses: Biblical Folk Scenes. 1931–1932. (Master's thesis, Eastman School of Music; rev. 1937; recorded: Silver Crest TAL 42868, Unique Opera Records UORC 113.)

"As by the Stream of Babylon." New York: Schirmer, 1933.

"Juba." Chicago, Ill.: Clayton F. Summy, 1934.

"O Lord, the Hard-Won Miles." New York: Schirmer, 1934.

"Iorana: Tahitian Maiden's Love Song." Chicago, Ill.: Clayton F. Summy, 1935.

"Now Rest Beneath Night's Shadows." New York: Fisher, 1938.

Further Reading

Brooks, Christopher. "R(obert) Nathaniel Dett." In *The New Grove Dictionary of Music and Musicians*, 2nd ed., Vol. 7., ed. Stanley Sadie. London: Macmillan, 2001.

McBrier, Vivian Flagg. *R. Nathaniel Dett, His Life and Works (1882–1943)*. Washington, D.C.: Associated Publication, 1974.

Perry, Frank Jr. "R. Nathaniel Dett." In *Afro-American Vocal Music: A Select Guide to Fifteen Composers*. Berrien Springs, Mich.: Van de Vere, 1991.

Ryder, Georgia A. "Harlem Renaissance Ideals in the Music of Robert Nathaniel Dett." In *Black Music in the Harlem Renaissance: A Collection of Essays*, ed. Samuel A. Floyd Jr. Knoxville: University of Tennessee Press, 1993.

———. "R(obert) Nathaniel Dett." In *Center for Black Music Research, International Dictionary of Black Composers*, Vol. 1, ed. Samuel Floyd Jr. Chicago, Ill.: Fitzroy Dearborn, 1999,

Simpson, Anne Key. *Follow Me: The Life And Music of R. Nathaniel Dett*. Metuchen, N.J.: Scarecrow, 1993.

Spencer, Jon Michael. "R. Nathaniel Dett's Views on the Preservation of Black Music." *Black Perspective in Music*, 10(2), 1982.

———. "Wild Dreams of Bringing Glory and Honor to the Negro Race." In *The New Negroes and Their Music*. Knoxville: University of Tennessee Press, 1997.

———. "The R. Nathaniel Dett Reader: Essays on Black Sacred Music." Special issue of *Black Sacred Music: A Journal of Theomusicology*, 5(2), Fall 1991.

Domingo, Wilfred Adolphus

Wilfred Adolphus (W. A.) Domingo, an Afro-Caribbean immigrant, was a businessman, journalist, and author and a participant in the Garveyite, socialist, and communist movements in Harlem. He and Marcus Garvey had met in Kingston, where they were members of the National Club, a political organization, and they remained in close contact in the United States. Domingo introduced Garvey to the works of the nineteenth-century proto-black nationalist Edward Wilmot Blyden, and later to several radical black intellectuals in Harlem, including Hubert Harrison, A. Philip Randolph, Chandler Owen, and Richard B. Moore.

Although Domingo never officially joined Garvey's United Negro Improvement Association (UNIA), he was an active participant in early meetings of the New York branch in 1917–1919; he also arranged for a local printer, Henry Rogowski, to publish UNIA's periodical *Negro World*, and from August 1918 to July 1919, Domingo was its founding editor, a position in which Garvey gave him considerable latitude. However, Domingo's use of *Negro World* to express his own socialist views troubled Garvey, who espoused Booker T. Washington's bootstrap capitalism and who wanted to avoid trouble during the "red scare" of 1919. In June 1919, during a raid on the Rand School, the Lusk Committee seized many socialist texts, including a work in progress by Domingo called *Socialism Imperiled*, and Garvey and Domingo's collaboration came to an acrimonious end. Garvey and the UNIA's executive committee put Domingo on "trial" for publicizing views and ideas inconsistent with Garveyism, and Domingo left *Negro World* in July 1919. In 1925, in an open letter to the editor of the *Jamaican Gleaner*, Domingo publicly denounced Garvey's practices as "medieval, obscure, and dishonest" and Garvey's steamship corporation, the Black Star Line, as virtually a swindle.

As a political essayist, Domingo contributed articles on racism, capitalist exploitation, and imperialism to various radical black journals. He worked for the *Messenger* during the early 1920s, when the black socialists A. Philip Randolph and Chandler Owen were attacking Garvey (who had held an infamous meeting with the

Ku Klux Klan); but Domingo parted ways with the *Messenger* in 1923 after Randolph and Owen's crusade against Garvey became anti–West Indian. At this time, Domingo shifted his affiliation from the Socialist Party to the Harlem branch of the Communist Party. He also joined the African Blood Brotherhood (ABB) and began handling its periodical, the *Crusader,* as well as guiding ABB's publicity and propaganda. He started a weekly magazine of his own, the *Emancipator,* during the late 1920s.

One of Domingo's emphases was the importance of West Indian immigration to racial uplift in America. Later in his life, he was a notable critic of the short-lived West Indian Federation, a pan-Caribbean nationalist entity founded in 1958. Aside from this, however, little is known about Domingo's last years.

Biography

Wilfred Adolphus Domingo was born on 26 November 1889, in Kingston, Jamaica. He left Jamaica for the United States in 1910, relocated from Boston to New York in 1912, and started a fruit and vegetable import business in Harlem in 1922. Domingo was an editor of *Negro World,* a columnist for *The Messenger* (1917–1923), and a founding member of the African Blood Brotherhood (1919–1924). He also worked on and contributed to other radical black periodicals. He and Marcus Garvey had a long friendship and collaboration but eventually broke with each other. The date of Domingo's death is unknown.

J. M. FLOYD-THOMAS

See also African Blood Brotherhood; Black Star Line; Garvey, Marcus; Harrison, Hubert; Messenger, The; Moore, Richard B.; Negro World; Owen, Chandler; Randolph, A. Philip; Riots: 2—Red Summer of 1919; United Negro Improvement Association

Further Reading

James, Winston A. *Holding Aloft the Banner of Ethiopia: Caribbean Radicalism in America, 1900–1932.* New York: Verso, 1997.

Johnson, James W. *Black Manhattan.* New York: Arno, 1968. (Originally published 1930.)

Kornweibel, Theodore Jr. *No Crystal Stair: Black Life and the Messenger, 1917–1928.* Westport, Conn.: Greenwood, 1975.

———. *Seeing Red: Federal Campaigns against Black Militancy, 1919–1925.* Bloomington: Indiana University Press, 1998.

Watkins-Owens, Irma. *Blood Relations: Caribbean Immigrants and the Harlem Community, 1900–1930.* Bloomington: Indiana University Press, 1996.

Who's Who in Colored America. 1933.

Douglas, Aaron

Aaron Douglas was the leading visual artist of the Harlem Renaissance. Within weeks of his arrival in Harlem in 1925, he was recruited by W. E. B. Du Bois, the editor of *The Crisis*; and by Charles S. Johnson, the editor of *Opportunity*, to illustrate their editorials and articles on lynching, segregation, political issues, theater, and jazz, as well as poems and stories. Douglas, a high school teacher in Kansas City, had decided to join the young artists of the Harlem Renaissance after seeing a copy of *Survey Graphic*, which had devoted a special issue to Harlem and had chosen the Bavarian artist Winold Reiss to create a cover for the magazine. Douglas was impressed by Reiss's dignified, forthright portrayal of blacks.

Douglas was hired to create a visual message about a largely literary movement, for a public that had grown dramatically with the increase of black migration to the North during World War I. Du Bois had complained often in *Crisis* about a lack of black patronage and of a black audience, most notably in his "Criteria of Negro Art." As he knew, black artists found that most support for their work came from whites, who were the main patrons of the Harlem Renaissance; and he believed that blacks needed to support their own artists. It was his hope that Douglas could reach a new, emerging black public across the United States, starting with Harlem. This was a role that only an illustrator could fill. *Crisis* had a wide national readership, and any illustration Douglas made would be seen in libraries, schools, and homes across the country. Douglas tried to reach this new black middle-class public by using the language of African art as one of his most important tools. Before Douglas, some American artists had begun to include African art in their work, but none had used it on a regular basis.

Du Bois realized that an artist could help relay a message; and art, according to Du Bois, should have a message. He stated: "I do not care a damn for any art that is not used for propaganda. But I do care when propaganda is confined to one side while the other is stripped and silent." Douglas, accordingly, tried to create a new, positive black image, influenced by Africa. He was tired of white people's depictions of blacks and believed that his work could touch the black audience in a unique way. He wanted to change the way blacks were depicted in art and to bring the language of African art to Harlem and then to the entire United States. In 1925, he explained in a letter to Alta Sawyer, his future wife: "We are possessed, you know, with the idea that it is necessary to be white, to be beautiful. Nine times out of ten it is just the reverse. It takes lots of training or a tremendous effort to down the idea that thin lips and a straight nose [are] the apogee of beauty. But once free you can look back with a sigh of relief and wonder how anyone could be so deluded."

Douglas's growth and experimentation can be seen in his magazine illustrations, in which he created some of his most forceful and interesting works and evolved his artistic language, a language immersed in African art to a degree that was unprecedented among American artists. These works are clean and bold, often consisting of just a few simple figures that illustrate a basic idea or just show images of African Americans.

Douglas's first illustration in *Crisis*, in the issue of February 1962, was "Invincible Music: The Spirit of Africa," which had been drawn specifically for the magazine but was not accompanied by any related text and did not accompany any article. "Invincible Music" consists of one figure, presumably male, in silhouette, with head raised in song to the sky and right arm holding a mallet that is used to beat a large drum. This figure is crouching and is clad in only a simple wrap around the waist; the position—with shoulders parallel to the picture plane rather than receding into space in correct perspective—and the figure's hair and entire bodily profile or silhouette are reminiscent of Egyptian art, in which Douglas had a great interest. Here Egypt stands for all of Africa. Douglas was also trying to simplify the human form. Two shield-like marquise shapes are implanted in the ground behind the figure; their jagged design resembles African-inspired patterning. These shapes symbolize plant life, as do three smaller versions, which look like leaves and are placed in front of the figure. At the top of the drawing are two large jagged shapes that represent sources of energy, perhaps the sun or stars, as well as a stylized stream of smoke on the right. At the bottom of the drawing are flat papyrus plants (resembling tulips), which appear to be inspired by art deco. This drawing is successful partly because it is so simple, with large expanses of solid black and a bright white background, highlighted by grayish outlines and details, and also because its format—a silhouette—is so forceful.

Douglas's next illustration for *Crisis*, "Poster of the Krigwa Players Little Negro Theatre of Harlem," appeared in the issue of May 1926. It was not related to any particular play but was rather a type of advertisement for Du Bois's theater project. This illustration is even more strongly influenced by Egyptian and African imagery. Like "Invincible Music," it is in solid black and white, and it is boldly executed, almost like a woodblock print. The poster shows a single figure, sitting cross-legged, with the face turned to the side so that it is shown in profile; the figure is angular, primarily rectilinear in form, with exaggeratedly thick lips, the appearance of geometric tribal makeup, an afro hairstyle, a large hoop earring dangling from the visible ear, and an African mask or ancestral head held in the left hand. Stylized plants and flowers, resembling African motifs and art deco patterning, surround the figure, and a palm tree is shown. Above the figure, the influence of Egypt is apparent in pyramids on the left, a sun form above, and a sphinx on the right. Wave patterns form the bottom third of the composition, perhaps representing the Nile. Although this picture may have little to do with actual African imagery, the viewer can immediately see that the inspiration is African. Du Bois wanted Douglas to remind the readers of *Crisis* of their African ancestry and to inspire in them an interest in their common heritage. Egypt provided a vocabulary for achieving this goal, although except for the fact that the discovery of Tutankhamen's tomb had prompted a renewed interest in African art, there was only a tenuous link between Egypt and sub-Saharan Africa.

In addition to *Crisis* and *Opportunity*, Douglas did illustrations for other journals, including *Theatre Arts Monthly*; for books, including Locke's *New Negro*; and for the poems of Langston Hughes. He also received several commissions for murals and portraits. He created a particularly innovative cover for *Fire!!*, a radical black publication edited by Wallace Thurman that attempted to break away from the confines of the traditional leaders of the Harlem Renaissance and create a new artistic voice. Douglas also did three interior drawings for *Fire!!* and wrote its artistic statement.

In 1930 Douglas was commissioned to execute a cycle of murals for the library of Fisk University, representing a panorama of the history of black people in the new world. He began with life in Africa, then depicted slavery, emancipation, and freedom, which he symbolized as Fisk's Jubilee Hall. Through this extensive mural project, Douglas hoped to make the students at Fisk realize the important contributions of black Americans in building America. The final murals in the cycle, still visible today, represent philosophy, drama, music, poetry, and science, with depictions of night and day.

Many artists of the Harlem Renaissance traveled to Paris, and Douglas was no exception: he lived in Paris and studied at the Académie Scandinave there for one year, in 1931. This sojourn was followed by a one-year fellowship at the Barnes Foundation in Merion, Pennsylvania.

In 1934, as a project for the Works Progress Administration (WPA), Douglas executed what many people consider to be his masterpiece: the large Marxist-inspired murals *Aspects of Negro Life*, now at the Schomburg Center in Harlem. As early as the 1920s, Douglas had been determined to awaken middle-class blacks to the important issues of their time, but the Great Depression—which affected the black middle class more severely than its white counterpart—radicalized both Douglas and his audience. In *Aspects of Negro Life,* Douglas chronicled the struggle of black men and women from Africa through slavery and emancipation to their role as workers in the machine age. These murals—individually titled *The Negro in an African Setting, Slavery through Reconstruction, An Idyll of the Deep South,* and *Song of the Towers*—appealed directly to a public suffering the hardships of unemployment and poverty.

Douglas was not the only illustrator during these years to develop the vocabulary of Africa; numerous artists who followed him and were influenced by him took great pride in their African heritage. However, Douglas remains unique in that he provided crucial links between the literary figures of the Harlem Renaissance, their ideas about Africa, and the thinking of blacks throughout the world. Working during a time of limited artistic freedom for African Americans, he also had to confront the problem of trying to reach—with limited patronage—a public that was still geographically isolated, difficult to locate, and difficult to define. Despite these challenges, Douglas successfully addressed issues of importance to a growing black middle class. He based his work on studies of the African heritage and was the first black artist in the United States to create racial art; and as an illustrator for black magazines, he was able to reach a large readership. Black leaders sought his work to illustrate their message, and he received regular commissions until his departure from Harlem in 1937. Douglas brought African art to Harlem in a new, accessible, immediate way and then, through his illustrations, brought it to Americans, both black and white, across the country. He never depended on white patronage: he created African-inspired works largely under his own direction and the influence of black leaders. His experience indicates that this group effort, however brief, was one of the most exciting aspects of the time. The artists of the Harlem Renaissance were a small band, but they opened doors and increased opportunities for black artists in the 1930s.

Douglas's works reflected pride, unity, strength, dignity, and self-awareness. He was a pioneer in American art, breaking away from the traditions of more famous white artists such as Robert Henri, Reginald Marsh, and Ben Shahn to create unique, sophisticated works that interpreted modernism in a new light. Moreover, Douglas's influence extended beyond his extensive commissions during the Harlem Renaissance. He was hired by Fisk University in 1940 to create a new art department, and he became its founding chairman, remaining in this position until his retirement in 1966.

Douglas recognized the similarity between the period of the Harlem Renaissance and the period of the civil rights movement. Both were times of rapid social, political, and economic change, and during both eras he had tremendous hope for a better life for African Americans. His art—depicting the history of Africa and of black Americans, and pervaded by African imagery—was a way to encourage racial pride and build blacks' self-esteem.

In his later years, Douglas often spoke of the Harlem Renaissance, reminding his students that it had been a time "fraught with hope, bitter frustration, and struggle against an indifferent and frequently hostile environment." Knowing that his students were in the midst of their own struggle in contemporary America, he urged them to remain optimistic and hopeful and to keep their eyes on the prize. When he was one of the few remaining figures from the renaissance, he assured his students: "We still rejoice that we were among those who were found able and willing to shoulder the heavy burden of the pioneer and the pathfinder, firm in the conviction that our labor was a

Aaron Douglas. (Schomburg Center for Research in Black Culture, New York Public Library.)

(1944). Douglas was founder and chair of the art department at Fisk University in Nashville, Tennessee (1937–1966). He retired from Fisk in 1966 and died in Nashville in 1979, at age eighty.

AMY KIRSCHKE

See also Artists; Crisis, The; Du Bois, W. E. B.; Fire!!; Hughes, Langston; Krigwa Players; New Negro, The; Opportunity: Reiss, Winold; Survey Graphic; Visual Arts

Major Exhibitions

D'Caz-Delbo Gallery, New York. 1934.
Howard University, Washington, D.C. 1937.
Fisk University, Nashville, Tennessee. 1948, 1952, 1953.
Newark Museum, New Jersey. 1971.
Studio Museum in Harlem, New York. 1982.

Further Reading

Aaron Douglas Papers. Special Collections Division, Fisk University.
Douglas Papers. Schomburg Center for Research in Black Culture, New York Public Library.
Gips, Terry, ed. *Narratives of African American Art and Identity: The David C. Driskell Collection*. 1998.
Kirschke, Amy H. *Aaron Douglas: Art, Race, and the Harlem Renaissance*. 1995.

small but withal an essential contribution to the continued flowering of the art and culture of the black people of this nation." In making their own contribution to black culture, these students could hardly find a better guide than Aaron Douglas. He ranks among the most important American artists of the twentieth century; and his experiences and insights—which were so essential during the civil rights era—remain valuable today, as artists of a new generation face many of the same obstacles and challenges.

Biography

Aaron Douglas was born in Topeka, Kansas, in 1899. He received a B.F.A. from the University of Nebraska at Lincoln, in 1922; studied under Winold Reiss in New York in 1924–1927; studied at the Académie Scandinave in Paris (1931); and received an M.A. from Columbia University Teachers College in New York

Draper, Muriel

Muriel Draper—a writer, social activist, and broadcaster—played a major role in the Harlem Renaissance through one of the most influential salons in New York. Noted for her unusual looks and inventive clothes, she moved in artistic circles in England and America. She married the lieder singer Paul Draper in 1909, and the couple relocated to Italy. The Drapers had a difficult marriage, and Paul Draper died in 1925 at age thirty-eight. Muriel Draper then moved to New York, where she worked as an interior decorator and magazine writer. She, Carl Van Vechten, and A. R. Orage formed a trio of white intellectuals who infused international cultural progressivism into Harlem.

Like the pioneering Harlem author Jean Toomer, Muriel Draper was a follower of the mystic G. I. Gurdjieff, who was based in Paris; for seven years, from 1924 to 1931, Draper served the Gurdjieff group in New York as an unofficial secretary. During that time, meetings of the Gurdjieff group, led by Orage, were held at her apartment. Draper was a close associate of another of Gurdjieff's disciples, Carl Van Vechten, whose novel *Nigger Heaven* (1926) contributed to making Harlem a fad. Through their mixed-race gatherings, Draper and Van Vechten crusaded to break down the color barrier. Draper's Tuesday teas were modest affairs; however, she brought together the Harlem avant-garde and white artists without regard for race at a time when this was highly exceptional. With Carl Van Vechten, she also assisted the black singer Taylor Gordon in writing and publishing his memoirs, *Born to Be* (1929).

While participating in a creative writing group (to which Jean Toomer also belonged) conducted at her home by Orage, Draper wrote *Music at Midnight* (1929). This was a memoir of her years as a saloniste in London from 1911 to 1914, during her marriage to Paul Draper. Regular members of her salon in London had included Pablo Casals, Henry James, and Arthur Rubinstein, and she had also received visits from such notables as Gertrude Stein and Nancy Cunard.

Following up on the renown she achieved through *Music at Midnight*, she became a lecturer, speaking on social issues that were related to her interest in the psychoanalyst Karen Horney and in Marxism. After a tour of the Soviet Union in 1934–1935, Draper became active in leftist politics. She visited Spain during its civil war in 1937 and subsequently lectured about and raised money for the Loyalists. In 1938 she had a radio program on NBC, "It's a Woman's World," presenting political and social analyses. She made two further visits to the Soviet Union but ceased her political activities after being attacked by the House Un-American Activities Committee in 1949.

Van Vechten preserved Draper's papers and clothes at the Beinecke Rare Book and Manuscript Library at Yale University, where Romaine Brooks's portrait of her also hangs.

Biography

Muriel Draper was born c. 1886 and attended public schools in Haverhill, Massachusetts. She was employed as an interior decorator by the architect Paul Chalfin in New York (1916–1920) and as assistant manager of the Chicago Opera Company (1920–1922); she then operated her own decorating business

(1922–1927). Draper published articles and sketches in *Harper's*, *Town and Country*, and *Vogue* (1920–1929) and had a radio program on NBC, "It's a Woman's World" (1938). She was a member of the National Council of American-Soviet Friendship (1942) and the Women's International Democratic Federation (WIDF), Congress of American Women (1945–1949), and served as its president (1949). Draper died in New York City on 26 August 1952.

Jon Woodson

See also Cunard, Nancy; Toomer, Jean; Van Vechten, Carl

Further Reading

Draper, Muriel. *Music at Midnight*. 1929.

Kellner, Bruce. *Carl van Vechten and the Irreverent Decades*. Norman: University of Oklahoma Press, 1968.

Moore, James. *Gurdjieff: The Anatomy of a Myth*. Rockport, Mass.: Element, 1991.

Welch, Louise. *Orage with Gurdjieff in America*. Boston, Mass.: Routledge and Kegan Paul, 1982.

Dreiser, Theodore

Theodore Dreiser gained his reputation as a major American novelist during the first half of the twentieth century, as the author of critically acclaimed works that include *Sister Carrie* (1900), *Jennie Gerherdt* (1911), and *An American Tragedy* (1925). He was born in Terre Haute, Indiana, and grew up in a large family that included four brothers and five sisters. Because of constant financial pressure, Dreiser's family moved continually and even separated for a period of time. However, Dreiser managed to receive schooling and even attended college for a year at Indiana University (thanks to the financial assistance of a former schoolteacher). Eventually, Dreiser found work as a reporter for Chicago's *Daily Globe* and then wrote for a succession of newspapers across the United States. His experiences with these newspapers educated him about the world and enabled him to work at his craft. After writing several short stories, Dreiser published his first novel, *Sister Carrie*. Following the controversy surrounding this novel, Dreiser suffered a nervous breakdown. His brother Paul, the writer of popular songs such as "On the Banks of the Wabash," helped him recover and go on writing.

Although he was not a major figure in the Harlem Renaissance, Dreiser was a prominent writer and an active participant in the New York literary world; and his social life placed him in the circles of several renowned contributors to the renaissance. At one party held by the Van Vechtens, Dreiser heard James Weldon Johnson read "Go Down Death" and Paul Robeson sing. Along with Robeson and others, Dreiser later received the Award of Merit Medal from the American Academy of Arts and Letters. Dreiser also attended the production of *Othello* in which Robeson starred. In 1945, Dreiser invited Robeson to one of his teas, at which the two discussed race relations and the possibility of writing an article on that topic; before leaving, Robeson sang a rendition of "Ol' Man River" for Dreiser. At this tea, Dreiser and Robeson also discussed Paul Robeson Jr.'s educational experiences in Russia. Dreiser had always been interested in the Soviet Union and had visited it in 1927. Throughout his life, he leaned heavily toward communism, although he did not join the Communist Party until shortly before his death.

Dreiser also spent time with Langston Hughes. In 1938, he and Hughes were selected as delegates to attend the International Convention for International Peace. Hughes had the difficult responsibility of looking after Dreiser, who had a reputation for unusual behavior. True to form, Dreiser failed to attend a lunch that was being given for the delegation by a group of British writers. Eventually, though, Dreiser came around and conducted himself well; Hughes even stated that he was glad Dreiser had been selected. Shortly after the conference, however, Dreiser proceeded to Spain at the invitation of the Loyalists and then went to London, bypassing his fellow American delegates and causing more anxiety for Hughes.

Dreiser served as an honorary chairman to the National Committee for the Defense of Political Prisoners (NCDPP), which actively sought funds to support the legal defense of the nine Scottsboro boys in Alabama, who had been unjustly accused of assaulting two white girls and imprisoned; NCDPP also wrote a letter to the governor of Alabama. In July 1931, Dreiser wrote to the Association of Southern Women for the Prevention of Lynching; his letter shows an acute sensitivity to the injustices related to the trial and conviction of the Scottsboro boys, and he places this case in the context of the larger racial problems plaguing the United States. Dreiser also wrote "They Shall Not Die" (1934) as a defense of the Scottsboro boys.

Dreiser's short story "Nigger Jeff" (1901) reflects his early thoughts about lynching. He based part of the narrative on incidents that he observed as a reporter in St. Louis, Missouri; and some critics believe that the story depicts Dreiser's own transformation from newspaper reporter to serious artist. Dreiser uses the perspective of a young reporter named Elmer Davies, who is sent to Pleasant Valley to cover the story of Jeff Ingalls, a black man accused of assaulting a white girl. The reporter witnesses a mob's effort to take Ingalls away from the local sheriff. Eventually, Ingalls is seized by the mob, which is led by the girl's father and brother; he is then brought to a bridge and hanged. This incident has a tremendous impact on the reporter. After the others leave, Davies does not rush back to the city but stays at the bridge with the body. He then returns to the Pleasant Valley and learns that the sheriff will not take action against the men who have killed Ingalls. Before he leaves, Davies walks out to Ingalls' cabin to see the body again, discovers Ingalls' mother weeping in the corner, and is moved to tears.

Theodore Dreiser, photographed by Carl Van Vechten in 1933.
(Library of Congress.)

He leaves the cabin understanding that "it was not always exact justice that was meted out to all."

Dreiser's body of work influenced younger writers such as Richard Wright. In particular, Wright discovered in *Jennie Gerhardt* and *Sister Carrie* a sense of suffering that he associated with his own mother. Dreiser's *An American Tragedy* also influenced Wright's *Native Son*. The poet Margaret Walker recalled that to construct his fictional narrative, Wright used Dreiser's techinique of collecting newspaper articles related to a specific crime. Several critics have since noted parallels between Dreiser's character Clyde Griffiths and Wright's Bigger Thomas. Wright eventually became friends with Dreiser, and in 1944 attended Dreiser's farewell party in New York.

Theodore Dreiser remains an intriguing figure in the historical context of the Harlem Renaissance. His association with prominent African American artists and his interest in civil rights are worthy of more critical exploration.

Biography

Herman Theodore Dreiser was born on 27 August 1871, in Terre Haute, Indiana. He attended high school in Warsaw, Indiana, and entered Indiana University in 1889. He was a reporter for a series of newspapers: the Chicago *Globe* (1892), St. Louis *Globe-Democrat* (1892–1893), St. Louis *Republic* (1893), Pittsburgh *Dispatch* (1894), and *New York World* (1894). He was also an editor for a series of publications: the New York *Daily News* (1901–1903), *Smith's Magazine* (1904–1905), *Broadway Magazine* (1906), the Butterick "trio" (*Delineator, Designer,* and *New Idea Woman's Magazine*, 1907–1910), and the *American Spectator* (1932–1934). He applied to the Communist Party in 1945. His awards included the Merit Medal of the American Academy of Arts and Letters (1944). Dreiser died in Hollywood, California, on 28 December 1945.

PAUL R. CAPPUCCI

See also Hughes, Langston; Johnson, James Weldon; Robeson, Paul; Scottsboro; They Shall Not Die; Van Vechten, Carl; Walker, Margaret

Selected Works

Sister Carrie, 1900. (2nd ed., 1907.)
Jennie Gerhardt. 1911.

The Financier. 1912.
A Traveler at Forty. 1913.
The Titan. 1914.
Free and Other Stories. 1918.
Twelve Men. 1919.
An American Tragedy. 1925.
Dreiser Looks at Russia. 1928.
Dawn. 1931.
Tragic America. 1931.
America Is Worth Saving. 1941.
The Bulwark. 1946.
The Stoic. 1947.

Further Reading

Griffin, Joseph. *The Small Canvas: An Introduction to Dreiser's Short Stories*. Rutherford, N.J.: Fairleigh Dickinson University Press, 1985.

Hakutani, Yoshinobu. *Young Dreiser: A Critical Study*. Rutherford, N.J.: Fairleigh Dickinson University Press, 1980.

Lehan, Richard. *Theodore Dreiser: His World and His Novels*. Carbondale and Edwardsville: Southern Illinois University Press; London and Amsterdam: Feffer and Simons, 1969.

Lingeman, Richard. *Theodore Dreiser: An American Journey 1908–1945*. New York: Putnam, 1990.

Matthiessen, F. O. *Theodore Dreiser*. New York: William Sloane, 1951.

Pizer, Donald. *The Novels of Theodore Dreiser: A Critical Study*. Minneapolis: University of Minnesota Press, 1976.

Shapiro, Charles. *Theodore Dreiser: Our Bitter Patriot*. Carbondale: Southern Illinois University Press, 1962.

Swanberg, W. A. *Dreiser*. New York: Scribner, 1965.

Du Bois, W. E. B.

Historian, sociologist, political activist, editor, essayist, novelist, poet, and prophet, William Edward Burghardt Du Bois stands as one of the towering figures in American history. In a public career encompassing three-quarters of a century, Du Bois delivered eloquent, trenchant, and occasionally contradictory commentary on what he called "the problem of the Twentieth Century . . . the problem of the color line." In the 1920s, he played a central role in the unfolding drama of the Harlem Renaissance, initially as an inspiration and patron and later as an increasingly captious critic.

Du Bois was born in Great Barrington, Massachusetts, in 1868. His origins were humble. His mother, Mary, worked odd jobs, mostly as a domestic servant, before suffering a paralytic stroke; he scarcely knew his father, Alfred, who had abandoned the family. Still, Du Bois remembered his childhood as happy, a more or less "typically New England" upbringing, only occasionally ruffled by the racial realities of post-Reconstruction America. He flourished in Great Barrington's public schools, exhibiting even in these early days the qualities that would distinguish his life and art: a voracious intellect, a romantic imagination, and an overweening (although, in retrospect, quite justified) sense of his own historical importance.

Du Bois graduated from Great Barrington High School in 1885 and proceeded to Fisk University, from which he graduated three years later. Fisk, the flagship of the American Missionary Association's post–civil war campaign to uplift the freedpeople, gave Du Bois not only a fine classical education but also his first exposure to black life in the South under Jim Crow. In *Darkwater* (1921), Du Bois would describe that experience in characteristically grandiloquent prose: "Consider, for a moment, how miraculous it all was to a boy of seventeen, just escaped from a narrow valley. I willed and lo! my people came dancing about me . . . riotous in color, gay in laughter, full of sympathy, need, and pleading."

From Fisk, Du Bois went to Harvard, where he earned a second bachelor's degree in 1890 and a doctorate in history five years later. Although excluded from the university's dormitories and most of its social life, he flourished academically, developing close relationships with some of America's premier intellectuals, including the philosophers William James, Josiah Royce, and George Santayana and the historian Alfred Bushnell Hart. Du Bois's Ph.D. dissertation, "The Suppression of the African Slave Trade to the United States of America," completed under Hart's direction, was published in 1896—the first of his more than two dozen books.

Du Bois's graduate education also included a two-year sojourn at the University of Berlin, where he immersed himself in the emerging discipline of sociology. Although he failed to earn the coveted German doctoral degree—his support from the white philanthropic Slater Fund dried up before he could complete the residency requirement—his years in Germany proved formative. The encounter with sociology not only shaped Du Bois's future academic career but also confirmed his political vocation, offering a framework for engaged intellectual activism. Although often frustrated by the sheer irrationality of racial prejudice, Du Bois remained convinced that it was possible to generate authoritative, objective knowledge about human life (and about Negro life in particular), and that this knowledge could be used to fashion a more rational, more just world. More broadly, his years in Germany established some of the signature tensions in his thought. Living in Germany sharpened his racialism, his conviction that each race or *Volk* possessed its own distinctive genius or "gift"; but at the same time, Germany confirmed the cosmopolitan in him who exulted in what he called "the world beyond the veil," that vast "kingdom of culture" unsullied by American racial madness.

Despite his peerless education, Du Bois had no chance of a permanent appointment at a white university when he returned to the United States in 1894. He accepted a position teaching classics at Wilberforce University, an African Methodist Episcopal church school in Ohio. (Ironically, in light of future events, Du Bois also applied for and was offered a position at Booker T. Washington's Tuskegee Institute, but the offer did not arrive until after he had accepted the post at Wilberforce.) Although he often waxed lyrical about African American Christianity, Du Bois had little patience with organized religion, and he soon became estranged from the dominant evangelical ethos at Wilberforce. In 1896, he left to accept a temporary research position at the University of Pennsylvania, from which came his second book, *The Philadelphia Negro*, which is still regarded as a classic of urban sociology. In retrospect, his years at Wilberforce are significant chiefly for introducing him to his future wife, a "doe-eyed," somewhat stolid student named Nina Gomer. Although grievously mismatched, the couple remained married for more than half a century, until Nina's death in 1950. They had two children: a son, Burghardt, whose death in infancy would later be poignantly rendered in "The Passing of the First Born," one of the essays in *The Souls of Black Folk*; and a daughter, Yolande.

In 1898, Du Bois joined the faculty of Atlanta University, where he spent the next decade teaching, writing, and overseeing the Atlanta Studies, an ambitious annual series of conferences and monographs designed to provide an exact sociological portrait of African American life. He also put the final touches on his masterwork, *The Souls of Black Folk*, a collection of essays, autobiographical fragments, and fiction intended to illuminate the subjective human reality of those who lived "within the veil." In the book's belletristic "Forethought," Du Bois made it clear that his imagined audience was white, but this work would have its most profound impact on African American readers, including virtually all of the writers and artists who later distinguished themselves in the Harlem Renaissance.

The Souls of Black Folk marked Du Bois's entrance into the arena of racial politics. Chapter 3, "Of Mr. Booker T. Washington and Others," offered a respectful but telling critique of the so-called wizard of Tuskegee, whose advocacy of "industrial" education and political accommodation had lent an apparent black seal of approval to the Jim Crow regime settling over the South. In 1905, Du Bois helped organize the Niagara Movement, an assembly of black leaders opposed to Washington's leadership and committed to fighting for full civil equality for African Americans. Although this movement never achieved a firm institutional foundation, it signaled a new black assertiveness and contributed directly to the establishment, four years later, of the National Association for the Advancement of Colored People (NAACP). In 1910, Du Bois moved to New York City, to take office as the director of publicity of NAACP and to edit its monthly journal, *The Crisis*.

Du Bois's relationship with the predominantly white leadership of NAACP was contentious from the outset and would eventually culminate in his resignation. But for the predominantly black readership of *Crisis*, Du Bois *was* the NAACP. Working with limited funds and a minimal staff, he turned the magazine into his personal broadsheet, offering news and commentary, edifying reading lists, book reviews, and, on more than a few occasions, scathing criticism of individuals or institutions that had neglected their responsibility to the race. The riot in east St. Louis, the savage practice of lynching, America's entry into World War I (which Du Bois, to his later regret, endorsed), the Bolshevik revolution, Garveyism, the biennial meetings of his own Pan-African Congress, the New Deal—all of these developments and more were discussed and digested in the columns of *Crisis*. In the words of Lewis (1993), Du Bois became the self-appointed "preceptor of the race." No debate in black American life could be considered complete until Dr. Du Bois had had his say.

Inevitably, Du Bois was drawn into debates swirling around the Harlem Renaissance. Initially, he expressed an almost paternal fondness for the writers of the "younger literary movement," whom he regarded as his heirs. That assessment was characteristically immodest but by no means unfair. Virtually all of the core contentions of the New Negro movement can be found in Du Bois's writing a generation before. Du Bois first insisted that the Negro was "primarily an artist," that the "rude melodies" of black slaves constituted the "only true American music," and that blacks' "gift of laughter and song" had enriched an otherwise impoverished, materialistic American culture. Du Bois also recognized, long before Alain Locke, James Weldon Johnson, and other progenitors of the Harlem Renaissance, that artistic and literary production could provide a powerful weapon in African Americans' continuing quest for justice and respect. Although his chief identity was as a scholar and editor, he occasionally wielded that weapon, most notably in the novel *The Quest of the Silver Fleece* (1911) and the sprawling historical pageant *The Star of Ethiopia* (1913).

Du Bois was quick to establish himself as a patron and mentor to the emerging New Negro movement. He hired the novelist Jessie Fauset as literary editor of *Crisis*, and together they launched one of the era's first competitions for black writers. Among the young writers "discovered" by *Crisis* was Langston Hughes, whose epochal poem, "The Negro Speaks of Rivers," dedicated to Du Bois, appeared in 1921. Du Bois attended the Civic Club dinner of 1924 that served as literary Harlem's downtown debut, and he was one of the first reviewers to hail the genius of Jean Toomer's *Cane*, although he seems to have been taken more with the book's lyricism than with its modernist conception, which left him frankly bewildered. "His art carries much that is difficult or even impossible to understand," Du Bois complained. "I cannot, for the life of me, for instance, see why Toomer could not have made the tragedy of 'Carma' something that I could understand instead of vaguely guess at; 'Box Seat' muddles me to the last degree and I am not sure that I know what 'Kabnis' is about."

Embedded in Du Bois's curious review of *Cane* were the seeds of his future estrangement from the New Negro movement. For someone who wrote so eloquently of the "souls" of black "folk," Du Bois had surprisingly conservative aesthetic tastes. In an era attuned to modernist experimentation and the possibilities of vernacular expression, Du Bois preferred the soaring flights of Byron and Tennyson or their German romantic antecedents, Goethe and Schiller.

313

(*The Souls of Black Folk* included epigrams from all four authors.) His taste in music was likewise classical and distinctly Eurocentric. Although he appreciated the majesty of the "sorrow songs," he regarded blues as vulgar and jazz as unrefined. Whereas Langston Hughes glimpsed a universe of beauty in the keening wail of a saxophone on a Harlem street corner, Du Bois thrilled to Beethoven and Wagner.

As these differences in aesthetic values and judgment became apparent, Du Bois's regard for the rising generation of black writers plummeted, as did their respect for him. By the mid-1920s, *Opportunity*, an upstart magazine launched by Charles Johnson and the National Urban League, had displaced *Crisis* as the premier outlet for New Negro writing, and figures like Johnson, Alain Locke, and Carl Van Vechten had usurped Du Bois's role as literary patron. Personal encounters between Du Bois and his imagined offspring typically left both parties disappointed. The poet Claude McKay detected no human warmth in the idol of his youth, only "a cold, acid hauteur of spirit, which is not lessened when he vouchsafes a smile." Although not mentioned by name, Du Bois was clearly one of the targets of *Fire!!*, a short-lived journal launched by "younger Negro writers" (including Langston Hughes, Wallace Thurman, Richard Bruce Nugent, and Zora Neale Hurston) as an artistic declaration of independence from the older generation of "respectable," "bourgeois" black writers and critics.

Disagreements over the direction of the New Negro movement exploded into the open in 1926, following the publication of Carl Van Vechten's notorious novel *Nigger Heaven*. Many black writers defended the novel—Wallace Thurman half-facetiously predicted that a statue in Van Vechten's honor would one day be erected in Harlem—but Du Bois decried it as a "slap in the face," a violation of the "hospitality" that black people had extended to its white author. The book's appearance confirmed Du Bois's belief that the New Negro movement had lost its way, that a movement begun to advance black claims to citizenship had degenerated into a modern-day minstrel show, purveying stereotypical images of black criminals, prostitutes, and buffoons for the amusement of white readers.

In the months that followed, Du Bois continued to rail against what he dubbed the "Van Vechten school" of black writing. In his eyes, younger black writers were guilty not only of political irresponsibility but also of artistic blindness, recycling tales of "low down" black people while ignoring the rich vein of artistic material to be found in the predicament of intelligent, upstanding Negroes. His reviews of New Negro writing ranged from disappointed (*Fine Clothes to the Jew*, Langston Hughes's second volume of poetry, contained "extraordinarily beautiful bits" but lamentably confined itself to "lowly types") to vicious (passages in Claude McKay's *Home to Harlem*, he reported, left him "wanting to take a bath"). In the end, only a handful of writers escaped his scorn, among them Jessie Fauset, Countee Cullen (who was briefly married to Du Bois's daugher, Yolande), and Nella Larsen.

Over the course of the 1920s, Du Bois made several attempts to redirect the Harlem Renaissance along more appropriate lines. In 1926, he launched a symposium in *Crisis*: contributors, white and black, were asked to respond to a series of seven questions on the theme "The Negro in Art: How Shall He Be Portrayed?" Although he circulated the questionnaire to a cross section of writers, editors, and publishers, his own opinions were obvious from the tone of the questions:

1. When the artist, black or white, portrays Negro characters, is he under any obligations or limitations as to the sort of character he will portray?
2. Can the author be criticized for painting the worst or the best characters of a group?
3. Can publishers be criticized for refusing to handle novels that portray Negroes of education and accomplishment, on the ground that these characters are no different from white folk and therefore not interesting?
4. What are Negroes to do when they are continually painted at their worst and judged by the public as they are painted?
5. Does the situation of the educated Negro in America with its pathos, humiliation, and tragedy call for artistic treatment at least as sincere and sympathetic as "Porgy" received?
6. Is not the continual portrayal of the sordid, foolish, and criminal among Negroes convincing the world that this and this alone is really and essentially Negroid, and preventing white artists from knowing any other types and preventing black artists from daring to paint them?
7. Is there not a real danger that young colored writers will be tempted to follow the popular trend in portraying Negro character in the underworld rather than seeking to paint the truth about themselves and their own social class?

For the next six months, Du Bois printed the replies in *Crisis*. Insofar as he had hoped, through the questionnaire, to recapture artistic leadership of the Harlem Renaissance, the results were disappointing. Although a few respondents answered in the intended spirit—Jessie Fauset's reply deserved perfect marks—most reacted with something between bemusement and dismissal. "What's the use of saying anything?" Langston Hughes asked. "The true artist is going to write what he chooses anyway regardless of outside opinion. . . . It's the way people look at things, not what they look at, that needs to be changed."

Du Bois concluded the symposium with a long essay of his own, "Criteria of Negro Art," in which he explicated his ideas about the universal attributes of "beauty" and the specific contributions that black writers and artists might make toward its realization. The essay included stern instructions on the political responsibilities of the black writer, suggesting in several places that the duty of vindicating the reputation of the race trumped the value of art for art's sake. "All art is Propaganda," he thundered. "I do not give a damn for art that is not Propaganda."

It is no disrespect to Du Bois, whose place in history is now secure, to say that this was not his finest hour. In the first place, his characterization of contemporary writing was factually incorrect. As James Weldon Johnson showed in a careful inventory published at the end of the 1920s, scarcely one-quarter of the works written by or about African Americans in the previous decade fell within what Du Bois called the "Van Vechten school." Even *Nigger Heaven*, after its admittedly lurid beginning, dealt chiefly with the predicament of educated middle-class black people. The unfolding debate had also pushed Du Bois into a position—art equals propaganda—that not only smacked of philistinism but also directly contradicted positions he had previously maintained. Just five years before, for example, Du Bois had defended Eugene O'Neill's controversial play *The Emperor Jones* against black critics who decried it for perpetuating racial stereotypes. To compel artists to represent only "the best and highest and noblest in us," to "insist that Art and Propaganda be one," betrayed a "complete misunderstanding . . . of the aim of Art," he wrote on that occasion. "We have criminals and prostitutes, ignorant and debased elements just as all folks have." Five years later, having seen his position as literary patron usurped, he was prepared to subject art to a more rigorous political test.

Du Bois's second novel, *Dark Princess* (1928), can also be read as an attempt to move African American literature in more responsible directions. The novel hewed closely to its author's political prescriptions, with middle-class characters debating the predicament of the world's darker races in impeccable English and with nary a prostitute or jazz club in sight. The main character, Matthew Towns, is a disillusioned black medical student who has fled the racism of the United States to live in Germany. There he meets the title character, a beautiful Indian princess who just happens to be the leader of a secret global movement of people of color. Alternately romantic and didactic, the book could scarcely have been more out of step with the artistic temperament of the 1920s, and it had little apparent impact on other black writers.

Although Du Bois surely lost the battle for the soul of the Harlem Renaissance, he may have won the war. As the Great Depression ravaged Harlem and popular enthusiasm for black people's arts ebbed, many prominent "New Negroes" began to look back at the 1920s with a certain embarrassment, renouncing not only the bohemian excesses of the decade but also their own naïve belief that art alone could conquer racial prejudice. Du Bois watched it all with more than

W. E. B. Du Bois, portrait by Laura Wheeler Waring, oil on canvas. (National Portrait Gallery, Smithsonian Institution Art Resource, N.Y.)

W. E. B. Du Bois, photographed by Carl Van Vechten. (Library of Congress.)

a little satisfaction. In 1933, in a speech at Fisk University, he pronounced an epitaph for the renaissance—an epitaph that continues, for better and for worse, to shape critical assessments of the movement:

> Why was it that the Renaissance of literature which began among Negroes ten years ago has never taken real and lasting root? It was because it was a transplanted and exotic thing. It was a literature written for the benefit of white people and at the behest of white readers, and starting out privately from the white point of view. It never had a real Negro constituency and it did not grow out of the inmost heart and frank experience of Negroes. On such an artificial basis no real literature can grow.

Although by 1933 Du Bois had settled comfortably into the role of curmudgeonly elder statesman, his public career had run scarcely half its course. He

survived for another three decades, remaining politically and intellectually engaged until the end. He resigned as editor of *Crisis* in 1934, but he continued to churn out articles, essays, and editorials on the issues of the day. He also published a steady stream of books, including *Black Reconstruction*, a classic work of radical history; *Dusk of Dawn*, a lyrical autobiography; and three more novels, the so-called Black Flame trilogy, which traced the movements of a thinly veiled autobiographical protagonist, Manuel Mansart, through the twentieth century.

As the shadow of McCarthyism darkened American political life, Du Bois found himself increasingly isolated and vulnerable. His passport was suspended, and he faced mounting harassment, an experience he recounted in the short book *In Battle for Peace*. In 1951, he was arrested for failing to register as an agent of a foreign principal, a politically motivated charge growing out of his involvement with an international Peace Information Center. In 1961, Du Bois accepted an invitation from Kwame Nkrumah, prime minister of the newly independent republic of Ghana, to spend his last years in Africa. On the day of his final departure from the United States, 1 October 1961, he formally enrolled as a member of the American Communist Party, a parting shot against the native land that had rejected his gifts.

Biography

William Edward Burghardt Du Bois was born on 23 February 1868, in Great Barrington, Massachusetts. He studied at public schools in Great Barrington; Fisk University, Nashville, Tennessee (A.B., 1888); Harvard University (A.B., 1890, A.M., 1991, Ph.D., 1895); and the University of Berlin (1892–1894). He taught at Wilberforce University, Xenia, Ohio (1894–1896); the University of Pennsylvania (1896–1897); and Atlanta University (1897–1910, 1934–1943). Du Bois was a participant in the Pan-African Conference of 1900 and the Universal Races Congress of 1911. He was a founding member of the Niagara Movement (1905), National Association for the Advancement of Colored People (1910), and Pan-African Congresses (1919, 1921, 1923, 1927, 1945). Du Bois was an editor at *Moon Illustrated Weekly*, Memphis, Tennessee (1906–1907); *Horizon*, Washington, D.C. (1907–1910); *Crisis*, New York City (1910–1934); and *Phylon*, Atlanta (1940–1944). He was a columnist for the Pittsburgh *Courier* (1936–1938), New York *Amsterdam News* (1938–1944),

Chicago *Defender* (1947–1948), and *People's Voice* (1947–1948). He was also vice-chairman of the Council on African Affairs (1949–1954) and a candidate for the U.S. Senate (Labor Party, 1950). He immigrated to Ghana in 1961 and became a Ghanaian citizen. His awards included Knight Commander, Liberian Order of African Redemption (c. 1907); Spingarn Medal (1920); International Peace Prize (1952); and Lenin Peace Prize (1959). Du Bois died in Accra, Ghana, on 27 August 1963.

JAMES CAMPBELL

See also Atlanta University Studies; Cane; Crisis, The; Crisis: The Negro in Art—How Shall He Be Portrayed? A Symposium; Dark Princess; Emperor Jones, The; Fire!!; Fauset, Jessie Redmon; Harlem Renaissance: 1—Black Critics of; Harlem Renaissance: 2—Black Promoters of; New Negro Movement; Niagara Movment; Nigger Heaven; National Association for the Advancement of Colored People; Pan-African Congresses; *specific individuals*

Selected Works

The Suppression of the African Slave Trade to the United States of America, 1638–1870. 1896.

The Philadelphia Negro: A Social Study. 1899.

The Souls of Black Folk: Essays and Sketches. 1903.

The Quest of the Silver Fleece: A Novel. 1911.

The Negro. 1915.

Darkwater: Voices from within the Veil. 1921.

The Gift of Black Folk: Negroes in the Making of America. 1924.

Dark Princess: A Romance. 1928.

Black Reconstruction in America: An Essay toward a History of the Part Which Black Folk Played in the Attempt to Reconstruct Democracy in America, 1860–1880. 1935.

Dusk of Dawn: An Essay toward an Autobiography of a Race Concept. 1940.

The Autobiography of W. E. B. Du Bois: A Soliloquy on Viewing My Life from the Last Decade of Its First Century. 1962.

Further Reading

Aptheker, Herbert. *The Literary Legacy of W. E. B. Du Bois.* White Plains, N.Y.: Kraus International, 1989.

Bell, Bernard W., Emily R. Grosholz, and James B. Stewart, eds. *W. E. B. Du Bois on Race and Culture.* New York: Routledge, 1996.

Lewis, David Levering. *W. E. B. Du Bois: Biography of a Race, 1868–1919.* New York: Holt, 1993.

———. *W. E. B. Du Bois: The Fight for Equality and the American Century, 1919–1963.* New York: Holt, 2000.

Rampersad, Arnold. *The Art and Imagination of W. E. B. Du Bois.* Cambridge: Harvard University Press, 1976.

Dudley, Sherman H.

Sherman H. Dudley, known for his rapid understated humor, was one of the leading black comedians of the early twentieth century and was also a manager and promoter. Although remarkably accomplished, he remains a neglected figure in the study of the Harlem Renaissance, partly because he often operated outside the Manhattan center of black art.

Early in his career, he performed with medicine shows and minstrel shows. He was the proprietor of a traveling tent show, Jolly Ethiopians; and he appeared with Richards and Pringle's Georgia Minstrels, Rusco and Holland Minstrels, McCabe and Young's Operatic Minstrels, P. T. Wright's Nashville Students, Sam Corker, and Will Marion Cook's *Clorindy* company; he also appeared with Billy Kersands in *King Rastus*. He had his own troupe, Dudley's Georgia Minstrels, in 1897–1898. In 1904 he joined the Smart Set Company, starred in its shows, and soon took over the productions.

Several companies used the name Smart Set between 1902 and 1924. Dudley's Smart Set Company produced musical comedies for mainly white audiences, including *The Black Politician, Dr. Beans from Boston,* and *His Honor the Barber,* featuring Dudley as principal comedian. These successful shows helped establish a format for black musical comedy: a variety show with a more structured plot usually involving hare-brained schemes, gambling, preposterous protagonists, and horse races. Dudley is perhaps best-known for his act with a trained mule in *His Honor the Barber.* This production was notable as well because black audience members were not relegated to the balcony ("nigger heaven"); rather, there were segregated seating areas throughout the house—a significant shift in the system. Also significantly, Dudley's shows were criticized by white and black reviewers for imitating white productions and for having performers who looked "too white" (some because of makeup). Their reaction suggests the complex racial situation at the time: performers had to strike a balance between black aesthetics and white audiences' stereotypes.

As an entrepreneur, Dudley was instrumental in creating unions and touring agencies for black

Dudley, Sherman H.

performers. He organized a vaudeville touring agency, Dudley's Theatrical Circuit, which operated from 1891 to 1916 and is considered the first black-controlled theater circuit and booking agency. It was based in Washington, D.C., and began with seven theaters there and elsewhere; by 1914 it had nineteen. In 1916, Dudley's Circuit and two other organizations merged into the Southern Consolidated Circuit (SCC), which had fierce battles with the Theater Owners' Booking Association (TOBA) and was eventually absorbed by TOBA (1921). The resulting touring circuit was complete and independent of the white circuits; although performers complained of mistreatment by TOBA, low pay, and southern racism, this circuit did guarantee work and increased exposure for black talent.

In 1921, Dudley helped found the Colored Actors' Union (CAU), the first African American theatrical union. In its first year, it had 800 individual members, 500 vaudeville acts, and twenty-seven stock companies. In 1926 it produced the *Colored Actors' Union Theatrical Guide*, a handbook containing a history of black theater, biographies of major players, a list of resources for performers, and articles about the national status of African Americans. In 1937, CAU was replaced by the Negro Actors Guild of America.

Biography

Sherman H. Dudley was born in 1880. He began his career in medicine shows and minstrel shows and had his own troupe, Dudley's Georgia Minstrels (1897–1898). He joined the Smart Set Company in 1904. His vaudeville touring agency, Dudley's Theatrical Circuit (1891–1916), is considered the first black-controlled theater circuit and booking agency. In 1916, Dudley's circuit and two other organizations merged to form the Southern Consolidated Circuit (SCC), which rivaled, but was later (1921) absorbed by, the Theater Owners' Booking Association (TOBA). Dudley helped found the Colored Actors' Union (CAU, 1921). He died in 1940.

NADINE GEORGE-GRAVES

See also Blacks in Theater; Minstrelsy; Musical Theater; Theater Owners' Booking Association

Further Reading

Bean, Annemarie, James V. Hatch, and Brooks McNamara. *Inside the Minstrel Mask: Readings in Nineteenth Century Blackface Minstrelsy.* Middletown, Conn.: Wesleyan University Press, 1996.
Hill, Anthony D. "Improving Conditions on the TOBA Black Vaudeville Circuit." In *Pages from the Harlem Renaissance: A Chronicle of Performance.* New York: Peter Lang, 1996.
Woll, Allen. *Black Musical Theatre: From Coontown to Dreamgirls.* Baton Rouge: Louisiana State University Press, 1989.

Dunbar Apartments

The Dunbar Apartments–located at the northeastern end of Harlem, at Seventh Avenue and 150th Street—were completed in 1928, just before the Great Depression. These apartments were named after the African American poet and novelist Paul Laurence Dunbar (1872–1906), who had achieved fame at the turn of the twentieth century for such works as *Lyrics of Lowly Life* (1896) and *The Sport of the Gods* (1902) and who is often considered an inspiration for the Harlem Renaissance, although he never actually lived in Harlem.

Two decades after Dunbar's death, the apartment complex bearing his name was erected. It was designed by Andrew J. Thomas and was a massive construction project. The final complex occupied an entire city block and consisted of six separate redbrick buildings, each six stories high. These buildings were situated around a common garden that included a playground.

John D. Rockefeller Jr. financed the development, initially operating it on a cooperative basis. Eventually, though, as the Depression worsened and as the payment defaults mounted higher and higher, Rockefeller foreclosed on the buildings. Soon thereafter, the Dunbar

Dunbar Apartments. (Brown Brothers.)

318

National Bank, located in one of the buildings, was liquidated. The Dunbar National Bank had been the sole bank in Harlem operated by African Americans. After dissolving the cooperative, Rockefeller reimbursed the former tenant-owners for their capital infusion and then converted the apartments to rental units.

The Dunbar Apartments still stood as of this writing.

JANICE TRAFLET

See also Dunbar, Paul Laurence; Harlem: 4–Housing

Further Reading

Anderson, Jervis. *This Was Harlem: A Cultural Portrait, 1900–1950*. New York: Farrar Straus, Giroux, 1991.

Jackson, Kenneth, ed. *Encyclopedia of New York City*. New Haven, Conn.: Yale University Press, 1995. (See "Paul Laurence Dunbar.")

The WPA Guide to New York City: The Federal Writers' Project Guide to 1930s New York. New York: Pantheon, 1982. (Originally published 1939.)

Dunbar, Paul Laurence

Paul Laurence Dunbar was a prolific and popular African American author whose works appeared in such noted literary magazines as the *Atlantic Monthly*, the *Century*, *Lippincott's Monthly*, and the *Saturday Evening Post* and were read and enjoyed by both whites and blacks. In his incorporation of political themes and his use of local color and dialect, he was an important precursor of the Harlem Renaissance.

Dunbar was born in Dayton, Ohio. His parents—Matilda and Joshua Dunbar—were former slaves; Joshua Dunbar had escaped from a plantation in Kentucky and served in the Massachusetts Fifty-Fifth regiment during the Civil War. Paul Laurence Dunbar was educated in Dayton's public schools; when he reached high school, he was the only African American student. During his high school years, he began to explore creative writing. At age sixteen, he began to write poetry, which appeared in the local newspaper and was largely influenced by British romantic poets such as Keats, Wordsworth, and Coleridge, and by Americans such as Whittier and Longfellow.

After graduating from high school, Dunbar entered a world that was sharply divided by race. Despite his education, he was unable to break through the racial barriers, and he accepted a job as an elevator operator in a hotel in Dayton. However, he was able to find time and financial support for his writing, and in 1892, he published *Oak and Ivy*, a book of poems largely influenced and inspired by Longfellow's style. Dunbar then went to Chicago's World Columbian Expedition, where he met two men who would be his literary patrons: Charles Thatcher and Henry Tobey. They advanced Dunbar money so that he would be able to write another volume of poetry; they also promoted his work and ensured that it would be reviewed by the prominent literary editor William Dean Howells. Their funding allowed Dunbar to produce *Majors and Minors*, a collection of poetry that was instrumental in making him famous.

Despite racism and segregation, the American public was hungry for a gifted African American author, and Dunbar became popular because his work fulfilled at least three desires of readers: (1) he was an eloquent poet and a highly skilled versifier; (2) his

Paul Laurence Dunbar, c. 1909. (Schomburg Center for Research in Black Culture, New York Public Library.)

fiction conformed to the public's need for local color; and (3) he was a writer who could provide and confirm the familiar, popular version of African Americans' experience under slavery and since emancipation. In many ways, *Majors and Minors* met all of these criteria; and Howells, in his review, proclaimed Dunbar the poet laureate of the Negro race. However, Howells also said that Dunbar was most authentic when writing in dialect rather than standard English—and this assessment, intended as praise, proved to be a double-edged sword. Dunbar did attract a tremendous following that moved past racial divisions, but his newfound reputation as a dialect poet in the "plantation tradition" obscured the political and social themes that actually dominated his work.

Later scholars would criticize Dunbar for perpetuating the racist concept of the "happy darky," a figure central to the plantation tradition. This tradition chronicled an antebellum South in which the butler and the mammy are shadowy counterparts of the white master and mistress; that is, the black characters reflect the virtues and graces of the ruling caste. Dunbar's work was widely interpreted as being part of the plantation tradition—an interpretation that made no allowance for the difficult circumstances in which Dunbar had to write, or for the fact that in his time, editorial control and criticism were almost exclusively in the hands of whites. Also, this interpretation ignores an important aspect of Dunbar's writing: he worked within limiting literary conventions in order to use them as a vehicle for offering a radical political alternative to the racial problems of the era.

For example, Dunbar's "Mr. Cornelius Johnson, Office-Seeker," published in *The Strength of Gideon and Other Stories* (his second volume of short stories, 1900), focuses on attempts by the title character to secure a patronage position in return for having done campaign work for a congressman and reveals the power of racism. Moreover, Johnson is unable to follow either Booker T. Washington's call for patience or W. E. B. Du Bois's call for aggressive political and social action. In many ways, Dunbar expands on this story's argument in his novel *The Sport of the Gods* (1902), which describes the difficulties of a southern African American family faced with the choice of staying in the South, and remaining loyal to the family that once owned them, or migrating to New York City, where racism is less but where there are many new, unforeseen dangers. In both of these works, Dunbar drew on the plantation tradition, but readers might also see how he used it for social protest.

Later commentators would also criticize Dunbar for his use of dialect in his poetry. In particular, African Americans such as Sterling Brown and Charles T. Davis—although they admitted that Dunbar had been the first American poet to treat African American life with any degree of fullness—also argued that Dunbar had willfully misrepresented black history. That is, in relying on dialect, and in adopting the plantation tradition, Dunbar had suggested that the "old time" African American was content to serve a white master and was out of place in postbellum America.

Still, some poets of the Harlem Renaissance, such as Langston Hughes and Countee Cullen, would find inspiration in Dunbar's work. Citing specific examples of Dunbar's poems—"We Wear the Mask," "When Malindy Sings," "Frederick Douglass," "The Colored Soldiers," "The Haunted Oak"—Hughes and Cullen argued that Dunbar had expressed pride in his African American heritage, and that his texts included passages where one might find his call for social action.

Dunbar was aware that his choice of dialect and the plantation tradition might lead to a misinterpretation of his intentions and vision. In fact, he predicted the critical reaction to his work and the damaging effects of Howells's praise. It is only more recently that readers and scholars have become fully aware of Dunbar's objectives and have been able to consider him an important forefather of African American literature.

Biography

Paul Laurence Dunbar was born on 27 June 1872, in Dayton, Ohio, and studied at public schools there. Dunbar edited at least three issues of the *Dayton Tattler*, a black district newspaper. He published *Oak and Ivy* in 1892, *Majors and Minors* in 1896, *Lyrics of the Hearthside* in 1899, *The Strength of Gideon and Other Stories* and *The Love of Landry* in 1900, *The Fanatics* in 1901, *The Sport of the Gods* in 1902, *Lyrics of Love and Laughter* and *In Old Plantation Days* in 1903, *The Heart of Happy Hollow* in 1904, and *Lyrics of Sunshine and Shadow* in 1905. Dunbar married Alice Ruth Moore, a teacher and writer, in 1898; they separated in 1902. Dunbar collaborated with Will Marion Cook on musical plays for black performers (1898–1900) and raised funds for the Tuskegee Institute in 1899; he also wrote a song for the Tuskegee Institute at Booker T. Washington's request in 1901. Dunbar's health problems began around 1900, with pneumonia and then tuberculosis; he died of tuberculosis on 9 February 1906.

GINA ROSSETTI

See also Authors: 5—Poets; Brown, Sterling; Cook, Will Marion; Cullen, Countee; Howells, William Dean; Hughes, Langston; Literature: 7—Poetry; Poetry: Dialect

Selected Works

Oak and Ivy. 1892.
Majors and Minors. 1896.
Lyrics of Lowly Life. 1896.
Folks from Dixie. 1898.
The Uncalled. 1898.
Lyrics of the Hearthside. 1899.
The Strength of Gideon and Other Stories. 1900.
The Love of Landry. 1900.
The Fanatics. 1901.
The Sport of the Gods. 1902.
Lyrics of Love and Laughter. 1903.
In Old Plantation Days. 1903.
The Heart of Happy Hollow. 1904.
Lyrics of Sunshine and Shadow. 1905.

Further Reading

Bone, Robert. *Down Home: A History of Afro-American Short Fiction from Its Beginnings to the End of the Harlem Renaissance.* New York: Putnam, 1975.

Brawley, Benjamin. *Paul Laurence Dunbar: Poet of His People.* Chapel Hill: University of North Carolina Press, 1936.

Cunninham, Virgina. *Paul Laurence Dunbar and His Song.* New York: Dodd, Mead, 1977.

Gayle, Addison Jr. *Oak and Ivy: A Biography of Paul Laurence Dunbar.* New York: Doubleday, 1971.

———. *The Way of the World: The Black Novel in America.* Garden City, N.Y.: Anchor, 1975.

Lawson, Victor. *Dunbar Critically Examined.* Washington, D.C.: Associated Publishers, 1941.

Martin, Jay, ed. *A Singer in the Dawn: Reinterpretations of Paul Laurence Dunbar.* New York: Dodd, Mead, 1975.

Metcalf, E. W. Jr. *Paul Laurence Dunbar: A Bibliography.* Metuchen, N.J.: Scarecrow, 1975.

Redding, Saunders. *To Make a Poet Black.* Chapel Hill: University of North Carolina Press, 1939.

Turner, Darwin. "Paul Laurence Dunbar: The Rejected Symbol." *Journal of Negro History*, 52, 1967, pp. 1–13.

Wagner, Jean. *Black Poets of the United States, from Paul Laurence Dunbar to Langston Hughes.* Urbana: University of Illinois Press, 1973.

Dunn, Blanche

Blanche Dunn was born in the West Indies in 1911 and left for the United States when she was fifteen years old. Very little is known about her early life in the West Indies or about her life when she first arrived in New York City. However, by 1927 she had attracted the affection of Wilda Gunn, a dress designer who was originally from Cleveland. Dunn's beauty, charm, and bravado gave her an entrée to opening nights on Broadway and to the best tables at Harlem's speakeasies, especially the very fashionable Hot Cha. Dunn also sought stardom as a singer and actress. She secured a small role in Dudley Murphy's film of *The Emperor Jones* (1933), which was moderately successful.

Dunn was a noteworthy figure at the legendary parties hosted by Carl Van Vechten—gatherings that were evidently designed to showcase Van Vechten's latest black artistic discoveries for a largely white audience. Langston Hughes attended some of these parties and recounted how Dunn captivated wealthy luminaries such as Salvador Dalí.

In 1940 Dunn began an affair with Marion "Joe" Carstairs, a British oil magnate who had set up a sort of oligarchy on the Bahamian island Whale Cay, where he was visited by celebrities such as Mabel Mercer and Marlene Dietrich. Dunn and Carstairs's tempestuous relationship ended in 1941, and Dunn returned to New York. That year, she posed for Carl Van Vechten's series *Portrait Photographs of Celebrities*.

In both of her portraits by Van Vechten, Dunn wears enormous silver hoop earrings, three strands of wooden beads, heavy beaded bracelets on both wrists, a very low-cut peasant-style blouse, a striped bustling skirt, and a matching head rag. This attire suggests some visual and racial editorializing on Van Vechten's part, but Dunn seems to overcome it: her mouth is defiantly set, and her eyes avoid engagement with the photographer, implying that she may have considered her own beauty a form of artful resistance.

At one time, there was speculation that Dunn was the basis of the character Audrey Denny in Nella Larsen's novel *Quicksand* (1928). However, this conjecture was unfounded: Denny—who is described as light-skinned, lives downtown, and seems to have no

Dunn, Blanche

West Indian connections—has little in common with Dunn, who was brown-skinned, spoke with a strong West Indian accent, and lived in Harlem. In fact, Denny was probably based on a friend of Larsen's named Anita Thompson.

Biography

Blanche Dunn was born in the West Indies in 1911. She immigrated to the United States in 1926 and met and was befriended by the dress designer Wilda Gunn in 1927. Dunn had a small role in a film adaptation of Eugene O'Neill's play *The Emperor Jones* in 1933. In 1940 she moved to Whale Cay, a Bahamian island purchased by a British oil magnate and speed boat champion, Marion "Joe" Carstairs; their affair (marked by an episode in which she chased him with a butcher knife and he escaped by leaping out of a window), ended in 1941. Also in 1941, Dunn posed for Carl Van Vechten's series *Portrait Photographs of Celebrities*.

HEATHER LEVY

See also Emperor Jones, The; Hughes, Langston; Quicksand; Van Vechten, Carl

Film and Portraits

The Emperor Jones. 1933. (United Artists, dir. Dudley Murphy.)

Van Vechten, Carl. *Portraits of Blanche Dunn, May 10, 1941.* (Lot 12735 Nos. 349–350. Library of Congress Prints and Photographic Division, Washington, D.C.)

Further Reading

Hughes, Langston. *The Big Sea: An Autobiography.* Toronto and New York: HarperCollins Canada and Hill and Wang, 1993.

Summerscale, Kate. *The Queen of Whale Cay.* New York: Viking, 1997.

Wirth, Thomas H., ed. *Gay Rebel of the Harlem Renaissance: Selections from the Work of Richard Bruce Nugent.* London: Duke University Press, 2002.

Duse Mohamed Ali

See Ali, Duse Mohamed

E

Eastman, Crystal

Crystal Eastman helped prepare the legal blueprints for the workers' compensation program, the American Civil Liberties Union, and the Equal Rights Amendment. She was nicknamed "the tigress" by Hazel Halliran, an equally fearless suffragist. Even Eastman's enemies were willing to concede her absolute fairness and persuasive eloquence. A condescending newspaper announcement of her appointment as the only woman on the New York Employers' Liability Commission in 1909 read: "Portia Appointed by Governor."

Eastman gave most of the credit for her own social insights to her progressive mother, Annis Ford Eastman, an ordained minister who was a granddaughter of the automobile magnate Henry Ford and who had inherited the family ingenuity, although none of Ford's capital, and who encouraged her children to be intellectually independent and physically strong. Crystal Eastman spent a great deal of time riding a mustang that she had been given (although she refused to ride sidesaddle, as women were then expected to; she also wore short skirts, for freedom of movement, and cut her hair short), and she grew up to be an athletic, self-possessed six-foot-tall woman. She dedicated her life to feminism, and she and her scholarly brother Max had a lifelong intellectual collaboration—early on, they seriously examined how to advance the status of women and were advocates of birth control, open sexuality, and wages for housework.

Crystal Eastman achieved academic success at Vassar, Columbia University, and New York City University Law School. After a careful study of the dangerous working conditions in industries in Pittsburgh, she drafted the first workers' compensation law. She was a peerless advocate not only of industrial safety but also of the antiwar movement: She was a founding member of the American Civil Liberties Union (1917) and the Women's Peace Party (1920); she also was one of the key writers of the Equal Rights Amendment in 1923. She developed friendships with a wide range of prominent people, such as the Roosevelt family.

Crystal Eastman was also—significantly for the Harlem Renaissance—a passionate advocate for the disenfranchised and was able to overcome public indifference about gender, race, sexuality, and class discrimination in order to achieve legal reforms. Her other gift to the Harlem Renaissance was her promotion of the poet Claude McKay, who became an associate editor of Eastman's journal *The Liberator*.

Biography

Crystal Eastman was born on 25 June 1881, in Marlborough, Massachusetts. At age three she had scarlet fever, which permanently affected her kidneys. As a girl, she rebelled against long skirts, wore a man's bathing costume, and with her brother Max Eastman founded the Apostles of Nakedness, a society dedicated to birth control and open sexuality, in 1893. In 1894, she wrote an essay, "Woman," advocating women's emotional and economic autonomy. She graduated from Vassar College, Poughkeepsie, New York, in 1899; went to Columbia University to study for a master's degree in sociology (1904); and graduated from New York University, where she had studied labor law, in 1907.

Crystal Eastman in 1916. (Photograph by Arnold Genthe. Library of Congress.)

helped draft the Equal Rights Amendment in 1923. Fuller died of a stroke in 1927, and Eastman died on 8 July 1928, of nephritis. She was inducted into the National Women's Hall of Fame in 2000.

HEATHER LEVY

See also Eastman, Max; Kellogg, Paul U.; Liberator, The; McKay, Claude; Villard, Oswald Garrison; Wise, Stephen Samuel

Selected Publications

"Employers' Liability in Pennsylvania." (Reprinted in 70 Alb. L.J. 68.)

Wisconsin Bureau of Labor and Industrial Statistics, Thirteenth Biennial Report, 85–85. 1909.

"Minutes of Evidence Accompanying the First Report to the Legislature of the State of New York, Commission Appointed Under Chapter 518 of the Laws of 1909 to Inquire into the Question of Employers' Liability and Other Matters." 16 March 1910.

"Work Accidents and Employers' Liability." *Survey,* 3 September 1910.

Work Accidents and the Law, from *The Pittsburgh Survey: Findings in Six Volumes,* ed. Paul U. Kellogg. Russell Sage Foundation, 1910. (Reprint, Arno, 1969.)

Further Reading

Ascher, Carol, et al., eds. *Biographer and Subject: A Critical Connection between Women—Biographers, Novelists, Critics, Teachers, and Artists about Their Work on Women*. New York: Routledge, 1993.

Cook, Blanche Wiesen. *Crystal Eastman on Women and Revolution*. New York: Oxford University Press, 1978.

———. *Toward the Great Change: Crystal and Max Eastman on Feminism, Antimilitarism, and Revolution*. New York: Garland, 1976.

Eckhaus, Phyllis. "Restless Women: The Pioneering Alumnae of New York University School of Law." *New York University Law Review*, 66, 1996.

Hackney, James. R. "The Intellectual Origins of American Strict Products Liability: A Case Study in American Pragmatism." *American Journal of Legal History*, 39, 1995, p. 443.

She taught high school English and history in Elmira, New York (1905); worked at the Greenwich Settlement House (1906); and took a job as a researcher with Paul Kellogg (1907). She was appointed by Governor Charles Evans Hughes as the only woman on the New York State Employers' Liability Commission and became a key member of the Wainwright Commission (1909). In addition to her careeer in labor law, she was an activist for woman's suffrage and later in antiwar and leftist causes. She married Wallace Benedict, an insurance agent, and moved to Milwaukee but decided that the marriage was a failure and returned to New York in 1913. With Lillian Wald, Jane Addams, Paul Kellogg, Rabbi Stephen Wise, and Oswald Garrison Villard, she organized the Anti-Preparedness Committee (later known as the American Union Against Militarism). In 1916, she married the British poet Walter Fuller; he too was an antiwar activist. In 1917, she formed the American Civil Liberties Union with Roger Baldwin and Norman Thomas. She was editor of the progressive left-wing journal *The Liberator* (1917–1921), was denounced during the "red scare" of 1920–1922, and

Law, Sylvia. "Crystal Eastman: Organizer for Women's Rights, Peace, and Civil Liberties in the 1910s. *Valparaiso University Law Review*, 28, 1994, p. 1305.

Eastman, Max

Max Forrester Eastman (1883–1969) was a prominent journalist, political activist, and literary figure, who edited influential radical periodicals (*The Liberator*, which he co-owned with his sister Crystal Eastman, and *The Masses*); wrote twenty-six books, including fiction, poetry, and translations from Russian; and edited two anthologies and a documentary film on the Russian revolution. He opposed America's entry into World War I and was a feminist and socialist, but he was critical of Marxism, Joseph Stalin, and the Soviet Union and eventually rejected communism. Eastman lived in Greenwich Village at a time when it was becoming known as a hub of intellectual and artistic activity.

Under Eastman's editorship, the socialist monthly *The Masses* emphasized both politics and art. Its contributors and editors included Randolph Bourne, Floyd Dell, Art Sloan, John Reed, Sherwood Anderson, George Bellows, Carl Sandburg, John Sloan, Boardman Robinson, and Stuart Davis. In *The Masses*, Eastman expressed his own antiwar sentiments and his views against entering World War I; as a result, in August 1917, the federal government denied the publication second-class mailing privileges and put it out of business. Moreover, Eastman, along with seven other editors and contributors, was indicted on charges of conspiring to obstruct military recruiting. Two trials ensued, which received national press coverage and were noteworthy for Eastman's eloquence on the stand and in his summations; they both ended with divided juries.

Max and Crystal Eastman founded *The Liberator* in 1918 to advance the cause of the Bolshevik revolution in Russia. In 1921, Eastman asked the poet Claude McKay to become an associate editor; soon afterward, Eastman made McKay and the writer Michael Gold coeditors. *The Liberator* published poetry by McKay in 1919, and one of Jean Toomer's poems in 1922. Langston Hughes was among its subscribers.

In 1922, Max Eastman went to the Soviet Union, where he learned Russian, conferred with Bolshevik leaders, and became a follower of Leon Trotsky. He then decided to go to western Europe, taking with

Max Eastman. (Brown Brothers.)

him a copy of "Lenin's Testament," in which V. I. Lenin named Trotsky as his political heir and warned against Stalin; Eastman published sections of it as *Since Lenin Died* (1925), and it served as a statement about the betrayal of the revolution under the new leadership of the Soviet Union. After returning to the United States in 1926, Eastman served as Trotsky's literary agent and translator. During the 1930s, Eastman supported himself as a lecturer and became the chief anti-Stalinist of the American political left (he was the only American writer to be personally attacked by Stalin, who called him a "gangster of the pen").

In later decades, Eastman moved further to the right, becoming an editor for *Reader's Digest* and a contributor to the *National Review*. During the 1950s, he supported the anticommunist crusader Senator Joseph McCarthy.

Biography

Max Forrester Eastman was born on 4 January 1883, in Canandaigua, New York. His parents, Samuel Elijah Eastman and Annis Ford Eastman, were both Protestant ministers. After attending Mercersburg Academy for two years, Max Eastman entered Williams College; he received his B.A. in 1905. He studied for a Ph.D. at Columbia University under the pragmatist John Dewey but did not complete his dissertation; later, he was a professor of logic at Columbia, and his book *The Enjoyment of Poetry* (1913) became a standard college text. In 1910, Eastman founded the Men's League for Woman Suffrage. He became Leon Trotsky's translator and literary agent in the 1920s; during the 1930s, he supported himself as a lecturer. He later moved to the right politically and was an editor of *Reader's Digest*. Eastman was married three times: to Ida Rauh in 1911 (they were divorced in 1922); to Eliena Vassilyenva Krylenko, a sister of the minister of justice of the Soviet Union, in 1924 (she died of cancer in 1956); and to Yvette Szekely in 1958. Eastman divided his time between residences in New York City, Martha's Vineyard, and the Caribbean. He died in Barbados on 25 March 1969.

MARTHA AVALEEN EGAN

See also Anderson, Sherwood; Eastman, Crystal; Greenwich Village; Liberator, The; McKay, Claude; Toomer, Jean

Selected Works

Enjoyment of Poetry. 1913.
Journalism versus Art. 1915.
Understanding Germany. 1916.
Colors of Life. 1918.
The Sense of Humor. 1921.
Since Lenin Died. 1925.
Marx and Lenin: The Science of Revolution. 1926.
The Literary Mind. 1931.
Kinds of Love. 1931.
Art and the Life of Action. 1934.
Artists in Uniform. 1934.
Enjoyment of Laughter. 1935.
Lot's Wife: A Dramatic Poem. 1940.
Stalin's Russia and the Crisis of Socialism. 1940.
Marxism, Is It Science? 1940.
Heroes I Have Known. 1942.
Enjoyment of Living. 1948.

Poems of Five Decades. 1954.
Reflections on the Failure of Socialism. 1955.
Great Companions. 1959.
Love and Revolution. 1964.
Seven Kinds of Goodness. 1967.

Further Reading

Cantor, Milton. *Max Eastman*. New York: Twayne, 1970.
O'Neill, William L. *The Last Romantic: A Life of Max Eastman*. New York: Oxford University Press, 1978. (Reprint, 1990.)

Ebony and Topaz

Ebony and Topaz (1927), a large single-issue anthology edited by Charles S. Johnson, was published by *Opportunity* under the aegis of the National Urban League. Described as a "collectanea," it was intended as a companion piece to Alain Locke's *The New Negro* (1925), to which it was similar in format; however, the black literary expression in *Ebony and Topaz* was less self-conscious and more self-assured. It included prose and poetry, which reflected, according to Johnson, a "venture in expression . . . a *faithful* reflection of current interests and observations in Negro life."

Johnson loosely classified the contents in five parts in which a broadly interdisciplinary approach is evident: Negro folk life, historical figures in careers and art, racial problems and attitudes, introspection, and articulation of intimate feelings. In his introduction, Johnson said that the anthology was characterized by spontaneity and humor (which perhaps had previously been suppressed in favor of sobriety), and—more important—that it had a new impetus: "A spirit has been quietly manifest of late which it would be a gentle treason to ignore." However, Alain Locke, in his own blunt contribution "Our Little Renaissance," observed that "the mellowness of maturity has not yet come upon us."

Ebony and Topaz was an interracial exercise: Literary contributions came from both black and white writers, including Arna Bontemps, Abram L. Harris, Francis Holbrook, Frank Horne, Helene Johnson, George Chester Morse, Julia Peterkin, Baron von Rucksteschell, and Dorothy Scarborough. There were also bold illustrations by Charles Cullen, Richard Bruce Nugent, and Aaron Douglas (Douglas's contribution had previously appeared in *Opportunity* in October 1926, accompanying poetry by Langston Hughes). Charles Cullen supplied the art for the cover, moderating his usual highly charged eroticism. However, Richard Bruce Nugent—whose art had sharpened considerably after his contribution to Wallace Thurman's periodical *Fire!!* (1926) gave him a taste for expression—seems to have had carte blanche and produced some of the most striking graphic images of the Harlem Renaissance: four illustrations titled *Drawings for Mulattoes*. Whereas Cullen's Negro body type is flawless and athletic, Bruce's figures have a flawed physicality and seem caught in cultural contortions. Additional illustrations, courtesy of Arthur Schomburg, reflected an interest in international high art: reproductions of works by Sebastian Gomez and the English court painters Thomas Gainsborough and Joshua Reynolds.

There are some parallels between *Ebony and Topaz* and *Fire!!*—for one thing, they had many of the same contributors. Still, their differences seem more significant. *Ebony and Topaz* lacked the edginess and independence of *Fire!!* and was perceived by critics as simply art for art's sake, but it tried to maintain realism, in which *Fire!!* was deficient. Retrospectively, *Ebony and Topaz* seems to have more in common with *Harlem: A Forum of Negro Life* (1928), Thurman's successor to *Fire!!*.

As a single volume, *Ebony and Topaz* may have had a negligible impact. Within the context of single-issue publications of the Harlem Renaissance, though, it represents a measured voice "stressing the black man's 'Americanism'" (Hayden 1968). It turned out to be Johnson's swan song at the National Urban League; he took up an academic career at Fisk University in 1928.

CATHERINE O'HARA

See also Bontemps, Arna; Douglas, Aaron; Fire!!; Harlem; Horne, Frank; Johnson, Charles Spurgeon; Johnson, Helene; Locke, Alain; National Urban League; New Negro, The; Nugent, Richard Bruce; Opportunity; Peterkin, Julia Mood; Schomburg, Arthur A.

Further Reading

Baker, Houston. *Modernism and the Harlem Renaissance.* Chicago, Ill.: University of Chicago Press, 1987.

Gilpin, Patrick J. "Charles S. Johnson: Entrepreneur of the Harlem Renaissance." In *The Harlem Renaissance Remembered*, ed. Arna Bontemps. New York: Dodd, Mead, 1972.

Hayden, Robert. "Preface to the Atheneum Edition." In *The New Negro*, ed. Alain Locke. New York: Atheneum, 1968, p. xiii.

Hutchinson, George. *The Harlem Renaissance in Black and White.* Cambridge, Mass.: Belknap, 1995.

Johnson, Charles S., ed. *Ebony and Topaz: A Collectanea.* New York: National Urban League, 1927.

Lewis, David Levering. *When Harlem Was in Vogue.* New York: Vintage, 1982, pp. 198–239.

Eclectic Club

The Eclectic Club was an active literary and artistic society in Harlem that met monthly starting in early 1922. Largely ignored by posterity and often mistakenly referred to as the "Electric Club," the group nonetheless provided an important forum in which poets, politicians, and patrons socialized and discussed future projects. Its existence is documented principally in the columns of *Negro World*; the accounts there suggest that the Eclectics were a peripatetic group.

From the outset, the projects of the Eclectic Club were predominantly, although not exclusively, distinguished by their focus on Afro-Caribbean works. As Claude McKay, one of the club's most noted guests, insisted, the Puerto Rican areas of Harlem had the greatest interest in literary culture during the early 1920s. McKay spoke to the Eclectic Club on at least two occasions. One of these was on 8 April 1922, when McKay read poems from his collection *Harlem Shadows*; Arthur Schomburg and Joel Augustus Rogers were present at this event. During 1922 Schomburg and Rogers both frequently attended the club's other events, occasionally speaking before the group. Their attendance was probably a result of the fact that the Eclectics shared their interest in popularizing black history. William H. Ferris attended more sporadically, but his presence also illustrates the favorable reception the club gave to black history.

Other prominent members with an Afro-Caribbean background included Eric Walrond, who was also in attendance when McKay read his work. Walrond was one of the club's most important recruiters, introducing Zora Neale Hurston to the group in mid-1925, as well as his fellow columnists at *Negro World*, Lester Taylor and E. V. Plummer. Some of the Eclectics advanced their careers through the club's events. For instance, in January 1922, Duse Mohamed Ali addressed the club at the Jackson School of Music on West 138th Street on the topic "Modern Egypt"; a few weeks later, Ali resumed a working relationship with Marcus Garvey, taking the position of foreign-affairs correspondent for Garvey's organization, the Universal Negro Improvement Association (UNIA). (However, although the club was sympathetic to Garveyism, it by no means fell under the aegis of UNIA.) Walrond maintained strong ties with the Eclectics long after he left his position as editor of Garvey's publications, and Hubert Harrison's occasional appearances indicate that even those who had repudiated Garveyism might still find sufficient attraction in the club.

The president of the Eclectic Club was a man of modest means who went by the name William Service Bell. McKay considered Bell a "cultivated artistic New England Negro." Bell was by no means just a figurehead; he took an active interest in the work of those around him and occasionally even read his own work before the group. By 1926 Bell was making a living as an actor and singer, and for a short period he lived in a bohemian apartment house at 237 West 136th Street known as "Niggerati Manor." It was because of Bell that a few copies of the failed publication *Fire!!* were saved from the fire in which most copies were destroyed.

Although its name may have suggested otherwise, the rank-and-file members of the Eclectic Club tended to be "ladies and gentlemen in *tenue de rigueur*" (McKay 1937–1970). Through societies such as the Eclectic Club, the White Peacock, and the Booklovers Club (the present-day Schomburg Center for Research in Black Culture), the "renaissance" became a part of everyday Harlem. Moreover, the early establishment of the Eclectic Club and its concern for Afro-Caribbean projects support a wider chronological and substantive definition of the Harlem Renaissance.

ANDREW MICHAEL FEARNLEY

See also Ali, Duse Mohamed; Booklovers Club; Ferris, William H.; Fire!!; Harrison, Hubert; Hurston, Zora Neale; McKay, Claude; Negro World; Rogers, Joel Augustus; Schomburg, Arthur A.; Walrond, Eric

Further Reading

Martin, Tony. *Literary Garveyism: Garvey, Black Arts, and the Harlem Renaissance.* Dover, Mass., 1983.

McKay, Claude. *A Long Way from Home.* New York and London, 1970. (Originally published 1937.)

Negro World. Schomburg Collections, New York Public Library.

Wintz, Cary. *Black Culture and the Harlem Renaissance.* Houston, Tex., 1988.

Edmonds, Randolph

During the Harlem Renaissance, musical stage productions were a common form of entertainment. Especially popular were shows that featured African Americans in song-and-dance routines; among these were such musicals as *Strut, Miss Lizzie* (1922); *Chocolate Dandies* (1924); and *Lucky Sambo* (1925). As the titles indicate, this form of entertainment often relied on stereotypes of African Americans and thus did little to aid blacks in their quest for equal rights. Many African American playwrights challenged these negative images by writing plays that depicted the discrimination confronting African Americans in their daily lives.

Fostered by W. E. B. Du Bois, the Negro "little theater" movement, which began in the 1920s, was a venue for exuberant activity among the nearly 300 African American dramatists writing in the 1920s and 1930s. To Du Bois, the stage was a platform for teaching about African American culture and history. Randolph Edmonds shared this view. Known as the "dean of black academic theater," Edmonds worked against stereotypes of African Americans by encouraging the development of drama based on their folk culture and history. Through his work with college and high school students, Edmonds promoted drama clubs and theater courses as part of the curriculum. His career was dedicated to teaching drama, administering theater organizations he had founded, writing more than fifty plays, and publishing three anthologies of his plays and some forty essays on the relationship between drama and education.

Edmonds began writing folk plays at Oberlin College, where he organized the Dunbar Forum, an African American group that produced several of his early plays. Through a fellowship he received from the Rockefeller Fund while attending Yale, Edmonds studied drama in England for one year. At that time he also took courses at Dublin University and attended productions at the Abbey Theater, which had promoted the development of folk drama.

Nearly all of Edmonds's plays focus on the life of working-class African Americans, the folk. Seldom light or joyous, his plays portray problems within black families—problems caused by migration to the North, by the suffering endured during slavery, and by the sacrifices these families make for their communities. His play *Breeders* (1930) reveals how his work differed from typical productions on Harlem stages. In this play, the master of a black slave woman attempts to force her to have sexual intercourse with a black man in order to produce strong slave children; rather than submit, she poisons herself.

From 1926 until 1934, Edmonds taught drama at Morgan College (later Morgan University) in Baltimore, Maryland, where he directed the Morgan College Players, an organization he had founded. At Morgan, he formed the Negro Intercollegiate Dramatic Association (NIDA), which held annual tournaments among five African American colleges to encourage the creation and production of black folk plays. At Dillard University, he founded the Southern Association of Dramatic and Speech Arts (SADSA) in 1936; it later became the National Association of Dramatic and Speech Arts (NADSA). At Florida A&M University, he served as the chairman of the Department of Speech and Drama for more than twenty years.

The S. Randolph Edmonds Theatrical Collection is housed in the Black Archives Research Center and Museum at Florida A&M University.

Biography

Sheppard Randolph Edmonds was born in 1900 in Lawrenceville, Virginia. He studied at Saint Paul Normal and Industrial School in Lawrenceville, Oberlin College in Ohio (A.B. 1926), Columbia University (A.M., 1934), Yale School of Drama (1936), Dublin University, and the London School of Speech Training and Dramatic Arts (1938). He taught at Morgan College (later Morgan University) in Baltimore, Maryland (1926–1934); Dillard University, New Orleans, Louisiana (1935–1947); and Florida A&M University, Tallahassee (1948–1968). Edmonds was a theater columnist for the Baltimore *Afro-American* (1930–1934) and founder of the Morgan College Players, Negro Intercollegiate Dramatic Association (NIDA, 1931), and Southern Association of Dramatic and Speech Arts (SADSA, 1936; it later became the National Association of Dramatic and Speech Arts, NADSA). He died in Lawrenceville, Virginia, in 1983.

CHRISTINE RAUCHFUSS GRAY

See also Community Theater; Literature: 3—Drama

Selected Works

"Black Drama in the American Theatre: 1700–1970." In *The American Theatre: A Sum of Its Parts*. New York: French, 1971, pp. 379–426.
Shades and Shadows. Boston, Mass.: Meador, 1930.
Six Plays for a Negro Theater. Boston, Mass.: Walter H. Baker, 1934. (Foreword by Frederick H. Koch.)
The Land of Cotton and Other Plays. Washington, D.C.: Associated Publishers, 1942.

Further Reading

Peterson, Bernard L., Jr. *Early Black American Playwrights and Dramatic Writers: A Biographical Directory and Catalog of Plays, Films, and Broadcasting Scripts*. Westport, Conn.: Greenwood, 1990.
Sanders, Leslie Catherine. *The Development of Black Theater in America: From Shadows to Selves*. Baton Rouge: Louisiana State University Press, 1988.

Elder Becton

See Becton, George Wilson

Ellington, Duke

No figure of the Harlem Renaissance achieved more of the goals set by leaders and intellectuals of the movement than Duke Ellington, who purposefully promoted black artistic expression as a way of breaking down prejudice, achieving racial uplift, and displaying and documenting black humanity and achievement. He was one of the most famous and widely disseminated black voices in the international mass media, commenting for more than four decades on black identity, history, and pride. However, although some modern-day accounts include jazz and blues artists as part and parcel of the Harlem Renaissance, this represents a revisionist view: Its leadership kept popular musicians at a distance and downgraded their cultural contributions. The intellectuals of the renaissance tended to apply the same elite standards to music as to literature—recognizing only music that embraced European criteria, hoping for great achievements by African Americans in classical music, and encouraging composers to transform supposedly primitive jazz, blues, and plantation melodies into conventional orchestrated works of Western art. This approach to music largely ignored the significant, decidedly nonprimitive contributions of jazz and blues musicians. "Renaissance leaders aspired to create a New Negro, one who would attend concerts and operas and would be economically and socially prepared to enter an ideally integrated American society" (Floyd 1990). Ellington, although he brought his music to concert halls, rarely waded into these academic and semantic battles; he concentrated on creating and performing what may have been the most accomplished oeuvre in the history of American music, much of it pointedly inspired by African American themes, and enjoyed by millions around the world.

Ellington's interest in black culture came largely from his upbringing in black middle-class Washington, D.C., which was considered the center of "respectable Negro society" from the end of the Civil War until World War II. African American students there received detailed instruction in black history and identity: "What used to happen was that they were concerned with you being representative of a great and proud race," Ellington recalled in the 1960s. "They used to pound it into you, you go to the English class, that [race pride] was more important than the English." The black community and schools also exposed students to African American music as well as European classical music, and there were elaborate pageants of black history using music, dance, and narration (Tucker 1991). One reason that Ellington gained national prominence and widespread respect—and earned millions of dollars—during the 1920s and 1930s, while the writers of the Harlem Renaissance were struggling to survive, is that a century-long tradition of successful black music productions and performers had preceded him, mostly centered in New York City. This tradition did not yet support long-form musical works or compositions that directly challenged American racism, but as early as the turn of the twentieth century, it provided a multiracial paying audience; and, as Ellington notes in his autobiography, he and his musical peers in Washington were part of that audience. He mentions dozens of acts that he followed avidly as a young man and whose success on a national level inspired him to leave a lucrative band business he had established in his hometown and venture North to New York City in 1923.

Ellington, though, took years to achieve success in the more competitive publishing and recording circles of New York; and he might never have attained it at all if not for his partnership with the Jewish manager, publisher, and entrepreneur Irving Mills from 1926 to 1939. To find a niche in the crowded, frequently anti-Semitic and racist music publishing industry, Mills decided to focus on black jazz and blues, music shunned by most Tin Pan Alley publishers. This earned him admiring notice in black newspapers; introduced him to his most significant client, Ellington; and thus drew him into band managing. Mills's main achievement for Ellington during the 1920s was the band's residency at the Cotton Club, which lasted more than three years and included national nightly radio broadcasts—the first time a black band had received so much national exposure. During this early period in their association, Mills and Ellington seemed more concerned with establishing the orchestra as a top show business attraction than with promoting Ellington as a serious artist.

The Cotton Club was a glamorous, expensive, and successful night spot, even during the Great Depression, but it was also segregated, featuring blacks onstage performing for an exclusively white audience. It was part of a lucrative market during the Harlem Renaissance that took advantage of a "Negro infatuation" among whites who wanted to expose themselves to the supposedly more licentious, primitive, authentic black culture. Ellington's music at this time was often (although not always) promoted as "jungle" music or advertised with strongly African connotations. The distinctive growling, shrieking, moaning sounds of the band instrumentalists Bubber Miley and Joe Nanton inspired this characterization, as did the club's penchant for skits set in Africa. These skits, usually featuring scantily clad light-skinned black women, often portrayed African Americans as one step removed (if that much) from the jungle, although Ellington and the band wore tuxedos, performed sophisticated music, and were not part of the jungle tableaux. Mills and Ellington, however, did not long adhere to emphasis on "primitive" and "weird" effects, which did not accord with Ellington's view of black music or with Mills's idea of the enormous commercial and artistic potential among white as well as black audiences for Ellington's compositions. Starting in 1930, Mills began a historic, nonstereotyped marketing campaign that provided the financial and artistic foundation for Ellington's nearly half-century career as a composer and popular entertainer.

Mills spent a decade churning out publicity that equated Ellington's compositions and personal bearing with "genius," "quality," and respectability. During the

1930s, Mills placed Ellington in major studio feature films more often and more respectfully than any blacks would be presented until after World War II, with Ellington always in formal clothing, befitting a serious composer and conductor. Mills conveyed the compelling impression that Ellington's shows and recordings constituted an invitation to understand popular music, African American music, and African Americans in a new way. Although it was true that Mills promoted his other black artists using the same stereotypical images that prevailed in show business, and that Mills claimed for himself what would now be considered an unethically disproportionate part of Ellington's earnings, Ellington never protested, privately or publicly. Ellington knew that Mills had given him an opportunity to create and present music that no black composer and few American composers of any color had previously enjoyed. For black and white artists of this period, it took high-powered management to launch a popular music career, and the artists' financial sacrifice was seen as a normal cost of doing business.

Of course, Mills's marketing of Ellington worked so well principally because Ellington's music more than lived up to it. Onstage and in the recording studio, Ellington reveled in his dual role as entertainer and serious composer, which reflected his own musical interests and background and attracted the wide audience he needed to support his writing and the orchestra that performed his compositions. The more rigid critics may have had trouble reconciling artistic quality with the top-forty charts, but Ellington proved equally accomplished at creating intriguing compositions and recordings that easily fit into commercial boundaries, and at composing more esoteric and adventurous works, such as his extended compositions and his compositions that programmatically illustrated African American culture. Often, Ellington's best pieces fulfilled both functions; examples are "Black and Tan Fantasy," "East St. Louis Toodle-Oo" (a musical impression of the lope of a tired black man walking home from work), "Black Beauty" (written for the Harlem singer and actress Florence Mills, who had recently died), and "A Portrait of Bert Williams." The marketing emphasis on Ellington as a composer, as well as his need to write for a listening as well as a dancing audience during the Cotton Club's radio broadcasts, allowed him to work in a larger variety of genres and styles than any other black performer of the period: "hot" jazz, vocal tunes, dreamy instrumentals, low-down blues, swinging riff-laden stompers, and more.

Ellington's extended works, which had the bearing and length of symphonic music, were unprecedented, and they upset listeners who insisted on a strict division between pop and classical forms. These relaxed, charming pieces broke through the three-minute barrier of pop and jazz recording in the 1930s and 1940s: *Creole Rhapsody* lasted nine minutes (on two sides of a 78-rpm record), and *Reminiscing in Tempo* lasted thirteen minutes (on four sides). Moreover, their shifting tempos and unpredictable transitions represented a musical adventure that expanded audiences' expectations for pop and jazz performers, and made for some of the freshest and most intriguing pieces in the Ellington canon. They remain examples of the emotional, intricately arranged music that rewards repeated listenings and careful attention, like the best music of any genre. In these longer works, Ellington revealed the nearsightedness of musical as well as racial segregation.

The first European tour of Ellington's orchestra, in 1933, solidified his reputation as an important American composer. Unlike their American counterparts, English critics and audiences did not hesitate to place his music on a high plane alongside Bach, Wagner, and Schoenberg, and they linked Ellington's inspiration and genius to his African American heritage. The Europeans' views were extensively reproduced in the American press (even in the South) and changed Americans' attitudes and expectations. Ellington's music and demeanor, and the way he was marketed, began a shift in the cultural hierarchy—in which only European classical music had been exalted as high art and indigenous American forms had been denigrated. Before Aaron Copland and Charles Ives rose to national prominence at the time of World War II, ushering in a widespread celebration of and search for American highbrow music, Ellington inspired a reevaluation of American music and black music, and new schools of criticism of popular music and jazz, on both sides of the Atlantic. After the war, American music, like American literature, would be studied more frequently and more seriously in the United States and abroad. Without issuing declamatory or inflammatory statements, Ellington had challenged and altered not just social and political attitudes concerning African Americans but also the standing of American artists of all colors.

On 23 January 1943, Ellington and his orchestra appeared in their first concert at Carnegie Hall, amid a crowd of interracial celebrities and the biggest media buildup ever assembled on Ellington's behalf. The highlight of the evening was the premiere of his longest extended work (lasting more than forty minutes), *Black,*

Brown, and Beige: A Tone Parallel to the History of the American Negro, an ambitious multipart work programmatically illustrating black history from the African continent to blacks' contribution in World War II. With this event, Ellington used his own power in the music business, and Americans' wartime patriotism, to bring the subject of black respectability, pride, and history into the national consciousness even more fully than he had ever done before. In numerous interviews, he eloquently discussed such issues as the "middle passage" and relations between blacks and whites during slavery, subjects that rarely received a hearing in the American mass media, let alone a serious or accurate one. Before it was common or even safe to confront American racism politically, Ellington used his art and his commercial success as a public arena, challenging the false suppositions of black inferiority that lay behind discrimination and bringing alternative messages about blacks to a national audience.

Eleven months after his debut in Carnegie Hall, Ellington continued these efforts to assemble a musical record of black life and history, with the premiere of his evocation of Roi Ottley's book *New World a-Comin'*

Duke Ellington. (Brown Brothers.)

(1943), which predicted better times for American blacks. Later additions to this part of the Ellington canon (often cowritten with his friend and writing partner Billy Strayhorn) include *A Tone Parallel to Harlem* (*Harlem Suite*), *My People*, and *New Orleans Suite*. In the 1960s, Ellington continued to release extended suites, such as *Afro-Bossa*, *Far East Suite*, and *Afro-Eurasian Eclipse*, that reflected the African diaspora and the internationalism of many blacks during that period. Ellington's "sacred concerts," which he considered his most important work, featured personal and historical treatments of religion, an important facet of African American history. But Ellington repeatedly stressed that no single genre or theme could define his work. *Such Sweet Thunder* and *Suite Thursday*, evocative multipart suites illustrating works by William Shakespeare and John Steinbeck, are two of the many examples of Ellington's determination to remain, as an artist, beyond any easy categorization other than "American composer."

Biography

Edward Kennedy ("Duke") Ellington was born in Washington, D.C., on 29 April 1899. He attended public schools there; studied piano with a local teacher, Marietta Clinkscales; attended Armstrong High School; and studied harmony with Henry Grant (1918–1919). Ellington formed his first band, the Dukes Serenaders, in Washington, D.C. (1918). He performed regularly with his group the Washingtonians at the Kentucky Club, New York City (1923–1927) and was then hired by the Cotton Club (1927–1931). He composed music for and appeared in many films, including *Black and Tan* (1929), *Check and Double Check* (1930), *Murder at the Vanities* (1934), *Belle of the Nineties* (1934), *Symphony in Black* (1935), *Cabin in the Sky* (1943), *Reveille with Beverly* (1943), *Anatomy of a Murder* (1959), and *Paris Blues* (1961). He toured in the United States (1931–1974) and in Europe (1933, 1939, 1950, 1958, 1960s). He gave annual concerts at Carnegie Hall, premiering long-form works, in 1943–1948. Ellington made more than 200 appearances on international television from 1949 to 1973; from 1963 to 1973, he made tours abroad sponsored by the U.S. State Department; and in 1965, 1968, and 1973, he gave three sacred concerts. His awards included the George Washington Carver Memorial Institute, Supreme Award of Merit (1943); the National Association for the Advancement of Colored People, Spingarn Medal

(1959); an Oscar nomination for the score of *Paris Blues*; eight Grammy awards (1962–1973); City of New York, Musician of Every Year, Gold Medal (1965); Paris Medal (1965); City of Chicago Medal (1965); City Club of New York Medal, Distinguished New Yorker Award (1966); Emmy Award for "Duke Ellington: Love You Madly" (1967); Ordem dos Musicos do Brasil (1968); Presidential Medal of Freedom (1969); special papal blessing from Pope Paul VI (1969); Yale University Duke Ellington Fellowship Program (established 1972); National Association of Negro Musicians, Highest Award for Distinguished Service in Music (1972); Eleanor Roosevelt International Workshop in Human Relations, International Humanist Award (1972); commemorative stamp issued by the U.S. Postal Service (1986); and honorary doctorates from numerous schools, including Wilberforce College (1949), Yale University (1967), Brown University (1969), Berklee College of Music (1971), Howard University (1971), and University of Wisconsin at Madison (1971). Ellington died in New York City, on 24 May 1974.

HARVEY COHEN

See also Cotton Club; Harlem: 3—Entertainment; Jazz; Music; Music: Bands and Orchestras; Musicians; Nightclubs; Nightlife

Selected Works

"Black and Tan Fantasy." 1927. (Cowritten with Bubber Miley.)

"East St. Louis Toodle-Oo." 1927. (Cowritten with Bubber Miley.)

"Black Beauty." 1928.

"Mood Indigo." 1930. (Cowritten with Irving Mills and Albany Bigard.)

Creole Rhapsody, Parts 1 and 2. 1931.

"It Don't Mean a Thing (If It Ain't Got That Swing)." 1932. (Cowritten with Irving Mills.)

"Solitude." 1934. (Cowritten with Eddie DeLange and Irving Mills.)

Reminiscing in Tempo. 1935.

Symphony in Black. 1935. (Film soundtrack.)

"Jack the Bear." 1940.

"Ko-Ko." 1940.

"Bojangles (A Portrait of Bill Robinson)." 1940.

"A Portrait of Bert Williams." 1940.

Black, Brown, and Beige. 1943.

New World a-Comin'. 1943.

Deep South Suite. 1946.

"On a Turquoise Cloud." 1947.

"The Clothed Woman." 1947.

A Tone Parallel to Harlem (*Harlem Suite*). 1951.

Such Sweet Thunder. 1957. (Cowritten with Billy Strayhorn.)

Suite Thursday. 1960. (Cowritten with Billy Strayhorn.)

My People. 1963.

Afro-Bossa. 1963. (Cowritten with Billy Strayhorn and Juan Tizol.)

Far East Suite. 1966. (Cowritten with Billy Strayhorn.)

Second Sacred Concert. 1968.

The River. 1970.

New Orleans Suite. 1970.

Afro-Eurasian Eclipse. 1971.

Further Reading

Ellington, Duke. *Music Is My Mistress*. New York: Doubleday, 1973.

Ellison, Ralph. "Homage to Duke Ellington on His Birthday." In *Going to the Territory*. New York: Random House, 1986.

Floyd, Samuel J. Jr., ed. *Black Music in the Harlem Renaissance*. New York: Greenwood, 1990.

Hasse, John Edward. *Beyond Category: The Life and Genius of Duke Ellington*. New York: Simon and Schuster, 1993.

Nicholson, Stuart. *Reminiscing in Tempo: A Portrait of Duke Ellington*. Boston, Mass.: Northern University Press, 1999.

Peretti, Burton W. *Jazz in American Culture*. Chicago, Ill.: Ivan R. Dee, 1997.

Stratemann, Klaus. *Ellington Day by Day and Film by Film*. Copenhagen: Jazz Media, 1992.

Tucker, Mark. *Ellington: The Early Years*. Urbana: University of Illinois Press, 1991.

———, ed. *The Duke Ellington Reader*. New York: Oxford University Press, 1993.

Ellis, Evelyn

Evelyn Ellis appeared in both film and theater during the Harlem Renaissance; although she was a minor actress, she was connected to significant networks of African American filmmakers, playwrights, and performers. She appeared in race films and in a few plays with black casts during this era. She is notable for having played the role of Crown's Bess in a successful production by the Theater Guild of Dorothy and DuBose Heyward's play *Porgy* (1927); and as a member of the Lafayette Players Stock Company, Ellis was part of a black artistic community on the East Coast. Community theater groups such as the Lafayette Players that were not constrained by the racial codes of the film and theater industries offered African American actresses greater creative possibilities; thus Ellis and her colleagues in community groups could appear in plays that were not originally intended for African American performers. The actors of the Lafayette Players also often worked in race films, which were conceived with black performers and black audiences in mind, and Ellis acted in two of these during the 1920s, the golden age of the genre.

One of her race films was a silent-era comedy, Reol Productions' *Easy Money* (1921), in which Sherman Dudley also appeared. The setting is Millbrook, a thrifty little southern town. The character Andy Simpson (played by Dudley) is looked on as slow, plodding, and lacking in ambition by everyone except his sweetheart, Margie Watkins (played by Edna Morton), who is the daughter of a bank president. Margie becomes attracted to J. Overton Tighe, who has recently arrived in town in an expensive car; and despite Andy's warnings against easy money, the townspeople eagerly buy shares in a phony stock promoted by Tighe. As a comedy, this film was an exception for Reol, which usually produced dramas (including *Burden of a Race, Secret Sorrows*, and an adaptation of Paul Laurence Dunbar's novel of 1902, *Sport of the Gods*).

Later, Ellis performed in Oscar Micheaux's controversial film *A Son of Satan* (1924), which starred Lawrence Chenault and featured the chorus from the original company of *Shuffle Along*. Micheaux was the most prolific director of race films and was known, according to one contemporary critic, for "giving us the real stuff." The scenes of drinking in *A Son of Satan* offended the censors, and Micheaux was forced to reedit the film for exhibition.

Biography

Evelyn Ellis was born on 2 February 1894, in Boston, Massachusetts. She was a member of the Lafayette Players Stock Company and appeared in *Othello* (Lafayette Theater, 1919). During the 1920s she had minor roles in the films *Easy Money* (1921) and *A Son of Satan* (1924) and in the plays *Roseanne* (1923), *Goat Alley* (1927), and *Porgy* (1927). She later had roles in *Native*

Son (1941), *Blue Holiday*, (1945), the play *Deep Are the Roots* (1945), *The Lady from Shanghai* (1948), *The Joe Louis Story* (1953), *Interrupted Melody* (1955), *Tobacco Road* (with an all-black cast, 1950), *The Royal Family* (at City Center in New York, 1951), *Touchstone* (1953), and *Supper for the Dead* (1954). Ellis died on 5 June 1958, in Saranac Lake, New York.

TERRI FRANCIS

See also Chenault, Lawrence; Dudley, Sherman H.; Lafayette Players; Micheaux, Oscar; Porgy: Play; Race Films; Shuffle Along

Further Reading

Bowser, Pearl, Jane Gaines, and Charles Musser, eds. *Oscar Micheaux and His Circle: African-American Filmmaking and Race Cinema of the Silent Era*. Bloomington and Indianapolis: Indiana University Press, 2001.

Hill, Anthony D. *Pages from the Harlem Renaissance: A Chronicle of Performance*. New York: Peter Lang, 1996.

Hottschild, Brenda Dixon. *Digging the Africanist Presence in American Performance Dance and Other Contexts*. Westport, Conn.: Greenwood, 1996.

Hughes, Langston, and Milton Meltzer. *Black Magic: A Pictorial History of the Negro in American Entertainment*. Englewood Cliffs, N.J.: Prentice-Hall, 1968.

Patterson, Lindsay, ed. *Anthology of the Afro-American in the Theatre: A Critical Approach*. International Library of Afro-American Life and History. Cornwells Heights, Pa.: Publishers Agency, 1976.

Sampson, Henry T. *Blacks in Black and White: A Source Book on Black Films*, 2nd ed. Landham, Md., and London: Scarecrow, 1995.

Tanner, Jo A. *Dusky Maidens: The Odyssey of the Early Black Dramatic Actress*. Westport, Conn.: Greenwood, 1992.

Thomas, Ireland D. "Motion Picture News." *Chicago Defender*, 31 January 1925, p. 6A.

Thompson, Sister Francesa. *The Lafayette Players, 1915–1932: America's First Dramatic Stock Company*. Ann Arbor, Mich.: University Microfilms, 1972.

Ellison, Ralph

Ralph Ellison, the author of *Invisible Man*, one of the most important twentieth-century American novels, owed much of his development as a writer to the Harlem Renaissance. Ellison was born in 1914 in

Oklahoma; he moved with his mother to Indiana just before the riots of 1921 in Tulsa. From 1933 to 1936 he studied music at the Tuskegee Institute; then, intending to earn money for his senior year, he moved to New York. In New York he met Richard Wright, began to write under Wright's guidance, and joined the Communist Party. Ellison remained in New York until 1955, three years after *Invisible Man* was published and two years after it had received the National Book Award. Thus Ellison's career was launched from New York and in particular from the social and artistic milieu of Harlem.

Invisible Man is a tale of self-discovery. The young African American protagonist escapes from his segregated southern hometown to a black college, only to be expelled and sent to "the big city" to find his own way in the world. Thereafter he experiences a series of disillusionments—episodes that he narrates from a hole, deep in the ground, illuminated by 1,369 lightbulbs. He explains how he slowly came to realize that he had badly misunderstood his world, that he was blind both to the intricate social and political machinery of democracy and to the real nature of African Americans' place in greater American society. As he does so, the metaphor of invisibility comes to signify the experience of being black in America but also, more broadly, the experience of being an ordinary citizen in a democracy. As a narrator, the protagonist takes a jazzy, ironic, tragicomic attitude toward reality and insists on his own power to remake reality through creative speech. Early critics of *Invisible Man* considered it an outstanding existentialist account of the human condition. With time, however, and with Ellison's many essays (in *Shadow and Act* and *Going to the Territory*) as a guide, it has become clear that this novel also makes a profound sociotheoretical argument about democracy and the place of minority cultures and minority viewpoints in a democracy.

Invisible Man was born, according to Ellison, in 1945, when his efforts to work on a war novel were "interrupted by an ironic, down-home voice that struck me as being as irreverent as honky-tonk trumpet blasting through a performance, say, of Britten's *War Requiem*" (1995, xv). Like other figures of the Harlem Renaissance, Ellison was powerfully influenced by the blues and jazz tradition as well as by African American folklore. He drew on these sources as he worked toward a novel that simultaneously criticizes American society and affirms the ability of that society to consolidate independent traditions. The novel jokes, puns, and riddles its way through the argument that in the

Ralph Ellison. (Library of Congress.)

United States there is no such thing as white culture separate from black culture, or black culture separate from white culture; democracy is a political regime in which the common experiences of diverse citizens are constituted out of the sacrifices of their fellow citizens. Ellison, as he said of his protagonist, was "forged in the underground of American experience and yet managed to emerge less angry than ironic. [He was] a blues-toned laugher-at-wounds who included himself in his indictment of the human condition" (1995, xviii).

Biography

Ralph Waldo Ellison was born on 1 March 1914, in Oklahoma City, Oklahoma, where he attended segregated public schools. He later studied at the Tuskegee Institute. Ellis worked for the New York Federal Writers' Project of the Works Progress Administration in New York City (1938–1941); served as a merchant marine in World War II until 1945; worked at odd jobs as a freelance photographer and installing audio systems in New York (1945–1955); and taught at Bard College (1961), Rutgers University in New Jersey (1962–1964), and New York University (1970–1980). He was editor of the *Negro Quarterly* (1942–1943) and wrote for it (1942–1943) and many other periodicals, including *New Masses* (1938–1942), *Tomorrow* (1944), *New Republic*,

Saturday Review, Antioch Review, Reporter, The Nation, New World Writing, Quarterly Review of Literature, Partisan Review, and *Iowa Review.* During his lifetime, he published short stories and essays, one novel (*Invisible Man,* 1952), and two essay collections (*Shadow and Act,* 1966; and *Going to the Territory,* 1986). His *Flying Home and Other Short Stories* (1996) and a second novel, *Juneteenth* (1999), were published posthumously. Ellison was a charter member of the National Council on the Arts and Humanities; a member of the Carnegie Commission on public television; and a trustee of the John F. Kennedy Center for the Performing Arts and Colonial Williamsburg. His awards included the National Book Award (1953), the Russwurm Award, a fellowship at the American Academy of Rome (1955–1957), an appointment to the American Academy of Arts and Letters (1964), the Presidential Medal of Freedom (1969), Chevalier de l'Ordre des Arts et Lettres (France, 1970), and the National Medal of Arts (1985). Ellison died in New York City on 16 April 1994.

DANIELLE ALLEN

See also Federal Writers' Project; Second Harlem Renaissance; Works Progress Administration; Wright, Richard

Selected Works

"Slick Gonna Learn." *Direction,* September 1939, pp. 10–11, 14, 16.

"The Birthmark." *New Masses,* 36, 2 July 1940, pp. 16–17.

"Afternoon." In *American Writing,* ed. Hans Otto Storm et al. Prairie City, Iowa: James A. Decker, 1940.

"Mister Toussan." *New Masses,* 41, 4 November 1941, pp. 19–20. (Reprinted in *Negro Story,* 1, July–August 1944, pp. 36–41.)

"That I Had the Wings." *Common Ground,* 3, Summer 1943, pp. 30–37. (Reprinted as "Mr. Toussaint." *Negro Story,* 1, 11, October 1944, pp. 3–4.)

"In a Strange Country." *Tomorrow,* 3, July 1944, pp. 41–44. (Reprinted in *I Have Seen War: Twenty-Five Stories from World War II,* ed. Dorothy Sterling. New York: Hill and Wang, 1960.)

"Flying Home." In *Cross Section,* ed. Edwin Seaver. New York: Fisher, 1944. (Reprinted in *Ten Modern Masters,* ed. Robert Gorham Davis. New York: Harcourt Brace Jovanovich, 1972. *Dark Symphony,* ed. James A. Emanuel and Theodore L. Gross. New York: Free Press, 1968. *The Best Short Stories of World War II: An Anthology,* ed. Charles A. Fenton. New York: Viking,

1957. *The Best Short Stories by Negro Writers,* ed. Langston Hughes. Boston, Mass.: Little, Brown, 1967. *Stories in Black and White,* ed. Eva Kissin. New York: Lippincott, 1970.)

"King of the Bingo Game." *Tomorrow,* 4, November 1944, pp. 29–33. (Reprinted in *Dark Symphony,* ed. James A. Emanuel and Theodore L. Gross. New York: Free Press, 1968. *Afro-American Literature: An Introduction,* ed. Robert Hayden, David J. Burrows, and Frederic R. Lapides. New York: Harcourt Brace Jovanovich, 1971.)

Invisible Man. New York: New American Library, 1952. (Reprint, New York: Random House, 1952.)

"Did You Ever Dream Lucky?" *New World Writing Number 5.* New York: New American Library, 1954, pp. 134–145.

"A Coupla Scalped Indians." *New World Writing Number 9.* New York: New American Library, 1956, pp. 225–236. (Reprinted in *Black Literature in America,* ed. Houston A. Baker Jr. New York: McGraw-Hill, 1971.)

"Out of the Hospital and Under the Bar." In *Soon, One Morning: New Writing by American Negroes, 1940–1962,* ed. Herbert Hill. New York: Knopf, 1963.

Shadow and Act. New York: New American Library, 1966. (Reprint, New York: Random House, 1964. Included in *The Collected Essays of Ralph Ellison,* ed. J. F. Callahan. New York: Modern Library, 1995.)

Going to the Territory. New York: Random House, 1986. (Included in *The Collected Essays of Ralph Ellison,* ed. J. F. Callahan. New York: Modern Library, 1995.)

Flying Home and Other Stories, ed. and intro. John F. Callahan. New York: Random House, 1996.

Juneteenth, ed. J. F. Callahan. New York: Random House, 1999.

Further Reading

Baker, Houston A. Jr. *Blues, Ideology, and Afro-American Literature: A Vernacular Theory.* Chicago, Ill.: University of Chicago Press, 1984.

Benston, K. W., ed. *Speaking for You: The Vision of Ralph Ellison.* Washington, D.C.: Howard University Press, 1987.

Ellison, R. Introduction. In *Invisible Man.* New York: Vintage International, 1995. (Originally published 1981.)

Locke, A. "From *Native Son* to *Invisible Man:* A Review of the Literature of the Negro for 1952." *Phylon,* 14, 1953, pp. 34–44.

Negro Quarterly, Spring 1942 / Winter–Spring 1943. (Early articles by Ellison.)

New Masses, 16 August 1938–20 October 1942. (Early articles by Ellison.)

O'Meally, ed. *New Essays on Invisible Man*. Cambridge: Cambridge University Press, 1988, pp. 95–122.

Schor, E. *Visible Ellison: A Study of Ralph Ellison's Fiction*. Westport, Conn: Greenwood, 1993.

Sundquist, E. J., ed. *Cultural Contexts for Ralph Ellison's Invisible Man*. Boston, Mass.: Bedford (St. Martin's Press), 1995.

Warren, K. "Ralph Ellison and the Reconfiguration of Black Cultural Politics." *Yearbook of Research in English and American Literature*, 1995, pp. 11, 139–157.

Watts, J. G. *Heroism and the Black Intellectual: Ralph Ellison, Politics, and Afro-American Intellectual Life*. Chapel Hill: University of North Carolina Press, 1994.

Emancipator

First published in March 1920, the *Emancipator* was a socialist weekly newspaper in Harlem, edited by Wilfred Aldophus (W. A.) Domingo. The mission of the *Emancipator* was to "provide a 'scientific chart and compass' for blacks, in relation to national and international, social and political movements" (Samuels 1977). Domingo advocated socialism as the answer to the oppression of blacks in the United States; he felt that black Americans were victims of capitalism and should be involved in the socialist revolution. The *Emancipator* sprang up in the context of other radical Harlem newspapers of the time (such as *Negro World* and the *Messenger*), with offices at 2295 Seventh Avenue in New York. It became famous in part because it was investigated by the Lusk Committee (the State of New York Joint Committee Investigating Seditious Activities), which was then looking into socialist and communist activities; but despite its fame, the *Emancipator* lasted only three months, publishing ten issues. Its last issue appeared in May 1920.

W. A. Domingo was born in Kingston, Jamaica, in 1889 and came to the United States in 1910. From August 1918 to July 1919, he edited *Negro World*, the newspaper of the United Negro Improvement Association (UNIA) led by Marcus Garvey. Domingo also contributed to another periodical of the Harlem Renaissance, the *Messenger*, edited by A. Philip Randolph and Chandler Owen. Randolph and Owen would later contribute articles to the *Emancipator*. However, the focus of the *Emancipator* differed from that of *Negro World* and the *Messenger* and their founders. Unlike Garvey's *Negro World*, the *Emancipator* emphasized class issues more than racial issues; and the *Emancipator* spoke to the common, uneducated black masses, whereas the *Messenger* appealed to black intellectuals.

These differences in philosophy were most pronounced in relation to Garvey. Domingo had first met Garvey when they were both living in Jamaica, and—as noted above—Domingo edited *Negro World* and was involved with UNIA. However, he never joined UNIA, and he eventually parted ways with it and with Garvey. This break came because Domingo's socialist views conflicted with Garvey's philosophy: Domingo opposed Garvey's teachings and believed that the welfare of black Americans depended on class equality rather than racial issues. Domingo expressed his opposition in the pages of the *Emancipator*, criticizing Garvey's practices and Garvey's narrow focus on black nationalism. In addition to attempting to discredit Garvey in the *Emancipator* and other periodicals of the time, Domingo, Randolph, Owen, and other black socialists supported Garvey's eventual deportation to Jamaica.

The *Emancipator*'s contributing editors included Richard B. Moore, Chandler Owen, A. Philip Randolph, Cyril Briggs, and Anselmo Jackson. Domingo and Moore, who was also a Caribbean-born activist, were members of the Twenty-First Assembly District Branch of the Socialist Party in New York City, and they used the *Emancipator* to promote socialist ideas. But like many other black socialists during the Harlem Renaissance, they became disenchanted with the Socialist Party of America (SPA) because of its inattention to the racial problems of blacks. In 1918, Domingo, Briggs, and Moore formed the African Blood Brotherhood (ABB), which advocated racial equality, freedom of blacks from capitalism, and an end to terrorism by the Ku Klux Klan and similar groups.

HEATHER MARTIN

See also African Blood Brotherhood; Briggs, Cyril; Domingo, Wilfred Adolphus; Garvey, Marcus; Messenger; Moore, Richard B.; Negro World; Owen, Chandler; Randolph, A. Philip; United Negro Improvement Association

Further Reading

Hill, Robert A., ed. *The Marcus Garvey and Universal Negro Improvement Association Papers*. Berkeley: University of California Press, 1983–1990.

Samuels, Wilfred D. *Five Afro-Caribbean Voices in American Culture 1917–1929: Hubert H. Harrison, Wilfred A. Domingo, Richard B. Moore, Cyril V. Briggs, and Claude McKay*. Boulder, Colo.: Belmont, 1977.

Turner, Joyce Moore. "Richard B. Moore and His Works." In *Richard B. Moore, Caribbean Militant in Harlem: Collected Writings, 1920–1972*, ed. W. Burghardt Turner and Joyce Moore Turner. Bloomington: Indiana University Press, 1988.

Emperor Jones, The

The Emperor Jones, a play by Eugene O'Neill, premiered at the Neighborhood Playhouse in New York City on 3 November 1920. A film based on O'Neill's play, with a screenplay by DuBose Heyward, was produced in 1933. An opera by Louis Gruenberg with libretto by Kathleen de Jaffa, based on the play, premiered at the Metropolitan Opera House in New York City, also in 1933.

Eugene O'Neill's play *The Emperor Jones* is the story of an African American, Brutus Jones, who has escaped prison to the West Indies. Over the course of eight scenes, Jones becomes the emperor of an island, and with the help of his Cockney aide-de-camp, the trader Henry Smithers, Jones rules with brutality and with an eye only to amassing a personal fortune. Jones and Smithers both categorize the "natives" of the island as backward and ignorant, but eventually Smithers alerts Jones that the "natives" are practicing witchcraft and preparing a rebellion. Jones flees the palace for the forest. He believes that he can be killed only by a silver bullet (the original title of the play was *The Silver Bullet*). In a series of flashbacks, brought about by his disorientation in the forest and the never-ending sound of drumming, Jones recalls incidents in his earlier life, which include being a Pullman porter, killing a man over a woman, going to and escaping from prison, and working on a ship and jumping overboard. He also hallucinates that he is being auctioned off in front of white planters, and he has encounters with a "Congo witch-doctor" and a crocodile. At the end of the play, Jones is killed by his own soldiers, who have made silver bullets.

O'Neill, the playwright, was greatly influenced by the expressionist work of two Europeans: August Strindberg and Frank Wedekind. *The Emperor Jones* was his own first attempt at this style of drama, which emphasizes a hero who experiences the world from the inside out. Jones's hallucinations are the prime example of expressionism in *The Emperor Jones*. In his atmospheric portrayal of the Caribbean island, O'Neill also taps into the early twentieth-century fascination with primitivism in art and performance, as well as into his own experiences prospecting for gold in Honduras. For the plot, O'Neill combined various sources: a story he had heard about a onetime ruler of Haiti, Vilbrun Guillaume Sam, who had claimed that he could be killed only by a silver bullet; a book he had read on the use of drums in religious rituals in the Congo; and Joseph Conrad's novel *Heart of Darkness*. Many critics of *The Emperor Jones*, at the time and subsequently, have emphasized that O'Neill was not trying to show a close connection between African Americans and Africa, but rather was trying to give a more universal commentary on the fearful, primitive beast in all of us. Nevertheless, O'Neill did choose to confront this aspect of humanity through the character of Brutus Jones.

The production was directed by George Cram Cook (known as "Jig"), and the set was designed by Cleon Throckmorton. The costuming was by Blanche Hays, who chose to dress Jones as a parody of Marcus Garvey, the Jamaican-born founder of the United Negro Improvement Association; Garvey sometimes appeared in marches in Harlem wearing British military regalia. Except for the role of Brutus Jones, white performers played the black-identified roles in blackface. O'Neill's choice of an African American protagonist presented some difficulty. By 1920, no African American actor had been cast in a serious drama written by a white American. The casting of an actual African American, the actor Charles S. Gilpin (1878–1930), was a radical move for the already left-leaning theater group. There was a heated discussion among the actors about whether a black man or a white man in blackface should play the role. O'Neill does not seem to have expressed an opinion, although he is documented as having played a black character in blackface in one of his early plays, *Thirst* (1916); but Jasper Deeter, the actor who originated the role of Smithers, had seen Gilpin's recent success in a small part as William Custis, an old servant, in John Drinkwater's play *Abraham Lincoln*.

Gilpin, who was originally from Richmond, Virginia, had begun his professional life working at newspapers in Richmond and Philadelphia. In Philadelphia, he began participating in music hall performances. Gilpin toured with the Canada Jubilee Singers and the Smart Set, where he first met Bert Williams and

George Walker. He then sang in the chorus of Williams and Walker's *Abyssinia* in 1906. In 1915, he and Anita Bush formed the Lafayette Players in Harlem. Like many actors, Gilpin also worked at other jobs—for instance, as a Pullman porter and an elevator operator—between roles, a point emphasized in newspaper articles after the success of *The Emperor Jones*. The notion that the Provincetown Players "discovered" Gilpin as a "natural" talent looms large in these accounts, including one, which was often repeated, that Gilpin had been working at Macy's as an elevator operator immediately before he read for the part of Brutus Jones. The true story is that Gilpin was one of the leading character actors of the time, and he also needed to make a living.

The critical acclaim for *The Emperor Jones* was instantaneous. The Provincetown Players immediately began running, in their own playbill, excerpts from positive reviews by Heywood Broun (New York *Tribune*, 4 November 1920), Kenneth Macgowan (New York *Globe*, 4 November 1920), and Alexander Woollcott (*New York Times*, 7 November 1920). After its two-week run in the West Village, *The Emperor Jones* was moved to Broadway by the producer Adolph Klauber for a total run of 240 performances. In the African American press, most critics and intellectuals praised Gilpin but were less laudatory toward O'Neill. In *New York Age*, the drama critic Lester A. Walton stated bluntly: "Had not Charles S. Gilpin essayed to appear as Brutus Jones in the season's dramatic success, 'The Emperor Jones,' this play would be slumbering in manuscript" (30 April 1921). Jessie Redmon Fauset wrote, in an essay in *The Crisis* on Bert Williams: "Among many colored theatergoers, Charles Gilpin's rendition caused a deep sense of irritation. They could not distinguish between the artistic interpretation of a type and the deliberate travestying of a race, and so their appreciation was clouded. . . . I need hardly add that the character of Emperor Jones is a class type" (May 1922).

Gilpin was surely aware of the debate in the African American community about his participation in O'Neill's play. When *The Emperor Jones* started touring with Gilpin in the title role in 1921, he began changing O'Neill's frequent use of the pejorative "nigger" to "Negro" or "colored man." O'Neill was not amused. Reportedly, he told Gilpin, "If you change the lines again, I'll beat the hell out of you" (Sheaffer 1973, 35). For two years, Gilpin spoke the word he felt so insulted by, and it continued to put him in an uncomfortable and ambivalent position in the

African American community. Gilpin began to drink, sometimes appearing onstage after a few too many. Ironically, O'Neill, who laid bare his own and his family's addiction in *Long Day's Journey into Night* (1956), proved very impatient with Gilpin's developing alcoholism. By 1923, O'Neill wrote to his friend Mike Gold:

> Yes, Gilpin is all "ham" and a yard wide. Honestly, I've stood for more from him than from all the white actors I've ever known—simply because he was colored! He played Emperor with author, play, and everyone concerned. . . . I'm "off him" and the result is he will get no chance to do it in London. . . . So I've corralled another Negro to do it over there . . . a young fellow with considerable experience, wonderful presence and voice, full of ambition and a damn fine man personally with real brains. (Sheaffer, 36–37)

The young fellow with brains was Paul Robeson, a graduate of Rutgers and Columbia Law School. Robeson had been cast in several amateur and professional plays, but he was also halfheartedly pursuing a career in law. In the autumn of 1923, Robeson became a subscriber to the Provincetown Players, and on his receipt one of its associate directors, Kenneth Macgowan, asked if he would be interested in auditioning for O'Neill's new play, *All God's Chillun Got Wings*. Rehearsals for that play began in March 1924, and, as a moneymaker, the company decided to revive *The Emperor Jones*, with Robeson in the leading role. Robeson opened in *The Emperor Jones* on 6 May, after a two-week rehearsal period. At the same time, he memorized his lines for *All God's Chillun* and dealt with the public uproar over that play (published in *American Mercury* three months before it premiered onstage), which was about a love affair between a white woman and a black man from the same poor New York neighborhood. For both roles, Robeson, the son of a preacher and highly educated, had to work with his wife, Essie, on making the black dialect, as written by O'Neill, sound natural (Duberman 1989, 59).

When the revival of *The Emperor Jones* opened on 6 May 1924, Robeson received a standing ovation and was asked to come out and bow five times. Gilpin was in the audience, and after the performance, he fought with Robeson backstage. Gilpin had acted in the role of Brutus Jones more than 1,500 times over the course of his association with it, which included several revivals at the Provincetown Playhouse; but with the casting of Robeson, Brutus Jones was forever identified as Robeson's breakthrough role. The difference between the portrayals was significant. Gilpin's Brutus Jones was a man with an intellect, however crude his articulation of that intellect might be. Gilpin, who was light-skinned, slight of stature, age forty-two, and balding, relied on a lifetime of acting technique to get a sense of Jones as a character. Robeson, a former All-American football player, over six feet tall, and physically beautiful, took over the small stage at the Neighborhood Playhouse. He played Brutus as a brute, probably because of his own relative inexperience as an actor; intellectually, he was certainly able to contextualize the role. In an article in *Opportunity*, "Reflections on O'Neill's Plays," Robeson wrote: "And what a great part is 'Brutus Jones.' His is the exultant tragedy of the disintegration of

Charles Gilpin in *The Emperor Jones*, 1920. (Brown Brothers.)

a human soul" (December 1924). Robeson took the position of many people in African American theater regarding the significance of *The Emperor Jones*. Montgomery Gregory, the founder of the Howard Players, a drama laboratory at Howard University in Washington, D.C., stated: "In any further development of Negro drama, *The Emperor Jones*, written by O'Neill, interpreted by Gilpin, and produced by the Provincetown Players, will tower as a beacon-light of inspiration. It marks the breakwater plunge of Negro drama into the main stream of American drama" (1925, 157).

The Emperor Jones was made into a film in 1933, again starring Robeson as Brutus Jones; the screenplay was by DuBose Heyward (author of the novel *Porgy*), and the director was Dudley Murphy. The structure of the film puts Jones's flashbacks in the forefront. The physical presence of Robeson is still arresting, but his skill as an actor makes his performance. In fact, some white critics complained that Robeson's style was too civilized for Brutus. By 1933, Robeson had seven more years of acting experience, including *Othello*, than when he had originated the role. He also had a heightened awareness that the character Brutus Jones, although, in Robeson's words, a masterpiece, was not an example of the triumph of a great African "emperor" but the sad story of a pretender to a throne.

Also in 1933, the Metropolitan Opera in New York produced the operatic adaptation of *The Emperor Jones* by Louis Gruenberg and Kathleen de Jaffa. A few minor parts were cast with African Americans, but Lawrence Tibbett played in the title role, in blackface. The Metropolitan Opera would not cast an African American in a principal role until 1955, when Marian Anderson sang Ulrica in Verdi's *Masked Ball*.

ANNEMARIE BEAN

See also Bush, Anita; Crisis, The; Fauset, Jessie Redmon; Garvey, Marcus; Gilpin, Charles; Gruenberg, Louis; Heyward, DuBose; Lafayette Players; Negro World; O'Neill, Eugene; Provincetown Players; Robeson, Paul; Walton, Lester

Works Discussed

The Emperor Jones. 1933. (Film, United Artists, dir. Dudley Murphy. Performance by Paul Robeson.)

Gruenberg, Louis. *Eugene O'Neill's The Emperor Jones: An Opera in Two Acts, a Prologue, an Interlude, and Six Scenes*, Op. 36, libretto Kathleen de Jaffa. Newton Center, Mass.: GunMar Music, 1990.

O'Neill, Eugene. *The Emperor Jones*. Published in *Anna Christie, The Emperor Jones, The Hairy Ape*. New York: Vintage, 1995.

Further Reading

Cooley, John R. "The Emperor Jones and the Harlem Renaissance." *Studies in the Literary Imagination*, 7(2), 1974, pp. 73–83.

Duberman, Martin. "The Provincetown Playhouse (1922–1924)" and "The Discovery of Africa (1932–1934)." In *Paul Robeson: A Biography*. New York: New Press, 1989, pp. 47–67, 156–183.

Gregory, Montgomery. "The Drama of Negro Life." In *The New Negro*, ed. Alain Locke. New York: Albert and Charles Boni, 1925, pp. 153–160.

Krasner, David. "Whose Role Is It, Anyway? Charles Gilpin and the Harlem Renaissance." In *A Beautiful Pageant: African American Theatre and Drama and Performance in the Harlem Renaissance, 1910–1927*. New York: Palgrave, 2002, pp. 189–205.

Sheaffer, Louis. "The Provincetown's Costly Success." In *O'Neill: Son and Artist*. New York: Little, Brown, 1973, pp. 25–46.

Ethiopian Art Players

The Ethiopian Art Players were a theater company of twenty-five African American performers based in Chicago and active in 1923–1925. Raymond O'Neil, a white man, was the founder and director of the company; reportedly, he was inspired to organize a black group (rather than a white group, as he had originally intended) after seeing how talented black nightclub performers in Chicago were. One of the group's sponsors was the wife of the playwright and novelist Sherwood Anderson.

O'Neil's goals for the Ethiopian Art Players were (1) to use dramatic material that had universal appeal to audiences, regardless of race; (2) to encourage whites and blacks to write plays about the black experience; and (3) if the Ethiopian Art Players were successful, to share what they had learned with other black community theater groups. The Ethiopian Art Players accepted not only professional performers but also amateurs who would be trained and developed, and O'Neil was particularly interested in presenting the performers in nonmusical plays. With regard to elements of production, O'Neil admired the English scene designer and producer Edward Gordon Craig, who used color, line, forms, and lighting to create atmosphere. O'Neil also worked with the German producer and director Max Reinhardt and with Jacques Copeau, a French critic who had founded the Vieux Colombier theater. Both Reinhardt and Copeau applied Craig's ideas in their work. The repertoire of the Ethiopian Art Players included Oscar Wilde's *Salome*, Shakespeare's *Comedy of Errors* and *The Taming of the Shrew*, and Molière's *The Follies of Scapin*, but it needed a work by a black playwright and requested help from *The Crisis*, the official publication of the National Association for the Advancement of Colored People (NAACP). W. E. B. Du Bois, the editor of *The Crisis*, recommended Willis Richardson, who had won two of its annual literary contests, and the company chose Richardson's one-act play *The Chip Woman's Fortune*.

When Harry H. Frazee, a theater entrepreneur and philanthropist, saw the Ethiopian Art Players perform in Chicago, he was so impressed that he invited them to play at his theater, the Frazee, on Broadway in New York City. The company opened there on 15 May 1923, presenting *The Chip Woman's Fortune* as the curtain-opener, then *Salome*, and then a condensed modern-dress version of *The Comedy of Errors* accompanied by a jazz band. Evelyn Preer played the title role in *Salome* and the female lead in *The Chip Woman's Fortune*; Sidney Kirkpatrick played King Herod in *Salome*, the male lead in *The Chip Woman's Fortune*, and the merchant Aegeon in *The Comedy of Errors*.

The Chip Woman's Fortune, which centered on a critical incident in the life of a poor African American family and was the first serious nonmusical play by an African American to be presented on Broadway, turned out to be the piece that was best received by critics and theatergoers. The critics were not comfortable with African American performers taking the roles of white characters, as they did in *Salome* and *The Comedy of Errors*, although the players did meet the standards of European theater—and, ironically, although at that time many white performers darkened their skin to play black characters.

Richardson's characters in *The Chip Woman's Fortune* are not stereotyped: They have dignity, pride, and a love of God, family, and neighbors. Nor did other works produced by the Ethiopian Art Players stereotype African Americans as drunks, prostitutes, criminals, or clowns who grin and sham their way through life. Thus the Ethiopian Art Players not only performed classical European works and opened the door of mainstream professional theater to African American performers, but the company also opened doors for realistic plays about African American life.

MARVIE BROOKS

See also Blacks in Theater; Kirkpatrick, Sidney; Preer, Evelyn; Richardson, Willis; Theater

Further Reading

Archer, Leonard C. (1973). *Black Images in the American Theatre*. Brooklyn, N.Y.: Pageant-Poseidon, 1973, pp. 15, 114–118.

"Colored Artists in Serious Drama on Broadway." *New York Amsterdam News*, 2 May 1923, p. 5.

"Colored Group Presenting 'Salome' to Make International Tour Soon." *New York Amsterdam News*, 25 April 1923, p. 6.

Corbin, John. "Jewels in Ethiope's Ear." *New York Times*, 20 May 1923, p. 11. (Online: *ProQuest Historical Newspaperes: New York Times Database*.)

Du Bois, W. E. B. "Opinion." *Crisis*, 25(6), April 1923, p. 251; 26(3), July 1923, pp. 103–104. (Columns.)

Harris, Abram L. "The Ethiopian Art Players and the Nordic Complex." *Messenger*, 5(7), July 1923, pp. 774–775, 777.

Henderson, Mary C. *Theatre in America*. New York: Abrams, pp. 269–270.

"How Colored Players in Serious Drama Are Received on Broadway." *New York Amsterdam News*, 16 May 1923.

Jackson, Wallace. "The Theatre: Drama." *Messenger*, 5(6), June 1923, pp. 746–748.

Johnson, James Weldon. *Black Manhattan*. New York: Da Capo, 1958, pp. 190–191.

Leiter, Samuel L., ed. *The Encyclopedia of the New York Stage, 1920–1930*. 1985, Vol. 1, pp. 145; Vol. 2, p. 793, note 2.

"Notable Cast in 'Salome.'" *New York Amsterdam News*, 18 April 1923, p. 5.

Peterson, Bernard L. Jr. *Early Black American Playwrights and Dramatic Writers: A Biographical Directory and Catalog of Plays, Films, and Broadcasting Scripts*. Westport, Conn.: Greenwood, 1990, pp. 165–169.

———. *Profiles of African American Stage Performers and Theatre People, 1816–1960*. Westport, Conn.: Greenwood, 2001, pp. 212–214.

"Salome Scores at Lafayette." *New York Amsterdam News*, 25 April 1923, p. 5.

Woll, Allen. *Dictionary of the Black Theatre*. Westport, Conn.: Greenwood, 1983, pp. 42–43, 243–244.

Europe and the Harlem Renaissance: 1—Overview

As its most common name suggests, the flowering of African American culture in the 1920s and early 1930s has usually been seen as centered in Harlem. Harlem was indeed of central importance to the Harlem Renaissance, but from the start, the movement was also tied to developments in Europe.

In the preface to the March 1925 issue of *Survey Graphic*, Alain Locke compares the growing cultural identity of African Americans to the rise of new, independent nations in Europe in the early twentieth century: "Harlem has the same role to play for the New Negro as Dublin has had for the New Ireland or Prague for the New Czechoslovakia." He is optimistic about Harlem's role as the center of an emerging political and cultural identity, like Dublin or Prague, "those nascent centers of folk-expression and self-determination." An even more significant connection between Harlem and Europe began with the entry of the United States into World War I. Many historians and literary critics cite the participation of black soldiers in this war as a stimulus for the Harlem Renaissance. Black soldiers wondered what a victory against oppression in Europe would mean for their own lives back in the still largely segregated United States. Once home, they marched down Fifth Avenue in protest against a segregated military; the spirit of the demonstration is recorded in W. E. B. Du Bois's essay "Returning Soldiers" (1919).

Numerous minor connections between the Harlem Renaissance and specific European countries can also be traced. In Germany, for example, some citizens who were opposed to the Nazi regime cultivated a taste for jazz and other forms of black art. Two leading intellectuals of the Harlem Renaissance, Alain Locke and W. E. B. Du Bois, studied at Humboldt University in Berlin; and the German artist Winold Reiss drew the illustrations for the special issue of *Survey Graphic*, including the cover image of Ronald Hayes, a singer who first rose to fame in Europe between 1921 and 1923, and then gained prominence in the United States. Claude McKay and the singer and actor Paul Robeson lived and worked for some time in England, and from there Nancy Cunard compiled an important anthology, *Negro* (1934). The most substantial connections to the Harlem Renaissance, however, are found in France and the Soviet Union.

Langston Hughes's autobiography, *The Big Sea* (1940), offers an extended meditation on the position of the African American in the United States and abroad. Hughes frequently contrasts his experiences with racial segregation in the United States to the more liberal modes of interaction in Europe and records intimate interactions between whites and blacks in France that would have been nearly impossible at that time in many parts of the United States. Some of the most glowing praise for France is found in Countee Cullen's poem "To France" (1935); the French people and culture, Cullen writes, "most have made me feel that freedom's rays / Still have a shrine where they may leap and sear." The poem implies that the project of racial equality has failed in the United States. However, African Americans were not treated as true equals in France. France still had its colonies, and black Americans who were not intellectuals or artists were easily grouped with Algerian laborers and thus not warmly welcomed. Hughes records this bias as he tells of his search for a job in Paris. Even there, his opportunities for employment were limited. A group of "colored musicians" told him: "There're plenty of French people for ordinary work. 'Less you can play jazz or tap dance, you'd just as well go back home."

Black artists able to "play jazz or tap dance," however, could often make a career of it. Josephine Baker is the best known of the African American performers who helped create *le tumulte noir*, the Parisian craze for African American music and dance in the mid-1920s. In prints designed by the French artist Paul Colin, Baker is famously portrayed wearing a skirt of palm leaves or yellow bananas. These illustrations reflect the French public's treatment of the black American performer as the exotic other; this fetishizing, however, was already implicit in much of the writing by Harlem Renaissance artists (see, for example, the Harlem poems of McKay and Hughes).

A parallel craze for the African American intellectual and artist was developing in the Soviet Union. Here, darker skin tones were also often fetishized, but the people of the Soviet Union in some ways played down racial difference and understood African Americans' drive for equality and self-determination in the United States more in terms of a shared class struggle. Many black artists were eager to visit the young Soviet Union. In the early 1920s, McKay spent several years there. He records an enthusiastic reception in the packed streets of Moscow in November 1922, but he shrewdly realizes that the welcome was not directed toward him as an individual: "I was welcomed thus as a symbol, as a member of the great American Negro group—kin to the unhappy black slaves of European Imperialism in Africa—that the workers in Soviet Russia, rejoicing in their freedom, were greeting through me." The twenty-two African Americans traveling to Moscow in 1932 to star in *Black and White*, a Soviet film on race and labor relations in the United States, received a similarly enthusiastic but problematic reception. The unsuccessful project was plagued by problems, including poor planning and a script so at odds with the realities of life in the United States that Langston Hughes—as he writes in his autobiography, *I Wonder as I Wander* (1959)—found it "improbable to the point of ludicrousness." Louise Thompson Patterson records that their hosts in the Soviet Union were extremely hospitable yet disappointed: Many of the educated black Americans making the journey did not seem dark enough and "didn't square with their concept of working class folk."

Although figures of the Harlem Renaissance traveled to Europe and attained a popularity abroad that often surpassed what they achieved in the United States, the European prejudice toward black Americans often limited the ways in which these artists and intellectuals were able to express themselves. Particularly in France, however, many ideas of the Harlem Renaissance did take root, and these ideas soon spread to other areas of the globe. A significant international legacy of the Harlem Renaissance is found among the key figures of the *négritude* movement. Three black poets who had been students together in Paris in the 1930s—Léopold Senghor (a president of Senegal), Aimé Césaire (a Martinican poet and statesman), and Léon Gontran-Damas (of French Guiana)—all mention Hughes and McKay as principal influences on them.

The Harlem Renaissance, in short, was not only about Harlem. Its limitations as well as its successes extended to Europe and beyond.

JAMES B. KELLEY

See also Baker, Josephine; Black and White; Césaire, Aimé; Cullen, Countee; Damas, Léon; Du Bois, W. E. B.;

343

Hayes, Roland; Hughes, Langston; Locke, Alain; McKay, Claude; Negro: An Anthology; Patterson, Louise Thompson; Senghor, Léopold; Survey Graphic; Reiss, Winold; Robeson, Paul

Further Reading

Blake, Jody. *Le Tumulte Noir: Modernist Art and Popular Entertainment in Jazz-Age Paris, 1900–1930*. University Park: Pennsylvania State University Press, 2003.

Cunard, Nancy, ed. *Negro: An Anthology*. London: Nancy Cunard with Wishart, 1934.

Hughes, Langston. *The Big Sea*. New York: Knopf, 1940.

———. *I Wonder as I Wander*. New York: Rinehart, 1959.

Lewis, David Levering, ed. *The Portable Harlem Renaissance Reader*. New York: Penguin, 1994.

Locke, Alain. "Harlem." *Survey Graphic*, 6(6), 1925.

Maxwell, William J. *New Negro, Old Left: African-American Writing and Communism between the Wars*. New York: Columbia University Press, 1999.

McKay, Claude. "Soviet Russia and the Negro." *Crisis*, 27, 1923–1924.

Patterson, Louise Thompson. "With Langston Hughes in the USSR." In *The Portable Harlem Renaissance Reader*, ed. David Levering Lewis. New York: Penguin, 1995.

Stovall, Tyler. *Paris Noir: African Americans in the City of Light*. Boston, Mass.: Houghton Mifflin, 1996.

Europe and the Harlem Renaissance: 2—Berlin

Although the Harlem Renaissance was a distinctly national phenomenon, it also crossed national borders, absorbing transnational influences and spreading its own creative message. Paris, so popular with white artists of the 1920s, has already been explored by scholars as a favorite place of writers of the renaissance, but the links of Berlin and Germany to the movement, less prominent and obvious, have not received much attention.

The connection between the Harlem Renaissance and Berlin began before the actual start of the renaissance. In October 1892, W. E. B. Du Bois, who was to become a leading figure of the renaissance, arrived in Berlin to seek a doctorate in economics, supported by a fellowship from the Slater Fund. Du Bois, then age twenty-four, began his studies at the Friedrich-Wilhelm III Universität at Berlin, generally known as the University of Berlin, one of Europe's most highly reputed universities. Germany was ruled by Kaiser Wilhelm II, and Berlin, as its capital, had a distinct Prussian style, so that Du Bois received an impression of military regimentation and obedience. Du Bois was fascinated by German culture. He had admired Goethe and Schiller even before coming to Berlin, and once there, he dedicated much of his spare time to the German classics. In September 1893, he recommended that students at Fisk University study European culture and Goethe's works in order to accelerate African Americans' uplift. Du Bois's German tutors left a strong impression on him, influencing his social and political outlook, which was fundamental to his role within the Harlem Renaissance. Taught by such famous professors as Gustav von Schmoller, Adolf Wagner, Heinrich von Treitschke, and Max Weber, Du Bois was guided in the direction of elitism; Wagner and von Schmoller, in particular, taught their vision of the top ranks of Prussian bureaucracy guiding the guardian state. From Weber, Du Bois acquired strong sociological skills, and it was also in Berlin that Du Bois developed a sense of leadership.

Alain Locke, another leader of the Harlem Renaissance, also enrolled at the University of Berlin. As the first African American Rhodes scholar, he had studied at Oxford University for three years before moving on to Berlin in 1910 for another year of studying philosophy. Although he arrived almost a decade later than Du Bois, Locke seems to have been inspired by the same intellectual ideas current in Berlin. Du Bois's later concept of the "talented tenth"—an educated African American elite that was to represent all African Americans and eventually elevate the race—seems to be directly connected to this strain in Berlin. Locke also clearly subscribed to the concept of the talented tenth, and it profoundly shaped the Harlem Renaissance movement.

Berlin also offered something very different: African art and culture. The Austrian Felix von Luschan became assistant director of the Museum für Völkerkunde in Berlin in 1885. Within a few years, he built up an extensive collection of African and especially Benin art, superior in size and quality to that of any other European museum. By highlighting the value of African art through his scientific appraisal, Luschan contributed greatly to the "discovery" of African art in Europe—a significant fact for the Harlem Renaissance.

Locke was aware of Luschan's work, and during the renaissance era he frequently focused on African art, presenting it as part of a highly valuable cultural heritage. Thus a redefinition of African art and, consequently, a foundation for the appreciation of African American art in the United States occurred through Europe.

Another indirect link between Berlin and the Harlem Renaissance is evident in the person of Rudolf Virchow, a scientist, anthropologist, and politician who taught at the University of Berlin and was its rector during Du Bois's stay in Berlin. Virchow also taught the anthropologist Franz Boas, whose scientific battle against racism was familiar to the participants in the Harlem Renaissance and significantly influenced the attitudes of the contemporary white publishing establishment. Zora Neale Hurston, one of the most prominent women of the renaissance, studied anthropology under Boas, concentrating on folklore.

Berlin also had an emotional impact on the Harlem Renaissance. When Du Bois returned to the United States from Berlin in1894, he had experienced a great disappointment: His grant from the Slater Fund had not been renewed, and as a result he had not earned his doctorate. Nevertheless, his stay in Berlin and his travels in Germany had a positive effect, similar to that documented by other African Americans who traveled to France. Du Bois noted, on his twenty-sixth birthday, that in Berlin he "felt free from most of those iron bands that bound me at home. Therefore, I have gained for my life work new hope and zeal—the Negro people shall yet stand among the honored of the world" (quoted in Lewis 1993, 145). In Berlin, the "veil of race" was, if only temporarily, lifted.

Locke, too, had felt liberated in Europe, not only because of the absence of racial constraints but also because, as a gay man, he apparently felt sexually liberated. Europe offered more sexual freedom than the United States even though homosexual contacts were against the law in Germany and England; and in Berlin and at Oxford, Locke joined well-structured homosexual subcultures. As is evident from Locke's correspondence with his friend C. Henry Dickerman, Berlin offered numerous opportunities for casual same-sex contacts. Locke clearly fell in love with Germany and Berlin, and throughout the 1920s he returned regularly not only to Berlin but also to other places, such as Dresden, admiring the culture, enjoying intimate friendships with numerous Germans with whom he corresponded intensely, and also using the renowned health resorts.

However, younger writers of the Harlem Renaissance reacted less favorably to Berlin and Germany. Locke attempted to persuade Countee Cullen (whom he guided along the path to gay self-discovery) to visit Germany and partake of the *Wandervogel* movement, which was well-known for its homosexual undercurrents. The planned trip never materialized, but Cullen eventually arrived in Berlin in 1929, when he had a Guggenheim fellowship for studies in Paris. Although Paris certainly was a better place for meeting fellow Americans, Berlin could also offer chance encounters, and Cullen ran into Marcus Garvey there. Cullen, like Du Bois, received an impression of Berlin as "an orderly, clean, regimented city, as if on dress parade" (1929, 119); otherwise, Cullen seems to have been largely unimpressed by the city.

Claude McKay, who first came to Berlin in the autumn of 1922, had an impression of wealth and stylishness. When he returned in 1923, however, the situation had changed dramatically: The Ruhr area was occupied by French soldiers as a consequence of provisions in the Versailles peace treaty, and inflation was skyrocketing. McKay had apparently been warned against returning to Germany because of allegations that black French soldiers on the Rhine had committed atrocities, and although he emphasized that he did not experience any form of racial hostility but was treated in a friendly way, Berlin seemed to have an atmosphere of depression, bitterness, and hostility. It thus seems fitting that McKay's poem "Berlin" conveys an image of a cold, harsh city. McKay stayed only from summer to autumn 1923 and then left Berlin for Paris.

Langston Hughes visited Berlin for only one night, in June 1932. He was on his way to the Soviet Union, where he, Louise Thompson Patterson, Dorothy West, and nineteen other African Americans were to take part in a movie about white supremacy in the southern United States. Hughes's impression of Berlin, although he only caught a glimpse of it, was one of misery and despair. Whereas the older generation of the Harlem Renaissance had been fascinated by Berlin, and more generally by German culture, the younger writers experienced a different place, with an atmosphere created by political and economic changes.

In Germany, despite these visits, little attention was paid to the initial development of the Harlem Renaissance. However, toward the middle to late 1920s African Americans began to be noticed in Germany. In 1925, a troupe called the Chocolate Kiddies performed in Berlin, followed by Josephine Baker and Louis Douglas in Nelson's theater. In 1927, Ruth Bayton, an associate of Josephine Baker and Florence Mills (who were at that point engaged in Paris and London), performed in Berlin. Moreover, several plays with African American themes were produced in Berlin in 1929. Literature about or by African Americans was also "discovered" in the late 1920s. In 1927, Carl Van Vechten's sensational novel *Nigger Heaven* was translated and serialized in the *Frankfurter Zeitung*. The book had been a best-seller a year earlier in the United States, and its exoticism and alluring themes—African Americans, Harlem, love, jealousy, sex—could be expected to interest German readers. *Nigger Heaven*, however, was not the type of literature that Locke wanted Europeans to become aware of. In a letter to Paul Huldermann of the *Deutsche Allgemeine Zeitung*, a major German newspaper published in Berlin, Locke described Van Vechten's novel as an appetizer and expressed a wish that more serious issues and works would be offered to German readers. Locke published two major articles about African Americans in Huldermann's newspaper in 1929, introducing Berliners and Germans in general to the Harlem Renaissance movement. As is evident from their correspondence, Huldermann also asked Locke for poems of the Harlem Renaissance, to be printed in a magazine produced by the major publishing house Ullstein. Apparently, Fischer Verlag, another major German publishing company, had considered translating Locke's seminal work *The New Negro*, although it eventually gave up the plan because of the work's length. Huldermann and Locke intended to publish a thinner version of *The New Negro*—tentatively called *Schwarzes Amerika* ("Black America")—specifically for a European audience. Huldermann also published articles on African Americans and planned to include this subject in a series of radio addresses in January and February 1929, but it remains unclear whether these projects were realized.

Around the same time, other figures of the Harlem Renaissance were approached by Germans and particularly Austrians who wanted to translate and publish their works. In fact, Jessie Redmon Fauset's novel *There Is Confusion* (1924) had evidently been translated into German by an unnamed Austrian the same year it was published, although her case was exceptional. In 1927, Countee Cullen was approached by an Austrian, Marie Murland, who asked for permission to translate some of Cullen's poems in order to publish them in German newspapers such as the *Berliner Tägliche Rundschau*; and in 1931, James Weldon Johnson was asked for permission to translate his *Autobiography of an Ex-Colored Man*. Johnson had to decline because the

Autobiography had already been translated in 1928; and it is not clear that these works were eventually published in Germany. Anna Nussbaum of Vienna did collect and translate poetry of the Harlem Renaissance with the permission of the authors, and in 1929, she published the anthology *Afrika Singt*. These efforts to introduce a German or German-speaking reading public to works of the Harlem Renaissance are impressive, but they apparently failed commercially: As Amy Spingarn informed James Weldon Johnson in 1930, *Afrika Singt* sold poorly, indicating a lack of interest in the literature of the renaissance.

In contrast to Paris, Berlin usually represented not much more than a stopover for the younger generation of the Harlem Renaissance. Still, the impact of Berlin, and of Germany, on the intellectual foundation of the movement and on the influential older figures who led the Harlem Renaissance should not be overlooked.

CHRISTA SCHWARTZ

See also Baker, Josephine; Boas, Franz; Cullen, Countee; Du Bois, W. E. B.; Garvey, Marcus; Homosexuality; Hughes, Langston; Hurston, Zora Neale; Fauset, Jessie Redmon; Johnson, James Weldon; Locke, Alain; McKay, Claude; Mills, Florence; Talented Tenth; There Is Confusion; Van Vechten, Carl; West, Dorothy

Further Reading

Alain Locke Papers. Moorland-Spingarn Research Center, Howard University, Washington, D.C.

Cooper, Wayne F. *Claude McKay: Rebel Sojourner in the Harlem Renaissance—A Biography*. New York: Schocken, 1990.

Cullen, Countee. "Countee Cullen to His Friends." *Opportunity*, April 1929.

Du Bois, W. E. B. "The Talented Tenth." In *Negro Protest Thought in the Twentieth Century*, ed. Francis L. Broderick and August Meier. Indianapolis, Ind.: Bobbs, 1965. (First published 1903.)

———. *The Autobiography of W. E. B. Du Bois: A Soliloquy on Viewing My Life From the Last Decade of Its First Century*. New York: International, 1968.

Fauset, Jessie. *There Is Confusion*. New York: Boni and Liveright, 1924.

Irek, Malgorzata. "From Berlin to Harlem: Felix von Luschan, Alain Locke, and the New Negro." In *The Black Columbiad: Defining Moments in African American Literature and Culture*, ed. Werner Sollors and Maria

Diedrich. Cambridge, Mass., and London: Harvard University Press, 1994.

———. "The European Roots of the Harlem Renaissance." *Berliner Beiträge zur Amerikanistik*, 1, 1994.

Johnson, James Weldon. *The Autobiography of an Ex-Coloured Man*. New York: Knopf, 1927. (Originally published 1912.)

Lewis, David Levering. *W. E. B. Du Bois: Biography of a Race, 1868–1919*. New York: Holt, 1993.

Locke, Alain. "The Art of the Ancestors." *Survey Graphic*, Harlem Number, March 1925.

McKay, Claude. *A Long Way From Home*. New York: Harcourt, 1970. (Originally published 1937.)

———. "Berlin." N.d. Claude McKay Papers, James Weldon Johnson Memorial Collection, Beinecke Rare Book and Manuscript Library, Yale University.

Nussbaum, Anna, ed. *Afrika Singt*. Vienna and Leipzig: Speidel, 1929.

Rampersad, Arnold. *The Life of Langston Hughes, Vol. 1, 1902–1941: I, Too, Sing America*. New York: Oxford University Press, 1988.

Van Vechten, Carl. *Nigger Heaven*. New York: Knopf, 1926.

Europe and the Harlem Renaissance: 3—London

As Europe's largest and most cosmopolitan city, London had attracted African Americans since the nineteenth century. The wealth of shared traditions, the many cultural ties, and the absence of a language barrier prompted a continuous migration of black Americans to London, which was home to the largest African-descended population outside of Africa before Harlem became the "capital of the black world" in the 1920s. London's black community consisted of immigrants and expatriates from Africa, the United States, and the West Indies. For many black American artists, writers, and performers, the city served as a hub before they moved on to Paris and other European locales. Black activists and intellectuals came to London, where they could exchange ideas with thinkers from different origins in the black diaspora.

Of course, London was not immune to racism. England's growing black migrant population experienced economic hardships and pervasive discrimination. During World War I, a shortage of white laborers temporarily shifted manufacturing jobs to blacks, but these blacks later found themselves in a worse economic situation as prewar conditions returned in 1918. The following year brought race riots in several cities. As a result, blacks founded the League of Coloured Peoples (LCP) in 1931, advocating social and legal change to improve their living conditions in Britain.

The significance of London to the Harlem Renaissance era lies in (1) its abolitionist heritage and anti-slavery traditions, which helped shape the political aspirations of blacks in the early twentieth century; (2) its function as a crossroads of black communities from Africa, the Caribbean, and the United States; (3) its vibrant cultural life and political traditions, which nurtured intellectual experimentation; and (4) its complex and often contradictory strands of the colonial legacy and progressive traditions, which both encouraged and hindered black emancipation. In short, London can be seen as "an important junction point or crossroads on the webbed pathways of black Atlantic political culture" (Gilroy 1993).

London's first Pan-African Congress in 1900 marked the beginning of universal black political agendas. Seeking to unite people of African descent in their shared pursuit of racial equality and political emancipation, the conferences generated a sizable pan-African presence in London. By the 1920s, prominent black figures in London included Jomo Kenyatta and Kwame Nkrumah from Africa; Aimé Césaire, C. L. R. James, and Marcus Garvey from the Caribbean; and Paul Robeson and many others from the United States.

For the American sociologist and historian W. E. B. Du Bois, London became closely associated with his lifelong commitment to pan-African causes. He participated in London's Pan-African Conference, which first introduced the term "pan-African." As a participant in and co-organizer of related events in London, such as the First Universal Races Congress (1911) and the subsequent Pan-African Conferences in 1919, 1923, and 1927, Du Bois gained critical insights into the continuing impact of colonialism on the black diaspora. Exchanges with other delegates allowed him to review his theories of black emancipation in a transnational context.

London also figured as a politically transformative place for the black nationalist leader Marcus Garvey, who lived and studied there between 1912 and 1914. In London, Garvey met Duse Mohamed Ali, a Sudanese-Egyptian actor, writer, and publisher who had launched pioneering black newspapers in London. Duse introduced Garvey to other Africans, thus providing opportunities for exchange of political ideas in

347

the context of the diaspora. Garvey's experiences in London inspired him to found the Universal Negro Improvement Association (UNIA) in his native Jamaica and later to establish branches in Harlem. During the brief success of his nationalist movement, Garvey hired Duse as a foreign affairs specialist for his own newspaper, *Negro World*.

London's vibrant cultural scene attracted leading artists, musicians, and performers of the Harlem Renaissance. The philosopher Alain Locke had a special connection to England: Support from the Quakers had enabled his grandfather Ishmael to study at Cambridge University. Locke spent time in London when he was the first African American Rhodes scholar to study at Oxford University, between 1907 and 1910. Claude McKay lived in Europe from 1919 to 1921, and then again from 1923 to 1934. During his first sojourn in London, McKay became involved with the communist movement, although he later abandoned this position. In literature, as in other areas of the Harlem Renaissance, texts were not created exclusively by African Americans; in this respect, the British socialite Nancy Cunard deserves mention for compiling and editing the illustrated anthology *Negro* in 1934.

Although London never had an artists' quarter like Montparnasse in Paris, it did become an important gateway for black American artists on their way to the continent. During the nineteenth century, black artists gravitated toward Britain, whose abolitionist groups had supported visits and grand tours by artists such as Robert M. Douglass Jr., Robert S. Duncanson, and Edmonia Lewis. For decades, London continued to serve as a first contact point with Europe for African American artists as they traveled to Paris, Rome, and other artistic centers. The painter Henry Ossawa Tanner, the sculptor Meta Warrick Fuller, the printmaker Albert Alexander Smith, and others passed through London, where they encountered artists from other countries. The British-born sculptor Edna Manley studied art in London before moving to Jamaica in 1922; in Kingston, she created works that would be exhibited in Britain from 1929 onward. Similarly, the Jamaican sculptor Ronald C. Moody exhibited at British galleries in 1935 and 1937. A Londoner, the white painter and stage designer Edward Burra spent almost a year in New York in 1933–1934, creating lasting impressions of Harlem street life.

During the 1910s and 1920s, London was a center for the dissemination of ragtime and early jazz in Europe, as African Americans came to London during World War I and afterward. The Original Dixieland Jazz Band toured England as early as 1919. For the bandleader and composer James Reese Europe, London became a springboard to France, where his 369th "Hellfighters" Infantry Band introduced military and civilian audiences to early jazz. At the same time, Will Marion Cook's Southern Syncopated Orchestra had many successes in London, including a performance at Buckingham Palace. Several members of Cook's band remained in London, Paris, Berlin, and other European locales; influential figures from his group included Sidney Bechet, Arthur Briggs, and Benny Peyton. Bechet spent formative years of his career in London between 1919 and 1923 and again after 1925, when he joined Josephine Baker and Louis Douglas in the wildly successful *Revue Nègre* in Paris. The itineraries of many jazz revues reveal that engagements in London often marked the starting point of larger European tours.

As black musicians brought jazz to London, they nourished an emerging local jazz culture during the 1920s. This influence became evident in the original jazz criticism of the English double bass player, composer, and writer Spike Hughes. Similarly, the English trumpeter, singer, and bandleader Nathaniel "Nat" Gonella was inspired by Louis Armstrong, who performed to enthusiastic audiences in London between 1932 and 1935.

American dancers and other entertainers were also successful in London. Many stars who had made their name in Noble Sissle's production of *Shuffle Along* in New York became even more famous in London: They included Florence Mills, Ethel Waters, and Adelaide Hall. Mills, a dancer and singer, had some of her most significant successes at London's Pavilion Theater, where she had already been acclaimed for her appearance in *Blackbirds* (1926). Hall, a scat singer, joined Sam Wooding's *Chocolate Kiddies* in 1925 for a tour of London and other European cities; by 1934, she and her husband, Willie Hicks, settled permanently in London, where they opened a nightclub. Paul Robeson made his London stage debut in 1922, in a production of *Taboo*; his subsequent engagements included leading roles in Eugene O'Neill's *The Emperor Jones* in 1924 and *Show Boat* in 1928. Robeson's experience in London is representative of that of many other African Americans: It gave him new political perspectives on historical interconnections. Other African Americans for whom London became synonymous with professional accomplishment included Lawrence Brown, Roland Hayes, and Marian Anderson. For them, London's wealth of professional opportunities often resulted in groundbreaking successes that eventually led to recognition at home as well.

Although Harlem became the world's new "black capital" in the 1920s, London remained an essential site of cultural production for the Harlem Renaissance. Either despite or because of its contradictory blend of colonial legacies and emancipatory traditions, London continued to attract black artists, writers, musicians, philosophers, and thinkers from different points of origin in the diaspora. Thus London during the time of the Harlem Renaissance anticipated much of the energy and spirit of London today, which is and always has been a multiethnic metropolis.

JÜRGEN HEINRICHS

See also Ali, Duse Mohamed; Anderson, Marian; Armstrong, Louis; Bechet, Sidney; Césaire, Aimé; Cook, Will Marion; Cunard, Nancy; Du Bois, W. E. B.; Europe, James Reese; Fuller, Meta Warrick; Garvey, Marcus; Hall, Adelaide; Hayes, Roland; Mills, Florence; Pan-African Congresses; Pan-Africanism; Robeson, Paul; Tanner, Henry Ossawa; Waters, Ethel

Further Reading

Gilroy, Paul. *The Black Atlantic: Modernity and Double Consciousness.* Cambridge, Mass.: Harvard University Press, 1993.

Leininger-Miller, Theresa. *New Negro Artists in Paris: African American Painters and Sculptors in the City of Light, 1922–1934.* New Brunswick, N.J.: Rutgers University Press, 2001.

Powell, Richard J., and David A. Bailey. *Rhapsodies in Black: Art of the Harlem Renaissance.* London and Berkeley: Hayward Gallery, University of California Press, 1997.

Rappolt, Mark, ed. "London: Postcolonial City." *AA Files,* 49, Spring 2003. (Special issue, Architectural Association, London.)

Schwarz, Bill. "Black Metropolis, White England." In *Modern Times: Reflections on a Century of English Modernity,* ed. Mica Nava and Alan O'Shea. London: Routledge, 1996, pp. 176–207.

Simon, Zoltan. "From Lenox Avenue to the Charlottenburg Palace: The Construction of the Image of Europe by Harlem Renaissance Authors." *British and American Studies,* 4(2), 1999, pp. 105–112.

Stephens, Michelle A. "Black Transnationalism and the Politics of National Identity: West Indian Intellectuals in Harlem in the Age of War and Revolution." *American Quarterly,* 50(3), September 1998, pp. 592–608.

Europe and the Harlem Renaissance: 4—Paris

By the time of the Harlem Renaissance, Paris had already been a cultural magnet for white Americans for centuries, symbolizing their European origins. African Americans were not entirely excluded from this contact. The story of Sally Hemings' sojourn there with Thomas Jefferson in the eighteenth century is well documented. During the nineteenth century the black Shakespearean actor Ira Aldridge toured France, and prominent blacks such as Frederick Douglass and Booker T. Washington visited Paris. The sculptor Meta Warrick Fuller (1877–1968) studied in Paris from 1899 to 1903, working with Auguste Rodin. In 1900, W. E. B. Du Bois organized an exhibition at the World Exposition in Paris to demonstrate "the history of the American Negro, his present condition, his education, and his literature." A few black entertainers, including Belle Davis, Louis Douglas, Will Garland, Ida Forsyne, and Ollie Burgoyne, also found their way to Paris in the early years of the twentieth century.

However, it was predominantly through World War I that black Americans discovered Paris as a haven of racial tolerance. The warm welcome that greeted black American troops in France made a lasting impression. It would be simplistic to suggest that France was free of racial and cultural prejudice; however, the French did not have the rigid notions regarding skin color that prevailed in the Anglo-Saxon tradition, and especially in America. The idea that it was possible to interact with white Europeans on an equal basis came as a culture shock—a pleasant one—to many black Americans, so much so that some actually stayed on, including the historian Rayford Logan and Eugene Bullard. Bullard had become the first black military aviator by joining the French forces and went on to become manager and part-owner of a popular nightspot, Le Grand Duc.

A more specific cultural impact came from contact between French musicians and their counterparts in black military bands, such as James Reese Europe's 369th Infantry Band (the Harlem Hellfighters) and Tim Brymn's 350th U. S. A. Artillery Band. Bands such as these entertained troops around France, amazing

French musicians with their ability to produce strange "jazz" effects from their instruments.

Encouraged by their welcome, many black musicians returned to Paris after the war. By 1918 Louis Mitchell and His Jazz Kings were established at the Casino de Paris. Other arrivals included the sensational drummer Buddy Gilmore and the trumpeter Arthur Briggs. Briggs came to Europe in 1919 with Will Marion Cook's Southern Syncopated Orchestra, which also included Sidney Bechet and the young classical genius Edmund Thornton Jenkins. Jenkins settled in Paris in 1922 and died there in 1926 at the early age of thirty-two. In 1923, Palmer Jones and his wife, the singer Florence Embry Jones, were featured at Le Grand Duc until Florence joined Louis Mitchell's new club, named—after her—Chez Florence. In 1924, Bricktop arrived to replace Florence at Le Grand Duc, staying on to become a Parisian legend for many years. In 1925, Josephine Baker arrived as part of the *Revue Nègre* to become the toast of Paris. In Bricktop's words, "Paris was having its own version of the Harlem Renaissance. It was called *le tumulte noir*."

These entertainers and musicians brought jazz-based dance music, with overtones of ragtime and blues. The classical conductor Ernest Ansermet's perceptive reviews of the Southern Syncopated Orchestra marked the origin of serious appreciation of jazz as an art form. Important French critics like Hugues Panassie and Charles Delaunay, and the Belgian Robert Goffin, soon followed. The exotic appeal of black jazz for French audiences was augmented by an interest in African art and motifs that had been sparked by artists such as Matisse, Picasso, and Braque.

Although jazz and the nightclubs around Montmartre epitomized black Americans for the Parisians, many African Americans in Paris had only a passing interest, if any, in jazz. Many were artists and writers who had come to soak up the rich heritage of the great galleries and institutions, such as the Louvre and the Sorbonne, and also—as in the case of Aaron Douglas and Palmer Hayden—to study African art. Paris offered an important symbolic link, with its physical proximity to Africa and contacts with French-speaking Africans from the colonies. In 1919, W. E. B. Du Bois organized the first Pan-African Congress in Paris, with fifty-seven delegates from fifteen nations and colonies, and sixteen African Americans. In 1921, when the second congress held one of its sessions in Paris, the writers Jessie Redmon Fauset and Walter White accompanied Du Bois.

Fauset had studied at the Sorbonne in 1914, becoming sufficiently fluent in French that she was asked to translate *Batouala*, a novel by the African writer René Maran; however, although this novel had won the Goncourt Prize, Fauset considered it inappropriate for her image. Fauset returned for another six months in 1924, and (as noted above) she had also attended the session of the Pan-African Congress in Paris in 1921. Her own novel *Plum Bun* was written in Paris.

Other blacks who lived in Paris were businesspeople or students who were happy to temporarily escape from segregation at home. Throughout the 1920s there was a steady procession of African Americans coming to Paris, some merely as tourists or for short stays, others for extended periods. In addition to Fauset, a surprising number of significant writers and artists of the Harlem Renaissance stayed in Paris for at least some months, as if on a pilgrimage. Claude McKay arrived in 1923 from Russia and spent many years in France, much of the time in the provinces; his novel *Banjo* is set in Marseilles. Langston Hughes arrived in 1924; he was told that he was wasting his time if he didn't play an instrument or tap dance, but he did get a job as a busboy at Le Grand Duc, with the help of Rayford Logan. Jean Toomer came in 1924 and again in 1926, becoming a disciple of the mystic philosopher Gurdjieff. Countee Cullen visited in 1926 and for a longer period in 1928–1929. Gwendolyn Bennett lived in the Latin Quarter during part of 1925–1926. J. A. Rogers did research for his book *Sex and Race* and lectured on anthropology at the Sorbonne in 1929. Other transient writers included Alain Locke (1927); Walter White (1927), negotiating a translation of his *Fire in the Flint*; Eric Walrond (1929); and Nella Larsen (1931).

Paris, of course, attracted African American painters. Henry Ossawa Tanner came as early as 1891; he lived and worked in Paris for most of the rest of his life and was awarded the French Legion of Honor in 1923. Many notable artists followed him. Laura Wheeler Waring studied expressionism and the Romantics at the Académie de la Grande Chaumière, a popular Parisian workshop and studio, in 1924. William Henry Johnson arrived in Paris in the autumn of 1926 and had a studio in Montparnasse; he returned to New York in late 1929. Hale Woodruff was inspired to go to Paris (where he would stay until 1931) by hearing stories of Henry Ossawa Tanner, who helped him get started there. Palmer Hayden received a grant to study in

Paris at the École des Beaux-Arts; he stayed until 1932. After winning a Guggenheim fellowship, Archibald Motley left for Paris in 1929, returning to Chicago in 1930. Aaron Douglas started a year's study at the Académie Scandinave in 1931. Lois Mailou Jones came just before World War II; she had a scholarship from Howard University to study at the Académie Julian during the school year 1937–1938.

Sculptors were also attracted to Paris, in the footsteps of Meta Warrick Fuller. One of the first after Fuller was Nancy Elizabeth Prophet, in 1922. Prophet's work was exhibited at the August Salon in Paris from 1924–1927 and at the Salon d'Automne in 1931 and 1932. Augusta Savage almost came to Paris in 1923, but, on racial grounds, she was denied the scholarship she had won. She finally arrived in 1929, having won a Julius Rosenwald fellowship that gave her an opportunity to study in Paris for one year. She stayed until 1931.

Although jazz and popular music dominated the black musical scene in Paris, there was also classical music. Edmund Thornton Jenkins was a resident composer and performer, and there were occasional recitals by notables such as Roland Hayes, Paul Robeson, and Marian Anderson. Some black classical performers found it easier to gain acceptance in France than in the United States: These included Lillian Evanti, who made her debut with the Paris Opera in *Lakmé* in 1925; Caterina Yarboro, who had to establish herself in Europe before obtaining operatic roles at home; and the clarinetist Rudolph Dunbar, who later achieved fame in Europe as a conductor.

The many artists of various disciplines who established temporary residence in Paris did not constitute a close-knit black artistic community, having widely differing aesthetic viewpoints. Their main link was the many clubs and cabarets with black musicians and entertainers. Bricktop always gave a warm welcome to lonely expatriates, as did Florence Embry Jones. Later, Adelaide Hall established her Big Apple nightclub. Josephine Baker established herself as a Parisian institution and made her first French sound film, *Zou Zou*, in 1934.

There was also a continuous stream of black entertainment troupes passing through Paris. Sam Wooding and the *Chocolate Kiddies* came in 1925; Florence Mills came with her *Blackbirds* for four months in 1926; and later versions of Lew Leslie's *Blackbirds* came in 1929, 1934, and 1936. These brought names like the Nicholas Brothers, Adelaide Hall, Valaida Snow, and Edith

Wilson, and first-rate jazz orchestras led by Will Vodery, Noble Sissle, and others. Some of the entertainers would opt to stay on in Paris. Johnny Hudgins had a mime act that became a popular favorite in Paris in the late 1920s, inspiring a short film by Jean Renoir. Valaida Snow was based in Europe for most of the 1930s. By the early 1930s, jazz performers such as Duke Ellington and Louis Armstrong were household names in France. Ellington and Armstrong toured and gave concerts there in 1933–1934; and Ellington's musicians were amazed how seriously the fans took their music—these French fans knew details of earlier recordings that the band members themselves had forgotten.

Although expatriate African Americans enjoyed their ability to interact freely with French people, relationships with traveling white Americans were more mixed. Many white Americans who traveled to Paris were cosmopolitan, with liberal social attitudes. Those who frequented Bricktop's and Chez Florence, like Cole Porter and F. Scott Fitzgerald, enjoyed the company of the black expatriates. Sinclair Lewis befriended Claude McKay; the English aristocrat Nancy Cunard made no secret of her affair with the pianist Henry Crowder and actively promoted contacts between blacks and whites; wealthy white American patrons courted the favors of Florence Embry Jones. For the painter Hale Woodruff, who was in Paris from 1927 to 1931, just knowing that the city was a center for writers such as Hemingway and artists such as Man Ray was exciting even though contact was limited and fortuitous.

However, there were also conservative Americans who reacted indignantly when black Americans were treated as equals. An incident reported in *Variety* had the headline, "Americans Protest at Negro Dancing With White Woman." This had occurred during the intermission of Florence Mills' *Blackbirds* show at the cabaret Les Ambassadeurs in 1926. A black professional dancer was dancing with a Frenchwoman at her husband's request, but the police had to be called to quiet the protesters. In 1927, Jimmy Walker, the mayor of New York, heatedly denied a story, reported in the Baltimore *Afro-American*, that he had behaved similarly in a Parisian cabaret.

By the late 1930s the Depression had taken its toll on the Harlem Renaissance at home, and the onset of fascism and a looming second world war effectively shut down its offshoot in Paris. Josephine Baker stayed on and became a hero of the French resistance;

Valaida Snow left Paris only to wind up in a Nazi detention center in Denmark. Although Paris was soon bereft of its contingent of black and white American expatriates, the memory of its hospitality was not lost. It would blossom again in a postwar black literary scene with figures such as Richard Wright, James Baldwin, and Chester Himes, and Josephine Baker would reclaim her status as a black superstar.

BILL EGAN

See also Artists; Authors: 2—Fiction; Authors: 5—Poets; Batouala; Blackbirds; Fire in the Flint, The; Francophone Africa and the Harlem Renaissance; Guggenheim Fellowships; Literary and Artistic Prizes; Music: Bands and Orchestras; Musicians; Pan-African Congresses; Pan-Africanism; Revue Nègre, La; Rosenwald Fellowships; Visual Arts; *specific artists, writers, and musicians*

Further Reading

"Americans Protest at Negro Dancing With White Woman." *Variety*, 9 June 1926. (For incident at Les Ambassadeurs.)

Andrews, William L., Francis Smith Foster, and Trudier Harris, eds. *The Oxford Companion to African American Literature*. New York and Oxford: Oxford University Press, 1997. (See especially Kenneth R. Janken, "Expatriatism.")

Fabre, Michel. *From Harlem to Paris: Black American Writers in France, 1840–1980*. Champaign: University of Illinois Press, 1991.

Fabre, Michel, and John A. Williams. *A Street Guide to African Americans in Paris*. Paris and Michigan: Belleville Lake Press and Cercle d'études Afro-Americaines, 1992, 1996. (Special edition printed for "April in Paris" Conference on African-American Music and Europe held at the Sorbonne 24–27 April 1996.)

Goddard, Chris. *Jazz Away from Home*. New York and London: Paddington, 1979.

Lotz, Rainer E. *Black People: Entertainers of African Descent in Europe and Germany*. Bonn, Germany: Birgit Lotz Verlag, 1997.

"Mayor Walker Likes Girls Extra White." *Baltimore Afro-American*, 1 October 1927.

Murray, Albert. *Oral History Interview with Hale Woodruff, November 18, 1968*. Smithsonian Archives of American Art, Washington, D.C.

Shack, William A. *Harlem in Montmartre: A Paris Jazz Story between the Great Wars*. Berkeley, Los Angeles, and London: University of California Press, 2001.

Stovall, Tyler. *Paris Noir: African Americans in the City of Light*. Boston, Mass., and New York: Houghton Mifflin, 1996.

Studio Museum in Harlem. *Harlem Renaissance: Art of Black America*. New York: Abradale and Abrams, 1994. (See especially "Chronologies of the Artists," p. 174.)

Europe and the Harlem Renaissance: 5—Soviet Union

Among the most striking features of the quest for cultural identity in the African diaspora in the early twentieth century was the extent to which it entailed travel abroad. Not just coincidentally, Langston Hughes's and Claude McKay's respective autobiographies were called *I Wonder as I Wander* and *A Long Ways from Home*, and the *nègritude* movement—created in the 1930s by African and Caribbean leaders who were directly inspired by the Harlem Renaissance—first emerged in France. It is not surprising, then, that the Harlem Renaissance also manifested itself as far east in Europe as Russia, and that both Hughes and McKay wrote poems about Moscow as well as Harlem. The lofty humanitarian ideals of the experiment in the Soviet Union were attractive to black intellectuals; and although the communist regime officially denounced nationalism of any kind, it actually provided material support to encourage assertion of black cultural identity in the Americas and Africa. The connections between the Soviet Union and the Harlem Renaissance illustrate, particularly, that the renaissance included music, theater, art, and politics as well as literature.

In Russia direct exposure to African American culture actually began at the very start of the twentieth century. For example, the concert singer Coretta Arli-Titz, formerly Coretta Alefred, had a career in Russia that spanned the czarist and Soviet periods. She came to Russia in 1904 as a member of a vaudeville troupe of seven Negro women called the Louisiana Amazon Guards; stayed through the revolution; eventually graduated from the Leningrad and Moscow conservatories of music; became one of the most popular singers in Moscow, performing in four languages, and a successful movie actress; and in the 1930s married a noted professor of music. Marian Anderson, on a tour in the 1930s, visited Arli-Titz. The avant-garde theater director Vsevelod Meyerhold was allowed to include a full jazz band, consisting entirely of Russians, in some of his productions in the early 1920s, although communist ideology required that jazz represent decadence in Meyerhold's plots. A steady stream of entertainment artists toured the Soviet Union, such as the Leland Drayton revue for six months in 1925; and Sam Wooding and his Chocolate Kiddies, featuring thirty-three black American jazz musicians, dancers, and singers, for three months in 1926. Benny Peyton's seven-piece New Orleans Jazz Band, including the saxophonist Sidney Bechet, also visited Russia in 1926.

The reaction of the Russian public to these artists attests to a growing popularity of African American culture, especially jazz, in defiance of the official communist attitude, summed up in Maxim Gorky's description of jazz as "degenerate, bourgeois music." Jazz was considered harmful because it presumably expressed capitalist values and because it celebrated artistic spontaneity and individual freedom, both of which the Soviet regime consistently tried to repress. However, the Soviet authorities acquiesced partly because they were unable to stop it and partly because they wanted to acknowledge this manifestation of African American genius. Several writers of the Harlem Renaissance, such as McKay, Hughes, and Richard Wright, had some of their early work published in communist periodicals. The Soviet government also paid tribute to American Negroes during this period through special awards. For instance, the novelist Arna Bontemps won the Pushkin Prize in 1926; others were elected as honorary members of the Moscow city council; and a mountain was eventually named after Paul Robeson, who first visited Russia in 1934. Although Russian society in general shared the negative stereotypes of blacks prevalent in all Western societies, the Soviet leaders systematically used such honors as propaganda to point out American racial inequality. They even relaxed their usual atheistic censorship to allow Robeson's music, including spirituals such as "Steal Away to Jesus," to be broadcast on Radio Moscow, although with commentary informing the audience that such language at times served as encoded exhortations to slaves to run away.

With directives from Moscow, the American Communist Party was also systematically active in Harlem. A notable black leader in this endeavor was Louise Thompson Patterson, a social worker who was a close friend of Langston Hughes and was briefly married to the novelist Wallace Thurman. In her apartment she held frequent informal gatherings of black artists and intellectuals, as well as specific discussions of the party's position on what was often called the "Negro question." Hughes was persuaded in 1930 to become president of a new party organization in Harlem, the League of Struggle for Negro Rights, that supported the antilynching crusade. In the 1930s, the Communist Party was also active in union organizing among unemployed artists and those working in New Deal relief programs that were constantly under fire from conservatives in the U.S. Congress. These programs included a branch of the Federal Writers' Project; the Harlem Community Art Center; a music project sponsoring orchestras, bands, and music appreciation classes; a puppet show; and an African dance troupe, all under the Works Progress Administration (WPA).

The founding of political schools in the 1920s "to promote universal communist brotherhood" brought a coterie of blacks to Russia, with ten places set aside in 1925–1926 for Africans and black Americans, including two for women, although none came that early. Nearly 100 African Americans would eventually train at these schools. Regarding the political dimensions of the Harlem Renaissance, it is noteworthy that many black artists and writers expressing cultural nationalism were also political figures. A closer look at the touring artists listed above reveals a number who were increasingly drawn into radical politics. One example is Claude McKay, the first prominent black American to visit the Soviet Union. He did so on his own, with no party affiliation, and when he arrived in 1922 he was welcomed as a poet rather than a politician. However, because the lone black American delegate to the fourth Communist International Congress in session there was the very light-complexioned Otto Huiswood, the Soviet leaders wanted McKay, who was very dark, to represent the American Negro to the Russian public. McKay was therefore photographed with the leaders of the Communist International (Comintern) and was introduced to luminaries such as the poet Vladimir Mayakovsky, Leon Trotsky, and V. I. Lenin's wife, Krupskaya, who was representing her mortally ill husband. McKay was also made an honorary member of the Moscow city council and was treated to a brief airplane ride while on an inspection of the Red Army. During several months' stay in Russia, McKay wrote articles and poetry that were published locally, including one reverent homage to Moscow and Lenin entitled "Moscow." The intense, if temporary, appeal of the Soviet dream can be appreciated if one considers the mood of that poem alongside McKay's earlier poem "If We Must Die," a cry of outrage against lynching in America.

McKay was just one of the contributors to the Harlem Renaissance who spent time in Russia as well as Harlem during that era. W. E. B. Du Bois, for one, had been drawn to socialism in the early 1890s, while studying in Germany; publicly expressed socialist sympathies in the first decade of the twentieth century; first visited Russia in 1926; and used a Marxian analytical framework in some of his historical writing, especially in *Black Reconstruction* in the 1930s but also in earlier articles. Du Bois was encouraged by friends such as the reformer Mary White Ovington, a moderate socialist and cofounder of the National Association for the Advancement of Colored People (NAACP).

Otto Huiswood is another example. The grandson of a slave, Huiswood was born in 1893 in Suriname, a part of the Dutch empire. In 1912—like many West Indian and South American black intellectuals in the early twentieth century—he moved to the United States. There he was a trader in tropical products and later a printer in Harlem, and he became involved with American socialist and Negro organizations. One was a group connected to *The Messenger*, an originally socialist monthly established by A. Philip Randolph and Chandler Owen that ran from 1917 to 1928. By 1920, Huiswood was reputed to be the first black member of the American Communist Party; consequently, in 1922, he became a member of the American delegation to the Fourth Comintern Congress. Despite being upstaged by McKay in public appearances, Huiswood also was elected an honorary member of the Moscow city council and had a rare audience with Lenin. In 1927, Huiswood studied at the Lenin School in Moscow, one of the political institutions founded to train elite communist leaders. He became an authority on conditions in the Caribbean region, where he was assigned by Comintern to be the primary organizer. He also succeeded the Trinidadian George Padmore as editor of the Comintern monthly *Negro Worker*. Padmore, another West Indian drawn to New York and then to radical politics, had been the Communist Party's main liaison with black Africa until he was expelled from the party for opposing colonialism, on which the party line was temporarily equivocal. In communist debates over how to address the "Negro question" in America, Huiswood was among a majority of black members who insisted that racial equality was as critical as the class struggle, sometimes noting that racism was a

problem even within the party. This is another instance in which the black consciousness of the Harlem Renaissance period may be seen as influencing Soviet policies.

The Soviet critique of the dominant Western civilization resonated with black intellectuals. Even the usually mild-mannered, good-humored Langston Hughes was inspired at times to bitter musing, as in "Goodbye Christ," written during his travels in Russia in 1932. Hughes had come to Russia as part of a group—including Henry Lee Moon, Ted Poston, and some twenty others—recruited in the United States for *Black and White*, a propaganda film that proved abortive. (Incidentally, during the transatlantic voyage on the ship *Bremen*, some members of this group, traveling in second class, encountered Alain Locke and Ralph Bunche, who were in first class, bound for Paris.) Hughes recounts this project, for which he was hired as a consultant, in detail in his autobiography.

Two members of the *Black and White* project made Russia their home for the rest of their lives and were major contributors to Soviet film. The first was Lloyd Patterson, a graduate of Hampton Institute (1931) who had come seeking adventure. After the project folded, he worked for a time on stage sets at Vsevolod Meyerhold's theater, where he met his future wife, Vera Ippolitovna Aralova, later one of the Soviet Union's leading theatrical costume designers, as well as a celebrated painter. Patterson eventually played minor roles in several films and became a journalist for Radio Moscow. He died during World War II while Moscow was under siege. Lloyd Patterson's son, James ("baby James"), born in Moscow in 1933, became an instant sensation as a child star in the classic Soviet film *Circus* in 1936.

The second veteran of *Black and White* who became a celebrity in the Soviet Union, although he was little known in the United States, was Wayland Rudd. He had been raised by foster parents in Nebraska and had shown early talent as an actor. He preceded Paul Robeson in the role of Othello (which was then rarely played by blacks), at Jasper Deeter's Hedgerow Theatre in Rose Valley, Pennsylvania. There, he also played the lead in *The Emperor Jones*, another role that would later be associated with Robeson. Rudd initially returned home after two years in Russia but then decided to settle in Russia, convinced that Russian directors were much freer to pursue their art than their American counterparts. He attended the Russian State College of Theatrical Arts; graduated as a director;

and won wide popularity with Soviet audiences for roles in such films as *Tom Sawyer*, *Without Prejudice*, and an adaptation by George Grebner of Jules Verne's *Fifteen-Year-Old Captain*. In a letter to Robeson in 1952, Rudd still expressed strong support for the Soviet Union. When Rudd died in 1953, in Moscow, the Union of Soviet Artists accorded him its highest honors; at his funeral, a baritone sang a Russian version of "Deep River."

However, archival materials that have recently become available show that all was not well regarding the attitude of the Soviet Union toward blacks, and that other blacks in Russia made observations directly contradicting flattering accounts such as Rudd's. There is a dramatic report of a protest by African and African American students in the political schools, against racism in artistic productions and other Soviet practices. Moreover, this inconsistency between theory and practice existed not only in Russia but also within the American Communist Party, as is attested to by numerous accounts, such as Richard Wright's essay "American Hunger." In general, black artists had few illusions about going abroad and did not consider it a panacea. In a letter to Langston Hughes dated 28 February 1944, Eslanda Robeson congratulated Hughes on his remarks about race relations on the radio "Town Meeting of the Air"—remarks that apparently included scathing derision of Soviet society along with his denunciation of inequality in America.

Still, the direct exposure of Russian society to blacks, black culture, and black thought served to dispel some stereotypes and to reveal the complexities entailed in applying Marxist-Leninist theory to actual human conditions. And for black artists, travel abroad provided a basis for comparison that they would otherwise have lacked in appraising their status as human beings and as artists. For instance, Claude McKay—in a long, undated letter sent from Nice, France—chided Eslanda Robeson for underestimating the inferior treatment of Negro artists in America as compared with Europe. One positive contribution to the Harlem Renaissance of exposure to Russia and its ideals was that the Soviet Union, a major world society, affirmed the respectability of oppressed groups and their cultures. Furthermore, the Russians' expression of confidence in black culture seems to have been needed. Paul Robeson initially shared the American establishment's contempt for jazz as a form of music; and black thinkers had differences of opinion concerning the worth of black culture, betraying lingering doubts and perhaps suggesting a division along class lines.

Zora Neale Hurston, in a letter of 18 April 1934, to Eslanda Robeson, said:

> One night, Alan [sic] Locke, Langston Hughes and Louise Thompson wrassled with me nearly all night long that folk sources were no [sic] important, nobody was interested, waste of time, it wasn't art nor even necessary thereto, ought to be suppressed, etc. etc., but I stuck to my guns and the world is certainly coming my way in regards to the Negro.

ALLISON BLAKELY

See also Antilynching Crusade; Bechet, Sidney; Black and White; Bontemps, Arna; Communist Party; Du Bois, W. E. B.; Hughes, Langston; McKay, Claude; Messenger, The; Ovington, Mary White; Patterson, Louise Thompson; Robeson, Paul; Wright, Richard

Further Reading

Blakely, Allison. *Russia and the Negro*. Washington, D.C.: Howard University Press, 1986.

Duberman, Martin. *Paul Robeson*. New York: Knopf, 1988.

Gorky, M. "O muzyke tolstykh" ("Degenerate Music"). *Pravda*, 18 April 1928.

Huiswood, Otto E. "World Aspects of the Negro Question." *Communist*, February 1930, pp. 132–147.

Lewis, David Levering. *W. E. B. Du Bois: The Fight for Equality and the American Century, 1919–1963*. New York: Holt, 2000.

McClellan, Woodford. "Africans and Black Americans in the Comintern Schools, 1925–1934." *International Journal of African Historical Studies*, 26, 1993, pp. 371–391.

McKay, Claude. "Soviet Russia and the Negro." *Crisis*, December 1923, pp. 61–64; January 1924, p. 117.

———. *Selected Poems of Claude McKay*. New York: Harcourt Brace, 1981. (Originally published by Bookman, 1953.)

Naison, Mark. *Communists in Harlem during the Depression*. New York: Grove, 1984.

Paul Robeson Collection, Correspondence. Moorland-Spingarn Research Center Archives, Howard University.

Poston, Ted. "Negroes in New York" Collection, New York City Works Progress Administration, Federal Writers' Project Records.

Rampersad, Arnold, ed. *The Collected Works of Langston Hughes*, Vol. 1. Columbia: University of Missouri Press, 2001.

Starr, S. Frederick. *Red and Hot: The Fate of Jazz in the Soviet Union*. New York: Oxford University Press, 1983.

Wright, Richard. *American Hunger*. New York: Harper and Row, 1977. (Originally published 1944.)

Europe, James Reese

The multitalented James Reese Europe excelled in bandleading, arranging, organization, business, publicity, and military command, and in offering the public an erudite vision of the history and role of black music. He also wrote hit songs (although his compositions, redolent of turn-of-the-century ragtime, marching bands, and nineteenth-century string bands, have mostly not survived the test of time); and he was the primary force in guiding orchestrated jazz, ragtime, and blues to a wider audience in the 1910s. Europe was a significant influence on the Harlem Renaissance and on later efforts to put African American music as an art form on the same cultural plane as classical music.

Europe spent most of his school years in Washington, D.C., one of the few American communities where black history and music were openly celebrated and extensively taught. He came to New York City in 1902

James Reese Europe's Clef Club Band, 1914. (Schomburg Center for Research in Black Culture, New York Public Library.)

or 1903, hoping to find a foothold in black Broadway productions—one of the few professional areas in which blacks competed on a high level with whites, although the two races did not perform together. Europe worked with all of the major creators of successful black musicals of the period, including Will Marion Cook, who advocated using black music to present a vision of black culture and history, an idea that Europe would promote more widely. In 1905, Europe performed with the Memphis Students, the group James Weldon Johnson credited with playing the first jazz heard in New York City. By 1910, Europe decided to devote himself to projects of his own devising.

Europe's leadership in the Clef Club brought about improved artistic and employment opportunities for black musicians. This organization, established in 1910, combated rampant discrimination in the musical world of New York City; it operated as a trade union, booking agency, and publicity service demonstrating the high standards and abilities of black classical and popular musicians and raising their profile and respectability. On 2 May 1912, Europe's Clef Club symphony orchestra became the first black orchestra to perform at Carnegie Hall, presenting a "serious and dignified program of African American music" to what was probably the first integrated audience for a concert in America. The program changed the perception not only of African American music but of all American popular music. According to one reviewer, this was the occasion when "popular music first invaded the concert auditorium." Europe believed that only a black orchestra could play black music, which diverged from classical music and represented a different identity and historical background. The orchestra's unorthodox 125-piece instrumentation included fourteen upright pianos that dominated the stage and were arranged to blend in unusual tonal colors and rippling rhythmic patterns; there were also banjos, mandolins, and harp guitars, as well as traditional orchestral instruments such as violins and cellos. The musicians occasionally sang and danced, adding to the dense, textured sound. Newspaper reviews praised the orchestra's "seductively rhythmic" jazz sound and its "soft and beautiful" qualities.

The enthusiastic reaction ensured a return to Carnegie Hall and numerous bookings in America and abroad, some for an upper-class clientele on yachts and in mansions. Europe also became the first black bandleader to receive a major recording contract. Yet a large segment of the critical community deemed music worthy of respect only if it adopted exclusively European forms, and a critic for *Musical America* accordingly advised the Clef Club orchestra to "give its attention in the coming year to a . . . Haydn symphony. If the composers . . . will write short movements for orchestra, basing them on classic models, next year's concert will inaugurate a new era for the Negro musician in New York and will aid him in being appraised at his full value and taken seriously." Europe replied: "We have developed a kind of symphony music that, no matter what else you think, is different and distinctive, and that lends itself to the playing of the peculiar compositions of our race." Black Americans, like Europeans, had to follow their own traditions. The music performed at Carnegie represented "the product of our souls; it's been created by the sufferings and miseries of our race," Europe explained to the *New York Post*. "Some of the old melodies we played . . . were made up by slaves of the old days, and others were handed down from the days before we left Africa."

One recording by Europe's Society orchestra, "Down Home Rag" (1913), gives a hint of what the Clef Club orchestra sounded like at Carnegie Hall. Although scaled down to eighteen pieces, the group in this recording has the same combination of traditional and less traditional string instruments, along with two pianos. The result is an exhilarating wall of sound with a rollicking beat, ominously droning backup vocals, and main melodies (led by the violin) that resemble reels; it brings nineteenth- and twentieth-century influences together into a wild and exciting mélange. "Down Home Rag" represents sophisticated African American music before musical rules were decided on in the young art form of jazz.

After his term as president of the Clef Club, Europe was important during the 1910s in bringing the controversial fad of social dancing to the American public, in a partnership with Vernon and Irene Castle. With the Castles (who were white) devising brisk dance steps and Europe and Ford Dabney writing and directing the music, several dance crazes were instigated, including the fox-trot and the turkey trot; and millions of records—frenetic, polyrhythmic renderings that were, for the time, particularly sexual and daring—were sold. These first efforts by black bands on major recording labels demonstrated that black music represented a new, exciting enterprise that could appeal to a multiracial, multiclass cross section of the American public. The recordings showed Europe's facility with commercial as well as more highbrow genres; they also helped form a link between black music and

the mildly rebellious youth culture of the 1910s and 1920s. Moreover, having a white married couple—celebrities—dancing in front of a black orchestra and openly praising the African American influence in music was an unprecedented and influential development, economically and in terms of American race relations.

During World War I, Europe continued to break down barriers while serving as a lieutenant in the famous all-black 369th U.S. Infantry Division. He was the first African American to lead troops under fire as an officer in a machine gun company. The 369th was the first American regiment to fight side by side with the French, and the black American troops expressed surprise at and appreciation for the respect accorded to them by the French, unlike many counterparts in the U.S. Army. But Europe was mainly noted during and after the war for his leadership of the military band. Originally, he wanted to serve in a purely military capacity, in order to benefit "the race" as well as his country; but a private donation of $10,000 and a formal request by the army persuaded him to take on the band as well. The group he created received a tumultuously affirmative response on both sides of the Atlantic; Europe was credited with exposing the European continent for the first time to the sounds of orchestrated ragtime, blues, and jazz. Lieutenant Noble Sissle, drum major for the band, recalled how the rendition of the "Memphis Blues" made the "dignified French officers . . . tap their feet, along with the American general, who temporarily had lost his style and grace" and that "even German prisoners forgot they were prisoners, dropped their work to listen and pat their feet to the stirring American tunes." Sissle said that Europe's band made him "satisfied that America's music would someday be the world's music"—a feeling shared by many contemporary observers and later commentators.

Biography

James Reese Europe was born in Mobile, Alabama, on 22 February 1880. He attended public schools in Washington, D.C.; studied composition, piano, and violin with Enrico Hurlei and Joseph Douglass (c. 1895); and studied in New York City with Melville Charlton and Harry T. Burleigh (c. 1903). Europe was a lieutenant and bandmaster in the 369th Infantry Regiment ("Hellfighters") in World War I. He established himself as a composer of popular songs and instrumentals and as musical director of major black theater productions, including John Larkin's *A Trip to Africa* (1904), S. H. Dudley's *The Black Politician* (1904–1908), Cole and Johnson's *Shoe-Fly Regiment* (1906–1907) and *Red Moon* (1908–1909), and Bert Williams's *Mr. Lode of Koal* (1909). He joined Ernest Hogan's Memphis Students in 1905. Europe founded the Clef Club, a union and booking agency for black musicians (1910) and organized and conducted annual concerts of African American music at Carnegie Hall by the large Clef Club Symphony Orchestra (1912–1913) and the National Negro Symphony Orchestra (1914). He was principal composer, orchestra conductor, and musical director, with Ford Dabney, for the dancers Irene and Vernon Castle (1913–1916). Europe obtained the first major recording contract for a black orchestra, with Victor, in 1913. He continued to compose marches, dances, and songs and to collaborate with artists such as Ford Dabney, Eubie Blake, Noble Sissle, Henry Creamer, and Bob Cole, from 1910 to 1919. He recorded for Pathé in 1919. Europe died in Boston, Massachusetts, on 9 May 1919, at age thirty-nine, after having been stabbed by a mentally disturbed member of his band during a postwar tour.

HARVEY COHEN

See also Clef Club; Cook, Will Marion; Fifteenth Infantry; Music; Music: Bands and Orchestras; Sissle, Noble

Selected Works

The Black Politician. 1904 (Musical comedy.)
"On The Gay Luneta." 1906. (Lyrics by Bob Cole.)
"Down Home Rag." 1913. (Composed by Wilbur Sweatman, performed on Victor by James Reese Europe's Society Orchestra.)
"Castle House Rag." 1913.
"Castle Walk." 1913. (Cowritten with Ford Dabney.)
"Hi! There!" 1915.
Darkydom. 1915. (Also, *Darkeydom*; musical revue, cowritten with Will Marion Cook.)
"On Patrol in No Man's Land." 1919.
"Memphis Blues." 1919. (Composed by W. C. Handy and W. George Norton, recorded by Lieutenant Jim Europe's 369th Infantry Band.)

Further Reading

Badger, Reid. *A Life in Ragtime: A Biography of James Reese Europe*. New York: Oxford University Press, 1995.
Kimball, Robert, and William Bolcom. *Reminiscing with Sissle and Blake*. New York: Viking, 1973.
Sissle, Noble Lee. "Memoirs of Lieutenant 'Jim' Europe." (Unpublished manuscript held at the Library of Congress.)

Farrow, William Mcknight

William McKnight Farrow was probably the best-known and most highly regarded African American printmaker of the early twentieth century. His printing medium of choice was etching; he was also an avid draftsman, watercolorist, and oil painter.

However, Farrow is important to the Harlem Renaissance not so much because of the works of art he made in the 1920s and 1930s but because he was an extremely important early source of inspiration and guidance for African American artists who became prominent in the mid-twentieth century. Farrow was an active supporter of African American artists and a promoter and advocate of their work, and he is perhaps most famous for this pivotal role in African American art. His teaching and curatorial positions at the Art Institute of Chicago made possible his considerable influence among African American artists.

Farrow was born in 1885 in Dayton, Ohio. He moved to Chicago, where he spent the rest of his life. He studied at the Art Institute of Chicago with Ralph Clarkson and Karl Buehr and was later hired to teach there, becoming the first black instructor at the Art Institute. At the Art Institute he taught etching and organized exhibits of contemporary art, including art by African Americans; he was also involved with other major curatorial projects, including reorganizing the Egyptian collection. Farrow was an early supporter of the study of African American visual arts. He wrote "Art for the Home," a weekly column for the *Chicago Defender*, and many articles on African American artists. He helped establish the Chicago Art League in 1925 and served as its president. The most important achievement of this organization may have been the exhibit "The Negro in Art Week" (1927), a major early exhibit of the art of African Americans; Farrow was one of the curators, and his own works were exhibited in it. Farrow knew some of the most famous artists associated with the Harlem Renaissance and was particularly close to Archibald J. Motley Jr., with whom he studied at the Art Institute.

Farrow's prints varied considerably in subject matter. He did portraits of contemporary people of importance, such as African American artists, and of historical figures such as Abraham Lincoln. His paintings and illustrations were used as covers for *Crisis*. He also did illustrations for textbooks used in trade courses in the public schools of Chicago.

Farrow's reputation has suffered in recent decades because much of his work was technical and commercial. Nevertheless, his important role as an advocate for African American art at the dawn of the Harlem Renaissance deserves further recognition.

Biography

William McKnight Farrow was born on 13 April 1885, in Dayton, Ohio. He was educated at the Art Institute of Chicago (1908–1917) and taught there (he was also supervisor of the print shop at the Art Institute and assistant to the curator of temporary and contemporary exhibitions) and at the Carl Shurz Evening School and Museum, Northwestern University. He won first honors in figures and still life at the Lincoln Exposition (1915), the Eames McVeagh Prize for Etching from the Chicago Art League (1928), and the Peterson Prize (1929). Farrow was a member of the Art Institute of

Chicago Alumni, Alliance of Society of Fine Arts, Chicago Art League (which he served as president), Society for Sanity in Art, YMCA in Chicago, Chicago Urban League, and National Association for the Advancement of Colored People. He died in 1967.

HERBERT R. HARTEL JR.

See also Chicago Defender; Crisis, The; Motley, Archibald J. Jr.

Exhibitions

1915. Lincoln Exposition.
1917. Arts and Letters Society of Chicago.
1922. Tanner Art League.
1924. New York Public Library, 135th Street branch.
1928–1945. Chicago Art League.
1930. National Gallery of Art, Washington, D.C.
1928, 1930, 1931, 1935. Harmon Foundation, New York.
1932. Howard University, Washington, D.C.
1933. Century of Progress, Chicago.
1939. Augusta Savage Studios
1940. American Negro Exposition, Chicago.
1945. South Side Community Center, Chicago.

Further Reading

Afro-American Paintings and Prints from the Collection of Judge Irvin C. Mollision: A Gift to the Atlanta University Art Collection. Atlanta, Ga.: Atlanta University, Waddell Gallery, 1985.

"Farrow, William McKnight." In *African-American Artists: A Bio-Bibliographical Dictionary*, ed. Theresa Dickason Cederholm. Boston, Mass.: Boston Public Library, 1973, p. 92.

Henderson, Harry, and Romare Bearden. *African-American Artists: From 1792 to the Present.* New York: Pantheon, 1993, pp. 116–117, 149, 153, 338.

Reynolds, Gary A., and Beryl J. Wright. *Against the Odds: African-American Artists and the Harmon Foundation.* Newark, N.J.: Newark Museum, 1989, pp. 14, 17, 172, 183–187.

Father Divine

Father Divine became one of Harlem's most recognizable figures during the 1930s. He created the Peace Mission Movement, founded on the principles of New Thought and Christian Science. Father Divine explained to his followers that he was God incarnate and that they could create heaven on earth. He also advocated a "raceless" society, believing that racial categories were not a legitimate way to classify people. In conjunction with his ministry, Father Divine established restaurants, boardinghouses, and stores, all of which offered affordable services and an integrated atmosphere. He and his Peace Mission became well known in Harlem for political activism and philanthropy. Estimates of Father Divine's followers during his heyday range from 10,000 to two million.

Although Father Divine and the Peace Mission did not acknowledge his prior incarnation, he had apparently been born in Rockville, Maryland, and his original name was George Baker. As a young man, he worked as a hedge cutter in Baltimore and taught Sunday school. In 1906 he met Rev. St. John Divine Bishop (John Hickerson) and Samuel Morris, two ministers who proclaimed their own divinity. He joined them and adopted the title "the Messenger." He eventually parted ways with these two men, but he had taken their message to heart.

When he arrived in New York City in 1914, he continued to preach his own divinity. He adopted a new name, Major Jealous Divine, which he had derived from the Bible (Exodus 34: 14): "For the Lord whose name is Jealous is a jealous God." In 1919, he and his wife, Penninah, moved with his followers to a home in an otherwise all-white neighborhood in Sayville, Long Island. From this home, he operated an employment service for his followers.

Father Divine and his followers coexisted fairly peacefully with their neighbors in Sayville until 1931. By then, his ministry had grown significantly, and more and more Harlemites were traveling to Sayville to visit him. In November 1931, neighbors filed a complaint regarding noise, and Father Divine and many of his followers were arrested. He believed that the complaint was racially motivated. The trial took place in May 1932, and afterward the presiding judge, Lewis J. Smith, gave Father Divine the harshest sentence possible, ignoring the jury's recommendation of leniency. Three days after handing down this severe sentence, Judge Smith died and Father Divine reportedly said, "I hated to do it." The attendant publicity spurred on the growth of the Peace Mission.

Although most of Father Divine's followers were African Americans, people of all races joined the Peace Mission. There were missions from New York to Los Angeles, but few were located in the southern

United States. Many of Father Divine's followers in Harlem committed themselves fully to the Peace Mission, turning over their belongings and living communally. They also had to lead a celibate life, even if they were married. This policy of celibacy led critics, including Marcus Garvey, to claim that Father Divine was advocating race suicide. Father Divine, despite his own marriage, believed that a celibate life was just as necessary for his followers as abstaining from alcohol, profanity, and untoward entertainment.

Worship at Father Divine's Peace Missions centered on huge banquets. Hundreds of followers attended these banquets and feasted on elaborate, multicourse meals. All of the food first passed through Father Divine's hands before it made its way around the table. At the banquets, followers would testify on his behalf, explaining how he had improved their lives. During the Depression, Father Divine and his Peace Mission also provided thousands of meals to residents of Harlem.

Father Divine encouraged his followers to make amends for wrongs they had committed in the past. Newspapers across the country carried stories of Father Divine's followers who paid off decades-old debts. Also, his followers took an active role in improving themselves and the communities in which they lived. For example, they enrolled en masse in New York City's night schools; and he urged members of the Peace Mission to intimidate drug dealers in Harlem.

Political activism was an integral part of the Peace Mission. Father Divine sponsored voter-registration drives and supported other organizations in protests and boycotts. This activism culminated in the Righteous Government Convention, held at the Rockland Palace in Harlem in 1936. With thousands in attendance, Father Divine and his followers passed a series of planks in support of antilynching laws, the abolition of capital punishment, and destruction of weapons of war. An antilynching bill written by the Peace Mission was introduced in the U.S. Congress but was defeated. Members of the "black bourgeoisie" generally criticized Father Divine's religious movement, but they did take note of the impact his political and philanthropic activities had on Harlem.

During the 1940s, Father Divine began to lose his appeal. The Peace Mission faced allegations of impropriety and financial mismanagement; and although neither Father Divine nor the mission was convicted of any charges, the scandals proved damaging. Some scholars also believe that the increasing prosperity in America detracted from the services Father Divine offered his followers: people could provide for themselves and no longer needed his assistance. Furthermore, his second marriage in 1946, to twenty-one-year-old Canadian Edna Rose Ritchings (Mother Divine), disillusioned some of his followers who had given up their marriages for the movement.

Father Divine eventually moved the headquarters of the movement out of New York and into Philadelphia. The remaining Peace Missions became more centralized, and many of the businesses associated with the Peace Mission closed.

Father Divine died in Philadelphia in 1965. His death was not just the passing of a leader but also an ideological stumbling block for some of his remaining followers. He had claimed that, being God, he was immortal, and he had instructed his followers that if they truly believed in him, they too would become immortal. The death of a follower could be understood as a failure of faith, but his own death was more troubling. The Peace Mission explained that Father Divine had made the ultimate sacrifice and "laid his earthly body down."

As of this writing, the Peace Mission still existed, but on a much smaller scale than at the height of Father Divine's fame.

Father Divine. (Brown Brothers.)

Biography

Father Divine (George Baker) was born in Rockville, Maryland, in 1879. He arrived in New York City in 1914 and moved to Sayville, Long Island, in 1919. In January 1936, he held a three-day Righteous Government Convention. In 1942 he established new headquarters in Philadelphia. He died in Philadelphia on 10 September 1965.

DANIELLE BRUNE

See also Antilynching Crusade; Religion; Religious Organizations

Further Reading

Burnham, Kenneth E. God Comes to America. Boston, Mass.: Lambeth, 1979.

Fauset, Arthur Huff. Black Gods of the Metropolis. Philadelphia: University of Pennsylvania Press, 1945.

Mother Divine. The Peace Mission Movement. Philadelphia, Pa.: Imperial, 1982.

New Day, 1936–1989. (Peace Mission newspaper containing transcripts of Father Divine's sermons, lectures, and letters.)

Watts, Jill. God, Harlem U.S.A. Berkeley and Los Angeles: University of California Press, 1992.

Weisbrot, Robert. Father Divine and the Struggle for Racial Equality. Chicago: University of Illinois Press, 1983.

Fauset, Arthur Huff

Arthur Huff Fauset left his mark on the Harlem Renaissance through his contribution to major works such as The New Negro and to the sole issue of Fire!!, as well as through his stories in Crisis and Opportunity. Unlike many writers involved in the renaissance, Fauset did not relocate to Harlem but remained in Philadelphia, where he taught in the public schools and was a major figure in local civil rights issues.

Fauset's first literary work appeared in 1922 in an issue of Crisis, the magazine of the National Association for the Advancement of Colored People (NAACP). Fauset's short piece retells a folktale that the narrator heard from the "queen of Sedalia" in North Carolina. Fauset's interest in folk literature was not lifelong, but this essay is indicative of his work to preserve African American folktales in the 1920s. While pursuing an undergraduate degree in anthropology, Fauset collected

Negro folktales in Nova Scotia under the guidance of the renowned anthropologist Elsie Clews Parsons. He later traveled throughout the southern United States collecting such material.

Alain Locke, who had been a mentor to Fauset, called on him to make a contribution to Locke's seminal collection, The New Negro. Fauset focused on his interest in African American folktales for his essay, "American Negro Folk Literature," and also compiled the bibliography of Negro folklore that appeared in the back of the book. In his essay, Fauset addressed the need for "scientific collection" of Negro folklore. Although he praised Joel Chandler Harris's efforts to collect "Uncle Remus" stories, Fauset pointed out that these were adaptations, not faithful representations, of traditional stories.

In April 1926, at an awards banquet held by Opportunity magazine, Fauset won first prize for his short story "Symphonesque." Other honorees on this occasion included Arna Bontemps, Zora Neale Hurston, and Dorothy West. Fauset was in equally impressive company when he joined with Wallace Thurman, Langston Hughes, Zora Neale Hurston, and other notables to produce Fire!!—"a quarterly devoted to the younger Negro artists." Fauset provided finanical support and also contributed the essay "Intelligentsia," in which he ridiculed the reverence accorded to intellectuals, suggesting that "the contribution of the Intelligentsia to society is as negligible as gin at a Methodist picnic."

Fauset's best-known work was the publication of his doctoral thesis, Black Gods of the Metropolis, in 1944. In this work he turned his anthropological eye on Negro religious cults in the urban North, documenting the practices, beliefs, and followers of cults such as Father Divine's Peace Mission and the Moorish Science Temple that had sprung up in the North amid the "great migration."

In part because of his distance from Harlem and in part because he was overshadowed by his well-known sister, Jessie Redmon Fauset, Arthur Huff Fauset has remained one of the relatively unknown participants in the Harlem Renaissance. David Levering Lewis's description of Claude McKay can also be applied to Arthur Huff Fauset: he was a man who was in the renaissance "but not of it."

Biography

Arthur Huff Fauset was born in Flemington, New Jersey, on 20 January 1899. He graduated from Central High

School in Philadelphia, the Philadelphia School of Pedagogy for Men, and the University of Pennsylvania (A.B., 1921; M.A.; Ph.D, 1942). He was an elementary school teacher in public schools in Philadelphia (1918–1926) and principal of the Joseph Singerly School there (1926–1946). Fauset died in Philadelphia, on 2 September 1983.

DANIELLE BRUNE

See also Bontemps, Arna; Crisis, The; Father Divine; Fauset, Jessie Redmon; *Fire!!*; Hughes, Langston; Hurston, Zora Neale; Locke, Alain; *New Negro*; Opportunity Literary Contests; Thurman, Wallace; West, Dorothy

Selected Works

"A Tale of the North Carolina Woods." *Crisis*, 23, 1922, pp. 111–113.

"American Negro Folk Literature." In *New Negro*, ed. Alain Locke, 1925.

"Symphonesque." *Opportunity*, June 1926, pp. 178–180, 198–200.

"Intelligentsia." *Fire!!*, 1926, pp. 45–46.

For Freedom, 1927.

"Jumby." In *Ebony and Topaz*, ed. Charles S. Johnson, 1927.

"Negro Folktales from the South." *Journal of American Folklore*, 40, 1927.

"Tales and Riddles Collected in Philadelphia." *Journal of American Folklore*, 41, 1928.

"Safe in the Arms of Jesus." *Opportunity*, October 1929, pp. 124–1128, 133.

Sojourner Truth: God's Faithful Pilgrim. 1938. (Reprint, 1971.)

Black Gods of the Metropolis. 1941. (Reprint, 1971.)

Further Reading

Carpenter, Carole. "Arthur Huff Fauset." In *African-American Pioneers in Anthropology*, eds. Ira E. Harrison and Faye V. Harrison. Urbana and Chicago: University of Illinois Press, 1999.

Lewis, David Levering. *The Portable Harlem Renaissance Reader*. New York: Penguin, 1995, p. 156.

Fauset, Jessie Redmon

As literary editor of and a major contributor to *Crisis*, Jessie Redmon Fauset played a principal role in the development of many key figures and issues of the Harlem Renaissance. As a novelist, she ranks with Zora Neale Hurston and Nella Larsen: She, Hurston, and Larsen were the three most respected female Harlem writers. Although Fauset's books have not seen quite as much of a revival over the past two decades as have those of Hurston and Larsen, many scholars consider her influence as mentor, essayist, and literary critic unparalled.

Although she identified her birthplace as Philadelphia, Fauset was born in Fredericksville, New Jersey; her family moved to Philadelphia while she was a child. She graduated from the Philadelphia High School for Girls in 1900 as valedictorian; she was probably the only African American at the school during that time. As an honors graduate, she was supposed to receive a scholarship to Bryn Mawr College, but it was never awarded. Instead, Fauset attended Cornell University; she was the first black woman to earn a degree there and the first black woman awarded membership in Phi Beta Kappa. She went on to pursue graduate work at the University of Pennsylvania, where she earned a master's degree in French; she also studied at the Sorbonne.

In 1903, shortly after the death of her father, Fauset wrote to W. E. B. Du Bois, asking his advice about what kind of summer work she might undertake that would help her learn about other classes of African Americans. This correspondence began a lifelong friendship and professional association. Du Bois helped Fauset obtain a teaching position at Fisk University for the summer of 1904. Fauset then went to work teaching French and Latin at the famous M Street High School (later renamed Dunbar High) in Washington, D.C., in 1906. She remained there until 1919.

In 1912 Fauset published her first short story, "Emmy," in *Crisis*, the magazine of the National Association for the Advancement of Colored People (NAACP). At this time she became active in the NAACP. Among other efforts, she was involved in an attempt to obtain dormitory space for black students at Smith College. She also began a regular column in *Crisis*, "The Looking Glass," which provided literary and other news gathered from various international journals. She was paid $50 per month for the column.

In 1919 Du Bois persuaded Fauset to become the literary editor of *Crisis*. She had regularly published short stories and essays there since her first contribution in 1912. Among the authors Fauset discovered and encouraged during her editorial tenure at *Crisis* are Langston Hughes, Countee Cullen, Jean Toomer, Nella Larsen, Georgia Douglas Johnson, Anne Spencer,

George Schuyler, Arna Bontemps, and Claude McKay. Langston Hughes recognized her contributions in his autobiography, *The Big Sea*: "Jessie Fauset at the *Crisis*, Charles Johnson at *Opportunity*, and Alain Locke in Washington were the people who midwifed the so-called New Negro Literature into being. Kind and critical but not too critical for the young, they nursed us along until our books were born." As Hughes implies, Fauset was a generation older than most of the Harlemites in the news; she was also much more reserved in demeanor. Although she was active in Harlem's literary and salon life, she was not a part of its nightlife. Also, although she lived in New York City, she maintained associations in Washington, D.C., where she met regularly with the Saturday Nighters Club at the home of Georgia Douglas Johnson.

Jessie Fauset was among those who believed firmly that arts and letters could help overthrow racial prejudice. In addition to her editorial work, she contributed to *Crisis* and other publications, providing essays, poems, short stories, literary criticism, and biographical sketches of prominent black Americans. She considered biography a genre of particular importance. In 1932, in an interview for *Southern Workman*, she argued that there was an urgent need for "ambitious Negro youth" to have reading materials on "the achievements of their race." Her essay production was prodigious; one of her most famous essays is "The Gift of Laughter," which appeared in Alain Locke's *New Negro*. Her poetry, on the other hand, has never been considered her strong point, remaining conventional in both form and themes.

In 1920 an offshoot of *Crisis* was developed for children, entitled *The Brownies' Book*. Fauset served as its editor and a major contributor. She described it as "designed for all children but especially for ours." The introductory issue began with Fauset's dedication: "To Children, who with eager look/Scanned vainly library shelf and nook/For History or Song or Story/That told of Colored Peoples' glory." However, the *Brownies' Book* lasted for only twenty-four issues.

In the June 1922 issue of *Crisis*, Fauset criticized the theme of primitivism that was so prevalent in attempts by white authors to write about African Americans. Her criticism was generated in part by her feelings on reading the white author T. S. Stribling's novel *Birthright*. Fauset doubted that "white people will ever be able to write evenly on this racial situation in America," and this reaction is thought to have motivated her decision to write a novel.

Fauset's *There Is Confusion*—often cited as the first Harlem novel—was published on 21 March 1924, a date that coincided with a famous dinner given by the New York Writers Guild. This dinner, also known as the Manhattan Civic Club Dinner of 1924, earned a place in literary history because it was attended by virtually all of Harlem's luminaries, including James Weldon Johnson, W. E. B. Du Bois, Countee Cullen, and Langston Hughes, as well as figures from the major publishing houses and editors of some of the most influential journals of the time. Charles S. Johnson, who had organized the dinner, suggested that it was meant to honor Fauset and her first novel, but much of the program was given over to introducing the upcoming stars of the Harlem Renaissance to those in positions to help them get published.

There Is Confusion has numerous characters and subplots, but the main focus is on the courtship of Joanna Marshall, who hopes to be a dancer; and Peter Bye, who plans on a career in medicine. In attempting to achieve their goals, both struggle against racism, and Joanna struggles against sexism as well. Eventually Joanna's career leads her to work in vaudeville, which she considers less than respectable, and she gives it up, deciding that the best use of her talents will be to help her husband further his career. Wall (1995) argues that Fauset's insistence on the fulfillment of the "marriage plot" impairs the aesthetic integrity and social integrity of the novel.

However, as a fiction writer—although she stayed within fairly traditional forms and styles—Fauset did break new ground through her depiction of middle-class African American life, a milieu that had not previously been represented. In "The Negro in American Literature" (1925), William Stanley Braithwaite praised Fauset's creation of an "entirely new milieu in the treatment of race in fiction. . . . In such a story, race fiction, detaching itself from the limitations of propaganda on the one hand and genre fiction on the other, emerges from the color line and is incorporated into the body of general and universal art."

In January 1925 Fauset traveled to North Africa; she was one of very few Harlem writers and artists to do so. She wrote about her trip in an article for *Crisis* entitled "Dark Algiers the White."

Fauset's second novel, *Plum Bun: A Novel without a Moral*, appeared in 1929, three years after she had resigned her editorship at *Crisis* and had returned to teaching. The protagonist of *Plum Bun*, Angela Murray, is a young African American living in Philadelphia. Realizing that racism is the only obstacle to her success and happiness, and discovering that she can pass as white, she moves to New York. She studies art and meets and pursues a wealthy white man, who—because of her class—refuses to marry her. After becoming his mistress and then being rejected by him, she comes to respect the choices of her sister, who has stayed in Harlem and has found a loving husband and established a rich family life. *Plum Bun* considers the problems of passing and the racial and gender barriers faced by a young woman seeking to make her way in the world; it also offers a kind of cultural history of the Harlem Renaissance, exploring the caprices of patronage. Wall has suggested that some characters in this novel are fictional representations of certain historical figures, including Du Bois and the sculptor Augusta Savage.

In 1929, Fauset married Herbert E. Harris, who worked for the Victory Insurance Company. Their wedding was preceded by numerous social events, acknowledging Fauset's status in her community.

Fauset's third novel, *The Chinaberry Tree*, published in 1931, traces the lives of two generations of African American women in a small black community. One of the characters is "Aunt Sal" Strange, a former slave, who loved the white Colonel Halloway and bore him a daughter. He bought Sal a home in New Jersey but did not see marriage as an option. Sal's daughter, Laurentine, must bear the stigma of having been born out of wedlock in a community where propriety is valued above all else. Although Sal's choice is understood and forgiven because the circumstances of slavery are taken into account, there is no leeway for Laurentine or her cousin Melissa. Whereas Fauset explored the intersections of race and gender in *Plum Bun*, in *The Chinaberry Tree* she focuses on the intersections of race and class.

Fauset published her fourth novel, *Comedy: American Style*, in 1933. In this work the focus is again on a light-skinned African American woman, Olivia Carey, but her role as a mother is most important. Very much an "anti-race woman," she marries a light-skinned man and seems happy until her third child turns out to have much darker skin than the rest of the family. Olivia's fixation on color leads her daughter into a bad marriage and eventually leads her darker-skinned son to suicide. Olivia ends up living meagerly in a very poor house in Paris.

From 1927 to 1944 Fauset taught primarily in the public schools in New York City, most notably at DeWitt Clinton High. After *Comedy: American Style*, her literary output was negligible. Herbert Harris died in 1959; and

Jessie Redmon Fauset, portrait by Laura Wheeler Waring. (National Portrait Gallery, Smithsonian Institution; Art Resource, N.Y.)

shortly thereafter, Fauset, whose own health was failing, took up residence with relatives. She died in 1961.

Biography

Jessie Redmon Fauset was born on 27 April 1882, in Fredericksville, New Jersey, the seventh child of Redmon and Annie Seamon Fauset. Her father was an African Methodist Episcopal minister. While she was still a child, her mother died, as did four of her siblings. She received a B.A. from Cornell University (1905) and an M.A. from the University of Pennsylvania (1919); she also studied at the Sorbonne. Fauset taught at Fisk University (1904); taught French and Latin in high schools (1905–1919); and taught in the New York City public schools (1926–1944). She was literary editor of *Crisis* (1919–1926) and editor of the *Brownies' Book* (1920–1921). She married Herbert E. Harris in 1929. Fauset died of heart disease on 30 April 1961, in Philadelphia, Pennsylvania.

KATHRYN WEST

See also Authors: 2—Fiction; Birthright; Braithwaite, William Stanley; Brownies' Book, The; Civic Club Dinner,

1924; Crisis, The; Du Bois, W. E. B.; Literature: 4—Fiction; Stribling, Thomas Sigismund; There Is Confusion; *specific writers*

Selected Works

There Is Confusion. 1924. (Reprint, 1989.)
Plum Bun: A Novel without a Moral. 1928. (Reprint, 1990.)
The Chinaberry Tree: A Novel of American Life. 1931. (Reprint, *The Chinaberry Tree and Selected Writings*, 1994.)
Comedy, American Style. 1933. (Reprint, 1995.)

Further Reading

Braithwaite, William Stanley. "The Negro in American Literature." In *The New Negro*, ed. Alain Locke. 1925.

Harris, Violet J. "Race Consciousness, Refinement, Radicalism: Socialization in *The Brownies' Book*." *Children's Literature Association Quarterly*, 14(3), 1989, pp. 192–196.

Hughes, Langston. *The Big Sea: An Autobiography*. New York: Knopf, 1940.

Johnson, Abby Arthur. "Literary Midwife: Jessie Redmon Fauset and the Harlem Renaissance." *Phylon*, June 1978, pp. 143–153.

Johnson-Feelings, Dianne, ed. *The Best of the Brownies' Book*, intro. Marian Wright Edelman. New York: Oxford, 1996.

McDowell, Deborah E. "The Neglected Dimension of Jessie Redmon Fauset." In *Conjuring: Black Women, Fiction, and Literary Tradition*, eds. Marjorie Pryse and Hortense J. Spillers. Bloomington: Indiana University Press, 1985, pp. 86–104.

McLendon, Jacquelyn Y. *The Politics of Color in the Fiction of Jessie Fauset and Nella Larsen*. Charlottesville: University Press of Virginia, 1995.

Pfeiffer, Kathleen. "The Limits of Identity in Jessie Fauset's 'Plum Bun.'" *Legacy*, 18(1), 2001, pp. 79–93.

Shockley, Ann Allen. *Afro-American Women Writers, 1746–1933: An Anthology and Critical Guide*. New York: Meridian, 1988.

Showalter, Elaine. *Sister's Choice*. New York: Oxford University Press, 1991.

Starkey, Marion L. "Jessie Fauset: An Interview." *Southern Workman*, May 1932, pp. 217–220.

Sylvander, Carolyn Wedin. *Jessie Redmon Fauset, Black American Writer*. Troy, N.Y.: Whitson, 1981.

———. "Jessie Redmon Fauset." In *Dictionary of Literary Biography*, Vol. 51, *Afro-American Writers from the Harlem Renaissance to 1940*, ed. Trudier Harris. Detroit, Mich.: Gale Research, 1987.

Wall, Cheryl A. *Women of the Harlem Renaissance*. Bloomington: Indiana University Press, 1995.

Federal Programs

During the 1930s, employment opportunities disappeared for many artists of the Harlem Renaissance. Federal government programs, however, provided some of these black Americans with jobs and a way to preserve their skills and self-esteem.

The Great Depression (1929–1939) represented the greatest economic failure in U.S. history. Roughly fifteen million people lost their jobs. By 1934, 17 percent of the white population and 38 percent of the black population were viewed as incapable of self-support. Many Americans turned to the national government for help.

Before Franklin D. Roosevelt assumed the presidency in March 1933, he promised a "New Deal" for the American people. In his first inaugural address, he stirred the nation with the words, "The only thing we have to fear is fear itself." With congressional collaborators, he shepherded through Congress an impressive body of initiatives that attacked industrial stagnation and unemployment. Eleven measures became federal law during the First New Deal in 1933. These statutes established administrative agencies to regulate and set policy.

The Civil Works Administration (CWA), one of the first relief agencies to assist blacks, sponsored the Public Works of Art Project. It commissioned artists to paint in public buildings. Following the demise of CWA in 1934, the Treasury Department's Section of Painting and Sculpture employed more than 5,000 artists. The Federal Emergency Relief Administration (FERA) provided checks to unemployed survivors. To ensure minority employment, FERA placed several blacks in positions of authority. One, Forrester Washington, served as director of Negro Works.

Roosevelt certainly had his critics. Taking issue with the initial results of his New Deal, they pointed out that more than 10 million Americans were jobless. This led the president to start a second wave of legislation in 1935. The National Youth Administration, with Mary McLeod Bethune as head of the Negro Affairs section, helped young blacks receive job training. However, many scholars view the creation of the Works Progress Administration (WPA) as the most far-reaching measure to revitalize the economy because it greatly reduced joblessness. Over an eight-year period, it employed more than 8.5 million people. WPA employees built roads, bridges, and public buildings. In 1936, from an initial funding of $1.4 billion, Congress earmarked $85 million for WPA to assist "educational, professional, and clerical persons."

Harry L. Hopkins proved to be an excellent choice to head WPA. A former social worker, he had earlier overseen FERA and had previously dealt with racial issues. Soon after the creation of WPA, W. E. B. Du Bois—the editor of *Crisis*—and other black leaders sent letters to the administration that argued for employment relief in proportion to the population. Ultimately, the president issued Executive Order 7046, which required WPA to hire qualified workers irrespective of race. Hopkins reiterated this point by issuing directives with provisions against discrimination. He also established a "black cabinet," which included Robert C. Weaver and William H. Hastie, to advise him on employment-related issues.

To help professional people, Hopkins set up a Professional Projects Division. The unit's main goal was to hire needy writers, actors, artists, and musicians. Federal One, the program's official name, consisted of four arts projects: Federal Writers', Federal Theater, Federal Arts, and Federal Music. Each project had a national director: Henry G. Alsberg (Writers'), Hallie Flanagan (Theater), Holger Cahill (Art), and Nikolai Sokoloff (Music).

With regard to artists of the Harlem Renaissance, the Federal Writers' Project is perhaps best known because of the many leading figures who participated in it. New York City alone had twenty Writers' Projects. During the 1930s, Richard Wright, Ralph Ellison, and Claude McKay did research on little-known achievements of blacks; their research later resulted in a work called *The Negro in New York* (1967). Zora Neale Hurston took part in the Florida Project. In Washington, D.C., Sterling Brown served as national editor of *Negro Affairs*. The Illinois Project nurtured the literary aspirations of Margaret Walker and Frank Yerby. The careers of many lesser-known African Americans were also favorably affected by the Federal Writers' Project.

When Hallie Flanagan became national director of the Federal Theater Project in 1935, she established nine black branches in major cities. She considered Harlem the pivotal location, appointing John Houseman, Orson Welles, and the black American actress Rose McClendon to manage the unit there. After they restored

the Lafayette Theater in Harlem, they employed 700 black actors, singers, dancers, and technicians. They envisioned the Lafayette as presenting plays that would deal with all aspects of black life. In 1936, Houseman opened the revived Lafayette with Frank Wilson's *Walk Together Chillun*. In 1939, he presented *Macbeth*, the first full-scale professional black Shakespearean production. Overall, the Lafayette produced nearly 1,200 plays, including many with black themes.

The Federal Arts Project sponsored classes for aspiring black artists and strengthened the skills of established ones. In major cities, more than 100 artists secured employment. They painted murals for public buildings, worked as sculptors, produced posters, and were mentors to other artists. In Harlem, Vertis Hayes, Aaron Douglas, and Augusta Savage offered instruction in their own studios. In 1937, the Arts Project financed the Harlem Community Art Center and Chicago's South Side Community Art Center. An impressive list of artists took advantage of government patronage, including Jacob Lawrence, Archibald Motley, Charles Sebree, Romare Bearden, and Dox Trash.

Under the leadership of Nikolai Sokoloff, the Federal Music Project created thirty-four new orchestras and offered music instruction throughout the nation. The orchestras and other programs provided jobs for nearly 10,000 musicians. The Music Project also established the Colored Concert Band, whose black musicians specialized in rhythm and blues; Norman L. Black directed the band. At one point, the Music Project employed nearly 6,000 teachers. Citizens received free lessons in music theory, history, and composition. Henrietta Robinson, a black teacher, participated in Philadelphia. In 1997, at age ninety-three, she published an account of the legacy of black musicians in southern New Jersey.

In 1942, believing that communists had infiltrated Federal One programs, the chairman of the House Committee on Un-American Activities, Martin Dies, persuaded his colleagues to halt funding. Clearly, the Great Depression had left the artists of the Harlem Renaissance with fewer opportunities; and even with federal programs, black artists, if they were employed, often received lower wages. Yet it cannot be denied that those who found jobs in federal programs not only gained economic relief but also earned self-respect through their work.

PAUL T. MILLS JR.

See also Bearden, Romare; Bethune, Mary McLeod; Brown, Sterling; Douglas, Aaron; Ellison, Ralph; Federal

Writers' Project; Hurston, Zora Neale; Lafayette Theater; Lawrence, Jacob; McLendon, Rose; McKay, Claude; Motley, Archibald; Savage, Augusta; Second Harlem Renaissance; Walker, Margaret; Wilson, Frank; Works Progress Administration; Wright, Richard; Yerby, Frank

Further Reading

Badger, Anthony J. *The New Deal: The Depression Years, 1933–1940.* New York: Hill and Wang, 1989.

Fraden, Rena. *Blueprints for a Black Federal Theatre, 1935 1939.* New York: Cambridge University Press, 1994.

Gates, Henry L. Jr., and Nellie Y. McKay, eds. *The Norton Anthology of African American Literature.* New York: Norton, 1997.

Harris, Jonathan. *Federal Art and National Culture: The Politics of Identity in New Deal America.* Cambridge, England: Cambridge University Press, 1988.

Hirsch, Jerrold. *Portrait of America: A Cultural History of the Federal Writers' Project.* Chapel Hill: University of North Carolina Press, 2003.

Kirby, John B. *Black Americans in the Roosevelt Era: Liberalism and Race.* Knoxville: University of Tennessee Press, 1980.

Mangione, Jerre. *The Dream and the Deal: The Federal Writers' Project 1935–1943.* Boston, Mass.: Little Brown, 1972.

Sitkoff, Harvard. *A New Deal for Blacks: The Emergence of Civil Rights as a National Issue.* New York: Oxford University Press, 1978.

Wolters, Raymond. *Negroes and the Great Depression: The Problem of Economic Recovery.* Westport, Conn.: Greenwood, 1970.

Federal Writers' Project

The Federal Writers' Project (FWP) began as a small, unique component of the larger Works Progress Administration (WPA), programs in the New Deal that were designed to employ portions of the nation's labor force. FWP, which was described as white-collar relief, provided work relief primarily to writers but also hired artists, actors, and musicians, all of whom were willing to work in aiding the arts. Many of the writers who were hired were placed in skilled and professional-technical positions. Before coming under the auspices of WPA, in 1934, FWP had been known as the Authors' League and had been under the Civil Works Administration (CWA), also a white-collar relief program. By 1935, WPA had incorporated FWP into its mission, and in November of that year, FWP hired Henry G. Alsberg, an editorial writer, to serve as the director.

The writers hired for FWP were not necessarily professional writers but rather unemployed professionals from different occupations: newspaper people, lawyers, teachers, librarians, recent college graduates, and even physicians and preachers. Very few were trained creative writers. In 1935, its first year, FWP employed more than 4,000 workers, and by 1936 its payroll rose to 6,700. By 1939, however, the number of workers declined to 3,600; and in 1941, the number fell to 3,000. On average, 4,800 people were on the payrolls during the four-year life of FWP.

FWP hired a large percentage of blacks, the greatest numbers for its projects in New York City and Louisiana. In selecting individuals, Alsberg gave preference to already established editors, journalists, and freelance writers, and these individuals primarily lived in large cities, including New York, Chicago, and Los Angeles. In rural areas, Alsberg had more difficulty hiring qualified writers, relying instead on volunteers who submitted their work to editors in the large cities. FWP was not specifically designed to promote writers' talents, but in effect it did so. Many young black writers, including Ralph Ellison and Richard Wright, began their careers with FWP; and many ambitious participants in FWP eventually returned to their careers with more self-assurance in their craft.

Alsberg had a passion for nonfiction and promoted it over other written genres, such as poetry and short stories. Under his direction FWP developed into an exceptional agency with regard to the utilitarian work produced by its writers; however, these professionals were not allowed to write their own works on FWP time, and some of them therefore felt frustrated. Still, Alsberg did encourage the participants to write on their own time, outside the office, so that their creativity could contribute to the FWP's literature.

The first, and major, contribution of Alsberg and his writers was the *American Guide Series* (AGS), which was loosely based on the Baedeker guidebooks in Europe, factual aids assisting travelers. Alsberg's goal for AGS was to inform and entertain the general reading public. Each book in the series contained three parts: Part 1 "offered essays on a variety of subjects important to a state—its history, people, the arts, economics, politics, and religion." Part 2 "consisted of up-to-date, fact-laced pieces on the state's cities." Part 3, "the longest, directed the reader throughout the state on motor tours." The books also contained points of interest (POIs); and the history sections also described architecture, encouraging Americans to seek out architectural sites. The writers of FWP asked for suggestions about what to include in AGS, and the public responded with family records; state highway agencies calculated tour mileages; and rail and bus companies and government agencies provided information about roads and tourist sites. In addition, the writers relied on knowledgeable volunteers from small towns for descriptions of less visited yet interesting sites. Lewis Mumford, the Librarian of Congress, called these guides "a great patriotic effort" in rediscovering America. With the success of AGS, FWP began to produce additional new series, including the *American Recreation Series* and *American Pictorial Guides*. Auxiliary projects included the *Life in America Series*, about 150 published titles covering diverse topics from zoo animals to ethnic and religious groups.

There were also transcontinental tour books and trail guides, romanticizing America's pioneer era. Other writing projects included indexing of local newspapers; works on local history; a national project of organizing old state and local records, commonly known as the Historical Records Survey; and the creation of black studies in which the authors of smaller local guides described black communities and their contributions to local and state efforts. The editors of FWP saw these black historical and cultural essays as offering an understanding of the country's racial problems.

Preserving the country's folk heritage later developed into the American Folklore Project. America's folklore was slowly vanishing, so John A. Lomax, the first folklore editor, working under Alsberg's direction, set out to collect and record tales and songs of an older generation. Lomax encouraged the collection and recording of ballads, oral histories, and poetry, and through these recordings, dialects and speech rhythms were preserved. Another FWP project, in 1936, was recording the stories of people who had been slaves. Alsberg and Lomax called on former slaves to describe their life before and after emancipation. Before the project ended, FWP collected some 2,000 stories of former slaves from seventeen states.

In 1939, FWP was accused of radicalism and waste, and shortly thereafter, Congress restricted its activities. In December 1942, President Franklin D. Roosevelt ordered all WPA projects closed; and FWP shut its doors in spring 1943. By 1943, FWP had created and published more than 1,200 pamphlets and books and had sold or given away some 3.5 million copies of its publications. It had also provided relief to white-collar professionals; had undertaken an artistic and literary effort to document America, the American people, and the American heritage; had observed and recorded unfamiliar parts of America; and had contributed to national self-awareness.

ANNE ROTHFELD

See also Ellison, Ralph; Federal Programs; Second Harlem Renaissance; Works Progress Administration; Wright, Richard

Further Reading

Mangione, Jerre. *The Dream and the Deal: The Federal Writers' Project, 1935–1943*. Boston, Mass.: Little, Brown, 1972.

McDonald, William F. *Federal Relief Administration and the Arts: The Origins and Administrative History of the Arts Projects of the Works Progress Administration*. Columbus: Ohio State University Press, 1969.

Penkower, Monty Noam. *The Federal Writer's Project: A Study in Government Patronage of the Arts*. Urbana and Chicago: University of Illinois Press, 1977.

Ferris, William H.

William Henry Ferris is often considered a minor figure among the black intelligentsia in the first half of the twentieth century, but he was a member of the "talented tenth" and an important contributor to the art and literature of the black nationalist movement in the 1920s.

Ferris was a graduate of Harvard and Yale universities and a charter member of the American Negro Academy, a sort of think tank founded by Alexander Crummell in 1897. He also took an active role in the debate between W. E. B. Du Bois and Booker T. Washington. Ferris supported the Afro-American Council, an early precursor of the National Association for the Advancement of Colored People (NAACP), and worked with William Trotter, the radical editor of the Boston *Guardian*—although a dispute with Trotter led him to a brief flirtation with the Washington camp. In 1913, Ferris published his magnum opus, *The African Abroad*.

Heavily influenced by the English writer Thomas Carlyle and the American Ralph Waldo Emerson, the book featured an eclectic mix of social, political, and economic commentary informed by literary and historical observations. *The African Abroad* is an excellent example of contributionist history. Its scope encompasses the evolution of Western civilization, locating cultures of Africa and the African diaspora within these developments. Ferris coined the term "Negro-Saxon," which highlights his belief in the connection between African American and European, especially Anglo-Saxon, culture.

In 1919 Ferris, after having worked briefly as editor of the *Champion* in Chicago and at the A.M.E. Book Concern, joined Marcus Garvey's movement as literary editor of *Negro World*. Garvey's movement gave Ferris an important outlet for his intellectual beliefs. To him, Garvey embodied the possibility of blacks' developing race art and literature. Throughout Ferris's journalistic contributions to *Negro World*, one finds consistent themes: celebratory assessments of ancient Africa, contributionist appraisals of black art and literature, and a balanced assessment of Marcus Garvey's Universal Negro Improvement Association (UNIA). A central component of Garvey's program was affirming the importance of history. Numerous historical articles in *Negro World*, no doubt written by Ferris, capitalized on this theme. His review in 1921 of John Cromwell's *Negro in American History* is an example. Ferris also brought an artistic component to *Negro World* through numerous assessments of "Negro art and literature," a topic not often associated with Garvey's movement. Perhaps most interesting was Ferris's discussion, in 1922, of the musical ability of the Black Star Line Band. Unlike W. E. B. Du Bois, whom he admired and whom he often presented as a paragon of black intellectual achievement, Ferris offered balanced and favorable assessments of Garvey's movement. In his article "Dr. Du Bois's Ten Mistakes" (1923), Ferris points out in a delicate, judicious tone numerous errors in Du Bois's article "Back to Africa" (also 1923) in *Century Magazine*.

The importance of Ferris's contribution lay in his attempts to link the components of civilization–art, literature, and music–to the nationalist discourse of Garvey's movement. This goal may have influenced Ferris's participation in the literary contest of UNIA, which was launched in 1921. The contest is significant because it preceded similar activities by mainstream organizations such as NAACP and the Urban League. Ferris raised blacks' art, literature, and music to levels of admiration and respect comparable to what was accorded to American and European artistic expression. His erudite commentary and astute observations laid the groundwork for deeper appreciation of black history and art during this period.

Biography

William Henry Ferris was born in New Haven, Connecticut, in 1874. He studied at Hillhouse High School there, at Yale University (A.B., 1899), and at Harvard University (M.A., 1900). He was editor of *The Champion* in Chicago (1916–1917); literary assistant at the African Methodist Episcopal Book Concern in Philadelphia (1917–1919), and literary editor of *Negro World* (1919–1923) and *Spokesman* (1925–1927). Ferris died in obscurity in New York City on 23 August 1941.

STEPHEN G. HALL

See also Du Bois, W. E. B.; Guardian, The; Negro World; Talented Tenth; Trotter, William Monroe; Universal Negro Improvement Association

Further Reading

Burkett, Randall. *Black Redemption: Churchmen Speak for the Garvey Movement*. Philadelphia, Pa.: Temple University Press, 1978.

Ferris, William Henry. *The African Abroad; Or His Evolution in Western Civilization, Tracing His Development under the Caucasian Milieu*, 2 vols. 1913.

Gaines, Kevin Kelley. *Uplifting the Race: Black Leadership, Politics, and Culture in the Twentieth Century*. Chapel Hill: University of North Carolina Press, 1996.

Martin, Tony. *African Fundamentalism: A Literary and Cultural Anthology of Garvey's Harlem Renaissance*. Dover, Del.: Majority, 1983.

Fetchit, Stepin

Stepin Fetchit, a vaudeville entertainer and pioneering black film actor, emerged near the end of the Harlem Renaissance as Hollywood's first African American movie star. He appeared in more than forty-five feature films and shorts between 1927 and 1976, including *Hearts in Dixie* (1929), *Judge Priest* (1934), *Stand Up and Cheer* (1934), *Charlie Chan in Egypt* (1935),

Miracle in Harlem (1948), and *The Sun Shines Bright* (1954). During the 1930s, his portrayals of stereotypical plantation "darkies," chicken thieves, lazy roustabouts, and other "coon" characters made him a national celebrity. His performances drew laughter and applause from white and black moviegoers alike, but they also increasingly sparked firestorms of protest and criticism from civil rights organizations and black newspapers, which objected to the demeaning and offensive roles that made him a star.

Fetchit (whose original name was Lincoln Theodore Monroe Andrew Perry) was born in Key West, Florida, in 1902 and grew up in Alabama. Around 1914, he joined the Royal American Shows carnival, performing as "Rastus the Buck Dancer" in its plantation minstrel revue. Over the next decade he toured the South and southwest with minstrel groups, carnival companies, and medicine shows. He eventually formed his own minstrel act, with Ed Lee, billed as "Step 'n' Fetchit, the Two Dancing Crows from Dixie." After the team split up in the mid-1920s, he retained the stage name Stepin Fetchit, and he soon became a successful solo entertainer on the Theater Owners Booking Association (TOBA) circuit. During this time he also moonlighted as an entertainment reporter for the *Chicago Defender*, writing a newspaper column that covered African American stage and vaudeville performers and, after his arrival in Hollywood, screen actors.

In 1927, Fetchit obtained his first screen role in MGM's silent melodrama of the old South, *In Old Kentucky* (1927); and over the next two years he appeared in supporting roles in several successful films, including *The Kid's Clever* (1929), *Salute* (1929), and *Show Boat* (1929). He gave his breakthrough performance as Gummy, a shiftless plantation laborer, in Fox Film Corporation's critically acclaimed *Hearts in Dixie* (1929), an early talking film with an all-black cast. Fetchit reportedly earned $1,500 per week for this film, making him one of the highest-paid black actors in Hollywood, and his performance led to a series of screen roles in which he portrayed lazy, dim-witted "coon" characters that represented then-current racist caricatures of African Americans.

Offered only a limited range of roles, Fetchit rose to stardom during the 1930s by essentially portraying the same shiftless, simple-minded character time and again. Onscreen, he sported a trademark shaved head and wore baggy clothing that accentuated his tall, lanky, loose-limbed frame. Bald and stoop-shouldered, his characters shuffled from place to place and, when confused, cast puzzled, bug-eyed stares and stammered in broken dialect. They added comic relief to the films, often serving as targets of verbal and physical abuse by the white characters. In time, Fetchit even had a host of imitators, most notably Willie Best (originally billed as "Sleep 'n' Eat") and Mantan Moreland.

Fetchit played his signature character in twenty-six feature motion pictures between 1929 and 1935, many of them for Twentieth-Century-Fox, including *Stand Up and Cheer* (1934), *David Harum* (1934), and *Judge Priest* (1934). In the mid-1930s, at the height of his popularity, he received featured billing with Shirley Temple and Will Rogers, and he was in such demand in Hollywood that, according to Bogle (1973), he often worked on several motion pictures simultaneously and had special roles written for him. Meanwhile, Fetchit continued to make stage appearances as a singer, dancer, and comedian, headlining at the Cotton Club, the Apollo Theater, and other major venues; he also composed at least two songs, "'Member Mandy" and "Step Fetchit Strut," both in 1929.

Fetchit led the extravagant lifestyle of a Hollywood movie star, described by the *Chicago Defender*, in 1936, as the "squire and lord mayor of Harlemwood." At the height of his career, he owned six houses staffed with sixteen Chinese servants; wore $2,000 cashmere suits imported from India; threw lavish cocktail parties; and had a fleet of twelve chauffeured automobiles, including a champagne-pink Rolls Royce, for cruising around town. But he was also plagued by personal problems. He became so temperamental and unreliable that in 1931 the exasperated executives of Fox released him; a three-year absence from motion pictures followed. His public fistfights, arrests for drunken driving and assault, and breach of contract suits were all regularly reported in the entertainment sections of black newspapers. Fetchit declared bankruptcy at least twice, once in 1930 and again in 1947, after squandering the more than $2 million he had reportedly earned in films and vaudeville.

During Fetchit's heyday in the 1930s—the midst of the Great Depression—his comedic film performances delighted both white and black audiences. Some film historians argue that his foolish, self-mocking characters particularly appealed to anxious white moviegoers in an America pervaded by Jim Crow practices and racial tension. But by the time of World War II, Fetchit's humiliating portrayals of African American characters had thoroughly alienated black moviegoers, and the National Association for the Advancement of Colored People (NAACP) and the black press increasingly condemned him for propagating negative racial

371

stereotypes. He made only a few motion pictures during the 1940s and 1950s; and eventually he moved to Chicago, where for much of the rest of his life he worked as a stand-up comedian and singer in nightclubs and strip shows. In 1970, he sued the Columbia Broadcasting System for $3 million, alleging that its documentary *Black History: Lost, Stolen or Strayed* (1968) had unjustly accused him of perpetuating shameful, degrading images of African Americans. The case was dismissed in 1974.

During the 1970s, after an absence of almost two decades, Fetchit returned to motion pictures, appearing in *Amazing Grace* (1974) with Moms Mabley, and in *Won-Ton-Ton, The Wonder Dog That Saved Hollywood* (1976), his final film appearance. In 1977, after suffering the first of a series of strokes, Fetchit entered the Motion Picture and Television Country House in Los Angeles, where he stayed until his death in 1985.

Stepin Fetchit remains a highly controversial figure in African American culture, but he nonetheless ranks as a pioneer of early African American cinema. Bogle defends him as an "immensely talented" actor and comedian who had "a legendary sense of timing" and "a strong visual presence" onscreen, and who opened the doors of movie studios to blacks in Hollywood.

Stepin Fetchit. (Photofest.)

The Hollywood chapter of the NAACP honored Fetchit with a Special Image Award in 1976, and he was inducted into the Black Film Makers Hall of Fame in 1978. Never apologetic, Fetchit always maintained that he had paved the way for succeeding black actors by portraying the first African American character that white moviegoers found "acceptable." "I became the first Negro entertainer to become a millionaire," he told an interviewer in 1968. "All the things that Bill Cosby and Sidney Poitier have done wouldn't be possible if I hadn't broken [racial barriers]. I set up thrones for them to come and sit on."

Biography

Stepin Fetchit (Lincoln Theodore Monroe Andrew Perry) was born on 30 May 1902, in Key West, Florida, the son of Joseph and Dora (Monroe) Perry, both of whom had been born in England, probably of West Indian ancestry. He attended St. Joseph's College in Montgomery, Alabama, until about age twelve. Beginning c. 1914 he toured professionally as Rastus the Buck Dancer with Royal American Shows, and as part of the vaudeville team Step 'n' Fetchit, the Two Dancing Crows from Dixie. He toured as a solo performer on the vaudeville circuit and later the nightclub circuit under the name Stepin Fetchit c. 1927–1975. He worked as entertainment reporter for the *Chicago Defender* c. 1924–1929 and appeared in more than forty-five feature films and shorts in 1927–1976. His awards included the Special Image Award of the Hollywood chapter of NAACP (1976) and induction into the Black Film Makers Hall of Fame (1978). He died in Los Angeles, California, on 19 November 1985, of congestive heart failure and pneumonia, at age eighty-three.

PATRICK HUBER

See also Chicago Defender; Film: Actors; Film: Blacks as Portrayed by White Filmmakers; Hearts in Dixie; Minstrelsy; Moreland, Mantan; Theater Owners Booking Association

Selected Works

In Old Kentucky. 1927.
Hearts in Dixie. 1929.
Salute. 1929.
Show Boat. 1929.
David Harum. 1934.

Judge Priest. 1934.

Stand Up and Cheer. (1934)

Marie Galante. 1934.

Charlie Chan in Egypt. 1935.

Dimples. 1936.

Big Timers. 1945.

Miracle in Harlem. 1947.

The Sun Shines Bright. 1954.

Amazing Grace. 1974.

Won-Ton-Ton, The Wonder Dog That Saved Hollywood. 1976.

Further Reading

Bogle, Donald. *Toms, Coons, Mulattoes, Mammies, and Bucks: An Interpretive History of Blacks in American Films*. New York: Viking, 1973.

———. *Blacks in American Films and Television: An Encyclopedia*. New York: Garland, 1988.

Cripps, Thomas. *Slow Fade to Black: The Negro in American Film, 1900–1942*. New York: Oxford University Press, 1977.

Hampton, Wilborn. "Stepin Fetchit, the First Black to Win Film Fame, Dies at 83." *New York Times*, 21 November 1985.

McBride, Joseph. "Stepin Fetchit Talks Back." *Film Quarterly*, 24(4), Summer 1971.

Peterson, Bernard L. Jr. "Stepin Fetchit." In *American National Biography*, eds. John A. Garraty and Mark C. Carnes. New York: Oxford University Press, 1999.

Regester, Charlene. "Stepin Fetchit: The Man, the Image, and the African American Press." *Film History*, 6(4), 1994.

Seiler, Michael. "Stepin Fetchit, Noted Black Movie Comic of 1930s, Dies." *Los Angeles Times*, 20 November 1985.

"Stepin Fetchit Dead at 83; Comic Actor in Over 40 Films." *Variety*, 27 November 1985.

Fields, Dorothy

Between 1926 and 1973, Dorothy Fields matched her colloquial, witty lyrics to more than 400 songs. Many of them have become pop and jazz standards: "On the Sunny Side of the Street," "Don't Blame Me," "Exactly Like You," "I'm in the Mood for Love," "A Fine Romance," "Pick Yourself Up," "The Way You Look Tonight," and "Big Spender." The list of her collaborators on Broadway and in Hollywood reads like a who's who of American popular song: Jimmy McHugh, Jerome Kern, Cole Porter, Sigmund Romberg, Irving Berlin, Arthur Schwartz, Cy Coleman, and her brother Herb Fields. Her songs have been performed by everyone from Louis Armstrong, Billie Holiday, Fred Astaire, and Ginger Rogers to Dizzy Gillespie, King Pleasure, Aretha Franklin, and a Brazilian leopard named Baby. In 1971, Fields was among the first ten members elected to the Songwriters Hall of Fame, and the only woman.

Fields most directly affected the Harlem Renaissance through the lyrics she wrote for floor shows at the Cotton Club during its heyday in the late 1920s. Her father, Lew Fields, a successful producer and veteran vaudeville comedian, discouraged his children from seeking careers in the theater. But in 1926 Fields, then age twenty-one, sent samples of her work to Jimmy McHugh, who had been retained by the Cotton Club to compose music for revues produced by Lew Leslie and later Dan Healey. A Fields-McHugh collaboration was performed on 4 December 1927, at the same opening in which Duke Ellington's orchestra made its debut as the Cotton Club's house band. Fields became a full writing partner for the revue of

Dorothy Fields, 1934. (© Bettmann/Corbis.)

spring 1928, which played on Broadway as *Lew Leslie's Blackbirds of 1928* and featured "I Must Have That Man," "Diga Diga Do," and "Doin' the New Low-Down." Adelaide Hall sang the show's biggest hit, "I Can't Give You Anything but Love" (interpolated from *Harry Delmar's Revels of 1927*, and sometimes rumored to have been composed by Fats Waller and Andy Razaf).

Cab Calloway, whose band began to substitute for Ellington's in 1929, maintained that Fields "wasn't really funky enough to write the kind of songs that would carry a Negro revue of that type" (Calloway and Rollins 1976, 93). Fields did quietly omit her name from the more risqué numbers demanded by Healey's formula for the Cotton Club and by the expectations of white audiences who were seeking authenticity, and she shared the ambivalence of many white participants in the Harlem Renaissance. For example, her lyrics for "You've Seen Harlem at Its Best" (recorded by Ethel Waters in 1934) stand uncertainly between the notion of Harlem as an uptown amusement destination for hip downtowners and a gender-conscious recognition of what James Weldon Johnson once described as a community of "ordinary, hardworking people" occupied with "the stern necessity of making a living" (1930, 161):

> When you've seen gals who wail,
> "Hello, baby, love for sale,"
> Pound the pavements east to west,
> Grabbing what they can to keep a handy man,
> You've seen Harlem at its best.

Fields wrote for the Cotton Club until late 1929, when she and McHugh left for Hollywood, and songwriting chores for the revues were taken over by Harold Arlen and Ted Koehler.

Biography

Dorothy Fields was born in Allenhurst, New Jersey, on 15 July 1905. She was a lyricist for revues at the Cotton Club and on Broadway in New York with the composer Jimmy McHugh in 1927–1933; was a lyricist for film scores with the composers Jimmy McHugh and Jerome Kern and others in Hollywood in 1929–1939; wrote the book, lyrics, or both for Broadway musicals in collaboration with Herbert Fields and the composers Arthur Schwartz, Cole Porter, Cy Coleman, and others in 1939–1973; and was a lyricist for the CBS DuPont Show of the Month, *Junior Miss*, with the composer Burton Lane (New York, 1957). Her honors included an Academy Award for Song of the Year ("The Way You Look Tonight") with the composer Jerome Kern (1936), a Tony Award for Musical Play (*Redhead*), and election to the Songwriters Hall of Fame (1971). Fields died in New York City, on 28 March 28, 1974.

RYAN JERVING

See also Blackbirds; Calloway, Cab; Cotton Club; Ellington, Duke; Hall, Adelaide; Leslie, Lew; Musical Theater

Selected Stage Works

Harry Delmar's Revels of 1927. (With Jimmy McHugh.)
Lew Leslie's Blackbirds of 1928. (With Jimmy McHugh.)
International Review. 1930. (With Jimmy McHugh.)
Something for the Boys. 1943. (Book only, with Herb Fields and Cole Porter, composer.)
Annie Get Your Gun. 1946. (Book only, with Herb Fields and Irving Berlin, composer.)
A Tree Grows in Brooklyn. 1951. (Book with Herb Fields and music with Arthur Schwartz.)
Sweet Charity. 1966. (With Cy Coleman.)

Films

Roberta. 1935. (With Jerome Kern.)
Swingtime. 1936. (With Jerome Kern.)

Further Reading

Calloway, Cab, and Bryant Rollins. *Of Minnie the Moocher and Me.* New York: Crowell, 1976.
The Chronological Ethel Waters, 1931–1934. Classics, 1994. (Recording; Ethel Waters, performer.)
Dorothy Fields. Smithsonian American Songbook Series, 1993. (Recording; various performers.)
Furia, Philip. *The Poets of Tin Pan Alley: A History of America's Great Lyricists.* Oxford and New York: Oxford University Press, 1990.
Haskins, Jim. *The Cotton Club.* New York: Random House, 1977.
Johnson, James Weldon. *Black Manhattan.* New York: Knopf, 1930.
Winer, Deborah Grace. *On the Sunny Side of the Street: The Life and Lyrics of Dorothy Fields.* New York: Schirmer, 1997.

Wilk, Max. *They're Playing Our Song: Conversations with America's Classic Songwriters.* New York: Atheneum, 1973. (See also New York: Da Capo, 1997.)

Yours for a Song: The Women of Tin Pan Alley. (Dir. Terry Benes; Fox Lorber, 1999.)

Fifteenth Infantry

The return of the Fifteenth Infantry to New York, in February 1919, after the end of World War I, is sometimes considered to mark the beginning of the Harlem Renaissance. Neither the return of the Fifteenth Infantry nor the Harlem Renaissance brought an end to violations of African Americans' civil liberties or to legally sanctioned segregation, but both did begin an awareness of African Americans' contributions in all segments of society.

The Fifteenth Infantry, a unit of the New York National Guard, was officially formed on 16 June 1916, with Colonel William Hayward as commander. With a few notable exceptions, such as the bandleader James Reese Europe, the regiment was predominantly led by white officers. Along with Reese, other famous African American men who enlisted with the Fifteenth Infantry, and encouraged others to do so, were Noble Sissle, Eubie Banks, and Horace Pippin. Before their enlistment, most of these African American men had been Pullman porters and waiters, hotel waiters, and doormen. They had little or no experience as soldiers. For the most part, their own officers conducted their training, with almost no assistance from either the National Guard or the regular army.

Arthur Little, a white officer of the Fifteenth Infantry, described it as "the self-made regiment of the American Army. It started without traditions, without education, and without friends" (1936). It did not even have a home base. The regiment began training in an old dance hall in Brooklyn; it also used a state training camp near the town of Peekskill and later at Camp Whitman in New York state. After performing guard duty in various parts of New York state, the regiment was sent to Spartanburg, South Carolina, for further training before embarking for France. Its contentious reception in South Carolina reflected the reality that even though these men were serving their nation, large segments of society refused to recognize their contribution and still wanted them to remain segregated.

When the United States officially entered World War I and the American Expeditionary Force was organized, the Fifteenth Infantry Regiment was redesignated as the 369th and, with other "colored" units of the National Guard, became the Ninety-Third Division (Provisional). This new division was activated at Camp Stuart, Virginia, in December 1917, and almost immediately the 369th was sent to France, with the remainder of the division following in later months. Ostensibly, the division was sent to France because the French army needed replacements. The 369th participated in various defensive and holding operations; its largest operation was the Meuse-Argonne offensive from 16 September 1918 through 11 October 1918—in which, according to some reports, one-third of the unit was killed or wounded. The 369th was credited with never having had a soldier captured and never giving up an inch of ground that it had taken. It spent 191 days in combat and was the first unit to reach the Rhine.

While serving with the French, the 369th fought with distinction and was decorated as a unit, and 170 individuals were awarded the Croix de Guerre. Corporal Henry Johnson and Private Needham Roberts were the first Americans awarded the Croix de Guerre. They had been on guard duty on 14 May 1918 when twenty Germans on a raid tried to take Roberts prisoner. Johnson, using a knife, freed Roberts; and between the two of them, they killed four Germans, wounded several others, and held their position as the rest of the Germans fled. This skirmish became known as the "battle of Henry Johnson." In the battle of the Meuse-Argonne, the 369th captured and held the town of Sechault while facing artillery fire, machine gun fire, and entrenched German soldiers.

One aspect of the history of the Fifteenth Infantry during the war is the story of Lieutenant James Reese Europe. Europe, a well-known bandleader in the United States, conducted a military band known as the 369th Infantry Hell Fighters, which included Noble Sissle and Eubie Blake and is credited with introducing American jazz to Europe. During the war, this band entertained French soldiers and officers in camps and hospitals, and also civilians. Reese composed songs about his wartime experiences and recorded these when he came back to the United States; however, he was killed soon after returning from the war.

Little discusses the hardships that his soldiers suffered at home before the war as a consequence of racism and "the cumulative prejudices of hundreds of

The 369th Colored Infantry returns home: members of this famous unit, formerly the Fifteenth New York regulars, arrive in New York City, 1919. (© Corbis.)

years," but he says that after the war they "were going home as heroes!" They had been denied a parade before departing for France; when they returned, however, the Fifteenth Infantry marched up Fifth Avenue to receive the plaudits of a million grateful citizens of New York, and then marched on for the full length of Lenox Avenue, through Harlem, cheered on by a quarter of a million black men, women, and children. Little reports that on this day, "New York City knew no color line."

SUSIE SCIFRES KUILAN

See also Blake, Eubie; Europe, James Reese; Sissle, Noble; World War I

Further Reading

Barbeau, Arthur E., and Florette Henri. *The Unknown Soldiers: Black American Troops in World War I.* Philadelphia, Pa.: Temple University Press, 1974.

Henri, Florette, and Richard Joseph Stillman. *Bitter Victory: A History of Black Soldiers in World War I.* Garden City, N.Y.: Doubleday, 1970.

Little, Arthur W. *From Harlem to the Rhine: The Story of New York's Colored Volunteers.* New York: Covici Friede, 1936.

Nalty, Bernard C. *Strength for the Fight: A History of Black Americans in the Military.* New York: Free Press, 1986.

Williams, Charles Halston. *Negro Soldiers in World War I: The Human Side.* New York: AMS, 1970.

Film

Whoever controls the film industry controls the most powerful medium of influence over the public. (Thomas Edison)

Background

During the era of silent films, before the advent of the Harlem Renaissance, black faces appeared in motion pictures, but few belonged to African Americans. As a rule, white actors blackened their faces with burnt cork to play blacks in roles that reinforced images immortalized in the novel *Uncle Tom's Cabin* (1852) by Harriet Beecher Stowe. This practice peaked in 1915 with the release of D. W. Griffith's *The Birth of a Nation*. Upset by the color prejudice manifest in this landmark movie, African Americans, such as Oscar Micheaux, stepped up efforts to organize film companies and produce their own pictures. An outpouring of group pride, which fostered creativity and collaboration by blacks throughout the jazz age, provoked the reaction to Griffith's work and gave rise to numerous films by African Americans. These "race movies" enchanted blacks from the beginning of the 1920s to the early 1930s.

Original Negatives

For nearly two decades after the dawn of motion pictures, African Americans had little influence in the film industry. To their dismay, a mood of nostalgia for antebellum times prevailed in popular culture. Most often, Hollywood movies presented black people as plantation slaves happy to serve their masters; otherwise, blacks were depicted as tramps, thieves, or tricksters. As noted previously, in general white actors played black parts with their faces painted dark, and this practice prevailed when Griffith cast *The Birth of a Nation*, a sweeping tale of the Civil War and Reconstruction.

The early movies in which whites performed black roles were continuing, or renewing, a custom. After the War of 1812, white minstrels began to make up with burnt cork and render impressions of blacks in song and dance. Out of their routines, a theatrical tradition was born. By the mid-nineteenth century, minstrel shows by whites in blackface were among the most popular pastimes in American society. Their popularity faded in the 1890s, though, as motion pictures emerged and adopted the convention.

In 1903, the first film narrative with a black lead premiered. It was an adaptation of *Uncle Tom's Cabin* directed by Edwin Porter, who had a white actor, in burnt cork, take the role of Uncle Tom. Like the character in the novel by Harriet Beecher Stowe on which the film was based, the cinematic Uncle Tom thrilled contemporary audiences by submitting piously to his plight as a slave. Six subsequent movie versions of the novel appeared in theaters between 1909 and 1927 and confirmed the public's fascination with black performances, which reprised the black figures developed in the book. In other films by whites, such as *The Chicken Thief* (1904), *The Octoroon* (1911), *Old Mammy's Charge* (1913), *A Slave's Devotion* (1913), and *Rastus's Riotous Ride* (1914), black leads copied the devout Tom or other stock characters created by Stowe, including hearty Aunt Chloe, half-witted Topsy, dazzling Eliza, and defiant George. Griffith inserted a form of each type acted by whites into *The Birth of a Nation*. In the process, he lowered blacks to new depths through characterizations that stripped them of dignity. But Griffith also took filmmaking to new heights through innovative editing; and President Woodrow Wilson, voicing the opinion of the national majority, found the movie an exhilarating account of the past.

African Americans had been protesting against their onscreen image for years before *The Birth of a Nation*. The "great migration," beginning in 1910, brought many blacks to the North from southern counties plagued by the violence of the Ku Klux Klan and the futility of sharecropping. As these African Americans settled in tight pockets in and around northern cities, their resistance to negative portraits gathered strength. The National Assocation for the Advancement of Colored People (NAACP), formed in 1909 under the leadership of W. E. B. Du Bois, reflected this mounting opposition. A short while after its inception, NAACP had launched a crusade against the use of stereotypes of blacks by the film industry. Other associations that were formed to promote the interests of African Americans—for example, the National Urban League—had soon followed suit. But *Birth of a Nation*, with its undignified blackface characters in menial or menacing roles, excited the most furious response; this film ignited an explosion of black cinema that contributed to the Harlem Renaissance.

Answer Prints

"Race movies" flourished in the black community before the Great Depression. They picked up a practice that had been initiated by William Foster, who founded a motion picture company in 1910 and produced *The Railroad Porter*, with an all-black cast and crew, two years later. Race movies were issued by more and more African American filmmakers and were presented in an increasing number of black theater chains. The actors in these movies were real blacks, and the plots were about timely matters relevant to the audiences. These productions often had inadequate capital and thus contained rough cuts and poor lighting; even so, they elicited pleasure as well as pride.

The spread of black film ventures became apparent in 1916 when the Lincoln Motion Picture Company, formed by Noble Johnson, produced *The Realization of a Negro's Ambition*. These ventures met a demand for businesses owned and operated by African Americans. Marcus Garvey, who emigrated from Jamaica and gained a large following, was an important advocate of black enterprises. Garvey insisted that blacks had to rely on their own resources to improve their standing in society, and the positive response to his rhetoric suggested that an emergent generation was primed to change its fortunes through these means.

The Brotherhood of Sleeping Car Porters, a union organized by A. Philip Randolph in 1925, was a sign of the times. It demonstrated the ascent of a social consciousness, involving an extensive commitment to cooperative economics, among African Americans; and this consciousness generated a market for race movies. In cities across the country, audiences filled movie houses to cheer *Body and Soul* (1925), which came from the Micheaux Film Corporation and starred Paul Robeson. Although this film about a wretched man who undergoes a radical transformation had an uneven narrative (as a result of poor funding and white censorship), it nevertheless delighted viewers. By its mere existence, the movie pleased blacks, for it assured them that, through collaborative activities, they could rise above the barriers of color prejudice.

Recognizing this climate of thought regarding the growth of black cinema, Alain Locke noted, in *The New Negro* (1925), that African Americans were moved by a fervor for unified action—and that he could hear a cry for arts respectful of black culture. Locke observed that this trend brought writers (such as Langston Hughes and Zora Neale Hurston) considerable patronage throughout the "roaring twenties." Other black artists also enjoyed broad support; some of the most noteworthy were the sculptor Selma Burke, the photographer James Van Der Zee, and the musician

Duke Ellington. Micheaux too found encouragement for more than three dozen motion pictures.

Before the stock market crashed in 1929, numerous black film companies appeared. They tended to dissolve in the following decade, but in their day these businesses produced features for a network of movie chains located in black neighborhoods. The time was right for them, and their target audiences greeted them with enthusiasm. These films were collaborative enterprises that promised relief from the usual Hollywood fare in which blacks were restricted to demeaning roles. Thus through their design and material, the film studios fortified current trends.

Key Light

Although black film companies were reacting against the color prejudice that was rife in the social order, the movies they shot upheld national ideals. Jim Crow, imposing racial divisions, haunted the country: blacks were forced into segregated housing, schools, and jobs; and there were glaring inequalities between public accommodations maintained for blacks and those reserved for whites. These disparities grieved African Americans, but they still believed in the American creed, and their favorite race movies advanced mainstream morals.

The Lincoln Motion Picture Company—the brainchild of Noble Johnson, a black actor with modest film credits in Hollywood—relied on themes that became typical of black independent producers. Lincoln's initial release, *The Realization of a Negro's Ambition* (1916), espouses faith in the prospect of upward mobility. Reminiscent of Horatio Alger's *Ragged Dick*, the film has a hero who, through his own intelligence and initiative, rises from a farm to fame and fortune. Lincoln's second feature, *The Trooper of Company K* (1916), is the story of a slouch who enlists in the Tenth Calvary, develops better habits, and honors himself fighting for his country; thereafter, he wins the girl of his dreams. The standard script for the Lincoln studio had a happy ending. Its later productions, such as *The Law of Nature* (1917), *A Man's Duty* (1919), and *By Right of Birth* (1921), end with a joyful family reunion attained through honest effort in the face of enormous hardship.

The Foster Photoplay Company, pioneered by William Foster, preceded Lincoln by six years. Foster's productions shunned drama in favor of comedy. Soon, joined by the Afro-American Film Company, the invention of Hunter Haynes, Foster was specializing in slapstick borrowed from popular vaudeville routines.

His *Pullman Porter* (1913), about a raucous romantic triangle, typified his projects, offering delight in lieu of discretion. *Lovie Joe's Romance* (1914), from the Afro-American Film Company, was in the same vein. Unlike their successors, neither Foster nor Haynes explored issues of racial uplift.

On the brink of the jazz age, there was a turn toward themes related to social accomplishment. The Frederick Douglass Film Company, named after the famous nineteenth-century abolitionist, was part of this shifting tide: its film *The Colored American Winning His Suit* (1916) had a protagonist who becomes a lawyer and saves his future father-in-law from injustice. Motifs of moral and social triumph soon characterized race movies. Time and again the heroes used brains and hard work to beat hard times. Examples include *The Slacker* (1917), from the Peter P. Jones Photoplay Company; *Loyal Hearts* (1919), from the Democracy Film Company; and *Reformation* (1920), from the Loyalty Film Company. Each such film inspired blacks to dream that they could climb high in society despite handicaps.

Micheaux adopted this approach in 1918 when he filmed *The Homesteader*, which was based on his own novel about his younger days on the prairie in South Dakota. During the 1920s, he produced a rapid succession of motion pictures. In general, they had subjects that aroused a sense of pride and possibility among blacks across the country, and they attracted large audiences and received rave reviews into the 1930s. In 1931 Micheaux made *The Exile* (1931), a talkie with a melodramatic plot in which the protagonist's diligence and virtue elevate him in society. Micheaux's successes persuaded white businessmen to finance black film companies that were devoted to dramas of human progress. Reol Productions, for example, distinguished itself with parables such as *Easy Money* (1921), *Secret Sorrow* (1921), and *The Call of His People* (1922), along with *The Sport of the Gods* (1921), adapted from a novel of the same name by Paul Laurence Dunbar. Another company funded by whites, the Colored Players Film Corporation, appropriated the recognized format in *Ten Nights in a Barroom* (1926), starring Charles Gilpin, and *The Scar of Shame* (1927). The Harlem Renaissance, then, encompassed the ascendancy of race movies encouraging black achievements undaunted by color prejudice.

Boom Operator

Beyond doubt, Oscar Micheaux (1883–1951) was the leader of the pack. He had the spirit of a pioneer at age seventeen, when he left his small family farm in rural Illinois to become a Pullman porter in Chicago. He held the job for six years, banking a good deal of his income, until he found an opportunity to buy land in South Dakota. Alone among whites on the prairie, he worked at agriculture and accumulated riches as well as respect from his fellow homesteaders. He married his hometown sweetheart, but the marriage failed because frontier life unsettled her. After their divorce, misfortune plagued Micheaux; his farm business dissipated, and he resorted to writing to make sense of his fallen state. A resulting series of novels, stories of redemption, got him back on his feet. By chance, the shift led him to shoot race movies and set the pace in the field.

In 1913, Woodruff Press printed Micheaux's first book, *The Conquest*, a veiled autobiography fictionalizing his life from his boyhood to his time as a homesteader. It sold well and justified the publication of a second novel, *The Forged Note* (1915). Micheaux's third work, *The Homesteader*, caught the attention of the Lincoln Motion Picture Company, which offered to make a movie out of it. The deal fell through because Micheaux wanted to direct the film and have it run longer than Lincoln's usual features. Nevertheless, with royalties from his book, he produced a cinematic version of the narrative. Reviewers showered the production with lavish praise; most of them deemed it a watershed in the history of black cinema, and their judgment proved valid.

Although Micheaux made films until 1948, he reached the crest of his career around the end of the Harlem Renaissance. In his heyday, he wrote, directed, and produced an average of two films per year; for instance, in 1920 he offered black moviegoers *Within Our Gates* and *The Brute*. During the 1920s, he had an unbroken string of films, including *Deceit* (1921), *The Dungeon* (1922), *The Ghost of Tolston's Manor* (1923), *Birthright* (1924), *Body and Soul* (1925), *Broken Violin* (1926), *The Millionaire* (1927), and *Wages of Sin* (1928). By the close of the decade, his output was unmatched. Micheaux's movies drew record crowds to black theaters before the onset of the Great Depression. After the Depression had begun, he made headlines with *The Exile* (1931), the first picture with sound from a black studio. But after that, his popularity waned during the 1930s, when he released *Easy Street* (1930), *Lem Hawkin's Confession* (1935), *The Underworld* (1937), *Temptation* (1938), *God's Stepchildren* (1938), and *Lying Lips* (1939). *The Betrayal* (1948), succeeding *The Notorious Elinor Lee* (1940), was his final production.

As yet, no black filmmaker has rivaled Hollywood to the same extent as Micheaux did. He made many accomplished black stage performers into stars of the screen. Laura Bowman, Shingzie Howard, Canada Lee, Ethel Moses, and Lorenzo Tucker are among the film celebrities associated with Micheaux. Also, an unprecedented number of African Americans came to see his films. He whetted their appetite with advertising campaigns that promised spectacular dramas with stellar black casts. To the audiences who packed the movie theaters, it mattered little that his films often suffered from bad lighting and jarring cuts resulting from budgetary constraints. Operating with a small amount of capital, he would take less than two months to shoot a film, in homes and nightclubs or on slapdash sets. The key to his success was his use of subjects and stars that conveyed a positive image of blacks—something that was absent in Hollywood productions.

As authors such as Hughes and Hurston won fame with folktales, Micheaux achieved distinction with movies that embodied black people's dreams. Beginning with *The Homesteader*, he gave top billing to dignified African Americans. He applied this principle to great effect in *The Birthright*; and for *Body and Soul*, he handed the lead to the legendary Paul Robeson, thereby bringing the first black superstar to the screen. When Micheaux switched to sound for *The Exile*, his style remained the same. He continued to put noble black characters in problematic situations that were familiar to African Americans, and in the process, he propelled the development of race movies.

Raw Stock

At the peak of the Harlem Renaissance, black cinema from Micheaux and his contemporaries received generous criticism. Ordinarily, the critics commended race movies for social reasons, avoiding any consideration of the aesthetics of the genre, because they felt that these movies filled a void in the film industry and should therefore be defended. On occasion, critics mentioned flaws such as erratic montages and uneven acting, but they attributed these problems to pressures imposed by creditors and censors, and they considered the flaws of little importance in light of the social function of race movies. These commentators stressed that the material gave African Americans a vital cinema of their own. Following the death of Micheaux, two decades passed before questions of form and content occupied very many critics. Then, galvanized by the black arts movement, various scholars and researchers began to say that the old productions were deficient in artistic and cultural value.

Cripps (1977) and Sampson (1995) established that early black cinema had been hampered by censorship. From the outset, for example, movies by blacks were subjected to bowdlerization. The following are other specific examples. A need to appease white backers prevented Emmett Scott (a secretary to Booker T. Washington) from realizing "Lincoln's Dream," his planned response to *Birth of a Nation*; he had to change the name of his project to *Birth of a Race* and add footage that rendered the finished product an incoherent mélange. The Chicago Board of Censors objected to a lynching scene in Micheaux's *Within Our Gates* and attempted (although unsuccessfully) to prevent this film from appearing; and white operators of theaters in the South that catered to blacks refused to book the film. *Body and Soul* was edited to please censors in New York, and this editing jumbled the plot. Because of a romantic episode involving a black man and a white woman, the Pennsylvania Board of Censors prevented *The Exile* from being shown in Pittsburgh. Time and again, such incidents frustrated black independents.

Moreover, there was never enough money for more than B movies. Lacking the resources for expensive features, black film companies had to settle for moderate productions. Money shortages beset the Foster Photoplay Company and the Lincoln Motion Picture Company. In the 1920s, Reol Productions, the Ebony Film Corporation, and the Democracy Film Corporation managed to assemble decent films, but they did so under the control of white investors. Micheaux, hounded by fiscal woes, had to cut corners. Of course, the tight budgets within which black filmmakers had to work affected the quality of their movies.

In the past few decades, critics have also assailed the content of race movies. Some researchers have noted that light-skinned blacks were consistently given leading roles and have therefore upbraided Micheaux and his peers for replicating the hierarchy of color that prevailed in white cinema. Similarly, some scholars have objected to plots that conformed to conventional Hollywood scripts with happy endings, and several have deplored themes extolling bourgeois conduct. According to scholars such as these, race movies placed the fortunes of blacks in their own hands, thus absolving whites of blame for the problems of African Americans. Now, however,

challenges to such critiques are emerging from scholars who suggest that the black pictures of the Harlem Renaissance era should be understood as expressions of a mood which that found favor in black circles.

Because few copies of race movies are extant, details about them are often little more than speculation. The available material does indicate that meager budgets caused these films to lack polish and that the films were vitiated by censorship. But audiences forgave their imperfections and packed halls such as the Lafayette Theater in Harlem to watch them. These films offered dreams of black achievement to an entire generation. They were right for the time.

Closing Credits

In 1927, *The Jazz Singer*, starring Al Jolson, introduced talking pictures and sounded the death knell for blackface actors and for race movies. Although Jolson played the part of a blackface vaudevillian in *The Jazz Singer*, the new sound technology aroused—and fed—an appetite for realism; as a result, Hollywood was forced to cast more African Americans in black roles. This technological advance also increased the cost of producing movies because the apparatus required for a synchronized soundtrack was so expensive. In addition, after the stock market crashed, black independents had increasing difficulty securing enough capital to compete in the new era. These factors combined to squeeze black film companies out of the market. Before World War II began, race movies had passed from the American scene. A few black independents remained in business beyond the 1930s: Micheaux was one of them; another one was Spencer Williams, who released *Tenderfeet* in 1928 and *Go Down Death* in 1944. But eventually even the survivors were undone by insolvency.

During the Great Depression, Hollywood, with the promise of big paychecks, lured black stars like Clarence Brooks, Paul Robeson, and Lena Horne away from black studios. At the same time, white companies enticed black audiences by developing black musicals, such as *Black and Tan* (1929) and *Saint Louis Blues* (1929), respectively featuring Duke Ellington and Bessie Smith. Nostalgia for the antebellum South returned and made hits of *Hallelujah* (1929) and *Hearts in Dixie* (1929), which had all-black casts. Hollywood also discovered that it was profitable to sprinkle comedies, mysteries, and westerns with African Americans in stereotypical roles. By the time *Cabin in the Sky* (1943) and *Stormy Weather* (1943)—both filled with African American actors—were made, the black independents had all gone out of business.

Race movies left a legacy for future black filmmakers. After Micheaux and his counterparts were gone, black cinema remained dormant for more than twenty-five years. Then, black film directors gained a foothold once again at the start of the black arts movement. This revival was initiated by films such as Melvin Van Peebles's *Sweet Sweetback's Baadasssss Song* (1971) and *Shaft*, directed by Gordon Parks (also 1971). During the 1970s, numerous revenge dramas called "blaxploitation" films—such as *Superfly* (1972) and *Foxy Brown* (1974)—featured black stars. There was a significant audience for comedians such as Richard Pryor, Eddie Murphy, and Whoopi Goldberg and for movies with racial themes; and during the 1980s, such movies made some black comedians superstars. However, black film companies were still scarce until Spike Lee organized Forty Acres and a Mule Filmworks, whose productions, such as *She's Gotta Have It* (1986) and *Do the Right Thing* (1989), were very successful at the box office and sparked a second resurgence of black cinema. The trend begun by Lee brought filmmakers such as John Singleton, Julie Dash, and Charles Burnett to the fore and lasted until the end of the twentieth century.

So far, though, no generation of black filmmakers has matched the volume of output of those who created the race movies. Prohibitive costs and Hollywood blockbusters with African American headliners have continued to thwart black independents. Those who have been notably successful have applied a formula devised by their forerunners during the Harlem Renaissance: they have taken the pulse of the black community and have treated that community agreeably onscreen. This approach constitutes a special part of the heritage bequeathed by figures such as Micheaux.

Wrap

The Birth of a Nation, with its blackface actors, set off a boom in black cinema that reverberated throughout the Harlem Renaissance. The resulting race movies met a demand for positive images of blacks onscreen. A host of black independents opened for business, and their films excited pride and ambition. Among these filmmakers, Oscar Micheaux produced forty features. Black filmmakers were constrained by scanty budgets and by censorship, and their productions were consequently impaired, but audiences packed the movie houses to see their films. Proponents of black aesthetics have frowned on the typical themes of race movies, but so little of these films remains available that commentary is often not much more than guesswork. After the *Jazz Singer* appeared, race movies faded from the scene, but they provided a lesson for future generations.

ROLAND L. WILLIAMS JR

See also Brooks, Clarence; Birth of a Nation, The; Birth of a Race, The; Colored Players Film Corportation; Film: Actors; Film: Black Filmmakers; Film: Blacks as Portrayed by White Filmmakers; Hallelujah; Hearts in Dixie; Lincoln Motion Picture Company; Micheax, Oscar; Race Films; Robeson, Paul; *other specific individuals*

Further Reading

Bogle, Donald. *Toms, Coons, Mulattos, Mammies, and Bucks.* New York: Viking, 1973.

Cripps, Thomas. *Slow Fade to Black.* New York: Oxford University Press, 1977.

Leab, Daniel. *From Sambo to Superspade.* Boston, Mass.: Houghton Mifflin, 1975.

Lewis, David Levering. *When Harlem Was in Vogue.* New York: Oxford University Press, 1981.

Locke, Alain. *The New Negro.* New York: Alfred and Charles Boni, 1925.

Nesteby, James. *Black Images in American Films.* New York: Lanham, 1982.

Sampson, Henry. *Blacks in Black and White.* Metuchen, N.J.: Scarecrow, 1995.

Stowe, Harriet Beecher. *Uncle Tom's Cabin.* Boston: John P. Jewett, 1852.

Film: Actors

In 2002, when Halle Berry became the first black woman to win an Academy Award as best actress, more than six decades had passed since the first black woman had won an Academy Award in any category: that was Hattie McDaniel, who had won as best supporting actress for her performance in *Gone with the Wind* (1939). In the years between, only one other black woman had won: Whoopi Goldberg, in 1990, for her supporting role in *Ghost*. Interestingly, responses in the black community to Berry's award (for her role in *Monster's Ball*, the story of a woman who falls in love with a recovering white racist who happens to be the man who executed her husband) were mixed. Recognition of this milestone was tempered by questions surrounding the range of roles offered by Hollywood to blacks and especially to black women. For some critics, Berry's character was contemporary evidence of the persistence of restrictions that had first been imposed on black actors at the dawn of American filmmaking.

The quarter-century from 1888 to 1915 that witnessed unprecedented technological advances in the newly established American film industry was also a period of perhaps unparalleled antiblack sentiment and violence. Somewhat ironically, the year 1896 saw both the first projection of moving images onto a large screen and a decision by the Supreme Court, in *Plessy v. Ferguson*, that helped usher in an era of legalized racial separation. Given its unquestioned power to shape public opinion—and despite its potential to challenge racial and other standards—American film during this period was implicated in the nation's subjugation and defamation of its black population. Black actors, during the heyday of the Harlem Renaissance, found themselves at the center of a people's struggle for accurate and humanistic representation onscreen.

Hollywood: Opportunity and Boundaries

During the 1920s, as reported by the black press and well documented in Hollywood's Central Casting Bureau, black actors made gains in terms of overall numbers employed by white studios, but those gains did not translate into improved status (Regester 1997, 95). Nor did their appearance in silent films during the 1920s significantly challenge long-standing stereotypes of black Americans. Black film actors, like members of other ethnic minority groups who responded to casting calls during this era, were consistently relegated to appearances as extras. Although employment opportunities generally were plentiful, black actors in the mid-1920s most often appeared as "backdrop": soldiers, slaves, members of crowds, and, frequently, natives in exoticized African or Pacific island settings. Although opportunities to challenge cinematic representations of race were clearly circumscribed, the black acting presence in Hollywood, at least in terms of sheer numbers, was firmly established by 1926 (Regester, 98).

With the transition to the sound era in film, blacks continued to be visible as extras, but they also began to secure a few major roles. In 1927, the same year that *The Jazz Singer* signaled the industry's transition to sound, and in the following year, several films—including *Louisiana*, *Jungle Gods*, *The Missing Link*, *The River*, *The Wedding March*, and *Diamond Handcuffs*—employed large numbers of blacks as extras and a few in substantial roles. In 1927, the famous black actor James Lowe obtained a leading role in a production of *Uncle Tom's Cabin*. And the end of the decade would bring the production of two major all-black feature films that showcased many of the most talented actors of the 1920s and 1930s. On the one hand, these gains represented a tremendous improvement in the financial viability of black acting, but on the other hand, black actors acquiesced in their own marginalization. Not until the late 1930s did blacks resort to strikes and other direct measures to gain higher wages and more dignified roles in film.

Hollywood: Black Actors and Comedy

Humor was ubiquitous in American films at the turn of the twentieth century. The silent film era may be best remembered for its comedies (Watkins 1994, 183). Unfortunately for blacks, the genre reinforced racial stereotypes for white audiences accustomed to laughing at the portrayals of black life provided by minstrelsy and vaudeville. Bogle (2001) and others have identified several black character types that appeared in minstrelsy and vaudeville and made an almost seamless transition to moving pictures: the fawning Tom, the self-mocking coon, the jolly but recalcitrant mammy (Aunt Jemima), the tragic mulatto, the brutal buck. Arguably, it was the figure of the coon, or Sambo, whose appearance in America cinema in the first half of the twentieth century had the most devastating impact on efforts to present an honest portrait of black life to American audiences.

Before his popularity began to wane in the late 1930s, Stepin Fetchit was the best-known and most successful black actor in Hollywood. He was, as well, the quintessential coon or Sambo figure in American film. He and his comic "stepchildren"—Willie Best, Mantan Moreland, and Fred "Snowflake" Toones, among others—would leave in the American psyche and memory an indelible image of a lazy, dull-witted, tongue-tied black man. Despite his efforts to inject some respectability into his film roles, Fetchit's characters were among the most demeaning figures in black film history. Ultimately, although he was tremendously popular among white moviegoers, he alienated significant numbers of blacks.

A lesser-known source for exploring images of blacks in films before the civil rights era is the collection *Our Gang* (renamed *The Little Rascals* in its television version, for legal reasons), film shorts produced between 1922 and 1944. Four black child actors had major roles in this popular series. Ernie Morrison portrayed, among other characters, "Sunshine Sammy" in the early, silent installments of *Our Gang*. Allen Hoskins, who bridged the gap between the silent and sound versions, was best known as "Farina." Matthew Beard's "Stymie" and William Thomas Jr.'s "Buckwheat" are the black characters most often associated with *Our Gang*. Throughout its run, the series contained racial jokes and reinforced stereotypes of blacks in general and of black children in particular. However, as has been noted by several critics, the gang's world—especially when compared with the adult black world depicted in films of the era—was one of "equal-opportunity buffoonery," because all of the children were the butt of jokes and because they generally related to each other with no regard to race (Watkins, 219–220).

Hollywood: Black Actors and Musicals

The advent of sound movies sparked Hollywood's interest in black performers for at least two reasons: the belief that black voices, with their "unmistakable resonance," were well-suited to the new medium; and the continued popularity of black music. *The Jazz Singer* (1927) launched the sound era in filmmaking, and the critical reception of its star, Al Jolson, prompted renewed interest in blackface productions. Some of the earliest beneficiaries of shifting technologies were black musicians who made appearances in all-black musical shorts. In the late 1920s and into the 1930s, some of the nation's greatest musicians appeared in one- and two-reelers that showcased their talents. Perhaps most notable were the performances of Bessie Smith in *Saint Louis Blues* (1929) and Duke Ellington in *Black and Tan* (also 1929). Black musicians also made cameo appearances, some quite unflattering, in white feature films of the period: for example, in Paramount's *Rhapsody in Black and Blue* (1932), Louis Armstrong was cast as a jungle king, complete with animal skins and native headdress (Watkins, 214).

Three notable all-black movies produced in the 1920s and 1930s—*Hearts in Dixie* (1929), *Hallelujah!*

(1929), and *The Green Pastures* (1936)—were striking departures from the musical shorts and cameo appearances. All three were lavish productions in which black musical talent was showcased along with black acting. *Hearts in Dixie* starred Clarence Muse and Stepin Fetchit, the former in a seemingly dignified role and the latter exhibiting his standard buffoonery. Set in the South during the plantation era, *Hearts in Dixie* offered standard antebellum stereotypes, but its all-black cast was the first to appear in a feature-length film. *Hallelujah!* was a morality play directed by King Vidor; its leading lady, Nina Mae McKinney, was the first recognized black film actress (Bogle, 33). *Green Pastures*, the cinematic adaptation of a successful Broadway play, highlighted the talents of Rex Ingram and Eddie "Rochester" Anderson. Despite their technical and narrative weaknesses, all three films gave black actors an opportunity to display their talents and helped pave the way for subsequent all-black productions.

Hollywood: Black Actors and Drama

D. W. Griffith's controversial production *The Birth of a Nation* (1915) was the first feature-length American film. A technological marvel, it was powerful evidence that history and drama could combine to produce a popular, influential, and—for black Americans—dangerous work of art. That this film would so successfully rewrite the history of the Civil War and Reconstruction was cause for alarm; that it would so unflinchingly reinforce stereotypes of blacks as socially and politically incompetent, and black men as bestial by nature, was an even greater motivation for black Americans to protest its release. But *Birth of a Nation* was not unique. Aside from black independent filmmakers' visions of black life, most cinematic drama marginalized rather than humanized black Americans.

While the stereotype of the coon, or Sambo, dominated portraits of blacks in comedy films, Hollywood drama in the 1920s and 1930s was replete with other black character types: the long-suffering, loyal Tom; the aggressive, asexual mammy; and the tragic mulatto. Dramatic film has always held the potential to question, if not subvert, the existing racial order, but the "New Negro" was seldom to be found in Hollywood cinema. Bogle (35, 53) notes that with regard to black film roles, the 1930s were an "era of servants," a period when even the most dignified black actors were relegated to subservient relationships with white leading actors. Thus the legendary actor and dancer Bill "Bojangles" Robinson became humorist Will Rogers's loyal servant in *In Old Kentucky* (1935), and most famously Shirley Temple's trusted "Uncle Billy" in a plantation melodrama, *The Littlest Rebel* (1935). Clarence Muse became the archetypal Tom, Nigger Jim, in *Huckleberry Finn* (1931). And the antebellum mammy or Aunt Jemima—a figure who often combined the loyalty of Tom, the comic affability of Sambo, and her own unique "sassiness" (i.e., bitchiness)—was resurrected as a maid in the twentieth century and portrayed by Louise Beavers and Hattie McDaniel, among others.

A mainstay of American film and literature in the first half of the twentieth century was the "tragic mulatto," almost always a woman. The actress Fredi Washington, whose facial features were racially ambiguous, was frequently cast as a black woman passing for white with tragic consequences. She appeared opposite Paul Robeson in *The Emperor Jones* (1933) and opposite Louise Beavers in 1934 in a version of *Imitation of Life*, a film that would become the archetypal statement of the consequences of racial passing. These films were seemingly vehicles for a sophisticated exploration of identity by biracial or multiracial Americans but were based on the faulty assumption that the mulatto's experience is inherently tragic.

Beyond Hollywood: Black Actors and Black Independent Film

Historically, black independent films have offered alternative images of black life and culture, and in the early twentieth century they provided much-needed work for black artists beyond the reach of Hollywood. William Foster, Oscar Micheaux, Noble and George Johnson, Spencer Williams, and a few other black independent filmmakers offered a working environment that generally allowed black actors to avoid the demeaning roles assigned to their Hollywood counterparts. These underground "race films" also provided a rapidly growing black moviegoing population with a form of entertainment of which they could be proud.

The earliest phase of race films—despite their technical flaws—challenged existing portraits of black Americans. This phase began with William Foster's *The Railroad Porter* (1912); continued with Biograph Pictures' *A Natural Born Gambler* (released in 1914 and starring the noted vaudevillian Bert Williams); and crystallized in *Birth of a Race* (originally called "Lincoln's

Dream"), the black community's response to *Birth of a Nation*.

The next phase of independent black filmmaking began with the incorporation of Noble and George Johnson's Lincoln Motion Picture Company in 1916. The Johnson brothers' films, which included *The Realization of a Negro's Ambition* (1916) and *The Trooper of Troop K* (1916), were conscious attempts to capture the achievements of black Americans and create heroes and heroines (Bogle, 341). In order to remain with Lincoln, actors such as Jimmie Smith and Beulah Hall would forgo other opportunities; perhaps these actors appreciated the control over image enjoyed by a black production crew and acting ensemble. However, by the late 1920s and early 1930s—because of a lack of capital and because the film industry was rapidly expanding and diversifying—many of the black companies had folded. White filmmakers, recognizing that films aimed at a black audience were commercially viable, began to dominate the market (this trend foreshadowed the emergence of "blaxplotation" films in the 1970s).

Beginning in 1918, the legendary independent filmmaker Oscar Micheaux produced pioneering works for three decades. His films included narratives that, like those of the Johnson brothers, were dedicated to the theme of black uplift. However, Micheaux consistently navigated dangerous thematic terrain, exploring interracial relationships and the "color complex"—a range of contentious issues related to gradations of skin color and to the resulting conflicts within the black community. Among the actors employed by Micheaux were Lorenzo Tucker, the "black Valentino"; Bee Freeman, the "sepia Mae West"; the sultry Ethel Moses; and Julia Theresa Russell and Paul Robeson, who had the leading roles in Micheaux's masterpiece *Body and Soul* (1925).

It might be argued that the cinematic counterpart to the New Negro in the literature of the Harlem Renaissance was to be found in the world of black independent filmmaking. Literature and film both argued for honest depictions of black life; each was uncompromising in its own way; both began to wane in the mid- to late 1930s; and both would leave an indelible imprint on black history and culture. Bogle (136) has suggested that the New Negro would not appear in Hollywood films until the 1940s, when a new generation of actors and their roles—outgrowths of the social spirit of the day—would help redefine the relationship between blacks and America.

C. C. HERBISON

See also Baker, Josephine; Beavers, Louise; Birth of a Nation, The; Birth of a Race, The; Blackface Performance; Blacks in Theater; Calloway, Cab; Colored Players Film Corporation; Ellington, Duke; Emperor Jones, The; Fetchit, Stepin; Film; Film: Black Filmmakers; Film: Blacks as Portrayed by White Filmmakers; Green Pastures, The; Hallelujah!; Hearts in Dixie; Johnson, Noble; Lincoln Motion Picture Company; Lowe, James B.; Madame Sul Te Wan; McKinney, Nina Mae; Micheaux, Oscar; Minstrelsy; Moreland, Mantan; Muse, Clarence; Race Films; Robeson, Paul; Robinson, Bill "Bojangles"; Vaudeville; Washington, Fredi; Waters, Ethel; Within Our Gates

Further Reading

Bogle, Donald: *Toms, Coons, Mulattoes, Mammies, and Bucks: An Interpretive History of Blacks in American Films*, 4th ed. New York: Continuum, 2001.

Bowser, Pearl, and Louise Spence. *Writing Himself into History: Oscar Micheaux, His Silent Films, and His Audiences.* New Brunswick, N.J.: Rutgers University Press, 2000.

Cripps, Thomas. *Slow Fade to Black: The Negro in American Film, 1900–1942.* New York: Oxford University Press, 1993.

Diawara, Manthia, ed. *Black American Cinema.* New York: Routledge, 1993.

Guerrero, Ed. *Framing Blackness: The African American Image in Film.* Philadelphia, Pa.: Temple University Press, 1993.

Regester, Charlene. "African American Extras in Hollywood during the 1920s and 1930s." *Film History*, 9(1), 1997, pp. 95–115.

Snead, James. *White Screens / Black Images: Hollywood from the Dark Side*, eds. Colin McCabe and Cornel West. New York: Routledge, 1994.

Watkins, Mel. *On the Real Side: A History of African American Comedy from Slavery to Chris Rock.* Chicago, Ill.: Lawrence Hill, 1994.

Film: Black Filmmakers

An African American appeared in the first motion picture copyrighted in the United States; this was a young laboratory assistant of Thomas Alva Edison's, Fred Ott, who pretended to sneeze, and made history with his silent, overacted, head-snapping atchoo.

From then on, black people were part of the film industry. Early white American filmmakers featured black vaudeville entertainers, among other subjects, in short silent films; one 35-mm film that survives from the early era shows a black male tap dancer.

During the early experimental phase of the film industry—a phase characterized by rapid progress through trial and error—black assistants worked behind the scenes, beside open-minded white inventors. These black laboratory assistants would sometimes be captured on laboratory demonstration films intended to depict human movement. They were often the inspiration or even the masterminds of cinematic breakthroughs, but because of cultural prejudice, their names were never registered on the patents.

In these early days, between 1888 and 1896, only a few black people other than those employed in laboratories were able to view movies. Edison's Kinetoscope machine accommodated only a single viewer at a time, and other technologies allowed only a few people to watch a film, in a small space (of course, these limitations also restricted the number of white people who could see a movie). In 1896, however, the first motion pictures were presented in a "movie theater" in New York City. The Edison Company had devised a projector known as the Projectoscope and started showing films to large, paying audiences on a regular basis. The first such film showed contemporary scenes of Herald Square in New York City and travelogues of more exotic places, including Niagara Falls in upstate New York and Passaic Falls in New Jersey.

The laboratory of the Edison Company, in West Orange, New Jersey (less than ten miles from New York City), began filming trains and train routes in *Black Diamond Express* in December 1896. Black men employed as porters, cooks, and skilled laborers on the trains were often seen in these films. Travelogues featuring train rides with scenic views were very popular, and black audiences particularly enjoyed seeing black workers in the background. But black moviegoers were segregated. In some localities, blacks were relegated to the balconies of white vaudeville theaters; in larger northern and southern cities that already had lucrative black vaudeville theaters with middle-class black patrons, the Edison films were shown to all-black audiences between burlesque comedy routines and party music.

Travelogues, newsreels, special events, crime, war, the Paris Exposition of 1900, and Native American cultural events were the typical subjects of most silent films at the turn of the twentieth century. There was also footage of black soldiers going off to fight the Spanish-American War. All of this made movies a very popular form of entertainment and a source of information, but the paying public soon began to demand fictional films with plots. Accordingly, white businesspeople, and soon afterward black business-people, scrambled to meet this demand. It was natural and convenient to adapt for the screen some of the vaudeville dramas that were being featured in the same theaters as the early films. Many popular vaudeville stories and stage actors and actresses found their way to silent movies between 1902 and 1915.

In 1903, a fourteen-minute film dramatization of Harriet Beecher Stowe's popular novel *Uncle Tom's Cabin* was released and shown to enthusiastic audiences in theaters all over the country. The black characters were portrayed by white actors in blackface, and this film proved very effective at transferring demeaning stereotypes of blacks from literature to the movies. At about this time, many other films were produced that also depicted black people in subservient and comic roles.

Not until 1912—when William Foster founded the Foster Photoplay Company—did a filmmaker challenge these onscreen images of black people or depict blacks as confronting complex issues. Foster, a publicity and booking agent for vaudeville in Chicago, was the first black to use the vast pool of African American talent and community drama as a resource for films. His Foster Photoplay Company was organized particularly to specialize in "non-degrading Black-cast comedies," as he wrote in *Freeman* (in the issue of 20 December 1913). He noted: "Nothing has done so much to awaken race consciousness of the colored man in the United States as the motion picture. It has made him hungry to see himself as he has come to be."

With a stock company of black actors from vaudeville and musical theater, Foster set out to represent in American movies the lifestyles of the black middle class. His debut film, in 1912, was a ten-minute comedy-drama, *The Railroad Porter*—America's first movie with an all-black cast. *The Railroad Porter* was in part a parody of railroad travelogue films, but it also included the complexities of what can happen when a man stays away from home too long: Foster's porter must cope with a cheating wife. In this film, Foster gave life to the black railroad porter, a figure who had previously appeared in movies only as serving white travelers. Foster produced at least eleven films before

his company folded in 1918 as a result of insufficient funding and distribution. His titles included *The Butler* and *The Fall Guy*. In 1914, he also produced a newsreel, *The Colored Championship Baseball Game*, which is the only known film documenting the Colored Baseball Leagues.

To a considerable degree, Foster's hope of uplifting the race was dashed when *Birth of a Nation* was released in 1915. This film, directed by D. W. Griffith, was a masterpiece, but it depicted American history in the aftermath of the Civil War from the viewpoint of those who sympathized with the Confederacy, and it portrayed black people as rapists, thieves, ignorant preachers, and cowering rascals. Foster responded with a screenplay that would eventually bear the title *Birth of a Race* and started production on it in 1916. After two years of production and financing from several backers—including Booker T. Washington's Tuskegee Circle, Universal Pictures, and Julius Rosenwald of Sears Roebuck—Foster's last film was a commercial failure.

As Foster's company in Chicago faltered, the brothers George Johnson (a black postal worker originally from Omaha) and Noble Johnson (an actor) founded the Lincoln Motion Picture Company in Los Angeles, California. According to its promotional literature, Lincoln "not only produced pictures entertaining to Negroes but to all races. Our market is as large as we make it; the world is our field."

In 1916, the Johnson brothers produced the country's first full-length black film drama, *A Realization of a Negro's Ambition*. This was the story of a black graduate of Tuskegee Institute who becomes an oil tycoon in California. Twenty years later, George Johnson said that the film had allowed "black actors to pursue performances liberated from the stereotypes of buffoonery promoted in the mainstream film business." The Lincoln Motion Picture Company produced films until it was forced out of business by a flu epidemic that closed movie theaters in 1921. Its titles included *A Trooper of Company K* (1917) and *By Right of Birth* (1921).

In 1918, another young black filmmaker, Oscar Micheaux, responded to Griffith's *Birth of a Nation*. Micheaux, an up-and-coming novelist who was originally from Chicago, dramatized his book *The Homesteader*, based on his own experience as a black farmer in South Dakota and financed by other farmers there, black and white. Micheaux had turned down an offer by the Johnson brothers, who wanted to buy his screenplay; he opened the Micheaux Book and Film Company in

Chicago and proceeded to produce his own films, of which *The Homesteader* was the first. Micheaux shot his early films on location in Chicago and in studios in New York. In 1926, he closed his Chicago operation and moved permanently to Harlem.

Micheaux became the most successful black filmmaker in American history. He produced more than thirty films between 1918 and 1951. Although he emphasized middle-class black America, he also addressed contemporary issues such as lynching. His titles include *Within Our Gates* (1919), *The Brute* (1920), *The Symbol of the Unconquered* (1920), *The Gunsaulus Mystery* (1921), *The House behind the Cedars* (1924), *The Son of Satan* (1924), *Birthright* (1924 and 1939), *Thirty Years Later* (1928), *The Daughter of the Congo* (1930), *The Exile* (1931), *Darktown Revue* (1931), *Temptation* (1936), *The Underworld* (1936), *God's Stepchildren* (1939), *The Notorious Elinor Lee* (1940), and *The Betrayal* (1948).

Despite Micheaux's success, many of his films seem to have been crudely produced with minimal funding. Members of his technical crew would double as extras—as would Micheaux, who also made cameo appearances in his own films. He was often criticized for using light-skinned black people to play the roles of whites and authority figures.

Micheaux marketed his pictures to black audiences on a circuit of black vaudeville theaters in the South and along the east coast—the "Chitterlings Circuit," as it was affectionately called by its patrons. His films were also shown in churches, community centers, and dance halls; and he would often exhibit his personal copy of a film as he drove from location to location in his own car. As soon as he completed the exhibition circuit, Micheaux would immediately start filming his next project.

Micheaux has been credited with keeping black stage actors working when times were hard during the Depression. He introduced Paul Robeson to the movies in 1924, in the silent drama *Body and Soul*. Micheax said in 1920, "The appreciation my people have shown my maiden efforts convinces me that they want racial photoplays depicting racial life, and to that task I have concentrated my mind and efforts." In his films, he was able to explore many topics that were unique to black America; for example, he often used the "tragic mulatto" as a theme in which his characters overcame life's difficulties. He emphasized the positive, praiseworthy qualities of black America, but he was not afraid to show the seedy aspects of black life as well—and as a result, the black press continually criticized him and his movies.

In 1928, Micheaux filed a voluntary bankruptcy petition in the U.S. Seventh District Court in New York City. In 1929, with new white partners, he reorganized his company in New York state under the name Micheaux Film Corporation. The president of this new company, Frank Schiffman, also owned several theaters in New York City that catered to black audiences. However, the partnership was short-lived and Micheaux ultimately ran his film production company without partners. By the 1930s, Micheaux was not the only producer interested in making films for black audiences: nearly 150 film companies were targeting the black community, although most of their films were poorly written, poorly acted, and poorly directed.

Another black filmmaker who was unsatisfied with Hollywood's depiction of his race was the actor and director Spencer Williams. Williams made his mark in black films during the 1930s. Films he directed include *Bronze Buckaroo*, *Harlem on the Prairie*, *Blood of Jesus*, *Dirty Girtie from Harlem*, and *Juke Joint*. Of these, *Blood of Jesus* is of particular interest. The main female character is faced with a traditional choice—life in the country versus the more exciting but also more sinful life of a big city—and Williams accordingly documented a river baptism; but he also introduced double exposure to black films, as an inexpensive special effect. In his films, Williams did not try to correct all that was wrong in America; he tended to show ordinary black life. Because his films were popular among audiences as well as critics, he was considered the most successful black film director of his era. (In his later years, Williams was even more famous as Andy in the popular television program *Amos 'n' Andy*. Although he was criticized for taking this role, he maintained that the character was not stereotypical but strong and intelligent.)

A few black actors and actresses who became famous in films produced by blacks also crossed over to white companies that produced "race films" with all-black casts for black audiences. Paul Robeson was one of the first black victims of white Hollywood's double-edged sword. Two white producers, John Krimsky and Gifford Cochran, recruited Robeson in 1933. Robeson's talent as an entertainer, athlete, and scholar was undisputed, and he had already made his film debut in Micheaux's *Body and Soul* and had starred in a Swiss film, *Boarderline*, in 1929; but he fell prey to filmmakers who had ultimate control over the final edit and could therefore remake his image and that of black people. Robeson, who made nine feature films between 1929 and 1942, said that he was never satisfied with their depiction of blacks and that he had been tricked into playing characters whose roles were reconstructed in the editing room without his knowledge. (One such film was *Sanders of the River* in 1937.) Robeson was an outspoken advocate of civil rights whose complaints to white producers were tolerated, perhaps because his appeal at the box office outweighed other considerations. Evidently, he was selected in preference to other black actors at least partly because he was able to pacify both black and white moviegoers. To blacks, he represented hope (his screen presence was very impressive); to whites, he was seen as being kept in his place as long as his screen characters were submissive to whites. Robeson said that he took questionable roles in order to strengthen his bargaining position; but he finally gave up his fight with Hollywood in 1942, when he joined a picket line protesting against his last movie, *Tales of Manhattan*—and in any case he had little effect on the white film industry, which refused to create the kind of scripts that would have complemented his talent. Other black actors had even less access to positive roles; most of them were grateful just to have a job and performed stereotyped roles in order to get a paycheck.

The most successful actor who crossed over from all-black films to Hollywood films was Stepin Fetchit (Lincoln Theodore Perry). As a vaudevillian, he had developed, with a partner, a routine called "Step 'n' Fetchit." After that act broke up in the mid-1920s, he took Stepin Fetchit as his stage name and created a new character based on his former partner. Perry perfected the lazy, stupid, subservient black stereotype onstage and carried it into movies. When black filmmakers fell on hard times, Stepin Fetchit found steady work in white Hollywood; he was the first black actor to achieve featured billing in movies with white stars, and he never bowed to objections about his character. He saw himself simply as a hardworking comic actor; claimed that he was the first black entertainer to become a millionaire; and believed that he had been influential in opening doors to the motion picture world for other blacks. Stepin Fetchit starred in at least forty films from 1927 to 1975; they included *In Old Kentucky* (1927), *Salute* (1929), *Judge Priest* (1934), and *Steamboat around the Bend* (1935). Other blacks who crossed over were Duke Ellington (who appeared with his orchestra in *Black and Tan*, an RCA Phonophone production of 1929), Mantan Moreland (who appeared in *Tall, Tan,*

and Terrific in 1946), and Bill Robinson (who appeared in *Harlem Is Heaven* in 1945).

Eventually, a lack of coordinated distribution, exhibition, and publicity caused black filmmakers, one by one, to stop producing. Another factor was film rationing during World War II. Moreover, exhibition space for black films was drastically reduced; many of the black vaudeville theaters that at one time had shown black films went out of business during World War II and abandoned their buildings. Black filmmaking could not recover from economic hardships, the loss of exhibition space, and the shortage of film stock available to nonwhite businesses in the early 1940s, and it succumbed during a flurry of wartime recruitment films for the U.S. Army. The first phase of black filmmaking was over by 1950.

SHARON ELIZABETH SEXTON

See also Amos 'n' Andy; Birth of a Nation, The; Birth of a Race, The; Ellington, Duke; Fetchit, Stepin; Film; Film: Actors; Film: Blacks as Portrayed by White Filmmakers; Johnson, Noble; Lincoln Motion Picture Company; Micheax, Oscar; Moreland, Mantan; Race Films; Robeson, Paul; Robinson, Bill "Bojangles"

Further Reading

"Actor Stepin Fetchit, 83, Dies in L.A. Hospital." *Jet*, 9 December 1985.

A Brief Analysis of Six Black Genre Films. Moorland-Spingarn Research Center.

Horowitz, Joy. "Hollywood's Dirty Little Secret." *Premiere*, March 1989.

Koppes, Clayton R., and Gregory D. Black. "The Second World War in Black and White: How Hollywood Lost the Battle for Racial Progress." *Washington Post*, 11 October 1987.

Oscar Micheaux and the Black Independents. Moorland-Spingarn Research Center.

"The Problem with Post-Racism." *New Republic*, 5 August 1985.

Sampson, Henry T. *Blacks in Black and White: A Source Book on Black Films*. Metuchen, N.J.: Scarecrow, 1977.

"Stepin Fetchit Dead at 83; Comic Actor in Over 40 Films." *Variety*, 27 November 1985.

Stewart, Jacqueline. "William Foster: The Dean of the Negro Photoplay." *Oscar Micheaux Society Newsletter* (University of Chicago), 9, Spring 2001.

Woll, Allen L., and Randall M. Miller. *Ethnic and Racial Images in American Film and Television: Historical Essays and Bibliography*. New York and London: Garland, 1987.

Film: Blacks as Portrayed by White Filmmakers

On the basis of his darkness he glowed. (Ralph Ellison)

Perspective

In the wake of World War I, a stream of hope surged through African American culture, but this wave clashed with the depiction of blacks presented in films made by whites. Thousands of black people aspiring to social equality and economic security poured into northern cities from the rural South; they were seeking a fair chance to demonstrate their true talents, and they swore that, given the opportunity, they could soar to new heights and in the process promote the general welfare. To their dismay, these migrants encountered Hollywood movies that mocked their ambitions by casting blacks in roles that simply perpetuated stereotypes formed during the era of slavery.

Alain Locke observed the postwar mood among African Americans. In *The New Negro* (1925), he described a spirit that was infusing blacks with a strong determination to leave the bottom of society, where slavery and segregation had stranded them, and climb up the social ladder. With regard to popular portrayals of black people, Locke discerned a growing intolerance for traditional depictions of blacks as servile characters such as Uncle Tom and Sambo in Harriet Beecher Stowe's novel *Uncle Tom's Cabin* (1852). Locke had identified the trend of a new generation, and his insight was verified by the angry reaction of the National Association for the Advancement of Colored People (NAACP) and the Urban League to D. W. Griffith's film *The Birth of a Nation* (1915), which slighted African Americans and supported the Ku Klux Klan.

By the beginning of the Harlem Renaissance, as African Americans sought to rise in society, protests against stereotypical portraits in motion pictures became a common topic of articles in *Crisis* and *Opportunity*, two journals that conveyed the perspective of the black community. This outcry, however, failed to stem the tide of unrealistic images of blacks that flowed from white film studios. In fact, the growing demand by blacks for fairness in movies effectively created a backlash: Hollywood habitually featured blacks as flat characters reminiscent of Stowe's verbal sketches of slaves.

Group Show

When it was first published, *Uncle Tom's Cabin* stirred the country. It was a sincere indictment of slavery, and it was widely credited with inciting the Civil War. Throughout the last half of the nineteenth century, this book inspired a variety of imitators, including novels and plays, that thrilled the general public; and its influence extended into the twentieth century, affecting the motion picture industry. In 1903, Edwin Porter adapted Stowe's novel for the screen, and several cinematic versions of the story arrived in theaters during the era of silent films. Before movies began to talk in 1927, white filmmakers settled on showing five types of blacks, each resembling a figure in *Uncle Tom's Cabin*: Uncle Tom, Topsy, Eliza, Aunt Chloe, and George Harris. Imitations of these five figures covered the complete range of black characters in white cinema. Like the figures in the book, blacks in mainstream movies evoked, respectively, a shaman, scamp, siren, shrew, and scoundrel. Bogle (1997) described the few black roles as "Toms, coons, mulattoes, mammies, and bucks." Moreover, these characterizations of blacks persisted long after *The Jazz Singer* (1927) introduced sound, continuing well beyond the stock market crash of 1929 that started the Great Depression.

Birth of a Nation contains the entire array of blacks featured in white productions. The faithful soul who serves the Cameron family to the end has the air of a shaman that distinguishes Uncle Tom in Stowe's novel; the film is full of derelict scamps akin to the pickaninny Topsy, particularly the barefoot blacks in Congress after the Civil War; Lydia Brown, the mulatto, has the allure of a siren and recalls Eliza; Mammy has the shrewish manner of Aunt Chloe; and Silas Lynch and the sinister Gus behave as scoundrels, displaying the defiance of George Harris. Every black figure in *Birth of a Nation* represents one of the five types.

Birth of a Nation fascinated President Woodrow Wilson, who proclaimed, "It's like writing history with lightning," but it appalled African Americans. Blacks in Boston rioted after its premiere there. The NAACP tried to have the film banned and picketed showings in New York and Chicago. W. E. B. Du Bois condemned it in *Crisis*. Across the country, black magazines and newspapers railed against it. A reviewer in the *Chicago Defender* called it despicable racist propaganda. Despite these protests from the African American community, however, *Birth of a Nation* remained in demand, and its treatment of black characters continued to find favor in American cinema.

Evidently, the formulaic roles of blacks in feature films satisfied a widespread desire to excuse slavery in early American society. Initially, around 1619, Africans had entered American culture as indentured servants, equal to the average white immigrant and with the right to gain their freedom. Two generations later, to stabilize the workforce, one region after another instituted bondage for blacks—contrary to the emergent social ethos whereby everyone was said to be born for liberty. This development entailed a dehumanization of blacks and a sense that blacks were at their best in service to whites, a concept that persisted into the nineteenth century, with two sides divided over the degree to which whites stood superior to blacks. That concept influenced Stowe. In *Uncle Tom's Cabin*, as James Baldwin once noted, she immortalized the most popular images of blacks at that time, placing blacks below whites but above slavery. Her work was appealing enough to impress the motion picture industry; and during the period of the Harlem Renaissance—to repeat—black characters in mainstream movies were variations of her five types, despite strong opposition from African Americans.

Primary Colors

The first "black" star in American cinema was actually white: an actor who painted his face black to play Uncle Tom in Edwin Porter's movie adaptation (1903) of Stowe's novel. Such portrayals were enormously popular; moviegoers welcomed a succession of imitators who appeared in silent movies. The next stars were also white: women who enacted fair black belles in dramas such as *Octoroon* (1911), in which a few drops of black blood make the title character a tragic figure. Not until the jazz age did black actors star in movies made by whites, but by the time the Harlem Renaissance was reaching a downturn, African Americans were in vogue in films, as fretful scoundrels and

full-bodied shrews. Paul Robeson became famous in *The Emperor Jones* (1933); Hattie McDaniel won a Academy Award for her role in *Gone with the Wind* (1939); and funny scamps, like the black lead in *Topsy and Eva* (1927), remained in style. Characters such as these appeared more or less frequently from time to time, but at no time did they disappear.

Several white actors wearing burnt cork played Uncle Tom before Sam Lucas, an African American, stepped into the role in 1914, to be followed by James Lowe (1927). Likewise, whites in blackface initially played loyal slaves in films such as *The Confederate Spy* (1910), *For His Master's Sake* (1911), and *A Slave's Devotion* (1913). Clarence Muse became the most celebrated authentic black performer of this type after his appearance as Jim in a screen version of *Huckleberry Finn* (1931). During the early era of silent films, the only other type that achieved the prestige of Uncle Tom was the star-crossed siren evocative of Eliza in *Uncle Tom's Cabin*. This spellbinder appeared in *The Debt* (1912), *The Octoroon's Sacrifice* (1912), and *In Slavery Days* (1913; in this film a white actor in makeup performed the black part). Nina Mae McKinney won renown for this kind of role when she starred as Chick in *Hallelujah!* (1929).

Another type, the renegade who defies white authority (reminiscent of George Harris in *Uncle Tom's Cabin*), took a while to earn applause in movie theaters. The conduct of Silas and Gus in *Birth of a Nation* was deplorable enough to check interest in their kind. Even the beloved black vaudevillian Bert Williams attracted little attention when—hidden by the minstrels' blackface—he imitated the notorious toughs in *A Natural Born Gambler* (1916). The round black shrew became popular long before the rogue. Figures based on Aunt Chloe in *Uncle Tom's Cabin* helped make hits of films such as *Old Mammy's Charge* (1913) and *Coon Town Suffragettes* (1914). Louise Beavers represented this type in *Imitation of Life* (1934) and received rave reviews.

Eventually, though, black scamps started to become prominent in silent films, and thereafter they never faded from motion pictures. This type, similar to Stowe's figure of Topsy and created for comic relief, originated in *Ten Pickaninnies* (1904); appeared in *Wooing and Wedding of a Coon* (1905) and *The Masher* (1907); and ensured the success of the Rastus Series, including *How Rastus Got His Turkey* (1910), *Rastus in Zululand* (1910), and *Rastus's Riotous Ride* (1914). Characters in this category are messy and mischievous, tantamount to capricious children. Stepin Fetchit (Lincoln Perry) perfected this role, beginning with the film *In Old Kentucky* (1927); and by the time he appeared in *Judge Priest* (1934), his rendition of a scamp had made him a top box-office attraction.

As pictures with sound became prevalent, Hollywood abandoned its habit of assigning black parts to whites in blackface. In *The Jazz Singer* (1927), the first talkie, Al Jolson played a vaudevillian who sang onstage with his face painted black, but this was the last major application of the practice. As the Harlem Renaissance ebbed, African Americans were performing most of the black roles in mainstream movies. However, films produced by whites still did not show the spirit of the New Negro heralded by Alain Locke, and African American actors stayed chained to the old stereotypes.

Trompe l'Oeil

Three prominent and popular film projects can serve to illustrate the modest range of parts reserved for blacks in American cinema during the "roaring twenties": the *Our Gang* series of comic shorts, started in 1922 by Hal Roach, presented a succession of black scamps; *Hearts in Dixie* (1929) had a scamp and a shaman in starring roles; and *Hallelujah!* (also 1929) had a siren opposite a scoundrel and a shrew. Each of these productions broke new ground in motion picture history, but none of the dramatic leads deviated from the old standards.

Our Gang brought the first black child superstar to the screen: a small boy (Allen Clayton Hoskins) who played Farina. Audiences adored him. Surrounded by a motley crew of white children, he seemed to stand equal in status to them; nevertheless, his appearance and attitude called Topsy to mind. Like Topsy, Farina wore a profusion of pigtails all over his head; and, again like Topsy, he cloaked a penchant for duplicity with a plaintive air of dignity. Therefore, although many fans thought that Farina constituted an improvement in racial representation, he actually reinforced low expectations for blacks—the attitude that sustained Jim Crow laws. After the first child actor outgrew the role, Roach replaced him with two other boys who became known as Stymie and Buckwheat, and they matched Farina in bearing and behavior.

Hearts in Dixie, directed by Paul Sloane, was the first all-black musical. Stepin Fetchit, playing Gummy in this film, resembled an older, bald Farina, and his performance recaptured the buffoonery that Stowe had attributed to Topsy. In the eyes of some critics, Clarence Muse dignified the film by his handling of the role of Nappus, but even this character perpetuated the traits of Uncle Tom. Like Stowe's hero, Nappus is portrayed as devout, deferential, docile, and self-sacrificing. The supporting roles in *Hearts in Dixie* were split between singing scamps and shrews, consorting with a fledgling siren and scoundrel. Although this film was revolutionary in content, then, it was routine in characterization.

Hallelujah!—a musical written and directed by King Vidor—was filled with blacks breaking into song at the drop of a hat. Overall, it was enthusiastically received, even by W. E. B. Du Bois; critics said that this movie gave black performers a chance to try their wings and that they did take flight in fine form. Nina Mae McKinney, in the role of Chick, won the most acclaim, becoming a screen goddess; but, as noted previously, her role too was a type—McKinney conveyed the allure of Eliza, the mulatto in *Uncle Tom's Cabin*. Chick turns Zeke, a good boy, into an outlaw and distresses his devout parents, Pappy and Mammy. Essentially, every role in this production approximated a plantation slave as imagined by Stowe; thus *Hallelujah!* kept racial representation within the bounds of convention.

In brief, with regard to the treatment of blacks in film, the increasing use of African Americans (rather than whites wearing blackface) in black parts was the sole innovation that came out of Hollywood during the 1920s. The characterization of blacks in *Hearts in Dixie* and *Hallelujah!* simply extended an established tradition; these two musicals, along with *Our Gang*, gave only an illusion of progress in racial representation. On the whole, stereotypes of blacks prevailed.

Picture Plane

On 19 February 1919, African Americans lined Fifth Avenue to watch the all-black 369th Infantry Regiment (Fifteenth Infantry), nicknamed the Hell Fighters by their French comrades in World War I, parade into Harlem after returning home from combat. As the marchers crossed 130th Street, the band broke into a popular tune and the crowd became almost frenzied: the uniformed soldiers symbolized African Americans' readiness for full participation in American society. At the end of that year, a black film company captured these soldiers' service to the country in *Our Colored Soldiers*. White filmmakers ignored their story.

The career of Noble Johnson demonstrates how blacks stayed shackled to stereotypes in mainstream movies against their wishes. Johnson's father was a rancher in Colorado who raised and raced horses and had won the Kentucky Derby in 1902, and Noble Johnson exuded confidence and charm. By chance, his familiarity with horses, plus his fair skin and sharp features, earned him the part of a Native American in a western called *The Eagle's Nest*. The experience inspired him to join in organizing the Lincoln Motion Picture Company, the second black studio in the United States. Lincoln, with Johnson in the leading role, produced *The Realization of a Negro's Ambition* (1916), echoing the faith of Booker T. Washington that decency and diligence never go unrecognized. Johnson's performance thrilled audiences; and after he played a complex hero in two additional films released by Lincoln, Universal Pictures offered him a contract. This contract required him to resign from Lincoln, but tight finances forced him to accept it; and Universal—a white studio—then proceeded to squeeze him into bit parts as a servant or savage of African, Asian, or Native American ancestry.

At the same time, though, Oscar Micheax, an African American, sought to develop movies with black stars playing dynamic heroes. He started his own studio in 1918, and it survived the Great Depression; before going out of business in 1948, he shot more than thirty pictures, such as *The Homesteader* (1918) and *Body and Soul* (1925), featuring many complicated black characters. Micheaux was the first of a wave of black filmmakers animated by the spirit of the black community. Like the others, though, he had to settle for a small share of the movie market. Jim Crow regulations confined his work to a few theaters open to blacks. Works by white producers played in far more locations; thus white producers controlled the general impression of blacks conveyed by movies.

Before and behind the cameras, blacks had a low profile in the motion picture industry. Everyone who was apparently rising in stature eventually came up against a low "glass ceiling," crashed, and fell into oblivion. For example, the glory that enveloped Nina Mae McKinney after her appearance in *Hallelujah!* disappeared in the blink of an eye. After making *Hallelujah!*, she went abroad for two years with a cabaret act that played at Chez Florence in Paris and the Palladium theater in London; during this time she appeared as a jungle siren in a British picture, *Congo Raid* (1930), and she came home to New York for its world premiere. Thereafter, she declined into obscurity, although she did star as a crafty charmer in *The Devil's Daughter* (1939), released by a black studio; and she played a terrible tramp in *Pinky* (1940), a Hollywood product. She later earned a living performing on the road with her own band; in 1967, barely remembered, she died at age fifty-four.

Given the confidence that prevailed among African Americans in the 1920s—a confidence noted by Alain Locke—one would expect blacks like McKinney, Micheaux, and Johnson to remain in the limelight for a long time. But events of the summer of 1919, which James Weldon Johnson called the "red summer," revealed a staunch impulse to restrict blacks' prestige. Although 1919 had begun with the prideful parade of the 369th Infantry Regiment, the summer brought race riots in two dozen cities, including Washington, Atlanta, Chicago, St. Louis, and Omaha. The turmoil was incited by the activities of the Ku Klux Klan opposing equality for African American citizens. The Klan's racist objectives had evolved from the rationale for black bondage in early American society, which in turn had set the stage for *Uncle Tom's Cabin*. Throughout the 1920s, its influence persisted, and Hollywood continued to cast blacks as figures from Stowe's novel, lacking in depth and limited in distinction.

Retrospective

At the height of the Harlem Renaissance, the New Negroes hailed by Alain Locke had come to big cities seeking success. Independent films by Oscar Micheaux and other blacks reflected the African American mind, but mainstream movies posed a challenge. Hollywood portrayed black people as five types of flat figures, all of whom were overshadowed by whites. Generally, the motion picture industry preserved a bias provoked by slavery and perpetuated by *Uncle Tom's Cabin*. It allotted blacks only a very narrow space for achievement and, figuratively speaking, compelled them to sing the blues during the jazz age.

ROLAND L. WILLIAMS JR.

See also Beavers, Louise; Birth of a Nation, The; Crisis, The; Emperor Jones, The; Fetchit, Stepin; Film; Film: Actors; Film: Black Filmmakers; Hallelujah!; Hearts in Dixie; Johnson, Noble; Lincoln Motion Picture Company; Locke, Alain; Lowe, James; McKinney, Nina Mae; Micheaux, Oscar; Muse, Clarence; New Negro,

The; Opportunity; Riots: 2—Red Summer of 1919; Robeson, Paul; Williams, Egbert Austin "Bert"

Further Reading

Bogle, Donald. *Toms, Coons, Mulattos, Mammies, and Bucks*. New York: Continuum, 1997.

Huggins, Nathan. *The Harlem Renaissance*. New York: Oxford University Press, 1971.

Leab, Daniel J. *From Sambo to Superspade*. Boston: Houghton Mifflin, 1975.

Noble, Peter. *The Negro in Film*. London: Skelton, 1948.

Stowe, Harriet Beecher. *Uncle Tom's Cabin*. Boston: John P. Jewett, 1852.

Fine Clothes to the Jew

Langston Hughes' second volume of poetry, *Fine Clothes to the Jew* (1927), was published at the height of the Harlem Renaissance. It followed his highly successful debut volume, *The Weary Blues* (1926), and was in turn followed by *The Negro Mother and Other Dramatic Recitations* (1931). This context is significant because *Fine Clothes to the Jew* remains Hughes' most controversial book of poetry, became a transitional work in his canon, and was a classic acknowledgment of his manifesto "The Negro Artist and the Racial Mountain" (1926).

Fine Clothes to the Jew derives its title from an observation Hughes had made: he noticed that many residents of Harlem pawned their own clothes in neighborhood shops, most of which were owned and operated by Jews. However, this meaning was often misunderstood, and Hughes eventually regretted that he had let the title stand.

It is a courageous volume. Hughes was attempting to broaden his thematic base and to bring something Whitmanesque to the setting of Harlem. In one poem, "Brass Spittoons" a young Negro sings "A bright bowl of brass is beautiful to the Lord" as he polishes a spittoon; the theme of "Ballad of Gin Mary" is evident, as is that of "The New Cabaret Girl." "Mulatto," "Prayer," "Feet o' Jesus," and "Song for a Dark Girl" were all very well received, and the blues component in these poems was highly praised. But the critics made little mention of originality, and *Fine Clothes to the Jew* is decidedly uneven, suffering in comparison with Hughes's later collections of poetry.

What made *Fine Clothes to the Jew* controversial was the reaction of some black intellectuals—readers or reviewers—who concluded that it was a sorry return to the dialect tradition and that it overemphasized the negative aspects of Negro life. A review in the Pittsburgh *Courier* bore the headline "Langston Hughes's Book of Poems Trash"; a review in the *New York Amsterdam News* bore the headline "Langston Hughes—The Sewer Dweller." The Harlem Renaissance promoted racial pride, and those who were perceived as naysayers were quickly confronted. Hughes was no exception. However, he stated that his poetry was an attempt to tell stories of Negroes who were "workers, roustabouts, and singers, and job hunters on Lenox Avenue in New York or Seventh Street in Washington or South Street in Chicago." Accordingly, *Fine Clothes to the Jew* contains poems about gambling, love, prostitution, drugs, religion, jealousy, and friendship, among other topics. The common theme is daily life in Harlem.

Hughes was deeply affected by the adverse criticism of *Fine Clothes to the Jew*, criticism generated primarily by the black press. In his first autobiography, *The Big Sea*, he says that "the Negro critics did not like it at all. . . . Certainly, I personally knew very few people anywhere who were wholly beautiful and wholly good. . . . [I didn't] write them protesting letters, nor in any way attempt to defend my book." Hughes subsequently notes that many of the controversial poems in *Fine Clothes to the Jew* were later used successfully in Negro schools and colleges. Nevertheless, Hughes mentioned *Fine Clothes to the Jew* in the collection *Anna Bontemps/Langston Hughes Letters 1925–1969* only very briefly, the most notable comment being that the volume was his sole work that was out of print in 1946. In 2002, first editions of *Fine Clothes to the Jew* sold for between $200 and $1,100.

BRIAN J. BENSON

See also Amsterdam News; Authors: 5—Poets; Hughes, Langston; Literature: 7—Poetry; Pittsburgh Courier

Further Reading

Berry, Faith. *Langston Hughes: Before and Beyond Harlem*. Westport, Conn.: Lawrence Hill, 1983.

Blake, Susan L. "The American Dream and the Legacy of Revolution in the Poetry of Langston Hughes." *Black American Literature Forum*, 14, 1980, pp. 100–104.

Dickenson, Donald. *A Bio-Bibliography of Langston Hughes*, 2nd ed. New York: Archon, 1972.

Gates, Henry Louis Jr., and K. A. Appiah. *Langston Hughes: Critical Perspectives Past and Present*. New York: Armistad, 1993.

Hughes, Langston. *The Big Sea: An Autobiography*. New York: Thunder's Mouth, 1986.

Rampersad, Arnold. *The Life of Langston Hughes, Vol. 1, 1902–1941: I, Too, Sing America*. New York: Oxford University Press, 1986.

Singh, Amritjit. "Beyond the Mountain: Langston Hughes on Race/Class and Art." *Langston Hughes Review*, Spring 1987, pp. 37–43.

Troutman, C. James, ed. *Langston Hughes: The Man, His Art, and His Continuing Influence*. New York: Garland, 1995.

Wintz, Cary D. *Black Culture and the Harlem Renaissance*. Houston, Tex.: Rice University Press, 1988.

Fire!!

Fire!! (1926) was a projected periodical, edited by Wallace Thurman; it was intended to appear quarterly, but only one issue was actually produced.

For younger artists, *Crisis* and *Opportunity* were crusty establishment publications; these artists' own métier was to debunk the genteel standards (which Thurman called "party-line art") espoused by the "talented tenth" and to position themselves as firebrand agitators for a modern black culture. Their subversive publication *Fire!!* came out in November 1926; it was inspired by Carl van Vechten's provocative novel *Nigger Heaven*, which had been published earlier that year and which W. E. B. Du Bois had found "neither truthful nor artistic." Although *Fire!!* consisted of only its first issue, it was immortalized in the annals of the Harlem Renaissance for having been "Devoted to Younger Negro Artists."

This new publishing venture aimed to be radical, provocative, and available to both the white and the black cultural establishment; and its contributors were expected to take their inspiration from not the bourgeoisie but the proletariat. Thurman, as the editor, had assembled an impressive array of artists and writers who were eager to define a true "Negro aesthetic"; they wanted to produce something genuinely modern and had no intention of splicing high and low art to make some kind of mongrel art. Like the talented tenth, they wanted a pure representation of the Negro experience—a way to "express our dark skinned selves without fear or shame"—and so they looked to the streets, where the worker could be found, as could the seedier side of black life with its illicit gratifications. Therefore, the topics covered in *Fire!!* would include sex, racism, androgyny, homoeroticism, the "primitive" Negro, prostitution, and interracial relations.

Contributions to *Fire!!* took the form of stories, essays, poetry, plays, editorials, and artwork. One piece, "Cordelia the Crude," Thurman's story about a sixteen-year-old prostitute, later appeared on Broadway and eventually in theaters in Chicago and Los Angeles. Langston Hughes, Countee Cullen, Edward Silvera, Lewis Alexander, Helene Johnson, Waring Cuney, and Arna Bontemps contributed poetry. Arthur Huff Fauset's sociological essay on the intelligentsia was a witty swipe at the pretentious acolytes whom Zora Neale Hurston called "Negrotarians" and "niggerati." Gwendolyn Bennett contributed a story on interracial relations, "Wedding Day." Hurston supplied a play in four scenes called "Color Struck" and a short story called "Sweat," about marital vengeance and regret.

Art came from Aaron Douglas and Richard Bruce Nugent; the latter made a literary contribution as well. The enigmatic cover was by Douglas, and the integrated title and the lean geometric strokes are characteristic of his work; perhaps in no other image from the Harlem Renaissance are the motifs so strikingly pared down. Douglas also supplied incidental art that is unmistakably African in style: three economically drawn figures of a pastor preaching, an artist painting, and a waitress serving. These three vignettes seem satirical, although they make no racial or political declamation except, possibly, as icons of Western materialism. Bruce was considered the *enfant terrible* of New Negro art (David Levering Lewis has described him as a "self-conscious decadent"), and his recurring themes were homosexuality and androgyny.

At the time, black critics hated *Fire!!* Even Douglas's artwork did not escape criticism. Rean Graves of the Baltimore *Afro-American* said: "Aaron Douglas who in spite of himself and the meaningless grotesqueness of his creations, has gained a reputation as an artist, is permitted to spoil these perfectly good pages and a cover with his pen and ink hudge pudge." Nugent's literary and artistic contributions were antithetical to the high culture embraced by the talented tenth and therefore attracted much attention. Referring to Bruce's homoerotic story in *Fire!!*—"Smoke, Lilies, and Jade"–W. E. B. Du Bois voiced a concern that the "Negro renaissance" was being turned "into decadence." In recent times, Cooke (1984) has described *Fire!!* as a "quasi-surrealisitic organ"; when compared with contemporary establishment publications, it is iconoclastic (particularly in its secularism) and simultaneously ironic and anguished. Lewis (1994) has described it as a "flawed, folk centered masterpiece," concisely suggesting a distinctive but tentative movement toward exploring black identity within a white hegemony.

In any case, the assertions of "younger" artists such as Thurman, Hurston, Nugent, and Hughes made *Fire!!* a pivotal moment in the Harlem Renaissance, because Negroes were being called on to reject the paternalism of the talented tenth and seek autonomy. However, autonomy came at a price: *Fire!!* left Thurman in considerable debt, despite appeals in the first issue for donations. Later, a fire destroyed unsold editions that were being kept in storage. Ultimately, *Fire!!* is important for its verve rather than for intellectual grandiloquence.

Thurman tried again in November 1928, with *Harlem: A Forum of Negro Life*, a magazine which was perhaps less subversive and less primitive than *Fire!!* However, *Harlem* ran for only two issues.

CATHERINE O'HARA

See also Baltimore Afro-American; Crisis, The; Douglas, Aaron; Harlem; Negrotarians; Nigger Heaven; Niggerati; Nugent, Richard Bruce; Opportunity; Talented Tenth; Thurman, Wallace; *other specific writers*

Further Reading

Cooke, G. Michael. *Afro-American Literature in the Twentieth Century: The Achievement of Intimacy.* New Haven, Conn.: Yale University Press, 1984.

De Jongh, James. *Vicious Modernism: Black Harlem and The Literary Imagination.* Cambridge: Cambridge University Press, 1990.

Hughes, Langston. "American Art or Negro Art?" *Nation*, 123, 18 August 1926.

Lewis, David Levering, ed. *The Portable Harlem Renaissance Reader.* New York: Viking Penguin, 1994.

Thurman, Wallace. "Negro Artists and the Negro." *New Republic*, 31 August 1927.

———. *Fire!!*, 2nd ed. Metuchen, N.J.: Fire, 1982. (Originally published 1926.)

Fire in the Flint, The

Walter White's novel *The Fire in the Flint* (1924) caused a stir because of its unflinching exploration of lynching in the American South. White was active in the antilynching crusade and directed the efforts of the National Association for the Advancement of Colored People (NAACP) to have Congress pass antilynching bills. White also published a nonfiction examination of lynching, *Rope and Faggot: A Biography of Judge Lynch* (1929).

White's novel tells the story of Dr. Kenneth Harper, who is clearly intended to stand in sharp contrast to the usual portrayals of victims of lynching as either depraved beasts or agitators seeking to destabilize the social structure. Harper's father has told him that "only bad Negroes ever get lynched." The book begins when Harper opens a medical practice in Central City, Georgia, and ends just a few months later with his death at the hands of a mob. Harper has attended Atlanta University, has attended medical school "in the North," and has served admirably in World War I. He returns from France to his hometown, where he believes he can do good; he assumes, naively, that he will not "have any trouble" with the local racists. Harper at first stays detached from the racial issues of the town, but inevitably he is drawn in—both professionally, because he is called on to save a white woman's life, and personally, because he falls in love with an activist, Jane Phillips. Jane inspires him to help organize sharecroppers into a collective which would allow them at least a chance of not going deeper into debt with each harvest. (White uses this love story to convey the message that black citizens need to organize themselves politically.) Still, Harper, despite his movement from idealistic indifference to engagement with programs for social change, remains convinced that through hard work and moral living, he can be accepted, if not respected, in the white community. Finally, however, after his sister is raped and his brother commits suicide to avoid being lynched, Harper loses his illusions. Nevertheless, he answers the call to attend his white patient, an act that leads to his own brutal murder.

The melodramatic details of the plot have led many critics to dismiss *The Fire in the Flint* as propaganda, but the book was widely read and generated many articles debating whether it gave a realistic account of race relations. White, in his autobiography, characterizes the reaction to the book as "gratifyingly prompt and vigorous." Today, the novel remains provocative, and the struggles Harper faces as a professional trying to succeed in a racist culture continue to offer insights. White suggested that after World War I, southern society became increasingly intolerant as a result of specific political and sociological events—an idea suggesting in turn that the attitudes leading to lynching and to racism in general can be changed if social conditions are changed. White (1948) wrote that although the novel ends with Harper's murder, "one senses that the spirit of revolt against bigotry which he symbolizes will be accelerated rather than diminished by his death."

NEIL BROOKS

See also Antilynching Crusade; White, Walter

Further Reading

Raper, Arthur. *The Tragedy of Lynching*. Chapel Hill: University of North Carolina Press, 1933.

Tolnay, Stewart, and E. M. Beck. *A Festival of Violence: An Analysis of Southern Lynchings, 1882–1930*. Urbana: University of Illinois Press, 1995.

Waldron, Edward E. *Walter White and the Harlem Renaissance*. Port Washington, N.Y.: Kennikat, 1978.

White, Walter. *Rope and Faggot: A Biography of Judge Lynch*. New York: Knopf, 1929.

———. *A Man Called White: The Autobiography of Walter White*. New York: Viking, 1948.

Fisher, Rudolph

Rudolph Fisher, who would become the chief chronicler of life in Harlem during the period of the Harlem Renaissance, initially gained recognition as a short-story writer while he was still a medical student at Howard University. With encouragement from Alain Locke, Fisher succeeded in placing his first (and most famous) short story, "The City of Refuge," in the February 1925 issue of the prestigious *Atlantic Monthly*. According to Arna Bontemps, this feat "created something of a sensation" among African American writers because none of them "had been able to break into that magazine" (Tignor 1982). Fisher would publish his work three more times in *Atlantic Monthly* as well as in other periodicals owned by whites, including *McClure's*, *Story*, *American Mercury*, and the New York *Herald Tribune*. Of course, he also published work in periodicals owned by blacks, such as *Opportunity* and *Crisis*; however, for African Americans at that time, literary success was measured largely in terms of gaining access to mainstream (white) readers. Fisher certainly achieved this, and his success was partly

the result of early efforts by Walter White, Carl Van Vechten, and others who recognized his promising talent. In March 1925 Fisher's "The South Lingers On" was included in a special issue of *Survey Graphic*; also in 1926, *Crisis* awarded Fisher first place in the Amy Spingarn Prize for fiction (for his "High Yaller"). Fisher's "The City of Refuge" was included in Edward J. O'Brien's *Best Short Stories of 1925*; and "Miss Cynthie" was included in *Best Short Stories: 1934*. During Fisher's brief literary career before his death at age thirty-seven, his work also appeared in three other anthologies. He published a total of fifteen short stories, all but one of which are set in Harlem.

Fisher likewise proved himself a gifted novelist, with *The Walls of Jericho* (1928). Alfred A. Knopf published this debut novel and reportedly contracted with Fisher for two additional ones. Reviews of *The Walls of Jericho* were generally positive, and several reviewers expressed relief that Fisher had provided a well-proportioned, propaganda-free alternative to the more sensational fare offered up in Carl Van Vechten's *Nigger Heaven* (1926) and Claude McKay's *Home to Harlem* (1928). *The Walls of Jericho* had been inspired by a wager with a friend, who had bet that Fisher could not write a novel effectively uniting Harlem's upper and lower classes. Fisher met the challenge and crafted a work unique among the novels of the period, because other authors predominantly focused on a single class. Fisher's seriocomic novel is also notable for his adroit social satire—a skill that had not so far been revealed in his short fiction. Fisher's satire, like his humor, succeeds in part because it is democratic, taking aim at blacks and whites alike as well as at all levels of society; and it differs noticeably from the more caustic, condemnatory, cynical satire of George S. Schuyler and Wallace Thurman.

In 1932 Covici-Friede published Fisher's second novel, *The Conjure-Man Dies: A Mystery Tale of Dark Harlem*. Reviews were generally encouraging, although this novel did not arouse the same enthusiasm as *The Walls of Jericho*. Fisher had been preceded in detective fiction by the African American serial novelists J. E. Bruce and Pauline Hopkins; however, *The Conjure-Man Dies* remains a watershed as the first detective novel by an African American author to be set in an all-black environment and to have an all-black cast of characters. Although of signal importance today, this accomplishment remained uncelebrated in Fisher's lifetime and for decades thereafter. Nevertheless, the plot was resurrected for a highly popular stage production by the Works Progress Administration (WPA) at the Lafayette Theater in Harlem in 1936. (Critics are divided regarding how much Fisher was involved in writing the stage adaptation.) Fisher intended to write at least two more novels with the same pair of detectives—Dart and Archer—but had only enough time to produce a follow-up short story, "John Archer's Nose," before he died.

For the better part of the twentieth century, literary critics classified Fisher as a talented also-ran of the Harlem Renaissance: a writer of merit, but one whose achievements were limitied and were worthy of only limited discussion. Some critics considered his short fiction to be his best work, and he received consistent praise for his ability as a humorist and satirist as well as for his objective realism and general craftsmanship. However, *The Walls of Jericho* received less attention over the years, and *The Conjure-Man Dies* rarely elicited any critical response at all. The 1980s and 1990s marked a turning point in studies of Fisher: the short fiction was collected and published for the first time in 1987; both of his novels were reprinted in paperback for the first time in the 1990s; and two new generations of critics brought a newfound enthusiasm to bear on Fisher's work, particularly the detective fiction. The growth in critical attention has been remarkable. Significant work on Fisher was done in the 1980s by John McCluskey Jr., Margaret Perry, Leonard J. Deutsch, and Eleanor Q. Tignor. Somewhat newer critics, such as Stephen F. Soitos, Adrienne Johnson Gosselin, and Maria Balshaw, have considered the complexities of Fisher's multifaceted representation of Harlem during the 1920s and 1930s, as well as his contribution to African American literature both during and after the Harlem Renaissance.

Biography

Rudolph John Chauncey Fisher was born on 9 May 1897, in Washington, D.C. He studied at public schools in Providence, Rhode Island; Brown University in Providence (A.B., 1919; A.M., 1920); Howard University in Washington, D.C. (M.D., 1924); Freedmen's Hospital in Washington, D.C. (1924–1925); and Columbia University (1925–1927). He was a lecturer at Howard University in 1920–1924; began a private medical practice in 1927; was a roentgenologist at Mount Sinai and Montefiore hospitals in New York City in 1927; was acting superintendent at International Hospital in New York City in 1929–1932; was an x-ray technician

for New York City Health Department in 1930–1934; was a first lieutenant in the medical corps of the New York National Guard, 369th Infantry, in 1931–1934; and was a book reviewer for the New York *Herald Tribune* in 1931–1932. His awards included a National Research Council Fellowship in 1925 and the Amy Spingarn Prize in 1927. Fisher was a member of the North Harlem Medical Association in 1927–1930, the Harlem Health Center (advisory board) in 1930–1933, the Manhattan Medical Society in 1930–1934, and the Queens Clinical Society in 1932–1934. He died in New York City on 26 December 1934.

CRAIG GABLE

See also American Mercury; Conjure-Man Dies, The; Crisis, The; Locke, Alain; Opportunity; Survey Graphic; Van Vechten, Carl; Walls of Jericho, The; White, Walter

Selected Works

"The Caucasian Storms Harlem." *American Mercury*, August 1927. (Reprinted in *The Portable Harlem Renaissance Reader*, ed. David Levering Lewis. New York: Penguin, 1994.)

The Walls of Jericho. 1928.

The Conjure-Man Dies: A Mystery Tale of Dark Harlem. 1932.

The City of Refuge: The Collected Stories of Rudolph Fisher, ed. John McCluskey Jr. 1987.

The Short Fiction of Rudolph Fisher, ed. Margaret Perry. 1987.

Joy and Pain. 1996. (Collected stories.)

Further Reading

Balshaw, Maria. "Space, Race, and Identity." In *Looking for Harlem: Urban Aesthetics in African-American Literature.* London: Pluto, 2000.

Chander, Harish. "Rudolph Fisher (1897–1934)." In *African American Authors, 1745–1945: A Bio-Bibliographical Critical Sourcebook*, ed. Emmanuel S. Nelson. Westport, Conn.: Greenwood, 2000.

Davis, Arthur P. "Rudolph Fisher." In *From the Dark Tower: Afro-American Writers 1900 to 1960.* Washington, D.C.: Howard University Press, 1974.

Deutsch, Leonard J. "Rudolph Fisher's Unpublished Manuscripts: Description and Commentary." *Obsidian*, 6(1–2), 1980.

Gable, Craig. "Rudolph Fisher: An Updated Selected Bibliography." *Bulletin of Bibliography*, 57(1), 2000.

McCluskey, John Jr. "Introduction." In *The City of Refuge: The Collected Stories of Rudolph Fisher*. Columbia: University of Missouri Press, 1987.

Perry, Margaret. "The Brief Life and Art of Rudolph Fisher." In *The Short Fiction of Rudolph Fisher*. New York: Greenwood, 1987.

Sinnette, Calvin H. "Rudolph Fisher: Harlem Renaissance Physician-Writer." *Pharos*, 53(2), 1990.

Soitos, Stephen F. "Detective of the Harlem Renaissance: Rudolph Fisher." In *The Blues Detective: A Study of African American Detective Fiction*. Amherst: University of Massachusetts Press, 1996.

Tignor, Eleanor Q. "Rudolph Fisher: Harlem Novelist." *Langston Hughes Review*, 1(2), 1982.

————. "Rudolph Fisher." In *Afro-American Writers from the Harlem Renaissance to 1940*, ed. Trudier Harris. Detroit, Mich.: Gale, 1987.

Tolson, Melvin B. "Rudolph Fisher." In *The Harlem Group of Negro Writers*. Westport, Conn.: Greenwood, 2000.

580 Saint Nicholas Avenue

Ethel Ray Nance, Regina Anderson (Regina M. Anderson Andrews), and Louella Tucker shared a fifth-floor apartment—sometimes called "Dream Haven"—in a stylish six-story building at 580 Saint Nicholas Avenue in Harlem, at the corner of 139th Street, near City College of New York. This apartment building, where Ethel Waters also lived, began welcoming black residents at the same time as nearby buildings on Saint Nicholas Avenue became home to W. E. B. Du Bois and to Saint James Presbyterian Church. Nance worked for Charles S. Johnson and *Opportunity* magazine; Anderson was a librarian at the 135th Street branch of the New York Public Library; and both women extended the work of these two important organizations to "580," as part of their commitment to racial uplift and women's independence and achievement. They brought home books to review; Anderson searched for potential programs to bring to the library, where readings and discussion groups were held; and because the apartment was within walking distance of the 135th Street library and the popular 135th Street YMCA, it became a place of rest and relaxation for people who had been attending events there and at other nearby locations. At "580," Nance hosted an evening meeting to discuss the format of the *Survey Graphic* issue on Harlem, introducing her own collection of Aaron Douglas's art to Charles Johnson, Winold Reiss, and the editor, Paul Kellogg; this was a factor in making Douglas the visual artist of choice during the Harlem Renaissance.

In fact, 580—which became so popular that cabdrivers could identify it just by that number—was central to virtually everything and everyone associated with the Harlem Renaissance. Countee Cullen would bring new poems there to read, and the women at 580 took him to his first cabaret. Eric Walrond loved to come to relate his downtown exploits. Gwendolyn Bennett was a frequent visitor. Carl Van Vechten, on his first visit, brought both a bottle of wine and Jean Toomer. Aaron Douglas, penniless and moving from Kansas to New York at Nance's urging, slept on the sofa at 580 until he found work and his own home. Zora Neale Hurston, who had also been impoverished, relinquished the sofa when a change of fortune made her Fannie Hurst's live-in secretary. At 580, W. E. B. Du Bois, Charles S. Johnson, James Weldon Johnson, and Jessie Fauset shared ideas and dreams with the younger artists whose work inspired *Opportunity* and *Crisis* to run literary contests. Following the first *Opportunity* awards program in 1925, many of the attendees assembled at 580, and a historic group photo that included Langston Hughes, Charles S. Johnson, E. Franklin Frazier, Rudolph Fisher, and Hubert Delany was taken on the roof.

Although 580 had an enduring impact, it was short-lived, lasting for less than two years before Nance returned home to Duluth, Minnesota, to take care of her ailing mother in late 1925 and Anderson married in 1926. A fictional relationship between two characters in Van Vechten's *Nigger Heaven*—Mary and Olive—was modeled on the supportive friendship between Nance and Anderson. Their sense of uplift found expression in numerous individual and group projects after the Harlem Renaissance: one of the most notable was *Black New Yorkers*, a project initiated by Anderson with research assistance from Nance. In 2000, their text inspired the book *Black New Yorkers* and an accompanying exhibition at Harlem's Schomburg Center for Research in Black Culture.

ONITA ESTES-HICKS

See also Anderson, Regina M.; Douglas, Aaron; Johnson, Charles Sprugeon; Kellogg, Paul U.; Nance, Ethel Ray;

135th Street Library; Opportunity; Reiss, Winold; Survey Graphic; *specific artists, writers, and others*

Further Reading

Bontemps, Arna. *The Harlem Renaissance Remembered.* New York: Dodd, Mead, 1972.

Huggins, Nathan Irvin. *Harlem Renaissance.* New York: Oxford University Press, 1971.

Hull, Gloria. *Color, Sex, and Poetry: Three Women Writers of the Harlem Renaissance.* Bloomington: Indiana University Press, 1987.

Kirschke, Amy Helen. *Aaron Douglas: Art, Race, and the Harlem Renaissance.* Jackson: University Press of Mississippi, 1995.

Lewis, David Levering. *When Harlem Was in Vogue.* New York: Knopf, 1981. (See also Penguin ed., 1997.)

———. *W. E. B. Du Bois: The Fight for Equality and the American Century, 1919–1963.* New York: Holt, 2000.

Shockley, Ann Allen. Interview with Ethel Ray Nance, 18 November 1970.

Smith, Jessie Carney. "Ethel Nance"; "Regina Anderson." In *Notable Black American Women.* Detroit, Mich.: Gale Research, 1992.

Taylor, David Vassar. Interview with Ethel Nance. 15 May 1974. (Transcript.)

Ulansky, Gene. "A Quiet Storm." *Excel,* Fall 1989, pp. 40–42.

Van Vechten, Carl. *Nigger Heaven.* New York, Urbana, and Chicago: University of Illinois Press, 2000.

Watson, Steven. *The Harlem Renaissance, Hub of American Culture, 1920–1930.* New York: Pantheon, 1995.

Wntz, Cary D. *Black Culture and the Harlem Renaissance.* Houston, Tex.: Rice University Press, 1988.

Fool's Errand

Fool's Errand, a play by Eulalie Spence (1894–1981), was first presented by the Krigwa Players Little Negro Theater, as part of its second production season in April 1927. Spence, a high school teacher who became an integral part of the "little theater" movement in Harlem, had been born in Nevis, West Indies, and had joined the Krigwa Players soon after this theater company was founded by W. E. B. Du Bois in 1925. She served the Krigwa Players in several capacities, as a performer, technician, and playwright.

Fool's Errand was a departure for Spence: her one-act plays usually explored some facet of contemporary urban life, but this was a folk comedy-drama set in a cabin in an "unprogressive Negro settlement" somewhere in the rural South. The cabin is occupied by Doug; his wife, Mom; and their teenage daughter, Maza. Mom has been called away to a temporary live-in job as a domestic, and the cabin has been tended by Aunt Cassie. When Aunt Cassie discovers some hidden baby clothes, she assumes the worst and calls in the church council to confront Maza and identify the father of her illegitimate child. Freddie and Jud, Maza's two suitors, are to be tricked into attending the council meeting; arriving too soon, Maza and Jud are sent on a trumped-up "fool's errand" until the council is ready. When the inquisition finally begins, Maza protests her innocence. Before a shotgun wedding can be arranged, Mom returns and reveals that it is she who is pregnant; nonplussed by having a second child so many years after the first, she hid the baby clothes she had made until she could tell her family. The real fool's errand has been performed by the church council, prodded by Aunt Cassie's snooping.

Du Bois selected *Fool's Errand* as the Krigwa Players' entry in the Fifth Annual International Little Theatre Tournament, sponsored by the New York Drama League. This was the Krigwa Players' first competition; and the Krigwa company was also the first entry by an African American troupe with an African American playwright. Spence took over as the play's director, took on the responsibility of preparing for the tournament, and led the cast in restoring for use in the tournament a discarded set her sister had found in Greenwich Village. During the tournament, which lasted from 2 to 7 May 1927, the Krigwa Players, competing against sixteen other groups, gave three performances at Broadway's Frolic Theater. Although the Krigwa Players did not win the David Belasco Trophy, they were awarded $200 for presenting one of the best unpublished plays. A short time later, *Fool's Errand* was published by Samuel French—another first for an African American playwright. During the contest, Spence had also been selected for second prize and a shared third prize in the playwriting competition sponsored by the Urban League's journal, *Opportunity,* for her plays *The Hunch* and *The Starter.* In 1926, she had taken second place in the Krigwa playwriting contest, supported by *Crisis* (the journal of the National Association for the Advancement of Colored People), for another one-act work, *Foreign Mail*.

Ironically, the fine showing in the tournament by Spence and the Krigwa Players, rather than strengthening the company, led to its demise. Du Bois refused to share the cash award with Spence or the cast, stating that the prize money was needed to cover the company's expenses. Many company members left, and Du Bois withdrew, taking with him the copyrighted name Krigwa.

FREDA SCOTT GILES

See also Crisis, The: Literary Prizes; Du Bois, W. E. B.; Krigwa Players; Little Theater Tournament; Opportunity Literary Contests

Further Reading

Brown-Guillory, Elizabeth, ed. *Wines in the Wilderness: Plays by African American Women from the Harlem Renaissance to the Present*. New York: Praeger, 1990.

Burton, Jennifer, ed. *Zora Neale Hurston, Eulalie Spence, Marita Bonner, and Others: The Prize Plays and Other One-acts Published in Periodicals*. New York: G. K. Hall, 1996.

Hatch, James V., and Ted Shine, eds. *Black Theatre U.S.A.: Plays by African Americans, 1847 to Today*. New York: Free Press, 1996.

Locke, Alain, ed. *Plays of Negro Life: A Source Book of Native American Drama*. Westport, Conn.: Negro Universities Press, 1970. (Reprint.)

Perkins, Kathy, ed. *Black Female Playwrights: An Anthology of Plays before 1950*. Bloomington: Indiana University Press, 1989.

Ford, Arnold Josiah

Arnold Ford's first career once he came to the United States in 1912 was as a musician. He performed jazz as a member of Harlem's Clef Club and was bandmaster for the New Amsterdam Musical Association. In 1917 he became musical director and choirmaster of Liberty Hall, the Harlem center of Marcus Garvey's Universal Negro Improvement Association (UNIA). Ford produced the group's *Universal Ethiopian Hymnal*, writing several of the songs himself. He was

a cowriter of UNIA's anthem, "Ethiopia, Land of Our Fathers." The hymns Ford composed drew on Christian, Jewish, Muslim, and African traditions and celebrated a future African redemption. UNIA was one of many groups that found parallels between the Old Testament stories of the Hebrews escaping from captivity in Egypt and the emancipation of American slaves.

Building on these connections, it was a relatively small step to the establishment of a new religion borrowing elements of Judaism. With a partner, Rabbi Wentworth Arthur Matthew, Ford founded the Black Jews of Harlem, recruiting members from among Garvey's followers. Members called themselves Ethiopian Hebrews or Hebrew Israelites, and they believed that the ancient Hebrews were black. White Jews, Ford believed, were offshoots of the original Hebrews, who had adopted their religion from Africans with whom they came into contact.

In 1923, Ford broke with UNIA; and in 1924 he established Beth Bnai Abraham (House, or Congregation, of the Sons of Abraham) in Harlem. Like Ford, many members of the congregation were from the West Indies. Ford was fluent in Hebrew and in Yiddish, had studied the Torah and the Talmud, and had made contacts with liberal white Jews who answered his questions about their faith. Calling himself Rabbi Ford, he led the congregation, set up an Ethiopian-Hebrew school, and worked to establish a black Jewish homeland in Ethiopia. Ford used his influence to found the Progressive Corporation, a mostly secular organization of black businessmen; and the Aurienoth Club, a group of black professionals who supported the idea of a black Jewish Zion.

In 1930, Ford traveled to Ethiopia to witness the coronation of Haile Selassie. Over the next few years he worked to accumulate enough land in Ethiopia for what he hoped would be a wave of immigrants, and in fact some sixty followers joined him there in 1931 and 1932. Little is known about the few remaining years of his life. Some have suggested that Ford reappeared in Detroit in 1930, and that as Wallace Fard he established the Nation of Islam, but most scholars find the theory unsupportable and believe he died in Ethiopia in 1935.

Biography

Arnold Josiah Ford was born in Barbados, West Indies, c. 1890 and was educated in public schools there. He served as a music teacher for the British navy. He emigrated to Harlem in 1912; was a jazz musician, 1912–1920; was musical director of UNIA, 1917–1923; and founded and led Beth Bnai Abraham, 1923–1930. Ford died in Addis Ababa, Ethiopia, in September 1935.

CYNTHIA BILY

See also Clef Club; Universal Negro Improvement Association

Further Reading

Berger, Graenum. *Black Jews in America*. New York: Federation of Jewish Philanthropies of New York, 1978.

Chireau, Yvonne. "Black Culture and Black Zion: African American Religious Encounters with Judaism, 1790–1930—An Overview." In *Black Zion: African American Encounters with Judaism*, eds. Yvonne Chireau and Nathaniel Deutsch. Oxford: Oxford University Press, 2000.

King, Kenneth. "Some Notes on Arnold J. Ford and New World Black Attitudes to Ethiopia." In *Black Apostles: Afro-American Clergy Confront the Twentieth Century*, eds. Randall K. Burkett and Richard Newman. New York: G. K. Hall, 1978.

Landes, Ruth. "The Negro Jews of Harlem." *Jewish Journal of* Sociology, 9, 1967.

Landing, James E. *Black Judaism: Story of an American Movement*. Durham, N.C.: Carolina Academic Press, 2002.

Scott, William. "Rabbi Arnold Ford's Back-to-Ethiopia Movement: A Study of Black Emigration, 1930–1935." *Pan African Journal*, 8(2), Summer 1975.

Ford, James William

James William Ford was a preeminent African American member of the Communist Party of the United States (CPUSA) and—as a vice-presidential candidate in the election of 1932—the first African American on a national ballot.

Ford was born in Alabama. After graduating from Fisk University, he moved to Chicago, where he worked as a parcel post dispatcher with the U.S. Post Office and joined the Chicago Postal Workers Union. His experiences in Chicago during the 1920s largely shaped his commitment to the American trade union movement. His trade unionism became more militant in reaction to Jim Crow employment policies and tyrannical union officials, and his reputation as a trade unionist grew steadily. He was an early supporter of the Brotherhood of Sleeping Car Porters and formed a lasting friendship with its founder, A. Philip Randolph. Ford joined the American Negro Labor Congress (ANLC) in 1925 and the Trade Union Educational League in 1926; he then joined CPUSA and rose rapidly through its ranks, serving as an elected delegate of the committee meeting of the Communist International (Comintern) in 1927 and 1928. His increasing radicalism caused problems with his job as a postal worker, and he was fired in 1927, reportedly having been framed.

Ford believed that victory against the ravages of capitalism could be achieved through the "unity of the Negro people and the white workers." In 1927, he was an elected delegate of the Trade Union Educational League to the International Labor Union's Fourth World Congress in Moscow. At this congress, he was elected to its executive committee. A year later, Ford returned to Moscow for the Sixth World Congress of the Comintern and traveled throughout the Soviet Union to observe how national minorities fared there. After returning to the United States, he relocated from Chicago to New York City and became part of Harlem's political scene. In 1929 he was arrested for protesting against the United States' military actions in Haiti; also in 1928, as a member of the American delegation to the Second World Congress of the League Against Imperialism in Frankfurt, Germany, he demanded the unconditional liberation of Ethiopia. Ford devoted much time and energy to forging solidarity between oppressed people in the United States and worldwide in a struggle against capitalism and imperialism; he wanted to merge Garveyite pan-Africanism and Communism, and he was instrumental in organizing the First International Conference of Negro Workers in Hamburg, Germany, in 1930. In 1931, at the League of Nations' conference on African children, he spoke against European colonial policy. In 1932, in the United States, he participated in the Bonus Army March, a protest by veterans of World War I who were seeking federal relief, and was again arrested.

During the 1930s, Ford was a major force within CPUSA. In 1932 he was nominated to run for vice-president on the Communist Party ticket alongside William Z. Foster. In 1933, Ford became the head of

CPUSA's Harlem branch. He was later a member of the Political Committee, New York State Committee, and National Committee of CPUSA; and he was influential in moving CPUSA toward a "united front" with the National Association for the Advancement of Colored People (NAACP), the Urban League, the National Negro Congress, and other civil rights organizations—a significant revision of communist policy toward race-based movements. By 1937, he was asserting that racial injustice and the class struggle could be dealt with in tandem because African Americans sought three goals: a decent and secure livelihood; human rights; and an equal, honorable, and respectable status in society. He was again nominated for vice president in 1936 and 1940. In 1938, Ford was the party's candidate for the U.S. Senate from New York.

During World War II, Ford still led the Harlem section of CPUSA, although he had less power nationally. By the 1950s, during the cold war, he was executive director of the National Committee to Defend Negro Leadership, a group organized to assist African American party members who were targeted by federal laws against presumed communists and subversives. He remained an active member of CPUSA until his death.

Biography

James William Ford was born in Pratt City, Alabama, on 22 December 1893, the son of Lyman and Nancy Reynolds Foursche. (The family's surname was changed to Ford when a racist policeman questioned the father and could not spell or pronounce Foursche.) Ford completed high school in 1913 and then went to Fisk University, where he became a campus leader as a scholar and an athlete. He joined the army in 1917, during World War I, before graduating from Fisk, but he returned there in 1919 after his honorable discharge and received a B.A. He then moved to Chicago, where he worked for the post office and became a trade unionist; he also joined the Communist Party. In 1927 his radicalism led to his dismissal from the post office. He attended labor congresses in Moscow and traveled in the Soviet Union. Around 1928 he relocated from Chicago to New York City and entered the political scene in Harlem. He became head of the CPUSA's Harlem Branch in 1933. In 1932, 1936, and 1940 he ran for vice-president on the Communist Party ticket; in 1938 he ran for the Senate as the Communist

Party's candidate from New York. Ford died on 21 June 1957.

JUAN FLOYD-THOMAS

See also American Negro Labor Congress; Brotherhood of Sleeping Car Porters; Communisty Party; Garveyism; Pan-Africanism; Randolph, A. Philip

Further Reading

Cunard, Nancy. *Negro: An Anthology*. London: Wishart, 1934.

Davis, Benjamin J. Jr. *Communist Candidate for Vice-President of the United States, James W. Ford, What He Is and What He Stands For*. New York: Workers Library, 1936.

Ford, James W. *Anti-Semitism and the Struggle for Democracy*. New York: National Council of Jewish Communists, n.d. (Possibly 1939.)

———. *The Communists and the Struggle for Negro Liberation: Their Position on Problems of Africa, of the West Indies, of War, of Ethiopian Independence, of the Struggle for Peace*. New York: Harlem Division of the Communist Party, n.d. (Possibly 1936.)

———. *Imperialism Destroys the People of Africa*. New York: Harlem Section of the Communist Party, n.d. (Possibly 1930s.)

———. *The Negro and the Democratic Front*. New York: International, n.d. (c. 1938.)

———. *The Negro People and the New World Situation*. New York: Workers Library, 1941.

———. *The Negroes in a Soviet America*. New York: Workers Library, 1935.

———. *The War and the Negro People*. New York: Workers Library, 1942.

———. *Win Progress for Harlem*. New York: Harlem Division of the Communist Party, 1939.

Ford, James W., Benjamin J. Davis Jr., William L. Patterson, and Earl Browder. *Communists in the Struggle for Negro Rights*. New York: New Century, 1945.

Ford, James W., and Harry Gannes. *War in Africa: Italian Fascism Prepares to Enslave Ethiopia*. New York: Workers Library, 1935.

"James W. Ford: A Tribute." *Political Affairs*, August 1957, pp. 14–29.

Kornweibel, Theodore Jr. *Seeing Red: Federal Campaigns against Black Militancy, 1919–1925*. Bloomington: Indiana University Press, 1998.

———. *"Investigate Everything": Federal Efforts to Compel Black Loyalty during World War I*. Bloomington: Indiana University Press, 2002.

Record, Wilson. *The Negro and the Communist Party.* Chapel Hill: University of North Carolina Press, 1951.

Forsyne, Ida

Although Langston Hughes named Ida Forsyne as one of the twelve best dancers of all time, she never achieved as much commercial or critical success in the United States as she did in Europe.

By age ten, Forsyne was dancing and singing for small sums of money at candy stores and house-rent parties, and she cakewalked for twenty-five cents a day at the Chicago World's Fair. She broke into professional theater when she joined Sissieretta Jones's *Black Patti's Troubadours*, a show in which she sang "You're Just a Little Nigger but You're Mine All Mine" while pushing a baby carriage across the stage. After the tour, she appeared in modified minstrel shows in Manhattan, Coney Island, and Atlantic City and had a solo act in the first interracial musical, Will Marion Cook's *The Southerners*. Forsyne went abroad with the Tennessee Students to perform at the Palace Theater in London, billed as "Topsy, the Famous Negro Dancer," a stock figure from minstrelsy based on the character in Harriet Beecher Stowe's *Uncle Tom's Cabin*. The tiny, exuberant Forsyne enthralled audiences and critics in London with her wild dance numbers. She continued to appear in major venues, such as the Moulin Rouge in Paris, where she began performing a dance routine in a potato sack, occasionally with a chorus of ballet dancers in blackface. By 1911, Forsyne's success led her to Moscow, where her routines included cakewalking as well as Russian dance steps. According to Stearns and Stearns (1994), Forsyne inspired a modest trend of Russian dancing on the vaudeville stage in the United States.

Forsyne's success in Europe lasted for nine years but was cut short by World War I. In 1914, she returned to the United States, where she faced difficulty getting jobs in theater as a result of the shifting aesthetic and social values ushered in by the Harlem Renaissance. The dance routines that had made her famous throughout Europe were considered stereotypical by most black New York audiences, whose interest had turned to jazz dancing. Of her brief appearance at the Lincoln Theater in Harlem, she said, "Lincoln audiences were terrible and always booed anything artistic. All they wanted was bumps and Shake dancing" (quoted in Stearns and Stearns, 254).

Also, she was considered too dark for the Harlem nightclub circuit, which tended to feature light-skinned women. She explained: "I couldn't get a job because I was black, and my own people discriminated against me" (Stearns and Stearns, 256). Forsyne did appear in the musical comedy *Darkydom* (1914) at the Lafayette Theater in Harlem.

By the early 1920s, Forsyne's career had stalled, although she toured with Sophie Tucker and later with Bessie Smith on the Theater Owners' Booking Association (TOBA) circuit. She also was cast in several minor film roles. In 1951, she assisted Ruthanna Boris with the choreography for New York City Ballet's "The Cakewalk." Little is known about her life after her theatrical career, except that for a brief time she worked as an elevator operator in a hotel in upstate New York. Soon thereafter, she lived at the Concord Baptist Nursing Home in Brooklyn, where she died in 1983.

Biography

Ida Forsyne (also known as Ida Forcen and Ida Forsyne Hubbard) was born in 1883 in Chicago. She toured with Black Patti's Troubadours, 1898–1902; performed in Europe, 1905–1910; performed in Russia, 1911–1914; toured with Sophie Tucker, 1920–1922; toured with Mamie Smith, 1924; and toured with Bessie Smith, 1927. Forsyne died in Brooklyn, New York, on 19 August 1983.

PAUL SCOLIERI

See also Cook, Will Marion; Lafayette Theater; Lincoln Theater; Mitchell, Abbie; Smith, Bessie; Smith, Mamie; Theater Owners' Booking Association

Selected Stage Credits

Smart Set. 1902. (Road show produced by Gus Hill.)
The Southerners. 1904. (Musical review produced by Will Marion Cook at the New York Roof Garden.)
Abbie Mitchell and Her Coloured Students. 1906. (Musical review at the Palace Theater, London.)
Darkydom. 1914. (Musical comedy at the Lafayette Theater, New York.)

Selected Films

The Emperor Jones. 1933. (United Artists.)
The Green Pastures. 1936. (Warner Brothers.)

Further Reading

Grimes, Sara. *Backwater Blues: In Search of Bessie Smith.* Amherst, Mass.: Rose Island, 2001.

Hughes, Langston. *Black Magic: A Pictorial History of the African-American in the Performing Arts.* New York: Da Capo Paperback, 1990. (Originally published Englewood Cliffs, N.J.: Prentice Hall, 1967.)

Ida Forsyne Oral History Tapes, Hatch-Billops Collection, New York.

Stearns, Marshall, and Jean Stearns. *Jazz Dance: The Story of American Vernacular Dance.* New York: Da Capo, 1994.

Tanner, Jo A. *Dusky Maidens: The Odyssey of the Early Black Dramatic Actress.* Westport, Conn.: Greenweed, 1992, p. 171.

Forsythe, Harold Bruce

Harold Bruce Forsythe was a prolific composer and writer, but except for some manuscript songs in the European tradition, now at the Huntington Library, his music—which included symphonic poems and an opera, among other works—is lost; and Harry Hay reported settings of spirituals with a strong blues character that as of the present writing remained unlocated. Forsythe's formal music training was largely in the European romantic tradition. On his own, however, he developed a strong interest in African and African American music as well as history, art, religion, and magic. More of Forsythe's writing than his music survives, also in manuscript form. A long manuscript novel, "Masks" (also "Frailest Leaves"), is partly autobiographical and probably descriptive of the New Negro movement in Los Angeles.

Forsythe found in the composer William Grant Still a compelling model who was exploring ways to use the European-American concert tradition in music to express aspects of African American culture. His writing on Still's music, which offers significant insights, may be the most important part of his output. Still and Forsythe probably met in New York City; they developed a professional friendship important to both during 1929–1930, while Still was working temporarily in Los Angeles. Forsythe's "A Study in Contradictions," the first serious critical essay on Still's music and the first to recognize the subtleties of Still's fusion of styles, came in 1930. Soon afterward, Forsythe provided a long essay, "The Rising Sun," intended as an introduction for Still's ballet *Sahdji.* Later, Forsythe wrote the libretto to Still's first opera, *Blue Steel,* and a scenario for a ballet, *The Sorcerer.* Still and Forsythe's friendship ended abruptly in 1935, however.

A combination of ill health, early deafness, and cultural isolation prevented Forsythe from pursuing the path he had laid out for himself of discovering, exploring, and explicating the African aspects of his heritage in both music and words.

Biography

Harold Forsythe went to Los Angeles with his parents in 1913 and remained there except for one period of study in New York City. He studied piano with Nada McCullough and William T. Wilkins at the Wilkins Conservatory concurrently with his high school education. He also studied music composition privately with Charles E. Pemberton, a faculty member at the University of Southern California. His introduction to literature and to the New Negro movement came through Wallace Thurman, who boarded with Forsythe's family while attending the University of Southern California in 1922. Forsythe graduated from Manual Arts High School, where he was recognized as a gifted pianist and composer, in 1926. The following fall, he enrolled at the Juilliard School of Music in New York, where he studied briefly with Rubin Goldmark. At Juilliard, Forsythe became aware of his growing deafness, which was probably why he withdrew before completing a full year of study. Returning to Los Angeles, he supported himself through odd jobs and a stint as a pianist on an offshore gambling ship during Prohibition. Advancing deafness brought his career as a musician to a halt by the late 1930s. He retrained himself as a nurseryman and worked at that occupation for more than two decades. He died in poverty. He had married Sara Turner, a former Cotton Club showgirl, in 1945; at the time of this writing, one of his two sons, Harold Sumner Forsythe, was a professor of history at Rancho Santiago College.

CATHERINE PARSONS SMITH

See also Still, William Grant; Thurman, Wallace

Further Reading

Forsythe, Harold Bruce. Papers. Huntington Library, San Marino, Calif.

Smith, Catherine Parsons. "An Unknown 'New Negro.'" In *William Grant Still: A Study in Contradictions*. Berkeley and Los Angeles: University of California Press, 2000, pp. 94–113. (See also Forsythe, Harold Bruce. "William Grant Still: A Study in Contradictions," pp. 274–303.)

Fortune, Timothy Thomas

Timothy (T.) Thomas Fortune—the most important black journalist of his time—founded the newspaper *New York Age* in order to speak out against racism and injustice in the United States, particularly in the South.

Fortune was born a slave in 1856; during Reconstruction he worked as a page in the Florida legislature. He began his career in journalism as a compositor for the Jacksonville *Daily Union*. During the late nineteenth century, he worked at several newspapers and magazines (including *People's Advocate, Weekly Witness*, and *Rumor*) and started the *Globe*. He came to New York around 1880 and became a leading proponent of black rights in the 1880s and 1890s. By the time of the *Globe*'s demise in 1883–1884, Fortune had a considerable reputation as a fearless editor. In 1884 he was the sole owner, editor, and chief printer of *Freeman*, speaking out against racism in the South. (Some white publishers and editors considered *Freeman* dangerous—evidence that people read it and took it very seriously.) In 1885 Fortune published a book, *Black and White: Land, Labor, and Politics in the South*, in which he focused on economic factors, discussing working conditions under capitalism and criticizing land grants to railroads. In 1887 he organized the National Afro-American League, a civil rights group. Throughout the 1880s and 1890s, he advocated mixed marriages, used the courts to fight racial discrimination, supported Ida B. Wells's protest against lynching, and urged that blacks be called Afro-Americans.

Fortune developed a lifelong friendship with Booker T. Washington, with whom—through the medium of *New York Age*—he would be very influential. Although the two men differed in temperament and disagreed over Washington's political philosophy of accommodation, Fortune supported Washington's programs in editorials in *New York Age*; and this support caused some of Washington's critics to accuse Fortune of expediency. (Those critics included W. E. B. Du Bois; J. Max Barber, publisher of *Voice of the Negro* in Atlanta; and William Monroe Trotter, editor of the Boston *Guardian*.)

Fortune used *New York Age* to fight against the disenfranchisement of African Americans and to urge them to become independent voters; he believed that political independence would strengthen their negotiating position. By nineteenth-century standards, Fortune's language was strikingly militant, caustic, and jolting, and it unsettled some readers, especially white southerners. But the editor of the Cincinnati *Afro-American* stated that Fortune was "without peer or superior as a colored journalist."

In 1904, Fortune, who was facing a personal financial crisis, sold *New York Age* to Frederick Randolph Moore but maintained his editorship. By then, Fortune was also doing work for other publications, including *Colored American Magazine*, which was published in Boston; and the *Amsterdam News*, which was published in New York. In 1914 Fortune moved to Washington, D.C., where he became publisher and editor of the Washington *Sun*. He continued to exhort black Americans to address their own political and economic conditions and to fight for equal rights and opportunities.

Fortune's work as an editor attracted the attention of Marcus Garvey, and Fortune served as the editor of Garvey's *Negro World* from 1923 until his death in 1928. However, there is no evidence that Fortune joined Garvey's Universal Negro Improvement Association (UNIA).

Fortune's career at *New York Age* and *Negro World* coincided with the Harlem Renaissance; during this period his efforts to promote change took on a new urgency. Fortune helped articulate blacks' demands for equality and renewed racial pride in a new urban environment.

Biography

Timothy (T.) Thomas Fortune was born a slave in Marianna, Florida, on 3 October 1856; his father, who was of mixed blood, was a shoemaker, tanner, and political leader. As a child during the Civil War, Fortune was taught by Union soldiers who were stationed in Marianna; he retained a lifelong interest in learning. He served as a page in the senate in Tallahassee during Reconstruction and received an appointment to West Point, which he could not accept because of his race. In the 1880s, he attended Stanton Institute, a school established by the Freedman's Bureau; he also attended Howard University. He got his start in journalism working as a compositor for the Jacksonville

T. Thomas Fortune, c. 1910. (Schomburg Center for Research in Black Culture, New York Public Library.)

See also Amsterdam News; Barnett, Ida B. Wells; Garvey, Marcus; Moore, Frederick Randolph; Negro World; New York Age; Trotter, William Monroe; Washington, Booker T.

Manuscript Collections

Emmett J. Scott Papers. Soper Library, Morgan State College.

Booker T. Washington Papers. Manuscript Division, Library of Congress.

Further Reading

Berry, Mary Frances, and John W. Blassingame. *Long Memory: The Black Experience in America*. 1982.

Calloway-Thomas, Carolyn. "T. Thomas Fortune on the 'Land of Chivalry and Deviltry.'" *Negro History Bulletin*, April–June 1979.

Duster, Alfreda M., ed. *Crusade for Justice: The Autobiography of Ida B. Wells*. 1970.

Franklin, John Hope, and August Meier, eds. *Black Leaders of the Twentieth Century*. 1981.

Franklin, John Hope, and Alfred A. Moss Jr. *From Slavery to Freedom: A History of Negro Americans*. 1988.

Fortune, T. Thomas. *Black and White: Land, Labor and Politics in the South*. 1884.

Harlan, Louis. *Booker T. Washington: The Making of a Black Leader, 1856–1901*. 1972.

Thornbrough, Emma Lou. "American Negro Newspapers, 1880–1914." *Business History Review*, 1966.

———. *T. Thomas Fortune: Militant Journalist*. 1972.

Daily Union; while he was in school, he worked as a printer for the *People's Advocate*, an African American newspaper, but then he returned to the *Daily Union*. He married Carrie C. Smiley of Florida while he was employed at the *Advocate*; they later separated. He came to New York c. 1880 and worked at the *Weekly Witness*, a religious paper; the *People's Advocate*; and *Rumor*. He also started the *Globe*, which lasted until 1883–1884, and was the owner and editor of *Freeman* (1884). He published a book, *Black and White: Land, Labor, and Politics in the South*, in 1885. He founded *New York Age* in 1887 and sold it to Frederick Randolph Moore in 1904. Fortune moved to Washington, D.C., in 1914 and became editor and publisher of the Washington *Sun*. He was the editor of Marcus Garvey's *Negro World* from 1923 to 1928. Fortune died on 2 June 1928.

CAROLYN CALLOWAY-THOMAS
THURMON GARNER

Four Saints in Three Acts

The opera *Four Saints in Three Acts* (1934), with libretto by Gertrude Stein and score by Virgil Thomson, occupies a unique position in American performance history. First produced in 1934, right after Stein's best-selling *Autobiography of Alice B. Toklas*, the opera was an immediate success. Its all-black cast, plotless libretto, opaque dialogue, and garish cellophane set alternately thrilled and shocked audiences. To this day it remains the longest-running opera in the history of Broadway. Its very singularity, however, precluded its having a broad, lasting influence in the arts. Attempts to revive *Four Saints in Three Acts* have tended to fail, and only recently have scholars begun to examine its cultural and historical significance.

Stein and Thomson conceived *Four Saints in Three Acts* as an opera about the contemplative life of the working artist, an existence which Stein likened to that of saints, who, in Stein's estimation, mostly sit around doing nothing. Hence, although the nominal setting was sixteenth-century Spain, the authors and producers did all they could to subordinate the historical context to the theme of creative meditation. Stein's libretto omits references to time and place; Thomson's score drew from American secular traditions; and Florence Stettheimer's brightly colored cellophane curtains and trees rendered the stage otherworldly.

Virgil Thomson's decision, approved by Stein, to cast African Americans in all of the parts was certainly part of this dissociative strategy. The black cast, more than any other aspect of the performance, cut against the ostensible setting. Although Thomson publicly insisted that black performers were necessary only for their rich voices and poise, he nevertheless rejected a proposal to have the cast perform in whiteface. Moreover, he conceded ulterior motives for his casting strategy in a newspaper interview: "Negroes objectify themselves very easily," he said. "They live on the surface of their consciousness" (quoted in Watson 1998, 202).

The disjunction between the opera's setting and its cast attracted much critical attention. By 1934, New York theater audiences had seen many all-black shows, among them Marc Connelly's *Green Pastures* and Hall Johnson's *Run Little Chillun*, but blacks had not yet penetrated the upper reaches of the fine arts. Most white critics praised the black cast, acknowledging the power of the voices even as they were struck by the performers' appearance. Significantly, black critics almost completely ignored *Four Saints in Three Acts*, focusing instead on *They Shall Not Die*, a play about the Scottsboro trial. To these black critics, Stein and Thomson's opera seemed a terrible waste of talent and opportunity. History bore out their viewpoint: audiences viewed the black cast as a gimmick not to be repeated, and of the performers, only Edward Matthews (Saint Ignatius) enjoyed much acclaim afterward.

Today, cultural critics question Stein's and Thomson's motives. Webb argues, for example, that *Four Saints in Three Acts* "deliberately situated black persons in a timeless realm devoid of history or stories" (2000, p. 449). Ironically, the renewed interest in this opera derives from scholarly attempts to locate Stein's racial and cultural politics—exactly the historically specific questions that Stein and Thomson tried to evade.

JUSTIN A. PITTAS-GIROUX

See also Green Pastures, The; Johnson, Hall; They Shall Not Die

Further Reading

Watson, Steven. *Prepare for Saints: Gertrude Stein, Virgil Thomson, and the Mainstreaming of American Modernism.* New York: Random House, 1998.

Webb, Barbara. "The Centrality of Race to the Modernist Aesthetics of Gertrude Stein's Four Saints in Three Acts." *Modernism/Modernity*, 7(3), 2000, pp. 447–469.

Francophone Africa and the Harlem Renaissance

The idea of Africa occupied a central place in the politics, aesthetics, art, and imagination of the Harlem Renaissance. However, the renaissance had an ambivalent attitude toward that idea. From one angle, Harlem's aesthetics reproduced the totalizing stereotypes of Africa as exotic and primitive. From another angle, Harlem's aesthetics reproduced idealized and positive images of Africa that exemplified the concern of the movement with nostalgia and its agenda of reclaiming roots and heritage. The presence of the idea of Africa underscores the international theme in Harlem's aesthetics, one that encapsulated the preoccupation of the movement with discourses of encounter and a black diaspora. Because its international theme incorporated a search for a common origin of the black diaspora, the Harlem Renaissance drew inspiration from Africa, first as a geographic monolith and second from the diverse geographic regions that were mostly under colonial rule. One such region was francophone Africa, which then consisted of French colonies primarily in the western, northern, and central regions of Africa. Francophone Africa gave imaginative energy to the political, artistic, and aesthetic focus of the Harlem Renaissance. Moreover, francophone Africa provided possibilities for imagining racial pride through cultural awareness and heritage.

Understanding the relationship of the Harlem Renaissance to francophone Africa requires, first, an understanding of its relationship to France. For many people, the Harlem Renaissance as a movement of self-affirmation had its beginnings in 1919, at a parade in Harlem by the men of the 369th Infantry (Fifteenth Infantry, the Harlem Hellfighters), a predominantly African American regiment in the then-segregated U.S. Army. The men of the 369th had served in France during World War I and had experienced no racial segregation, oppression, bias, or prejudice there. The French had treated the soldiers as equals, an experience the U.S. Army denied them. This valuing of France and French ideas about liberty started the long relationship between the Harlem Renaissance and France. However, the racial equality experienced by African American soldiers blinded some intellectuals and political activists of the Harlem Renaissance to France's colonial policies in Africa, which were oppressive and antithetical to the French liberal tradition. Significantly, many writers and intellectuals of the Harlem Renaissance "met" and confronted their African heritage in and through France—through interaction with francophone African intellectuals and politicians who were mostly based in Paris.

In Harlem, there was an expanded awareness and consciousness aptly captured by the idea of the "New Negro," a term that Alain Locke used as the title of the most representative text of the movement, *The New Negro* (1925), which became influential among francophone Africans in France. The New Negro espoused black pride and power, a bold declaration that called into question the oppression of blacks, including colonialism in Africa, and resonated with francophone African politicians and intellectuals. W. E. B. Du Bois, in "The Negro Mind Reaches Out" (a piece in *The New Negro*), spelled out France's relationship with its African colonies. Using the central metaphor of shadow to talk about European colonialism generally, Du Bois portrayed the shadow of France in francophone Africa as a systematic mode of political oppression, economic exploitation, and cultural domination. Du Bois highlighted the paradox of France, with its ideals of equality and liberty, subjugating and suppressing Africans in its colonies. French industry exploited African colonies for the economic development of France. Educational and cultural systems promoted French in the colonies instead of African languages and customs.

Other writers in Harlem produced creative and ethnographic work to represent Africa and its traditions and customs. Magazines and newspapers such

as *Opportunity*, *Crisis*, and Marcus Garvey's *Negro World* published articles and editorials on French colonial policies in Africa, championed the liberation of francophone Africa, and highlighted the problems of Africans under French colonial rule. At times these publications focused on art and aesthetics from francophone Africa. Alfred G. Barnes's article "Negro Art, Past and Present" (in *Opportunity* of May 1926) focused on the francophone African territories of Gabon, Ivory Coast, and Sudan-Niger. Lawrence Buermyer's article "The Negro Spirituals and American Art" focused on the francophone region of the Bushongo and Baluba of francophone Congo (*Opportunity*, 1926). In his article "The Art of the Congo" (*Opportunity* of May 1927), Melville Herskovits examined the francophone territories of the Congo basin in order to comment on the sophistication of African art. Also, publications in Harlem reviewed texts on francophone Africa such as André Gide's *Voyage au Congo* (1927) and *Retour du Tchad* (1928) and Paul Morand's *Magie noire* (1928).

The relationship between Harlem and francophone Africa was partly intellectual. Francophone African writers in the 1930s read the work of writers of the Harlem Renaissance such as Langston Hughes, Countee Cullen, James Weldon Johnson, Claude McKay, Jean Toomer, and Sterling Brown in English and in translation. Mercer Cook, an African American professor of French at Howard University, first publicized in the United States the work of French-speaking blacks, among them francophone Africans. Publications by blacks in France, such as *Revue du Monde/Review of the Black World* (1931–1932), *Depeche Africaine* (1928–1930), and *Les Continents* (1924), promoted race consciousness and Afrocentric aesthetics and philosophy. *Revue du Monde/Review of the Black World* published works by writers of the Harlem Renaissance such as Hughes and McKay; excerpted *The New Negro*; and published articles that focused on art, aesthetics, philosophy, and literature of the black diaspora.

Perhaps the most dramatic entry of francophone Africa into the consciousness of Harlem came through a significant personality, René Maran, who lived in France and Africa as a colonial administrator for France; and a significant publication, Maran's novel *Batouala* (1921). *Batouala*, which won Maran a prestigious French literary award, the Prix Goncourt, exposed the exploitative and racist practices of French colonialism in central Africa, the former Africaine Equatoriale Française. Publications such as *Opportunity*, *Crisis*, and *Negro World* reviewed Maran's novel positively. For example, in *Negro World*, Eric Walrond's "*Batouala*, Art, and Propaganda" (1922) and William H. Ferris's "The Significance of René Maran" (1922, editorial) focused on the political purposes of the novel; Ferris's "World's Ten Greatest Novels: Why René Maran's *Batouala* Won Goncourt Prize; Novels for Propaganda" (1922) and Alain Locke's "The Colonial Literature of France" (1923) provided in-depth analyses of francophone colonial literature in Africa. Maran became an inspirational figure who promoted the Harlem Renaissance in France. His friendship with Alain Locke in the 1920s and 1930s promoted intellectual, aesthetic, and scholarly interest in Africa. Maran participated symbolically in the literary Harlem Renaissance through his contributions to *Opportunity* and *Crisis*. With the Dahomean Kojo Tovalou-Houenou, he edited *Les Continents*, a publication devoted to black cultural, aesthetic, and political concerns. It published works by Harlem's writers, such as Hughes, Cullen, and Locke; published Garvey's speeches; and reported the activities of Garvey's Universal Negro Improvement Association (UNIA).

Another dimension of the relationship between francophone Africa and the Harlem Renaissance was the international political realm, as represented by the pan-African organization that had been partly conceptualized and realized by Du Bois. It advocated equal rights and political rights for blacks and whites and also called for political freedom, education, and land and economic resources for Africans under colonial rule. This organization fostered relations that emphasized the commonality of the black experience. Paris was the site of the first Pan-African Congress in 1919. Among the participants were Du Bois; Blaise Diagne, the Senegalese and black representative to the French National Assembly; and Gratien Candace, the black deputy from Guadeloupe. At the time of the second Pan-African Congress in 1921, there was a deep ideological fissure in the organization over Du Bois's open call for an end to colonial rule in Africa versus Diagne's advocacy of retaining a French colonial system that recognized the role of Africa within French colonial hegemony. The distrust between Du Bois and Diagne had severe consequences for the pan-African organization. Diagne abandoned it, and with him francophone African leadership and support. The rift also prevented the convening of the fourth Pan-African Congress in 1925. Opposition by colonial powers also hindered the vision of the organization. The Pan-African Congress considered holding its fifth assembly in Tunis (North Africa), which was then a French colony, but the French government would not allow the congress to be held on francophone African soil, for fear of political turmoil in its other African colonies.

Francophone Africans responded favorably to Marcus Garvey, who in the early 1920s popularized the slogan "back to Africa," promoting ties between African Americans and Africa. Kodjo Tovalou-Houenou, who was based in Paris and was associated with Garvey, sent copies of *Negro World* to Dahomey, and in 1924 created in Paris the Ligue Universelle pour la Défense de la Race Noire, which articulated pan-Negroism as promoted by Garvey's UNIA. The organization later became known as the Comité de Défense de la Race Nègre, and its first president was Lamine Senghor, a cousin of Léopold Senghor. Race consciousness and pride as articulated by Garvey and other figures of the Harlem Renaissance permeated the work of francophone African writers, who began to define themselves in terms of their race—a development that later was transformed into the full-fledged *négritude* (negritude) movement.

In fact, the negritude movement was the most significant contribution of Harlem's aesthetics to francophone Africa. Harlem provided the fundamental philosophical and aesthetic concepts of negritude, and the founders of the movement—Aimé Césaire, Léopold Senghor, and Léon Gontran-Damas—spoke of their indebtedness to the Harlemite writers of the 1930s, mostly Hughes, Cullen, Toomer, and McKay. Senghor openly credited McKay as the spiritual founder of negritude. McKay's novel *Banjo* was a favorite of many francophone African writers, who in turn explored its themes and style in their own work. The expressiveness and spontaneity of Harlem's aesthetics influenced francophone African writers such as Senghor, Birago Diop, Sembene Ousmane, and Ousmane Soce Diop, author of *Mirages du Paris* (1937). Negritude poetry, in particular Senghor's oeuvre, gave an important place to feelings, music, song, and rhythm—elements that came directly from Harlem's aesthetics. Negritude writers learned from the writers of the Harlem Renaissance about the power of poetry for self-expression, self-exploration, and social change. In addition to this literary influence, the central tenets of negritude were based on Garvey's black nationalism—which was opposed to racial assimilation and prized a pure, unadulterated African culture–and on the philosophical underpinnings of the pan-African movement. Thus the themes of self-assertion, rebellion, and racial pride articulated by the Harlem Renaissance influenced francophone African writers in their conceptualization of negritude aesthetics and the eventual political mobilization against French colonial rule in Africa.

PATRICK S. BERNARD

See also Batouala; Césaire, Aimé; Crisis, The; Damas, Léon; Fifteenth Infantry; Garvey, Marcus; Herskovits, Melville; Locke, Alain; Maran, René; McKay, Claude; Negritude; Negro World; Opportunity; Pan-Africanism; Pan-African Congresses; Senghor, Léopold

Further Reading

Brown, Lloyd W. "The African Heritage and the Harlem Renaissance: A Re-Evaluation." *African Literature Today*, 9, 1978, pp. 1–9.

Cook, Mercer A. "Some Literary Contacts: African, West Indian, Afro-American." In *The Black Writer in Africa and the Americas: Conference on Comparative Literature*, ed. Lloyd W. Brown. Los Angeles: University of South California Press, 1973, pp. 120–121.

Daye, Pierre. "Le Mouvement Pan-Nègre." *Flambeau* (Brussels), 7, July–August 1921, pp. 359–375.

"The Decorated Colors of the French Colonial Troops." *Crisis*, 19, November 1919, p. 346.

Du Bois, W. E. B. "Memorandum to M. Diagne and others on a Pan-African Congress to Be Held in Paris in February 1919." *Crisis*, 4, March 1919, pp. 224–225.

———. "The Negro Mind Reaches Out." In *The New Negro*, ed. Alain Locke. New York: Simon and Schuster, 1992. (Originally published 1925.)

Du Bus, de Warnaffe.—"Le Garveyism en Action dans Notre Colonie." *Congo*, June–December 1921, pp. 575–576.

———. "Le Mouvement Pan-Nègre aux États-Unis et Ailleurs." *Congo*, May 1922.

Edwards, Brent Hayes. *Practice of Diaspora: Literature, Translation, and the Rise of Black Nationalism*. Cambridge, Mass.: Harvard University Press, 2003.

Fabre, Michel. "Rene Maran, the New Negro, and Negritude." *Phylon*, 36, 1975, pp. 340–351.

———. "The Harlem Renaissance Abroad: French Critics and the New Negro Literary Movement (1924–1964)." In *Temples of Tomorrow: Looking Back at the Harlem Renaissance*, eds. Geneivieve Fabre and Michael Feith. Bloomington: Indiana University Press, 2001, pp. 314–332.

"French Colonial Policy." *Opportunity*, 2, September 1924, pp. 261–263. (An exchange between René Maran and Alain Locke.)

Geiss, Imanuel. *The Pan-African Movement*, trans. Ann Keep. London: Methuen, 1974.

Ikonne, Chidi. "Rene Maran and the New Negro." *Colby Library Quarterly*, 16(4), December 1979, pp. 224–239.

Janken, Kenneth R. "African American and Francophone Black Intellectuals during the Harlem Renaissance." *Historian*, Spring 1998, pp. 1–17.

Kestleloot, Lilyan. *Black Writers in French: A Literary History of Negritude*. Philadelphia, Pa.: Temple University Press, 1974.

Langley, Jabez Ayodele. "Pan-Africanism in Paris, 1924–1936." *Journal of Modern African Studies*, 7(1), April 1969.

Logan, Rayford W. "France Will Not Betray Her Subjects." *Chicago Defender*, National Edition, 22 November 1924, part 2, p. 9.

McKay, Claude. *Banjo: A Story without a Plot*. New York: Harcourt, 1929.

Mudimbe-Boyi, Elisabeth. "African and Black American Literature: The 'Negro Renaissance' and the Genesis of African Literature in French," trans. J. Coates. In *For Better or Worse: The American Influence on the World*, ed. Allen F. Davis. Westport, Conn.: Greenwood, 1981, pp. 157–169.

———. "Harlem Renaissance and Africa: An Ambiguous Adventure." In *The Surreptitious Speech: Presence Africaine and the Politics of Otherness, 1947–1987*, ed. V. Y. Mudimbe. Chicago, Ill.: University of Chicago Press, 1992, pp. 174–182.

Tovalou-Houenou, Prince Kojo. "The Problem of Negroes in French Colonial Africa." *Opportunity*, 2, July 1924, pp. 203–207.

Francophone Caribbean and the Harlem Renaissance

The influence of the Harlem Renaissance on the cultural dynamics of the francophone Caribbean is inestimable. Franco-Caribbean literature was born with negritude (*négritude*), and negritude was a diasporic offshoot of the Harlem Renaissance. World War I and the international political events in its aftermath brought African Americans and French-speaking blacks together in Paris, the capital of France. Besides black soldiers, many musicians and intellectuals of the Harlem Renaissance made their way to France.

In this *après-guerre* France, jazz and primitivism became the rage of Paris, perhaps in an attempt to block out the horrors wrought by the war. And blackness was linked to cosmopolitanism, becoming a source of creative inspiration in literature and the arts among Europeans, with their exoticist tracts and tableaux, and cultural workers of the Harlem Renaissance.

W. E. B. Du Bois, editor of *Crisis* and author of the classic *The Souls of Black Folk* (1903), was among the first of the Harlem Renaissance coterie to coalesce with elite francophones of color. With the help of Blaise Diagne (the Senegalese deputy in the French parliament) and Gratien Candace, Du Bois was able to organize the first Pan-African Congress, held in Paris from 19 to 21 February 1919. Because Du Bois was (in the words of David Levering Lewis) the "impresario of pan-Africanism," his theories on the "talented tenth," on the uneasy symbiosis of blackness and Americanness, and on the cultural histories of Africa and its diaspora found currency among a cadre of elite francophones in Paris at the time, some of whom were committed to reconciling France's discourse on humanism with its slipshod colonial practices. Such encounters helped make the worldview of French-speaking blacks more global and also expand their understanding of racial inequality and oppression. Hitherto, they had lacked a language imbued with the complexities of race and racialism to articulate the malaise many of them experienced in France. They were citizens of France but—curiously, considering the color blindness implied by the French ideal of *liberté*, *fraternité*, and *egalité*—they were treated as outsiders.

Du Bois's vigorous anticolonialism and anti-imperialism were moderated with respect to France. His admiration for the principles of Jacobin France and his own personal ability to exist in France unfettered by the "accursed veil" clouded his radicalism. Nevertheless, the tenuous alliance that he established with these *métropolitains de couleur* under the rubric of the "Pan African Association" proved no match for the fruits offered by the French policy of assimilation. His vision of a black international community eventually came to be considered "dangerously internationalist" and threatening to French colonial policy, with its *mission civilisatrice* and its assimilationist dicta. Most elite francophones believed that France held out the only hope for the cultural advancement of the "backward races in Africa," as the rhetoric on civilization went.

Marcus Garvey, with his Universal Negro Improvement Association (UNIA), also cast his eye on France. He even channeled funds to the fledgling newspaper *Dépêche Africaine*, whose colonial reformist radicalism perturbed French government officials sufficiently to make them begin a campaign of dogged monitoring. However, Garvey's vision of global black solidarity and "Africa for the Africans" failed to appeal widely to *les français noirs*. His failure to overcome the idea of a color-blind France is perhaps more obvious than Du Bois's, as Kojo Tovalou, editor of the newspaper *Les Continents*, emphasized during a visit to UNIA's headquarters in New York in 1924: "Mr. President Garvey . . . France is the only country that does not have race prejudice, but struggles for its disappearance." In the end, colonial reforms, which would facilitate assimilation into Frenchness rather than the eventual decolonization proposed by both Garvey and Du Bois, were the marching orders followed by French-speaking blacks. As the editors of *Dépêche Africaine* definitely surmised, "the methods of colonization by civilized nations are far from perfect; but colonization itself is a human and necessary project."

However, the Harlem Renaissance had its most lasting impact not in politics but in the cultural realm, particularly in literature. In salons set up in Paris by the author René Maran (who was a winner of the Prix Goncourt) and in Clamart, a suburb of Paris, by Andrée, Jane, and Paulette Nardal, and in the pages of newspapers, reviews, and magazines like *Continents*, *Dépêche Africaine*, and *Revue du Monde Noir*, francophone and Harlem Renaissance writers, intellectuals, and journalists discussed issues of race, culture, identity, and internationalism. Although jazz was in vogue, literary ideas and ideals professed in such texts as Alain Locke's anthology *The New Negro*, Langston Hughes's poetry, and Claude McKay's novel *Banjo* would become the cultural legacy exported to the French West Indies in the years preceding World War II.

Black self-expression, racial pride, and cultural exploration embodied in the works mentioned previously instigated calls for an authentic black literature in the French Caribbean rather than the usual imitation of French literary masters. "Race-conscious literature" became the battle cry. Langston Hughes' proletarian literature, lacking the exoticist themes characteristic of McKay's *Banjo*, served as a model. Like the New Negro in America, francophone writers also endeavored to invoke a "race spirit," in accordance with Alain Locke's theories in his introduction to *The New Negro*, to create a francophone New Negro in a new world.

411

The New Negro spawned the term *néo-nègre* in the francophone context—a concept that would later be transformed into the cultural movement *négritude*. The most readily identifiable proponents of the francophone New Negro movement that began in France are Aimé Césaire of Martinque, Léon-Gontron Damas of Guyana, and Léopold Sédar Senghor of Senegal. The ideological content of *néo-nègre* and *négritude* were conceived at Maran's salon and the salon in Clamart and on the pages of *Revue du Monde Noir* under the stewardship of Paulette and Jane Nardal. The poet Aimé Césaire coined the neologism in *Cahier d'un retour au pays natal* (1936). He, Damas, and Senghor— as attendees at those salons and as avid readers of *Revue du Monde Noir*, whose six issues were decidedly diasporic in content, including translations of poetry and prose by Harlem Renaissance writers—would make their distinctive marks on this burgeoning movement in the francophone world in subsequent literary and philosophical works.

Although *Cahier d'un retour au pays natal* was neither conceived nor written in Martinique, Césaire's *pays natal* became the muse for his reflections on the cultural vapidity of the Antilles, a condition he saw as caused by French colonial imposition and solipsism. This cultural void was a result of a defective system of formation whereby Antilleans were "crammed to splitting open with white morality, white culture, white education, white prejudice," as the poet Étienne Léro wrote in the surrealist manifesto *Légitime défense* (1932), and succinctly represented in the deleterious phrase *nos ancêtres les gaulois*. Also in this text, in the fashion of Langston Hughes, Césaire proposes to become the *porte-parole* of the proleteriat, where his "tongue" as poet "will serve those miseries which have no tongue"; "his voice the liberty of those who founder in the dungeons of despair."

And so as another world war loomed, Aimé Césaire, his philosopher wife Suzanne Césaire, and the Marxist and surrealist René Ménil returned to Martinique. With their newfound understanding of Africa, a global race consciousness, and a profound respect for Haiti (where black consciousness directly manifested itself as a result of the Haitian revolution and international isolation through indigenism and such writers as Jean-Price-Mars and the anthropologist Antènor Firmin), they undertook a mission—to urge Antillean artists to shed cultural sterility through their literary and cultural review *Tropiques*.

Tropiques emerged in the Antillean cultural landscape in April 1941. René Ménil had already taken West Indian writers of color to task some nine years earlier in *Légitime défense*. Describing works by these authors as "bored and boring; depressed and depressing," he suggested that they use the New "American" Negro writer as an inspiration for what Caribbean literature could become. In his debut essay "Naissance de notre art" (1941) in *Tropiques*, Ménil continued to accuse Martinican artists in particular of mediocrity, of coming to "courts of Culture empty-handed . . . with borrowed graces." In the first anniversary issue of *Tropiques*, Suzanne Césaire lamented, in the tellingly titled essay "Malaise d'une civilisation" (1942), that Martinican cultural workers lived inauthentically, in imitation, and hence had produced no "original" styles.

Both Césaire's and Menil's criticisms echoed Paulette Nardal's prophetic words in "The Awakening of Race Consciousness among Black Students" (1932), published in the last issue of *Revue du Monde Noir*. Nardal recognized that, because of the processes of French acculturation and assimilation, Caribbean writers were uneasy in their black skin. This malaise led to feelings of inferiority and made their creative works mere "tributaries of Latin culture." Evoking the Harlem Renaissance as a model and citing Langston Hughes, Nardal concluded that the "Americans, having thrown off all inferiority complexes, tranquilly 'express their individual dark-skinned selves without fear or shame.'" This purging of inferiority complexes and coming to terms with the particularity of the "land, race, and economic forms, etc." of the Caribbean, as Ménil writes in "Naissance," would allow for the development of fecund, inimitable cultural productions. Such was the challenge of the Negro writer in the francophone Caribbean *entre deux guerres*; the road map for the realization of this cultural awakening was the Harlem Renaissance.

TRACY DENEAN SHARPLEY-WHITING

See also Césaire, Aimé; Damas, Léon; Du Bois, W. E. B.; Garvey, Marcus; Hughes, Langston; Locke, Alain; Maran, René; McKay, Claude; Negritude; New Negro, The; Pan-African Congresses; Senghor, Léopold

Further Reading

Archer-Straw, Petrine. *Negrophilia: Avant-Garde Paris and Black Culture in the 1920s*. New York: Thames and Hudson, 2002.

Cunard, Nancy. *Negro: An Anthology*. New York: Continuum, 1996.

Fabre, Michel. *From Harlem to Paris: Black American Writers in France, 1840–1980*. Champaign-Urbana: University of Illinois Press, 1991.

Kesteloot, Lilyan. *Black Writers in French: A Literary History of Negritude*, trans. Ellen Conroy Kennedy. Washington, D.C.: Howard University Press, 1991.

Richardson, Michael. *Refusal of the Shadow: Surrealism and the Caribbean*. London: Verso, 1996.

Sartre, Jean-Paul. "Black Orpheus." In *What Is Literature? and Other Essays*. Cambridge, Mass.: Harvard University Press, 1988.

Shack, William. *Harlem in Montmartre: A Paris Jazz Story between Great Wars*. Berkeley: University of California Press, 2001.

Sharpley-Whiting, T. Denean. *Negritude Women*. Minneapolis: University of Minnesota Press, 2002.

Stovall, Tyler. *Paris Noir: African Americans in the City of Light*. New York: Houghton Mifflin, 1996.

Frank, Waldo

In *Our America* (1919), Waldo Frank claimed, as had Van Wyck Brooks in *America's Coming of Age* (1915), that America was culturally split between genteel idealism (highbrow) and material obsession (lowbrow). In Frank's words, modern America was "externalized." What was most needed was an awakened sense of cohesion and purpose, a sense of collective identity, that only the artist and the intellectual could provide. Initially, in the first issue of *Seven Arts* (a journal Frank founded with Brooks, Floyd Dell, and James Oppenheim) and in an essay titled "Emerging Greatness," Frank saw in Sherwood Anderson this promise of a renaissance of the imagination that would help create a new sense of "national self consciousness." However, if Anderson ultimately proved disappointing, Frank detected in Jean Toomer "the spiritual power to hoist himself wholly into a more essential plane: the plane in which the materials of the phenomenal world are re-created into pure aesthetic forms." As a result, Toomer, who thought that "art had a sort of religious function," felt that he and Frank were united "in the dual task of creating an American literature."

Hutchinson (1995) has argued that the Harlem Renaissance is best understood as a search for an American national identity commonly pursued and contested by black and white intellectuals: "The issue of American national identity was, in any case, the dominant problematic structuring the literary field

relevant to the Harlem Reniassance. . . . The attempt, overall, came down to an effort to expand the notion of 'the people' who compose the national community." Through his relationship with many of the young intellectuals who made up what Blake (1990) called the "beloved community," Frank was indirectly linked to the cultural renaissance symbolically focused in Harlem, but Frank was most directly linked with the imaginative concerns of African Americans through the person of Jean Toomer.

In 1921 Toomer accepted the job of acting principal of a small black industrial school in Sparta, Georgia. This experience led him to write several stories that would eventually make up *Cane*, the novel many people consider to be the greatest artistic achievement of the Harlem Renaissance. One year later, Toomer returned to the South (this time to Spartanburg, South Carolina), together with Frank—who, after having spent time in Virginia and the deep South, was drawn by Toomer's insistence that the South and the southern Negro offered "the opportunity for a vivid symbolism" for a world fast becoming homogenized by "machines, motor cars, phonographs, [and] movies." Out of this experience came Toomer's *Cane* and Frank's *Holiday*. Each novel was unquestionably the work of its author, but the two novels would not have been the same without the other's criticism and encouragement. In Toomer's "Bona and Paul," for example, Frank found "a certain loss of intensity—a certain amount of mere writing" in much of the imagery. But "Kabnis," he suggested, was "quite perfect as an expression of the man who wrote it." And Frank, whose novel centers on a lynching in a small southern town, eagerly asked for Toomer's critical comments: "I shall send you the other parts in quick order. You can help me INESTIMABLY, Jean, if you will go through the whole thing carefully—take what time you need for that and mark all the 'stiffnesses' and give me your suggestions of improvements." Even after the publication of *Holiday*, Frank continued to consult Toomer regarding the validity of the critical comments.

Frank's aphorism "The person is the individual made real" expresses the code he shared with Jean Toomer in their attempt to overcome, through art, the alienation they saw in modern life.

Biography

Waldo Frank was born on 25 August 1889. He studied at De Witt Clinton High School, New York (1902–1906);

Waldo Frank. (Brown Brothers.)

at a private preparatory school in Lausanne, Switzerland (1906–1907); and at Yale University (1907–1911). He was a reporter for the New York *Evening Post* and *New York Times* (1911–1913), an associate editor for *Seven Arts* (1916–1917), a contributing editor for *New Masses* (1926), chairman of the League of American Writers (1936), and a delegate to the Congress of Revolutionary Writers and Artists of Mexico in Mexico City (1937–1938). His awards included membership in the National Institute of Arts and Letters. Frank died on 9 January 1967.

Mark Helbling

See also Anderson, Sherwood; Cane; Toomer, Jean

Selected Works

Our America. 1919.
The Dark Mother. 1920.
Rahab. 1922.
City Block. 1922.
Holiday. 1923.
Chalk Face. 1923.
Salvos. 1924.
Virgin Spain. 1926.
Time Exposures. 1926.
In the American Jungle. 1925–1936.
Rediscovery of America. 1929.
Memoirs of Waldo Frank. 1973.

Further Reading

Carter, Paul. *Waldo Frank.* New York: Twayne, 1967.
Bittner, William. *Novels of Waldo Frank.* Philadelphia: University of Pennsylvania Press, 1958.
Blake, Casey Nelson. *Beloved Community: The Cultural Criticism of Randolph Bourne, Van Wyck Brooks, and Lewis Mumford.* Chapel Hill: University of North Carolina Press, 1990.
Helbling, Mark. *The Harlem Renaissance: The One and the Many.* Westport, Conn.: Greenwood, 1999.
Hutchinson, George. *The Harlem Renaissance in Black and White.* Cambridge, Mass.: Harvard University Press, 1995.
Ogorzaly, Michael. *Waldo Frank: Prophet of Hispanic Regeneration.* Lewisburg, Pa.: Bucknell University Press, 1994.
Perry, Robert. *Shared Vision of Waldo Frank and Hart Crane.* Lincoln: University of Nebraska, 1966.

Frazier, E. Franklin

E. Franklin Frazier was one of the leading cultural critics during the maturation of the Harlem Renaissance. This black American—who would go on to become chairman of the department of sociology at Howard University, president of the American Sociological Society (later Association), and one of the most acclaimed authorities on the black family, the black middle class, and race relations—established a reputation during the "Negro movement" as someone who wanted to combine the essential insights of two diametrically opposed orientations: integration and separatism. During the 1920s, Frazier's popular articles were published in *Southern Workman, Crisis, Opportunity*, and *Nation*; his scholarly articles appeared in *Journal of Social Forces, Howard Review, Annals of the American Academy of Political and Social Science*, and *Current History*. At the first *Opportunity* fete in May 1925, Frazier's essay on social equality was awarded first prize—a tribute to his critical acuity. As early as 1925, Frazier published an article, "Durham: Capital of the Black Middle Class," in Alain Locke's classic anthology *The New Negro*. In this essay, Frazier argued unequivocally, as Moses has observed, for the necessity of "black economic self-reliance as a basis for ethnic regeneration of black Americans" (1990, 108). Three years later, in an essay entitled "La Bourgeois Noire," which appeared in V. F. Calverton's *Anthology of American Negro Literature*, Frazier went so far as to applaud Marcus Garvey's movement for its attempt to develop "nationalistic aims with an economic program" (108). In other words, Frazier thought that the black American question was not solely economic; for Frazier, as Cruse observed, the question "was, and is, also a cultural one" (1967, 155). The Harlem Renaissance lacked directionality, Frazier suggested, at least partly because it represented a type of cultural nationalism that was supported by white rather than black capitalists. Furthermore, Lewis has argued with regard to the New Negro movement that Frazier "exposed its deficiencies from the vantage point of one of its presumed agents" (1994, 173). Frazier succinctly summed up the shortcomings of the Negro Movement when he argued that "it knows nothing of . . . Work and Wealth" (181).

Although Frazier preached a variant of economic nationalism, his views on black cultural nationalism were far more complex. As Platt (1991) has noted, Frazier argued that the African past had no relevance for black culture in the United States. Nonetheless, Frazier thought that it would be good to nurture black racial identity by teaching and developing courses in black history, and by the artistic exploitation of themes from the vital black folk culture of the United States. As a consequence, Frazier abhorred some black peoples' imitation of whites—the use of skin-bleaching creams, the vogue of hair straightening, and other current fashions. Still, he argued that social equality would eventually destroy both racial identity and racial consciousness. In short, Frazier thought that integration and eventual assimilation were inevitable.

Frazier's critiques were an integral part of the New Negro movement during the 1920s. Thus, although his professional relationship with the sociologist Charles S. Johnson would eventually sour in the 1930s, during the Harlem Renaissance the two had a mutually beneficial relationship. In fact, during the years 1924 to 1929 Johnson published eight of Frazier's articles in the National Urban League's organ *Opportunity*; three of these articles were the genesis of some of Frazier's later work on the black family. Subsequent historians

and cultural critics, such as Cruse and Platt, have applauded Frazier's work during the 1920s. For example, Cruse notes that Frazier knew "The unique literary and cultural revival of the 1920s turned out to be a directionless movement . . . because it was divorced from the politics and economics of Negro culture as a group concept" (156). Platt has written that during the Harlem Renaissance, "At stake was the content of culture, which, Frazier argued, could not be separated from issues of class and politics" (128).

At least one critic, in contradistinction to Cruse's and Platt's analyses of Frazier's nationalist cultural examinations, has described Frazier as an assimilationist; however, this label ignores the critiques that Frazier wrote during the 1920s. It is more likely that Frazier's writings during this period were characterized by an ambiguity and openness that left them

E. Franklin Frazier. (Schomburg Center for Research in Black Culture, New York Public Library.)

subject to more than one interpretation. As mentioned previously, Frazier's writings were inspired by his yearning to combine the insights of two opposed positions—color-blind universalism and racially exclusive nationalism. In other words, he desired the integration of diverse racial groups on an equal basis, but without the complete loss of each group's own cultural identity. Thus, although Frazier believed that the world's races and peoples would eventually merge, he was not an assimilationist during the 1920s. Throughout his career, he felt that in the foreseeable future it would be necessary for blacks to reconstruct a communal and institutional life capable of accomplishing the arduous task of black uplift—a mission that he felt the artists of Harlem had failed to perform.

Biography

Edward Franklin Frazier was born on 24 September 1894, in Baltimore, Maryland. He studied at public schools in Baltimore; Howard University, Washington, D.C. (B.A., 1916); Clark University, Worcester, Massachusetts (M.A., 1920); New York School of Social Work (research fellow, 1920–1921); American-Scandinavian Foundation (fellow, 1921–1922); and the University of Chicago (Ph.D., 1931). He taught at Tuskegee Institute in Alabama (1916–1917); Saint Paul's Normal and Industrial School, Lawrenceville, Virginia (1917–1918); Baltimore High School (1918–1919); Morehouse College, Atlanta, Georgia (1922–1927); Atlanta School of Social Work (1922–1927); Fisk University, Nashville, Tennessee (1929–1934); and Howard University (1934–1962). Frazier was director of the Harlem Riot Commission (1935), a Guggenheim fellow (1940), consultant for *An American Dilemma* (1942), president of the American Sociological Association (1948), and chief of the Division of Applied Social Sciences in UNESCO (1951–1953). He died on 16 May 1962.

VERNON J. WILLIAMS

See also Calverton, V. F.; Johnson, Charles Spurgeon; New Negro, The; New Negro Movement; Opportunity

Selected Articles

"A Note on Negro Education." *Opportunity*, 2, March 1924, pp. 213–214.

"Some Aspects of Negro Business." *Opportunity*, 2, August 1924, p. 239.
"Social Equality and the Negro." *Opportunity*, 3, June 1925, pp. 165–168.
"Durham: Capital of the Black Middle Class." In *The New Negro*, ed. Alain Locke. New York: A. and C. Boni, 1925, pp. 333–340.
"Three Scourges of the Negro Family." *Opportunity*, 4, July 1926, pp. 210–213, 234.
"The Garvey Movement." *Opportunity*, 4, November 1926, pp. 147–148.
"Is the Negro Family a Unique Sociological Unit?" *Opportunity*, 5, June 1927, pp. 165–168.

Selected Longer Works

The Free Negro Family. 1932.
The Negro Family in Chicago. 1932.
The Negro Family in the United States. 1939. (Reprinted abridged ed., 1966.)
Negro Youth at the Crossways. 1940.
Bourgeoisie Noire. (American ed. published as *Black Bourgeoisie*, 1957.)
The Negro in the United States. 1949. (Rev. ed., 1957.)
Race and Culture Contacts in the Modern World. 1957.
The Negro Church. 1964. (Published posthumously.)

Further Reading

Cruse, Harold. *The Crisis of the Negro Intellectual*. New York: Morrow, 1967.
Edwards, G. Franklin. *E. Franklin Frazier on Race Relations*. Chicago, Ill.: University of Chicago Press, 1968.
Lewis, David Levering, ed. *The Portable Renaissance Reader*. New York: Penguin, 1994.
Moses, Wilson. *The Wings of Ethiopia*. Ames: Iowa State University Press, 1990.
Platt, Anthony. *E. Franklin Frazier Reconsidered*. New Brunswick, N.J.: Rutgers University Press, 1991.

Fuller, Meta Warrick

Meta Vaux Warrick is sometimes seen as a precursor of the Harlem Renaissance. Although she did not live in New York, she was inspired by the ideals of

W. E. B. Du Bois, whom she met in Paris. Her long career began at a time when the art world was just beginning to open up to women and lasted until her death at age ninety.

Warrick grew up in a comfortable middle-class family in Philadelphia and later spent summers on Martha's Vineyard. In 1894, she won a three-year scholarship to the Pennsylvania School for Industrial Arts. In the fall of 1899, she traveled to Paris, where she studied with Rodin, met several other important artists, and exhibited at Samuel Bing's Art Nouveau Gallery. She also studied in Rome at the Colarossi Academy. Later she was included in shows in Philadelphia, New York, Boston, and Washington, D.C.

After returning to the United States in 1902, she became engaged with issues affecting blacks. The following year, she made a plaque commemmorating Emperor Menelik II of Abyssinia. She married the first black psychiatrist in America, Dr. Solomon Fuller, who was originally from Liberia. They moved to Framingham, Massachusetts, where she set up a studio. In 1907, Meta Warrick Fuller became the first black female artist hired by the federal government.

All of the work Fuller did before 1910 was destroyed in a fire. Her surviving work, however, reflects her increasing involvement in black culture. She was impressed by an anticolonial movement called Ethiopianism, which combined black American traditions with those of Africa. That movement inspired Fuller's best-known sculpture, *Ethiopia Awakening* (1914, or more probably 1921). Although this work was made before the heyday of the Harlem Renaissance, it merges the two cultures—African and black American. The lower half represents a wrapped mummy, and the upper half is an Egyptian princess who is very much alive. The theme of birth as a metaphor for artistic creation is used here in the context of the legendary land of the queen of Sheba, who is considered black by traditon.

In 1917, blacks protested against the lynching of Mary Turner, a black woman from Georgia who had been accused of plotting the murder of a white man. The protests were publicized in the magazine *Crisis*. To commemorate this event, in 1919 Fuller produced *Mary Turner*, subtitled *Protest against Mob Violence*. It shows a woman quietly gazing down at heads embedded in the painted plaster from which it was modeled. Like *Ethiopia Awakening*, although in a very different style, this sculpture depicts a woman immobilized below the waist (here, because she is embedded in the material itself) but able to move above the waist.

Fuller's *Talking Skull* (1937) is a contemplative work, showing an African man meditating on a skull. It reflects the artist's lifelong interest in themes of death as well as birth and rebirth.

By the 1950s, following the march of African Americans' progress in the United States, Fuller was creating several works inspired by the civil rights movement. In 1957, the Afro-American Women's Council in Washington, D.C., commissioned her to execute ten sculptures of famous black women. Fuller died eleven years later, in 1968.

Biography

Meta V. W. Fuller was born on 9 June 1877, into a comfortable Philadelphia family. She is considered a precursor of the Harlem Renaissance, and although she lived and worked around Boston, she was sympathetic to the ideals of the renaissance. After graduating from art school, she studied in Paris, where she

Meta Warrick Fuller. (Schomburg Center for Research in Black Culture, New York Public Library.)

417

Fuller, Meta Warrick

met and was influenced politically and culturally by W. E. B. Du Bois and artistically mainly by Rodin. When she returned to the United States, Fuller became involved in black issues, which are reflected in the themes of her sculpture. She died in 1968, at age ninety.

LAURIE ADAMS

See also Artists; Visual Arts

Selected Works

Ethiopia Awakening. 1914. (Schomburg Center for Research in American Sculpture, New York Public Library.)

Mary Warner. 1919. (Museum of Afro-American History, Boston.)

Talking Skull. 1937. (Museum of Afro-American History, Boston.)

Further Reading

Bearden, Romare, and Harry Henderson. *A History of African-American Artists from 1792 to the Present*. New York: Pantheon, 1993.

Heyd, Milly. *Mutual Reflections: Jews and Blacks in American Art*. New Brunswick, N.J., and London: Rutgers University Press, 1999.

Lewis, Samela. *African-American Art and Artists*. Berkeley: University of California Press, 1990.

Patton, Sharon F. *African-American Art*. New York: Oxford University Press, 1998.

Studio Museum in Harlem. *Harlem Renaissance: Art of Black America*. New York: Abrams, 1987.

G

Garland Fund

The Garland Fund—so named for its benefactor, Charles Garland, but more properly called the American Fund for Public Service—was unique among American philanthropies in the 1920s and 1930s. The fund was directly set up to counter the ruling class's domination, especially in education, labor organizing, the media, and race relations.

Ironically, radicalism was aided by a rising stock market. The fund had an initial capitalization of $800,000; and not quite twenty years later its directors had disbursed almost $2 million. With the libertarian Roger Baldwin, founder of the American Civil Liberties Union (ACLU), as secretary and the socialist Norman Thomas as president, the fund's board provided an unusually cooperative meeting ground of the American left. Almost every radical cause and campaign applied to the Garland Fund for money during the 1920s and 1930s, including striking workers, the American Birth Control League, and the ACLU.

Among the first applicants to the Garland Fund was A. Philip Randolph, who sought a loan to help his struggling journal, *The Messenger*. A loan of $500 was made by the fund to the paper in 1923, followed by a grant of $2,000. The fund lent money to the National Association for the Advancement of Colored People (NAACP) the same year and later made a donation to its antilynching campaign. The next year, the National Urban League received $1,000 to fund a study titled "Negro Relations to the Trade Unions." When A. Philip Randolph was initially contacted to head the effort to establish the Brotherhood of Sleeping Car Porters in 1925, the Garland Fund voted to give $1,200 for the

production of organizational materials. Eventually, the fund gave $11,200 for the brotherhoood's general organizing fund, enough to pay the salaries of several field organizers.

At the same meeting, the fund's board voted $26,000 to NAACP to defend Dr. Ossian Sweet, who had been accused of murder as a result of a riot in the all-white Detroit neighborhood into which his family attempted to move after buying a home. The money, which was conditional on the raising of matching funds, led eventually to the establishment of a permanent defense fund by NAACP. It was a very important aid in a developing strategy to obtain legal equality. Money from the Garland Fund also made possible, in 1927, the pursuit of *Nixon* v. *Herndon* that resulted at least temporarily in the invalidation of the all-white primary.

The influence of the Garland Fund was not welcome in all quarters. In 1926, Robert L. Vann, publisher of the *Pittsburgh Courier*, attacked James Weldon Johnson in print, accusing Johnson—who was a member of the fund's board—of occupying palatial offices on Fifth Avenue and of using the fund's money as a personal slush fund.

Johnson's membership on the fund's board, however, paid dividends for NAACP. In 1930, after the stock market crash reduced income, the fund decided on a major investment in a strategy of NAACP—a legal campaign to achieve racial equality. The NAACP's decision in 1931 to focus its efforts on ending segregation in schools paved the way for the eventual landmark decision by the Supreme Court in *Brown* v. *Board of Education* in 1954. The Garland Fund had given some $30,000 to the campaign during the 1930s.

The Garland Fund also aided other campaigns for black equality in America: the successful appeal of Lloyd L. Gaines to attend the University of Missouri, the defense of the Scottsboro boys, and the interracial Southern Tenant Farmers Union.

After slowing its activities in 1937 and 1938, the fund finally liquidated itself in June 1941, a victim of its success and of the inability of board members to overcome factional political differences in order to continue to work together.

STEPHEN BURWOOD

See also Brotherhood of Sleeping Car Porters; Johnson, James Weldon; Messenger, The; National Association for the Advancement of Colored People; National Urban League; Philanthropy and Philanthropic Organizations; Pittsburgh Courier; Randolph, A. Philip; Vann, Robert L.

Further Reading

Curti, Merle. "Subsidizing Red Radicalism: The American Fund for Public Service, 1921–1941." *Social Science Review*, 33, September 1959.

Freeman, Joseph. *An American Testament: A Narrative of Rebels and Romantics.* New York: Farrar and Rinehart, 1936.

Lamson, Peggy. *Roger Baldwin, Founder of the American Civil Liberties Union: A Portrait.* Boston, Mass.: Houghton Mifflin, 1976.

Samson, Gloria Garrett. *The American Fund for Public Service: Charles Garland and Radical Philanthropy, 1922–1941.* Westport, Conn.: Greenwood, 1996

Garvey, Marcus

Marcus Garvey was the dominant African American figure in the era of the Harlem Renaissance, especially from about 1919 to 1925. His Universal Negro Improvement Association (UNIA) was the largest African American mass movement ever. More than any single individual, he provided the radical political underpinning to the Harlem Renaissance, known as the New Negro movement. Garvey also significantly affected the purely literary and cultural aspects of the Harlem Renaissance through his encouragement of literature and the arts. From his headquarters on 135th Street in Harlem, Garvey presided over a multifaceted and far-flung empire that encompassed millions of followers

and sympathizers all over the world. There were about 1,200 branches of the UNIA spread over more than forty countries, from Australia to the United States. Most of these branches and most members were in the United States. New York City, as befit the headquarters, had the largest single branch, with 35,000 to 40,000 members.

Garvey arrived in the United States in March 1916, after several early years of agitational work in Costa Rica, Panama, Jamaica, and Europe. He had led a printers' strike in Jamaica. He had published newspapers and fought for better treatment for the Caribbean immigrants in Costa Rica and Panama. He had traveled through several European countries and had worked in London for an important pan-African journal, *Africa Times and Orient Review.*

Garvey was born in 1887 in St. Ann's Bay, Jamaica. As a youth, he excelled at the printing trade. He also participated in anticolonialist political activity and in the nascent Jamaican labor movement. He founded UNIA in 1914 shortly after his return home from four years of travel. The organization was a response to the suffering that Garvey encountered everywhere among the African masses. Garvey came to the United States in March 1916, after UNIA had been active for almost two years in Jamaica. His immediate purpose was to raise funds for his work in Jamaica. He had hoped to meet Booker T. Washington, founder of Tuskegee Institute, the most famous institution of African American education, but Washington, whom he admired, died a few months before Garvey's arrival.

Garvey toured the United States and Canada in 1916 and 1917. On his return to his new base in Harlem, he joined a corps of open-air speakers and stepladder orators who abounded on Harlem's street corners. Harlem had only recently become the major African American section of New York City, but by the time of Garvey's arrival, less than a decade after its transformation into an African American enclave, it was already well on the way to becoming a veritable capital of the African world. Its population was cosmopolitan, with recent immigrants from the South accounting for about half its population and immigrants from the Caribbean making up 20 percent.

Garvey was by this time a polished speaker. He had won a prize for public speaking in Jamaica and had spoken at Speakers' Corner in Hyde Park in London. He quickly built a following on the streets and moved into a rented hall when his audiences became too large for the street. By 1918 he had made the decision to relocate his headquarters from Kingston, Jamaica, to Harlem. He incorporated the Universal Negro Improvement Association and African Communities League, as the organization was officially called, and moved ahead with great speed. His newspaper, *Negro World*, appeared in 1918. It would soon be the most widely circulated newspaper in the African world. It would also be one of the best. Its editors over the next few years would include some of African America's most talented journalists: T. Thomas Fortune, a former aide to Booker T. Washington and the generally acknowledged "dean" of African American journalists; John Edward Bruce ("Bruce Grit"), perhaps second only to Fortune in the hall of African American journalistic fame; Amy Jacques Garvey, the talented wife of Marcus Garvey; William H. Ferris, author of a two-volume work *The African Abroad*, who had a B.A. from Yale and an M.A. from Harvard in journalism; and Eric Walrond, author of *Tropic Death*, one of the outstanding collections of short stories of the Harlem Renaissance.

At the end of World War I in November 1918, Garvey could already attract a crowd of 5,000 to a meeting celebrating the armistice. In this year he also established the Negro Factories Corporation, which in turn established restaurants; a millinery factory, black doll factory, tailoring establishment, hotel, trucking business, and job printing press; and other enterprises in Harlem. By the early 1920s the Negro Factories Corporation was employing more than 1,000 people. In 1919, only three years after his arrival in the United States, Garvey—who was then thirty-two years old—began his most spectacular undertaking, the Black Star Line Steamship Company. This steamship line was plagued with difficulties and eventually collapsed, but its ships had sailed up and down the eastern seaboard of the United States and to several Caribbean islands and Central America. The line's appearance was everywhere met with jubilant demonstrations from African Americans and Afro-Caribbeans, who greeted it as an expression of hope for a suffering people.

In 1920 Garvey held the largest convention in African American history to that time. UNIA's First International Convention of the Negro Peoples of the World met on 1 August 1920 at Madison Square Garden in New York, with 25,000 people in attendance—an overflow crowd. Delegates came from many countries. After the ceremonial opening, the deliberations continued at the organization's Liberty Hall in Harlem for the rest of the month.

Garvey was by now the best-known figure in the African world. The king of Swaziland is said to have

admitted that he knew of only two African Americans, namely Marcus Garvey and Jack Johnson, the heavyweight boxing champion. Garvey's exploits were being reported, often with exaggeration and even hysteria, in the newspapers of Europe and farther afield. British and other colonial governments were banning his newspaper and imprisoning his followers in an attempt to curb his influence. The U.S. government kept him under intense surveillance. By 1919 J. Edgar Hoover, later famous as head of the Federal Bureau of Investigation (FBI), had begun plotting to have Garvey deported, a plot that was realized in 1927. In 1919 Garvey also survived an attempted assassination said to have been instigated by a district attorney in New York.

Meanwhile Garvey's physical presence in Harlem had become inescapable. His weekly meetings at Liberty Hall on 138th Street attracted thousands. UNIA and the Black Star Line boasted some of the best choirs and orchestras in New York, and UNIA's convention parades were spectacular affairs, with numerous brass bands, uniformed auxiliaries of UNIA, and thousands of spectators. The opening parade of the convention of 1920 is said to have been ten miles long. Garvey rode in an open car, wearing the plumed hat and military uniform favored by powerful leaders of the day. By contrast, his day-to-day attire could be plain and even shabby on occasion.

Garvey's physical presence was matched by his ideological presence. Harlem was an area of radical ideas and influential personalities. Between World War I and 1920 A. Philip Randolph published the socialist magazine *The Messenger*. Hubert H. Harrison, a "race man" and sometime socialist, published *The Voice* and in 1917 founded the Liberty League of Negro Americans. Cyril Briggs led the African Blood Brotherhood. He published the magazine *Crusader* and led a small cadre into the Workers (Communist) Party. Downtown, on the white side of New York, the integrationist and exponent of protest politics W. E. B. Du Bois published *Crisis*, which was the organ of the National Association for the Advancement of Colored People (NAACP) and African America's largest magazine.

Garvey distinguished himself from this crowded field by championing the ideology of African nationalism, which in due course would become known as Garveyism. Like Booker T. Washington he felt that Africa's descendants should become economically self-reliant. He went much farther than Washington, however, in eschewing financial assistance from whites, in building a racially exclusive organization, and in adopting a confrontational attitude toward the white power structure.

There were three facets to his nationalist ideology: "race first," self-reliance, and nationhood. "Race first" was a term used earlier by Hubert H. Harrison, who later joined forces with Garvey for a while. It suggested that African people must put their racial self-interest first. Garvey thought that despite the class difference among Africa's descendants, they were all beset by the problem of race, which therefore became a common denominator. He hoped to turn the disability of race into a positive factor by rallying his followers around the reality that they had in common. By politically organizing around the concept of race, he would turn it into a powerful force for mobilization and empowerment.

Only people of African descent could join UNIA. African descent was defined liberally to include people of mixed African and other races, as long as they acknowledged and identified with their African origin. Garvey was hostile to those for whom light skin encouraged disdain for their darker brethren. Although he recruited the darker masses like none other, there was a fair representation of members of all hues within the organization.

Race first meant that African people should see beauty in themselves. Racially demeaning ads for beauty products were frowned on, and Garveyites were encouraged to display racially appropriate pictures in their homes. Garvey's framed essay, "African Fundamentalism," was a favorite wall decoration. Race first also meant putting the racial interest first in literature, historical writing, religion, and every sphere of life. It did not mean unwarranted antagonism toward other races, but Garvey was adamant that all other peoples put their racial self-interest first and that African peoples must learn to aggressively pursue theirs. He therefore urged his followers to scrutinize critically the works of other historians on the African past. He argued that other historians could never write with true love or feeling for the African. Garvey's Afrocentric vision led him to challenge the assertions of European historians that King Tut, whose tomb was discovered in Egypt in 1922, was white.

Race first also meant that God had to be depicted as black. People have always depicted their gods in their own image and likeness, Garvey argued, and African people should not be exceptions to that rule. Race first also made necessary independent media capable of injecting the perspectives of the race into the marketplace of ideas. UNIA's *Negro World* performed this task admirably.

It was in literature and the arts that race first had the most direct impact on the Harlem Renaissance, which was essentially a literary and cultural movement. By the time that the renaissance became fully conscious of itself in the mid-1920s, Garvey and UNIA had already anticipated its activity by several years. *Negro World* was UNIA's single most important contribution to the renaissance. Under the direction of Hubert H. Harrison, it introduced the first regular book review section in an African American publication. From the early 1920s it published "Poetry for the People," a section that showcased the poems, both good and bad, of hundreds of contributors. Important literary figures such as Zora Neale Hurston and important political figures such as T. Albert Marryshow of Grenada and Kobina Sekyi of Ghana were among the aspiring poets, as was Garvey. Poetic submissions were supplemented by contributions on poetics (usually entitled "What Is Poetry?"), music, drama, and the like. In the period 1920 to 1925 *Negro World* was in all likelihood the most important literary outlet for pan-African writing. It also pioneered literary competitions, later a notable feature of the renaissance. With a weekly publication schedule and a circulation much larger than that of Du Bois's *Crisis*, *Negro World* reached more readers in more countries and published more aspiring writers than many of its rivals combined. Most of Garvey's own poetry was published from 1927 to the late 1930s, after the heyday of literary activity by *Negro World*. His collected poems are enough to fill a work of respectable size, *The Poetical Works of Marcus Garvey*.

Garvey's second major idea, self-reliance, was exemplified by the Negro Factories Corporation and the Black Star Line, as well as in *Negro World*, which was in addition to everything else a successful business. His famous admonition "do for self" later became a staple in the ideas of the Nation of Islam, led by a former Garveyite, Elijah Muhammad.

Nationhood postulated the building of independent political power, whether in the United States or abroad. Garvey's ambitious Universal Political Union attempted to enlist the voting strength of his followers to influence politics in the United States. It was, however, unable to develop to its full potential because of Garvey's imprisonment in 1925 and the consequent slow decline of UNIA.

By the early 1920s Marcus Garvey was indisputably the most powerful leader in African America and the pan-African world. His UNIA had approximately 1,200 branches (called divisions) in more than forty countries. There were divisions in thirty-eight states, with the South being far and away the most intensely organized region. Louisiana alone had seventy-four branches, according to surviving records, and in actuality the number was somewhat larger. Large cities throughout North America had large branches with thousands of members, and these branches owned substantial amounts of real estate. The cities included New York, Chicago, Detroit, Boston, Philadelphia, Cleveland, Los Angeles, Toronto, Montreal, Miami, and New Orleans.

Garvey's success and his well-defined ideology brought forth a host of adversaries. Some, such as communists and integrationists, opposed him on ideological grounds. Communists preached the primacy of class over race and saw the united workers of the world as the most potent force for political change. Garvey countered that white workers were as infected as anyone else with the virus of racism and that while interracial working-class solidarity might be good as an ideal, it was premature to adopt this as a practical strategy to lift the African race out of oppression. Integrationists, led by NAACP, resented Garvey's ability to mobilize a vast number of people and to amass more money than the integrationists could, despite their access to white philanthropy. Du Bois became the major unofficial spokesman for the integrationist group. Du Bois, who had been trained at Harvard and was still fresh from a serious conflict with Garvey's mentor Booker T. Washington, considered Garvey poorly educated, uncouth, and dishonest. He described Garvey as black and ugly and called him a lunatic or a traitor. Garvey responded with similar vitriol, suggesting that Du Bois hated the small amount of African blood that flowed through his veins.

The most damaging of Garvey's opponents, however, were the European colonialist governments and the United States. Colonial powers such as Great Britain and France banned *Negro World*, arrested Garveyites, sometimes prevented Garvey from landing in their territories, and generally tried to frustrate the work of UNIA. The United States arrayed its security apparatus against Garvey, planted agents in his organization, and eventually sent him to prison on a dubious charge of mail fraud in connection with the failure of the Black Star Line.

After serving almost three years of his five-year sentence, Garvey was released early when President Calvin Coolidge commuted his sentence in 1927. By this time millions of people around the world had appended their names to petitions asking for Garvey's release. The timing of his release may also have been influenced by an impending presidential year in the United States. Presidential commutation was, however, made contingent on deportation, and Garvey was shipped to Jamaica in December 1927. There he arrived to the greatest hero's welcome in the history of that country. He again published newspapers and held a grand international convention. In 1929 he founded the People's Political Party, Jamaica's first modern political party. He was once more imprisoned, however, this time by Jamaica's British rulers. He relocated to England in 1935 in an effort to rebuild his declining movement, now weakened by a schism.

Garvey died in London in 1940. Although UNIA never regained the dominance it had held during the 1920s, it remained an important organization in several places as late as the 1950s. An impressive array of later leaders in African America and throughout the pan-African world had roots in Garveyism. They included such children of Garveyites as Congressman Charles Diggs of Detroit, Congresswoman Shirley Chisholm of Brooklyn (New York), and Malcolm X. Garvey's ideas also permeated the "black power" era

Marcus Garvey, 1926. (Library of Congress.)

Marcus Garvey, c. 1920. (Library of Congress.)

of the 1960s and 1970s and the later Afrocentric movement in academia. After two decades during which Garvey had been nearly expunged from the historical record, the black power movement of the 1960s rediscovered him as a precursor and a hero. He has since become, in addition, a very popular object of academic inquiry. The centenary of his birth in 1987 was an occasion for large-scale celebrations around the world.

Biography

Marcus Garvey was born on 17 August 1887, in St. Ann's Bay on Jamaica's north coast. He founded UNIA in 1914; he arrived in the United States in March 1916. By 1918 he had decided to relocate his headquarters from Kingston, Jamaica, to Harlem; his newspaper, *Negro World*, appeared in 1918. He began the Black Star Line in 1919. UNIA's First International Convention of the Negro Peoples of the World met on 1 August 1920, at Madison Square Garden in New York. Garvey championed African nationalism (Garveyism), and his Universal Political Union attempted to mobilize voters to

influence politics in the United States. Garvey was imprisoned in 1925 (on a charge related to the failure of the Black Star Line); he was released in 1927 but was deported to Jamaica in December of that year. In 1929 he founded the People's Political Party in Jamaica, but he was imprisoned again in Jamaica and in 1935 went to Great Britain. Garvey died in London in 1940, at age fifty-two.

TONY MARTIN

See also Black Star Line; Garveyism; Negro World; New Negro Movement; Pan-Africanism; Universal Negro Improvement Association; *specific individuals*

Further Reading

Garvey, Amy Jacques. *Garvey and Garveyism*. Kingston, Jamaica: Author, 1963.

Garvey, Amy Jacques, ed. *The Philosophy and Opinions of Marcus Garvey, Or, Africa for the Africans*. Dover, Mass.: Majority, 1986. (First published, 1923, 1925.)

Garvey, Marcus. *The Poetical Works of Marcus Garvey*, comp. and ed. Tony Martin. Dover, Mass.: Majority, 1983.

Martin, Tony. *Literary Garveyism: Garvey, Black Arts, and the Harlem Renaissance*. Dover, Mass.: Majority, 1983a.

———. *Marcus Garvey, Hero: A First Biography*. Dover, Mass.: Majority, 1983b.

———. *Race First: The Ideological and Organizational Struggles of Marcus Garvey and the Universal Negro Improvement Association*. Dover, Mass.: Majority, 1986. (First published 1976.)

———. *African Fundamentalism: A Literary and Cultural Anthology of Garvey's Harlem Renaissance*. Dover, Mass.: Majority, 1991.

Negro World. (Available on microfilm.)

Garveyism

Garveyism is the term applied to the ideology of Marcus Moziah Garvey (1887–1940), leader of the largest African American and pan-African mass movement ever. Garveyism flourished in the 1920s, the peak period of Garvey's Universal Negro Improvement Association (UNIA). It has remained a vital force in pan-African life. The term is probably as old as his UNIA (founded in Jamaica in 1914), but it was further popularized by *Garvey and Garveyism* (1963), the biography written by his wife, Amy Jacques Garvey.

Garveyism was essentially what has variously been called African or black nationalism. It was therefore not a new ideology, although it received arguably its most definitive articulation from Marcus Garvey. This idea has been a staple of African American thought since the inception of political activity in that community. In UNIA, Garvey was able to fashion a mass instrument to implement his ideas on a scale without precedent or parallel.

Black nationalism has traditionally been articulated in contradistinction to integrationism. Whereas integrationists have preferred to stress the Americanness of African Americans, nationalists have emphasized the African aspect. Integrationists have therefore worked within interracial organizations, often, like the National Association for the Advancement of Colored People (NAACP), founded and led by Euro-Americans. Nationalists have tended toward racially exclusive organizations, preferring independent endeavor rather than dependence on the goodwill of others.

Among Garvey's distinguished nationalist precursors can be counted David Walker, whose *David Walker's Appeal* (1829) remains one of the most celebrated polemics of African American history. Walker refuted the pseudoscientific theories that considered Africans to be an inferior species. He denounced American slavery as the harshest in history and saw the white perpetrators of this evil as devils. He encouraged the African American population to rise up against its oppressors. Martin Delany, author of *The Condition, Elevation, Emigration, and Destiny of the Colored People of the United States* (1852), is another precursor, as are Bishop Henry McNeal Turner of the African Methodist Episcopal Church and Edward Wilmot Blyden, an intellectual of the late nineteenth century and the early twentieth who was born in the Caribbean and based in West Africa. Delany, Turner, and Blyden all exalted their blackness, sought to rescue African history from the distortions of others, and advocated emigration to Africa as the ultimate salvation for African Americans in a hostile land. Bishop Turner insisted that God be portrayed as black. All of these ideas would later be incorporated into Garveyism.

The ideology of Garveyism was systematically developed by Garvey in hundreds of speeches, supplemented by essays, poems, and other writings, throughout his political life. The major tenets of the ideology revolved around three very straightforward concepts: "race first," self-reliance, and nationhood. In his early readings and in his travels in the Caribbean, Latin America, and Europe between 1910 and 1914, Garvey noticed, with great alarm, the universal suffering of the African race. The race was everywhere subjugated and weak, and Garvey grappled with the problem of how to turn its fortunes around and save it, as he assessed the situation, from reenslavement or even extinction. For a people lacking political or economic power, he saw the power of organization, buttressed by an appropriate ideology of empowerment, as the solution to their predicament.

"Race first" postulated the necessity for African-descended peoples to put their own racial self-interest first. The precise expression was initially popularized by a Harlemite intellectual, Hubert H. Harrison, a sometime collaborator with Garvey. Garvey argued that all other races put their interests first, often to the detriment of others. Africans would have to be equally solicitous of their own welfare, although not necessarily to the extent of oppressing others. "Race first," Garvey said, freely acknowledged the right of others to safeguard their interests, although not the right to oppress others.

"Race first" permeated all aspects of his people's existence. It meant that African people should see physical beauty in themselves. This needed to be emphasized after several hundred years of slavery and its aftermath, which had stereotyped African hair, skin color, and phenotypes as ugly. Garvey urged his followers to remove white pinups from their walls. He frowned on racially demeaning advertisements for beauty products. He also praised the beauty of black women in poetry:

> Black queen of beauty, thou hast given color to the world!
>
> Among other women thou art royal and the fairest!
>
> Like the brightest of jewels in the regal diadem,
>
> Shin'st thou, Goddess of Africa, Nature's purest emblem!

Garvey's newspaper, *Negro World*, published a gala Christmas edition in 1921 showcasing beautiful African women of various tints and phenotypes, from all over the world. One of the beauties was Amy Jacques, soon to be Garvey's second wife.

But "race first" went well beyond physical considerations. Garvey was adamant that African people, alternatively dictated to and paternalistically led for so long, should now define their own reality. This must be the case in historical studies. Garvey, a keen amateur student of history, would have agreed with the famous assertion of the first editorial in African America's first newspaper, *Freedom's Journal*, in 1827: "Too long have others spoken for us," wrote the editors, John Brown Russwurm and Rev. Samuel Cornish. "We wish to plead our own cause." Garvey thought that other historians showed little love for the African. He stressed that only the suffering African could definitively interpret the experience of his or her people. "Mr. H. G. Wells may divert civilization for the benefit of his Anglo-Saxon group," he said on one occasion, "but that does not make it a fact that the people who laid claims to the civilization he attributed to others are going to give up easily. The black man knows his past."

Several prominent historians accordingly gravitated toward UNIA or were sympathetic to its aims. J. A. Rogers, the great discoverer of little-known facts of African history, on occasion wrote for *Negro World*. Carter G. Woodson, who was the second African American to receive a Ph.D. in history at Harvard University (1912), wrote a weekly column for the paper.

"Race first" also extended to religion. Garvey had a Christian upbringing, and his speeches and writings were laced with Christian allusions. Yet he advocated widespread religious tolerance within UNIA. Christians, Muslims, atheists, African Hebrews, and later Rastafarians were among those accommodated within the organization. All those who believed in a god probably accepted Garvey's insistence that God for African people must be portrayed in their own image and likeness (that is, as black). Two of the most important organizations growing out of UNIA after its decline in the 1930s made this idea a focal point of their new theologies. Elijah Muhammad's Nation of Islam proclaimed Islam the black man's religion, with a black God and a white devil. The Rastafarian movement accepted His Imperial Majesty Haile Selassie of Ethiopia as the "living God."

Garveyism's strong advocacy of "race first" brought it into a symbiotic relationship with white supremacists such as Earnest Sevier Cox of the White America Society. Garvey was as hostile as anybody to the pseudoscience of supremacists, but he also distrusted white liberals, such as those running NAACP. In his rejection of miscegenation and in his desire for a separate state, he shared at least two crucial preferences with white supremacists. It was presumably on this basis that Garvey accepted a request from the Ku Klux Klan for a summit meeting in Atlanta in 1922. Neither side had any illusions about the other's position. "I was speaking to a man who was brutally a white man,"

Garvey picturesquely put it, "and I was speaking to him as a man who was brutally a Negro."

When UNIA was founded in 1914, Garvey was already an accomplished printer and journalist. He had by then edited his own publications in Jamaica, Costa Rica, and Panama and had worked for the foremost pan-African journal of the day, Duse Mohamed Ali's *Africa Times and Orient Review*, which was based in London. He was therefore acutely aware of the power of the media. Uncompromisingly independent media thus became an indispensable adjunct to the idea of "race first." A struggling race had to inject its point of view into the marketplace of ideas. "We are not afraid of the word 'propaganda,'" Garvey explained, "for we use the term in the sense of disseminating our ideas among Negroes all the world over. We have nothing stealthy in this meaning." Garvey's *Negro World*, published in Harlem from 1918 to 1933, became the African world's most widely circulated newspaper in the 1920s. In addition to general news, its editorials, transcribed speeches, creative writing, and letters all reflected UNIA's doctrine of race first. The potency of this message was not lost on imperialist governments, which banned *Negro World* in several countries in Africa, Central America, and the Caribbean.

"Race first" helped provide the underpinning of racial pride and awareness that permeated the Harlem Renaissance. Garvey's influence on the renaissance was also more direct, because his activities inserted themselves into Harlem's literary and cultural life. Garvey's movement nurtured such well-known fledgling writers and artists as Zora Neale Hurston, Eric Walrond, Claude McKay, and the sculptor Augusta Savage, together with others less well known. Some of these did their earliest apprentice work in the pages of *Negro World*, which practically doubled as political newspaper and literary organ.

Garvey encouraged an explosion of literary and cultural activity that actually anticipated the "official" dates (c. mid- to late 1920s) usually given for the Harlem Renaissance. *Negro World*, in its section "Poetry for the People," published many bards, known and unknown, from all over the world. It also provided a rich fare of literary vignettes, short stories, literary criticism, articles on poetics, thoughts on music appreciation, and the like. *Negro World* also pioneered the literary competitions of the Harlem Renaissance era. African America's first regular book review column appeared in *Negro World*, edited by Hubert H. Harrison.

Garvey applied his idea of "race first" to literary work, in what in hindsight might be called the Garvey aesthetic. Black writers should approach their task responsibly. They should maintain a certain racial decorum. They should not "prostitute" their talent, as Garvey put it, to titillate white audiences desirous of confirming their negative stereotypes of the race. Garvey accordingly criticized Claude McKay's blockbuster novel *Home to Harlem* (1928). He similarly criticized Paul Robeson for acting in films such as *The Emperor Jones*, which held the race up to ridicule.

Garvey practiced what he preached and produced a substantial corpus of poems and plays, in addition to many memorable speeches and essays. Many of the prose items were collected by Amy Jacques Garvey in the famous *Philosophy and Opinions of Marcus Garvey, Or, Africa for the Africans* (1923 and 1925). The literary aspect of Garveyism was also articulated by the accomplished corps of editorial workers at *Negro World*. These included T. Thomas Fortune, the generally acknowledged "dean" of African American journalists; William H. Ferris, a graduate of Harvard and Yale; John Edward Bruce (popularly known as "Bruce Grit"), a highly respected veteran journalist; Eric Walrond, a major short-story writer; and Amy Jacques Garvey, an associate editor at *Negro World*.

The second major principle of Garveyism was self-reliance. Garvey stressed the psychological benefits to be derived from "doing for self." Although he favored reparations, he refused to accept financial assistance from white philanthropists for the mature UNIA. UNIA's monuments to self-reliance were exceedingly successful for a time and astounded friend and foe alike. The Negro Factories Corporation operated restaurants, groceries, a printing press, a trucking business, a millinery establishment, and a factory where black dolls were made, and manufactured UNIA uniforms, among other things. It employed more than 1,000 people in Harlem. Divisions of UNIA in cities such as New York, Chicago, Cleveland, Detroit, Toronto, and Montreal owned valuable real estate. *Negro World* was, in addition to everything else, a hugely successful business enterprise. In the Black Star Line Steamship Company, UNIA produced the most spectacular African American business undertaking of the period. The line's three acquired ships (it paid down on a fourth) sailed between the eastern seaboard of the United States and the Caribbean and Central America. Thousands assembled to see the ships in such places as New York and South Carolina. In Port Limon, Costa Rica, workers stopped work for the day and showered a Black Star Line ship with fruit and flowers. Garvey collected more money from the shareholders of Black Star Line than white-funded organizations such as the NAACP and National Urban League were able to dream of.

The spirit of self-reliance permeated every aspect of UNIA. A publishing house produced *Philosophy and Opinions of Marcus Garvey*, although it became one of the casualties of Garvey's imprisonment in 1925 and the consequent slow demise of UNIA.

The third major tenet of Garveyism was what Garvey called "nationhood." Nationhood was essentially a quest for political self-determination. Despite his emphasis on African regeneration and his effort to relocate his headquarters to Liberia, Garvey did not advocate neglect of local politics wherever African people found themselves. He was acutely aware of the universal political powerlessness of African people and sought to address this in many ways. UNIA conceived of itself as a provisional prototype of a future African government. Delegates to a convention held by UNIA accordingly bestowed the title "provisional president of Africa" on Garvey. At its annual international conventions (the convention of 1920 attracted 25,000 people to the opening ceremonies), UNIA had a provisional parliament, in which delegates from many countries, such as England and South Africa, debated issues affecting the race.

The first convention, of 1920, was responsible for the adoption and popularization of several important symbols of nationhood. These included the "Universal Ethiopian Anthem," composed especially for UNIA and designated the anthem of the race. Red, black, and green were declared the official colors of the race—red for blood and sacrifice, black for the sons and daughters of Africa, and green for the luxuriant land of their forebears. These colors have endured among the mass of Africa's descendants in North America, the Caribbean, and elsewhere. They have also been incorporated into the flags of some independent African countries.

One of the most ambitious manifestations of nationhood coming out of the convention of 1920 was the important Declaration of Rights of the Negro Peoples of the World. The assembled delegates produced a historically significant document outlining the main grievances of African people everywhere and also making demands for improved treatment. They declared in the document's preamble:

> Be it Resolved, That the Negro people of the world, through their chosen representatives in convention assembled in Liberty Hall . . . protest against the

wrongs and injustices they are suffering at the hands of their white brethren, and state what they deem their fair and just rights, as well as the treatment they propose to demand of all men in the future.

The document deplored racism in public transportation, including international travel by sea. It deplored the racism of court systems and the use of African and Caribbean soldiers in white people's wars. It condemned lynching as the most revolting barbarity visited on African Americans. It condemned the unusually cruel treatment of African people in prisons. It wanted Africa's descendants everywhere to be made "free citizens of Africa." It deplored Jim Crow and denial of voting rights in the United States. It called for the capitalization of the word "Negro" and the teaching of black history in schools. "We also demand," the delegates said, "Africa for the Africans at home and abroad." The document proclaimed the determination of the men of the race to defend their women from the depredations of white men.

All of these multifarious trappings of nationhood were reinforced by the UNIA's diplomatic service, which sent ambassadors and commissioners to Great Britain, Liberia, and the League of Nations, among other places.

For the United States, Garvey planned an ambitious foray into nationhood through his Universal Political Union (UPU). Like much else, UPU failed to reach maturity because of Garvey's imprisonment in 1925. It was an attempt to harness the vast following of UNIA for political ends. UPU would endeavor to control the votes of its constituency to reward those politicians who were good to African America. It would likewise seek to punish, by withholding support, those who reneged on their promises. For the few short months of its existence, UPU showed itself willing to oppose African American candidates and support white ones, when that seemed necessary to ensure its objectives.

Nationhood could also be seen in Garvey's view of Africa in general. He advocated the recovery of African independence, which had been comprehensively lost in the European "scramble for Africa" from the mid-nineteenth century to World War I. UNIA's own plan to relocate its headquarters from Harlem to Liberia was an effort to plant itself in almost the only African nation enjoying a semblance of independence at the time. (Ethiopia was the only other independent country on the African continent.) Everywhere that UNIA implanted itself, its advocacy of nationhood bore political fruit. The African National Congress in South Africa, the Workingmen's Association in Trinidad and Tobago, and the Lagos Youth Movement in Nigeria were among the political entities permeated with Garveyites. In Cuba the British diplomatic representatives came close to formally acknowledging UNIA as a quasi-representative body for the large immigrant British West Indian population. After his deportation from the United States to Jamaica in 1927, Garvey founded Jamaica's first modern political party, the People's Political Party. Garvey served several terms on the Kingston and Saint Andrew Corporation Council.

That Garvey's message of nationhood was heard can be seen from the figures who claimed that he was their political inspiration. These include Kwame Nkrumah, first president of independent Ghana; Nnamdi Azikiwe, first governor-general of Nigeria; and Jomo Kenyatta, independence leader of Kenya. In the United States, Malcolm X and Congresswoman Shirley Chisholm, the first African American woman in Congress, were children of activist Garveyites.

The ideology of Garveyism energized the largest pan-African mass movement of all time. Its appeal was as universal as the UNIA's name. Garveyism was propagated in Garvey's *Negro World*, in the spoken words of official and unofficial emissaries of the movement, in official or quasi-official publications and documents such as the *Universal Negro Catechism*, and through UNIA's *Constitution and Book of Laws*.

In the 1930s, after his deportation from the United States, Garvey distilled his wisdom into a secret course of lessons administered both by correspondence and in person in Toronto. These lessons, later published as *Message to the People: The Course of African Philosophy*, summarized the main ideas of Garveyism, together with practical advice for organizers on self-education, personal deportment, diplomacy, fund-raising, and other pertinent subjects. Prominently restated here was Garvey's concept of God, an important corollary of his ideas of "race first" and self-reliance. God, Garvey said, endowed all human beings equally and then left them to their own devices to fight the battle of life. Any race that fell behind could blame itself at least in part for not fulfilling its God-given potential to be the equal of other races.

The spread of Garveyism was nothing short of phenomenal. Within three years of his obscure landing in the United States, Garvey had started *Negro World* and the Black Star Line. One year later he had convened the largest convention to date in African American history. The spread of the idea and the movement that gave it concrete expression can be attributed to many factors. Among these are Garvey's charisma as a speaker and writer and the fact that he was an indefatigable organizer. An important element in UNIA's success was also the clarity of Garvey's articulation of his ideology. Garveyism appealed equally to the Aborigines of Australia and the congregation of the local African Methodist Episcopal Church in Colorado Springs, Colorado, which formed the nucleus of UNIA in that city. Moreover, although undoubtedly a mass movement like few others, UNIA and its ideology of Garveyism also attracted many distinguished intellectuals.

As a successful ideology, Garveyism inevitably attracted opponents as well. The major organizational battles fought by Garvey and UNIA were in essence ideological battles against those who disagreed with, hated, or feared Garveyism. The integrationist elite, especially in the United States, were implacable foes and collaborated with the government to hasten Garvey's ultimate trial and deportation. W. E. B. Du Bois and other members of NAACP and other anti-Garvey organizations, wrote, either in concert or individually, to the attorney-general, the secretary of state, and other officials offering their services in the campaign against Garveyism. The United States and European colonialist governments feared Garvey's impact on the African masses as they became radicalized and decided that they needed to throw off their yoke. The Communist International resented Garvey's ability to organize the proletarians and peasants the communists coveted. The communists also opposed their doctrine of "class first" to Garvey's ideology of "race first." For a communist, the white worker was the best friend of his fellow black proletarian. For Garvey, class distinctions within the race were real but of less significance than the racial oppression that indiscriminately bound all African peoples together.

All of these adversaries took their toll on UNIA, but the organization might have survived as a major force if the state power of the United States had not been deployed against it. Despite Garvey's deportation in 1927, UNIA was still an influential, although not overwhelmingly important, entity into the 1950s in places such as New York, Toronto, Montreal, Philadelphia, and Detroit.

The slow demise of UNIA did not mean the demise of Garveyism, which remains an important expression of the African nationalism that has always been a major force in African America and elsewhere. The "black power" movement of the 1960s and 1970s was a peak manifestation of Garveyism and African na-

tionalism. This period brought Garvey to the forefront once again, both as an icon of the movement and as a subject of serious historical scholarship. His popularity has tended to grow on both fronts ever since.

After all is said and done, Garveyism was simply an expression of racial uplift for a downtrodden people who, Garvey asserted, had it within them to regain their God-given right to equality with the rest of the world. He summarized his ideology in the short and beautiful essay "African Fundamentalism." The subtitles proclaimed the Garveyism that the essay expounded: "A Racial Hierarchy and Empire for Negroes"; "Negro's Faith Must Be Confidence in Self"; "His Creed: One God, One Aim, One Destiny." Garvey began the essay as follows:

> The time has come for the Negro to forget and cast behind him his hero worship and adoration of other races, and to start out immediately to create and emulate heroes of his own. We must canonize our own saints, create our own martyrs, and elevate to positions of fame and honor black men and women who have made their distinct contributions to our racial history.

Never, however, was his summary of Garveyism so succinct as in his poem "Blackman!" (1934):

> What Is In Thy Bosom? Pluck It
> Out—Is It Genius, Is It Talent
> For Something? Let's Have It.

TONY MARTIN

See also Black Star Line; Emperor Jones, The; Garvey, Marcus; Harrison, Hubert; Hurston, Zora Neale; McKay, Claude; Negro World; Pan-Africanism; Robeson, Paul; Rogers, Joel Augustus; Savage, Augusta; Universal Negro Improvement Association; Walrond, Eric; Woodson, Carter G.; *other specific individuals*

Further Reading

Burkett, Randall. *Garveyism as a Religious Movement*. Metuchen, N.J.: Scarecrow, 1978.

Garvey, Amy Jacques. *Garvey and Garveyism*. Kingston: Author 1963.

Garvey, Amy Jacques, comp. and ed. *The Philosophy and Opinions of Marcus Garvey, Or, Africa for the Africans*. Dover, Mass.: Majority, 1986. (Originally published. in two vols., 1923, 1925.)

Garvey, Marcus. *The Poetical Works of Marcus Garvey*, comp. and ed. Tony Martin. Dover, Mass.: Majority, 1983.

———. *Message to the People: The Course of African Philosophy*, ed. Tony Martin. Dover, Mass.: Majority, 1986.

Hill, Robert A., Carol A. Rudisell, et al., eds. *The Marcus Garvey and Universal Negro Improvement Association Papers*. Berkeley: University of California Press, Vol. 1, 1983. (See also subsequent volumes.)

Lewis, Rupert, and Patrick Bryan, eds. *Garvey: His Work and Impact*. Trenton, N.J.: African World, 1991.

Martin, Tony. *Literary Garveyism: Garvey, Black Arts, and the Harlem Renaissance*. Dover, Mass.: Majority, 1983a.

———. *Marcus Garvey, Hero: A First Biography*. Dover, Mass.: Majority, 1983b.

———. *The Pan-African Connection*. Dover, Mass.: Majority, 1984. (Originally published 1983.)

———. *Race First: The Ideological and Organizational Struggles of Marcus Garvey and the Universal Negro Improvement Association*. Dover, Mass.: Majority, 1986. (Originally published 1976.)

Martin, Tony, comp. and ed. *African Fundamentalism: A Literary and Cultural Anthology of Garvey's Harlem Renaissance*. Dover, Mass.: Majority, 1991.

Gershwin, George

George Gershwin, a son of Russian Jewish immigrants, earned a reputation as America's first generally recognized great composer, a writer adept at long-form serious works, Broadway musicals, popular songs, and folk opera. A large part of the reason his oeuvre remains so vibrant, lasting, and controversial was that Gershwin incorporated black musical influences and devices more frequently and effectively than his peers. Classical music critics expressed discomfort that he studied and openly loved black musical forms and Tin Pan Alley pop as much as classical practice and theory, but the public embraced the amalgam, which helped shape the definition of serious American music and highlighted how it differed from European forms. During the jazz age of the 1920s, when blacks were almost entirely shut out of the most popular sectors of the radio and recording industries and white interpretations of jazz ruled the airwaves, primary innovators such as Bessie Smith and Louis Armstrong were relegated to appearances on "race records" and in segregated clubs. With his witty use, in his compositions, of African American musical devices from blues and jazz, Gershwin recognized the centrality of the black contribution to American music and life. He did not water down jazz as much as other white bandleaders and composers of the day, and he helped create an eventual multiracial market for the black jazz and blues artists who would break through the segregation of the entertainment industry in the late 1920s and become internationally revered. There was also a significant amount of cross-pollination between Gershwin and jazz artists throughout the twentieth century: his compositions were among the most covered by them, and some of Gershwin's ideas, especially the chord sequence for "I Got Rhythm," became popular source material for new compositions by artists including Duke Ellington ("Cotton Tail," 1940) and Charlie Parker ("Moose the Mooche," 1946).

Gershwin's career began when he quit high school to work as a song plugger in the Tin Pan Alley publishing house of Jerome H. Remick. The work disillusioned him when he found that most songs he promoted were written to make a quick buck, rather than to match the sophisticated musical quality Gershwin admired in the songs Jerome Kern wrote for Broadway musicals. Gershwin's attempts to breathe interest into these hoary commercial pieces improved his piano and arranging skills, and by 1916 he was composing his own works while embarking on a successful side career as a performer on piano rolls. In early 1917, he left Remick and the song plugging business behind for a job closer to the world he wanted to inhabit, becoming a rehearsal pianist for a new musical by Kern. Within a year, Gershwin landed his first publishing deal. A year after that, four months before his twenty-first birthday, he composed his first full Broadway score, *La La Lucille*.

Al Jolson's over-the-top rendition of "Swanee" was Gershwin's first hit song; it earned Gershwin $10,000 in royalties in 1920 alone. While he spent the next four years learning the mechanics of Broadway musical production by composing and arranging ten shows for Broadway and London stages, the money and fame he received from "Swanee" allowed him to begin composing and presenting long-form serious works. Although little known, *Blue Monday* (1922) was the first of these, an early unsuccessful attempt at a "miniature" American opera about black life. Gershwin and the lyricist B. G. DeSylva completed it in five days, and it played for only one night as part of *George White's Scandals of 1922*. This twenty-five-minute piece included actors in blackface and "an unabashed 'mammy song,'" according to Jablonski (1987), who describes its "stereotypical racism" as "no worse than the standard treatment of the Negro by white writers" of the period. *Blue Monday* featured a gambler as the central character, and much of the action takes place in a bar. Critics mostly savaged it, although it was revised and restaged in later decades. The next time Gershwin attempted an opera based on the lives of black Americans, he would show more care and conduct more research. His next foray into more serious realms occurred on 1 November 1923, during a "Recital of Ancient and Modern Music for Voice" by the mezzo-soprano Eva Gauthier at Aeolian Hall in New York City. Gauthier had been searching for fresh material, and Carl Van Vechten suggested that she sample the best of the popular American songwriters whose works were informed by jazz. The program featured works by Bartók and Schoenberg alongside an "American" section dedicated to works by Irving Berlin, Kern, and Gershwin, with Gershwin providing piano accompaniment. The reaction of the audience and critics proved wildly enthusiastic. The new masters of American popular song had never been placed in such a rarefied atmosphere; the event marked the beginning of a highbrow respect for their craft that would increase during the course of the century.

The main event that transformed Gershwin into a major composer in the eyes of the American public was the premiere of *Rhapsody in Blue* at Aeolian Hall on 12 February 1924, as part of a program called "An Experiment in Modern Music." The rapturous reception that greeted the composition overshadowed newspaper commentary concerning the show the next day, and transcended the somewhat crass publicity for the program. Paul Whiteman, the famous bandleader who concocted the event and conducted *Rhapsody in Blue*, had marketed the concert as an overview of American musical history, with judges from the classical field (such as Jascha Heifetz and Sergey Rachmaninoff) issuing opinions after the performances about what constituted the true identity of American music. Whiteman had so much enthusiasm for his idea that he had never asked Gershwin to participate before allowing newspapers to report that "Gershwin is at work on a jazz concerto." Whiteman was lucky. Gershwin came through with what remains the most famous American concert composition.

Numerous theories have emerged to explain the excellence and continuing popularity of *Rhapsody in Blue*. Gershwin's facility with melody and arranging, honed by his classical music studies, and his experience in writing memorable songs in the competitive milieus of Tin Pan Alley and Broadway were certainly important. But, as is the case with much enduring American music (such as spirituals, bluegrass, and country music), the resonance of this piece had a great deal to do with Gershwin's ability to fuse disparate black and white sources into a compelling whole. Within *Rhapsody in Blue*, Gershwin combined classical forms and textures with the syncopation and "blue" thirds and sevenths of African American blues and jazz, the frenetic rhythms of urban America of the 1920s, and the keening sounds and minor-key modes of Jewish and Russian music. The black bandleader and composer James Reese Europe had made forays into Carnegie Hall in the mid-1910s; but aside from those, American music, by whites or blacks, was rarely heard in major concert halls. *Rhapsody in Blue* marked the beginning of a trend toward considering American music worthy of such exposure. After the financial and artistic success of *Rhapsody in Blue*, Gershwin spent more time developing concert music and receiving instruction from classical music teachers. The acclaimed *Concerto in F* and *An American In Paris* followed, along with the more academic and less appealing *Second Rhapsody for Piano and Orchestra* (1931).

Months after the premiere of *Rhapsody in Blue*, Gershwin and his brother and lyricist Ira Gershwin made their first success in establishing their own approach to the Broadway musical—*Lady Be Good!* The romantic plots and song themes of the Gershwins' musicals during the 1920s differed little at first from the competition, but their musical and lyrical sophistication were usually well above average and kept rising throughout the decade. As the brothers assembled more successful shows, they grew more adventurous in their choice of settings. The original production of *Strike Up the Band*, with a book by the humorist George S. Kaufman, and a carefully integrated score that developed the plot, was a step closer to Gershwin's dream of developing a great American opera. (Usually, Broadway musicals were more haphazard in their construction, adding new hit songs whether or not these songs coalesced with the plot.) *Strike Up the Band* playfully but sharply criticized aspects of the 1920s: the embrace of materialism, American jingoism, profiteering by big business in World War I, and the meaninglessness of the war for many Americans—all themes shared by prominent writers of the Harlem Renaissance. Yet audiences did not support this step away from Broadway's usual escapism, even if it did include "The Man I Love," one of the most enduring of the Gershwins' songs; the brothers and Kaufman were too far ahead of their time. A revival of the show in 1930, with the most controversial lyrics removed, did become a hit, though. *Of Thee I Sing* was a more auspicious attempt to bring the Broadway musical into new realms, winning a Pulitzer Prize for its book and libretto, which lightly satirized the American political system. While it did make some jabs at authority figures and included some talk of impending impeachment, its primary focus on presidential love and childbearing in the White House made for a far less threatening premise than *Strike Up the Band*. What was innovative about *Of Thee I Sing*, as Bowers (1995) has written, was the Gershwins' score: "a masterful progression of straight songs, recitatives, and extended musical scenes; it stormed the boundaries of conventional musical theater and charted new territory for the genre."

The lessons learned by the Gershwins in their Broadway years were brought to bear and heightened with their next production, the American "folk opera" (as Gershwin liked to call it) *Porgy and Bess*. It was based on a novel of 1925 by DuBose Heyward, who closely collaborated with the Gershwins on the opera. He viewed the project as a piece of folklore based on the experiences of poor blacks he knew well and studied extensively while working as a cotton checker for years on the wharves of Charleston, South Carolina. Like *Blue Monday* before it, *Porgy* dealt with themes of love and intense jealousy in the lives of gamblers, prostitutes, and other less-than-respectable blacks. In *Porgy*, however, an all-black cast played the roles, not whites in blackface, and the characterizations were deeper and more nuanced. The characters interacted in a community whose members were obviously devoted to one another and were hard workers attempting to do the best they could in a difficult environment. Heyward and Gershwin purposely sought to avoid the stereotypes of "Negro vaudeville" found in most depictions of blacks on American stages, including the stage play of *Porgy* (1927). Gershwin, at Heyward's urging, spent two months in Charleston, interacting with the black community. He found himself particularly inspired by the spirituals, as is heard in "Prayer," a piece using six different prayers sung simultaneously, in a revolving, hypnotic fashion similar to that of a black choir he heard in Charleston. Once again, Gershwin infused African American musical devices within a genre where they were usually not present— an operatic score. Many critics were initially put off by this hybrid, but the peculiarly American combination has been a main source of the appeal of *Porgy and Bess* through the generations.

Although *Porgy and Bess* is now considered a classic, its initial reception in New York was disappointing. After years of preparation, the three-hour opera had opened in Boston to a fifteen-minute ovation and glowing reviews, and the black composer and scholar J. Rosamond Johnson had declared that Gershwin was the "Abraham Lincoln of Negro music." The director and producers, however, found the length excessive and asked for cuts. Gershwin and his collaborators cooperated, shearing off one-quarter of the work, including many of the more challenging and intricate sequences. Two weeks later, the reviews in New York were mostly scathing, although some noted the power of the music and the historic nature of the production. *Porgy and Bess* closed prematurely, unable to earn back its principal. Besides the ill-advised cuts, which were restored in performances after Gershwin's death, another possible reason for the show's failure was the decision to use white opera stars to record the score for its initial release, instead of the black stars who had been carefully chosen by Gershwin. Lawrence Tibbett and Helen Jepson gave fine, if somewhat histrionic, performances, but they reflected too much of a European opera sensibility, whereas Gershwin had aimed for warmth and personality in his decidedly American opera by casting Todd Duncan and John W. Bubbles. Those in charge may have assumed that using the actual cast would have doomed the commercial prospects for the recordings, but five years later, when recordings of *Porgy and Bess* by the original cast were released, the opera finally began to catch on with the American mass public. Hundreds of recordings followed, by a multitude of artists in various genres.

Porgy and Bess engendered controversy over the decades, even as its reputation as the premier American opera solidified. The Gershwins and Heyward never insisted that it was an authentic portrait of black culture, but other observers suggested this, and some blacks expressed unhappiness that another major artistic success had risen from a vision of uneducated, morally suspect working-class blacks, no matter how much respect was paid to black culture and music in the construction of the show. The creators of *Porgy and Bess* had tried to avoid clichés from minstrelsy, but the subject matter still cut too close for some people, perhaps understandably. In 1953 the Eisenhower administration decided to send a state-sponsored tour of the opera to various foreign locales, including the Soviet Union, as an example of the positive state of American race relations, and this too angered many blacks. Some in the black musical community expressed resentment as well: they knew that, since the early 1920s, no black composers could receive the backing to stage a similarly expensive production concerning black life in a major opera or Broadway venue.

Gershwin spent most of his last months writing for films in Hollywood. Studio bosses worried about his recent immersion in highbrow material, but Gershwin assured them that he was as anxious to write million-sellers as they were to promote them. Any concerns on the studio's part were unwarranted. As no less an authority than Irving Berlin declared a half-century later, "no one wrote greater songs than George and Ira did during the last year of George's life." The brothers once again reached for and attained new heights with compositions such as "Nice Work If You Can Get It," "They All Laughed," and "They Can't Take That Away from Me." With their relaxed swing, their sophisticated romantic patter, and their humor (in both words and music) based on the seemingly real-life trials of lovers, these songs are perennially charming expositions of high art on the jukebox. When Gershwin began his career, such notions of high art concerning American popular music were incongruous; by the time he succumbed to a brain tumor in 1937, this idea was well on the way to worldwide acceptance, thanks in large part to his contributions.

George Gershwin, 1938. (Library of Congress.)

Biography

George Gershwin (Jacob Gershvin) was born in Brooklyn, New York, on 26 September 1898. He studied at public schools and received musical instruction from Charles Hambitzer (1912–1914); Edward Kilenyi, Sr. (1919–1921); Henry Cowell (1927–1929); and Joseph Schillinger (1932–1936). Gershwin was a song plugger for Jerome H. Remick, a music publishing firm in New York City (1914–1917); a performer on piano rolls for various companies (1916–1926); and a rehearsal pianist and concert organizer and accompanist at the Century Theater (1917). He secured a contract with the Harms musical publishing company in 1918. His first full Broadway score was *La La Lucille* (1919). He composed the scores for ten shows on Broadway and in London, including five for the producer George White in 1920–1924. Gershwin was accompanist and composer for Eva Gauthier's program at Aeolian Hall featuring songs by European classical and American popular composers (1923). He composed and premiered several long-form serious works, including *Rhapsody in Blue*, 1924; *Concerto in F*, 1925; *An American in Paris*, 1928; and *Second Rhapsody for Piano and Orchestra*, 1931. He composed the music for several highly successful Broadway musicals, with his brother Ira as lyricist, including *Lady, Be Good!* 1924; *Tell Me More*, 1925; *Tip-Toes*, 1925; *Oh, Kay!* 1926; *Funny Face*, 1927; *Treasure Girl*, 1928; *Show Girl*, 1929; *Girl Crazy*, 1930; *Strike Up the Band*, 1930; and *Of Thee I Sing*, 1931. He composed songs for major motion pictures, including *Delicious*, 1931; *Shall We Dance*, 1937; *A Damsel in Distress*, 1937; and *The Goldwyn Follies*, 1938. He hosted, performed on, and produced the nationally broadcast CBS radio program *Music by Gershwin*, 1934–1935. He composed the music for the folk opera *Porgy and Bess*, 1935. Gershwin died in Hollywood, California, on 11 July 1937.

HARVEY COHEN

See also Bubbles, John; Ellington, Duke; Europe, James Reese; Heyward, DuBose; Johnson, John Rosamond; Porgy and Bess; Porgy: Novel; Porgy: Play; Van Vechten, Carl

Selected Works

Gershwin Plays Gershwin: The Piano Rolls. 1993. (Collection of Gershwin's piano roll performances from 1916 to 1926, Elektra/Nonesuch.)

"Swanee." 1919. (Lyrics by Irving Caesar.)

Lullaby for String Quartet. 1919.

Rhapsody in Blue. 1924.

Lady, Be Good! 1924. (Lyrics by Ira Gershwin, book by Guy Bolton and Fred Thompson.)

Concerto in F. 1925.

"Sweet and Lowdown." 1925. (Lyrics by Ira Gershwin.)

Strike Up the Band. 1927. (Lyrics by Ira Gershwin, book by George S. Kaufman.)

"The Man I Love." 1927. (Lyrics by Ira Gershwin.)

An American in Paris. 1928.

"But Not for Me." 1930. (Lyrics by Ira Gershwin.)

"I Got Rhythm." 1930. (Lyrics by Ira Gershwin.)

Of Thee I Sing. 1931. (Lyrics by Ira Gershwin, book by George S. Kaufman and Morrie Ryskind.)

Porgy and Bess. 1935. (Lyrics by DuBose Heyward and Ira Gershwin, libretto by Hayward.)

"Nice Work If You Can Get It." 1937. (Lyrics by Ira Gershwin.)

"They All Laughed." 1937. (Lyrics by Ira Gershwin.)

"They Can't Take That Away from Me." 1937. (Lyrics by Ira Gershwin.)

Further Reading

Bowers, Dwight Blocker, Larry Starr, and Herb Wong. Liner notes. *I Got Rhythm: The Music of George Gershwin.* Washington, D.C.: Smithsonian Collection of Recordings, 1995.

Jablonski, Edward. *Gershwin: A Biography.* Garden City, N.Y.: Doubleday, 1987.

Jablonski, Edward, and Lawrence D. Stewart. *The Gershwin Years.* Garden City, N.Y.: Doubleday, 1973.

Kimball, Robert, ed. *The Complete Lyrics of Ira Gershwin.* New York: Knopf, 1993.

Rosenberg, Deena. *Fascinating Rhythm: The Collaboration of George and Ira Gershwin.* New York: Dutton, 1991.

Schiff, David. *Gershwin: Rhapsody in Blue.* New York: Cambridge University Press, 1997.

Schwartz, Charles. *Gershwin: His Life and Music.* New York: Da Capo, 1973.

Wilder, Alec. *American Popular Song: The Great Innovators 1900–1950.* London: Oxford University Press, 1972.

Gilpin, Charles

Charles Sidney Gilpin (1878–1930) began his acting career by performing in saloons and theaters at night, and as a temporary performer for traveling shows, to earn extra money; he also sharpened his talents by working as a singer or dancer at fairs, restaurants, and variety theaters. Even in his early teens, his baritone voice was distinctive.

Gilpin moved with his mother to Philadelphia in the early 1890s. He continued to expand his talent for song, dance, and comedy while working with vaudeville and minstrel companies, including the Big Spectacular Log Cabin Company and Perkus and Davis Great Southern Minstrel Barn Storming Aggregation. After the latter folded in 1896, Gilpin moved back to Philadelphia and worked at several jobs. He joined the Canadian Jubilee Singers of Hamilton, Ontario, in 1903, and stayed with the group for two years.

Gilpin's first significant role arrived in 1905 in "The Two Real Coons," a vaudeville act starring Bert Williams and George Walker based on a scene from their musical *In Abyssinia.* Gilpin next worked for the Smart Set Company, a black minstrel group. In 1907 he performed with the Pekin Stock Company of Chicago and attracted attention for his work in a three-act musical, *The Husbands.* Gilpin engaged in blackface comedy and sometimes acted as white characters in white makeup during his tenure with Pekin. He worked sporadically with the Pan-American Octette from 1911 to 1913. Over the next few years he performed briefly in *The Girl at the Fort* with the Anita Bush Company and was one of the founding members of the Lafayette Players in 1916. Later that year, Gilpin resigned from the troupe, reportedly over a salary dispute. His pioneering work at the Lincoln and Lafayette theaters helped usher in an era of artistic presentations open to black audiences.

In 1920, Gilpin impressed audiences and critics with his spellbinding performance as Brutus Jones—a Pullman porter and former convict who becomes the dictator of a Caribbean island—in Eugene O'Neill's play *The Emperor Jones.* In this drama, Gilpin appeared alone in six of the eight scenes; and he was the first African American actor to star in a dramatic production in an all-white theater. The play had its debut in Greenwich Village in New York City, at what later became known as the Provincetown Playhouse. Because the audiences were so large, the production then moved uptown to the Princess Theater. On 4 November 1920, Heywood Braun wrote in the New York *Tribune* that Gilpin "gives the most thrilling performance we have seen any place this season" and underscored Gilpin's power to reduce stereotypes and racist perspectives: "if *The Emperor Jones* were taken elsewhere we have little doubt that the manager would engage a white man with a piece of burnt cork to play Brutus Jones." In 1921 Gilpin was received at the White House and was awarded the Spingarn Medal for distinguished achievement by the National Association for the Advancement of Colored People (NAACP). In February 1921 he attended the annual awards dinner of the Drama League of New York, despite protests by some whites, after being named one of ten people who had contributed most to American theater the previous season.

During the Harlem Renaissance, Gilpin used his fame to motivate black performers around the United States. In January 1922 he attended a rehearsal of the Dumas Dramatic Club in Cleveland, Ohio. Afterward, he challenged members to create one of the best black theater groups in the world and made a donation of $50. Members recast themselves as the Gilpin Players and began several years of outstanding performances at the distinguished Karamu House.

Artistic differences among O'Neill, the production managers, and Gilpin led to the casting of Paul Robeson as Brutus Jones when *The Emperor Jones* was revived. Gilpin had changed some lines that he found offensive, and O'Neill was critical of this action and also accused Gilpin of heavy drinking. Gilpin did play the role of Brutus again in a Broadway revival in 1926, however. Also in 1926, he starred in the film version of *Ten Nights in the Barroom*, produced in Philadelphia by the Colored Players Film Corporation. His final performance of Brutus Jones was in Woodstock, New York, in 1929.

After that, Gilpin was reported to have suffered an emotional breakdown, losing his ability to sing. He died on 6 May 1930, and was buried at Lambertville, New Jersey, in a quiet ceremony. His friends and former coworkers held a second ceremony—for a huge crowd—on 1 June 1930, at Duncan Brothers funeral parlor on Seventh Avenue in New York City. Gilpin's body was exhumed, and he was reburied in Woodlawn Cemetery.

In 1941, Richmond's first low-income housing project, Gilpin Court, was named in honor of Gilpin. Five years later, O'Neill delivered a belated accolade. During a reflective interview, he stated, "As I look back now on all my work, I can honestly say there was only one actor who carried every notion of a character I had in mind. That actor was Charles Gilpin."

Biography

Charles Sidney Gilpin was born on 20 November 1878, in Jackson Ward in Richmond, Virginia, to Peter Gilpin (a laborer in a steel mill) and Caroline White (a nurse in Richmond City Hospital); he was the youngest of fourteen children. Gilpin attended the Saint Francis School for Catholic Colored Children until he quit at age twelve to become a printer's apprentice; he also performed in saloons, at fairs, and in variety theaters. He moved to Philadelphia in the early 1890s and worked with theatrical companies and at other jobs; over his life he was an elevator operator, printer, barber, janitor, and trainer of prizefighters. In 1897 he married Florence Howard; they had a son, Paul Wilson, in 1903. In 1905 Charles Gilpin had a significant role in "The Two Real Coons"; he next worked for the Smart Set Company, a black minstrel group; in 1907 he performed with the Pekin Stock Company of Chicago; in 1911–1913 he worked with the Pan-American Octette; he then worked with Anita Bush's company and was a founding member of the Lafayette Theater. He played Brutus Jones in *The Emperor Jones* (1920) and in some revivals (although the role was to become associated mainly with Paul Robeson). Gilpin was awarded a Spingarn Medal in 1921. In 1926

Charles Gilpin, c. 1920–1930. (Library of Congress.)

he starred in the film version of *Ten Nights in the Barroom*. He retired to Eldridge Park, New Jersey, c. 1929 and was cared for by his second wife, Alma Benjamin, until his death on 6 May 1930, at age fifty-one. He was first buried at Lambertville, New Jersey, but was later reburied at Woodlawn Cemetary.

R. JAKE SUDDERTH

See also Anita Bush Theater Company; Colored Players Film Corporation; Emperor Jones, The; Karamu House; Lafayetter Theater; Lincoln Theater; Minstrelsy; Vaudeville

Further Reading

Anderson, Jervis. *This Was Harlem*. New York: Farrar Straus Giroux, 1982.

Beckerman, Bernard, and Howard Siegman, eds. *On Stage*. New York: Arno with Quadrangle/New York Times Book Company, 1973.

Bishop, Helen. "Gilpin Wants to Play Comedy." *Boston Transcript*, 1922.

Fletcher, Tom. *One Hundred Years of the Negro in Show Business*. New York: Da Capo, 1954.

Haskins, James. *Black Theater in America*. New York: HarperCollins, 1982.

Johns, Robert L. "Charles S. Gilpin." In *Notable Black American Men*, ed. Jessie Carney Smith. Detroit, Mich.: Gale Research, 1999.

Klotman, Phyllis Rauch. *Frame by Frame—A Black Filmography*. Bloomington: Indiana University Press, 1979.

Kneeborne, John D. "It Wasn't All Velvet: The Life and Hard Times of Charles S. Gilpin, Actor." *Virginia Cavalcade Magazine*, Summer 1988.

Logan, Rayford W., and Michael R. Winston, eds. *Dictionary of American Negro Biography*. New York: Norton, 1982.

Mroczka, Paul. "Charles Sidney Gilpin." In *American National Biography*, Vol. 9, eds. John A. Garraty and Mark C. Carnes. New York: Oxford University Press, 1999.

New York Times, 7 May 1930, 2 June 1930. (Obituaries.)

Oppenheimer, Priscilla. "Anita Bush." In *The Harlem Renaissance: A Historical Dictionary of the Era*, ed. Bruce Kellner. New York: Methuen, 1984.

Thompson, Sister M. Francesca. "The Lafayette Players, 1917–1932." In *The Theater of Black Americans*, ed. Errol Hill. Englewood Cliffs, N.J.: Prentice-Hall, 1980, Vol. 2.

Who's Who in Colored America. New York: Who's Who in Colored America, 1927.

"Godmother"

See Mason, Charlotte Osgood

God's Trombones

God's Trombones: Seven Negro Sermons in Verse is only fifty-six pages long, but this brief book reflects some of the issues that interested participants of the Harlem Renaissance: the preservation and appreciation of African American culture, the role of literature and the arts in shaping attitudes about African Americans, the incorporation of distinctive elements of African American culture into literature and visual art, and the complementary nature of literature and the arts. The main components of the book, published in 1927 by Viking, are an opening prayer and seven sermons transcribed into poems by James Weldon Johnson. But there is also a preface by Johnson in which he explains his intentions for the book, and each poem is accompanied by a black-and-white illustration by Aaron Douglas and a title page lettered by the calligrapher C. B. Falls.

In content, the sermons follow what Johnson identifies as a pattern often followed and innovated on by African American preachers. The cycle begins with an opening prayer, moves from "The Creation" through several Old Testament and New Testament stories, and ends with "The Judgment Day." Johnson, as he explains in the preface, wanted the book to draw attention to the importance of African American preachers as leaders in the African American community and as artists. He used his poems to preserve the sermons they delivered and to demonstrate the manner in which they delivered these sermons; he hoped that the book would increase the respect granted to the preachers.

The book was widely reviewed in the 1920s, attracting attention in *Crisis* and *Opportunity* and also in mainstream publications such as *Poetry*, *Nation*, and the *New York Times Book Review*. Reviewers were overwhelmingly positive, praising the quality of Johnson's poems and his tribute to the preachers. Only a few reviewers mentioned Douglas's contributions, but those who did, including W. E. B. Du Bois and Alain Locke, complimented them warmly. Since the 1920s, the book has inspired a range of adaptations, including numerous audiorecordings of performances by preachers and actors, many of them accompanied by music;

scores for choral dramas and orchestral performances; and even a claymation video narrated by James Earl Jones and Dorian Harewood. Scholarly attention to *God's Trombones* has been more limited, but it reveals aspects of the book that deserve further study.

Several literary scholars who have focused on *God's Trombones* have addressed Johnson's decision not to use dialect in these poems. In his preface, Johnson defends this choice, arguing that his diction reflects the preachers' technique of blending biblical language with black idioms. He also asserts that the conventions and ideas associated with black dialect made it too limited a form to express the complexities of African Americans' experiences, an argument he made repeatedly in the 1920s. Some critics of the book, such as Gates (1987), argue that Johnson's dismissal of dialect was misguided and shortsighted; others, such as Jones (1991), insist that Johnson was able to record a self-affirming black vernacular through his use of the imagery, syntax, and rhythms characteristic of the black preachers.

A related issue worth further exploration involves Johnson's transformation of these oral sermons into written poems. In his preface, Johnson discusses the difficulty of this act of transcription and explains his strategies. For example, he used several poetic techniques, including strategically placed line breaks and punctuation, to indicate the rhythm of the preachers' delivery. But, he admits, his transcripts are clearly unable to fully communicate the experience of hearing these sermons. In fact, Johnson argues that the sermons should be "intoned," rather than read, and he often demonstrated the preachers' delivery style at parties and on radio performances. His consideration of the potential and limitations of his written form and his discussion of his techniques invite consideration of the implications of transcription and of his stylistic choices.

Several art historians mention Douglas's contributions to *God's Trombones*, but often only in passing. The most extensive consideration of his illustrations is by Ater (1993) and Kirschke (1995). Each of them points out that these illustrations incorporate the posturing and facial features Douglas would have seen in Egyptian art and demonstrate his interest in modernism and cubism; they position these works as steps toward the mature style Douglas would use in the mural series he created in the 1930s.

The collaboration between Johnson and Douglas in *God's Trombones* also is worth analysis, particularly because it reveals parallels between literature and the other arts. For example, just as Johnson was experimenting with form and language to capture the intricacies of preachers' oral performances, Douglas was developing a style that reflected both African and American aesthetics. Furthermore, Johnson's poetry and Douglas's illustrations also complement one another in content. For instance, Douglas modernized the setting of "The Prodigal Son." In the poem, Johnson describes a young man traveling to Babylon, where he squanders his fortune and becomes involved with women and gambling before returning to his father's house. In Douglas's drawing, dancers wear fashions of the 1920s, and a trombone, gin bottle, and playing card stretch from the corners of the picture. The downfall of Douglas's Prodigal Son could easily have happened in Harlem. By updating the tale, Douglas implicitly demonstrates the relevance of these biblical stories and the preachers' renderings of them to African Americans in the 1920s. Carroll (2002, the present author) analyzes in more depth the relations between the written and visual texts, arguing that they complement one another in important ways and that the implications of the book as a whole exceed those of either its written or its visual elements.

God's Trombones is an important but underappreciated part of both Johnson's and Douglas's oeuvre; it also is an important example of the collaboration between writers and artists during the Harlem Renaissance. *God's Trombones* was only one of many illustrated books produced during the Harlem Renaissance, and it suggests the value of studying the renaissance as a broad cultural movement involving many different forms of expression.

ANNE CARROLL

See also Douglas, Aaron; Johnson, James Weldon

Further Reading

Ater, Renee Deanne. "Image, Text, Sound: Aaron Douglas's Illustrations for James Weldon Johnson's *God's Trombones: Seven Negro Sermons in Verse.*" M.A. thesis, University of Maryland, College Park, 1993.

Carroll, Anne. "Art, Literature, and the Harlem Renaissance: The Messages of *God's Trombones.*" *College Literature*, 2002.

Cooper, Grace C. "Black Preaching Style in James Weldon Johnson's *God's Trombones.*" *MAWA Review*, 4(1), 1989.

Fleming, Robert E. "Johnson's Poetry: The Two Voices." In *James Weldon Johnson.* Boston Mass.: Twayne—G. K. Hall, 1987.

Gates, Henry Louis Jr. *Figures in Black: Words, Signs, and the "Racial" Self*. New York: Oxford University Press, 1987.

Jones, Gayl. *Liberating Voices: Oral Tradition in African American Literature*. Cambridge, Mass.: Harvard University Press, 1991.

Kirschke, Amy Helene. *Aaron Douglas: Art, Race, and the Harlem Renaissance*. Jackson: University Press of Mississippi, 1995.

Koprince, Susan J. "Femininity and the Harlem Renaissance: A Note on James Weldon Johnson." *CLA Journal*, 1985. (See also *Critical Essays on James Weldon Johnson*, eds. Kenneth M. Price and Lawrence J. Oliver. New York: G. K. Hall—Simon and Schuster Macmillan, 1997.)

Rogal, Samuel J. "The Homiletic and Hymnodic Elements in the Poetry of James Weldon Johnson." *Marjorie Kinnan Rawlins Journal of Florida Literature*, 7, 1996.

Sundquist, Eric. *The Hammers of Creation: Folk Culture in Modern African-American Fiction*. Athens: University of Georgia Press, 1992.

Grace, Charles Manuel

See Daddy Grace

Great Migration

"Great migration" refers to a massive exodus of African Americans from the South to the North, beginning in 1890 and culminating at the onset of World War I in 1914. During this period roughly 500,000 African Americans left their southern homeland for Baltimore, Chicago, New York, and Philadelphia, shifting much of the black population from rural settings to urban centers. The presence of African Americans in these cities had a significant impact on the changing political, economic, and social landscape; thus the great migration has been described as a pivotal time in twentieth-century American history.

The great migration, however, was not the first instance of black mobility. Since the forced migration of Africans to the Americas in the seventeenth century, people of African descent have been consistently on the move. Throughout the nineteenth century, the North represented hope and opportunity for both runaway and newly emancipated slaves. After the Civil War, more than 40,000 former slaves, known as "exodusters," headed to Kansas for economic and social opportunity. Still, at the close of the nineteenth century, the largest number of African Americans fled the South to begin new lives in the North.

While the motivations for migration were as varied and distinct as each of the migrants who made the journey north, there are, nonetheless, a few major themes. One such theme was safety. In the 1890s, the increasing restrictions of Jim Crow compounded with the lynchings and violence that ensued prompted many African Americans to leave the South in hope of finding a safer life in the North. For example, articles written by Ida B. Wells warned African Americans of the lynching spectacles that took place throughout the South; and cartoons depicted the North as a place of hope and the South as a place of terror. A second theme had to do with the environment. The late nineteenth century and the early twentieth were a time of severe environmental destruction. Floods and droughts destroyed the livelihood of many small farmers throughout the South, and the onslaught of the boll weevil devastated cotton production. As a result, tenant farmers, sharecroppers, and owners of small farms looked to the North for economic opportunity. A third, related theme was economics. African American farmers began to consider the North as a new place of settlement not only because of the environmental devastation that was sweeping across the South but also because of the industrialization that was developing in the North, because this created a demand for a black labor force. A fourth theme, related to the labor force, was World War I. During the war, restrictions were placed on immigration to the United States, leading to a labor shortage in many new factories in the North. Also, many American workers, virtually all of whom were white males, left their jobs and joined (or were drafted into) the armed forces; this exacerbated the labor shortage. Corporations responded by sending labor agents to the South; the agents actively recruited African American men to work and live in the burgeoning northern cities. A fifth theme was social equality, which seemed more likely in the North. In sum, African Americans were pushed out of the South by violence, Jim Crow, and the erosion of their farms and were pulled to the North by the promise of economic opportunity and social equality.

Relatively recent research on the history of African American migration to the North has not only explored the reasons why so many African Americans fled from the South but also uncovered provocative details about their experiences as migrants. A significant number of southern migrants never made it to their northern destinations, but instead settled in urban parts of the South and in the Upper South. Many migrants found seasonal work while on their journey to the North and ended up following the seasonal labor patterns instead of traveling farther north. Other migrants never made it to the big urban centers, such as Philadelphia, Chicago, or New York, but instead settled in Pittsburgh, where they found jobs in the steel plants.

The emphasis on economic opportunity and labor as the impetus for migration has, according to some historians, obscured our understanding of who the migrants were. Although most migrants were African American men in search of work, there were also a significant number of African American women. Current research on issues relating to gender challenges our understanding of the migration narrative and provides us with more insight into the migratory experience of many southern African Americans. Women, like men, went north for economic opportunity, hoping to find jobs as domestics, department store clerks, and teachers. Yet because many of the opportunities were first offered to men, women were often last to leave the South. Also, as mothers and caretakers of the family, they often felt obliged to remain in the South until they had enough money to establish a new life in the North. Studies of boardinghouses, sororities, and personal diaries reveal that African American women created social networks connecting southern migrants to northerners, who helped facilitate their journey to and settlement in the North.

By taking their analyses in new directions, historians have been redefining our understanding of the great migration. As the new research indicates, to focus only on economic motivations would be to underestimate the social and cultural forces that influenced many African Americans' decision to move to the North. Settling in Chicago or New York was not only an economic matter but also a cultural and social matter. The Chicago *Defender*, a newspaper that circulated throughout the South, gave many African Americans their first glimpse of life in the North. Articles on the newly developing grassroots black community formed the bulk of the paper, but there were also articles on the cultural activities of the newly settled migrants; there were even reports on the black baseball team. Chicago certainly attracted a huge number of migrants to its emerging black community, and one can only imagine the incalculable effects that the blossoming world of music, art, poetry, and dance had on the many migrants who chose to come to New York City.

The influx of African Americans to New York as part of the great migration is a central component in the development of the Harlem Renaissance. For many migrants, Harlem represented the culmination of their artistic imagination, creative energy, and intellectuality; it was, therefore, a popular destination. In addition to its creativity and art, Harlem was for many migrants their new capital; they called it the "promised land" or the "mecca of the New Negro." In Harlem, there were black police officers, black doctors, a black basketball team, black millionaires, black intellectuals, and black political leaders. Artistic energy, combined with a new sense of pride and protest, contributed to a new identity that transformed rural southern migrants into the "New Negro." No longer would African Americans simply be perceived as sharecroppers and tenant farmers; the Harlem Renaissance, nourished by the great migration, radically altered their identity as citizens in the United States.

The dazzling artistic innovation in Harlem attracted southern migrants such as Zora Neale Hurston (who came from Florida) and Rudolph Fisher (who came from Washington, D.C.). Moreover, although the Harlem Renaissance certainly appealed widely to southern migrants, it was a unique destination in that it also transcended the traditional migratory pattern—south to north—and enticed people of African descent from all over the United States and the Caribbean. Billie Holiday came from Philadelphia; the poet Claude McKay and the political leader Marcus Garvey migrated from the West Indies. Their arrival in Harlem has not usually been considered part of the great migration, but it does reveal the migratory impulses that shaped and influenced the experiences of African Americans in the United States, and more specifically the Harlem Renaissance.

The new presence of African Americans in the North transformed the character of the United States. The migrants left their mark not only as laborers in northern factories and as domestics in other people's homes, but also—and indelibly—on cultural expression, such as Jacob Lawrence's painting *Migration of the Negro*, and a possible return hinted at in the lyrics of Gladys Knight and the Pips' "Midnight Train to Georgia." The great migration has perhaps not yet ended; it has just taken a different direction.

JAMES T. DOWNS JR.

See also Barnett, Ida B. Wells; Chicago Defender; Fisher, Rudolph; Great Migration and the Harlem Renaissance; Hurston, Zora Neale; Lawrence, Jacob

Further Reading

Adkins, LaTrese Evette. "Dangers Seen and Unseen: Black Women's Mobility, Community, and Work during the Migration Era, 1915–1940." M.A. thesis, Michigan State University, 1998.

Garber, Eric. "A Spectacle of Color: The Lesbian and Gay Subculture of the Jazz Age in Harlem." In *Hidden from History: Reclaiming the Gay and Lesbian Past*, eds. Martin Duberman, Martha Vicinus, George Chauncy Jr., et al. New York: Penguin, 1989.

Gottlieb, Peter. *Making Their Own Way: Southern Blacks' Migration to Pittsburgh, 1916–1930*. Chicago: University of Illinois Press, 1987.

Griffin, Farah Jasmine. *Who Set You Flowin'? The African-American Migration Narrative*. New York: Oxford University Press, 1995.

Grossman, James R. *Land of Hope: Chicago, Black Southerners, and the Great Migration*. Chicago, Ill.: University of Chicago Press, 1989.

Painter, Nell Irvin. *Exodusters: Black Migration to Kansas after Reconstruction*. New York. Knopf, 1977.

Trotter, Joe, et al. *The Great Migration in Historical Perspective: New Dimensions of Race, Class, and Gender*. Bloomington: Indiana University Press, 1991.

Great Migration and the Harlem Renaissance

Following the Civil War and emancipation, southern blacks, mostly former slaves, forged new lives in the South. In the 1870s, however, race relations in the South began to deteriorate. By 1890 white voters had largely driven blacks from southern politics and had imposed a pervasive system of racial apartheid that reduced all African Americans in the South to servility. In the 1890s a prolonged agricultural crisis threatened the livelihood of all rural southerners, touching off a new wave of racial violence. Lynchings of blacks by white vigilantes became common and widespread throughout the rural South. The arrival of the boll weevil after 1900 undercut cotton production, the mainstay of southern agriculture, making life even more desperate for rural southern blacks. By 1910 tens of thousands of southern blacks, despairing of life in the South, left the region altogether, setting in motion the great migration. From 1917 to 1960 between three million and five million African Americans left the South for northern cities. Several hundred thousand of these rural southern migrants came to Harlem, most from the South Atlantic states of Virginia, North and South Carolina, Georgia, and Florida, forming in New York the largest and most vibrant African American community in the nation. Before World War I, northern cities offered only marginal opportunities for African Americans. European immigrants and their children claimed most of the unskilled and semiskilled jobs in the nation's factories, and white labor unions systematically barred blacks from membership. In New York City most African Americans accepted low-paying, insecure menial work as cooks, porters, domestic servants, laundry workers, and day laborers. Only a few found well-paid employment on the railroads, in the post office and the civil service, and on the city's docks.

Northern working-class whites saw the growing tide of impoverished black migrants as a threat to their own precarious livelihood. White laborers treated blacks as racial inferiors who degraded their neighborhoods. Angry and afraid, in city after city, white mobs vented their frustrations on any and all nonwhites who crossed their path, setting off a wave of urban race riots as violent and destructive as the lynchings in the rural South. World War I momentarily moderated this violence and also offered unprecedented economic opportunity to southern blacks. The outbreak of war in 1914 cut off European immigration to the United States and created an enormous demand for American manufactured war material. The United States' entry into World War I in 1917 increased the demand for factory labor even as conscription forced millions of able-bodied males into military service, creating a labor shortage throughout the nation. Northern employers sent employment agents throughout the South, promising blacks good jobs in the North. By 1920 hundreds of thousands of southern blacks had come to northern cities.

The wartime migration of rural African Americans to cities changed American urban life. In the 1920s, for the first time, every American city contained significant numbers of African Americans. Before 1900, African Americans had been primarily a rural and southern people. In 1920 they had also become an urban and northern people. In most cities the arrival of thousands of poor black southerners destabilized residential patterns. With the end of unrestricted European immigration, African Americans became the fastest-growing ethnic group in the urban North. When black migrants pushed into new neighborhoods, working-class whites fought to contain them, often resorting to the southern whites' strategy of racial segregation, enforced by police and mob violence. New York escaped the worst of this violence. Harlem's isolation from the rest of the city provided African Americans with a safe haven.

By 1920 about 21 percent of Harlem's African Americans were native New Yorkers, about 20 percent came from the British West Indies, and 55 percent came from the South. Ninety percent of the 180,000 native-born blacks who lived in Harlem in 1920 came from the five-state south Atlantic region. Southerners came to Harlem primarily to find work. The remaining native-born Americans were largely native New Yorkers, largely educated and middle-class. Most formed households of a husband and wife, several children, a relative or two, and, frequently, a boarder from back home. Nearly all were either illiterate or semiliterate and settled for low-paying menial jobs. About half of the women worked, most in the needle trades, in laundries, or as domestic help. A few found employment in beauty shops, in restaurants, and in department stores as stock clerks, and according to welfare agencies, several thousand resorted to prostitution. Males often worked as janitors, day laborers, porters, and elevator operators. About 5 percent obtained middle-class employment as undertakers, ministers, teachers, doctors, lawyers, and shop owners; 5 percent worked as skilled craftsmen such as masons, carpenters, barbers, cabinetmakers, and plumbers; about 5 percent worked either for the railroads or as postal clerks; another 5 percent worked in factories or at the Brooklyn Naval Yard; and about 10 percent worked on the West Side and Brooklyn piers.

Not all of Harlem's black migrants came from the South. About 20 percent came from the West Indies. In the 1890s the Ward Steamship Line established regular runs between the West Indies and New York. By World War I Jamaicans formed one of the largest immigrant groups in New York and by far the city's largest nonwhite immigrant community. In 1930 nearly 100,000 Jamaicans lived in New York, most in Harlem between Central Park and 115th Street, east of Lenox Avenue. The Jamaicans who arrived in New York were nearly all literate, spoke British public school English, belonged to the Anglican church, and included large numbers of middle-class professionals and merchants. They also brought with them a highly developed political consciousness and extensive experience with democratic politics, providing Harlem with much of its political leadership.

Many first-generation southern migrants tried desperately to assimilate to northern white culture. The wealthiest individual in Harlem, Madame C. J. Walker, made her fortune by selling her hair-straightening formula to black southerners. She lived in a brownstone on West 136th Street in Harlem, elbow to elbow with Harlem's poor, but she also owned a palatial mansion on the Hudson River. Southern and West Indian migrants dreamed of becoming New Yorkers. The young, especially, dressed as New Yorkers, spoke urban slang, adopted new foods, applied bleaches to their skin, and patronized beauty and barber shops that promised to remake them into stylish urban people. The jazz clarinettist Garvin Bushell observed that in the 1920s most of the Negro population in New York either had been born there or had been there so long that they were fully acclimated:

> They wanted you to forget the traditions of the South and were trying to emulate the whites. . . . You weren't allowed to play blues and boogie woogie in the average Negro middle class home . . . . You could only hear the blues and real jazz in the gutbucket cabarets where the lower class went. The term 'gutbucket' came from the chitterlings bucket. (1988, p. 19)

Still, African Americans retained important aspects of their southern and Jamaican identity: their cuisine, their music, important elements of style, their sense of racial identity, and most of all their religion. According to Bushell (20–21), "Gradually, the New York cabarets began to hear more of the real pure jazz and blues by musicians from Florida, South Carolina, Georgia, Louisiana and other parts of the South." Harlem and its music remained essentially African American; in the jargon of the era, "it swung." Bushell explained: "They called it 'shout' in those days, from the church when the Baptist minister would start preaching and the congregation would get all worked up emotionally. Negro church music had a great influence on jazz. They sang the blues in church; the words were religious, but it was the blues. They often had a drummer and a trumpet player there."

In the 1920s migration from Georgia, North Carolina, and South Carolina reached 400,000; in the 1930s it dropped to 230,000; in the 1940s it jumped to 477,000. In 1930 more than 75 percent of Harlem's African American migrants had come from the five south Atlantic states. One-quarter of Harlem's black residents were native New Yorkers, and 15 percent were British West Indians. In the depression years of the 1930s, southern migration to Harlem slowed, but beginning with World War II it accelerated again. The Census

Bureau did not compile figures specifically for Harlem. For New York City as a whole, however, the bureau calculated that in the 1940s the African American population in the city increased by 300,000, and that it increased by another 300,000 in the 1950s. Almost all of the increase derived from migration from the South Atlantic states, from natural increase, or from Puerto Rico. After 1924 restrictions on immigration barred most people of African descent from entering the United States. After World War II, however, large numbers of African Americans from the American territory of Puerto Rico immigrated to Harlem. In 1910 New York City's African American population stood at about 2 percent. In 1960 it exceeded 15 percent.

At the close of the great migration in the late 1960s, Harlem had become a southern and Caribbean city. Most of its people spoke with southern or Caribbean accents, they prepared and ate traditional southern and Caribbean foods, their worship services conformed to southern and Caribbean conventions, and their nightclubs, dance halls, and theaters offered the same fare as African American communities in the South and Puerto Rico. At the same time, Harlem's residents had also adopted many northern ways. Most noticeably, they had become an urban people. They worked at city jobs, not as farmers; they lived among neighbors, not relatives; the clock, not the calendar, governed their lives; and they answered to themselves, not to their community. These changes occurred slowly, one person at a time, day by day.

The rapid rise in the number of Pentecostal and Holiness churches in Harlem after World War II, and the increasingly southern, sanctified features of its old-line Protestant and Catholic congregations, reflected this influence. Even Harlem's formal institutions of culture—the Schomberg Library, the Young Men's and Young Women's Christian Associations (YMCA and YWCA), the Urban League, the National Association for the Advancement of Colored People (NAACP), the *Amsterdam News,* and its socially prominent churches—increasingly defined their role in Harlem in the language of southern migrants' sanctified religion and music. But Harlem's migrants also carried back to their homelands Harlem's political militancy and city ways, sowing seeds of change in the South and in Puerto Rico. Appropriately, the legendary Harlem Globetrotters basketball team warmed up their worldwide audiences with down-home music: "Sweet Georgia Brown." By the 1970s Harlem and "Sweet Georgia Brown" had become interrelated pieces in a much larger, complex African American mosaic that came from the South, the Caribbean, and Africa itself—an artifact of the great migration.

PETER RUTKOFF

WILLIAM SCOTT

See also Anglophone Caribbean and the Harlem Renaissance; Great Migration; Walker, Madame C. J.

Further Reading

Bushell, Garvin, with Mark Tucker. *Jazz from the Beginning.* Ann Arbor: University of Michigan Press, 1988.

Devlin, George. *South Carolina and Black Migration, 1860–1940.* New York: Garland, 1989.

Hawkins, Homer. "Trends in Black Migration from 1863–1960." *Phylon,* 34, 1973.

New York Urban League. "Twenty-Four Hundred Negro Families in Harlem." 1927. (Unpublished manuscript, New York Urban League files.)

Scott, Emmet. *Negro Migration during the War.* New York: Oxford University Press, 1920.

Trotter, Joe William Jr. *The Great Migration.* Bloomington: Indiana University Press, 1991.

U.S. Census Bureau. *United States Census, New York City.* Washington, D.C.: U.S. Government Printing Office, 1900, 1910, 1920, 1930.

Watkins-Ownes, Irma. *Blood Relations: Caribbean Immigrants and the Harlem Community, 1900–1930.* Bloomington: Indiana University Press, 1996.

Green Pastures, The

As the framework for his play *The Green Pastures* (1929), which is a deliberately naive retelling of stories from the Old Testament, Marc Connelly depicts an elderly black Sunday school teacher explaining the mysteries of the Bible to a group of curious, fidgety black children in the deep South during the Depression. The play stresses the analogy between the children of Israel in the Old Testament and blacks in the rural South: God, the angels, and the biblical characters resemble the sort of adult figures that the children would recognize. As Connelly explained in the preface to the printed version of the play, "*The Green Pastures* is an attempt to present certain aspects of a living religion in the terms of its believers." For some readers now, as for the original audience, the sincerity, affection, and good humor of this play make it consistently enjoyable; for its critics, it is sentimental, condescending, and racist. *The Green Pastures* opened on Broadway in February 1930, had a six-year run, and won a Pulitzer Prize for its author. But a revival in 1951 failed, partly because of the shift in racial attitudes after World War II.

The first act consists of a series of dramatizations of familiar scenes from the Old Testament, with poor southern blacks taking on the roles of God and the biblical characters. The stage directions explain that the angels "look and act like a company of happy negroes at a fish fry." God, known throughout the play as "De Lawd," has a taste for boiled custard and "ten-cent seegars." The first act moves from the creation and Adam to Noah and the flood; the second act jumps briskly from the patriarchs Abraham, Isaac, and Jacob to Moses and Exodus and a newly invented character, "Hezdrel," who is about to be killed defending the Temple in Jerusalem from Herod's attack. At the play's conclusion, the angels comment sympathetically on the plight of an unseen Jesus, who is being sent off to his crucifixion.

The popularity of *The Green Pastures* among white audiences during the Depression is understandable. As in the American melodramatic tradition, the poor and humble are shown as keeping their dignity (Richards 1997), and sympathy for others is displayed in highly emotional situations (Mason 1993). Connelly, who had earned his reputation as the coauthor with George S. Kaufman of several successful Broadway comedies, provided his characters with charm and earthy good sense. The view of Miller and Frazer (1991) that the play's "sincerely religious atmosphere" actually "overcomes the condescending view of ignorant folk" is open to question, as is the suggestion of Berkowitz (1992) that the play's charm, humor, and emotional power cover the implicit racism. Craig (1980) cites a contemporary viewer who dismissed the play's "inauthentic black folklore" and complained that it treated blacks as stereotypical figures.

A modern reading of the play reveals certain paradoxes. The structure of the play is loose and episodic, but anyone raised on these stories will find Connelly's retelling fresh and amusing, with no knee-jerk piety. (God wearily admits to one of the archangels that "Even bein' Gawd ain't a bed of roses.") To counter the charge of sentimentality, the play can be shown to contain a deeply pessimistic streak. God lives up to his Old Testament reputation of being bad-tempered and aloof. Outraged at human misbehavior but neglectful of injustice, De Lawd withdraws out of unhappiness

with his own creation: "I repent of dese people dat I have made and I will deliver dem no more."

That the play adopts the racist attitudes of its time is undeniable. As in the "jungle" numbers that were featured in Duke Ellington's programs at the Cotton Club in Harlem, the talented African American performers in the first production were asked to present a false impression of black life. The supposed dialect of poor blacks in Louisiana owes more to racist stage tradition than to observation of actual speech. (Audiences continue to forgive George Gershwin's opera *Porgy and Bess* for using such unrealistic speech, but not *The Green Pastures*.) It also seems undeniable, though, that the play is sympathetic to the plight of impoverished blacks in the deep south during the Depression. Certain figures are deeply sympathetic, such as Adam, Hosea, and Hezdrel.

By making all the villains—such as Pharaoh and "Cain the Sixth"—black, as well as the other characters, the play forgoes the opportunity to put the blame for black people's suffering outside the local black community. But as a measure of its dramatic sophistication, the play's most admirable character is also shown to be its most defective. "De Lawd," like the other characters, needs to learn the lesson of mercy as a reward for suffering, and in the course of the play, he learns to abandon wrath in favor of compassion. As the theologian Karen Armstrong explains in her study of Genesis (1996), the Old Testament God "is omnipotent but powerless to control humanity." De Lawd has to come to terms with his own neglect of his creation. In the climactic scene, De Lawd is impressed

Scene from *The Green Pastures* showing Moses and Aaron before Pharaoh. (Photofest.)

Marc Connelly. (Library of Congress.)

by the steadfast faith of Hezdrel, who explains that he worships the God of Hosea the prophet, not the wrathful God of Moses. Pleased, but not a little discomforted by Hezdrel's earnest faith, De Lawd tells Hezdrel, "If dey kill you tomorrow I'll bet dat God of Hosea'll be waitin' for you." In the short final scene, De Lawd tells the archangel Gabriel that people on earth have earned mercy through suffering. "Did he mean dat even God must suffer?" he asks himself about his encounter with Hezdrel.

Like the stage versions of *Uncle Tom's Cabin* in the 1850s, *The Green Pastures* showed sympathy for the struggles of the African Americans depicted onstage (Richards 371). Although it is probably not performable today because of its racial stereotyping, *The Green Pastures* shows energy, wit, irreverence, and a willingness to ask difficult questions.

BYRON NELSON

See also Cotton Club; Porgy and Bess

Further Reading

Armstrong, Karen. *In the Beginning: A New Interpretation of Genesis.* New York: Knopf, 1996.

Berkowitz, Gerald M. *American Drama of the Twentieth Century.* London and New York: Longman, 1992.

Connelly, Marc. *The Green Pastures.* New York: Holt, Rinehart, and Winston, 1929.

Craig, E. Quita. *Black Drama of the Federal Theatre Era.* Amherst: University of Massachusetts Press, 1980.

Mason, Jeffrey D. *Melodrama and the Myth of America.* Bloomington: Indiana University Press, 1993.

Miller, Jordan Y., and Winifred Frazer. *American Drama between the Wars: A Critical History.* Boston, Mass.: Twayne, 1991.

Richards, Jeffrey, ed. *Early American Drama.* New York: Penguin, 1997.

Green, Paul

Paul Green's black and white folk literature—written throughout 1919–1937, the years of the Harlem Renaissance—secured his place as a white writer who depicted black life in America. Green was the son of a southern white farmer and from childhood was aware of the ills that beset blacks; he used literature to express his ardent belief in freedom and equality for all. Green wrote controversial one-act plays focusing on southerners to illuminate harsh race relations. His inclusion of black themes and his presentation of black life offered a greater understanding of black culture. In literature earlier in the century, black characters were commonly portrayed as villains or relegated to the background; Green, by contrast, introduced blacks as humans who were as true to life as possible.

Although Green aroused much opposition and resentment, this reaction did not prevent him from attempting to fully represent the lives of people cast off by mainstream society, and he addressed humanitarian issues and social problems. Green did not write solely about blacks; he included in his works the people he knew most about, typically white tenant farmers, convicts, mill workers, field laborers, teachers, and poor blacks and whites. Common themes in his work include the social aspirations and fate of blacks, love between blacks and whites, malice and discrimination inflicted by whites, issues relating to mulattoes, freedom and equality, and religious conflicts. Green integrated vernacular speech, poetry, pantomime, and various forms of music into his literature.

Green's *White Dresses*, his first characteristic play centered on blacks, is the tragic story of a mulatto woman living in a black environment. It was produced in White Plains, New York, in 1923. In 1927 Green received a Pulitzer Prize for his play *In Abraham's Bosom*, a tragedy about a black educator who attempts to establish a school for blacks in North Carolina. *In Abraham's Bosom* was produced in New York by the Provincetown Players and staged by Jasper Deeter in

1926. Later in his career, Green became known for his symphonic dramas, plays that incorporated music for dramatic effect. His symphonic history plays took up events in American history and culture—for example, events involving the founding fathers. The four most popular of these plays were *The Lost Colony* (1937), celebrating the first British settlement in America, Raleigh's colony at Roanoke Island; *The Highland Call* (1941), about the Scottish settlement in North Carolina; *The Common Glory* (1948), about Jefferson's role as well as the state of Virginia throughout the American Revolution; and *Faith of Our Fathers* (1950), about George Washington. In 1941 Green worked with Richard Wright on an adaptation of Wright's *Native Son* for Broadway.

Green is largely unrecognized today, but he was a prominent figure throughout the Harlem Renaissance. His efforts to introduce blacks into realistic modern literature and theater helped pave the way for black actors. He also expressed progressive ideals and a sense of cultural pride during what was a delicate time for blacks.

Biography

Paul Eliot Green was born on 17 March 1894, in Lillington, North Carolina. He was educated at Buie's Creek Academy in North Carolina, graduating in 1914, and at the University of North Carolina in Chapel Hill (1921); he did graduate study in 1921–1922 and had a Kenan Philosophy Fellowship to study philosophy at Cornell University in 1922–1923. He was a school principal in Olive Branch, North Carolina, in 1914–1917; served in the U.S. Army Corps of Engineers in 1917–1919; was an instructor and then an assistant professor of philosophy at Chapel Hill in 1923–1936, and later taught in the department of dramatic arts in 1936–1944; was editor of the *Reviewer* magazine, Chapel Hill, in 1925; was a contributing editor at *Contempo* magazine in 1931–1932; and wrote for Fox, Warner Brothers, and others in Hollywood in 1932–1936. He married Elizabeth Atkinson Lay in 1922. Five one-act plays by Green were produced by the Carolina Play-makers in Chapel Hill in 1920. His characteristic Negro play *White Dresses* was produced in 1923. He completed his first music drama, *Potter's Field: A Symphonic Play of the Negro People,* in 1931; and two novels, *The Laughing Pioneer* and *This Body the Earth,* in 1932 and 1936, respectively. His symphonic plays include *The Lost Colony* (the most popular, first produced at Roanoke

Island in 1937), *The Highland Call* (1939), *The Common Glory* (1947), and *Faith of Our Fathers* (1950). He worked with Richard Wright on an adaptation of *Native Son* for Broadway in 1941. Green was president of the National Theatre Conference (1940–1942) and a member of the National Institute on Arts and Letters (1941), the U.S. Executive Committee, and the National Commission, UNESCO (1950–1952); he participated in the International Conference for the Performing Arts in Athens (1962). His awards included the New York City Belasco Cup for a one-act play, *The No 'Count Boy* (1925); a Pulitzer Prize for *Abraham's Bosom* (1927); and a Guggenheim fellowship (1928, 1929). Green died on 4 May 1981, at his home in Chapel Hill. The Paul Green Foundation was formed in 1982.

LISA A. CZERNIECKI

See also Contempo; Provincetown Players; Wright, Richard

Selected Works

The Lord's Will and Other Carolina Plays. New York: Holt, 1925.
Contemporary American Literature: A Study of Fourteen Outstanding American Writers. Chapel Hill: University of North Carolina Press, 1925.
Lonesome Road: Six Plays for the Negro Theatre. New York: McBride, 1926.
Wide Fields. New York: McBride, 1928.
The House of Connelly and Other Plays. New York: French, 1931.
Shroud My Body Down. Iowa City, Iowa: Clio, 1935.
The Lost Colony. Chapel Hill: University of North Carolina Press, 1937.
Out of the South: The Life of a People in Dramatic Form. New York: Harper, 1939.
Native Son. (With Richard Wright, adaptation.) New York: Harper, 1941.
The Highland Call: A Symphonic Play of American History. Chapel Hill: University of North Carolina Press, 1941.
The Common Glory: A Symphonic Drama of American History. Chapel Hill: University of North Carolina Press, 1948.
Five Plays of the South. New York: Hill and Wang, 1963.

Further Reading

Adams, Agatha Boyd. *Paul Green of Chapel Hill.* Chapel Hill: University of North Carolina Press, 1951.

Clark, Barrett Harper. *Paul Green*. New York: McBride, 1928.

Green, Paul. *Paul Green's Wordbook: An Alphabet of Reminiscence*, ed. Rhoda H. Wynn. Chapel Hill: Appalachian Consortium, 1990.

———. *A Paul Green Reader*, ed. Laurence G. Avery. Chapel Hill: University of North Carolina Press, 1998.

Kenny, Vincent S. *Paul Green*. New York: Twayne, 1971.

Greene, Lorenzo

Lorenzo Johnston Greene, an early promoter of black history, wrote the first scholarly history of blacks in colonial New England.

Greene entered Howard University to study medicine but became interested in history after taking courses with two notable African American historians: Walter Dyson, a Europeanist; and William Leo Hansberry, a pioneer in the study of African civilizations. Greene decided to pursue graduate training in history; and when he was initially rebuffed by Yale because he had taken so few history courses at Howard, he was encouraged to enter Columbia University to take additional courses. There, he met the Americanist Dixon Ryan Fox and developed an interest in the black colonial experience in the United States. Greene completed his M.A. in 1926, but in 1928 he encountered financial difficulties that interrupted his doctoral studies at Columbia. For assistance, he turned to a fellow alumnus of Howard, Charles Wesley, who had received a Ph.D. from Harvard and was an investigator for the Association for the Study of Negro Life and History (ASNLH). Wesley persuaded Carter G. Woodson, the founder of ASNLH, to retain Greene to assist in a national survey of the black church, and Woodson hired Greene as a part-time associate and field investigator. In this capacity, Greene assisted in the production of several seminal studies of the black experience.

Much of what we know about Greene's involvement with ASNLH during the Harlem Renaissance comes from a diary he kept between 1928 and 1930. Greene's entries were meticulous and provide valuable personal and professional insights into the organization's early years. In addition to recounting his work with the national church survey, Greene also detailed his contributions to several publications of ASNLH, including *African Myths*, *The Negro in Our History*, and *The Negro Wage Earner*. The diaries also give us a glimpse of the inner workings of ASNLH. Greene noted his interactions with other investigators for ASNLH, such as Charles Wesley and Alrutheus Ambush Taylor. He described the quality of their scholarship as well as stories Woodson related to him. Most important, he revealed how exacting Woodson was with regard to the publication of scholarly work. Woodson often made Greene correct or proofread a work several times before accepting it. In the case of the national church survey, Woodson's criticism of the original draft led to the abandonment of the project, and Greene was reassigned to a project that culminated in the production of *The Negro Wage Earner*. Greene described the tabulation and interpretation of statistics that went into this work, as well as research at the Library of Congress and other institutions. He also described the national convention of ASNLH in 1928 and 1929, as well as Woodson's work with Negro History Week, instituted in 1926.

In addition to exposing the inner workings of ASNLH, Greene, in his second diary, covering 1930–1933, described his own role in promoting ASNLH and its work. He and four other men left Washington, D.C., in 1930 to sell books issued by Associated Publishers. This trip, which encompassed much of the upper and lower South as well as Pennsylvania, Oklahoma, Missouri, and Illinois, demonstrates the length to which the organization went to promote its work. Greene's diary also reveals much about the respect and admiration that Woodson's work stimulated in black communities throughout the United States. On several occasions, the mere mention of Woodson's name was enough to secure lodging, food, and assistance with transportation.

Although Greene is not as well known as many of his contemporaries, his contributions to the growth of African American history as a historical specialty are immeasurable. His early editorial work, his fundraising, and his scholarship helped define the mission of ASNLH in the first half of the twentieth century.

Biography

Lorenzo Johnston Greene was born on 16 November 1899, in Ansonia, Connecticut. He was educated in public schools; at Howard University in Washington, D.C. (A.B., 1924); and at Columbia University in New York City (A.M., 1926; Ph.D., 1942). Greene was a part-time research associate and field investigator for the Association for the Study of Negro Life and History

(1928–1933); taught history at Lincoln University in Jefferson City, Missouri (1933–1972); and was an editor of *Midwest Journal* (1947–1956). He was chairman of the Subcommittee on Education, Missouri Advisory Committee to U.S. Commission on Civil Rights (1959–1961); president of the Association for the Study of Negro Life and History (1965–1966); director of the Institute for Drop-Out Prevention and Teacher Orientation, Jefferson City, Missouri; and director of the Institute to Facilitate Desegregation in Kansas City Public Schools, Missouri (1972–1974). Greene died in Jefferson City on 24 January 1988.

STEPHEN G. HALL

See also Association for the Study of Negro Life and History and Journal of Negro History; Black History and Historiography; Woodson, Carter G.

Selected Works

The Negro Wage Earner. 1930.
The Negro in Colonial New England, 1620–1776. 1942.
Missouri's Black Heritage. 1980. (As editor.)

Further Reading

Selling Black History for Carter G. Woodson: A Diary, 1930–1933, ed. Avrah Strickland. 1996.
Working with Carter G. Woodson, the Father of Black History: A Diary, 1928–1930, ed. Avrah Strickland. 1989.

Greenwich Village

Renowned for its rich and diverse literary, intellectual, and artistic heritage, Greenwich Village—often called simply the Village—is an old residential neighborhood located in the lower section of downtown Manhattan that is bounded by First Street, Fourteenth Street, Houston Street, Broadway, and the Hudson River waterfront.

During the early nineteenth century, new institutions arose in Greenwich Village to serve the spiritual, educational, and cultural needs of the growing community. Religious denominations commissioned elaborately decorated buildings; New York University grew on the east side of Washington Square from 1836 on; and the neighborhood soon became the site of art clubs, private picture galleries, learned societies, literary salons, and libraries. Fine hotels, shops, and theaters also flourished. However, the character of the neighborhood changed markedly at the close of the century, when German, Irish, and Italian immigrants found work in the breweries, warehouses, and coal and lumber yards near the Hudson River as well as in the manufacturing lofts in the Southeast corner of the neighborhood. Older residences were either subdivided into cheap lodging hotels and multiple-family apartment houses or demolished to build tenements. Plummeting real estate values prompted nervous retailers and genteel property owners to move farther uptown.

At the turn of the twentieth century, Greenwich Village—much like Harlem—was a quaintly picturesque and ethnically diverse neighborhood. By the time World War I began, it was widely known as a bohemian enclave with secluded side streets, low rents, and a tolerance for radical political views and nonconformist lifestyles. Attention became increasingly focused on artists and writers noted for their boldly innovative work: books and irreverent "little magazines" were published by small presses, art galleries exhibited the work of the avant-garde, and experimental theater companies ignored the financial considerations of Broadway. A growing awareness of its idiosyncrasies helped make the Village an attraction for tourists. Entrepreneurs provided amusements ranging from evenings in artists' studios to bacchanalian costume balls. During Prohibition, local speakeasies attracted patrons from uptown. Decrepit rowhouses were remodeled into "artistic flats" for the more affluent residents, and luxury apartment towers appeared at the Northernmost edge of Washington Square by 1926—although the stock market crash of 1929 halted the momentum of new construction in this area of the city. During the 1930s, galleries and collectors promoted contemporary art. The sculptor Gertrude Whitney Vanderbilt opened a museum dedicated to modern American art on West Eighth Street, now the New York Studio School. The New School for Social Research, on West Twelfth Street since the late 1920s, inaugurated the "university in exile" in 1934.

From 1920 until about 1930, an unprecedented outburst of creative activity among African Americans occurred in all manner of artistic endeavors. Beginning as a series of literary discussions in lower Manhattan (Greenwich Village) and upper Manhattan (Harlem), this African American cultural movement became known as the "New Negro movement" and later as the Harlem Renaissance. African Americans were encouraged to celebrate their heritage and to become the "New Negro," a term coined in 1925 by the sociologist and critic Alain Locke. This movement was more than a literary phenomenon and more than a social revolt against racism. Adventurous participants in the Greenwich Village scene, most notably Carl Van Vechten, were very excited by the Harlem Renaissance. Also, many artists and writers in Greenwich Village found great inspiration in the formative years of the Harlem Renaissance because it exalted the unique cultural expression and racial heritage of African Americans and magnificently redefined African American expression.

JUAN FLOYD-THOMAS

See also Black Bohemia; Locke, Alain; New Negro Movement; Van Vechten, Carl

Further Reading

Beard, Rick, with Leslie Cohen Berlowitz. *Greenwich Village: Culture and Counterculture.* New Brunswick, N.J.: Rutgers University Press, 1997.

Bender, Thomas. *New York Intellect.* Baltimore, Md.: Johns Hopkins University Press, 1988.

Binder, Frederick M., and David M. Reimers. *All the Nations under Heaven: An Ethnic and Racial History of New York City.* New York: Columbia University Press, 1995.

Harris, M. A. *A Negro History Tour of Manhattan.* New York: Greenwood, 1968.

Jackson, Kenneth T., ed. *The Encyclopedia of New York City.* New Haven, Conn.: Yale University Press, 1995, pp. 506–509.

Katz, William L. *Black Legacy: A History of New York's African Americans.* New York: Atheneum, 1997.

Lewis, David Levering. *When Harlem Was in Vogue.* New York: Oxford University Press, 1988.

Ottley, Roi, and William Weatherby, eds. *The Negro in New York.* New York: New York Public Library Press, 1967.

Stansell, Christine. *American Moderns: Bohemian New York and the Creation of a New Century.* New York: Metropolitan, 2000.

Ware, Caroline F. *Greenwich Village, 1920–1930: A Comment on American Civilization in the Post-War Years.* Berkeley and Los Angeles: University of California Press, 1994.

Watson, Sherrill D. *New York City's African Slaveowners.* New York: Garland, 1994.

Wetzsteon, Ross. *Republic of Dreams, Greenwich Village: The American Bohemia, 1915–1950.* New York: Simon and Schuster, 2002.

Wilder, Craig Steven. *In the Company of Black Men: The African Influence on African American Culture in New York City.* New York: New York University Press, 2001.

Griggs, Sutton E.

The novelist, essayist, and minister Sutton Elbert Griggs (1872–1930) is important in the African American literary tradition as one of the earliest voices of black nationalism; he was also one of the earliest African American writers to establish a publishing company, Orion, in Nashville, Tennessee. He distributed his own thirty-three books primarily through Orion; and because they were distributed throughout the African American community, he probably had a larger African American readership than his contemporaries Charles Chesnutt and Paul Laurence Dunbar. Among Griggs's published works were five novels: *Imperium in Imperio* (1899), *Overshadowed* (1901), *Unfettered* (1902), *The Hindered Hand* (1905), and *Pointing the Way* (1908). Little is known about Griggs's personal life, but his professional achievements indicate his lifelong commitment to racial justice, racial solidarity, and self-determination.

His first novel, *Imperium in Imperio*, because of its radical nature and its emphasis on ideology, is especially pertinent to studies of the Harlem Renaissance. This protonationalist text advocates a violent overthrow of the U.S. government through the efforts of an underground black political organization, the Imperium. Bell (1987) describes this work as "one of the most thematically radical Afro-American novels of the nineteenth century" (61). Although it was published twenty-six years before *Survey Graphic* helped publicize the inception of the Harlem Renaissance, *Imperium in Imperio* prefigures ideological issues that were of extreme importance to artists of the renaissance era. The text is immediately concerned with the utilitarian purpose of early African American literature, the state of African American leadership, and the emergence of a new, militant concept of black masculinity. The novel is both sensationalist and didactic, and it anticipates the tension between aesthetics and ideology in many renaissance texts. The fantastic plot turns indicate that Griggs wanted to entertain his readers, but his primary aim is to impel them to pursue racial justice. Griggs's two protagonists, Bernard Belgrave and Belton Piedmont, are loosely modeled on W. E. B. Du Bois and Booker T. Washington, respectively—representing the divergent methods of African American leaders.

The conflicted relationship that develops between them is a metaphor for the complexities of attempting to unite African Americans from diverse backgrounds under a single model of leadership. Perhaps most significantly, Griggs uses the "New Negro" to symbolize the growing militancy of African Americans at the turn of the twentieth century, prefiguring the association of this term with the literature of the Harlem Renaissance.

Griggs's other four novels all center on the related issues of African American uplift and equality. His second novel, *Overshadowed*, focuses on the conflicted nature of the emergent black middle class. Griggs's growing interest in international politics and the black diaspora is at work in *Unfettered* and *The Hindered Hand*; in both novels, Griggs focuses on the timely issues of imperialism and African Americans' complicated relationship to the African past. By the time his last novel, *Pointing the Way*, was published, Griggs had begun to temper his radical ideology with the rhetoric of interracial cooperation. Accordingly, during World War I he spoke in the African American community in support of Liberty Bonds.

After publishing his final novel, Griggs devoted his attention to the ministry. He was secretary of the Education Department of the National Baptist Convention in Nashville, Tennessee, and in 1920 he became pastor of the Tabernacle Baptist Church in Memphis. The pastorate gave Griggs another venue for his interest in interracial cooperation; he remained active in the ministry and was president of the American Baptist Theological Seminary from October 1925 to January 1926. He then moved to Houston, Texas, to establish the National Religious and Civic Institute.

MICHELLE TAYLOR

See also Chesnutt, Charles Waddell; Dunbar, Paul Laurence; Survey Graphic

Biography

Sutton Elbert Griggs was born on 19 June 1872, in Chatfield, Texas. He studied at public schools in Dallas, Texas; at Bishop College, Marshall, Texas; and at Richmond Theological Seminary, Richmond, Virgina. He was the founder of Orion Publishing Company, Nashville, Tennessee; president of the American Baptist Theological Seminary; and pastor of Tabernacle Baptist Church, Memphis, Tennessee. Griggs died in Houston, Texas, on 3 January 1933.

Selected Works

Imperium in Imperio. 1899.
Overshadowed. 1901.
Unfettered. 1902.
The Hindered Hand: or, The Reign of the Repressionist. 1905.
The One Great Question. 1907.
Pointing the Way. 1908.
Needs of the South. 1909.
The Race Question in a New Light. 1909. (Enlarged as *Wisdom's Call,* 1911.)
The Story of My Struggle. 1914.
How to Rise. 1915.
Life's Demands; or, According to the Law. 1916.
The Reconstruction of a Race. 1917.
Light on Racial Issues. 1921.
Guide to Racial Greatness; or, The Science of Collective Efficiency. 1923.
The Negro's Next Step. 1923.
Kingdom's Builders' Manual: Companion Book to Guide to Racial Greatness. 1924.
Paths of Progress; or, Cooperation between the Races. 1925.
Triumph of the Simple Virtues; or, the Life Story of John L. Webb. 1926.
The Winning Policy. 1927.

Further Reading

Bell, Bernard. *The Afro-American Novel and Its Tradition.* Amherst: University of Massachusetts Press, 1987.

Elder, Arlene. *The "Hindered Hand": Cultural Implications of Early African American Fiction.* 1978.

Kinney, James. *Amalgamation: Race, Sex, and Rhetoric in the Nineteenth-Century American Novel.* 1985.

Moses, William. *The Golden Age of Black Nationalism, 1850–1925.* New York: Oxford University Press, 1978.

Thompson, Betty Taylor. "Sutton Griggs." In *Dictionary of Literary Biography,* Vol. 50, *African American Writers before the Harlem Renaissance,* eds. Trudier Harris and Tahdious Davis. Detroit, Mich.: Gale Group, 1986.

Tracy, Steven. "Saving the Day: The Recordings of the Reverend Sutton E. Griggs." *Phylon,* 47(2), 1986.

Grimké, Angelina Weld

Angelina Weld Grimké is important to the Harlem Renaissance both as a writer and as a member of an influential, aristocratic Bostonian family. Because she did not produce much work after the mid-1920s, she is often overlooked in present-day critical analysis; however, her drama *Rachel* (1920) is significant as one of the first uses of the stage to directly confront the evil of lynching, and her poetry is significant for its artistry and its themes, including the sometimes repressed expression of lesbian desire.

Grimké was born in Boston in 1880; she was the only daughter of Archibald Henry and Sarah Stanley Grimké, who separated some time in her early childhood, around 1883. Archibald Grimké was the nephew of the famous abolitionist sisters Sarah Moore Grimké and Angelina Grimké Weld; he was an escaped slave and found these aunts after traveling north toward freedom and education. Scholars speculate that Sarah Stanley's prominent white family was against her interracial marriage and that this opposition might have contributed to the separation. After a brief time with her mother, Angelina Weld Grimké returned to her father, a lawyer who was prominent in Boston's elite black community, and never again saw her mother, who died in 1898.

Grimké was exposed to political activism at a young age, in her family circle. She was very much attached to her father and remained so throughout his life. A writer from early childhood, she composed poems dedicated to her family, including her aunt, Charlotte Forten Grimké; and when she was only thirteen years old, her "Tribute to Theodore Weld—On His Ninetieth Birthday" appeared in a local newspaper. After grammar school, she attended several elite academies before graduating in 1902. She started a teaching career at the Armstrong Manual Training School in Washington, D.C., but was unhappy teaching in her major field, physical education. She took classes in English at Harvard during the summers of 1904–1910, switched to teaching English, and in 1907 transferred to the M Street School, where she taught English until she retired in 1933. This school, which became Dunbar High School in 1916, was well known for its academic and artistic training of young black students; Grimké wrote a poem dedicated to it: "To the Dunbar High School," which was published in *Crisis* in 1917.

Grimké was older than many of the most significant writers of the Harlem Renaissance and is distinct in that she lived outside Harlem for most of her life and in that she was already established as a poet before the dates which are generally accepted as the flowering of the renaissance. She was embraced by the renaissance literary community as a poet whose work had gained attention in local black journals, and her recognition escalated during the Harlem Renaissance: her work appeared in journals such as *Crisis* and *Opportunity* and in anthologies published during and after the renaissance, including *Negro Poets and Their Poems* (1923), *The New Negro* (1925), *Caroling Dusk* (1927), and *Negro Caravan* (1941). Perhaps because of her early success publishing poems in journals—according to Hull (1979, 1987), her elegy "El Beso" was called "as perfect as an antique gem in its genre"—Grimké had high hopes for her dramatic writing, most of which remains unpublished. The exception is her play *Rachel*, which is significant not only because of its poignant treatment of lynching but also because it was considered at the time to be the first use of the stage to directly confront racism. Grimké is perhaps best known for this play, which was sponsored by the drama committee of the local National Association for the Advancement of Colored People (NAACP) and was first performed on 3–4 March 1916. Even for its time the play was controversial; some critics held that Rachel's response, on learning that her absent father has been lynched, is exaggerated. Rachel—expressing Grimké's own position—vows never to have children of her own and breaks off her romantic relationship. Despite its dark tone, after its publication in book form in 1920, *Rachel* received many positive reviews and came to be seen as a tragic portrayal of the horror of lynching. In more recent times, the play's characters have seemed overly romanticized, although *Rachel* is still recognized as a historically significant work. Today's audiences tend to dislike the depressing plot and the conclusion—the play ends with a dark stage and a weeping child.

Besides *Rachel* and some nonfiction pieces, including a loving tribute to her father published in *Opportunity* in 1925, Grimké continues to be known for her beautiful, muted lyric poetry. She specialized in imagistic presentations of the natural world to present a mood or theme; and although some of her poetry—such as "Tenebris" and "Beware Lest He Awakes"—addresses racial themes, most of it is about love. Hull (1979, 1987) speculates that the hushed tones and muted colors of Grimké's love poetry, as in "A Mona Lisa" and "When the Green Lies Over the Earth," are a consequence of repressed lesbianism. Many of Grimké's unpublished or recently published works contain explicit references to female lovers and broken romances with women. This repression of her homosexuality appears to have been encouraged by her father, and critics consider the silencing of Grimké's erotic life to have been an influence on the silencing of her artistic life.

Shortly after her father's death in 1930, Grimké retired from teaching and moved to New York City. Her letters indicate that she hoped to return to writing, but she never published again, although she did continue to be a public representative of the Grimké family. Letters indicate also that she became reclusive and somewhat asocial, distrusting even close friends. She died in 1958 after a long illness.

Biography

Angelina Weld Grimké was born on 27 February 1880, in Boston, Massachusetts. She attended public grammar schools in Boston and Hyde Park, Massachusetts, 1887–1994; and several private secondary schools, including Fairmount School in Boston, Carleton Academy in Northfield (Minnesota), Cushing Academy in Ashburnham (Massachusetts), and Girls' Latin School in Boston. She received a degree in physical education from Boston Normal School of Gymnastics in 1902; took summer courses in English at Harvard University, 1904–1910; taught physical education and later English in Washington, D.C., at Armstrong Manual Training School, 1902–1907; and taught English at the M Street High School (renamed Dunbar High School in 1916) from 1907 until her retirement in 1933. She died in New York City on 10 June 1958.

SHARON BARNES

See also Crisis, The; Opportunity; Rachel

Selected Works

"To Keep the Memory of Charlotte Forten Grimké." *Crisis*, 9, January 1915, p. 134.
"To the Dunbar High School." *Crisis*, 13, March 1917, p. 222.
"The Closing Door." *Birth Control Review*, 3, September 1919.
Rachel: A Play in Three Acts. 1920.
"The Black Finger." *Opportunity*, 1, September 1923, p. 343. (Also in *The New Negro: An Interpretation*, ed. Alain Locke. 1925.)
"Little Grey Dreams." *Opportunity*, 2, January 1924, p. 20.
"Dusk." *Opportunity*, 2, April 1924, p. 99.
"I Weep." *Opportunity*, 2, July 1924, p. 196.

"A Biographical Sketch of Archibald H. Grimké." *Opportunity*, 3, February 1925, pp. 44–47.
"Death." *Opportunity*, 3, March 1925, p. 68.
Caroling Dusk, ed. Countee Cullen. 1927.
Readings from Negro Authors, eds. Otelia Cromwell, Lorenzo Dow Turner, and Eva B. Dykes. 1931.
Negro Poets and Their Poems, rev. enlarged ed., ed. Robert T. Kerlin. 1935.
Negro Caravan, eds. Sterling Brown, Arthur P. Davis, and Ulysses Lee. 1941.
Poetry of the Negro, 1746–1949, eds. Langston Hughes and Arna Bontemps. 1949.
Black Writers of America: A Comprehensive Anthology, eds. Richard K. Barksdale and Keneth Kinnamon. 1972.
Poetry of Black America: Anthology of the Twentieth Century, ed. Arnold Adoff. 1973.
New Negro Renaissance: An Anthology, eds. Michael W. Peplow and Arthur P. Davis. 1975.
Black Sister: Poetry by Black American Women, 1746–1980, ed. Erlene Stetson. 1981.
Afro-American Women Writers, 1746–1933, ed. Ann Allen Shockley. 1988.
Selected Works of Angelina Weld Grimké, ed. Carolivia Herron. 1991.
The Sleeper Wakes: Harlem Renaissance Stories by Women, ed. Marcy Knopf. 1993.

Further Reading

Bradley, Gerald. "Goodbye, Mister Bones." *Drama Critique*, 7, Spring 1964, pp. 83–84.
Greene, Michael, "Angelina Weld Grimké." In *Dictionary of Literary Biography*, Vol. 50, *Afro-American Writers before the Harlem Renaissance*, ed. Trudier Harris. Detroit, Mich.: Gale Group, 1986.
Herron, Carolivia, ed. and intro. *Selected Works of Angelina Weld Grimké*. New York and Oxford: Oxford University Press, 1991.
Hull, Gloria T. "Under the Days: The Buried Life and Poetry of Angelina Weld Grimké." *Conditions: Five, Black Women's Issue*, 1979, pp. 17–25.
———. Hull, Gloria T. *Color, Sex, and Poetry: Three Women Writers of the Harlem Renaissance*. Bloomington and Indianapolis: Indiana University Press, 1987.
McKinney, Ernest R. "Rachel: A Play by Angelina W. Grimké." *Competitor*, 1, 1920, pp. 51–52.
Miller, Jeanne-Marie A. "Angelina Weld Grimké." In *Dictionary of Literary Biography*, Vol. 54, *American Poets, 1880–1945, Third Series*, ed. Peter Quatermain. Detroit, Mich.: Gale Group, 1987.

Mollette. "They Speak: Who Listens? Black Women Playwrights." *Black World*, 25, April 1976, pp. 28–34.

Roses, Lorraine Elena, and Ruth Elizabeth Randolph. *Harlem Renaissance and Beyond: Literary Biographies of 100 Black Women Writers, 1900–1945.* Boston, Mass.: G. K. Hall, 1990.

Shockley, Ann Allen. *Afro-American Women Writers, 1746–1933.* Boston, Mass.: G. K. Hall, 1988.

Gruenberg, Louis

The composer Louis Gruenberg, a European-American Jew of prodigious talent, training, and output, is rarely thought of as being part of the Harlem Renaissance. Whether by intent or coincidence, though, Gruenberg's use of jazz and Negro spirituals in his concert music paralleled the hot debates about such use among Harlem Renaissance intellectuals. Furthermore, his most famous work, the controversial opera *The Emperor Jones*, was based on Eugene O'Neill's 1920 play, which had starred the iconic African American performer Paul Robeson.

One of a now-forgotten generation of American "modernist" composers, Gruenberg was a pioneer in his efforts to energize American music through an infusion of rhythms and melodies derived from folk and popular musics of American blacks, whites and "Indians." He believed that a vibrant nationalistic style would result from the inclusion of these "primitive" elements, provided that they were handled with skill and sophistication. He expounded his theories in prominent interwar music journals such as *Modern Music*. He also wrote a good deal of music to prove his point.

Gruenberg was not alone in his attraction to "high-brow jazz." George Gershwin, John Alden Carpenter, Aaron Copeland, and William Grant Still among American composers and Igor Stravinsky, Kurt Weill, Paul Hindemith, Darius Milhaud, and Ernst Krenek among the Europeans were enchanted by the uses of jazz in concert music.

Beginning in 1923, Gruenberg wrote music in the "American idiom" for a wide range of instrumental and vocal forces. His setting of "jazz poet" Vachel Lindsay's poem *Daniel Jazz*, which spoofs the biblical tale of Daniel in the lion's den, was a critical success at its 1925 premier in Venice. *The Creation: a Negro Sermon* tells the familiar Bible story in a colloquial way using a male narrator and eight instrumentalists. Its text, by James Weldon Johnson, was published a year later, in 1927, part of *God's Trombones—Seven Negro Sermons in Verse*. The Gruenberg—Johnson collaboration created a bold and theatrical impact and launched the career of the hitherto unknown African American baritone, Jules Bledsoe.

The pinnacle of Gruenberg's popular success was the opera *The Emperor Jones*, based on Eugene O'Neill's play of a decade earlier. Gruenberg wrote his own libretto with the blessing of O'Neill. Although scheduled to be premiered in Berlin in 1932, it was deemed neither the time nor the place for an opera by a Jew about a black man. Instead, the 77-minute "monodrama" had its premier on 7 January 1933, on a double bill with *Pagliacci* at the Metropolitan Opera House in New York, where *The Emperor Jones* had the longest continuous run of any opera in the Met's history. The white baritone, superstar Lawrence Tibbett, was the protagonist, Brutus Jones, in blackface. Despite that throwback to an American theatrical tradition despised by African Americans, the production did provide jobs, perhaps for the first time, to African American singers. Critical reaction was mixed. Olin Downes of the *New York Times* greatly admired the work, as did Paul Robeson; influential modernist critic Paul Rosenfeld hated it. The opera's reputation for politically incorrect language and plot—a black man's brutality toward other blacks—guarantees that the opera will not be revived often, if at all.

Biography

Louis Gruenberg was born on 22 July/3 August 1884, near Brest-Litovsk, Russia, and emigrated to the United States in 1885. He attended public schools in New York, quitting at age fifteen to become the sole support of his family. He was a child piano prodigy whose earliest music studies were with his father, then at the National Conservatory of Music, New York. He returned to Europe as a teenager to study at the Vienna Conservatory of Music, then at the Berlin State Academy of Music, 1905. He was a piano and composition student of Ferruccio Busoni in Berlin, starting in 1908, but his studies were interrupted by World War I. He made his European debut as a pianist in Berlin, 1912. He abandoned his career as a performer to devote his life to composing and championing modern music in the United States from 1919 on, eventually composing six symphonies, thirty-six other instrumental works, eighteen operas and operettas, and thirteen other vocal works. He helped establish the American Music Guild in 1921 and the League of Composers in 1923. He conducted the American premier of Arnold Schoenberg's *Pierrot Lunaire*, 1923. He was president of the U.S. chapter of the International Society for Contemporary Music during the 1920s. He achieved international fame as composer of the cantata *The Daniel Jazz*, 1925. His best-known work was *The Emperor Jones*, performed eleven times at The Metropolitan Opera, New York, 1933. He was chairman of the Department of Composition at Chicago Musical College, 1933–1936. He moved to California in 1937, where he composed nine film scores and was nominated unsuccessfully for Academy Awards for *The Fight for Life*, 1940; *So Ends Our Night*, 1941; and *Commandos Strike at Dawn*, 1942. He was commissioned by the violin virtuoso Jascha Heifetz to compose *Violin Concerto*, 1944. Awards he received include the New York Philharmonic Flagler Prize for *Hill of Dreams*, 1920; RCA Victor Prize for *Symphony no. 1*, 1930; Bispham Memorial Medal for *The Emperor Jones*, 1933; and Lake Placid Club Prize for *Piano Quintet*, 1937, an award he could not accept in person because the Club barred Jews as members and guests. Gruenberg died in Beverly Hills, California, on 10 June 1964.

HONORA RAPHAEL

See also Emperor Jones, The

Selected Works

Polychromatics, Op. 16. 1923.
The Creation, Op. 21. 1925. (Text by James Weldon Johnson.)
The Daniel Jazz, Op. 23. 1926. (Text by Vachel Lindsay.)
Jazzberries, Op. 25. 1925.
Jazzettes, Op. 26. 1925.
Twenty Negro Spirituals. 1926.
Jazz-Suite, Op. 28. 1929.
Jazz-Masks, Op. 30a. 1929.
Jazz Epigrams, Op. 30b. 1929.
The Emperor Jones, Op. 36. 1931. (After Eugene O'Neill.)
"For an American Gesture." *Modern Music*, 1, June 1924.

Further Reading

Metzer, David. "A Wall of Darkness Dividing the World: Blackness and Whiteness in Louis Gruenberg's 'The Emperor Jones.'" *Cambridge Opera Journal*, 7(1), 1995.
Nisbett, Robert Franklin. "Louis Gruenberg: His Life and Works." Dissertation, Ohio State University, 1979.
———. "Louis Gruenberg's American Idiom." *American Music*, 3(1), 1985.
Oja, Carol. *Making Music Modern*. New York: Oxford University Press, 2000.
Saminsky, Lazare. *Music of the Ghetto and the Bible*. New York: Bloch, 1934.

Guardian, The

In 1901, William Monroe Trotter began a weekly newspaper, the Boston *Guardian*, to add an editorial voice that would speak freely and courageously for the equality of Negro people. The *Guardian* reinvigorated a muted Negro press: editors of other Negro newspapers, who had recently abandoned their militant stances, were inspired and mobilized. The *Guardian* led to the establishment in 1908 of the National Association for the Advancement of Colored People (NAACP).

The *Guardian* was born during what has been described as an "era of reaction and adjustment (1877–1915)" that started when President Rutherford B. Hayes pulled Union soldiers from the South and became the "most dangerous and brutal period for Afro-Americans" (Hughes et al. 1983, 215). This period overlaps with what NAACP has called the "lynching era," from 1889 to 1939; during that period, 2,522 African Americans were lynched. As a result, many editors of the African American press, who had once been outspoken in favor of racial equality, chose to tone down their comments; those who did not were fired or run out of town. One exception was Ida B. Wells, who in 1889 became an editor of the newspaper *Free Speech and Headlight* in Memphis, Tennessee, and made it well known for editorial veracity. She wrote against lynching, but mob violence closed *Free Speech and Headlight* in 1892. The number of lynchings of African Americans reached 115 in 1900 and 130 in 1901, according to the Tuskegee Institute. While lynchings were taking place in the South, race riots broke out as a form of protest in the North. During this chaotic time for African Americans, Booker T. Washington disappointed other Negro leaders by professing "accommodation" and "conciliation," policies that effectively weakened the editorial vigor of the Negro press except for the handful of militant newspapers located in the North.

Trotter's *Guardian*, in a sense, freed the restrained Negro press. Trotter's editorials were scathing attacks on Booker T. Washington: "What man is a worse enemy to a race than a leader who looks with equanimity on the disenfranchisement of his race in a country where other races have universal suffrage by constitutions that make one rule for his race and another for the dominant race" (Toppin 1971, 168). Trotter also attacked other Negro politicians and leaders, such as W. E. B. Du Bois, for failing to speak in unison with him against Washington's philosophy. At that time, Du Bois—a teacher, an author, and editor of *The Crisis*—was considered by many to be "*the* Negro leader," and he believed that Washington's philosophy of accommodation and patience would work if given adequate time. Less than a year later, according to some accounts, Trotter persuaded Du Bois to change that position and become opposed to Washington; although according to other accounts, Du Bois had concluded on his own that Washington's philosophy was not working. In any case, the *Guardian* had allies in the Negro press in its criticism of Washington: the Cleveland *Gazette*, the Chicago *Conservator*, the Richmond *Planet*, the Washington *Bee*, and the *Christian Record*. Trotter died in 1934, but the *Guardian* continued to be published into the 1950s.

GERI ALUMIT

See also Antilynching Crusade; Barnett, Ida B. Wells; Black Press; Du Bois, W. E. B.; National Association for the Advancement of Colored People; Trotter, William Monroe; Washington, Booker T.

Further Reading

Hughes, Langston, Milton Meltzer, and C. Eric Lincoln, *A Pictorial History of Black Americans*. New York: Crown, 1983.

Meier, August. "Booker T. Washington and the Negro Press: With Reference to the *Colored American* Magazine." *Journal of Negro History*, 38, 1953.

Meier, August. *Negro Thought in America, 1880–1915*. Ann Arbor: University of Michigan Press, 1969.

Newkirk, Pamela. *Within the Veil: Black Journalists, White Media*. New York: New York University Press, 2000.

Pride, Armistead S., and Clint C. Wilson II. *A History of the Black Press*. Washington, D.C.: Howard University Press, 1997.

Shannon, Samuel. "Tennessee." In *The Black Press in the South, 1865–1979*, ed. Henry Lewis Suggs. Westport, Conn.: Greenwood, 1983.

Simmons, Charles A. *The African American Press: A History of News Coverage during National Crises, with Special Reference to Four Black Newspapers, 1827–1965*. Jefferson, N.C.: McFarland, 1998.

Toppin, Edgar A. *A Biographical History of Blacks in America since 1528*. New York: David McKay, 1971.

Guggenheim Fellowships

The Guggenheim Fellowships, sponsored by the John Simon Guggenheim Memorial Foundation, are competitive grants (not scholarships) available to advanced professionals pursuing interests in the humanities, the creative arts, and science. A Guggenheim fellowship may be used for a span of six to twelve months and is determined according to the individual needs of the scholar and the scholarly project. These fellowships are intended to provide advanced scholars with financially assisted time to closely examine, do research on, or create an individual endeavor in order to, according to Simon Guggenheim, the father of John Simon Guggenheim, encourage "the advancement and diffusion of knowledge and understanding and the appreciation of beauty." Other Guggenheim foundations also provide substantial monetary gifts: for example, the Solomon Guggenheim Foundation provides grants to support studies of nature and causes of aggression, and the Daniel Guggenheim Foundation provides grants to support aviation and rocketry.

The Guggenheim family has a tradition of humanitarian interests expressed through assistance to artists, scientists, and scholars. Meyer Guggenheim came to America from Switzerland in 1848 and acquired his wealth by importing lace and investing in silver mining in North and South America. John Simon Guggenheim, the grandson of Meyer Guggenheim, died suddenly while he was in college, and a fellowship was then established in his name by his parents. The John Simon Guggenheim foundation was incorporated on 16 March 1925, with an initial endowment of $3 million by Simon Guggenheim. Initially, the Guggenheim fellowships were intended for American citizens only, but Simon Guggenheim expanded eligibility to include Latin Americans by providing additional funding for more fellowships in 1929.

Because of Guggenheim fellowships, several exceptional figures of the Harlem Renaissance were able to develop their talents fully and were able to complete specific artistic and scholarly endeavors. Some of the Guggenheim Foundation's most distinguished fellows were participants in the Harlem Renaissance. Countee Cullen, the second African American fellow, received the award in 1928. He used the fellowship during 1928–1934 to travel back and forth between France and the United States, study, and write. In 1929, shortly after receiving the fellowship, he published *The Black Christ and Other Poems*. The folklorist, novelist, and playwright Zora Neale Hurston received a fellowship in 1936 and 1938 to complete research on folk religions in Jamaica and Haiti. A detailed account of her studies and experiences is represented in *Tell My Horse* (1938). The artist Jacob Lawrence was awarded a Guggenheim fellowship after serving as a steward's mate and combat artist for the U. S. Coast Guard during World War II; in 1946–1947, he painted a series called *War*.

GENYNE HENRY BOSTON

See also Cullen, Countee; Hurston, Zora Neale; Lawrence, Jacob; Philanthopy and Philanthropic Organizations

Further Reading

Bontempts, Arna. *The Harlem Renaissance Remembered.* New York: Dodd, Mead, 1972.

Davis, Arthur. *From the Dark Tower: African-American Writers 1900–1960.* Washington, D.C.: Howard University Press, 1974.

Davis, John Hagy. *The Guggeheims: An American Epic.* New York: Morrow, 1978, p. 276.

Hoyt, Edwin Palmer. *The Guggenheims and the American Dream.* New York: Funk and Wagnalls, 1967.

Hurston, Zora Neale. *Dust Tracks on a Road: An Autobiography.* Philadelphia, Pa.: Lippincott, 1971.

O'Connor, Harvey. *The Guggenheims: The Making of an American Dynasty.* New York: Covici, Friede, 1937.

Gumby Book Studio

In 1926, Levi Sandy Alexander Gumby strutted down Fifth Avenue with "fancy clothes, a perennial walking stick, pale yellow kid gloves, and a diamond stick-pin" (Nugent 2002, 223). Gumby—a onetime butler, bellhop, and songwriter, and at that time a postal clerk—had just moved to "the Avenue," into an enormous second-floor studio between 131st and 132nd streets. Gumby needed a space to accommodate his growing collection of

"rare editions and manuscripts and items for my fast-growing scrapbooks" purchased with "the generosity of [a] staunch friend"—Charles Newman, a wealthy white stockbroker whom Gumby had known since 1910 (Gumby 1951, 5). Gumby's "Book Studio," decorated with a grand piano and Persian carpets, matched the grandeur he admired in things associated with the New Negro. Gumby's salons attracted "friends who brought their friends, regardless of race or color—those who were seriously interested in arts and letters. . . . I daresay that [it] was the first unpremeditated interracial movement in Harlem" (Gumby, 5).

Gumby was also involved in another interracial movement: he and Newman were lovers. Their relationship was evidently tumultuous; in a letter of 1917 Gumby explains, "When I say you're a bitch it's only half what you are." However, such outbursts seem to have complemented Gumby's precise charm (Wirth 2002). Richard Bruce Nugent, whom Gumby called "the one person I don't hafter [sic] pull my punches with," explains that Gumby could "go into fits of rage, of majestic and pompous ire" just as easily as he could deliver one of his raucous, explicit sonnets to great applause" (Nugent 2002, 225; Wirth, 29). Gumby's studio was a magnet for Harlemites, male and female, and their guests. Samuel Steward, a gay white writer and a friend of Gertrude Stein's, remembered "being taken to Gumby's one evening by a lesbian friend and enjoying a delightful evening of 'reefer,' bathtub gin, a game of truth, and homosexual exploits" (Garber 1989, 322).

Gumby was "one of Harlem's reigning dandies"; however, he was also recognized for his meticulous scrapbooks, in which he gave accounts of aspects of black culture that were typically overlooked (Kellner 1987, 147). Aubrey Bower (1930, 20), the book critic of the *New York Amsterdam News*, lauded Gumby as an "indispensable" documentarist "whose patient and unselfish labors fertilize the soil from which grow the flowers of history and letters." In September 1930, a "stag reception" for Countee Cullen, held to celebrate his return to the United States, was also reported in the *Amsterdam News*, complete with a list of attendees, as if they were "movable fixtures in his bright and social art collection" (Nugent, 225).

But this party was one of Gumby's last. He had already sold several first editions because Newman had lost millions in the stock market crash of 1929 and could no longer bankroll soirees. Soon after Gumby closed the Book Studio, he contracted tuberculosis, and although he survived, after four years in the hospital, not all of his collection did. A "gentleman's agreement" to house the collection led to pilfering and partial damage: "two bottom cases were practically paper-mud" (Gumby, 8). Restoring what he could, Gumby continued the collection; he donated it to Columbia University in 1951.

SETH CLARK SILBERMAN

See also Cullen, Countee; Gumby Book Studio Quarterly

Further Reading

Bowser, Aubrey. "English Critic Lauds American Negro Art." *New York Amsterdam News*, 13 August 1930, p. 20.

Garber, Eric. "A Spectacle in Color: The Lesbian and Gay Subculture of Jazz Age Harlem." *Hidden from History: Reclaiming the Gay and Lesbian Past*, eds. Martin Bauml Duberman, Martha Vicinus, and George Chauncey Jr. New York: New American Library, 1989, pp. 318–331.

Gumby, L. S. Alexander. "The Gumby Scrapbook Collection of Negroana." *Columbia Library World*, 5(1), January 1951, pp. 1–8.

Kellner, Bruce. "Gumby, [Levi Sandy] Alexander." In *The Harlem Renaissance: An Historical Dictionary for the Era*. New York: Methuen, 1987, p. 147.

Nugent, Richard Bruce. "On Alexander Gumby." In *Gay Rebel of the Harlem Renaissance: Selections from the Work of Richard Bruce Nugent*, ed. Thomas H. Wirth. Durham, N.C., and London: Duke University Press, 2002, pp. 223–226.

Wirth, Thomas H. "Introduction." In *Gay Rebel of the Harlem Renaissance: Selections from the Work of Richard Bruce Nugent*, ed. Thomas H. Wirth. Durham, N.C., and London: Duke University Press, 2002, pp. 1–61.

Gumby Book Studio Quarterly

Gumby Book Studio Quarterly stands with *Fire!!* and *Harlem* as single-issue literary journals of the Harlem Renaissance appearing during the mid-1920s to early 1930s. The *Gumby Book Studio Quarterly* was a project of the avid bibliophile, scrapbook creator, and popular Harlemite personality Alexander Gumby. Contributors included George Schuyler, Arthur Schomburg, and Richard Bruce Nugent, who submitted the short fictional work "The Tunic with a Thousand Pleats." Gumby was supported by a New York stockbroker who made it possible for him to enhance his book and scrapbook collections. However, that support evaporated after the stock market crash of 1929. This lack of funding, coupled with Gumby's four-year hospitalization for tuberculosis, meant that the *Gumby Book Studio Quarterly* made it only as far as galley proofs, with no distribution. Gumby continued his voluminous scrapbook collection after recovering from tuberculosis, but he abandoned the idea of the journal.

HEATHER MARTIN

See also Gumby Book Studio; Nugent, Richard Bruce

Further Reading

Garber, Eric. "Richard Bruce Nugent." In *Dictionary of Literary Biography*, Vol. 51, *Afro-American Writers from the Harlem Renaissance to 1940*, ed. Trudier Harris. Detroit, Mich.: Gale Research, 1987.

"L. S. Alexander Gumby Is Dead; Compiled Scrapbooks on Negro." *New York Times*, 18 March 1961.

Nugent, Bruce. *Gay Rebel of the Harlem Renaissance: Selections from the Work of Richard Bruce Nugent*, ed. and intro. Thomas H. Wirth. Durham, N.C.: Duke University Press, 2002.

Hall, Adelaide

Early in her career, Adelaide Hall was a member of J. Homer Tutt and Salem Tutt Whitney's troupe, appearing in several of their original musicals. Her first appearance on Broadway was in Sissle and Blake's *Shuffle Along* (1921); she sang and danced as one of eight Jazz Jasmines, and also sang a solo in the up-tempo number "Bandana Days." Her success in that musical led to a featured role in Miller and Lyles's hit *Runnin' Wild* (1923), in which she sang James P. Johnson's "Love Bug," "Old-Fashioned Love," and "Ginger Brown." In 1925, Hall had a major success at the famous Club Alabam in New York City. She then joined the cast of Sam Wooding's *Chocolate Kiddies*, which toured in Europe for about a year and was especially well received in London. During her European tour, Hall met Bert Hicks, a Trinidadian who was an officer in the merchant navy; he became her husband and manager. On their return to the United States in 1926, Hall joined the cast of *Tan Town Topics*, where she appeared with Florence Mills's sister Maude, Ralph Cooper, and Thomas "Fats" Waller and his band. Hall's next show, *Desires of 1927*, with music and lyrics by J. C. Johnson and Andy Razaf, toured from October 1926 through early 1927 and reunited her with J. Homer Tutt. During the latter part of that year, she joined the RKO circuit and appeared with Duke Ellington and his band in *Jazzmania* and *Dance Mania*. Hall's first recording, a wordless obligato to Ellington's "Creole Love Call," was the result of her humming a counter-melody during a performance of the piece. Ellington liked her improvisation and recorded it several days later.

After the tragic and unexpected death of Florence Mills, Hall was chosen to star in Lew Leslie's *Blackbirds of 1928*, with a cast that included Bill Robinson, Mantan Moreland, Aida Ward, Tim Moore, and the Cecil Mack Choir. Hall sang several of Jimmy McHugh and Dorothy Fields's hit songs, including "Diga, Diga, Do" and "I Can't Give You Anything but Love." She toured with the show in Europe and remained in Paris after it closed, to star at the Moulin Rouge and at the Lido. Hall rivaled Josephine Baker as the leading African American entertainer in Paris. In 1930, she returned to New York to appear in *Brown Buddies*. On returning to Paris in 1936, she and her husband opened La Grosse Pomme, a club on Rue Pigalle. After they moved to London in 1938, they opened the Florida Club, which was destroyed during the blitz in World War II.

Hall appeared in several film shorts, including *Dancers in the Dark* (1932), *All Colored Vaudeville Show* (1935), and *Dixieland Jamboree* (1935). Although her later career was based mainly in London, she returned to New York to appear with Lena Horne in *Jamaica* (1957). On her return to London, she and her husband opened another club, the Calypso. During the last decade of her life, Hall toured in a one-woman show, which was seen in New York in 1988 and 1992.

Biography

Adelaide Hall was born in Brooklyn, New York, possibly on 20 October 1901. Hall's birth date is not certain; in 1991, in an interview, she said she was ninety years old, but several sources list her birth date as 1904. Her father was a German and African American music teacher (he taught at Pratt Institute); her mother, Elizabeth Gerrard, was African American and American Indian. During the 1910s, the family moved to Harlem. As children, Hall and her younger sister, Eileen, sang at various events. Early in her career, Hall was a member of J. Homer Tutt and Salem Tutt Whitney's troupe; she made her Broadway debut in *Shuffle Along* (1921) and appeared in Miller and Lyles's *Runnin' Wild* (1923). She performed at Club Alabam (1925) and in *Chocolate Kiddies*. Her other shows included *Tan Town Topics* (1926), *Desires of 1927*, and *Blackbirds of 1928*. Hall performed and recorded with Duke Ellington and appeared in several film shorts. She was married to Bert Hicks. She died on 7 November 1993.

JOHN GRAZIANO

See also Baker, Josephine; Blackbirds; Ellington, Duke; Europe and the Harlem Renaissance: 3—London; Fields, Dorothy; Musical Theater; Shuffle Along; Singers

Further Reading

Bourne, Stephen. *Sophisticated Lady: A Celebration of Adelaide Hall*. London: Lilla Huset, 2001.

Commire, Anne, ed. *Women in World History: A Biographical Encyclopedia*. Detroit, Mich.: Gale Group, 1999.

Garraty, John A., and Mark C. Carnes, eds. *American National Biography*. New York: Oxford University Press, 1999.

Hine, Darlene Clark. *Women in America: An Historical Encyclopedia*. Brooklyn, N.Y.: Carlson, 1993.

Smith, Jessie Carney, ed. *Notable Black American Women*. Detroit, Mich.: Gale Research, 1992.

Southern, Eileen. *Biographical Dictionary of Afro-American and African Musicians*. Westport, Conn.: Greenwood, 1982.

Tucker, Mark. *Ellington: The Early Years*. Urbana: University of Illinois Press, 1991.

Hallelujah

King Vidor and Metro-Goldwyn-Mayer released the film *Hallelujah* (or *Hallelujah!*) in 1929, on the heels of *Hearts in Dixie*, the first musical from a major Hollywood studio that had an all-black cast. Writing years later, Vidor said of *Hallelujah*, "I wanted to make a film about Negroes, using only Negroes in the cast. The sincerity and fervor of their religious expression intrigued me,

as did the honest simplicity of their sexual drives." Both of these essentialist beliefs are readily apparent in the film. Nonetheless, *Hallelujah* broke away from the stock character roles generally reserved for African American actors, and this encouraged black leaders, including W. E. B. Du Bois, to comment favorably that the production had moved away from "buffoonery."

Hallelujah tells the story of a young man from the country, Zekiel, or Zeke (played by Daniel Haynes), who goes to the city to sell his family's cotton crop. There he meets a slick city woman named Chick (Nina Mae McKinney), who—along with her lover, Hot Shot (William Fountaine)—conspires to relieve Zeke of the money he has just been paid for his family's cotton. A fixed crap game leads to a fight between Hot Shot and Zeke, culminating in the accidental death of Zeke's brother Spunk (Everett McGarity). Filled with remorse, Zeke repents and, with the guidance of his father (Harry Gray), a pastor, becomes a minister himself.

Zeke and his family take to the road, holding revival meetings and baptisms. When Zeke encounters Chick in the midst of his crusade, he convinces her of her own sinful nature. Chick repents, but her religious ecstasy is reminiscent of her sexual ecstasy, and Zeke again falls under her spell. Zeke attempts to escape his lust by proposing to a "good girl," Missy Rose (Victoria Spivey). Missy Rose's purity, however, is not enough to keep Zeke from Chick. During one of his own evening services, he runs off to the city with Chick. Months later, Chick is restless and attempts to leave with Hot Shot. In the subsequent chase, Chick is thrown from her carriage and dies; Zeke then hunts down Hot Shot and strangles him. Following his prison sentence, Zeke returns to his country home, where his family welcomes him with open arms and he is reunited with Missy Rose.

Vidor used several traditional songs—"Swing Low, Sweet Chariot," "Let My People Go," "Ol' Time Religion"—as a musical backdrop for the film. The songs themselves usually echoed the onscreen action, but they rarely forwarded the plot. Vidor hired the Dixie Jubilee Singers to perform these standards. He relied on the leading actors, however, to sing two tunes by George Gershwin. Zeke sings "At the End of the Road" while waiting to gin his family's cotton, and Chick sings "Swanee Shuffle" in a local club. Only the youngest actors (Milton Dickerson, Robert Couch, and Walter Tait), playing Zeke's siblings, showcase their talent as dancers in a spontaneous celebration outside their home.

Vidor recruited the actors for his film in Chicago and Harlem. The *New York Times* found the subject captivating enough to devote a story to the process of "Finding Screen Negroes." Unable to secure Paul Robeson for the lead, Vidor turned to another actor, Daniel Haynes, who had graduated from Morris Brown University before appearing in several roles on Broadway. Haynes's voice and physique fit Vidor's conception of Zeke, and he was cast. For the role of Chick, Vidor had originally selected Honey Brown. When she became ill on the set of the film, Vidor sent for Nina Mae McKinney, his second choice. McKinney's performance impressed Vidor, and she was retained by MGM.

Most of *Hallelujah* was filmed on location in Tennessee and Arkansas. Vidor captured footage of his actors in local cotton fields, cotton gins, and sawmills to provide the background for the story. He also utilized the human resources of his locations, calling on African-Americans to help him design and implement the mass baptism scene. Four pastors answered Vidor's call and brought their congregations to serve as extras. Vidor also hired Harold Garrison, an African American employee of MGM, as an assistant director to help shape the production.

The actors and the film received generally positive reviews. W. E. B. Du Bois wrote of *Hallelujah*:

> It is the sense of real life without the exaggerated farce and horseplay . . . which most managers regard as inseparable from the Negro character that marks *Hallelujah* as epoch-making. . . . The music was lovely and while I would have preferred more spirituals instead of the theme-song, yet the world is not as crazy about Negro talk songs as I am. Everybody should see *Hallelujah*.

The reviewer for the *New York Times*, Mordaunt Hall, said that *Hallelujah* was a "most impressive audible film" and in a separate article praised the "clever negro cast."

Nonetheless, Vidor and MGM had difficulty finding theaters to show the film. Southern theater owners were hesitant to show the "all-black" musical, and northern theater owners were concerned that a "preponderance" of African-Americans might drive away white customers. Vidor offered to give the owner of a large theater chain in Florida a check for $1,000 if the owner showed *Hallelujah* and it did not perform well. The owner agreed, and the film succeeded. Despite these small victories, MGM struggled to distribute the film, and the financial returns were limited.

Some of the religious and sexual themes Vidor explored in this film had previously been examined by

an independent black filmmaker, Oscar Micheaux. In his film *Body and Soul* (1924), Micheaux told the story of a corrupt minister. Micheaux's film, however, was much darker than *Hallelujah*, and his minister (named Jenkins), in contrast to Zeke, is not misguided but evil. *The Green Pastures*, first as a play on Broadway (1930) and then as a Hollywood movie (1936), followed in the tradition of *Hallelujah* with its fascination with and romanticization of "Negro religion."

DANIELLE BRUNE

See also Film; Film: Actors; Film: Blacks as Portrayed by White Filmmakers; Gershwin, George; Green Pastures, The; McKinney, Nina Mae; Micheaux, Oscar

Further Reading

Cripps, Thomas. *Slow Fade to Black*. New York: Oxford University Press, 1977.

Kisch, John, and Edward Mapp. *A Separate Cinema*. New York: Farrar, Straus and Giroux, 1992, p. xx.

Vidor, King. *A Tree Is a Tree*. New York: Garland, 1972, p. 175. (Originally published 1952, 1953.)

Hamid, Sufi Abdul

In 1932, Bishop Amiru Al-Minin Sufi Abdul Hamid—after having succeeded with a similar campaign in Chicago earlier that year under the alias Bishop Conshankin—formed the Negro Industrial and Clerical Alliance in Harlem and began once again to publicize the slogan "Don't buy where you can't work." Hamid captured the attention of Harlemites with his outrageous dress, appearing beturbaned and in a mélange of national costumes; and he earned the appellation "black Hitler" in both the black and the white press with his rhetoric of black nationalism and virulent anti-Semitism. (According to some reports, "black Hitler" was a title he gave himself.)

Hamid achieved success in 1934 with his boycotts of jobs, which had the objective of procuring positions for black clerks in department stores and five-and-ten stores owned and operated by whites in Harlem. The same year, however, he lost control of the coalition of groups of activists that had been formed for these campaigns to the more respectable Harlem Citizens League for Fair Play. Shortly thereafter, in October 1934, Hamid faced charges of disorderly conduct, brought against him by the Jewish Minutemen of America and the white Harlem Merchants' Association for allegedly advocating "war against the Jews" (McDowell 1998, 228). Although Hamid was cleared of these charges, he was unofficially blamed for a riot that took place in Harlem on 19 March 1935. Claude McKay (1935a) then took up Hamid's cause in an article in *The Nation*, "Harlem Runs Wild." McKay believed that the riot and the condemnation of Sufi Abdul Hamid indicated pressure points—points at which a combination of black and white liberals and radicals were attempting to suppress a positive, nationalist black labor movement. During the 1930s, McKay wrote often and passionately on Hamid and Hamid's cause.

Biography

Sufi Abdul Hamid was born in the shadow of an Egyptian pyramid on 6 January 1903—a fact for which his parole officer produced documentation at one of Hamid's many legal trials. Actually, his origins are obscure. Police at the scene of his death, a plane crash on Long Island on 31 July 1938, gave his real name as Eugene Brown and his address as Lombard Street, Philadelphia. Lewis (1981, 300) traced Hamid to Lowell, Massachusetts. In 1930, Hamid founded, in Harlem, the Universal Temple of Tranquillity; in 1932, he led a successful boycott of jobs in Chicago and began boycotting merchants in Harlem; in February 1934, as part of a coalition of activist groups, he organized a successful boycott of Blumstein's department store. However, he had legal woes, and among African American intellectuals he developed a reputation (perhaps deserved) as a charlatan and a racketeer; both his legal difficulties and this reputation effectively neutralized him as a force in Harlem's labor politics. During the late 1930s, he turned to experiences as a cultist, relying on the mystical and hoping to challenge Father Divine's standing as the premier cultic figure in Harlem.

MARK CHRISTIAN THOMPSON

See also Father Divine; McKay, Claude; Riots: 4—Harlem Riot, 1935

Further Reading

Greenberg, Cheryl Lynn. *"Or Does It Explode": Black Harlem in the Great Depression*. New York: Oxford University Press, 1997.

Hunter, Jerome. "'Don't Buy Where You Can't Work': Black Union Boycott Movements During the Depression, 1929–1941." Ph.D. dissertation, University of Michigan, 1977.

Lewis, David Levering. *When Harlem Was in Vogue*. New York: Random House, 1981.

McDowell, Winston C. "Keeping Them 'In the Same Boat Together'? Sufi Abdul Hamid, African Americans, Jews, and the Harlem Jobs Boycotts." In *African Americans and Jews in the Twentieth Century*. Columbia, Mo., University of Missouri Press, 1998, pp. 208–236.

McKay, Claude. "Harlem Runs Wild." *Nation*, 140, 3 April 1935a, pp. 382–383.

———. Interview with Sufi Abdul Hamid. *Nation*, 140, 3 April 1935b, p. 383.

———. *Harlem: Negro Metropolis*. New York: Dutton, 1940.

Ottley, Roi. *New World a-Comin': Inside Black America*. New York: Arno, 1968. (Originally published 1943.)

Solomon, Mark. *The Cry Was Unity: Communists and African Americans, 1917–1936*. Jackson: University Press of Mississippi, 1998.

Weisbrot, Robert. *Father Divine*. Boston, Mass.: Beacon, 1984.

Handy, W. C.

William Christopher (W. C.) Handy was born in Florence, Alabama, in 1873. His early musical education was exclusively in vocal music—traditional hymns and classical sacred works rather than Negro spirituals. Instrumental music was disallowed, but the vocal training gave him a very keen ear. By the time Handy finished school, he had secretly learned to play the cornet and found casual work with a local dance band.

In 1896, after various odd jobs, he joined the band of a white-owned black troupe, Mahara's Minstrels, that introduced him to the world of black minstrelsy, ragtime, and black popular music. Handy soon became an established bandleader in this field. Extensive travel brought him into contact with leading black musicians and entertainers and gave him an opportunity to visit Cuba, where he absorbed elements of local Latin music. He stayed with Mahara's Minstrels until 1903, apart from an interlude as musical director of the Agricultural and Mechanical College in Huntsville, Alabama, a forerunner of Tuskegee College.

Handy married Elizabeth Price in Kentucky in 1898. By 1903, with young children to support, they needed to settle down. Handy felt drawn to the South and settled, as musical director of the local black band, in Clarksdale, Mississippi, in the heart of the Delta region, a home of traditional blues.

Handy now considered himself a composer as well as a bandleader. He traveled widely in the region, and his sharp ear recognized a unique music style among nomadic blues singers of the Delta. He also observed the excitement that these "blues" aroused in people who merely listened politely to his own conventional music. He decided to use blues motifs in his own compositions, and he met with instant success.

His first blues piece, "Mr. Crump" (1909), was a satirical comment on a politician in Memphis, Boss Crump, who adopted it as the theme song of a successful mayoral campaign. Handy was inundated with requests for copies and had sheet music published in 1912 as "Memphis Blues." It sold hugely, but he was duped into selling his copyright for a mere $500. This experience taught him a lifelong lesson; one result was the establishment of the Pace and Handy Music Company, publishers of sheet music.

Handy had been friendly with the banker Harry Pace since 1907, and Pace had supplied words to several of Handy's compositions. Their first publication, in 1913, was Handy's "Jogo Blues," later rewritten as the phenomenally successful "Saint Louis Blues." Before long it was followed by "Beale Street Blues," and then by many more works over the next decade. In 1917, Handy's Memphis Orchestra went to New York for a recording session at Columbia.

New York was a growth area for black music, with pre-jazz orchestras like that of James Reese Europe. Harlem was its musical center, with stride pianists like James P. Johnson. Handy's music was well known there. In 1918, Pace and Handy moved to Harlem, taking up residence in swanky Strivers' Row. Handy played an active role in the musical life of Harlem and became a respected figure, but his business had its ups and downs.

In 1921, Pace was frustrated by the unwillingness of white-owned record companies to record black artists. He resigned from Pace and Handy to found Black Swan Records, intending to record black performers exclusively. Handy, who was not part of the recording company, re-formed the publishing company with his brother Charles. Handy Brothers Music Company had heavy debts, and Handy developed

serious eye problems that temporarily blinded him and left him severely visually impaired for the rest of his life. However, with his music rights, and with some help from friends, the company survived its problems.

Handy remained an active composer and performer. In 1926 he cowrote a book, the comprehensive survey *Blues: An Anthology*. In 1928 he presented a concert representing the "full spectrum of black music" at Carnegie Hall. In later years he turned to spirituals as a source of inspiration, publishing a *Collection of Negro Spirituals* in 1938.

Throughout the 1930s Handy toured and performed; he played at the Apollo Theater in Harlem in 1936. A concert was held at Carnegie Hall to commemorate his sixty-fifth birthday. In 1937 he became a founding member of the Negro Actors' Guild. He published his autobiography, *Father of the Blues*, in 1941. In 1943 he suffered a fall on a subway in New York and was seriously injured; this injury reduced his activities. Handy died in 1958.

Handy was much honored during his lifetime and afterward. In 1931, Memphis constructed Handy Park on Beale Street, and a statue was erected in 1960. There was a film, *Saint Louis Blues* (1958), based loosely on his life; and a commemorative postage stamp was issued in 1969. The Blues Foundation established the W. C. Handy Blues Awards in 1980. Handy's hometown—Florence, Alabama—built a museum in his honor.

Some lovers of blues question Handy's credentials in this area, accusing him of copying and commercializing music that was already in the public domain. Although he adopted the title "father of the blues," Handy never claimed to have "invented" blues. He always acknowledged that he had drawn on an existing folk heritage, considering himself a composer in that idiom. He adapted elements of traditional blues and transformed or embellished them—as in his subtle use of Latin motifs in "Memphis Blues" and "St. Louis Blues"—to create a blues-based variant of the American popular song.

Handy's successful commercial exploitation of the blues idiom paved the way for later breakthroughs by black female blues singers. This development began with Mamie Smith's recording of "Crazy Blues" in 1920 and culminated with the successes of Bessie Smith. By succeeding in business, Handy showed that black composers and artists could be masters of their own destiny in a world dominated by whites. He was a staunch champion of the talents of black musicians.

W. C. Handy, C. 1940s; the sheet music on the piano is "Saint Louis Blues." (Schomburg Center for Research in Black Culture, New York Public Library.)

In 1935, he wrote and published *Negro Authors and Composers of the United States*, and in 1944 he published *Unsung Americans Sung*, a tribute to underappreciated black musical figures. He contributed greatly to the status of black music as a major factor in American—and world—popular culture during and after the Harlem Renaissance. "Saint Louis Blues" is perhaps the world's best-known piece of American music.

Biography

William Christopher Handy was born on 16 November 1873, in Florence, Alabama, to Charles Bernard Handy, a minister, and Elizabeth Brewer, both freed slaves. He studied at the Florence District School for Negroes. He was a schoolteacher in Birmingham, Alabama (1892) and held various other jobs (1892–1896). He joined Mahara's minstrel troupe in 1896, married in 1898, and visited Cuba with the Mahara troupe in 1900. Handy was musical director at Agricultural and Mechanical College, Huntsville, Alabama (1900–1902), then rejoined Mahara as bandleader (1902). He was director of the Knights of Pythias Band in Clarksdale, Mississippi, in 1903. He moved to Memphis c. 1906. He established Pace and Handy Music Company in 1913; this company moved to New York in 1918. When Pace and Handy split up, Handy formed Handy Brothers Music Company (1921). He presented a concert of black music at Carnegie Hall in 1928. Handy Park was opened in Memphis in 1931. Handy was a founding member of the Negro Actors' Guild

(1937). His sixty-fifth birthday was commemorated at Carnegie Hall in 1938. Handy died in New York City on 28 March 1958; he is buried in Woodlawn Cemetery, Bronx, New York.

BILL EGAN

See also Black Manhattan; Black Swan Phonograph Company; Blues; Blues: An Anthology; Clef Club; Covarrubias, Miguel; Europe, James Reese; Hunter, Alberta; Jazz; Music; Music: Bands and Orchestras; Pace, Harry H.; Pace Phonographic Company; Saint Louis Blues; Smith, Bessie; Smith, Mamie; Still, William Grant; Strivers' Row

Selected Works

Blues: An Anthology. 1926. (Rev. ed., 1972.)
Negro Authors and Composers of the United States. 1935.
W. C. Handy's Collection of Negro Spirituals. 1938.
Father of the Blues: An Autobiography. 1941.
Unsung Americans Sung. 1944.

Further Reading

Carlin, Richard. "Handy, W. C." In *The American National Biography*, Vol. 10, ed. John A. Garraty and Mark C. Carnes. New York: Oxford University Press, 1999.

Davis, Francis. *The History of the Blues*. London: Secker and Warburg, 1995.

Floyd, Samuel A. Jr. *The Power of Black Music*. New York and Oxford: Oxford University Press, 1995, pp. 108–109.

Handy, D. Antoinette, "W. C. Handy." In *Black Heroes of the Twentieth Century*, ed. Jessie Carney Smith. Detroit, New York, Toronto, and London: Visible Ink, 1998.

Handy, W. C. *Father of the Blues: An Autobiography*, New York: Handy Brothers, 1941. (Also, New York: Collier, 1970. Includes a full list of Handy's musical compositions and arrangements up to 1940.)

Locke, Alain. *The Negro and His Music: Negro Art Past and Present*. New York: Arno and New York Times, 1969, ch. 9.

Southern, Eileen. *The Music of Black Americans: A History*, 3rd ed. New York and London: Norton, 1997.

Stearns, Marshall W. *The Story of Jazz*. London, Oxford, and New York: Oxford University Press, 1956. (Rev. ed. 1972.)

Vincent, Ted. *Keep Cool: The Black Activists Who Built the Jazz Age.* London, and East Haven, Conn.: Pluto, 1995, ch. 2. (See "W. C. Handy, the Blues, and Black Struggle.")

Harcourt Brace

Harcourt Brace was founded on 29 July 1919, in New York City, by Alfred Harcourt and Donald Brace, both of whom had worked for Henry Holt and Company for fifteen years. Harcourt had managed to bring Carl Sandburg, Robert Frost, and W. E. B. Du Bois to Holt, but had struggled to do so in an environment that he felt stifled creativity. Having developed a contentious relationship with the Holt family and having become convinced that he would not be able to publish books exploring "new ideas" if he remained at Holt, Harcourt decided to leave. He was encouraged to start his own publishing house by Sinclair Lewis, whom he had known through Holt and whose novels became some of Harcourt Brace's best-sellers during the 1920s.

Along with the publishing houses run by Alfred A. Knopf, Ben Huebsch, and Boni and Liveright, Harcourt Brace sought to rewrite American culture through the publication of texts that would move the seat of American literature from Boston to New York and counter the Anglocentricity that dominated the publishing industry, even in older New York houses. Because the editors at Harcourt Brace were committed to change and diversity, they embraced African American writing from the inception of the firm. Harcourt Brace had fewer connections with the avant-garde than Boni and Liveright or Knopf but nonetheless was committed to pushing the boundaries of current publishing trends.

Harcourt's plan for developing a list of titles was based on the personal taste and connections of his top staff members. Each staff member would attract writers in his or her own area of interest, and these areas would eventually become focus areas for the house as a whole. Joel Spingarn, who served as vice president and literary adviser for Harcourt Brace, was instrumental in its development as a firm dedicated to publishing African American texts. Spingarn had been a professor at Columbia University, was a civil rights activist, and was a founding member of the National Association for the Advancement of Colored People (NAACP). Promoting the works of new African American writers through Harcourt Brace fit well with Spingarn's personal mission of national cultural advancement through a multicultural agenda.

Notably, Spingarn's vision of African American writing was not limited by the distinction between high art and propaganda that motivated the choices made by some other publishing houses. Spingarn did support the publication of books that excelled as propaganda, even if they were less than successful aesthetically, but under his guidance Harcourt Brace became known for publishing a wide variety of texts by black writers. James Weldon Johnson's *Book of American Negro Poetry*, Claude McKay's *Spring in New Hampshire* and *Harlem Shadows*, Arna Bontemps' *God Sends Sunday*, and Sterling Brown's *Southern Road* are among the books Harcourt Brace published during the Harlem Renaissance. However, as Hutchinson (1995, 377) comments, a listing of works published by Harcourt Brace during this period cannot adequately convey the extent of the firm's intertextual commitment to African American art. More than any other firm, Harcourt Brace was committed to representing the rich intertextual diversity of the Harlem Renaissance.

AMANDA M. LAWRENCE

See also Boni and Liveright; Bontemps, Arna; Brown, Sterling; Johnson, James Weldon; Knopf, Alfred A.; McKay, Claude; Publishers and Publishing Houses; Spingarn, Joel

Further Reading

Dzwonkoski, Elizabeth. "Harcourt Brace." In *American Literary Publishing Houses, 1900–1980*, 2 vols., ed. Elizabeth Dzwonkoski. Detroit, Mich.: Gale Research, 1986, pp. 180–183.

Hutchinson, George. *The Harlem Renaissance in Black and White.* Cambridge, Mass.: Belknap Press of Harvard University Press, 1995.

Wintz, Cary D. *Black Culture and the Harlem Renaissance.* Houston, Tex.: Rice University Press, 1988.

Harlem: 1—Overview and History

On 17 February 1919, the black 369th Regiment (Fifteenth Infantry), returning home after heroic service in France in World War I, marched up Fifth Avenue and through Harlem to the cheers of thousands of Harlemites. African-Americans to a great extent had taken the advice of W. E. B. Du Bois, who, in an editorial in *The Crisis*, had urged them to "close ranks" and support the war effort, with the idea that their country would no longer deny their claim to equal rights. For many African-Americans, their wartime sacrifices, their move into the heretofore middle-class white preserve of Harlem, and even the retaliatory self-defense of black communities attacked by white mobs signaled the birth of a "New Negro." Many people in Harlem found cause for optimism during the ensuing decade, as white publishing houses discovered talented young black writers, Broadway discovered African American culture, and white tourists discovered Harlem's nightlife.

Harlem was the unofficial political and cultural capital of Afro-America in the first half of the twentieth century, and especially in the 1920s. During this decade, Harlem became America's most populous urban center; was the headquarters of black nationalism, embodied in Marcus Garvey's Universal Negro Improvement Association (UNIA); and was a magnet for black artists from the southern United States, South America, the Caribbean, and other parts of the world. Its artistic productions generated audiences throughout the Americas, the Caribbean, Africa, and Europe, as they still do today; and the writers, musicians, and visual artists of the Harlem Renaissance have become part of the American cultural canon. In many ways, the period of the Harlem Renaissance, although it was filled with promise, could provide only partial deliverance from racial barriers, or from the stereotypes and oppressive conditions that were tolerated by what some people called "Old Negro" thinking. The glittering popular image of Harlem in the 1920s was a reality for some residents but a more complicated situation, or even a mirage, for many others, especially the ordinary working population. But blacks still came to Harlem. For southern black migrants seeking relief from segregation, political disenfranchisement, and grinding rural poverty, Harlem was an oasis. For the growing foreign-born black population of New York, Harlem held out the possibility of greater economic advancement than they could achieve in their various Caribbean homelands.

The African presence in New York dates back to the era of Dutch control and the naming of the city, New Amsterdam, in the 1620s; but blacks' residence in Harlem was relatively new. By 1840, the center of the black population shifted from the lower tip of Manhattan between Cedar and Canal streets to the infamous squalor of the Five Points district. Twenty years later, Five Points had become overwhelmingly Irish, and most New York blacks were living in the southern portion of Greenwich Village. By 1900, this part of the Village had become predominantly Italian, and most of its black population had continued to move northward up the West Side to the Tenderloin district, which extended from the West Twenties to the West Fifties; and to the San Juan Hill neighborhood, in the West Sixties. Then, black real estate agencies, like Philip Payton's Afro-American Realty Company and Nail and Parker's firm, seized the opportunity when landlords in Harlem needed to fill vacancies in their apartment buildings—a situation that was created by a housing boom in conjunction with the extension of the subway system to Harlem. Soon black churches, such as Abyssinian Baptist, were following their parishioners and acquiring or building edifices in Harlem.

It was a source of pride for African-Americans to move into a previously all-white area with housing stock far superior to what was available anywhere they had lived before in New York City. The writer James Weldon Johnson—who was also a diplomat and an official of the National Association for the Advancement of Colored People (NAACP)—reflected the optimism to be gained from living in an area "situated in the heart of Manhattan," which "is not a slum, nor is it a 'quarter' consisting of dilapidated tenements." Harlem, according to Johnson, had "streets as well paved, as well lighted, and as well kept as any other part of the city." This was a significant difference from earlier black neighborhoods in Manhattan. For blacks—to repeat—housing in Harlem was clearly an improvement over their previous living conditions. Yet although Johnson hoped that by moving uptown, blacks had left the slums behind, regression and stagnation would eventually create slum conditions in parts of Harlem too.

By 1920, 70 percent of the African American population of Manhattan lived between 118th Street and 144th Street, from the Harlem River to the Hudson River. Ten years later, half of the city's black population would live in Harlem. The black community grew in numbers from 83,000 in 1920 to 204,000 in 1934. Between 1910 and 1930, while Manhattan's white population decreased by 633,249, the black population increased by 154,135. Eventually, black New Yorkers found it extremely difficult to obtain housing outside Harlem; consequently, they would pay more for housing than their white counterparts. In Manhattan, the density rate for blacks was 336 people per acre—significantly higher than the rate for whites, 222 per acre. The high population density in Harlem contributed to the deterioration of the housing stock, as apartments were cut into smaller units to accommodate demand and maximize the building owners' profits. By 1938, the median rental for vacant apartments in Harlem had reached $30 per month, compared with $18 per month for Manhattan in general.

Housing congestion took its toll on the health of Harlemites, who had higher rates of communicable diseases and higher mortality rates. For example, for New York City as a whole, the death rate from tuberculosis was 76 per 100,000 people, but the rate for Harlem was 183 per 100,000 between 1923 and 1927. For New York City, the mortality rate from pneumonia was 124 per 100,000; the rate for Harlem was 244 per 100,000. Thus health and life expectancy were considerably reduced for blacks in Harlem—as they had been in earlier decades for blacks in other parts of the city. No doubt, a lack of access to better health care and the exclusion of black patients and physicians from New York's hospitals, other than Harlem Hospital, contributed to this problem. Pressure from the black community had forced a reorganization of Harlem Hospital and the integration of its medical staff. But this change, like so many changes in Harlem, did not transform the delivery of health services, which remained inadequate and unequal.

For black migrants, wages and employment conditions in urban America were an improvement over their occupations in the South as sharecroppers, tenant farmers, and low-wage workers. Yet the situation in the North for many African-Americans proved ambiguous during the 1920s. The number of black professionals in New York doubled in the 1920s, and from 1910 through 1930, black males in Manhattan consistently had a higher rate of employment than their white counterparts. In 1930, 88.6 percent of black males living in Manhattan had jobs, compared with 87.1 percent of white males. In the 1920s, then, the lack of a job was not a great problem; rather, the low-paying jobs that many African-Americans found themselves in made it difficult to make ends meet and pay the rent. The people who held "rent parties" in Harlem in the 1920s, to raise money to pay their landlords, were often employed, but their wages were insufficient to meet the cost of housing and food.

As late as 1935, businesses owned by blacks constituted only 18.6 percent of the total number of businesses in Harlem. Black enterprises tended to be services such as barbershops, beauty salons, and funeral parlors, and they tended to be smaller and less profitable than the larger individually owned white businesses or white chain stores. Department stores in Harlem's main business districts, such as 125th Street, did not hire black managers or even black sales clerks. African Americans were excluded from all but janitorial jobs with the city subways, bus companies, utility companies, and telephone companies; and blacks were nearly totally excluded from the police and fire departments. Thus many people came to regard black Harlemites as, in a sense, a colonized people banned from the colonizers' institutions and economic life.

Similarly, many residents of Harlem felt excluded from the political life of the city, and even from the political life of their own community. Black members of the Democratic Party in New York City had no significant influence. In 1898, the Democratic leadership—known as Tammany Hall—formed a segregated auxiliary exclusively for African Americans, called the United Colored Democracy. It was a citywide organization, however, and therefore was unable to compete for political power and patronage, which remained at the district level, in the hands of white district leaders. The Republican Party did not segregate blacks in a separate auxiliary, but neither did it allow any black district leaders to emerge in Harlem. African American Republicans, discontented with their exclusion, organized the United Civic League in 1913 to push for greater inclusion in the party and black candidates for elective office. Two of the league's candidates were elected to office: Edward A. Johnson, a black lawyer, was elected assemblyman from Harlem's Nineteenth District; and in 1918, another black lawyer was elected from the Twenty-first District. In 1919, Charles H. Roberts, a Republican, became New York City's first black alderman. However, not until 1929 did Charles Fillmore become Harlem's first black Republican district leader, and not until 1935 did Herbert Bruce become its first Democratic district leader.

Another response by blacks who felt alienated from a segregated society was radicalism. Black socialists included A. Philip Randolph and Chandler Owen, editors of *The Messenger*, a socialist publication opposed to the United States' involvement in World War I. In 1918, Cyril Briggs began publication of *The Crusader*, a monthly periodical advocating black nationalism, Marxism-Leninism, and violent revolution. Also appearing in 1918 were two literary and cultural magazines, *Challenge* and *Negro Voice*, published by William Bridges and Hubert Harrison, respectively. *Negro World*, a publication of the Jamaican immigrant Marcus Garvey, captured the imagination of the masses in Harlem and of blacks throughout the diaspora. Garvey was able to recruits numerous black followers in the United States, the Caribbean, and Africa—and in Harlem, where nearly one-quarter of the population was foreign-born blacks from the Caribbean, and where he had many devout black American supporters.

Garvey had his first speaking engagement before a large audience in Harlem in the summer of 1917 and quickly outdistanced his black radical competitors in attracting a mass following. In 1920 he spoke before thousands in Madison Square Garden at a huge convention of UNIA, after an enthusiastic parade through Harlem. He advocated a nationalistic agenda emphasizing the need for diasporic blacks to create their own economic institutions—black-owned retail businesses, factories, steamship lines, and so on—that would unite blacks in an international web of commerce and advancement, leading eventually to a decolonized, independent, united Africa. Garvey came to believe that blacks would never obtain either political or economic equality in the United States and sooner or later would have to repatriate themselves to Africa, rebuild it, and make it strong.

Eventually, UNIA—which had grown into the largest black mass movement in the world in less than ten years of existence in the United States—began to unravel, partly because of the petty jealousy of Garvey's rivals within and outside the organization. Moreover, UNIA had relied heavily on his charismatic leadership, and it declined rather rapidly when he was imprisoned for mail fraud (a charge that may have been based on a technicality). By the late 1920s, Garvey had been released but was in exile, and UNIA continued to decline.

The decline of Garvey's movement, however, did not diminish the reputation of Harlem as the capital of the black world. That reputation rested on the cultural developments of the "Negro Renaissance"—developments in literature, music, and the visual arts. White cultural critics discovered black themes and black artists as downtown audiences attended musicals such as *Dixie to Broadway* and *Blackbirds* or more serious dramas such as *The Emperor Jones* and *The Green Pastures*. Through the efforts of black scholars—including Charles S. Johnson at *Opportunity* magazine and W. E. B. Du Bois at *The Crisis*—black artists were put in contact with white publishing houses and editors. James Weldon Johnson and Walter White of the NAACP, along with Alain Locke, a professor of philosophy at Howard University, served as literary and artistic shepherds to a flock of young writers, painters, and

sculptors who flourished in the 1920s and 1930s and in many cases have become part of the canon. James Weldon Johnson said that their artistic achievements brought about an "entirely new national conception of the Negro . . . placing him in an entirely new light before the American people. Indeed they placed the Negro in a new light before himself." For Johnson and many cultural critics, the Harlem Renaissance was not simply a rebirth of black artistic production but the birth of a new identity and self-definition for African Americans. Locke said: "Harlem has the same role to play for the New Negro as Dublin has had for the New Ireland or Prague for the New Czechoslovakia."

However, black writers were by no means unified with regard to the role of Harlem—or their own role or that of their artistic products—in this redefinition. The works published during the decade reflected assimilationist and antiassimilationist themes, and bourgeois and antibourgeois values. Claude McKay praised the instinctive unassimilated black man in *Banjo* (1929). Langston Hughes heralded the black common man and the black working class in his prose and poetry. Jean Toomer praised the spirituality of rural southern blacks in *Cane* (1923). Other works focused on black bourgeois heroes and heroines; examples are Jessie Redmon Fauset's *There Is Confusion* (1924) and Nella Larsen's *Passing* (1929).

But despite the lack of thematic and stylistic unanimity—or probably in great part because of it—the Harlem Renaissance, like Harlem itself, had a dynamism and a diversity that were widely attractive. The Great Depression dried up private patronage for black creative artists, and in the succeeding decade, these artists embraced more leftist themes related to class and found a new patron in the Federal Arts Project. But the Harlem Renaissance had laid the foundation for black writers and artists for generations to come: from James Baldwin and Amiri Baraka to Alice Walker and Maya Angelou.

During its renaissance, Harlem was, in terms of class, a heterogeneous community; in the decades that followed, it would be transformed into a more homogeneous, low-income, working-class community as much of its former middle-class population became suburbanized after World War II. As of the present writing, Harlem was undergoing further change: Gentrification was attracting a new middle class to Harlem's affordable brownstones, and national chain stores were opening new branches in locations that had once been thought undesirable. Whether these changes would revitalize the economy and employment or merely move the poor from one geographic area to another within the city remained to be seen. Yet Harlem continued to be the best-known black community in the world, and even its current changes were occuring, in great part, because of its historic reputation as the capital of Afro-America—a reputation established during the era of the Harlem Renaissance.

Larry A. Greene

See also Afro-American Realty Company; Briggs, Cyril; Crisis, The; Fifteenth Infantry; Garvey, Marcus; Harlem Hospital; Harrison, Hubert; House-Rent Parties; Negro World; New Negro; Opportunity; Owen, Chandler; Randolph, A. Philip; United Colored Democracy; Universal Negro Improvement Association; White, Walter; *specific artists and writers*

Further Reading

Capeci, Dominic J. *The Harlem Riot of 1943*. Philadelphia, Pa.: Temple University Press, 1977.

Greenberg, Cheryl Lynn. *Or Does It Explode: Black Harlem in the Great Depression*. New York: Oxford University Press, 1991.

Greene, Larry. "Harlem in the Great Depression: 1928–1936." Ph.D. dissertation, Columbia University, 1979.

———. "Harlem, The Depression Years: Leadership and Social Conditions." *Afro-Americans in New York Life and History*, 17, July 1993.

Huggins, Nathan I. *Harlem Renaissance*. New York: Oxford University Press, 1971.

Naison, Mark. *Communists in Harlem During the Depression*. Urbana: University of Illinois Press, 1983.

Osofsky, Gilbert. *Harlem: The Making of a Ghetto—Negro New York, 1890–1930*. New York: Harper and Row, 1963.

Harlem: 2—Economics

At the apex of the Harlem Renaissance, Harlem experienced a rapid increase in population and business growth, a sign of a vibrant economy. The area received new capital, people, and ideas. Immediately before its renaissance, Harlem had been a large residential neighborhood populated by eastern European Jews and African Americans, who moved uptown after excessive residential capacity impelled landlords to recruit new tenants.

Increasing public transportation, federal spending on infrastructure, and foreign conflict perpetuated the boom. The rise of the stock market in the 1920s and mobilization for World War I created more efficient manufacturing and distribution throughout the United States. Harlem's proximity to Wall Street was advantageous, as the value of common stocks and railroad bond yields produced consistent returns. Harlem benefited from growth in jobs and from the disposable income that industrial professionals spent in the neighborhood.

Economic geography separated Harlem from other American urban neighborhoods. By marketing Harlem as a place, business leaders and boosters showcased the area's international flair, artistic heritage, and famous residents. This commodification of the area resulted in increasing returns during the Harlem Renaissance. The region drew aficionados of art and music, and visitors came to sites that were significant for the African American cultural heritage. In fact, Harlem has continued to draw capital resources (net benefits) to the City of New York for years for these reasons.

Before the residential boom in Harlem, local land was considered unproductive. During the 1840s and 1850s, many farms were deserted and used by Irish squatters. Horsecar lines and a steamboat that ran during the summer from 125th Street to Peck Slip were the only transportation links available for travel to New York's business district. In 1873, New York City annexed Harlem, and new, elevated rail service was proposed. Over the next twenty-five years, rail service was extended, and land in Harlem became valuable. Building trades and municipal officials infused the area with capital, subsidizing jobs and buying goods.

Because the Harlem River was a navigable eight-mile tidal straightaway between Manhattan and the Bronx, connecting the East River with Spuyten Duyvil Creek and the Hudson River, the waterway was considered valuable for shipping in the nineteenth century. The first section of the Harlem River Ship Canal (U.S. Ship Canal), a waterway designed to connect the Hudson and Harlem rivers, was completed in 1895. Afterward, Manhattan was successfully circumnavigated so that Long Island Sound was accessible to shipping traffic from the Hudson. By the end of the twentieth century, six swing bridges, one lift bridge, and three arch bridges spanned the river, which served as a transportation link joining the boroughs of New York City.

In Harlem, new apartment buildings were strategically placed to take advantage of this prime location, near rail lines, burgeoning roads, and waterways. However, extensive building in the late nineteenth century created excess capacity during sporadic recessions in the 1890s, so landlords in Harlem sought new tenants. Many eastern European Jews moving from tenements in lower Manhattan and African Americans willing to pay higher prices than their white counterparts were recruited. The former primarily moved into buildings between 110th and 125th streets; the latter moved near 135th Street. Many black New Yorkers arrived from the Tenderloin district of Manhattan after witnessing brutal race riots or being displaced by the construction of Pennsylvania Station in 1906–1910. Some longtime residents of Harlem fled as the newcomers arrived, but the new residents were determined to stay. Even as organizations like the West Side Improvement Association tried to exclude black residents, companies like Philip A. Payton's Afro-American Realty Company courted black tenants.

Before its renaissance, Harlem supported thousands of domestic and personal service jobs and employees, and some manufacturing employment, primarily in the garment and masonry industries. Professional service jobs, public employment, and trade and transportation jobs increased rapidly after 1900. Some local manufacturers and distributors specialized in finished and semifinished nondurable consumer goods such as clothing, printed materials, textiles, and leather. Sales of beauty-care products and professional services grew rapidly, as did retail businesses specializing in imported products. Harlem's economy gained measurably from a constant infusion of capital and people during the first twenty years of the twentieth century. The success of local proprietors transformed Harlem into a national headquarters for black businesses, a trend that continued for years afterward.

General migration to Harlem slowed immediately after World War I, when the large supply of unskilled European labor ceased to flow into New York City. When the U.S. Congress passed the Emergency Quota Act (1921), the nation's first quantitative immigration law, immigrants were restricted in number on the basis of their country of origin. The Immigration Act of 1924 made the quota system permanent. A growing need for labor in New York provided opportunities for vast numbers of African Americans recruited by agents to leave the American South and move to Harlem. These new arrivals further invigorated Harlem with people, ideas, and capital. Alain Locke

wrote in 1925: "The wash and rush of this human tide on the beach line of the Northern city centers is to be explained primarily in terms of a new vision of opportunity, of social and economic freedom, of a spirit to seize, even in the face of an extortionate and heavy toll, a chance for the improvement of conditions."

Jazz musicians and writers drew visitors "uptown" and transformed the neighborhood into a recreational destination. The Cotton Club (formerly Jack Johnson's Club Deluxe) and Connie's Inn were owned by whites and catered to a white clientele, but both clubs built Harlem's reputation as a neighborhood of entertainment during Prohibition. According to the census of 1920, there were approximately 152,467 people living in Harlem, up from 91,709 in 1910. Service employment remained constant. James Hubert of the New York Urban League published a study (*Living Conditions of Small Wage Earners*, 1927) of approximately 2,400 tenants in the neighborhood, which confirmed that this employment had persisted for years. Hubert's report also showed a trend in Harlem: Gainfully employed families were earning slightly less than four times the amount of their rent in gross pay. The average weekly income for a family was $19.75, and the average monthly rent was $41.14.

Harlem's growth as a business district during the Renaissance drew capital from across the nation, boosting local financial institutions. As Harlem gained new residents and capital, *New York Age* and *Amsterdam News* promoted the community's new business leaders. The Carver Savings and Loan Association and the United Mutual Life Insurance Company employed several local residents and were regionally powerful firms. Several funeral homes, law firms, and medical practices were founded during the 1920s, and Apple Bank for Savings, originally named Harlem Savings Bank, accumulated vast capital. Patrons of the arts, both black and white—including the wealthy A'Lelia Walker, who operated a popular salon, the Dark Tower, from her home—merged business interests and art.

The literature of the Harlem Renaissance promoted economic independence. Black residents no longer regarded themselves as subservient and sought grand economic projects in Harlem. However, a division emerged between more conservative black business owners and new leaders, who promoted a self-assertive image of what came to be called the "New Negro." This new philosophy was described in periodicals such as *The Crisis* (1910), published by the National Association for the Advancement of Colored People (NAACP) and edited by W. E. B. Du Bois with help from the novelist and literary editor Jessie Redmon Fauset; and *Opportunity* (1923), published by the Urban League and edited by the sociologist Charles S. Johnson. Cultural independence was described as the ideal way to sustain economic independence: "Harlem's New Negroes employed a strategy of self-empowerment through cultural ascendancy rather than direct economic or political protest" (Douglas 1995).

More radical publications in Harlem questioned the economic authority of contemporary American business leaders. *The Messenger*, established by A. Philip Randolph and Chandler Owen in 1917, held that the oppression of blacks was not racial but economic in origin. This periodical denounced the American Federation of Labor, which largely excluded African Americans, and black America's involvement in World War I. In March 1922, Randolph began advocating the pooling of black business resources, citing an increase in bankruptcies in Harlem. His astute theories on cooperative economic power were proved in 1925, when he organized the Brotherhood of Sleeping Car Porters. Randolph drew support from the numerous black fraternal lodges and social clubs that dotted Harlem. Economic independence movements began at Saint James Presbyterian Church, Abyssinian Baptist Church, Canaan Baptist Church, and Saint Philip's Protestant Episcopal Church.

Marcus Garvey's Universal Negro Improvement Association (UNIA) was another example of an organization promoting economic independence, although Garvey went about this differently from most entrepreneurs in Harlem. Garvey sought to return Harlemites to their African homelands in a "back to Africa" program to restore worldwide economic equality. His weekly newspaper, *Negro World*, was widely read in America and abroad. In 1919, Garvey founded the Black Star Line Steamship Corporation in Harlem to achieve his goal. Shares valued at $5 each were sold at meetings of UNIA and through mailed circulars; and nearly $200,000 was raised in less than four months. Harlem was the headquarters of Garvey's ventures; much of the capital came from the working poor of the Caribbean and the United States. Numerous owners of businesses and real estate in Harlem, and the labor leader Randolph, were critical of Garvey's managerial skills and considered his behavior divisive. He was denounced as an opportunistic social and political leader who was promoting unrealistic economic development plans for Harlem for his own benefit.

Booker T. Washington and his close business associates had founded the National Negro Business League (NNBL) in Boston, Massachusetts, in 1900, and many of the leaders of this organization cast their projects from Harlem. T. Thomas Fortune, editor and publisher of *New York Age*, was appointed chairman of the executive committee of NNBL and tirelessly encouraged black economic growth. The secretary of NNBL, Albon L. Holsey, founded the Colored Merchants' Association (CMA); and the banker Richard Wright, a Philadelphian, established the National Negro Bankers Association and played a vital role in financing small bakeries, groceries, and cleaning firms in Harlem.

However, when the stock market crashed in 1929 and the Great Depression followed, Harlem's economy was badly damaged. The Depression displaced millions of jobs, and in this regard, Harlem was particularly vulnerable. Thousands of the working poor lived in the district, and their jobs disappeared when infrastructure and retail sales suffered. According to federal data, Harlem had rates of unemployment three to four times greater than neighborhoods with primarily white residents. In the face of economic decline—and racism—few African American families prospered. Numerous adults in Harlem began working as street peddlers or vendors in order to survive. Neighborhood "cotton pickers" were famous for finding marketable goods by searching through refuse. Moreover, patrons of the arts reduced their financial support. Some writers in Harlem fell out of favor with publishers when their works were accused of promoting communist ideals; some performers also fell from favor because of their communist leanings.

Many workers and artists based in Harlem were eventually absorbed into other areas of American society, including universities and the U.S. government's Works Progress Administration (WPA). But in the summer of 1934, more than 19,000 families were on relief. The unemployed would gather at the "Tree of Hope" (near the Lafayette Theater) at 132nd Street and Seventh Avenue to touch its trunk for luck. In March 1935, a riot resulted in widespread looting and symbolized the economic plight of the neighborhood. To combat the problem of scarce jobs, officials of the National Urban League in Harlem adopted a slogan, "Don't buy where you can't work," that had been developed in St. Louis; its point was to boycott chain stores operated by whites.

In 1929, in an essay in *Modern Quarterly*, the sociologist E. Franklin Frazier argued that the Harlem Renaissance was divorced from the politics and economics of black culture as a group concept. This issue is debatable, but clearly the ideals and leaders of the Harlem

Renaissance influenced collective and group economic development across the United States. Harlem still remains a center of African American business. A survey by *Black Enterprise* in 2004 of the 100 largest African American businesses in the United States found that 29 percent were located in New York state, and several had germinated in Harlem.

SANDY SUMMERS HEAD
R. JAKE SUDDERTH

See also Abyssinian Baptist Church; Afro-American Realty Company; Amsterdam News; Black Star Line; Brotherhood of Sleeping Car Porters; Cotton Club; Crisis, The; Fortune, Timothy Thomas; Frazier, E. Franklin; Garvey, Marcus; Messenger, The; Negro World; New York Age; Nightclubs; Nightlife; Opportunity; Owen, Chandler; Randolph, A. Philip; Riots: 4—Harlem Riot, 1935; Saint Philip's Protestant Episcopal Church; Universal Negro Improvement Association; Walker, A'Lelia

Further Reading

Anderson, Jervis. *A. Phillip Randolph: A Biographical Portrait*. New York: Harcourt, 1972.

Black Enterprise. (Archives of this magazine list African-American firms and their locations.)

Douglas, Ann. *Terrible Honesty: Mongrel Manhattan in the 1920s*. New York: Farrar, Straus and Giroux, 1995.

Draper, Theodore. *The Rediscovery of Black Nationalism*. New York: Viking, 1970.

Foner, Philip S., and James S. Allen, eds. *American Communism and Black Americans: A Documented History, 1919–1929*. Philadelphia, Pa.: Temple University Press, 1987.

Garvey, Amy Jacques, ed. *Philosophy and Opinions of Marcus Garvey*. Dover, Mass.: Majority, 1986.

Gurock, Jeffrey S., and Calvin B. Holder. "Harlem." In *The Encyclopedia of New York City*, ed. Kenneth T. Jackson. New Haven, Conn.: Yale University Press, 1995, pp. 523–525.

Hill, Robert A., ed. *The Marcus Garvey and Universal Negro Improvement Association Papers*. Berkeley: University of California Press, 1983.

Hutchinson, George. "Mediating 'Race' and 'Nation': The Cultural Politics of *The Messenger*." *African American Review*, 28(4), 1994, pp. 531–548.

Ingham, John N., and Lynne B. Feldman. *African-American Business Leaders: A Biographical Dictionary*. Westport, Conn.: Greenwood, 1994.

Johnson, James Weldon. *Black Manhattan*. New York: Da Capo, 1991.

Lewis, David Levering. *When Harlem Was in Vogue*. New York: Vintage, 1982.

Locke, Alain LeRoy. *The New Negro*. New York: Atheneum, 1970. (Reprint with new preface by Robert Hayden. Originally published 1925.)

Schuyler, George. *Black No More*. New York: Macaulay, 1931.

U.S. Bureau of the Census. *Census of Population*, 1900, 1910, 1920, 1930.

Harlem: 3—Entertainment

The Harlem Renaissance is often treated as primarily a literary movement, but music and entertainment were at the center of the cultural productivity and social optimism associated with the period. Black migrants from around the country, a category that included many of the artists celebrated as key figures in the creative life of the renaissance, along with whites, flocked to Harlem to participate in the cultural milieu of the cabarets, nightclubs, and theaters as observers and participants. Music is often celebrated as a medium that transcends social divisions such as class and race, but the entertainment history of Harlem illustrates the extent to which such divisions determined the conditions of the culture being produced there.

The New Negro movement was primarily a middle-class phenomenon; its artists and intellectuals came mostly from educated, relatively privileged backgrounds. Secular music and dance were considered to be mere popular culture, often vulgar and distinct from the high culture—such as sculpture, painting, classical music, and literature—being produced in literary salons and artistic parlors. Nonetheless, it was the vernacular culture of the masses of working-class black people—their songs, dance, and music—from which the "talented tenth" drew inspiration. That said, class distinctions were not easily transcended. The affluent—W. E. B. Du Bois, Roy Wilkins, Walter White, and other renaissance leaders and artists—lived on Sugar Hill along with doctors, lawyers, and successful businesspeople. The up-and-coming and middle-class artists and writers, like Paul Robeson, Countee Cullen, Clarence Cameron White, W. C. Handy, and Fletcher Henderson, lived on Strivers' Row; and the black poor and working classes lived in "the Valley." Social circles were just as circumscribed by class as residential patterns were. For example, the upper classes congregated in the "Dark Tower," the third floor of A'Lelia Walker's home, for intellectual conversation. In contrast, jazz musicians and entertainers gathered at the Rhythm Club to socialize and jam together. Elite fraternities and sororities held dances at the Renaissance Casino, while working people came together at basement parties to raise money to pay their high rents. At these informal gatherings, musicians such as Fats Waller and Duke Ellington honed their craft and proved themselves to their peers.

Although class distinctions clearly informed the creative outlets that particular entertainers pursued, the distinctions were also frequently blurred and crossed. George Gershwin was known to frequent Harlem rent parties, for example, and he invited jazz musicians to his own parties downtown, where they gained entry to and employment in mainstream musical productions. Moreover, although critics emphasize the "talented tenth's" designation of spirituals as the classical music of black America, in contrast to what was then considered to be the more vulgar secular music, the status of spirituals as high culture did not gain widespread acceptance until composers and performers such as Harry T. Burleigh and Roland Hayes began to perform this music in public concerts and James Weldon and John Rosamond Johnson anthologized it. "New Negro" composers strove to elevate the race's music, while establishing themselves within European musical traditions. In addition to Burleigh and the Johnson brothers' compositions in both spiritual and secular traditions, other breakthroughs in African American concert music included Roland Hayes' concert of lieder and spirituals at Town Hall in 1923, the organization of the Hall Johnson Choir in 1924, and the "First American Jazz Concert" at Aeolian Hall in 1924.

The strides made in musical concert halls were significant, but it is also true that most curiosity seekers flocked to Harlem to hear jazz and blues, musical forms that they believed expressed the sexual, exotic, and uninhibited. These characteristics of jazz and blues appealed to many people who had a new turn-of-the-century attitude toward modern society. Everyone, white and black, went to Harlem to hear black music. Racial and gender conventions were viewed—at least in lore if not in reality—as being more easily transgressed in Harlem. Just as important, Harlem was viewed as a hotbed of musical creativity.

Musical pioneers such as W. C. Handy, Ford Dabney, James Reese Europe, and Will Marion Cook made significant contributions in the early years of the twentieth century, formalizing black music, orchestrating it, and paving the way for future generations of musicians. Bandleaders such as Fletcher Henderson and Duke Ellington popularized the music and went on to assume the title of jazz composers. Henderson's orchestra worked as the house band at the Roseland Ballroom on Broadway, a segregated club that excluded blacks. Henderson is credited with initiating the transformation of ragtime from its roots in Dixieland into the more urbane sounds of the big band movement. He accompanied the blues singers Ethel Waters and Bessie Smith, and he collaborated with other musicians. His band's hit "Sugar Foot Stomp" came to signify both "hot" and "sweet" styles of New York jazz.

Ellington moved from Washington, D.C., to Harlem in 1923 and worked his way up through the ranks until he and his orchestra were hired for a long-term gig at the prestigious Cotton Club in 1927. The four-year run at the Cotton Club gave Ellington national exposure—there were weekly broadcasts on the CBS radio network—as well as the opportunity to collaborate on compositions and arrangements that would become classics, such as "Black and Tan Fantasy" (1927) and "Black Beauty" (1928). By 1928, the Ellington Orchestra became the premier jazz ensemble. Its members had honed their characteristic styles, such as "growling" solos, blue notes, and hot rhythms, that helped define what would come to be known as the orchestra's trademark "jungle" style. By the early 1930s, Ellington had gained fame as the composer of "Mood Indigo" and "Sophisticated Lady" and was living on Sugar Hill.

In 1930, Cab Calloway replaced Ellington's orchestra at the Cotton Club, where he introduced "Minnie the Moocher" (1930), a song that featured the scat singing which that would become his trademark. Before that he appeared at Harlem's Savoy Ballroom, as well as in the all-black Broadway revue Connie's Hot Chocolates. Individuals such as Fats Waller played at rent parties and nightclubs and composed music for shows and revues throughout the 1920s.

The Savoy proved to be a central meeting place, because, unlike the Cotton Club, the Roseland, Connie's Inn, and numerous other establishments, it did not discriminate against African Americans, and unlike A'Lelia Walker's Dark Tower, it did not exclude the working classes. A cross section of people came together at the Savoy Ballroom, and many entertainers reaffirmed their allegiance to the black community by performing in black and integrated venues like the Savoy whenever possible. The heterogeneous environment cultivated group creativity; in addition to the musical richness to be found there, many of the dances of the period were invented at the Savoy, including the lindy, black bottom, shimmy, truckin', snakehips, and Suzy Q. After long days of laboring hard for low wages, black people congregated at spaces like the Savoy, and especially in the more intimate places like the jook joints and rent parties, in order to reclaim their humanity. In such places, the cellar clubs and jooks, before a working-class clientele, Ethel Waters performed as a teenager and became known for her shimmy dance. Bill "Bojangles" Robinson showed off his footwork on Lenox Avenue, and in 1918, he premiered at New York's Palace Theater. At this performance, Robinson performed his trademark "stair dance," in which he tap-danced up and down a five-step staircase. The talented tenth may have associated vernacular dances such as these with stereotypical images of the lower classes, and such performances were certainly not regarded as theatrical art, but the dances created and performed in the cabarets and clubs, and at house parties, captured and embodied the optimism and escapism of the time.

If the early history of jazz in Harlem showcases the talent of men, the history of blues during the period puts the spotlight on women. Mamie Smith made the first blues recording by a black singer in 1920. The success of Smith's rendition of "You Can't Keep a Good Man Down" for Okeh records was quickly followed by the release of "Crazy Blues," which became a huge hit. Because of the trend set by Smith, record companies focused on developing the careers of female blues singers in the first decade of the commercialization of blues. During this period the recording industry played a central role in disseminating blues music, producing "race records" to market to an African American audience. Individuals such as Alberta Hunter, Ida Cox, Ethel Waters, Lucille Hegamin, Edith Wilson, Victoria Spivey, Rosa Henderson, Clara Smith, Trixie Smith, and Sippie Wallace all found success singing blues. Audiences could listen to these women singing not only in nightclubs and theaters but also on records, for labels such as Paramount, Columbia, and Black Swan, the only black-owned record company.

African American migrants from the rural South carried blues with them when they came, during the "great migration," to urban centers like Harlem. The recordings of classic blues singers such as Mamie Smith, Gertrude "Ma" Rainey, and Bessie Smith illustrate the extent to which the music reflected the new social realities of its creators. Thus themes such as individual love, sexual and economic independence, alcoholism, drugs, and travel all figure prominently in the lyrics and speak in different ways of their makers' relatively recent emancipation. Moreover, because women blues singers—who came from poor and working-class roots—were assumed to deviate from the norms of appropriate female behavior, their lyrics dealt explicitly with topics such as sexuality that could not be openly explored in the middle-class narratives of most black women writers.

Whereas Ma Rainey recorded most of her songs in Chicago between 1923 and 1928, Bessie Smith was closely identified with Harlem during her recording career. She performed at nightclubs in Harlem and attended and performed at Carl Van Vechten's parties on the West Side, which brought together wealthy white connoisseurs of black culture, black entertainers and intellectuals, and white artists. Van Vechten, a chronicler of the Harlem Renaissance, wrote about and photographed Smith, creating some of the most enduring images of her.

If Smith was regarded as singing a more urbanized blues than Rainey, Ethel Waters was known for a style of blues that was even smoother, more precise, and therefore considered more "sophisticated" than the bluesy vocalizations of Rainey and Smith. Singers affecting this more urbanized style were thought to appeal more to whites, who frequented "sophisticated" cabarets run by mobsters, such as Connie's Inn and the Plantation Inn. Edith Wilson, like Waters, was one such performer. She opened at the Cotton Club in 1925 and also appeared at the Lafayette Theater, the Lincoln Theater, and other New York cabarets in song and comedy skits. Her style was polished and upbeat, and it traveled easily outside African American circles. Wilson also performed in the Broadway hits *Shuffle Along* and *Blackbirds of 1926*, among others.

About forty musical shows and revues were produced during the 1920s and 1930s, including *Shuffle Along* (1921), *Chocolate Dandies* (1924), *Runnin' Wild* (1924), and *Hot Chocolates* (1929). Many of these shows, which featured comedy sketches, singing, dancing, and rent-party skits, were produced in downtown theaters. Harlem did have some influential African American theaters, though. Chief among them was the Lafayette, between 131st Street and 132nd Street on Seventh Avenue. From its opening in 1915, the Lafayette catered to black audiences, often staging plays from Broadway at more affordable prices and tailoring them to suit the taste of the black audience. Its repertoire consisted of a range of plays, such as *Othello, Madame X, The Servant in the House, The Count of Monte Cristo, Dr. Jekyll and Mr. Hyde*, and *On Trial*. The Lafayette was also known to feature wild shows that were memorialized by Arthur P. Davis, Regina Andrews, Arna Bontemps, and Langston Hughes. The company ran successfully and profitably for a dozen years.

W. E. B. Du Bois founded the Krigwa Players' Little Theater in 1926, and this troupe produced more sober fare in the basement of the New York Public Library's 135th Street branch. Du Bois and the playwrights featured by the Krigwa Players strove to produce dramas aimed toward Negro communities and to convey something of the truth of Negro life.

DAPHNE LAMOTHE

See also Blues; Blues: Women Performers; Cotton Club; House-Rent Parties; Jazz; Krigwa Players; Lafayette Theater; Lincoln Theater; Madame X; Music; Musical Theater; On Trial; 135th Street Library; Renaissance Casino; Roseland Ballroom; Savoy Ballroom; Servant in the House, The; Singers; Van Vechten, Carl; *specific entertainers, musicians, singers, and writers*

Further Reading

Collier, James Lincoln. *The Making of Jazz: A Comprehensive History.* Boston, Mass.: Houghton Mifflin, 1978.

Davis, Angela. *Blues Legacies and Black Feminism.* New York: Vintage, 1998.

Floyd, Samuel A. *Black Music in the Harlem Renaissance.* New York: Greenwood, 1990.

Harrison, Daphne Duval. *Black Pearls: Blues Queens of the 1920s.* New Brunswick, N.J.: Rutgers University Press, 1988.

Hughes, Langston. *The Big Sea.* New York: Hill and Wang, 1997. (Originally published 1940.)

Lewis, David Levering. *When Harlem Was in Vogue.* New York: Oxford University Press, 1979.

Southern, Eileen. *The Music of Black Americans: A History.* New York: Norton, 1971.

Harlem: 4—Housing

Part I

A headline in the New York *Herald* in December 1905—"Negroes Move Into Harlem"—announced that Harlem was changing. A search for better housing was the basic motivation for the move of African Americans to Harlem before the Harlem Renaissance. This move started in 1904 with the relocation of just a few black families to West 134th Street between Lenox and Fifth avenues.

Harlem had originally been a small, dispersed farming community. Then, in the late 1700s, New York City's wealthy, prominent citizens began to regard it as an ideal location for their estates. With the passage of time, Harlem was considered a suburb of the central city. By the early 1800s, the soil no longer supported farming, and many families had moved to better land. Some black slaves lived in Harlem as early as 1752. Once freed, many continued to live and work as servants in the Harlem area. The Village of Harlem was annexed to the rest of New York in 1873.

Although the building of a train line to Harlem spurred some development in the 1830s, much of Harlem was covered with shantytowns by the start of the Civil War. At the end of the Civil War, three more Harlem-bound elevated train lines were in operation. These in turn spurred development in the 1880s, which resulted in overbuilding that attracted new black residents.

Into this scenario walked the black real estate broker Philip Payton, who bought up five-year leases from white building owners and leased apartments to black tenants, beginning with a building on West 134th Street. White businesses and civic community organizations in Harlem protested against this infusion of black renters and home owners; they urged white owners to hold tight and not sell or rent to blacks. But for landlords who were facing financial ruin, renting to black tenants was too profitable a deal to refuse.

Following the "draft riots" of 1865, in which blacks were a target of violence, many blacks moved from Manhattan to Brooklyn. However, thousands of black families remained in shanties and tenements in two mid-Manhattan areas, known then as the Tenderloin (West Twentieth to West Forty-second or West Fifty-third Street between Sixth and Seventh avenues) and San Juan Hill (West Sixtieth to West Sixty-fourth Street between Tenth and Eleventh avenues). Another riot in 1900 made it easier to consider a move away. At that time, New York had 60,666 black residents.

When plans were announced to clear the area around Thirty-third Street in order to build the original Pennsylvania Station, black residents began to worry about where they would live. Their plight and desperation coincided with the overbuilding that had taken place recently in Harlem. In addition to the black people who moved uptown from lower Manhattan, other blacks who had heard of Harlem or had family or friends already there began coming from the American South and from the Caribbean West Indies.

White flight did not occur seriously until 1920, as blacks started the move west across Lenox Avenue, breaking the color line that this avenue had marked. By 1925, blacks lived from West 110th Street up to West 145th Street. Black churches followed—or sometimes led–their congregations to Harlem. Saint Philip's Protestant Episcopal Church, which before 1911 had been located in the Tenderloin area, bought tenements along West 135th Street to rent apartments to black tenants.

For most of the new residents, the housing in Harlem represented an unprecedented improvement. Civil reformers, for their part, considered improvements in housing vital to overall improvement in the life of the city. Thus, beginning in 1901, they had passed "tenement house laws" that tried to address the worst ills of poorly designed urban dwellings—and of dwellings that had not been designed at all, such as those in the abandoned factory buildings and cellars inhabited by some of the poorest New Yorkers before 1900.

Part II

The housing that existed in Harlem at the time of the renaissance included mansions that had been built as much as a century before the move by blacks to Harlem; row houses, of which some of the finest examples were to be found in Harlem; brick tenements; apartment buildings, some of which were elegant, luxurious elevator buildings comparable to the best in the city; and various alternative kinds of housing. The most prevalent and distinctive form of housing in Harlem was the row house, in which the dominant visible building material was brownstone, limestone, or brick. By the end of the nineteenth century, builders considered tenements and apartment buildings more profitable to build, but African Americans were routinely denied occupancy in some luxury apartment buildings until after this period.

Although many of the early black migrants to Harlem were the wealthiest of the black populace, who could afford the steep rents, they represented just a small fraction of the black residents of New York who moved to Harlem. They were followed by working-class people who could not afford the exorbitant rents

found in Harlem. Often, therefore, several families would pool their money and live together as a huge extended family, dividing up the space to suit each nuclear family.

When real estate brokers realized what was happening, they would sometimes divide a building themselves, creating layouts in which each individual occupant got a single room with access to a toilet and cooking facilities on the same floor of the building, or on a nearby floor. Some row houses originally intended for one family were eventually subdivided to provide as many as twenty small rooming units.

Hotels such as the Libya at 149 West 139th Street and the Cecil at 210 West 118th Street represented one short-term alternative form of housing. Another alternative was the Young Men's Christian Association (YMCA). The nation's first black YMCA relocated from West Fifty-third Street to West 135th Street. At various times, it was the home of the writers Claude McKay, Langston Hughes, and Ralph Ellison.

Following are some examples of the various forms of housing.

Two mansions are the Morris-Jumel Mansion (1764), a Georgian house that George Washington used as his headquarters in 1776; and Hamilton Grange (1802) on Convent Avenue, a Federal-style house that was built for Alexander Hamilton.

Harlem's best-known row houses are those on Strivers' Row (1891), consisting of 106 luxurious brownstones on West 138th Street and West 139th Street between Seventh and Eighth avenues; they were first leased to African Americans in 1919. Numbers 330 to 336 Convent Avenue (1892) are a colorful array of Queen Anne–style row houses. Astor Row (1880)—a group of twenty-eight three-story brick semiattached houses on West 130th Street with large, graceful wooden porches and large front yards—was built by a son of the Astor family as working-class housing. Hamilton Terrace (1899) was a semiprivate street of three-story row houses. Sylvan Terrace (1882) had wood-sided working-class row houses, on a street that ran through the gardens of the Jumel estate. Numbers 133 to 143 West 122nd Street (1887) were distinctive terra-cotta row houses.

Apartment buildings included the Paul Laurence Dunbar Apartments (1928), built with financing from John D. Rockefeller Jr. as cooperatives for middle-class black families. The complex, which included 511 apartments, had its own savings bank. It was once the home of W. E. B. Du Bois, Countee Cullen, and Paul Robeson.

Graham Court (1901) at Seventh Avenue and 116th Street was built by William Waldorf Astor and was considered the most luxurious apartment building in Harlem; it was first leased to African Americans in 1933. Number 409 Edgecombe (1917), a twelve-story apartment building, was the most popular address in Sugar Hill for black leaders and artists.

The architects of most of the housing that black residents found on arriving in Harlem around 1904 had been hired by speculative developers. Although most of these architects were not well known, a few were among the most notable in New York. The famous firm of McKim, Mead and White (Stanford White, the architect of Pennsylvania Station) led the design of Strivers' Row. William B. Tuthill designed a series of handsome bay-windowed buildings at 4 to 16 West 122nd Street (he went on to design Carnegie Hall). Francis Kimball, who designed row houses on West 122nd Street, also designed one of New York's first high office buildings.

By the time the Harlem Renaissance started, most of the lots in Harlem's grid up to 145th Street were already built up. Thus most of the construction work in this area during the period of the renaissance involved the renovation of existing buildings and the occasional demolition of an existing large house to make way for apartment buildings.

Most architects working in Harlem during this period were not black. However, at least three African American architects were prominent and very productive. Vertner Tandy, who had been trained at Tuskegee and Cornell, was New York's first black registered architect. He and his partner, George W. Foster, one of the first black architects in New Jersey, designed the new Saint Philip's Protestant Episcopal Church on West 134th Street; they also undertook residential projects, including a house for Madame C. J. Walker at 108 to 110 West 35th Street. (Walker, America's first black female millionaire, who made her fortune through the manufacturing and distribution of black hair-care products, also commissioned Tandy to design a thirty-five-room mansion in Westchester County, New York.) John Louis Wilson worked for Tandy in 1924–1926, became the first black architecture graduate of Columbia University in 1928, and was licensed in New York state in 1930. Wilson undertook substantial renovation of dozens of houses during and after the Harlem Renaissance. He is best known as the only black among seven architects who were selected in 1934 to design the Harlem River Houses, a 574-unit redbrick building complex that is recognized as the first newly constructed public housing project in New York City and in the United States.

Part III

By 1932, Harlem, like the rest of the nation, had slumped into the Depression; perhaps 50 percent of the families in Harlem were on welfare. Hard times, of course, impaired people's ability to pay for housing. Even though 60 percent of black women worked (compared with only 20 percent of white women), they still did not make enough to pay rent, or to buy food and clothing for themselves and their children. As early as 1927, according to a survey by the Urban League, 48 percent of families in Harlem were spending more than twice as much of their income for rent as comparable white families. This situation was exacerbated by the Depression. Rent parties, which became popular in Harlem during this period, were a necessity for hundreds of tenants—a way to raise money for the rent that was due on the first of the month. Also, 25 percent of 2,326 renters surveyed had at least one roomer within their space. Evictions became common. Even people in luxury buildings were hit by the Depression: Rockefeller foreclosed on the Dunbar Apartments in 1936.

At the time of the Urban League's report in 1927, real estate in Harlem was firmly in the hands of white absentee landlords. As had been the case before black people came to Harlem, black families looking for better housing were severely restricted by racial discrimination as to where they could move or live. The Harlem Tenants' League was formed in 1928 to fight rigid segregation and the lack of options available to tenants who had been presented with rent increases. The first protest by the Tenants' League was against the expiration of the Emergency Rent Laws, which controlled rent ceilings. The rent strike was one strategy used; such strikes were of limited value, but they did catch the attention of local politicians. By 1934, however, redlining of areas where most residents were black became a standard practice. This policy made it difficult or impossible for blacks and whites to refinance homes they owned in Harlem or to buy homes there.

The decline of housing in Harlem would continue into the late 1960s, when the population decreased drastically, many buildings were left abandoned, and—as a result of tax defaults—the city became the principal owner of residential properties in Harlem. From the 1990s on, though, the renovation of old residential buildings and the construction of new buildings made Harlem a magnet for those in search of what was still fundamentally some of the best housing in Manhattan. Today, remnants of housing from the days of the Harlem Renaissance remain as witnesses to Harlem's most glorious era.

ROBERTA WASHINGTON

See also Afro-American Realty Company; Dunbar Apartments; House-Rent Parties; Saint Philip's Protestant Episcopal Church; Strivers' Row; Sugar Hill

Further Reading

Adams, Michael Henry. *Harlem Lost and Found*. New York: Monacelli, 2002.

Anderson, Jervis. *Harlem: The Great Black Way*. London: Orblis, 1982.

Doklart, Andrew S., and Gretchen S. Sorin. *Touring Historic Harlem: Four Walking Tours in Northern Manhattan*. New York: Oliphant, 1997.

Johnson, James Weldon. *Black Manhattan*. New York: Knopf, 1930.

Lewis, David Levering. *When Harlem Was in Vogue*. New York, Random House, 1982.

Mitchell, Melvin L. *The Crisis of the African-American Architect: Conflicting Culture of Architecture and (Black) Power*. New York: Writer's Advantage, 2003.

Osofsky, Gilbert. *Harlem: The Making of a Ghetto, 1890–1930*. New York: Harper and Row, 1966.

Plunz, Richard. *A History of Housing in New York*. New York: Columbia University Press, April 1992.

Harlem: 5—Neighborhoods

Negro Harlem's three broad highways form the letter H, Lenox and Seventh Avenues running parallel northwards, united a little above their midpoints by east-and-west 135th Street. . . . These two highways, frontiers of the opposed extreme of dark-skinned social life, are separated by an intermediate any-man's land, across which they communicate chiefly by way of 135th Street. Accordingly 135th Street is the heart and soul of black Harlem; it is common ground, the natural scene of unusual contacts, a region that disregards class. It neutralizes, equilibrates, binds, rescues union out of diversity. (Fisher, 1987)

By the 1920s, Harlem was identified as a "city within a city" (Johnson 1930) and as the "Negro capital of the world" (Locke 1925 / 1968). Migration to Harlem in the early decades of the twentieth century transformed an ethnically mixed community into an almost wholly African American community within a generation. Speculation in property before the construction of the Lenox Avenue subway in the first decade of the century had resulted in large numbers of apartments and not enough tenants. In an effort to protect (and ultimately maximize) profits, buildings were let to African Americans, who subsequently paid higher rents for poorer facilities than tenants in any other part of the city. The landlords got a return on their investment, and Negro Harlem was born. From 1910 to 1920, the African American population expanded by 66 percent (from about 90,000 to 150,000); and from 1920 to 1930, it increased by 115 percent (from about 150,000 to 325,000). The development of this community, as Rudolph Fisher noted, was as internally diversified as it was extraordinary. Outsiders saw Harlem as an entertainment capital characterized by bars, dance halls, and speakeasies; but in reality Harlem was a complex community with distinct neighborhoods organized according to use and class stratification. The descriptions that follow of famous locales that were recognizable by the mid-1920s suggest the class-driven intraracial organization of Harlem.

Lenox Avenue

Lenox Avenue from 125th Street up to around 147th Street represented the center of Harlem's street life, restaurants, and entertainment. In any number of accounts of life in Harlem during this period (such as Fisher's), emerging from the subway at Lenox and 135th Street is cited as the paradigmatic urban experience. Lenox Avenue was associated in the popular imagination with the most notorious aspects of life in Harlem; Fisher depicts it as "the boulevard of the unperfumed; 'rats' they are often termed." In part this was because of the economic conditions affecting housing in the area. Apartments built for a property boom that never happened were let at increasingly exorbitant rents, and tenants made ends meet by subdividing and subletting their space, often many times over. The problems attendant on this overcrowding included poor sanitation, bad services, criminality, and lack of employment opportunities. But the reputation of Lenox as the "low-down" section of Harlem has far more to do with the kinds of services that were offered to Harlemites and to white visitors. As Anderson (1981) describes it, Lenox provided the most famous, the most outrageous, the best-loved, and the most notorious of Harlem's nightspots.

In an era when Harlem was recognized as the nightclub capital of New York, if not of the world, Lenox reigned supreme. To Lenox belonged the Lenox Club at Lenox and 143rd Street, which had a largely African American clientele; the Plantation Inn at 126th Street; and the Savoy Ballroom at 140th Street. The Savoy was the largest dance hall and the most significant mixed-race venue in Harlem; all of the major balls and other events were held there, and it was perhaps best known as the home of the lindy hop. Lenox's most famous nightspot, the Cotton Club, had white audiences only. Its reputation, built on the legendary performances of Cab Calloway and his band, Duke Ellington, Ethel Waters, Lena Horne, and Bill "Bojangles" Robinson, accounted for much of the stereotype of wild after-hours Harlem. The most famous of Harlem's nighttime venues was just off Lenox, on West 133rd Street between Lenox and Seventh avenues. This block had so many nightclubs that it was known as Jungle Alley. Here one could find Tillie's Chicken Shack for after-hours eating, Pod and Jerry's for stride piano from some of Harlem's most famous names, jazz contests at Mexico's, and the cross-dressing "mannish woman" Gladys Bentley singing at the Clam House.

Seventh Avenue

Seventh Avenue, often known as the "great black way," stood for all that was handsome and best about Harlem. It was the widest and most beautiful of Harlem's avenues, with an uninterrupted vista stretching from 125th Street up to 145th Street, and with a median that was given over to plantings of trees and flowers. It too was home to nightclubs and dance halls, including Connie's Inn at Seventh Avenue and 131st Street, which presented cabaret revues with music by Fats Waller and lyrics by Andy Razaf; and Small's Paradise at Seventh and 135th Street. Seventh Avenue was the site of many important theaters, including the Alhambra, the Lafayette, and the Roosevelt. Left-wing magazines such as the *Liberator* had their offices here, as did the Blyden and the National bookstores, which specialized in African and African American books. Harlem's best hotel, the Teresa, was at the corner of Seventh and 125th Street. The most prestigious churches in Harlem

were also located on Seventh Avenue (and a funeral procession up some part of Seventh was a mark of one's social standing).

Seventh Avenue was the prime location for both formal and informal parades. It was the route of parades by many of Harlem's fraternal organizations, protest marches, and celebrations. Parades by Marcus Garvey's Universal Negro Improvement Association (UNIA) and the followers of Father Divine went along Seventh Avenue; and in 1947, there was a parade in honor of the boxer Joe Louis. The Easter parades and Sunday afternoon promenades along Seventh Avenue were famously recorded by James Weldon Johnson; on these occasions, all classes of Harlemites donned their best and most fashionable clothes and came out to stroll: "This was not simply going out for a walk; it is like going out for an adventure" (Johnson 1930).

135th Street

Fisher said that 135th Street was the "common ground" mediating between Seventh and Lenox avenues. In many ways this was the symbolic home of the "New Negro" and the New Negro Renaissance. Here one could find the Harlem Young Men's Christian Association (YMCA), where Langston Hughes and other famous figures of the Harlem Renaissance lived for a time. The YMCA also provided rooms for literary groups; at their meetings, one might hear, for example, Hughes or Countee Cullen reading from his recent work. It was, and still is, an imposing landmark in Harlem. Even more important was the 135th Street Library (later renamed the Schomburg Center for Research in Black Culture, after Arthur Schomburg deposited his extensive collection of materials on African Americans and Africa there). This library—which was the Harlem branch of the New York Public Library—provided a locus for many activities associated with the Harlem Renaissance: readings, meetings, and performances as well as research. At one time or another virtually every literary African American of note spent time writing or doing research at the 135th Street Library. In the 1920s and 1930s, the library sponsored and promoted diverse cultural activities by and for residents of Harlem. In the 1930s, it also commissioned for its own walls some of the most famous works of African American visual art—Aaron Douglas's murals *Aspects of Negro Life*. And 135th Street, as Fisher noted, had the lion's share of a rather more popular form of cultural capital; it was legendary for its barbershops and beauty salons, which were recorded by photographers such as James Van Der Zee and Morgan and Marvin Smith. These shops and salons were an important community space, where information about parties, literary gatherings, and political meetings would be exchanged. They played a crucial role in the development of cultural self-esteem as well as making the fortune of more than one African American.

125th Street

If 135th Street was the locus of literary Harlem, 125th Street was (and to a considerable extent has remained) its commercial hub. At one end of 125th Street there was a stop on the Eighth Avenue elevated railway (another of Harlem's iconic, often photographed gateways); at the other end was a stop on the Lenox Avenue subway. African Americans came to 125th Street later than to the upper portions of Harlem; this street did not have a black majority until the mid-1920s. Once in residence, though, blacks took advantage of the department stories and other commercial outlets available there. Also on 125th Street were the Harlem Opera House, Loew's Victoria, and the Apollo Theater, which became perhaps the most important and most prestigious venue for black entertainment. Success at the Apollo became the sign of having arrived as an African American performer. Louis Armstrong and his orchestra, Billie Holliday, and Ella Fitzgerald all appeared there. Most notably, however, the Apollo was a resolutely populist institution. Its clientele, numbering in the thousands, were ordinary African

Americans whose approval or disdain could make or break a performer's reputation.

Sugar Hill and Strivers' Row

Sugar Hill and Strivers' Row were the antithesis of the populism represented by the Apollo Theater. These were two distinct residential areas of Harlem where one found the most desirable town houses and the wealthiest and best-educated African Americans. Strivers' Row consisted of two leafy blocks—138th and 139th streets—between Seventh and Eighth avenues. Its town houses were designed in 1891 by Stanford White, among others, for the developer David H. King Jr and were intended as homes for wealthy white Harlemites. The white clients evaporated as the surrounding areas were taken over by African Americans; and although the two blocks held out for some time against black tenants and owners, they became home to a largely upper-class black coterie by the mid-1920s. Writers such as Wallace Thurman railed against the snobbishness of this community, which was seen as slavishly imitating the white upper classes, and it is true that many of the residents manifested a class prejudice built on intraracial prejudice—nearly all of the residents of Strivers' Row were light-skinned.

Sugar Hill became a neighborhood to aspire to sometime later than Strivers' Row, but its location on a hill overlooking Harlem soon made it a metaphor of the good life for African Americans. It lay roughly between Amsterdam Avenue to the west and Edgecombe Avenue to the east, running northward from 145th Street to 155th Street. Like Strivers' Row, it had

Harlem, 125th Street, c. 1915–1920s. (Brown Brothers.)

Harlem Savings Bank at 124 East 125th Street, in the 1920s. (Brown Brothers.)

once been a white neighborhood, but as wealthy African Americans made inroads into the area, its luxurious brownstones and apartments became the choice of black celebrities, socialites, intellectuals, politicians, civic leaders, and churchmen. The journalist and writer George S. Schuyler, the painters Aaron Douglas and Hale Woodruff, Langston Hughes, Ralph Ellison, A'Lelia Walker, Duke Ellington, Paul Robeson, and Walter White were among those who made Sugar Hill their home.

MARIA BALSHAW

See also Alhambra Theater; Apollo Theater; Cotton Club; Douglas, Aaron; Father Divine; Fisher, Rudolph; Jungle Alley; Lafayette Theater; Liberator, The; Nightlife; 135th Street Library; Savoy Ballroom; Small's Paradise; Strivers' Row; Sugar Hill; Van Der Zee, James; *specific entertainers and writers*

Further Reading

Anderson, Jervis. *This Was Harlem: A Cultural Portrait*. New York: Farrar, Straus and Giroux, 1981.

Fisher, Rudolph. "City of Refuge" and "Blades of Steel." In *City of Refuge: The Collected Stories of Rudolph Fisher*, ed. John McCluskey Jr. Columbia and London: University of Missouri Press, 1987. ("City of Refuge" originally published 1925; "Blades of Steel" originally published 1928.)

Huggins, Nathan. *Harlem Renaissance*. London, Oxford, and New York: Oxford University Press, 1971.

Johnson, James Weldon. *Black Manhattan*. New York: Knopf, 1930. (Reprint, New York: Da Capo, 1991.)

Lewis, David Levering. *When Harlem Was in Vogue*. New York and Oxford: Oxford University Press, 1981.

Locke, Alain. *The New Negro*. New York: Atheneum, 1968. (Originally published 1925.)

Osofsky, Gilbert. *Harlem: The Making of a Ghetto—Negro New York, 1890–1930*. New York: Harper and Row, 1963. (See also 2nd ed., 1971.)

Harlem: 6—Public Health

Significant, rapid migration of blacks from the southern United States and the Caribbean before World War I radically changed what had been predominantly Irish, Jewish, and Italian communities in Harlem. This influx of black people—most of whom were poor—took place against a background of racial prejudice supported by pseudoscientific theories of genetic inferiority, social Darwinism, and eugenics. The numbers and the health needs of the population created a severe strain on the medical services available in Harlem. Moreover, two other factors also contributed to inadequate health care: One of these was misperceptions about black culture; the other was the attitude of organized American medicine, which militated against government support for what were considered expensive state-sponsored medical programs. In this context, efforts to integrate the medical staff at Harlem Hospital—the only public facility in the community—and the founding of the Harlem Hospital Nursing School to train black women nurses were important innovations. Nevertheless, the quality and kind of medical services available to the black community were adversely affected by the distribution of funding for health care, by discrimination in the allocation of medical resources and personnel, and by racial prejudice that limited access to professional medical societies and research positions.

During the period of the Harlem Renaissance, most medical care was offered through various fee-for-service providers, including homeopaths, physicians, midwives, pharmacists, and purveyors of folk remedies. Although this range of providers did not differ from those used by European immigrants, poor blacks—as a consequence of both their race and their poverty—relied mostly on folk medicine or became patients at public facilities. Public outpatient facilities soon became inadequate to meet the needs of the black community, a population that increased by more than 300 percent between 1920 and 1932. Inpatient facilities at Harlem Hospital were also consistently unable to meet the demands of the community. Despite efforts by African American physicians who tried to draw attention to public health issues, preventive medicine was rare, poor sanitary conditions were widespread, and infectious diseases proliferated. There was an increased incidence of venereal disease, consumption, malnutrition, heart disease, and substance abuse. Psychiatric services were almost nonexistent and remained so until the founding of the Lafargue Clinic just after World War II.

Moreover, under a "justification for scientific research," many poor and ill-informed blacks became subjects of experiments (such as the infamous Tuskegee study of untreated syphilis), were subjected to unnecessary procedures, or were treated negligently because their complaints were routine or fell outside the scope of research protocols. Middle-class black Harlemites sometimes adopted racial stereotypes, demanding white physicians, or they sought treatment in private clinics owned by blacks; both reactions encouraged a segregated system and deprived public institutions of important political support. For example, these attitudes among the middle class hampered the efforts led by Louis T. Wright, an African American graduate of Harvard Medical School, to integrate black physicians at Harlem Hospital. Another impediment was the attitude of private foundations, such as the Rosenwald Fund, that proposed to strengthen African American medical institutions. These foundations were well meaning, and they did achieve some practical success in funding programs to combat infant mortality, sexually transmitted diseases, and tuberculosis; ironically, however, they slowed the pace of integration and hindered well-trained black physicians from obtaining staff positions at largely white institutions. Instead of creating opportunities for black health care professionals, these foundations helped perpetuate a stereotype of black doctors and nurses as less well trained or less competent.

By 1923, most African American physicians earned their medical degrees at Howard University or Meharry; few blacks gained admittance to the predominantly white medical schools that received the most funding, benefited most from current scientific research, and largely supervised specialist training. There was a shortage of practitioners willing to treat inner-city patients, and so the ratio of black physicians to patient visits fell. The American Medical Association controlled the politics of medicine, although the black National Medical Association worked to raise standards and respect for black physicians. Nationwide, the medical establishment was characterized by "separate and unequal" health care for blacks and whites, and this situation obviously influenced health care in Harlem.

Extreme poverty and social dislocation exposed the need for psychiatric services based in Harlem. An epidemic of juvenile crime, thwarted aspirations, discrimination in housing and employment, and limited educational opportunities created despair; as a result, the black community in Harlem was afflicted by anxiety bordering on neurosis, but there were few openings for black physicians to receive psychiatric training in New York City. In 1946, after having worked for a decade on the project, Fredric Wertham, one of the nation's most distinguished psychiatrists, organized the Lafargue Clinic in the basement of the parish house of

Saint Philip's Church, with the encouragement and advice of Ralph Ellison, Richard Wright, Earl Brown, Marion Hernandez, and Father Sheldon Hale Bishop. Wertham enlisted and trained a multiracial volunteer staff to establish this mental health clinic, dedicated to alleviating the "free-floating hostility" of many people in Harlem and to understanding the reality of black life in America—a reality shaped by oppression. The clinic, which was named in memory of Karl Marx's son-in-law Dr. Paul Lafargue (a Cuban-born black French physician, social reformer, and politician), became one of the most noteworthy institutions in the United States, serving the poor and promoting civil rights.

JAMES E. REIBMAN

See also Ellison, Ralph; Harlem Hospital; Saint Philip's Protestant Episcopal Church; Tuskegee Experiment; Wright, Richard

Further Reading

Bailey, A. Peter. *The Harlem Hospital Story: 100 Years of Struggle against Illness, Racism, and Genocide.* Native Sun, 1991.

Byrd, W. Michael, and Linda A. Clayton. *An American Health Dilemma: A Medical History of African Americans and the Problem of Race: Beginnings to 1900.* New York and London: Routledge, 2000.

———. *An American Health Dilemma: Race, Medicine, and Health Care in the United States, 1900–2000.* New York and London: Routledge, 2002.

Maynard, Aubre de L. *Surgeons to the Poor: The Harlem Hospital Story.* New York: Appleton-Century-Crofts, 1978.

Myrdal, G. *An American Dilemma: The Negro Problem and Modern Democracy.* New York: Harper and Row, 1944.

Reibman, James E. "Ralph Ellison; Fredric Wertham, M.D.; and the Lafargue Clinic: Civil Rights and Psychiatric Services in Harlem." *Oklahoma City University Law Review*, 26(3), Fall 2001, p. 1041.

Reynolds, P. Preston. "Dr. Louis T. Wright and the NAACP: Pioneers in Hospital Racial Integration." *American Journal of Public Health*, 90(6), June 2000, p. 883.

Harlem Community Players

During the 1920s, Harlem was a magnet not only for African American artists but also for many white New Yorkers. Many middle-class Americans attended black vaudeville shows, dramas, and Broadway productions and also expressed great interest in community-based "little theater" groups and amateur dramatic clubs of the day, such as the Harlem Community Players.

In the late 1920s, the Harlem Community Players produced Edward Smith's drama *Release* in the Harlem Library Little Theater at the 135th Street branch of the New York Public Library. This little theater space had been converted from a lecture room in the basement of the library and was active from the mid-1920s until the mid-1940s. The first resident group to use the Harlem Library Theater was the Krigwa Players, led by W. E. B. Du Bois (the founder of the group) and the artistic director Charles Burroughs.

Such dramatic societies served as a cultural resource for the community. The Lafayette Players, the first theater group in Harlem, was formed in 1916, and there were several other black theater groups during the Harlem Renaissance, such as the Krigwa Players, the Negro Art Theater, the Utopia Players, and the Harlem Community Players. Most of them were small amateur groups that produced classics or melodramas about middle-class life. Many of their plays dealt with black life and were performed by blacks, but had been written by whites.

FELECIA PIGGOTT-MCMILLAN

See also Community Theater; Krigwa Players; Lafayette Players; Negro Art Theater; 135th Street Library; Utopia Players

Further Reading

Peterson, Bernard L. *The African American Theatre Directory, 1816–1960: A Comprehensive Guide to Early Black Theatre Organizations, Companies, Theatres, and Performing Groups.* Westport, Conn.: Greenwood, 1997.

Harlem: A Forum of Negro Life

Harlem: A Forum of Negro Life (1928) was a literary journal edited by Wallace Thurman. He undertook this new publication two years after the demise of *Fire!!*, a magazine that in its single issue had devoted itself to artistic expression unfettered by racial propaganda. Thurman's reasons for the new venture—which was intended as a successor to *Fire!!*—were, first, that

black artists in New York had no journal of their own and thus could not reach their primary audience (since few African Americans would consistently buy a white publication just for the sake of contributions by black artists); and, second, that the black editors of *The Crisis* and *Opportunity*, according to him, hampered artistic freedom. Thurman envisioned *Harlem: A Forum of Negro Life* as a way to make up for these deficiencies and give a voice to the young black artist, who was rebelling "against shoddy and sloppy publication methods, . . . against the patronizing attitudes his elders assumed toward him, . . . against their editorial astigmatism and their intolerance of new points of view" (Thurman 1928, 21).

As chief editor, Thurman carefully organized what turned out to be the only issue of *Harlem*, published in November 1928. He balanced the bohemian pieces of Richard Bruce Nugent, Roy de Coverly, and George W. Little with the more conservative contributions of Alain Locke, Walter White, and George Schuyler. *Harlem* lacked the fiery spirit of its predecessor, but, appealing to a wider audience and costing only twenty-five cents a copy, it seemed to have a better chance of surviving. During its short existence, it nearly achieved its goal of being "a wholly new type of magazine, one which would give expression to all groups" (Thurman, 21). It included illustrations by Nugent and Aaron Douglas; political advice from White, who was the chairman of the National Association for the Advancement of Colored People (NAACP); discussions of theater by Theophilus Lewis and Nugent; poems by Helene Johnson, Alice Dunbar Nelson, and Langston Hughes; and short stories by Hughes, Schuyler, de Coverly, and Little. By presenting so many different opinions and values, Thurman was trying to sever any links between his new magazine and *Fire!!*, which had been a one-sided affair: "If you are in doubt as to which side of a public argument you agree with—look for both sides in *Harlem*." In an editorial, he reassured the reader that *Harlem* was entering the field "without any preconceived editorial prejudices, without intolerance, without a reformer's cudgel" (22).

After a single issue, and without having been reviewed in any other periodicals, *Harlem: A Forum of Negro Life* folded. There are no official records that reveal the specific reasons for its failure, but one explanation might be that the black public lacked interest in literary magazines and was unready to support yet another black periodical. Theophilus Lewis (1932) seems to believe that financial difficulties led to the downfall of the new journal; another, and more probable, cause may have been the poor quality of the material in the first issue.

Nikolas Huot

See also Crisis, The; Douglas, Aaron; Fire!!; Hughes, Langston; Johnson, Helene; Lewis, Theophilus; Locke, Alain; Nelson, Alice Dunbar; Nugent, Richard Bruce; Opportunity; Schuyler, George S.; Thurman, Wallace; White, Walter

Further Reading

Bontemps, Arna, ed. The Harlem Renaissance Remembered. New York: Dodd, Mead, 1972.

Huggins, Nathan Irvin, ed. Voices from the Harlem Renaissance. New York and Oxford: Oxford University Press, 1976.

Hughes, Langston. The Big Sea. New York: Knopf, 1940.

Johnson, Abby Arthur, and Ronald Maberry Johnson. Propaganda and Aesthetics: The Literary Politics of African-American Magazines in the Twentieth Century. Amherst: University of Massachusetts Press, 1979.

Lewis, David Levering. When Harlem Was in Vogue. New York: Knopf, 1981.

Lewis, Theophilus. "Wallace Thurman Adores Brown Women Who Have Beauty Mark on Shoulder; Prefers Sherry to Gin." Journal and Guide, 5, 5 March 1932, p. 7.

Notten, Eleonore van. Wallace Thurman's Harlem Renaissance. Amsterdam: Rodopi, 1994.

Thurman, Wallace. Editorial. Harlem: A Forum of Negro Life, 1(1), November 1928, pp. 21–22.

Harlem General Hospital

Harlem General Hospital emerged from the Harlem Dispensary (1868), a charitable foundation that had been formed to provide medical care for the poor of Harlem. The dispensary not only dealt with immediate medical issues but also became a pioneer in public health efforts against contagious and epidemic diseases. However, it was eclipsed by the foundation of Harlem Hospital on 18 April 1887.

Harlem General Hospital began as a twenty-bed facility; later, it was expanded to fifty-four beds. It was run by the Department of Public Charities and Correction in a rented wooden building at 120th Street and the East River and served as a center for transferring patients to hospitals on Ward's and Randall's islands and as an emergency unit of Bellevue Hospital. Eventually, as a result of a population boom that included a large influx of Negroes, a new Harlem Hospital was built on Lenox Avenue between 136th and 137th streets. This new facility, which had 150 beds, was opened on 13 April 1907. In turn, it became too small, so in 1915 a nurses' wing was opened and an additional 240 beds became available.

In 1917, during World War I, Harlem General Hospital sent a medical unit—which served with distinction—overseas. Also as part of the war effort, the hospital trained army medical personnel, especially in the use of X-ray technology. In 1918, medical students at Fordham University rotated through the hospital, which had been recognized as a teaching hospital. In addition, its professional quality was attested to by the fact that several attending physicians also held positions in other medical faculties in the area.

Military service during World War I created a severe shortage of personnel in city hospitals and enabled black physicians to join the house staff at Fordham and Bellevue hospitals. This precedent provided an impetus for integrating hospitals in New York City. Because Harlem had a large black population that was gaining political power, and because there was evidence that blacks were being treated indifferently and inadequately at Harlem General Hospital, a demand arose to admit Negroes to its house staff. In 1919, Louis T. Wright, who was a veteran and a graduate of the Harvard medical school, was appointed as a provisional clinical assistant visiting surgeon, the lowest rung of the medical staff. Wright's appointment was greeted with discontent by the rest of the medical staff, and it became a cause célèbre in the growing black community of Harlem. As a result of widespread political pressure and a campaign in the black press, abuses suffered by black patients were revealed, as was a predominant racist animus among many white physicians. In 1920, several Negro physicians obtained affiliation with the outpatient staff. In 1925, after additional political and legal pressure, the derogatory designation "provisional" was removed from the appointments of these physicians.

Until 23 January 1923, when the nursing school at Harlem General Hospital opened, black women could be trained only at Lincoln Hospital School for Nurses in the Bronx. When black nurses and nursing students appeared at Harlem General Hospital, many white nurses either resigned or transferred to other hospitals; but a notable exception was Sadie O'Brien, who lent her expertise as first principal of the School of Nursing and as superintendent of nurses for the hospital. The graduates of the nursing school encountered problems when they sought additional training or staff positions at other medical institutions. Finally, in 1937, training became available at Willard Park Hospital for communicable diseases and at Bellevue Hospital for psychiatry.

In 1930, there was a reorganization of the medical staff; this provoked bitterness, and a multiracial group of physicians led by Wright and John Fox Connors emerged. Thereafter, a policy of "full and equal opportunity" based on merit guided the appointments of both black and white physicians. Ties to the community of Harlem were strengthened, and by 1935 the hospital's census was nearly 85 percent black. However, although the hospital was the primary medical facility in Harlem, its outpatient and bed services were inadequate to meet the demands of the community; it faced continual underfunding that strained its resources, and it was also affected by persistent racism.

JAMES E. REIBMAN

See also Harlem: 6—Public Health; Wright, Louis T.

Further Reading

Bailey, A. Peter. *The Harlem Hospital Story: 100 Years of Struggle against Illness, Racism, and Genocide*. Native Sun, 1991.

Linden, Diana L., and Larry A. Greene. "Charles Alston's Harlem Hospital Murals: Cultural Politics in Depression Era Harlem." *Prospects, Annual*, 26(31), 2001, p. 391.

Maynard, Aubre de L. *Surgeons to the Poor: The Harlem Hospital Story*. New York: Appleton-Century-Crofts, 1978.

Reynolds, P. Preston. "Dr. Louis T. Wright and the NAACP: Pioneers in Hospital Racial Integration." *American Journal of Public Health*, 90(6), June 2000, p. 883.

Harlem Globetrotters

The Harlem Globetrotters were one of two exceptionally talented black professional basketball teams that began playing in the 1920s. At first, the Globetrotters were the less successful of the two teams; the New York Renaissance Five (better known as the New York Rens) were considered the premier black professional squad until the late 1930s, playing before large audiences of both black and white fans. In time, however, the Globetrotters would become one of the best-known sports entertainment franchises not only in the United States but around the world—in part by relying on carefully orchestrated comedy routines during games.

Ironically, the original Harlem Globetrotters were neither from Harlem nor particularly well-traveled. The team was organized in 1927 by a twenty-five-year-old entrepreneur, Abe Saperstein, initially as a splinter squad of another team, the Savoy Big Five, which Saperstein coached in Chicago. Saperstein was a Jewish immigrant who had been born in London; he had realized, in the early 1920s at the University of Illinois, that he was too slight to play varsity sports, and so he had turned to coaching. By the mid-1920s, he was running a successful youth league team called the Chicago Reds. Impressed by his success, a former baseball star in the Negro Leagues—Walter Ball—hired Saperstein in early 1926 to coach an all-black American Legion basketball team. Later in 1926, the business manager of that team persuaded the owners of Chicago's Savoy Ballroom (modeled after the famous Savoy in Harlem) to sponsor evening basketball games, offering Saperstein's unit as the main attraction. The team was renamed the Savoy Big Five and began playing in November 1926. But disappointing crowds, coupled with an intractable salary dispute, led three of the Big Five players and Saperstein to leave the Savoy soon thereafter to form their own team.

This new team was first called Saperstein's New York, then simply New York, then Saperstein's Harlem New York. Although it would not officially be called the Harlem Globetrotters until the mid-1930s, these earlier names also implied cosmopolitanism. That was a deliberate strategy: Saperstein wanted midwestern spectators to think the team had, in his words, "been around" (Zinkoff and Williams 1953, 25). Saperstein also chose a barnstorming schedule rather than staying in Chicago, where he would have had difficulty booking large arenas regularly.

The team—consisting of Walter "Toots" Wright, Byron "Fats" Long, and Willis "Kid" Oliver (the three former members of the Savoy Big Five), plus Andy Washington and Bill Tupelo (who had been newly signed by Saperstein)—played its first game on 7 January 1927, in Hinckley, Illinois. According to Zinkoff and Williams, Saperstein and the players traveled in a secondhand Model T, with Saperstein at the wheel. In these lean early years, Saperstein was simultaneously the team's driver, owner, coach, manager, and trainer, and an on-court substitute when a regular player was injured or fatigued. By the end of the first barnstorming season, the team had a total of 101 wins against only 16 losses, although steady profits were still many years away.

In 1929, Saperstein signed Inman Jackson to replace Andy Washington, signaling a shift from traditional basketball to a mix of serious play and gimmicky clowning. Jackson was the team's first "superclown," the predecessor of such famous later figures as Reece "Goose" Tatum, who joined the Globetrotters in the early 1940s, and Meadowlark Lemon, who arrived in 1954. The comedy routines first made popular by Jackson—which included no-look passing, bouncing the ball off his head into the basket, and lining his teammates up in mock football formations—accomplished three purposes: They entertained the crowd, gave the players a rest (because clowning, although often fast-paced, required less running), and kept the final score close. The score was crucial in getting future bookings: During this era, all such barnstorming teams understood that they should not completely dominate their opponents, although this feat could be easily accomplished by skilled professional athletes. Local fans wanted to believe that their amateur squad had a chance to defeat the professional touring club; otherwise, they would lose interest in staging rematches.

During the 1930s the Globetrotters extended their barnstorming, eventually playing throughout the upper Midwest and even, by the mid-1930s, as far west as Washington state. They were also now beginning to play in larger urban centers, including Detroit, where the Globetrotters often began their season with a game on Thanksgiving Day. The real competition with the New York Rens also began in the 1930s, as the Globetrotters gained a more national reputation. Despite the challenge of constant travel, often on poor roads (a strain exacerbated by the great physical distances between top teams), and the persistent exclusion of black squads from professional leagues, the black teams thrived during the Depression. According to Ashe, "the addition of the Globetrotters enhanced all of black basketball; fans took it more seriously and a sort of intra-racial rivalry began" (1993, 48). Despite their rivalry, or perhaps because of it—Robert Douglas, the owner of the Rens, was said to have resented the Globetrotters' clowning as racially demeaning—the Rens and Globetrotters

Early members of the Harlem Globetrotters. Standing, left to right: Abe Saperstein, Toots Wright, Byron Long, Inman Jackson, and William Oliver. Seated: Al Pullins. (Photofest.)

did not meet on the court until 1939 at the Chicago World Professional Tournament, when they faced each other in the second round. That year, the Rens defeated the Globetrotters 27–23 and went on to win the tournament title. However, the following year, the Globetrotters defeated the Rens in the semifinals and won their own first tourney championship. From 1940 on, Saperstein's team soared in popularity as the Rens declined. Today, the Globetrotters are the franchise best remembered for their association, however nominal, with Harlem.

WILLIAM GLEASON

See also Professional Sports and Black Athletes

Further Reading

Ashe, Arthur R. Jr. *A Hard Road to Glory: A History of the African-American Athlete, 1919–1945*, rev. ed., Vol. 2. New York: Amistad, 1993.

Bjarkman, Peter C. *The Biographical History of Basketball*. Lincolnwood, Ill.: Masters, 2000.

Henderson, Edwin B. *The Black Athlete: Emergence and Arrival*. Cornwells Heights, Pa.: Publishers' Agency, 1976.

Hollander, Zander, ed. *The Modern Encyclopedia of Basketball*. New York: Four Winds, 1969. (See also rev. ed., 1973.)

Peterson, Robert W. *Cages to Jump Shots: Pro Basketball's Early Years*. Oxford and New York: Oxford University Press, 1990.

Rayl, Susan. "African American Ownership: Bob Douglas and the Rens." In *Basketball Jones*, ed. Todd Boyd and Kenneth L. Shropshire. New York and London: New York University Press, 2000.

Zinkoff, Dave, and Edgar Williams. *Around the World with the Harlem Globetrotters*. Philadelphia, Pa.: Macrae Smith, 1953. (An account of the team's silver-anniversary international tour.)

Harlem: Negro Metropolis

Claude McKay's *Harlem: Negro Metropolis* (1940) is a community study. McKay, taking a cross section of Harlem, provides a profound historical examination of the major movements and figures that affected Harlemites in the 1920s and 1930s. This study is a direct descendant of W. E. B. Du Bois' sociological studies of Philadelphia (1899) and blacks in the North (1901), and of James Weldon Johnson's history of Harlem (1930).

McKay takes a close look at both the famous and the notorious aspects of Harlem's social geography and concludes that Harlem is neither the shining star nor the scourge of urban Negro communities. He focuses primarily on group phenomena, describing activities that bring people together for some common goal or interest. The Marxist approach that he adopts precludes the excessive attention to an intellectual or monied elite so often found in accounts of Harlem in the early twentieth century. McKay's concern is with the life of the masses, and his lively prose makes their exuberance and originality leap off the page. For McKay, religion, individualism, and personal wealth have no intrinsic value; they exist to structure society and, in this case, to allow Harlem to express its public culture. Thus his study is not an organizational history of religious or political movements but rather a social history of ordinary people in which he traces the careers of specific figures.

The opening chapters chronicle Harlem's development into a black neighborhood. McKay describes the origins of sections such as Strivers' Row and Sugar Hill from the acquisition of property to the letting of overpriced rooms, and the mixing of diverse black immigrant groups, races, and classes in Harlem. McKay uses this introductory material to identify Harlem as a sort of melting pot whose challenge was to fit the "Aframerican" minority into American society.

McKay's study of Father Divine is of particular interest. With humor and contempt, McKay discusses the beginnings of Father Divine's mass movement and its inner workings as a religion, a community, a social program, and a real estate enterprise. What McKay finds most notable is Father Divine's system of communal living, sustained by doctrines such as the nonexistence of sex, race, color, and money. Father Divine's followers acquiesced in sexual segregation at home and at work; those who worked turned their earnings over to the organization, while those who were out of work shared the maintenance of its rooming houses. The organization looked out for the health and well-being of its members and also provided ten-cent meals to hundreds of Harlemites every day. Father Divine's followers—an interracial, multiclass group who believed him to be God—had independent churches around the country. McKay characterizes Father Divine as an odd little man who was a brilliant, if mysterious, capitalist.

McKay is also interested in African American occult religion, which he traces to the inherent "magic" of Africa. He describes the practices of occultists as similar to fetishism in Guinea and to West Indian obeah and voodoo. These practitioners met in homes and storefronts, burning incense, oils, and candles and selling various cures and talismans.

Cultists in Harlem were different from the voodooists, psychics, and soothsayers of the occult. They were more like the adherents of Father Divine, following individual leaders who developed, and traded on, a doctrine of themselves based on some form of Christianity. Many of these leaders were attractive and dynamic and had significant influence over the people of Harlem.

McKay also considers various efforts by propertied persons and businesspeople to stimulate black commerce in Harlem. Blacks' move into retail, service, and manufacturing was slow and sparse. Cafeterias, pushcarts, and laundries were representative of the small ventures; larger successful businesses included a Negro doll factory, the Brown Bomber Baking Company, and Madame C. J. Walker's beauty empire. McKay also describes the development of "the numbers"—a gambling game—explaining its complicated operation and appeal. The importance of trust and community in running the numbers in Harlem provided a lesson in black consumerism when outsiders tried to take over the operation. The numbers game promoted the numerology of the occultists, and bootlegging by numbers runners stimulated the entertainment business in Harlem. Speakeasies and clubs provided recreation and social life for blacks, although few of these places were owned by black people. McKay mentions several popular clubs and the bands that played there, noting that cabaret acts were subjected to exploitation and received low pay.

In studying politicians, McKay names Harlemites in city government, education, medicine, and so on from whom political types could be drawn. This elaborate list reveals an infrastructure of professionals who served and supported the community in Harlem. McKay describes the arduous and complex efforts of blacks to infiltrate Tammany Hall, elect officials, and obtain appointive positions in government. In detailing political mobilization, McKay describes community politics between Puerto Ricans, immigrant blacks, and native-born blacks in Harlem. There were elaborate efforts to gain representation in city assemblies, in state government, on the board of education, and in the judiciary; McKay attributes these efforts to the independent spirit stirred up by Marcus Garvey's movement.

McKay describes the development and popularity of Garvey's controversial "back to Africa" movement in the United States in some detail. The account of Garvey's life and exploits indicates that despite his energy and imagination, he lacked organizational ability—a shortcoming that precipitated the failure of the Universal Negro Improvement Association (UNIA). Still, his movement cultivated racial pride, internationalism, and a sense of the potential of mass politics in black America.

A full third of *Harlem: Negro Metropolis* is taken up by the final chapter: "Sufi Abdul Hamid and Organized Labor." Hamid, a former cultist, attempted to bring his successful labor campaign—with its slogan "Don't buy where you can't work"—to New York from Chicago. Boycotts and picketing forced local businesses to pay attention to this campaign and actually to hire black clerks and other staff members. Hamid did politicize the notoriously blasé young people of the black middle class, but despite this, his efforts were largely unsuccessful. He and his supporters were wrongfully labeled anti-Semites in the press and were opposed by various groups, including the Communist Party, that were loath to see blacks organizing on their own. Hamid's program to provide service jobs for Harlemites crumbled, and Harlem was left with a dubious legacy of anti-Jewish sentiment. McKay, in describing how black labor activism was

thwarted, condemns the role of the Communist Party in the life and politics of Harlem. He believes that the pervasive, although unseen, power of the party was responsible for failures in Negro organizations and labor activism. He particularly notes the negative effect of the party's interracial policies on the Negro community and black political activism within the American social and political structure.

Harlem: Negro Metropolis is enjoyable to read: interesting, amusing, and full of surprising explanations and facts. McKay emphasizes that even though most of the major movements of the 1920s and 1930s failed, they had a lasting constructive effect on Harlemites' political sensibilities and sense of possibilities, and on other black communities; moreover, less organized versions of the various practices and belief systems often survived. Adopting a dry, critical tone throughout, McKay refuses to take his subject too seriously. He emphasizes his own theory of Harlem's status—that Harlem was merely a place in upper Manhattan, New York City, U.S.A., where black people managed to make a living within a complicated racist society.

STEPHANIE L. BATISTE

See also Black Manhattan; Communist Party; Du Bois, W. E. B.; Father Divine; Garveyism; Hamid, Sufi Abdul; Home to Harlem; McKay, Claude; Numbers Racket; Strivers' Row; Sugar Hill; Universal Negro Improvement Association; Walker, Madame C. J.

Further Reading

Blary, Liliane. "Claude McKay and Black Nationalist Ideologies (1934–1948)." In *Myth and Ideology in American Culture*, ed. Regis Durand and Michel Fabre. Villeneuve d'Ascq: Université de Lille, 1976.

Cooper, Wayne F. *Claude McKay–Rebel Sojourner in the Harlem Renaissance: A Biography*. Baton Rouge: Louisiana State University Press, 1987.

———. *The Passion of Claude McKay: Selected Poetry and Prose, 1912–1948*. New York: Schocken, 1973.

Du Bois, W. E. B. *The Black North in 1901: A Social Study*. New York: Arno, 1969. (Originally published 1901.)

———. *The Philadelphia Negro*. Millwood, N.Y.: Kraus-Thomson, 1973. (Originally published 1899.)

Giles, James R. *Claude McKay*. Boston, Mass.: Twayne, 1976.

Johnson, James Weldon. *Black Manhattan*. New York: Knopf, 1930.

Lewis, David Levering. *When Harlem Was in Vogue*. New York: Knopf, 1981.

Timothy, Helen P. "Claude McKay: Individualism and Group Consciousness." In *A Celebration of Black and African Writing*, ed. Bruce King, Kolawole Ogungbesan, and Iya Abubakar. Oxford: Oxford University Press, 1975.

Warren, Stanley. "Claude McKay as an Artist." *Negro History Bulletin*, 40, 1977, pp. 685–687.

Harlem: Play

Harlem (1929), a drama by Wallace Thurman and William Jourdan Rapp, was chosen as one of the best plays of the 1928–1929 season and was considered one of the most important plays of the Harlem Renaissance era. It was originally called *Black Belt* and was advertised under that title before its opening. As *Harlem*, it was first produced on Broadway at the downtown Apollo Theater, where it opened on 20 February 1929. After ninety-three performances, it went on the road; it then returned to Broadway for a short run. *Harlem* proved successful enough for a second company to produce it.

The plot concerned the devastating effects of adversity on a black family that migrated to Harlem from the South expecting to find a better life but discovered instead a den of debauchery, racketeering, prostitution, drugs, and murder. The play examined, especially, the experiences of a distracted migrant mother who was caught in the whirlpool of life on the streets and was struggling to save herself, her husband, and her children from being submerged.

The original cast of *Harlem* numbered sixty. It included Inez Clough, Lew Payton, and Isabel Washington, but the revival had a completely different cast. In general, the reviewers thought that the acting was quite realistic. A reviewer for the *New York Times* also mentioned the intense dramatic appeal of the play, noting its treatment of themes such as love and murder. Another critic mentioned its authenticity, which was a result of its frank portrayal of black life; in fact, *Harlem* is significant because it dealt with some of the less desirable political and social aspects of the city. *Harlem* relied to a considerable extent on strong language, and some audience members considered that offensive.

In addition to this play, Thurman wrote several novels that received considerable attention from influential

Harlem, scene from the stage production. (Billy Rose Theatre Collection, New York Public Library, New York City. © The New York Public Library / Art Resource, N.Y. Keysheet Box 44, Image 58. Photographer: White Studio, anonymous.)

figures of the Harlem Renaissance, including *The Blacker the Berry*, *Infants of the Spring*, and *The Intern*. He also contributed to some of the most popular periodicals of the Harlem Renaissance, such as *Fire!!*, *The Messenger*, and *The World Tomorrow*.

CARMEN PHELPS

See also Clough, Inez; Thurman, Wallace; Washington, Isabel

Further Reading

The African-American Theatre Directory, 1816–1960. Westport, Conn.: Greenwood, 1997.

Johnson, James Weldon. *Black Manhattan*. New York: Da Capo, 1930.

Kellner, Bruce, ed. *The Harlem Renaissance: A Historical Dictionary for the Era*. Westport, Conn.: Greenwood, 1984.

Mapp, Edward. *Directory of Blacks in the Performing Arts*. Metuchen, N.J.: Scarecrow, 1978.

Peterson, Bernard. *Profiles of African American Stage Performers and Theatre People, 1816–1960*. Westport, Conn.: Greenwood, 2001.

Harlem Renaissance: 1—Black Critics of

The literary and cultural flowering of the Harlem Renaissance is a source of pride for many African Americans. However, the renaissance has also received its share of skepticism and criticism. Critics charged that the promoters of the Harlem Renaissance had an inflated sense of its significance or had vastly overestimated what arts and letters could achieve; such critics also charged that the renaissance was simply cosmetic or irrelevant, or that the early literature of the renaissance was too elitist and was devoted to proving that black people were just like white people.

One must bear in mind that the Harlem Renaissance passed through at least three phases. Lewis (1979) suggests that its first phase began in 1917 and lasted until 1923. In this period, whites began to take an interest in black life and subjects, and whites dominated publication. In 1917, Ridgely Torrence and Emily Hapgood (who were white) presented three one-act plays with all-black casts: *The Rider of Dreams*, *Simon the Cyrenean*, and *Granny Maumee*. Then, in 1919, came the poem "If We Must Die" by Claude McKay (1889–1948), an immigrant from Jamaica. In 1920, there was a production of *The Emperor Jones*, by Eugene O'Neill, starring the African American actor Charles Gilpin. Black creative energy was emerging into the open, and in 1922, McKay published a collection of poems, *Harlem Shadows*, and James Weldon Johnson (1871–1938) published *The Book of American Negro Poetry*. Also in 1922, the white writer Thomas Stribling published a novel, *Birthright*, about an African American physician, educated at Harvard, who returns to the South and is killed there. In 1923, Boni and Liveright published *Cane*, by Jean Toomer (1894–1967), a writer whose work had been promoted by Sherwood Anderson. These developments stimulated a desire by African Americans to take a greater role in shaping and controlling their own literary representation. Blacks wanted to write literature about black people rather than passively sitting back and leaving literature about black people to be written by white people.

That desire in turn ushered in the second phase of the Harlem Renaissance, from 1924 to 1926, presided over by Charles Spurgeon Johnson (1893–1956) of the National Urban League and by individuals such as James Weldon Johnson (1871–1938) and Walter White (1893–1955) of the National Association for the Advancement of Colored People (NAACP). In March 1924, Charles Johnson arranged a dinner at the Civic Club in Manhattan, ostensibly to honor the publication of *There Is Confusion* by Jessie Redmon Fauset (c. 1882–1961). This dinner launched the term "Negro renaissance." Alain Locke (1885–1954) also played a prominent role at this time. The second phase of the Renaissance was dominated by the optimistic premise that arts and letters could achieve or help achieve a breakthrough in the struggle for racial equality. James Weldon Johnson said the world does not know that a people are great until they produce great literature and art. Literary and cultural achievement would be a means to the end of promoting civil rights. Lewis calls this perspective "civil rights by copyright." The approach of the Urban League and the NAACP, however, seemed to be based on the idea that in order to "win acceptance" by whites, black people had to prove that they were "just like" elite white people, sharing the same sense of propriety and convention. The result was a genteel literature about prim and proper light-skinned black people who seemed to be plastic imitations of elite whites, or about tragic mulattos struggling with racial ambivalence and the dilemmas of racial identity.

By 1926, the younger generation of African American writers rebelled against the censorship and "control" imposed by the older generation; these younger figures pushed the Harlem Renaissance into its third—populist—phase. The young insurgents reacted against what they perceived as an elitist, condescending view of black life, a view taken by people who were ashamed of the black working class, the ghetto, and the rural South. These younger writers of the renaissance included Claude McKay, Langston Hughes (1902–1967), Wallace Thurman (1902–1934), and Zora Neale Hurston (1891–1960).

Consequently, in discussing the Harlem Renaissance, it is crucial to specify what phase of the renaissance one is referring to. Furthermore, there were at least two different segments of the black community seeking to push or pull the renaissance in the direction they thought it should go: The "talented tenth" pulled in the direction of genteel culture as a means to the end of racial equality, and the young rebels pulled in the populist direction of art for art's sake. And always, in the background, the publishing companies and the patrons who supplied the fellowships and paid the bills were white–they had their own agendas, too. The result was a complex, many-sided tug-of-war, which gave rise to criticism of the Harlem Renaissance from many different quarters.

The most caustic critic of the Harlem Renaissance was George Schuyler (1895–1977). For the most part, he was criticizing its second phase. From 1923 to 1928, he served on the staff of *The Messenger*, edited by A. Philip Randolph and Chandler Owen. Schuyler married a white woman from Texas and was an integrationist. For many years he wrote a column called "Views and Reviews" in the *Pittsburgh Courier*. In June 1926, he published an article in *The Nation*, called "The Negro-Art Hokum," ridiculing the pretensions of the renaissance. Schuyler rejected the thesis that there was any distinctive "Negro" culture, seeing "Aframerican" music and culture as simply black versions of white American music and culture. Schuyler described the spirituals as merely slave songs based on Protestant hymns and biblical texts. Blues was nothing more than work songs and secular songs of "sorrow and tough luck." Jazz was but an outgrowth of ragtime. This music reflected the peasantry of the South and a caste of a certain section of the country, but it was foreign to northern Negroes and West Indian Negroes. The music and dancing were no more expressive or characteristic of the Negro race than the music and dancing of Appalachian highlanders or Dalmatian peasants were expressive of the Caucasian race. There was no distinctly African American culture or psychology. The African American was merely a "lampblacked Anglo-Saxon."

Schuyler's criticism cut two ways. He rejected the idea of a unique African American culture. But he also condemned the apparent need of some Caucasians to write about black Americans merely to suggest that no matter how civilized the African American appeared to be, "it is only necessary to beat a tom-tom or wave a rabbit's foot and he is ready to strip off his . . . suit, grab a spear and ride off wild-eyed on the back of a crocodile." In 1931, Schuyler wrote a satire, *Black No More*, that parodied leading figures of the Harlem Renaissance. In this novel, Dr. Junius Crookman develops a method of turning black people into white people. The National Social Equality League (standing for the NAACP) is horrified because it no longer has a need to exist. The hair-straightening business is pushed to the brink of collapse. Schuyler mocked the preoccupation of W. E. B. Du Bois and the NAACP with the "Negro problem" and suggested that they made a living from continually agitating about the issue of segregation and race. If the issue of race prejudice and discrimination were actually solved, Schuyler seemed to say, the NAACP would go out of business.

Schuyler also mocked the NAACP and the African American writers of the second phase of the Harlem Renaissance for striving so furiously to show that black people were "just like (elite) white people." Apparently he had Jessie Redmon Fauset's *There Is Confusion* (1924) in mind. In 1924, he described an African American fashion show held at Madison Square Garden. He described the crowd as consisting of mostly light-skinned people ("A genuine Negro was conspicuous"). They were doctors, lawyers, undertakers, dentists, members of college fraternities, all well-dressed, orderly, and cultured. He dismissed them as "manikins." In effect, this polished assemblage of the talented tenth was little more than a black imitation of the white elite. Its great mission was to achieve respectability and present itself as educated, cultivated, and refined. By being as much like the white elite as possible, black people could "prove" that they were worthy of respect and deserving of equality, and that they should be accepted by the white community. This model behavior would also distance them from the stereotype that all black people were loud, vulgar, and ignorant. Schuyler dismissed the debutante balls and glittering social occasions as a make-believe fantasy world.

Schuyler's observation about the light complexion of much of the African American intelligentsia of the 1920s, and some of the writers of the first and second phases of the Harlem Renaissance, was quite accurate. Jean Toomer, Jessie Fauset, and Nella Larsen (1891–1963) were light-complexioned people of African ancestry, and all three wrote about the dilemmas of mulatto or biracial identity. Toomer was the grandson of P. B. S. Pinchback, the biracial acting governor of Louisiana during Reconstruction. His "prose poem" *Cane* (1923) explores the theme of the tragic mulatto, caught between two worlds, black and white, and not fitting entirely into either one. The book seems to be a meditation on the meaning of racially mixed identity, or the search for identity, as if the author were trying to find (or understand) an enigmatic part of himself or his past or his ancestry. By 1930, Toomer would renounce his "blackness," deciding that he was no longer a Negro but "simply an American." He turned to the mysticism of Georgi Gurdjieff (and perhaps to the hope of a futuristic utopian society beyond race and color). In *There Is Confusion* (1924), by Jessie Fauset, the main characters are well-born black Philadelphians struggling against racism. Her second novel, *Plum Bun* (1929), also explores the problems of light-complexioned people who can "pass for white." Nella Larsen wrote *Passing* (1929), which directly confronts the choices made by biracial people who are light enough to "pass." Like Schuyler, many other African Americans ridiculed what they saw as snobbery, elitism, classism, and pretentiousness on the part of the "black bourgeoisie" and some of the early writers of the Harlem Renaissance, as well as the obsession with the theme of mulattos and racial ambivalence.

Many of the critics of the Harlem Renaissance bear a complex relationship to it because they were participants. Thus they criticized some particular aspect or phase of the renaissance. For example, W. E. B. Du Bois initially felt that arts and letters could be used as propaganda, to advance the cause of breaking down negative stereotypes and promoting racial equality. However, Du Bois intensely disliked works such as *Nigger Heaven* (1926), by the white author and patron of the renaissance Carl Van Vechten. He also hated Claude McKay's *Home to Harlem* (1928), which described ghetto life. Du Bois wrote that after reading *Home to Harlem* he felt "distinctly like needing a bath." He warned that the renaissance was deteriorating into art without politics, no longer serving the cause of advancing the struggle for racial equality. It ran the risk of sliding into mere decadence and vulgarity. He proclaimed:

> Thus all art is propaganda and ever must be, despite the wailing of purists. I stand in utter shamelessness and say that whatever art I have for writing has been used always for propaganda for gaining the right of black people to love and enjoy. I do not care a damn for any art that is not used for propaganda.

Du Bois charged that some whites who praised the Harlem Renaissance had an ulterior motive for doing so: "The recognition accorded to Cullen, Hughes, Fauset, White and others shows that there is no real color line. Keep quiet! Don't complain! Work! All will be well!" Thus the recognition and acclaim given to the literary movement could be used as proof of "progress" and could therefore be used to deny or minimize the reality of continuing racial oppression. In November 1926, Du Bois asked how the NAACP, as a radical, fighting organization, struggling for the rights of black people to be ordinary human beings, could turn aside to talk about mere art. He asked, "What have we who are slaves and black to do with art?" For Du Bois, art for art's sake, devoid of political content, was useless and even counterrevolutionary. It was little more than an evasion.

From a very different direction, as early as 1926, younger writers rebelled against the confining strictures and the prim, proper, puritanical conventions of their elders. This rebellion ushered in the third (populist) phase of the Harlem Renaissance. Claude McKay, Langston Hughes, Wallace Thurman, and Zora Neale Hurston were among those who rejected the strategy of "civil rights by copyright" and a literature of genteel, well-mannered, assimilated black people who were "just like" elite white people. The younger writers rejected a literature about "whitewashed" black people who seemed to feel that they were "better" than other black people because they were more "cultured" or lighter in color. The dissidents seem to have reacted viscerally to the hypocritical snobbery and elitism of a class of relatively privileged black people who felt entitled to judge and look down on and feel ashamed of and superior to other black people. After all, was this not precisely what racist whites had done to blacks as a whole for centuries?

Langston Hughes was one of the great populist rebels of the Harlem Renaissance. He defended art for art's sake. He sought to describe the full range of black life, as it actually was, without shame or apology. Hughes relentlessly ridiculed the illusion that arts and letters would change the cruel realities of racial domination and subordination. In *The Big Sea*, he said:

> Some Harlemites thought the millennium had come. They thought the race problem had at last been solved through Art plus Gladys Bentley. They were sure the New Negro would lead a new life from then on in green pastures of tolerance created by Countee Cullen, Ethel Waters, Claude McKay, Duke Ellington, Bojangles, and Alain Locke.

Furthermore, most blacks hadn't heard of the Harlem Renaissance, and it hadn't raised their wages any. Hughes's most devastating critique is given by the fictional character Oceola, in *The Ways of White Folks* (1934):

> And as for the cultured Negroes who were always saying art would break down color lines, art could save the race and prevent lynchings! "Bunk!" said Oceola. "Ma ma and pa were both artists when it came to making music, and the white folks ran them out of town for being dressed up in Alabama."

Another defiant critic of "proving how white and proper we can be" was Wallace Thurman. His relationship to the Harlem Renaissance is complex because he was novelist, editor, promoter, and critic all in one. He was a dark-skinned man, from Salt Lake City, Utah. As a novelist, he wrote *The Blacker the Berry* (1929) and *Infants of the Spring* (1932). The former explores the taboo subject of color stratification within the black community. The main character of the book is a dark-skinned black woman who is shunned and rejected by light-skinned black people and who struggles to find self-acceptance. The book reveals how color bias has been reproduced within the black community as internalized self-hatred. In November 1926, Thurman also founded and edited a literary magazine called *Fire!!*, a quarterly "Devoted to the Younger Negro Artists." As an editor, he was a promoter of a new (third) phase of the Harlem Renaissance. *Fire!!* included the poems "Elevator Boy" by Langston Hughes, "From the Dark Tower" by Countee Cullen, and "Southern Road" by Helene Johnson. It also included the short story "Sweat" and the play *Color Struck* by Zora Neale Hurston, and Thurman's own short story "Cordelia the Crude," about a young prostitute. The most shocking and sensational entry was "Smoke, Lilies, and Jade," by Richard Bruce Nugent. Nugent was controversial because he was openly homosexual, and the story describes an encounter between Alex and a man (Beauty) he meets on the street after a party in Greenwich Village. The story is written as if from an intoxicated haze, in which everything blurs together, and Alex's fiancée (Melva) and Beauty also blur together in Alex's mind. Readers have interpreted this as androgynous and homoerotic. It certainly scandalized the talented tenth, the guardians of the renaissance.

Thurman deliberately intended to shock traditional sensibilities and social conventions, and to portray all of African American life, warts and all. Thus he included literature about street life, ordinary working people, and sexuality. In November 1928, Thurman tried again with a new magazine; this successor to *Fire!!* was called *Harlem*. Thurman symbolizes the revolt of the younger generation against the censorship and snobbery of the older generation. At the same time, class dynamics appear to have been at work: The younger writers identified with the working class and the black urban masses rather than the elite. Thurman's marriage to Louise Thompson ended in divorce, amid accusations that he was a homosexual. And he was, in fact, an alcoholic. Thurman was a manifold "outsider." He was from Utah (not the Northeast or South). He was dark, not light. He had not attended one of the historically black colleges that educated the children of the black elite. And he was gay (or bisexual). He seems to have been destined to be one of the great rebels of the renaissance even as he was a significant participant in it. He criticized the elitist, bourgeois wing and the second phase of the renaissance, while advocating a more egalitarian and unapologetic approach.

Like Thurman, Zora Neale Hurston was a member of the populist wing and the third phase of the Harlem Renaissance. She humorously referred to the white patrons and allies of the civil rights movement and the renaissance as "Negrotarians," and to the writers, artists, and literati as the "niggerati." She drew inspiration from the rural South and its folklore and dialect. She was not ashamed of what the "highbrow" crowd would consider to be the ignorant, embarrassing, or superstitious folkways of the South.

In the inevitable tug-of-war between generations, time is on the side of youth. The most enduring literary symbol of the Harlem Renaissance is Langston Hughes. He would become the most beloved poet of the period, the poet laureate of the renaissance. In the end, the loving criticism of the rebels prevailed, and it would go on to inspire later generations and the literary awakening of the black arts movement and the black aesthetics of the 1960s.

WAYNE GLASKER

See also Du Bois, W. E. B.; Fauset, Jessie Redmon; Fire!!; Hughes, Langston; Hurston, Zora Neale; Johnson, Charles Spurgeon; Johnson, James Weldon; Larsen, Nella; Locke, Alain; McKay, Claude; Messenger, The; Nation, The; Nugent, Richard Bruce; Pittsburgh Courier; Schuyler, George S.; Talented Tenth; Thurman, Wallace; Toomer, Jean; White, Walter

Further Reading

Baker, Houston, Jr. *Modernism and the Harlem Renaissance.* Chicago, Ill.: University of Chicago Press, 1987.

Huggins, Nathan. *The Harlem Renaissance.* New York: Oxford University Press, 1971.

Hutchinson, George. *The Harlem Renaissance in Black and White.* Cambridge, Mass.: Belknap, Harvard University Press, 1995.

Lewis, David Levering, ed. *When Harlem Was in Vogue.* New York: Knopf, 1979. (With new preface, New York: Penguin, 1997.)

———. *The Portable Harlem Renaissance Reader.* New York: Penguin, 1994.

Rampersad, Arnold. *The Life of Langston Hughes*, 2 vols. New York: Oxford University Press, 1986.

Wall, Cheryl. *Women of the Harlem Renaissance*. Bloomington: Indiana University Press, 1995.

Harlem Renaissance: 2—Black Promoters of

Several African Americans, along with the National Association for the Advancement of Colored People (NAACP) and the National Urban League, played a significant role in promoting the Harlem Renaissance. The involvement of African Americans in promoting literature by and about blacks began in earnest in 1924. It had been preceded, in 1923, when Jean Toomer's novel *Cane* was published by Boni and Liveright. Toomer's work had been promoted by Sherwood Anderson. Thereafter, African Americans consciously sought a greater role in shaping the representation of their own image to the wider public.

One of the foremost African American promoters of the Harlem (or African American) Renaissance was Charles Spurgeon Johnson (1893–1956). He was born in Virginia and earned a Ph.D. in sociology from the University of Chicago in 1918. He came to New York as the director of research for the Urban League in 1921, and in 1923, he began to edit its magazine, *Opportunity*. In 1924, Johnson sponsored a literary gathering at the Civic Club in Manhattan. The event took place on 21 March 1924, and a week later the New York *Herald Tribune* referred to it as evidence that America was on the "edge . . . of a Negro renaissance." The idea of a Negro renaissance was born, and Johnson had been a midwife in the process. Beginning in 1925, *Opportunity* sponsored an annual literary competition, awarding prizes and steering promising talent to publishing houses (which at that time were owned entirely by Caucasians). Johnson compiled information on talented artists and writers who could be recruited and promoted. For example, he encouraged Aaron Douglas (1898–1979), an artist from Kansas, to come to New York. Johnson was one of the great middlemen in the process of linking black talent to white publishers and sponsors from 1924 to 1926. In 1926, Johnson left New York for Fisk University, where he served as chairman of the sociology department, and in 1946, he became the first African American president of Fisk.

The NAACP also sponsored a literary contest and awarded prizes. W. E. B. Du Bois (1868–1963) was the editor of the NAACP's magazine, *The Crisis* (beginning in 1910), and Jessie Redmon Fauset (1882–1961) served as literary editor (1919–1926). Fauset had graduated with honors from Cornell and had received an M.A. in French from the University of Pennsylvania. She was one of the first people to recognize the talent of Toomer and Langston Hughes. In 1921, Fauset published Hughes's famous poem "I've Known Rivers" in *The Crisis*. Funds for the NAACP's literary prize came from Amy Spingarn, the wife of Joel Spingarn. The Spingarn Award, begun in 1915, was not originally for literary, artistic, or creative endeavor, but four of the eight awards given from 1924 to 1931 went to performing artists or writers (Roland Hayes, Charles Chesnutt, the actor Richard B. Harrison, and James Weldon Johnson).

Walter White (1893–1955), the assistant executive director of the NAACP (1918–1930), also promoted the careers of promising writers and actors. For instance, he urged Paul Robeson to give up a career in law to pursue acting. Also, White was a friend of Carl Van Vechten and the publisher Alfred Knopf. Thus he was in a position to commend talented writers to the attention of Knopf. James Weldon Johnson (1871–1938), executive secretary of the NAACP (1920–1930), was another promoter of the Harlem Renaissance. In 1922, he published *The Book of American Negro Poetry*. He is most famous, perhaps, as the author of the song "Lift Every Voice and Sing" (1900).

The premier promoter of the renaissance was Alain Locke (1885–1954). Locke, a lifelong bachelor, was a graduate of Harvard and the first African American Rhodes scholar (1907–1910). He earned a Ph.D. from Harvard in 1918 and served on the faculty at Howard University beginning in 1912. Locke edited the special edition of *Survey Graphic* (May 1925) and the anthology *The New Negro* (1926). As an editor, he was in a unique position to select which authors and works to publish. He is credited with helping to advance the careers of Countee Cullen, Claude McKay, Richmond Barthé, Aaron Douglas, and Langston Hughes, among others. Locke was also influential because of his friendship with Charlotte Osgood Mason ("Godmother"), a wealthy white widow who used her fortune to become a patron of the arts. She was interested in preserving the "purity" of "primitive" peoples and cultures, uncontaminated by the corruption of modern Western civilization. Locke was in a position to recommend gifted writers and artists to Mason, and she could provide them with financial support. She served as benefactor to Langston Hughes, Claude McKay, and Zora Neale Hurston.

Arthur (Arturo) Schomburg (1874–1938) was Puerto Rican, not African American. However, it should be noted that he collected literature, art, and material on Africa and Africans in the new world. Over time he amassed more than 5,000 books, 3,000 manuscripts, and several thousand etchings, drawings, and pamphlets. These items formed the basis of the famous Schomburg Collection.

Perhaps the most ostentatious of the African American promoters of the Harlem Renaissance was A'Lelia Walker (c. 1885–1931), daughter of the millionaire Madam C. J. Walker (who was famous for her hair treatment process and her empire of beauty salons). A'Lelia Walker inherited her mother's estate on the Hudson River and maintained residences on Edgecombe Avenue and 136th, Street. Her apartment on Edgecombe Avenue has been described as a combination retreat and pleasure dome, where she threw lavish parties and entertained artists, writers, and dignitaries. Although she did not support the writers and artists financially, no account of the promoters of the renaissance would be complete without her.

Finally, as part of the effort to promote the renaissance, even a "numbers king" in Harlem, Casper Holstein (who came from the Danish West Indies), donated money for *Opportunity*'s literary prizes.

It is crucial to ask, however, what the promoters of the Harlem Renaissance *believed* they were doing. What were their motives? What ends did they hope to achieve, and what means were they using to reach those ends? Although scholars debate these questions, the writings of some of the "promoters" suggest that they saw the production of "great" literary and cultural work as a way to elevate the status of African Americans and improve the treatment of blacks by the white majority. The individuals who expressed the view that the demonstration of artistic merit would help improve the position of black people within American society are sometimes referred to as the "arts and letters school." James Weldon Johnson, who had studied literature at Columbia, wrote in *The Book of American Negro Poetry* (1922):

> The final measure of the greatness of all peoples is the amount and standard of the literature and art they have produced. The world does not know that a people are great until that people produces great literature and art. No people that has produced great literature and art has ever been looked upon by the world as distinctly inferior. . . . And nothing will do more to change the mental attitude and raise

his status than a demonstration of intellectual parity by the Negro through the production of literature and art.

The African American literary critic Benjamin Brawley expressed to James Weldon Johnson the view that "we have a tremendous opportunity to boost the NAACP, letters, and arts, and anything else that calls attention to our development along the higher lines." For Brawley, Fauset, Du Bois, and the so-called talented tenth, however, development along the "higher lines" seems to have meant development by the "right type" of African American: the college-educated, white-collar professionals, the middle class, the "bourgeoisie." It meant activity by black people who were refined, educated, polished, and well-mannered. It probably did not mean the untutored masses—the rural peasantry, the sharecroppers, or the residents of the ghettos and slums.

In praising the ideal of the power of culture to promote the cause of racial equality, Alain Locke proclaimed that African Americans' "more immediate hope rests in the revaluation by white and black alike of the Negro in terms of his artistic endowments and cultural contributions, past and prospective." Furthermore, the writers and artists found themselves "acting as the advance guard of the African peoples in their contact with twentieth-century civilization." In "Harlem: Mecca of the New Negro," the special number of *Survey Graphic* (1926), Locke wrote: "Harlem has the same role to play for the New Negro as Dublin has had for the New Ireland or Prague for the New Czechoslovakia." And W. E. B. Du Bois consistently defended art and literature as "propaganda" that should serve a cause.

Some scholars have interpreted these statements by James Weldon Johnson, Charles S. Johnson, Brawley, Fauset, and Locke as evidence that the promoters of the Harlem Renaissance hoped to achieve a breakthrough in civil rights and use culture for political purposes. They hoped to use culture as a political weapon, as a means to the end of achieving better treatment and conditions for African Americans. Somehow, if only African Americans could "prove" that they were talented human beings with a worthwhile culture, each poem or novel or sculpture would undermine the old images of black people as inherently and immutably ignorant, illiterate, and inferior. If only black people could prove how refined and cultured they could be or were becoming, their works of genius would change white supremacists' opinions and overturn racial prejudice. Racism would be overthrown and broken down by means of displaying the cultural brilliance of Afro-America. Arts and letters would become alternatives to the blocked paths to the voting booth and the workplace. Lewis (1994) describes this approach as "civil rights by copyright."

At worst, some promoters of the renaissance may have naively fallen into the trap of imagining that if only African Americans could show and prove that they were "just like white people," could compose sonnets and rhyming couplets, and could create works of subtle beauty and elegance, "white people" would begin to regard them as human beings and not savages whose heathen ancestors swung (naked) through the trees in Africa. If only African Americans exhibited the same manners and "refined" sensibilities as the white elite, and spoke with proper diction and conjugated foreign verbs, Caucasians would abandon racism and begin to accept African Americans as fellow citizens worthy of all the same rights and opportunities as everyone else. This strategy of trying to show that black people could be "just like white people," and thereby earn respect and win sympathy, would lead some individuals to a quest for assimilation and mindless imitation of the British-American elite and its culture.

Some African American promoters of the Harlem Renaissance had a second motive. They wanted to present positive images of black people. They were concerned that literature *about* black people was being written *by* whites. As an equal and opposite reaction, African Americans sought greater control over the literary representation of black people. They felt that black people were better qualified to provide a genuine, authentic, informed account of black life. They believed black people would benefit if they were in a position to present positive images that "uplifted" the race and presented its "best face." One of the best examples of this perspective is Jessie Redmon Fauset. Describing her expectations of what might come of the renaissance, she wrote: "Here is an audience waiting to hear the truth about us. Let us who are better qualified to present that truth than any white writer, try to do so." One might add that Fauset's writing tended to focus on light-complexioned biracial African Americans who were educated and refined, struggling to win "acceptance" in the face of irrational and undeserved hostility from whites.

Charles S. Johnson exemplifies a third (and rather opportunistic) approach toward promoting the Harlem Renaissance. In contrast to those who adopted an uncritical strategy of blind imitation, Johnson perceived that white America, at the time, was taking an unprecedented interest in black America. In 1917, Ridgely Torrence and Emily Hapgood had staged three one-act plays with all-black casts at the Provincetown Playhouse: *The Rider of Dreams, Simon the Cyrenean*, and *Granny Maumee*. In 1920, there was a production of *The Emperor Jones*, by Eugene O'Neill, starring the African American actor Charles Gilpin. In 1922, a white writer, Thomas Stribling (1881–1965), wrote the novel *Birthright*, about an African American who is a Harvard-educated physician and is killed after his return to the South. In 1923 (as noted previously), Boni and Liveright published *Cane*, by Jean Toomer, whose work had been championed by Caucasians such as Sherwood Anderson and Waldo Frank. Johnson realized that this interest by Caucasians in African Americans presented an opportunity for African Americans *to promote their own agenda*. Capitalizing on the interest of white publishers could be a way for African Americans to pursue their own quest for respect, civil rights, and improved opportunities and conditions. Thus the interest of white publishers in using black writers and their culture could be used by African Americans to advance the cause of resisting white supremacy. Johnson realized that the "game" was one of mutual use: use and be used. Far better that each side get something out of the exchange than that the exchange be entirely one-sided. Obviously this exchange was taking place in a context where the relationship of power was very asymmetric.

Some of the African American promoters of the renaissance may have overestimated what culture (arts and letters) could achieve. They may have had an inordinate faith in the power of poetry, novels, and pretty paintings of landscapes and sunsets to combat negative stereotypes about African Americans. Ultimately, some promoters of the renaissance may have expected more from arts and letters than arts and letters could achieve or deliver. There is no substitute for organized struggle, and one cannot realistically expect culture to do the work of politics. Nor will an elite movement be enough. There is no substitute for an organized *mass* movement, springing up from the grassroots.

But one must be careful not to imagine that all the promoters of the Harlem Renaissance bought into the idea of using arts and letters as an alternative means of advancing the political struggle for racial equality. Wallace Thurman (1902–1934), who was both a participant (as a novelist and editor) and a promoter, illustrates a fourth approach to the renaissance. This approach may be described as populist. Thurman was one of the enfants terribles of the period. He was dark-skinned; had been born in Salt Lake City, Utah; had attended the University of Utah and the University of Southern California; and had worked at the Los Angeles post office with Arna Bontemps. Leaving California in 1924, he came east and worked with A. Philip Randolph's publication *The Messenger*. He was also circulation manager of *The World Tomorrow*, a liberal white monthly. Thurman rejected the bourgeois pretensions and respectability of the black middle class. In 1926, he founded and edited a short-lived journal called *Fire!!* that included works by Langston Hughes, Richard Bruce Nugent, and Zora Neale Hurston. It shocked the civil rights establishment by including depictions of prostitutes, street life in the ghetto, and even ruminations of an androgynous or bisexual nature. Thurman, whose marriage to Louise Thompson ended in divorce and accusations that he was a homosexual, reflected the views of the younger generation of artists. He rebelled against the elders and their snobbish sense of social convention, and he promoted art for art's sake. His novel *The Blacker the Berry* (1929) exposed the taboo subject of color stratification *within* the black community, with lighter-complexioned African Americans ostracizing and looking down on those who were darker. In "The Negro Artist and the Racial Mountain" (1926), Langston Hughes, very much in accord with Thurman's defiant stance, insisted:

> We younger Negro artists who create now intend to express our individual dark-skinned selves without fear or shame. If white people are pleased, we are glad. If they are not, it doesn't matter. We know we are beautiful. And ugly too. . . . If colored people are pleased, we are glad. If they are not, their displeasure doesn't matter either.

For inspiration, Thurman and Hughes looked to ordinary black people and to everyday life in the ghetto. Zora Neale Hurston looked to the folklore of the rural South. Thurman, Hughes, Hurston, and others like them represented a phase of the renaissance that refused to worship at the altar of arts and letters as a means to the end of improving racial conditions. They rejected the strategy of "sanitizing" black life and putting only the best foot forward at all times and trying to prove how much black people could mimic the image of (elite) white people. Instead, they articulated

the value of self-acceptance as they struggled to combat self-hatred within the black psyche and within the black community.

The Harlem Renaissance was a seed that would grow into a mighty tree, and eventually bring forth much fruit. It was also a stepping-stone or a bridge to—or a foundation for—later developments. It inspired African Americans, giving them a new sense of their own abilities and possibilities, and it helped create a psychological revolution. Only fifty years after the end of slavery, African Americans could take pride in the genius of Du Bois; the poetry of Cullen, McKay, Hughes, and Bontemps; the stories of Toomer, Fauset, Larsen, and Hurston; the art of Aaron Douglas and Palmer Hayden. These achievements, from a people who were supposedly incapable of producing literature or culture, proved that the ideology of inborn, immutable black inferiority was a lie. Although the renaissance is criticized for having been confined to a few (mostly) elite writers, this small cadre dared to raise its voice to defend the honor and aspirations of a despised and victimized people. It is remarkable that an oppressed people managed to produce so much beauty and talent despite the terrorism of lynching, serfdom, sharecropping, and incarceration in the ghettos.

The renaissance is also sometimes criticized as artificial and merely ornamental or cosmetic. After all, it did not change the grim realities of the ghetto, the high rates of infant mortality, or the lower life expectancy of African Americans. It did not raise wages or give jobs to the unemployed. It did not alter the relationship of domination and subordination. The relationship between the black promoters of the Harlem Renaissance, black writers, and the whites who financed them, patronized them, and owned the publishing companies was a decidedly unequal one. However, the renaissance was a stage in the development of a people. It was a rung on a ladder. The miracle is that it happened at all. Whatever its shortcomings, the Harlem Renaissance became a beacon of inspiration whose light illuminated a dark hour and whose legend endures to this very day.

WAYNE GLASKER

See also Anderson, Sherwood; Boni and Liveright; Brawley, Benjamin; Civic Club Dinner, 1924; Crisis, The: Literary Prizes; Du Bois, W. E. B.; Fauset, Jessie Redmon; Fire!!; Holstein, Casper; Johnson, Charles Spurgeon; Johnson, James Weldon; Knopf, Alfred A.; Locke, Alain; Mason, Charlotte Osgood; National Association for the Advancement of Colored People;

National Urban League; New Negro, The; Opportunity Literary Contests; Schomburg, Arthur A.; Spingarn, Joel; Survey Graphic; Thurman, Wallace; Van Vechten, Carl; Walker, A'Lelia; White, Walter; *specific artists and writers*

Further Reading

Baker, Houston, Jr. *Modernism and the Harlem Renaissance.* Chicago, Ill.: University of Chicago Press, 1987.

Huggins, Nathan. *The Harlem Renaissance.* New York: Oxford University Press, 1971.

Hutchinson, George. *The Harlem Renaissance in Black and White.* Cambridge, Mass.: Belknap, Harvard University Press, 1995.

Lewis, David Levering. *When Harlem Was in Vogue.* New York: Knopf, 1979. (With new preface, New York: Penguin, 1997.)

———. ed. *The Portable Harlem Renaissance Reader.* New York: Penguin, 1994.

Rampersad, Arnold. *The Life of Langston Hughes,* 2 vols. New York: Oxford University Press, 1986.

Wall, Cheryl. *Women of the Harlem Renaissance.* Bloomington: Indiana University Press, 1995.

Harlem Renaissance: 3—Legacy of

Until the early 1970s, most students of the literature of the United States could not have been terribly concerned with the legacy of the New Negro or Harlem Renaissance. They were barely aware of this historical phenomenon, which had extensive implications for all Americans' understanding of culture, citizenship, artistic production, and the intricate ways in which they define one another. But since the 1970s, the Harlem Renaissance has gained prominence in our sense of social, cultural, and literary history, as well as in the college and university curriculum. One can approach the legacy of this movement and period from various angles, and perhaps the best way to gauge the range of possibilities is to recount the reception of the Harlem Renaissance in recent American cultural history.

In the 1970s, when scholars such as Nathan Huggins, James O. Young, Margaret Perry, and Amritjit Singh (the present writer) extended and revised the earlier surveys of the period by Sterling A. Brown, Hugh M. Gloster, and Robert Bone, they were concerned mostly with remedying the absence of the renaissance from books such as Hoffman (1962). Such scholars had hoped to include the Harlem Renaissance in what Van Wyck Brooks, in the 1920s, saw as America's coming-of-age and to link their examination of this historical phenomenon to their new concern with shaping a multiethnic consciousness of American literature—a project we associate today with the beginnings and the impact on our curriculum and pedagogy of organizations such as the College Language Association (CLA), the Society for the Study of Multi-Ethnic Literature of the United States (MELUS), and the National Association of Ethnic Studies (NAES) and with anthologies such as the two-volume *Heath Anthology of American Literature* (1990). In fact, Huggins (1971), in the first major study of the "black 1920s," regards black Americans' confusion over identity as uniquely American and describes it in the post–World War I context as symbiotic with that of white Americans: "White Americans and white American culture have no more claim to self-confidence than black. . . . Blacks have been essential to white identity (and whites to black). . . . They cannot be understood independently." Huggins notes that "whenever Americans do come of age, they will have gained true insight into themselves" by claiming their interdependence, but he also recognizes that blacks' willingness to be used for the sake of whites' "psychic dependency" defines "deep moral tensions" in American race relations.

Many scholars—notably Cruse (1967)—have argued that the Harlem Renaissance failed at precisely the project it had set out to accomplish: to extend the civil and human rights of African Americans by demonstrating the quality and quantity of their artistic contributions. Cruse, the harshest of the critics, blames the failure of the renaissance to define its own nationalist aesthetic on the "ludicrous" integrationist goals of its protagonists and on its dependence on white institutions. Huggins's seemingly simple statement—near the conclusion of his book—that "the true Negro renaissance awaits Afro-Americans' claiming their *patria,* their nativity"—militates against his more complex analyses throughout his book of the interrelatedness of black and white identities during the 1920s. In contrast to Cruse, who views the powerlessness and imitativeness of the writers and intellectuals of the Harlem Renaissance as a direct consequence of their individualism, Huggins sees their obsession with group identity as a source of debilitating provincialism. Huggins places considerable faith in what he extrapolates as Wallace Thurman's point in *Infants of the Spring*: "Artistic production was an extremely personal, individualistic thing, not to be turned on or off by nationalism of any kind." Singh (1976) describes Cruse's charges as having been made from the vantage point of the 1960s and 1970s and argues that "the failure or success of any literary movement cannot be directly related to the acceptance or rejection of a well-defined ideology." He finds that the patronage of the black middle class was "as mixed a blessing as the white patronage" and asserts that "the majority of Harlem Renaissance novels did not deal with issues central to the black masses." Baker (1987) notes that Lewis (1987), in focusing on the "tragically wide, ambitious, and delusional striving" of black intellectuals, takes a view of the failures of the renaissance that is contrary to Huggins's. For Lewis, as Baker puts it, "the architects of the Renaissance believed in ultimate victory through the maximizing of the exceptional. They deceived themselves into thinking that race relations in the United States were amenable to the assimilationist patterns of a Latin country."

So until well into the 1980s, the Harlem Renaissance was viewed mostly as an exciting period for the arts—a period that produced many fascinating works of poetry, fiction, music, painting, and sculpture but whose major promoters and participants made remarkably naive arguments about the sociopolitical possibilities of art and had naive expectations for American legal and political institutions. Baker attempted to interpret the period more positively and has been credited by Helbling (1999) and others with moving the discussion of its failure or success to a new plane. Baker sees as inadequate to the (discursive) history of Afro-American modernism any *"histories* that are assumed in the chronologies of British, Anglo-American, and Irish modernisms." Detecting a distinctively "Afro-American *sounding*" in the texts and figures of the Harlem Renaissance (his choices include Booker T. Washington, Charles W. Chesnutt, and W. E. B. Du Bois), he offers "what is perhaps *sui generic* definition of modern Afro-American sound as a function of a specifically Afro-American discursive practice." Hutchinson (1995), attempting to establish the Harlem Renaissance as a successful project, focuses on "interracialism" and underplays the often colonial nature of relations between American whites and blacks in the 1920s. Hutchinson chastises Baker for a lack of historical complexity and suggests that Baker, like Huggins, fails to notice that the writers of the Harlem Renaissance looked more to the "low modernism" of Whitman, Sinclair Lewis, Sandburg, Shaw, and Synge than to the "high modernism" of Eliot, Joyce, Yeats, Stein, or Pound—a point made earlier by Rampersad (1989).

An important aspect of the historiography of the Harlem Renaissance during the 1980s and 1990s is feminist scholarship, which has revised and expanded our sense of the renaissance. Feminist scholars of these decades examined how issues of genre, periodization, class, and gender had been treated earlier, during the 1970s, and also brought to the fore many neglected women writers of the 1920s and 1930s. For example, Hull (1987) argues that women writers are "tyrannized by periodization, the hierarchy of canonical forms, critical rankings of major and minor, and generalizations about literary periods." The new feminist consciousness allowed many black women scholars to offer a fresh, sometimes empathic examination of the challenges faced by women artists of the 1920s and 1930s regarding gender, race, and class. This scholarship is embodied in Hull et al. (1982) and in the cumulative work of dozens of other writers and scholars, such as Alice Walker, Audre Lorde, Mary Helen Washington, Barbara Christian, Henry Louis Gates Jr., Nellie McKay, Toni Morrison, Gloria Naylor, Gayl Jones, Sherley Ann Williams, Hortense Spillers, Cheryl Wall, Hazel Carby, Michael Awkward, Deborah McDowell, Gloria Hull, Thadious Davis, Maureen Honey, Karla Holloway, and Marcy Knopf. Walker, in particular, through essays such as "In Search of Our Mothers' Gardens" and "Looking for Zora" (originally published in the mid-1970s in *Ms.*), helped establish Zora Neale Hurston as a central figure of the period. Walker argued for a radically new view of black female creativity while recounting her search for Hurston—her life; her grave in the marshes of Eatonville, Florida; and the meaning of her narratives, especially *Their Eyes Were Watching God*. In these essays, which have inspired scores of other scholars, Walker made the point that Hurston had not received her due from other writers of the Harlem Renaissance writers or from later critics, primarily because of her strong individuality, her uninterest in becoming either white or bourgeois, and her devotion to black folk culture. Walker noted: "That Hurston held her own literally against the flood of whiteness and maleness that diluted so much other black art of the period in which she worked is a testimony to her genius and her faith." Walker also wrote forewords to Hemenway's biography (1977) and Washington's anthology (1978) of Hurston—two books that brought further attention to Hurston's importance in the Harlem Renaissance.

Since the 1980s, we have benefited immensely not only from the social and cultural histories of the period by Jervis Anderson, Cary Wintz, and David Levering

Lewis but also from the revisionist readings of the "modern" by Houston Baker Jr., James de Jongh, Michael North, Sieglinde Lemke, and others. There is also extensive and still growing new scholarship on music, theater, and the fine arts and on literary and cultural activity away from New York City, as well as several essays on gay and lesbian issues. Smith (1977) presaged much of the work by black feminists, and Nero (1991) took another new direction in African American literary study. Extending the arguments of Smith and Nero to the Harlem Renaissance, many scholars continue to offer important new readings and rereadings of texts and figures. With the availability of previously unpublished writings by Richard Bruce Nugent in *Gay Rebel of the Harlem Renaissance* (2002) and by Wallace Thurman in *The Collective Writings of Wallace Thurman* (2003), the interrelated processes of recovery and rereading are likely to accelerate.

The aesthetic legacy of the Harlem Renaissance is indicated best by latter-day understandings of the triangular relationship among the positions taken by Du Bois, Alain Locke, and the younger writers such as Langston Hughes, Thurman, and Hurston, most of whom were associated with the magazine *Fire!!* (1926). Sharing the optimism of white American cultural pluralists and progressive reformers, Locke recognized that "the conditions that are molding a New Negro are [also] molding a new American attitude." In terms of art and literature, Locke saw no conflict between being "American" and being "Negro," but rather an opportunity to enrich both through cultural reciprocity. In a way, Locke was reinterpreting Du Bois's concept of "double consciousness" for aesthetic and cultural uses, and Locke's view seems to have had room for many different talents to exist and thrive together. Locke did not see any direct connection between African American artists and the African arts that had influenced the works of many Europeans such as Picasso. For Locke, the most important lesson the Negro artist in the United States could derive from African art was "not cultural inspiration or technical innovations, but the lesson of a classic background, the lesson of discipline, of style, of technical control." He wanted the younger writers to create a cohesive artistic movement that would—through a responsible and pluralistic exploration of "race"—contribute to Negroes' struggle for civil equality. Like James Weldon Johnson, Locke stressed the importance of racial expression in African American writing, linking Negroes' civil rights to their artistic output. And like Charles S. Johnson, he rejected cultural separatism

and endorsed a hybrid of black experiences and Euro-American aesthetic forms. Thurman and others often found Locke's well-intentioned but overbearing views a challenge to their artistic independence, and they were even more vehemently opposed to the programmatic and promotional ideologies of leaders and intellectuals such as Du Bois, Allison Davis, Aubrey Bowser, and Benjamin Brawley. In fact, Thurman's consuming passion was arguing against the older generation's insistence on representational didacticism and idealism, which for him was indistinguishable from the bourgeoisie's obsession with uplift and respectability. Thurman not only wrote more forcefully and persistently than others on these issues, but he also tried to organize the opposition of the younger generation through the publication of *Fire!!* and *Harlem*. These two magazines did, as intended, shock the older generation, but for financial reasons neither lasted beyond the first issue.

The central debate of the period—the incidence of racial expression in African American writing and art—is probably best summed up in Schuyler (1926) and Hughes (1926), two articles published in consecutive issues of *The Nation*, along with some further correspondence from these two authors. Schuyler considers Negro art simply an African phenomenon, rejecting the possibility of any such development among black Americans. He considers spirituals, blues, jazz, and the Charleston not racial expression but "contributions of a caste in a certain section of the country." Otherwise, in literature, painting, sculpture, and drama, the American Negro has produced hardly anything racially distinctive, because "the Afro-American is merely a lampblacked Anglo-Saxon." Hughes, in turn, finds the taint of self-hatred in Schuyler's view of black art and culture. In his own essay, Hughes projects a culturally pluralistic view of black art, emphasizing the integrity of the artist. He observes that for most blacks and black artists, "the word white comes to be unconsciously a symbol of all the virtues. It holds for the children beauty, morality, and money." For Hughes, issues of racial expression converge on the issue of class within the black community. The "lowdown folks," he says, "furnish a wealth of colorful, distinctive material for any artist because they still hold their own individuality in the face of American standardizations. And perhaps these common people will give to the world its truly great Negro artist, the one who is not afraid to be himself." As a black artist, Hughes welcomes a growing middle-class black audience for his work but regards this audience as a potential threat to his artistic integrity. Using his own poems and Jean Toomer's *Cane* as examples of the kind of racial expression he approves and cherishes, Hughes asserts his artistic independence of both whites and blacks: "We younger Negro artists who create now intend to express our individual dark-skinned selves without fear or shame. . . . We build our temples for tomorrow, strong as we know how, and we stand on top of the mountain, free within ourselves."

As of the present writing, there had been no serious study of the effect of the Harlem Renaissance on later African American authors. It would appear, though, that what is important for latter-day culture and literature is the New Negro's insistence, in so many spheres, on self-definition, self-expression, and self-determination—a striving after what Locke called "spiritual emancipation." The many debates that took place during the Harlem Renaissance on art and propaganda, representation and identity, assimilation versus militancy, and parochialism versus globalism enriched the perspectives on issues of art, culture, politics, and ideology that have emerged on the African American scene since the 1930s, especially the perspectives offered by Richard Wright, Ralph Ellison, and Toni Morrison. In the 1920s, journals such as *The Crisis*, *Opportunity*, and *The Messenger* helped interpret for their growing readership the powerful impact of World War I and the "great migration" on the African American masses. Since the late 1970s, Zora Neale Hurston has received wide recognition for her feminist consciousness. Sharing an interest in issues of class and color with male writers such as McKay, Hughes, Toomer, and Rudolph Fisher, women writers such as Hurston, Jessie Redmon Fauset, Nella Larsen, Dorothy West, Marieta Bonner, and Gwendolyn Bennett—each in her own way—explored female lives and the politics of gender. Today, the women writers of the Harlem Renaissance have become a major literary presence and a source of inspiration. Jean Toomer appears to have been read and admired by most African American writers since the 1920s. Langston Hughes, a major figure of the Harlem Renaissance, continued to support and influence the careers of many black writers until his death in 1967. The renaissance can certainly be credited with initiating discussions on many artistic and cultural concerns of African Americans that have caused heated controversy since the 1960s—such as the treatment of black themes and characters by white writers and the aesthetic criteria for black writing. The novelist John A. Williams has written: "For me . . . the

real meaning of the Harlem Renaissance was that it gave us an example, and having had that example, we do not need to make the same mistakes its members made" (Fuller 1970). From comments by Richard Wright and Ralph Ellison, it appears that they learned from the mistakes of their predecessors in the renaissance, especially in being aware of the dangers inherent in gearing their artistic impulses to the needs and demands of a primarily white audience. Also, the many clear-headed pronouncements on race, gender, and art by Hughes, Locke, Hurston, and McKay probably paved the way for Toni Morrison's unabashed rejection of false dichotomies between being a "black" and a "woman" novelist, as well as between being an "American" and a "global" writer.

Later African American writers have perhaps learned more from the failings of the Harlem Renaissance than from its achievements, but by the late 1920s, black authors in the West Indies and Africa were already taking inspiration from the spirit and individual works of the New Negro movement. Léopold Senghor of Senegal and Aimé Césaire of Martinique had read poetry and fiction of the Harlem Renaissance in translation while they were still students at the Sorbonne. Under its influence, these two poets developed their variant concepts of *négritude*, which, according to them, expressed the unifying essence of black experience and culture throughout the world. These and other African intellectuals such as Sembene Ousmane and Ousmane Soce, who have articulated African nationalism, were inspired by Claude McKay's *Banjo*. The South African writer Peter Abrahams has written in his autobiography, *Tell Freedom*, about how, as a teenager at the Bantu Men's Social Center in Johannesburg, he discovered writers of the renaissance such as Claude McKay, Langston Hughes, Georgia Douglas Johnson, Countee Cullen, and W. E. B. Du Bois, and how they gave him hope for the future and faith in "color nationalism." In the 1990s, the Harlem Renaissance began to be seen as an important manifestation of nationalist stirrings in the early twentieth century that led to a fuller postcolonial consciousness in global literature and politics.

Many writers of the Harlem Renaissance who remained active after the 1920s—such as Hughes, Nugent, West, and Arna Bontemps—talked and wrote about the period, but Thurman provided, in his roman à clef *Infants of the Spring* (1932), the only detailed contemporary account of the movement. This work, a thinly veiled satire on the major figures of the renaissance, presents mediocre artists caught in a web of frivolity and recalcitrance without purpose or privacy, unable to achieve anything worthwhile. Raymond, Thurman's protagonist, is disgusted at attempts to romanticize Harlem and offers a harsh judgment of himself and his colleagues, almost all of whom in his view are warped by either "propaganda" or "decadence." Although many people today would hesitate to accept Thurman's judgment uncritically, *Infants of the Spring* symbolized a coming-of-age of the renaissance literati. It demonstrated the ability of the movement to evaluate and possibly modify its direction. However, there was little opportunity for Thurman's criticism to be absorbed. The stock market had crashed in 1929, and white Americans' ability to sustain and enjoy the "Negro fad" had been severely hampered. Perhaps, as Ralph Ellison noted, the black writers of the 1920s "had wanted to be fashionable and this insured, even more effectively than the approaching Depression, the failure of the 'New Negro' movement." By the mid-1930s, exotic and genteel novels about black life were no longer popular with publishers and were being attacked by a new breed of black writers and critics. In early 1934, Eugene Saxton, who had handled McKay's work at Harper Brothers, bluntly informed McKay that his popularity had been part of a passing fad. In 1940, Langston Hughes spoke for many when he said of the Harlem Renaissance, "I had a swell time while it lasted. But I thought it wouldn't last long. . . . For how could a large number of people be crazy about Negroes forever?"

If Thurman's assessment is harsh and lopsided, it is equally unfair to evaluate the Harlem Renaissance according to the hindsight of Hughes, Nugent, and McKay—or according to the aesthetic criteria of Du Bois and Brawley or the theoretical constructs and reviews of Locke, who was accused by women writers such as Fauset of maliciously misreading their work. Intense intellectual and artistic activity created fruitful controversy over basic issues relating to art and its appreciation. The racial matrix of artistic expression received serious critical attention, and some later concepts—such as the "black aesthetic"—were prefigured in discussions among renaissance artists. This is an important part of the legacy of the Harlem Renaissance, even though the attitude of many individual artists toward these matters seems to have been characterized by ambivalence and tension, conflicting impulses as well as tentative solutions.

AMRITJIT SINGH

See also Bontemps, Arna; Brawley, Benjamin; Césaire, Aimé; Crisis, The; Du Bois, W. E. B.; Ellison, Ralph; Fauset, Jessie Redmon; Fire!!; Johnson, Charles Spurgeon; Johnson, James Weldon; Harlem: A Forum of Negro Life; Harper Brothers; Hughes, Langston; Hurston, Zora Neale; Infants of the Spring; Locke, Alain; McKay, Claude; Messenger, The; Negritude; Nugent, Richard Bruce; Opportunity; Schuyler, George S.; Senghor, Léopold; Thurman, Wallace; Toomer, Jean; West, Dorothy; Wright, Richard; *other specific writers*

Further Reading

Baker, Houston A. *Modernism and the Harlem Renaissance.* 1987.

Bone, Robert. *The Negro Novel in America.* 1958. (Rev. ed. 1965.)

Bontemps, Arna, ed. *The Harlem Renaissance Remembered.* 1972.

Cruse, Harold. *The Crisis of the Negro Intellectual.* 1967.

Fuller, Hoyt, ed. *Black World.* November 1970. (Special number on the Harlem Renaissance.)

Gloster, Hugh. *Negro Voices in American Fiction.* 1948.

Helbling, Mark. *The Harlem Renaissance: The One and the Many.* 1999.

Hemenway, Robert. *Zora Neale Hurston: A Biography.* 1977.

Hoffman, Frederick. *The Twenties.* 1962.

Huggins, Nathan. *Harlem Renaissance.* 1971.

Hughes, Langston. "The Negro Artist and the Racial Mountain." *Nation,* June 1926.

———. *The Big Sea.* 1940.

Hull, Gloria. *Color, Sex, and Poetry: Three Women Writers of the Harlem Renaissance.* 1987.

Hull, Gloria, Patricia Bell Scott, and Barbara Smith, eds. *All the Women Are White, All the Blacks Are Men, but Some of Us Are Brave.* 1982.

Hutchinson, George. *The Harlem Renaissance in Black and White.* 1995.

Lewis, David Levering. *When Harlem Was in Vogue.* 1987.

Nero, Charles I. "Toward a Gay Black Aesthetic: Signifying in Contemporary Black Gay Aesthetic." In *Brother to Brother: New Writings by Gay Black Men,* ed. Essex Hemphill. Boston, Mass.: Alyson, 1991, pp. 229–252.

Perry, Margaret. *Silence to the Drums: A Survey of the Literature of the Harlem Renaissance.* 1976.

Rampersad, Arnold. "Langston Hughes and Approaches to Modernism." In *The Harlem Renaissance: Revaluations,* ed. Amritjit Singh, William S. Shiver, and Stanley Brodwin. 1989.

Renaissance in the United States: 1—Boston

Schuyler, George S. "The Negro-Art Hokum." *Nation*, June 1926.

Singh, Amritjit. *The Novels of the Harlem Renaissance.* 1976.

Singh, Amritjit, and Daniel M. Scott III, eds. *The Collected Writings of Wallace Thurman: A Harlem Renaissance Reader.* New Brunswick, N.J.: Rutgers University Press, 2003.

Smith, Barbara. "Toward a Black Feminist Criticism." In *Conditions: Two.* 1977, pp. 25–44.

Thurman, Wallace. *Infants of the Spring.* 1932. (Reprint, 1992 with foreword by Amritjit Singh.)

Wall, Cheryl A. *Women of the Harlem Renaissance.* 1995.

Washington, Mary Helen, ed. *I Love Myself When I Am Laughing.* 1978. (Anthology of writings by Zora Neale Hurston.)

Wintz, Cary D. *Black Culture and the Harlem Renaissance.* 1988.

Wirth, Thomas H., ed. *Gay Rebel of the Harlem Renaissance: Selections from the Work of Richard Bruce Nugent.* Durham, N.C.: Duke University Press, 2002.

Young, James O. *Black Writers of the Thirties.* 1973.

Harlem Renaissance in the United States: 1—Boston

Many commentators have described Boston as ambivalent toward its black citizens. On the one hand, Crispus Attucks died for American independence there, Phillis Wheatley wrote there, the abolitionist movement thrived there, and some of the nation's most important black writers and thinkers lived there. On the other hand, African Americans in Boston have over the course of centuries faced numerous obstacles to access to housing, education, and jobs. If the history of blacks in Boston is ambiguous, so too is the identity of the black community. On the one hand, the black community in Boston can be identified with a tradition of freedom predating the Civil War and with a level of sophistication rivaling that of any other African American community. On the other hand, this freedom and sophistication characterized a black elite representing only a small part of the community as a whole.

Regardless of its actual size, though, this black elite exerted a considerable influence on black intellectual and cultural life throughout the United States before the Harlem Renaissance. In 1914, Daniels noted that,

because of their educational advantages, Boston's black elite in some ways identified more readily with whites than with rank-and-file blacks. And yet in the first two or three decades of the twentieth century, the black upper class in Boston took a step away from identification with whites and began to agitate for real social change. Once this change took place, the black Brahmins of Boston—in the 1910s and 1920s—promoted some of the most progressive elements of African American political thought.

By the first part of the twentieth century, black Boston was moving from its traditional location in the West End (Beacon Hill) and into the South End. During these decades the cultural life of black Boston began to be dominated by social clubs, cultural organizations, and a few individual activists. The network of settlement houses (South End House, Robert Gould Shaw House) that had been developed to celebrate black civic pride and to provide social services was augmented by the work of groups such as the Woman's Era Club (founded in 1892), the Wendell Phillips Club, the Bachbends, Prince's African Masonic temple, and Greek-letter organizations. For example, the Aristo Club (founded in 1924) encouraged the teaching of African American history in the schools and increased educational and cultural opportunities for Boston's youth. At the same time that social groups increased civic-mindedness in Boston's black community, arts and cultural organizations led the way in terms of literature, music, and visual arts. Two of the most prominent—the Boston Literary and Historical Society (1901) and the Saint Mark Musical and Literary Union (1902)—promoted cultural activity and sponsored local writers and performing artists.

The most visible political activist in the early decades of the twentieth century was William Monroe Trotter (1873–1934), who founded the Boston Equal Rights League in 1901—nine years before the establishment of the National Association for the Advancement of Colored People (NAACP). W. E. B. Du Bois, who received his Ph.D. from Harvard in 1895, was inspired by Trotter not only in developing the NAACP but also in developing his concept of the "talented tenth" and the New Negro movement. Trotter's newspaper *The Guardian* was a source of information and black progressive opinion in Boston. In 1903, Trotter and his followers disrupted a speech being delivered by Booker T. Washington. In 1915, Trotter organized a protest campaign against D. W. Griffith's *Birth of a Nation.* Black Bostonians such as William Henry

Lewis, William H. Ferris, Josephine St. Pierre Ruffin, Angelina Weld Grimké, Maria Baldwin, and George Washington Forbes joined Trotter in extending the tradition of black activism in Boston (initiated by Attucks and running through the black abolitionists) into the twentieth century. Boston, then, was the home of an educated black elite that laid a social, cultural, and political foundation for insistence on equality for black citizens.

Art and literature within the black community in Boston took many different and sometimes competing forms. In theatrical circles, figures such as Ralf Coleman and his Negro Repertory Theater made a considerable impression on the community. The play *The Rider of Dreams* by Ridley Torrence was a great success in February 1927. In dance, Stanley E. Brown, Mildred Davenport, and Jimmy Slyde won national acclaim. The painter Allan Rohan Crite (b. 1910) was one of the most influential visual artists from Boston. Although recognition for Crite was slow in coming, his work—especially in the 1930s and 1940s—documents places and people that made the black community in Boston a thriving and productive cultural center.

The literature that came from Boston tended to be traditional—unlike that of New York (which was often experimental) or that of Chicago (which celebrated the working man). As early as in Wheatley's poetry, decorousness and shapeliness were hallmarks of Boston's literary taste. Boston produced a great many important black literary figures. Besides Wheatley, there were Lucy Terry Prince, the first black poet in the United States; David Walker, author of the famous *Appeal to the Coloured Citizens of the World*; and William Wells Brown, the first published black novelist and the author of *Clotel* (1853).

During the 1920s and 1930s, the main figures associated with Boston were the extremely influential poet and editor William Stanley Braithwaite; the protest writers Pauline Hopkins and Angelina Weld Grimké; and three writers of the younger generation: William Waring Cuney, Helene Johnson, and Dorothy West.

Braithwaite (1878–1962), who was largely self-educated, was a major force in American literature during much of the first half of the twentieth century as a poet and even more as an editor. He published two books of his own lyric poetry—*Lyrics of Life and Love* (1904) and *The House of Falling Leaves* (1908)—which adhered to nineteenth-century ideas concerning subject matter and form; and his *Anthology of*

Magazine Verse, a collection of the best magazine poetry of the year, was published annually from 1913 to 1929. These collections brought poetry into American homes and influenced the literary tastes of the public (Braithwaite is especially recognized for bringing Robert Frost into public prominence). Unlike some of his black contemporaries, Braithwaite was reluctant to treat racial experiences in his own poetry or to choose poems with this theme in his anthologies, feeling that such content interfered with the universality of the work and only accentuated the differences between whites and blacks. Braithwaite also published *The Book of Elizabethan Verse* (1906), *The Book of Georgian Verse* (1908), *The Book of Restoration Verse* (1909), the history *The Story of the Great War* (1919), and *The Bewitched Parsonage: The Story of the Brontës* (1950), a biography. In his long and illustrious career, he was one of the most influential editors of poetry in the United States. However, he had a tense relationship with many figures of the Harlem Renaissance. Claude McKay writes:

> [Braithwaite] said that my poems were good, but that, barring two, any reader could tell the author was a Negro. And because of almost insurmountable prejudice against all things Negro, he said, he would advise me to write and send to magazines only such poems as did not betray my racial identity. . . . So, I thought, that was what Boston made of a colored intellectual.

Although Braithwaite has often been criticized for having no apparent interest in furthering the New Negro movement, it is an error to assume that Braithwaite did not identify with black writing. He served on the board of *The Crisis* for many years; he was the author of critical essays on black literature ("Some Contemporary Poets of the Negro Race," which appeared in *The Crisis* in 1919; and "The Negro in American Literature," which appeared in Alain Locke's *The New Negro* in 1925); and he left at his death an unpublished *Anthology of Negro Authors: Prose and Verse*.

The poet, playwright, and short-story writer Angelina Weld Grimké (1880–1958) is traditionally read as an adherent of the "black genteel" school of writing; she was raised in a elite family in Boston, and she grew up surrounded by intellectuals and activists. Nevertheless, her writing addresses some crucial themes and issues of her time. In the aftermath of the "red summer" of 1919, when lynchings of blacks rose sharply, her stories "The Closing Door" (1919) and "Goldie" (1920) described lynching in harrowing detail and suggested very little hope for future generations. Her play *Rachel* (1916) examines the effect of lynching on family members who must live on after the horror of the event. Recently, her diaries have come under scrutiny because they reflect the frustration she felt as a woman who loved women in the early decades of the twentieth century. Her poetry, with its themes of death and unfulfilled love, is read today in light of the details of her life.

A forerunner of Grimké and of many aspects of the Harlem Renaissance, Pauline Hopkins (1859–1930) wrote for *The Colored American*—one of the first magazines aimed at African Americans. Her articles in the early 1900s and her "magazine novels" were important protest literature in which she addressed problems and issues of race relations that were thought to be unspeakable and were not touched by other journals. She used the form of the romantic novel to explore and challenge prevailing racial and gender representations that were foremost in the minds of middle-class African Americans in the early part of the twentieth century.

The *Saturday Evening Quill*, published from 1928 to 1930, was a product of Boston's literary atmosphere that gained recognition among and attracted the interest of writers in Harlem. It was edited by Eugene Gordon, and its contributors included William Waring Cuney, George Reginald Margetson, Florida Ridley, Alvirah Hazzard, Helene Johnson, and Dorothy West. The *Quill* was a proponent of the New Negro movement. Unlike Braithwaite—but like their counterparts in Harlem—the young black intellectuals who wrote for the *Quill* wanted to depict racial experience, through which they felt black art distinguished itself and became meaningful for all its readers. Unlike Grimké, these writers were not so much interested in protest as in creating literary expressions of black experiences. In September 1928, in *The Crisis*, Du Bois praised the *Saturday Evening Quill* for its interesting content and consistent quality.

The poet William Waring Cuney (1906–1976) attended the New England Conservatory of Music (an institution whose first black student, Rachel Washington, graduated in 1876). While he was at school in Boston, he wrote for the *Saturday Evening Quill*. He had also attended Lincoln University, where he and Langston Hughes were classmates, and he maintained a friendship with Hughes for decades. Although Cuney's poetry has been largely overlooked by scholars (his first

collection of poems, *Puzzles*, was published in 1960), he is a minor Harlem renaissance poet deserving of more attention. His poem "No Images" is a compact statement and analysis of the lack of positive racial images in American society.

The short-story writer and novelist Dorothy West (1907–1998) was raised in an upper-middle-class home in Boston. She is known widely for her reminiscences of Harlem in the 1920s and 1930s. West moved to New York in 1927 with her cousin Helene Johnson (1907–1995), and the two women soon became part of a group of younger writers and poets principally centered on Wallace Thurman. Johnson published several poems (including one in the single issue of *Fire!!*) but stopped writing poetry after her marriage in 1933. West, after her arrival in New York, was a member of the cast in the traveling production of DuBose Heyward's *Porgy* with Richard Bruce Nugent. West became involved in the film project *Black and White* and traveled to the Soviet Union with Langston Hughes and others during 1932 and part of 1933.

When she returned to the United States, West became the editor of *Challenge: A Literary Quarterly* (which later became *New Challenge*). Like the *Saturday Evening Quill*, *Challenge* published younger black poets and writers. *Challenge* is important, too, as a transition between the Harlem Renaissance and the generation of writers who emerged in the late 1930s and who found fault with the faddishness of the 1920s. The associate editor of the new journal, Richard Wright, would publish his "Blueprint for Negro Writing" in the first issue of *New Challenge* in 1937. West published her first novel, *The Living Is Easy*, in 1948. This novel was prized for its characterizations and for its depiction of life among Boston's upper middle class, and social historians continue to read it as a source of information about the lifestyles of Boston's black elite. West, who was still alive during the revival of interest in the Harlem Renaissance in the late twentieth century, provided valuable information about the 1920s and 1930s in Harlem and Boston through her letters, interviews, and memoirs. Her papers are a significant source of information about the Harlem Renaissance.

It is estimated that between 1899 and 1936, approximately 145,000 foreign-born blacks came to the United States, and many of them came to Boston. This shift in populations highlighted differences and exacerbated disagreements between native-born blacks and those from other parts of the world—a phenomenon included in many depictions of Harlem by writers of the renaissance, such as Wallace Thurman, Eric Walrond, Rudolph Fisher, Claude McKay, and Langston Hughes. In the early decades of the twentieth century, too, the black community in Boston underwent considerable changes: An influx of immigrants from the South and Midwest (including the young Malcolm X) and from the West Indies and Cape Verde (islands off the coast of west Africa) meant that the community grew quickly and diversified considerably. By the 1920s, Boston's black community was expanding beyond the South End and into Roxbury. The city became a center of entertainment and culture for blacks, with nightclubs like the Storyville Café and the Hi Hat Club.

Diversified by immigration, more extended geographically than before, and no longer focused on the tastes and influence of the black elite, Boston's black community underwent tremendous alterations in the latter half of the twentieth century. Intimately involved with the very beginnings of the United States, the African American community in Boston has faced obstacles with intelligence and creativity. It is indisputable that Boston played a major role in black cultural expression in the years before, during, and after the Harlem Renaissance.

DANIEL M. SCOTT III

See also Black and White; Braithwaite, William Stanley; Challenge; Cuney, Waring; Ferris, William H.; Grimké, Angelina Weld; Guardian, The; Johnson, Helene; Rachel; Saturday Evening Quill; Trotter, William Monroe; West, Dorothy; Wright, Richard

Further Reading

Braithwaite, William Stanley. *The William Stanley Braithwaite Reader*, ed. Philip Butcher. Ann Arbor: University of Michigan Press, 1972.

Cromwell, Adelaide M. *Boston's Black Upper Class: 1750–1950*. Fayetteville: University of Arkansas Press, 1994.

Daniels, John. *In Freedom's Birthplace: A Study of the Boston Negroes*. New York: Arno, 1969. (Originally published 1914.)

Grimké, Angelina Weld. *Selected Works of Angelina Weld Grimké*, ed. Carolivia Herron. New York: Oxford Unversity Press, 1991.

Hayden, Robert C. *African Americans in Boston: More Than 350 Years*. Boston, Mass.: Public Library of the City of Boston, 1991.

West, Dorothy. *The Living Is Easy*. Boston, Mass.: Houghton Mifflin, 1948. (Reprint, Old Westbury, N.Y.: Feminist, 1982.)

———. *The Richer, the Poorer: Stories, Sketches, Reminiscences*. New York: Doubleday, 1995.

Harlem Renaissance in the United States: 2—California and the West Coast

California, and particularly the West Coast cities of Los Angeles, San Francisco, and Oakland, played an important if generally unrecognized role in the migrations that were fundamental to the New Negro movement. There were significant contributions in many fields, but the most important were in music.

Although African Americans participated in the exploration, conquest, and settlement of the American West, the actual number of blacks there remained relatively small until after the United States entered World War II, when the New Negro movement was mostly over. As late as 1940 San Francisco had about 4,800 blacks (this number rose to 43,500 in 1950), and Oakland had about 8,400 (it had 47,600 in 1950). The largest concentration of blacks in West Coast cities before and during the New Negro movement was in Los Angeles. The black population there generally doubled in each succeeding census, going from about 8,000 in 1910 to more than 64,000 in 1940 (there were 171,000 in 1950). Los Angeles was also the only city on the West Coast in which a clearly defined black neighborhood had developed before World War II. The black population was subjected to formal housing restrictions, limiting it mainly to the vicinity of the Central Avenue business corridor, in the late 1920s.

In addition to the relatively late formation of black neighborhoods, several other features are important for understanding the New Negro movement on the West Coast. Emigration to the West Coast was limited because it was much farther away and more expensive to reach than such cities as Chicago, Kansas City, or New York. The black population was relatively stable, prosperous, and conservative. Residential areas were shared with ethnic Mexicans, whites, and, to a lesser extent, Asians. (Overt racial hostility from whites often focused on ethnic Chinese and Japanese, who outnumbered African Americans in San Francisco, Seattle, and Portland.) Racially mixed schools were the rule. Literacy was more widespread than in black communities in other parts of the United States. Although conditions were far from perfect, cities on the West Coast were seen as relatively less repressive than eastern cities throughout the New Negro period. Nevertheless, opportunities in the arts and literature for African Americans and other minorities were much more limited than opportunites for the white population.

Although this article concentrates on Los Angeles, individual blacks achieved distinction in other places as well from the mid-nineteenth century on. Judge Mifflin Wistar Gibbs, who came to California in 1850, published the first black newspaper in California and later became consul to Madagascar. Nelson Primus (1842–1916) and Grafton Tyler Brown (1841–1918) came to the West and worked as painters. In the New Negro period after World War I, Horace Roscoe Cayton Jr. (1903–1970), son of a newspaper publisher in Seattle and grandson of a U.S. senator, graduated from the University of Washington and studied at the University of Chicago; he became a distinguished sociologist, producing a memoir that eloquently sets forth his personal conflicts as a member of the "talented tenth" (*Long Old Road*, 1965) as well as important studies of Chicago's black community. The sculptor Sargent Johnson (1888–1967) was born in Boston but made most of his career in San Francisco, where he created striking modernist figures of African Americans and taught at the California College of Arts and Crafts, important to the training of later generations of black artists. Ralph Bunche (1904–1971) went east from Los Angeles to Harvard and achieved distinction at the United Nations. The architect Paul Revere Williams (1894–1980) was born in Los Angeles and established his own firm there; he designed and built mansions for both white and black movie stars as well as commercial buildings. Wallace Thurman and Arna Bontemps are well-known writers of the Harlem Renaissance who were raised in the West and lived in Los Angeles for significant periods before they migrated eastward to Harlem. (Thurman's *The Blacker the Berry*, 1932, set in Los Angeles, satirizes the destructive hierarchy of color he found within the black community there.) William Grant Still (1895–1978) used his Guggenheim fellowship to move permanently to Los Angeles in 1934. Early jazz musicians from New Orleans spent significant time in both San Francisco and Los Angeles. Many popular entertainers found their way to the film colony in Hollywood, where they struggled to maintain their personal integrity despite the white filmmakers' expectation that they would

play stereotyped, often menial roles. Noble Johnson founded the Lincoln Motion Picture Company, one of the earliest and most successful of the black film companies, in 1916, although he abandoned it in 1921 in favor of a more economically viable career as a bit player in stereotyped black and Native American roles. Among the many well-known entertainers who remained in California were the arranger Will Vodery, the actor Clarence Muse, the dancer Bill "Bojangles" Robinson, and the Nicholas brothers.

Artists and writers who remained in the West but were not associated with Hollywood are much less well known. Artists often worked as amateurs and did not receive recognition until the 1960s. For example, Leonard Cooper (b. 1899) worked in Salinas as a painter and music teacher; and Alice Gafford (1886–1981), who had been born in Kansas, was a painter in Los Angeles. The more immediately successful painters Charles White (1918–1979) and Beulah Woodard (1895–1964) spent most of their careers elsewhere, but they had substantial influence, partly as teachers at the Otis Art Institute in Los Angeles.

Mexican art was shown in Los Angeles in major exhibitions in 1923 (the first such exhibit in the United States), and again in 1925 and 1931, and it had both political and aesthetic influence on American artists. Diego Rivera and Jorge Juan Crespo (who taught at the Chouinard Art Institute from 1930 to 1938) were particularly influential. Their politics were far to the left of the generally more conservative black newspaper editors discussed as follows. The Mexican muralists Rivera and José Clemente Orozco executed influential works in San Francisco and at Pomona. Artists in the West were inhibited by a lack of a market for their work and even a lack of galleries for its display; when the National Association for the Advancement of Colored People (NAACP) presented Eugene Burk's *The Slave Mother* to the Oakland Museum in 1931, it was a breakthrough for that institution. The various federal relief projects in the 1930s offered some slight change, especially encouraging the production of outdoor and indoor murals. This activity sowed the seeds for the blossoming of black art in the 1960s and later.

Fragmentary runs survive of at least fifteen black newspapers published in Los Angeles, and five published in Oakland, at some point in the 1920s or 1930s. Of the black writers who remained in the West, most that we know about were journalists. The self-educated, pioneering writer Delilah M. Beasley did research for her landmark history of blacks in California for eight years before publishing it in 1919. Later she provided a column, "Activities Among Negroes," for the (white) *Oakland Tribune*, partly intended as a way to counter the negative stereotypes that were common in the white press. During most of the New Negro period, Charlotta Bass edited the dominant *California Eagle*, a black weekly published in Los Angeles that dates back to 1879; the surviving run of this paper (from 1914) provides invaluable coverage of black activity in southern California. *Flash*, a weekly literary magazine that survived for a little more than the year 1929, was edited by the writer Fay M. Jackson, an enterprising and outspoken graduate of the University of Southern California; Jackson later was the Hollywood reporter for the Associated Negro News Service. Harold Bruce Forsythe was the most important writer to emerge in *Flash*.

Music making was widespread in the black communities. Concert music had a prominent place. In Los Angeles, John S. Gray and William T. Wilkins operated music schools that trained generations of African Americans to read and perform so-called serious music. In 1936, Samuel Browne began teaching at Jefferson Middle School, which trained the generation of black studio musicians who emerged after World War II. There were large choirs in the churches and in the community; Jester Hairston, Hall Johnson, Eva Jessye, Freita Shaw Johnson, and Mrs. A. C. Bilbrew (also an organist) were among their directors. Bilbrew and Elmer Bartlett were prominent church organists. An independent gospel style developed, replaced after World War II by Thomas A. Dorsey's Chicago gospel style. Concerts and musicales were abundant; the famous tenor Roland Hayes performed in Los Angeles very early in his career—in 1918, before an integrated audience. W. E. B. Du Bois's pageant *The Star of Ethiopia*, first produced in New York in 1913, was produced at the Hollywood Bowl in 1925. Among other exceptional performers were the pianist Lorenza Jordan-Cole, the violinist Bessie Dones, and the singer Ivan Harold Browning. William Grant Still came to Los Angeles in 1934 (as noted previously) and composed most of his symphonies and all eight of his operas there; other works from his years in Los Angeles include film music, arrangements for radio and television, ballets, and chamber music. Alain Locke wrote to Still about his second symphony in 1937: "It is so strange that nowhere among Negro musicians do you find any really intellectual interest in new works and experimenting." Blacks' involvement with concert music in the New Negro period was vital but was, as Locke's words suggest, already being ignored by most intel-

lectuals. Harold Bruce Forsythe (whom Locke did not know) is an exception. Forsythe's extensive music training and writing skills led him to understand the challenge of expressing the African American experience in terms of so-called classical music.

The best-documented activity in the cities of the West Coast, however, was in jazz. Bert Williams had formed his partnership with George Walker in San Francisco in the 1890s; they reached stardom, bringing the cakewalk to Broadway in 1898. Black musicians from New Orleans and elsewhere found their way to San Francisco, at least by 1908. The so-called Barbary Coast—a few blocks along Pacific Street—became a center for dance music with a New Orleans flavor. The shimmy or shim-me-sha-wobble had originated there as early as 1900. After 1908, in short order, came the turkey trot, bunny hug, chicken glide, Texas Tommy, pony prance, grizzly bear, "and many other varieties of close and semi-acrobatic dancing, which swept the country during the half dozen years that preceded the world war" (Stoddard 1982, 127). Sid Le Protti's So Different Orchestra was the most active performing group on the Barbary Coast, gradually incorporating features of the new style. In San Francisco in 1913, the word "jazz" was first applied to the black dance music that had previously been known as ragtime. (The style was probably somewhere in between what we now think of as ragtime, which had crystallized in 1895, and Dixieland jazz, which emerged in the early 1920s.) A large proportion of the (relatively few) blacks listed as "professionals" in San Francisco in the census of 1910 were musicians and entertainers—an indication of the importance of these performance venues. (Labor unions excluded black workers for most of this period.) When the Barbary Coast was closed down in 1921, some of its musicians emigrated to the Central Avenue area in Los Angeles, which was already a center for black music.

In the relatively conservative atmosphere of Los Angeles, musicians were expected to read music with facility and perform in many styles, because most local musicians and much of the audience had some classical training. Many jazz leaders required their musicians to play from written arrangements. Of the New Orleans musicians who came to Los Angeles, formally trained musicians (many of them Creole) were more successful than the pure improvisers who did not read. Bill Johnson and Ernest Coycault had played in Los Angeles as early as 1908; Coycault remained and Johnson returned in 1912, possibly with Jelly Roll Morton. Freddie Keppard had arrived by

1914, when he formed the Original Creole Band, made up of six musicians from New Orleans. This group was "discovered" while entertaining at a boxing match in Los Angeles and hired to perform on the Pantages vaudeville circuit in that year. For the next four years, the Original Creole Band toured the United States, playing in vaudeville houses and making their version of the New Orleans style (still often called "ragtime") known to a wide audience. In 1917, Jelly Roll Morton began what turned into a stay of five years, pursuing a variety of business interests as he discovered his forte as a composer and arranger. The trombonist Kid Ory, who arrived in 1919 and also stayed for five years (before joining Louis Armstrong in Chicago), organized a series of recordings on the Sunshine label in 1921. These are usually considered to be the first recordings of instrumental jazz by an African American band; their style is clearly Dixieland.

Several bands and musicians stayed in the Los Angeles area, anchoring the Central Avenue music scene and launching the careers of many well-known musicians. The Spikes Brothers ran a music business on Central Avenue from 1919 that served as a booking agency for black musicians. The black union (Local 767 of the American Federation of Musicians) was eventually integrated into Local 47, expanding opportunities and leading to the end of highly discriminatory pay scales, but this did not happen until 1953. (Black musicians worked for much lower wages than white musicians, whether they played for all-white, all-black, or racially mixed audiences.) One of Reb Spikes's bands was the Legion Club 45. Other important bandleaders and bands included Mutt Carey, Harry Southard's Black and Tan Jazz Orchestra, Sonny Clay's Stompin' Six, Charlie Lawrence's Sunnyland Jazz Band, Paul Howard's Quality Serenaders, Les Hite, and Curtis Mosby's Dixieland Blue Blowers. Lionel Hampton, who achieved international fame for his vibraphone playing in the late 1930s, got his start as a drummer with Hite, Howard, and Mosby.

With the start of World War II, the black population of Los Angeles soared, bringing further change and a new set of issues. Whether there was a distinct, laid-back "West Coast style" associated with jazz in the years of the New Negro movement is still not clear. What is clear is that, in a lively jazz scene that fostered the early careers of many famous musicians, the groundwork had been laid for the emergence in Los Angeles of cool jazz, such as Miles Davis's "Birth of Cool," and postwar rhythm and blues (R&B).

CATHERINE PARSONS SMITH

See also Bontemps, Arna; Forsythe, Harold Bruce; Hayes, Roland; Johnson, Hall; Johnson, Noble; Johnson, Sargent Claude; Lincoln Motion Picture Company; Morton, Jelly Roll; Muse, Clarence; Ory, Edward "Kid"; Robinson, Bill "Bojangles"; Still, William Grant; Thurman, Wallace; Williams, Egbert Austin "Bert"

Further Reading

Cox, Bette Yarbrough. *Central Avenue: Its Rise and Fall (1890–c. 1955), Including the Musical Renaissance of Black Los Angeles*. Los Angeles, Calif.: Beem, 1993.

DjeDje, Jacqueline Cogdell, and Eddie Meadows, eds. *California Soul: Music of African Americans in the West.* Berkeley and Los Angeles: University of California Press, 1998.

Reed, Tom. *The Black Music History of Los Angeles: Its Roots—A Classical Pictorial History of Black Music in Los Angeles from the 1920s to 1970.* Los Angeles, Calif.: Black Accent on L.A., n.d. (Published in 1992.)

Stoddard, Tom. *Jazz on the Barbary Coast.* Chigwell, Essex: Storyville, 1982.

Harlem Renaissance in the United States: 3—Chicago and the Midwest

Although the Harlem Renaissance was centered in New York, it helped shape the lives and careers of people in literature, the fine arts, and the performing arts across the country during the 1920s and 1930s. In the Midwest, this was clearly evident among creative artists in Ohio, Illinois, and Missouri as well as other places. The work of these individuals continues to testify to the lively and significant discourse among artists nationwide.

At the turn of the twentieth century, Ohio was home to two giants of African American literature: Paul Laurence Dunbar (1872–1906) and Charles Waddell Chesnutt (1858–1932). Because both men focused on the experiences of African Americans, they served as important role models for many younger, nationalistic writers who would follow their example during the Harlem Renaissance.

Dunbar was the first African American writer to achieve national renown in the modern era. He was a native of Dayton, Ohio, and was the son of former slaves. Dunbar was educated in the public schools of Dayton and became active in literary circles before he had earned his high school diploma. He went on to publish six volumes of poetry, beginning with *Oak and Ivy* in 1893; and several novels, librettos, and essays. He is probably best remembered—and has been alternately praised by both African Americans and whites—for his "dialect verse," in poems such as "Little Brown Baby" and "When Malindy Sings." Through both his dialect poems and his poems in "standard" English (including "Sympathy"—"I know why the caged bird sings"), Dunbar tried to capture the full range of African American experiences.

Chesnutt was a native of Cleveland, Ohio, and in his life and work we also find threads that weave together much of the story of early twentieth-century life among African Americans there and elsewhere. In addition to being a successful writer, Chesnutt was a successful buisnessman and engaged in benevolent and volunteer work. Because of his honest, forthright portrayal of life "along the color line" and his ability to deal with such controversial subjects as color and class prejudice among well-to-do "colored" Americans, his works were well received by African American and white readers. By the turn of the twentieth century, Chesnutt had several works in print, including *The Conjure Woman* (1899), *The House Behind the Cedars* (1900), and *The Wife of His Youth and Other Stories of the Color Line* (1899). In his fiction, Chesnutt always dealt skillfully with controversial issues, but in real life he exercised caution before publicly supporting radicals who were calling for social, political, or educational reform. Information about his early life suggests that he was well aware of the injustices suffered by African Americans of his day because of their race, and by early adulthood he was well prepared to be a race leader. Most important, Chesnutt—like W. E. B. Du Bois—understood the value and limitations of self-help programs, through his work with the Cleveland Association of Colored Men and the National Association for the Advancement of Colored People (NAACP). In Cleveland, as across the nation, the NAACP was the primary organization through which African Americans would agitate for social and educational reforms. the NAACP also supported cultural programs during the Harlem Renaissance.

Langston Hughes was an alumnus of Central High School in Cleveland (class of 1920) and a longtime associate of the city's Karamu House theater. Hughes frequently acknowledged that his writing was influenced by Dunbar and Chesnutt. His early work reflected the nationalistic focus of Dunbar's poetry; and long after leaving high school, Hughes corresponded with Chesnutt—and with Chesnutt's daughter and biographer, Helen Chesnutt, who was an educator in Cleveland. Interestingly, Hughes's poetry was also influenced by the free verse of another midwesterner, Carl Sandburg. Hughes came to New York to enroll in undergraduate courses at Columbia University, and to position himself, as he said, to become an active member of Harlem's cultural community.

At this time, the work of the composer, lyricist, and bandleader Noble Sissle (1889–1975) was transforming popular entertainment for blacks and whites in Manhattan. Sissle was a native of Indianapolis, Indiana; he moved to Cleveland with his family in 1909 and graduated from Central High School in 1911. As a young man, Sissle formed a very successful songwriting team with Eubie Blake, touring America's vaudeville circuit and Europe in the 1920s. They were the cowriters of the Broadway musical *Shuffle Along* (1921), which was a smash hit.

Chicago, Illinois, had a vibrant artistic community during this era, and writers in particular found a great deal of material there. Richard Wright, who moved to Chicago in 1927 (he had been born in Mississippi), experienced his most prolific period of publishing during the "Chicago renaissance" of the 1930s. Strongly influenced by the social, political, and economic movements of his day, he wrote "Blueprint for Negro Writing" (1937), a radical call for African American writers to free themselves from the restrictions imposed by the current dominant literary forms. His other celebrated works include *Uncle Tom's Children* (1938) and *Native Son* (1940).

While working for the Federal Writers' Project of the Works Progress Administration (WPA), Wright met and befriended Margaret Walker (1915–1998), who was then a student at Northwestern University in Evanston, Illinois. Walker too went on to become a celebrated writer; she won the Yale Younger Writers' award in 1942 for her volume of poetry *For My People*, and she had a long teaching career at the postsecondary level before publishing her novel *Jubilee* (1966).

The poet and novelist Arna Bontemps (1902–1973) moved to Chicago and joined Wright, Walker, and others in the South Side writers' group there. While he was living in Chicago, Bontemps completed *Black Thunder* (1936), *Drums at Dusk* (1939), and other works. After receiving his master's degree in library science from the University of Chicago in 1943, Bontemps became librarian at Fisk University in Nashville, Tennessee.

The African American community in South Side Chicago also provided many performance opportunities for budding and established musicians. In the 1930s, blues and jazz artists such as Louis Armstrong, Duke Ellington, and Billie Holiday, and the modern dancer Katherine Dunham, performed before enthusiastic crowds of recent migrants to the city; they also took their music to St. Louis.

In addition to these secular forms of African American music, Chicago was a center for some of the nation's most important sacred music. The gospel vocalist Mahalia Jackson and the composer-pianist Thomas Andrew Dorsey (the "father of gospel music") are examples. Jackson and Dorsey were both pioneering artists in a tradition known as gospel-blues—sacred music with secular influences. The presence of secular elements in Dorsey's music is not surprising: He was a former pianist for the blues singer Gertrude "Ma" Rainey. With support from the local Baptist churches and others belonging to the National Baptist Convention, Dorsey established a broad base of support for his choral music and eventually, in 1932, founded the National Convention of Gospel Choirs and Choruses.

In addition to organizations within and outside the religious and artistic communities, individual patronage and philanthropy were important sources of support for activities of the renaissance in the Midwest. One philanthropist was the entrepreneur and self-made millionaire Madame C. J. Walker, who established a phenomenally successful hair-care business in St. Louis and later Indianapolis. Until her death in 1919, she supported African American educational programs championed by Booker T. Washington and Mary McLeod Bethune, and the activities of the National Association of Colored Women. After Walker's death, the national headquarters of the family business was established in Indianapolis. Walker's daughter A'Lelia Walker, who had a home in New York, used the family fortune to become a popular patron of the African American arts community. She was the hostess of the short-lived "Dark Tower" gatherings, where literati, book lovers, and others engaged in numerous multicultural social exchanges in 1927 and 1928. Langston Hughes called A'Lelia Walker the "joy-goddess of Harlem's 1920s."

With the onset of the Great Depression in 1929, many sources of financial patronage dried up, but public arts programs—especially the Federal Arts Program, which was part of the New Deal—encouraged creative artists to continue working.

With few exceptions, most of the "younger Negro artists" described in Langston Hughes's essay "The Negro Artist and the Racial Mountain" (1926) would not live to see the black arts movement of the 1960s and 1970s. Nevertheless, their legacy would live on in Harlem, Chicago, Cleveland, and other African American population centers and artistic communities.

REGENNIA N. WILLIAMS

See also Armstrong, Louis; Blake, Eubie; Bontemps, Arna; Chesnutt, Charles Waddell; Dunbar, Paul Laurence; Ellington, Duke; Harlem Renaissance in the United States: 4—Cleveland; Holiday, Billie; Hughes, Langston; Karamu House; Shuffle Along; Sissle, Noble; Walker, Madame C. J.; Walker, Margaret; Wright, Richard

Further Reading

Bundles, A'Lelia. *On Her Own Ground: The Life and Times of Madam C. J. Walker*. New York: Scribner, 2001.

Gates, Henry Louis Jr., et al., eds. *The Norton Anthology of African American Literature*. New York: Norton, 1997.

Grabowski, John J., and David D. Van Tassel. *The Dictionary of Cleveland Biography*. Bloomington: Indiana University Press, 1996.

Hine, Darlene Clark, et. al. *The African American Odyssey*. Upper Saddle River, N.J.: Prentice Hall, 2003.

Hughes, Langston. *The Big Sea*. New York: Thunder's Mouth, 1986. (Reprint.)

Kramer, Victor A., ed. *The Harlem Renaissance Re-Examined*. New York: AMS, 1987.

Lewis, David Levering, ed. *The Portable Harlem Renaissance Reader*. New York: Viking Penguin, 1994.

Rampersad, Arnold. *The Life of Langston Hughes*, Vol. 1, *1902–1941: I, Too, Sing America*. New York: Oxford University Press, 1986.

Rampersad, Arnold, and David Roessel, eds. *The Collected Poems of Langston Hughes*. New York: Knopf, 1995.

Wintz, Cary D. *The Harlem Renaissance: A History and an Anthology*. Maplecrest, N.Y.: Brandywine, 2003.

Harlem Renaissance in the United States: 4—Cleveland

The stage was set for the development of the arts in Cleveland as early as 1883, when Charles Waddell - Chesnutt—who is considered the first African American writer of fiction—settled there. Several artists in a variety of genres followed him, including the poet Langston Hughes.

Chesnutt was born in Cleveland. As a child, he moved to Fayetteville, North Carolina, with his parents; but as a young man he returned to Cleveland, passed his bar examination, and opened a court reporting business. Writing was his first love, and he developed into a recognized author of short stories and novels, publishing in the prestigous *Atlantic Monthly*. Chesnutt became a member of Booker T. Washington's "committee of twelve" in 1905 and helped establish the Playhouse Settlement when it came to Cleveland in 1914. Chesnutt's daughter, Helen, was Langston Hughes's English teacher at Central High School in Cleveland.

Russell Wesley Jelliffe and Rowena Woodham Jelliffe, who were associated with the settlement house movement of the 1920s, and particularly with Karamu House, had a profound impact on the arts in Cleveland; in the early twentieth century, black arts in Cleveland and the Karamu Theater were virtually synonymous. The Jelliffes had graduated from Oberlin College in 1910 and had undertaken graduate study in sociology at the University of Chicago. They did fieldwork at Chicago Commons, a local settlement house where they lived, as well as at Jane Addams's Hull House. In 1914, as newlyweds who had recently completed their master's degrees, they moved to Cleveland to conduct a survey and remained there. Significantly, at about that time—1915—Cleveland's Negro population included eight doctors, three dentists, two nurses with professional training, twelve lawyers, and thirty teachers, who contributed to a cultural milieu in which the arts could be introduced and could thrive.

P. Dudley Allen and the Second Presbyterian Church Men's Club provided seed money to establish a center for activities and recreation for the expanding African American population in the Central Avenue district, known also as the "Roaring Third." The center was incorporated in 1917 as the Playhouse Settlement Neighborhood Association and would become known, nationwide, as Karamu House. Karamu has been described as the nation's oldest multiracial metropolitan center for the arts, the outstanding Negro community theater in America, the oldest and best organization of colored actors in America, and the country's first interracial theater.

In Karamu's early days, most of its activities were geared toward children and the assimilation of new immigrants to the city. The Playhouse Settlement was dedicated to helping all racial groups, but more blacks than others were settling in the neighborhood: In 1910, African Americans were 1.5 percent of the population of Cleveland; a decade later, they were 4.3 percent. Although Rowena Jelliffe aimed her arts program toward youngsters, a few young adults were soon drawn to the theater. The adult theater began as an informal group for reading and discussing plays but soon began performing onstage as the Dumas Players (named after Alexandre Dumas *père* and *fils*). Their first production was *The Little Stone House*, performed at Cleveland's Central High School in the autumn of 1921, and subsequently in nearby Oberlin.

The Dumas Players were not the only amateur black theater group in Cleveland in the 1920s. The Aldridge Players were formed through the Phillis Wheatley Association, and other groups were formed through the Cleveland Association of Colored Men, the Council of Women, and churches. Specific groups such as the Federal Theater and the Robeson Players, Harrison and Taylor Players, Vagabond Players, Charity Players, and Richard B. Harrison Players were active at various times during that period and later.

There was some dispute concerning the Dumas Players. For one thing, settlement houses in white neighborhoods tended to discriminate against blacks; for another, some blacks protested vehemently against the works the Dumas Players chose to perform. There were objections because works by white playwrights were being presented almost exclusively (this controversy began with a production of *Stevedore*); and more serious dissent developed in the spring of 1922, when Charles Gilpin, manager of the Lafayette Theater in Harlem, came to Cleveland to appear in *The Emperor Jones*. Harry C. Smith, editor of the Negro weekly the *Cleveland Gazette*, praised Gilpin's acting but attacked the play; he also attacked the Jelliffes, who were white. The Dumas Players were not swayed by Smith's review and in fact invited Gilpin to their rehearsal of *Wolves* by John Jay Bell. Gilpin's encouraging words and the $50 he donated for future scholarships inspired the group to change their name to the Gilpin Players. Smith continued his attacks even after works by black playwrights were performed.

In 1927, some members of the Gilpin Players decided to change their name again, this time to Karamu, a Swahili word meaning "a place of joyful gathering." This name reflected the group's interest in Africa and seemed appropriate for an organization in the heart of Cleveland's black community; also, it was in accordance with the philosophy of Alain Locke, who was encouraging American Negroes to reflect on their heritage. With the new name came a more intense focus on performing plays by African Americans, notably those of Langston Hughes, who was by then emerging as a luminary in Cleveland and who lived around the corner from Karamu. It is worth mentioning here that Hughes's experiences at Central High School had been very important to his early artistic development: He had been encouraged in grammar and literature by Helen Chesnutt and Ethel Weimer, and in art by Clara Dieke. Hughes had talent for the visual arts, and at the Playhouse Settlement he taught lettering and block prints to youngsters.

Most of Hughes's plays were previewed during the 1930s at the Karamu Theater; and his farce *Joy to My Soul*, set in Cleveland, had its world premiere there on April Fool's Day 1937. Silver (1961) notes that *Joy to My Soul* received mixed reviews, being described variously as "rollicking," "amusing," "lusty, lightly diverting burlesque," "boisterously slangy," "not Hughes at his best," and "the finest by Hughes." New York was the site of the world premiere of Hughes's *Mulatto* (an outgrowth of a poem with the same title), but he had first offered it to Karamu. The actors were busy with productions in other cities, and it was put off until 1939. Controversy arose when *Mulatto* opened in New York, and although Hughes thought that using the original version for the production in Cleveland would dispel the criticism, it did not. The play aroused such intense anger that the theater was destroyed by arson on 22 October 1939—but the Karamu and the Jelliffes carried on.

According to Silver, "*Mulatto* was the end of the Langston Hughes 'decade,' but not the end of his 'era.' He remains the 'king' of Karamu playwrights, with more of his works produced there than those of any other writer." During Hughes's lifetime, the mutual admiration between him, Karamu, and Cleveland was very evident. Western Reserve University gave Hughes an honorary doctorate in 1964. Hughes, for his part, said that the Karamu was "immensely valuable" both to him and to the community, and he wrote glowingly about the theater on several occasions. Also, in his autobiography, *The Big Sea* (1940), Hughes acknowledged Charles Chesnutt's influence, calling Chesnutt "my fellow Clevelander." On the centenary of Hughes's birth in 2002, Cleveland held a citywide celebration in his honor.

Two of Hughes's students in printmaking at Karamu were Hughie Lee-Smith and Charles Sallee Jr. In 1934, the Karamu Theater set aside a substantial amount of money to establish an Art Scholarship Fund for a Karamu student to attend the Cleveland School of Art (later the Cleveland Institute of Art). Sallee was the first winner and Lee-Smith the second. Lee-Smith and Sallee organized a group known as the Karamu Artists and were praised by James A. Porter in his landmark book *Modern Negro Art*. Porter wrote that Sallee was "the leader of a powerful group of artists that would make a difference in the quality of WPA prints." The group, of course, exhibited at Karamu House; they also exhibited at other venues in Cleveland, and eventually on tour. When their show opened in New York at the American Artists' Gallery on 7 January 1942, the critic for the New York *Post* said that it was "the largest Negro art exhibition ever held in this city." It included work by twenty-five Karamu artists, in various media: painting, sculpture, ceramics, jewelry, and prints. Another venue for artists in Cleveland was the Cleveland Museum, which held annual May Shows.

Finally, Karamu was also a venue for musicians and dancers. Musicians such as Hale Smith (who composed settings of Hughes's poems) were influenced by, and contributed to, the programs at Karamu, and dance found strong artistic expression there.

Black art has continued to thrive in Cleveland, and Karamu House has continued to nurture talent. The unique atmosphere of this artistic community may be partly a result of the interracial foundation on which the Playhouse Settlement was created.

MARIANNE WOODS

See also Chesnutt, Charles Waddell; Emperor Jones, The; Gilpin, Charles; Harlem Renaissance in the United States: 3—Chicago and the Midwest; Hughes, Langston; Karamu House; Locke, Alain; Mulatto; Porter, James Amos; Stevedore

Further Reading

Abookirie, Noerena. "Children's Theatre Activities at Karamu House in Cleveland, Ohio, 1915–1975." Ph.D. dissertation, New York University, 1982.

Benson, Carol Angela. "Hull House and Karamu House." M.A. thesis, University of Wisconsin, 1965.

Blood, Melanie Nelda. "The Neighborhood Playhouse, 1915–1927: A History and Analysis." Ph.D. dissertation, Northwestern University, 1994.

Christy, Denis Rachel. "The Contributions of the Gilpin Players of Karamu Theatre to Cleveland's Interracial

Unit of the Federal Theatre Project." M.A. thesis, Kent State University, 1976.

Looman, Glen. "Karamu House: The Establishment and Evolution of a Settlement House for Cleveland's African-American Community, 1914–1923." Ph.D. dissertation, Cleveland State University, 1995.

Miller, Henry. "Art or Propaganda: A Historical and Critical Analysis of African-American Approaches to Dramatic Theory, 1900–1965." Ph.D. dissertation, City University of New York, 2003.

Patterson, Linsay. *Anthology of the American Negro in the Theatre: A Critical Approach*. London and New York: Publishers Company, 1967.

Silver, Reuben. "A History of the Karamu Theatre of Karamu House, 1915–1960." Ph.D. dissertation, Ohio State University, 1961.

Harlem Renaissance in the United States: 5—Kansas and the Plains States

In June 1925, Aaron Douglas, who had been born in Kansas, arrived to take his place in an artistic community recently acknowledged in a special edition of *Survey Graphic*—"Harlem: Mecca of the New Negro." Fifty years later Douglas recalled what had inspired him to leave a secure teaching job in Kansas City: "The most cogent single factor that eventually turned my face to New York was the publication of the spectacular issue of 'Survey Graphic' magazine with the splendid portrait of a black man on the cover drawn by Fritz Winold Reiss" (Patterson 1999, 2). Once in New York, Douglas set to work immediately, producing illustrations for both *The Crisis* (the magazine of the National Association for the Advancement of Colored People, NAACP) and *Opportunity* (the magazine of the National Urban League). He reflected later: "I began to feel like the missing piece that all had been looking for to complete or round out the idea of a Renaissance" (Patterson, 7).

Alain Locke, one of the mentors of the Harlem movement, in his introduction to *The New Negro*—a subsequent book version of the special issue of *Survey Graphic*—speaks of the renaissance of the New Negro as a flourishing of cultural production by young artists self-consciously contributing to racial uplift. Although Locke refers to Harlem as the most important gathering of a growing movement of black artists and intellectuals, he recognizes, too, the influence of earlier migrations by African Americans from the rural

South to the more urban North and Midwest in creating this community of artists. Scholars often refer to this cultural moment as the Harlem Renaissance, thereby locating it geographically, whereas Locke locates it in a historically specific people, the New Negroes. For most artists who developed this new consciousness, sites far from Harlem nurtured their social and artistic activities. Individuals like Aaron Douglas grew up in Kansas and the surrounding plains states. Distinctive black cultures thrived outside Harlem in places like St. Louis, Kansas City, Minneapolis, Omaha, Topeka, and Wichita, and throughout Oklahoma, where considerable numbers of African Americans had previously settled.

During the closing decades of the nineteenth century, freedmen and freedwomen had been impelled to leave their homes in the South by several factors: Reconstruction ended; "Jim Crow" laws were passed; and the North promised greater economic opportunities. In Kansas, for instance, the flood of migration from the border states of Missouri, Kentucky, and Tennessee peaked in the summer of 1879; and the black population in Kansas swelled by about 26,000 people in the decade between 1870 and 1880. An estimated 6,000 black migrants, called Exodusters in contemporary newspapers, traveled through St. Louis, Missouri, during the one-month period of mid-March through mid-April 1879. These new immigrants created new towns; they also added to populations of African Americans already settled in midwestern cities. Some migrants founded black towns such as Nicodemus in Kansas and Langston in Oklahoma. Poor rural migrants settled into segregated communities in Omaha (Nebraska), Chicago (Illinois), and Tulsa (Oklahoma)—places that would erupt with violence in the early twentieth century.

Several factors shaped a New Negro renaissance in Kansas and other plains states well before Locke defined the renaissance in Harlem. The racial politics that divided some followers of Booker T. Washington and W. E. B. Du Bois in the East influenced black midwesterners too, sometimes differently. Two factors—race consciousness and segregation—led to the creation of separate black newspapers, schools, and social clubs. Essays by Du Bois in local black-owned newspapers and in national magazines influenced readers. Aaron Douglas, for instance, was a regular reader of *The Crisis* (which was edited by Du Bois) during his college years in Lincoln, Nebraska. But unlike some national publications that strongly supported one viewpoint or the other, midwestern newspapers covered both Du Bois and Washington.

Black-owned newspapers such as the *Iowa Bystander* in Des Moines, the *Call* in Kansas City (Missouri), the *Black Dispatch* in Oklahoma City, and the *Negro Star* in Wichita (Kansas), brought news of Harlem and Chicago's South Side to local communities. Nick Chiles, a businessman in Topeka, began publication of *The Plaindealer* in 1899, just two years after Booker T. Washington had made a well-received speech in Topeka advocating racial support for black businesses. In 1914, black political leaders, influenced by Du Bois, formed the Topeka chapter of the NAACP; Aaron Douglas's future father-in-law was a founding member of this chapter. A year after its inception, protesters associated with the NAACP succeeded in having the film *The Birth of a Nation* banned in Topeka. (Forty years later, of course, Topeka would be a focus of national attention when members of the NAACP challenged segregated schools in *Brown* v. *Board of Education of Topeka, Kansas*.)

Black newspapers also communicated information about local social events and individual artistic achievements. Reports on educational and social clubs appeared regularly in the columns of such newspapers. Women's literary societies such as the Pierian Club in Kansas City and the Dunbar Society in Topeka flourished throughout the early twentieth century and beyond. Social and artistic events at elite black schools—such as Sumner High School in Kansas City, Kansas, and Lincoln High School in Kansas City, Missouri—also received considerable attention in these newspapers. Although these schools were segregated, their facilities rivaled those of neighboring white schools, and they employed excellent teachers who served as race leaders. Such schools functioned as centers of creativity and intellectual life in African American communities.

Families and the community both emphasized education, and this emphasis further supported the next generation of African American high school and college graduates. For instance, Langston Hughes (who moved to Harlem in 1924) lived from 1909 to 1915 with his grandmother in Lawrence, Kansas, where he excelled in elementary school. Early in life, Hughes developed a sense of family honor and community responsibility, on which he drew throughout his career. From his grandmother, Mary Langston, in particular he acquired a sense of responsibility to his family and to African Americans. Several of his ancestors had fought slavery and segregation; for instance, his grandfather Charles Langston—Mary Langston's second husband—had been an abolitionist and an active member of the community. (Mary Langston's first husband, Lewis Sheridan Leary, had died after being seriously wounded when he joined the abolitionist John Brown's assault against the federal arsenal at Harpers Ferry, Maryland, in 1859.) Hughes also learned an appreciation for theater from his mother, Carrie Langston, who shared her passion with her son and took him on trips to nearby Kansas City to see performances.

Aaron Douglas was born a few miles west of Lawrence in Topeka, Kansas, in 1899. Douglas attended a segregated elementary school and graduated from the integrated Topeka High School in 1917. While he was a high school student, Douglas established a reputation among his peers and teachers as an excellent artist and a serious student, forming an early taste for, in his words, the "heavy" literature of writers such as Emerson, Bacon, Dumas, and Shakespeare. In 1915 and again in 1917, Douglas designed the cover images for the high school yearbook. The caption under his image in the yearbook of 1917 noted: "He is one of the most talented artists in school and he has specialized in Art ever since he entered." Despite his poverty, Douglas graduated from the school of fine arts at the University of Nebraska in 1922; he was the first African American to receive such a degree there. Through his art, writing, teaching, and public speaking, Douglas challenged antiblack racism and the resulting barriers that the average African American faced in mainstream American society.

Education promised unique opportunities to young black women and men. In *Shadow and Act*, for instance, Ralph Ellison explains how a "frontiersmen" atmosphere in Oklahoma during the 1920s encouraged him to read and grow intellectually. Ellison recalled that this prevailing attitude of wide-open freedom offered him an opportunity to imagine himself in the roles of the figures—white, black, and other—he read about and saw in early movies. The writer, poet, and editor Frank Marshall Davis grew up combing the stacks of the library in Arkansas City, Kansas, and then studied journalism at Kansas State University in Manhattan before moving east to Chicago.

Like education, music—especially blues and jazz—was an important aspect and source of the cultural renaissance. In their later writings, Frank Marshall Davis, Ralph Ellison, and Langston Hughes all note how important it was for them to hear blues and jazz in local venues as they were growing up. Great jazz musicians such as Charlie "Bird" Parker (born in 1920 and raised in Kansas City) and Coleman Hawkins (born in 1904 in St. Joseph, Missouri, and raised in Topeka, Kansas) were part of coteries of musicians who had created their sound in Kansas City and Chicago.

In the 1920s and 1930s, clubs and theaters in Kansas City were centered on the jazz district at Eighteenth and Vine. Hot spots such as Club Reno, Gem Theater, and Lyric Hall earned national reputations. In Kansas City, as in Harlem during the renaissance, the jazz scene supported black artists who were expressing themselves in their own unique styles. The pianist William "Count" Basie came to Kansas City in 1927, and in 1935, he led the Barons of Rhythm, a group that included Walter "Hot Lips" Page, Lester "Pres" Young, Buster Smith, and, a year later, Eddie Durham. The saxophonist Charlie Parker—whose own nickname, "Bird," initiated the name "Birdland" for the scene in Kansas City—joined Jay McShann's band in Kansas City in 1938 and then toured throughout the nation, including New York. The talent and ambition of musicians in Kansas City led them to develop a regional cultural renaissance and also propelled them to success in Chicago and New York, the national centers of black culture.

Even before jazz gained broad popularity in the 1920s and 1930s, however, vaudeville acts with roots in the plains states had toured the country. George Walker, who was born in Lawrence, Kansas, c. 1873, performed throughout Kansas before taking his act on the road from San Francisco to New York. While he was in San Francisco, Walker teamed up with Bert Williams; these two men would bring the cakewalk to mainstream white audiences. Similarly, Hattie McDaniel, who was born in 1895 in Wichita, Kansas, left school in 1910 to perform on the traveling vaudeville circuit. (In 1940, McDaniel became the first African American to win an Oscar, for her portrayal of Mammy in *Gone With the Wind*.)

In expressing their talents, black artists had to overcome many obstacles. Langston Hughes's white seventh-grade teacher, for instance, remembered him fifty years later only as a troublemaker with "no talent, much less promise" (Rampersad 1986, 17). Such a comment, half a century after the fact, suggests the difficulties many potential artists and scholars in Kansas and throughout the plains states must have faced at the time as they struggled for achievement. Yet Hughes, Douglas, and countless other African American artists contributed enormously to the flowering of black culture known as the Harlem, or New Negro, Renaissance.

CHERYL R. RAGAR

See also Blues; Crisis, The; Douglas, Aaron; Ellison, Ralph; Hughes, Langston; Jazz; Survey Graphic; Williams, Egbert Austin "Bert"

Further Reading

Cox, Thomas C. *Blacks in Topeka, Kansas, 1865–1915: A Social History*. Baton Rouge: Louisiana State University Press, 1982.

Davis, Frank Marshall. *Livin' the Blues: Memoirs of a Black Journalist and Poet*, ed. John Edgar Tidwell. Madison: University of Wisconsin Press, 1992.

Early, Gerald. *Black Heartland: African American Life, the Middle West, and the Meaning of American Regionalism*, 2 vols. St. Louis, Mo.: Washington University, 1996–1997.

Ellison, Ralph. Introduction. In *Shadow and Act*. New York: Random House, 1967. (Reprint, New York: Vintage, 1995.)

Jackson, Carlton. *Hattie: The Life of Hattie McDaniel*. Lanham, Md.: Madison Books, 1990.

Meier, August. *Negro Thought in America 1880–1915: Racial Ideologies in the Age of Booker T. Washington*. Ann Arbor: University of Michigan Press, 1963. (Reprint, 1988.)

Morgan, Thomas L., and William Barlow. *From Cakewalks to Concert Halls: An Illustrated History of African American Popular Music from 1895 to 1930*. Washington, D.C.: Elliott and Clark, 1992.

Painter, Nell Irvin. *Exodusters: Black Migration to Kansas after Reconstruction*, 2nd ed. Lawrence: University Press of Kansas, 1986.

Patterson, Cheryl R. "Aspects of Negro Life, from Topeka to Harlem, Forming Aaron Douglas." Master's thesis, University of Kansas, 1999.

Rampersad, Arnold. *The Life of Langston Hughes*, Vol. 1, *1902–1941*. New York: Oxford University Press, 1986.

Russell, Ross. *Jazz Style in Kansas City and the Southwest*. Berkeley: University of California Press, 1968.

Tidwell, John Edgar. "Coming of Age in a Land of Uncertainty." *Cottonwood*, 56, Fall 2000, pp. 43–59.

Tidwell, John Edgar, et al. "Plateaus of Uncertainty: Symposia on Legacies and Future of the Race—Part 2: Legacy of the Harlem Renaissance." *Cottonwood*, 57, Spring 2001, pp. 45–61.

Harlem Renaissance in the United States: 6—Philadelphia

Philadelphia's contribution to the Harlem Renaissance has traditionally been defined in terms of cultural center (Harlem) versus periphery (Philadelphia). For instance, the landmark exhibition "Harlem Renaissance:

Art of Black America" (1987) positioned Philadelphia in opposition to Harlem:

> Indeed, the artistic migration to Harlem would have been modest to negligible without the efforts of a half dozen or so prominent figures. Otherwise the Harlem cultural scene would have become little more than a larger version of Washington, D.C., or Philadelphia, places where arts and letters meant Saturday night adventures in tidy parlors, among mostly tidy-minded literati.

Recent scholarship has deemphasized the notion of Harlem as an exclusive site of this cultural phenomenon, instead viewing it as "a geopolitical metaphor for modernity and an icon for an increasingly complex black diasporal presence in the world" (Powell 1997).

Although less significant than New York, Philadelphia did play an essential role in advancing the black cultural movement of the 1920s. As the nation's first capital, as one of America's oldest settlements, and as Pennsylvania's largest city, Philadelphia was linked to the plight of African Americans, their cultural aspirations, and their quest for political emancipation. Also, its seaport and central geographic location on the eastern seaboard made it a center of commerce and trading where the arts, literature, and music could flower.

In the early twentieth century, Philadelphia, like other large cities, provided a community of increasingly mobile artists, musicians, and writers with an urban-centered experience of modernity. Philadelphia's impact on the Harlem Renaissance manifested itself in three areas: (1) in a spirit of tolerance and cultural experimentation stemming from the city's abolitionist heritage and deep-rooted religious traditions; (2) in a community of innovative artists, writers, and musicians whose works explored the nexus of modernity and African American identity; and (3) in the advancement of educational opportunities for blacks in prominent local institutions.

Philadelphia was one of the few American cities with significant black populations as early as 1790; and in Philadelphia (unlike, say, New York and Baltimore, which had a large number of slaves), most blacks were free. Quaker settlers had rejected the institution of slavery early on, although they maintained segregation. Also, Philadelphia had a long history of independent black churches that advanced cultural and social endeavors. Bishop Richard Allen's African Methodist Episcopal (AME) Church in Philadelphia became the country's first black congregation. As early as 1831, Allen coordinated black conventions advocating literacy and education. Building on the abolitionist heritage and strong religious traditions, Philadelphia's black populace developed a resilient spirit of cultural autonomy and self-determination. Abolitionist patronage supported the production of art and material culture. Philadelphia was not a haven from racism, but its diverse ethnic communities and varied social composition differed from the harsh realities of segregation in the South. Its uniquely positioned black population is also evident in W. E. B. Du Bois's landmark sociological study *The Philadelphia Negro* (1899). Jones (1995) characterizes Philadelphia as "the artistic apex of 19th century African America in terms of its visual arts production, exhibits, collecting and documentary efforts. In this context, it also functions as a model of both the major accomplishments of, and obstacles to, African American artistic expression."

In the early twentieth century, Philadelphia offered African Americans the economic and political conditions that engendered the Harlem Renaissance. Blacks in Philadelphia, as in other industrialized cities of the Northeast and Midwest, experienced a series of demographic and social transformations. In the first two decades of the new century, the city attracted large numbers of blacks from a predominantly rural South. Philadelphia also functioned as a stopover for those continuing their artistic and intellectual journey to Harlem. Like New York, Philadelphia had an economic and social infrastructure to accommodate the influx of new migrants and the social and cultural impulses that accompanied them. Throughout the 1920s, then, numerous writers, artists, musicians, and performers lived or worked in Philadelphia, creating a convergence of artistic practice that has come to characterize the Harlem Renaissance. Some artists had been born and raised in Philadelphia; others had formative educational experiences there before moving away; still others spent their most productive years there.

Philadelphia's heritage of nineteenth-century black cultural associations fostered the emergence of literary societies during the Harlem Renaissance era. In the 1920s, various literary currents came together in *Black Opals*, a prestigious journal featuring prose, poetry, and reviews by local black writers who had formed a society of the same name. Contributors to *Black Opals* included Lewis Grandison Alexander (1900–1945), who was from Washington, D.C., but was based in Philadelphia and had studied at the University of

Pennsylvania; and Effie Lee Newsome (Mary Effie Lee, 1885–1979), who was a native of Philadelphia and had extensive educational experience at Wilberforce University, Oberlin College, the Pennsylvania Academy of Fine Arts, and the University of Pennsylvania. Newsome also contributed regularly to the children's column in *Opportunity*.

Alain Locke (1886–1954) was also a native of Philadelphia, and he maintained close ties with the city even though he lived in Washington, D.C., and taught at Howard University for most of his life. His influential book *The New Negro* (1925) laid out the vision of the renaissance as a black contribution to American music, art, and literature that would simultaneously embrace a uniquely African American heritage. Another pivotal figure, the novelist, poet, biographer, and literary critic Jessie Redmon Fauset (1882–1961), had been schooled in Philadelphia; she received a scholarship to attend Cornell University as the first black woman there, before pursuing another degree in classical languages from the University of Pennsylvania. Fauset became the literary editor of *The Crisis* in 1919. Besides writing significant literary works about black middle-class life, she was a mentor to younger, more bohemian writers, including Jean Toomer, Langston Hughes, and Countee Cullen. Fauset was part of Harlem's literary scene but kept up an ongoing involvement with *Black Opals* in Philadelphia—and also with the Saturday Nighters Club in Washington, and with other literary clubs, underscoring the mobility of figures of the Harlem Renaissance. The writer Idabell Yeiser was also based in Philadelphia and deserves mention for her insightful accounts of her extensive journeys in Europe and Africa.

A sizable number of painters, printmakers, and sculptors created a visual counterpart to the evolving body of literature during 1918–1935, the period associated with the Harlem Renaissance. Well-known artists whose work and legacies point to Philadelphia as a place of artistic formation include Henry Ossawa Tanner, Meta Warrick Fuller, Laura Wheeler Waring, Jacob Lawrence, and Dox Thrash. Philadelphia's black artists owed much of their success to the city's excellent art schools, universities, and museum collections, which provided opportunities for artistic inspiration, professional networking, and exchanges of ideas.

The Philadelphia Centennial Exhibition had recognized leading black artists such as Edward Mitchell Bannister and Edmonia Lewis as early as 1876, when Henry Ossawa Tanner (1859–1937) was beginning his studies at the Pennsylvania Academy of Fine Arts.

Frustrated by racial prejudice and harassment, Tanner later studied in France and became an expatriate there, but he remained an important figure at home. In 1899, the Philadelphia Museum of Art bought his painting *The Annunciation* (1897); this was the first acquisition of his work by an American institution. Tanner's growing international success drew other Philadelphian artists to Paris, where they sought his advice and academic guidance.

The sculptor Meta Warrick Fuller (1877–1968), a native of Philadephia, also went abroad for training; after attending the Philadelphia Museum School of Industrial Art (later the Philadelphia College of Art), she spent three years in Paris, where Tanner looked after her. Fuller returned to Philadelphia in 1903 as a fairly well-established artist. She exhibited frequently at the Pennsylvania Academy of Fine Arts and earned a gold medal at the Tercentennial Exposition of 1907 for *Jamestown Tableau*, a sculptural ensemble recounting the settlement of the first black community in colonial America in 1607. Fuller moved to Massachusetts after her marriage in 1909 but left an influential legacy in Philadelphia. Her career, spanning several decades and two continents and embracing emancipation and liberation, anticipated the spirit of the Harlem Renaissance. Fuller's well-known bronze sculpture *Ethiopia Awakening* (1914) foreshadowed the emergence of a new cultural consciousness among African Americans at the onset of the renaissance era.

The painter Laura Wheeler Waring (1887–1948), who was from Connecticut, arrived in Philadelphia in 1907 to attend the Pennsylvania Academy of Fine Arts. She moved on to found the art department at nearby Cheyney State Teachers College, where she would remain until 1945. During the 1920s, a scholarship enabled her to study in Paris, where Tanner introduced her to a group of expatriates constituting a who's who of the Harlem Renaissance: the artists Palmer Hayden, Malvin Gray Johnson, Nancy Elizabeth Prophet, Augusta Savage, and Hale Woodruff; the writers Countee Cullen, Langston Hughes, and Jessie Redmon Fauset; and the performers Lillian Evanti, Roland Hayes, and Paul Robeson.

The Philadelphian sculptor May Howard Jackson (1877–1931) also attended the Pennsylvania Academy of Fine Arts, between 1895 and 1902. Declining an invitation from Fuller to go to Europe for advanced academic training, Jackson instead accepted a teaching position at Howard University in Washington, D.C., where she continued to produce portrait busts of prominent African Americans such as W. E. B. Du Bois and Paul

Laurence Dunbar. She also produced an important series of sculptures representing women and children during the 1910s and 1920s; these works explored issues of racial identity, a subject at the heart of the Harlem Renaissance. At this time another sculptor, Augusta Savage, who was already working for the periodical *Fire!!*, exhibited her work at Philadelphia's Sesquicentennial Exhibition of 1926. The Philadelphian Allan R. Freelon (1895–1960), a painter and printmaker who was the artistic director of *Black Opals*, frequently exhibited at the Harmon Foundation; his works also appeared as covers and illustrations in *The Crisis* and *Opportunity*. Freelon was a graduate of the Philadelphia Museum School of Industrial Arts, the University of Pennsylvania, and the Tyler School of Arts, and later became supervisor of Philadelphia's art education program. Jacob Lawrence (1917–2000) spent part of his childhood in Philadelphia before moving to Harlem at age thirteen. His family's experience of the great migration from the rural South to the industrialized North later figured prominently in his sixty-painting work *Migration of the Negro* (1941).

Others artists—building on the legacy of Philadelphia's visual culture of the 1920s—began their careers during the mid-1930s, just as the Harlem Renaissance was declining. This new cohort of young and highly productive African American printmakers and painters worked under the auspices of the graphic arts division of the Works Progress Administration (WPA) and the Federal Arts Project. Dox Thrash (1893–1965) experimented with the limitations print as a medium and consequently developed the carborundum print process, a technique that allowed for a wider range of tints and tonal variations. Thrash's expertise in technique complemented the powerful social commentary of the printmaker Raymond Steth (1916–1997). Other significant members of the graphic arts group included Claude Clark (b. 1915), Samuel Joseph Brown (b. 1907), and Humbert Lincoln Howard (1906–1990). Howard studied with James A. Porter at Howard University before transferring to the University of Pennsylvania. Like many other black artists in Philadelphia, Howard advanced his studies at the legendary Barnes Foundation. He frequently exhibited at the Pennsylvania Academy of Fine Arts, the Philadelphia Art Alliance, and the Pyramid Club, a social organization for black professionals.

The architect Julian F. Abele is a captivating yet frequently overlooked figure of Philadelphia's Harlem Renaissance. He was the first black architecture graduate of the University of Pennsylvania (in 1902), and he then studied at the École des Beaux Arts in Paris with financial support from his patron, Horace Trumbauer.

Howard joined Trumbauer's architectural firm in 1906 and later became its chief designer. Abele and Trumbauer developed a symbiotic working relationship that compensated for their individual difficulties—Trumbauer lacked formal training; Abele, although outstandingly talented, was hampered by the racially charged climate of Philadelphia's architectural association—and they succeeded in obtaining important commissions, such as the residence of James B. Duke in New York City and the architectural master plan for Duke University.

Philadelphia was a principal center of music in the United States and had a range of excellent concert halls. Its role as a center of music publishing in the nineteenth century preceded its role as a site of popular music. During the 1920s, its black churches produced internationally successful gospel choirs such as the Clara Ward Singers. This was also the time when Philadelphia emerged as a center for jazz. Important figures included the pianist Sam Wooding (1895–1985), a native of Philadelphia, whose band played at hotels in Atlantic City in 1919 before moving on to New York. By the mid-1920s, Wooding's jazz band and dance revue *Chocolate Kiddies* conquered European stages. In 1921, the dancer Josephine Baker (1906–1975), who was then still unknown, arrived in Philadelphia with a traveling show; she met and married her second husband, William Howard Baker, there. The opera singer Marian Anderson (1897–1993) was a Philadelphian, although she first gained fame in Europe before receiving belated recognition at home. Other important figures with ties to Philadelphia include the singer and actor Paul Robeson (1898–1976), the singer Ethel Waters (1896–1977), and, later, the trumpeter Dizzy Gillespie (1917–1993). Still later, the tenor saxophonist John Coltrane (1926–1967) chose Philadelphia for studies: He attended the Ornstein School of Music and Granoff Studios during his formative years.

Another aspect of Philadelphia's role during the Harlem Renaissance era was its educational institutions. In addition to leading art schools and museum collections, the greater Philadelphia area had some of the nation's oldest black colleges and universities. Cheyney State Teachers College and Lincoln University, originally established by Quakers to educate free blacks and runaway slaves, attracted African Americans from Philadelphia and beyond. The celebrated art collection and educational foundation of Albert C. Barnes in Merion turned out to be another cultural magnet. Established in 1922 as a nonprofit organization to promote appreciation of and education in the fine arts, the Barnes Foundation contributed signifi-

517

cantly to the formation of Philadelphia's black cultural movement. Barnes's interest in both Western and African art proved particularly attractive to many black artists; and his belief in egalitarian causes, his commitment to education as a tool for social change, and his financial support created a welcoming environment for Aaron Douglas, Claude Clark, Horace Pippin, and others. In 1926, the Barnes Foundation established close ties with Lincoln University—a collaboration that epitomizes the cultural synergy of Philadelphia's black renaissance.

JÜRGEN HEINRICHS

See also Anderson, Marian; Baker, Josephine; Barnes, Albert C. Black Opals; Fauset, Jessie Redmon; Federal Programs; Fire!!; Fuller, Meta Warrick; Harmon Foundation; Jackson, May Howard; Lawrence, Jacob; Locke, Alain; Porter, James Amos; Robeson, Paul; Savage, Augusta; Tanner, Henry Ossawa; Waring, Laura Wheeler; Waters, Ethel; Works Progress Administration

Further Reading

Blockson, Charles L. *African Americans in Pennsylvania: Above Ground and Underground—An Illustrated Guide.* Harrisburg, Pa.: RB, 2001.

Campbell, Mary Schmidt, David Driskell, David Levering Lewis, and Deborah Willis Ryan. *Harlem Renaissance: Art of Black America.* New York: Studio Museum in Harlem/Abrams, 1987.

Jones, Steven Loring. "A Keen Sense of the Artistic: African American Material Culture in Nineteenth-Century Philadelphia." *International Review of African American Art*, 12(2), 1995, pp. 4–29.

Powell, Richard J. *Black Art and Culture in the Twentieth Century.* New York: Thames and Hudson, 1997.

Tomlinson, Glenn C., and Rolando Corpus. "A Selection of Works by African American Artists in the Philadelphia Museum of Art." *Philadelphia Museum of Art Bulletin*, 90(382–3), Winter 1995.

Willis, Arthur C. *Cecil's City: A History of Blacks in Philadelphia, 1638–1979.* New York: Carlton, 1990.

Harlem Renaissance in the United States: 7—The South

During the Harlem Renaissance, the South was not a place for African Americans to remain in, raise families, and prosper but, as in the days of slavery, a "prison-house of bondage"—a place to leave. Actually, though, the South was a region of contradictions for its black residents. Patterns such as vigorously enforced race-based segregation, economic exploitation, suspension of civil rights, political disenfranchisement, and relentlessly brutal suppression of dissent existed alongside influential black institutions: newspapers, churches, and schools. These black institutions, formed by and within African American communities, nurtured a new leadership and new strategies for resisting oppression and effecting social change. Southern artists, entertainers, musicians, and writers mined black sacred and secular traditions in order to introduce new forms and themes to national and international audiences, meanwhile debating over the enduring value of these traditions and over daring pronouncements about legitimately African American aesthetics. Nevertheless, for about fifteen years during the "great migration," hundreds of thousands of black farm families did move to the North or West, leaving the boll weevil infestation and their own second-class citizenship and grinding losses as sharecroppers for a more prosperous urban life, factory jobs, and promises of social equality. The South, for its part, struggled to reconcile its dismal history of enslavement, and the aftermath of enslavement, with the new directions in religion, education, activism, and the arts that the Harlem Renaissance offered.

Religion

Because of the "black codes" that prevented slaves from gathering to worship communally, or that allowed services for slave congregations to be led only by ministers hand-picked to reinforce notions of racial inferiority, African American religion developed a subversive element throughout much of the South. Both free and enslaved blacks devised coded expressions of an African past manifested in the movements, sermons, spirituals, rituals, and icons of both Protestants and Catholics; thus religion became an expression of rebellion against bondage and an indicator of a distinctly African American culture. For example, in Louisiana—as in other states where large numbers of slaves had been imported from the Caribbean—*santería* flourished alongside Catholicism; and Catholicism and west African religions were reassembled into a new belief system. It thus is not surprising that during the Harlem Renaissance black churches in the South continued to represent the heart and soul of African American culture. They were incubators for political and educational leaders, sources of relief and renewal to communities besieged by Jim Crow, and affirmative symbols to artists, regardless of race.

African American churches in the South were essential in educating black youth and organizing political assaults against racism. They raised money to send their brightest students to the segregated colleges and normal schools that served them, and created networks of families to house, feed, and pay teachers who traveled to their communities. W. E. B. Du Bois, in his *Souls of Black Folk* (1903), recalls such assistance when he finished matriculating at Fisk University in Nashville and begin teaching in a one-room schoolhouse in rural Tennessee. Many students would return to their southern homes as ministers, to ask local whites for calm and humanity in times of racial tension, and to develop "bully pulpits" from which they called for immediate or gradual relaxation of racial apartheid. In addition to their spiritual functions, African American churches in the South performed services as mundane, and as specific to the region, as providing safe havens and meals for black travelers when all-white hotels and restaurants refused their patronage.

In rural as well as urban communities in the South, African American churches offered a release valve for pressures built up by racial stereotyping, financial hardships, and so on. Church members fraternized at picnics, weddings, funerals, ice cream socials, tent meetings, revivals, and other events; and they published newspapers disseminating political opinions as well as announcing the locations of places of worship and the hours of services. In all this, they found freedom from the surveillance by the master that had characterized the religious practices of an earlier generation. As the nation became urbanized and industrialized, some of the creative productions of the Harlem Renaissance—such as Langston Hughes and Zora Neale Hurston's play *Mule Bone: A Comedy of Negro Life* (1931) and Hurston's novel *Their Eyes Were Watching God* (1937)—celebrated southern black churches or satirized them, or both.

Education

During the Harlem Renaissance, the South was a site for the education of professional and working-class African Americans, despite the obstacles raised by the "separate and unequal" Jim Crow system, which impaired the quality of instruction, limited the availability of institutions, and weakened the power of black communities to define their own educational agenda.

Shoddy buildings, shortages of teachers, inadequate instruction, and poor equipment plagued segregated rural schools especially. Even when teachers could be found to accept the low or inconsistent pay that such communities offered, and these communities' remoteness from cities, the pupils often stayed away from school to help in the fields or otherwise assist their families financially. Rural areas were dotted by Bible colleges, funded primarily by such denominations as the African Methodist Episcopal Church and the Baptists, that developed pastors and teachers for such communities. However, the most visible symbols of black people's educational progress in the region were industrial schools such as Booker T. Washington's "experiment" in Tuskegee, Alabama, and Hampton Institute in Virginia.

The industrial schools were funded by a combination of contributions from white northern philanthropists (the Carnegies, Rockefellers, Rosenwalds, and Phelps-Stokeses, for example), religious organizations, and African American individuals and communities. The curriculum emphasized practical skills, discipline, hard work, and self-help, along with cultural awareness and racial pride. Whites who suspected that too much education and literacy would stir up restlessness and dissatisfaction among blacks in the region were reassured that the students would return to their communities with marketable trades such as carpentry, bricklaying, dressmaking, and laundering. With buildings constructed by the students and dining halls stocked with food that the students prepared, industrial schools modeled thrift, self-sufficiency, morality, persistence, deferred gratification, and cooperation—qualities that proved crucial to arguments for extending the full rights of citizenship to African Americans.

Yet these schools did have detractors. Many critics complained, for example, about the preponderance of white faculty members and presidents, although by the 1920s black administrators and instructors were being hired more routinely than had been the case in the nineteenth century. And the novelist Nella Larsen—after an unhappy experience living at Fisk with her husband, a physics teacher—invented a fictional institution, Naxos, in her novel *Quicksand* (1928), to skewer the industrial model for promoting conformity, snobbery, and self-hate. In response to such criticism, institutions including Fisk and Atlanta University added liberal arts tracks to their vocational offerings in order to prepare the best and the brightest to enter such professions as law, teaching, and medicine.

Despite such objections, southern black educational institutions at all levels were crucial to the establishment of a black middle class in the region and to the development of innovative individuals. For instance, the chemist George Washington Carver spent his career teaching at Tuskegee University, where he made internationally recognized discoveries regarding paint dyes and soybean, peanut, and potato production. James Weldon Johnson served as principal of the Central Colored Grammar School in Jacksonville, Florida, before he began his celebrated creative career in New York City. Similarly, African American women found opportunities to rise to leadership positions by establishing and directing all-female schools, such as—in Georgia—Spelman Seminary (later Spelman College) in Atlanta and Haines Normal and Industrial School in Augusta; or by taking positions as "lady principals" at coeducational schools. And black families in rural areas benefited from agricultural extension and community outreach services, libraries, health care programs, and primary schools staffed by the faculty and students of educational institutions.

Activism

Black southerners during the Harlem Renaissance confronted a hostile social and political climate and entrenched Jim Crow policies. They were subjected to literacy tests and poll taxes that denied them the vote; to sharecropping and low-wage agricultural labor that created economic inequities; and to a legal system that encouraged false arrests of law-abiding African Americans and the exploitation of convict labor by wealthy whites. Additionally, social control often took the form of mob violence. Particularly in rural areas, lynching was practiced indiscriminately; the victims were men, women, and children whose offenses were frequently more imaginary than real. In the cities, especially after black soldiers who had served in World War I returned from overseas to compete for jobs and agitate for social justice, angry whites incited riots that devastated African American communities and caused the death of many residents—most notoriously in Longview, Texas, and Washington, D.C., during the "red summer" of 1919.

The National Association of Colored Women (NACW) and National Association for the Advancement of Colored People (NAACP) responded to such oppression by campaigning through the legal and political systems. They pressed at the local, state, and national levels for antilynching legislation, increases

in teachers' pay, and additional resources for public health and educational institutions in African American communities. Sometimes black citizens armed themselves against lynch mobs and rioters. As a final recourse, they could leave the South as part of the great migration—which thus was a way of actively resisting their disempowerment and of asserting their dignity as much as it was a way to find more lucrative industrial jobs or to find better housing and schools.

Culture

Southerners were central figures in the artistic flowering that African Americans initiated. The South as a romantic "land of cotton" was still quite prominent in the national imagination. However, African American artists of the Harlem Renaissance doubted that the region held pleasant associations for their people, and their artistic expression influenced mainstream popular and commercial culture.

Writers and visual artists stood at the forefront of a movement to remove stereotypes of black southerners and to assert the complexity and beauty of these black people's lives. They also challenged the notion that Harlem was the only black space rich enough to produce enduring artistic contributions. The South inspired northern black artists to visit, live there, and produce honest portrayals, and it inspired native southern artists to capture their insiders' views for posterity.

Jean Toomer's experimental novel *Cane* (1923), for example, derived from his brief residence as a teacher in Georgia. It contrasted vivid landscapes, alluring mulatto beauties, and the haunting sounds of spirituals, work songs, and blues with the terrors of lynching and the stark economic hardships that characterized the rural black South. James Weldon Johnson, in his *Autobiography of an Ex-Colored Man* (1912), fictionalized the life of a light-complexioned protagonist in Georgia during the Jim Crow period. Langston Hughes's poems in his *Weary Blues* (1926) relied on musical rhythms that could be traced to the days of slavery in the South. Zora Neale Hurston, in *Mules and Men* (1935), collected folklore from the region. Johnson's sermons in *God's Trombones* (1927), along with the spirituals he and his brother anthologized (1925, 1926), brought attention to additional creative forms. Walter White, a longtime official of the NAACP, could pass for white and occasionally infiltrated meetings of the Ku Klux Klan to gather information on lynching. Out of these experiences came his *Rope and Faggot: An*

Analysis of Judge Lynch (1929), as well as *Fire in the Flint* (1924), on African American life in Georgia; and *Flight* (1926), a portrait of mulatto life and the black middle class in Atlanta.

The painter Jacob Lawrence, who was based in Harlem, captured the many ways in which flight and its symbols—the train, the North Star—recur as motifs in black southern history. African American schools, most notably Fisk and Tuskegee, commissioned such visual artists to design and decorate buildings and to train students.

Singers such as Bessie Smith and Gertrude "Ma" Rainey and musicians such as Louis Armstrong, Joseph "King" Oliver, Sidney Bechet, and Jelly Roll Morton refined blues and jazz in cities like Memphis and New Orleans. Frequently, they resettled in the North to perform in larger venues and record for the nascent "race record" industry but would then come to the South again on the "chitlin' circuit" to perform in black-owned vaudeville houses or traveling tent shows. These musicians further demonstrate the rich contribution of the South to the Harlem Renaissance.

BARBARA MCCASKILL

See also Armstrong, Louis; Artists; Autobiography of an Ex-Colored Man; Bechet, Sidney; Du Bois, W. E. B.; Fire in the Flint, The; God's Trombones; Great Migration; Hughes, Langston; Hurston, Zora Neale; Johnson, James Weldon; Johnson, John Rosamond; Jim Crow; Larsen, Nella; Lawrence, Jacob; Morton, Jelly Roll; Oliver, Joseph "King"; Quicksand; Rainey, Gertrude "Ma"; Riots: 2—Red Summer of 1919; Smith, Bessie; Toomer, Jean; Vaudeville; Washington, Booker T.; White, Walter

Further Reading

Anderson, James D. *The Education of Blacks in the South, 1860–1935.* Chapel Hill and London: University of North Carolina Press, 1988.

Brundage, W. Fitzhugh, ed. *Under Sentence of Death: Lynching in the South.* Chapel Hill: University of North Carolina Press, 1997.

Franklin, John Hope, and Alfred A. Moss Jr. *From Slavery to Freedom: A History of African Americans.* New York: McGraw-Hill, 1947. (See also 8th ed., New York: Knopf, 2000.)

Griffin, Farah Jasmine. *"Who Set You Flowin'?": The African American Migration Narrative.* New York: Oxford University Press, 1995.

Harris, Trudier. *Exorcising Blackness: Historical and Literary Lynching and Burning Rituals.* Bloomington: Indiana University Press, 1984.

Harrison, Alferdteen, ed. *Black Exodus: The Great Migration from the American South.* Jackson: University Press of Mississippi, 1991.

Johnson, Alonzo, and Paul T. Jersild, eds. *Ain't Gonna Lay My 'Ligion Down: African American Religion in the South.* Columbia: University of South Carolina Press, 1996.

Litwack, Leon F. *Trouble in Mind: Black Southerners in the Age of Jim Crow.* New York: Knopf, 1998.

Marks, Carole. *Farewell—We're Good and Gone: The Great Black Migration.* Bloomington and Indianapolis: Indiana University Press, 1989.

Neverdon-Morton, Cynthia. *Afro-American Women of the South and the Advancement of the Race, 1895–1925.* Knoxville: University of Tennessee Press, 1983.

Taylor, Arnold H. *Travail and Triumph: Black Life and Culture in the South Since the Civil War.* Westport, Conn.: Greenwood, 1976.

Tolnay, Stewart Emory, and E. M. Beck. *A Festival of Violence: An Analysis of Southern Lynchings, 1882–1930.* Urbana: University of Illinois Press, 1995.

Harlem Renaissance in the United States: 8—Texas and the Southwest

The Harlem Renaissance influenced and promoted creative efforts of African Americans in Texas and the Southwest, although output was sometimes more restricted in the Southwest (as in the western United States in general) than in New York. Many prominent participants in the Harlem Renaissance had grown up in the West before moving to Harlem. Many other black westerners were prevented from relocating to New York because of the distances and the expense involved, and because (especially in the case of black women) they were reluctant to break family ties; these creative artists participated in regional and local renaissances in their home communities, despite numerous obstacles that were often imposed by whites.

The Harlem Renaissance was manifested in an increase in the artistic productivity of blacks in Texas and the Southwest, and it took place in a more tolerant social climate than had existed in previous years. Blacks' artistic endeavors and expressions were fostered by organized drama groups, theaters, nightclubs, galleries, schools, and newspapers. Avenues for artistic expression were opened not only by the Harlem Renaissance but also by a growing middle class, better educational opportunities, and the growth of cities. The cities of the region—for example, Albuquerque, Amarillo, Dallas, El Paso, Fort Worth, Houston, Phoenix, and San Antonio—served as vital outlets for black artistic expression during the renaissance.

But not all African American artists in the Southwest found a ready path to success. In white Texas, for instance, opportunities for black painters were limited; few black artists are recorded, and the works of those few were seldom given prominence. However, in September 1930, seventy-three examples of painting and sculpture, selected from more than 200 hundred nationwide entries for the Harmon Award, were exhibited in Houston. A black Houstonian, Samuel Countee, was one of the prominent exhibitors. Countee's painting *My Guitar*, a life-size portrait of a black man with a guitar, was later hung in the Negro Hall of Life at the Texas Centennial Exposition in 1936 and became a very popular piece in the collection. Frank Sheinall, an elevator operator from Galveston who was a self-taught painter in oils, also had a painting in the centennial exhibit, and the following year he was featured at the Fifth Annual Exhibit of the Negro Carnegie Branch Library in Houston.

Black dramatists in Texas also faced difficulties, because the opportunities that existed in theater were limited to actors rather than playwrights. Few, if any, plays written by black Texans of the period appear to have survived, but actors in the cities of the Southwest found new opportunities. Three examples are Clarence Brooks, Dick Campbell, and Arthur Wilson, who were all born in Texas. Campbell and Wilson both performed in Harlem during the renaissance: Campbell at the Cotton Club and Wilson in productions of the Lincoln and Lafayette theaters. In Houston, Texas, as early as 1919, the American Theater advertised that it would offer the best of colored professionals playing in colored houses. In 1931, blacks in Houston and San Antonio established Negro "little theater" troupes that presented shows throughout Texas. Black actors in Dallas organized the Dallas Negro Players, who gave their first performance in December 1928 to a racially mixed audience. The Dallas Negro Players experienced considerable financial difficulties, but in the autumn of 1930 presented *Jute*, a three-act play on race relations written by a white Dallasite, Kathleen Witherspoon.

It was in music—particularly blues, gospel, ragtime, and jazz—that Texan African Americans excelled and contributed most significantly to the national cultural milieu during the 1920s and 1930s. Their music grew out of the unique experience of black Texans and became a permanent part of the national musical heritage. The musicians wrote, performed, and ultimately recorded their work. The most successful example during this period was Blind Lemon Jefferson, a blues singer from Dallas who recorded for Paramount; during the late 1920s he was the best-selling black musician in the nation.

The most versatile black Texas musician was Huddie "Leadbelly" Ledbetter. Leadbelly began singing early in his life; spent the years 1918–1925 and 1930–1934 in prisons in Texas and Louisiana, where he became the lead man, or caller, for the work gangs; and eventually gained national recognition with songs such as "Goodnight Irene," "Midnight Special," and "Jail-House Blues." Leadbelly shared certain characteristics with many blues singers—intense vitality, a roving spirit, independence, and arrogance. Other talented black Texas performers included Texas Alexander, "Whistlin'" Alex Moore, Aaron Thibeaux "T-Bone" Walker, Mance Lipscomb, Sam "Lightning" Hopkins, and "Ragtime" Henry Thomas. Beulah "Sippie" Wallace, who was born in Houston, combined boogie-woogie with gospel, blues, and jazz; she had a successful career singing throughout Texas and touring with Louis Armstrong. Another vocalist, Victoria Spivey from Houston, sang in clubs and shows, acted in films, and wrote songs, including "Black Snake Blues."

The career of the singer and writer Penman Lovinggood indicates the opportunities for educated, talented black Texans in music during the Harlem Renaissance. He was born in Austin, the son of the founder and longtime president of Samuel Huston College. By 1925 he became a noted tenor in New York; in the 1930s, he performed with John Rosamond Johnson's quartet and the W. C. Handy orchestra. Lovinggood also wrote an opera and the book *Famous Modern Negro Musicians* (1921).

As more blacks moved into Texas cities, outstanding black bands also emerged. The bands directed by Troy Floyd of San Antonio and Alphonso Trent of Dallas achieved a national reputation. In Fort Worth, King Holston and Frank Bonapartes led highly popular black bands. Other musical groups included the Blues Syncopaters in El Paso, the Real Jazz Orchestra of Laredo, and Gene Coy's Happy Black Aces in Amarillo. These bands toured the state, playing to enthusiastic audiences in major cities and in more remote areas.

The singer Julius Bledsoe, who was born in Waco in 1899 and was educated at Bishop College, left Texas for New York in 1924. Four years later he was acclaimed for his rendition of "Ol' Man River" in the musical *Show Boat.* Maud Cuney-Hare, who was also born in Texas, said in her book *Negro Musicians and Their Music* that Bledsoe was the most versatile African American singer on the current stage. The swing pianist Teddy Wilson was born in Austin in 1912, studied music theory at Tuskegee and Talladega colleges, joined the Benny Goodman Trio in 1935, and left the Goodman trio four years later to form his own swing band, which he reduced to a sextet in 1940. The contralto Etta Moten was a native Texan (although she left Texas early in her life) who studied at Paul Quinn College; she became a successful singer on radio and appeared in movies and onstage during the 1930s.

In 1925, the Texas Association of Negro Musicians was organized, with headquarters in Fort Worth (where it was host to a national convention of Negro musicians in 1929); it was an affiliate of the National Association of Negro Musicians, which had started in 1919. The Texas Association published a journal, *The Negro Musician,* whose editor (and the guiding hand of the association) was Manet Harrison Fowler. Fowler, a dramatic soprano, had been born and educated in Fort Worth; at one time she operated a school in New York, the Nawlimu School for the Development of African Music and Creative Arts, before returning to Texas.

During the period of the renaissance, Texas also had an articulate group of poets, most of whom were middle-class and college-educated. Their poetry ranged widely in content, philosophy, and approach. In 1925, Bernice Love Wiggins published a volume of poetry, *Tuneful Tales,* in El Paso, but she later moved to California and was heard from no more. In 1933, the folklorist J. Mason Brewer published his first book of poems, *Negrito: Negro Dialect Poems From the Southwest.* Brewer (who was the Texas counterpart of Alain Locke) also collected the work of other black poets in Texas during the renaissance, in *Heralding Dawn: An Anthology of Verse* (1936). In his introductory essay, he argued that Texas poets should use materials drawn from the life of the urban and rural masses and should focus on African American culture, superstitions, customs, and traditions. Most of the black Texans included in his anthology did draw from that traditional base.

Among these poets was Clarence F. Carr, who wrote "When Dad Cooks Soda Biscuits." Carr had studied at Wilberforce University, where he came under the influence of Paul Laurence Dunbar. Another poet in the anthology was Lawrence Carlyle Tatum, a resident of Limestone County who also lived for a time in Los Angeles, where he published two volumes of verse. Brewer also included his own poetry, such as "Deep Ellum and Central Tracks," a vivid portrayal of the red-light district in Dallas. Some of the poets, such as J. Austin Love and Josie B. Hall, drew on the spiritual life of blacks in Texas. "The Will to Do," a poem by J. W. Fridia (a physician from Waco who wrote poetry for the Houston *Informer*), expressed a middle-class belief in self-help. Black Texas poets also expressed some criticism of the black community. Hypocritical behavior is castigated in Richard T. Hamilton's delightfully sarcastic "Sister Mandy Attends the Business League." Hamilton was a native of Alabama who had earned a medical degree at Howard University and had come to Dallas in 1901.

Two poets—Malcolm Christian Conley and Lauretta Holman Gooden—were openly critical of the segregated, racist society in Texas. Conley, who was from Tyler, began to appear in national publications in 1930: His "Four Walls" was published in *The Messenger* and his "Nineveh" and "American Ideals" in *The Crisis.* Gooden lived in Dallas, where she and her husband operated a grocery store. In "Questions to a Mob," she inveighed against lynching. The writings of these black poets marked an increasing willingness by black Texans in the 1930s to speak out against the inequities of their position.

Although poetry in Texas was equal to that of other parts of the nation in output and nature, African Americans in Texas and the Southwest—with one notable exception—were less successful in fiction. Melvin B. Tolson (who was later to become an acclaimed poet) wrote a novel, *Beyond the Zaretto,* in 1924, but was unable to have it published. He did publish a short story in 1926, "The Tragedy of the Yarr Karr," in the *Wiley Wild Cat.* Jennie V. Mills, a homemaker in Waco, also published a short story, "Doomed to Despair," in the *Waco Messenger* in 1933. However, the predominant writer of fiction at this time was Anita Scott Coleman of New Mexico.

Coleman's heritage was varied and unique. She was born in Guaymas, Sonora, Mexico, in 1890, the child of a Cuban man and a woman whom he had bought as a slave, most likely in order to free her. He later fought for the Union during the Civil War, and afterward he gravitated to Mexico and the Southwest. Anita Scott grew up in New Mexico, graduated from New Mexico Teachers College in Silver City, taught school, married, and later moved to Los Angeles. In

1920, in a biographical sketch for *The Competitor*, she was referred to as Miss Coleman from Silver City, so she seems to have been married and in New Mexico at that time; evidently her career as a teacher ended because of her marriage. She and her husband raised four children in Los Angeles, where she also managed a boardinghouse for children and continued writing. The impact of marriage on a working woman is reflected in her stories, especially "Peter and Phoebe Up North" and "The Little Grey House." Coleman was a polished and successful author by the time she was in her mid-twenties; she received many awards, and her work was sought by editors such as Wallace Thurman. Her twenty-one short stories and essays were published in national magazines, including *Half-Century*, *The Crisis*, *The Messenger*, *The Competitor*, and *Opportunity*; they reflect concerns of women and African Americans during the early twentieth century. Until relatively recently, her work has been mostly ignored by critics, despite its initial favorable reception, but she was a significant participant in the Harlem Renaissance.

The Hall of Negro Life at the Texas Centennial Exposition of 1936 was a culmination of the activities of the renaissance. It was funded by the federal government and had some 400,000 visitors, approximately 60 percent of whom were white. The Hall of Negro Life contained four murals by Aaron Douglas; featured music, dance, and educational and economic programs; and included an exhibit of artists of the Harlem Renaissance sponsored by the Harmon Foundation. Thomas (1938) provides a valuable tool for understanding the role of blacks in Texas culture during the 1930s.

The Texas Centennial Exposition fostered a renewed interest in the history of African Americans in Texas. In 1935, L. V. Williams had published "Teaching Negro Life and History in Texas High Schools" in the *Journal of Negro History*. The following year, three short works were published either in connection with the exhibition or as a result of this renewed interest: Ira B. Bryant Jr., *The Texas Negro Under Six Flags*; W. E. B. Du Bois, *What the Negro Has Done for the United States and Texas*; and Charles E. Hall, *Progress of the Negro in Texas*.

Finally, to gain further insight into this period in Texas, it is useful to give some more detail about two figures previously discussed briefly—J. Mason Brewer and Melvin B. Tolson. Brewer, who compiled the anthology of poetry *Heralding Dawn* and published a volume of his own poems, *Negrito*, was born in Goliad, graduated from Wiley College, took a graduate degree at Indiana University, and taught at the high school and college levels. Brewer sought diligently to portray black culture and (like his contemporary Zora Neale Hurston) included folklore in his work. His first published writing, in 1932, was forty folktales under the title "Juneteenth" in *Tone the Bell Down*, a publication of the Texas Folklore Society. The next year, 1933, the society published Brewer's "Old Time Negro Proverbs." He also published a historical-political study, *Negro Legislators of Texas and Their Descendants*, in 1935.

Tolson was the Texan scholar and artist with the closest personal ties to the Harlem Renaissance. He was born in Missouri in 1898, accepted a teaching job at Wiley College in 1923, and remained at Wiley for twenty-four years. During the summers, though, he visited New York City, where he became friends with leading renaissance writers such as Langston Hughes. Hughes traveled to Texas on numerous occasions, and one of his visits resulted in the poem "West Texas." Tolson also attended Columbia University in New York, and in 1940 he completed his master's thesis, "The Harlem Group of Negro Writers," which was the first scholarly study of renaissance writing.

BRUCE A. GLASRUD

See also Bledsoe, Jules; Brooks, Clarence; Campbell, Dick; Cuney-Hare, Maud; Douglas, Aaron; Harmon Foundation; Hughes, Langston; Johnson, John Rosamond; Lovinggood, Penman; National Association of Negro Musicians; Show Boat; Spivey, Victoria; Thurman, Wallace; Wilson, Arthur "Dooley"

Further Reading

Beeth, Howard, and Cary D. Wintz, eds. *Black Dixie: Afro-Texan History and Culture in Houston*. College Station: Texas A&M University Press, 1992.

Brewer, J. Mason, ed. *Heralding Dawn: An Anthology of Verse*. Dallas, Tex.: June Thomason, 1936.

Christian, Garna L. "Texas Beginnings: Houston in the World of Jazz." *Houston Review*, 12(3), 1990, pp. 144–156.

Clayton, Lawrence, and Joe W. Specht, eds. *The Roots of Texas Music*. College Station: Texas A&M University Press, 2003.

Farnsworth, Robert M. *Melvin B. Tolson, 1898–1966: Plain Talk and Poetic Prophecy*. Columbia: University of Missouri Press, 1984.

Fowler, Manet Harrison. "History of the Texas Association of Negro Musicians." *Negro Musician*, August 1929, pp. 114–116.

Glasrud, Bruce A. "From Griggs to Brewer: A Review of Black Texas Culture, 1899–1940." *Journal of Big Bend Studies*, 15, 2003, pp. 195–212.

Glasrud, Bruce A., and Laurie Champion. "Anita Scott Coleman (1890–1960)." In *American Women Writers, 1900–1945: A Bio-Bibliographical Critical Sourcebook*, ed. Laurie Champion. Westport, Conn.: Greenwood, 2000, pp. 77–81.

Govenar, Alan B., and Jay E. Brakefield. *Deep Ellum and Central Track: Where the Black and White Worlds of Dallas Converged*. Denton: University of North Texas Press, 1998.

Hales, Douglas. *A Southern Family in White and Black: The Cuneys of Texas*. College Station: Texas A&M University Press, 2003.

Hare, Maud Cuney. *Negro Musicians and Their Music*. Washington, D.C.: Associated Publishers, 1936.

Lovinggood, Penman. *Famous Modern Negro Musicians*. Brooklyn, N.Y.: Press Forum, 1921. (Reprint, New York: Da Capo, 1978.)

Sapper, Neil Gary. "Black Culture in Urban Texas: A Lone Star Renaissance." *Red River Valley Historical Review*, 6, Spring 1981, pp. 56–77.

Thomas, Jesse O. *Negro Participation in the Texas Centennial Exposition*. Boston, Mass.: Christopher, 1938.

Tolson, Melvin B. *The Harlem Group of Negro Writers*, ed. Edward J. Mullen. Westport, Conn.: Greenwood, 2001.

Wiggins, Bernice Love. *Tuneful Tales*. El Paso, Tex.: privately printed, 1925. (Reprint, Lubbock: Texas Tech University Press, 2002.)

Harlem Renaissance in the United States: 9—Washington, D.C.

The 1920s marked a cultural awakening among blacks in which more of them were actively involved in the arts. Their creative endeavors extended to all realms of the arts—fiction, poetry, drama, music, dance, and the visual arts. This time was unlike any other period before the 1920s in that white American publishers began to recognize black self-expression and issue it in books, magazines, and journals. The 1920s also gave rise to all-black literary quarterlies and "little magazines" that became major vehicles for the expression of the New Negro.

This new literary genius was not confined to Harlem, a section of New York City widely considered to be the "mecca" of black culture in the 1920s. Black com-munities in many cities experienced similar, although sometimes less extensive, literary and artistic activity. Washington, D.C., was no exception. Washington was the home of many cultural leaders, writers, musicians, performers, and visual artists. Some of them had been born there, and others were a part of the "great migration," in which an estimated 700,000 to 1 million blacks left the South between 1917 and 1920. According to the census of 1920, there were approximately 109,966 blacks living in the District of Columbia, making it the city with the third-largest population of blacks in the nation.

The rise of the "New Negro" movement in Washington brought an increased interest in the life and character of blacks. There was a new degree of frankness, openness, and self-awareness. The Harlem Renaissance transformed blacks as subject and artists from the old stereotype into the New Negro, who was more militant and embraced all facets of the black experience, including African heritage, social protest, folk songs, blues, jazz, lynching, race riots, and social injustice. Three writers—Langston Hughes, Jean Toomer, and Rudolph Fisher—effectively captured the spirit, energy, and experiences of the urban masses. Their imagery conjured up the moods of city streets filled with the naturalness of ordinary people.

During the early years of the twentieth century, an increasing number of blacks settled on and near Seventh and U streets in Washington. This neighborhood, which was populated by recent migrants, was a place where writers could gather rich material for stories. Washington had a dynamic social scene; and during the 1920s and 1930s, U Street—with its supper clubs, cabarets, jazz venues, and cafés—was the undisputed entertainment capital of black Washington. Bohemian Caverns, which opened in 1926, was the queen of U Street. In the early years, evening attire was mandatory—ladies wore gowns, and gentlemen wore tuxedos. Club Bengasi was upscale and a magnet for café society. At the Dance Hall at Ninth and V streets, one could regularly hear Louis Armstrong. Patrons at the Jungle Inn jived to the music of Jelly Roll Morton. Oriental Gardens, the oldest black cabaret in the city, catered to a racially mixed crowd, and Duke Ellington worked with the legendary Bricktop. Phoenix Inn also drew racially mixed audiences. Other points of interest in the general vicinity included the Casbah, Rocky's, Cecelia's, the Capitol Pleasure Club, the Rendezvous, and the Bali Club. The big three movie houses were the Lincoln Theater, the Booker T, and the Republic.

At Seventh and U streets, there was more of a "down-home" atmosphere, bustling and full of energy. Ninth Street divided the genteel and prosperous to the west and the poorer residents to the east. The action was on Seventh Street, especially for those who had migrated from points farther South. Noise and music from the traffic, pool rooms, storefront churches, barbershops, beauty salons, and liquor stores mingled together excitingly. In fact, the pool halls were second only to barbershops as important community gathering places. There was Club Off Beat, and just a few doors down one could hear the latest sounds at the University Record Shop. The Dunbar, at Seventh and T streets, was known as a family theater; it was black-owned and featured short subjects and universal news. There were evening performances at the Howard Theater, which had a seating capacity of 1,500 and was the first legitimate theater for blacks in the nation. Its location near Seventh Street placed it at a focal point in the black community. During the 1920s, the Howard Theater and the Howard University Players collaborated to present about two plays a year. In the late 1920s and early 1930s, programming gravitated toward big bands such as those of Duke Ellington, Cab Calloway, Jimmie Lunceford, and Earl "Fatha" Hines. Also, in the 1930s, the Howard Theater began its amateur-night contests. The winners included performers such as Bill Kenny of the Ink Spots and Billy Eckstein. During the period of the Harlem Renaissance, programming was geared toward jazz and blues, and there was an impressive schedule that included Ella Fitzgerald.

Langston Hughes was one of the major figures who were greatly influenced by Seventh Street. Hughes claimed that while he was living in Washington, the "cultured colored society" of the northwest section ignored him. Because he had a dislike of middle-class blacks in Washington, he explored Seventh Street for the themes and characters that he portrayed in his writing. He found inspiration in the dynamic and vibrant black life that was located there, and he incorporated the stories he heard into his own work, creating fresh, racially sensitive poetry. Most of the poems he wrote in Washington appeared in *Fine Clothes to the Jew* (1927). In Hughes's poetry, as in that of others of the younger generation, black life was artistically celebrated. Because the subjects of Hughes's works were simply themselves, he created a new racial consciousness that focused on everyday black life, elevating it to a new meaning.

The community just north of Seventh and U streets was a vast contrast to the happenings at that intersection. This community was home to Howard University, Freedmen's Hospital, Miner Normal School, and LeDroit Park, a neighborhood of strong black middle-class standing. Howard University was fertile ground for a black renaissance in the Washington area. The dean of the Harlem Renaissance, Alain Locke, was a member of the philosophy department. Illustrious faculty members in other disciplines included Kelly Miller, Ralph Bunche, Ernest Just, and T. Montgomery Gregory. Locke played an instrumental role both locally and nationally. On a local level, he helped organize the art gallery and the music department at Howard University. He and Gregory, who was a member of the drama department, collaborated to put together a student writers' group, which became known as the Stylus Society. There was a little magazine, *The Stylus*, which served as the organ for this group. As a student at Howard University, Zora Neale Hurston was a member of the Stylus Society, and she later said it had been an important part of her early writing career. Gregory also played a pioneering role at Howard University in developing drama as an art form in the lives of blacks and in black theater. Gregory's interest in creating a national Negro theater movement was the seed for the establishment of the Howard Players, which became a renowned college theater troupe. As director of the drama department, Gregory inspired a national interest in black drama, and he collaborated with playwrights such as Willis Richardson, Paul Green, and Eugene O'Neill. In 1927, Gregory and Locke published *Plays of Negro Life*, which included works by several playwrights connected to Washington: Thelma Myrtle Duncan, Georgia Douglas Johnson, Jean Toomer, Willis Richardson, and Richard Bruce Nugent. On a national level, Locke served as guest editor for a special issue of *Survey Graphic* (March 1925) that was devoted to "Harlem: Mecca of the New Negro." This special issue was organized and edited from Washington, and on its release it sold an unprecedented 40,000 copies. The success of this special issue led Locke to edit *The New Negro* (1925), in which perhaps sixteen of the thirty-seven contributors had some connection to Washington.

During the Harlem Renaissance, numerous social clubs and small cultural groups were active in and around Washington. Some of these were organized simply as literary study groups; others had a broader base that included the study of history and culture. The most inclusive of these groups that met on a regular basis was the Saturday Nighters, which met at the home of Georgia Douglas Johnson. On Saturday nights, her home became the social hub for the Washington group of the Harlem Renaissance—established Washingtonians as well as younger writers and artists who would later make a name for themselves. These gatherings were especially popular among the young writers but were also frequented by older writers who served as their mentors. The Saturday Nighters Club began when Jean Toomer asked Georgia Douglas Johnson to "hold weekly conversations among writers in Washington." The group met continually for about ten years and was still holding intermittent gatherings as late as 1942. In 1926, the Saturday Nighters Club was mentioned in Gwendolyn Bennett's "Ebony Flute" column in *Opportunity* magazine. The Saturday Nighters, through their longevity and the contributions they made, demonstrated that a common interest in the arts and culture could create a community.

A small sampling of those who were involved in the scene in Washington includes Richard Bruce Nugent, Waring Cuney, and Rudolph Fisher. Nugent, a native Washingtonian with close ties to Alain Locke and Langston Hughes, was a true bohemian, a nonconformist who rejected middle-class norms. His short story "Smoke, Lilies, and Jade" was the first literary work on a purely homosexual theme to be published by a black. Although Nugent was a gifted writer and artist, little of his work is currently in print. He was known to present his writings to Locke on scraps of newspaper, paper bags, or anything else he could find. In fact, Langston Hughes rescued what became Nugent's first published poem, "Shadow," from the trash. Because Nugent wrote under many aliases, a compilation of his writings might be unexpectedly large.

Waring Cuney was known by his contemporaries as one of the favorites of the young writers. Cuney studied briefly at Howard University and eventually graduated from Lincoln University, where he was a classmate of Langston Hughes. Cuney did further study at the New England Conservatory of Music and at the Conservatory in Rome. His most frequently anthologized poem, "No Image," was written when he was eighteen years old, and he won an award for it in *Opportunity*'s literary contest when he was twenty. This poem is considered a minor classic of the New Negro movement.

Rudolph Fisher was a true renaissance man—physician, novelist, short-story writer, musician, and orator. His short life (thirty-seven years) was filled with many academic, oratorical, and literary accomplishments. By all accounts, Fisher is considered one of the major literary figures of the Harlem Renaissance. His stories appeared regularly in *Atlantic Monthly*, *The Crisis*, *Opportunity*, and *Story*, and he was said to be the wittiest of the New Negroes. In his works, Fisher gave the reader a glimpse of ordinary blacks living and working in their community. His *Conjure Man Dies* (1932) was the first black detective story.

To sum up, Washington's role in the Harlem Renaissance was clearly defined by the activity that occurred in the city and by the number of literary figures and other creative artists who either were in the area or maintained ties to it as active participants in its cultural scene. In addition to Alain Locke and other mentors (T. Montgomery Gregory, Kelly Miller, Georgia Douglas Johnson, Edward Christopher Williams, and Carrie Williams Clifford), there were numerous creative spirits from the younger generation. These included Waring Cuney, Richard Bruce Nugent, Lewis G. Alexander, Rudolph Fisher, Langston Hughes, Jean Toomer, James L. Wells, Sterling Brown, Clarissa M. Scott Delaney, May Miller, Richard Goodwin, Albert Rice, Thelma Myrtle Duncan, and James A. Porter.

GEORGE-MCKINLEY MARTIN

See also Armstong, Louis; Bennett, Gwendolyn; Brown, Sterling; Conjure Man Dies, The; Cuney, Waring; Ellington, Duke; Fine Clothes to the Jew; Fisher, Rudolph; Green, Paul; Howard University; Hughes, Langston; Hurston, Zora Neale; Johnson, Georgia Douglas; Locke, Alain; Miller, Kelly; Morton, Jelly Roll; Nugent, Richard Bruce; O'Neill, Eugene; Opportunity Literary Contests; Porter, James Amos; Richardson, Willis; Stylus; Survey Graphic; Toomer, Jean; Williams, Edward Christopher

Further Reading

Catchpole, Terry. "Some of the Sounds of the Howard." *Washingtonian Magazine*, 2(9), June 1967.

Fisher, Rudolph. *The Conjure-Man Dies: A Mystery of Dark Harlem*. Ann Arbor: University of Michigan Press, 1992.

Gardner, Bettye, and Bettye Thomas. "The Cultural Impact of the Howard Theatre on the Black Community." *Journal of Negro History*, 55(4), October 1970.

Hughes, Langston. *Fine Clothes to the Jew*. New York: Knopf, 1927.

————. *The Big Sea: An Autobiography*. New York: Knopf, 1940.

Johnson, Richard M. "Those Who Stayed: Washington Black Writers of the 1920s." In *Records of the Columbia Historical Society of Washington, D.C.*, Vol. 50, ed. Francis Coleman Rosenberger. Washington, D.C.: Columbia Historical Society, 1980.

Locke, Alain. "Beauty and the Provinces." *Stylus*, June 1929.

————, ed. *The New Negro*. New York: Atheneum, 1968. (Originally published 1925.)

Locke, Alain, and Montgomery Gregory, eds. *Plays of Negro Life*. New York: Harper, 1969.

Martin, George-McKinley, et al. *Black Renaissance in Washington, D.C., 1920s–1930s*. Washington, D.C.: District of Columbia Public Library, June 2003. (Web site.)

Miller, Kelly. "Where Is the Negro's Heaven?" *Opportunity*, 4(48), December 1926.

Rubin, Lawrence. "Washington and the Negro Renaissance." *Crisis*, 78(3), April–May 1971.

Harlem Shadows

Harlem Shadows (1922) was Claude McKay's first book of poetry published in the United States. This collection of poems follows rigid structures but also explores a variety of themes, including McKay's famous protest sonnets.

Many of the poems in *Harlem Shadows* were first published in the literary journals *Seven Arts*, *Pearson's Magazine*, and *Liberator*. This fact, as well as the beginning of McKay's autobiography *A Long Way From Home*, indicates that McKay was dependent on white editors. In contrast to this image of McKay, however, critics of the 1960s and later hailed McKay as a protester—an artist who was willing to confront white racist practices. Their evaluation challenges the idea of McKay's dependency and suggests that he was a pioneer because he was able to get published in such white literary journals without compromising his racial politics.

Before coming to New York City, McKay had published two volumes of dialect poetry in Jamaica: *Songs of Jamaica* and *Constab Ballads* (both 1912). In 1919, McKay went to England for three years; there, he published *Spring in New Hampshire* (1920). *Harlem Shadows* was an expanded version of McKay's poetry from *Spring in New Hampshire*, including many of the protest poems. McKay's most famous poem, "If We Must Die," was excluded from the English publication but appeared in *Harlem Shadows*. "If We Must Die" is a militant poem urging black people to fight lynch mobs and dogs, so that if blacks must die, they will die with dignity. The reference to black people is only implied, though, and during World War II, Winston Churchill made this poem known to an international audience as a call to arms for British troops. In September 1971, the poem was circulated among inmates at Attica State Prison in New York before an uprising by these prisoners. Other poems excluded from *Spring in New Hampshire* also reflected McKay's militancy, but "If We Must Die" more than any other poem made McKay one of the most important poets of the Harlem Renaissance and established his reputation as a militant. Unlike McKay's novel *Home to Harlem*, *Harlem Shadows* was praised by most black intellectuals at its time of publication.

Interestingly, "If We Must Die" instigated a debate, which is still going on, about McKay's protest sonnets. The problem is how to reconcile the protest with the sonnet form. Sonnets consist of fourteen lines, with various rhyme schemes. In the early twentieth century, the sonnet was still closely associated with the romantic poets of the early nineteenth century. To most critics of McKay's poetry, the militant subject matter seems inconsistent with a form associated with love and beauty. For example, with regard to "The Lynching," another militant sonnet in *Harlem Shadows*, Giles (1976) thinks that the self-consciousness of the imagery of Christ interferes with the horror aroused by the lynchers. The final couplet reads: "And little lads, lynchers that were to be, / Danced round the dreadful thing in fiendish glee." In 1918, Frank Harris, the editor of *Pearson's Magazine*, had rejected this poem, arguing that it did not do justice to its historical parallel, the race riot of 1917 in St. Louis. However, Harris published "To the White Fiends," a poem that, according to Gayle (1972), casts the speaker as a Christlike figure and thus continues the powerless pleading of Dunbar's poetry. In the middle of the poem, the tone changes to humility and calm: "But the Almighty from the darkness drew / My soul and said: Even thou shalt be a light / Awhile to burn on the benighted earth." Keller (1994) sees the poem as a tour de force of restraint: The speaker offers the specter of violence but then withdraws it as a favor to those who mistreat him. However, Gayle prefers the militancy of the sonnet "The White House," which appeared in *Liberator* in 1922. In "The White House," the speaker is seething with anger, and only self-restraint keeps it from bubbling over:

Oh, I must search for wisdom every hour,
Deep in my wrathful bosom sore and raw,
And find in it the superhuman power
To hold me to the letter of your law!

Alain Locke included five of McKay's poems in the groundbreaking anthology of the Harlem Renaissance, *The New Negro*. However, McKay selected only two of those poems—"Baptism" and "Tropics in New York"—for inclusion in *Harlem Shadows*, perhaps because Locke tended to favor the romantic poems of the spirit rather than the angry protest sonnets. In "Baptism," McKay uses baptism by fire as a metaphor for confronting racist oppression; such confrontation produces "A stronger soul within a finer frame." "Tropics in New York" highlights themes of migration, focusing on the tropical fruit available in New York that elicits a longing for home; the speaker says, "I turned aside and bowed my head and wept." McKay would turn to this subject—love and longing for Jamaica—again and again. In such poems as "Flame-Heart," "Home Thoughts," "North and South," "After the Winter," "My Mother," "In Bondage," and "Winter in the Country," McKay recalls the beauty of Jamaica and contrasts it with the manmade, stultifying industrial world. Virtually every critic who has written about his Jamaican-inspired poems has described them as nostalgic, romantic, or pastoral.

Other widely anthologized poems are "America," "Outcast," "Spring in New Hampshire," "Harlem Shadows," and "The Harlem Dancer." The last two of these focus on jobs available to black women in urban centers. In "Harlem Shadows," the job is prostitution. In the three stanzas of this poem, the speaker focuses on the "slippered feet," "tired feet," and "weary feet" of these young women. "The Harlem Dancer" focuses on the spectacle of a black female dancer in a cabaret but ends with a denial of complete objectification: "But looking at her falsely-smiling face, / I knew her self was not in that strange place."

KIMBERLY J. BANKS

See also Liberator, The; McKay, Claude; New Negro, The; Seven Arts

Further Reading

Brown, Lloyd W. *West Indian Poetry*. London: Heinemann, 1984.
Cooper, Wayne F., ed. *The Passion of Claude McKay: Selected Poetry and Prose, 1912–1948*. New York: Schocken, 1973.
———. *Claude McKay: Rebel Sojourner in the Harlem Renaissance—A Biography*. Baton Rouge: Louisiana State University Press, 1987.
Gayle, Addison Jr. *Claude McKay: The Black Poet at War*. Detroit, Mich.: Broadside, 1972.
Giles, James R. *Claude McKay*. Boston, Mass.: Twayne, 1976.
Huggins, Nathan Irvin. *Harlem Renaissance*. New York: Oxford University Press, 1971.
Keller, James R. "'A Chafing Savage, Down the Decent Street': The Politics of Compromise in Claude McKay's Protest Sonnets." *African American Review*, 28, 1994, pp. 447–456.
Locke, Alain, ed. *The New Negro*. New York: Atheneum, 1992. (Originally published 1925.)
Wagner, Jean. *Black Poets of the United States: From Paul Laurence Dunbar to Langston Hughes*, trans. Kenneth Douglas. Chicago: University of Illinois Press, 1973. (Originally published 1962.)

Harleston, Edwin A.

Edwin Augustus Harleston is best known for his many portraits of African Americans. He was born in 1882 in Charleston, South Carolina. Throughout his childhood he showed an aptitude for art (although also for science and singing) and was an avid draftsman. After graduating from Atlanta University in 1904, he studied medicine at Harvard University, but eventually he gave up that career path to pursue his interest in art.

Harleston went north and studied art at the school of the Museum of Fine Arts in Boston from 1906 to 1912. While living in an African American neighborhood in Boston, he was surrounded by people who were willing and able to speak openly about racial injustice. Later, he would become an outspoken civil rights activist, perhaps as a result of this experience. He eventually returned to Charleston, where he lived for the rest of his life. Harleston was never able to earn a living from his painting, although he strove for many years to get publicity for his work and to obtain portrait commissions. In order to earn a living, he operated a funeral home in Charleston that his father, an undertaker, had started. As a successful African American businessman, he became an influential civic leader in Charleston. In 1916, he helped establish the Charleston branch of the National Association for the Advancement of Colored People (NAACP); this was one of its first branches in the South, and he was its first president. He was active in efforts to improve education for African Americans in the South.

Harleston depicted African American business-people, professionals, artists, writers, and musicians. He also painted many portraits of poor rural African Americans. In addition to working in oil and charcoal, he was a photographer, and he took many portrait photographs over the years. Perhaps his most famous portrait is of the African American painter Aaron Douglas, which was done in 1930 and is now in the Gibbes Museum. His portrait *The Soldier* (1919) depicts a young African American man in military garb with arms folded across the chest and with a countenance of annoyance and disappointment directed at the viewer. This has been interpreted as indicative of what many African Americans felt about their service in the military during World War I—that their efforts, heroism, and risks were not appreciated, because of their race. In this and other paintings, such as *The Honey Man*, *The Charleston Shrimp Man*, and *The Old Servant*, Harleston's depictions of African Americans are noteworthy for the sense of humanity and dignity he conveyed.

Harleston died in 1932. His recognition as an artist increased in the years after his death. Because he created paintings of great sincerity and honesty and depicted African American people and life, he was an important precursor of the artists of the Harlem Renaissance before artists, who were a generation younger but founded their art on goals and ideals that were the same as his.

Biography

Edwin Harleston was born in 1882 in Charleston, South Carolina, the third of six children; his father was a rice planter and then an undertaker. Harleston was educated at the Avery Institute (graduating in 1900), Atlanta University (A.B., 1904), Boston Museum of Fine Arts School (1906–1912), and Harvard University. His awards included the Amy E. Springarn Prize, 1925, for *Crisis of Ouida* (a portrait of his wife); and the Alain Locke Portrait Prize, Harmon Foundation, New York, 1930, for *The Old Servant*. He died of pneumonia in 1932.

HERBERT R. HARTEL JR.

See also Artists; Douglas, Aaron

Exhibitions

1921–1923: New York Public Library, 135th Street branch.
1928, 1931, 1936: Harmon Foundation, New York.

1930, 1933: National Gallery of Art, Washington, D.C.
1936: Texas Centennial Exhibition, Museum of Fine Arts, Dallas.
1935, 1937: Howard University, Washington, D.C.
1941, 1945: South Side Community Art Center, Chicago.
1942: Downtown Gallery, New York.
1967: City College of the City University of New York.

Further Reading

Driscoll, David. *Two Centuries of Black American Art*. New York and Los Angeles: Knopf and Los Angeles County Museum of Art, 1976, pp. 57, 136.

"Edwin A. Harleston." University of South Carolina–Aiken Web site. (Biography page.)

"Harleston, Edwin." In *African-American Artists: A Bio-Bibliographical Dictionary*, ed. Theresa Dickason Cederholm. Boston, Mass.: Boston Public Library, 1973.

Henderson, Harry, and Romare Bearden. *African-American Artists: From 1792 to the Present*. New York: Pantheon, 1993.

McDaniel, Maurine Aku. *Edwin Augustus Harleston, Portrait Painter 1882–1931*. Atlanta, Ga.: Emory University, 1994.

Powell, Richard J. *Black Art and Culture in the Twentieth Century*. New York: Thames and Hudson, 1997.

Reynolds, Gary. *Against the Odds: African-American Artists and the Harmon Foundation*. Newark, N.J.: Newark Museum, 1990, pp. 14, 17, 20, 31, 199–200.

Severens, Martha R. *The Charleston Renaissance*. Spartanburg, S.C.: Saraland, 1998.

Harmon Foundation

The Harmon Foundation, or William E. Harmon Foundation, was the most important institution involved in promoting African American visual art during the Harlem Renaissance. Harmon, a real estate professional, created it in 1922 to encourage self-improvement among disadvantaged peoples by rewarding individual achievements. It had various programs but became best known for the Harmon Foundation Awards for Distinguished Achievement Among Negroes, which began in 1926 and received widespread press coverage in the late 1920s. During 1926–1930, the awards program was administered by Dr. George E. Haynes, chair of the Commission on Race Relations of the

Federal Council of Churches. The foundation was directed for many years by Mary Beattie Brady, who counted among her close advisers Haynes and also Alain Locke.

The foundation gave awards in eight categories: (1) literature, (2) music, (3) fine arts, (4) business and industry, (5) science and innovation, (6) education, (7) religious service, and (8) race relations. With regard to the fine arts, there was also, starting in 1928, an exhibition program of works entered by African Americans; separate prizes were awarded in conjunction with these annual exhibitions, which generated a good deal of interest among critics and others. From 1928 to 1933, largely because of the activities of the Harmon Foundation, African Americans emerged as a distinct presence in the American art world. After 1933 the awards program was discontinued, and the foundation devoted itself primarily to promoting African American artists through educational programs, publications, and exhibitions. By the time it closed down in 1967, the Harmon Foundation had acquired a significant body of work, some of which was dispersed to the art collections of historically black colleges. The archives of the Harmon Foundation, housed in the Library of Congress, remain a major repository of information on the development of early twentieth-century African American artists.

The Harmon Foundation encouraged discourse about the work of black American artists that shaped much subsequent criticism and scholarship, and its promotional materials and its policies regarding the exhibitions powerfully influenced viewers' response. The group shows opened in New York and traveled throughout the country. George Haynes was instrumental in organizing these shows, and he stipulated as a condition for bringing them into a particular community that the exhibition must be displayed in a place where both races could view it without discrimination. Exhibitions were thus typically sponsored by regional interracial councils and committees on race relations and displayed in black churches, libraries, public schools, and local branches of the Young Men's Christian Association (YMCA). In 1930, the Federal Council of Churches sent questionnaires to the various organizations that had sponsored the show, asking for statistics on the number of white and black visitors. Host institutions were also asked to report on the effect of the show on white people who saw it and to note if there appeared to be any significant change in community race relations afterward. All this tended to encourage a sociological rather than an aesthetic

approach to African American art—a situation that continued to vex the artists for the remainder of the twentieth century.

Although the Harmon Foundation was not commercial, one of its stated goals was financial self-sufficiency among black artists, and works in the traveling shows were offered for sale. Nominally, the foundation was committed simply to excellence and to cultivating creativity, but the purity of these objectives was bound to be undermined by its multiple roles as museum, agent, benefactor, and critical authority. Its opponents, then and later, regarded such conflicts of interest in a non-black philanthropic agency as a hindrance to the artists' growth and development. This climate of trade stimulated (and to an extent controlled) by well-meaning advocacy characterized a great deal of the cultural activity of the Harlem Renaissance.

Recent scholarship suggests that with respect to African American art, the efforts of the Harmon Foundation, however commendable, contributed to critical confusion and contradictory values. The foundation's official promotional literature insisted that the works entered in the competitions were judged solely on technical and aesthetic criteria (separate juries of arts professionals were convened for the fine arts awards and the exhibitions prizes), but spokesmen associated with the foundation (such as Alain Locke) stressed conspicuous racial identity as a criterion. Similarly, Haynes rejected the frequent suggestion by progressive artists and critics that the most powerful, "authentic" racial expression would come from naive or unschooled black artists, but the foundation stressed that many of the exhibiting artists were nonprofessionals.

In a well-known essay of 1934, "The Negro Artist and Modern Art," Romare Bearden accused the Harmon Foundation of taking a patronizing attitude toward black artists by encouraging them to exhibit prematurely. This accusation may seem unduly harsh, given that the foundation was then involved in establishing the professional credentials of black artists seeking employment in the Federal Arts Project. Nevertheless, the condescension Bearden described was conspicuous in press coverage of the foundation's awards and of the traveling exhibitions. In 1928 to 1933, accounts of the awards in newspapers were filled with hard-luck stories about aspiring black artists who supported themselves through manual labor and who showed remarkable creative ability despite their inexperience. Press releases on award winners always included biographical information that the foundation called "human interest" material.

Sometimes the press repeated this material verbatim, but often the information was used selectively, with an emphasis on the artists' humble circumstances rather than their training or experience.

Historians have also asked to what extent the foundation deliberately promoted essentialist notions of black aesthetics. Haynes's own belief in universal artistic standards was evident in the makeup of the juries, but the foundation's literature sent mixed and even conflicting messages. Officials were concerned about the technical proficiency of African American art, or "Negro art," but were also aware that they could best stimulate interest in it by identifying it as distinctive. Thus some scholars have concluded that the foundation actively encouraged exhibiting artists to make characteristically racial art, and certainly Locke's close association with the foundation supports this belief. However, the foundation's catalogs and publicity represented both the universalist and the essentialist positions. Press packets for the traveling shows, for example, quoted reviews of past exhibitions in which the affirmation of characteristically racial artistic qualities and the mastery of prevailing conventions were both acknowledged.

The Harmon Foundation's group shows had their greatest success in the early 1930s, when the fascination with primitivism and black culture generated by Harlem Renaissance was in decline. In 1931, the foundation shifted the site of its shows in New York from International House, a kind of multicultural center, to the Art Center; this move resulted in a significant change in the press coverage and in the promotional materials. Before 1931, the foundation's catalogs had been essentially illustrated checklists, but in 1931 and again in 1933, Locke contributed substantial essays positioning the works in an explicit critical and historical context. Although Locke rehashed many issues that had emerged in his early treatises of the Harlem Renaissance, these catalog essays reveal a subtle but strategic new emphasis. In the context of the cultural nationalist rhetoric of the 1930s, it began to appear that the Harmon Foundation had reinforced traditional inequalities of race and power by constructing the black artist as a distinct category, who then was driven into the margins as the "Negro vogue" dissipated. During these years Locke, and also James Porter, worked to integrate black artists into a cultural mainstream preoccupied with the Depression and normative "Americanism."

Because the Harmon Foundation had a virtual monopoly on promoting black visual artists, it played a crucial role in the subsequent formation of the canon. Through its awards and exhibitions, the foundation systematically introduced a critical mass of black artists to the American public. The foundation carefully constructed a narrative of black artistic progress, which in turn created an informed public that could chart its course by following the activities of the foundation. Press releases each year speculated on the future promise of prizewinners and often mentioned that the prize money facilitated trips abroad for education and development. By 1930, critics in the mass media prefaced their reviews of the foundation's shows with comments implying that the names of the black artists had become household words. With a few notable exceptions, the Harmon Foundation launched—and to an extent managed—the career of nearly every African American artist who emerged in the years between the two world wars. The black artistic canon that emerged from the Harmon Foundation has endured a very long time; to this day, most of the African Americans represented in Harlem Renaissance art exhibitions were introduced to the general public through the foundation's shows, and many were prizewinners.

MARY ANN CALO

See also Cultural Organizations; Harmon Traveling Exhibition; Haynes, George Edmund; Locke, Alain; Porter, James Amos

Further Reading

Bearden, Romare. "The Negro Artist and Modern Art." *Opportunity*, 12, December 1934.

Breaking Racial Barriers: African Americans in the Harmon Foundation Collection. Washington, D.C., and San Francisco, Calif.: Smithsonian Institution and Pomegranate Artbooks, 1997.

Leininger-Miller, Theresa. *New Negro Artists in Paris: African American Painters and Sculptors in the City of Light, 1922–1934.* New Brunswick, N.J.: Rutgers University Press, 2001.

Malloy, Erma Meadows. "African-American Visual Artists and the Harmon Foundation." Ph.D. dissertation, Columbia University Teacher's College, 1991.

Negro Artists: An Illustrated Review of Their Achievements. New York: Harmon Foundation, 1935.

Reynolds, Gary, and Beryl J. Wright, *Against the Odds: African-American Artists and the Harmon Foundation*. Newark, N.J.: Newark Museum, 1989.

Harmon, Pappy

Pappy Harmon was a native New Yorker, born in Greenwich Village shortly after the mid-nineteenth century. He moved to Harlem after his wife and children died of influenza during the Spanish-American War. He had been in show business—as a ventriloquist—until 1910, when theater doors were closed to black performers. Needing work, he acquired a small wagon and a horse he called Maude and rode up and down 131st Street peddling vegetables, fruit, fresh fish, and assorted junk. He must have been quite a sight, with his long, lanky frame wrapped in a threadbare pair of old-fashioned overalls and topped by a shock of gleaming white hair against his dark black face. His beloved Maude was not his only pet; he also kept pigeons, which he called his children, on the roof of his apartment building. Although he was an entertainer by trade, many chose to label him crazy, eccentric, or just a "little too much" to take (Mitchell 1967, 73). In reality, however, Pappy Harmon was more than just an entertainer and crazy local junk dealer. He was a sort of street philosopher, a sage of Harlem.

Harmon was deeply interested in human psychology, current events, and cultural movements—in truth, he was simply interested in understanding human beings. He said that he enjoyed peddling junk and produce on the street because it afforded him an opportunity to be among the people. He told the young Loften Mitchell, "You never know unless you're out there among people just what's going to happen next. You go and hide someplace and you can find yourself kicked right out of a lot of places—like the theatre" (74). It was said that Harmon's two-room apartment was lined with books and the walls were lined with newspaper clippings telling the story of African American drama: articles about Bert Williams, Charles Gilpin, *The Emperor Jones*, and other contemporary developments in black theater. Once, Harmon happened on a street-corner conversation about Florence Mills's place in American theater, and after listening for just a moment, he chimed in: "What's the matter with you all? Someone here was just looking for a white person to compare Florence with? Why do we always have to

have a white person to remind us of ourselves? . . . Why can't we say there ain't no words for Florence Mills? Let's just say—she's Florence Mills," and he stormed off (Mitchell, 78). Despite this kind of straightforward, insightful thinking, Harmon was often ridiculed or dismissed as a lunatic. However, for those who took the time to listen to him, he made perfect sense, and he left a lasting impression. Mitchell recalls, "In those days—like most kids on my block—I thought Pappy Harmon knew everything. If Pappy said the Yankees would win the pennant, that Babe Ruth would hit a homer, and that there'd be no war this year, I believed him" (77).

Biography

Pappy Harmon was born c. 1860 in Greenwich Village. He lost his wife and children to influenza during the Spanish-American War and thereafter moved to Harlem. He worked as a ventriloquist and all-around showman until 1910. He became a street vendor and junk dealer on 131st Street. Harmon died in the summer of 1929 in his apartment on Fifth Avenue.

STEPHEN CRINITI

See also Emperor Jones, The; Gilpin, Charles; Mills, Florence; Williams, Egbert Austin "Bert"

Further Reading

Kellner, Bruce, ed. *The Harlem Renaissance: A Historical Dictionary for the Era*. Westport, Conn.: Greenwood, 1984, p. 156.
Mitchell, Loften. *Black Drama: The Story of the American Negro in the Theatre*. New York: Hawthorn, 1967.

Harmon Traveling Exhibition

In 1922, William E. Harmon began the Harmon Foundation, and by 1925 he teamed up with George Haynes of the Federal Council of Churches and Alain Locke of the New Negro movement to sponsor an awards ceremony. The Harmon Foundation awards offered both recognition and a monetary gift to Negroes who excelled in their field and who worked for the betterment of race relations in America. After the awards of 1927, which saw a significant number of entries in the fine arts category, the director of the foundation, Mary Beattie Brady, suggested that it sponsor an exhibition of the fine arts submissions in conjunction with the annual awarding of medals. In January 1928, the first annual "Exhibit of Fine Arts Productions of American Negro Artists" opened at International House on Riverside Drive in New York City. Although International House was small and awkward, Brady chose it mainly because she wanted "a place where the two races would meet under the most harmonious circumstances" (Reynolds 1989, 34). The modest exhibit of 1928 lasted only about ten days, but a seed had been sown for the more extensive exhibitions to come.

Over six years from 1928 to 1933, the Harmon Foundation held five such exhibitions (there was none in 1932), giving 125 black artists an opportunity to display their work. These exhibitions were the first of their kind to showcase only black artists. Some of the notable artists featured (often in multiple exhibitions) were Palmer Hayden, Laura Wheeler Waring, William H. Johnson, Sargent Johnson, Richmond Barthé, Hale Woodruff, Malvin Gray Johnson, and Aaron Douglas. Beginning in 1929, the exhibition toured the country after closing in New York. By the end of 1930, it had reached almost twenty cities, including Atlanta, Baltimore, Boston, Nashville, Oakland, San Diego, Denver, Houston, Minneapolis, and New Orleans. Not only did the exhibition grow, but the accompanying catalog grew as well. The catalog began as nothing more than a glorified checklist, but it was expanded in 1931 to include essays by Alain Locke, Arthur Schomburg, and Alon Bemont, among others. As a result of the expanded catalog and the considerable attention the exhibits received in the press, the Harmon exhibition grew into more than simply a display of black artwork; it became the primary occasion for discussions of Negro art.

Each exhibition catalog included some form of the following statement of goals, which appeared in 1931: "It was hoped through this assembling to acquaint and interest the public more generally in the creative accomplishments in fine arts by Negroes, thereby assisting this group to a more sound and satisfactory economic position" (4). The original catalog, in 1928, had added to these two goals a third: "stimulating [the Negro] to aim for the highest standards of achievement" (quoted in Bennett 1928, 111). George Haynes echoed this sentiment when he referred to the exhibited works as "not 'Negro Art' but universal art" (quoted in Reynolds, 108). Such statements can easily be read as

a call for black artists to strive for a Eurocentric set of standards—in other words, they sound as if the Harmon Foundation had asked the entrants to "paint white." There was some confusion, however, about the foundation's standards, as the administrators not only called for a "universal" art but also—led by Locke— began to solicit art that would explicitly address Negro subjects and tap into a perceived vital primitiveness. These statements of goals as well as the somewhat confusing set of criteria for judging sparked considerable controversy among critics and raised serious questions about the definition and nature of "Negro art."

Critics reacted strongly to the exhibition for a variety of reasons. One notable criticism was that the foundation's administrators were showcasing artists who had not yet matured enough in their craft. The work of professionals often hung next to that of amateurs, causing the artists' technical handicraft to be questioned. Describing the selection process, Aaron Douglas said, memorably: "Harlem was sifted. Neither streets, homes nor public institutions escaped. When unsuspecting Negroes were found with a brush in their hands they were immediately hauled away and held for interpretation. . . . Every effort to protest their innocence was drowned out with big-mouthed praise" (quoted in Dover 1960, 31). Another frequent criticism, notably voiced by Cyril Kay-Scott of the Denver Art Museum, was that without the exhibition title above the door, viewers might believe they were looking at an exhibition of white artists. But other critics argued that, on the contrary, the artists were trying too hard to draw on primitive roots, when they had never truly experienced this kind of primitivism in their own lives. Henderson (1928, 123) observed: "The Negro artist of today is likely to meet two chief dangers—that of self-consciously trying to return to the primitive art of his race and that of imitating the products of white artists. By either of these routes he fails to express himself as a modern Negro in a modern environment."

The most scathing and most famous criticism of the Harmon Foundation's exhibitions, however, came from Romare Bearden, in an article in *Opportunity*. Bearden essentially gathered all of the objections mentioned previously into one concentrated condemnation of the foundation: "First, we have no valid standard of criticism; secondly, foundations and societies which supposedly encourage Negro artists really hinder them; thirdly, the Negro artist has no definite ideology or social philosophy." He went on to lament a lack of feeling in the black artworks and concluded: "An intense, eager devotion to present day life, to study it, to help relieve it, this is the calling of the Negro artist" (1934, 372).

Still, the Harmon Foundation's exhibitions, however flawed, promoted the careers of nearly all of the artists of the Harlem Renaissance and thereby made a future for black art possible. Also, the criticisms leveled at these exhibitions were themselves necessary to the life of black art. The exhibitions provided, for the first time, a platform for vitally important conversations about the nature and role of black art in America—conversations that were long overdue and that continue to propel American art today.

STEPHEN CRINITI

See also Harmon Foundation; Haynes, George Edmund; Locke, Alain; Schomburg, Arthur A.; *specific artists*

Selected Publications (Harmon Foundation)

Exhibit of Fine Arts by American Negro Artists. New York, 1929.

Exhibit of Fine Arts by American Negro Artists. New York, 1930.

Exhibit of Fine Arts: Productions of American Negro Artists. New York, 1928.

Exhibition of Productions by Negro Artists. New York, 1933.

Exhibition of the Work of Negro Artists at the Art Center. New York, 1931.

Negro Artists: An Illustrated Review of Their Achievements. New York, 1935.

Further Reading

Bearden, Romare. "The Negro Artist and Modern Art." *Opportunity*, December 1934, pp. 371–372.

Bennett, Gwendolyn B. "The American Negro Paints." *Southern Workman*, 57(3), 1928, pp. 111–112.

Dover, Cedric. *American Negro Art*. New York: New York Graphic Society, 1960.

"Editorials: American Negro Art." *Opportunity*, August 1926, pp. 238–239.

"Exhibit Raises Question Whether Negro Should Paint 'White'." *Art Digest*, 15 February 1931, p. 7.

Henderson, Rose. "First Nation-Wide Exhibit of Negro Artists." *Southern Workman*, 57(3), 1928, pp. 121–126.

———. "Exhibit of Painting and Sculpture by Negro Artists." *Southern Workman*, 58(4), 1929, pp. 165–169.

———. "American Negro Exhibit at International House." *Southern Workman*, 59(4), 1930, pp. 166–170.

———. "Negro Artists in the Fifth Harmon Exhibition." *Southern Workman*, 62(4), 1933, pp. 175–181.

"The Negro Annual." *Art Digest*, 15 May 1934, p. 18.

Reynolds, Gary A., and Beryl J. Wright. *Against the Odds: African-American Artists and the Harmon Foundation*. Newark, N.J.: Newark Museum, 1989.

Harper Brothers

Harper Brothers publishing company began in New York in March 1817, when the brothers James and John Harper, who had both been apprentices for printing firms, joined to start their own printing firm, J. and J. Harper. Their two younger brothers joined them—one in 1823 and the other in 1825—and with all four working together, they began to see themselves as publishers instead of just printers. The Harper brothers' approach to publishing was innovative in several ways. They were the first to introduce to the United States the concept of a series of books, which were published as "libraries." They were also the first publishing house to deal in a general list. In 1833, the firm switched to a steam press and changed its imprint to Harper and Bros. The firm continued to change with the times, introducing British authors and titles and publishing respected names, so that by the end of the nineteenth century, Harper Brothers was the leading publishing house in America.

During the 1890s the firm began to experience financial difficulties and had to borrow large sums of money from J. P. Morgan and Company. In consequence, for the first time, the firm was not under family control. The change in control led to several unfortunate and nearly devastating choices that prolonged the company's financial struggles into the early 1920s. Ultimately, two vice presidents—Thomas B. Wells and Henry Hoyns—were able to implement a plan to relieve the company of its two-decade cycle of debt. This plan included moving the firm from Franklin Square to East Thirty-third Street and finally resolving the issue of control by instituting Douglas Parmentier as president of the company in 1924. With these changes, then, Harper Brothers began a new era.

In 1925, the company made several dramatic changes in order to keep up with new publishers such as Knopf, Boni and Liveright, and Harcourt Brace. For one thing, the firm revamped *Harper's* magazine, evidently in an effort to make it look more like Knopf's *American Mercury*. The changes included a new editor with "modern" preferences and an updated look for the magazine, developed with the help of W. A. Dwiggins, who was chief designer at Knopf. The contents of the magazine were remodeled, and the cover also underwent a transformation so as to resemble *American Mercury*. This version of *Harper's* came out in September 1925, and circulation doubled quickly thereafter. All of this helped transform one of America's oldest publishing houses in such a way that it was in line with the new tastes reflected by other publishers in New York.

With regard to the Harlem Renaissance, one of the most significant changes made by Harpers at this time was to bring in Eugene Saxton as book editor. Saxton soon began to attract African American authors, including Countee Cullen. Harpers published Cullen's first volume of poetry, *Color*, and Frederick Lewis Allen, who was chief editor at the time, nominated the collection for a Pulitzer Prize. Harpers kept in close contact with Cullen after this first volume and supported him in other endeavors as well. Allen asked Cullen to represent the company at a book celebration week at the Jordan Marsh department store in Boston, and Harpers also assisted Cullen in negotiations to set several of the poems from *Color* to music. Additionally, Harpers arranged a lecture tour for Cullen and asked him to contribute poems to *Harper's* magazine. In 1927, Harpers published *Caroling Dusk*, an anthology of black poetry edited by Cullen. That year the company also published his second and third volumes of poetry, *Copper Sun* and *The Ballad of the Brown Girl*. In 1930, Saxton asked Cullen to write a book-length poem about the history of blacks in America. Cullen expressed interest, but this project was never undertaken, because he began to focus his efforts on a novel, *One Way to Heaven*. Nevertheless, Harpers remained Cullen's lifelong publisher.

Harpers also supported Claude McKay. The firm published his first novel, which was an expanded version of his short story "Home to Harlem," as well as his next novel, *Banjo*, which appeared in 1929. Although there was a loss in the demand for McKay's works after the stock market crash of 1929, he and Harpers continued their relationship. However, Harpers lost money publishing McKay's collection of short stories, *Gingertown* (1932), and his novel *Banana Bottom* (1933); and Saxton then told McKay that he no longer wanted to publish a novel entitled "Savage Loving," which he had earlier asked McKay to revise for publication in place of *Gingertown*. McKay's agent, Max Lieber, reportedly told McKay that this decision was based on Saxton's opinion that the Harlem Renaissance was

a fad and that people no longer cared about black authors. But it seems questionable that this was actually Saxton's opinion. Max Lieber was a member of the Communist Party, and the comment he attributed to Saxton was actually the party's position on the Harlem Renaissance; also, Lieber may have had political reasons for attacking McKay, because McKay had become disillusioned with the Communist Party. More probably, both Saxton and Lieber were reluctant to publish "Savage Loving" because of its overt homosexual content.

Whatever Saxton's opinion was regarding the Harlem Renaissance, Harpers continued to publish writings by African American authors. The firm published *The Medea and Some Poems* by Countee Cullen in 1935, Claude McKay's autobiography *A Long Way From Home* in 1937, and Richard Wright's *Uncle Tom's Children* in 1938 and *Native Son* in 1940. During the 1930s, the number of works by African American authors waned, but Harpers does not seem to have given up publishing black authors simply because the Harlem Renaissance was said to be a "fad." Instead, Harpers maintained its relationship with the two prominent black authors it had begun publishing in the 1920s, and it took on Richard Wright, the next important African American author to emerge after the Depression.

APRIL CONLEY KILINSKI

See also American Mercury; Boni and Liveright; Color; Copper Sun; Cullen, Countee; Harcourt Brace; Knopf, Alfred A., Inc.; McKay, Claude; Publishers and Publishing Houses

Further Reading

Hutchinson, George. *The Harlem Renaissance in Black and White*. Cambridge, Mass.: Belknap Press of Harvard University Press, 1995.
Tebbel, John. *Between Covers: The Rise and Transformation of Book Publishing in America*. New York: Oxford University Press, 1987.
Wintz, Cary D. *Black Culture and the Harlem Renaissance*. Houston, Tex.: Rice University Press, 1988.

Harrington, James Carl "Hamtree"

Hamtree (James Carl) Harrington was born in 1889 and was one of many comedians of his generation who aspired to take on the mantle of the great Bert Williams. Harrington joined a traveling carnival at age fourteen and soon established himself as a black-face comedian in Williams's mold; in fact, he was billed as "the vest pocket Bert Williams." The name Hamtree came from a sketch in which he hid a stolen ham in a tree.

An early romance with a chorus girl, Edna Murray, produced a son. By 1916, Harrington had teamed up with Maude Mills, the sister of Florence Mills. In March 1916, they were married onstage at Gibson's Standard Theater in Philadelphia. They toured the black vaudeville circuits with modest success until 1920. Reviewing their act in 1920, Sime Silverman of *Variety* found Harrington's imitation of Williams competent but "cold" beside the original.

In 1921, Harrington and Mills separated, and he found a new female partner, Cora Green. She had previously been a member of the Panama Trio singing group with Florence Mills. The new partnership was featured in the first black show to follow *Shuffle Along*, *Put and Take* (1921), a clever revue that was, however, panned for imitating white shows. Then followed Creamer and Layton's *Strut Miss Lizzie* (1922), which was not much more successful despite numbers like "Dear Old Southland" and "Way Down Yonder in New Orleans."

Greater success came when Harrington and Green spent a year with Florence Mills's *Dixie to Broadway* (1924–1925); audiences loved Harrington's haunted house scene, although sophisticates deplored it. Their success earned them a four-year contract on the prestigious Keith-Albee vaudeville circuit in 1925, starring in a show called *Nobody's Gal*. They made some records on the Brunswick label. In 1927, they were summoned to London to replace the ailing Florence Mills in the provincial tour of *Blackbirds of 1927*.

By 1930, Harrington was again on his own. He continued in black shows, *Change Your Luck* (1930) with Alberta Hunter, *Old Kentucky* (1932) with Clara Smith, and then with Ethel Waters in an otherwise all-white success on Broadway, *As Thousands Cheer* (1933). With vaudeville and live entertainment withering during the Depression, he found a place in black movies. These included *Rufus Jones for President* (1933), with Ethel Waters and a very young Sammy Davis Jr.; *The Devil's Daughter* (1934), with the beautiful Nina Mae McKinney; and *Keep Punchin'* (1938), a vehicle for the boxing champion Henry Armstrong.

Mainly these movies, plus some musical shorts, keep Harrington's name in the public memory, but his stage career was not yet over. He played in Lew Leslie's last comeback attempt, *Blackbirds of 1939*, a flop that nevertheless helped launch Lena Horne's career. Harrington was a founding member of the Negro Actors' Guild in 1937. After he had retired to live in Harlem, he returned one last time in another unsuccessful revival, *Shuffle Along of 1952*.

Hamtree Harrington died in 1956. His career, spanning the era of the Harlem Renaissance, epitomized the opportunities available for black comedians of the time if they were prepared to occupy approved niche roles.

Biography

James Carl "Hamtree" Harrington was born in Columbia, South Carolina, in 1889. He left school at age fourteen, performed in vaudeville before 1920, and then performed in stage shows: *Put and Take* (1921), *Strut Miss Lizzie* (1922), *Dixie to Broadway* (1924), *Nobody's Gal* (1926), *Blackbirds of 1927* (England, 1927), *Harlem Girl* (1930), *Change Your Luck* (1930), *Old Kentucky* (1932), *As Thousands Cheer* (1933), *Blackbirds of 1939* (1939), and *Shuffle Along of 1952* (1952). His film appearances included *Gayety* (Vitaphone short, 1929), *His Woman* (1931), *Rufus Jones for President* (1933), *The Devil's Daughter* (1934), and *Keep Punchin'* (1938). Hamilton was a founding member of the Negro Actors' Guild in 1937. He died in Harlem in 1956.

BILL EGAN

See also Blackbirds; Blackface Performance; Film: Actors; McKinney, Nina Mae; Mills, Florence; Racial Stereotyping; Vaudeville; Williams, Egbert Austin "Bert"

Further Reading

Kellner, Bruce. *The Harlem Renaissance: A Historical Dictionary for the Era.* New York: Methuen, 1987.

Peterson, Bernard L. Jr. *A Century of Musicals in Black and White.* Westport, Conn.: Greenwood, 1993.

———. *Profiles of African American Stage Performers and Theatre People, 1816–1960.* Westport, Conn.: Greenwood, 2001.

Sampson, Henry T. *Blacks in Black and White: A Source Book on Black Films.* Metuchen, N.J., and London: Scarecrow Press, 1977.

———. *Blacks in Blackface: A Source Book on Early Black Musical Shows.* Metuchen, N.J., and London: Scarecrow Press, 1980.

Woll, Allen. *Black Musical Theatre: From Coontown to Dreamgirls.* New York: Da Capo, 1991, pp. 102–104.

Harrison, Hubert

Hubert Harrison—a writer, orator, editor, educator, and radical political activist—lived in Harlem from 1907 until his death in 1927. A. Philip Randolph called him the father of Harlem radicalism; J. A. Rogers considered him the foremost Afro-American intellect of his time and the political leader with the sanest and most effective program; James Weldon Johnson considered him a "walking cyclopedia," especially of history and literature.

Harrison played a major role in the largest class-radical movement (socialism) and the largest race-radical movement (the "New Negro" and Garveyism) in American history. In the 1910s and 1920s, when Harlem became the international center of radical black thought, he profoundly influenced people such as Randolph, Chandler Owen, Cyril Briggs, Richard B. Moore, W. A. Domingo, and Marcus Garvey. Many of his ideas became the stock in trade of the black left in the twentieth century.

Harrison was also a cultural and literary force who wrote book and theater reviews, articles, and editorials; lectured (his series for the Board of Education, "Literary Lights of Yesterday and Today," is especially notable); edited five publications based in Harlem; aided black writers and artists (including Rogers, Andy Razaf, Walter Everette Hawkins, Claude McKay, Lucian B. Watkins, Anselmo Jackson, Solomon Plaatje, Charles Gilpin, and Augusta Savage); and helped develop the 135th Street Public Library into an international center for research in black culture.

In 1900 to 1910, Harrison was active in lyceums at Saint Benedict's and Saint Mark's churches; in educational programs at the Young Men's Christian Association (YMCA) and the White Rose Home for Colored Working Girls; in literary societies, discussion groups, and workers' circles; and with several small black periodicals. He worked with Arthur Schomburg, John Bruce, the actor and activist Charles Burroughs, the social worker and activist Frances Reynolds Keyser, and the bibliophile George Young. In this period Harrison broke from organized religion and was attracted to free thought, socialism, scientific humanism, and the protest philosophy of W. E. B. Du Bois.

From 1911 to 1914, Harrison was America's leading black socialist writer, theoretician, campaigner, and speaker, and the initiator of the party's first major effort at organizing African Americans, the Colored Socialist Club. In 1917 he founded the first organization and first newspaper of the militant "New Negro" movement: the Liberty League (which prepared the groundwork for Garvey's Universal Negro Improvement Association, UNIA) and *The Voice*. In 1919, Harrison edited the monthly *New Negro*; in January 1920 he became the principal editor of Garvey's *Negro World*, which he reshaped into an international political and literary force with pointed editorials, regular book reviews, a magazine section devoted to poetry for the people, and later a column, "West Indian News Notes." In the 1920s, after leaving the *Negro World*, Harrison lectured on literary, historical, scientific, and political topics for the Board of Education's "Trends of the Times" series and other organizations; wrote book and theater reviews and articles; was an activist against censorship; and helped build the Department of Negro Literature and History at the 135th Street Public Library, the International Colored Unity League, and *Voice of the Negro*.

Politically and in his literary work, Harrison focused on the common people, and his race-conscious mass appeal marked a shift from the leadership approaches of Booker T. Washington and Du Bois. He rejected Washington's reliance on white patrons and a black political machine and Du Bois's reliance on the "talented tenth." He was a candid critic of the creative arts who preferred objective assessments to the notion that blacks had to be presented in a favorable light, and he believed that the critic should not dictate to the artist. His mass-based "New Negro" movement preceded and was qualitatively different from the more middle-class, more arts-based, and more apolitical movement associated with the publication of Alain Locke's *New Negro* in 1925. Harrison's life and work suggest important issues about the Harlem Renaissance. He openly questioned the genuineness of the "literary renaissance," the willingness to take "standards of value ready-made from white society," and the claim of a significant new rebirth. He maintained that there had been an uninterrupted, although ignored, stream of literary and artistic products by blacks from 1850 into the 1920s and that what was called a renaissance was mostly a creation of whites who overlooked such contributions. He envisioned a true literary renaissance that would express the true values and aspirations of black people, and he challenged the role of many prominent gatekeepers of culture who he felt depended on whites and were unable or unwilling to form their own opinions.

Harrison died unexpectedly at age forty-four, leaving a wife and five children. His funeral, in Harlem in December 1927, was attended by thousands, but within months of his death the Harlem activist Hodge Kirnon noted an ominous "concerted silence" about his life. Many prominent African American and leftist leaders, particularly those, like Du Bois, who had been stung by his criticism, were noticeably silent. This situation was intensified by the fact that Harrison had been poor, black, foreign-born, and from the Caribbean; had opposed capitalism, racism, and the Christian church; had supported socialism, "race consciousness," racial equality, women's equality, free thought, and birth control; and had been more of a "freelance" educator and activist than an "organization man." As the twenty-first century opened, however, a rapidly growing interest in Harrison was evident.

Biography

Hubert Harrison was born on 27 April 1883, in Estate Concordia, Saint Croix, Danish West Indies, and emigrated to New York City in 1900 (he was naturalized in 1922). He studied in public schools in Saint Croix and New York City and was self-educated thereafter. He worked as associate editor, *Unique Advertiser,* New York, 1904; editor, *St. Mark's Mirror,* New York, 1906; editor, *Fair Play,* New Rochelle, New York, 1906; post office clerk, New York, 1907–1911; public speaker, Socialist Party of New York, 1911–1914; editor, *The Masses,* New York, 1911; instructor, Modern School, New York, 1915; columnist, *New York News,* 1915; contributing editor, *Colored American Review,* New York, 1915; editor, *The Voice,* New York, 1917–1919; organizer, American Federation of Labor, Philadelphia, Atlantic City, and Washington, D.C., 1918; cochair, National Liberty Congress, Washington, D.C., 1918; editor, *New Negro,* New York, 1919; editor, *Negro World,* New York, 1920, then associate editor and contributing editor, 1920–1922; lecturer, New York City Board of Education, 1922–1926; columnist, *Boston Chronicle,* 1924; columnist *New York Inter-State Tattler,* 1924; speaker, La Follette for President Committee, Milwaukee, Chicago, and Indianapolis; speaker, American Negro Labor Congress, New York, 1926; editor, *Embryo of the Voice of the Negro,* New York, 1927;

and editor, *Voice of the Negro,* New York, 1927. He also wrote for numerous periodicals and founded several organizations. He died in New York City, on 17 December 1927.

JEFFREY PERRY

See also Briggs, Cyril; Domingo, W. A.; Garvey, Marcus; Johnson, James Weldon; McKay, Claude; Moore, Richard B.; Negro World; 135th Street Library; Owen, Chandler; Randolph, A. Philip; Rogers, Joel Augustus; Saint Mark's Methodist Episcopal Church; Savage, Augusta; *other specific individuals*

Selected Works

The Negro and the Nation. 1917.
When Africa Awakes: The "Inside Story" of the Stirrings and Strivings of the New Negro in the Western World. 1920.
A Hubert Harrison Reader, ed. Jeffrey B. Perry. 2001.

Further Reading

Foner, Philip S. *American Socialism and Black Americans: From the Age of Jackson to World War II.* Westport, Conn.: Greenwood, 1977.

Gaines, Kevin K. *Uplifting the Race: Black Leadership, Politics, and Culture in the Twentieth Century.* Chapel Hill: University of North Carolina Press, 1996.

Jackson, John G. *Hubert Henry Harrison: The Black Socrates.* Austin, Tex.: American Atheist, 1987.

James, Portia. "Hubert H. Harrison and the New Negro Movement." *Western Journal of Black Studies,* 13, 1989.

James, Winston. *Holding Aloft the Banner of Ethiopia: Caribbean Radicalism in Early Twentieth-Century America.* New York: Verso, 1998.

———. "Being Red and Black in Jim Crow America: Notes on the Ideology and Travails of Afro-America's Socialist Pioneers, 1877–1930." *Souls,* 1(4), Fall 1999, pp. 45–63.

Moore, Richard B. "Hubert Henry Harrison (1883–1927)." In *Dictionary of American Negro Biography,* ed. Rayford W. Logan and Michael R. Winston. New York: Norton, 1982.

Perry, Jeffrey B. "Hubert Henry Harrison 'The Father of Harlem Radicalism': The Early Years—1883 through the Founding of the Liberty League and *The Voice* in 1917." Ph.D. dissertation, Columbia University, 1986.

———. "An Introduction to Hubert Harrison, 'the Father of Harlem Radicalism.'" *Souls*, 2(1), Winter 2000, pp. 38–54.

———, ed. *A Hubert Harrison Reader*. Middletown, Conn.: Wesleyan University Press, 2001.

Rogers, Joel A. *World's Great Men of Color,* 2 vols., ed. with intro. John Henrik Clarke. New York: Collier, 1972.

Samuels, Wilfred D. "Hubert H. Harrison and 'The New Negro Manhood Movement.'" *Afro-Americans in New York Life and History*, 5, January 1981.

Harrison, Richard

Richard Berry Harrison is best known for his first and only professional theatrical role, which he secured at age sixty-five: De Lawd in Marc Connelly's *The Green Pastures*. Harrison was reluctant to take the part, fearing that the play would be a version of Uncle Tom in heaven and that he would be betraying his race; but he overcame his doubts and dedicated the remaining five years of his life to portraying an anthropomorphic God made in the image of a southern black preacher for the 1,657 performances of the show on Broadway and the company's three-and-a-half-year national tour.

A graduate of the Detroit Training School of Art (1887), Harrison was proficient in elocution and a talented actor but was prevented by the color line from developing a career on the legitimate stage. Supporting himself as a bellhop, Pullman porter, and dining car waiter throughout the 1890s, he took his public readings of poetry and Shakespeare on tour. He also teamed up with his good friend the poet Paul Laurence Dunbar, serving as a reader of dialect poems from the collection *Oak and Ivory* in an effort to sell Dunbar's books. Eventually Harrison found employment as a reader with the Lyceum Bureau of Los Angeles and toured in Mexico, California, and the Midwest and throughout the South giving performances and lectures at colleges and in churches.

Noting that young African Americans had no access to theatrical training, Harrison began his career as an educator in dramatics at the start of World War I. This was the era of the "great migration," and Harrison spent these years campaigning for funds to institute training programs for church schools, setting up summer lyceum courses in New York City, and teaching elocution and drama at Branch Normal in Arkansas, Flipper Key College in Oklahoma, and Haines Institute

in Augusta, Georgia. During the 1920s, he ran a summer-school dramatics curriculum for teachers at North Carolina Agricultural and Technical College and served as a lecturer for the Greater New York Federation of Churches, directing church festivals, training church dramatic groups, and giving recitals. By the time he appeared on Broadway as a humane, dignified God who "walked the earth like a natural man," he had trained more than 300 teachers and scores of students who otherwise would have had little access to formal education in theater and drama.

Although Harrison did not fit the usual profile of the New Negro as outlined by Alain Locke, it is clear that his commitment to racial pride and to providing access to the professional skills of theater and public speaking for young African Americans was in line with the movement. He, like Locke and Montgomery Gregory, determined that technique and training in the arts would - become an important resource for successful race relations through which the acceptance of African Americans as equal and productive citizens could be secured.

Biography

Richard Berry Harrison was born on 28 September 1864, in London, Ontario. He attended the Training School of Art, in Detroit, from which he graduated in 1887. He founded the summer dramatic school for teachers at North Carolina Agriculture and Technical State University in Greensboro, which he ran 1922–1929. He performed in one-man versions of *Macbeth* and *Julius Caesar* for the Lyceum Bureau; helped write and played the lead in Frank Wilson's *Pa Williams' Gal* (1923) for the Lafayette Theater; toured as Shylock and Othello in one-man versions of *The Merchant of Venice* and *Othello*, respectively; appeared in the films *How High Is Up* (1923) and *Easy Street* (1930); and played De Lawd in *The Green Pastures* for the Broadway productions and on the national tour (1930– 1935), a role for which he won the Springarn Award in 1931. He received an honorary master's degree from Howard University and a doctorate in dramatic literature from North Carolina Agriculture and Technical College and Lincoln University in 1934. Harrison was the first actor to be awarded the Sigma Society Key from Boston University. He died in Harlem on 14 March 1935.

ANDREA J. NOURYEH

See also Dunbar, Paul Laurence; Green Pastures, The; Lafayette Theater; Pa Williams' Gal

Further Reading

Daniel, Walter C. "'Absolution': An Unpublished Poem by Richard B. Harrison." *Negro History Bulletin*, 37, 1974, pp. 309–311.

———. "*The Green Pastures*: Religiosity in the American Theatre." *Journal of American Culture*, 5(1), Spring 1982, pp. 51–58.

———. "*De Lawd*": *Richard B. Harrison and The Green Pastures*. New York: Greenwood, 1987.

Haskins, James. *Black Theater in America*. New York: HarperCollins, 1982.

Hatch, James V. "Theatre in Historically Black Colleges: A Survey of 100 Years." In *A Sourcebook of African-American Performance: Plays, People, Movements*, ed. Annemarie Bean. New York: Routledge, 1999, pp. 151–164.

Hill, Errol. *Shakespeare in Sable: A History of Black Shakespearean Actors*. Amherst: University of Massachusetts Press, 1984.

Mapp, Edward. *Directory of Blacks in the Performing Arts*, 2nd ed. Metuchen, N.J.: Scarecrow, 1990.

Hayden, Palmer C.

Palmer Hayden showed artistic talent at an early age, but after failing to set himself up as an artist, he joined two circuses as a roustabout; there he drew advertisements and portraits of the performers, and it was perhaps through this experience that he sharpened his powers of observation and developed the directness that would be characteristic of his later work. During World War I, in the army, he made maps. (His experiences in the army would provide the subject for a series of paintings in the 1960s and 1970s, and in 1973, he was awarded a Creative Arts Project grant in New York City to develop a series of paintings of the history of the black soldier in America.) After his discharge from the army in 1920, Hayden moved to New York City, where he studied painting and drawing at Columbia University and worked in the post office. He eventually settled in Greenwich Village. He supported himself as a janitor at Cooper Union and began working with Victor Perard, one of the teachers there; he captured his experience in *The Janitor Paints a Picture* (1936, National Museum of American Art). The city would become an important source for his paintings; he executed views of street scenes, the environs of New York City public housing, and landmarks such as

the Brooklyn Bridge. During the summers he worked at the Boothbay Art Colony in Maine with A. C. Randall, executing marine scenes that earned a Harmon Foundation Gold Award for painting in 1926. Along with the financial support of a patron whose identity has been lost to history, the Harmon Foundation award allowed Hayden to study in Europe.

He set up a studio in Paris and spent his summers in Brittany. In Paris, at the suggestion of the painter Laura Wheeler Waring, he visited Henry Ossawa Tanner; he also befriended Hale Woodruff—who described him as a bon vivant and dandy. (He introduced himself to Woodruff with the words, "A buzzard laid me and the sun hatched me.") Hayden and Woodruff associated with a group of expatriate African Americans; Hayden's watercolor *Nous à Quatre Paris* (c. 1930, Metropolitan Museum of Art, New York) shows Hayden, Woodruff, the poet Countee Cullen, and another member of the group, Ernest Dupré, playing cards in a café similar to the Café La Coupole, which Hayden painted several times.

In Paris, Hayden developed a figural style that shows the influence of current trends such as art deco and cubism and is related to the stylizations of Aaron Douglas and the posters and illustrations of French artists such as Paul Colin and Roger Perot depicting musicians and dancers in plush interracial settings. Hayden studied at the École des Beaux Arts and constantly visited the Louvre. Like many of his contemporaries, he grappled with the notion of developing a uniquely African American art based on African art. Alain Locke, in the essay "The Legacy of Ancestral Arts" (1925), noted that "a younger group of Negro artists" were "beginning to move in the direction of a racial school of art." Although he admitted that African Americans experienced as much alienation and misunderstanding as Europeans when they first encountered African art, he said that "there is the possibility that the sensitive artistic mind of the American Negro, stimulated by a cultural pride and interest, will receive from African arts a profound and galvanizing influence." Hayden, who met Locke in Paris, would acknowledge that influence in *Fetiche and Fleurs* (1926, Fisk University, Nashville, Tennessee), in which a head from the Fang group is placed in a traditional still life arrangement. Hayden also produced witty depictions of reconstructed African villages and dancers at the Paris Exposition Coloniale of 1930, conveying the artificiality of fabricated reconstructions of "native" life but also the dignity of the "natives" caught in this anomalous situation. Hayden never visited

Africa, but in the 1960s he would return to African themes.

When Hayden came back to New York in 1932, he found employment in the Federal Arts Project and was assigned to paint scenes along the Hudson River. After leaving this project in 1940, he began to concentrate on various aspects of the life he observed around him.

Many critics have noted that Hayden's work eludes specific classification because he imitated no teacher or master. Usually, his art is characterized as naive, folkloric, or satiric—and the last characteristic has sometimes put him out of favor with serious-minded people. He developed an exceptional skill at narrative that draws us into a scene. He retains relatively flat color areas defined within strong, elegant linear elements, and his work now teases the distinction between so-called fine art and illustration. Hayden's approach is not unlike that of a photographer who captures people at unguarded moments. Whether it is a woman caught by a gust of wind lifting her skirt (*Gusting to Thirty-five Degrees*) or a little girl in her Sunday best admiring her new red shoes, the individuals respond to Hayden's scrutiny with an unself-consciousness, ease, and trust that any photographer would envy. In *Gusting to Thirty-five Degrees,* the woman's knowing smile as she struggles against the wind tells us that she is fully aware of being observed at an embarrassing moment. Hayden's portrayal is exact in all details, letting us see a bit of lace panty and a shapely leg framed by the curve of the woman's billowing coat.

Biography

Palmer Cole Hayden (originally named Peyton Cole Hedgeman) was born in Widewater, West Virginia, on 15 January 1890. By age four he showed artistic ability. At age sixteen he left Widewater for Washington, D.C., working as a drugstore errand boy and porter and enrolling in a correspondence course in drawing. After failing to set himself up as a professional artist, he joined the Buffalo Bill Circus and then the Ringling Brothers' Circus as a roustabout. Members of the circus had him do portraits of themselves and advertisements for the show. With the outbreak of World War I, he joined the army; he was stationed in the Philippines and later at West Point. He moved to New York after his discharge in 1920 (eventually settling in Greenwich Village); he worked in the post office and as a janitor at Cooper Union, studied art at Columbia

University, and worked at the Boothbay Art Colony in Maine during the summers. He won an award from the Harmon Foundation in 1926 that enabled him to study in Europe, and he set up a studio in Paris. In 1932, having returned to New York, he worked for the Federal Arts Project. Hayden married Miriam Hoffman, a schoolteacher, in 1940. They settled on West Fifty-sixth Street in midtown Manhattan, where he spent the rest of his life. He died in New York City in 1973.

LOWERY STOKES SIMS

See also Artists; Douglas, Aaron; Federal Programs; Harmon Foundation; Locke, Alain; Tanner, Henry Ossawa; Waring, Laura Wheeler; Woodruff, Hale

Further Reading

Bearden, Romare, and Henry Henderson. *A History of African-American Artists from 1792 to the Present.* New York: Pantheon, 1993.

Sims, Lowery S. "Palmer Hayden." New York: Just Above Midtown Gallery, 1975. (Exhibition catalog.)

Hayden, Robert

Robert Earl Hayden (1913–1980) was a poet and educator influenced by the Harlem Renaissance. His early writing, in particular, evinces an apprenticeship to poets like Langston Hughes and Countee Cullen; but even in his later writings and outlook, Hayden, like many artists inspired by the Harlem Renaissance, believed that the cultivation of a shared aesthetic and humanity would help remove the color line.

Hayden's original name was Asa Bundy Sheffey; at the age of eighteen months, he was taken in and renamed by William and Sue Ellen Westerfield Hayden after first his father and then his mother abandoned him, although he maintained a relationship with his mother. He was raised by the Haydens in an impoverished area of Detroit, Michigan, nicknamed Paradise Valley. Severe myopia precluded a physically active life, but the young Hayden found a refuge in reading and writing.

After majoring in Spanish at Wayne State University, but still one credit short of his B.A., Hayden found employment during the Great Depression with the Federal Writers' Project of the Works Progress

Robert Hayden. (Library of Congress.)

Administration (WPA). His research into the settlement of African Americans in Michigan would later find expression specifically in poems such as "Runagate Runagate" and, more generally, in his overall engagement with history in his poetry.

In time, Hayden's conversion to the Baha'i World Faith in 1942 also found expression in the themes of his poetry. Baha'i tenets, such as the belief that humankind's quest for truth is cyclical but progressive, permeate the poetry in *Words in the Mourning Time* (1970). Initially, however, Hayden's poetry was beholden to Cullen and Hughes. His first published poem, "Africa" (*Abbot's Monthly*, 1931), was in many ways a response to the question posed by Countee Cullen in "Heritage": "What is Africa to me?" Hayden's speaker replies: "Dear Africa, you're more to me / Than reeking jungle. / In thee I take undying pride." On meeting Cullen in 1941, Hughes was delighted to learn that his mentor had read and enjoyed his poetry. However, Langston Hughes's earlier response to Hayden's poetry had been less flattering: Over a lunch, Hughes had encouraged Hayden to find his own voice—Hayden's first published poetry collection having been pervaded by Hughes's voice in its use of dialect and blues.

Evidently, Hayden followed Hughes's advice as a graduate student in English at the University of Michigan where, under the tutelage of W. H. Auden,

he cultivated a restrained, economical style that is poignant without being maudlin. This approach is best exemplified in "Those Winter Sundays," one of Hayden's most lauded and most frequently anthologized poems.

In 1966, at the first Black Writers' Conference held at Fisk University, Hayden was attacked for being critical of the black nationalist school of writers, but Hayden, like Cullen before him, preferred to be a poet rather than a black poet. He was redeemed when that same year an international panel of judges, including Langston Hughes, awarded him the Grand Prix de la Poésie for *A Ballad of Remembrance*. During the last decade of his life, Hayden achieved recognition: He gave frequent poetry readings, received numerous honorary degrees, and was twice appointed the poetry consultant for the Library of Congress, an unprecedented honor.

Biography

Robert Earl Hayden (originally named Asa Bundy Sheffey) was born on 4 August 1913, in Detroit, Michigan; he married Erma Inez Morris in 1940. He was educated at Northern High School in Detroit (1930); Wayne State University (B.A., 1942); and the University of Michigan, Ann Arbor (M.A. in English, 1944). He was a writer and researcher for the Federal Writers Project, Works Progress Administration, in Detroit (1936–1939); director of Negro Research, Detroit Federal Writers' Project (1939–1940); researcher, Federal Historical Records Survey, WPA (1940); professor of English, Fisk University, Nashville, Tennessee (1946–1969); appointed poetry editor, *World Order* (1967); poet in residence, Indiana State University, Terre Haute (1967); visiting professor of English, University of Michigan (1968); Bingham professor, University of Louisville, Kentucky (1969); visiting poet, University of Washington, Seattle (1969); professor of English, University of Michigan (1969); writer and editor for Scott, Foresman (1970); on the poetry staff, Breadloaf Writers' Conference, Middlebury College, Vermont (1972); and visiting poet, Connecticut College, New London (1974). His awards included the Hopwood Minor Award for Poetry (1938); the Hopwood Major Award for Poetry (1942); a Rosenwald fellowship in creative writing (1947); a Ford Foundation grant for travel and writing in Mexico (1954); the Grand Prix de la Poésie, First World Festival of Negro Arts, Dakar, Senegal (1966); a nomination for a National Book Award

(1970); the Russell Loines Award for Poetry, National Institute of Arts and Letters (1970); election as a fellow of the Academy of American Poets (1975); appointment as consultant in poetry, Library of Congress (1976–1978); membership in the Academy of American Poets and Institute of Arts and Letters (1979); and an invitation to President Jimmy Carter's "White House Salute to American Poetry" (1980). He recorded poetry for the Library of Congress archives (1968). "A Tribute to Robert Hayden" was held on 24 February 1980, at the University of Michigan. Hayden died in Ann Arbor, Michigan, on 25 February 1980.

VALARIE MOSES

See also Cullen, Countee; Federal Writers' Project; Hughes, Langston

Selected Works

Heart-Shape in the Dust. 1940.
The Lion and the Archer: Poems, with Myron O'Higgins. 1948.
Figure of Time: Poems. 1955.
A Ballad of Remembrance. 1962.
Selected Poems. 1966.
Kaleidoscope: Poems by American Negro Poets. 1967. (As editor.)
"Preface." In *The New Negro*, ed. Alain Locke. 1968. (Originally published 1925.)
Words in the Mourning Time. 1970.
Afro-American Literature: An Introduction. 1971. (As editor, with David J. Burrows and Frederick R. Lapides.)
How I Write, with Paul McCluskey. 1972.
The Night-Blooming Cereus. 1972.
Angle of Ascent: New and Selected Poems. 1975.
The Legend of John Brown, with screen prints by Jacob Lawrence. 1978.
American Journal. 1978. (Expanded version reprinted 1982.)
Collected Prose, ed. Frederick Glaysher. 1984.
Collected Poems, ed. Frederick Glaysher. 1985.

Further Reading

Conniff, Brian. "Answering 'The Waste Land': Robert Hayden and the Rise of the African American Poetic Sequence." *African American Review*, 33(3), 1999.
Fetrow, Fred M. *Robert Hayden*. Boston, Mass.: Twayne, 1984.

Gallagher, Ann M. "Hayden's Those Winter Sundays." *Explicator*, 51(4), 1993.
Gayle, Addison Jr. *Black Expression: Essays by and about Black Americans in the Creative Arts.* New York: Weybright and Talley, 1969.
Genge, Susan. "Hayden's Homage to the Empress of the Blues." *Explicator*, 57(2), 1999.
Gibbons, Reginald. "Robert Hayden in the 1940s." *TriQuarterly*, 62, 1985.
Goldstein, Laurence, and Robert Chrisman, eds. *Robert Hayden: Essays on the Poetry.* Ann Arbor: University of Michigan Press, 2001.
Harper, Michael S. "Remembering Robert Hayden." *Michigan Quarterly Review*, 21, 1982.
Hatcher, John Southall. *From the Auroral Darkness: The Life and Poetry of Robert Hayden.* Oxford: George Ronald, 1984.
Layman, Richard. "Robert Hayden." In *Conversations With Writers*, 1. Detroit, Mich.: Gale Research, 1977.
Pool, Rosey E. "Grand Prix de la Poésie for Robert Hayden." *World Order*, 17(4), 1983.
Potter, Vilma Raskin. "Reconsiderations and Reviews: A Remembrance for Robert Hayden, 1913–1980." *MELUS*, 8(1), 1981.
Rashid, Frank. "Robert Hayden's Detroit Blues Elegies." *Callaloo*, 24(1), 2001.
Richards, Phillip M. "Robert Hayden (1913–1980): An Appreciation." *Massachusetts Review*, 40(4), 1999–2000.
Stepto, Robert B. "After Modernism, after Hibernation: Michael Harper, Robert Hayden, and Jay Wright." In *Chant of Saints: A Gathering of Afro-American Literature, Art, and Scholarship*, ed. Robert B. Stepto, Michael S. Harper, and John Hope Franklin. Urbana: University of Illinois Press, 1979.
Williams, Pontheolla T. *Robert Hayden: A Critical Analysis of His Poetry.* Urbana and Chicago: University of Illinois Press, 1987.
Zabel, Darcy. "Hayden's Runagate Runagate." *Explicator*, 60(2), 2002.

Hayes, Roland

The distinguished and distinctively brilliant African American tenor Roland Hayes (1887–1976) was known not only for his artistry but also for his unique way of fighting racism and bigotry in America and in Europe. He was the first African American concert artist to achieve international prominence, and he had many other "firsts" in his long career. He was hailed as one of the great voices of the twentieth century, and he mastered the music of not just America but much of the world. In order to perform the music of other nations, he made a point of learning to sing in the language of each country he visited and in which he concertized. His preparation for this monumental task was supplemented by intensive study with several prominent teachers and coaches; he always seemed to be able to find just the right person to train him or guide him. The important teachers and coaches with whom Hayes studied in Europe were George Henschel in London, Theodore Lierhammer in Vienna, and Gabriel Fauré in Paris. His association with Henschel—who had studied with Johannes Brahms—led to a lifelong friendship, and it was through Henschel that Hayes polished his art and solidified his singing technique. Because of his concept of universality as well as his vocal art, Hayes falls easily into the category of the "New Negro" of the Harlem Renaissance.

Hayes was in a sense a self-made man and artist. He had been rather late in developing academically; he arrived at Fisk University, and was allowed to enroll, with the equivalent of only a sixth-grade education. He soon encountered personal problems that eventually cut short his studies at Fisk; one reason for these problems was that he was performing with the famous Jubilee Singers, which were not actually associated with the university's music department. However, he remained loyal to Fisk and often returned there to perform. (The present writer had the good fortune to hear Hayes in recital at Fisk in the early 1960s.)

After his experience at Fisk, Hayes moved from Nashville to Louisville, where he met Arthur Calhoun, one of many white associates who would assist him with his training and help him to get gainful employment. Eventually, he went to Boston, where he had a summer residency with the Jubilee Singers in 1911. He then began serious study with Arthur Hubbard, meanwhile supporting himself by working as a messenger at the John Hancock Life Insurance Company. (His many supporters from this company contributed much to the success of his professional debut at Symphony Hall in Boston.) After settling in Boston, he sang at every opportunity, to demonstrate his vocal artistry.

In 1914, Hayes was chosen to go on one of Booker T. Washington's lecture tours to sing with the noted baritone Harry T. Burleigh, who was the first African American concert artist and a close friend of Washington's. Not only was this a great boost for the aspiring young Hayes, but Burleigh also became an inspiration to him as well as a conduit to sources of indigenous American music. Moreover, news of this tour reached Nashville and, at Fisk University, reached a Miss Robinson—a teacher from whom Hayes had been estranged. She wrote to Hayes, suggesting a reconciliation, and his response was to go back to Fisk and sing the tenor role in Mendelssohn's *Elijah*, with Burleigh singing the baritone lead. On this trip to Nashville, Hayes also visited his cousin Helen Alzada Mann, who would become his wife in 1932.

From the time when he first began to sing in public, Hayes realized that he had a unique talent; he believed that this talent was God-given and that it was something to be nurtured and shared with the world. He also realized that his beloved mother, Fannie, whom he called Angel Mo, had given him a special upbringing. (The title of Hayes's autobiography is *Angel Mo and Her Son Roland Hayes*, and Chapter 2 is called "I Worship My Mother.") Although his mother was a former slave, on one of his tours when she traveled with him, she was able to critique his performance—telling him how important it was not only to hear but also to understand the message he wanted to impart to his audience. Hayes described Fannie as "an indomitable woman whose high standards of personal honesty and dignity had exerted" a profound effect on him. He said that "next to our souls, Mother Fannie cherished our minds. She wanted us to have an education so that we could do good in the world."

But in the early twentieth century, despite his talent and his inspirational upbringing, Hayes, as an African American, could not find professional sponsorship or management. He tried to engage as his manager William H. Brennan of the management staff at Symphony Hall in Boston—this was an audacious move for a black man at the time, and the attempt failed. (Not until 1923, when Hayes returned from Europe as a celebrity, would Brennan accept the position of his manager.) Hayes was not deterred from persisting with his career; he decided to be his own manager and promoter. He did hire a secretary, and between them they compiled mailing lists and other promotional literature. Also, Hayes had an entrée to the news media, which he used. Against the advice of his friends and his teacher, Arthur Hubbard, he pursued his dream of renting Symphony Hall for his professional debut in 1917. This debut recital drew an overflow crowd and earned him a $2,000 profit. (In retrospect, though, there had already been a minor debut: Hayes had sung the tenor arias in a performance of *Messiah* at Howard University c. 1910.)

Early on, tours were important in Hayes's career. He planned and managed them carefully and felt that overall they were successful. In 1915, for example, in order to earn money for his future endeavors, Hayes made a tour of several southern cities, singing in Negro churches with the aid of the American Missionary Association (AMA); in later years, he would reciprocate with a benefit performance for AMA. Early in 1918, Hayes and his accompanist, Lawrence Brown, set out on a tour that extended all the way to the West Coast. Hayes's mother went with them and took a liking to Brown. (Brown, who came from Charlestown, South Carolina, was later an accompanist for Paul Robeson.) There was a second transcontinental tour late in 1918, covering basically the same territory but with some additions and under "Negro auspices."

One factor in the success of Hayes's tours was the distinctiveness of his art. He recounted that "an elderly gentleman of aristocratic bearing came to me and said, 'Mr. Hayes, you seem to me to sing with all the art of the master singers I have heard and yet with some new emotional quality of your own. I wish you would tell me how you have come by that special quality.'" Hayes was a masterful communicator and a masterful interpreter of song. He has been described as an "expressor of the soul in song" (Carter 1977)—"soul" being understood here as deep inner expressiveness and genuine conviction. Hayes considered his voice a tool for a mission that was more important than art: racial harmony. Hayes pursued this mission in his own unique manner, which was quiet but strong. An example is a concert he gave in Vienna to a hypercritical audience that greeted him with hisses; called him, with blatant disrespect, the *Negertenor*; and seemed to be asking, Who gives him the right to sing our music? Hayes waited patiently for about twenty or twenty-five minutes, then nodded to his accompanist. They began a rendition of a piece that was a favorite of the Viennese, Schubert's *Du bist die Ruh*. Hayes sang in perfect German and with solid artistry, and he finally silenced the audience. By the end of the concert, he had won the audience over and received tremendous bravos of acclaim.

Work and studies abroad were also important to Hayes. The $2,000 he earned from his debut recital in Boston made possible a trip to Europe "in search of the roots of French and German art songs." He had studied the French and German languages and French and German art songs assiduously, and he was already familiar with the singing of Enrico Caruso—in fact, while Hayes was in Louisville (where, as noted previously, his benefactor was Arthur Calhoun), he had learned many arias and other works by listening to Caruso's recordings. In addition to his most important teachers and coaches (Henschel in London, where he spent most of his time; Lierhammer in Vienna; and Fauré in Paris), Hayes met and became friends with many international artists who recognized his genius; these figures included Pablo Casals, Ignacy Paderewski, Myra Hess, and Fritz Kreisler. Kreisler urged Pierre Monteux to engage Hayes for an appearance with the Boston Symphony on 16 November 1923—perhaps the first time that an African American was engaged to sing with a major American orchestra. Furthermore, during the three years that he spent in London (1920–1923), Hayes came into contact with his roots. There were many black residents in London at the time, including some who were British, some from the Caribbean, and some from West Africa, and Hayes benefited from the assistance of these primary sources. He studied their folklore and also learned to sing in their native languages. With the help of the West African community in London, for instance, Hayes studied and performed the folk music of West Africa. (Hayes's father, William, was of black and Indian heritage and may well have also been an influence in this regard.)

A source of support for Hayes—and subsequently a source of information about him—was the news journal *West Africa*, which was founded in early 1917 in London for a black and white readership in Britain and in Africa; Albert Cartwright was its editor and music critic. *West Africa* strongly promoted Hayes's career in London, reporting on all of his recitals and performances in Europe; and Hayes would usually list in this journal his programs as well as reviews of his recitals and other performances. In addition, he announced a command performance at Buckingham Palace for the king (George V) and queen in April 1921. Cartwright chided the London *Times* and other news media for their cool response to Hayes, and the *Times* later changed its stance.

Hayes's ability to sing in many languages—such as those of West Africa, as mentioned previously—was significant. Hayes was a fast learner; he had a command of French, German, and Italian, and he also sang in Russian on his tour of Russia. He knew several languages before coming to Europe and continued his study of languages during his stay there. This mastery of languages was one aspect of his general versatility: He was very universal in his approach and presented

Roland Hayes, photographed by Carl Van Vechten.
(Library of Congress.)

a marvelously varied repertoire. For instance, his recital programs included some works dating back as early as the fifteenth century.

Hayes was the first of his race to make a comfortable living as a concert artist. During the 1920s, he made seven hugely successful transcontinental tours of the United States; and in 1924, the *New York Times* reported that Hayes had earned $100,000. Hayes bought a villa in France and a 623-acre farm in Georgia, where his mother had been a slave. He also had a residence in Brookline, Massachusetts, where he spent the end of his life with his wife and his only child—his daughter, Afrika, who sang recitals with him in Boston.

Hayes was an impeccable artist and a rare human being, a humanitarian with a universal spirit and a remarkable personality. One friend may have touched the essence of Hayes's spirit: "Roland has achieved great things. But he's one in a million. He could have been anything he put his mind to, because he has that kind of intelligence and drive." At the peak of his career, Hayes was said to be the only concert artist who could

fill both Carnegie Hall in New York and Symphony Hall in Boston three times in the same season. The Boston *Post* called him "the greatest recitalist in the world."

Biography

Roland Hayes was born in 1887 in Curryville, Georgia; his mother was a former slave. He was educated at Fisk University; performed with the Jubilee Singers (summer 1911) in Boston, Massachusetts; and began serious study with Arthur Hubbard in Boston. Hayes made his professional debut at Symphony Hall in Boston in 1917. He made several coast-to-coast tours in 1916–1919 and went to London in 1920–1923 (his debut in London was at Aeolian Hall in 1920). On his return to the United States, his recital of 2 December 1923 began his long, illustrious career, throughout which he would tour internationally. Hayes received numerous honorary degrees and, in 1924, the Spingarn Medal. He was probably the first black artist to sing with a major symphony orchestra (Boston, 1923) and one of the first blacks to make a good living through a concert singing career: He was able to buy a French villa, a large farm in Georgia, and a beautiful home in Brookline, Massachusetts. Hayes died in Boston in 1976.

MALCOLM BREDA

See also Burleigh, Harry Thacker; Singers; Washington, Booker T.

Further Reading

Abdul, Raoul. *Blacks in Classical Music: A Personal History.* New York: Dodd, Mead, 1977.

Carter, Mavra Griffin. "Roland Hayes: Expressor of the Soul in Song (1887–1977)." *Black Perspective in Music,* 5(2), Fall 1977.

Green, Jeffrey P. "Roland Hayes in London, 1921." *Black Perspective in Music,* 10(1), Spring 1982.

Hayden, Robert C. *Singing for All People: Roland Hayes— A Biography.* Boston, Mass.: Little, Brown, 1989.

Hayes, Roland. *My Songs: Afroamerican Religious Folk Songs Arranged and Interpreted by Roland Hayes.* Boston, Mass.: Little, Brown, 1948.

Helm, MacKinley *Angel Mo' and Her Son, Roland Hayes.* Boston, Mass.: Little, Brown, 1942.

Marr, Warren, II. "Conversation with Roland Hayes." *Black Perspective in Music,* 2(2), Fall 1974.

Woolsey, F. W. "Conversation with Roland Hayes." *Black Perspective in Music*, 2(2), Fall 1974.

Haynes, George Edmund

George Edmund Haynes was a pioneering black sociologist and social worker, a passionate advocate of education and self-improvement, and a founder and first executive secretary of the National Urban League (NUL).

The child of a domestic worker, Haynes was born in Pine Bluff, Arkansas, in 1880. He earned a B.A. at Fisk in 1903 and an M.A. in sociology at Yale a year later. Over the next six years he studied at the University of Chicago, the New York School of Philanthropy, and Columbia University, all while supporting his mother and sister by working as secretary of the Colored Men's Department of the International Committee of the Young Men's Christian Association (YMCA). In 1912, he became the first African American to earn a Ph.D. from Columbia University. His dissertation, *The Negro at Work in New York City: A Study in Economic Progress*, was published the same year.

At a time when most political leaders, black and white, urged African Americans to remain in the rural South, Haynes saw black urbanization as an inevitable by-product of modernization. He stressed the need for careful, nonpartisan investigation of the actual conditions of black urban life, including health, housing, vice, family life, and above all employment. He also stressed the vital need for a cadre of trained black social workers, to aid new southern migrants in their "adaptation" to the demands of urban life. Both convictions were embodied in the Committee for Improving Industrial Conditions of Negroes in New York, which he and Ruth Standish Baldwin, a wealthy white philanthropist, founded in 1910. A year later, he and Baldwin engineered the merger of their committee and several other social welfare agencies to create the National League on Urban Conditions Among Negroes, which became known as the National Urban League. Haynes became its first executive secretary. In 1918, he accepted a position as director of the Department of Negro Economics, a wartime agency within the U.S. Department of Labor. At the same time, he held a professorship at Fisk University, where he introduced the first program in social work at a black university.

Haynes played little of a direct role in the Harlem Renaissance. His commitment to scientific investigation, incremental reform, and "interracial cooperation" was distinctly out of step with the temper of the "New Negro" movement, with its emphasis on bold self-assertion and social transformation through art. He did contribute an essay, "The Church and the Negro Spirit," to *Survey Graphic*'s special issue on Harlem in 1925, but the essay was one of those that Alain Locke excised in preparing *The New Negro*.

Over the remaining decades of his life, Haynes devoted his energies to numerous liberal social welfare agencies, including the Federal Council of Churches, the Commission on Interracial Cooperation, and the YMCA. In 1930, he traveled under the auspices of the YMCA to South Africa, whose problems of urbanization and "race friction" seemed to resemble those he had confronted in the United States. He returned to Africa in 1947, undertaking a continent-wide survey, the fruits of which appeared in his final book, *Africa: Continent of the Future*. He died in New York in 1960.

Biography

George Edmund Haynes was born in 1880 in Pine Bluff, Arkansas. He studied at Fisk University in Nashville, Tennessee (B.A., 1903); Yale University (M.A., 1904); the University of Chicago; the New York School of Philanthropy; and Columbia University (Ph.D., 1912). He was a cofounder of the Committee for Improving Industrial Conditions of Negroes in New York (1910) and the National Urban League (1911) and the first executive secretary of the National Urban League; a professor of education and sociology at Fisk University; and director of the Department of Negro Economics, U.S. Department of Labor (1918–1921). Haynes was a member of the President's Commission on Unemployment (1921), the Commission on Interracial Cooperation, the Federal Council of Churches, and the World Committee of the Young Men's Christian Association. He died in Mount Vernon, New York, in 1960.

JAMES CAMPBELL

See also National Urban League; New Negro, The; Survey Graphic

Selected Works

The Negro at Work in New York City: A Study in Economic Progress. 1912.

The Trend of the Races. 1922.

"The Church and the Negro Spirit." *Survey Graphic*, March 1925.

Africa: Continent of the Future. 1950.

Further Reading

Carlton-La'Ney, I. "George Edmund Haynes's Impact on Social Work Education." In *From Vision to Action: Social Workers of the Second Generation*, ed. Janice Edwards. St. Thomas, Virgin Islands: University of St. Thomas Press, 1992.

Perlman, Daniel. "Stirring the White Conscience: The Life of George Edmund Haynes." Ph.D. dissertation, New York University, 1972.

Weiss, Nancy J. *The National Urban League, 1910–1940*. New York: Oxford University Press, 1974.

Hearts in Dixie

Hearts in Dixie (1929), directed by Paul Sloane II and released by Fox Films, was the first feature-length Hollywood film with an almost exclusively black cast. Previously, most black roles in films were played by white actors in blackface, a long-standing theatrical tradition that gained popularity in the nineteenth century with the development of the minstrel show. *Hearts in Dixie*, by contrast, eschewed the use of blackface. By employing black actors, its makers sought to achieve a more realistic depiction of black life in the South.

With a script written by Walter Weems (a former southern minstrel performer), *Hearts in Dixie* narrates the story of an old black farmer named Nappus. His daughter Chloe is married to Gummy (played by Stepin Fetchit), a ne'er-do-well who suns himself by day and dances by night, leaving Chloe to perform all of the housework and manual labor. When Chloe and one of their two children fall ill, Gummy calls a voodoo woman instead of the white doctor, and both die. Determined to make a better life for his surviving grandchild, Nappus sells his mule and farm to raise enough money to send the boy north to become a doctor. The film ends with Nappus's wish that someday his grandson will return to the South to help their people.

On its release early in 1929, *Hearts in Dixie* was lauded by the mainstream white press. Mordaunt Hall, reviewer for the *New York Times*, described the

Eugene Jackson and Clarence Muse in *Hearts in Dixie*, 1929. (Photofest.)

film as "a talking and singing production that is gentle in its mood and truthful in its reflection of the black men of those days down yonder in the cornfields" (1929, 30). However, the film met with a lukewarm response in the black press. A reviewer for the Chicago *Defender*, an important African American newspaper, was ambivalent about the depiction of black life, complaining that the film "dragged" and referring sarcastically to its "occasional spark of darky humor" ("Hearts in Dixie" 1929, 6).

Despite its historical significance, *Hearts in Dixie* has attracted little critical attention in recent scholarship. Much of the criticism that does exist has focused on the ideologies the film seems to endorse. First, the film participates in what has been called the "plantation myth," which painted an idealized and nostalgic vision of slavery. Furthermore, by depicting the voodoo woman as impotent, the film values white science and medicine over African or folk tradition. Bogle argued that because the film was written and directed by whites, "the actor becomes a black man in blackface" (1973, 27), depicting black life as it was imagined by whites. Some commentators would argue that this is particularly true of Stepin Fetchit. The first African American actor to receive top billing in the movies, he was at once a talented performer and an embarrassment to some blacks who felt that the role of the "plantation coon" (Bogle, 28), which he perfected, reinforced white stereotypes of blacks. Still, despite the flaws in *Hearts in Dixie*, Cripps maintains that Nappus has a "quiet patriarchal dignity" and that the action "flows from black ambition, not white instigation" (1993, 239). *Hearts in Dixie* remains a milestone in the vexed history of African Americans in Hollywood cinema.

ALISON LANDSBERG

See also Fetchit, Stepin; Film

Further Reading

Bogle, Donald. *Toms, Coons, Mulattos, Mammies, and Bucks*. New York: Viking, 1973.

California Eagle, 14 and 21 December 1928. (Review.)

Cripps, Thomas. *Slow Fade to Black: The Negro in American Film, 1906–1942*. New York: Oxford University Press, 1993.

Hall, Mordaunt. "Way Down Yonder." *New York Times*, 28 February 1929, p. 30. (Review.)

"'Hearts in Dixie' Opens in New York." *Chicago Defender*, 16 March 1929, part 1, p. 6.

Variety, 6 March 1929, p. 15. (Review.)

Hegamin, Lucille

The blues singer Lucille Hegamin was most prominent in the early 1920s. She began her professional career around 1909, touring with a Leonard Harper revue. In 1914 to 1918, she was a cabaret and café singer in Chicago, billed as the "Georgia peach." She worked extensively with the legendary New Orleans pianist Tony Jackson at the Elite No. 2 Theater on Chicago's south side, popularizing his classic song "Pretty Baby" and W.C. Handy's "Saint Louis Blues." She also worked with Jelly Roll Morton and others before marrying the pianist Bill Hegamin, who then became her accompanist.

In 1918 to 1919, the Hegamins traveled to Los Angeles; they worked there and also in San Francisco and Seattle. Around November 1919, they moved to New York, where they worked at cafés in Harlem (the Dolphin, Connor's) while Lucille Hegamin established herself in New York. By the spring of 1920, she had graduated to singing at major events, such as the spectacular dances put on by Happy Rhone's Orchestra at the Manhattan Casino. The Manhattan Casino was a large room, unkind to singers, and Rhone's ensemble often numbered thirty players or more. Hegamin's voice, although not large, had an edge that penetrated; she proudly recalled her ability to "wail."

Voices of this type were much in demand during the early commercial fad for blues, and Hegamin soon became a popular recording artist, the second African American woman blues singer to record. Her initial recordings, on the Arto label, featured her husband on piano and several fine jazz musicians, and sold well. Among the most important was "He May Be Your Man but He Comes to See Me Sometimes." After touring extensively to support her record sales, she began a stint at Harlem's Shuffle Inn on 131st Street. In January 1922, she took part in a legendary four-way blues contest in New York, placing second behind Trixie Smith. Around February to May 1922, she toured the eastern United States with the number-two company of the show *Shuffle Along*. In the autumn of 1923, she appeared in the musical comedy *Creole Follies* in New York and Washington, D.C.

From December 1923 through 1926, she worked primarily as a solo act, now with the pianist Cyril Fullerton, her marriage and partnership with Bill Hegamin having failed. She briefly led her own jazz band from November 1925 to February 1926. She continued as a prolific recording artist, making more than forty sides for Cameo Records from September 1922 to the autumn of 1926 (she was dubbed the "Cameo girl"). In early 1925, she performed frequently on the radio station WHN, broadcasting from the Cotton Club with Andy Preer and his Cotton Club Syncopators. From January to March 1927 she was active primarily in Philadelphia.

After the late 1920s, Hegamin's career began to fade. She eventually found work as a nurse and put show business behind her, but she was rediscovered during the blues revival of the 1960s; in August 1961, she recorded alongside Alberta Hunter and Victoria Spivey, accompanied by an old-timers' jazz band, for the Prestige "Bluesville" label. Although these were her first recordings in almost thirty years, they found her in good voice and were well received. She made a few personal appearances in clubs during the early 1960s, as a revered elder of the blues.

Biography

Lucille Nelson Hegamin was born in Macon, Georgia, on 29 November 1894. She had no formal musical training; she sang in church and local theatricals as a child and entered professional show business c. 1909, touring with a Leonard Harper revue. She became a cabaret and café singer in Chicago. She married the pianist Bill Hegamin, who became her accompanist; they worked together on the West Coast, then moved to New York c. 1919. She worked in cafés in Harlem and then moved up to major venues and recordings. After her marriage to Bill Hegamin failed, she worked mostly solo (1923–1926), continued recording, and did radio broadcasts. When her performing career faded (late 1920s), she became a nurse; she was rediscovered during a blues revival in the 1960s. She died on 1 March 1970, in New York City.

ELLIOTT S. HURWITT

See also Blues: Women Performers; Cotton Club; Handy, W. C.; Hunter, Alberta; Manhattan Casino; Shuffle Along; Singers; Spivey, Victoria

Further Reading

Harris, Sheldon. *Blues Who's Who.* New Rochelle, N.Y.: Arlington House, 1979.

Jazz Journal (UK), July–August 1967.

Kunstadt, Leonard. *Record Research*, November 1961– January, February, March 1962.

Henderson, Fletcher

James Fletcher Hamilton Henderson, known as Fletcher Henderson and as Fletch Smack Henderson, is among the most important figures in the emergence of jazz during the 1920s and 1930s. As musical director for Black Swan Records, piano accompanist for hundreds of early blues recordings, leader of an innovative ensemble that began as a polished dance orchestra and became crucial to the development of big band jazz, and chief arranger for Benny Goodman during the height of his popularity in the mid-1930s, Henderson helped shape many elements of American popular music between the world wars. He had a remarkable eye for talent, hiring and shepherding the careers of numerous sidemen, soloists, and arrangers who profoundly influenced the direction of jazz. Although his upbringing made him an unlikely candidate to help develop and popularize a revolutionary new musical form, he came as near as any black jazz musician to the "New Negro" ideal as established by the leaders of the Harlem Renaissance, providing a model for the talented, striving, professional black musician that many African Americans could follow.

Fletcher Henderson was born into an upstanding middle-class family in Cuthbert, Georgia. His grandfather James, born a slave, served as a delegate to South Carolina's Constitutional Convention of 1868 and in the state legislature during Reconstruction. Both his parents were college-educated and were respected teachers at the Howard Normal School, where his father was also principal. Young Fletcher Henderson grew up surrounded by music, but exclusively in classical rather than popular forms. Even after his success in jazz, his parents forbade the playing of jazz in their house. His well-rounded childhood education included compulsory piano lessons, which he reportedly resented, from age six to thirteen.

While earning a B.S. in chemistry at Atlanta University, his father's alma mater, Henderson played the organ for university church services, performed in several musical stage shows, and led the Georgia Student Army Training Corps band during World War I. Although he earned money playing piano at a resort in Woods Hole, Massachusetts, during the summers while he was in college, he as yet showed no signs of a professional interest in music.

In June 1920, Henderson traveled to New York intending to enroll at Columbia University for graduate work in chemistry, but from his first days in the city he found himself drawn, by chance and a lack of financial resources, toward work in New York's vibrant music scene, and increasingly toward popular music styles. After playing piano on a riverboat orchestra, he was hired by Pace and Handy Music Company as a song plugger, performing tunes the company published to increase sales of its sheet music. When the coproprietor Harry Pace, a fellow alumnus of Atlanta University, split from Handy to form the Black Swan Phonograph Company in 1921, he hired Henderson as music director, recording manager, and piano accompanist.

The years 1921 through 1923 were vital in Henderson's musical development. Black Swan's determination to record both classical and popular music brought Henderson, as pianist on many of the label's early recordings, into contact with a wide variety of music, including blues and dance styles. The success of the blues singer Ethel Waters also prompted Black Swan to send Waters and Henderson on tour with a small ensemble, the Black Swan Troubadours, in 1921 and 1922. The sophisticated Henderson was so uncomfortable at the prospect of touring with a blues singer that he felt compelled to obtain permission from his family beforehand. Ultimately, however, Waters's influence on Henderson in 1921 and 1922 was

551

crucial. Frustrated at his lack of a feel for blues and jazz rhythm, Waters coached Henderson in left-hand technique, even buying him piano rolls by James P. Johnson as a model. Henderson quickly absorbed the new blues and dance styles, and his versatility, talent, reliability, and organizational skills made him one of the most sought-after piano accompanists in New York. By 1923, he had performed on more records than any other African American artist, accompanying singers such as Bessie Smith, Rosa Henderson, Trixie Smith, and Turner Layton.

Fletcher Henderson formed his first dance orchestra late in 1922. The musicians were primarily a recording ensemble until Club Alabam, an elite white-only downtown dance venue, hired them for steady work in January 1924. When a dispute with the management led them to quit in June, they were quickly hired at the Roseland Ballroom (the "Home of Refined Dancing") on Broadway, where they would make their home until 1928. A live radio broadcast from the Roseland Ballroom on WHN increased their exposure, and Henderson was on his way to national prominence.

With these engagements and recording contracts on numerous labels, including the prestigious Columbia, the Henderson orchestra became one of the premier black ensembles in New York in the mid-1920s. Henderson's unit was the only black orchestra competing directly with white dance bands such as Sam Lanin's and Paul Whiteman's for work in elite, whites-only downtown clubs and for market share among both black and white consumers of recorded music. His success in these venues was based on several factors. The Henderson orchestra was a disciplined, sophisticated, musically educated unit of young black instrumentalists who could read virtually any music put in front of them. Their talent and versatility made it possible not only to play "sweet music" (waltzes, foxtrots, and other "refined" dances) for their audience, but also to adapt quickly to trends, such as orchestrating increasingly popular blues songs into a polished, danceable form, or including "hot" jazz and blues-inflected solos in an otherwise "sweet" repertoire. Thus the Henderson band of 1923 and 1924 was not a jazz ensemble but a dance ensemble that could perform at the highest levels of the profession and attract black and white audiences alike.

Nevertheless, in this early ensemble there were two men who would move Henderson toward the new jazz style in the mid-1920s and significantly influence the direction of jazz. Coleman Hawkins, a brilliant young soloist who would become the most important

tenor saxophonist during the first half of the twentieth century, joined the band in 1923. More important, that same year Don Redman, a college-educated multi-reed player from West Virginia, began his four-year stint as chief arranger with Henderson. Redman laid the foundation for jazz arranging by his inventive use of call-and-response patterns between brass and reed sections and his ability to integrate ensemble playing and improvised solos.

In the autumn of 1924, the Roseland Ballroom gave Henderson money to expand his orchestra to include four brass and three reeds. The additions allowed Redman to experiment with a larger ensemble and brought to the band the clarinetist Buster Bailey and the cornet player Louis Armstrong, both from King Oliver's Creole Jazz Band in Chicago. Armstrong's effect was immediate and profound, for both the commercial and the musical fortunes of the band. Both men, especially Armstrong, were wildly popular with the crowd at Roseland. From the first night, dancers and even people passing on the street stopped to listen to Armstrong's brilliant sound. When Henderson introduced his orchestra with Armstrong to Harlem at the Lafayette Theater later that year, Armstrong established himself as the new trumpet king of New York. The demand for the band grew nationally, and Henderson began touring one week per month during the autumn of 1925. Moreover, Armstrong's melodically innovative and driving jazz improvisations influenced virtually all who heard him. Trumpet players tried to imitate his fire and style. Coleman Hawkins and other instrumentalists moved toward more modern jazz performance, and Don Redman incorporated Armstrong's ideas into his arrangements for the ensemble.

Armstrong's departure in the autumn of 1925 did not at all hinder the band's musical or commercial development. Henderson added new musicians who were more familiar with jazz improvisation and began increasing the number of jazz pieces, as opposed to popular dance numbers, in the repertoire. This indicated not only musical maturity but also an increased interest in jazz among consumers of popular music, both in nightclubs and on records. By 1928, the Henderson orchestra had shifted from a versatile dance ensemble with "hot" jazz soloists to becoming one of the top jazz bands of the era. Although Redman left in 1927, Henderson attracted some of the best talent in the business, including the trumpeters Rex Stewart, Tommy Ladnier, and Cootie Williams and the saxophonist Benny Carter, who soon became principal arranger. While the band maintained a home base at

Roseland, frequent tours took it across the East and Midwest. The demand for the Henderson orchestra was such that Henderson established a band under his brother's leadership to cover any dates for which he was already booked.

Fletcher Henderson and his orchestra, at their peak, represented the closest approximation to "New Negro" ideals found in jazz. After his marriage in 1924, Henderson and his family moved to Strivers' Row and often took in young, aspiring musicians as boarders. He consistently demonstrated a commitment to improving his race, performing benefits for African American charities, including the Defense Fund of the National Association for the Advancement of Colored People (NAACP) and the Brotherhood Fraternity, which raised funds for the education of young black men. Also, following the example of the Clef Club (a black musicians' union that had been formed in 1910), Henderson insisted on discipline, professionalism, and excellent skills in reading music, none of which had been associated with the improvisatory, bawdy, "uncivilized" nature of early jazz. Henderson had filled his orchestra primarily with young, professional, educated black musicians of middle-class origins who shared his aspirations for musicianship and respectability, aspirations that included work in the elite downtown dance clubs. It was a model of a striving, professional, musical organization that many others, including the young Duke Ellington, would follow.

The reaction among African Americans to the Henderson orchestra, however, was mixed. It was a great source of pride for most, and in 1927 the Chicago *Defender* identified Henderson's outfit as "the greatest orchestra of the Race." Members of Ellington's band feared battles with the Henderson outfit, knowing that their defeat was virtually preordained. Yet its success among white audiences and its more polished sound led to charges that its music was "adulterated" and was meant "for the white man's consumption" after Henderson opened the Savoy Ballroom in 1926. For the "talented tenth," embarrassed by the cultural and musical rough edges of jazz, Henderson's more composed music and sophisticated image were a comfort; the African American professional was assured that he could, in the words of David Levering Lewis, still enjoy the jazz of the Henderson band "at the Savoy without being downright savage about it."

After 1928, the band's fortunes began to decline. Following a serious automobile accident in August

Fletcher Henderson. (Brown Brothers.)

1928, Henderson lost interest in the business of running an orchestra, and he began to fall into debt in 1930. Forced to disband in 1934, he reconstituted his outfit the next year, attracting but failing to hold several of the most talented young jazz musicians of the period. A six-week stand at the Grand Terrace Ballroom in Chicago, including a contract with NBC radio, provided the band with one final commercial success, a release of the song "Christopher Columbus" in 1936.

In 1930, Henderson began to write arrangements for his orchestra; and when Benny Goodman needed jazz material for his big band's radio program "Let's Dance" in 1934, the producer John Hammond introduced him to Henderson, who sold twenty-seven of his arrangements to Goodman. These pieces formed the foundation of Goodman's repertoire during his rise to stardom in 1935. In all, Henderson probably contributed between 300 and 400 arrangements to Goodman's orchestra, and many bandleaders, including Count Basie, Chick Webb, Ray Noble, and Tommy Dorsey, performed Henderson's music. At the height of the swing era, Henderson was recognized as among the greatest arrangers in jazz.

Henderson's work behind the scenes in helping Goodman, a white clarinetist, become the "king of swing," and his competition with the bandleader Paul Whiteman, known as the "king of jazz," a decade before has been central to the academic debates over the place of African American music in twentieth-century America. Caught among competing visions of African American culture in a racially divided America, however, Henderson and his orchestra responded as so many other jazz musicians did—by simply revolutionizing American music above the din of academic arguments.

Biography

James Fletcher "Smack" Henderson was born in Cuthbert, Georgia, on 18 December 1897. He was educated at Atlanta University College Prep (1911–1912, 1913–1916) and Atlanta University (as a chemistry major, 1916–1920). He was a song plugger for Pace and Handy Music Publishing Company (1920–1921); was musical director and pianist for Black Swan Records (1921–1923); toured with Ethel Waters and the Black Swan Troubadours (1921–1922); made recordings with Waters, Rosa Henderson, Alberta Hunter, Turner Layton, Bessie Smith, Trixie Smith, Lena Wilson, J. Arthur Gaines, and Ravella Hughes (1921–1924); made recordings on the Black Swan, Paramount, Emerson, Brunswick, Columbia, Victor, Vocalion, and Decca labels; led the Henderson Dance Orchestra (1922–1923); was featured at Club Alabam (1924); had Louis Armstrong in his orchestra (1924–1925); performed at Roseland Ballroom (steadily, 1924–1928; intermittently, 1929–1936); had a contract with WHN radio (1924–1930); made regional and national tours (1924–1934); played at the grand opening of the Savoy Ballroom (March 1926); had a six-week engagement at the Pompeiian Room, Congress Hotel, Chicago (1927); conducted the orchestra for the musical *Great Day* (1929, but never made it to Broadway); had a contract with WABC radio (1930–1932); moved from Roseland to Connie's Inn (1930–1931); disbanded his orchestra because of financial difficulties (1934); formed a new orchestra (1935–1939); had his last commercial success, the song "Christopher Columbus" (1936); began arranging for Benny Goodman (1934); was a staff arranger with Goodman (1937–1941); was a pianist with the Benny Goodman Orchestra (1939); performed in the concert "Spirituals to Swing" (December 1939); formed another new band, which played intermittently (1941–1947); and appeared in reunion concerts with Ethel Waters (1948–1950). Henderson died in Harlem on 29 December 1952.

WILLIAM J. NANCARROW

See also Armstrong, Louis; Black Swan Phonograph Corporation; Clef Club; Music: Bands and Orchestras; Jazz; Lafayette Theater; Pace, Harry H.; Roseland Ballroom; Savoy Ballroom; Waters, Ethel; *other specific musicians*

Selected Recordings of the Fletcher Henderson Orchestra

"The Dicty Blues." 1923.
"Go Long Mule." 1924.
"Shanghai Shuffle." 1924.
"Copenhagen." 1924.
"Sugarfoot Stomp." 1925. (Arranged by Henderson, 1931.)
"The Stampede." 1926. (Composed by Henderson.)
"Henderson Stomp." 1926. (Composed by Henderson.)
"Whiteman Stomp." 1927.
"Variety Stomp." 1927. (Co-composed by Henderson.)
"King Porter Stomp." 1933. (Arranged by Henderson.)
"Down South Camp Meeting." 1934. (Composed and arranged by Henderson.)
"Wrappin' It Up." 1934. (Composed and arranged by Henderson.)
"Christopher Columbus." 1936.

Further Reading

Allen, Walter C. *Hendersonia: The Music of Fletcher Henderson and His Musicians—A Bio-Discography*. Highland Park, N.J.: Walter C. Allen, 1973.

Audibert, Michel. *Fletcher Henderson et son orchestre 1924–1951: sa place dans l'histoire du jazz*. Bayonne, France: Michel Audibert, 1983.

Charters, Samuel, and Leonard Kunstadt. *Jazz: A History of the New York Scene*. Garden City, N.Y., 1962.

Driggs, Frank, and John Hammond. Liner notes. *A Study in Frustration: The Fletcher Henderson Story, Thesaurus of Classic Jazz*. Columbia/Legacy Records, 1961 (LP), 1994 (CD).

Lewis, David Levering. *When Harlem Was in Vogue*. New York: Knopf, 1981.

Magee, Jeffrey Stanford. "The Music of Fletcher Henderson and His Orchestra in the 1920s." Ph.D. dissertation, University of Michigan, 1992.

Schuller, Gunther. *Early Jazz: Its Roots and Musical Development*. Oxford and New York: Oxford University Press, 1968.

Stewart, Rex. "Smack! Memories of Fletcher Henderson." *Down Beat*, 32, 3 June 1965.

Herskovits, Melville

In 1896, nine years after his arrival from Germany, Franz Boas received a permanent appointment in anthropology at Columbia University. Almost immediately, he became the leading anthropological voice in America, and his students Melville Herskovits, Margaret Meade, Ruth Benedict, Alfred Krober, and Edward Sapir would become dominant authorities as well far into the twentieth century. Boas was important for his criticism of the "scientific racism" that dominated European and American thought and his argument that cultures (the "genius of a people") were diverse, were independent, and had an internal integrity of their own. As a result, such prominent black intellectuals as W. E. B. Du Bois, Alain Locke, Walter White, Carter G. Woodson, Charles S. Johnson, Arthur Schomburg, and Zora Neale Hurston all sought his counsel throughout the 1920s and 1930s. As Hutchinson (1995) has noted, Boas's concepts "became bedrock assumptions among 'New Negro' authors of virtually every persuasion." Melville Herskovits had nearly the same importance, especially in his relationship with Locke and Hurston. Whereas most of Boas's students focused their attention on Native American cultures, Herskovits devoted his life to the study of Africa and the transmission of African culture to the new world.

In 1924, after completing his dissertation "The Cattle Complex in East Africa," Herskovits met Locke in New York City; the two soon became friends as well as intellectual collaborators. Herskovits's anthropometric studies in Harlem (the measuring of African Americans to help disprove the argument that race was a fixed and unvarying constant) and such articles as "The Cultural Approach to Sociology" (1923) helped clarify for Locke theoretical distinctions between race and culture that he would make in "The Concept of Race as Applied to Social Culture" (1924). As a result, it was now possible for Locke to turn his attention to the symbolic dimensions of racial identity. Thus the genesis of Locke's *The New Negro* (1925) was, in part, in this understanding that race "determines the stressed values which become the conscious symbols and tradition of culture." At the same time, Locke was of assistance to Herskovits, helping him obtain a teaching position at Howard University in Washington, D.C., where he gave the course "Introduction to Physical Anthropology" and was able to continue gathering anthropometric evidence to extend his studies of race. Also, at Locke's invitation, Herskovits contributed to *The New Negro* an essay called "The Negro's Americanism," in which he argued that Harlem was "essentially not different from any other American community" but was "the same pattern, only a different shade." Locke was not entirely pleased with this argument; he structured *The New Negro* to emphasize that culturally and temperamentally, blacks were distinguished from whites and that Harlem was not just like any other American community.

As a result of his relationship with Locke and Ernest Just at Howard, the vitality and diversity of *The New Negro*, and his own observation that blacks were consolidating as a social group, Herskovits began to revise the assimilationist emphasis he had made in "The Negro's Americanism." In *The American Negro* (1928), Herskovits argued that a race was not so much a homogeneous biological group as a cultural group. This shift in point of view eventually led to his classic work *The Myth of the Negro Past* (1941), in which he explored the African cultural heritage of African Americans. As a consequence, Herskovits increasingly turned his attention to cultural factors to help explain what science had revealed but could not fully explain. In 1926, Herskovits outlined to the National Research Council his hope of tracing the cultural roots of African Americans by returning to "the great African collections of the major European ethnological museums." Later, with the help of Boas and Elsie Clews Parsons, he did research in West Africa (Dahomey, Nigeria, and the Gold Coast), Suriname, and the Caribbean (Trinidad and Haiti). His work in the Dutch colony of Suriname on descendants of runaway slaves, the Saramaka, led to *Rebel Destiny* (1934), an almost novelistic rendering intended to help capture the "temperamental base" that Locke had emphasized, and *Suriname Folklore* (1936). Throughout these years Herskovits kept in touch with Locke. Their shared interest in Africa and African culture had long been a major strand of their friendship.

When Herskovits first began measuring in Harlem in 1924, Zora Neale Hurston was one of his

Melville and Frances Herskovits. (Schomburg Center for Research in Black Culture, New York Public Library.)

assistants. For the next ten years, however, they saw little of each other. During that time, Hurston had been doing fieldwork in the South and in the Bahamas and kept in close contact with Boas and Ruth Benedict, and Herskovits had taken a position at Northwestern University in 1927. Then Hurston was persuaded by Boas that she should study with Herskovits for a Ph.D. in anthropology, so she and Herskovits were once again in contact. Although Hurston's plans for graduate work failed to materialize, Herskovits would play a significant role as an adviser and personal friend as she expanded the research she had begun in the American South into the Caribbean. As their correspondence suggests, her interest in African American culture and in the African diaspora—in particular, the complex spiritual world of the African maroon communities in Jamaica and Haiti—was what she shared most directly with Herskovits. In *Tell My Horse*, her study of these two islands, she praised him as the one person who had written about voodoo (in his *Life in a Haitian Village*) and actually knew something about it.

Herskovits taught at Northwestern until the end of his life. He became the first chair of the Department of Anthropology in 1938, and ten years later he established the program of African studies. In 1961, he was appointed to the chair of African studies, the first position of its kind in the United States.

Biography

Melville Jean Herskovits was born on 10 September 1895, in Bellefontaine, Ohio. He studied at the University of Chicago (A.B., 1920), Columbia University (Ph.D., 1923), and the New School of Social Research in New York. He taught at Columbia University (1924 and 1927); Howard University, Washington, D.C. (1925); and Northwestern University (1927–1963). Herskovits was a founding member and first president of the African Studies Association (1957–1958) and an officer in other organizations, including the American Anthropological Association, American Association for the Advancement of Science, American Folklore Society, International Anthropology Congress, and First International Congress of Africanists, 1962. He was an adviser to the Mayor's Committee on Race Relations (Chicago, 1945) and the U.S. Senate Foreign Relations Committee (1959–1960). He died on 25 February 1963.

MARK HELBLING

See also Boas, Franz; Hurston, Zora Neale; Locke, Alain; New Negro, The

Selected Works

"The Cattle Complex in East Africa." *American Anthropologist*, 1926.
The American Negro: A Study in Racial Crossing. 1928.
"Race Relations in the U.S." *American Journal of Sociology*, 1928.
Rebel Destiny. 1934.
Suriname Folklore. 1936.
Life in a Haitian Village. 1937.
The Economic Life of Primitive People. 1940.
The Myth of the Negro Past. 1941.
Man and His Works. 1948.
Continuity and Change in African Culture. 1959.
The Human Factor in Changing Africa. 1962.
Economic Transition in Africa. 1964.
The New World Negro: Selected Papers in Afroamerican Studies. 1969.

Further Reading

Helbling, Mark. *The Harlem Renaissance: The One and the Many*. Westport, Conn.: Greenwood, 1999.
Hemenway, Robert. *Zora Neale Hurston: A Literary Biography*. Urbana: University of Illinois Press, 1977.

Hutchinson, George. *The Harlem Renaissance in Black and White*. Cambridge, Mass.: Harvard University Press, 1995.

Jackson, Walter. "Melville Herskovits and the Search for Afro-American Culture." In *Malinowski, Rivers, Benedict, and Others: History of Anthropology*, ed. George Stocking. Madison: University of Wisconsin Press, 1986.

Heyward, DuBose

DuBose Heyward was an unlikely figure to become associated with the Harlem Renaissance, but his novel *Porgy* (1925) was the first major work of fiction by a white southerner to depict African Americans in non-stereotypical ways. It won him the respect and admiration of James Weldon Johnson, Nella Larsen, Jean Toomer, and many others in Harlem's intellectual circles.

Heyward was born in Charleston, South Carolina, in 1885, into a once aristocratic southern family that had been dispossessed and wrecked financially by the Civil War. His widowed mother, Janie, did what she could to keep the family afloat, taking in piecemeal sewing work, operating a boardinghouse on a nearby barrier island, and eventually becoming a local-color writer of some repute. Her subject was the lives and lore of the Gullah Negroes—an ethnically homogeneous subculture that throve on the sea islands in the Southeast. The Gullahs were said to have originated in Angola (hence, "gullah") and to have been imported as a tribe to Georgia and South Carolina rather than split up as most slaves at the time were; thus the Gullahs more than other slaves retained an unusually strong sense of their customs, origins, and tribal bonds. Speaking a glittering metaphorical language that brought to life their myriad folktales and folk songs, the Gullahs appealed to Janie Heyward as a subject for art. She subsequently wrote several books, transcriptions of Gullah tales, for white audiences and later performed them orally as a parlor-room speaker for ladies' afternoon teas up and down the eastern seaboard.

Janie Heyward and John Bennett, who was a local author of children's books and an avid researcher into the ways of the Gullahs, urged Heyward in the early 1920s to give up the work for which he had had to settle—that of an insurance agent—and pursue his dream of a life in art. Together with Heyward's new wife, Dorothy Hartzell Kuhns, they collectively pointed him toward the rich storehouse of untapped artistic material in the Gullah culture of Charleston.

Thus was born *Porgy*, a critical and popular sensation in 1925 because of its honest and undiluted view of the African American—not as the ignorant or shifty darky of nineteenth-century writing, but as a person with the same aims and dreams, thoughts and emotions, as white people, simply emanating from a different culture. Reviewers in both the North and the South uniformly applauded the novel, seeing it as revolutionary for its time.

Heyward was mildly ostracized by some quarters of Charlestonian society for his progressive views. He began to spend less time in Charleston and more time in the mountains of western North Carolina, where he did the bulk of his writing, and in New York, where his wife, a professional playwright, got him interested in theater. Dorothy Heyward drafted a script for a play of *Porgy*, Heyward helped her refine it, and the resulting work was performed in New York in October 1927, once again to great critical acclaim. Many reviewers said that the lush Negro spirituals, which set the emotional mood of the play, were worth the price of admission alone, and the Heywards found themselves adopted by wealthy white New Yorkers and the elite of Harlem as well. Most important, the play *Porgy* helped energize the nascent black theater movement at the time, for the Heywards insisted that the cast be all-black, not white actors in blackface as was the custom. As a result, more headlining roles began to open up for black actors.

Heyward, now famous, continued to pursue this vein of then-new material—the white modernists' interest in primitivism—in his next major novel, *Mamba's Daughters* (1929). This book, a longer and more complex work than *Porgy*, tells the story of three generations of Gullah women and the successive generations' striving to rise above their social and cultural destiny. In this novel, Heyward abandoned the somewhat aloof voice of the white outsider in *Porgy* and adopted instead a much more sympathetic narrative voice, one that clearly champions the attempts of the Gullah women to better their lot in life.

Much of Heyward's fame resulted from the stage dramatizations of his work. In 1939, *Mamba* was performed on Broadway, where it made a star of Ethel Waters in her first major dramatic role. And *Porgy*, of course, became *Porgy and Bess* in 1935—the first American folk opera. Heyward collaborated with George Gershwin and Ira Gershwin in all possible ways on this production. He wrote the libretto single-handedly, carving it out of the play version of the story. Either by himself or in collaboration with Ira Gershwin, he wrote half the arias for the opera. And he also scouted for talent, assisted in rehearsals, and performed other production chores. *Porgy and Bess*, however, was a relative failure, commercially and critically, when it first opened: Black critics objected to what they considered to be the stereotyped portrayal of African Americans; white critics carped over whether the work was a legitimate opera or a Broadway musical.

Despondent and embittered by New Yorkers' insensitivity to *Porgy and Bess*, into which he had poured nine years of labor and love, Heyward beat a retreat from the glitterati and returned to his roots in Charleston. He published some more novels, taking a more overt social-critical angle; and he involved himself in local

DuBose Heyward, 1931. (Library of Congress.)

historic preservation efforts and in a playwriting group that had attached itself to a newly restored eighteenth-century theater.

Heyward died of a heart attack at age fifty-four in 1940, just three years after George Gershwin's death. Both men died thinking that *Porgy and Bess* had been a failure, but it was actually their greatest success; it has since achieved literary and musical immortality.

Biography

Edwin DuBose Heyward was born on 31 August 1885, in Charleston, South Carolina, and studied at Boys' High School there. He was a cofounder of the Poetry Society of South Carolina (1920), was editor of its *Year Book* (1921–1923), was elected its president in 1924, and resigned in 1925. He toured Europe in 1927. He received a D.Litt. from the University of North Carolina in 1928. He took a second trip abroad, to the Mediterranean and the Holy Land, and was made an honorary doctor of letters by the College of Charleston in 1929. He attended the Southern Writers Conference in Charlottesville, Virginia, with Faulkner, Glasgow, and others (1931). Heyward was the first South Carolinian elected to the National Institute of Arts and Letters. He was awarded an honorary degree from the University of South Carolina and cruised to the Virgin Islands in 1937. He was named resident director of the Dock Street Theater in Charleston in 1939. Heyward died at age fifty-four in Tryon, North Carolina, on 16 June 1940.

JAMES M. HUTCHISSON

See also Gershwin, George; Johnson, James Weldon; Larsen, Nella; Porgy and Bess; Porgy: Novel; Porgy: Play; Toomer, Jean; Waters, Ethel

Selected Works

"Poetry South." *Poetry*, 20, April 1922, pp. 35–48. (With Hervey Allen.)
Carolina Chansons, Legends of the Low Country. 1922. (With Hervey Allen.)
Skylines and Horizons. 1924.
Porgy. 1925.
"The New Note in Southern Literature." *Bookman*, 61, April 1925, pp. 153–156.
Porgy: A Play. 1927. (With Dorothy Heyward.)
Mamba's Daughters. 1929.

The Half Pint Flask. 1929.

Jasbo Brown and Selected Poems. 1931.

Peter Ashley. 1932.

Porgy and Bess. 1935. (With George Gershwin and Ira Gershwin.)

Lost Morning. 1936.

Star Spangled Virgin. 1939.

Mamba's Daughters: A Play. 1939. (With Dorothy Heyward.)

Further Reading

Alpert, Hollis. *The Life and Times of Porgy and Bess.* New York: Knopf, 1989.

Durham, Frank. *DuBose Heyward: The Man Who Wrote "Porgy."* Columbia: University of South Carolina Press, 1954.

Hutchisson, James M. *DuBose Heyward: A Charleston Gentleman and the World of Porgy and Bess.* Jackson: University Press of Mississippi, 2000.

Higher Education

Ever since Alain Locke's seminal essay "Enter the New Negro" (1925), the term "New Negro" has usually been reduced to its linkage with the authors and literature of the Harlem Renaissance. As used in the 1920s, however, the term referred to more than the active writers of the Harlem Renaissance: it also included the African American masses and especially the young. "For the younger generation," Locke wrote, "is vibrant with a new psychology" (1969, 3). This new spirit, which Locke attributed to a renewal of self-respect and independence, was nowhere more evident during the 1920s than on black college and university campuses.

The 1920s represented the real beginnings of modern public as well as private black higher education, although that aspect of the decade is usually overlooked in most discussions and analyses. These years witnessed the first significant growth in the population of African American as well as African college students in the United States, ongoing efforts at the modernization of the curriculum, the emergence of modern intercollegiate spectator sports such as football, and increased personal freedom for students on campus. The decade also witnessed the appearance of students who were not only better prepared academically for the academic rigors of college, but also more mature, assertive, expressive, and militant

at black institutions of higher education—all traits that characterized the New Negro of the Harlem Renaissance.

The new confidence that characterized students of color specifically and members of their race generally in the 1920s resulted from many forces. Before World War I, militant new leaders, such as W. E. B. Du Bois, had emerged, demanding full civil rights and an immediate end to racial segregation and thereby inspiring greater self-assertiveness among African Americans. The "great migration" to the urban North further disrupted old patterns of life and created new hopes as well as new problems. The fight abroad to make the world safe for democracy during World War I led to greater expectations at home, despite the bloody race riots of 1919. As African Americans entered the 1920s, it was clear that their long journey down the desert years of history had strengthened, not weakened, their resolve to improve their lives.

Important changes occurred in black higher education during the decade. An essential characteristic of black colleges and universities during the 1920s was their first emergence as institutions of higher education after nearly half a century as poverty-stricken elementary and secondary schools. The chief factor that brought them into existence was the growth of a system of public education for African Americans in the South. This system, by creating a demand for teachers, made their preparation the focus of the black colleges' mission. The education of teachers set in motion a complex supply—demand chain in which the availability of teaching positions drew students into the colleges to qualify for these positions. The growth of this total system of racially segregated public education not only was responsible for the development of black higher education but also ascribed to it an indispensable role as the source of manpower for black education and, ultimately, placed it in intellectual and pedagogical control over that system—defining the content, establishing methods, setting standards, and, as the sole outlet for the system, serving as a criterion for its success.

Many forces converged to make this happen. Among these was a change in the economic fortunes of black higher education after 1900. This is attributable to the appearance of two large and purposeful private philanthropic agencies—the Rosenwald Fund and the General Education Board—which were concerned with the improvement of educational opportunities for African Americans. Moreover, there was some improvement in public support for black schools as a result of the positive effect that World War I had on the nation's economy. In educational terms, this meant that the demand for education rose and more public money from rising taxes and private charitable dollars went into schools. As the demand for teachers rose, the educational requirements for teachers rose too, and public funds had to be used to improve teacher training—some of which was directed toward the African American community. These conditions led to the growth of black colleges and an improvement in both physical plants and faculties as well as the academic quality of students who enrolled in these institutions.

Improved economic conditions also made higher education a goal for more African American young people during the 1920s. Between 1919–1920 and 1929–1930, the undergraduate enrollments at fifty-seven four-year black colleges and universities grew from 9,589 to 16,392. During this period, the largest increase in enrollments occurred at thirty black four-year colleges, more than doubling from 4,473 to 10,222. Significantly, the total undergraduate enrollment at these schools was about equally divided among male and female students: 5,116 and 5,110, respectively. This growth in enrollment at private black colleges would continue uninterrupted until 1953. A similar increase occurred at twenty-seven black public colleges, where enrollments grew from 3,720 in 1919–1920 to 6,170 by 1929–1930—an upward trend that would continue uninterrupted to the present day (Bowles and De Costa 1971, 52, 55).

The publication of the Phelps-Stokes Fund's *Jones Report* in 1916 also helped bring about the demise of many marginal and substandard black institutions, which were colleges or universities in name only, and led to the termination of many of the elementary and secondary education divisions in black colleges. As a result, the average age of students at these institutions increased. Thus, by 1920, the average age of the student body at black colleges began to approach the modern norm of seventeen to eighteen years for college freshmen. Moreover, because of the great migration, a larger proportion of students not only came from urban areas and from improved public school systems but also were high school graduates and so were better prepared for the academic rigors of college. Finally, a higher number of students came from families in which one or both parents had received some postsecondary schooling. All of these changes had, by the 1920s, created a type of student who was less willing than his or her predecessors to tolerate the all-encompassing petty restrictions on stu-

dent life on campus that characterized the traditional system of discipline at black colleges.

The 1920s were also noteworthy for the appearance of African Americans on the scholarly scene, in the pages of *Journal of Negro History*, *Opportunity*, and *Survey Graphic,* who would contribute to the future intellectual growth of black higher education as well as the modernization of its curriculum and mission. Their names read like a who's who of twentieth-century scholars. They included the director of Tuskegee University's Bureau of Records and Research and editor of *The Negro Yearbook*, Monroe N. Work; the historians Luther P. Jackson, Lorenzo J. Greene, William Leo Hansberry, and Rayford Logan; the English professor Benjamin Brawley; the folklorists Miles Mark Fisher and Lorenzo D. Turner; and the sociologists E. Franklin Frazier and Charles S. Johnson.

Alain Locke, who is usually credited with playing a major role in defining and promoting the Harlem Renaissance, began his career as a scholar at the nation's premier black educational institution of the 1920s—Howard University. At Howard, Locke was accepted and acclaimed by its dean of arts and sciences, Kelly Miller. Along with his former classmate Montgomery Gregory, Locke organized the Howard Players. In addition, African American scholars organized into a group known as the Sanhedrin under the joint leadership of Locke and Miller. Locke organized Howard's first literary journal, *Stylus*. He helped in the organization of Howard's art gallery and the music department, for he believed strongly that general and cultural education was a desirable goal for African American students. Locke devoted much of his own teaching to the new science of anthropology, social conflict, and social theory during this period.

Before the 1920s, the system of rules and regulations governing students at black colleges and universities was an all-encompassing web of Victorian paternalism that intruded on nearly every aspect of student life. Students were told when to rise in the morning, when to retire at night, and even what to wear. Daily attendance at campus convocations or chapel services was mandatory. Students and their dormitory rooms were required to be neat and clean. The use of alcohol and tobacco by students as well as card-playing, dancing, and whatever else teachers and administrators considered immoral or opposed to true culture was forbidden. Fraternities and sororities were also prohibited.

Some African American students had naturally objected to the regimentation imposed by these campus rules and regulations even before the 1920s, but such discipline was tolerable in the late nineteenth century, when it was thought to be prompted by Christian piety and was applied to white and black students alike. Yet the tradition of piety remained in force at black institutions of higher education long after the leading white colleges deemphasized their concern for the moral uplift of students and began to stress secular scholarship. African American students suspected that the continuation of the strict discipline governing their lives at black colleges during the 1920s was prompted by the belief that Africans were especially sensuous beings who lacked self-discipline and restraint and were incapable of exercising free will. Behind this view, they believed, lay the fear that if African Americans were allowed to exercise personal freedom, they would become a threat to white civilization.

The spirit of W. E. B. Du Bois—editor of the magazine *The Crisis*—hovered over the black college rebellions of the 1920s. He instigated the confrontation at Fisk University and publicized and celebrated African American student protests nationwide. Throughout the 1920s Du Bois wrote editorials and articles excoriating the so-called corrupt bargain between philanthropists and the white South, which forced black institutions of higher learning to compromise both their mission and their principles in return for money. He lamented the fact that African Americans' dependence on the rich for donations to absolutely necessary causes made it increasingly difficult for them to exercise intelligence, apply frank and honest criticism, and achieve freedom and self-respect. African Americans' fear of retribution for challenging the system, in Du Bois's opinion, sapped the manhood of the race, bred cowards and sycophants, and crucified honest men and women. For Du Bois, therefore, black college student protests of the 1920s involved nothing less than the tremendous question of whether African American young people were to be trained as they and their parents wished or as white southerners and their northern allies demanded.

Yet Du Bois believed that African American students of the 1920s had come of age. They should no longer tolerate the sort of petty dictation that had seemed natural in the early days of black higher education when African Americans were no more than a generation removed from slavery. Du Bois considered African American students free men and women. While acknowledging that African American parents wanted their children reared under all necessary con-

straints, he noted that at the same time they demanded for young people the equally necessary freedom and self-respect which were essential to the development of responsible adults.

The challenge to parietal rules and regulations governing student life at black colleges broke forth with unprecedented force following World War I. In the spring of 1920, students at Wilberforce University boycotted classes to protest a faculty resolution restricting social intermingling between male and female students on campus. Two years later, students at Storer College struck to protest the expulsion of three males who had been involved in an altercation with local whites. In 1923, most of the student body at Livingstone College went on strike during much of May; some students left the college for good. Demanding more "freedom of choice," students at Howard University went on strike in 1925 to protest compulsory Reserve Officers' Training Corps (ROTC) for males and overly strict enforcement of military requirements by university officials. That same year students at W. E. B. Du Bois's alma mater, Fisk University, began a classroom boycott to demand fewer social restrictions and demonstrate support for fellow students who had been expelled for allegedly participating in an earlier campus protest. In 1927, students at Hampton Institute staged a bitter and protracted boycott to protest the arbitrary enforcement of parietal rules and regulations, which led to the expulsion of sixty-nine undergraduates and to probation for hundreds more. Student unrest at Wilberforce, Howard, Fisk, and Hampton received the most attention in the African American press, but there were reports of at least ten additional student protests and boycotts at black institutions of higher education, including Knoxville College, Lincoln University in Pennsylvania, Shaw, Alcorn A&M, Lincoln University in Missouri, Saint Augustine, and Johnson C. Smith.

Another correlative of the mentality of the New Negro, which manifested itself at black colleges and universities during the 1920s, was an increased demand for competitive sports. Although attempts to develop intercollegiate athletics in black higher education had begun in the 1890s, such efforts did not bear real fruit until after World War I. By the 1920s, nearly every black college and university sponsored teams in football, baseball, basketball, and track and field. The jubilation and pageantry of these contests were exemplified in a ritual unique to football games at black colleges in the 1920s that was known as the "rabbles," in which well-dressed students poured out of the stands at halftime and—to the accompaniment of music provided by some of their peers—danced around the field in a free-flowing exhibition. Significantly, female students at black colleges began participating in intercollegiate basketball and track contests during the 1920s; in this regard, black colleges not only afforded women more opportunities to compete but also accorded more prestige to their accomplishments than white institutions of higher education (P. Miller 1995, 119–120). Thus, as a response to prevailing notions of blacks' and women's inferiority, organized athletics at black colleges constituted a telling assertion of pride and accomplishment.

The 1920s were also noteworthy for the appearance of an appreciable number of African students in the United States, many of whom were enrolled at black colleges and universities. In a program initiated by the Phelps-Stokes Fund, Hampton and Tuskegee institutes were selected as hosts for African students from British colonies in Africa in the early 1920s. Although the goal of the program was to train Africans who would passively accept colonial rule in their homelands, the results were quite the opposite. At Tuskegee, the African history classes of Professor Simbini M. Nkomo—who was variously described as being from present-day Madagascar, Zimbabwe, and South Africa—deliberately attempted to communicate the spirit of incipient nationalism or racial-self-evaluation, which he regarded as the foundation of true progress for Africans. One observer of Tuskegee's African students remarked that all of them displayed a pan-African consciousness, an attitude assisted, in no small part, by the African American milieu in which African students could immerse themselves. Nkomo's efforts led to the founding of the African Student Union of America (ASU). The agenda of the organization's fourth annual conference at Tuskegee Institute included items ranging from misrepresentations of African life and history to cooperation between African and African American students. "The ASU presented its members with the concrete need to prepare themselves for leading their own people, and inspired them with the determination to take independent action if need be" (King 1971, 221). In 1925, the future leader of independent Nigeria, Benjamin Nmandi Azikwe, arrived in the United States to begin his undergraduate studies. As a student, Azikwe not only learned everything he could about political science from his American professors but also participated in a brief student protest at Lincoln University.

Although most African and African American youths attended black institutions of higher education, a small number were enrolled at northern white private and public colleges and universities during the 1920s. The exact number of students of color who attended these institutions will probably never be known, but it is possible to identify some of them. The historians William Leo Hansberry, William M. Brewer, Alrutheus A. Taylor, and Charles H. Wesley received bachelor's or graduate degrees or both from Harvard between 1919 and 1925. The first African American cabinet member and secretary of the Department of Housing and Urban Development, Robert C. Weaver, graduated from Harvard University in 1929. The teacher and anthropologist Caroline Bond Day, the composer and writer Marieta Bonner, the singer Lola Wilson Hayes, and the future chairman of Howard University's French department, Theodora R. Boyd, all received bachelor's degrees from Radcliffe College. Both Zora Neale Hurston and Langston Hughes attended Columbia University. Hughes left after a year, finding the atmosphere uncongenial to his tastes, but Hurston remained at Columbia, where she was a student of the anthropologist Franz Boas. Under Boas's guidance she began research on African American folklore and religion, much of which was later incorporated into her novels, such as *Mules and Men*, *Jonah's Gourd Vine*, and *Their Eyes Were Watching God*. Countee Cullen attended New York University, from which he graduated in 1923, and received a master's degree from Harvard University. The African American educator William Allison Davis attended Williams College; he graduated summa cum laude in 1924 and was the class valedictorian. Wallace Thurman, author of *The Blacker the Berry* (1929) and *Infants of the Spring* (1932), attended the University of Utah and the University of Southern California.

The matriculation of African American students at white colleges was, at best, only tolerated during the 1920s. "A dozen little discriminations annoy you," one African American undergraduate confessed in 1927, "discriminations that you have known all your life, but you hoped to escape" at college. You can "never hope to play" on your college's team or "belong to literary societies or pep organizations or any other extracurricular activities," he complained. The white students "shun you except when they want something." Nor could they "refer to you in the singular." An African American student was "always addressed as one of 'you fellows.' You can't understand why you can never be an individual" (L. Miller 1927, 138). In what was perhaps one of the most egregious instances of racial harassment during the decade, Halston V. Eagleson, an African American undergraduate at Indiana University–Bloomington, was kidnapped by three white students in 1922 and taken to Spencer, Indiana. There he was arrested and jailed briefly to prevent him from earning his letter in band. Despite efforts by the Eagleson family to press charges against the perpetrators, the case was dismissed for lack of evidence (Halsell Gilliam 1985, 41).

African Americans of the 1920s stood in opposition to the tradition of paternalism that characterized black colleges and the unapologetic racism of white institutions of higher education. Prompted by a growing racial consciousness and greater ambition, African American students demanded greater respect and independence for themselves as well as a better quality of life on their campuses. They discarded past notions of what type of education was best suited for them and demanded a greater say in their own lives as well as the educational institutions that were supposed to prepare them for the challenges of modern society and advance the race. They wanted to escape from the backwaters of American life and join the mainstream. In their struggle to do so, students and faculties not only helped reform the curriculum of black institutions of higher education but also transformed the extracurricular activities of these schools. African American students attending the nation's white colleges put those schools on notice as well that they were no longer willing to accept racial discrimination in silence. In these and countless other ways, black colleges, students, and faculty members both reflected and contributed to the mythos of the New Negro during the 1920s.

MONROE LITTLE

See also Association for the Study of Negro Life and History and Journal of Negro History; Boas, Franz; Brawley, Benjamin; Crisis, The; Cullen, Countee; Du Bois, W. E. B.; Frazier, E. Franklin; Greene, Lorenzo; Historically Black Colleges and Universities; Howard University; Hurston, Zora Neale; Johnson, Charles Spurgeon; Locke, Alain; Miller, Kelly; Opportunity; Stylus; Survey Graphic; Thurman, Wallace; Work, Monroe Nathan

Further Reading

Bowles, Frank, and Frank A. De Costa. *Between Two Worlds: A Profile of Negro Higher Education*. New York: McGraw-Hill, 1971. (Fifth of a series of profiles sponsored by the Carnegie Commission on Higher Education.)

Halsell Gilliam, Frances V. *A Time to Speak: A Brief History of the Afro-Americans of Bloomington, Indiana, 1865–1965*. Bloomington, Ind.: Pinus Strobus, 1985.

Holmes, Eugene C. "Alain Locke and the New Negro Movement." *Negro American Literature Forum*, 2(3, Protest and Propaganda Literature), Autumn 1968, pp. 60–68.

Jones, Maxine D., and Joe M. Richardson. *Talladega College: The First Century*. Tuscaloosa: University of Alabama Press, 1990.

King, Kenneth James. *Pan-Africanism and Education: A Study of Race, Philanthropy, and Education in the Southern States of America and East Africa*. New York: Oxford University Press, 1971.

Locke, Alain. "The New Negro." In *The New Negro*, ed. Alain Locke. New York: Atheneum, 1969.

Logan, Rayford W. *Howard University: The First Hundred Years, 1867–1967*. New York: New York University Press, 1969.

Miller, Loren. "College." *Crisis*, 33(3), January 1927, pp. 138–140.

Miller, Patrick B. "To 'Bring the Race Along Rapidly': Sport, Student Culture, and Educational Mission at Historically Black Colleges during the Interwar Years." *History of Education Quarterly*, 35(2), Summer 1995, pp. 111–133.

Sollors, Werner, et al., eds. *Blacks at Harvard: A Documentary History of African American Experience at Harvard and Radcliffe*. New York: New York University Press, 1993.

Wolters, Raymond. *The New Negro on Campus: Black College Rebellions of the 1920s*. Princeton, N.J.: Princeton University Press, 1975.

Historically Black Colleges and Universities

In 1927, 13,580 students were enrolled at predominantly black colleges and universities, while another 1,500 black students were enrolled at predominantly white colleges. This was a sixfold increase over the 2,132 African Americans who had been enrolled in college only a decade earlier ("Enrollment" 1928). As their numbers increased, the black college students and alumni of the 1920s demanded a different and higher type of education. These demands were manifest in many student strikes and alumni revolts.

These rebellions should be understood in context. The "New Negroes" on campus were responding to the growing racial consciousness and the larger ambition that also gave rise to the Harlem Renaissance. This new consciousness was also influenced by a more assertive ethos that developed as a result of blacks' participation in World War I, and it came to the fore against the background of the "great migration" of blacks from the rural South to urban areas. Looming in the more distant background was a long-simmering revolt against the paternalistic spirit and the industrial emphasis that had characterized much of black college education in the past.

Part I

During and after the Civil War, northern benevolent societies and denominational bodies, the Negro church, and the Freedmen's Bureau began the heroic task of educating the freedmen. These missionaries rejected southerners' demands that they begin with industrial and manual training to prepare blacks for skilled work, later add the sequence of elementary and secondary schools, and still later add colleges. They thought they would be wasting money if they established elementary or vocational schools without also providing a college education for teachers. Hence they founded colleges—Fisk, Howard, Hampton, Talladega, Atlanta, and others—which together trained a few thousand teachers who then instructed the masses in the fundamentals of reading, writing, arithmetic, and life.

Yet many white southerners feared that any education of blacks beyond the vocational level would lead to increased dissatisfaction with the inferior status accorded to African Americans in the South. The editor of the New Orleans *Times-Democrat* warned that "the higher education of the Negro unfits him for the work that it is intended that he shall do, and cultivates ambitions that can never be realized" (quoted in "A Blow" 1904). Throughout the South, planters feared that college education would undermine the willingness of blacks to work in the fields and would make African Americans less deferential, submissive, and dependent. Some of them heartily endorsed the contention of Senator James K. Vardaman of Mississippi: "What the North is sending South is not money but dynamite; this education is ruining our Negroes. They're demanding equality" (quoted in Baker 1964).

Many white southerners also said that the missionary teachers had ignored the limited aptitude and capabilities of the Negro. At a time when social Darwinism was in vogue, even some black people thought that the races were at different stages of cultural evolution

and that the educational curriculum should be adjusted accordingly. "The educational requirements of the people who are only a few hundred years out of the jungle are not the same as those of people who have had thousands of years of civilization," the black president of Georgia Normal College explained. "The great mass of our people need to be trained in agriculture, the mechanical arts, the trades and industries, and in the art of homemaking" (Holley 1948).

Given the prevalence of these views, many black colleges proceeded cautiously. Following the example set at Hampton and Tuskegee institutes, they renounced agitation and added vocational courses that promised to make black students more efficient workers. This vocational emphasis was then reinforced with support from secular northern philanthropists associated with the Slater, Jeanes, Phelps-Stokes, and Rosenwald foundations; the Southern Education Board; and the Rockefeller General Education Board. The secular philanthropists took care to avoid alienating the white South. Rather than follow the egalitarian example of the Yankee missionaries, the secular philanthropists fostered vocational training as especially suited to a predetermined, subordinate role for black people in American society.

The trend in this direction was heightened when Congress, through the Smith-Lever and Smith-Hughes acts of 1914 and 1917, rounded out the program of vocational and agricultural training and established a county-agent bureaucracy. The county agents then assumed responsibility for seeing that the land-grant colleges, and especially black institutions, did not stray from the gospel of vocationalism. Together the combination of secular philanthropy and federal aid altered the course of the black colleges and initiated a vocational phase in the history of Negro higher education.

In retrospect it seems inevitable that black college students, even those trained at vocational institutes, would eventually challenge the subordination of their race. Segregation, after all, required that blacks provide their own leaders, and this meant that a critical minority of African Americans had to be trained in medicine, law, journalism, theology, and other professions. Moreover, as it happened, teaching eventually became the most reliable source of employment for black college graduates. Thus even the land-grant A&M colleges, while offering a veneer of vocational courses, enrolled most of their students in teacher-training programs that resembled the studies then in vogue at most white colleges. The black students were segregated, of course, and generally received inferior training, but the ideal of aspiration was preserved.

As a result of World War I and the great migration, many blacks of the 1920s also enjoyed larger social and economic opportunities, and consequently felt a greater need for higher education and professional training. Far from being grateful for the financial aid that the government and secular philanthropy had showered on vocational schools, many black students, professors, and alumni feared that the higher aspirations of the race had been sacrificed in order to obtain money from the ruling powers. They were not prepared to adjust to a subordinate status but instead demanded the right to full participation in American life.

The challenge to subordination broke forth with unprecedented force when blacks returned from the "war to make the world safe for democracy" with a fierce determination to battle against discrimination in their own land. The rising tide of Negro protest was manifest in many ways—in the warfare of the "red summer" of 1919; in Marcus Garvey's black nationalist movement; in the resurgence of black pride celebrated by the artists of the Harlem Renaissance; and in the growth of the National Association for the Advancement of Colored People (NAACP), the Urban League, and the black press. It was evident during the 1920s that "New Negroes" were ascendant in the black community, and they were determined to enjoy all the rights and privileges of American citizens.

The wave of rebellion that engulfed most of the leading black colleges was one of the most significant aspects of the New Negro protest movement. It began at one of the leading vocational institutes. In 1922, when the governor of Florida shifted the emphasis at Florida A&M from teacher training to trade training, students not only went on strike but also burned down the Mechanical Arts Building. Similarly, at Lincoln Institute in Missouri, there was a decade-long struggle between one faction that emphasized vocational training and another that stressed the importance of traditional liberal arts and sciences. And at Hampton Institute, several hundred students were suspended in 1927 after demanding that more emphasis be given to academic subjects. "The complaints with regard to education are possibly unique in the annals of student strikes," the Hampton administration noted, "demanding as they did more and better education" ("The Strike" 1927). One of the suspended students explained that the students had a "Du Bois ambition" that would not mix with a "Booker T. Washington education" (Robert A. Coles, quoted in Baltimore *Afro-American*, 1927).

"Du Bois protest" was also on display at Fisk University, the nation's most prominent liberal arts college for blacks. In 1925, students at Fisk took exception to the suspension of the student newspaper, the *Fisk Herald*, and to the denial of a request for a campus chapter of the NAACP; they also complained about the university's sponsoring of segregated Jim Crow entertainments, and they protested against a draconian code of student discipline that was rigorously enforced and was justified with statements to the effect that black young people were particularly sensuous beings who would abandon themselves to indulgence if they were not subjected to firm control.

To Du Bois it seemed that Fisk had devised a plan that was intended to persuade the elite of black youth to accept a subordinate status, to make them know "their place." He was delighted when, in February 1925, more than one hundred students from Livingstone Hall ignored the ten o'clock curfew and instead sang, yelled, smashed windows, and told the faculty that it would not be safe for any authorities and that they were "going to keep up this sort of thing until the President's hair was white." According to the dean of women, "The disorderly students overturned chapel seats, broke windows, . . . all the while keeping up a steady shouting of 'Du Bois!' 'Du Bois!'" (Scriber 1925). Police were called to the campus to restore order, but this precipitated a student strike of ten weeks' duration. Eventually, a new administration was inaugurated, after the trustees conceded that it was impossible to operate a college without students.

Part II

The black students and alumni of the 1920s aimed at control of their colleges. This did not necessarily mean that the colleges had to be headed by African Americans. In 1925, the rebellious students and alumni at Fisk had demanded only that their white president be ousted, because they thought he had compromised too much with white segregationists and supremacists; they accepted another white man as a replacement, because they found him in sympathy with their basic ideals. The same scenario was repeated at Lincoln University in Pennsylvania in 1926. In each instance, however, the protests on campus elicited elements of racial pride and confidence that some Negroes were capable of presiding over the college.

Going beyond their brothers and sisters at Fisk and Lincoln, who had demanded only that they be given a larger role in the management of their schools, the faculty and alumni at Howard University insisted that an African American should be in charge of their school. They did so because they, like some of the artists of the Harlem Renaissance, were stirred by a new sense of racial pride and self-consciousness. Thus the historian Carter G. Woodson of Howard was convinced that the absence of black leaders, along with the presence of textbooks that emphasized the primitive quality of the African background and the servile character of the black American experience, left many African Americans with the conviction that they were inferior and should accept an underprivileged status. If elite black students were given the impression that the Negro race and its leaders would never amount to much, Woodson said, they would not be prepared to uplift the group. Such students could "hardly find delight in undertaking what [their] education has led [them] to think impossible" (1933).

Similarly, Alain Locke, who was then a professor of philosophy and literature at Howard, concluded that blacks must take control of the university if the students were to develop the confidence needed for leadership. In scores of articles and especially in a remarkable anthology that gave its name, *The New Negro*, to the black arts movement of the decade, Locke celebrated black poetry, fiction, drama, scholarship, music, and art as the necessary foundation for building a self-confident race that could face whites with equanimity (1925a). He feared that if whites remained in control of black colleges, African American young people would succumb to an atmosphere of "spirit-dampening condescension" and would leave the campus as a talented tenth committed not to group service but to bourgeois individualism (1925b).

Like Woodson and Locke, Howard's dean of arts and science, Kelly Miller, and its most prominent sociologist, E. Franklin Frazier, also insisted that the university needed black leaders to inspire its students with enthusiasm for racial service and uplift. They thought that white leadership left many black students with the impression that the Negro race would never measure up and that black collegians consequently would settle for the "materialistic individualism of middle-class American life." They lamented that, instead of preparing "for the uplift of a downtrodden people," black students were "preparing themselves for the professions as a means to wealth and enjoyment" and not as a prerequisite for racial uplift.

Thus these professors joined with the leaders of the Howard Alumni Association in 1925 and 1926 and demanded that James Stanley Durkee, the eleventh in an

Howard University, 1942. (Photograph by John Collier. Library of Congress.)

almost unbroken line of white clergymen-presidents, should be replaced by an African American. Eventually, Mordecai W. Johnson was chosen in 1926 as the first black president of Howard University—a choice that the journal *Christian Century and Christian Work* hailed as "a new milepost in the long pilgrimage of a race" (quoted in "Howard's New President" 1926).

The New Negroes on campus were in revolt against both the industrial emphasis and the paternalistic spirit that had characterized an earlier era of black college education. Prompted by a larger ambition and a growing racial consciousness, the black students and alumni of the 1920s demanded a higher type of curriculum and a greater degree of control over their colleges. They turned their backs on the limited educational program of trade training and, as Du Bois (1921) put it, proposed "to speak for ourselves and to be represented by spokesmen whom we elect. And whenever in any case this policy is contravened we are going to fight that decision in every civilized way, and to the last ditch."

RAYMOND WOLTERS

See also Du Bois, W. E. B.; Frazier, E. Franklin; Garveyism; Higher Education; Howard University; Locke, Alain; Miller, Kelly; Riots: 2—Red Summer of 1919; Woodson, Carter G.

Further Reading

Baker, Ray Stannard. *Following the Color Line*. New York: Harper Torchbook, 1964, p. 247.
Baltimore Afro-American, 19 November 1927.

"A Blow at Negro Education." *Current Literature*, 36, January–June 1904, pp. 491–492.

Du Bois, W. E. B. "Thomas Jesse Jones." *Crisis*, 22, October 1921, p. 256.

"Enrollment in Negro Universities and Colleges." *School and Society*, 28, 29 September 1928, pp. 401–402.

Holley, Joseph Winthrop. *You Can't Build a Chimney From the Top*. New York: William-Frederick, 1948, p. 82.

"Howard's New President." Pamphlet, 1926. (Howard University Archives.)

Locke, Alain, ed. *The New Negro*. New York: Albert and Charles Boni, 1925a.

———. "Negro Education Bids for Par." *Survey*, 54, September 1925b, pp. 570, 593.

Scriber, Dora. Communication to alumni, 14 February 1925. Du Bois Papers, reel 15, frame 0447.

"The Strike at Hampton." *Southern Workman*, 56, 1927, pp. 569–572.

Wolters, Raymond. *The New Negro on Campus: Black College Rebellions of the 1920s*. Princeton, N.J.: Princeton University Press, 1975.

Woodson, Carter G. *The Mis-Education of the Negro*. Washington, D.C.: Associated Publishers, 1933, pp. xxxiii, 6, 55–56.

Hobby Horse

Douglas Howe opened the Hobby Horse bookstore in Harlem some time around 1928, at a time when interest by both blacks and whites in African American literature was at a zenith, yet there were few avenues for making this literature available to the public.

At the time, Harlem was considered the national hub of black culture and artistry. African Americans who were seriously interested in becoming writers, performers, and musicians were eventually likely to make their way there. In Harlem, they found a supportive group of other writers and artists with whom to share their work and ideas. And in the cultural mosaic made up of blacks who had migrated from the South and the Caribbean, they found characters and images that would inhabit their work.

The Hobby Horse, considered the nation's first African American bookstore, was a combination bookstore and tearoom. It was a place where young African American writers and artists could congregate and publicly share their work and where many of Harlem's noted black society matrons met for lunch and afternoon tea. These social gatherings were often reported in black newspapers such as the Chicago *Defender*.

The Hobby Horse was originally located at 205 West 135th Street. This site was in the heart of Harlem's social activity, and Howe had access to many of the established literary and artistic luminaries of the Harlem Renaissance, as well as up-and-coming figures. Not only did the Hobby Horse stock and display books by African Americans, but Sunday evening book discussions were also held there, and—more important—black writers and poets gave readings from their own work. At the Hobby Horse, poets and writers such as Langston Hughes and Zora Neale Hurston found a public venue for both their published works and their works in progress. Howe also exhibited paintings and photographs by many popular visual artists of the day at the Hobby Horse. Among these artists was James Allen (b. 1907), whose photographic portraits of African American and white celebrities of the Harlem Renaissance were often reprinted in the popular black press.

Howe had not been the first to conceive of a bookstore featuring the works of African American writers: Many other literati of the Harlem Renaissance had also sensed a need for such an enterprise and contemplated the idea. Among them was Nella Larsen (the author of *Passing* and *Quicksand*), who began to seek financing for a bookstore in 1926, two years before Howe opened the Hobby Horse. Like Howe, Larsen envisioned a bookstore that would do more than just sell books—a place where Harlem's fashionable set could gather, buy books, and discuss literature, and where black authors could read from their work. Larsen was especially concerned about the scarcity of venues for public display and promotion of the works of African American writers, because she was nearing completion of her own first novel. Larsen sought financing for her venture from her friend Carl Van Vechten, but he was unable to supply it.

Howe's Hobby Horse was in operation until 1930.

JANICE TUCK LIVELY

See also Chicago Defender; Hughes, Langston; Hurston, Zora Neale; Larsen, Nella; Van Vechten, Carl

Further Reading

Anderson, Jervis. *This Was Harlem*. New York: Farrar, Straus and Giroux, 1982.

Andrews, William. *Classic Fiction of the Harlem Renaissance*. New York: Oxford University Press, 1994.

Hobby Horse

Davus, Thadious M. *Nella Larsen, Novelist of the Harlem Renaissance.* Louisiana, 1994, pp. 217–219.

Harlem Renaissance: Art of Black America. New York: Studio Museum in Harlem, 1987.

"The Hobby Horse." In *The Harlem Renaissance: A Historical Dictionary of the Era*, ed. Bruce Kellner. New York, 1987, p. 170.

Hughes, Langston. *Selected Poems.* New York: Vintage, 1987.

Hurston, Zora Neale. *Their Eyes Were Watching God.* New York: Harper and Row, 1990.

Larsen, Nella. *Quicksand and Passing.* New Brunswick, N.J.: Rutgers University Press, 1986.

Lewis, David Levering. *When Harlem Was in Vogue.* New York: Knopf, 1981.

Holiday, Billie

Billie Holiday's triumph was to take the American popular song and use it to claim her place in the world. She was probably the most complete, unadulterated jazz singer of all time, although that fact has been overshadowed because of a quirk in the human condition that makes us fascinated with those who gamble with life and lose. But even if her life was like a long, tortuous sentence struggling to express itself, to attempt to reconstruct it as that of an ordinary woman beset by trials and tribulations is to misunderstand her with a degree of perversity equal to her own.

Many of the personality problems Holiday grappled with throughout her life could well have had their roots in her traumatic childhood. She was continually abandoned to friends and relatives, and her rape at age eleven wrought emotional havoc; these experiences could have contributed to the diminished sense of self that those close to her spoke of. This feeling of rejection would also go some way toward explaining her abnormally dependent personality, her desire to attach herself to someone who would love and care for her—and then, once she was in a relationship, her willingness to do anything and accept anything to maintain it. Equally, a lack of parental supervision might have had a bearing on her shaky moral discipline, expressed at an early age through truancy and uninterest in academic activities. Yet such calm after-the-fact rationalization can never fully explain the dark, destructive forces that inhabit human nature. From her early teens, Billie Holiday associated marijuana and alcohol with good times. As

a young woman, she lived it up with a vengeance. Yet she found something within herself that enabled her to create some of the great classics of jazz during the 1930s, in the company of some of the finest jazz musicians of the day.

In pickup bands led by the pianist Teddy Wilson, her songs included "I Wished on the Moon," "What a Little Moonlight Can Do," "I Cried for You," "Summertime," and "This Year's Kisses." With Teddy Wilson and under her own name she also created a series of recordings with Lester Young on tenor saxophone that convey a degree of mutual inspiration epitomizing jazz at its highest level of creativity—"Sun Showers," "I'll Get By," "Me Myself and I," "A Sailboat in the Moonlight," "He's Funny That Way," "When You're Smiling," "Back in Your Own Backyard," and "All of Me." These recordings reveal a singer of broad emotional range able to narrow her focus at will, able to seize the pressure points of a song to reshape the music so profoundly that once heard it goes on to enjoy a second life, a life within memory; many of her songs from this period are truly unforgettable.

Although she enjoyed considerable success and admiration for her recording of "Strange Fruit" (1939), which portrayed a southern lynching, few listeners realize how Billie Holiday took the tradition of the previous generation of female blues singers and applied it to the American popular song. By careful use of material, she performed these songs in a way that invoked a blues mood without actually being blues. Bessie Smith and her contemporaries all sang in the first person about sex, infidelity, and broken relationships. Billie Holiday carefully chose sophisticated popular songs with lyrics that dealt with similar issues, often expressing yearning and pain. In effect, she created a character part for herself that evolved directly out of the blues tradition, without being a blues singer per se. The "character" she chose to portray was a woman unlucky in love whose experience of life appeared to be mirrored in the text of her songs. Even when singing in the big bands of Count Basie and Artie Shaw, she refused to perform songs that did not conform to the role she created for herself. Frequently she sang "I" songs, addressed to "you," but changed the "I" from positive to negative: "*I* Cover the Waterfront," "The Man *I* Love," "*I* Can't Get Started," "*My* Old Flame," "*I'll* Get By," and so on. In the 1940s, she created a series of enduring classics for the Decca label that included "Lover Man," "Good Morning Heartache," and "That Old Devil Called Love," the latter two especially written to frame her great talent to considerable effect. Through the mediation of her "character" with the songs she performed, audiences gradually began to read her real-life history into her performances. In the late 1940s, when she never seemed far from the clamor of the tabloid headlines, she chose songs that interacted with her real-life image, such as "Tain't Nobody's Business If I Do." This song, recorded a year after she was released from prison after being convicted of possessing drugs, triumphantly reinforced her notoriety while defiantly justifying her indulgence of the self.

As her voice deteriorated in the 1950s, it ironically became the source of her authenticity on albums for Norman Granz's Clef and Verve labels (1952–1957), and in the album *Lady in Satin* (1958), in which the dues she had paid, the wrong associations she had made, and the collapse of a promising career all seemed to be refracted in the flaws of her latter-day voice. Even today the way her image interacts with her music remains the least understood aspect of her art. But

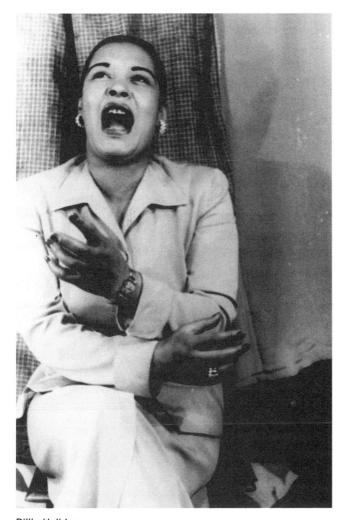

Billie Holiday. (Library of Congress.)

equally, this image of Billie Holiday as an all-purpose victim, part a romantic martyr and part a heroine of excess, has gradually tended to overwhelm her artistry. When in November 1956 she performed a concert in which readings from her autobiography *Lady Sings the Blues* (ghostwritten by William F. Dufty) alternated with songs that had become associated with her, she was consciously erecting the legend into which she would finally step, closing the doors behind her, when she died in 1959. Yet the essential truth about Billie Holiday is that she was a great artist, not because of her hedonistic and much publicized lifestyle, but despite it.

Biography

Billie Holiday (also Eleanora Fagan, Eleanora Gough, Eleanora Monroe, Eleanora McKay, Eleanora Gough McKay, Lady Day) was born on 7 April, 1915, in Philadelphia (although her birthplace has long been given as Baltimore). She was the illegitimate daughter of Sarah Julia "Sadie" Harris and Clarence Holiday, who would later play banjo and then guitar and become a member of the Fletcher Henderson Orchestra (1928–1933). For the first eighteen months of her life, she was raised by Martha Miller in Baltimore. She began her education at Public School 102, the Thomas Hayes Elementary School, at 601 Central Avenue in Baltimore, in 1920. That year her mother married Philip Gough, but by 1923, the marriage was over and the daughter returned to Martha Miller. In 1925, persistent absence from school resulted in her being sent to the House of the Good Shepherd, a juvenile house of correction; after nine months she was paroled to Sadie Gough. On 24 December 1926, Wilbert Rich was arrested for raping her, and she was returned to the House of the Good Shepherd as a witness for the prosecution. (Rich went on trial on 18 January 1926 and was convicted.) She was returned to the custody of her mother on 2 February 1927. Around this time, while employed as a cleaner at a brothel, she discovered jazz through recordings and a wind-up Victrola and was attracted to the singing of Louis Armstrong. In 1928, her mother went to Harlem, leaving her once again in the care of Martha Miller. She had now begun singing in public for tips. Her mother—who was then a prostitute at 151 West 140th Street—sent for her at the end of the year. On the night of 2 May 1929, mother and daughter were arrested for vagrancy, a charge then associated with solicitation. Sadie Gough was discharged, but the daughter was sentenced to 100 days at Blackwell's Island. She was released in October 1929 and moved with her mother to Brooklyn. The mother was now employed as a domestic, and the daughter began singing with the saxophonist Kenneth Hollon in clubs. Around this time she changed her name to Billie Holiday. She worked as a waitress in Mexico's on 133rd Street in Harlem in 1930, singing for tips while serving customers. An audition with Charlie Johnson's band at Small's Paradise ended in failure. Around this time, Holiday began smoking marijuana. She opened at Covan's on West 132nd Street in 1932; the following year she was spotted by the entrepreneur John Hammond. Her other admirers included Paul Muni and Charles Laughton. She sang at Pod's and Jerry's and then at the Hot Cha Restaurant at 2280 Seventh Avenue; next, she worked the "bar and grill" circuit. In November 1933, she made her recording debut with Benny Goodman's pickup unit. In 1934, she began a friendship with Lester Young, then a member of the Fletcher Henderson band. She made her debut at the Apollo Theater on 125th Street on Friday, 23 November 1934; she was then in a relationship with the pianist Bobbie Henderson, with whom she performed. Through John Hammond, she was given a role in Duke Ellington's *Symphony in Black* (1935). She had stints with the Mills Blue Rhythm Band and Ralph Cooper's band, and while she was working at Clark Monroe's Uptown House, Hammond negotiated a record deal with Brunswick, whereby Holiday was to be vocalist for a series of sessions under the leadership of the pianist Teddy Wilson, beginning 2 July 1935. She worked at the Famous Door on Fifty-second Street in September 1935. Joe Glaser became her manager, and from October 1935 to January 1936, she appeared in the musical *Stars Over Broadway*, starring Louis Armstrong. She appeared with Eddie Condon in Sunday afternoon jam sessions at the Famous Door in February–March 1936, and briefly with Jimmie Lunceford and Fletcher Henderson. Her records with Wilson led to a contract in her own right in 1936 with Vocalion, although she continued to work with Wilson. She worked with a band led by the trumpeter Louis Metcalfe that included her father and Lester Young in October 1936. She joined Count Basie on 13 March 1937, and had an affair with Basie's guitarist Freddie Green. She left Basie in February 1938. She joined Artie Shaw's orchestra on 9 March 1938, and left on 19 November 1938, having made one record— "Any Old Time"—with the band. She opened at Café Society in Greenwich Village on 22 December 1938, and was an immediate hit with the café crowd. She became

associated with a song by Abel Meeropol (who wrote under the name Lewis Allen) called "Strange Fruit." Columbia refused to record it because the lyrics depicted a lynching in the South, but it was put out by Commodore Records and became a minor hit (1939). Holiday had an affair with the pianist Sonny White, then met James Monroe (Jimmy, b. 1911), the brother of Clark Monroe (of Monroe's Uptown House). In April 1940, she opened at Kelly's Stables on Fifty-second Street with a band led by Roy Eldridge, then at Café Society with Art Tatum. She married Jimmy Monroe on 25 August 1941. She played at the Apollo with Lionel Hampton and had a season at the Famous Door with Benny Carter. Her final session for Columbia was on 10 February 1942. She made a theater tour with Benny Carter and orchestra. In May 1942, Jimmy Monroe was arrested on the West Coast for drug smuggling. To pay for his defense, Holiday traveled to Hollywood and opened at Trouville with Lester Young, but Monroe was convicted (receiving a one-year sentence), and lawyers' fees took much of Holiday's money. She recorded with Paul Whiteman on 12 June 1942, "Trav'lin Light." She opened in Chicago in August 1942 with Red Allen. In February 1943, she opened at Kelly's Stables on Fifty-second Street; by now she was becoming known as the "queen of Fifty-second Street." Her marriage to Monroe was effectively over, and he took a job at the Douglas plant on the West Coast. Holiday became a mainstay at the Onyx Club on Fifty-second Street throughout 1943 and 1944. An affair with the bassist John Simmons ended in 1943. At this time, Holiday became a heroin user. She recorded with Commodore records, toured to Chicago, returned to New York, and opened at the Downbeat Club. She signed with Decca records on 7 August 1944. She recorded classics such as "Lover Man" and "That Old Devil Called Love." She had a relationship with the trumpeter Joe Guy, an early swing-into-bebop musician. In January 1945, she appeared in the Second Annual Esquire Magazine Jazz Concert. She toured widely at this time. Her mother, Sadie, died on 6 October 1945—many people say that Holiday never recovered from this blow. She spent most of 1946 at Downbeat. She performed in a concert at Town Hall in February 1946; *Downbeat* magazine called it "a startling success." In May 1946, she played with Norman Granz's Jazz at the Philharmonic. She appeared in the film *New Orleans*, but her drug addiction created problems during the filming. She returned to Fifty-second Street. She was made to confront her addiction by her manager, Joe Glaser, and spent a period of rehabilitation in a private nursing home, but she continued to use drugs at the behest of Joe Guy, her boyfriend. Glaser betrayed her to the Federal Bureau of Narcotics, and she was arrested after a week at the Earle Theater in Philadelphia, on 16 May 1947. The prosecution had only flimsy evidence, but Glaser refused her legal representation. Joe Guy, who had legal representation, was freed; Holiday received a sentence of a year and a day on 27 May 1947, and was sent to the Federal Reformatory for Women in Alderston, Virginia. She remained in custody until 16 March 1948, and then gave a concert at Carnegie Hall on 27 March 1948. Because of her prison sentence, she was denied a cabaret card. She played in the revue *Holiday on Broadway* in April 1948, then at the Ebony Club, where she became involved with the owner, John Levy (not the bass player). Her life was now beginning to collapse around her; without the prestige of playing at New York clubs, her asking price began to drift down. She played on the West Coast at Billy Berg's club. An incident with a knife was reported in the newspapers, and then she was arrested for possession of narcotic drugs. She was acquitted in May 1949 and continued to tour extensively outside New York, but she was dropped by Decca in 1950. That year, she made a film short with Count Basie. Her life was now a daily round of club work and a daily struggle to get drugs. In 1951, she began a relationship with Louis McKay. In 1952, she began recording for Norman Granz's Clef label. In early 1954, she toured Europe with the group Jazz Club USA. In 1955, the West Coast became the center of her activities. She was arrested while playing in Philadelphia on 23 February 1956, for possession of drugs. In the summer of 1956, her ghostwritten autobiography, *Lady Sings the Blues,* was published, and there was a concert at Carnegie Hall in November to relaunch her career. On 28 March 1957, she married Louis McKay in Chihuahua, Mexico. She continued to record for Norman Granz, creating what many critics claim are latter-day classics, but in 1957 he decided not to renew their contract, because she had become increasingly difficult to work with. An appearance on television in *The Sound of Jazz* in December 1957 provided an indelible picture of Holiday at work. In 1958, she recorded *Lady in Satin* for Columbia, but it was clear that the ravages of her lifestyle had caught up with her. In September 1958, she played at the Blackhawk Restaurant in San Francisco; on 5 October, she played at the Monterey Jazz Festival. In November 1958, she made a brief European tour. In February 1959, she flew to London for an appearance on television. Her final album, *Billie Holiday* (March 1959), was a very sad affair. On 30 May 1959, she collapsed and was admitted to a hospital in New York. Holiday died on 15 July 1959. A requiem mass was held at Saint Paul's Roman Catholic Church on Columbus Circle on 22 July 1959.

STUART NICHOLSON

See also Armstrong, Louis; Blues: Women Performers; Ellington, Duke; Henderson, Fletcher Jazz; Nightclubs; Nightlife; Singers

Further Reading

Blesh, Rudi. *Combo USA: Eight Lives in Jazz.* Philadelphia, Pa., 1971.
Dance, Stanley. *The World of Swing.* New York, 1974.
Friedwald, Will. *Jazz Singing.* New York, 1990, p. 126.
Giddins, Gary. *Faces in the Crowd.* New York, 1992, p. 65.
Hodier, Andre. *Toward Jazz.* New York, 1962, p. 191.
Holiday, Billie, and William F. Dufty. *Lady Sings the Blues.* New York, 1956.
James, Burnett. "Billie Holiday and the Art of Communication." *Jazz Monthly,* 5, June 1959, p. 9.
———. *Essays on Jazz.* London, 1961, p. 45.
Jones, Max. "The Trouble with Billie." *Wire* (7), 1984.
———. *Talking Jazz.* London, 1987, p. 244.
Kuehl, Linda, and E. Schokert. *Billie Holiday Remembered.* New York, 1973.
Lyttelton, Humphrey. *The Best of Jazz 2.* London, 1981, p. 196.
Nicholson, Stuart. *Billie Holiday.* London, 1994.
O'Meally, Robert. *Lady Day: The Many Faces of Billie Holiday.* New York, 1991.
Pleasants, Henry. *The Great American Popular Singers.* London, 1974, p. 157.
Widgery, D. "The Woman Who Moved the World." *Wire* (7), 1984, p. 2.
Williams, Martin. *The Jazz Tradition.* New York, 1962, p. 191.
———. "Billie Holiday: Actress without an Act." *Jazz Journal,* 21, October 1968, p. 22.

Holstein, Casper

Casper Holstein—a staid, abstemious businessman and investor—owned the elite Turf Club in Harlem (at 111 West 136th Street), apartment buildings, a stable of horses in Canada, a farm in Virginia, and a house on

Long Island. He was also involved in "the numbers," or policy, a form of gambling that was popular in Harlem. An individual could place a bet with a local numbers runner, for as little as ten cents, on a combination of three numbers (e.g., 709); the runners were employed, and the winners were paid by a "bank" or "banker." Holstein was one of the "big six" policy bankers in Harlem during the 1920s and was known for his reliability in paying bettors who had "hit" the winning number. According to Redding (1934) and Hansen (1996), tradition credits Holstein with the idea of getting the three winning digits from the daily Clearinghouse totals of the New York Stock Exchange; this method assured bettors that the winning number would not be fixed.

Holstein came to the attention of the American public when he was kidnapped by white gangsters in September 1928 and held for ransom ($50,000). The public also became aware that the numbers game, which white gangsters had derisively dismissed as "nigger pennies," was actually a gold mine and that some black policy bankers were rich. Later, when Prohibition was repealed (1933) and their bootlegging operations ceased, white gangsters such as Dutch Schultz took control of numbers gambling in Harlem. Judge Samuel Seabury's commission exposed corruption in the numbers (including bribery or fixes for numbers operators), and numbers bankers were investigated for tax evasion. Holstein left the numbers when he saw circumstances turning against it; however, as late as 1937, he was convicted of operating a numbers game.

Holstein became a patron of the Harlem Renaissance by donating $1,000 for cash prizes for the second literary contest held by *Opportunity* (1925–1926) and another $1,000 for the third contest (1926–1927). In his honor, the prizes were called the Casper Holstein Awards. The Holstein awards were given for essays, plays, poetry, personal narrative sketches, art, and musical composition. Holstein's financial support enabled the managers of the contests to seek out more talented applicants and to give more prizes. Charles S. Johnson, the editor of *Opportunity*, wanted to introduce the creative works of African Americans to the American public and to get publishers interested in them. He also wanted talented African Americans to be able to express Negro life in their own terms, and he hoped to use black culture to promote interracial understanding. Contest applicants (who did not have to be American citizens) were expected to focus on subjects relating directly or indirectly to Negro life.

Holstein served as an "angel"—that is, a financial backer—for Johnson and for the Harlem Renaissance at a critical moment, when the movement was just getting off the ground. As a "race man," Holstein had faith in the abilities of the Negro, and he demonstrated this faith by using his money to support the uncovering of creative talent. In this regard, he and Charles Johnson were in accord. Holstein favored Johnson's goals, as he noted in a letter that Johnson read at the awards dinner for the first contest and published in *Opportunity* in 1927: "I honestly think [the contest] will go far towards consolidating the interests of, and bridging the gap between the white and black races in the United States today, and particularly will it encourage among our gifted youth the ambition to scale the empyrean heights of art and literature."

Holstein's philanthropy took other forms as well. He was unstinting in giving funds for the education, at colleges and technical schools, of young people from the Virgin Islands and the United States. He also donated money to historically black colleges in the United States. He sent money, clothes, and food to people in the Virgin Islands and set up a relief fund of $100,000 when the islands were devastated by hurricanes in 1924; he also sent lumber and workmen to help the islanders rebuild. After the U.S. government bought the islands in 1917, Holstein used his position as president of the Virgin Islands Congressional Council and his personal wealth to get the United States to redress certain social and political ills there.

Despite his successes, Holstein made some enemies in political circles. Law enforcement officials watched him constantly, and he was arrested in 1937 for operating a small-time numbers game. He was convicted, received an indeterminate sentence, and remained in prison for about a year.

Holstein died penniless in 1944, in New York City. Thousands attended his funeral at the Memorial Baptist Church in Harlem, and he was buried at Woodlawn Cemetery in the Bronx, New York. The University of the Virgin Islands established a scholarship in his honor, and a library collection, with books by and about black people, was named after him. An annual celebration commemorating his philanthropy and his achievements was decreed in the islands.

Holstein and Charles Johnson have been called midwives of the Harlem Renaissance. Johnson said of Holstein: "There is a faith and service deserving of more than casual appearance. A Negro who is by no means a millionaire has faith enough in the future

Casper Holstein, 1926. (Schomburg Center for Research in Black Culture, New York Public Library.)

of his own developing race to give of his means to support it."

Biography

Casper Holstein was born on 6 December 1876, in Christiansted, St. Croix, Virgin Islands. At age twelve he came to the United States with his mother. He graduated from Boys High School in Brooklyn, New York, served in the U.S. Navy, and then worked for a prominent stockbroking family, the Christies (or Chrysties). He became engaged in business, real estate, and investing, and in "the numbers" as a "banker." He was kidnapped in 1928 and held for ransom. Later, when conditions became unfavorable, he left the numbers racket. In 1925–1927, he donated money for prizes in *Opportunity*'s literary contests. In 1937, he was arrested, convicted, and jailed for operating a small-time numbers game. Holstein died penniless in New York City on 5 April 1944.

MARVIE BROOKS

See also Johnson, Charles Spurgeon; Numbers Racket; Opportunity Awards Dinner; Opportunity Literary Contests; Organized Crime; Race Men

Further Reading

Boyer, William W. *America's Virgin Islands: A History of Human Rights and Wrongs.* Durham, N.C.: Carolina Academic, 1963.

"Casper Holstein Dies a Pauper." *New York Amsterdam News,* 15 April 1944, p. 2-A.

"Casper Holstein Dies After Long Illness; Several Thousand Present at Last Rites." *New York Age,* 15 April 1944, pp. 1, 5.

Drake, St. Clair, and Horace R. Cayton. "Business Under a Cloud." In *Black Metropolis: A Study of Negro Life in a Northern City,* rev. enlarged ed. New York: Harcourt Brace and World, 1970, Vol. 2, pp. 470–491.

"Former Policy King in Harlem Dies Broke." *New York Times,* 9 April 1944, p. 34.

Gill, Jonathan. "Numbers Game." In *Encyclopedia of African-American Culture and History,* ed. Jack Saltzman, David Lionel Smith, and Cornel West. New York: Simon and Schuster Macmillan, 1996, Vol. 4, pp. 2032–2034.

Haller, Mark H. "The Changing Structure of American Gambling in the Twentieth Century." *Journal of Social Issues,* 35(3), Summer 1979, pp. 87–114.

Hammer, Richard. *The Illustrated History of Organized Crime.* Philadelphia, Pa.: Courage, 1989.

Hansen, Axel C. *From These Shores.* Nashville, Tenn.: Hansen and Francois, 1996.

Fleming, G. James. "Law Regards Holstein as Menace While Throngs Recall Good Deeds." *New York Amsterdam News,* 15 February 1936, pp. 1, 3.

Holmes, Eugene C. "Alain Locke and the New Negro Movement." *Negro American Literature Forum,* 2(3), 1968, pp. 60–68.

"Holstein Faces Term in Prison." *New York Amersterdam News,* 8 February 1936, p. 1.

"Holstein Seized in a Policy Raid." *New York Times,* 24 December 1935, p. 3.

Kelly, Robert J. "Casper Holstein." In *Encyclopedia of Organized Crime in the United States: From Capone's Chicago to the New Urban Underworld.* Westport, Conn.: Greenwood, 2000, pp. 157–158.

Lawrence, Carl Dunbar. "Casper Holstein Dies at Sixty-Seven; Colorful Harlem Sportsman." *New York Amsterdam News,* 15 April 1944, pp. 1–2A.

Light, Ivan. "Numbers Gambling Among Blacks: A Financial Institution." *American Sociological Review,* 42, December 1977, pp. 892–904.

Moolenaar, Ruth. *Profiles of Outstanding Virgin Islanders,* Vol. 2. U.S. Virgin Islands: Department of Education, 1992.

"Mystery Surrounds the Kidnapping and Return of Holstein." *New York Amsterdam News*, 26 September 1928, pp. 1–2.

Opportunity: A Journal of Negro Life. 1925–1927. (See editorials about the literary contests; accounts of the awards dinner; articles by Holstein.)

"Prison Term for Holstein." *New York Amsterdam News*, 15 February 1936, p. 3.

Redding, Saunders J. "Playing the Numbers." *North American Review*, December 1934, pp. 238, 533–542.

"Rudolph Brown Tells His Story." *New York Amsterdam News*, 3 October 1928, pp. 1–2.

Schatzberg, Rufus. *Black Organized Crime in Harlem, 1920–1930*. New York: Garland, 1993.

———. *African-American Organized Crime: A Social History*. New York: Garland. 1996.

Turnbull, Charles W., and Christian J. Lewis. *Casper A. Holstein: Unusual Humanitarian*. St. Thomas: Virgin Islands Department of Education. 1974.

Willensky, Elliot. *When Brooklyn Was the World, 1920–1957*. New York: Harmony, 1986.

Holt, Nora

Nora Holt was one of the most fascinating personalities of the Harlem Renaissance, as well known for her musical abilities as she was for her vibrant, adventurous personal life. She was a good friend of Carl Van Vechten and other luminaries of the period.

Nora Lena Douglas was born in Kansas. The exact year of her birth is unknown; it was either 1895 or 1890. Her parents encouraged her musical talent, and she studied at Chicago Music College, becoming one of the first African Americans to receive a master's degree in music. In January 1921, she began editing her own periodical, *Music and Poetry*, a "monthly music magazine of high standard" that also offered her an opportunity to publish her own compositions and spotlight new artists. Holt cofounded the National Association of Negro Musicians, an association that is still active as of the present writing. She was the music critic for several African American newspapers and was one of the earliest African American women to produce her own radio show.

Holt was intelligent, witty, and fashionable, and her personal life attracted the public eye. She married at least five times, and she was known for her rendition of the sexually suggestive song "My Daddy Rocks Me (With One Steady Roll)." Van Vechten used

Holt as a model for the character Lasca Sartoris in his controversial novel *Nigger Heaven* (1926). This novel offers one of the best descriptions of Holt:

> The nose was delicate, the mouth provocative and sensual. Pear-shaped pearls depended from the lobes of the tiny ears. The black, wavy hair was combed severely back from the forehead, above the ears, and shingled. The lady was dressed in the smartest mode of the moment; moreover, . . . she wore her clothes with that manner which is rare with women of any race or colour. (79–80)

On 29 July 1923, Holt married the wealthy Joseph L. Ray, a secretary and attendant to Charles Schwab, head of Bethlehem Steel Corporation in Pennsylvania. Three years later their divorce made the headlines of several black newspapers. Ray charged his wife with infidelity, but according to Holt, Ray disliked being known as "Mr. Holt" and wanted to retrieve the money and real estate he had given her on their marriage (Dannett 1966). Holt demonstrated her poise in

Nora Holt, photographed by Carl Van Vechten. (Library of Congress.)

her public response to the charges, reprinted on the front page of the *Chicago Defender* in 1926:

> I have never, to any person or newspaper, made a statement against Mr. Ray and there is plenty I could and may have to say, but I maintain that only crude and uncultured people fight out their domestic differences in public. In the divorce court, yes; in newspapers, never.

Nora Holt was the embodiment of contradictions, and as other commentators have noted, her life resists easy summarization. Gracious and assertive, artistic and attractive, she exhibited many of the feminist qualities associated with other women of this period, yet she has not been as frequently studied.

Biography

Nora Holt (Nora Lena Douglas) was born 1895 (or 1890) in Kansas City, Kansas, to Rev. Calvin N. Douglas, an African Methodist Episcopal minister, and Gracie Brown Douglas. She studied at Western University in Quindaro, Kansas (1915), and at Chicago Music College (B.A., 1917; master's, 1918). She was married five or more times. Holt was a music critic for the Chicago *Defender* (1917–1921) and for the *Amsterdam News* (1943–1956). She cofounded, with Nathaniel Dett and Clarence White, the National Association of Negro Musicians (1919) and was its vice president (1919–1922). She was editor and publisher of *Music and Poetry* (1921); a music teacher in public high schools in Los Angeles, California (1937–1943); owner or operator of a beauty parlor in Los Angeles (1940s); and producer of *Nora Holt's Concert Showcase*, a weekly classical radio program on WLIB, New York (1953–1964). Holt was a member of the New York Music Critics Circle (1945). She died in Los Angeles on 25 January 1974.

MIRIAM THAGGERT

See also National Association of Negro Musicians; Nigger Heaven; Van Vechten, Carl; White, Clarence Cameron

Selected Works

"Rhapsody on Negro Themes." Master's thesis (symphonic), Chicago Music College, 1918.
Music and Poetry. January–October 1921.

Further Reading

Dannett, Sylvia G. L. *Profiles of Negro Womanhood*. Yonkers, N.Y.: Educational Heritage, Vol. 1, 1964; Vol. 2, 1966.
Johns, Robert L. "Nora Holt." In *Notable Black American Women*, ed. Jessie Carney Smith. Detroit, Mich., and London: Gale Research, 1992.
Kellner, Bruce. *Carl Van Vechten and the Irreverent Decades*. Norman: University of Oklahoma Press, 1968.
———, ed. *Keep A-Inchin' Along: Selected Writings of Carl Van Vechten about Black Art and Letters*. Westport, Conn., and London: Greenwood, 1979.
———. *Letters of Carl Van Vechten*. New Haven, Conn., and London: Yale University Press, 1987.
"Mrs. Nora Holt Ray's Silence Ends." *Chicago Defender*, 6 February 1926, p. 1.
Reed, Bill. *Hot from Harlem: Profiles in Classic African-American Entertainment*. Los Angeles, Calif.: Cellar Door, 1998.
Van Vechten, Carl. *Nigger Heaven*. New York: Knopf, 1926.

Home to Harlem

Claude McKay's novel *Home to Harlem* (1928)—his first venture into fiction—was a best-seller when it was released. However, it received a mixed reaction from the black community. Langston Hughes praised it as the first fruit of the Harlem Renaissance, basing his evaluation on McKay's willingness to represent urban working-class black life. W. E. B. Du Bois, by contrast, found the book disgusting and said that he felt in need of a bath after reading it. He associated its focus on sex and sensuality with a controversial novel by Carl Van Vechten, *Nigger Heaven* (1926); moreover, he thought that both novels perpetuated stereotypical images of blacks.

Home to Harlem opens with its protagonist, Jake Brown, abandoning a tour of military duty in Brest, working his way to London on a ship, and then deciding to go back to Harlem after a two-year absence. He returns to Harlem and spends the night with a part-time prostitute, Felice, who returns his money in the morning with a note. Ostensibly, Jake spends the rest of the novel searching for Felice, having forgotten her address, but his journeys in Harlem and the Northeast provide occasions for reflecting on black urban life. The scenes of the novel take place in cabarets, saloons, and boardinghouses, and among dock and train workers. Jake tries to maintain a sense of honor and nobility as he encounters employers who try to exploit him and women who want to take care of him. Memorable characters include Zeddy, Rose, Miss Curdy, Susy, Billy Biasse, and Ray. Zeddy is an old friend of Jake's but becomes his enemy at the end of the novel because Felice—who was Zeddy's girlfriend—prefers Jake. Zeddy threatens to reveal that Jake is absent without leave from the army, so Jake and Felice leave for Chicago. Rose is a bisexual singer who wants to take care of Jake and wants him to beat her as a sign of his masculinity. Jake escapes from Rose; this escape is similar to a later escape by Zeddy from Miss Curdy and Susy, who live in Brooklyn and give parties with free alcohol in the hope of finding sexual partners. Billy Biasse owns a saloon where Jake keeps his suitcase for two years and is part of the male company to which Jake constantly retreats.

In *Home to Harlem*, Ray vies with Jake for importance. The second section opens by introducing Ray and closes with his departure from the United States and from this story, although Ray became the protagonist of McKay's second novel, *Banjo*. Traditionally, Ray's intellectuality has been understood as the opposite of Jake's physicality, but more recently Ray and Jake have been seen as complementary, learning from each other and growing through their relationship. Ray, a Haitian immigrant to the United States, raises questions about the United States as a colonial power and about images of Africa in the Western imagination. At the same time that he brings a critical perspective to bear on racial and colonial relationships, he also envies the physical and sensual aspects of Jake's life and the lives of most people. Ray sees working-class people as animal-like in their simplicity, working and loving without caring about the hows and whys of the world. Many critics interpret Ray as a fictional projection of McKay's own sensibility and philosophy. Ray's thoughts about the world occasionally interrupt the development of the novel for several pages at time; that is, McKay sacrifices the plot for reflections and ideas that are not integral to it. Although Ray envies working-class people, his attitude toward them and the black middle class moves between stereotypes, challenges to stereotypes, and seeming disdain. The ambiguity of McKay's language and especially his doubtful use of irony have made it difficult, despite numerous attempts, to settle Hughes's and Du Bois's debate over whether the novel is pathbreaking or tawdry.

The complexities of *Home to Harlem* have led to analyses of widely varied elements such as its homoerotic subtext, its cosmopolitanism, its primitivism, its critical use of racist vocabulary, and even its punctuation. Throughout *Home to Harlem*, McKay uses devices such as ellipses and exclamation marks, and critics have tried to relate them to meaning in this novel. Ramchand (1970) takes these punctuation devices as reflective of jazz and argues that McKay intended them to create rhythm and texture but did not always succeed; but Spencer (1998) argues that many of the ellipses in *Home to Harlem* appear at points where McKay is implying unspeakable homoeroticism. Ramchand initiated a discussion of cultural dualism that other critics, such as Chauhan (1990) and Nelson (1992), have built on. These critics call attention to McKay's heritage as a Jamaican educated under an English system, who then migrated to the United States; to England; back to the United States; to Russia, France, Spain, and Morocco; and then again to the United States (where he died). Huggins (1971) argues that *Home to Harlem* (unlike Van Vechten's *Nigger Heaven*) represents an insider's view of black life and enmeshes the reader in the confusion and struggles of the characters. Priebe (1972) argues that rather than being a happy-go-lucky character, Jake is alienated, and that his alienation accounts for his continual wanderings. Some critics have offered discussions about primitivism and masculinity in the 1930s. Lively (1984) argues that McKay uses primitivism as a form of protest against racial and colonial oppression. McCabe's study (1997) is part of a fairly widespread effort to reevaluate the importance of primitivism in the development of modernism and its aesthetics. Hathaway (1999) suggests that McKay should be understood as someone who resisted categories of race, class, nationality, and political affiliation. In general, the criticism has become more varied as manhood becomes less important and issues of sexuality, gender, interracial relationships, and colonialism become more important.

KIMBERLY J. BANKS

See also Du Bois, W. E. B.; Hughes, Langston; McKay, Claude; Nigger Heaven

Further Reading

Carby, Hazel. "Policing the Black Woman's Body in an Urban Context." In *Identities*, ed. Kwame Anthony Appiah and Henry Louis Gates Jr. Chicago, Ill.: University of Chicago Press, 1995. (First published 1992.)
Chauhan, P. S. "Rereading Claude McKay." *CLA Journal*, 34(1), 1990, pp. 68–80.

Hathaway, Heather. *Caribbean Waves: Relocating Claude McKay and Paule Marshall*. Bloomington and Indianapolis: Indiana University Press, 1999.

Huggins, Nathan Irvin. *Harlem Renaissance*. New York: Oxford University Press, 1971.

Lively, Adam. "Continuity and Radicalism in American Black Nationalist Thought, 1914–1929." *Journal of American Studies*, 18, 1984, pp. 207–235.

McCabe, Tracy. "The Multifaceted Politics of Primitivism in Harlem Renaissance Writing." *Soundings*, 80, 1997, pp. 475–497.

Nelson, Emmanuel S. "Community and Individual Identity in the Novels of Claude McKay." In *Claude McKay: Centennial Studies*, ed. A. L. McLeod. New Delhi: Sterling, 1992.

Priebe, Richard. "The Search for Community in the Novels of Claude McKay." *Studies in Black Literature*, 3(2), 1972, pp. 22–30.

Ramchand, Kenneth. *The West Indian Novel and Its Background*. New York: Barnes and Noble, 1970.

Spencer, Suzette A. "Swerving at a Different Angle and Flying in the Face of Tradition: Excavating the Homoerotic Subtext in 'Home to Harlem.'" *CLA Journal*, 42, 1998, pp. 164–193.

Van Vechten, Carl. *Nigger Heaven*. New York: Harper and Row, 1971. (Originally published 1926.)

Homosexuality

Many scholars regard Richard Bruce Nugent's short story "Smoke, Lilies, and Jade" (1926)—about a vagabond artist named Alex who beds a Latino man late one night after a literary salon—as the first extant publication by an African American to "openly depict" homosexuality, even though Alex is technically bisexual. They assert that Nugent is one of the few beacons of what the gay black poet Essex Hemphill calls "evidence of being," proof of black gay men's experiences; or what Garber describes as "a homosexual subculture, uniquely Afro-American in substance, [found] throughout the so-called Harlem Renaissance" (1989, 318). Woods says that "Nugent was the exception," cautioning: "When reading the writers of the Negro Renaissance we should not expect, nor be disappointed by the lack of, the kind of openness we now reasonably demand of gay writers" (1993, 139). Nugent, however, never understood "what the fuss was about. Even today some ask him: 'How could you write anything gay in 1926?' His reply is "I didn't

know *it was gay* when I wrote it'" (Smith 1986, 214). Nugent "wore his bohemianism and homosexuality like a badge of honor"; he felt that "everybody he met was 'in the life,' especially if he found them physically attractive. He [had] the belief that 'if you can't take me the way I am, it's your problem. It's certainly not mine'" (Smith, 209). Nugent's attitude was by no means singular; it reflects the attitude of many black men and women "in the life." One of these, Nugent reveals, was the "truly named" Philander Thomas, a fellow actor Nugent met in 1927 during the Broadway production of *Porgy*. Thomas embodied the free attitude toward sexuality, including homosexuality, that characterized Harlem's nightlife. Thomas's talent was finding "bedmates": "People who came to Harlem did so to vent their pleasures. Everybody thought that they could and Philander saw to it that they did. . . . He was much more outgoing than I. I liked his random freedom" (Smith, 216). The "random freedom" of philandering Thomas and Nugent are but two contributions made to bohemian Harlem's language and network of institutions sustaining its community "in the life."

The relative freedom of Harlem's bohemians can be overlooked by those reading for contemporary gay, lesbian, bisexual, or transgendered communities. During the Harlem Renaissance, black men and women did not always use the word "gay," "lesbian," or "homosexual" to reflect what is now a distinct identity. Sexuality, Nugent assures us, was just one part of black peoples' lives:

> Harlem was very much like [Greenwich] Village. People did what they wanted to do with whom they wanted to do it. You didn't get on the rooftops and shout, "I fucked my wife last night." So why would you get on the roof and say, "I loved prick." You didn't. You just did what you wanted to do. Nobody was in the closet. There wasn't any closet. (Kisseloff 1989, 288)

Regardless of the degree to which black men and women publicly proclaimed their sexuality, the laissez-faire attitude Nugent identifies can be found in how Harlem's own *did* express bohemian experiences through black vernacular. Although words naming homosexuality had been used since 1862, different ones were needed to reflect black men and women "in the life." As Jeanne Flash Gray, who lived in Harlem in the 1930s, remembers, "There were many places in Harlem run by and for Black Lesbians and Gay Men, when we were still Bull Daggers and Faggots and only whites were lesbians and homosexuals" (Garber, 331). Numerous blues songs revel in this black bohemian vernacular: They include Lucille Bogan's "B. D. Women Blues," in which she warns "B. D. women sure is rough / They drink up many a whiskey and they sure can strut their stuff"; Gertrude "Ma" Rainey's "Sissy Blues" and "Prove It on Me Blues"; and George Hanna's "Freakish Blues" and "Sissy Man Blues," in which he confides, "If you can't bring me a woman, bring me a sissy man." Writers, in turn, used blues as a kind of homosexual shorthand. For example, Claude McKay first refers to homosexuality in *Home to Harlem* (1928) with Bessie Smith's "Foolish Man Blues": "And there is two things in Harlem I don't understan' / It is a bulldyking woman and a faggoty man." Another word used by Harlem's writers is "queer," applied since the 1910s by cosmopolitan male New Yorkers "who identified themselves as part of a distinct category [based on] their homosexual interest" (Chauncey 1994, 15). The writers McKay, Eric Walrond, Wallace Thurman, Zora Neale Hurston, and Jean Toomer—as well as others—used "queer" because it could also mean "different" or "odd." Such double meanings define black vernacular, which historically has been contextual rather than direct, in order to conceal meaning from potentially hostile outsiders. Harlem's bohemians, Chauncey maintains, crafted their vernacular for protection as well: "The visibility of bulldaggers and faggots in the streets and clubs of Harlem during the late 1920s and early 1930s does not mean they enjoyed unqualified toleration throughout Harlem society" (253).

How Harlem society tolerated bohemian culture fluctuated. Harsh reactions to Nugent's story, to other queer literature, and to bawdy blues songs were simply a public defense, reflecting Nugent's admonition against proclaiming "I love prick" on the rooftops. Sometimes these defenses came from people who were participating in the bohemian culture they presumably condemned. For example, Alain Locke, who is often called the intellectual godfather of the Harlem Renaissance, argued strongly that any black literature highlighting sexuality would only confirm racist, reductionist ideas of blacks as promiscuous. Locke wrote negative reviews of work by McKay and of *Fire!!: Devoted to Younger Negro Artists* (1926), the publication in which Nugent's story first appeared. Still, Locke was known in some circles for taking more than a literary interest in Langston Hughes, and he contributed to Harlem's bohemian network like any other "in the life." His written reprimands are not necessarily

hypocritical, though. Locke felt that black art which reached a reading or viewing public should not air private affairs. Moreover, such art should not revel in "sexual taboos" that whites publicly damned. The black artists should forgo references to black bodies (as sexual, or as violent) so that black art could be aesthetically appreciated just like white art, away from racism. According to Locke, social appreciation of black people would follow from aesthetic appreciation of black art. Because of this focus on the social potential of art, Locke, W. E. B. Du Bois, and others confined themselves mainly to aesthetics in their public criticism of art, never trespassing on an individual's private life. In a review, Du Bois wrote that he needed to take a bath after reading *Home to Harlem*, but he "spent heavy days regretting" firing Augustus Granville Dill, a close associate and business manager of Du Bois's magazine *The Crisis*, after Dill was arrested for having sex with a man in a public rest room (Silberman 2001, 258). In the editorial column of *The Crisis*, Du Bois briefly mentioned Dill's departure but without explaining the reason for it. A similar silence followed Wallace Thurman's arrest for the same "offense"; Ma Rainey's arrest for running an "indecent party" at her home, an orgy involving the women in her chorus; and the dissolution of the poet Countee Cullen's marriage to Du Bois's daughter, Yolande. Publicly, she made sure that "the Harlem press reported Cullen was infatuated with another woman, but she confided to her father that Cullen's homosexuality was the problem" (Chauncey, 265).

Not a problem was Harlem's bohemian nightlife. Notwithstanding the minister Adam Clayton Powell's "scathing and bitter denunciation of perversion" and other reproaches published in *New York Age*, Harlem's evening bohemians were well known and celebrated. One of the most visible was Gladys Bentley, "'huge, voluptuous [and] chocolate colored,' according to one fan" (Chauncey, 252). Bentley was as famous for her notorious shows at Hansberry's Clam House on 133rd Street, in which she performed in a white tuxedo and top hat, as she was for her girlfriends; she ad-libbed popular ballads, turning the Broadway tunes "Sweet Georgia Brown" and "Alice Blue Gown" into odes for anal sex. She inspired the writer Blair Niles to create Sybil, an openly lesbian singer, in *Strange Brother* (1931). Also famous was the drag queen Gloria Swanson (originally named Winston), who was "so perfect a woman [people] came and left never suspecting his true sex" (Chauncey, 251). As Dr. Herman Warner remembered:

Gladys and Gloria were extremely popular. Gloria Swanson used to sing a song called "Hot Nuts." . . . As soon as you would enter [the club], he would make you sing the song: "Hot nuts, tell it to the peanut man. You see that man walking there in green? He has good nuts but he won't keep 'em clean. (Kisseloff, 323)

Such participation was not limited to those in one of Harlem's many bohemian institutions, like 267 House on 136th Street, Edmond's Cellar on 132nd Street and Fifth Avenue, or Lulu Belle's on Lenox Avenue near 127th Street. As Howard "Stretch" Johnson, a dancer at the Cotton Club, recalled, bohemian culture spread farther:

There was another place, where they had a chorus of all homosexuals, who used to come out and dance in drag. That was the 101 Ranch [on 140th Street], which is where they invented a dance called the Shim-Sham Shimmy, which became a kind of a national anthem for dancers. Practically every dancer in Harlem could do the Shim-Sham Shimmy. (Kisselhoff, 323)

The 101 Ranch—or the Daisy Chain, as it was also called—became so well known that both Fats Waller and Count Basie commemorated it in songs. Harlem's bohemian culture became so popular that many black performers "in the life" such as Bessie Smith, Alberta Hunter, Josephine Baker, Ethel Waters, and the comedienne Jackie "Moms" Mabley, who regularly wore men's clothes, flirted with bisexual imagery in their work.

However, it was at private parties that "flirting" became more forthright. As the dancer Mabel Hampton explained, "We used to go to parties every other night. . . . The girls all had the parties" (Garber, 321). The hostess of one of these parties on 137th Street described it as a "freakish party, everybody in here is supposed to be a bull dagger or a c—" (Chauncey, 280). Parties thrown by A'Lelia Walker, Clinton Moore, and others were as notorious and as well attended. Moore's parties were said to have attracted Cole Porter and Cary Grant, and boasted sexual entertainment. Another famous gathering place was Alexander Gumby's studio on Fifth Avenue between 131st and 132nd streets, known as Gumby's "bookstore" or "book studio" for the many books lining its walls. A white author, Samuel Steward, recalled "being taken to Gumby's one evening by a lesbian friend and enjoying a delightful evening of 'reefer,' bathtub gin, a game of truth, and homosexual exploits" (Garber, 322).

In Harlem, bohemian parties were one setting for interracial mixing, and the white gay writer and patron Carl Van Vechten—whose articles in *Vanity Fair* are often credited with introducing the Harlem Renaissance to the white public—became Harlem's interracial ambassador. Like Locke, Van Vechten had more than a literary interest in many black writers he helped publish. Van Vechten's parties were legendary, and his photographs document many of Harlem's bohemians. According to Garber, interaction between whites and blacks "in the life" at Van Vechten's parties and elsewhere came from an "identification and feeling of kinship [which] may have been the beginnings of homosexual 'minority consciousness'" (329).

Another interracial meeting place was Harlem's most public bohemian institution, the Hamilton Lodge drag ball held at Rockland Palace Casino on Eighth Avenue and 155th Street, "the largest annual gathering of lesbians and gay men in Harlem—and the city" (Chauncey, 257). It soon became known as the "Faggots' Ball," and its complex spectacle and public presence provoked negative reactions in the press, which nonetheless praised the queens' beautiful and sometimes astonishing outfits. Even writers celebrating it, like Langston Hughes in *The Big Sea* (1940), are careful to position themselves as observers of, not like, the "faggots." Its interracial character led some writers to blame blacks' homosexuality on infiltration by "the discarded froth of Caucasian society" (Chauncey, 260). But the race of the ball's winning queen reflected racial divisions despite any "minority consciousness." The *Amsterdam News* noted that "considerable rivalry exists between the ofay chicks and the Mose broods"; and Bonnie Clark, the first black contestant to win (in 1931 and again in 1932), complained that the ball was "arranged for the white girls to win. They never had no Negro judges" (Chauncey, 263). Nonetheless, the social networks reflected in the Faggots' Ball and other Harlem institutions were a sometimes ignored but hardly hidden aspect of being "in the life."

SETH CLARK SILBERMAN

See also Baker, Josephine; Black Bohemia; Cullen, Coutee; Fire!!; Gumby Book Studio; Hughes, Langston; Hunter, Alberta; Locke, Alain; Mabley, Jackie "Moms"; McKay, Claude; New York Age; Nugent, Richard Bruce; Rainey, Gertrude "Ma"; Smith, Bessie; Thurman, Wallace; Van Vechten, Carl; Walker, A'Lelia; Waters, Ethel

Further Reading

Chauncey, George. *Gay New York: Gender, Urban Culture, and the Making of the Gay Male World, 1890–1940*. New York: Basic Books, 1994.

Garber, Eric. "A Spectacle in Color: The Lesbian and Gay Subculture of Jazz Age Harlem." In *Hidden From History: Reclaiming the Gay and Lesbian Past*, ed. Martin Bauml Duberman, Martha Vicinus, and George Chauncey Jr. New York: New American Library, 1989, pp. 318–331.

Kisseloff, Jeff. *You Must Remember This: An Oral History of Manhattan From the 1890s to World War II*. New York: Schocken, 1989.

Silberman, Seth Clark. "Lighting the Harlem Renaissance *AFire!!*: Embodying Richard Bruce Nugent's Bohemian Politic." In *The Greatest Taboo: Homosexuality in Black Communities*, ed. Delroy Constantine-Simms. Los Angeles, Calif.: Alyson, 2001, pp. 254–273.

Smith, Charles Michael. "Bruce Nugent: Bohemian of the Harlem Renaissance." In *In the Life: A Black Gay Anthology*, ed. Joseph Beam. Boston, Mass.: Alyson, 1986, pp. 209–220.

Woods, Gregory. "Gay Re-Readings of the Harlem Renaissance Poets." In *Critical Essays: Gay and Lesbian Writers of Color*, ed. Emmanuel S. Nelson. New York, London, and Norwood, Australia: Harrington Park, 1993, pp. 127–142.

Horne, Frank

Frank Smith Horne (1899–1974) was an optometrist, a public administrator, and an important minor poet of the Harlem Renaissance. He is best known for "Letters Found Near a Suicide," a set of short poems that he worked on throughout the 1920s; it won second prize in 1925 in the Amy Spingarn contest of *The Crisis* magazine. Although Horne was influenced by the racial consciousness of his contemporaries, much of his work focuses on more general themes—in particular, the fear that God might be absent from the modern world and the difficulty of maintaining faith.

Horne was born and grew up in Brooklyn. He received a bachelor's degree from City College in 1921, and he was made a doctor of optometry by the Northern Illinois College of Optometry. He practiced in New York and Chicago until 1926, when he was stricken by a severe illness. The exact nature of the condition is not clear, but Horne called it his "mean illness," and many of his later poems speak of having difficulty walking and having restricted use of one arm. On medical advice, Horne moved to Georgia, where he taught at the Fort Valley Normal and Industrial School from 1926 to 1936. He was very successful, coaching the track team and advancing from teacher to acting president.

Early in his life, Horne was interested in writing, but he did not begin to publish until he was urged to do so by Gwendolyn Bennett and Charles S. Johnson. Throughout the late 1920s, Horne appeared frequently in *Opportunity*, reviewing books and providing anecdotes for Bennett's column "The Ebony Flute." "Letters Found Near a Suicide" was first published in *Opportunity* in 1925, and then added to in 1929. Parts of it also appeared in *Caroling Dusk* (1927), Countee Cullen's anthology of poetry by black Americans. "Letters Found Near a Suicide" is written in a sparse, stripped-down style, but in "Harlem" (1928), Horne also experimented with the jazz style then in vogue among young poets. In 1932 he won honorable mention in *Opportunity*'s literary contest for his essay "Concerning White People."

In 1936, Horne went to work for the U.S. Housing Authority in Washington. There he was a participant in President Franklin Roosevelt's "black cabinet," an advisory group led by Mary McLeod Bethune. In 1938, he returned to New York, where he worked for the City Commission on Inter-Group Relations and for the Housing Redevelopment Board.

Horne had no book published until his *Haverstraw* was issued by an Englishman named Paul Bremen in 1963. That volume has additions to "Notes Found Near a Suicide" but dates these changes back to the 1920s. The new section in *Haverstraw* is largely autobiographical, ending with a poem addressing God as uncaring, and showing much concern for the pain and difficulty of living with a disability. *Haverstraw* was kept to an extremely small printing of 300 numbered copies and so seems to have been meant for an elect few rather than as a serious attempt to establish a reputation for Horne. By the time of his death in 1974, Horne had once again returned to writing and had published additional poems in *The Crisis* in 1965, 1966, and 1970.

Biography

Frank Smith Horne was born in Brooklyn, New York, on 18 August 1899. He attended the College of the City of New York (B.S., 1921); Northern Illinois College of Optometry (earning a degree in 1922 or 1923); and the University of Southern California (A.M., c. 1932). He practiced optometry in Chicago and then New York City (1922–1926). He was at Fort Valley High and Industrial School from 1926 to 1936, beginning as a teacher and ending as dean and acting president. From 1938 to 1955, he served in various administrative capacities for agencies of the U.S. Housing Authority in Washington, D.C., and then New York. He was on the New York City Commission on Inter-Group Relations (executive director from c. 1956–1962) and the New York City Housing Redevelopment Board (consultant, c. 1962–1974). He was a member and board member of the American Civil Liberties Union and a member of the National Association for the Advancement of Colored People (NAACP), National Housing Conference, and National Association of Inter-Group Relations Officials. Horne died in New York City, on 7 September 1974.

STEVEN NARDI

See also Bennett, Gwendolyn; Bethune, Mary McLeod; Crisis, The: Literary Prizes; Johnson, Charles Spurgeon; Opportunity; Opportunity Literary Contests

Selected Works

Haverstraw. 1963.
Bontemps, Arna, ed. *American Negro Poetry*. 1963.
Bontemps, Arna, and Langston Hughes, eds. *The Poetry of the Negro: 1746–1949*. 1949.

Further Reading

Brown, Sterling. *Negro Poetry and Drama*. Washington, D.C.: Associates in Negro Folk Education, 1937.
Metzger, Linda, ed. *Black Writers*. Detroit, Mich.: Gale Research, 1989.
Primeau, Ronald. "Frank Horne and the Second Echelon Poets of the Harlem Renaissance." In *Remembering the Harlem Renaissance*, ed. Cary D. Wintz. New York: Garland, 1996, pp. 371–391.

Hot Chocolates

Hot Chocolates (1929), originally titled *Tan Town Topics*, helped define an important era in musical theater and confirmed the shift from vaudeville formulas to jazz-centered productions. It was one of the most piquant Broadway shows of the late 1920s. Connie and George Immerman, proprietors of the famous Harlem cabaret

Connie's Inn at 131st Street and Seventh Avenue, produced *Hot Chocolates*; and their former delivery boy, Thomas "Fats" Waller, wrote the music, along with Harry Brooks and Andy Razaf, who also wrote the lyrics. The crowd at Connie's Inn was white; the only blacks allowed in the establishment were waiters and entertainers. Many black Harlemites railed against this practice; an article in *The Age* deplored the Immerman brothers' policy of selling cheap liquor and banning even the most elite blacks from a club in their own neighborhood while admitting all types of white patrons, including disreputable sorts. Still, the black musical revue found an early home here, with productions such as *Hot Feet, Connie's Inn, Harlem Hotcha*, and *Hot Chocolates*. Even after *Hot Chocolates* moved to the Hudson Theater on Broadway, where it had a run of 219 performances, it kept its hot Harlem nightclub flavor, and the opening number, "At Connie's Inn," re-created the uptown scene. (When *Hot Chocolates* first moved to Broadway, each night after the performance, members of the company would trek back uptown to Connie's Inn to perform the same numbers. Eventually, however, this proved too much for the cast, and they stopped doing it.)

There were eighty-five performers in *Hot Chocolates*, which starred the singers Baby Cox and Edith Wilson. Leroy Smith's orchestra provided the music, and the dancing was highly praised. *Hot Chocolates* was an early success for the show's trumpeter, Louis Armstrong, who, although he did not receive billing, was praised by reviewers. He (and later Fats Waller) played during intermission. Billy Higgins was a singer, composer, and blackface comedian. Leonard Harper was a dancer, choreographer, and producer. Jazzlips Richardson had been a carnival comedian; he danced as a filler in *Hot Chocolates* and became one of the show's smash hits. His routine was filled with gymnastics (especially splits and back flips), eccentric dancing, rubbery contortions, and minstrel comedy. Baby Cox's snakehips routine along with Louise "Jota" Cook's gyrations stopped the show. At one point, the Immermans tried to get Bill "Bojangles" Robinson to join the show, but he was too busy with vaudeville; instead, they booked Roland Holder to perform a clean, sophisticated soft-shoe routine in top hat and tails to the tune of "Swanee River." Paul and Thelma Meeres were in their heyday as good-looking, sophisticated waltz dancers; bronze-complexioned Bahamians, they were considered to be the most beautiful couple in Harlem. Their elegant performance was a contrast to the blue humor, suggestive lyrics, double entendres, and scantily attired showgirls, all of which raised a few eyebrows. On the whole, though, audiences and critics did not seem to mind the raunchy material. After all, breaking away from the prudishness of the Victorian era was part of the appeal of the Harlem Renaissance.

Waller wrote several of his most renowned songs for this production, including "Black and Blue" and "Can't We All Get Together." "Ain't Misbehavin'," which became a classic, solidified Waller's reputation as a masterful composer. Most reviewers thought that the score would be an instant hit, although the *New York World* felt that too much emphasis was placed on this one song, which was repeated often in the show.

NADINE GEORGE-GRAVES

See also Armstrong, Louis; Musical Theater; Razaf, Andy; Waller, Thomas "Fats"; Wilson, Edith

Further Reading

Balliett, Whitney. *Jelly Roll, Jabbo, and Fats: Nineteen Portraits in Jazz.* London: Oxford University Press, 1983.

Dictionary of the Black Theatre: Broadway, Off-Broadway, and Selected Harlem Theatre. Westport, Conn.: Greenwood, 1983.

Harrison, D. D. "Edith Goodall Wilson." In *American National Biography*, ed. John A. Garraty and Mark C. Carnes. New York: Oxford University Press, 1999, Vol. 23, pp. 563–564.

Kirkeby, W. T., with Duncan P. Scheidt and Sinclair Traill. *Ain't Misbehavin': The Story of Fats Waller.* New York: Da Capo, 1975.

Machlin, Paul S. *Stride: The Music of Fats Waller.* Boston, Mass., and London: G. K. Hall, 1985.

Shipton, Alyn. *Fats Waller: His Life and Times.* New York: Universe, 1988.

Singer, Barry. *Black and Blue: The Life and Lyrics of Andy Razaf.* New York: Schirmer, 1992.

Vance, Joel. *Fats Waller: His Life and Times.* Chicago, Ill.: Contemporary, 1977.

Waller, Maurice, and Anthony Calabrese. *Fats Waller.* New York: Schirmer, 1977.

Woll, Allen. *Black Musical Theatre: From Coontown to Dreamgirls.* Baton Rouge: Louisiana State University Press, 1989.

House-Rent Parties

Although house-rent parties once flourished in the black neighborhoods of Chicago, Detroit, Washington D.C., and other cities, they have become most closely associated with Harlem. During the 1920s and 1930s (and even into the 1940s), such parties formed the backbone of Harlem nightlife and became for many working people not only an enjoyable and affordable way to dance and socialize but also an economic necessity. For the reasonable admission price of between ten cents and a dollar, plus the cost of liquor and food, guests could dance, drink, flirt, and gamble, while the hosts collected enough money to pay the landlord for another month.

The house-rent party evolved out of traditions that were several generations old by the beginning of the Harlem Renaissance. Since the late nineteenth century, African American families in the rural South had enjoyed Saturday night barbecues and fish fries, complete with music and dancing, at events called "frolics" or "breakdowns." By the turn of the twentieth century, African Americans in southern cities were throwing dance parties expressly to raise money. Dozens of couples would cram into tiny apartments, and the sometimes painful results of dancing in such confined spaces led to the term "shin-digs" to describe these events, although they were also referred to as "stomps," "boogies," "breakdowns," "skiffles," "scuffles," "struggles," "shake-me-downs," "chitterling rags," and "struts."

African Americans who came north during the great migration brought with them their fondness for a good shin-dig. This social custom served them well, for instead of finding plentiful and profitable work in northern cities, many migrants instead found relentless economic exploitation by employers, landlords, and merchants. Wages for black workers were disproportionately low in New York, and rents in Harlem were exorbitantly high. Limited economic options forced residents of Harlem to find creative ways to supplement their income, and so many families transformed the southern shin-dig into the modern house-rent party.

To prepare for a rent party, hosts would clear all furniture (except for the piano) from the front rooms of the apartment, take up the rugs, replace regular lightbulbs with more sensuous colored ones, and sometimes rent folding chairs from a local undertaker. Some hosts would even hire "home defense officers" (HDOs), to bounce unwelcome guests and squelch incipient brawls. The highlight of any rent party was the music, often provided by a single piano player, a series of pianists, or even a three- or four-piece musical ensemble. Well-known pianists such as "Fats" Waller, James P. Johnson, and Willie "the Lion" Smith regularly made the rounds at rent parties, where musicians competed in "cutting contests" to determine who was the most talented. Bootleg liquor, usually homemade corn whiskey (called "King Kong") or bathtub gin, was sold by the pint or in quarter-pint portions called "shorties." For an additional price, guests could purchase southern-style meals that usually included some combination of hoppin' John, fried chicken, fried fish, chitterlings, mulatto rice (rice and tomatoes), gumbo, chili, collard greens, potato salad, and sweet potato pone. The party would often last until dawn, or until someone summoned the Black Maria (the police patrol wagon) to break it up.

In order to attract a large number of paying guests, hosts advertised their parties using "rent party tickets." Often, they enlisted the help of the "Wayside Printer," a middle-aged white man who walked the streets of Harlem with his portable press. For a modest fee, he stamped the party information onto tickets about the size of a business card. Interestingly, these tickets always identified rent parties using such terms as "Social Party," "Social Whist Party," "Parlor Social," or "Matinee Party." Other, less elevated terms included "Too Terrible Party," "Boogie," and "Tea Cup Party." Tickets often incorporated popular slang phrases, lyrics from current songs, or bits of poetry. One ticket from 1927 implored: "Save your tears for a rainy day, / We are giving a party where you can play / With red-hot mammas and too bad She-bas / Who wear their dresses above their knees / And mess around with whom they please." Another reasoned: "You Don't Get Nothing for Being an Angel Child, So You Might As Well Get Real Busy and Real Wild."

Hosts would distribute these tickets to friends, neighbors, and even strangers on the street corner. Sometimes, hosts targeted a specific population, such as Pullman porters, interstate truck drivers, or black tourists. Other hosts simply tucked the tickets into elevator grilles or apartment windows. Drumming up a good crowd was important, for competition was fierce; as many as twelve parties in a single block and five in an apartment building, simultaneously, were not uncommon in Harlem during the 1920s. Although rent parties raged every night of the week, the most popular evening was Saturday, because most day laborers were paid on Saturday, and few had to work on Sunday. The next favorite party night was Thursday, when most sleep-in domestic workers were off-duty. The only population generally not invited to rent parties was white people. During Prohibition (1920–1933), any white man in Harlem could potentially be a rev-

enuer or a cop, who would certainly appreciate the opportunity to raid a rent party for violating liquor laws, or to extort money from the hosts in order to keep them out of jail. But even without that threat, black hosts seldom welcomed the presence of unfamiliar, inquisitive white people in their homes.

During the Harlem Renaissance, house-rent parties essentially amounted to a kind of grassroots social welfare. However, their general atmosphere was far more sordid than the average neighborhood block party. Frequently, back rooms were reserved for gambling or drug use, and sometimes hosts would offer the private use of the back bedrooms to couples for a price. Before long, gangsters and small-time racketeers had also entered the rent-party business, staging nightly parties that served as a front for their more illegitimate business ventures. Not surprisingly, some Harlem residents were ashamed of or appalled by rent parties, especially those who firmly believed in the immorality of jazz, liquor, and gambling. Certain black intellectuals and writers also scorned these gatherings, believing that such rowdy displays of passion and intemperance reflected poorly on the black race. No accounts of rent parties appear in the works of Jessie Redmon Fauset, Nella Larsen, or W. E. B. Du Bois, for instance, and in his sociological description of Harlem, *Black Manhattan* (1930), James Weldon Johnson simply ignores them. We do, however, get enthusiastic depictions of rent parties in the works of Langston Hughes, Wallace Thurman, and Claude McKay.

KATHLEEN DROWNE

See also Hughes, Langston; Johnson, James P.; McKay, Claude; Smith, Willie "the Lion"; Thurman, Wallace; Waller, Thomas "Fats"

Further Reading

Anderson, Jervis. *This Was Harlem: A Cultural Portrait, 1900–1950*. New York: Farrar, Straus and Giroux, 1981.
Byrd, Frank. "Rent Parties." In *A Renaissance in Harlem*, ed. Lionel C. Bascom. New York: Avon, 1999.
Hughes, Langston. *The Big Sea*. New York: Hill and Wang—Farrar, Straus and Giroux, 1997. (Originally published 1940.)
Oliver, Paul. *Blues Fell This Morning: Meaning in the Blues*. Cambridge and London: Cambridge University Press, 1990. (Originally published 1960.)
Osofsky, Gilbert. *Harlem: The Making of a Ghetto—Negro New York, 1890–1930*, 2nd ed. New York: Harper and Row, 1971.

Ottley, Roi. *New World a-Coming*. New York: Arno and New York Times, 1968.

Reid, Ira DeA. "Mrs. Bailey Pays the Rent." In *Ebony and Topaz: A Collectanea*, ed. Charles S. Johnson, in *The Politics and Aesthetics of "New Negro" Literature*, ed. and intro. Cary D. Wintz. New York and London: Garland, 1996.

Schoener, Allon, ed. *Harlem on My Mind: Cultural Capital of Black America, 1900–1968*. New York: Random House, 1968.

Watson, Steven. *The Harlem Renaissance: Hub of African-American Culture, 1920–1930*. New York: Pantheon, 1995.

Howard University

In November 1866, representatives of the First Congregational Society of Washington, D.C., met to discuss plans for establishing a seminary for the training of black ministers. Their interest in creating "Howard Theological Seminary" stemmed from a sense of commitment and obligation to the formerly enslaved men and women of the nation. Prominent among the group of Congregationalists was General Oliver Otis Howard, a Civil War hero and commissioner of the Freedmen's Bureau. In his capacity as an official of the Freedmen's Bureau, Howard had a significant interest in the welfare and education of the formerly enslaved. He became a natural leader in the group's effort, and consequently the university was named for him. As their proposal gained momentum, the school's founders soon saw fit to broaden their vision from theological seminary to Howard Normal and Theological Institute for the Education of Teachers and Preachers. Ultimately, they went a step further and obtained congressional support for the incorporation of Howard University, an institution dedicated to "the education of youth in the liberal arts and sciences." The charter of Howard University was enacted by the U.S. Congress on 2 March 1867.

Since its inception, Howard University has distinguished itself as a training ground for countless African Americans who would make significant contributions to American society. Among them are prominent civil rights lawyers, such as Supreme Court Justice Thurgood Marshall, who were trained under the tutelage of Charles Hamilton Houston, the influential dean of Howard's law school. Other distinguished graduates include Debbie Allen (actress and choreographer), Edward Brooke (former U.S. senator), Ralph Bunche (political scientist, first African American Nobel laureate), David Dinkins (former mayor of New York City), Elaine R. Jones (first woman to head the NAACP Legal Defense Fund), Vernon Jordan (former president, National Urban League), Toni Morrison (author, recipient of Pulitzer and Nobel prizes), Jessye Norman (opera star), Phylicia Rashad (actress), L. Douglas Wilder (first African American governor of Virginia), and Andrew Young (former ambassador to the United Nations, mayor of Atlanta). Howard is also well known for its exceptional faculty. Benjamin Brawley, Sterling Brown, Ralph Bunche, Charles Drew, Rudolph Fisher, John Hope Franklin, E. Franklin Frazier, Francis Grimké, Lois Maillou Jones, Alain Locke, Rayford Logan, Kelly Miller, James Nabrit, Dorothy Porter, James Porter, Robert Terrell, Howard Thurman, Charles Wesley, and Carter G. Woodson are an abridged list of significant African American intellecual leaders who have served Howard University as pedagogues.

The Moorland-Spingarn Research Center (MSRC), a division of the university's library system, is yet another reason for Howard's prestige among American institutions of higher education. MSRC is an extensive repository of documentation and memorabilia relating to the history and culture of African Americans. Its holdings include the Alain Locke papers and the Rose McClendon Memorial Collection of photographs by Carl Van Vechten. In addition, MSRC houses manuscripts of W. E. B. Du Bois, E. Franklin Frazier, Angelina Weld Grimké, Georgia Douglas Johnson, Rayford Logan, Kelly Miller, and Carter G. Woodson, as well as correspondence by Countee Cullen, Langston Hughes, Zora Neale Hurston, Charles S. Johnson, and others.

The period of the Harlem Renaissance indelibly influenced African Americans' interest in the liberal arts. By extension, the artistic movement also had an influence on African American higher education, and Howard University is no exception. The ideological thrust of the university during that period is evident in Howard's theoretical stance with respect to the lingering debate on higher education between Booker T. Washington and W. E. B. Du Bois. Recognizing the severe limitations of Washington's philosophy, Howard stood squarely in Du Bois's camp. Under the influence of humanist scholars, such as Alain Locke, Mercer Cooke, Frank Snowden, Arthur P. Davis, and Sterling Brown, who helped identify the intellectual life of the university, Howard conformed to a pedagogy best defined by Du Bois: "The curriculum of Higher Education which must underlie true life is intelligence, broad sympathy, knowledge of the world that was and is and the relation of men to it." Howard's proponents of the liberal arts engaged in an outright assault against the industrialist camp. They made clear that in advocating a liberal arts orientation, they were not seeking to create an elite which would be alienated from the larger African American community, as Washington had feared. Rather, they concurred with Du Bois's observation that "what black men need is the broader and more universal training so that they can apply the general principles of knowledge to the particular circumstances of their condition." Mordecai Wyatt Johnson, Howard's first black president, echoed Du Bois's dictum in his inaugural address of 1926:

> The great danger that confronts Howard University and all Negro institutions of learning is not that we shall have too much liberal education, but that we shall have too little of it—that we shall turn out competent physicians, competent lawyers, competent teachers in their several specialties, who are at the same time incompetent, shallow sympathied men, ignorant of the fundamental human relations and not knowing how to take their part in the general development of a community. . . . It is absolutely necessary that there shall [be] studies which fit a man sympathetically to understand the kind of country that he is living in, the progress which that country has made, the direction in which it is moving, the nature of the institutions with which he has to deal, and the relations and possibilities of his own people to his government and to the progress of his country. This is what is meant by a liberal education—not the preparation of a leisured aristocracy, simply spending its time in the discussion of things of cultural interest to incompetent men, but the broadening of the sympathies, and that deepening of the understanding which make the experienced minister, the lawyer, and the teacher for the public good, together endeavoring to develop a country which shall have a deep sense of community and of brotherly cooperation.

This concept of "broad sympathy" remains at the core and is the sine qua non of Howard University's mission, which states in part: "Howard University is dedicated to attracting, sustaining, and developing a cadre of faculty who, through their teaching and research, are committed to producing distinguished and compassionate graduates who seek solutions to human and social problems in the United States and throughout the world."

Howard University, c. 1900. (Library of Congress.)

With regard to Howard University's profound legacy, and its continued humanistic vision, Zora Neale Hurston's reflections on her time as a student at Howard offer an eloquent tribute to the institution and its significance to African American life and culture. She recalled that when the students sang the alma mater, "my soul stood on tiptoe and stretched up to take in all that it meant. So I was careful to do my class work and be worthy to stand there under the shadow of the hovering spirit of Howard. I felt the ladder under my feet." Howard University had a significant impact on African American life during Reconstruction and through the Harlem Renaissance, and the tradition and influence of the institution continue today.

NATASHA COLE-LEONARD

See also Higher Education; Historically Black Colleges and Universities; *specific faculty members and alumni*

Further Reading

Battle, Thomas C. "The Moorland-Spingarn Research Center." *Library Quarterly*, 58, 1988, pp. 143–163.

Du Bois, W. E. B. *The Souls of Black Folk: Essays and Sketches.* Boston, Mass.: Bedford, 1997. (Originally published 1903.)

Dyson, Walter. *Howard University, the Capstone of Negro Education—A History: 1867–1948.* Washington, D.C.: Graduate School, Howard University, 1941.

Howard University Home Page. Howard University, August 2001. (Web site, www.howard.edu)

Logan, Paul, ed. *A Howard Reader: An Intellectual and Cultural Quilt of the African-American Experience.* Boston, Mass.: Houghton Mifflin Custom Publishing, 1997.

Logan, Rayford. *Howard University: The First Hundred Years, 1867–1967.* New York: New York University Press, 1969.

Traylor, Eleanor, Alphonso Frost, and Leota Lawrence, eds. "Foreword." In *Broad Sympathy.* Needham Heights, Mass.: Simon and Schuster Custom Publishing, 1997.

Howells, William Dean

From his stint as the editor of *Atlantic Monthly* in the 1870s to his death in 1920, William Dean Howells was arguably the most powerful man in American publishing. Merely by mentioning a book in one of his monthly magazine columns, the "dean of American letters" could bring fame and greatly increased sales to the author. From this eminent position, he brought the works of African American writers to the attention of a white reading public. He was also the most outspoken proponent of literary realism. According to his theories of writing, a work of fiction should portray the world as it is and faithfully record the way people commonly speak and act. To achieve this, the work must accurately reflect the experience and environment of the writer. It should come as no surprise that Howells encouraged most what he imagined to be authentic expressions of the African American experience, sometimes favoring works written in dialect over those written in standard English.

Raised in the radical Republican politics of Ohio, Howells hoped for a peaceful reconciliation between the races and social equality for African Americans. He renounced any aggressive solutions to racial oppression, favoring instead gradual betterment based on increased economic power for African Americans and the exposure of the African American experience through the arts. In his "An Exemplary Citizen," Howells praised Booker T. Washington for a speech that Washington gave at the Atlanta Exposition of 1895. Howells did not see submission in Washington's speech; instead, he admired Washington's ability to maintain good-natured patience in the face of overwhelming injustice. In 1909, William Dean Howells, along with forty-two other prominent American liberals, signed a letter drafted by Oswald Garrison Villard, editor of the New York *Post*, on the hundredth anniversary of Abraham Lincoln's birth to protest a recent race riot in Springfield, Illinois. Howells later joined the National Association for the Advancement of Colored People (NAACP) when it began in 1910.

Howells was an early champion of African American literature, advancing the careers of Paul Laurence Dunbar and Charles Chesnutt by proclaiming the literary merits of their work to a white audience. He believed in the importance of artistic expression in the greater cause of civil rights. Achievement through the arts demonstrated the talent and genius of a people. He had faith that the sympathy generated through works of art would eventually lead to understanding between the two races and raise the status of African Americans.

Through his review of Paul Laurence Dunbar's second book of poetry, *Majors and Minors* (1896), Howells introduced Dunbar to a popular readership. Although he praised the more traditional poems written in standard English, he maintained that the verse written in dialect was more faithful to and representative of the African American experience. True to the tenets he set for realism, Howells praised Dunbar as "the first man of his color to study his race objectively, to analyze it to himself, and then to represent it in art as he felt it and found it to be." On the basis of this one review, Dunbar became a household name. Howells continued his support by contributing a laudatory introduction to Dunbar's third book, *Lyrics of Lowly Life* (1896). Dunbar appreciated the attention he received from Howells, but he felt that his ability to express himself freely was hampered by Howells's public call for dialect pieces.

Charles Chesnutt was already nationally known through his stories in *Atlantic Monthly* by the time Howells reviewed two volumes of his work, *The Conjure Woman* (1899) and *The Wife of His Youth and Other Stories of the Color Line* (1899), in 1900, but Howells's endorsement of these books established Chesnutt as a major literary figure and a preeminent African American voice. Howells's reaction to Chesnutt's work was similar to his reception of Dunbar's—Howells applauded Chesnutt's command of his materials and the "unerring knowledge" of his subject matter. He further advised Chesnutt to write from experience as a light-skinned African American and "acquaint us with those regions where the paler shades dwell as hopelessly, with relation to ourselves, as the blackest negro." Although he praised the dramatic power of *The Marrow of Tradition* (1901) the following year, Howells could not contain his ultimate disappointment. In his review "A Psychological Counter-Current in Recent Fiction," in which he chastised literature he called "morally false and mentally despicable," Howells described the tone of Chesnutt's novel as "bitter, bitter." The anger Howells detected in Chesnutt disturbed his dream of reconciliation between the races. After this harsh criticism, the relationship

William Dean Howells, 1877. (Library of Congress.)

between Howells and Chesnutt cooled and eventually dissolved.

Howells's fascination with the condition of the "paler shades" found its way into his own work well before his exposure to the work of Chesnutt. In his novella *An Imperative Duty* (1891), a young woman discovers the secret of her parentage, that her mother had been African American, a member of a group which the young woman had always considered inferior and ugly. The doctor of nervous disorders who falls in love with her overcomes his own initial repulsion and racism to wed her and escape to Europe. Chesnutt kept a copy of this exploration into the psychological effects of racism in his personal library, where it may have provided some literary context for his own work.

Howells was greatly responsible for the popular reception of African American writers at the turn of the twentieth century. In his own way, he also tried to influence the direction of African American literature, fostering in its writers a faith in realistic portrayals of African American life and a confidence in the development of a distinctive African American voice.

Biography

William Dean Howells was born in Martinsville (later Martin's Ferry), Ohio, on 1 March 1837. He had occasional formal schooling in Hamilton, Ohio, 1842–1847. He was a printer's apprentice for the *Ohio State Journal*, 1851–1852; a printer at the *Ashtabula Sentinel*, 1852– 1856; city editor of the *Cincinnati Gazette*, 1857; city editor of the *Ohio State Journal*, 1858–1860; U.S. consul for Venice, 1861–1864; assistant editor at *Atlantic Monthly*, 1866–1870; editor at *Atlantic Monthly*, 1871– 1880; editor at *Cosmopolitan*, 1891–1893; and president, American Academy of Arts and Letters, 1908– 1920. His awards included the Howells Medal for Fiction, 1915. Howells died in New York City on 11 May 1920.

CHARLES D. MARTIN

See also Chesnutt, Charles Waddell; Dunbar, Paul Laurence; Villard, Oswald Garrison

Selected Works

Their Wedding Journey. 1871.
A Foregone Conclusion. 1874.
The Undiscovered Country. 1880.
A Modern Instance. 1882.
The Rise of Silas Lapham. 1885.
Indian Summer. 1886.
Annie Kilburn. 1888.
A Hazard of New Fortunes. 1890.
A Boy's Town. 1890.
An Imperative Duty. 1891.
Criticism and Fiction. 1891.
A Traveler From Altruria. 1894.
"Life and Letters." *Harper's Weekly*, 1896. (Review of Paul Laurence Dunbar's *Majors and Minors*.)
"Introduction." In *Lyrics of Lowly Life,* by Paul Laurence Dunbar. 1896.
Their Silver Wedding Journey. 1899.
"Mr. Charles Chesnutt's Stories." *Atlantic Monthly,* May 1900.
"An Exemplary Citizen." *North American Review*, August 1901.
"A Psychological Counter-Current in Recent Fiction." *North American Review*, December 1901.
The Leatherwood God. 1916.
Years of My Youth. 1916.

Further Reading

Andrews, William. "William Dean Howells and Charles W. Chesnutt: Criticism and Race Fiction in the Age of Booker T. Washington." *American Literature*, 48(3), 1976.

Cady, Edwin H. *The Road to Realism: The Early Years 1837–1885 of William Dean Howells.* Syracuse, N.Y.: Syracuse University Press, 1956.

————. *The Realist at War: The Mature Years 1885–1920 of William Dean Howells.* Syracuse, N.Y.: Syracuse University Press, 1958.

Lynn, Kenneth S. *William Dean Howells: An American Life.* New York: Harcourt Brace Jovanovich, 1970.

McElrath, Joseph R. Jr. "W. D. Howells and Race: Charles W. Chesnutt's Disappointment of the Dean." *Nineteenth-Century Literature*, 51(4), 1997.

Stronks, James B. "Paul Laurence Dunbar and William Dean Howells." *Ohio Historical Quarterly*, 67(2), 1958.

Hughes, Langston

Langston Hughes was one of the most influential, prolific, and beloved writers to emerge from the Harlem Renaissance. Over the course of a professional writing career that spanned nearly five decades, Hughes gained international attention and acclaim in nearly every genre of writing, including poetry, the short story, the essay, drama, the novel, history, autobiography, journalistic prose, children's literature, literature for adolescents, the libretto, and song lyrics. He was also a popular speaker, reading his poetry and prose to audiences of all ages around the world. Just as eclectic as his interests in numerous genres were the subjects on which Hughes chose to focus his creative talents. Keenly aware of both his own sociocultural milieu and issues affecting people worldwide, Hughes wrote as powerfully about jazz, blues, and the African American working and middle classes as he did about imperialism in Haiti or the effects of revolutionary socialism on Soviet central Asia. Whatever his subject or genre, Hughes wrote with passion, clarity, and a great deal of humanity, blending a critical awareness and condemnation of oppressive ideologies and institutions with a subtle, ironic, blues-toned sense of humor that sought the comic in the tragic and celebrated the healing power of laughter.

Hughes's artistic presence in Harlem, the burgeoning center of African American artistic and intellectual activities, actually preceded his physical arrival. In the autumn of 1920, when he was only eighteen years old, he had drawn the attention of Jessie Redmon Fauset—who was the literary editor of the youth-oriented *Brownies' Book* and of *The Crisis*, the prestigious magazine of the National Association for the Advancement of Colored People (NAACP)—with several poems written for children that he submitted for publication. Fauset was impressed with the submissions, promised to publish one poem in a coming issue of *Brownies' Book*, and asked whether Hughes had written any children's articles or stories about Mexico (he was living with his father in Toluca at this time). Hughes responded by sending a brief piece on Mexican games, an essay about daily life in Toluca, and a third article about a Mexican volcano, all of which Fauset accepted and published, respectively, in the January, April, and December 1921 issues of *Brownies' Book*. Fauset published a fourth essay by Hughes, "The Virgin of Guadalupe," in *The Crisis* that same year.

Although these pieces gave hints of a youthful literary talent, the publication of his poem "The Negro Speaks of Rivers" in *The Crisis* in 1921 helped establish Hughes as a significant voice in African American literature. The poem's unique blend of self-revelation and historical consciousness reflected a young poet with firm control of the English language and a deep appreciation of the culture on which he would subsequently focus his creativity. The poem also introduced Hughes to important contacts in New York City. Having arrived in New York in September 1921, to enroll for classes at Columbia University, Hughes was soon invited by Fauset to visit the offices of the NAACP and to meet W. E. B. Du Bois, whose eloquent words of strength, protest, and defiance in *The Souls of Black Folk* and in editorials in *The Crisis* were among the earliest Hughes remembered from his childhood. Fauset and Du Bois would prove to be very important to Hughes at the start of his career, publishing his writings in *The Crisis* and introducing him to many dignitaries at the NAACP, especially those who were part of the literary and artistic community at the center of the Harlem Renaissance.

If "The Negro Speaks of Rivers" signified Hughes's maturing literary vision, "The Weary Blues"—published in *Opportunity* magazine in May 1925—cemented his reputation as one of the preeminent poets of the Harlem Renaissance. "The Weary Blues" blended blues lyrics that Hughes remembered from his childhood with a syncopated narrative that captured the actions and emotions of a blues musician. The poem's innovative appropriation of the blues form would serve Hughes well, earning him first prize in a literary contest sponsored by *Opportunity*. The poem also impelled Carl Van Vechten, a novelist and patron of the arts, to approach Hughes and ask to see other examples of his work. Van Vechten was impressed by what he read and urged his own publisher, Alfred A. Knopf, to consider one of Hughes's manuscripts. The result was *The Weary Blues*, published in 1926 to nearly unanimous critical acclaim. Reviewers noted the lyrical quality of Hughes's verses but focused more intently on the ways in which the young poet seemed to be doing something never before attempted in poetry—convincingly representing in print the rhythm, tone, and emotive qualities of jazz and blues. The poems in *The Weary Blues*, to many reviewers, also captured the sheer excitement and energy that characterized Harlem during the mid-1920s. Here, some readers suggested, was clearly a poet who loved African American culture and was unafraid to represent aspects of that culture in his writings.

Hughes's reputation as a poet was certainly made secure by *The Weary Blues*, but during the Harlem Renaissance he also established himself as a talented writer in other genres. Most notably, the publication of "The Negro Artist and the Racial Mountain" (1926) in *The Nation* signaled Hughes's transformation from a promising writer of nonfiction to one of America's most engaging essayists. At stake in the essay was no less than the very existence of a distinct African American aesthetic, an art originating in the confluence of African folk culture and the black experience of the "middle passage," slavery, Reconstruction, and the long era of segregation. Hughes had touched on this subject implicitly in "The Negro Speaks of Rivers," but it would take a controversial essay by another African American writing for *The Nation*, George S. Schuyler, to provoke a more explicit articulation of a distinct black art. Schuyler's "The Negro-Art Hokum" (1926) challenged the premise that art produced in the United States was in any way influenced by race. In the midst of the intense excitement surrounding the publication of Alain Locke's anthology *The New Negro* (1925), which heralded an awakening in African American visual arts, literature, music, and scholarship, Schuyler registered strong and bitingly sarcastic doubt that the movement known as the Harlem Renaissance was anything more than racial propaganda and self-promotion by a small elite. Central to Schuyler's argument is the idea that "race" is a cultural construct, a product of social class, caste, and physical environment rather than a biological determinant. Schuyler pointed out that, historically, the concept of fundamental differences among the races had been used in the United States to develop a white supremacist ideology in which African Americans were

cast as inherently inferior to white Americans. Schuyler insisted that celebrations of a distinct African American art—which might be translated by whites as a "peculiar art"—could only legitimize such an ideology.

Hughes understood the merits of Schuyler's argument concerning "fundamental differences" among races, but he was incensed by Schuyler's suggestion that African Americans were merely "lampblacked" Anglo-Saxons. In a letter to the editor of *The Nation* that appeared shortly after Schuyler's essay was published, Hughes made his own position clear:

> For Mr. Schuyler to say that "the Negro masses . . . are no different from the white masses" in America seems to me obviously absurd. Fundamentally, perhaps, all peoples are the same. But as long as the Negro remains a segregated group in this country he must reflect certain racial and environmental differences which are his own.

Hughes had enumerated these differences two months before this letter, in "The Negro Artist and the Racial Mountain," his finest essay and a virtual declaration of independence for the younger artists and writers of the Harlem Renaissance. Troubled by what he perceived to be a reliance on dominant white standards of art and culture among the African American middle class and intelligentsia, Hughes challenged black artists and writers to embrace a racial aesthetic and a source of creativity generated from within black communities in the United States rather than from without. In creating a truly racial art, the black artist could not be swayed by critiques of his or her subject matter or techniques, nor could fears of revealing aspects of black life that the standard-bearers of propriety frowned on stand in the way of artistic inspiration. "An artist must be free to choose what he does," Hughes insisted in the essay, "but he must also never be afraid to do what he might choose." In this respect, Hughes believed that there was a vast storehouse of largely untapped artistic material in the culture of the African American working masses. Jazz, spirituals, and blues offered the artist a wealth of resources for the creation of a distinct black aesthetic, and the often conflicted relations between black and white people in the United States furnished an "inexhaustible supply of themes" for the writer and dramatist. In utilizing these resources, the black artist could—indeed, must—begin to challenge and overturn dominant white standards of beauty that limited the representation of blackness to stereotypes associated with minstrelsy. Hughes dismissed Schuyler's argument that environment and economics had transformed African Americans into darker Anglo-Saxons, and he issued in its place a code of responsibility to the artists of his generation: "It is the duty of the younger Negro artist, if he accepts any duties at all from outsiders, to change through the force of his art that old whispering 'I want to be white,' hidden in the aspirations of his people, to 'Why should I want to be white? I am a Negro—and beautiful!'"

"The Negro Artist and the Racial Mountain" anticipated themes Hughes would pursue in his writings for the next decade, particularly in its strong critique of white racial prejudice but also in its condemnation of the black bourgeoisie's complicity in perpetuating racist attitudes. Uncompromising in his belief that the younger generation of African American artists and writers were being held back by timeworn attitudes, Hughes chastised "the best Negroes" in another powerful essay, "These Bad New Negroes: A Critique on Critics" (1927), for rejecting the work of writers such as Jean Toomer and Rudolph Fisher because these writers had described conflict and violence within African American communities. In this essay, he also took a controversial stance on Carl Van Vechten's sensationalistic novel *Nigger Heaven* (1926), which had caused a firestorm among the black literati and intelligentsia for its grossly stereotypical depictions of Harlem society and nightlife. A combination of his friendship with Van Vechten, a desire to shock the black bourgeoisie, and perhaps a sincere conviction that he was correct compelled Hughes to pronounce the novel "true to the life it pictures." In the essay, Hughes also addressed charges by critics that his own second book of poems, *Fine Clothes to the Jew* (1927), was mired in the lives of the lowest classes of African America. "Is life among the better classes," Hughes asked, "any cleaner or any more worthy of a poet's consideration?"

As the nation headed toward economic collapse, Hughes's response to this question was a resounding "no." The Great Depression brought to an abrupt halt the sense of joy and hope with which he had proclaimed, in "The Negro Artist and the Racial Mountain," a new and shining moment in African American art. The gaiety of the Harlem Renaissance had given way to the stark reality of economic crisis, and Hughes responded by focusing his work on the broader racist and classist attitudes that he perceived to be increasing in the United States. The Scottsboro trials of 1931 especially reinforced in Hughes's mind the connections between race and class, further convincing the

young writer that conservative thinking among blacks and whites alike was leading the nation, and particularly its millions of black citizens, toward disaster. The Scottsboro case involved nine African American youths—called the "Scottsboro boys" in the media—who had been arrested in Alabama and charged with the rape of two young white women on an open railroad freight car. Eight of the youths were quickly convicted by all-white juries and sentenced to death; the ninth was sentenced to life imprisonment. As Hughes journeyed through the South on a reading tour in the winter of 1931, the nine youths imprisoned at Kilby State Penitentiary in Montgomery, Alabama, were frequently on his mind. Concerned that the Scottsboro boys would perish by actual or legal lynchings, Hughes published a poem, "Scottsboro" (1931), and two powerful essays—"Southern Gentlemen, White Prostitutes, Mill-Owners, and Negroes" (1931) and "Brown America in Jail: Kilby" (1932)—which dramatized the vagaries of a racist southern justice system and implicitly criticized black leaders who remained silent about the trials.

This critique was implicit in poems such as "To Certain Negro Leaders," which Hughes published in the radical *New Masses* in 1931, and was extended in "Cowards From the Colleges" (1934), a scathing essay that took black college administrators to task for bowing down to the demands of white philanthropists. Hughes's personal experiences with white patronage during the 1920s certainly contributed to the honest conviction with which he criticized such philanthropy in the 1930s. He had been supported by a wealthy white woman, Charlotte Mason, while writing his first novel, *Not Without Laughter* (1930), and had thoroughly enjoyed the opportunity to focus on his art without having to worry about where his next paycheck would come from. As soon as Hughes's work took on a radical edge of social critique, however, Mason withdrew her patronage. This kind of hypocrisy, which seemed to fester behind philanthropic fronts, troubled Hughes long after the end of the Harlem Renaissance and the largesse of wealthy patrons who supported it. Addressing in absentia the first American Writers' Congress (1935), which was organized by politically committed writers on the left and out of which grew the radical League of American Writers, Hughes called on African American writers to reveal through their art

the lovely grinning face of philanthropy—which gives a million dollars to a Jim Crow school, but not one job to a graduate of that school; which builds a Negro hospital with second-rate equipment, then commands black patients and student-doctors to go there whether they will or no; or which, out of the kindness of its heart, erects yet another separate, segregated, shut-off, Jim Crow Y.M.C.A.

In this radical statement, which was published in essay form under the title "To Negro Writers," Hughes championed the transformative powers of the written word and urged writers to use their art to effect social change. Black writers must use their talents, Hughes argued, to overturn minstrel stereotypes and establish racial unity "on the *solid* ground of the daily working-class struggle to wipe out . . . all the old inequalities of the past." They must reveal, he continued, "the sick-sweet smile of organized religion" and the false leaders within black communities who fear to speak out against injustice.

Concerned as he was with issues affecting black communities in the United States, Hughes was no provincial; his increasing engagement with the political left in the late 1920s and 1930s was motivated as much by an active awareness of global class and racial oppression as it was by his commitment to representing the voices of the African American working masses. A trip to Haiti in 1931, for example, confirmed for Hughes the extent to which U.S. imperialism had cast an ugly net of racism and economic exploitation over a once proud people. When Hughes arrived in Haiti, signs of the American occupation were to be found everywhere. The U.S. military intervention, purportedly undertaken for humanitarian reasons after a coup d'état in 1915 had resulted in the overthrow and death of the Haitian president and the execution of political prisoners, had stripped the Haitian government of all vestiges of independence; the Haitian military, finances, and legislative powers were firmly under the control of the United States. Hughes's love of foreign travel was fed in part by a desire to temporarily escape racial prejudice and discrimination at home. The discovery that soldiers of the American occupation enforced Jim Crow in Haiti was thus a painful blow to him, as was the color line drawn between mulattoes and blacks and the fact that the Haitian ruling class segregated itself from the workers. Moving further away from the themes that characterized his writings of the 1920s, Hughes documented these sad realities in essays such as "People Without Shoes" (1931) and "White Shadows in a Black Land" (1932).

Langston Hughes, 1931. (Library of Congress.)

A trip to the Soviet Union in 1932 gave Hughes a sense of renewed optimism about the possibility of an egalitarian society. The contrast between the Soviet Union and the American South, where Hughes had spent more than four months on his speaking tour, could not have been more pronounced. Hughes was warmly greeted by white Muscovites gathered at the train station to meet him and was then whisked across Red Square in a luxurious sedan to the Grand Hotel, where he found courteous attendants and a clean, comfortable room. "Everything that a hotel for white folks at home would have," Hughes remarked in "Moscow and Me" (1933), "except that, quite truthfully, there was no toilet paper. And no Jim Crow." In essays and poems written during this trip, Hughes embraced revolutionary socialism as a viable alternative to the class and race antagonism that characterized life in the United States. "Put one more s in the U.S.A.," Hughes boldly proclaimed in a poem of 1934, "To make it Soviet." Such sentiments were characteristic of Hughes's writings of the 1930s. Discontented with the policies and practices of his own nation,

Hughes turned to others to seek the ideals of democracy that had been so badly compromised in the United States. Thus, while he was hailed as the "poet laureate of Harlem," Hughes was, by the close of the Harlem Renaissance, truly an international man of letters and a spokesperson for oppressed peoples worldwide.

Biography

James Mercer Langston Hughes was born on 1 February 1902, in Joplin, Missouri. He studied at public schools in Topeka, Kansas; Lincoln, Illinois; and Cleveland, Ohio. He then attended Columbia University (1921–1922) and Lincoln University, Pennsylvania (B.A., 1929). He worked as a crew member aboard a freighter headed for Africa (1923); worked in a Parisian nightclub (1924); collaborated with Zora Neale Hurston on *Mule Bone*, a play (1930); traveled through the South on a reading tour with support from the Rosenwald Foundation (1931); traveled to the Soviet Union to make *Black and White*, a motion picture about race relations in the United States (1932); wrote a series of articles for *Izvestia*, a Russian newspaper (1932); was a war correspondent in Spain for the Baltimore *Afro-American* (1937); founded the Harlem Suitcase Theater (1938); wrote a Hollywood script (1939); founded the Skyloft Players in Chicago (1941); was a columnist for the Chicago *Defender* (1942–1966); taught at the University of Chicago Lab School (1949); was a columnist for the *New York Post* (1962–1967); and traveled to Europe for the U.S. State Department (1965). His awards included the *Opportunity* prize for poetry (1925), a Guggenheim Foundation fellowship (1936), a Rosenwald Fund fellowship (1941), the NAACP Spingarn Medal (1960), and induction into the National Institute of Arts and Letters (1961). Hughes died in New York City on 22 May 1967.

CHRISTOPHER C. DE SANTIS

See also Black and White; Brownies' Book; Crisis, The; Du Bois, W. E. B.; Fauset, Jessie Redmon; Fine Clothes to the Jew; Mason, Charlotte Osgood; Mulatto; Not Without Laughter; Opportunity Literary Contests; Schuyler, George S.; Scottsboro; Van Vechten, Carl; Weary Blues, The

Selected Works

The Weary Blues. 1926.
Fine Clothes to the Jew. 1927

Not Without Laughter. 1930.
The Negro Mother and Other Dramatic Recitations. 1931.
Dear Lovely Death. 1931.
The Dream Keeper. 1932.
Scottsboro Limited. 1932.
Popo and Fifina. 1932. (With Arna Bontemps.)
The Ways of White Folks. 1934.
Mulatto. 1935.
Little Ham. 1935.
Troubled Island. 1936.
A New Song. 1938.
The Big Sea. 1940.
Shakespeare in Harlem. 1941.
The Langston Hughes Reader. 1958.
Good Morning, Revolution: Uncollected Social Protest Writings, ed. Faith Berry. 1973.
Mule Bone: A Comedy of Negro Life, ed. George Houston Bass and Henry Louis Gates Jr. 1991. (With Zora Neale Hurston.)
The Political Plays of Langston Hughes, ed. Susan Duffy. 2000.
The Poems: 1921–1940, ed. Arnold Rampersad. 2001.
Remember Me to Harlem: The Letters of Langston Hughes and Carl Van Vechten, 1925–1964, ed. Emily Bernard. 2001.
Essays on Art, Race, Politics, and World Affairs, ed. Christopher C. De Santis. 2002.
Works for Children and Young Adults: Poetry, Fiction, and Other Writing, ed. Dianne Johnson. 2002.
The Short Stories, ed. R. Baxter Miller. 2002.
The Plays to 1942: Mulatto to The Sun Do Move, ed. Leslie Sanders and Nancy Johnston. 2002.

Further Reading

Barksdale, Richard. *Langston Hughes: The Poet and His Critics*. Chicago, Ill.: American Library Association, 1998. (first published, 1977.)

Berry, Faith. *Langston Hughes: Before and Beyond Harlem*. Westport, Conn.: Lawrence Hill, 1983.

Bloom, Harold, ed. *Langston Hughes*. New York: Chelsea House, 1989.

Bloom, Harold. *Langston Hughes: Comprehensive Research and Study Guide*. Broomall, Pa.: Chelsea House, 1998.

Dace, Tish. *Langston Hughes: The Contemporary Reviews*. New York: Cambridge University Press, 1997.

Gates, Henry Louis Jr., and K. A. Appiah. *Langston Hughes: Critical Perspectives Past and Present*. New York: Amistad, 1993.

Jemie, Onwuchekwa. *Langston Hughes: An Introduction to Poetry*. New York: Columbia University Press, 1976.

McLaren, Joseph. *Langston Hughes: Folk Dramatist in the Protest Tradition, 1921–1943*. Westport, Conn.: Greenwood, 1997.

Miller, R. Baxter. *The Art and Imagination of Langston Hughes*. Lexington: University Press of Kentucky, 1989.

Mullen, Edward J. *Critical Essays on Langston Hughes*. Boston, Mass.: G. K. Hall, 1986.

———, ed. *Langston Hughes in the Hispanic World and Haiti*. Hamden, Conn.: Archon, 1977.

Ostrom, Hans. *A Langston Hughes Encyclopedia*. Westport, Conn.: Greenwood, 2001.

O'Daniel, Therman B. *Langston Hughes: Black Genius—A Critical Evaluation*. New York: Morrow, 1971.

Rampersad, Arnold. *The Life of Langston Hughes*, Vol. 1, *1902–1940: I, Too, Sing America*. New York: Oxford University Press, 1986.

Tracy, Steven C. *Langston Hughes and the Blues*. Urbana: University of Illinois Press, 1988.

Hunter, Alberta

The versatile blues and jazz singer Alberta Hunter was born in Memphis on 1 April 1895. In 1907 she ran away from home, accompanying her Chicago-bound music teacher (who was under the mistaken impression that Hunter had asked her mother for permission). At age fifteen she obtained her first job as a singer, in an exceedingly disreputable club called Dago Frank's, where she stayed for two years. Long-running engagements at Hugh Hoskins's and, especially, the Panama Café brought her more attention; Sophie Tucker, Eddie Cantor, and Al Jolson regularly stopped by to hear her sing. Soon Hunter was performing at Dreamland, Chicago's most prestigious club. "The South Side's sweetheart," as she was then being called, performed there with such jazz musicians as King Oliver, Sidney Bechet, and Tony Jackson. She was known for her rich contralto voice and excellent diction; her style was alternately earthy and sophisticated.

Hunter's initial recordings, for the Black Swan label in New York in 1921, featured Fletcher Henderson. She wrote and recorded "Down Hearted Blues" for Paramount in 1922 (because Hunter did not read music and therefore could not set down the score, the house pianist Lovie Austin received credit as a cowriter). A year later, Bessie Smith recorded it as her debut, with great success.

Hunter achieved fame in New York when she replaced Smith as a featured singer in the stage show

How Come? Advertised as a "girlie musical darkomedy" (Taylor 1987), *How Come?* was the most expensive black production to date. Hunter joined the cast, which also included Bechet, on 18 April 1923, and the show ran at the Apollo Theater for five weeks before going on the road (to Philadelphia, Baltimore, and the Lafayette Theater in Harlem). Meanwhile, Hunter's recording career accelerated. She was probably the first black singer to record with an all-white group (the Original Memphis Five, including Miff Mole, in 1923). In 1924 she made five records for the Gennett label with Louis Armstrong and the Red Onion Jazz Babies, including "Everybody Loves My Baby" and "Texas Moaner Blues"; because she was under contract with Paramount, Hunter used the name of her half sister, Josephine Beatty. That same year, she recorded as Alberta Prime on the Biltmore label, with Duke Ellington's band. Other notable recordings include "Chirpin' the Blues" (1923), "Your Jelly Roll Is Good" (1925), "I'm Hard to Satisfy" (1926), and three songs with Fats Waller on pipe organ for Victor ("Sugar," "Beale Street Blues," and "I'm Going to See My Ma," all 1927). Hunter also worked for Okeh, Decca, and Bluebird with musicians such as Eubie Blake, Clarence Williams, and Earl Hines. Most of her recordings during the 1930s were with orchestras, most notably Jack Johnson's society orchestra in London. She had her own radio show on NBC in 1938–1939.

In between recording dates, Hunter remained active on the circuit. Following an unsuccessful marriage in 1927 (Hunter was homosexual), she spent more and more time in Europe. Oscar Hammerstein and Jerome Kern heard her perform in 1927 at a benefit for victims of a flood in London, and they subsequently cast her as Queenie in a production of *Show Boat* with Paul Robeson at the London Palladium (1928–1929). One of the first female blues singers to tour Europe, she was especially well received in Paris, where she replaced Josephine Baker at the Casino de Paris.

During World War II, Hunter headed the first black USO show, completing twenty-five tours to various sites in Europe and the South Pacific. Soon after her mother died, Hunter retired from show business; she worked for the next twenty years as a nurse at Goldwater Memorial Hospital on Welfare Island (renamed Roosevelt Island in 1973). Renewed interest in the blues led to a successful comeback in 1977, when Hunter was eighty-two. She performed and recorded until her death in New York on 18 October 1984.

Biography

Alberta Hunter was born in Memphis, Tennessee, on 1 April 1895. In Chicago, she sang at Dago Frank's (1911–1913), Hugh Hoskins's (1913–1915), Panama Café (1915–1917), and Dreamland Ballroom (1917–1921); she also appeared in musical comedy revues in Chicago (1921–1922). Hunter made her first recording in New York City in 1921; joined the Broadway show *How Come?* in 1923; made the first of many European tours in 1927; performed in *Show Boat* at the London Palladium and in New York in 1928–1929; sang with Jack Johnson's orchestra throughout the 1930s; had her own show on NBC radio in 1938–1939; entertained troops during World War II on USO tours; joined ASCAP in 1952; and understudied three roles in the Broadway show *Mrs. Patterson* in 1954–1955. She passed the New York City elementary school equivalency examination, received a diploma (1955), attended the YMCA School for Practical Nurses (1956), and worked at Goldwater Memorial Hospital on Welfare Island (1956–1977). She returned to music in 1977. Hunter died in New York City on 18 October 1984.

GREGORY MILLER

See also Armstrong, Louis; Bechet, Sidney; Black Swan Phonograph Company; Blake, Eubie; Blues: Women Performers; Ellington, Duke; Henderson, Fletcher; Homosexuality; Oliver, Joseph "King"; Robeson, Paul; Show Boat; Singers; Smith, Bessie; Waller, Thomas "Fats"; Williams, Clarence

Selected Works

"Down Hearted Blues." 1922.
"Chirpin' the Blues." 1923.
"Down South Blues." 1923.
"You Got to Reap Just What You Sow." 1923.
"I'm Hard to Satisfy." 1926.

Recordings on CD

Complete Recorded Works, Vols. 1–4. Document 5422–5425.
The Legendary Alberta Hunter: DRG 5195.

Further Reading

Balliett, Whitney. *American Singers: Twenty-Seven Portraits in Song*. New York and Oxford: Oxford University Press, 1988.

Friedwald, Will. *Jazz Singing: America's Great Voices From Bessie Smith to Bebop and Beyond*. New York: Scribner, 1990; New York: Da Capo, 1996.

Harrison, Daphne Duval. *Black Pearls: Blues Queens of the 1920s*. New Brunswick, N.J.: Rutgers University Press, 1988.

Placksin, Sally. *American Women in Jazz: 1900 to the Present—Their Words, Lives, and Music*. New York: Seaview, 1982.

Sackheim, Eric. *The Blues Line: A Collection of Blues Lyrics*. New York : Schirmer, 1969. (See also 2nd ed., 1975.)

Southern, Eileen. *The Music of Black Americans: A History*. New York: Norton, 1971. (See also 3rd ed., 1997.)

Taylor, Frank C., with Gerald Cook. *Alberta Hunter: A Celebration in Blues*. New York: McGraw-Hill, 1987.

Winter, Kari J. "On Blues, Autobiography, and Performative Utterance: The Jouissance of Alberta Hunter." In *Creating Safe Space: Violence and Women's Writing*, ed. Tomoko Kuribayashi and Julie Tharp. Albany: State University of New York Press, 1997.

Hunter, Eddie

Eddie Hunter, a fast-talking comedian, was born in 1888 on New York's East Side, to a black father and a white mother. He left school in 1903. An early exposure to Bert Williams fired him with ambition to write vaudeville and musical comedy sketches. While working as an elevator attendant, he caught the attention of a regular passenger, the great tenor Enrico Caruso, who read his material and encouraged him.

Hunter's first public productions occurred in 1905–1906, when his parents rented a hall for him to perform his comedy sketches locally. He soon graduated to the Lincoln Theater in Harlem, sandwiching comedy acts between silent movies. When the Crescent Theater was founded in 1909, the owners invited him to write for them. The Crescent was Harlem's first true theater, the Lincoln being considered a movie house. Teamed with Thomas Chappelle, Hunter contributed highly successful stock pieces for several years, drawing crowds away from the rival Lincoln.

In 1912, when the owners of the Crescent leased the newly built Lafayette Theater, Hunter worked with Lester Walton, drama editor for *New York Age,* on productions similar to those at the Crescent. In 1915, when the Lafayette switched to straight drama, becoming the home of the Lafayette Players, Hunter returned to vaudeville. In 1920–1921, he toured as far as Salt Lake City, Utah, with his successful act—Hunter, Randall, and Senorita (his sister, Katherine), in their presentation *On the Border of Mexico*. In 1921, Hunter became the manager of the stock company of the Standard Theater in Philadelphia. He wrote and produced several shows there, which toured with his wife, Nina, in the cast.

In 1923, he produced his most famous show, *How Come?* Although its Broadway run was short and was treated harshly by the critics, it had already enjoyed long runs in Philadelphia and Washington, D.C., with a cast that included Alberta Hunter, Sidney Bechet, and, briefly, Bessie Smith. Revived in 1925, *How Come?* gained Hunter much attention, including a recording contract with Victor. This resulted in six sides during 1923–1924, including collaborations with the songwriter Alex Rogers, a veteran writer of material for Bert Williams. The association with Rogers enhanced Hunter's reputation as one of a group aspiring to inherit Williams's mantle.

Hunter collaborated with Rogers on two touring shows in 1924, *Struttin' Time* and *Steppin' Time*. Their coproduction of 1926, *My Magnolia*, starring Adelaide Hall, was a flop; but *Struttin' Hannah From Savannah* (originally *4–11–44*) toured successfully. In 1928 Hunter was invited to play in the English version of Lew Leslie's *Blackbirds of 1927*, after the original star, Florence Mills, withdrew because of ill health. He rejoined Lew Leslie for *Blackbirds of 1933*, which was a flop on Broadway but had some success on tour.

Eddie Hunter continued performing into the early 1940s, when he retired and became a property manager in Harlem's Sugar Hill area. However, he occasionally made special appearances; and in 1968, he was the recipient of a presentation by the people of Harlem, honoring his contributions to the black theater movement. He died in New York in 1980.

Biography

Edward (Eddie) Hunter was born in New York, on Ninety-seventh Street between Second and Third avenues, on 4 February 1888. He finished his education in 1903. He was a production manager with the Crescent Theater (1909), Lafayette Theater (1912), and the Standard Stock Company, Philadelphia (1921). Hunter died in New York in February 1980.

BILL EGAN

See also Bechet, Sidney; Blackbirds; Crescent Theater; Hall, Adelaide; Hunter, Alberta; Lafayette Players; Lafayette Theater; Leslie, Lew; Lincoln Theater; Mills, Florence; Musical Theater; Smith, Bessie; Sugar Hill; Walton, Lester

Productions and Performances

1909–1912. Short sketches, Crescent Theater. (Including *Going to the Races*, *The Battle of Who Run*, *What Happens When the Husbands Leave Home*, *The Railroad Porter*, *Subway Sal*.)
1920. *On the Border of Mexico*. (Vaudeville sketch.)
1921. *The Insane Asylum*. (Philadelphia.)
1922. *Abraham the Barber*. (Philadelphia.)
1923. *How Come?*
1924. *Steppin' Time*; *Struttin' Time*.
1925. *How Come?* (Revival.)
1926. *My Magnolia*; *4–11–44*.
1927. *Struttin' Hannah From Savannah*; *Darktown Scandals*.
1928. *Blackbirds of 1928*. (English provincial version.)
1933. *Blackbirds of 1933*. (Later toured as *Blackbirds of 1934*.)
1941. *Here 'Tis*.

Recordings

Vocal Blues and Jazz, Vol. 3, *1921–1928*. (DOCD-1015; with Alex Rogers.)
DOCD-5528: George Williams and Bessie Brown, Vol. 2, *1925–1930*. (DOCD-5528, with Alex Rogers.)

Further Reading

Albertson, Chris. *Bessie: Empress of the Blues*. London: Abacus (Sphere), 1975, p. 34.
Kellner, Bruce, ed. *The Harlem Renaissance: A Historical Dictionary for the Era*. New York: Methuen, 1984, pp. 175, 179.
Mitchell, Loften. *Black Drama*. New York: Hawthorn, 1967.
———. *Voices of the Black Theatre*. Clifton, N.J.: James T. Whit. 1975. (See "The Words of Eddie Hunter," pp. 35–57.)
Peterson, Bernard L. Jr. *The African American Theatre Directory, 1816–1960*. Westport, Conn.: Greenwood, 1993.
———. *A Century of Musicals in Black and White*. Westport, Conn.: Greenwood, 1993.

———. *Profiles of African American Stage Performers and Theatre People, 1816–1960*. Westport, Conn., and London: Greenwood, 2001. (See "Eddie Hunter," p. 132.)

Sampson, Henry T. *Blacks in Blackface: A Source Book on Early Black Musical Shows*. Metuchen, N.J., and London: Scarecrow, 1980. (See especially pp. 108, 119–120.)

Hurst, Fannie

Today Fannie Hurst is known primarily as the writer behind such films as *Imitation of Life*, *Back Street*, and *Humoresque*. Yet during the 1920s and 1930s, she was one of America's most popular and prolific novelists and short-story writers; she was the highest-paid writer in the nation. She also made her mark as a champion of many causes, especially workers' rights, women's rights, and civil rights for African Americans. Her significance to the Harlem Renaissance comes primarily from her support of Zora Neale Hurston and Dorothy West, among others; her championing of racial causes; and her work for publications such as *Opportunity*—but particularly from her friendship with Hurston.

Hurst was born in 1889 in Ohio and was raised primarily in St. Louis, Missouri, where she attended Washington University; she later did graduate work at Columbia University. Her ambition to be a writer developed early in her life, and she published numerous stories in student magazines while she was in school. In New York City, partly in order to study people for her writing, Hurst attended night court, observed people on the street, and took jobs as a waitress and a sales clerk. By 1913 her stories were appearing regularly in many popular magazines, most notably the *Saturday Evening Post*, whose editors had told her they would take anything she wrote.

Hurst married the pianist Jacques Danielson in 1915, but they kept their marriage secret for several years, living in separate houses, in part so that she could write without interruption and he could pursue his music. When news of the marriage broke on the front page of the *New York Times* in 1920, it became a cause célèbre, with both Hurst and Danielson writing defenses of their choices. In answer to one editorial in the *New York Times* that had castigated them for maintaining two separate residences during a housing shortage, Hurst asserted the right of a married woman to retain her name, life, and personal liberty. Later, though, Hurst and Danielson did share a home until his death in 1952.

Hurst's short stories were so popular that she was called the female O. Henry, and her publishers and her public urged her to write novels as well, although most critics agree that she was better in the short form. She wrote eighteen novels, more than 300 short stories, twelve films, numerous radio scripts and articles, and pamphlets about civil rights. Her stories tended to feature immigrants, shop girls, and people living in boardinghouse. She was frequently criticized for her sentimentality and uneven writing, but she was praised for her skill at rendering the emotional lives of women. Some thirty films have been made from her writings.

Among her novels, Hurst's own favorite was *Lummox* (1923), about a Polish immigrant domestic worker. Her greatest popular success was *Back Street* (1931). *Imitation of Life* (1933), probably her most recognizable title today, was filmed in 1934 and again in 1959. This story of a friendship between a white woman and a black woman and their two daughters, one of whom chooses to pass for white, met with great acclaim nationwide. In Harlem, it received general approval as a novel by someone who deeply deplored racial prejudice. There was, however, a notable exception: After the first wildly successful film version in 1934, starring Louise Beavers and Claudette Colbert, Sterling Brown published a review in *Opportunity* entitled "Imitation of Life: Once a Pancake." Brown said that the film and the novel indulged in stereotypes—the contented mammy, the tragic mulatto—and perpetuated archaic ideas about the mixture of the races. Langston Hughes, however, sent a note in 1937, thanking Hurst for having helped bring to the screen "the first serious treatment of the Negro problem in America." The next year, Hughes parodied Hurst's novel in "Limitations of Life" for the Harlem Suitcase Theater, but the two remained warm friends.

Hurst met Zora Neale Hurston on 1 May 1925, when she presented Hurston with second prize for a short story called "Spunk" at the first *Opportunity* awards dinner; Hurst had served as one of the judges. In September, Hurst invited Hurston to tea. In November, Hurston, needing tuition for Barnard and money for living expenses, moved into Hurst's house as her secretary. Hurston had no talent for the job. In "Zora Neale Hurston: A Personality Sketch" (1961), Hurst noted that Hurston's "shorthand was short on legibility, her typing hit-or-miss, mostly the latter, her filing a game of find the thimble." Hurston's job description was changed from secretary to chauffeur and companion.

We also have Hurston's description of her friendship with Fannie Hurst in her autobiography *Dust*

Tracks on a Road (1942). Hurston describes Hurst as "a curious mixture of little girl and very sophisticated woman." On one of their many driving trips, Hurst used the occasion to integrate a restaurant in Vermont by having Hurston dress as an Indian princess and accompany her. In the personality sketch of Hurston, Hurst applauded her "blazing zest for life" and noted, "Regardless of race, Zora had the gift of walking into hearts." As Wall (1995) points out, "Both accounts make much of the fact that Hurst employed Hurston as a secretary; . . . Hurston was actually in Hurst's regular employ for less than a month. Clearly the idea of the two, both writers, with strikingly similar names, appealed to the imagination of both." In 1934, Fannie Hurst wrote the introduction for Hurston's first novel, *Jonah's Gourd Vine*.

On 4 August 1946, after the Harlem Renaissance and the Harlem riots, Hurst wrote a piece for the *New York Times* Sunday magazine entitled "The Other and Unknown Harlem," in which she reminded her readers that "the large majority of Harlem, who lead ordered, backbone-of-the-nation lives, are seldom heard of. . . . [They are] the immense section of unhonored and unsung Harlem which represents decency, family unity, and social stability."

Hurst published throughout her life, and eventually she appeared frequently on radio and television programs. She remained involved in numerous reform movements, especially during the presidency of Franklin Roosevelt; she became a close friend of Eleanor Roosevelt, with whom she often campaigned for various issues. Hurst served as chair of the National Housing Commission in 1936–1937; chaired a national committee on workmen's compensation; was a member of the National Committee to the Works Progress Administration (WPA) in 1940–1941; and was a delegate to the World Health Organization Assembly of 1952. She also served as a member of the board of directors of the New York Urban League. She argued for equal pay for equal work and the right of a woman to retain her name after marriage. During World War II, she worked for the relief of oppressed Jews in eastern Europe and raised funds for refugees from Nazi Germany.

Most of Hurst's work was out of print at the time of the present writing, but Kroeger (1999) argues that she was a literary trendsetter who used her own celebrity to promote racial equality and women's rights. Hurst left instructions for her estate and her papers to be divided between Washington and Brandeis universities, with much of the money going to endow chairs in creative writing. In addition to those collec-

Fannie Hurst, c. 1931. (Library of Congress.)

tions, the bulk of her manuscripts and correspondence is at the Harry Ransom Humanities Research Center, University of Texas at Austin.

Biography

Fannie Hurst was born in Hamilton, Ohio, on 18 October 1889, to Rose Koppel Hurst and the shoe manufacturer Samuel Hurst—American Jews of Bavarian descent who had immigrated to the United States in 1860. She graduated from Washington University (B.A., 1909) and did graduate work at Columbia University. She had various part-time work in New York City, including as a waitress and in retailing. In 1915, she secretly married Jacques Danielson; he died in 1952. Her awards included an honorary degree from Washington University in 1953. Hurst died in New York City, on 23 February 1968.

KATHRYN WEST

See also Beavers, Louise; Brown, Sterling; Hughes, Langston; Hurston, Zora Neale; Opportunity; Opportunity Awards Dinner; West, Dorothy

Selected Works

Just Around the Corner. 1914.
Every Soul Hath Its Song. 1916.
Gaslight Sonatas. 1918.
Humoresque: Short Stories. 1919.
Star-Dust: The Story of an American Girl. 1921.
Lummox. 1923.
Appassionata. 1926.
A President Is Born. 1928.
Back Street. 1931.
Imitation of Life. 1933.
Lonely Parade. 1942.
Hallelujah. 1944.
Man With One Head. 1954.
Anatomy of Me: A Wonderer in Search of Herself. 1958.
Family! 1959.
God Must Be Sad. 1961.

Further Reading

Brown, Sterling. "Imitation of Life: Once a Pancake." *Opportunity*, April 1935, pp. 87–88.

Hemenway, Robert. *Zora Neale Hurston: A Literary Biography.* Urbana: University of Illinois Press, 1942.

Hurst, Fannie. "Zora Neale Hurston: A Personality Sketch." *Yale Gazette*, July 1961, p. 17.

Hurston, Zora Neale. *Dust Tracks on a Road.* Urbana: University of Illinois Press, 1942. (Reprint, 1984.)

Koppelman, Susan. "Fannie Hurst." In *The Oxford Companion to Women's Writing in the United States*, ed. Cathy Davidson and Linda Wagner-Martin. New York: Oxford University Press, 1994.

Kroeger, Brooke. *Fannie: The Talent for Success of Writer Fannie Hurst.* New York: Random House, 1999.

Shaughnessy, Mary Rose. *Myths About Love and Woman: The Fiction of Fannie Hurst.* New York: Gordon, 1980.

Wall, Cheryl A. *Women of the Harlem Renaissance.* Bloomington: Indiana University Press, 1995.

Hurston, Zora Neale

As a folklorist, ethnographer, novelist, short-story writer, storyteller, galvanizing personality, and emblematic figure of the celebration of black culture by the Harlem Renaissance, Zora Neale Hurston not only wrote about but also lived the quest of twentieth-century blacks to pursue beauty, individuality, and affirmation. Her writings, and her life, are characterized by a spirit of humor, contradiction, and imagination.

Hurston was born in Alabama in 1891. She grew up in Florida, and in her writings she refers repeatedly to her childhood and adolescence there: *Jonah's Gourd Vine*, for instance, is a veiled fictionalization of her parents' lives. Whereas many of the other major writers of the Harlem Renaissance focused on urban scenes and situations in Harlem, Hurston—primarily because of her parallel interest in customs and folklore—found her literary inspiration in the lives, language, and storytelling strategies of southern blacks.

In 1925, in search of the "New Negro" Renaissance, she arrived in New York and quickly distinguished herself as a storyteller and a source of entertainment at parties. But more than this, Hurston quickly translated her talent for storytelling to the written page—first by publishing "Spunk" in Alain Locke's *The New Negro* in 1925 and then by publishing "Sweat" and "Color Struck: A Play in Four Scenes" in *Fire!!* (November 1926). All three of these early works announce themes which would continue to occupy her writing for her entire career: storytelling, the relations between men and women, and the struggle for an independent sense of self. As part of a group that included Aaron Douglas, John P. Davis, Bruce Nugent, Gwendolyn Bennett, Langston Hughes, and Wallace Thurman, Hurston found herself among like-minded iconoclasts who were opposed, in various ways, to the more established figures: W. E. B. Du Bois, James Weldon Johnson, and Alain Locke. Wallace Thurman, in his passages on literary salons in *The Blacker the Berry* (1929) and *Infants of the Spring* (1934), highlights the bold, outspoken, and sometimes outrageous personality of Hurston (who is called Sweetie Mae Carr). Similarly, Langston Hughes, in his autobiography *The Big Sea* (1940), devotes a great deal of space to explaining Hurston:

> Of this "niggerati," Zora Neale Hurston was certainly the most amusing. Only to reach a wider audience, need she ever write books—because she is a perfect book of entertainment in herself. In her youth she was always getting scholarships and things from wealthy white people, some of whom simply paid her just to sit around and represent the Negro race for them, she did it in such racy fashion.

Such depictions of Hurston are not entirely complimentary, but they indicate the impression she made on Harlem in the 1920s.

Hurston's talent for storytelling may have been behind her decision to study anthropology at Columbia University and Barnard College with Franz Boas, Gladys Reichard, and Ruth Benedict. Like many of the younger generation of Harlem Renaissance writers, Hurston embraced the constructivist idea that race was a social convention rather than a biological necessity, but she also asserted her own "Negroness"—in such essays as "How It Feels to Be Colored Me" (1928)—and celebrated the distinctiveness of black culture, as in her "Characteristics of Negro Expression" (1934). Like Wallace Thurman and Rudolph Fisher, for example, Hurston held that for African Americans race was a burden that held them back from asserting their human individuality but was also a source of unique and delightful aspects of American life. Hurston celebrated that uniqueness in a series of sketches she published in *The Messenger* in late 1926, "The Eatonville Anthology."

Hurston was caught up in the particularly vicious social history of the African American, and she wrote her own story within the prescribed space of the divided self: just enough space to sustain one's "Negroness," but not enough space to move beyond the limitations of racial identification into self-determination. In "How It Feels to Be Colored Me," she says:

> At certain times I have no race, I am me. When I get my hat at a certain angle and saunter down Seventh Avenue, Harlem City, feeling as snooty as the lions in front of the Forty-Second Street Library, for instance. So far as my feelings are concerned, Peggy Hopkins Joyce on the Boule Mich with her gorgeous raiment, stately carriage, knees knocking together in a most aristocratic manner, has nothing on me. The cosmic Zora emerges. I belong to no race nor time. I am the eternal feminine with its string of beads.

Robert E. Hemenway, in his introduction to the second edition of Hurston's autobiography, *Dust Tracks on a Road*, discusses her sense of self as belonging to two distinct categories: private and public. The former is instinctive, folklorish, and Negro-centered; the latter is learned, literary, and "at home" in the wide white world. Applying this categorization to the autobiography, one begins to read it as a dialogue—somewhat heated and personal in places—between two selves who strive for identity and personhood by different means. These two selves appear throughout Hurston's work.

During the 1920s, however, much of that work was not under Hurston's own control. By agreement, Hurston ceded ownership of her writing to a wealthy patron, Charlotte Osgood Mason, who had offered the same agreement to Langston Hughes. As a result of her relationship with Mason, her research on folklore in the South (pursued in particular after she graduated from college in 1927), and the relative eccentricity of her focus on the rural South and on black female protagonists, a considerable amount of Hurston's writing in the 1920s remained unpublished and unrecognized, despite her personal triumphs and the success of her short stories.

Hurston came into her own as a folklorist and a novelist in the 1930s. With the publication of her books of folktales *Mules and Men* (1935) and *Tell My Horse* (1938) and the release of her novels *Jonah's Gourd Vine* (1934), *Their Eyes Were Watching God* (1937), and *Moses, Man of the Mountain* (1939), she became a major figure in African American literary and cultural expression. *Mules and Men* and *Tell My Horse* had resulted from ethnographic research that Hurston did as part of her studies with Boas and as the recipient of two Guggenheim fellowships, but *Jonah's Gourd Vine* heralded the emergence into American literature of a unique combination of narrative verve and inventiveness. In that work and her other novels of the 1930s, Hurston combined her research on folklore with the psychological possibilities of fiction. She exposed the inner life of black characters in all their creative, erotic, and personal depth and complexity through inventive language, unusual metaphors, natural imagery, and attention to the humorous and profound realities of rural southern life. In *Jonah's Gourd Vine* (which, as noted previously, is loosely based on the lives of her mother and father), Hurston juxtaposes the adventurous self-discovery of a philandering man against the complex self-diminishment of a long-suffering woman—chronicling what she called, in a letter to James Weldon Johnson, "the common run of us who love magnificence, beauty, poetry and color so much that there can never be too much of it."

These themes reappear in Hurston's second novel, *Their Eyes Were Watching God*, which is widely regarded as a very successful melding of storytelling with a focus on an independent woman's life. The opening paragraphs announce an interest in distinguishing the ways of men from those of women. As Janie Mae Crawford walks into town, her neighbors watch and comment from their porches, establishing an opposition between individual experience and social opinion.

The primacy of oral styles in this novel is indicated by its structure—it starts and ends with Janie's recounting of her life story to her friend Phoeby as the Florida night descends—and by the extensive use of images, similes, and metaphors derived from the black storytelling tradition. Chronicling Janie's girlhood and early womanhood in flashbacks, the novel traces her search for her own way of describing her life, for her own voice, for love, and for the world of people. Hurston's vivid use of black dialect shows that this dialect can convey complex, realistic characters—contrary to the proclamations of several black writers. (One example is James Weldon Johnson, in the introduction to *God's Trombones*; another is Richard Wright, in his review of *Their Eyes Were Watching God*—Johnson had decided not to use dialect, and Wright took Hurston to task for using it.) Hurston describes Janie and her world with a sympathy and an intimacy that are rare in American literature.

To her biographers, Hurston has seemed eccentric, elusive, and at times completely baffling; in her autobiography, she is doubly so. Autobiography is a genre caught in the cross fire between truth and fiction, and *Dust Tracks on a Road* is no exception. Walker (1975) concedes that Hurston "is probably more honest in her fieldwork and her fiction than she is in her autobiography, but only because she was hesitant to reveal how different she really was"; and in fact, Hurston took considerable liberties with the particulars of her life—as she admits in the text ("anybody whose mouth is cut cross-ways is given to lying"). This approach moves Hurston's autobiography away from strictly "objective" truth, freeing it to be more accurate about the directions Hurston's life took and about her perceptions of herself. Critics, too, have more freedom to read this autobiography as a work of the imagination in which the author's inventiveness may actually reveal much that she failed to see. Hurston offered this observation: "People are prone to build a statue of the kind of person that it pleases them to be. And a few people want to be forced to ask themselves, 'What if there is no me like my statue?' The thing to do is to grab the broom of anger and drive off the beast of fear."

Hurston's final book published during her lifetime, *Seraph on the Suwanee* (1948), depicts the rural South (like most of her previous works) but sets the action among white characters. Some critics consider this setting a rejection of black cultural traditions; others see it as an intentional reversal meant to highlight the flaws and foibles of a society that ascribes so much to categories like race and gender. In any case, though,

during the late 1940s and the 1950s, there was clearly a growing distance between Hurston's work and her readers. Hurston's conservative views about race, which had always troubled her colleagues in the Harlem Renaissance, stood out more prominently toward the end of her life. In the late 1940s and the 1950s, she wrote some articles for newspapers and magazines in the South, but for the most part she lived in obscurity; she worked occasionally as a librarian, teacher, or maid, and died in poverty in 1960.

The appearance of significant critical studies—particularly those by Walker (1975) and Hemenway (1977)—renewed interest in Hurston. To the writers and critics who rediscovered her in the 1970s and 1980s, she seemed to anticipate feminism, to embody the love of a distinctively African American culture, and to present a complicated, multilayered concept of the challenges facing black writers. In particular, there was a great deal of interest in *Their Eyes Were Watching God*, which has become part of the canon and a central text in American classrooms; and in *Mules and Men*, which is a classic of African American folklore. In 1991 *Mule Bone: A Comedy of Negro Life in Three Acts*, a play that Hurston cowrote with Langston Hughes and that caused a falling-out between them, was produced for the first time—nearly sixty years after its composition. Kaplan (2002) presents Hurston's correspondence with, among others, Countee Cullen, Langston Hughes, Fannie Hurst, Charlotte Osgood Mason, Carl Van Vechten, and Dorothy West. These letters reveal a sophisticated, complex woman who is very much aware of her considerable talents; they include her reactions to Hughes's depiction of her in *The Big Sea* and to the antipathy of the black press and the black public during the 1950s. Along with the stories, essays, and novels, the letters fill in the picture of a protofeminist, iconoclastic, down-home, politically conservative woman who wrote some of the most alluring prose of the twentieth century.

Hurston's complex, never fully comprehensible personality has made her infinitely attractive to critics. The contradictions and revisions in her work suggest how mobile and shifting her ideas of identity were. Hurston, rather boldly, stages herself, the South, and the situation of being a black woman in the United States for her audience. Finally, she was a master of the story. Her self-invention is inseparable from her love of storytelling and from the way she used language. Her celebration of black culture, her rebellious and independent spirit, and her determination to tell her story in her own voice (and with a sense of humor) continue to inspire writers and readers.

Zora Neale Hurston in Florida, 1935. (Library of Congress.)

Biography

Zora Neale Hurston was born in Notasulga, Alabama, on 7 January 1891 (but would later claim to have been born in 1901). She grew up in, and is particularly identified with, Eatonville, Florida. After the death of her mother in 1904, Hurston traveled with a theatrical troupe. She completed school in Baltimore, Maryland, and then enrolled at Howard University in Washington, D.C. (1923–1924). She came to New York in 1925 and began publishing that same year. She studied anthropology at Columbia University and Barnard College with Franz Boas, Gladys Reichard, and Ruth Benedict. Hurston became a major figure in African American literature in the 1930s. Her awards included two Guggenheim fellowships. In the late 1940s and the 1950s, Hurston did some writing for newspapers and magazines but lived mostly in obscurity, sometimes working as a librarian, teacher, or maid. She died in poverty in Fort Pierce, Florida, on 28 January 1960.

DANIEL M. SCOTT III

See also Bennett, Gwendolyn; Boas, Franz; Douglas, Aaron; Fire!!; Fisher, Rudolph; Hughes, Langston; Hurst, Fannie; Johnson, James Weldon; Mason, Charlotte Osgood; Messenger, The; New Negro, The; Nugent, Richard Bruce; Their Eyes Were Watching God; Thurman, Wallace; West, Dorothy

Works: Fiction

Jonah's Gourd Vine. Philadelphia, Pa.: Lippincott, 1934. (Reprint, New York: HarperPerennial, 1990.)
Their Eyes Were Watching God. Philadelphia, Pa.: Lippincott, 1937. (Reprints, Urbana: University of Illinois Press, 1979; New York: Harper, 1990.)
Moses, Man of the Mountain. Philadelphia, Pa.: Lippincott, 1939. (Reprint, New York: HarperPerennial, 1991.)
Seraph on the Suwanee. New York: Scribner, 1948. (Reprint, New York: HarperCollins, 1991.)
Spunk: The Short Stories of Zora Neale Hurston. Berkeley, Calif.: Turtle Island Foundation, 1984.
The Complete Stories. New York: HarperCollins, 1995.

Works: Nonfiction

Mules and Men. Philadelphia, Pa.: Lippincott, 1935.
Tell My Horse: Voodoo and Life in Haiti and Jamaica. Philadelphia, Pa.: Lippincott, 1938.
Dust Tracks on a Road. Philadelphia, Pa.: Lippincott, 1942. (Reprint, New York: HarperPerennial, 1995.)
I Love Myself When I Am Laughing . . . And Then Again When I Am Looking Mean and Impressive: A Zora Neale Hurston Reader, ed. Alice Walker. Old Westbury, N.Y.: Feminist, 1979.

Further Reading

Boyd, Valerie. *Wrapped in Rainbows: The Life of Zora Neale Hurston*. New York: Scribner, 2002.
Hemenway, Robert E. *Zora Neale Hurston: A Literary Biography*. Urbana: University of Illinois Press, 1977.
Howard, Lillie P. *Zora Neale Hurston*. Boston, Mass.: Twayne, 1980.
Kaplan, Carla, ed. *Zora Neale Hurston: A Life in Letters*. New York: Doubleday, 2002.
Lowe, John. *Jump at the Sun: Zora Neale Hurston's Cosmic Comedy*. Urbana: University of Illinois Press, 1994.
Walker, Alice. "In Search of Zora Neale Hurston." *Ms. Magazine*, March 1975, pp. 74–79, 85–89.

Infants of the Spring

Wallace Thurman's novel *Infants of the Spring* (1932) is an extraordinary work offering insights into the Harlem Renaissance from the perspective of a key figure in a younger group who called themselves or were called the niggerati (also spelled "niggeratti"). The events and discussions in *Infants of the Spring* are all set in "Niggeratti Manor," the home of the protagonist, Raymond Taylor—a meeting place of Harlem's black bohemia. Most of the characters seem to be thinly veiled real-life figures, and Taylor is evidently Thurman's persona. Similarly, the setting can be identified as Thurman's home at 267 West 136th Street, where he lived from 1926 to 1928. Except for its top floor (where an actress with two daughters, and another tenant, lived), the house was offered to young African American writers and artists by a black businesswoman, Iolanthe Sidney. In order to help talented young black people, Sidney asked for only a very low rent—or none, when (as frequently happened) her tenants were unable to pay anything at all.

The main focus of the fictional residence is Taylor's studio, where the niggerati gather for work, discussions, and parties. Two characters who live in Niggeratti Manor with Taylor are the artists Paul Arbian (modeled on Richard Bruce Nugent) and Pelham Gaylord (based on Rex Goreleigh), and the singer Eustace Savoy (based on William Service Bell). The story begins with the arrival of a white Canadian, Stephen Jorgenson (who is clearly modeled on Thurman's intimate friend Jan Harald Stefansson). Taylor and Jorgenson quickly become friends, and Jorgenson eventually moves in. Throughout the novel, the all-pervading issue of "race" is discussed. Racial tensions soon develop, as African American women compete for Jorgenson's attention: There are episodes of jealousy and continual arguments. Although Taylor is involved in the events, he is essentially the voice of reason, whose comments and insights—often in the form of an internal monologue—give the story its structure.

A significant aspect of the plot is the development of relationships. In this regard, the focus is on Taylor. His relationship with Jorgenson is described as intimate but platonic, giving the reader the impression that Thurman has intentionally excluded sexual attraction between these two men. The interracial experiment represented by Jorgenson's living in the center of Harlem does not succeed, and he and Taylor eventually split up. Taylor's relationship with Lucille (modeled on Thurman's wife, Louise Thompson) is also important. Here, too, sex is absent, yet it remains a continual point of discussion and tension between Taylor and Lucille, whose closeness intensifies toward the end of the novel.

Art constitutes a central issue in *Infants of the Spring*. The group of young African Americans who have gathered at Niggeratti Manor are actually creative failures: the writer Taylor and the painter Arbian represent unfulfilled talent, the poet Gaylord represents mediocrity at best, and the singer Savoy suffers from problems of racial identity. This failure is meant to reflect flaws that presumably hampered the development of the actual Harlem Renaissance. The niggerati—the "infants of the spring" of the title—suffer from stunted growth, as is suggested by the epigraph of the novel, two lines from *Hamlet*: "The canker galls the infants of the spring / Too oft before their buttons be disclosed."

The characters all seem to waste their talents or misinterpret their abilities: Taylor, deeply involved in discussions about race, relationships, and art, is unable to concentrate on his writing; Arbian, although clearly talented, does not work at his art but instead opts for decadent poses (his last pose being his craftily staged suicide); the vocalist Savoy has a penchant for white music, dislikes any type of African American music, fails dramatically, and ends up in the mental ward of a hospital in New York; Gaylord writes crude love poetry dedicated to one of the daughters of the actress living on the top floor, and is jailed for alleged rape—his poems, although they are metaphorical, are used as evidence against him. The most famous passage in the novel is a scene of a literary salon at which all of the great figures of the Harlem Renaissance are gathered, including a Dr. Parkes (who represents Alain Locke), DeWitt Clinton (representing Countee Cullen), and Sweetie May Carr (representing Zora Neale Hurston). There is a heated discussion—ending in shouting matches and chaos—about race and art and the direction the movement is to take. The message seems clear: The Harlem Renaissance could not succeed, because it was too narrowly defined, was defined in terms of race, and left no space for individualism.

When *Infants of the Spring* was published in 1932, the Harlem Renaissance had long since passed its height, and the nation had entered an economic depression. Consequently, the novel never received much critical attention. Thurman had actually developed the main body of the book in 1929–1930 during a one-year absence from Manhattan, when he stayed with a friend, the theater critic Theophilus Lewis, in Jamaica, Queens, and was supported by a grant from Elisabeth Marbury, a rich American literary agent who was also a patron of the arts. The text had apparently already been accepted by a publishing company in March 1930, but the name of the publisher is not known; nor is it clear why publication was deferred. It is certain, though, that Thurman reworked the novel several times, and this may have been one reason for the delay. Another factor in the delay in publication may have been the fact that Richard Bruce Nugent, Thurman's intimate friend at the time, also wrote an account of the Harlem Renaissance period, "Gentleman Jigger." Nugent claimed that Thurman had stolen chapters from "Gentleman Jigger" and had used them in *Infants of the Spring*. This alleged plagiarism has never been proved, and it seems that if Thurman actually did copy such material, he later removed these passages.

The few contemporary critics who reviewed *Infants of the Spring* at the time of its publication almost all dismissed it as poorly written. Thurman was always highly critical of his own work and seems to have concurred with this assessment; in 1932, in a letter to Langston Hughes, he said that the novel was "lousy." For many years, *Infants of the Spring* was out of print, but in a foreword to the 1992 edition, Singh reclaims its significance and holds that its themes are relevant in modern times. Even if the novel suffers from a rather thin story line and an overemphasis on monologue and discussions, it remains a unique, insightful, and entertaining insider's perspective on the Harlem Renaissance movement.

A. B. Christa Schwartz

See also Cullen, Countee; Hughes, Langston; Hurston, Zora Neale; Lewis, Theophilus; Locke, Alain; Nugent, Richard Bruce; Patterson, Louise Thompson; Thurman, Wallace

Further Reading

Abbott's Monthly Review, April 1932. (Review of *Infants of the Spring*.)

Fisher, Rudolph. "Harlem Manor." *New York Herald Tribune Books*, 21 February 1932. (Review of *Infants of the Spring*.)

Notten, Eleonore van. *Wallace Thurman's Harlem Renaissance*. Amsterdam: Rodopi, 1994.

Nugent, Richard Bruce. "Gentleman Jigger." N.d. (Unpublished typescript, Richard Bruce Nugent Papers, private collection of Thomas H. Wirth, Elizabeth, N.J.)

Singh, Amritjit. "Foreword to the 1992 Edition." In Wallace Thurman, *Infants of the Spring*. Boston, Mass.: Northeastern University Press, 1992.

Taylor, Lois. In *Opportunity*, March 1932. (Review of *Infants of the Spring*.)

Thurman, Wallace. *Infants of the Spring*. New York: Macaulay, 1932.

Inter-State Tattler

Although the *Inter-State Tattler* (1925–1932) was the most-maligned and shortest-lived example of Harlem's "chocolate drop press," it was more than just a "gossipy black weekly" (Watson 1995, 136). It offered a window onto the nightlife north of 125th Street, a scene enlivened by performers such as Bessie Smith and by clubs such as Small's Paradise, a regular advertiser. And in addition to columns called "Social Snapshots," "About People You Know," "Club Scribblings," and "Between Puffs," the *Inter-State Tattler* provided sports coverage as well as advice on finances, health, and fashion. Another column, "The World, the Flesh, and the Devil"—supposedly written by the "Three Moral Monkeys"—gave readers an opportunity to write in and redress, within limits, wrongs that anyone had done to them. Still, the playfulness of the *Tattler* led Lewis, for example, to describe it as "Afro-America's most frivolous newspaper . . . a sometimes viperous weekly hissing with gossip about 'sheiks' and 'shebas' at play in Harlem, Chicago, and on the West Coast" (1981, 126).

In focusing on the more social aspects of the New Negro, the *Tattler* was not entirely misguided. In fact, by ascribing a social element to the vibrant, yet sometimes too polished, psychology that Alain Locke and others wanted to project onto a new generation of black writers, the *Tattler* demonstrated how Harlem's "vogue and [its] literature were inextricably linked: Harlemania trained publicity's spotlight on black culture" (Watson, 106). Even Lewis concedes that the *Tattler* "excelled as a well-written gossip sheet with a racial conscience, and was even capable of serious literary commentary" (2000, 171).

The *Tattler*'s star columnist was its managing editor, Geraldyn Dismond Major, who doubled as "Lady Nicotine" for the column "Between Puffs" and appeared on the cover when she won first place among society writers in the Survey of the Negro Press of 1927. She was fond of A'Lelia Walker's wild parties: She said of one held in 1929 that "Bacchus himself passed out before midnight and along about two o'clock the shade of Rabelais returned to its tomb with its head hanging low in defeat." Major was also a regular at the annual Hamilton Lodge drag ball, known in the 1920s as the Faggots' Ball. In a column of February 1929, she observed that "a costume ball can be a very tame thing, but when all the exquisitely gowned women on the floor are men and a number of the smartest men are women, ah then, we have something over which to thrill and grow round-eyed."

Some of Harlem's luminaries were indeed round-eyed when they read Major's commentary. Her frank descriptions of bohemian venues such as the Hobby Horse, "which out-Villages the Village" with "exotic drawings . . . and a flock of artists," made it difficult for anyone to party anonymously. Neihart explains,

"Hell, some of the most committed faggots in Harlem were ambivalent about being seen [out], lest their names be celebrated in tomorrow's gossip columns" (2003, 8).

Coincidentally or pointedly, the *Tattler*'s use of blue ink reflected the off-color quality often associated with this periodical and with some undeniable aspects of the renaissance age.

SETH CLARK SILBERMAN

See also Hobby Horse; Homosexuality; Small's Paradise; Smith, Bessie; Walker, A'Lelia

Further Reading

Lewis, David Levering. *When Harlem Was in Vogue*. New York and Oxford: Oxford University Press, 1981.

———. *W. E. B. Du Bois: The Fight for Equality and the American Century, 1919–1963*. New York: Holt, 2000.

Neihart, Ben. *Rough Amusements: The True Story of A'Lelia Walker, Patroness of the Harlem Renaissance's Down-Low Culture*. New York and London: Bloomsbury, 2003.

Watson, Steven. *The Harlem Renaissance: Hub of African-American Culture, 1920–1930*. New York: Pantheon, 1995.

Isaacs, Edith

Edith Juliet Rich Isaacs began her career in theater in 1904 as a critic for *Ainslee's Magazine*. By 1918, she became editor of the influential magazine *Theatre Arts*. It was then that she established herself as one of the most important and influential members of the American theater community. One of Isaacs's main projects was the promotion of a national theater. She believed very strongly in the connection between theater and life; accordingly, she felt that a rich national American theater, rooted in American folk traditions, could enrich American life. She did not believe that theater in New York was fulfilling this purpose because it was too commercial, largely inartistic, and dull in general. Instead of following the uninspired paradigm of theater in New York, Isaacs urged Americans to go to "the four corners of the country and begin again, training playwrights to create in their own idiom, in their own theatres" (quoted in Martin 1996, 26). Also, Isaacs believed that in order for there to be a national theater—a national anything, for that matter—the American Negro must have an important role. Not only must black Americans be included in a national theater, she asserted, but the folk tradition she saw as vital to the existence of a national theater was most alive in black communities. In the June 1935 issue of *Opportunity*, Isaacs said that "the American theatre and the American Negro had a world of good things to place at each other's service if the road between them could be cleared. And . . . these things, rightly used, would enrich not only the theatre, but the whole of life" (174). With that, she set out to clear the road.

In August 1942 Isaacs devoted an entire issue of *Theatre Arts* to "The Negro in the American Theatre." The forty-nine-page feature included Isaacs's narrative along with copious photographs of actors (Ira Aldridge as Othello, Charles Gilpin in *The Emperor Jones*), productions (*Porgy and Bess*, *The Green Pastures*), and the like. Five years later, in 1947, Isaacs used this project as the basis for a landmark book-length study, also called *The Negro in the American Theatre*. In the introduction to this book, she stated her goal, again with an eye toward a unified national theater, and added: "The goal may not be reached until it is no longer possible to isolate the story of the Negro from the much broader panorama of the American theatre as a whole, in which the Negro plays his part as actor, dramatist, citizen. But at least the road is open now" (17). Alain Locke praised this goal, remarking: "*The Negro in the American Theatre* is all the more important because [it is] told in the overall context of the development of the drama of American life. . . . The story of the Negro's part in all this and of his progressive integration with it profits greatly through being told as an integral part of the general story." Locke also said that Isaacs was the most "consistent and constructive" friend of Negro drama (1948, 8–9). Isaacs was indeed a constructive friend; almost single-handedly, she opened the previously locked door of American theater to African Americans.

Biography

Edith Juliet Rich Isaacs was born on 27 March 1878, in Milwaukee, Wisconsin; her parents were Adolph Rich and Rose (Sidenberg) Rich. She graduated from Downer College (later Lawrence University) in 1899 and became a reporter for the *Milwaukee Sentinel*; she became literary editor of the *Sentinel* in 1903. She

married Lewis M. Isaacs, a lawyer, in 1904 and moved to New York. She wrote for *Ladies' Home Journal* and was a drama critic for *Ainslee's Magazine*; she was named editor of the magazine *Theatre Arts* in 1918 and served in that capacity until 1946. She worked with Alain Locke to sponsor the Blondiau Theatre Arts Collection of Primitive African Art. She edited *Theatre: Essays on the Arts of the Theatre* (1928), *Plays of American Life and Fantasy* (1929), *The American Theatre in Social and Education Life: A Survey of Its Needs and Opportunities* (1932), and *Architecture for the New Theatre* (1935). Isaacs aided in the creation of the National Theater Conference in 1925 and the American National Theater and Academy (ANTA) in 1935; she also served as ANTA's first vice president. In the mid-1930s, she was often consulted by Hallie Flanagan of the Federal Theater Project. Isaacs devoted the August 1942 issue of *Theatre Arts* to "The Negro in the American Theatre" and made this short narrative into a book of the same title in 1947. She relinquished the editorship of *Theatre Arts* to Rosamond Gilder in 1946. Isaacs died on 10 January 1956, at age seventy-seven.

STEPHEN CRINITI

See also Emperor Jones, The; Gilpin, Charles; Green Pastures, The; Locke, Alain

Selected Writings and Edited Works

Theatre: Essays on the Arts of the Theatre. Boston, Mass.: Little, Brown, 1927.

Plays of American Life and Fantasy. New York: Coward-McCann, 1929.

Architecture for the New Theatre. New York: Theatre Arts, 1935. (As editor.)

"The Negro and the Theatre: A Glance at the Past and a Prophecy." *Opportunity*, 13(6), 1935, pp. 174–177.

"The Negro in the American Theatre: A Record of Achievement." *Theatre Arts*, 26(8), 1942, pp. 494–543.

The Negro in the American Theatre. College Park, Md.: McGrath, 1947.

Further Reading

Bryant, H. Edward, III. "Edith Juliet Rich Isaacs." In *Notable Women in the American Theatre: A Biographical Dictionary*, ed. Alice M. Robinson, Vera Mowry Roberts, and Milly S. Barranger. New York: Greenwood, 1989, pp. 459–462.

"Edith J. R. Isaacs." In *Who Was Who in the Theatre: 1912–1926*, Vol. 3. Detroit, Mich.: Gale, 1978, p. 1274.

Locke, Alain. "A Critical Retrospective of the Literature of the Negro for 1947." *Phylon*, 9(1), 1948, pp. 3–12.

Martin, Carol. *A Sourcebook of Feminist Theatre and Performance: On and Beyond the Stage.* London: Routledge, 1996.

"Mrs. Isaacs Dies; Stage Expert, 78." *New York Times*, 11 January 1956.

Oppenheimer, Priscilla. "Edith (Juliet Rich) Isaacs." In *The Harlem Renaissance: A Historical Dictionary for the Era*, ed. Bruce Kellner. Westport, Conn.: Greenwood, 1984, pp. 186–187.

Tabor, Catherine Ann. "Edith Juliet Rich Isaacs: An Examination of Her Theories and Influence on the American Theatre." Ph.D. dissertation, University of Wisconsin–Madison, 1984.

Jackman, Harold

Harold Jackman, teacher, model, muse, and patron, is best known for being the best friend of poet Countee Cullen. Yet Jackman was himself a central figure of the Harlem Renaissance—though Arna Bontemps singled him out as one whose contributions to the renaissance had been ignored. Jackman had a collection of African American cultural artifacts; in addition, he was a witty and gossipy letter writer, and his correspondence with such figures as Countee Cullen, Langston Hughes, Nella Larsen, Zora Neale Hurston, Claude McKay, and Carl Van Vechten provides insight into his role in encouraging and supporting their literary efforts. Jackman was the physical model for the character Bryon Kasson in Van Vechten's novel *Nigger Heaven*, and he also appears in Wallace Thurman's novel *Infants of the Spring*.

Jackman met Countee Cullen in high school, and the two men remained close friends until Cullen's death in January 1946. They shared a love of theater, travel, and gossip. While Cullen was abroad, Jackman kept him and others informed of theatrical productions, literary news, and general goings-on in New York City. Their correspondence provides a context for and little-known details of many key events of the Harlem Renaissance. A discreet and humble man, Jackman was a member of Harlem's gay community. He frequented the famous Hamilton Lodge Balls, and his correspondence is filled with references, some coded, to other prominent gay men.

Jackman was active in the artistic and political communities in New York City. He directed Georgia Douglas Johnson's play *Plumes* in June 1929, was an associate editor of Dorothy West's journal *New Challenge* in 1937, and participated in political and literary groups that continued after the Harlem Renaissance. Throughout the 1930s and 1940s, he belonged to civic organizations including the Urban League and the American Theater Wing Stage Door Canteen. Jackman subsequently served as a contributing editor to *Phylon*, a literary journal published by Atlanta University (later Clark Atlanta University).

Jackman, a handsome man with prematurely gray hair, was a socialite in Harlem. He was a frequent escort of single women and was customarily king of the Urban League's Beaux Arts Ball. (The *New York Amsterdam News* reported his death with a headline on the front page: "Long Live the King!") He was also a model for Ophelia DeVore and Grace De Marco's legendary agency; he began modeling in the 1920s, appeared in advertisements in *Ebony* magazine through the late 1950s, and was featured in the historic special issue of the *Survey Graphic* (March 1925) in Winold Reiss's drawing *A College Lad*.

Jackman helped Carl Van Vechten obtain documents and other materials for the James Weldon Johnson Memorial Collection at Yale University. He also established what is now the Countee Cullen–Harold Jackman Memorial Collection at Clark Atlanta University, donating his own collection—including his correspondence with many well-known people—to Atlanta University. The collection, which also includes theater programs, drafts and manuscripts, sheet music, and audiotapes, has facilitated the study of African American culture.

Harold Jackman. (From "Harlem: Mecca of the New Negro," *Survey Graphic*, Vol. 6, No. 6, March 1925, F128.9.N3 H3 1925. Special Collections Department, University of Virginia Library, http://etext.virginia.edu/harlem/.)

Biography

Harold Jackman was born in England in 1901. He was raised in New York City and attended DeWitt Clinton High School, where he met Countee Cullen, who would become his close friend. Jackman earned a bachelor's degree from New York University and a master's degree from Columbia University. He was employed as a teacher by the New York City Public School System for his adult life. He was also active in the arts and politics; was a model; was an associate editor of *New Challenge* and a contributor to *Phylon*; and a correspondent with notable figures such as Langston Hughes, W. E. B. Du Bois, Gwendolyn Bennett, Dorothy West, Claude McKay, Countee Cullen, Richmond Barthé, Carl Van Vechten, and Owen Dodson. Jackman died in 1961.

JACQUELINE C. JONES

See also Barthé, Richmond; Bennett, Gwendolyn; Cullen, Countee; Homosexuality; Hughes, Langston; Hurston, Zora Neale; Infants of the Spring; Johnson, Georgia Douglas; McKay, Claude; New Challenge; Nigger Heaven; Survey Graphic; Thurman, Wallace; Van Vechten, Carl; West, Dorothy

Further Reading

Bontemps, Arna. "The Awakening: A Memoir." In *The Harlem Renaissance Remembered*, ed. Arna Bontemps. New York: Dodd, Mead, 1972.

Chauncey, George. *Gay New York*. New York: Basic Books, 1994.

Early, Gerald. *My Soul's High Song: The Collected Writings of Countee Cullen, Voice of the Harlem Renaissance*. New York: Doubleday, 1991.

Ferguson, Blanche. *Countee Cullen and the Negro Renaissance*. New York: Dodd, Mead, 1966.

Hawkeswood, William G. *One of the Children: Gay Black Men in Harlem*. Berkeley: University of California Press, 1996.

Lewis, David Levering. *When Harlem Was in Vogue*. New York: Random House, 1981.

———. *W. E. B. Du Bois: The Fight for Equality and the American Century 1919–1963*. New York: Holt, 2000.

Reimonenq, Alan. "Countee Cullen's Uranian 'Soul Windows.'" *Journal of Homosexuality*, 26(2–3), pp. 143–165.

Shucard, Alan. *Countee Cullen*. Boston, Mass.: Twayne, 1984.

Van Notten, Eleonore. *Wallace Thurman's Harlem Renaissance*. Atlanta, Ga.: Rodopi, 1994.

Jackson, May Howard

May Howard Jackson was a proponent of racial representation in art, and her neoclassical portrait sculptures reflected the positive self-image of black Americans during the Harlem Renaissance. In technique, she is considered a traditionalist; and her style was not entirely indicative of the "New Negro," since she neither experimented widely nor looked to Africa for ancestral roots; however, her later works were more angular and abstract, hinting at modernism.

Jackson's realistic portrait busts of black American leaders captured their psychological character and were a significant departure from the stereotypes, caricatures, and exotic images of blacks that prevailed at the time. Her sitters included W. E. B. Du Bois, Paul Laurence

Dunbar, Reverend Francis J. Grimke, W. H. Lewis, Kelly Miller, and Jean Toomer. During the late 1920s, perhaps because of a lack of commissions, Jackson turned to the theme of mother and child, in *Head of a Negro Child* (1929), *Shell-Baby in Bronze* (1929), and *Mulatto Mother and Her Child* (1929). These works are more abstract and less neoclassical.

In 1895, Jackson was first black American woman to receive a scholarship at the Pennsylvania Academy of the Fine Arts, where her teachers included John Joseph Boyle, William Merritt Chase, and Charles Grafly. She moved to Washington, D.C., in 1902 when she married William T. Sherman Jackson. Between 1899 and 1931, she had a studio in Washington and exhibited both there and in New York. She also taught art to black children in Washington and lectured at Howard University; one of her students at Howard was the artist and art historian James A. Porter. Another notable student of Jackson's was her nephew Sargent Johnson, who lived with her at one time; their work was shown in some of the same exhibitions of the Harmon Foundation, a philanthropic organization that promoted the work of black American artists.

Jackson was occasionally mentioned in *Crisis*; was cited in Benjamin Brawley's *Women of Achievement* (1919); was praised in a poem by Georgia Douglas Johnson (1922); and was invited by Mary Beattie Brady, organizer of the Harmon Foundation exhibition in New York in 1927, to serve as a judge (although Jackson was delayed and had to view the works separately after selections had been made).

Because of her race, Jackson was denied membership in the Washington Society of Fine Arts and eventually received no further invitations to exhibit at the National Academy of Design (where her work had been included in group shows in 1916 and 1928); moreover, many people thought that her interest in the physiognomy of black people, combined with her neoclassical sculptural style, was outmoded. Nevertheless, in 1928 she received a bronze medal from the Harmon Foundation in recognition of her work as a whole. When Jackson died, Du Bois wrote in *Crisis* (October 1931) that her death was "a loss to art." He added that she had "met rebuffs in her attempts to study, and in her attempts at exhibition, in her chosen ideal of portraying the American mulatto type; with her own friends and people she faced continual doubt as to whether it was worthwhile" but that she had "accomplished enough to make her fame firm in our annals."

Biography

May Howard Jackson was born 12 May 1877 in Philadelphia, Pennsylvania. She studied at public school and in J. Liberty-Tadd's Art School in Pennsylvania; and at the Pennsylvania Academy of the Fine Arts (A.B., 1895–1898, 1900–1902.) She married William T. Sherman Jackson, 1902; had a studio in Washington, D.C., 1902–1931; and was an instructor in the department of fine arts at Howard University, 1922–1924. Her awards included a scholarship to the Pennsylvania Academy of Fine Arts, 1895–1899; and a bronze medal from the Harmon Foundation, 1928. She died in Long Beach, New York, 12 July 1931.

CLAUDIA HILL

See also Brawley, Benjamin; Crisis, The; Du Bois, W. E. B.; Dunbar, Paul Laurence; Harmon Foundation; Johnson, Georgia Douglas; Johnson, Sargent Claude; Miller, Kelly; Porter, James Amos; Toomer, Jean

Selected Exhibitions

1912: Verhoff's Galleries, Washington, D.C.
1913: National Association for the Advancement of Colored People, New York.
1915: Corcoran Gallery of Art, Washington, D.C.
1916: Verhoff's Galleries, Washington, D.C. (Individual.)
1916: National Academy of Design, New York.
1919: Verhoff's Galleries, Washington, D.C.
1919: Tanner Art Students Society, Washington, D.C.
1919: Dunbar High School, Washington, D.C.
1928: National Academy of Design, New York.
1929: Harmon Foundation, New York.

Further Reading

Brawley, Benjamin. *Women of Achievement*. Chicago, Ill.: Woman's American Baptist Home Mission Society, 1919.
Benjamin, Tritobia Hayes. "May Howard Jackson and Meta Warrick Fuller: Philadelphia Trailblazers." In *Three Generations of African American Women Sculptors: A Study in Paradox*, ed. Carolyn Shuttlesworth. Philadelphia, Pa.: Afro-American Historical and Cultural Museum, 1996.
Cederholm, Theresa Dickason. *Afro-American Artists: A Bio-Bibliographical Directory*. Boston, Mass.: Trustees of the Boston Public Library, 1973.

Du Bois, W. E. B. "Postscript: May Howard Jackson." *Crisis*, October 1931.

Igoe, Lynn, with James Igoe. *250 Years of Afro-American Art: An Annotated Bibliography.* New York: Bowker, 1981.

Johnson, Georgia Douglas. *Bronze: A Book of Verse.* Boston, Mass.: B. J. Brimmer, 1922.

King-Hammond, Leslie. "Jackson, May Howard (1877–1931). "In *Black Women in America: An Historical Encyclopedia*, ed. Darlene Clark Hine, with Elsa Barkley Brown and Rosalyn Terborg-Penn. Brooklyn, N.Y.: Carlson, 1993.

Lewis, Samella. *Art: African American.* New York: Harcourt Brace Jovanovich, 1978.

Riggs, Thomas, ed. *St. James Guide to Black Artists.* Detroit, Mich.: St. James, 1997.

Stewart, Jeffrey C. ed. *The Critical Temper of Alain Locke: A Selection of His Essays on Art and Culture.* New York: Garland, 1983.

Jazz

On 6 April 1917, the Original Dixieland Jass Band opened at the Paradise Room of Reisenweber's Café on Columbus Circle in New York City. Through these white imitators of New Orleans–style novelty bands, the term "jass" or, later, "jazz" and the music known as jazz came to New York. By 1918, the term had become common usage; for example, in World War I black regimental bands were called "jazz bands." Another common term was "hot" music, as opposed to "sweet" music. Sweet music was the music played for ballroom dancing downtown; hot music became associated with the music of Harlem. The movement from sweet to hot was a major transformation and was significant to the concepts of jazz that developed during the Harlem Renaissance.

Musical Life in Harlem

Benny Carter, the noted jazz arranger, player, and composer, moved to Harlem in 1923 when he was sixteen years old. As he later remembered, "There was music everywhere—from dusk to dawn. And I was privileged to be right in the midst of it. I was encouraged to sit in with people like Willie 'the Lion' Smith and Bill Basie, that was before he became 'Count.' If you could play passably well you were welcome, as long as the proprietor didn't have to pay you" (Berger 1992).

The musical life that Carter described was a result of several factors. One was the rapid migration of blacks from the South to New York. A second factor was segregation. The policies of segregation forced many blacks to live in the upper-northeastern part of Manhattan, the area called Harlem; also, many African American musicians were barred, because of their race, from entering music conservatories and classical musical organizations such as symphony, opera, and ballet orchestras. A third factor, related to the second, was the fact that musicians had to commute from their homes in Harlem to their work downtown in Broadway theaters, recording studios, ballrooms, and clubs. To accommodate them when they returned to Harlem late at night, "after-hours" clubs developed; these clubs proved to be the real conservatories for black musicians. Duke Ellington and Billy Strayhorn's "Take the 'A' Train"—"the quickest way to get to Harlem"—reflects this pattern of travel from downtown to uptown. Ellington (1973) recounted how, after playing a show downtown at the Kentucky Club, he and drummer Sonny Greer would play special requests for patrons and receive $100 to $200 in tips. Then they would go to Harlem and spend it all in the after-hours clubs.

The typical jazz musician of Harlem would be exposed to a variety of musical styles and would have to master them in order to make a living. This situation produced a very capable type of musician who could perform many genres but who had little time and few opportunities to develop as a soloist. In the words of one musician, "You did your 'woodshedding' before you came to New York if you were a solo jazz player." Louis Armstrong, Sidney Bechet, and Duke Ellington were all accomplished soloists before coming to New York.

Still, despite the overcrowded, segregated conditions and the competition among musicians for work, Willie "the Lion" Smith said, "I'd rather be a fly on a lamppost in Harlem than a millionaire anywhere else."

What Is This Thing Called Jazz?

At the beginning of the Harlem Renaissance, jazz was defined by performances and performers from the New Orleans tradition. Nick La Rocca, the leader of the Original Dixieland Jass Band, explained: "Jazz is the assassination of the melody and the slap of syncopation." Melodic decoration, instrumental timbral effects, and syncopation were among the characteristics of this style. In 1925, Eubie Blake—composer of *Shuffle*

Along (1921), the first all-black show in a Broadway theater—described the public taste as follows: "What the public wants today are lively, jazzy songs, not too jazzy, with love interest, but without the sickly sentimentality in vogue a generation ago."

One characteristic distinguishing jazz from other music is that it is primarily a vocal style imitated by instruments. For instance, all the colors and nuances of the Negro voice were transferred into the plunger mutes of Bubber Miley's trombone and Cootie Williams's trumpet, into the slurs and growls of Johnny Dodds's clarinet, and into the trap sound effects of drummers Sonny Greer and Chick Webb. Another unique timbral effect was achieved by James Reese Europe, who replaced the second violins, violas, and cellos in his Society Orchestra with banjos to give a strumming, murmuring sound. Also, because ballrooms in New York were so large, bands and orchestras had to add more brass instruments and saxophones, which produced a much larger, louder sound.

The jazz of this time had a strong, and significant, emphasis on individualism. It was not what you played but how you played it. Bill Evans, a jazz pianist of the 1970s, said of jazz history: "Jazz is not a 'what'; it's a 'how'—and if you do things according to the 'how' of jazz, it's jazz." The jazz improviser became at the same time an interpreter and composer in relationship to the surrounding musicians and the listeners. Short preexisting forms such as blues and pop tunes from Tin Pan Alley formed the basis of the musical material from which the skilled jazz player could improvise.

The oral tradition provided the means of transmission for this music. It was the music heard in recordings, in after-hours clubs, and on the street that formed the ideas heard in jazz improvisations. Also, the "call and response" aspect of conversation, which came from the oral tradition, was adapted for jazz. The blues form consisting of statement, restatement, and result allows an instrumental response to the vocal music at the end of each couplet; this dialogue between soloist and accompaniment is based on call and response. Later, as the big bands emerged, call and response between the brass section and the saxophone section would become an important aspect of this type of jazz.

The "slaying of syncopation," as described by Nick La Rocca, was also an essential ingredient in jazz. A basic dance movement in many west African communities is to lift the foot up off the ground and place it down gently; the upbeat of the African dancer is reflected in the offbeat of the music. In European dances, the entire leg is used to give a stomping effect; thus the downbeat of the military march emphasizes the soldier's footfall. In other words, the African dance will accent beats two and four of a four-beat pattern, allowing the lifting of the foot and leg, whereas a march will place the emphasis on the first and third beats of the pattern. This concept of syncopation, introduced in ragtime ("ragged time"), was developed in jazz to superimpose one beat pattern over another simultaneously. As Ellington expressed this: "It Don't Mean a Thing If It Ain't Got That Swing"—"Doo-wah, doo-wah, doo-wah, doo-wah, doo-wah, doo-wah, doo-wah, doo-wah." Here, Ellington provides the call-and-response pattern but places the response in a pattern of nine over a pulse beat of eight. This throws the beat out of sync—syncopation. In this regard, too, the faster tempo of the new dances such as the fox trot and the Charleston (sixty and ninety beats per minute) seemed to reflect the hectic pace of the times.

William C. Handy, the composer of "Saint Louis Blues" and "Memphis Blues," taking a more philosophical and social viewpoint, believed that ragtime, blues, jazz, and spirituals all "came from the same strain of Negro creation." Alain Locke, a social philosopher, described jazz as "first a reaction from Puritan repressions and then an escape from the tensions and monotonies of machine-ridden, extroverted form of civilization" (1936). Locke also said: "Jazz is basically Negro, then, although fortunately, also human enough to be universal in appeal and expressiveness."

The journalist Joel Augustus Rogers, of the *Amsterdam News*, wrote in 1925 that the racial component of jazz was "one part American and three parts American Negro, and was nobody's child of the levee and the city slum. . . . It is really at home in its humble native soil wherever the modern unsophisticated Negro feels happy and sings and dances to his mood."

Performers of Jazz and Their Influence

Among the early venues for jazz performers were "rent parties." In the urban environment of Harlem, low wages and a lack of housing led to overcrowding—and to insufficient funds to pay landlords. One solution was the rent party, which often included a player of a "band in a box," the parlor piano. Rent parties would begin on a weekend afternoon and last until the next morning. At first, the music was ragtime, waltzes, popular tunes, and dances. Later, a style known as

"Harlem stride" piano playing became popular. In stride piano, the left hand played a note in the bass register on the downbeat and then a chord in a higher octave on the offbeat; the right hand played syncopated melodic patterns. Talented players would often syncopate the left hand as follows: 1 2 | 1 2 | 1 1 | 2 1 | (with 1 as the bass note and 2 as the chord). James P. Johnson, Willie "the Lion" Smith, and Thomas "Fats" Waller were all stride pianists and were in demand for rent parties.

When piano rolls were cut of these performances—such as James P. Johnson's "Carolina Stride"—a young player like Duke Ellington or Fletcher Henderson would learn to play the pieces by placing his fingers on the keys as they were depressed by the mechanical piano rolls. James Weldon Johnson observed in *Autobiography of an Ex-Colored Man* that these pianists were "making 'serious' or 'famous' work in the Negro vein an aim of the professional career."

Blues bands usually featured a small combo of trumpet, banjo or piano, and clarinet. W. C. Handy transported blues to New York, and specifically to Tin Pan Alley, to develop more of an urban feel instead of the rural tradition. In the early "race records," these small ensembles would provide accompaniment and occasional solos.

Between 1921 and 1939, forty black musicals were presented in New York City. Beginning in 1921 with *Shuffle Along*, by Eubie Blake and Noble Sissle, the Broadway theaters provided opportunities for African American musicians. The typical theater orchestra had violins, flutes, oboes, saxophone, trumpets, piano, banjo, and drums; sometimes a tuba or bass would be added. In 2002, this long tradition was continued when *Harlem Song*, a black musical recalling the Harlem Renaissance, played at the Apollo Theater in Harlem. (In June of that year, President George W. Bush invited the producers of *Harlem Song* to give a performance at the White House in honor of Black Music Month.)

Although few recording companies were owned by blacks (Black Swan, for which Ethel Waters was a featured singer, was an exception), even white owners were quick to realize that they could find a large market by making "race records." After a record of Mamie Smith singing "Crazy Blues" sold a million copies in less than a year, recording companies scrambled to record African American blues singers and instrumentalists. (Not until 1947 would *Variety* change the category "race music" or "Harlem Hit Parade" to "rhythm and blues.") Duke Ellington said of this period,

when he was employed at the Kentucky Club: "We recorded once a week, sometimes three or four times a week, for almost every existing label under different names: Duke Ellington on Victor, Jungle Band on Brunswick, Washingtonians on Harmony, Whoopee Makers on Perfect and Harlem Foot Warmers on Okeh."

Because of the technological limitations of the time, however, jazz was recorded in conditions that made a true representation of the music impossible. A record could hold only three minutes of music, which meant extended compositions and performances were severely curtailed. Certain instruments such as bass drums and string basses were omitted because of lack of space in the recording studios and because the acoustical range was limited. Also, the repertoire was restricted to what the owners thought they could sell. Therefore, Fletcher Henderson's waltz medleys from the Roseland Ballroom were not recorded, nor was Fats Waller playing Chopin's études. Nevertheless, jazz musicians were an important component of "race records."

One important influence on jazz that is not well documented during this period is music from the Caribbean and South America, called "Latin music." Roberts (1998) notes that more than half of James Reese Europe's 180 musicians were listed in the Clef Club Booking Agency as Puerto Ricans. This was evidently because they had a higher level of musical skills such as sight reading and playing different styles. The "tango craze" was imported uptown; "tango teas"—at which people would dance to ragtime as well as tangos—were popular in Harlem. In both "Saint Louis Blues" and "Memphis Blues," W. C. Handy included "habanera" sections reflecting a Cuban influence. In 1929 Juan Tizol, a Puerto Rican valve trombonist, joined the Ellington Band at the Cotton Club, where he wrote a famous piece of "jungle music" called "Caravan." Classy nightspots usually had one band or orchestra for dancing, a second for the shows, and a third to play Latin music and particularly tangos. The musicians of Harlem also knew calypso. Okeh Records made recordings of calypso in the 1920s, and Sam Manning recorded "My Little West Indian Girl."

Dance bands and show bands were probably the most influential aspect of jazz. In 1924, *Variety* listed 900 dance bands, with more than 7,200 musicians, in the United States. Paul Whiteman had sixty-eight bands and orchestras using his name, including eleven in New York City. The five- or six-piece New Orleans–style bands had to be increased to play in the larger clubs and ballrooms, which needed more sound. Duke Ellington, for instance, had to increase the number of his musicians from the six who played at the Kentucky Club to the eleven who played at the larger Cotton Club in 1927. (Ellington was an exception to the usual practice of hiring musicians on a per-service basis. By establishing his orchestra at the Cotton Club, he was able to keep the same musicians in the band and could compose for their individual musical qualities.) Because the dance bands also had to play for shows, musicians who could sight-read and play in many styles were preferred. Few outstanding solo players emerged from the ranks of New York's dance bands.

Hot versus Sweet

Many of the early jazz groups were known as "hot": Louis Armstrong's Hot Five and Hot Seven, Fletcher Henderson's Hot Six, and the like. The term "hot" seemed to distinguish these groups from musical ensembles that called themselves orchestras and played more sophisticated "sweet" music. The contrast between hot and sweet is suggested in the lyrics to Duke Ellington's "Don't Mean a Thing": "Makes no difference if it's sweet or hot. Just keep that rhythm, give it all you've got!"

An anecdote about the famous Fletcher Henderson Orchestra, which played at the Roseland Ballroom downtown, illustrates this conflict. When Louis Armstrong joined the Henderson orchestra in 1924, he arrived in the middle of a rehearsal of waltzes and started playing along quite loudly. Henderson stopped the music and asked what the dynamic marking was; Armstrong replied that it was "pp." Henderson said that this meant *pianissimo*—that is, play softly. Armstrong answered that he thought it meant "pound plenty!" This story indicates not only the difference between styles but also Armstrong's limited ability to read music. Armstrong played in the New Orleans style, an oral tradition in which he had developed his skill as a soloist rather than skill in reading music.

When Henderson became the recording director for Black Swan Records, he accompanied Ethel Waters on a successful tour with his Black Swan Dance Masters. Waters complained that he wouldn't play the "damn-it-to-hell" bass lines (stride piano style) that she preferred. She bought him some piano rolls of James P. Johnson, and Henderson learned to play in Johnson's hot style.

A notable comment about the sweet style that was preferred in the downtown ballrooms and shows comes from Duke Ellington, describing the style of Paul Whiteman. Ellington said that Whiteman "dressed

her in woodwinds and strings and made a lady out of jazz." However, the hot bands could parody sweet orchestras. Fletcher Henderson recorded "Dicty Blues" in 1922, and Duke Ellington recorded "The Dicty Glide" in 1929 "Dicty" was a slang word in Harlem indicating snobbishness or "putting on airs."

A distinguishing feature of hot bands and orchestras was their ability to relate to the responses of the dancers. Duke Ellington describes this feature in discussing Chick Webb, who led the Savoy Ballroom Orchestra: "The reason why Chick Webb had such control, such command of his audience at the Savoy Ballroom, was because he was always in communication with the dancers and felt it the way they did." This was the era of dances such as the Charleston, black bottom, and lindy hop.

Another aspect of hot versus sweet music is suggested by the number of white musicians who came to the dance clubs and after-hours joints to learn hot music. Paul Whiteman, George Gershwin, Darius Milhaud, and others came to listen and incorporate this style into their own music. For example, in 1924, in a concert called "Experiment in Modern Music" at Aeolian Hall, the Paul Whiteman Orchestra presented both the premiere of Gershwin's *Rhapsody in Blue* and a piece that had become famous in a recording the Original Dixieland Jass Band, "Livery Stable Blues." Later, the Whiteman Orchestra added such white jazz performers as Bix Beiderbecke on trumpet, Jack Teagarden and Frank Teschmaker on trombone, and Eddie Lang on guitar. Gene Krupa learned much of his drumming style from Chick Webb; and Benny Goodman not only learned his clarinet licks in Harlem but he also was the first important white bandleader to hire black musicians.

Jazz and the Harlem Renaissance

The writers and philosophers who developed the idea of the "New Negro"—W. E. B. Du Bois, Alain Locke, James Weldon Johnson—had little regard for "entertainment" music. They appreciated the qualities of the "sorrow songs," the Negro spirituals as sung by Harry T. Burleigh and Roland Hayes, but they felt that blues, jazz, and jazz dance did nothing to uplift the Negro race. One writer, Samuel Floyd (1995), states: "Initially, entertainment music, including jazz, was ignored or dismissed by Renaissance leaders in favor of concert music; the blues and other folk forms (except for the Negro Spiritual, which was held in high esteem) were rejected as decadent and reminiscent of the 'Old Negro.'" Benny Carter writes: "Jazz was viewed either ambivalently or with outright hostility by many of the leading figures of the movement. We in music knew there was much going on in literature, for example, but our worlds were far apart. We sensed that the Black cultural as well as moral leaders looked down on our music as undignified." An example of the ambivalence Carter mentions comes from the composer William Grant Still, who wrote the *Afro-American Symphony*: "Some forms of jazz are cheap, monotonous. No one can be blamed for scorning them. But there are also forms of jazz that are valuable additions to music; forms upon [which] great symphonies can be built."

By contrast, the younger literary talents of the Harlem Renaissance—Langston Hughes, Zora Neale Hurston, and Sterling Brown—embraced the new music and used it in their writings. Hughes wrote in one poem:

I'm going down to de river

And take me a rockin' chair

If the blues overcome me

I'm gonna' rock away from here.

Interestingly, in this poem Hughes uses an encapsulated version of the blues form by omitting the repetition of the first stanza. Benny Carter praises Hughes as "the poet laureate of the Renaissance and a man who had much respect for and understanding of this music"— that is, jazz. Hughes himself said, regarding the conflict over how to define the New Negro: "Let the blare of Negro jazz bands and bellowing voice of Bessie Smith singing Blues penetrate the closed ears of colored near-intellectuals until they listen and perhaps understand."

The Legacy of Jazz in the Harlem Renaissance

A significant development in jazz was the incorporation of the styles of ballroom and nightclub orchestras. Jazz, or some jazz, evolved from the New Orleans tradition of a small combo featuring solo players to big bands reading prepared arrangements and contrasting musical phrases between sections: brass, saxes, and rhythm. Harlem's musicians had to play in many ensembles and venues—tango tea dances, rent parties, Broadway theater orchestras, show clubs, military bands, "sweet" orchestras, and so on. As a result, a type of musician developed who could sight-read music and could play in many styles, but this often precluded the development of a personal soloistic style. Louis Armstrong came to New York as an established soloist, was acclaimed for his ability as an improviser, and was sought after for recordings; yet, in order to

play in Fletcher Henderson's dance orchestra, he had to improve his ability to read music.

A large number of retrospective art exhibitions, literary publications, theater reviews, and jazz performances have reflected the Harlem Renaissance. A number of jazz clubs around the world are named "Cotton Club"; bus tours of Harlem are offered every night in New York; and jazz is still recorded with homage to the Harlem traditions. Moreover, the eventual acceptance of jazz by the younger writers of the Harlem Renaissance assured it a place in the artistic and cultural legacy of the era.

JOHN K. GALM

See also Autobiography of an Ex-Colored Man; Blues; Brown, Sterling; House-Rent Parties; Hughes, Langston; Hurston, Zora Neale; Johnson, James Weldon; Locke, Alain; Music; Music: Bands and Orchestras; Rogers, Joel Augustus; Roseland Ballroom; Savoy Ballroom; Shuffle Along; Spirituals; *specific musicians*

Further Reading

Anderson, Paul Allen. *Deep River: Music and Memory in Harlem Renaissance Thought.* Chapel Hill: Duke University Press, 2001.

Berger, Ed. Liner notes to *Benny Carter: Harlem Renaissance.* 1992. (Sound recording.)

Ellington, Edward Kennedy. *Music Is My Mistress.* 1973.

Floyd, Samuel L., Jr. *The Power of Black Music: Interpreting Its History from Africa to the United States.* 1995.

Kirchner, Joe, ed. *The Oxford Companion to Jazz.* 2000.

Locke, Alain. *The Negro and His Music.* 1936.

Lowe, Allen. "Foot Stompers, Cross Dressers, and Swingers: The Big Bands, Singers, and Musicians of the Harlem Renaissance." In *Rhapsodies in Black: Music and Words from the Harlem Renaissance.* Rhino, 2000.

Ramsey, Guthrie P. *Race Music: Black Cultures from Bebop to Hip Hop.* Berkeley: UC Press, 2003.

Roberts, John Storm. *Black Music of Two Worlds*, 2nd ed. 1998.

Schuller, Gunther. *Early Jazz: Its Roots and Musical Development.* New York: Oxford UP, 1968.

Skipwith, Joanna, ed. *Rhapsodies in Black: Art of the Harlem Renaissance.* Berkeley: UC Press, 1997.

Spencer, Jon Michael. *The New Negros and Their Music: The Success of the Harlem Renaissance.* 1997.

Southern, Eileen. *The Music of Black Americans*, 3rd ed. 1997.

Smith, Willie. "The Lion." *Music on my Mind.* 1964.

Tracy, Steven. *Langston Hughes and the Blues.* Champaign: University of Illinois Press, 2001.

Ward, Geoffery C., and Ken Burns. *Jazz: A History of America's Music*. New York: Knopf, 2000.

Jessye, Eva

Eva Jessye was playing the piano by the age of five and organizing singing groups by the age of twelve, already on her way to becoming the "dean of black female musicians," as she would eventually be known. Jessye attended public schools in Coffeyville and Iola, Kansas, as well as in St. Louis and Seattle, living with various relatives. After graduating from Western University in Kansas in 1914, she spent three summers getting her teacher's certificate at Langston University in Oklahoma. Her long career included teaching, journalism, composing, radio production, film acting, and, most notably, choral conducting. Eva Jessye is best known for her central role as choral director in two important operas of the 1930s: Virgil Thomson and Gertrude Stein's *Four Saints in Three Acts* (1934), and George Gershwin and DuBose Heyward's *Porgy and Bess* (1935). By the mid-1930s, Jessye's choir was one of the preeminent black choral groups in the country, hailed for its eclectic repertoire and its full-throated sound.

The Eva Jessye Choir began as the Dixie Jubilee Singers, performing spirituals and popular songs. In 1926, Jessye moved to New York and formed the choir. The organization first worked singing "mood music" before movies began at the Rivoli Theater on Broadway. In 1926, the choir was hired for a radio show at the Capitol Theater. Jessye soon was asked to write her own radio shows, featuring her choir, now the Eva Jessye Choir, mostly performing spirituals that Jessye herself arranged. (The choir also performed in one of the first singing commercials on radio, for Van Heusen shirts.) In 1927 Jessye published *My Spirituals*, her arrangements interspersed with text describing the place of this music in her life. In 1929, her choir appeared in King Vidor's *Hallelujah*, Hollywood's first all-black talkie, for which she wrote some original music as well.

Although she championed black musical styles and forms, particularly spirituals, Jessye rebelled against the idea that she should produce only "black music." She was a choral director at Morgan College in Baltimore, but she resigned in protest when its president, a white southerner, insisted that her singers perform only "their own music." Her most notable

composition, *Paradise Lost and Regained* (1943), crosses racial boundaries by setting John Milton's work to the sounds and styles of black spirituals in what she called a "folk oratorio." Jessye's choir participated in numerous events of the civil rights movement, most notably as the official choir of Martin Luther King's March on Washington in 1963.

Jessye devoted the final decades of her long life to education. In 1972 she formed a new Eva Jessye Choir at the University of Michigan, where she organized a major archive on black musicians and entertainers. In 1979 she became an artist in residence at Pittsburg State University in Kansas, to which she contributed a large collection of her personal memorabilia. She received numerous honors and awards, including honorary doctorates from the University of Michigan and Eastern Michigan University. Eva Jessye died in 1992.

Biography

Eva Jessye was born 20 January 1895 in Coffeyville, Kansas. She studied at Western University, Quindaro, Kansas; graduated in 1914; received a teaching certificate from Langston University in Oklahoma in 1917; taught in public schools in Taft, Haskell, and Muskogee, Oklahoma, in 1917–1920; directed the music program at Morgan State College in Baltimore, Maryland, in 1920–1925; was a reporter for the Baltimore *Afro-American* in 1925; joined the Dixie Jubilee Singers (later the Eva Jessye Choir) in 1926; and sang on radio in 1926–1929. She appeared in *Hallelujah* (MGM, 1929), Virgil Thomson and Gertrude Stein's *Four Saints in Three Acts* (1934), George Gershwin and DuBose Heyward's *Porgy and Bess* (1935), and numerous revivals including a tour sponsored by the U.S. State Department in 1952. She composed three oratorios: *Paradise Lost and Regained* (1934), *Chronicle of Job* (1936), and *The Story of the Black Wise Man* (1958). She was awarded honorary doctorates by the University of Michigan (1976) and Eastern Michigan University (1987). Jessye died on 21 February 1992 in Ann Arbor, Michigan.

CRISTINA L. RUOTOLO

See also Four Saints in Three Acts; Hallelujah; Porgy and Bess; Spirituals

Selected Works

My Spirituals. New York: Robbins, 1927.
Selected Poems. Pittsburg, Kan.: Little Balkans, 1978.

Further Reading

Black, Donald F. "The Life and Work of Eva Jessye and Her Contributions to American Music." Dissertation, University of Michigan, 1985.

Robinson, Florence, "Eva Jessye." In *Notable Black American Women*. Detroit, Mich., and London: Gale Research, 1992.

Southern, Eileen. *Music of Black Americans*. New York: Norton, 1983.

Wilson, Doris Louise Jones. "Eva Jessye: Afro-American Choral Director." Dissertation, University of Washington at St. Louis, 1989.

Jim Crow

In the late 1820s, a blackface minstrel performer named T. D. Rice introduced a new character he claimed to have patterned after an elderly slave he had observed while traveling in Kentucky. Rice, a white man, delighted audiences with the song-and-dance routine, the lyrics of which were:

Wheel about and turn about and do just so;

Ev'ry time I wheel about I jump Jim Crow.

By the 1830s, "Jim Crow" had become a popular term describing a particular African American stereotype: the slow-witted, clownish, deferential, contented slave. By the late nineteenth century, Jim Crow had become synonymous with the entire culture of formal and legal separation of the races that pervaded American society in both the South and the North.

Beginning during the waning days of Reconstruction, southern whites began to construct a system of legally sanctioned discrimination in which African Americans were generally prohibited from inhabiting the same physical spaces as whites and from interacting with whites on an equal basis. This segregation took place not merely in private establishments such as restaurants, stores, theaters, hotels, and nightclubs, but also in virtually all areas of public life—education, housing, employment, organized labor, religion, the armed forces, transportation, health care, and marriage law—as well as facilities such as swimming pools, parks, rest rooms, and drinking fountains.

The establishment of Jim Crow in the South testified to the social and political strength of white supremacy after the Civil War. Under the Reconstruction Act of 1867 and the Civil Rights Act of 1875, southern blacks were formally given freedoms that had been only dreamed of during slavery: the right to participate in political and legal institutions as citizens; and the right to travel, dine, shop, and work alongside whites. Scholars have argued over the degree to which newly freed blacks were able to exercise these rights in the postwar years against the tide of white resentment and an entrenched code of deference. To whatever degree these rights and freedoms were exercised, they were short lived, as over the next three decades the integrationist gains of Reconstruction would be rolled back by powerful forces of white supremacy.

Scholars have also differed over whether Jim Crow laws merely reflected prejudices widely held among white southerners, or whether the laws were instrumental in nurturing a new and virulent ideology of white supremacy. Whatever the case, there can be little doubt that the architects of Jim Crow used the power of the law to affirm and naturalize the subordinate position of African Americans. Beginning in the 1870s with statutes enacted across the South against intermarriage between the races—whites had long considered such intermarriage an abomination—the prohibition on the physical union of black and white was soon expanded to an increasing number of social situations. The Civil Rights Act of 1875 was struck down by the Supreme Court in 1883, enabling a range of business establishments to discriminate on the basis of race. By the mid-1880s, segregated educational facilities had become mandatory by law in most southern states.

In conjunction with the relegation of African Americans to a separate social realm, Jim Crow also entailed the disenfranchisement of African American men (who had been given the vote in 1870) through various means, including poll taxes, literacy tests, intimidation, violence, and whites-only referenda. These techniques, however fraudulent and unconstitutional, proved highly effective: by 1900, registered black voters in the South had dwindled to 3 percent of the eligible population, making the possibility of remedies for African Americans through political representation more and more remote.

Jim Crow received its highest sanction in 1896, when the Supreme Court heard the case of a young Creole man who had been arrested for riding in a whites-only railway car in New Orleans. In this landmark case, *Plessy v. Ferguson*, the Court affirmed the constitutionality of racial segregation in public facilities and institutions, with the dubious proviso that the separate facilities for blacks were also "equal" to those reserved for whites. The ruling in *Plessy v. Ferguson* granted a powerful and lasting legitimacy to Jim Crow and set a template for race relations until the mid-twentieth century. Perhaps the most egregious effect of *Plessy* was the system of separate and substandard (with a few exceptions) educational institutions for African American children, a handicap that perpetuated poverty among blacks as well as political and social inequalities.

The endorsement of segregation by the highest court in the land demoralized the opponents of Jim Crow and made resistance to its codes unlawful. Yet law was only one means of enforcing white supremacy under Jim Crow; the threat of extralegal racial violence was ever present. Transgressions of segregation laws and of Jim Crow etiquette by African Americans (and, in some cases, by whites), especially those codes prohibiting sexual contact between the races, were met with the most extreme punitive measures. According to recent estimates, more than 3,200 African Americans were victims of lynch mobs in the period from 1880 to 1930. Violence was used systematically to enforce obedience to Jim Crow and to remind African Americans of their status as "outsiders," beyond the protections the law afforded white citizens.

Some scholars have argued that Jim Crow, despite placing African Americans at the margins of American society, also created spaces in which black culture flourished. Especially in the northern cities, where a somewhat milder form of Jim Crow was in force, African Americans made a virtue of their forced isolation from whites, cultivating self-sufficient and dynamic communities, educational institutions, newspapers, academic journals, political organizations, and artistic movements. New York's Harlem was such a community, both a result of the social, political, and spatial conditions of Jim Crow and a refuge from them. Yet the refuge was not total, because Jim Crow still largely governed the interactions between the races in daily life even in the cosmopolitan urban centers; its powerful sway could be observed, for example, in the all-white clientele of nightclubs in Harlem, such as the famous Cotton Club, where the artists and employees were African American.

Jim Crow described the system under which, as W. E. B. Du Bois wrote, African Americans spent their lives behind a "veil," a barrier that kept them from participating fully in American society, and that kept blacks and whites from recognizing each other's humanity. That veil began to tear in the mid-twentieth century with the rise of the civil rights movement and its explicit challenges to white supremacy and to Jim Crow.

COTTEN SEILER

See also Cotton Club; Lynching; Minstrelsy; Nightclubs

Further Reading

Dailey, Jane Elizabeth, Glenda Elizabeth Gilmore, and Simon Bryant, eds. *Jumpin' Jim Crow: Southern Politics from Civil War to Civil Rights*. Princeton, N.J.: Princeton University Press, 2000.

Dees, Jesse Walter, and James S. Hadley. *Jim Crow*. Ann Arbor, Mich.: Ann Arbor, 1951.

Franklin, John Hope, and Alfred A. Moss. *From Slavery to Freedom: A History of Negro Americans*. New York: Knopf, 1980.

Gilmore, Glenda Elizabeth. *Gender and Jim Crow: Women and the Politics of White Supremacy, 1896–1920*. Chapel Hill: University of North Carolina Press, 1996.

Kennedy, Stetson. *Jim Crow Guide to the U.S.A.: The Laws, Customs, and Etiquette Governing the Conduct of Non-whites and Other Minorities as Second-Class Citizens*. London: Lawrence and Wishart, 1959.

Litwack, Leon F. *Trouble in Mind: Black Southerners in the Age of Jim Crow*. New York: Knopf, 1998.

Woodward, C. Vann. *The Strange Career of Jim Crow*. New York: Oxford University Press, 1955.

Johnson, Charles Spurgeon

Charles S. Johnson—along with W. E. B. Du Bois, James Weldon Johnson, and Alain Locke—was an important black American promoter and patron of black essayists, graphic artists, fiction writers, and poets (both male and female) of the Harlem Renaissance.

Johnson was born, raised, and educated in Virginia. He had established himself as a major researcher and sociologist after his graduate studies at the University of Chicago from 1917 to 1918 (although he did not receive a doctorate from that university), before moving to Harlem in 1921. His reputation rested primarily on his immeasurably valuable contribution to a report by the Chicago Commission on Race Relations: *The Negro in Chicago: A Study of Race Relations and a Race Riot*, published in 1922. This careful, detailed 672-page study, which was funded by the philanthropist Julius Rosenwald, described the underlying causes of the bloody and disastrous riot that had taken place in Chicago during the "red summer" of 1919—foremost among them the "great migration" and the subsequent dislocations that resulted from the influx of black southern migrants in the North. The study also offered recommendations for a public policy that would prevent the recurrence of such rioting. Johnson had been appointed only associate executive secretary of the commission (the executive secretary was Graham Romeyn Taylor, the son of the "social gospel" prophet Graham Taylor); but Richard Robbins (1998) has concluded that Johnson wrote "at least seven" of the chapters in the study. The work, Robbins has also noted, "was a striking document for its time, whatever the criticism of its caution in coming to terms with the part played by the white power structure in sustaining discrimination."

Of more significance for the Harlem Renaissance is the fact that, while Johnson was enrolled in the graduate program in sociology at the University of Chicago, he was influenced by Robert E. Park, one of the nation's most distinguished students of sociology and the leading authority on race relations. From Park, as Wintz (1988) has noted, Johnson adopted the concept of the "marginal man," a concept first applied by Park's close friend and colleague at Chicago, William I. Thomas. To Johnson, the concept meant that African Americans were caught between their indigenous folk culture in the rural South and the urban industrial culture to which they migrated. Blacks were segregated and discriminated against in urban industrial areas; Johnson felt that it was essential to enhance their self-esteem by educating them about and preparing them to appreciate the distinctive value not only of their urban culture but also their indigenous folk culture. Furthermore, as Hutchinson has observed, Johnson thought that the press could nourish the "growth of a communal African American consciousness, which was a necessary stage in the development of an integrated America," as well as "create a national New Negro community" (1995, 179–180). In other words, through the revitalization of their folk culture, black Americans would be able to become more cohesive in the struggle for their inevitable integration into the American mainstream in the distant future.

In 1921, Johnson moved from Chicago to New York City, where he headed the research team of the National Urban League and founded and edited its monthly, *Opportunity: The Journal of Negro Life*, which he brought out during the years 1923–1928. Johnson was always committed to publishing articles containing political and socioeconomic data that he made accessible to sophisticated laypeople; he soon also turned to publishing essays, poetry, and short fiction by black writers who were then still unknown, such as

Countee Cullen, E. Franklin Frazier, Zora Neale Hurston, Langston Hughes, Nella Larsen, and Eric Walrond. Furthermore, during what Hurston called the "Negrotarian" phase of the Harlem Renaissance, Johnson developed a structure for *Opportunity*'s literary awards, which were presented at banquets in 1925 and 1926.

Johnson left New York in 1926 to become head of the department of sociology at Fisk University in Nashville, and subsequently became its first black American president. He continued to be a vital presence in the "New Negro" movement, however, publishing what is now a classic work of the Harlem Renaissance, the anthology *Ebony and Topaz*. It contained semi-popular sociology by such experts on race and race relations as E. Franklin Frazier, Ellsworth Faris, Ira D. A. Reid, and Edward B. Reuter, and creative work by Arna Bontemps, Countee Cullen, Rudolph Fisher, Zora Neale Hurston, James Weldon Johnson, Claude McKay, and several others; it rivals Alain L. Locke's *The New Negro* as a major manifesto of the 1920s.

Johnson was admired by many writers and graphic artists who credited him with having ignited the Harlem Renaissance: Bontemps, Hughes, Hurston, and the painter Aaron Douglas praised him highly. Hughes's statement that Johnson "did more to encourage and develop Negro writers during the 1920s than anyone else in America" (quoted in Lewis 1981, 125) indicates the respect that Harlem's black intellectuals paid to Johnson. During the 1920s, few people dared to criticize Johnson publicly.

During the past three decades, however, historians such as David Levering Lewis, Cary Wintz, and George Hutchinson have subjected Johnson to critical scrutiny, especially regarding whether or not he was a proponent of art for art's sake and whether he was a pluralist or an integrationist. Lewis argues that Johnson promoted unknown black artists primarily because art, in contrast to skilled labor, offered a path to upward mobility and could be used as a "weapon against old racial stereotypes." According to Lewis, Johnson assumed that black artists could acquire a power equivalent to economic power and thereby "redeem through art . . . the standing of his people" (1981, 48). That is, for Johnson art was utilitarian: its function was to elevate black people to first-class citizenship so that they would eventually be integrated into American society.

Wintz, though, finds Johnson far more enigmatic. He believes that Johnson was enthusiastic about the work of young black artists primarily because of their a proponent of a "pragmatist" aesthetic theory that sought to achieve pluralistic integration.

Despite the controversies surrounding Johnson's motivations and his theory of art, we do know that he saw art as a means of accomplishing a larger purpose: integration. After five years at the center of the artistic activities of the Harlem Renaissance, Johnson returned to the South in order, once again, to use social science to affect public policy in reference to blacks.

Biography

Charles Spurgeon Johnson was born 24 July 1893. He studied at Wayland Academy, Richmond, Virginia; Virginia Union in Richmond (A.B., 1916); and the University of Chicago (Ph.B., 1917). He was employed at the Chicago Commission on Race Relations, 1919–1921; and the National Urban League in New York, 1921–1928. He was the founder and editor of *Opportunity* in 1923–1928. He taught at Fisk University in Nashville, Tennessee, 1928–1947; and was its president from 1947 to 1956. Johnson died on 27 October 1956.

VERNON J. WILLIAMS

See also Bontemps, Arna; Cullen, Countee; Douglas, Aaron; Ebony and Topaz; Fisher, Rudolph; Frazier, E. Franklin; Great Migration; Hughes, Langston; Hurston, Zora Neale; Johnson, James Weldon; Larsen, Nella; McKay, Claude; National Urban League; Opportunity; Opportunity Literary Contests; Riots: 2—Red Summer of 1919; Walrond, Eric

Selected Works

The Negro in Chicago. 1922.
Ebony and Topaz. 1927.
The Negro in American Civilization. 1930.
A Preface to Racial Understanding. 1936.
Shadow of the Plantation. 1934.
Growing Up in the Black Belt. 1941.
To Stem This Tide. 1943.
Education and the Cultural Process. 1951.

Further Reading

Huggins, Nathan. *Harlem Renaissance.* New York: Oxford University Press, 1971.
Hutchinson, George. *The Harlem Renaissance in Black and White.* Cambridge, Mass.: Harvard University Press, 1995.

Charles S. Johnson, photographed by Bachrach. (Schomburg Center for Research in Black Culture, New York Public Library.)

realistic appraisal of the black experience: "They were investigating through their literature the very issues that Johnson had identified as crucial to the understanding of the black experience through his studies in sociology and his work in the Urban League" (1988, 122). According to Wintz, Johnson saw the Harlem Renaissance as an avenue by which blacks could gain acceptance into the American mainstream. Yet, despite his preoccupation with the "political and social position" of blacks in American letters, Johnson (unlike W. E. B. Du Bois) did not advocate art as propaganda, and he supported the artistic freedom of blacks. In short, Johnson regarded black artistic expression as a means to achieve integrationist ends.

Hutchinson takes a position between Lewis's depiction of Johnson as a pluralist and Wintz's depiction of Johnson as an integrationist. Hutchinson argues that the development of a "New Negro aesthetic" was a vital part of Johnson's vision for achieving an "art for life" adequate to the needs of black Americans and also for achieving the "integration and spiritual invigoration of a pluralistic and truly American civilization" (1995, 59–60). Thus Hutchinson describes Johnson as

Lewis, David Levering. *When Harlem Was in Vogue.* New York: Oxford University Press, 1981.

Robbins, Richard. *Sideline Activist.* Jackson: University Press of Mississippi, 1998.

Wintz, Cary D. *Black Culture and the Harlem Renaissance.* Houston, Tex.: Rice University Press, 1988.

Johnson, Fenton

Fenton Johnson was born in 1888 in Chicago. He went through the public school system there and attended Chicago University. After teaching for one year, Johnson moved on to work as a writer, poet, reporter, editor, publisher, and activist. Although he was involved in the literary circles of Chicago, Johnson remained distanced from his African American peers, and his poetry also remained somewhat distant. Some critics would argue that Johnson's new poetic style linked him more directly with the emerging white poets of the time, such as Carl Sandburg. Because Johnson used dialect in his poetry, however, some critics align him with black poets such as Paul Laurence Dunbar and Claude McKay. Still others place Johnson at the vanguard of the Harlem Renaissance, or they even believe that he stands alone as a precursor or an adjunct.

Actually, because of his time, location, style, and subject matter, it is difficult to place Johnson in the period or in the movement. While in Chicago, he was removed from Harlem and the growing number of black artists who began to congregate there between the turn of the twentieth century and World War I. Yet it was during this time that Johnson published three volumes of poetry: *A Little Dreaming* (1913), *Visions of the Dusk* (1915), and *Songs of the Soil* (1916). He also published works in the magazines *Crisis* and *Poetry*. He started *The Favorite Choice*, which first appeared on 17 August 1918 as "the first and only weekly magazine published by and for colored people" and went under three years later. Johnson was the editor and writer for most if not all of *Favorite Choice*. In 1920, Johnson published a collection of short stories, *Tales of Darkest America*, and a collection of essays, *For the Highest Good.* By the time the Chicago renaissance developed and was in full stride, between 1935 and 1950, Johnson seems to have disappeared.

The focus of much of Johnson's work is the common man. Like Dunbar and McKay, Johnson wrote some verse in dialect, particularly in his third volume, *Songs of the Soil.* Yet within this collection and even more so in the two earlier collections, Johnson wrote in a style akin to the emerging "new poetry" of the era; his style was new in its free form, with irregular rhythm and rhyme schemes, as well as in his use of plain speech. The result was his unique position relative to the emerging periods and movements. He portrays the real world in simple, direct language, and a sense of bitterness and disillusionment permeates his poetry—as is perhaps best revealed in "Tired." Johnson's sense of despair preceded that of the Harlem Renaissance. Another common theme is Ethiopia as a place of origin, or refuge, or both. Celebrating black culture, artists often incorporated different locations within Africa as the homeland or as an idyll. Johnson, whose racial consciousness is mixed with a radical and different poetic voice, demonstrates the struggle of the black artist in the early twentieth century.

Biography

Fenton Johnson was born in Chicago on 7 May 1888 and was educated in the public school system there, and at Chicago University. He taught for one year before becoming a writer, poet, reporter, editor, publisher, and activist in Chicago. Johnson died in 1958.

Brooke Carlson

See also Harlem Renaissance in the United States: 3—Chicago and the Midwest

Selected Works

A Little Dreaming. 1913.
Visions of the Dusk. 1915.
Songs of the Soil. 1916.
For the Highest Good. 1920.
Tales of Darkest America. 1920.

Further Reading

Bell, Bernard W. "Fenton Johnson." In *Dictionary of American Negro Biography*, ed. Rayford Logan and Michael R. Winston. New York: Norton, 1982.

Chapman, Abraham. *Black Voices: An Anthology of Afro-American Literature.* New York: Mentor, 1968.

Creadick, Anna. "Fenton Johnson." *Appalachian Journal: A Regional Studies Review*, 22(2), Winter 1995.

Cullen, Countee, ed. *Caroling Dusk: An Anthology of Verse by Black Poets of the Twenties.* New York: Harper, 1927.

Harrington, Joseph. "A Response to Lisa Wooley." *Langston Hughes Review*, 14(1–2), Spring—Fall 1996.

Hayden, Robert, ed. *Kaleidoscope: Poems by American Negro Poets*. New York: Harcourt, Brace, and World, 1967.

Hutchinson, James P. "Fenton Johnson: Pilgrim at the Dusk." *Studies in Black Literature*, 7(3), 1976.

Hughes, Langston, and Arna Bontemps, eds. *The Poetry of the Negro, 1746–1949: An Anthology*. New York: Doubleday, 1949.

Johnson, James Weldon, ed. *The Book of American Negro Poetry*. New York: Harcourt, Brace, and World, 1922.

Kreymborg, Alfred, ed. *Others for 1919*. New York: Nicholas L. Brown, 1920.

Long, Richard A., and Eugenia W. Collier, eds. *Afro-American Writing: An Anthology of Prose and Poetry*, 2nd enlarged ed. University Park: Pennsylvania State University Press, 1985.

Schafer, William J. "The Bridges of Fenton Johnson." *Appalachian Journal: A Regional Studies Review*, 22(2), Winter 1995.

Wooley, Lisa. "From Chicago Renaissance to Chicago Renaissance: The Poetry of Fenton Johnson." *Langston Hughes Review*, 14(1–2), Spring–Fall 1996.

Johnson, Georgia Douglas

Georgia Douglas Johnson is often considered the first black female poet of the twentieth century, preceded in popularity only by the nineteenth-century poet Frances Harper. Of Johnson's four collections of poetry, three were published or received recognition during the Harlem Renaissance: *The Heart of a Woman and Other Poems* (1918), *Bronze: A Book of Verse* (1922), and *An Autumn Love Cycle* (1928). All three were published at Johnson's own expense, since she had been unable to obtain financial support or find a commercial publisher.

Johnson was born in Atlanta, Georgia; her father was George Camp and her mother (whose maiden name she later took) was Laura Douglas Camp. Johnson spent her early years in Rome, Georgia; after her parents separated, she moved to Atlanta with her mother. She studied at Atlanta University and later taught school for nearly a decade. She married attorney and politician Henry Lincoln Johnson on 28 September 1903; the Douglases had two sons, Henry Lincoln Jr. (1906–c.1990) and Peter Douglas (1907–1957) before relocating to Washington, D.C., in 1910. During these "silent" years—despite the disapproval of her husband, who believed "a woman should take care of her home and her children and be content with that" (Hull 1987, 159–160)—Georgia Johnson fine-tuned her craft, often drawing on her musical background; she wrote several poems that she sang for visiting friends, and she frequently published poems as well as children's stories in magazines such as *The Liberator*, *The Messenger*, *The Crisis*, and *Opportunity*. She also became very active socially and politically, occasionally speaking on topics concerning women and minorities.

The appointment of Henry Johnson Sr. to a four-year term as recorder of deeds by President William Howard Taft in 1912 had propelled the Johnsons into a black social elite. After her husband's death in 1925, Johnson remained socially prominent, opening her home at 1461 S Street in northwest Washington, D.C., to literary figures such as Gwendolyn Bennett, William Stanley Braithwaite, Countee Cullen, W. E. B. Du Bois, Jessie Fauset, Waldo Frank, Zona Gale, Angelina Weld Grimké, Langston Hughes, Zora Neale Hurston, James Weldon Johnson, Vachel Lindsay, Alain Locke, Alice Dunbar Nelson, Richard Bruce Nugent, Anne Spencer, Wallace Thurman, and Jean Toomer; as well as to some social and political figures. During these Saturday soirées, her guests would share their most recent works. Johnson would later call her home "Half-Way House" because she considered herself "half-way between everybody and everything and I bring them together" (Shockley 1988, 350).

The years following her husband's death, although difficult for Johnson, had a liberating effect on her literary career. On the one hand, she had to assume the financial burden of maintaining a home and sending her two sons to college, which restricted the amount of time she could devote to writing. On the other hand, she had more creative freedom, since she no longer needed to contend with the silent disapproval of her spouse.

Johnson said that William Stanley Braithwaite had inspired her to write poetry; because she was influenced by him, critics have generally classified her raceless poetry as "genteel." In addition, Johnson's lyricism and her exploration of love and femininity have frequently led critics to compare her poetry to that of Sara Teasdale. By 1922, however, when Johnson published her second volume, *Bronze: A Book of Verse*, it became evident that she had been affected by the spirit of the Harlem Renaissance and its emphasis on racial consciousness.

As its title suggests, *Bronze* (unlike her first collection) exposed not the heart of all women but the heart of the "colored" woman. Johnson would later explain that "some one said—she has no feeling for the race. So I wrote *Bronze*—it is entirely racial" (quoted in Hull 1987, 160). Present-day scholars and biographers have tended to consider this volume Johnson's weakest, owing to its "obligatory" conception. However, critics of her time, such as W. E. B. Du Bois in his introduction to *Bronze*, commended Johnson for her "revelation of the soul struggle of the women of a race." Nevertheless, in her third collection, *An Autumn Love Cycle*, which includes the frequently anthologized poem "I Want to Die While You Love Me," Johnson reverted to the raceless themes she had explored in *The Heart of a Woman*. Some critics, such as Dover (1952), preferred a concentration on racial awareness and considered Johnson's decision unfortunate; but others considered *An Autumn Love Cycle* Johnson's strongest collection. Dover acknowledges that this volume expresses "the aching maturity of a sensitive woman in her forties" (1952, 634).

Johnson worked in other genres besides poetry. From 1926 to 1932 she wrote "Homely Philosophy," a weekly newspaper column consisting of tidbits of wisdom; it was syndicated to some twenty Negro publications. She also wrote plays during this time, under the influence of Zona Gale (the writer to whom *An Autumn Love Cycle* is dedicated). Johnson is said to have written twenty-eight scripts, but most of these were destroyed by workers clearing away her home after her death in 1966. Johnson's published dramas represent the social problems and themes with which she was concerned: lynching (*A Sunday Morning in the South*, c. 1925), miscegenation (*Blue Blood*, 1926), folk culture (*Plumes*, 1927), and history (*Frederick Douglass*, 1935; *William and Ellen Craft*, 1935). Johnson was an undoubtedly skillful dramatist. *Blue Blood* received honorable mention in *Opportunity*'s literary contest of 1926 and was performed later that year by the Krigwa Players of New York City; *Plumes*, her most famous play, received first prize the following year, firmly establishing her as a playwright.

Nevertheless, despite her other works, in 1950 Johnson would ask to be called the "mother of the Negro poets" (Tate 1997, xxxv). This seems appropriate, not only because of her willingness to provide a nurturing environment for budding writers, but also because of her own artistic talents and sensibilities.

Biography

Georgia Blanche Douglas Camp Johnson was born 10 September 1877 in Atlanta, Georgia. She studied at public and private schools there and in Rome, Georgia; at Atlanta University's Normal School, 1893; at Oberlin Conservatory of Music in Ohio, 1902; and at Howard University, c. 1965. She taught and served as an assistant principal in the Atlanta school system, 1903; was a substitute teacher and librarian in the public schools in Washington, D.C., c. 1924; was a file clerk in the civil service, c. 1924; and was commissioner of Conciliation, Department of Labor, 1925–1934. She received an honorary doctorate from Atlanta University in 1965. Johnson died in Washington, D.C., 14 May 1966.

VERONICA ADAMS YON

See also Braithwaite, William Stanley; Harlem Renaissance in the United States: 9—Washington, D.C.; Krigwa Players; Opportunity Literary Contests; Salons; *specific literary figures*

Selected Works

The Heart of a Woman and Other Poems. 1918.
Bronze: A Book of Verse. 1922
A Sunday Morning in the South. c. 1925.
Blue Blood. 1926.
Plumes. 1927.
An Autumn Love Cycle. 1928.
Frederick Douglass. 1935.
William and Ellen Craft. 1935.
Share My World. 1962.
The Selected Works of Georgia Douglas Johnson, ed. Henry Louis Gates Jr. 1997.

Further Reading

Brown-Guillory, Elizabeth. *Wines in the Wilderness: Plays by African American Women from the Harlem Renaissance to the Present*. Westport, Conn.: Greenwood, 1990.
Dover, Cedric. "The Importance of Georgia Douglass Johnson." *Crisis*, 59, 1952.
Fletcher, Winona L. "Georgia Douglas Johnson." In *Notable Women in the American Theatre: A Biographical Dictionary*, ed. Alice Robinson, Vera M. Roberts, and Milly S. Barranger. Westport, Conn.: Greenwood, 1989.
Hull, Gloria. *Color, Sex, and Poetry*. Bloomington: Indiana University Press, 1987.
Miller, Jeanne-Marie A. "Georgia Douglas Johnson and May Miller: Forgotten Playwrights of the New Negro Renaissance." *College Language Association Journal*, 33(4), 1990.

Shockley, Ann Allen. *Afro-American Women Writers, 174–1933: An Anthology and Critical Guide.* Boston, Mass.: G. K. Hall, 1988.

Stephens, Judith. "'And Yet They Paused' and 'A Bill to Be Passed': Newly Recovered Lynching Drama by Georgia Douglas Johnson." *African American Review,* 33(3), 1999.

Tate, Claudia. "Introduction." In *The Selected Works of Georgia Douglas Johnson,* ed. Henry Louis Gates Jr. New York: G. K. Hall, 1997.

Johnson, Hall

Hall Johnson, along with Eva Jessye, was a pioneer in the organization and development of professional concert ensembles. His great mission was to perform African American spirituals properly and meaningfully, without pretension but with beauty and simplicity, preserving the integrity of this music as it had developed during the era of slavery. His passion was to acquaint the world with the true and distinctive quality of spirituals. The objective of the Hall Johnson choirs, under his leadership, was to demonstrate how spirituals should be sung. These choirs became the first African American choral groups to win national and international distinction, and they had considerable influence. Many outstanding white choral directors, including Robert Shaw, came to the Harlem Young Men's Christian Association (YMCA) to watch Johnson's Hall rehearsals.

Johnson had been trained professionally as an instrumentalist and had a significant role, in 1923, in organizing the Negro String Quartet, for which he played violin and viola alternately. (The other members of this quartet were Arthur Boyd and Felix Weir, violins; and Marion Cumbo, cello.) Johnson also played in orchestras led by James Reese Europe, in the orchestras of various Broadway musicals, and in Will Marion Cook's Southern Syncopated Orchestra. In these orchestras, he met many important jazz musicians and classical musicians of the Harlem Renaissance period. In 1925, Johnson organized his preeminent choral ensemble, the Hall Johnson Choir; its major goal was to perform, legitimately, the spirituals and folk music of African Americans.

Johnson composed a number of original art songs, including *The Courtship* (1956); these works were sung by such professional artists as Marian Anderson and Roland Hayes. However, he is especially noted for his arrangements of African American spirituals and folk songs, in which his intention was to honor the authenticity and beauty of the music in its original form and style. Johnson also composed several large works based on spirituals; one of these was his sacred cantata *Son of Man* (1946).

After Johnson moved to California in 1938, he organized the Festival Choir of Los Angeles, a group that was formed to sing in the film version of *The Green Pastures.* Johnson remained in California for a number of years, directing choruses in the films *Lost Horizon*, *Way Down South*, and *Cabin in the Sky*. He also organized the 200-voice Festival Choir of Los Angeles, among other community-based groups. In 1946, Johnson resettled in New York, where he organized the Festival Negro Chorus of New York.

In 1951, the State Department chose Johnson and the Hall Johnson Choir to represent the United States at the International Festival of Fine Arts in Berlin—probably the most prestigious honor to be bestowed on the ensemble. At this time the choir also made an extensive tour of major European cities. After returning to New York, Johnson inaugurated an annual concert series called "New Artists," featuring a number of promising young African Americans. Johnson died in 1970 after a long and productive career.

Biography

Francis Hall Johnson was born in Athens, Georgia, 12 March 1888. He received a B.A. degree from the University of Pennsylvania. Beginning in 1910, he played the violin professionally. He organized the Negro String Quartet (1923), the first Hall Johnson Choir (1925), the Festival Choir of Los Angeles (1938–1946), and the Festival Choir of New York (1946). He and his choir represented the United States at the International Festival of Fine Arts in Berlin (1951). His awards included two Holstein prizes (1925, 1927); the Harmon Award (1930); an honorary doctorate from the Philadelphia Academy of Music (1934); and the City of New York Handel Award (1970). Johnson died in New York City on 30 April 1970.

MALCOLM BREDA

See also Anderson, Marian; Cook, Will Marion; Europe, James Reese; Hayes, Roland; Jessye, Eva; Spirituals

Further Reading

Carter, Marva Griffin. "Hall Johnson: Preserver of the Old Negro Spiritual." Master of Arts thesis, Boston University, 1975.

Harris, Carl Gordon, Jr. "A Study of Characteristic Stylistic Trends Found in the Choral Works of a Selected Group of Afro-American Composers and Arrangers." Unpublished D.M.A. dissertation. University of Missouri at Kansas City, 1972.

Johnson, Hall. "Notes on the Negro Spiritual." In *Readings in Black American Music*, 2nd ed., ed. Eileen Southern. New York: Norton, 1971.

Roberson, Leroy Alfred. "Hall Johnson: A Biography and an Analytical Study of Selected Songs for Solo Voice and Piano." D.M.A. dissertation, University of Southern Mississippi, 1992.

Johnson, Helene

At age eighteen, Helene Johnson won first prize in a short-story competition sponsored by the *Boston Chronicle*. In 1926 she came to New York to study journalism at Columbia University; when she arrived in Harlem, she was nineteen years old.

Johnson was one of a group of young women who came to Harlem in 1926 and 1927, including Mae Cowdery and Johnson's cousin Dorothy West, and she was acknowledged as an important voice among the emerging young poets. Particularly after her poem "Bottled" was published in *Vanity Fair* in May 1927, Johnson was lionized and was considered a peer of the most promising young writers, such as Langston Hughes and Countee Cullen. She made such a favorable impression on Wallace Thurman that, in his novel *Infants of the Spring* (1932), which was otherwise savagely cynical, he portrayed her as having real talent and a freshness and naïveté that the rest of the characters had lost. Johnson won several honorable mentions in *Opportunity*'s literary contests of 1925 and 1926 and second prize in 1927. Her poetry was also published in *Fire!!*, a short-lived journal edited by Wallace Thurman, Hughes, and Richard Bruce Nugent; and in the *Anthology of Magazine Verse* edited by William Stanley Braithwaite in 1927.

In New York, Johnson was in constant company with her cousin Dorothy West. The two became close friends with the young literary circle of the time. West and Johnson would become particularly good friends

of Zora Neale Hurston, and even take over Hurston's apartment for a summer. After Cullen read "Bottled" to one of his audiences, Johnson sent him a packet of other work, writing, "you'll like them Countee, because one of them is a sonnet." Johnson, like Cullen, was deeply interested in Percy Bysshe Shelley and the Romantic poets; in Braithwaite's anthology, she listed Shelley, Alfred, Lord Tennyson, Walt Whitman, and Carl Sandburg as her primary influences. Her poem "Fulfillment," in fact, ends with the poet swearing to "die bleeding—consummate with Life," a phrase that is reminiscent of the line "I fall upon the thorns of life! I bleed!" in Shelley's "Ode to the West Wind." Many of Johnson's other poems dwell on the beauty of nature and contrast it with the harsh reality of human society.

Despite an auspicious beginning, Johnson never lived up to her early promise. Exactly why is hard to say, in part because she shrouded her life in extreme privacy. Until her death in 1995—well after interest in the women poets of the Harlem Renaissance had been revived—Johnson resisted publicity. Biographical details about her are so scarce that even her married name was not published until 1970. We do know that after 1929 she moved out of Harlem and fell into obscurity. She was still writing, however, and around that time she sent some of her new work to Cullen, but nothing came of it. Her work next appeared in print in *Challenge*, a journal edited by Dorothy West (later *New Challenge*). But that contribution amounted to only a handful of poems which were criticized in some quarters as showing no significant development. After these publications, until her death, Johnson lapsed into public silence, although she continued to write. Her later poems, along with others from the 1920s that had not been published at the time, were collected in *This Waiting for Love* (Mitchell 2000) along with an extensive introduction.

Biography

Helene Johnson was born in Boston, Massachusetts, on 7 July 1907, and brought up in Boston, where she lived at 470 Brookline Avenue and attended the Boston Clerical School. She attended Columbia University in 1926–1927, studying journalism. She won honorable mentions and an award in *Opportunity*'s literary contests in 1925–1927; her poetry was published in *Vanity Fair*, *Fire!!*, and William Stanley Braithwaite's anthology. After 1929, she left Harlem and fell into obscurity, though her work appeared in *Challenge* and *New Challenge*. Johnson died in New York City on 6 July 1995.

Steven Nardi

See also Challenge; Cowdery, Mae Virginia; Cullen, Countee; Fire!!; Hurston, Zora Neale; Infants of the Spring; New Challenge; Opportunity Literary Contests; Thurman, Wallace; Vanity Fair; West, Dorothy

Selected Works

In *Caroling Dusk: An Anthology of Verse by Negro Poets*, ed. Countee Cullen. 1927.
In *Shadowed Dreams: Women's Poetry of the Harlem Renaissance*, ed. Maureen Honey. 1989.

Further Reading

Dictionary of Literary Biography, Vol. 51, *Afro American Writers from the Harlem Renaissance to 1940*. Detroit, Mich.: Gale, 1987.
Ferguson, Sally Ann H. "Dorothy West and Helene Johnson in *Infants of the Spring*." *Langston Hughes Review*, 2(2), 1983.
Mitchell, Verner D., ed. *This Waiting for Love: Helene Johnson, Poet of the Harlem Renaissance*. Amherst: University of Massachusetts Press, 2000.
Redmond, Eugene B. *Drumvoices: The Mission of Afro-American Poetry*. Garden City, N.Y.: Anchor Doubleday, 1976.

Johnson, James P.

Although unheralded, even during his lifetime, outside a small group of jazz aficionados and performers, James P. Johnson was among the most important and versatile American musicians of the twentieth century. Johnson was an innovative and virtuosic performer of "stride," a style of piano playing that featured a vigorous left hand and lively melodies that was a foundation of jazz; a talented songwriter for musical theater during the 1920s and 1930s who wrote "The Charleston," the anthem of the jazz age; and a composer of classical works for piano and orchestra.

Johnson was exposed to a remarkable variety of music during his youth in New Jersey and New York.

He absorbed the music and culture of black migrants from the American southeast, featuring lively songs for folk dances. He also frequented clubs in New York where he heard great ragtime pianists. But Johnson listened to classical music as well, on recordings, in cafés, and at performances of the New York Symphony. While honing his phenomenal piano skills entertaining at clubs and parties during his teens, Johnson studied harmony and composition in the hope of someday writing "serious" music.

By the late 1910s, he was recognized as the dean of the New York stride pianists. Johnson's presence at a "rent party," a social event held to help tenants in need of rent money, guaranteed attendance among dancers and musicians alike. Through the release of several piano rolls beginning in 1917, Johnson's music began to attract wider attention, and his influence spread. "Carolina Shout" was introduced in this period and soon became the piece by which all other stride pianists were measured. Many young pianists, including Duke Ellington and Thomas "Fats" Waller, learned piano by slowing the action on player pianos that were performing Johnson's music and then fingering the automatically depressed keys. In 1921, Waller became a student and lifelong friend of Johnson's, thus guaranteeing that Johnson's innovations would spread to the numerous jazz musicians who performed with Waller.

During the 1920s and 1930s, although Johnson continued to develop and perform as a pianist, he expanded into new musical territory. Beginning with *Runnin' Wild*, which made "The Charleston" a national sensation, and then in *Keep Shufflin'*, his most important collaboration with Fats Waller, he emerged as one of the premier songwriters for black musical theater. He also began to explore compositions using classical forms. Among composers writing in popular idioms, Johnson was most committed to the ideal expressed by leaders of the Harlem Renaissance that African American music achieved its highest expression in orchestral, chamber, or traditional vocal compositions. With a performance at Carnegie Hall of his *Yamekraw: A Piano Rhapsody*—and with numerous concerts that included his orchestral works—Johnson fulfilled his lifelong ambition to write "serious" music.

Johnson always shunned the showmanship favored by many of his colleagues in jazz, and he worked increasingly in classical forms when most jazz musicians were moving toward swing bands; as a result, he virtually ensured his own obscurity. Yet his crucial jazz innovations, his versatility as a composer and performer, and his influence on generations of pianists must give him a place among the leading American musicians of the twentieth century.

Biography

James Price Johnson was born 1 February 1894 in New Brunswick, New Jersey. He was educated in public schools in New Jersey and New York City; studied piano with his mother Josephine Johnson, Ernest Green, and Bruto Giannini; and studied composition with Jan Chiapuse at Toledo University, 1919. Pianists who influenced Johnson include Eubie Blake, Luckeyeth "Lucky" Roberts, and Richard "Abba Labba" McLean. Johnson had jobs as a dancer, vaudevillian, and nightclub performer in New York City and in Jersey City, Newark, and Atlantic City, New Jersey, 1912–1914; and he performed with James Reese Europe's Clef Club musicians, 1914–1920. Johnson's first published song was "Mamma's and Pappa's Blues," with his songwriting partner William Farrell, 1917; he cut piano rolls for Aeolian and other companies, 1916–1920; he made a tour of the east coast with *Smart Set Revue*, a black vaudeville show, 1918; he cut piano rolls for QRS Music, including "Carolina Shout," 1921; he was a mentor to Thomas "Fats" Waller, 1921; his first recorded performance, accompanying the singer Alice Leslie Carter on the Arto label, was in 1921; also in 1921, he made his first recording for Black Swan, "Harlem Strut"; he was musical director for *Plantation Days*, a touring revue in the United States and London, 1922–1923; he was an accompanist for singers including Eva Taylor, Spencer Williams, Bessie Smith, and Ethel Waters, 1920s; he performed at rent parties, nightclubs, and socials, 1920s–1940s; he contributed to black musicals, including *Runnin' Wild* (1923) and *Keep Shufflin'* (1928); his *Yamekraw: A Negro Rhapsody* (performed by Fats Waller) had its debut at Carnegie Hall in 1928; he performed in "From Spirituals to Swing" at Carnegie Hall in 1938 and 1939; the first performance of his blues opera, *The Organizer* (with libretto by Langston Hughes), was in 1940; "Jazzfest and Pop Concert Presenting James P. Johnson: Composer-Pianist" was presented at Carnegie Hall in 1945. Johnson was a member of ASCAP (1926). He died in New York City, 17 November 1955.

WILLIAM J. NANCARROW

See also Ellington, Duke; House-Rent Parties; Jazz; Musical Theater; Runnin' Wild; Waller, Thomas "Fats"

Selected Works: Musicals

Plantation Days. 1922–23, 1925. (As music director.)
Runnin' Wild. 1923. (With Cecil Mack.)
Negro Nuances. 1924. (With Sidney Bechet, Will Marion Cook, and Abbie Mitchell.)
Moochin' Along. 1925. (With Cecil Mack and Jessie Shipp.)
Keep Shufflin'. 1928. (With Fats Waller, Andy Razaf, and Harry Creamer.)
Messin' Around. 1929. (With Perry Bradford.)
Shuffle Along of 1930. (With Fats Waller.)
Harlem Hotcha. 1932. (With Andy Razaf.)
Policy Kings. 1938.

Other Works

"Carolina Shout." 1917.
"Charleston." 1923.
Yamekraw: Negro Rhapsody. 1927. (Premiere 1928.)
"Snowy Morning Blues." 1927.
"'Sippi." 1928.
Saint Louis Blues. 1929. (Film soundtrack; as musical director.)
"You've Got to Be Modernistic." 1930.
Harlem Symphony. 1932. (Orchestral work.)
"Hungry Blues." 1939.
The Organizer. 1939. (One-act blues opera with libretto by Langston Hughes.)

Further Reading

Blesh, Rudi, and Harriet Janis. *They All Played Ragtime*, 4th ed. New York: Oak, 1971.

Brown, Scott E. *James P. Johnson: A Case of Mistaken Identity*. Metuchen, N.J.: Scarecrow, and Institute of Jazz Studies, Rutgers University, 1986.

Hammond, John. "Talents of James P. Johnson Went Unappreciated." *Down Beat*, 28, December 1955.

Jasen, David A., and Gene Jones. *Spreadin' Rhythm Around: Black Popular Songwriters, 1880–1930*. New York: Schirmer, 1998.

Kirkeby, W. T., ed. *Ain't Misbehavin': The Story of Fats Waller*. New York: Da Capo, 1975.

Schuller, Gunther. *Early Jazz: Its Roots and Musical Development*. Oxford, U.K., and New York: Oxford University Press, 1968.

Johnson, James Weldon

To consider the career—or more properly the careers—of James Weldon Johnson is to throw a spotlight on someone who characteristically shunned the spotlight. Johnson was arguably the most versatile of all the figures associated with the Harlem Renaissance, and he blended quiet integrity, forceful ideas, and natural modesty. He crowded into sixty-seven years a series of remarkable achievements—as educator, lawyer, diplomat, poet, essayist, novelist, and songwriter—that would seem to require several lifetimes.

Johnson was born on 17 June 1871, the first son of Bahamians who had immigrated to Jacksonville, Florida. His mother, the former Helen Louise Dillet, was a schoolteacher who instilled in Johson and his brother, John Rosamond Johnson, a love of learning, with special interests in reading, drawing, and music. His father, James Sr., held a secure position of middle-class respectability as the headwaiter at a resort hotel, the Saint James. Both parents were hard workers, and both were civic minded. The family was unusual compared with many southern African Americans; it was an educated, cultured, and financially secure household. In comparison with many of the writers and artists who led the Harlem Renaissance, Johnson could arguably be said to have come from a privileged background.

Such opportunities smoothed the way for future success, but it would be a mistake to think that Johnson had a path free of obstacles throughout his life. He had to contend with virulent racial prejudice; to his great credit, he made the project of eradicating it his life's work.

As a youth he attended the Stanton School in Jacksonville, a segregated institution where his mother taught and where he learned much under the demanding tutelage of its principal, James C. Walter. Johnson graduated from Stanton in 1887, at the age of sixteen, and left the area to attend the preparatory division of Atlanta University (later Atlanta Clark University), because the high schools in Jacksonville were closed to African Americans. Two years later, he graduated from the preparatory division and entered the freshman class at Atlanta. He excelled in all his subjects, especially writing and speech. He began to write poems on African American themes (mostly dialect verse, which was the accepted mode for black poetry at the time), and in 1891 he won the university's prize for oratory for his address, "The Best Methods of Removing the Disabilities of Caste from the Negro."

The material in that speech was derived largely from Johnson's experiences during his summers when he taught school in rural Henry County, Georgia, and witnessed much that revealed to him the racial inequities in the United States—incidents that he later recalled in his autobiography, *Along This Way* (1933). The unspoken attitude of many whites on encountering "a strange Negro on a backcounty road" reminded him that he was "not entirely secure, not even in daylight." From that point on, he made it his life's philosophy that he "would not allow one prejudiced person or one million or one hundred million to blight my life. I will not let prejudice or any of its attendant humiliations and injustices bear me down to spiritual defeat. My inner life is mine, and I shall defend and maintain its integrity against all the powers of hell."

Johnson graduated from Atlanta University in 1893 with honors. Wanting to help improve the struggles and aspirations of African Americans, he returned to Jacksonville to teach at Stanton, where he took over as principal one year later. He expanded the curriculum to include high school classes, and at the same time undertook heavy additional responsibilities when he founded, in 1895, the *Daily American*, the first African American newspaper. As its editor, Johnson quickly acquired an image in the southeast as a spokesperson for African American advancement, although its particular brand of "radicalism," derived from the conservative views of Booker T. Washington (whom Johnson agreed with more than he agreed with the more liberal W. E. B. Du Bois), seems mild by today's standards. The *Daily American* failed after only a year; Johnson had tried to keep it afloat almost single handedly, and its failure gave him his "first taste of defeat in public life." But the newspaper did bring him to the attention of Washington, Du Bois, and others—connections which would later serve him well in his work as a political activist.

Undeterred, and spurred on by his strident ambition, Johnson started to study law with the encouragement of a local white attorney, and in 1898 he passed the bar, becoming the first African American in Florida to do so since Reconstruction. He continued to administer the Stanton School and to write poetry while setting up a successful law practice in Jacksonville with a former classmate from Atlanta University.

Around this time, Johnson also began to try his hand at song writing. His brother, John Rosamond, had been a gifted musician from early boyhood and had gone to the New England Conservatory of Music. On graduation in 1897, Rosamond returned to Jacksonville, discovered that his brother had been writing poetry, and convinced him that the lyrics could be set to Rosamond's music. Their greatest composition was an early work that James Weldon Johnson had written for a celebration of Abraham Lincoln's birthday at Stanton School: "Lift Every Voice and Sing." The brothers published it and forgot it, but it lived on in the minds of Stanton's students, who taught it to other students throughout the South; some twenty years later, it was officially adopted by the National Association for the Advancement of Colored People (NAACP) as the "Negro national anthem."

Their collaborative talents took the brothers out of Jacksonville and up to New York, where, at the turn of the century, they teamed with Bob Cole, a talented musician, to form a songwriting and producing trio. James Weldon worked in the background, supplying lyrics. Cole and Rosamond put together vaudeville material, which they performed onstage as "Cole and Johnson," placing them in the company of entertainers such as Will Marion Cook and Williams and Walker.

The Johnsons and Cole were enviably energetic and stunningly successful. Between 1901 and 1905, they composed some 200 songs for musical productions on Broadway and elsewhere. Their goal was to make the lyrics of Negro songs more sophisticated. The team's first collaboration was "Louisiana Lize," a love song written in a new lyrical style "which left out the watermelons, razors, and hot mamas typical of coon songs." For $50, they sold the singing rights to a popular white entertainer, May Irwin, who was known as a performer of coon songs. Irwin used it in her next show, *The Belle of Bridgeport*. Its success encouraged the team to experiment a bit, and they developed a successful method of collaboration in which they took turns writing words, composing melodies, and critiquing works in progress.

Under an exclusive three-year contract with the Broadway producers Klaw and Erlanger, the trio turned out many such songs, including such hits as "The Congo Love Song," "I've Got Troubles of My Own," "Tell Me, Dusky Maiden," "The Old Flag Never Touched the Ground," and "Oh, Didn't He Ramble."

Probably the most famous of these tunes was "Under the Bamboo Tree," which according to Rosamond had its origins in an unusual incident. He and Cole were walking uptown after a performance one day when he began to hum the African American spiritual "Nobody Knows the Trouble I've Seen." Hearing the song, Cole got the idea of rearranging it and working it into their act. When Rosamond objected that this was sacrilegious, Cole responded, "What kind of a musician are you anyway? Been to the Boston Conservatory and can't change a little old tune around." By the time Rosamond finally conceded, Cole had already written the words. "Under the Bamboo Tree" sold more than 400,000 copies, making it one of the biggest sellers ever. With James Weldon Johnson as their manager, the trio toured throughout the United States and also performed in Paris and London. Legend has it that "Under the Bamboo Tree" was the last thing they heard as they set sail from New York and the first thing they heard when they arrived in Paris.

Following their successful tour, Cole and Rosamond Johnson started their own theatrical company. In 1906, they produced and starred in a musical called *The Shoo-Fly Regiment*. After helping to write the songs for this show, James Weldon Johnson decided that it would be the last piece of work they would do together. Their song writing had been lucrative, netting them more than $25,000 a year in salary and royalties, but, as Johnson later reflected, "Success is a heady beverage" and "is safe only when it comes slowly." Their prosperity had been sudden, and Johnson had begun to feel that he was forsaking his avowed life's goal of helping to advance the ambitions of the race. He also found distasteful the tradition of the coon song within which he had to work as a writer, and even the dialect poetry he had earlier begun now seemed to him an inadequate form for expressing what he felt in his heart and thought in his mind. He had recently read Walt Whitman's *Leaves of Grass* (1855), and he saw that his own earlier poems had relied on white stereotypes of the African American.

Johnson had accelerated his study of literature beginning in 1904, when he started to take courses in creative writing at Columbia University taught by Brander Matthews, the well-known critic and anthologist. At this time an idea for a novel began to gestate in Johnson's mind, an innovative statement on African American identity that would lay to rest much of the white-generated writing about black life of the nineteenth century. While he was working with Bob Cole and Rosamond, however, Johnson did not have the time to devote to the book; he shelved the idea until 1906, when he left the trio to enter the diplomatic service.

For some time, Johnson had been active in New York political circles. He had become treasurer of the city's Colored Republic Club in 1904. He had also become friends with Charles W. Anderson, the most influential black Republican in the city, who was in turn a close friend of Booker T. Washington. When the black civil rights leadership split into conservative and radical factions, Johnson backed Washington, who used his connections to have the Theodore Roosevelt administration appoint Johnson as the U. S. consul in Puerto Caballo, Venezuela. Such posts had often gone to writers, and traditionally they were considered little more than sinecures that gave the writer time to reflect and work on writing.

In 1909 Johnson assumed his post in South America, where he expected to have time to work on his book; his duties turned out to be unusually demanding, however, and he could not finish the book until 1911, after a year's leave of absence. *The Autobiography of an Ex-Colored Man*, published anonymously in 1912, is arguably the central text of the Harlem Renaissance and by most reckonings one of the dozen key documents that best reflect the American experience. It tells the story of a light-skinned black man who drifts rather aimlessly throughout the South, then to New York, where he becomes involved with gambling and playing ragtime piano. Eventually he is "adopted" by a wealthy white man who takes him to Europe and broadens his musical abilities. On returning to the United States, the protagonist samples the life of the black middle class in different cities on the eastern seaboard, ending up in rural Georgia; after witnessing a lynching, he decides to return to the North and pass for white. The novel is a complex psychological portrait of a weak, self-indulgent man who is alienated by both races and ultimately succumbs to and is victimized by the racist values of American society. The novel created a stir in intellectual circles in New York, but Johnson did not admit that he was its author until 1927, when it was republished. Even then, after a well-documented public career, Johnson had to deny that the novel was based on his own life, and in fact he published *Along This Way* in part to set the record straight.

On leave in 1910, Johnson married Grace Nail, the daughter of a prosperous businessman in Brooklyn. He also took up a new consular post in Nicaragua, another difficult diplomatic assignment. In 1912, after much political turmoil in Nicaragua, U. S. troops landed at Corinto in response to an assassination and an attempted coup. When Woodrow Wilson, a Democrat, became president in 1914, Johnson resigned from the foreign service, citing race prejudice and the likelihood that party politics would bar him from securing a desirable new post.

Thus began the most famous and personally rewarding phase of Johnson's multifaceted public life: politics. He returned to New York to become an editorial writer for *New York Age*, the city's oldest and most distinguished black newspaper. Johnson's editorials were fiery and passionate, but they also reflected his basically conservative view that African Americans could improve their lot through self-education, hard work, and many of the middle-class white values that were the cultural norm.

In the summer of 1916, Joel E. Spingarn asked Johnson to attend the important Amenia Conference on racial issues, and a few months later Spingarn asked Johnson to become field secretary for NAACP, which had been organized in 1910 by blacks and whites in order to break down racial barriers. Johnson proved to be an immensely efficient administrator and an effective spokesperson for NAACP's platform. He organized local branches throughout the country and expanded the membership substantially. During his early tenure, he monitored and responded to the riots in East St. Louis, where 6,000 African Americans were driven from their homes; atrocities against black soldiers in World War I; the great Fifth Avenue March for civil rights; and the bloody race riots in Chicago and elsewhere during the "red summer" of 1919. The following year he went on an investigatory trip to Haiti and exposed the abuses of the American occupation there in a series of articles for *The Nation*.

The year 1920 also saw Johnson assume the role that destiny had seemed to carve out for him—general secretary, or chief executive, of NAACP. With typical modesty, Johnson claimed in his autobiography that he "got immense satisfaction" out of his work for NAACP, yet that understates his achievements by great lengths. In fact, it is difficult to single out for special mention one event that he orchestrated or one advance that was gained, so numerous were the organization's accomplishments during the decade when Johnson steered its course. Probably the most dramatic episode, though, was the attempt to get Congress to pass the Dyer antilynching bill in the summer of 1921, a measure behind which Johnson had placed the full force of NAACP and for which he had personally lobbied in the halls of the Capitol, literally camping out on the benches in front of senators' offices to wait for a chance to speak in its favor. The bill was defeated, but the campaign for its passage nevertheless brought the nation's attention to the issue of race prejudice as never before.

Throughout his years of political activism, Johnson was determined not to let his creative muscles atrophy, and he produced much literary work in the 1920s. For instance, he compiled three important anthologies of African American literature: *The Book of American Negro Poetry* (1922), *The Book of American Negro Spirituals* (1925), and *The Second Book of American Negro Spirituals* (1926). He also brought out a series of collections of verse, culminating with *God's Trombones: Seven Negro Sermons in Verse* in 1927. The book is a paean to the soulful richness of black Christianity—ironically so, since Johnson himself professed no religious faith except an optimistic dream of man's humanity to his fellow man and an acknowledgment of an unknowable spiritual presence permeating the material world.

Fatigued by his work in the political arena, Johnson left in 1930 to accept an appointment as a professor of creative writing at Fisk University, a position that gave him time to complete two more prose works: *Black Manhattan* (1930), a copiously researched but lively and engaging history of the African American presence in New York; and his autobiography, *Along This Way* (1933), a book of which John Hope Franklin has said, "It is impossible to understand the place of African Americans in the life of this country without *Along This Way*." The following year, some of the positions Johnson presented on race and politics in the autobiography were outlined in a slim volume called *Negro Americans, What Now?* At this time, he moved back to New York to become a professor of literature at New York University, where he remained until his death in an automobile accident in Maine in June 1938.

More than 2,500 people, black and white, filled the largest church in Harlem to attend Johnson's funeral, where, for more than an hour, a succession of the brightest and most celebrated figures of the era extolled his achievements. Even these eulogies seem inadequate, for Johnson lived so full a life, touching so many other people and influencing their thoughts and actions, that it may not be possible to gauge the degree to which he guided African Americans' awareness of their identity and of their place in American society. His greatest legacy may be that he lives on, not just in the histories of the NAACP, in the biographies of its members, or in the anthologies of African American literature, but in an unusually large number of books

James Weldon Johnson, c.1900–1920. (Library of Congress.)

for children and adolescents that tell of a life grounded in the bedrock of unwavering moral principle. In the words of another African American writer, Johnson symbolized what it meant "to be gifted, young, and black. We must begin to tell our young, there's a world waiting for you, yours is the quest that's just begun."

Biography

James Weldon Johnson was born in Jacksonville, Florida, 17 June 1871; his parents were James and Helen Louise Dillet Johnson. He studied at Stanton School; received an A.B. from Atlanta University, 1894; and did further study at Columbia University, 1903–1906. He was principal at Stanton School, 1893–1900. Johnson was founder and editor of the *Daily American*, 1895–1896. He received an honorary A.M. from Atlanta University, 1904. Johnson was U. S. consul to Venezuela, 1906–1908; and consul to Corinto, Nicaragua, 1909–1912. He married Grace Nail, 10 February 1910. He was a field secretary for the

National Association for the Advancement of Colored People (NAACP), 1916–1920; and its general secretary, 1920–1930. His awards included the following: Litt. D., Talladega College, 1917; Litt.D., Howard University, 1923; Spingarn Medal, 1925; Rosenwald Grant, 1929; an appointment as professor of creative writing, Fisk University, 1930; W. E. B. Du Bois Prize for Negro Literature, 1933; and Lewis Carroll Shelf Award for "Lift Every Voice and Sing," 1971. Johnson died in Wiscasset, Maine, 26 June 1938.

JAMES HUTCHISSON

See also Amenia Conference, 1916; Anderson, Charles; Antilynching Crusade; Autobiography of an Ex-Colored Man; Black Manhattan; Cole, Bob; God's Trombones; Johnson, John Rosamond; New York Age; Spingarn, Joel

Selected Works

The Autobiography of an Ex-Colored Man. 1912. (Republished, 1927.)

Fifty Years and Other Poems. 1917.

"Self Determining Haiti." *Nation*, 111, August 1920, pp. 236–238, 265–267, 295–297, 345–357.

The Book of American Negro Poetry. 1922.

"Lynching: America's National Disgrace." *Current History*, 19 (January 1924): 595–601.

The Book of American Negro Spirituals. 1925.

The Second Book of American Negro Spirituals. 1926.

God's Trombones: Seven Negro Sermons in Verse. 1927.

Black Manhattan. 1930.

Along This Way: The Autobiography of James Weldon Johnson. 1933.

Negro Americans, What Now? 1934.

Further Reading

Fleming, Robert E. *James Weldon Johnson and Arna Wendell Bontemps: A Reference Guide*. Boston, Mass.: G. K. Hall, 1978.

———. *James Weldon Johnson*. Boston, Mass.: Twayne, 1987.

Levy, Eugene. *James Weldon Johnson: Black Leader, Black Voices*. 1973.

Mason, Julian. "James Weldon Johnson: A Southern Writer Resists the South." *CLAJ*, 31(2), December 1987, pp. 154–169.

Oliver, Lawrence J., and Kenneth M. Price, eds. *Critical Essays on James Weldon Johnson*. New York: G. K. Hall, 1997.

Wilson, Sondra Kathryn, ed. *The Selected Writings of James Weldon Johnson*, Vols. 1 and 2. New York: Oxford University Press, 1995.

Johnson, John Arthur "Jack"

Jack Johnson was the first black man to win the world heavyweight boxing championship and is considered by many boxing enthusiasts to be the greatest heavyweight boxer of all time. More than a boxing legend, he symbolized open defiance to the unjust social order evident during the first half of the twentieth century.

Johnson was born into the first generation of free blacks in the United States. His father, a former slave, provided for the family admirably despite the limited opportunities afforded in Galveston, Texas. Galveston was an economically challenged city devastated by natural disaster and living under the yoke of the Jim Crow system. Essentially raised in poverty and with little formal education, Johnson turned to fighting as a means to transcend his constricted circumstances. He began fighting in degrading battle royals, which customarily featured numerous blacks against one another in a free-for-all to entertain white spectators. Around 1897, he began fighting professionally, experienced modest success, and earned a modest living.

By 1903, Johnson had developed as a boxer, winning the Negro heavyweight title from Denver Ed Martin in Los Angeles, in a twenty-round decision. He then focused on the world heavyweight champion, James J. Jeffries; but Jeffries, a white man, adhered to the established color line in professional fighting, which discouraged whites from fighting blacks. This was an age of prevalent racism, and blacks in the boxing world—like blacks in the larger society—were perceived by whites as inferior. As a result, Johnson's attempts to win the world heavyweight championship were frustrated. Circumstances changed, however, when Jeffries retired in 1904, amid a general lack of interest in boxing; the championship subsequently passed to other white boxers, first to Marvin Hart and then to Tommy Burns.

Burns, facing the problem of a declining sport, agreed to fight Johnson in 1908. The fight, which took place in Sydney, Australia, was stopped in the fourteenth round after Johnson had thoroughly punished the outmatched Burns. The color line had been broken, and a determined black man was the world heavyweight champion. White fans and sports commentators reacted to Johnson's victory by attempting to discount its significance, saying that boxing had deteriorated in recent years and that the best boxers were retired. But Johnson remained undaunted by the negative press, as was evident in his increasingly brazen attitude. When asked about the fight, Johnson discussed his opponent's athletic inferiority instead of offering the traditional commendation. Johnson was resolved, through his actions and his words, to defy American boxing as well as social etiquette. This was unsettling to the white community, which reacted with contempt for the new champion and demanded a match in which Johnson would be defeated and, presumably, the pseudoscientific theory of social Darwinism would be vindicated.

James J. Jeffries was called out of retirement as the "great white hope" to defeat and silence Johnson. Despite the protests of progressive reformers and the usual controversy surrounding a fight between a white and a black man, the match was held in Reno, Nevada, in 1910. Jeffries, previously undefeated, was the betting favorite; as the fight developed, however, it was apparent that he was outclassed. Moreover, Johnson demonstrated that he was more interested in humiliating Jeffries than in simply defeating him. He savored his victory as he physically punished and verbally taunted the helpless Jeffries. After Johnson had knocked Jeffries down three times in the fourteenth round (before this match, Jeffries had never been knocked down at all), the fight was stopped and Johnson retained his championship. The black community largely perceived Johnson's victory as a victory for all blacks; the white community reacted with malevolence and disdain, exasperated not only by the notion that a black man was the undisputed world champion but also by Johnson's arrogance. As a result, incidents of rioting and racial violence against blacks (including some murders) took place in many parts of the United States.

Johnson's lifestyle outside the ring further enraged whites. He was a wealthy entrepreneur who owned a prosperous nightclub, the Café de Champion in Chicago; he was also an egotist who flaunted his money, wearing flashy clothes and enjoying the high-life. The most intense controversy was centered on his public relationships with numerous white women at a time when miscegenation was considered taboo. Aside from the white girlfriends and prostitutes with whom he surrounded himself, Johnson married three white women: Etta Terry Duryea in 1911, Lucille Cameron in 1913, and Irene Marie Pineau in 1924. Even as he challenged white America, however, he realized that he was not immune to the nation's deep-seated racism.

White America, unable to defeat Johnson in the boxing ring, sought to defeat him through the judicial system. He was charged with violating the Mann Act, an outdated and infrequently applied federal law that prohibited the transportation of women across state lines for immoral purposes. In 1913, after a trial before twelve white male jurors, Johnson was found guilty, fined, and sentenced to a prison term of a year and a day. Rather than be imprisoned, he decided to flee the United States.

In exile, Johnson traveled through Europe, where he continued to fight. However, he encountered numerous difficulties including proposals to strip him of his title, financial troubles, and racism. In 1915, he journeyed to Cuba to defend his title against a white American, Jess Willard. In a match that is still controversial, Willard knocked Johnson out in the

Jack Johnson, c. 1910. (Library of Congress.)

twenty-sixth round. Johnson, no longer the heavy-weight champion, continued boxing in Spain and then in Mexico. In 1920, he returned to the United States, where he was arrested and imprisoned for his earlier conviction.

After serving his prison term, Johnson returned to boxing, but his best years were behind him. He fought his last professional match in 1928. After that, he participated in exhibition matches and also did some acting, managing to earn a humble living. In 1946, Johnson died in a car crash near Raleigh, North Carolina.

Biography

John Arthur ("Jack") Johnson was born 31 March 1878 in Galveston, Texas. He had a limited elementary school education. He began professional boxing in 1897; won the Negro heavyweight boxing championship title from Denver Ed Martin on 3 February 1903; won the world heavyweight championship from Tommy Burns in December of 1908; defended the world heavyweight championship against James J. Jeffries on 4 July 1910; and lost the world heavy-weight championship to Jess Willard on 5 April 1915. Johnson died near Raleigh, North Carolina, on 10 June 1946. He was inducted into the International Boxing Hall of Fame in 1954 and into the World Boxing Hall of Fame in 1980.

JOHN MARINO

See also Professional Sports and Black Athletes

Further Reading

Batchelor, Danzil. *Jack Johnson and His Times*. London: Phoenix Sports, 1956.

DeCoy, Robert H. *The Big Black Fire*. Los Angeles, Calif.: Holloway House, 1969.

Farr, Finis. *Black Champion: The Life and Times of Jack Johnson*. Greenwich, Conn.: Fawcett, 1969.

Gilmore, Al-Tony. *Bad Nigger: The National Impact of Jack Johnson*. Port Washington, N.Y.: Kennikat, 1975.

Odd, Gilbert, ed. *Jack Johnson: In the Ring and Out—The Classical Autobiography by the First Black Champion*. London: Proteus, 1977.

Roberts, Randy. *Papa Jack: Jack Johnson and the Era of White Hopes*. New York: Free Press, 1983.

Johnson, John Rosamond

John Rosamond Johnson was one of the most prolific composers and musicians of the early twentieth century and the Harlem Renaissance. He composed "Lift Every Voice and Sing" (the "Negro national anthem," 1900) and was also a successful arranger and vaudevillian. Rosamond changed the face of early black theater and was not only the first black composer to be signed by a white music company on Broadway (Joseph W. Stern, 1901) but also the first to compose music for white Broadway shows and conduct an all-white orchestra. He was among those who awakened interest in spirituals; he made arrangements of spirituals and published two volumes of these songs. Johnson studied for six years at the New England Conservatory of Music in Boston and was influenced by the nationalist composer Antonín Dvořák, who was then dean of the conservatory; Dvořák inspired Johnson's interest in black folk and popular traditions. As one of the few conservatory-trained musicians of the Harlem Renaissance, Johnson brought substance, style, and uniqueness to its music.

Johnson was introduced to musical theater in 1896, when he toured with John Isham's *Oriental America*; Isham had specifically recruited him because of his classical training and his familiarity with black popular rhythms. In 1897, Jackson returned to his hometown, Jacksonville, Florida, and began to give private piano lessons; he was also appointed music supervisor for the Jacksonville public schools. During that period Johnson (as composer) and his brother, James Weldon Johnson (as lyricist), wrote their first opera, *Toloso*. This was the beginning of a collaboration that would have a strong influence on musical theater. During the summer of 1899, the Johnson brothers traveled to New York and met some members of the black elite there: Harry Burleigh, Will Marion Cook, Paul Laurence Dunbar, George Walker, and Bert Williams—as well as Bob Cole, with whom they soon formed an alliance. On their return to Jacksonville, the brothers wrote "Lift Every Voice and Sing" to be sung by schoolchildren for a celebration of Abraham Lincoln's birthday in February 1900. The song became popular in schools throughout Jacksonville; was distributed as handwritten copies; was sung in black churches and schools, at graduation ceremonies, and at meetings of the National Association for the Advancement of Colored People (NAACP) across the nation. By the 1920s it was being recognized as the "Negro national anthem." It was finally published by the Edward B. Marks Company in 1921.

In 1900 the Johnson brothers returned to New York, where they worked with Bob Cole. With John Rosamond Johnson as composer, James Weldon Johnson as lyricist, and Cole as arranger, they wrote four songs for the show *Belle of Bridgeport* and one for the show *Rogers Brothers in Central Park*. These songs began to earn them a reputation. In 1901—because of this initial success and also because a fire had devastated the Stanton School, where they had worked in Jacksonville—the Johnsons decided to move to Harlem. Rosamond and Bob Cole completed the musical *Cannibal King*, with a libretto by Paul Laurence Dunbar, and they continued to gain popularity in the theatrical community. Their musical style, with its syncopation, its sophistication, and its varied use of dialect, became so popular that they took a collection of songs to the publisher Joseph Stern, who signed a three-year contract with them. This arrangement, the first for any black composers, established their professional career. The two Johnsons and Cole began contributing songs to Broadway musicals such as *Sleeping Beauty and the Beast*; and in 1902 Rosamond composed one of their biggest hits, "Under the Bamboo Tree," for the musical *Sally in Our Alley*. Its funny, catchy style and lyrics initiated a new type of popular music.

Also in 1902, John Rosamond Johnson and Bob Cole formed a vaudeville duo that soon became renowned as a "class act" because of their sophisticated charm and their avoidance of buffoonery. Johnson would often interject classical themes and art songs into their syncopated dance tunes, and he and Cole gradually overcame the image of the black minstrel entertainer and created a new image for future black performers. By 1903 they had become the hottest duo on Broadway. They enhanced their reputation with songs for the popular Broadway musicals *Mother Goose* and *Humpty Dumpty*.

In 1906 Johson and Cole composed and performed their own first show, *The Shoo-Fly Regiment*, which included one of Johnson's best songs, "L'il Gal," based on a poem by Dunbar. After touring in the west and midwest with modest success, the show opened on Broadway on 3 June 1907, but it was unsuccessful there, evidently because Johnson and Cole were out of their usual element and because their show, unlike their songs, lacked the financial support and advertising that their publishers usually provided.

In their next show, *Red Moon*, based on an Indian theme, Johnson had his first stage role as a comedic actor. The show began in Delaware in 1908 and traveled throughout the northeast and midwest before coming to the Majestic Theater in New York in 1909. As a result of the financial hardships, the strenuous schedule, and the numerous setbacks of the touring season, Cole suffered a mental and physical breakdown; he died on 2 August 1911 in a boardinghouse in the Catskills, New York.

Johnson formed another vaudeville act, with Dan Avery and Charles Hart, and this trio became part of a revue in London in 1912. Oscar Hammerstein appointed Johnson as musical director of the London Grand Opera House; Johnson remained in England for two years. When he returned to New York in 1914, Johnson became the founder and music director of the Harlem Music School Settlement for Colored People. During World War I, he served as a second lieutenant with the National Guard's Fifteenth Infantry. He returned to his musical and theatrical career in the 1920s, focusing more on black themes. His most notable contribution was *The Book of American Spirituals* in 1925, followed by *The Second Book of American Spirituals* in 1926. He had composed the arrangements, and James Weldon Johnson had provided the historical and musicological background, as well as an introductory preface.

Johnson turned to film in 1929, as conductor of a forty-voice choir for *Saint Louis Blues*, starring Bessie Smith. In 1933 he wrote the score for the film version of *The Emperor Jones*, starring Paul Robeson; this film was the first with a score by a black composer. Johnson continued to write songs for Broadway shows in the 1930s but primarily concentrated on collecting and arranging spirituals. In 1928 he appeared in a revue, *American*, which ran briefly; and in 1935 he acted in

Left to right: Bob Cole, James Weldon Johnson, and J. Rosamond Johnson, 1900s. (Schomburg Center for Research in Black Culture, New York Public Library.)

the original production of *Porgy and Bess*, as "Lawyer Frazier." His last role as an actor was in 1940, in the film *Cabin in the Sky*, starring Ethel Waters.

Biography

John Rosamond Johnson was born 11 August 1873 in Jacksonville, Florida. His parents were well educated and encouraged him and his brother, James Weldon Johnson, to read and study music. His father was a headwaiter at the Saint James hotel in Jacksonville and later became pastor of the Ebenezer Methodist Church; his mother was the first black woman to teach in a public school in Florida and was his first piano teacher. Johnson studied at the Stanton School in Florida and the New England Conservatory of Music in Boston, 1890–1896. He was music supervisor of the Jacksonville public schools, 1897–1901; musical director of London's Grand Opera House, 1912 (he married his childhood sweetheart, Nora Floyd, during his stay in London); musical director of the Harlem Music School Settlement for Colored People, 1914; and a second lieutenant in the National Guard's Fifteenth Infantry in World War I. After the war he returned to his musical career, focusing on spirituals and eventually working in films. Johnson died in Harlem, 11 November 1954.

BRENDA ELLIS

See also Cole, Bob; Dunbar, Paul Laurence; Emperor Jones, The; Fifteenth Infantry; Johnson, James Weldon; Musical Theater; Porgy and Bess; Saint Louis Blues; Spirituals

Selected Works

Toloso. 1898.
"Louisiana Lize." 1899.
"Lift Every Voice and Sing." 1900.
"Under the Bamboo Tree." 1901.
The Shoo-Fly Regiment. 1906.

Further Reading

Caldwell, Hansonia L. *African-American Music: A Chronology, 1619–1995*. California: Ikoro Communications, 1996.

Floyd, Samuel, ed. *Black Music in the Harlem Renaissance: A Collection of Essays*. Westport, Conn.: Greenwood, 1990.

Jasen, David A., and Gene Jones. *Spreadin' Rhythm Around: Black Popular Songwriters, 1880–1930*. New York: Schirmer, 1998.

Johnson, James Weldon. *Along This Way*. New York: Viking, 1933.

Johnson, James Weldon, and John Rosamond Johnson. *The Books of American Negro Spirituals*. New York: Viking, 1925, 1926.

Riis, Thomas. *Just before Jazz: Black Musical Theater in New York, 1890 to 1915*. New York: Smithsonian Institution, 1989.

Southern, Eileen. *Biographical Dictionary of African American and African Musicians*. Westport, Conn.: Greenwood, 1982.

———. *The Music of Black Americans: A History*. New York: Norton, 1983.

Johnson, Malvin Gray

In his short life, Malvin Gray Johnson, usually called Gray, became one of several artists whose work reflects the complexities of the Harlem Renaissance at its pinnacle. Johnson's range of subjects was wide and included portraits and figures, Harlem street life, African American folklore, and Negro spirituals. His modernist-inspired style was characterized by vigorous brushwork, intense areas of color, flattened and angular forms, and a lack of painterly finish. His work has the subtlety, charm, and sensitivity of his African American contemporaries in the early years of the Harlem Renaissance. Along with Aaron Douglas, William H. Johnson, and Hale Woodruff, Johnson was among the numerous painters and sculptors of the early 1930s who created a truly African American art by combining the basics of early modern styles with distinctly African American subjects, themes, and concerns.

Johnson was born in 1896 in Greensboro, North Carolina. He moved to New York City as a young man and studied at the National Academy of Design with Francis Coates Jones in the 1920s. In order to survive financially, he worked as a commercial artist and did various menial chores. He first gained widespread recognition when, in 1929, he received the Otto H. Kahn Prize from the Harmon Foundation for his painting *Swing Low, Sweet Chariot*, which was reproduced on the cover of *Crisis* in February 1929.

In the next five years, Johnson built his reputation with many paintings of his typical themes. In 1933 he painted murals for the Public Works of Art Projects

(PWAP). Critics responded to his works in various ways. While some admired the authenticity and sincerity with which he explored African American subjects, others disliked his quick, loose handling of paint and his modernist sensibility.

Johnson's finest portraits include his late *Self-Portrait*, *Postman*, and *Negro Soldier*, all from 1934. In the *Self-Portrait*, two African masks are seen behind the painter; they reflect his own countenance and allude to his African heritage at a time when this rediscovery was a broad concern of African American artists in the wake of the New Negro movement. In contrast, *Postman* is much less expressively curvilinear and more cubist in the description of forms. *The Old Mill* of 1934 is a vigorously painted cubist scene of rural industry. His *Negro Masks* is a sharply angular, dark-toned cubist still life of African tribal masks, a theme that African American artists of the era sometimes explored. Johnson's most compelling scenes of African American history and folklore include *Roll Jordan, Roll* (1930).

Johnson died suddenly at the age of thirty-eight, at the height of his career.

Biography

Malvin Gray Johnson was born 28 January 1896, in Greensboro, North Carolina. He studied at the National Academy of Design, New York City. He was awarded the Otto H. Kahn Prize, Harmon Foundation, New York, 1929, and was a member of the Society of Independent Artists. Johnson died 4 October 1934.

HERBERT R. HARTEL JR.

See also Crisis, The; Douglas, Aaron; Harmon Foundation; Johnson, William H.; Woodruff, Hale

Exhibitions

1928–1933, 1935: Harmon Foundation, New York City.
1934: Nicholas Roerich Museum, New York City.
1934: Corcoran Gallery of Art, Washington, D.C.
1935: New Jersey State Museum, Trenton.
1936: Texas Centennial Exhibition, Museum of Fine Arts, Dallas.
1939: Baltimore Museum of Art.
1940: American Negro Exposition, Chicago.
1940: Library of Congress, Washington, D.C.
1943: Institute of Contemporary Art, Boston.

1971: Newark Museum, Newark, N.J.
1976: Los Angeles County Museum of Art.

Further Reading

Driscoll, David. *Two Centuries of Black American Art.* New York and Los Angeles, Calif.: Knopf and Los Angeles County Museum of Art, p. 149.
Henderson, Harry, and Romare Bearden. *African-American Artists: From 1792 to the Present.* New York: Pantheon, 1993.
Lewis, Samella. *African-American Art and Artists.* Berkeley: University of California Press, 1990.
Patton, Sharon F. *African-American Art.* New York: Oxford University Press, 1998.
Powell, Richard J. *Black Art and Culture in the Twentieth Century.* New York: Thames and Hudson, 1997.
Reynolds, Gary. *Against the Odds: African-American Artists and the Harmon Foundation.* Newark, N.J.: Newark Museum, 1990, pp. 18, 23, 111, 114–116, 208–212.

Johnson, Noble

Noble Johnson was one of the most successful black supporting actors in Hollywood during the silent-film era and remained an important figure in film throughout his career. His career extended from 1914, when he filled in for an injured actor in a film produced by the Lubin Company, to 1950, when he appeared in *North of the Great Divide* as a Native American chief. During the 1920s—the period of the Harlem Renaissance—Johnson appeared in at least forty-five films. He officially retired in 1950, though he appeared again in an unmemorable black-and-white television movie, *Lost Island of Kioga*, in 1966. Johnson—who was 6 feet 2 inches tall, weighed more than 200 pounds, and was light skinned—is best known for playing formidable nonwhite characters, including Native Americans, Egyptians, Mexicans, and generic "exotics" (such as the chief on Skull Island in *King Kong* in 1933). Rarely did he have a role as an African American.

Johnson was raised on his father's ranch in Colorado Springs, where he trained race horses. He left in 1896 and traveled extensively in the American west, working as a cook and a cowboy, before involving himself with motion pictures with the Lubin Company on his return to Colorado Springs. During the next ten years,

Johnson established himself as a bit actor with Universal Studios. In 1916, Johnson joined with his brother, George P. Johnson, and the actor Clarence Brooks to form the Lincoln Motion Picture Company (incorporated 1917), the first black-financed film company dedicated to producing all-black films. Noble Johnson was its (unsalaried) president and ran the studio in Los Angeles; George Johnson controlled marketing and distribution in Omaha, where he held a full-time job with the post office. The Lincoln Motion Picture Company produced three films—*The Realization of a Negro's Ambition* (1916), *A Trooper of Troop K* (1917), and *The Law of Nature* (1918)—all starring Noble Johnson, before Universal demanded that Noble Johnson discontinue his association with Lincoln to avoid a conflict of interest. Primarily, Universal feared Johnson's successes in acting with Lincoln and wanted him to discontinue race films. Rather than lose his secure career at Universal for the instability of a fledgling company, Johnson resigned from Lincoln in September 1918. Clarence Brooks succeeded him as Lincoln's president; in 1923, after only seven films, the company folded because of financial difficulties.

Johnson, sometimes billed in the black press as "the race's daredevil movie star," was consistently given roles commensurate with his stature. He remained apart from the demeaning stereotyped roles to which black actors were usually relegated; rather, he presented to African American moviegoers an image of power and professional success. The *Chicago Whip* declared in 1919, "Johnson is a fair actor . . . and we trust he some day will be allowed to play a stellar role" (Bowser and Spence 2000, 235). As it happened, Johnson's only leading roles were in his own pictures with Lincoln. Although he appeared in numerous films and played some significant characters, such as Uncle Tom in *Topsy and Eva* (1927) and Queequeg in *Moby Dick* (1930), his career at Universal never included any major roles. His success lay more in the sheer volume of his films.

Biography

Noble Johnson was born 18 April 1881 and was raised on his father's ranch in Colorado Springs. He left Colorado Springs in 1896, traveled in the West, and then returned to Colorado Springs and joined the Lubin Company. He became a bit actor with Universal Studios, formed the Lincoln Motion Picture Company with his brother George P. Johnson and Clarence

Brooks in 1916, and (under pressure from Universal) resigned from Lincoln in 1918. During the 1920s and later he appeared in many films. The date of Johnson's death is unknown.

DAN MOOS

See also Brooks, Clarence; Film; Film: Actors; Film: Black Filmmakers; Lincoln Motion Picture Company; Race Films

Selected Filmography

The Eagle's Nest. 1915. (As a stagecoach driver and an Indian.)
The Realization of a Negro's Ambition. 1916.
Intolerance. 1916. (As a chariot driver.)
A Trooper of Troop K. 1917.
The Law of Nature. 1918.
The Four Horsemen of the Apocalypse. 1921. (As Conquest, uncredited.)
Tracks. 1922. (As Leon Serrano and also wrote the scenario.)
The Loaded Door. 1922. (As Blackie Lopez.)
The Adventures of Robinson Crusoe. 1922. (As Friday.)
The Ten Commandments. 1923. (As the Bronze Man in prologue.)
The King of Kings. 1927. (As a chariot driver.)
Vanity. 1927. (As a ship's cook.)
Topsy and Eva. 1927. (As Uncle Tom.)
The Mysterious Dr. Fu Manchu. 1929. (As Li Po.)
Moby Dick. 1930. (As Queequeg.)
Murders in the Rue Morgue. 1932. (As Janos.)
The Mummy. 1932. (As the Nubian.)
King Kong. 1933. (As a native chief.)
The Son of Kong. 1933. (As a native chief, uncredited.)
Dante's Inferno. 1935. (As Devil, uncredited.)
The Plainsman. 1936. (As Indian, uncredited.)
Drums Along the Mohawk. 1939. (As Indian, uncredited.)
The Ghost Breakers. 1940. (As the zombie.)
Jungle Book. 1942. (As a Sikh.)
She Wore a Yellow Ribbon. 1949. (As Red Shirt.)

Further Reading

Bowser, Pearl, and Louise Spence. *Writing Himself into History: Oscar Micheaux, His Silent Films, and His Audiences.* New Brunswick, N.J.: Rutgers University Press, 2000.
Cripps, Thomas. *Slow Fade to Black: The Negro in American Film 1900–1942*, 2nd ed. New York: Oxford University Press, 1993.

Gaines, Jane M. *Fire and Desire: Mixed-Race Movies in the Silent Era.* Chicago, Ill.: University of Chicago Press, 2001.

Leab, Daniel J. *From Sambo to Superspade: The Black Experience in Motion Pictures.* Boston, Mass.: Houghton Mifflin, 1975.

Richards, Larry. *African American Films through 1959: A Comprehensive, Illustrated Filmography.* Jefferson, N.C.: McFarland, 1998.

Sampson, Henry T. *Blacks in Black and White: A Source Book on Black Films,* 2nd ed. Metuchen, N.J.: Scarecrow, 1995.

Johnson, Sargent Claude

Sargent Claude Johnson was a visual artist who worked with great success in a range of media, producing lithographs, etchings, chalk drawings, large-scale murals, enamel metalwork, mosaic, and ceramics. Johnson made his artistic home in the Bay Area of California, rather than among the African American artists of the Harlem Renaissance. Nevertheless, he was a much-admired figure in the larger African American art world and won a number of awards in the influential shows sponsored by the Harmon Foundation. In 1935, the Harmon Foundation featured his work as part of a three-man exhibition at the Delphic Studios in New York City with the painter Malvin Gray Johnson and the sculptor Richmond Barthé, and he received an award for the wood polychrome *Forever Free*, now his most acclaimed work. This is a redwood sculpture covered with several coats of gesso and fine linen, sanded between layers. The piece is highly polished, with the flesh areas colored copper brown and the clothed portions painted black and white. The female figure looks obliquely upward, embodying strength and self-possession; at her feet she embraces and protects her young children.

Forever Free demonstrates an abiding preoccupation in Johnson's work: the relationship of the modern African American artist to his folk and African roots. The sculpture finds technical and stylistic inspiration in ancient Egypt, but Johnson is also inspired by ancient Asian, Mexican, and Native American plastic art. One can see in his work a relationship to west African tribal art, as well as to art deco, cubism, and the Mexican muralist tradition. His personal quest was to develop what he called, in 1935, a strictly Negro art; in common with other artists of the 1920s and 1930s, he took ideas

Mask of a Girl, 1926, by Sargent Claude Johnson (1888–1967); copper repoussé, 9 by 6 by 2½ inches. (© The Newark Musuem/Art Resource, N.Y. Collection of the Newark Museum, Newark, New Jersey, 92.108.)

from so-called primitive art. This engagement with nonwestern art led Johnson to spend time in Mexico, and through the 1940s he produced a number of pieces using the black clay of Oaxaca. One can also see the influence of a radically pared-down African style in the lithographs he produced in the late 1930s, which were inspired by his love of African American music. *Lenox Avenue* (1938) in particular evokes Harlem's most famous thoroughfare, through references to its musical and artistic output expressed as a clearly Africanist racial physiognomy.

Johnson continued to experiment with form and medium throughout his career. When the Works Progress Administration art project began in California in 1936, Johnson was hired, and the well-equipped studios gave him an opportunity to produce much larger works. Over the next few years he produced large-scale public projects. Later in the 1940s he worked with the Paine-Mahoney Company, producing massive porcelain enamel-on-steel murals and relief sculptures. In the 1950s he made a long visit to Japan. He continued to live in the Bay Area until his death in 1971. He stands as one of the most versatile artists to have come out of the Harlem Renaissance period.

Biography

Sargent Claude Johnson was born 7 October 1887 in Boston, Massachusetts. He attended public school in Worcester, Massachusetts, and the A. W. Best School of Art and California School of Fine Arts in 1915. He worked as a fitter for Schlussers and Brothers, 1917; and as a framer for Valdespino Framers, 1921. He was hired by the Works Progress Administration in 1936; he worked as a commissioned artist for the rest of his life. His awards included the following: Harmon Foundation; Otto H. Kahn Prize for *Sammy*, $250, 1927; Bronze Award, $100, 1929; Robert C. Ogden Prize, 1933; and San Francisco Art Association medals in 1925, 1931, 1935, 1938. Johnson died in San Francisco, 10 October 1967.

MARIA BALSHAW

See also Barthé, Richmond; Federal Programs; Harmon Foundation; Harmon Traveling Exhibition; Johnson, Malvin Gray; Works Progress Administration

Selected Exhibitions: Individual

1967: "Photos and Works by Sargent Johnson." San Francisco Negro Historical Society.
1971: "Sargent Johnson—Retrospective." Oakland Gallery, California.

Selected Exhibitions: Group

1925–1931, 1933, 1935, 1937: Harmon Foundation Exhibitions of Negro Art.
1935: Three-artist exhibition, Harmon Foundation, Delphic Studios, New York.
1945: "The Negro Artist Comes of Age." Albany (New York) Institute of History and Art.
1966: "The Negro in American Art." UCLA Fine Arts Gallery, Los Angeles.
1970: "Dimensions of Black." La Jolla (California) Museum of Art.
1997: "Rhapsodies in Black: Art of the Harlem Renaissance." Hayward Gallery, London, and tour.

Further Reading

Bearden, Romare, and Harry Henderson. *A History of African-American Artists: From 1792 to the Present.* New York: Pantheon, 1993.
Patton, Sharon. *African American Art*. London and New York: Oxford University Press, 1998.
Powell, Richard. *Black Art and Culture in the Twentieth Century*. London: Thames and Hudson, 1997.
Rhapsodies in Black: Art of the Harlem Renaissance. London: Hayward Gallery; and Berkeley: University of California Press, 1997.
Sargent Johnson: Retrospective. Oakland, Calif.: Oakland Museum, 1971.

Johnson, William H.

William Henry Johnson (1901–1970) was a major American artist of the twentieth century but has tended to be neglected. He was born in Florence, South Carolina. In 1918 he moved with his uncle to New York, where he underwent a rigorous training in art at the School of the National Academy of Design; he also studied at the Cape Cod School of Art, before relocating to Paris in 1926. In Europe, Johnson developed a turbulent style based on the paintings of Chaim Soutine, Edvard Munch, and Vincent Van Gogh, expressing his emotional reactions in exaggerated distortions and squeezing colors from the tube directly onto the canvas. After winning the Harmon Foundation Gold Medal in 1930, Johnson married Holcha Krake, a Danish tapestry weaver and ceramicist, and settled in Scandinavia for the next eight years.

In 1938, Johnson returned to Harlem and began to modify his expressionist style to depict scenes celebrating the black experience. Inspired by the work of Horace Pippin and Jacob Lawrence, Johnson simplified his painting, emphasizing flatness, heavy outlines, and jarring color contrasts in a style that has often been described as primitive, naïve, or folk oriented. Johnson painted a variety of subjects, from urban scenes of cafés and Harlem's nightlife, street musicians, and jitterbugs to rural scenes of farm life, chain gangs, churchgoers, and baptisms to biblical scenes and portraits. In the 1940s, Johnson's work became overtly religious and political, especially in his historical series *Fighters for Freedom*. Johnson was determined "to give, in simple and stark form, the story of the Negro as he has existed" (Powell 1991).

Johnson exhibited in several major shows and won accolades from both black and white critics, but his life then turned tragic: his wife died of cancer, and he himself began suffering the effects of a debilitating mental deterioration that eventually left him unable to

William H. Johnson (1901–1970), *Art Class*, c. 1939–1940; oil on plywood. (© Smithsonian American Art Museum, Washington, D.C./Art Resource, N.Y.)

work, confined to Central Islip State Hospital in New York for the remainder of his life. He had initially been considered one of the up-and-coming painters of the Harlem Renaissance; the strange circumstances of his illness, however, combined with a lack of gallery support, his expatriate status, and what many critics considered his stylistic fickleness, contributed to a widespread neglect of his art. This situation has been redressed only relatively recently, as several posthumous exhibitions returned Johnson to his status as a major black modernist.

Taylor (1971) notes that Johnson's primitivism, eclecticism, and spirituality made him a "forceful and original" painter; Driskell (1987) has argued that, by integrating religious and social messages, Johnson "changed the course of artistic interpretations of Black American themes in Christianity" and "enlightened the Black community about their own history and heritage." Powell (1991) has attempted to redefine Johnson as a "world-class citizen" rather than as an isolated and tragic figure; according to Powell, Johnson's lifelong search for "home" imbued his work with a powerful empathy for "the folk life and the cultural expressions of marginalized peoples."

Johnson was a professed "primitive," and his work corresponds to similar attempts by artists of the Harlem Renaissance to capture the innate power and spirituality of the folk heritage of common people. With his brilliant sense of design, coupled with a strong sensibility for rhythmic color and form, Johnson was able to create powerful visual narratives of African American life that celebrated the New Negro's deep reservoir of spirituality and humanity.

Biography

William H. Johnson was born 18 March 1901 in Florence, South Carolina. He studied at the Wilson School for Negroes in Florence, 1907–1917; at the School of the National Academy of Design, New York, 1921–1923; at the Cape Cod School of Art in Provincetown, Massachusetts, under Charles Webster Hawthorne, 1924–1926; and at the studio of George B. Luks in New York City, 1926. Johnson taught at WPA/FDA, Harlem Community Arts Center, in 1939–1942. His awards included the Cannon Prize for Painting, School of the National Academy of Design, 1924 and 1926; the Hallgarten Prize for Painting, Cape Cod School of Art, 1925; a Harmon Foundation Gold Medal, 1930; and a Certificate of Honor, National Negro Achievement Day, 1942. Johnson was confined to Central Islip State Hospital in 1948–1970. He died 13 April 1970 of acute pancreatitis.

RANDALL SHAWN WILHELM

See also Artists; Lawrence, Jacob

Selected Exhibitions: Individual

1927: "William H. Johnson: Paintings." Students and Artists Club, Paris, France.
1928: "William H. Johnson." Galerie Alban, Nice, France.
1929: "Exhibition of Paintings by William H. Johnson." Peter White Public Library, Marquette, Michigan.
1930: "William H. Johnson." Trondeim (Norway) Art Society.
1931: "Paintings: William H. Johnson." Alma Reed Galleries, New York.
1932: "Tempera Paintings by William H. Johnson." Wakefield Gallery, New York.
1946: "William H. Johnson." 135th Street Branch, New York Public Library.
1957–1961: "William H. Johnson: An Artist of the Work Scene." (Traveled nationally.)

1971–1973. "William H. Johnson, 1901–1970." National Collection of Fine Arts, Smithsonian Institution, Washington, D.C. (Posthumous; traveled to Africa and Europe.)

1982: "William H. Johnson: The Scandinavian Years." National Museum of American Art, Smithsonian Institution, Washington, D.C. (Posthumous.)

Further Reading

Bearden, Romare, and Harry Henderson, eds. "William H. Johnson." In *A History of African-American Artists from 1792 to the Present*. New York: Pantheon, 1993, pp. 185–199.

Driskell, David. "The Flowering of the Renaissance: The Art of Aaron Douglas, Meta Warwick Fuller, Palmer Hayden, and William H. Johnson." In *Harlem Renaissance: Art of Black America*. New York: Studio Museum in Harlem and Abradale, 1987.

Hammond, Leslie King. "The Life and Work of William Henry Johnson, 1901–1970." Ph.D. dissertation, Johns Hopkins University, 1975.

Powell, Richard J. "William H. Johnson's 'Minde Kertiminde.' *Siksi: The Nordic Art Review*, 1, 1986: 17–23.

———. *Homecoming: The Art and Life of William H. Johnson*. New York: Norton, 1991.

Taylor, Joshua C. "Introduction." In Adelyn D. Breeskin, *William H. Johnson: 1901–1970*. Washington, D.C.: Smithsonian Institution Press for the National Collection of Fine Arts, 1971.

Jones, Eugene Kinckle

Eugene Kinckle Jones was born in Richmond, Virginia, in 1885, during the post-Reconstruction era; his parents were Joseph Endom and Rosa Kinckle Jones. He earned a bachelor's degree from Virginia Union College in 1905 and that autumn enrolled in the master's program at Cornell University in mathematics and engineering. He refocused his studies on economics and sociology, in order to have more impact on African Americans, and received a master's degree in those two areas in 1908. At Cornell, he was a founding member of Alpha Phi Alpha fraternity, the first intercollegiate Greek-letter fraternity for African Americans. Jones was denied the opportunity to pursue a career in social work; he then worked as a teacher in Louisville,

Kentucky. He married Blanche Ruby Watson on 11 March 1909; they would have two children.

In 1911, Jones met the noted black sociologist George Edmund Haynes, who during that year brought him to New York City to work as a field secretary at the League of Urban Conditions among Negroes, which later became the National Urban League (NUL). In this position Jones helped to address the role of black migrants as well as the professional development of black social workers. In 1917, he became the first executive secretary of NUL; he served in this post until 1941, the longest tenure of any leader in the organization.

Jones wrote articles in *Opportunity*, the magazine of NUL, about the education of African American social workers; he also helped implement NUL's social work fellowship program to enable young black students to pursue graduate studies at various participating universities. According to Armfield (1999), this was part of Jones's initiative to improve the professional status of black social workers, whose services were needed in black communities in both the North and the South. Jones is credited with developing the first successful approach to professional training for black social workers; he helped to train a number of individuals with regard to health care, housing, industry, and fieldwork.

During the period of the Harlem Renaissance—the 1920s—Jones became the first African American elected to the executive committee of the National Conference of Social Work (he was elected treasurer in 1925). Additionally, he became vice president and chairman of the Harlem Adult Education Committee, chairman of Associates in Negro Folk Education, and a trustee of Virginia Union University and president of its alumni association. During the Great Depression he became a member of President Franklin Delano Roosevelt's unofficial "black cabinet"—a group of leading African Americans who gave the president input on the New Deal programs intended to improve employment opportunities for African Americans.

Jones's leadership was in the tradition of "race men" who were committed to using their education and position to advance the cause of the African American masses.

Biography

Eugene Kinckle Jones was born in Richmond, Virginia, 30 July 1885. He studied at Wayland Academy; Virginia Union College (A.B., 1905); and Cornell University

(M.A., 1908). He was a founding member of Alpha Phi Alpha Fraternity; an adviser to Mayor James J. Walker of New York City; treasurer of the executive committee, National Conference of Social Work; American delegate at the International Conference of Social Work in Paris; a participant in the International Conference of Human Relations in Cambridge, England; a member of President Franklin D. Roosevelt's "black cabinet"; a member of the executive board of the National Conference of Social Workers; vice president and chairman of the Harlem Adult Education Committee; chairman of Associates in Negro Folk Education; a trustee of Virginia Union University; and president of the Virginia Union alumni association. Jones was employed as a teacher in the public school system of Louisville, Kentucky (1909–1911); he was a field secretary of the National Urban League in New York City (1911–1917) and an executive secretary in New York City (1917–1941). He died in Flushing, New York, 11 January 1954.

ANDREW P. SMALLWOOD

See also Haynes, George Edmund; National Urban League; Opportunity; Race Men

Further Reading

Armfield, Felix L. "Jewel Eugene Kinckle Jones and the Development of Early African-American Social Work." *Sphinx*, 84(1), Spring 1999.

Battle, Marc Kevin. "Legendary Brothers Establish Place in History through Contributions to Humanity." *Sphinx*, 84(1), Spring 1999.

Lively, Tarron. "Eugene Kinckle Jones: Moving the Urban League to the Streets." *Washington Afro-American and Washington Tribune*, 28 July–3 August 2001. (Commemorative section of "Afro Chronicles.")

Walker, Wallace L. "Alpha Phi Alpha and the Founding of African-American Civil Rights Groups." *Sphinx*, 84(1), Spring 1999.

Wesley, Charles H. *The History of Alpha Phi Alpha: A Development in College Life*. Baltimore, Md.: Foundation Publishers, 1996. (16th printing.)

Jones, Lois Mailou

The story of Lois Mailou Jones (1905–1998) as an artist and teacher is perhaps told best through her own recollections and those of her students, in particular Benjamin (1994, 1995) and Driskell (1998). Her life spanned most of the twentieth century, and her work encompassed many stylistic changes.

Jones was born and educated in Boston, which was a center for the visual arts; it was the first American city to embrace impressionism, then considered a radical movement. At her family's summer home in Martha's Vineyard, she met the sculptor Meta Warrick Fuller and the musician and composer Harry T. Burleigh, both of whom had lived and worked in Paris and encouraged Jones to go there; she was also inspired by Fuller's stories about working with the sculptor Auguste Rodin. Jones obtained teaching positions at the Palmer Memorial Institute in Sedalia, North Carolina, in 1928; and at Howard University in Washington, D.C., in 1930. In 1937, when she had her first sabbatical leave, she received a General Education Board fellowship and left the United States to study at the Académie Julian in Paris. In the United States, Jones had endured her share of discrimination: for example, she was turned down for an assistantship at the School of the Museum of Fine Arts in Boston, even though she was one of its brightest graduates. The climate in America was such that Jones asked her friend Céline Tabary, whom she met at the Académie Julian, to deliver a number of her works to museums and galleries for her; she assumed that if she delivered them herself, they would probably be rejected because of her race.

Jones, Tabary, and Lillian Evanti—an opera singer who was introduced to Jones by Burleigh—were very close, calling themselves the "three blind mice." In 1953, Jones and the Haitian artist and graphic designer Louis Vergniaud Pierre-Noël were married at Tabary's summer home in Cabris, France. (Jones and her future husband had met at Columbia University in 1934.) Another of Jones's friends, the historian and philosopher Alain Locke, had a definite influence on the direction Jones took in her art. During a summer session at Columbia University in 1934, Jones had studied its ethnographic collection of masks from nonwestern cultures; while she was in France, she explored African themes in her own work (*Les Fétiches*, 1938), having seen original art—considered artifacts at the time—in museums and galleries and then having seen these images as reworked by Pablo Picasso and other avant-garde artists. When Locke became acquainted with Jones, he suggested that she explore these themes further, telling her that she had more right to Africa than, say, Picasso did.

Jones had a long-standing interest in design, emanating from her early education at the High School of Practical Arts (HSPA) in Boston; through her apprenticeship to Grace Ripley (Ripley Studios), she designed theater costumes and masks. However, she made a conscious decision to separate herself from design so that she could be regarded as a serious artist. At the time, "design" was associated with crafts, and those executing "patterns" were primarily women who remained anonymous—whereas Jones was explicit about wanting to be an artist and be known. She did, however, return to design later in life, exploring the theme of the mask and taking inspiration from her experiences in Haiti and Africa. In the 1970s and 1980s, she experimented with transforming this traditional three-dimensional medium onto a two-dimensional surface. Examples of her work during this period are *Moon Masque* (1971), *Sudanesia* (1970), *Ubi Girl from Tai Region* (1972), *Damballah* (1980), *Symbols d'Afrique I* (1980), *Petite Ballerina* (1982), and *Initiation, Liberia* (1983). Jones once recalled, "Very early I was introduced to Africa through creating the masks with the Ripley studios."

From time to time, Jones explored political themes in her work. *Meditation (Mob Victim)* (1944) is an empathic treatment of a single black man, representing the thousands of black men who had been lynched in the American South. Jones was not acquainted with the model for this work and had chosen him more or less by chance; it turned out, however, that his brother had been lynched in his presence. During the turbulent 1960s, Jones turned to images that included such notable figures as Martin Luther King Jr., John Kennedy, and Lyndon Johnson.

Although Jones spent her adult life mainly in Washington, D.C. (where she taught at Howard University) and in Paris (where she maintained a studio), her hometown, Boston, never forgot her. Jones's first individual show was held at the Robert Vose Galleries in Boston in 1939. At the time of this exhibition, the *Christian Science Monitor* described her as the "leading Negro artist." In 1973 the Boston Museum of Fine Arts organized "Reflective Moments," Jones's first major solo retrospective. Other important exhibitions were held in Washington. In 1972 Howard University honored Jones with a retrospective show, "Forty Years of Painting, 1932–1972." Another solo exhibition was held at the Phillips Collection in Washington in 1979.

During the last two decades of her life, Jones received many awards, and her works were exhibited throughout the world. She was extremely proud of her African American heritage, although she said that wanted to be remembered simply as an American artist. She also took pride in having taught for forty-seven years at Howard University, where she said she had "guided and taught many of today's major black artists." She summed up her career as having been "long and rich"; she noted that her style and subject matter showed "the unmistakable influence of the countries and cultures in which she has traveled and lived: France, Haiti, Africa, America."

Biography

Lois Mailou Jones was born in Boston, Massachusetts, on 4 November 1905; her parents, Thomas Vreeland Jones and Carolyn Dorinda Adams, had moved from Paterson, New Jersey, to Cambridge shortly after their marriage, and then to Boston. She was educated in Boston, studying at the High School of Practical Arts there, and was an apprentice of Grace Ripley (Ripley Studios). Jones taught at Palmer Memorial Institute in Sedalia, North Carolina (beginning in 1928), and—for forty-seven years—at Howard University in Washington, D.C. (beginning in 1930). In 1937 she went to Paris on a sabbatical to study at the Académie Julian. She married the Haitian artist and graphic designer Louis Vergniaud Pierre-Noël in 1953. Jones spent most of her adult life in Washington, D.C., and Paris. After a long career, she died in Washington, D.C., in 1998.

Marianne Woods

See also Artists; Burleigh, Harry Thacker; Fuller, Meta Warrick; Locke, Alain

Further Reading

Benjamin, Tritobia Hayes. *The Life and Art of Loïs Jones*. San Francisco, Calif.: Pomegranate Artbooks, 1994.
———. "Color, Structure, Design: The Artistic Expressions of Lois Mailou Jones." *International Review of African American Art*, 9, c. 1995, pp. 28–40.
Benjamin, Tritobia Hayes, E. J. Montgomery, and Joellen El-Bashir. "A Tribute to Lois M. Jones: Three Remembrances." *International Review of African American Art*, 15, 1998, pp. 39–43.
Driskell, David C. "A Tribute: Lois Mailou Jones (1905–1998)." *American Art*, 12, 1998, pp. 86–88.

LaDuke, Betty. "Lois Mailou Jones: The Grande Dame of African-American Art." *Woman's Art Journal*, 8, 1988, pp. 28–32.

Rowell, Charles H. "Interview with Lois M. Jones." *Callaloo*, 12, 1988, pp. 357–378.

Joplin, Scott

Scott Joplin, the child of a former slave and a freeborn black woman, grew up in the town of Texarkana on the Texas-Arkansas border. His often-cited birth date, 24 November 1868, is incorrect. He had no formal education as a youth, although the members of his family were very musical and played several instruments. A German immigrant musician (perhaps Julius Weiss) seems to have played a significant role in Joplin's musical and artistic development.

During the 1880s, Joplin probably moved to and lived in Sedalia, Missouri, where he worked as a traveling musician and became a close friend and associate of Tom Turpin of St. Louis, a pioneer in the early development of ragtime. In 1893, Joplin probably played in a band at the World's Columbian Exposition in Chicago, where the explosion of interest in ragtime began. Returning to Sedalia in 1894, he joined the Queen City Cornet Band and led his own dance band. He also traveled with a vocal group called the Texas Medley Quartette. During this period, he attended music classes at George R. Smith College in Sedalia, at the same time teaching piano and composition to several younger ragtime composers, including Scott Hayden and Arthur Marshall. From 1898 to 1899 Joplin performed as a pianist at the Maple Leaf Club; he issued his first piano rag, "Original Rags," in 1899. His next publication, "Maple Leaf Rag," sold more than half a million copies by 1909 and provided Joplin with a small but steady income for the remainder of his life. "Maple Leaf Rag" is probably the most famous of all piano rags; it formed the basis for Joplin's success in ragtime and for his title "king of ragtime."

In 1901 Joplin and his first wife, Belle, moved to St. Louis, where he spent more time composing and teaching than performing. Rags published during this time period were "The Easy Winners" (1901), "Sunflower Slow Drag" (1901), "The Entertainer" (1902), and "The Strenuous Life" (1902), a tribute to President Theodore Roosevelt.

Joplin's interests went beyond ragtime to serious music for lyric theater and classical European art forms. He composed a ballet called *The Ragtime Dance*, depicting a black American ball and incorporating a singer-narrator, which was first performed on 24 November 1899 in Sedalia and was published in 1902. *A Guest of Honor* was an opera depicting the black leader Booker T. Washington's dinner at the White House with President Theodore Roosevelt in 1902; this opera went on tour in 1903. Joplin's life work, however, was the composition of his opera *Treemonisha* (1911), and his subsequent efforts to publish and produce it. He moved to New York in 1907 to further his efforts to find a reputable publisher. Joplin claimed that Irving Berlin had access to the score of *Treemonisha* at this time and had stolen one of Joplin's themes for use in Berlin's hit song "Alexander's Ragtime Band." During his first year in New York, Joplin befriended and encouraged Joseph F. Lamb, a young white man who eventually became one of the foremost composers of ragtime, and one of the most successful.

Although *Treemonisha* received several favorable reviews from critics after Joplin published the score himself, he was never able to stage the work successfully

Scott Joplin as shown on the sheet music of "The Entertainer."
(© Bettmann/Corbis.)

in its entirety. Joplin published his last work, "Magnetic Rag," in 1914, through his own publishing company. After his death, it was apparent that he had been a prolific composer; he left behind numerous unpublished manuscripts and compositions of stage works and orchestral music, most of which appear to have been destroyed or lost in legal proceedings in 1961.

Joplin was the preeminent composer of piano ragtime, and he strove to be recognized as a composer of artistic merit above and beyond his popular acclaim. He called his piano rags "classic rags," meaning that they were comparable to European artistic music. The care that he took to create and subsequently publish and have performed accurate representations and renderings of his scores justifies his position.

Joplin's influence on the Harlem Renaissance movement specifically stems from his time in New York from 1907 to 1917. Ragtime as an American art form and a popular idiom flourished from about 1896 to 1918, and it has widely been identified as a precursor of jazz—that musical art form which is uniquely American in both its development and its subsequent influence and success throughout the twentieth century.

Biography

Scott Joplin was born between July 1867 and mid-January 1868 in northeastern Texas. He had few early educational opportunities, but most members of his family played musical instruments. Evidently, he moved to Sedalia, Missouri, in the 1880s, and he attended music classes at George R. Smith College in Sedalia in the 1890s. He worked as a traveling musician, and he may have played in a band in Chicago in 1893 for the World's Columbian Exposition. He issued his first piano rag, "Original Rags," in 1899; this was followed by the immensely popular "Maple Leaf Rag." Joplin moved to St. Louis, Missouri, in 1901. He devoted his time to teaching and composition and continued to publish piano rags. He had an ambition to write for lyric theater, and he wrote a number of ballets and short operas, most of which have not survived. He moved to New York City in 1907 and tried to publish and produce his opera *Treemonisha*. He completed *Treemonisha* in 1910 and published the score himself in 1911; thereafter, a few stagings and performances were done, none of any substance. Joplin continued to compose until his death in New York City on 1 April 1917. Most of his unpublished

manuscripts and scores were apparently lost or destroyed in 1961.

BRAD EDEN

See also Jazz

Selected Works

"Maple Leaf Rag." 1899.
"The Entertainer." 1902.
The Ragtime Dance. 1902. (Ballet.)
A Guest of Honor. 1903. (Opera, lost.)
"Rose Leaf Rag." 1907.
"Wall Street Rag." 1909.
Treemonisha. 1911. (Opera.)
"Magnetic Rag." 1917.

Further Reading

Berlin, Edward A. *Ragtime: A Musical and Cultural History.* Berkeley: University of California Press, 1980.
———. *King of Ragtime: Scott Joplin and His Era.* New York: Oxford University Press, 1994.
———. "Joplin, Scott" and "Ragtime." (Grove's Web site, ed. Laura Macy.)
Blesh, Rudi, and Harriet Janis. *They All Played Ragtime.* New York: Knopf, 1950. (See also 2nd ed., Grove, 1959; 3rd ed., Jazz Book Club, 1960; 4th ed., Music Scales, 1971.)
Curtis, Susan. *Dancing to a Black Man's Tune: A Life of Scott Joplin.* Columbia: University of Missouri Press, 1994.
Frew, Tim. *Scott Joplin and the Age of Ragtime.* New York: Friedman-Fairfax, 1996.
Gammond, Peter. *Scott Joplin and the Ragtime Era.* New York: St. Martin's, 1975.
Lawrence, V. B., ed. *The Collected Works of Scott Joplin.* New York, 1971. (Rev. 1981 as *The Complete Works of Scott Joplin.*)
Ping-Robbins, Nancy R. *Scott Joplin: A Guide to Research.* New York: Garland, 1998.

Jordan, Joe

Joe Jordan, a noted ragtime pianist, arranger, composer, and musical director, became renowned through his tenure at Robert T. Mott's Pekin Theater (formerly Pekin Music Hall) in Chicago in 1906–1909 and

1911–1913. When he was hired as musical director in 1906, Jordan immediately began supplying the new all-black stock company with his own works (*The Man from 'Bam*, 1906; *Mayor of Dixie*, 1906). As the first theater in the nation owned and operated by blacks, the Pekin quickly became a major center for black entertainment during the 1910s and 1920s.

In May 1905, the first "syncopated music" concert performed by the Memphis Students featured Jordan's work and the talents of Ernest Hogan, James Reese Europe, and Will Dixon (the group later featured Will Marion Cook).

During the 1920s and 1930s, Jordan was a much sought-after director and conductor of musical revues. *Strut Miss Lizzie* (1922), advertised as "Glorying the Negro Beauty," portrayed racial pride through a series of songs (mainly composed by Jordan), dances, and comedy scenes. *Rarin' to Go* (1925–1926), a touring musical revue, had a score by Jordan and an integrated cast who performed separately; it received little attention. *Deep Harlem* (1928–1929), another musical revue with a score by Jordan, chronicled the progress of the Negro from Ethiopian royalty to Harlem's cabarets in song, dance, and comedy. Jordan also composed most of the score for the musical comedy *Brown Buddies* (1930), which starred Bill "Bojangles" Robinson and ran for 111 performances at the Liberty Theater in Harlem. This acclaimed show, full of riveting dance sequences, looked at black soldiers in France during World War I. *Fast and Furious* (1931), which lasted for only seven performances at the New Yorker Theater, had music composed by Jordan and J. Rosamond Johnson as a team; it also included a rare appearance by Zora Neale Hurston, who acted in a few skits and sang. During the 1930s Jordan conducted the Negro Unit of the Works Progress Administration (WPA) Federal Theater Project, a project intended to help employ artists during the Great Depression.

A proponent of self-empowerment and self-help, Jordan was also a sought-after businessman. Early in 1917, he brought legal action against the Original Dixieland Jazz Band for copyright infringement: the band had used his tune "That Teasin' Rag" in its "Original Dixieland One-Step." The band's records were quickly recalled and redistributed as "Introducing 'That Teasin' Rag' by Joe Jordan." In 1920 and 1923, as the vice president and manager of the Chicago Production Company, Jordan produced revisions of *The Man from 'Bam*. Jordan was also a financial manager for Will Marion Cook's New York Symphony Orchestra in 1918 and a staff arranger for the Clarence Williams

Publishing Company during the 1920s. Meanwhile, Jordan toured the United States and Europe with his group, the Ten Sharps and Flats.

Jordan retired from music in 1944 after serving as director for the Army Specialist Corp's black orchestra, with the rank of captain. He relocated to Tacoma, Washington, and continued his real estate enterprises.

Biography

Joseph Zachariah Taylor Jordan was born 11 February 1882 in Cincinnati, Ohio. He learned violin, piano, and drums primarily by ear and briefly studied music at Lincoln Institute (later Lincoln University), Jefferson, Missouri, around 1899–1900. He taught private students in his studio in Tacoma, Washington, 1944–1971; and was on the faculty of the Modern Institute of Music in Tacoma, 1949. Jordan played violin, double bass, and drums in the band Georgia-Up-to-Date (St. Louis, Missouri), 1899; played violin and drums in the Taborin Band (St. Louis), 1900; was music and stage director of the vaudeville show *Dandy Coon* (Chicago), 1903; performed ragtime piano at Tom Turpin's Rosebud Café (St. Louis), 1904; was conductor and director of the Pekin Music Hall (Chicago), 1904; organized and wrote music for the Memphis Students (New York City), 1905; was musical director of the Pekin Theater (Chicago), 1906–1909; organized and produced the new Memphis Students, 1908; returned to the Pekin Theater as musical director, 1911–1913; directed an orchestra for the new States Theater (Chicago), 1913; organized the YMCA symphonic orchestra (Chicago), 1913; was musical director for the prizefighter Jack Johnson's European tour, 1915; was financial manager and assistant director of Will Marion Cook's New York Syncopated Orchestra, 1918; was vice president and manager of Chicago Production Company, 1920 on; was staff arranger for Clarence Williams Publishing Company, 1920s; was musical director and conductor for *Keep Shufflin'*, 1928; conducted the Negro Unit Orchestra of the WPA Federal Theater Project, 1930s; conducted a seventy-five-member symphony orchestra to accompany a choir of 350 for the ASCAP Silver Jubilee Festival (Carnegie Hall), 1939; directed an orchestra of black musicians in the Army Specialist Corps (ASC) at Huachuca, Arizona, as a captain, 1943–1944; and retired from active performance to continue his career in real estate, 1944. Jordan was the first African American elected to the board of directors of American Federation of Musicians (AFM) Local 208 of Chicago 1932; he joined ASCAP in 1939. He died in Tacoma, Washington, 11 September 1971.

EMMETT G. PRICE III

See also Cook, Will Marion; Europe, James Reese; Federal Programs; Hurston, Zora Neale; Johnson, John Rosamond; Musical Theater; Robinson, Bill "Bojangles"; Works Progress Administration

Selected Works

"Morocco Blues." 1926. (Piano; recorded, Arpeggio ARP 1205.)
"Hop Off." 1927. (Dance orchestra; recorded, Classics 580; Riverside SDP-11.)
"Betty Lou." New York: Harms, 1930.
"Don't Leave Your Little Blackbird Blue." New York: Harris, c. 1930. (Cocomposers, Porter Grainger and Shelton Brooks.)

Musical Theater

The Man from 'Bam. 1920, 1923. (Original, 1906–1907.)
Strut Miss Lizzie. 1922.
Rarin' to Go. 1925–1926.
Deep Harlem. 1928–1929.
Brown Buddies. 1930.
Fast and Furious. 1931.

Further Reading

Bauman, Thomas. "Jordan, Joseph Zachariah Taylor ('Joe')." In *Center for Black Music Research: International Dictionary of Black Composers*, ed. Samuel A. Floyd Jr. Chicago, Ill.: Fitzroy Dearborn, 1999.

Blesh, Rudi, and Harriet Janis. *They All Played Ragtime*, 4th ed. New York: Oak, 1971.

Fletcher, Tom. *100 Years of the Negro in Show Business*. New York: Burdge, 1954.

Morgan, Thomas L., and William Barlow. "Joe Jordan." In *From Cakewalks to Concert Halls: An Illustrated History of African American Popular Music from 1895 to 1930*. Washington, D.C.: Elliot and Clark, 1992.

Oppenheimer, Priscilla. "Jordan, Joe." In *The Harlem Renaissance: A Historical Dictionary for the Era*, ed. Bruce Kellner. Westport, Conn.: Greenwood, 1984.

Peterson, Bernard L., Jr. *A Century of Musicals in Black and White: An Encyclopedia of Musical Stage Works by, about, or Involving African Americans*. Westport, Conn.: Greenwood, 1993.

Southern, Eileen. "Jordan, Joe." In *The Greenwood Encyclopedia of Black Music: Biographical Dictionary of Afro-American and African Musicians*. Westport, Conn.: Greenwood, 1982.

Zimmerman, Richard. "Jordan, Joe." In *The New Grove Dictionary of American Music*, Vol. 2, ed. H. Wiley Hitchcock and Stanley Sadie. New York: Macmillan, 1986.

Journalists

Whether as newspaper and magazine publishers, editors, reporters, columnists, or critics, black journalists made vital contributions to African American politics and culture during the Harlem Renaissance. Black newspapers and magazines provided the institutional base for black journalists as well as publicizing and providing outlets for black essayists, poets, playwrights, and novelists. Without black journalists and the newspapers and magazines that supported them, the Harlem Renaissance would have had little impact.

By the 1920s, black newspapers had been in existence for more than one hundred years. From the establishment of the first black newspaper, *Freedom's Journal*, by John Russwurm in 1827 to the 1920s, black newspapers gathered and delivered news and opinion to black communities throughout the United States. During this time, because of the limited, if not biased, coverage in the general press, blacks found their newspapers the only source of news and opinion about their activities and concerns. The black press was one of the few segments of the American news media that actively campaigned for black equality in the United States. In that sense, the black press, along with civil rights organizations and black community groups, was an agent of protest. In some communities the black press, as the only medium of black protest, helped to create and influence other agents of change.

The black press not only expressed dissatisfaction with American racism but also helped create, maintain, and mold the black communities it served. In doing so, through its coverage of black organizations, social functions, personalities, issues, events, and achievements, it helped define the black community. According to Gunnar Myrdal in *An American Dilemma*:

The press defines the Negro group to the Negroes themselves. The individual Negro is invited to share in the sufferings, grievances, and pretensions of the millions of Negroes outside the narrow local community. This creates a feeling of strength and solidarity. . . . The [black] press is also the chief agency of group control. It tells the individual how he should think and feel as an American Negro and creates a tremendous power of suggestion by implying that all other Negroes think and feel in this manner. (171)

Although other black institutions, such as churches, were also significant agencies for group control, Myrdal correctly assessed the role of the black press. To a far greater extent than the white press during the Harlem Renaissance era, the black press showed the world to the black community, showed that community to itself, and showed the black community to the world.

Black newspapers and magazines were open to all within the black community who had something to say. Aspiring black journalists were barred from most if not all journalism schools in the 1920s, so black newspapers could not tap that source. They had to train their own reporters, columnists, and critics and in so doing tapped the rich source of black literary talent that surfaced during the Harlem Renaissance. Black publishers, for the most part, were highly literate and educated people who wanted to introduce to the world the black writers of the Harlem Renaissance. Quite a few saw the 1920s as a time of radical social change, so they gave a voice on their editorial pages to black radicals of the era. Many black newspapers had feature sections in which writers and journalists of the Harlem Renaissance published their works. In that sense, black newspapers served as literary magazines as well as purveyors of news and opinion. Such a role was necessary, because few if any black literary journals survived for very long, and only a few white journals published black writers.

Here, we examine the leading black journalists of the Harlem Renaissance. These include Carl Murphy of the Baltimore *Afro-American*, Robert S. Abbott of the Chicago *Defender*, Robert L. Vann of the Pittsburgh *Courier*, P. B. Young of the *Norfolk Journal and Guide*, John Mitchell of the *Richmond Planet*, and C. A. Franklin of the Kansas City *Call*. Among the most important editors of the period were T. Thomas Fortune, the "dean" of black journalists, who in the 1920s edited Marcus Garvey's newspaper *The Negro World*; W. E. B. Du Bois, who edited *The Crisis*, the house organ of the National Association for the Advancement of Colored People (NAACP); A. Philip Randolph and Chandler Owen, editors of *The Messenger*; and Charles S. Johnson, editor of *Opportunity*, the magazine of the Urban League.

Robert S. Abbott (1868–1940)

The black press flourished during the 1920s: more than 500 black newspapers had a total circulation of more than 1.5 million. Of all these newspapers, none prospered more than the Chicago *Defender*. Its publisher and editor was Robert Sengstacke Abbott. Abbott was born in 1868 on Saint Simons Island, Georgia, to a butler and a hairdresser; he grew up in Savannah, Georgia, and was raised by his mother and his stepfather, John Sengstacke. Sengstacke was a newspaperman himself, and this encouraged his stepson to enter the newspaper business. Abbott attended Hampton Institute, where he was trained as a printer. Printing jobs were hard to find, however, so he studied law. Despite completing a law course, Abbott was not admitted to the Georgia bar, so he returned to journalism.

In 1905, Abbott decided to start his own newspaper and chose Chicago as the place to start it. That year, Chicago's black population was 40,000 and growing. Three newspapers were already serving the black community in Chicago, but that did not stop Abbott, who called his newspaper the *Defender*. From an initial press run of 300 copies in 1905, the *Defender* grew to a circulation of more than 200,000 during World War I. The newspaper was distributed throughout the Midwest and the middle and deep South. Its popularity came from its constant publicizing of and crusading against local and national racial oppression, especially in the South. Along that line, it constantly encouraged its southern readers to migrate North, preferably to Chicago. In no small part because of the *Defender*'s encouragement, Chicago became a magnet for black migration from the South; its black population increased 144 percent to 110,000 by 1920. Many of these newcomers became readers of the *Defender*, thereby increasing the newspaper's circulation, wealth, and influence.

During the Harlem Renaissance, Abbott's Chicago *Defender* was the most widely read black newspaper, with a circulation approaching 250,000. Abbott put out a lively, sensationalist newspaper that appealed to all segments of the black community. Like its contemporaries in the white press of the "roaring twenties," the *Defender* featured lurid headlines and stories focusing on crime and sex. This appealed to the newspaper's numerous working-class readers. Still, the *Defender* gave comprehensive coverage to the day-to-day life of Chicago's black community and crusaded against local and national racism. The *Defender* was divided into twelve sections, including local, national, and international news; sports; entertainment; society; editorials and opinion; and a features section that spotlighted black writers and artists, especially those of the Harlem Renaissance. The features section offered poetry, short stories, and serialized novels. The *Defender*'s layout was imitated throughout the rest of the black press, and by the late 1920s most black newspapers had adopted its sensationalistic, comprehensive format. For good reason, the *Defender* called itself the "world's greatest weekly."

Politically, the *Defender* differed little from its contemporaries in the black press in that it generally supported the Republican Party locally and nationally. Abbott, as befitted his status as a successful entrepreneur, was moderate to conservative on most issues besides race. However, in 1928, annoyed by the Republican Party's neglect of issues concerning black people, Abbott and the *Defender* endorsed the presidential candidate of the Democratic Party, Alfred E. Smith.

Abbott and the *Defender* fell on hard times during the Great Depression. The newspaper's circulation decreased by 75 percent, and Abbott was forced to dip into his personal assets to keep the paper afloat. Then his health began to fail in the late 1930s. In 1939 he turned over control of the *Defender* to his nephew John Sengstacke. Shortly thereafter, in February 1940, Robert S. Abbott died.

Under Sengstacke's leadership, the *Defender* revived itself during World War II, reaching new heights in circulation and influence because of its extensive coverage of and advocacy for equitable participation by blacks in the war. Although the *Defender* continued to be a powerful voice of the black community during the civil rights era and beyond, it fell on hard times again during the 1990s and passed out of the control of Abbott's descendants. The *Defender* is still being published today, however, and is highly likely to continue to be as influential in the twenty-first century as it was during the twentieth.

Robert L. Vann (1879–1940)

Robert L. Vann—like his contemporary and rival Robert S. Abbott—was a lawyer who was interested in journalism. He is forever linked to the Pittsburgh *Courier*, which he ran from 1910 until his death in 1940. Vann, one of the few black attorneys in Pittsburgh, was asked by the founders of the *Courier* to organize their legal affairs. When they were unable to keep the newspaper going, Vann took it over and in ten years built it to equal the *Defender* in circulation and influence. The *Courier*'s layout followed that of the *Defender* but was less sensational. Also, the *Courier*'s columnists and writers tended to be of higher quality than those of the *Defender*. Prominent among Vann's writers was George Schuyler, who wrote most of the *Courier*'s editorials and a widely renowned column, "Views and Reviews." There was also J. A. Rogers, who contributed numerous articles and columns on ancient and contemporary Africa. Walter White, head of the NAACP, had his novel *The Fire in the Flint* serialized in the *Courier* and then became a book reviewer for the newspaper, reviewing the works of such writers of the Harlem Renaissance as Countee Cullen, Alain Locke, and Langston Hughes. Later, the *Courier* employed the distinguished black journalists P. L. Prattis and Wendell Smith. In the 1940s, Smith was instrumental in the effort to integrate major league baseball.

Unlike Abbott, Vann was very active in local and national politics. He was a "kingmaker" in Pittsburgh, controlling the black vote in the 1920s for the Republican Party. As such he was very influential in the Republican Party in Pennsylvania, and in the national party, during the 1920s. As time went by, however, Vann became disenchanted with the Republicans' lack of interest in black people's concerns; in the 1930s he switched to the Democratic Party, taking thousands of black votes with him. For this he was rewarded with an appointment as a special assistant to the attorney general in Washington, D.C.—a job with little power.

Because it had a politically active publisher, the *Courier* was an activist newspaper. It crusaded for racial equality in Pittsburgh, in Pennsylvania, and nationwide. It was one of the few black newspapers that supported the labor movement by giving news coverage and editorial support to A. Philip Randolph when he was organizing the Brotherhood of Sleeping Car Porters. During the 1920s, the *Courier*, while not the most widely read black newspaper (the *Defender* had a higher circulation), was perhaps the most influential, owing to its high-quality leadership and staff.

The Great Depression damaged the *Courier*, as it did other black newspapers. Vann found himself spending as much time back in Pittsburgh trying to keep the paper afloat as he spent in Washington. In the late 1930s, however, the newspaper's health improved. The *Courier*'s coverage of the impending world war, and its tireless advocacy of full participation by blacks in the war effort, restored it to national prominence. It led the black community's "double V" campaign for victory over racism at home and victory over fascism abroad. Vann himself, though, did not live long enough to see this revival; he died of cancer in 1940.

In the postwar years, the *Courier* continued to prosper, as its coverage and advocacy of the civil rights and "black power" movements helped it retain its readership. The Sengstacke family (the owners of the Chicago *Defender*) acquired it in 1965. Although, like black newspapers in general, it experienced hard times in the 1980s and 1990s, the *Courier* still publishes today as the *New Pittsburgh Courier* and is still a tireless advocate for racial justice.

Carl Murphy (1889–1967)

Carl Murphy was the gifted and charismatic publisher-editor of the Baltimore *Afro-American* from 1922 to 1967. One of the nine children of the *Afro-American*'s owner John H. Murphy, Carl Murphy joined the newspaper in 1918 and was picked by his family to take it over in 1922 after his father's death. He had been educated at Howard University, had received a graduate degree in German from Harvard University, and was a professor of German at Howard University when he joined the *Afro-American*. His academic and scholarly background manifested itself in the extremely high quality of the editorials—most written by him—carried in the newspaper. In general, the Baltimore *Afro-American* was very highly regarded, and it dominated the black media markets along the eastern seaboard.

Throughout the 1920s, Carl Murphy had his *Afro-American* crusade continuously for racial justice and advancement in Baltimore, in Maryland, and elsewhere. Among the issues were equalization of teachers' salaries in Baltimore, efforts to maintain and increase black membership in the Baltimore city council, the struggles for representation of blacks on the local school board and in the police department, and antilynching crusades. Nationwide, the *Afro-American* supported antilynching legislation, and it called for increased federal patronage for black Republicans. The newspaper tended to be a maverick concerning national politics, however. Carl Murphy was very progressive for his time and was attracted to leftist

views and politicians. Unlike his peers in the black press, Murphy was not afraid to go out on a limb politically. For example, in 1924 he endorsed the third-party candidate, Robert La Follette, for the presidency. In 1928 he had the *Afro-American* support the Democratic Party candidate, Alfred E. Smith, instead of the Republican, Herbert Hoover. In the 1930s the newspaper gave covert endorsements to Communist Party and Socialist Party candidates for local, state, and national offices. During that time, Murphy described himself as a "red."

Carl Murphy's literate background was reflected in the high quality and wide range of columnists and feature writers who appeared in the *Afro-American*. Among others, Walter White of the NAACP; Kelly Miller, dean of Howard University; and James Weldon Johnson all had columns in the newspaper. The *Afro-American* also had homegrown columnists such as William N. Jones and Ralph Matthews. Jones wrote a column, "Day-by-Day," that was a fixture of the *Afro-American* from 1922 until his death in 1940. In this column, which was almost an editorial page in itself, he commented on local and national issues. Jones had joined the *Afro-American* in 1921, after a stint as a social worker and field investigator for the Urban League; he became the city editor and then the managing editor. As a man of the left, he was subjected to red-baiting during the 1930s. His ideology was congruent with Carl Murphy's, however, so he never lost influence within the *Afro-American*. Ralph Matthews, a witty and acerbic writer, was the *Afro-American*'s answer to H. L. Mencken. Matthews had one or two columns in each issue of the *Afro-American* from the 1920s on. In these columns he lampooned various sacred cows in the black community, such as the black church and its ministers, black politicians, black "society," and the institutions of marriage and family. Matthews also wrote short stories and plays, and he contributed many of these pieces, usually expressing his worm's-eye view of male-female relationships, to the *Afro-American*'s feature pages. One interesting aspect of the *Afro-American* was that, while its editorial columns, written mostly by Carl Murphy, upheld the church, society, and the family, Matthews's columns satirized these institutions. It is to Carl Murphy's credit that, despite his forceful opinions, he tolerated and even encouraged those who disagreed with him. This tolerance of diversity was one of Murphy's greatest strengths and in turn strengthened the *Afro-American*.

More so than most of his peers, Carl Murphy appreciated the Harlem Renaissance and encouraged it by serializing the works of local and nationally known black novelists, publishing the poems and essays of Countee Cullen, Langston Hughes, and Claude McKay. The newspaper encouraged young black writers by publishing serials and short stories in its magazine section. Eventually these stories were published in an anthology edited by Nick Aaron Ford: *Best Short Stories by Afro-American Writers*.

Unlike its competitors the *Defender* and the *Courier, the Afro-American* expanded and prospered during the Great Depression. It established branch offices and editions in Washington, Philadelphia, Richmond, and Newark. By 1940 Carl Murphy presided over a newspaper chain that blanketed the East Coast. The *Afro-American* reached unprecedented highs in circulation, income, and influence during World War II, becoming a million-dollar company in 1945. It remained at that level for many years afterwards.

Carl Murphy died in 1967, full of years and success. He left a prosperous and powerful media voice, as well as descendants who have kept the newspaper alive and well during the hard times that have befallen the black press. Today the *Afro-American*, in continuous operation since 1892, is still a powerful voice for African Americans in Baltimore, Washington, and elsewhere on the east coast.

Charles S. Johnson (1893–1956)

A renowned sociologist, Charles S. Johnson was also a major player in the Harlem Renaissance due to editorship of *Opportunity*, published by the National Urban League. Johnson was the director of research for the Urban League and at their request founded *Opportunity* in 1923. From 1923 to 1927, when Johnson left the magazine to head Fisk University's Sociology Department, *Opportunity* not only published news of the Urban League but it also published most of the poets and essayists of the Harlem Renaissance. Johnson strongly believed that African Americans could achieve racial equality through literary and artistic accomplishments. Consequently he encouraged and mentored nearly every prominent literary figure of the Harlem Renaissance. Among Johnson's protégés were Arna Bontemps, Countee Cullen, Aaron Douglas, Jessie Fauset, and Langston Hughes. In 1925 Johnson's *Opportunity* began awarding literary prizes. That year Countee Cullen, Langston Hughes, and Zora Neale Hurston were the first recipients. *Opportunity* prizes gave needed recognition to Harlem Renaissance

artists and helped jump-start the movement. The NAACP's *Crisis* followed with awards of its own. In 1926 Countee Cullen joined *Opportunity* as the assistant editor. In that capacity he wrote a column "The Dark Tower."

After joining Fisk in 1927, Charles S. Johnson established the Race Relations Institute in 1944. In 1947 he became Fisk University's first black president. Under his stewardship Fisk prospered, increasing its enrollment and endowment. Johnson died in 1956. As for *Opportunity*, it still publishes today as the Urban League's house organ.

W. E. B. Du Bois (1868–1963)

A true man for all seasons W. E. B. Du Bois spent some of his most productive years as a journalist. In 1909 he left his faculty position at Atlanta University, where he established their Sociology Department, to join the National Association for the Advancement of Colored People (NAACP) as their director of research and publications. In that capacity, Du Bois founded and edited *Crisis*, the NAACP's magazine. During the 1920s the *Crisis* provided an outlet for Du Bois' developing Pan-Africanist and Socialist ideologies, as well as a platform from which he could denounce Marcus Garvey, with whom he feuded. Besides Du Boisian ideology and NAACP news, *Crisis* kept abreast of the artistic accomplishments of the Harlem Renaissance by publishing many black poets and essayists. The noted black writer Jessie Fauset was the *Crisis*'s literary editor. She made sure *Crisis* promoted and published Harlem Renaissance writers. Among those whose works appeared in the *Crisis* were Sterling Brown, Langston Hughes, and Claude McKay. In 1924, Du Bois had *Crisis* offer prizes for artistic excellence. In the late 1920s, Du Bois became disenchanted with the Harlem Renaissance, especially is growing emphasis on ghetto realism, so *Crisis* suspended its awards competitions.

Du Bois ran the *Crisis* as his own fiefdom and frequently clashed with the NAACP's leadership, who did not often appreciate Du Bois' criticism of the organization and his ideological meandering. In 1934, Du Bois published articles in the *Crisis* calling for blacks to build self-sufficient communities separated from whites. This was too much for Walter White and the NAACP board, who fervently believed in a racially integrated society. They dismissed Du Bois, who then rejoined the faculty of Atlanta University. There he established the sociological journal *Phylon*. As time went by, he became more and more active in leftist politics and organizations, believing that socialism offered the surest path for black advancement. For that stand, he was Red-baited during the 1950s. In 1959, Du Bois, disgusted with the slow pace of racial and social reform and his own persecution, joined the Communist party USA, then migrated to Ghana. There he began work on the *Encyclopedia Africana*, a task that occupied him until his death at 95 in 1963. As for the *Crisis*, the NAACP publishes it today as the organization's house organ.

P. B. Young (1884–1962)

Plummer Bernard Young, was born in North Carolina, migrated to Norfolk, Virginia, and in 1907 joined the staff of the Norfolk *Journal and Guide*. The *Journal and Guide* had been established in 1901 as a church journal. In 1910 Young bought out the owners, and along with his family, ran the paper until his death in 1962. Young and his *Journal and Guide* were second only to Carl Murphy and the *Afro-American* in readership and influence on the eastern seaboard. The *Journal and Guide* was especially influential in Norfolk and Virginia politics. Young was somewhat more conservative than his peers in the black press, preferring a conciliatory approach toward racial problems. Still, when black interests were threatened locally or nationally, Young's voice of protest could be heard loud and clear. In the 1920s, the newspaper campaigned against lynching and called for better schools, improved housing, and jobs for its readers. It also took a strong stand on crime reduction within the black community

The *Journal and Guide*'s format was not sensational, as were its contemporaries. This tended to limit its circulation though not necessarily its influence. In fact, its nonsensational format caused it to be taken more seriously than its competitors. Like other black newspapers, the *Journal and Guide* published Harlem Renaissance black poets, novelists and essayists. It also carried columns written by such black journalists as T. Thomas Fortune.

P. B. Young died in 1962, and his son Thomas W. Young succeeded him at the helm, only to die five years later. The *Journal and Guide* passed out of the control of the Young family in the 1970s and is now owned and operated by Brenda Andrews. Today the Norfolk *Journal and Guide* carries on in the tradition set by P. B. Young.

John Mitchell (1863–1929)

P. B. Young's main rival for journalistic dominance in Virginia was John Mitchell and the Richmond *Planet*. Mitchell took over the *Planet* in 1884 and ran it until his death in 1929. Mitchell was more militant in racial matters than P. B Young, and the two were frequently at odds during the 1920s. Mitchell from the beginning crusaded against the disenfranchisement of black voters in the South and led boycotts of streetcar companies that segregated black riders. He was far more active in politics than Young, serving in the Richmond City Council in the 1890s, as a delegate to Republican National Conventions, and running for governor of Virginia in 1921. Mitchell in his editorial policies represented the more militant "New Negro" of the 1920s than P. B. Young, who harked back to the more accommodationist ways of Booker T. Washington.

John Mitchell died in 1929. The Richmond *Planet* declined under his successors and was taken over Carl Murphy in 1938. The newspaper became the Richmond *Afro-American and Planet*. It followed the parent Baltimore *Afro-American* in layout, but its news coverage and editorials were localized to Richmond. The Richmond *Afro-American* lasted until 1996.

C. A. Franklin (1880–1955)

Chester A. Franklin was one of the most important publishers in the midwest. He started the Kansas City *Call* in 1919 and in a few short years built it into one of the more important black newspapers of the era. Franklin had run newspapers in Omaha and Denver before he moved to Kansas City during World War I. After a rocky early start, Franklin by the mid-1920s had the *Call* on a firm financial and journalistic footing. Like other black newspapers of the time, it campaigned for racial equality locally and nationwide. It led crusades against lynching, the Ku Klux Klan, and police brutality. It also campaigned for desegregated education and housing and increased job opportunities for blacks.

The *Call* rejected sensationalism as a means to sell newspapers. In that, it followed the example of the Norfolk *Journal and Guide*. It constantly presented the local and national black community in the most positive light, emphasizing news about black religious, social, and cultural activity. Along those lines, it provided an outlet for local and national black poets, novelists, and essayists. The *Call* also employed a distinguished roster of reporters and columnists. The most important of these was Roy Wilkins, later the head of the NAACP, who started his career as a reporter columnist for the *Call* in the late 1920s.

C. A. Franklin died in 1955; his wife, Ada Crogman Franklin, succeeded him as the owner and publisher of the *Call*. The Kansas City *Call* publishes today and is still the primary media voice for Kansas City's African Americans.

Marcus Garvey (1887–1940)

Marcus Garvey is not often remembered today as a newspaper publisher. However, he did establish a newspaper, the *Negro World*, to publicize the activities of the Universal Negro Improvement Association (UNIA). During the early 1920s, the UNIA was the most powerful black organization in the United States. Its membership numbered in the millions, and it established numerous subsidiaries, which included a church (African Orthodox Church) the Black Cross Nurses, the Black Star Line, an auditorium, and a laundry. Garvey preached a black nationalism built around a powerful Africa free of white colonial domination. This message resonated with black working-class folk in Harlem and elsewhere in the North, who attended UNIA meetings, patronized UNIA enterprises, bought stock in UNIA businesses, and read the *Negro World*.

For a time, the *Negro World* was the most important black newspaper in Harlem. At it is peak it had a circulation approaching 200,000. An aged T. Thomas Fortune, who had published the *New York Age* and who was considered to be the most important black journalist at the turn of the century, edited it. Along with hard news, the *Negro World* promoted Garveyite Black Nationalism in its editorials and features, serializing fictional stories of Africans overthrowing white colonialists. The *Negro World* along with other black newspapers of the era published poems, essays, and short stories by Alain Locke, Claude McKay, and Zora Neale Hurston. In fact, it was the first newspaper to publish her poems, doing so in 1922. After a while Garvey lost interest in promoting the Harlem Renaissance, believing that black artistic activity should be subordinate to Black Nationalist protest politics. Therefore, the *Negro World* became solely a propaganda organ for the UNIA.

The *Negro World* flourished as long as Marcus Garvey did. When Garvey was imprisoned for mail fraud in 1925 and deported to Jamaica in 1927,

the UNIA faded away. So did the *Negro World*. Still, during its heyday it was the strongest voice for Black Nationalism during this era.

A. Phillip Randolph (1889–1979)

Primarily known as a great labor leader due to his organizing black Pullman porters into the Brotherhood of Sleeping Car Workers, Randolph also was a noted journalist during the Harlem Renaissance. He cofounded with Chandler Owen (1889–1967) and edited the *Messenger*, which existed from 1917 to1928. This magazine became the leading black radical publication of the era. The *Messenger* promoted socialism as the road to black freedom and called for solidarity between black and white workers. It also harshly criticized Marcus Garvey and the UNIA.

The *Messenger*, like *Crisis* and *Opportunity*, promoted the Harlem Renaissance, though not to the extent of the latter two. The Renaissance was incidental to its mission of promoting black socialism. It did publish Arna Bontemps, Countee Cullen, Langston Hughes, and Claude McKay. and The *Messenger's* drama critic was Theophilus Lewis, who wrote for the magazine from 1923 to 1927. Lewis's reviews of black plays and other fiction were the *Messenger's* main contribution to the Harlem Renaissance.

Plagued by consistently low circulation, the *Messenger* folded in 1928. Randolph later became one the most powerful labor and civil rights leaders of the twentieth century, founding the Brotherhood of Sleeping Car Workers and organizing the 1941 and 1963 Marches on Washington.

Conclusion

Black journalists and the newspapers and magazines they published and edited provided one of the main outlets for the artists of the Harlem Renaissance. At the same time, they were themselves part of the explosion of black creativity that characterized that era. The 1920s were a golden age for black journalism, as circulation, advertising, and income reached new heights. This firm financial foundation enabled them to publish and publicize Harlem Renaissance artists. By supporting local black artists of the era, black newspapers ensured that the Harlem Renaissance would be a national phenomenon, not one limited to just New York City.

The Harlem Renaissance witnessed an outpouring of black literary and political magazines, which had not been seen before and has not been seen since. The most important of these—*The Crisis, Opportunity*, and the *Messenger*—were among the main publishers, critics, and employers of such Harlem Renaissance figures as Jessie Fauset, Zora Neale Hurston, Countee Cullen, Langston Hughes, and others. While white patronage and outlets were important to the success of the Harlem Renaissance, without black journalists the Harlem Renaissance would have had little impact.

HAYWARD "WOODY" FARRAR

See also Abbott, Robert Sengstracke; Baltimore Afro-American; Black Press; Chicago Defender; Crisis, The; Du Bois, W. E. B.; Fortune, Timothy Thomas; Johnson, Charles Spurgeon; Johnson, James Weldon; Messenger, The; Miller, Kelly; Murphy, Carl J.; Negro World; Opportunity; Owen, Chandler; Pittsburgh Courier; Randolph, A. Philip; Rogers, Joel Augustus; Schuyler, George S.; Vann, Robert L.; White, Walter

Further Reading

Buni, Andrew. *Robert L. Vann of the Pittsburgh Courier.* Pittsburgh, Pa.: University of Pittsburgh Press, 1974.

Detweiler, Frederick G. *The Negro Press in the United States.* Chicago, Ill.: University of Chicago Press, 1922.

Farrar, Hayward. *The Baltimore Afro-American 1892–1950.* Westport, Conn.: Greenwood, 1998.

Ford, Nick A. *Best Short Stories by Afro-American Writers.* Baltimore, Md.: Afro-American, 1950.

Huggins, Nathan Irvin. *Harlem Renaissance.* New York: Oxford University Press, 1971.

Johnson, Abby Arthur, and Ronald Mayberry. *Propaganda and Aesthetics: The Literary Politics of Afro-American Magazines in the Twentieth Century.* Amherst: University of Massachusetts Press, 1979.

Johnson, James Weldon. *Black Manhattan.* New York: Knopf, 1940. (Reprint, New York: Arno, 1968.)

Kornweibel, Theodore, Jr. *No Crystal Stair: Black Life and the Messenger.* Westport, Conn.: Greenwood, 1975.

Lewis, David Levering. *When Harlem Was in Vogue.* New York: Knopf, 1981.

Myrdal, Gunnar. *An American Dilemma: The Negro Problem and Democracy.* New York: Harper and Row, 1944.

Osofsky, Gilbert. *Harlem: The Making of a Ghetto.* New York: Harper and Row, 1966.

Ottley, Roi. *The Lonely Warrior: The Life and Times of Robert S. Abbott.* Chicago, Ill.: Regnery, 1955.

Pride, Armistead. *A History of the Black Press.* Washington, D.C.: Howard University Press, 1997.

Stein, Judith. *The World of Marcus Garvey: Race and Class in Modern Society.* Baton Rouge: Louisiana State University Press, 1986.

Suggs, H. Lewis, ed. *The Black Press in the South, 1865–1979.* Westport, Conn.: Greenwood, 1983.

Suggs, H. Lewis. *P. B. Young, Newspaperman: Race, Politics, and Journalism in the New South.* Charlottesville: University Press of Virginia, 1988.

Suggs, H. Lewis, ed. *The Black Press in the Middle West, 1865–1985.* Westport, Conn.: Greenwood, 1996.

Thornbrough, Emma Lou. *T. Thomas Fortune: Militant Journalist.* Chicago: University of Chicago Press, 1972.

Vincent, Theodore G. *Voices of a Black Nation: Political Journalism in the Harlem Renaissance.* Trenton, N.J.: Africa World, 1973.

Weiss, Nancy J. *The National Urban League, 1910–1940.* New York: Oxford University Press, 1974.

Wintz, Cary. *Black Culture and the Harlem Renaissance.* Houston, Tex.: Rice University Press, 1988.

Wolseley, Roland E. *The Black Press U.S.A.* Ames: Iowa State University Press, 1971.

Jungle Alley

Jungle Alley, also known as The Street, Paradise Valley, Beale Street, and The Stroll, was the part of 133rd Street between Lenox and Seventh avenues. It was the locale for many expensive, white-owned, segregated nightclubs and cabarets such as the Cotton Club, Connie's Inn, and Small's Paradise, and for extravagant rent parties and speakeasies. As a center of Harlem's social scene, Jungle Alley functioned as a setting where upper-class white Americans who wanted to transcend the rigid rules of the color line could visit Harlem and gaze on the African American culture and people "without actually descending into it" (Watson 1995). In many ways, the economic, social, and artistic activities associated with the residents and businesses of Jungle Alley made it a microcosm of the cultural vibrancy that characterized the Harlem Renaissance.

The vogue of Harlem contributed to the popularity of the pricey nightclubs and cabarets in Jungle Alley. In addition to the Cotton Club, Connie's, and Small's, its popular nightspots and jazz clubs included the Apartment, Minton's Playhouse, Crawford's, and the Beehive. African American performers such as Duke Ellington, Ethel Waters, Cab Calloway, and Bessie

Smith appeared frequently in these establishments. Wealthy white Americans who were intrigued by the image of the African American as a primitive exotic unabashedly journeyed to Jungle Alley to see shows featuring scantily clad performers while being served by dancing waiters. To become acquainted with Harlem's nightlife and the world of the presumed primitive exotics, a visit to Jungle Alley was an essential part of a nighttime foray into Harlem, "race capital of the world."

Despite the allure and excitement of Jungle Alley, and despite the fact that this specific area of Harlem was a place where the races could congregate and socialize, the realities of racism and segregation prevented it from functioning in a genuinely color-blind way. For example, the Cotton Club—the largest and most popular nightspot in Jungle Alley—aimed its advertising at a predominantly if not wholly white clientele. The owners of clubs, who were often affiliated with the mob, strictly enforced the rules of segregation; they also carefully selected and hired young, light-skinned women whose physical appearance would be nonthreatening to a white audience. Moreover, there was seldom any social interaction between audiences and performers. Thus, although the establishments in Jungle Alley provided an income and commercial recognition for many African American performers, the exclusionary and racist practices of club owners were a reminder that white Americans had "infiltrated" Harlem and would maintain the status quo.

It should be noted, however, that the status quo varied within Jungle Alley, in terms of the clientele and reputation of the businesses there. Some establishments, such as the Sugar Cane on 135 Street at Fifth Avenue, attracted a more racially diverse crowd and provided a setting for the sale and distribution of cocaine, marijuana, and bootleg liquor. At such nightspots, sultry torch singers would perform while the customers reveled and danced into the early morning hours. Although businesses like the Sugar Cane were less elegant than the Cotton Club, they represented an adventurous fringe of Jungle Alley and appealed to the black working class.

Similarly, speakeasies, also known as "lap joints," and rent parties were a common aspect of life in Jungle Alley. The rent party, originally designed to raise money to forestall a tenant's impending eviction, became a common social gathering and communal event for working-class African Americans. Speakeasies and black-owned nightclubs provided a venue for social interaction between blacks on the one hand and white curiosity seekers (particularly tourists) and white patrons of black artists on the other. Some establishments of this kind were used for more private events. The Bamboo Inn, for instance, was often used for young women's coming-out parties and for society matrons' luncheons; parties that began in someone's home would often conclude in a cabaret in Jungle Alley.

To some degree, the atmosphere of the speakeasies and rent parties allowed Harlemites to transcend barriers of race and class. As Wintz (1988) writes, "There all of Harlem converged: the prostitute, the washwoman, the petty gangster, the poet, and the intellectual shared the blues and swayed to the beat of the jazz musicians." Jungle Alley also appealed to gay and lesbian Harlemites. The Harlem Renaissance, in general, was a time of sexual as well as artistic freedom and exploration; moreover, the idea that African Americans were primitive exotics led, predictably, to a view of blacks as sexually uninhibited. Gay, lesbian, and bisexual Harlemites such as the novelist Wallace Thurman and the white patron Carl Van Vechten found Jungle Alley a zone of safety where they could express their sexuality. Gay establishments such as the Clam House, described as "a popular house for revelers but not for the innocent young" (Watson 1995), featured performers like Gladys Bentley and Bessie Smith, whose songs had double-entendre lyrics about same-sex love. Drag and costume balls, vividly depicted in Langston Hughes's autobiography *The Big Sea* (1940), were held at places such as the Rockland Palace and the Garden of Joy Club. Gays, lesbians, and bisexuals of all races also expressed their sexuality in private homes, apartments, and "buffet flats" such as Hazel Valentine's Daisy Chain. Jungle Alley, then, was a magnet for the sexually uninhibited.

Jungle Alley's commercial and social enterprises played a significant role in the development of the thriving Harlem community. Intellectuals, black artists and their patrons, gays, lesbians, bisexuals, working-class African Americans, and upper-class whites all converged on Jungle Alley in pursuit of good times, stimulating conversation, and hours of partying and drinking to the accompaniment of jazzy or soulful music. Despite the constraints of a racially divided society in the 1920s, the atmosphere of Jungle Alley enhanced the appeal of Harlem to a larger—and even a global—community.

LARNELL DUNKLEY JR.

See also Black Bohemia; Cotton Club; Harlem: 5—Neighborhoods; Homosexuality; House-Rent Parties; Nightclubs; Nightlife; Small's Paradise; *specific performers*

Further Reading

Coleman, Leon. "Carl Van Vechten Presents the New Negro." In *Harlem Renaissance Re-Examined*, ed. Victor A. Kramer and Robert A. Russ. New York: Whitston, 1997.

Garber, Eric. "A Spectacle in Color: The Lesbian and Gay Subculture of Jazz Age Harlem." In *Hidden From History: Reclaiming the Gay and Lesbian Past*, ed. Martin B. Duberman, Martha Vicinus, and George Chauncey Jr. New York: NAL, 1989.

Hughes, Langston. *The Big Sea: An Autobiography*. New York: Knopf, 1940.

Lewis, David Levering. *When Harlem Was in Vogue*. New York: Penguin, 1997.

Watson, Steven. *The Harlem Renaissance: Hub of African-American Culture, 1920–1930*. New York: Pantheon, 1995.

Wintz, Cary D. *Black Culture and the Harlem Renaissance*. College Station: Texas A&M University Press, 1996.